THE
ENCYCLOPEDIA
of the
INDIAN
DIASPORA

SPONSORS

The publisher would like to thank the following companies for their generous support.

Gold Sponsor

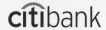

Other Sponsors

WARBURG PINCUS
JET AIRWAYS (INDIA) LTD

KEWALRAM CHANRAI GROUP
AMTEL INVESTMENT HOLDINGS PTE LTD
TEMASEK HOLDINGS

SAT PAL KHATTAR
SINGAPORE BUDDHIST LODGE

© 2006 Editions Didier Millet
All rights reserved
First published in Singapore by
Editions Didier Millet

www.edmbooks.com

In association with **National University of Singapore**

Published in North America by
University of Hawai'i Press
2840 Kolowalu Street, Honolulu, HI 96822 USA

www.uhpress.hawaii.edu

Printed in Singapore by Tien Wah Press Pte Ltd

Library of Congress Cataloging-in-Publication Data

The encyclopedia of the Indian diaspora / Brij V. Lal, general editor; Peter Reeves,
executive editor; Rajesh Rai, assistant editor.
p. cm.
Includes bibliographical references and index.
ISBN-13: 978-0-8248-3146-2 (hardcover: alk. paper)
ISBN-10: 0-8248-3146-2 (hardcover: alk. paper)
1. East Indian diaspora—Encyclopedias. I. Lal,
Brij V. II. Reeves, Peter, 1935- III. Rai, Rajesh.
DS432.5.E53 2006
909'.0491411003—dc22

2006024690

THE ENCYCLOPEDIA
of the
INDIAN DIASPORA

General Editor
BRIJ V. LAL

Executive Editor
PETER REEVES

Assistant Editor
RAJESH RAI

University of Hawai'i Press
Honolulu

ABOVE: *The flourishing Llandovery sugar estate in St. Ann, Jamaica, depended on indentured labour, 1891.*
PAGE 6: *An Indian woman in Martinique. By the early 20th century, the migration of women and of entire families was encouraged in an effort to foster the permanent settlement of Indians in the French colonies of the Caribbean.*
PAGE 7: *A number of emigration depots were located on the banks of the Hooghly at Calcutta. Migrants thus had to face a long journey upriver before the sea voyage had even begun.*

FOREWORD

HISTORY IS REPLETE with stories from time immemorial of Indian civilisation and its expanded influence far beyond India's shores. Today's Indian diaspora is one that extends to the four corners of the world. It is made up of Indian descendants of ancestors who, through trade and emigration, settled in various parts of the world. They can trace their ancestry to bonded labourers, 'political' deportees, tradesmen and business entrepreneurs, among others. Many Indian communities have graduated from being mostly plantation labourers to being skilled workers in manufacturing, construction and transportation. Their members have gone on to make a name in the modern world as 'knowledge workers'—IT and service specialists—and as prominent professionals in academia, medicine, science and law. The diaspora also boasts numerous illustrious figures in literature, film and the arts.

The Encyclopedia of the Indian Diaspora attempts to capture in a single volume the varied nature of the Indian diaspora with its cultural and linguistic diversity, a feature resulting from the many different locations where Indians have settled; the careers or professions in which Indians have excelled; and the many other ways in which Indians have flourished in over 60 communities worldwide. The diverse origins of the Indian diaspora, the development of its distinctive communities, and the talented and often gifted people which it comprises, are insightfully depicted in this book.

It is a story that is worthy of attention, especially in today's globalised world, in which the diaspora has come to play a significant and ongoing role wherever it has settled, creating for itself a niche in most of the countries it calls home. The endeavours and achievements of the diaspora through the years, the roles of its members and their contributions to contemporary society are laudable and make for compelling reading.

In facilitating the publication of both this volume and an earlier one on the overseas Chinese, Singapore has made a small contribution to increasing awareness of the rich history and modern dynamics of these diasporas, helping readers appreciate the processes by which the descendants of the great civilisations of India and China have migrated and settled around the world. It is important that future generations have a sense of historical perspective and are able to appreciate the contributions that these two traditions have made to the many nations in which the Indian and Chinese diasporas have made their homes.

The Encyclopedia of the Indian Diaspora brings together well-researched and authoritative accounts by scholars who specialise in the study of the Indian diaspora. The work was coordinated by the South Asian Studies Programme of the Faculty of Arts and Social Sciences at the National University of Singapore, under Professor Peter Reeves. Professor Brij V. Lal of The Australian National University, the book's General Editor, and all who have helped to put this book together deserve our sincere thanks. In particular, I must give special thanks to Mr Sat Pal Khattar, who took on the responsibility of finding financial support for this project and personally spent much time and effort quietly driving the project and seeing it through. Many sponsors have helped to ensure that the book was published: Citibank deserves special mention here. Above all, our thanks must go to Editions Didier Millet for coming up with this comprehensive work.

S. R. NATHAN
President
Republic of Singapore

CONTENTS

CONTRIBUTORS

CLARE ANDERSON, *Senior Lecturer, School of Historical Studies, University of Leicester, UK.*

FREDERIC ANGLEVIEL, *Professor, University of New Caledonia.*

MARTIN BAUMANN, *Professor, The Study of Religions, University of Lucerne, Switzerland.*

SURENDRA BHANA, *Professor of History, University of Kansas, US.*

MARINA CARTER, *Research Fellow, Centre for South Asian Studies, University of Edinburgh, UK.*

CHAN CHOENNI, *Co-ordinator for Strategy, Research and Communication, Ministry of Justice, the Netherlands.*

VIJAY DEVADAS, *Lecturer, Communication Studies, Division of Humanities, School of Social Science, University of Otago, New Zealand.*

ASSA DORON, *Post Doctoral Fellow, South Asian Studies Programme, National University of Singapore.*

RAJINDER DUDRAH, *Senior Lecturer in Screen Studies, Department of Drama, University of Manchester, UK.*

FRANK FANSELOW, *Lecturer, Department of Sociology and Anthropology, University of Brunei Darussalam.*

TILMAN FRASCH, *Assistant Professor, Department of History, South Asia Institute, University of Heidelberg, Germany.*

URMILA GOEL, *Visiting Scholar, Asia Centre, University of New England, Armidale, Australia; Researcher in Social and Cultural Anthropology, European University Viadrina, Frankfurt/Oder, Germany.*

RUBEN GOWRICHARN, *Professor of Social Cohesion and Transnational Issues, Tilburg University, the Netherlands.*

WAJIHAH HAMID, *Research Assistant, South Asian Studies Programme, National University of Singapore.*

KUSHA HARAKSINGH, *Associate Fellow, Department of History, University of the West Indies, Trinidad and Tobago.*

ROSEMARIJN HOEFTE, *Head of the Department of Collections and Coordinator of the Caribbean Expert Centre of KITLV/Royal Netherlands Institute of Southeast Asian and Caribbean Studies, Leiden, the Netherlands.*

KNUT A. JACOBSEN, *Professor, Department of the History of Religions, University of Bergen, Norway.*

VIRINDER KALRA, *Senior Lecturer, Sociology Department, School of Social Sciences, University of Manchester, UK.*

LAAVANYA KATHIRAVELU, *Research Assistant, Asia Research Institute, National University of Singapore.*

NATHAN KATZ, *Professor of Religious Studies, Florida International University, US.*

AMARJIT KAUR, *Professor of Economic History, School of Economics, University of New England, Australia.*

BINOD KHADRIA, *Professor of Economics, Zakir Husain Centre for Educational Studies, School of Social Sciences, Jawaharlal Nehru University, India.*

NANDITA KHADRIA, *Editor, Manpower Journal, Institute of Applied Manpower Research, India.*

IRENA KNEHTL, *Economist, researcher and writer on business and investment opportunities and prospects in Yemen.*

IGOR KOTIN, *Associate Professor, St. Petersburg State University; Senior Research Fellow, Russian Academy of Sciences, St. Petersburg, Russia.*

GYANESH KUDAISYA, *Assistant Professor, South Asian Studies Programme, National University of Singapore.*

MEDHA KUDAISYA, *Assistant Professor, Department of History and University Scholars Programme, National University of Singapore.*

SALIM LAKHA, *Senior Lecturer, School of Anthropology, Geography and Environmental Studies, University of Melbourne, Australia.*

BRIJ V. LAL, *Professor of Pacific and Asian History, Research School of Pacific and Asian Studies, The Australian National University.*

VINAY LAL, *Associate Professor, Department of History, University of California Los Angeles (UCLA), US.*

JACQUELINE LECKIE, *Senior Lecturer, Department of Anthropology, School of Social Sciences, University of Otago, New Zealand.*

JAMES D. LESLIE, *Professor (retired), Department of Physics, University of Waterloo, Canada.*

SCOTT LEVI, *Assistant Professor, Department of History, University of Louisville, US.*

AMARJIVA LOCHAN, *Reader in History, University of Delhi, India.*

KENNETH MCPHERSON, *Fellow, South Asia Institute, University of Heidelberg, Germany; Adjunct Professor, La Trobe University, Australia.*

KUMUD MERANI, *Head of the Hindi Programme, SBS Radio Sydney, Australia.*

RAJEND MESTHRIE, *Professor and Head of Linguistics, University of Cape Town, South Africa.*

VIJAY MISHRA, *Professor of English and Chair, School of Social Sciences and Humanities, Murdoch University, Australia.*

JOSEPHINE C. NAIDOO, *Professor Emerita, Department of Psychology, Wilfrid Laurier University, Canada.*

P. R. GOPINATHAN NAIR, *Honorary Fellow, Centre for Development Studies, Thiruvananthapuram, India.*

ULRIKE NIKLAS, *Professor and Director, Institute of Indology and Tamil Studies, University of Cologne, Germany.*

GIJSBERT OONK, *Lecturer, Department of History, Erasmus University of Rotterdam, the Netherlands.*

NATASHA PAIRAUDEAU, *Ph.D. candidate, School of Oriental and African Studies, University of London, UK.*

MICHAEL PEARSON, *Adjunct Professor of Humanities, University of Technology, Australia.*

ROSA MARIA PEREZ, *Professor, Department of Anthropology, Instituto Superior de Ciências (ISCTE), Portugal; Visiting Professor, Brown University, US.*

CAROLINE PLUSS, *Assistant Professor, Division of Sociology, School of Humanities and Social Sciences, Nanyang Technological University, Singapore.*

B. A. PRAKASH, *Professor and Head, Department of Economics, University of Kerala, India.*

RAJESH RAI, *Research Fellow, South Asian Studies Programme, National University of Singapore.*

ASHWIN AVINESH RAJ, *Ph.D. candidate, Division of Pacific and Asian History, Research School of Pacific and Asian Studies, The Australian National University.*

SUSHMA RAJ, *Ph.D. student, School of Geosciences, University of Sydney, Australia.*

S. IRUDAYA RAJAN, *Professor, Research Unit on International Migration, Ministry of Indian Overseas Affairs, Centre for Development Studies, Thiruvananthapuram, Kerala, India.*

PETER REEVES, *Visiting Professor and Head, South Asian Studies Programme, National University of Singapore.*

CLEM SEECHARAN, *Professor and Course Leader, Caribbean Studies, Department of Humanities, Arts and Languages, London Metropolitan University, UK.*

TERENJIT S. SEVEA, *MA candidate, London School of Economics, UK.*

VERENE A. SHEPHERD, *Professor, Department of History, University of the West Indies, Jamaica.*

BILVEER SINGH, *Associate Professor, Department of Political Science, National University of Singapore.*

VINEETA SINHA, *Associate Professor, Department of Sociology, National University of Singapore.*

KRIPA SRIDHARAN, *Senior Lecturer, Department of Political Science, National University of Singapore.*

BRIAN STODDART, *Vice-Chancellor and President, La Trobe University, Australia.*

TIN MAUNG MAUNG THAN, *Senior Fellow, Institute of Southeast Asian Studies, Singapore; Associate Editor, Contemporary Southeast Asia.*

GOOLAM VAHED, *Associate Professor, Department of History, University of KwaZulu-Natal, South Africa.*

FAIZAL YAHYA, *Assistant Professor, South Asian Studies Programme, National University of Singapore.*

GUIDE TO THE USE OF THE
ENCYCLOPEDIA AND EDITORIAL CONVENTIONS

STRUCTURE OF THE VOLUME

The encyclopedia has been divided into several sections. Parts I–IV survey the Indian setting and the causes, processes and patterns of migration from 'classical' times to the modern movements of people. The diaspora in the 'Age of Merchants' was concerned overwhelmingly with the movement of traders and merchants, religious and other specialists, seafarers and slaves. Migration in the 'Age of Colonial Capital' involved the forced movement of people (convicts) and the movement of indentured labourers from India to all parts of the British Empire, particularly those with plantation economies. It also saw the beginning of free migration and the continuation of merchant activity in both traditional areas and in territories newly opened by the expansion of the Empire. The mid-20th century post-colonial movement of people to Western countries and the related migration (and re-migration) of business people and professionals to new (and in some cases, formerly prohibited) areas, such as Australia, are covered in the 'Age of Globalisation'. That section also begins to address issues arising from the reappearance of migration on the basis of 'contract labour'. This has brought back some of the features of labour migration from the earlier period, which were considered important to the 'old' diaspora.

Part V looks at the changing relationship of the 'homeland' and the diaspora during the colonial and post-colonial periods, showing the ways in which perceptions of the diaspora and involvement with it have undergone change and reassessment. Part VI deals thematically with the cultural and social life of the diaspora, looking at ways in which language and religious values and practices have adapted and transformed, how popular culture—theatre, cinema, music, dance and fashion—and cuisine have evolved, and the important role of a wide range of sports that both link different areas of the diaspora and reconnect people in the diaspora with India; cricket being the most obvious example.

In Part VII, 'Voices from the Diaspora', we look at the evolution and character of the 'diasporic imaginary', which is best exemplified in the creative literature of the diaspora. The Indian diaspora has produced a very large and distinguished corpus of literary works, some of which are among the very best in the contemporary world. This creative endeavour may be the diaspora's most defining characteristic.

The final and largest section of the volume, Part VIII, 'Regions and Communities', provides 'country profiles' of the Indian diaspora across the globe, giving a synoptic view of their historical origins and evolution, their social and political experience and, where possible, their contemporary concerns and challenges. Important episodes and events which capture the essence of the community's experience are highlighted. There are some common threads across certain clusters—the plantation colonies, for example, with their history of indenture and subsequent struggle for social and political equality, and their continuing marginalisation and exclusion from power. Indian diasporic communities in the West share certain commonalities in terms of their origins, migration patterns, encounters with the culture of their countries of residence, their relative affluence and closeness to centres of power. It is the individual distinctiveness of the various diasporic communities, however, that stands out and underlines the enormous complexity and variation in experience.

The geographic dimension of the Indian diaspora is also staggering. It is worldwide and it varies in different periods and phases. The Indian Ocean littoral, Southeast and East Asia, plus Central Asia and the Middle East were traditional areas of movement. Further expansion went beyond traditional destinations: the colonial plantation outposts in the Caribbean, Malaya, Ceylon, Fiji, Mauritius and Natal; and commercial outposts with opportunities for trade and labour, such as Singapore, Hong Kong and East Africa. The latter half of the 20th century saw movement to North America and Europe, and also to former settler colonies, such as Australia, New Zealand and Canada. In more recent times, contract labour in Saudi Arabia and the Gulf States has shown a reversion to older forms of labour migration.

THE MATERIALS PRESENTED

The encyclopedia contains signed articles by the authors, who are named in the list of contributors. The largest body of material in both the 'Context' (Parts I–VII) and 'Regions and Communities' (Part VIII) sections of the volume is presented in essay form. In both sections there are also boxed features, which allow certain topics or illustrative examples to be looked at closely. Each authorial signature relates to all the text in the article or boxed feature—some small, others quite large—with which it is associated, except where indicated.

Every attempt has been made to ensure that the structure and content of the encyclopedia are clear by arranging the material according to both chronological and geographical indicators. Moreover, the volume has a comprehensive and detailed thematic index.

The encyclopedia is illustrated with a wide-ranging selection of photographs, both historical and contemporary, and examples of documents, dust jackets and other illustrative materials. Statistical data are presented throughout in figures and tables. In addition, there is a full set of maps—both to locate communities in terms of region and territory and to illustrate historical aspects of the growth and development of the community or the contextual factors to do with migration, settlement and socio-economic activities. For the maps, the intention has been to mark and name places mentioned in the accompanying text, together with additional features, to assist in terms of context and reference. The key to the features used in all the modern maps is as follows:

Area/areas under discussion	—— International boundary
Area/areas beyond scope of discussion	----- Provincial/state boundary

The bibliography is intended purely as a source for further reading on the subjects of each of the main sections of the 'Context' and 'Communities' sections of the volume. This means that rather than being presented as a single, consolidated list of bibliographical material (books, book chapters, articles and, where appropriate, websites), the bibliography is divided into relevant sections following the structure of the encyclopedia. Therefore, some titles may appear more than once.

LANGUAGES, MATERIALS AND AIDS

The editorial approach has been to use English as far as possible. However, the nature of the material is such that Romanised non-English vocabulary, including Indian terms and idioms with no exact English equivalents, occasionally appear. We have included a glossary which defines a large number of Indian words and names, along with some variants. Besides Indian languages, there is a sprinkling of Asian (Bahasa Melayu, Bahasa Indonesia, Thai and Chinese), Central Asian, Middle Eastern and European (French, Spanish, Portuguese, Dutch, German and Russian) terms. There are also words and phrases from the creole languages of some territories, and words arising from the diasporic versions of Indian languages carried to their new homes by Indian migrants; these are usually explained in the text.

The spelling of English words is based on The Concise Oxford Dictionary (Ninth Edition), which does not regard as foreign, and, therefore, does not italicise many words which have been absorbed into English from other languages, including Indian languages.

INTRODUCTION

'INDIANS ARE UBIQUITOUS', the Calcutta-based newspaper *The Statesman* claimed in August 1980. There were then only five countries where Indians had 'not yet chosen to stay'. These were Mauritania, North Korea, Romania, Guinea Bissau and the Cape Verde islands. It is a safe guess, 25 years later, that even these unlikely places have their own small sprinkling of Indian communities, complete with curry shops selling tandoori chicken, *tikka masala*, *idli* and *dosa*; video outlets; temples and mosques; and community organisations celebrating such festivals as Diwali, Id and Dussehra, and organising weekend and evening language classes for children, and musical evenings to keep the fraying memories of the ancestral culture alive. The government of India estimates the size of the Indian diaspora to be around 20 million, while other estimates vary; but whatever the figure, the size and spread of the Indian diaspora is staggering, especially in view of the conventional wisdom about Indians' general dislike of crossing the *kalapani*, the dark dreaded seas, for foreign lands. There was a time, a little over a hundred years ago, when migration was frowned upon, when it was widely believed that in most circumstances only the desperate departed their homeland for strange places, and then, too, under compulsion or false advertising by those who enlisted them for various jobs. There is no such fear now. Crossing the *kalapani* has become an enviable, much sought after symbol of success.

Like other movements and displacements of people, the Indian diaspora grew out of many causes and several crossings. In pre-European times, Indian traders crossed the Indian Ocean to the east coast of Africa and overland to Central and West Asia, while others, over many centuries, reached and colonised the heartland of many Southeast Asian cultures. In the 19th century, European commercial and colonial expansion and the abolition of slavery in the British Empire led to the large-scale recruitment of Indian indentured labourers for the 'King Sugar' colonies in the Atlantic, Pacific and Indian oceans, and under the *kangani* system to destinations in Southeast Asia. The third major crossing occurred from the mid-20th century onwards as Indians from the subcontinent sought new homes in the United Kingdom (UK), Europe, North America and Australasia. In the latest phase, a new kind of diaspora is emerging, the diaspora of the 'twice-banished', made up of people from the former colonies of Indian settlement (Trinidad, Guyana, Surinam, Fiji, Mauritius and East Africa) who now live in the West. Due to its varied origins, divergent patterns of migration and settlement, and different degrees of absorption or integration into the culture of their new homeland, the Indian diaspora defies easy categorisation. It is a complex confluence of many discreet cultures, languages and histories.

India's relations with its diaspora evolved haphazardly over time. In the 19th century, there was little public comment about the migration of its people to distant parts of the globe beyond the occasional complaint about abuses in the system of recruitment. In the early years of the 20th century, Mahatma Gandhi's struggle for racial equality in South Africa bore fruit in the form of scathing enquiries, by C. F. Andrews among others, which led to the abolition of the indenture system. In the inter-war period, India sought to use its influence with London to secure better political rights for 'Indians Overseas'. This active engagement and concern turned into passive interest after independence in 1947 as India got embroiled in regional conflicts and as it championed the cause of non-alignment. Overseas Indians were explicitly urged to identify themselves with the interests and aspirations of the countries of their residence. This pragmatic and sensible advice, self-evident and perhaps even self-serving, acknowledged the growing cultural and political distance between India and its diaspora.

The period of disengagement, lasting from the 1950s to the late 1980s or the early 1990s, coincided with two significant developments of great relevance to India's relationship with the diaspora. One was the phenomenal growth in the population of the diaspora in Western countries and its position in strategic sectors of the economy and public life: information technology, business, finance, the professions and academia, and in the upper reaches of national and international politics. The UK's House of Lords had Indian peers; Canada had provincial premiers and federal ministers of Indian origin; and Shridath Ramphal of Guyana was elected as secretary-general of the Commonwealth. The list of people of Indian descent in prominent positions globally is long and distinguished.

The other major development was the phenomenal growth of the Chinese economy, fuelled in no small part by the huge financial investment the overseas Chinese made in it. The lesson was clear and it was there to be learned: if China could successfully court overseas Chinese investment and appeal to the patriotism of its people abroad, why not India? The coincidence of these two developments at the end of the 20th century prompted Indian policy-makers to rethink India's own engagement with its diasporic community and to seek ways of reconnecting with it.

INDIA'S ENGAGEMENT WITH ITS DIASPORA

The result was the appointment in 2000 of a High Level Committee on Indian Diaspora headed by Dr L. M. Singhvi, a distinguished politician and former Indian high commissioner to the UK. The committee was charged with exploring ways in which non-resident Indians (NRI) and other persons of Indian origin (PIO) could play a role in India's economic development and, more broadly, with connecting India to its diaspora through cultural exchange. The committee proposed to 'acquaint the Indian public with the depth, variety and achieve-ments of the Indian Diaspora, sensitize it to their problems and their expectations from their mother country, propose a new policy framework for creating a more conducive environment in India to leverage these invaluable human resources—and thus to forge stronger ties between the two.' To that end, it recommended 'an overhaul of bureaucratic procedures and deep administrative and economic reforms [to] remove unnecessary obstacles standing in the way of optimal utilization of these resources.' The symbolic launching of this new policy took place on 9 January 2003—the date on which Mahatma Gandhi returned to India from South Africa in 1915. More than 2000 delegates from various parts of the diaspora attended the inaugural Pravasi Bharatiya Divas and 10 of its distinguished members were awarded the Pravasi Bharatiya Samman. The glitzy annual event is an opportunity for India to showcase its wares and celebrate the achievements of its diaspora. Much of the talk, however, is still about money and investment, and the growth and development of the Indian economy.

India's courting of the Indian diaspora has been encouraged, even prompted, by the emergence of global organisations based in Western countries. Perhaps the most visible and active among them is the Global Organisation of People of Indian Origin (GOPIO), formed in New York in 1989 to promote cooper-ation, communication and understanding within the Indian diaspora and to act as a lobby group for causes of particular concern to the diaspora, such as violations of human rights and political discrimination. Within each country with a substantial Indian population, there are hundreds of local and national organisations centred around religious affiliation, cultural background, language, regional origin in India or particular interests, such as music, art, dance or sport. These organisations may not be advocates for or on behalf of India, nor be directly political, but their social and cultural significance is profound. They share with non-Indians their cultural and religious heritage through music, dance and food, for example, which helps to break down the barriers of prejudice and misunderstanding. They also impart to children the fundamentals of their culture, though with varying degrees of success.

The Mumbai-based Indian film industry, popularly known as Bollywood, has played its part in globalising Indian culture and connecting the subcontinent to the diaspora. Its contribution has been immense and long-standing. Hindi films played a vital role in preserving the Hindi language in the far-flung sugar colonies from the 1930s onwards, admittedly with greater success in some places than others. Several years ago, in Georgetown, Guyana, I was deeply moved to meet a young Indian girl, Boodhia, who knew no Hindi at all but was glued to the television watching a black and white grainy film from the 1950s. 'I would like to go there one day', she said to me with deep longing, knowing full well that for her it was an impossible dream. Today, Bollywood movies, or at least the best of them, are screened in mainstream theatres in Western countries and watched by people from various cultural backgrounds. Bollywood movies are also screened in the most unlikely of places, such as Tonga, which has a long-standing, unwritten policy of keeping PIOs out of the tiny kingdom. In Fiji, Bollywood movies are sometimes dubbed in Fijian and enjoyed by families because reportedly they do not have sex scenes and are family-oriented.

Over the years, Bollywood cinema has become more sophisticated. No longer confined almost exclusively to syrupy romance musicals, they now deal with themes of critical relevance to contemporary society, problems of ageing, mental illness, communal violence, sexual exploitation and cross-cultural relationships. Furthermore, matching Hollywood in cinematic wizardry, they have wide appeal among people of all ages: films such as *Black*, *Baghban*, *Dev* and *Mr and Mrs Iyer* come to mind. Members of the Indian diaspora, too, are making movies and television sitcoms which are screened worldwide and are hugely popular not only with the diasporic community but with a much broader audience: *Bend It Like Beckham*, *Monsoon Wedding*, *Mississippi Masala* and *The Kumars at No. 42* are some examples.

CONNECTING THE DIASPORA

The diasporic imaginary has also played a huge role in globalising Indian culture and connecting the diaspora. The names of Indian writers of international distinction are legion, so much so that today it would be considered mildly remiss for a person of some learning not to know the names, if not the works, of the most famous of them, such as V. S. Naipaul, Salman Rushdie, Hanif Kureishi, Rohinton Mistry, Amitav Ghosh, M. G. Vassanji and Vikram Seth. *A House for Mr. Biswas*, *Midnight's Children*, *My Beautiful Laundrette*, *A Fine Balance*, *The Circle of Reason*, *The Book of Secrets* and *A Suitable Boy*, among dozens of others, would be on most lists of significant novels of the 20th century.

In subtle and sensitive ways, the writers of the Indian diaspora bring to the international literary consciousness the lived experience of Indian communities scattered across the globe. Once, this experience was deemed unworthy of serious literary engagement; now it finds its way into the heart of the former Empire's literary culture. It is literature to which children of the diaspora can relate, and of which they are justly proud. Great works of literature do not always have to be Western texts, the diasporic creative endeavour is saying. As a descendant of the 'old' diaspora, I find it particularly poignant that *A House for Mr. Biswas*, a novel about a proud but struggling man of unfulfilled literary ambition, from the rural sugar cane town of Chaguanas in Trinidad, marginalised and humiliated in his own extended family, is now considered a literary classic.

More recently, the Internet has connected not only the diaspora but the world in ways unimaginable a decade or so ago. We are deluged daily with requests from complete strangers for donations for this cause or that, invited to invest in some firm in Africa, and offered cures for imaginary ailments or shortcomings. Often we can deal with unwanted or unwarranted information quickly by resorting to the delete key; but sometimes we cannot or do not want to, because the new information captures our imagination, arouses our curiosity or promises a journey of discovery and adventure.

A piece called 'Hindu Rituals and Routines—Why Do We Follow Them?' came my way recently. It tells us why we light a lamp, have a prayer room, gesture *namaste*, prostrate before parents and elders, wear the *tilak* mark on our foreheads, consider the lotus position special, offer coconut milk to the gods and so on. Things which we once did automatically without understanding their meaning or purpose are illuminated with the click of the mouse. All of a sudden, a whole vanished world comes alive and childhood puzzles are solved. You can google the Ramayana and read the essence of that great epic in simple, accessible English. Whether you are an Indian living in Montréal, Melbourne, Japan or Jamaica, you are reading the same text, and are part of a network—part of the global Indian family, as some would like to have you believe. The Internet is a vast source of new enriching information, but it can just as easily be turned into an instrument of cultural propaganda and xenophobia, fanning the flames of fundamentalism and fanaticism with catastrophic effect. Just visit some of the websites of fundamentalist groups (of all faiths) and the picture becomes clear. The vitriol they display is frightening. Many who engage in cyberspace warfare over cultural and religious issues are, it seems, members of the new diaspora based in the West, not the old one.

It is understandable why India has recently taken much interest in cultivating links with its diaspora. A more difficult question is why Indians who have never been to India continue to nurture links with the subcontinent. For post-war migrants and others descended from them, the link with India is real and tangible. They keep in touch out of a sense of duty, responsibility and affection, or have networks formed by family and friends. For others, investment opportunities open up new connections. The decline, indeed the discrediting, of the either-or, us-or-them assimilationist ideology of the 1960s and 1970s has helped. Now, one can be a British citizen and at the same time be a proud Indian. Lord Dholakia is a British peer but he proudly proclaims his continuing emotional attachment to Gujarat, his ancestral homeland. Fatima Meer, the distinguished South Africa-born intellectual and anti-apartheid activist, can proclaim publicly, 'I am proud to be related to all these countries [where people of Indian origin have settled] and particularly to India to whom we have always referred to as Mother India.'

The acceptance of diversity, difference and pluralism, the increasing porousness of national boundaries, and the globalisation of culture has complicated the once narrow understanding of citizenship. Some turn to India for cultural and spiritual reasons, finding its civilisational values more pertinent to their lives. Elsewhere, political persecution and cultural denigration (as in some West Indian societies) have encouraged Indians to retain their cultural heritage and renew their links with India both as a potent act of resistance and as a powerful affirmation of their distinctiveness. India's emergence as a global power—a contender for a seat on the United Nations Security Council, a world leader in information technology, an exporter of skills and talents of the highest order, and no longer a producer of only shoddy goods for the mass market—and the triumph of its democracy, its deep respect for the verdict of the ballot box, enhances in the diasporic Indian a sense of pride in India's achievements. There is, somewhere within us, a deep desire to know who we are, where we have come from, and our place in the larger scheme of things. Naipaul once described India as *An Area of Darkness*, but has kept returning to it, kept renewing his links, and kept writing about it. 'We [Indians] have to develop a new sense of history', he said, accepting the Pravasi Bharatiya Samman. Perhaps some matters of the heart and soul remain beyond the reach of reason.

The Indian diaspora is large and growing, becoming ever more visible and powerful; but we should be cautious about speaking of the Indian diaspora in the singular. There are, in truth, diasporas of so many kinds—the 'dollar' diaspora of the West and the 'desperate' diaspora in the developing world, those which were formed by the 'brawn' drain and those formed by the 'brain' drain. There are also diasporas within diasporas, whose relationships with India are marked by myriad memories and different distances. Personal circumstance, proximity to the subcontinent, the timing, nature and purpose of the initial departure, and the political situation prevailing in the country of residence, all affect the relationship. There are points of convergence and divergence which influence relationships among members of the diaspora. Certain things bring us together—food, faith, fashion, art and music—and then it does not matter whether you have recently arrived from Surat or are a long-term resident of Surrey or Sydney.

An overarching sense of a shared culture forges bonds that transcend time and space. It is the common interest that matters. At other times, our Indianness takes second place to our local or national identities. Then we become Australian Indians or South African Indians or British Indians, demonstrating other social and cultural influences which have formed our identity. There may be other occasions when, say, Perth-based Indo-Fijians and other Indians may have more in common than with their counterparts on the east coast of Australia. One may consider oneself to be a part of the Tamil, Sikh or Gujarati diaspora first, but not necessarily at the expense of a wider identification. Such permutations and combinations are endless, conveying the complexity of the diaspora. Generally, relations among diasporic Indians from different backgrounds—Indians from India and Fiji Indians, for example, or Singaporean and Malaysian Indians—are harmonious, though occasional friction and misunderstandings occur, caused by different historical experiences and contrasting perceptions of culture, when 'hybrid' notions clash with 'essentialised' notions of what is right and proper. One purpose of this volume will have been served if it promotes a more nuanced understanding of the enormous diversity of the Indian diaspora.

ABOUT THIS BOOK

Now to the volume itself. The three key words in the title need brief comment: 'Encyclopedia', 'Diaspora' and 'Indian'.

ENCYCLOPEDIA

The conventional definition of an encyclopedia—from the Greek word *enkukliospaideia*—is that it is a comprehensive work of reference, usually in several volumes, on a particular subject or a range of connected topics arranged alphabetically. The emphasis is on compiling dry, incontestable facts about important dates, names and events, and the achievements of a life completed. It is intended, as far as possible, to be the last, most authoritative word on the subject. Its underlying principle is consensus about, not contestation over, established truths. This definition is from another era and seems hopelessly old-fashioned in the current intellectual climate. We live in a different world now, where the fundamental unknowability of the past is readily acknowledged, and where tentativeness and a sense of the partial (in both senses of the word) guide our search for the truth of the human experience. Facts do not speak for themselves; they speak when they are spoken to. Modern technology blurs old notions of time, space and boundaries. That is the inescapable reality of the bewildering world in which we live. That said, we have made every effort to be as comprehensive as possible within the constraints of the resources at our command. We have done everything in our power to check the accuracy of the facts in the text, but we placed no restriction on the way in which our contributors interpreted them. They are experts in their respective fields and we have respected their judgment. A more liberal definition of the word 'encyclopedia' is, 'a compendium for general education'. This volume meets that definition. It is an introduction to a subject and does not pretend to be anything else. We have tried to capture the lived experience of the Indian diaspora in all its confusing variety and complexity, and we see that as a real strength of the volume.

DIASPORA

The word derives from the Greek words *dia* ('through' or 'over') and *speiro* ('dispersal' or 'to sow'), and is a complex and contested word—understandably so, given its specific historical association with the dispersions of the Jewish people. The word carried connotations of violence, catastrophe, alienation, loss, exile and return; but words and concepts never remain static, they evolve in time to acquire expanded meanings in response to historical, cultural and social developments. Slavery, for example, once stood for a particularly violent form of labour recruitment in Africa, but it now includes all kinds of labour recruitment systems, including Indian indenture. Globalisation, in common knowledge, is a phenomenon of the late 20th century, but some people include the first phase of European expansion in the 15th and 16th centuries in its definition. There is now a similar expansiveness associated with the word 'diaspora'.

We do not have to accept all the meanings associated with the word historically to deploy it usefully for our purposes. In the Indian case, there is a common ancestral homeland from which people left for various reasons, voluntarily and involuntarily, heading to all corners of the globe. Many in the diaspora, particularly descendants of those who moved during the 'age of merchants' and the 'age of colonial capital', may have never been to India, but the country retains its place in their consciousness as a marker of their distinctiveness and difference, reinforced perhaps by the sense of exclusion and marginality in their home country. However fractured or frayed, ossified or fluid, there is a sense of cultural, religious and historical ties with India, in various combinations of longing and nostalgia.

Recall the case of the Guyanese girl Boodhia, who has never been to India and probably never will, but who longs for the land of the Hindi movies she watches in a language she cannot understand; or, take the proud Indo-Mauritian who wept at the news of Indira Gandhi's assassination, as if he had lost someone in his own family; and the Indian Australian who has never been to India and has a faltering acquaintance with Indian culture, but who passionately supports the Indian cricket team against Australia. There is, to use Stuart Hall's words, an 'imaginary coherence' to a set of disparate, distinctive collection of identities that gives the Indian diaspora its particular character.

INDIAN

We use the word in the generic sense to refer to a person from the Indian subcontinent. Before 1947, the definition was straightforward: everyone was an Indian, whether Muslim, Hindu, Tamil or Sikh. When we refer to the pre-Partition period and talk about, say, the descendants of indentured labourers, we use the word 'Indian', as we do when referring to historically more distant trade-related migration and settlement in pre-European times. Post-1947, the word has a politically restricted meaning, referring to Indian nationality. We have entries on Indians in the UK and the United States (US), for example, but not on Pakistanis and Bangladeshis, although we have no doubt that the Indian experience of migration and settlement in these countries would resonate in other South Asian experiences as well. There is also the matter of self-definition. The Jaffna Tamils consider themselves a people who have a distinctive history and cultural heritage in Sri Lanka. Their long-standing claim for a separate homeland is based on that self-definition. For that reason, they are not included in this volume as a separate category, but the Indian Tamils in Sri Lanka are, because of the particular history of their migration and their present predicaments, and because they define themselves as Indian Tamils. Common sense, flexibility and inclusiveness have guided our criteria for selection. However, there are cases in Southeast Asia, for example, where Jaffna Tamils have identified themselves closely as Indians and have thus pressed their claim for inclusion as part of the larger Indian category. There are other complicated cases as well. PIOs in the old diaspora may object to being called 'Indians Overseas'. They might prefer to call themselves Indo-Guyanese or Indo-Mauritian, which, for them, may reflect more accurately their sense of identity. We hope they will have no strong objection to being included in the larger overarching category of the Indian 'diaspora', and we hope, too, that the people of Bangladesh and Pakistan in particular will not object to our inclusion of them in our discussion of pre-Partition India.

There is the further matter of emphasis and the length of entries on the different communities in the Indian diaspora. In commissioning entries, we were not swayed by the contemporary size of the diaspora in the various countries today, nor by their current economic power and status. By that criteria, this volume would focus overwhelmingly on the Indian diaspora in North America and Europe. Rather, we have been guided by the principle of balance, for instance, in the coverage of the old and the new diaspora. The Indian population of Guyana, to take just one example, would be less than that of the borough of an American city, yet, Indians there once constituted nearly half of the population and played a vital role in its economic development. They deserve a fair share of our attention, just as those who live in Western countries do. The vanquished and the victors, the subalterns and the sahibs, all have equal claim on our attention. We have sought to provide extensive treatment of particular communities where Indians have been prominent in their countries; but clearly there are areas where Indian communities have been settled for a long period of time as traders, merchants or professionals without having a significant effect on the countries of their residence. These communities have been allocated less space but have been included in the volume because they, too, are an integral part of the diaspora.

We have also tried to be even-handed in the coverage of the different phases of Indian migration and settlement. Much of recent public and scholarly attention has been on the contemporary, post-war period. This is understandable given the recent explosion in the size of the diaspora, the focus on its relevance to India's economic needs and imperatives, and the ongoing debates in academia about questions of identity and culture. However, one purpose of this volume is to show that Indian migration and settlement has a long and complex history, which explains our attention to the historical evolution of the Indian diaspora. We hope that the encyclopedia will show just how rich, varied, contradictory and confusing the subject is, defiantly rejecting the easy grasp of smug theory.

With the completion of this project, our own editorial journey has come to an end. It has been an exhilarating journey of exploration and discovery. We now present the fruits of our collective endeavour to our readers, wherever they are, in the hope that this volume will introduce them to the accomplishments, setbacks, triumphs, tragedies and fascinating experiences of a community of people scattered around the world. At the end of our journey is, we hope, the beginning of yours.

Brij V. Lal

THE CONTEXT

Parts I–VII provide the basis for understanding the development of the Indian diaspora through the 19th and 20th centuries, and its character and functioning as seen in the first decade of the 21st century. It does this through an overview of the historical context in which the diaspora grew; an analysis of the political, social and administrative conditions within which the diaspora operated; and an account of the cultural life and achievements of the diaspora by the 21st century.

This photograph, taken in 1910, provides one of many iconic views of the diaspora. It shows The Grange at Agra Patna, a tea plantation in the central uplands of Ceylon. These plantations were one of the diaspora's many settings, since the entire workforce of the plantations was filled by labourers recruited from southern India.

THE INDIAN CONTEXT

The Indian diaspora is a representation of India: its peoples, regions, values, and diverse and appealing range of cultures. Through the movement of people and ideas, Indian influence was important throughout Asia and Europe before the 19th century. However, it was in the 19th and 20th centuries that large-scale migration from India across the world took place. It is from this migration that the diaspora was formed and it is crucial, therefore, to understand the circumstances in India that led to this major movement of Indian people who created the communities which comprise the diaspora.

The people who migrate and settle carry with them 'cultural artefacts'—ideas and values in terms of religion, artistic endeavour, social norms, political thought, ethical suppositions and organisational attitudes from the country in which they have been born and raised, in this case India. Understanding how particular diasporic communities work, their nature and organisational form, requires a sense of the India from which people came and the 'cultural baggage' that they brought with them to their new homes.

INDIA AS 'HOMELAND'

A DIASPORA EXISTS precisely because it remembers the 'homeland'. Without this memory, the image of 'their' India, these migrants and settlers would be simply people in a new setting, into which they merge, bringing little or nothing to the new 'home', accepting in various ways and forms the mores and attitudes that already exist in their new country and society.

The people of the diaspora, however, do not merely settle in new countries: they recreate in their socio-economic, political and cultural institutions a version of India, and they maintain perceptions of that homeland they remember.

Map 1.1 shows the five geographical zones of the Indian subcontinent: the Himalayas; the plains of the major northern river systems; the Vindhya range; the southern plateau; and the southern river valleys and coastal plains.

Map 1.1

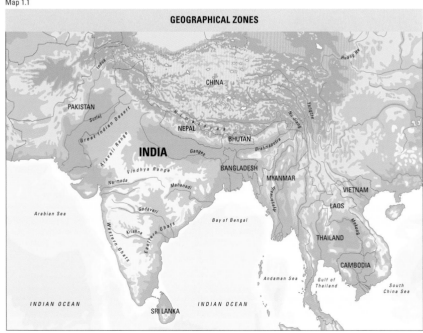

GEOGRAPHICAL ZONES

Later generations will have their ideas of India formed by their upbringing in host societies, views passed on from their parents and the wider diasporic society. Their perceptions of India can also come from their reading of the literature or art of India that is available to them. They may reconstruct their own position in terms of the great 'legends' of Indian society, for example, that of the exile or 'banishment' of Rama, in which they see their own fate visualised. In more modern times, their vision of India may be refreshed through return visits, travellers' tales or representations in various forms of media—cinema, cable television or cyberspace.

Even if steps are never taken to return, the longing to be once more in the homeland, to be again the people they see themselves as having been, is an important trait of the diaspora. It does not matter that the return may bring disillusionment, an experience of 'an area of darkness' rather than the 'remembered' or 'imagined' homeland.

India, on the other hand, has a changing or evolving set of perceptions and responses to the diaspora and its people. Diasporic communities may become valued as extensions of India, as a marker of Indian influence, a source of pride and of investment. Expressions of interest or concern, and indications of involvement from India, will vary over time, according to India's own position in the world and/or the particular sections of India and Indian society involved.

There have been differing views of India from the diaspora as well, shaped by the particular circumstances of their movement from the subcontinent. Colonial, nationalist or business diasporas, for example, will differ in their perceptions depending on time and political circumstances. Whatever the differences in attitude, from complete disinterest to feelings of superiority, or from concern for the condition of diasporic people to demands for diasporic involvement in India, an understanding of the links between India and the diaspora depends on an understanding of the Indian context.

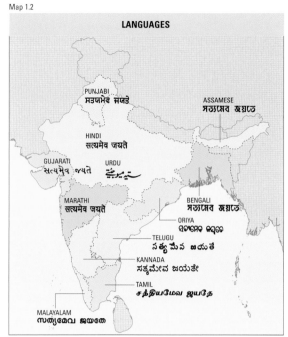

Map 1.2

LANGUAGES

Source: Robin Jeffrey, India's Newspaper Revolution, *2000.*

Figure 1.1

LANGUAGE FAMILIES REPRESENTED IN SOUTH ASIA

Indo-European family: Iranian and Indic branches

Iranian branch Pashtho (Pakistan) Baluchi (Pakistan)	**Indic branch** Urdu (Pakistan), Dvivehi (Maldives), Sinhala (Sri Lanka), Nepali (Nepal) ***Classical languages:*** Sanskrit, Pali ***Modern languages:*** Hindi, Bengali, Oriya, Assamese, Marathi, Gujarati, Punjabi, Maiyhili, Kashmiri, Sindhi, Konkani, etc.

Sino-Tibetan family: Tibeto-Burman branch

Jonkha and Tibetan (Bhutan), Newari and Sherpa (Nepal), Mizo and Manipuri (Northeast India)

Dravidian: North, Central and Southern branches

Northern and Central branch Brahui, Gondi, Kurukh, Kui	**Southern branch** Tamil, Telugu, Kannada, Malayalam, Tulu, tribal languages of the Nilgiris

Austro-Asiatic family: Munda branch

Tribal languages of Northern and Eastern India

Courtesy of Ulrike Niklas, Director, Institute of Indology and Tamil Studies, University of Cologne, Germany.

Map 1.2 shows the scripts of the major regional languages in India. The text on the map is India's national motto, 'Satyameva Jayate', which means 'truth alone triumphs'.

THE LAND

India is a complex land with marked regional variations and a rich history. This section introduces the main geographical and historical elements of the subcontinent from which, over time, Indian migrants moved to regions around the world.

Relationship with Asia

The Indian subcontinent has clear lines of communication with West Asia, Central Asia and Tibet, China and Southeast Asia through the Indian Ocean and the mountain passes of the Hindu Kush and the Himalayas, which mark its northern frontier. Historically, it has been active in reaching out to these neighbouring regions and, in turn, received people from and was influenced by them.

Geographical zones

The subcontinent has five major geographical zones: the high mountain ranges and their foothills in the north; the plains of the major river systems, Indus, Ganga (or Ganges) and Brahmaputra; the uplands and forest areas of central India; the southern plateau known as the Deccan; and the river valleys and coastal plains of the southern peninsula.

The northernmost frontier with Asia lies along the massive mountain range of the Hindu Kush and the Himalayas, running some 2500 km from Iran and Afghanistan in the west, along the border with Tibet, to southern China and Myanmar in the east. There has always been traffic across the mountains; nonetheless, the mountain range allowed the development of distinctively 'Indian' social, economic and cultural features within the subcontinent.

The great riverine plains of the north were regions of agricultural development. The Indus and Ganga valleys were the initial sites of sustained agrarian and urban growth. The central uplands, the Vindhyas, marked off the plains from the southern peninsula. The Deccan was drier and had less favoured soils than the river valleys, but it provided important linkages between the 'North' and the 'South'. The peninsula had its major agricultural regions and urban centres in the western and eastern coastal plains, in the river valleys, and the fertile deltas of the great southern rivers, such as the Godavari, Krishna and Kaveri.

Regions

The Indian subcontinent is divided into regions which have distinctive social and cultural formations. These are closely correlated to the regional languages of historic India. The regions are drawn together by overarching 'Indian' civilisational ties which are expressed, for example, in the traditional importance of pilgrimages to sacred sites in the 'four quarters', which mark the cultural frontiers of India.

Language

Language has been the clearest way to distinguish regions and identify people and culture. India has 14 regional languages as well as hundreds of languages with smaller groups of followers. Regional languages embody the culture of its people, acting as a repository of literary forms and folk knowledge. The languages affirm and reinforce regional distinctions of dress, food, music, dance and other art forms. In independent India, the states were reorganised in 1956 along linguistic lines (see Map 1.9), although Hindi and its related dialects spread over a number of northern states. In some states, more than one language is spoken, but the dominant language provides the basis of the state's borders.

Indian languages are members of separate 'language families'. The largest of these are the Indo-Aryan and Dravidian groups. There is linguistic influence in some areas of Sinic and Austronesian languages. Arabic has also had considerable influence on the development of Urdu and other regional languages.

Script is an important way of distinguishing language families. The Devanagari script (with regional variants) is used in the case of the Indo-Aryan languages: Sanskrit, Hindi, Rajasthani, Punjabi, Kashmiri, Bengali, Oriya, Assamese, Gujarati and Marathi. Dravidian scripts are used in the Dravidian languages: Tamil, Telugu, Kannada and Malayalam. Arabic-Persian script is used in Urdu, and also by Muslims writing some regional languages.

The elephant-headed deity Ganesh has ties to language and writing. Legend has it that he broke off his own tusk and used it to write the epic Mahabharata.

The ancient city of Mohenjo Daro was one of the largest Bronze Age cities in the world. It was built on baked mud-brick platforms to protect the city from the flood waters of the Indus.

This sculpture of a 'Priest King' gives some idea of the religious beliefs of Mohenjo Daro. Though the names of their gods are unknown and their language has yet to be deciphered, it is believed that a king who was worshipped like a god ruled the city of Harappa.

The Buddhist caves of Ajanta, carved into the face of a horseshoe-shaped gorge along the Waghore River, feature well-preserved paintings.

HISTORIC INDIA

The frontiers of historic India are co-terminus with the Indian subcontinent. India's history is a record of development from prehistoric time. The growth of agrarian and urban societies; the rise of important regional cultures; and the waxing and waning of great empires make this history a rich tapestry of human endeavour and cultural formation.

The Indus Valley civilisation
Urban civilisation in the subcontinent began with the Indus Valley civilisation, centred on the cities of Harappa and Mohenjo Daro. Archaeological exploration has shown that urban settlement extended beyond the Indus Valley. This civilisation declined because of climatic changes in the 2nd millennium BC. Its decline was also linked to the arrival of the nomadic Indo-Aryan pastoralists around 1500 BC.

Opening the Gangetic plain
The Indo-Aryans settled first in the Indus region and then in Punjab. With the development of iron tools after 1000 BC, this northern society began clearing substantial forests of the Ganga Valley. This created a base for the expansion of new urban cultures in the north.

The peninsula
Developments of a similar kind were also to be seen in the peninsula from the 6th century BC in the northwest Deccan (what is now Maharashtra), in the area of the northeast Deccan that was to become Andhra Pradesh, and in the southern Tamil, Kannada and Malayalam regions. By the 4th century BC in the Tamil regions, the Sangam Tamil poems speak of Chola and Pandya kings on the Coromandel Coast (Cholamandalam), the Pandyan domains centred on Madurai, and the Chera domains in what is now Kerala. What was distinctive of this area was the importance of maritime trade and the development of ports on both the eastern and western coasts. It was in the southern regions, between 50 BC and 50 AD, that there is evidence of India's trade with the Roman Empire and the beginnings of trade with Southeast Asia.

Imperial aspirations
While there were, in early societies, forms of tribal 'republics', the nature of the Indian polity overall took the monarchical form. In time, some of these kingdoms reached a stage where—in terms of their economic strength, state control and the provision of armies—they could undertake the task of merging large parts of India into an empire under their control. The first expression of an imperial pan-Indian ambition was that of Magadha under the Mauryas (c. 323–185 BC). Drawing on their control of trade along the Ganga, invaluable resources of iron and the development of a strong state apparatus, the Mauryans were able to bring much of North India—from Magadha to the Indus, the Vindhyan uplands, the Deccan and Kalinga (present-day Orissa)—into their empire. The Mauryan emperor Ashoka addressed several of his edicts to people in the Deccan and the more southerly areas.

This imperial ambition would be repeated under the Guptas (c. 3rd–6th centuries AD), the Delhi Sultanate (c. 13th–16th centuries AD) and the Mughals (c. 16th–18th centuries AD). There were important empires in the central and Deccan regions too, such as the Chalukyas (c. 5th–8th century AD) and the Rashtrakutas (c. 8th–10th century AD). Similarly in the south, major kingdoms included the Pallavas (c. 3rd–8th century AD), the Pandyas (c. 3rd–10th century AD), the Cholas (9th–13th centuries AD), and the Vijayanagara Empire (14th–16th centuries AD), which aspired to unite the southern peninsula. The imperial regimes ensured that India was seen and understood to be a major state within Asia and, at its strongest, predominant in southern Asia.

RELIGION AND SOCIETY
The religious systems of so-called tribal people represent the earliest religious forms in the subcontinent. The earliest urban cultures in the Indus Valley (4th to 2nd

Map 1.3

THE MUGHAL EMPIRE

Mughal Empire in 1605
Expansion to 1707

Kabul • Srinagar •
Kandahar • Lahore •
Multan •
Delhi •
Fatehpur Sikri • Agra • Lucknow •
SIND Allahabad • Patna •
BUNDELKHAND Tanda •
Ahmadabad • Ujjain • Palamau •
Burhanpur • CHOTA
Ellichpur • NAGPUR Cuttack •
Daulatabad •
Ahmadinagar • Bay of Bengal
Arabian Sea BIJAPUR • Golconda (nominally independent)
Pernukanda •
Calicut •
Madura •

Source: K. J. Schmidt, Atlas and Survey of South Asian History, *1999.*

millennia BC) provide evidence of other evolving systems and suggest that the Indus Valley culture had important influences on the later development of Hinduism.

Vedic religion and the development of Hinduism

The origins of the major religious system that developed in India, which came to be known as Hinduism, were the religious ideas and practices of the Indo-Aryan peoples. They brought with them, as oral texts, the religious ideas enshrined in the Vedas—collections of hymns to a pantheon of gods. These texts structured society to ensure the influence of the *brahmanas* ('those who prayed and who knew the secrets of ritual'). The Vedas were also the source for the development of a poetic and philosophical basis from which was to come important fundamental aspects of the nascent Hindu system. Supported by the social hegemony of the *brahmanas* and the Kshatriya ('those who ruled and fought'), that system developed over the millennium from 1500 BC to 500 BC.

The later Vedic period saw the development of a corpus of sacred texts, the Upanishads and the Puranas, and the formulation of the earliest versions of the epics, the Ramayana and the Mahabharata. Many of the incipient ideas in the Vedas were commented and elaborated upon in these texts, laying the foundation for the development of the caste system as well as the Hindu concepts of dharma (social and sacred obligations), karma (action), samsara (rebirth), and the atman (soul) seeking unity with the brahman (universal soul).

Buddhism and Jainism

In the 6th century BC came the reforming movements. The most significant were Jainism and Buddhism. Based on Mahavira's teachings, Jainism emphasised the purification of the soul through ahimsa (non-violence) and frugality. Initially confined to the Ganga plain, it was particularly popular among trading groups and became dominant in western India between the 11th and 14th centuries AD.

Buddhism, which was founded by Gautama Buddha, a contemporary of Mahavira, rejected caste and taught a 'Middle Way' between asceticism and ritual. It had widespread appeal. Buddhism was further strengthened when it was embraced by Emperor Ashoka and adopted as the religion of the Mauryan Empire. From the 3rd century BC to the 5th century AD, Buddhism became the dominant religious form in northern and eastern India and in what is today Maharashtra.

In the 5th century AD, however, Hinduism returned to strength under the Gupta Empire in the north. With this, a reassertion of brahman influence began to articulate 'Hinduism' in ways that would lead to its dominance in both the north and the south. It became, through its many forms and assimilationist character, the religion of a great majority of the people. Buddhism, which was carried to Sri Lanka, Southeast and East Asia, began to fade as a separate religion in India.

The formation of Indian Islam

Islam arrived in the subcontinent in the 8th century AD as part of the early expansion of Islam beyond Arabia. The Arabs brought with them the religious ideas of the Prophet Muhammad and established the first Muslim societies in Sind and the Multan region of Punjab. In other parts, notably the Malabar and Coromandel regions, the establishment of the northwestern Muslim societies was matched by the growth of Muslim communities as a result of contact with Arab seafarers and merchants.

Even so, these Indian Muslim communities represented relatively isolated outposts of Islam until the beginning of the more decisive movements from 1000 AD of Muslim warriors from Central Asia and Iran to North India. Muslim sultanates developed from bases in Delhi, Agra and Lahore. Islam also moved across the north to establish a stronghold in the east in Bengal. The Delhi sultans and the Mughal emperors also had visions of penetrating the south. Though these plans were never fully realised, Islam did move throughout the subcontinent, bringing with it other influences. The Sufi preachers, in particular, combined Indian and Islamic mysticism to create new schools of Indian Sufism that aided the spread of the religion and created new Muslim communities.

Sikhism

The spread of Islam led some to conceive not of 'conversion' but of syncretic developments to blend elements from different religions. Both within the *bhakti*

The Mughal Empire was founded by Babur in 1526. During the reign of his grandson, Akbar (1556–1605), the empire stretched from present-day Afghanistan in the west to Bengal in the east. Akbar's successors extended Mughal rule to southern India.

The original Guru Granth Sahib, the holy text of the Sikhs, is housed in Amritsar's Golden Temple.

Christianity is best given architectural expression in Goa, once a Portuguese enclave. Pictured here is the Church of Our Lady of the Immaculate Conception at Panaji, consecrated in 1541.

(devotional) traditions of Hinduism and the Sufi traditions of Islam, such syncretism awakened possibilities of new, more egalitarian religious practice. One of the most significant products of such thinking was the development of Sikhism and the idea of the Khalsa, based on Guru Nanak's teachings in the 16th century AD.

Christianity, Judaism and Zoroastrianism

Additional elements in India's religious landscape derived from religions outside the subcontinent. In a number of cases, these movements remained and became important, if minor, religious traditions. The earliest was Christianity, brought in its Syrian form by St. Thomas in the 1st century AD to southern India. Judaism also arrived, initially as a result of the Jewish 'dispersal' after 70 AD. This became the foundation of the Jewish community in Cochin, Kerala, and the Bene Israel's preferred explanation for their community's existence in western India.

The other small but very influential group were the Zoroastrians (Parsis) who fled Iran in the face of Islamic persecution. They brought Zoroastrianism to Gujarat, and from there, as Bombay developed, to the city in which they were highly successful in trade, manufacturing and business.

Historic India's influence

India gained much from interactions with other cultures. At the same time, through merchants, monks, envoys and adventurers, peaceful cultural exchanges and conflict, historic India was able to extend a considerable influence on the development of 'sacred' and social ideas and philosophies, art, architecture, mathematics and science in neighbouring cultures, and from there to other parts of the world.

The expansion of Buddhism

In terms of religious ideas, India was responsible for the expansion of Buddhism. Through Buddhist envoys sent by Emperor Ashoka in 250 BC, Buddhism gained widespread acceptance in Ceylon. From there it spread in the Theravada form to Burma and the rest of Southeast Asia. From the northernmost regions of the Mauryan Empire in Taxila, Buddhism also spread to Central Asia and, following that route, to Tibet, China, Korea, Japan, Vietnam and Mongolia. As a result of this expansion, sacred Buddhist sites in India became places of pilgrimage for Buddhists in other Asian lands.

Indian influence in Southeast Asia

In Southeast Asia, Indian religious specialists played an important role in the development of ideas of monarchy and the construction of state power in the early empires. Until the 4th century AD, Sanskrit was recognised as an official language in many parts of Southeast Asia. The Khmer capital of Angkor shows very strong Hindu influences. In addition to the mainland Southeast Asian states (Thailand, Cambodia and Myanmar), Hindu ideas were important in the archipelago as well. In Java, the Prambanan temple and the magnificent Buddhist stupa of Borobudur in Yogyakarta remain testimonies of this influence. In addition, the great Indian epics, the Mahabharata and the Ramayana, have had enduring cultural effects in terms of folk, popular and high culture, and in the development of the arts, dance and drama of this region. Like Hinduism and Buddhism before, Islam too was brought to Southeast Asia from India.

Cambodia's Angkor Wat is a repository of Hindu-influenced carvings and architecture.

Mathematics

India's most significant influence is possibly in the development of mathematics. The decimal system of numeral notation is believed to have first been used in India, from where it spread to other parts, as did the use of the number 'zero', which may have come into use in India even before the 6th century AD. Medieval Indian mathematicians, such as Aryabhata (c. 5th century AD), Brahmagupta (c. 7th century AD), Mahavira (c. 9th century AD) and Bhaskara (c. 12th century AD), made several mathematical discoveries, including infinity and the approximate value of π (pi), before similar developments elsewhere.

RELIGION AND THE SOCIAL ORDER

Religion played a social role in defining the community in which people grew up and in guiding life choices, lifestyles and life chances for most people. It also became the basis of social interaction and, on occasion, social conflict, if the values or interests of a particular community were threatened.

Caste and social power

Religion's relation to the social order in India is very clear. The first and most obvious sign is the importance of the institutions of caste and the relationship of caste to social power. From the Vedic period onwards, Hinduism, throughout its development up to the modern period, was based upon the system of caste. Firstly, this was in the form of *varnashramadharma*—the proper conduct of one's life in relation to one's position in society (varna) and the stage of life that one has reached (*asrama*). The nature of social and sacred obligations was tied to the occupation, marriage and civil conditions resulting from one's birth in a *jati* (birth group). The *jati*, which has a rank within the varna system, became the operative caste group for practical matters such as endogamy, occupation, kinship and commensality. Caste, moreover, brought hierarchical elements into play in Hindu—and to some extent even in Muslim, Sikh and Christian—communities, linked as it was to the *jati* system, occupation and to practices that had a bearing on ritual purity.

Sectarianism

A further aspect of religious social concern was the sectarian divisions within such communities. Hinduism could be conceived of as 'one' religion, but it also could be divided between those devoted to a particular deity (such as Shiva or Vishnu) or those who followed particular teachings. The Muslim community was split into Sunni and Shia, and divided in some places and periods by competing Sufi brotherhoods and by particular sectarian bases of communities, such as the Ismailis. Christians and Jews, even though much smaller in size, also had similar divisions. Christians were divided into Catholic, Orthodox and Protestant, and those different 'churches' made claims with regard to priority in faith and the correct understanding of the Word.

MODERN INDIA: COLONIAL RULE AND ITS EFFECTS

European colonial intrusion in India caused a major disjuncture in the history of the subcontinent. It brought about fundamental changes in some areas and led to the reformulation of tradition in others. The effects of colonial rule were among the most basic reasons for the large-scale migration of Indians from the subcontinent in the 19th and 20th century.

European contact and expansion

By the end of the 15th century, the Indian Ocean maritime route to India was open to Europeans. Portuguese, Dutch, English, French and Danish maritime traders established settlements in India from which they could trade. The rivalries of these European powers led to involvement and conflict in local politics. It was from such struggles that the English eventually emerged as the imperial rulers of India.

The East India Company

The British East India Company (EIC) arrived in India in 1600, when India was under Mughal power. Through a charter put in place by Queen Elizabeth I, the EIC had a monopoly on British trade from Asia to Europe. To facilitate this trade, the company established offices and warehouses, known as factories, in India and elsewhere along this maritime route. These factories enabled participation in Asian 'country trade', which provided part of the 'investment' needed for the purchase of homeward-bound cargoes of Indian textiles and spices, Chinese tea and Yemeni coffee.

By the mid-18th century, the political situation in India had fragmented considerably. The decline of Mughal power was paralleled by the rise of new regional powers in North India, the expansion of Maratha power in the Deccan and political changes in South India. These developments, a source of insecurity for the rising European powers, intensified the rivalry between the British EIC and its French counterpart, leading to the reinforcement of their military capabilities in India as they vied to form alliances with local powers.

Victory over the French in South India saw the British strengthen their position at Madras. More significantly, following the battles of Plassey (1757) and Buxar (1764), where the armies of Siraj-ud-daulah and Mir Kasim were routed by the EIC's forces, the British were placed in a novel position, as the Diwan, of administering Bengal's land revenues, nominally at the behest of the Mughal ruler. These battles marked a watershed. They entrenched the EIC further in local politics, leading to wider conflict with Indian states and ultimately transforming the trading company into a colonial empire that would come to rule most of India.

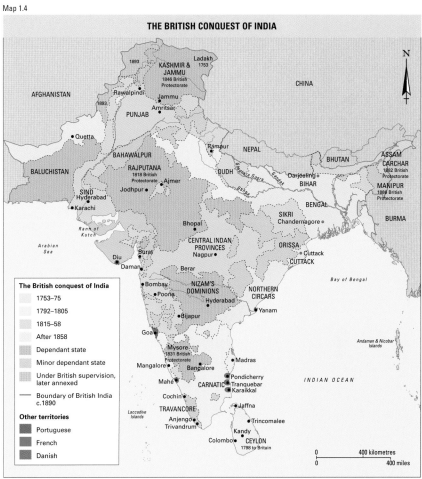

Map 1.4

THE BRITISH CONQUEST OF INDIA

The British conquest of India
- 1753–75
- 1792–1805
- 1815–58
- After 1858
- Dependant state
- Minor dependant state
- Under British supervision, later annexed
- Boundary of British India c.1890

Other territories
- Portuguese
- French
- Danish

Source: Ian Barnes and Robert Hudson, The History Atlas of Asia, *1998.*

Acquisition of territories (1757–1856)

The acquisition of territories which came to constitute British India by the end of the 1850s began with grants in Madras in the 1750s and the acquisition of Bengal, Bihar and Orissa by 1765. The remainder of the Madras Presidency was acquired in the 1790s and the first decade of the 19th century. Expansion through the Ganges Valley and into Orissa and Gujarat occurred in the period between 1801 and 1805. The Maratha territories, which would constitute the larger part of the Bombay Presidency, were annexed between 1817–22. Assam was taken in the mid-1820s, Sind in 1843 and Punjab in 1849. The final major annexation in 1856 was that of Avadh (Oudh), which comprised, by then, the central districts of the vital Ganges Valley.

The great revolt

By the 1850s, the results of EIC rule had begun to affect various social groups. The 'mutiny' by sepoys in the Bengal Army, following the annexation of Avadh, triggered a protest movement in many parts of North India against the EIC. This had the effect of rolling back EIC rule temporarily.

The British government, however, had the resources to

reinforce their position, crush the revolt and return to power; but they did so by coming forward in a clear imperialist position. With the EIC bankrupt as a result of the revolt, India was now placed directly under the Crown government.

Jewel in the crown

By the end of the 1850s, the British were in complete control of the subcontinent. The Indian empire was established as the 'the brightest jewel in the Crown'. In the 1870s, Victoria became 'Queen-Empress' to emphasise the British succession to the earlier empires and to exploit the Indian monarchical tradition to the utmost.

British India included the three original presidencies of Madras, Bengal and Bombay. Madras comprised the southeastern areas along the Coromandel Coast and its hinterland, and was made up of districts in which the southern languages of Tamil and Telugu were spoken, plus some smaller Kannada- and Malayalam-speaking areas. Bengal included Bihar and Orissa. The Bombay Presidency linked Bombay city to the territories in Maharashtra and Gujarat. Administrative areas which were distinguished from the presidencies were called 'provinces'. These comprised the North-Western

After 1858, the British directly controlled about 60 per cent of the Indian subcontinent. The remaining 40 per cent were states ruled by Indian princes subject to British 'paramountcy'.

The coat of arms of the British East India Company, c. 1730.

Following the Sepoy Mutiny, India was placed under direct Crown rule, as proclaimed by Queen Victoria in this document, dated 1858.

23

Provinces and Oudh (later the United Provinces), the Central Provinces, Punjab, Sind and Assam. Altogether, British India occupied some 60 per cent of the subcontinent.

Not all territories in India were directly ruled. Some rulers became allies or were accommodated by the British. In effect, a system of protected, though subordinated, 'princely states' developed. They were subject to the paramount power of the British and they were liable, if they did not follow British prescription, to be unseated. These princely states, over 500 in total, made up much of the remainder of the subcontinent, alongside small pockets such as Pondicherry, under the control of the French, and Goa, Daman and Diu under the Portuguese.

British 'Raj' in India

British imperial rule, 'the Raj', lasted until 1947. Colonial rule in India was underpinned by Britain's 'civilising mission', the idea of racial hierarchy and the superiority of the West. Within this context, there were different approaches taken depending on the influence of debates and developments in Britain and India. The initial view of India and Indians in Orientalist discourse acknowledged that India was once a great civilisation, yet British rule was justified as necessary in order to elevate Indians from their degraded state. Other ideologies were less sympathetic. Evangelicalism, for example, viewed Indian civilisation as essentially barbaric and saw British rule as necessary to change the very nature of Indian society. After the revolt of 1857, the dominant ideology, Victorian liberalism, emphasised British paternalism and limited reform as active change was deemed both 'dangerous', in that this would catalyse opposition, and 'pointless', since Indians, it was believed, would never reach the level of Englishmen.

The colonial administrative structure in India evolved over time. During the EIC period, difficulties in communication meant that officials had considerable leeway in administering local areas. There were governors at each of the presidencies and, until 1853, the governor of Bengal was also the governor-general. During this period, provinces had lieutenant-governors or chief commissioners as head of the administration. At the capital there was a secretariat staffed by EIC servants. From 1793, these servants had no commercial or trading functions; they became full-time administrators dealing with affairs from the district level as administrators—collectors and district magistrates or deputy-commissioners—and at higher levels as commissioners.

Following the revolt, Crown rule replaced the EIC Raj. The Government of India Act of 1858, passed by the British government at Westminster, resulted in the establishment of the India Office, headed by a secretary of state for India. In India itself, power resided in the governor-general of India, who became known as the viceroy. While answerable to the secretary of state, the viceroy controlled the administration, which was manned by the agency of the Indian Civil Service (ICS), 'the steel frame' of the Raj as the British prime minister, Lloyd George, called it.

In addition to this steel frame, control of the Raj depended on various pillars such as the army and police.

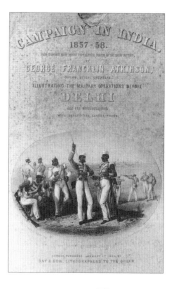

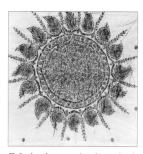

Fabric showcasing kamdani *work in a classical motif, a traditional craft of India.*

Painting depicting two men seated on the floor weaving baskets, c. 1840–50. The de-industrialisation of India in the 19th century forced many artisans to search for new work opportunities elsewhere.

From the earliest times, the EIC needed elements of military power and had developed the base of an army, drawn from the military labour markets that were important in various regions. In the process of acquiring control over the subcontinent, that army had grown considerably. It numbered 100,000 by 1789 and expanded to some 214,000 at the time of the revolt in 1857. From that period onwards, an army of approximately a quarter of a million troops was maintained, effectively making the Raj a 'garrison-state'. In addition, the police force was expanded during the period between 1857 and 1947 and became the key instrument of repression in containing peasant rebellions and growing political dissatisfaction in India.

The agrarian base and agrarian change

Colonial India was overwhelmingly an agrarian society, although artisanal manufactures were always important in terms of both domestic and international markets. The basic income of the state was derived from land revenue—the 'king's share' of the harvest—and the system under which this was assessed and collected was vital in all Indian systems of government and control. The effect of British rule was thus felt most widely in this area of revenue collection. In very general terms, variants of *zamindari* (landlord) were used in the north and *raiyatwari* (peasant proprietor) in the south.

British officials in different provinces experimented with such systems, usually without a full understanding of the system or its likely effects. Important changes in property rights, landholding patterns and relations between peasants and those who exacted the revenue share from them were thus effected.

The results were marked: the level of assessment was often too high and the demand on revenue payers was therefore heavy and difficult to meet regularly, particularly in poor harvest conditions. British rigidity in administering the law for arrears brought widespread changes of tenure and a noticeable increase in the control of land by moneylenders and financiers. Peasants, who now found themselves in the position of 'tenants', came under pressure as rent levels increased both directly and indirectly, leading to a growth in rural debt, the loss of land and an increase in rural migration to other parts of India; and for some, even beyond India as they looked for alternative work opportunities.

Artisanal production and manufacture

One of the original attractions for the British was access to high-quality textiles in India for new markets in Britain and Europe. However, the industrial changes that had taken place in England by the 19th century undermined the position of Indian producers in this trade—the

spinners, weavers and decorators of traditional fabrics—particularly as the changes affected textile manufacturing in the new mills. India experienced de-industrialisation as its artisanal spinners found it difficult to compete with mill-spun yarn in terms of the quality of the yarn and handloom, and weavers found it increasingly difficult to compete in terms of quality or price in the mass market that was opening up. Once again, therefore, in the Indian countryside, pressure on traditional occupations increased the mobility of artisans, who had to search for new work opportunities. India's international trading position changed radically. By the 1870s, it was transformed, as Peter Robb puts it, 'from being an exporter of processed goods and an importer of bullion to being an exporter of raw materials and an importer of manufactures.'

Education and the role of the English language

English education became a profound influence in the Indian empire because of the role it played in shaping new generations of Indian public men. With the move in the 1850s to establish the first universities in the three presidency towns of Calcutta, Madras and Bombay, the professional education of generations of Indian civil servants, lawyers, doctors and journalists was cast in the English format. Primary and secondary education largely took second place to higher education so far as the Raj was concerned, and so, one required an urban base and entrance to higher levels of education in order to advance in this new imperial context. Reinforcing this Englishness was the strength of the pull from educational institutions in Britain itself: the 'cramming' schools for the 'competition-wallahs' who wished to compete with their British counterparts in the ICS entrance examination introduced in 1853; the public schools and venerable universities for students from the Indian elite; and the Inns of Court for those who sought the status of barristers-at-law.

The importance of this English education in India was enhanced by the fact that English, despite some recognition of Indian languages in some lower level courts and provincial school systems, became the language of administration, the courts, political comment and debate, and, to some extent, of 'modern' Indian culture. By the late 19th century, English and English education had a strong position in modern, urban India.

Religion in colonial India

At the advent of colonialism, the EIC tended to avoid questions of religion in public policy. It did not, for example, permit missionaries to operate in the company's territories. However, this situation began to change in a number of ways. After the renewal of its charter in 1813, which took away the company's monopoly status in India, missionaries were able to travel to EIC territories. A number did come, and this started a more public discussion of Hinduism and raised questions of reform and conversion. The growth of Evangelicalism in the Anglican Church in the 1820s, moreover, sharpened this discussion since even EIC servants espoused the importance of asserting Christianity's inherent superiority and the need to encourage conversion. Missionary activity to convert Indians to Christianity was a major aspect of religious development in the colonial period, firstly under the Portuguese and Dutch, and again during the British period in the 19th and 20th centuries.

Religious developments were important in other ways as well. Colonial power, religious institutions and juridical

Missionaries in Mysore distributing food to seated children, c. 1890s–1900s.

beliefs of the colonial state and its officials challenged, often very directly, the religious values of the colonised people, calling for 'reform' and changes in the treatment of women, lower-caste people, and members of other communities. Imperialism insisted on the superiority of the 'Empire', and this meant that a Christian or quasi-Christian questioning of colonised people and their religious values was implicit in the colonial relationship. This also meant that there was the possibility of religious competition, especially around the question of 'conversion', but also related to the implementation of new social and cultural doctrines. As a result, Indian religious groups themselves tended to become more assertive to better compete not merely with official church or sectarian groups but also with the other communities.

Change and 'reform'

In the colonial period, there were also reform movements within the major Indian religious groups. These movements often questioned established practices, believing them outdated and harmful to the position of Indian Hindus or Muslims. The Brahmo Samaj drew together an influential group of Bengali intellectuals and reformers, notably Raja Ram Mohan Roy, from the 1820s onwards. Later in the 19th century, Swami Dayanand Saraswati in Punjab organised the Arya Samaj with a programme of returning to the Vedic basis of Hinduism and strengthening the community through reforms and education.

Religion and colonial politics

Religious developments necessarily became linked with political life and activity. In the 19th and 20th centuries, as nationalist and anti-colonial political activities grew, at least parts of such activities became linked with religious elements and religious ideas. Muslim, Hindu or Sikh nationalism naturally developed in this competitive situation because the victory or success of one group could adversely affect the status or interest of another group. Moreover, the political struggle was for power in the society that would be freed. Religious groups felt the need to secure their place in the new power structure. In the Indian case, this would lead eventually to the partition of the country because Muslim groups were unable to accept their future within a Hindu-dominated nation.

THE DEVELOPMENT OF NATIONALISM

Because colonialism was so intrusive, Indian nationalism grew in protest against India's subjection to imperial rule and to refute imperialist claims of the benefits of this rule.

The concept of the Indian nation

In the colonial period, British administrative measures drew India together to a greater extent than had been possible earlier. Regional diversity remained, but the Raj exerted control across the whole of the subcontinent. In British India, the directly administered provinces of the Empire, that control, through the ICS, was patently clear. In the territories of princely India, the 'indirectly-ruled' princely states, which comprised two-fifths of the Indian territory and about a third of the population of the Indian subcontinent, its power was real, although it operated largely behind the throne, under the veil of 'paramountcy'.

This imperial control made united Indian political action more possible than at any previous time. Indian public life in the 1850s and 1860s was regionally framed—in the arenas provided by the presidencies and provinces—but by the 1870s, the concept of an 'Indian' arena began to be viable.

The Indian Association, formed in 1871 in Calcutta, was the beginning of united action. In 1885, the Indian National Congress (INC), comprising India's leading public figures, held its first meeting in Bombay. Following its establishment, a range of organisations arose—the All-India Muslim League (1906) and a decade later, the All-India Hindu Mahasabha.

The INC was the most significant of these Indian parties because it deliberately set out to overcome the boundaries of presidencies and provinces, and foster an Indian common ground for all who lived in India. The INC reinforced this vision by having no permanent meeting place: each annual congress moved to a new city so that each region, over time, had the chance to host

representatives from all other regions and all representatives had the opportunity to travel through 'the nation'.

Anti-colonial nationalism

Indian nationalism was born of the hurt caused by the loss of freedom, identity and traditional forms—a feeling that good government could never replace self-government. It was influenced by nationalist ideas elsewhere, in the US, Europe (France, Germany, Italy and Ireland) and Latin America. While these ideas and concerns had been expressed before in writing, by the late 19th and early 20th century, they came to the fore in India as the nationalist movement provided a new vehicle for their expression. 'Swaraj [self-rule] is my birthright,' said 'Lokamanya' Bal Gangadhar Tilak; no British notion of a 'civilising mission' could replace it.

Such discontent was added to by still more tangible concerns: the drain of India's economic and fiscal resources to pay for foreign rule; the de-industrialisation of the country to increase the industrial strength of British mines and mills; and the telling signs of political 'divide and rule' forcing communities and regions apart through favouritism and administrative connivance.

What developed were different inflections and competitive positions: 'moderate' and 'extremist' nationalism; Muslim and Hindu nationalism; and regional concerns for nationality and language. There were movements of violent opposition in the *anushilan samitis* ('revolutionary' group); but stronger than these was the steady move towards mass nationalism, a nationalism of the people beyond the cities, universities and the English-educated arena.

The INC was the major player in the rise of nationalism and it bore the brunt of nationalist development—the clash of moderates and extremists and the debate over strategy and tactics. Nonetheless, this strengthened the nationalist argument for recognition of the need for Indians to have more representative and responsible government in India. The Indian Councils Act of 1892 somewhat broadened representation, and the 1909 Morley-Minto reforms took the process further forward

Gandhi adopted the traditional turban (top, c. 1916) of the Gujarati bania upon his return to India, but feeling that an emphasis on caste distinction was dangerous to national unity, he adopted what came to be known as the 'Gandhi cap' (below, 1921), the typical headgear of people throughout Gujarat regardless of caste. He later abandoned this practice as well.

The first meeting of the Indian National Congress, in Bombay, December 1885. It was founded by retired British civil servant Allan Octavian Hume.

with an enhancement of the role of the legislative councils and an increase in the number of Indian representatives.

Mass nationalism: the return of Mahatma Gandhi

On the nationalist front, World War I (1914–18) saw a strengthening of more radical forces. In 1915, Tilak and Annie Besant developed the more direct tactics of the Home Rule Leagues, which marked the beginning of the move of the INC from elite politics to mass mobilisation.

That same year, Mohandas Karamchand Gandhi, who came to be known as Mahatma ('Great Soul') Gandhi, returned to India after 23 years in South Africa. There, he had mobilised Indian settlers in Natal and developed his major political weapon, satyagraha (truth force), which centred on non-violent resistance. His arrival in the Indian political scene marked a watershed in the development of a truly mass-based nationalist movement.

From 1915 to 1919, Gandhi began his involvement with Indian protest movements—peasants in Champaran, millworkers in Ahmedabad and farmers in Kheda—and began to build the INC into a mass movement of resistance to imperial rule on the basis of non-violent opposition through the concept of satyagraha. The first major test came with the Rowlatt satyagraha, denouncing the Rowlatt Acts, which restricted political activity through the continued employment of wartime anti-terrorist measures such as preventive detention. The Rowlatt satyagraha had its dreadful denouement in the Jallianwala Bagh massacre (1919) overseen by General Reginald Dyer.

The key period of mass nationalism was from the 1920s to the 1940s. Led by the Mahatma, a series of major campaigns—'Non-Cooperation', 'Civil Disobedience', 'Individual Satyagraha' and 'Quit India'—marshalled popular forces against imperial power and increasingly called into question the legitimacy of British rule. Combined with broader changes internationally, Britain's own position and the inability of the imperial power to do more than hold down the situation, particularly during World War II (1939–45), the stage was set by the early 1940s for the British to begin to concede that their position in India was untenable.

DIVIDED NATION

The development of nationalism in India and the call for complete independence (*Purna Swaraj*) was a prospect that alarmed many leaders of the Muslim community. The demand from such leaders became sharply focused: if independence was to come, it should be accompanied by the 'partition' of historic India so that the Muslims, who they claimed were a separate nation, would have their own homeland in which to govern themselves securely.

The origins of division

British colonial policies had encouraged divisions within the nation-in-the-making. The first overt signs came with the formation of the All-India Muslim League in 1906 and the British acceptance, in the Morley-Minto reforms of 1909, of the league's argument that Muslims needed a secure place in the Indian political system. The reforms saw the first moves to divide the Indian nation by giving separate recognition for the representation of Muslims. That move was part and parcel of the 'divide and rule' tactics that had been inherent in the partition of Bengal in 1905.

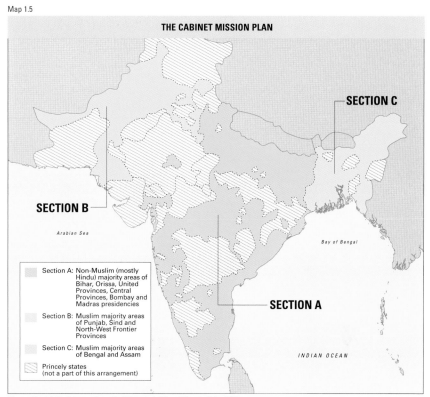

Map 1.5

THE CABINET MISSION PLAN

SECTION C

SECTION B

SECTION A

Arabian Sea

Bay of Bengal

INDIAN OCEAN

Section A: Non-Muslim (mostly Hindu) majority areas of Bihar, Orissa, United Provinces, Central Provinces, Bombay and Madras presidencies

Section B: Muslim majority areas of Punjab, Sind and North-West Frontier Provinces

Section C: Muslim majority areas of Bengal and Assam

Princely states (not a part of this arrangement)

Source: Joseph E. Schwartzberg, An Historical Atlas of South Asia, *1978.*

The division built into the legislatures in 1909 was strengthened by the nationalists themselves. In 1916, the Lucknow Pact, which sought to combine the efforts of the INC and the All-India Muslim League, sealed an agreement of separate electorates in Indian legislatures. Consequently, the Montagu-Chelmsford reforms, which produced the Government of India Act of 1919, built the complete system of legislatures on the basis of separate electorates. In fact, this act extended the principle to provide separate electorates for other groups, such as the Sikhs in Punjab, Anglo-Indians and Christians.

During the 1920s, there were numerous communal riots between Hindus and Muslims, especially in northern India. Election campaigning took on a communal tone. Political groups berated each other for protecting or advancing their own community's interests. On the Hindu side, the period saw the strengthening of political bodies such as the Hindu Mahasabha and the creation of the still more virulent Rashtriya Swayamsevak Sangh, which thought in terms of more militant Hindu political action. For many Muslims, the situation was increasingly one of frustration with the INC, which they felt was ignoring their concerns. This was especially so for a politician such as Muhammad Ali Jinnah, who saw his early hopes of Hindu-Muslim unity ebbing away to such an extent that he went into self-imposed exile in London.

'Pakistan' and the 'Pakistan movement' (1929–40)

By the end of the 1920s, the legacy of communal divisions experienced over the decade heightened the belief, in some circles, that India's Muslims needed a separate homeland. The idea had its first authoritative expression at the 1929 session of the All-India Muslim League, when the poet and intellectual from Punjab, Sir Muhammad Iqbal, called for a Muslim homeland in northwestern India, comprising the

The Cabinet Mission proposed a plan which would maintain the unity of India while allowing Muslim autonomy in areas where they were a majority (sections B and C on the map). Nehru opposed the plan because of the limited powers of the proposed central government.

Leaders of the INC and the Muslim League meeting with Viceroy Lord Louis Mountbatten on 2 January 1947 to discuss the transfer of power and the partition of India. CLOCKWISE FROM TOP: *Lord Mountbatten, M. A. Jinnah, Liaquat Ali Khan, Abdur Riab Nishtar, Baldev Singh, J. B. Kripalani, Vallabhbhai Patel and Jawaharlal Nehru.*

Symbols were allocated to political parties and independent candidates to enable illiterate segments of the population to vote. The INC's symbol is at the top left, two bulls with a yoke.

British Indian provinces of Punjab, Sind, Baluchistan and the North-West Frontier Province (NWFP). At the time, this call was an isolated one, seemingly merely the thoughts of a poet, and there was no immediate response by Muslim or other political groups.

The idea was reiterated in 1933 when a group of Indian Muslim students at Cambridge University published a pamphlet calling for a Muslim state, to which they gave the name 'Pakistan', derived from the names of the provinces to be included—P̲unjab, A̲fghania (by which they meant the NWFP), K̲ashmir, S̲ind and Baluchis̲tan—although it could also be construed as 'the land (-*stan*) of the pure (*pak*)'. Once again, the idea fell on deaf ears. Jinnah, in London, rejected it because he still hoped for an alliance between the All-India Muslim League and the INC. In 1934, he returned to India in response to calls from Muslim political groups to help strengthen the Muslim League in anticipation of the political reforms that would follow from the Government of India Act of 1935.

The coming of independence and Partition

The 1935 act introduced major electoral reforms. Legislatures at the central and provincial levels were expanded and the franchise widened considerably. At the 1937 elections, the INC won an overwhelming majority in Hindu-majority provinces, although it did not fare as well in seats reserved for the Muslim electorate. The Muslim League, which captured one-quarter of the Muslim seats it contested, expected that the INC would be open to sharing power in some provinces. That expectation was not fulfilled. In all the provinces where it had a clear majority, the INC took power in its own right and firmly turned away any suggestion of power sharing.

In fact, the INC went even further. Chastened by its showing in the Muslim seats, it resolved to gain the support of Muslims through a 'Muslim Mass Contact' campaign. Jinnah, who had assumed leadership of the Muslim League, saw this as a further hostile act that would impact directly on the party's position in the Muslim electorate. In response, the Muslim League increasingly emphasised that the dominance of the INC would endanger Muslims. It charged that blatantly Hindu

policies were adopted in Hindu-majority provinces in areas such as education and concluded that Muslims would not be safe under INC government.

In this state of mounting Muslim perception of political danger, the idea of a Muslim homeland gained support. The concerns came to a head at the 1940 meeting of the All-India Muslim League at Lahore. The Bengal Muslim leader, Fazlul Haq, moved a resolution for the formation of two groups of Muslim-majority provinces: one in the northwest comprising Punjab, Kashmir, Sind, Baluchistan and the NWFP; and the other in the east, encompassing Bengal. The Lahore resolution did not mention 'Pakistan' but came to be recognised as the Pakistan Resolution because from the time of its adoption, it dominated all discussions on the future of British India.

The decision to divide

By the time of the Pakistan Resolution, India was fully engaged in the 1939–45 war. The war was certainly one reason why the resolution was adopted, because given Britain's position early in the war and the INC's hostility to India's involvement (which had been done without consultation), there was a real possibility that Britain could be forced to withdraw from India, thus leaving the Muslims without adequate political safeguards. The INC, which had resigned its government position in protest against the war, mounted two major campaigns in 1940–41 and 1942 to put pressure on the British: 'Individual Satyagraha' in 1940–41 and 'Quit India' in 1942. As a result, the leadership of the INC spent the greater part of the war in gaol. INC leaders did meet Sir Richard Stafford Cripps when he came to negotiate what Gandhi termed 'a post-dated cheque on a failing bank' in 1941; otherwise, the war years were left to Jinnah to negotiate for 'Pakistan'.

Jinnah used the war years to strengthen the position of the All-India Muslim League, of which he became 'the Sole Spokesperson'. He built up the position of the party in Muslim-majority areas and had the ear of the British in the Hindu-majority provinces where governor's rule was in force. This paid off in the elections to the Indian legislatures that were held in 1945–46, after the end of the war. The Muslim League emerged as a political force to be dealt with; and with that strength, 'Pakistan', that is to say, the partition of India, became the main issue.

The British made two attempts to handle the partition issue: the first, in 1944, was the so-called Wavell Plan, to get agreement between the Muslim League and the INC; and the second was in 1946, when a Cabinet Mission attempted to find a compromise. Neither provided a base for a lasting agreement and, with growing communal tension stirred by rioting, partition was only a matter of time.

In fact, in February 1947, Lord Louis Mountbatten replaced Lord Wavell as the viceroy, and he came with instructions that the British would leave India by June 1948—'…united if possible, divided if necessary.' By 3 June 1947, Mountbatten published his plan that the partition would take place in August 1947. According to his plan, Bengal and Punjab would also be divided so that the Hindu-majority districts in both would be included in India and the Muslim-majority districts would be part of Pakistan. The drawing of the boundaries of Pakistan and India in Punjab, Bengal and Assam would be undertaken by a boundary commission headed by Sir Cyril Radcliffe after independence.

A polling station.

INDEPENDENCE AND PARTITION

Independence came to the Dominion of Pakistan on 14 August 1947 and India on 15 August 1947. In spite of the festivities, the attainment of independence was overshadowed by the colossal violence and displacement brought about as a result of Partition.

Partition brought two new national entities into being on the Indian subcontinent. As boundaries changed, older and long-standing arrangements became unsettled. Lines of communication, trading patterns and the movement of people and goods which had been traditionally related were now divided by new international boundaries. Partition also brought about the need for the division of assets between the new nations in terms of both infrastructure and monetary assets. A further set of changes arose as the princely states joined India and Pakistan. The existing boundaries were retained initially; however, in India, these states were quickly integrated into the new nation.

The impact of Partition

The major impact of Partition was the movement of people. In fact, around 18 million people moved: Hindus and Sikhs from West Punjab, Sind and the NWFP to India; Muslims from northern and western India to West Pakistan; Hindus from East Pakistan to West Bengal; and Muslims from Bihar and West Bengal to East Pakistan. This 'Transfer of Populations' began well before Partition was put into place; there were people certainly moving from early 1947 but this intensified after 14–15 August. This was especially true of Bengal, Assam and Punjab because of the partitioning of those provinces after the Radcliffe Award. The flight of Muslims from the United

The effects of Partition were widespread and devastating, and resulted in one of the largest mass transfers of populations in the world. Pictured here is the border city of Amritsar, where Hindus from Pakistan await the train bringing them further into India.

Provinces (UP), Bihar, Gujarat and Bombay, who in Pakistan came to be known as *muhajirs*, also increased after the formation of the new nations.

The movement of people was traumatic. As many as a million people were killed in this two-way movement, in many cases brutally murdered. Many more were assaulted, raped and abducted. Others took their own lives to avoid falling into the hands of aggressors.

In addition to redrawing cartographic boundaries, Partition called for the redrawing of nationality laws.

The Radcliffe Commission was required to demarcate the Muslim-majority areas in Punjab, Bengal and Assam which would be included in Pakistan.

Map 1.6

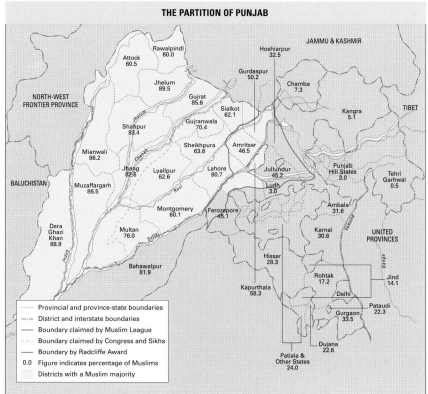

THE PARTITION OF PUNJAB

JAMMU & KASHMIR

Rawalpindi 60.0
Attock 60.5
Hoshiarpur 32.5
Gurdaspur 50.2
Jhelum 89.5
Chamba 7.3
Gujrat 85.6
Sialkot 62.1
Kangra 5.1
TIBET
NORTH-WEST FRONTIER PROVINCE
Gujranwala 70.4
Shahpur 83.4
Sheikhpura 63.6
Amritsar 46.5
Mianwali 86.2
Jhang 82.6
Lyallpur 62.6
Lahore 80.7
Jullundur 45.2
Punjab Hill States 3.0
Tehri Garhwal 0.5
BALUCHISTAN
Muzaffargarh 86.5
Ludh 3.0
Ambala 31.6
Dera Ghazi Khan 88.9
Montgomery 60.1
Ferozepore 45.1
Multan 76.0
Karnal 30.6
UNITED PROVINCES
Hissar 28.3
Bahawalpur 81.9
Rohtak 17.2
Jind 14.1
Kapurthala 58.3
Delhi
Pataudi 22.3
Gurgaon 33.5
Dujana 22.6
Patiala & Other States 24.0

········ Provincial and province-state boundaries
─·─·─ District and interstate boundaries
───── Boundary claimed by Muslim League
─ ─ ─ Boundary claimed by Congress and Sikhs
───── Boundary by Radcliffe Award
0.0 Figure indicates percentage of Muslims
▒ Districts with a Muslim majority

Source: O. H. K. Spate, The Partition of India and the Prospects of Pakistan, *1948.*

Map 1.7

THE PARTITION OF BENGAL AND ASSAM

BHUTAN
NEPAL
Darjeeling 24.0
Jalpaiguri 23.0
Goalpara 46.3
Kamrup 29.1
Cooch Behar 37.9
Dinajpur 50.2
Rangpur 71.4
Garo Hills 4.4
Khasi and Jaintia Hills 1.2
Malda 36.6
Bogra 64.0
Mymensingh 77.4
Sylhet 60.7
Cachar 37.9
BIHAR
Rajshahi 74.5
Murshidabad 56.6
Pabna 77.0
Dacca 67.3
Tripura 24.2
Birbhum 27.4
Faridpur 64.7
Tippera 27.1
Lushan Hills 0.0
Burdwan 17.8
Nadia 61.2
Jessore 60.2
Bankura 4.3
Noakhali 61.4
Hooghly 16.0
Khulna 49.3
Howrah 20.0
Calcutta 23.0
Midnapore 7.7
24 Parganas 32.5
Backergunge 72.3
BURMA
Chittagong 75.0
Chittagong Hill Tracts 3.0

········ Provincial and province-state boundaries
─·─·─ District and interstate boundaries
───── Boundary claimed by Muslim League
─ ─ ─ Boundary claimed by Congress and Sikhs
───── Boundary by Radcliffe Award
0.0 Figure indicates percentage of Muslims
▒ Districts with a Muslim majority

Source: O. H. K. Spate, The Partition of India and the Prospects of Pakistan, *1948.*

'Indian' now had to be distinguished from 'Pakistani'. Indians overseas, as in the diaspora, now had to take note of changes in their place of origin, and the new governments of India and Pakistan had to decide where to draw the line in granting nationality to those outside the country. (It is from these considerations that terms such as 'person of Indian origin' and 'non-resident Indian' had to be applied.)

Partition also saw the start of a phase of migration which started, for many, with movement to one of the new dominions, but often triggered further movement on to other parts of the Commonwealth or even to new destinations altogether. For some groups, such as the people of mixed descent who called themselves Anglo-Indians, it was clear that they had to leave, in many cases, to find a 'home' that they had often cherished even if they had not seen it directly.

The meaning of 'India'

Independence and Partition produced fundamental changes. These changes did not all take place neatly on 14–15 August 1947. The full repercussions, in fact, took years to work through in some cases. What this meant, on one level, was that those who had migrated from India had to assess their new position in light of the reshaping of the subcontinent and the new notions of nationality that were introduced if they wished to link themselves with the new nations of divided India.

These changes in the subcontinent from Partition and the formation of India and Pakistan, the accession and integration of the princely states into these two new nation states, and the later separation of Bangladesh from Pakistan in 1971, means that it is necessary to recognise that historic India, which embraced the entire Indian subcontinent, does not exist today as it did in the past. The different parts of the subcontinent are not now regions within India, but separate nation states whose relations are now of an international character. Thus, Indians in the diaspora, whose forebears came from historic India, may now identify themselves as Pakistanis or Bangladeshis, and newer migrants moving into areas where the diaspora already existed come from specific nations within the space of the Indian subcontinent.

THE INDIAN UNION
SINCE 1950

Independent India became the Indian Union in 1950 with the adoption of a new constitution. The record of the Union is important because the new India has had to deal with the diaspora in the late 20th century and into the 21st century.

The political system

There are 25 states in the union and seven union territories. These were formed from the integration of the princely states with the former British Indian provinces. Their boundaries were redrawn in 1956 on linguistic lines.

The parliament of the Indian Union works on the basis of a Westminster model, in which the government is formed by the party with a majority in the lower house of the bicameral legislature, the Lok Sabha (House of the People). The Lok Sabha is fully elected on universal adult suffrage. There are 530 members elected directly from the states and 13 directly elected from the union territories.

Prime Minister Manmohan Singh and President Vladimir Putin of Russia meeting in New Delhi in December 2004.

'South Asia': the term and its applicability

One way in which the realities of the emergence of 'new' nation states in the subcontinent have been recognised is by the use of the term 'South Asia'. The term is used to describe the entire region, which includes Nepal and Bhutan in the Himalayas, and Sri Lanka and the Maldives to the southeast and southwest of the Indian peninsula, in addition to Pakistan, India and Bangladesh. These seven nation states have separate national identities, but from the 1980s onwards, they have worked to establish a regional association known as the South Asian Association for Regional Cooperation (SAARC).

The upper house, the Rajya Sabha (Council of States), has not more than 250 members, 12 of whom are nominated by the president because of their special knowledge or practical experience; the remainder are elected indirectly by members of the legislative assemblies of the states in a system of proportional representation. The union is a federal republic with a president as head of state; the president is elected by an electoral college comprising members of the Houses of Parliament (Rajya Sabha and Lok Sabha) and the legislatures of the states.

With the exception of the period between 1975 and 1977, the years of Indira Gandhi's use of the 'Emergency' provisions of Article 356 of the constitution, India has been a democratic state since independence. The parliamentary system has been maintained and elections have taken place on a five-year basis for the most part. The rule of law and the fundamental rights of free speech, expression, belief, assembly and association, migration and choice of occupation or trade have been upheld by an independent judiciary. The constitution also protects Indians from discrimination on the grounds of race, religion, creed or sex, and these rights are enforceable by law.

The economic record

The economic record since independence was dominated for the first 40 years by policies of planned 'Import Substitution Industrialisation' (ISI), implemented through a series of five-year plans from 1950 onwards. These plans maintained a mixed economy in which the state had control of the 'commanding heights of the economy' through the operations of large public sector enterprises. These policies brought a measure of industrial growth and, through the 'Green Revolution', agricultural change in certain regions, which enriched many of the stronger agrarian elements—landlords and rich peasants.

The ISI basis of the economic programmes, which meant heavy protection for domestic industries through tariff barriers, meant that international trade declined relatively. These policies also produced a bureaucratic system of controls—the so-called 'Licence-Permit-Quota Raj'—which limited the rate of growth. Critics spoke pejoratively of a 'Hindu rate of growth' of about 3 per cent per annum. From the 1960s, a special economic relationship developed with the Union of Soviet Socialist Republics (USSR), which gave India trading advantages that helped bypass to some extent the need for hard currency and also gave the country access to oil at favourable rates.

The beginnings of liberalisation in the latter years of Indira Gandhi's prime ministership from 1980–84 were somewhat strengthened after her death by Rajiv Gandhi,

Map 1.8

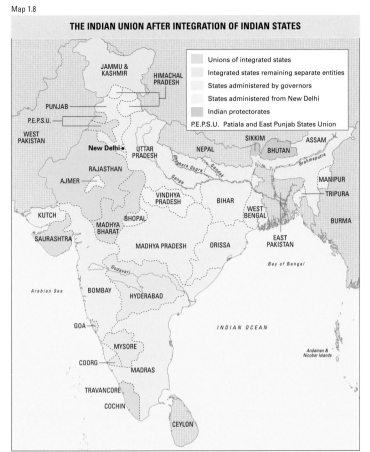

THE INDIAN UNION AFTER INTEGRATION OF INDIAN STATES

Unions of integrated states
Integrated states remaining separate entities
States administered by governors
States administered from New Delhi
Indian protectorates
P.E.P.S.U. Patiala and East Punjab States Union

Source: K. J. Schmidt, Atlas and Survey of South Asian History, *1999.*

Map 1.9

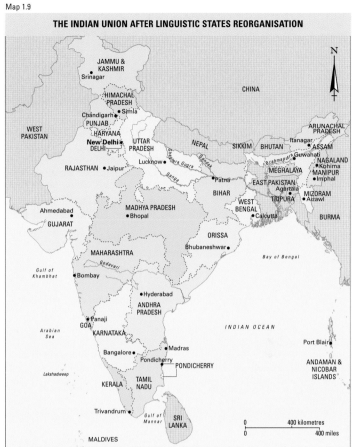

THE INDIAN UNION AFTER LINGUISTIC STATES REORGANISATION

Source: K. J. Schmidt, Atlas and Survey of South Asian History, *1999.*

who succeeded her. These changes, however, were not enough to protect the Indian economy from the difficulties brought about, firstly, by the end of the Cold War, with the changes this produced in the USSR and, therefore, in the special economic relationship. Two years later, India was again adversely affected by the Gulf War of 1991, which resulted in disruptions to migrant labour and remittances, and a drastic rise in oil prices.

The Indian economic crisis of 1991–92, when foreign exchange reserves fell to a critical level, produced a more comprehensive and far-reaching round of economic reform under the aegis of Prime Minister Narasimha Rao and Finance Minister Dr Manmohan Singh. This reform came as a consequence of the International Monetary Fund and World Bank's structural adjustment package: 'deflate, devalue, denationalise, deregulate' in return for the funding essential to save the economy. These reforms continued throughout the 1990s and into the 21st century, raising GDP growth to 6–8 per cent per annum by the late 1990s and even higher in the new millennium. Reforms of customs barriers and trade policies as part of an export-oriented industrialisation policy, a more energetic search for equity and foreign direct investment (FDI), the encouragement of joint ventures and participation by MNCs, and the beginnings of divestment in the public sector were the markers of the new economic order.

In the 1990s, moreover, the Indian economy began to exercise increasing strength in areas where its educational policies and skilled engineers gave it considerable advantage. Skilled software engineers produced by the Indian Institutes of Technology (IITs) and employed by more active entrepreneurs brought about advances in

Information Communication Technology (ICT), especially with regard to advances in software. The availability of an educated middle-class workforce fluent in English provided a basis for the development of 'outsourcing' of 'back-office' operations. Even in manufacturing, in areas such as pharmaceuticals and precision components, there were developments. The small and medium enterprise (SME) sector also showed considerable resilience. Investment in agriculture remained a concern, and rural poverty, though declining, was still a major weakness in the overall economy.

INDIA AND THE WORLD ORDER

By the early 21st century, India had consolidated its place as an important actor in the world political scene. With a population of more than a billion people, burgeoning economic strength and capacity in higher-level technological areas, it began to figure, alongside China, as part of the coming Asian powerhouse of world economic development. India, moreover, had important leadership qualities due its increasing strength and its record as a leader of the 'South', the 'developing world' in the later 20th century. It made new links with areas that it had neglected in the past—Southeast Asia and the US—and was in turn courted by those regions and the European Union. It also began to heal its relationship with China while maintaining links with Russia. In the early years of the 21st century, India has established itself as a power in world councils and a contributor to economic and political change. Once again it is a major civilisational force in the worlds of literature and the arts, science and technology, and in international trade and business.

Peter Reeves and Rajesh Rai

The integration of the princely states into the Indian Union was completed by January 1950. In 1956, the states of the Indian Union were reorganised along linguistic lines.

A Pakistani bus driver shakes hands with an Indian Border Security Force soldier after the bus, carrying Pakistani officials from the city of Lahore, crossed the border at Wagah, on its way to Amritsar, December 2005. This was the third such service launched by the two nations as part of a slow-moving peace process.

31

THE AGE OF MERCHANTS

From the earliest times, Indians have traded across the Indian Ocean and over the Asian landmass. This provided the setting for movement and settlement in lands beyond India—by admittedly small numbers of Indians—well before the period of European colonial intervention brought disruptive new patterns.

Part II focuses on four aspects of pre-colonial movement. Firstly, it outlines a range of Indian maritime communities and their activities up to c. 1800. Crossing the *kalapani*—the dark waters of the ocean—was not without risks, but trade provided the crucial incentive for merchants to move. It then looks at the caravan trade in the Central Asian zone during the same period. This was an area of great importance due to its connections to the Silk Road and linkages to China and Russia. Trade was not the only determinant for movement during the 'Age of Merchants'. Also highlighted is the haj—the Muslim pilgrimage to Mecca and Medina to retrace the Prophet's movements while establishing Islam in the 7th century. Finally, the section describes the almost wholly involuntary movement of Indians to Europe or the islands of the Indian Ocean as slaves or bonded servants.

❖

INDIAN MARITIME COMMUNITIES

A kotia being built at Cuddalore. Indian coastal communities aided the development of shipping technology.

MORE THAN 4000 years ago, coastal communities emerged in India sustained by occupations associated with the sea: fishing, shell collecting, salt making, sailing, trade, shipbuilding and piracy. The earliest maritime communities comprised fisherfolk. The growth of water-borne trade and communication saw increasing occupational specialisation in maritime communities. Fishermen became the first sailors and their settlements were nodal points for the first trading voyages and the evolution of shipping technology. The fishermen also contributed items for trade, such as cured and salted fish, salt, pearls, shells, seaweed, coral, ambergris and turtle shell. Archaeological findings at Harappan sites provide evidence from the earlier period. Evidence for 1st-century India is provided by one of the earliest extant commercial-cum-navigational guides, the *Periplus of the Erythraean Sea*, compiled by a Graeco-Egyptian merchant.

THE MARITIME SETTING

The development of occupational specialisation in maritime communities transformed fishermen into sailors and traders. A hierarchy emerged in some maritime communities based on control of larger trading vessels and particular resources. Most fishermen and sailors became the servants of the trader and shipowner as sailing craft grew larger and more capital intensive; but while many sailors were now wage earners, many did take small caches of trade goods with them to peddle en route. Evidence of this specialisation within Indian maritime communities can be found at Harappan and other sites along the shores of the Persian Gulf and Gujarat, dating back at least 4000 years.

By the time of the *Periplus of the Erythraean Sea*, Indian seamen and traders had emerged as distinctive,

if anonymous, historical figures. There is evidence of their presence in ports stretching from the Red Sea to Southeast Asia. The ubiquitous Indian sailors and traders were already the vital link in the passage to markets around the Indian Ocean and beyond, to China and imperial Rome. They were also the lifeblood of India's thriving coastal trade, linking the west and east coasts of India—and by extension Ceylon, and the Maldives and Lakshadweep islands—in a complex system of commercial exchanges.

MARITIME REGIONS

Where marine resources were plentiful and matched by resource-rich hinterlands, there developed particular maritime regions focusing on maritime trade. Millennia ago, Gujarat, the Malabar and Coromandel coasts, Orissa and Bengal formed distinctive maritime regions in the Indian Ocean. Within these regions were clusters of maritime communities of varying size and prosperity, and often with a limited lifespan, being subject to the vagaries of river flows, sea levels and the political and economic stability of their hinterlands. By the beginning of the present era in India, the fortunes of these regions were

Hindu fishermen on the beach near Azhikal, along the northern Malabar Coast, 1936.

Map 2.1

MARITIME TRADE IN THE INDIAN OCEAN (C. 12TH CENTURY AD)

Source: Kenneth McPherson, The Indian Ocean: A History of People and the Sea, *1993.*

subject to geographic and human forces over which they had minimal control. Consequently, the life of individual communities ranged from short and brutal to long and glorious, from communities marked today only by archaeological remains, such as Lothal and Dwarka, to extant ancient coastal cities such as Cambay, Broach and Calicut. However, whatever the vicissitudes of fate, these regions were sustained by the continuing long-term wealth of their hinterlands.

Gujarat was disrupted periodically by invaders, including the Huns, Arabs, Turks and Mughals, but its prosperity was maintained by a combination of agricultural wealth and its position as a portal to the great cotton textile wealth of the Indus and the upper Ganges valleys. It was this economic stability of Gujarat that sustained vigorous local trading and seafaring communities over the millennia.

The situation was the same for the two great coastal regions of southern India: the Malabar and Coromandel coasts. Less ravaged by invaders than northern India, the hinterlands of these coasts were rich in export commodities, principally rice and cotton textiles on the Coromandel Coast and pepper in Malabar. These items made the fortunes of many local trading groups and supported large communities of traders and sailors, ranging from the Muslim Mappilas of the Malabar Coast to the Hindu Chettiars, Paravas and the Muslim Chulias of Coromandel. An extension of this southern maritime zone incorporated Ceylon, with its valuable elephants and gemstones, the pearl and chank beds of the Gulf of Mannar and the Palk Strait. The Lakshadweep and Maldives archipelagos, which supplied coir, dried fish and cowries as well as sailors, were connected to the southern maritime zone.

While the prosperity of coastal communities was anchored in their access to maritime and terrestrial resources, the long-term rhythms of their lives were, until the coming of steamships, dictated by the pattern and regularity of wind systems. In the Indian Ocean, the monsoons determined sailing times, the duration of the voyage and the route. Other oceans and seas had less spectacular wind systems but they were all seasonal. This not only shaped travelling and fishing schedules but also encouraged the development of communities of traders and sailors. The need to collect cargoes and refit vessels prompted the formation of communities of Indian sailors, traders and shipowners in many maritime regions across the Indian Ocean by the beginning of the present era. In later centuries, similar communities spread around the Indian Ocean from the Red Sea to eastern Africa, across the Arabian Sea, and eastward to the ports of southern China.

CULTURAL EXCHANGE

The expansion of Hinduism and Buddhism in Southeast Asia followed the footsteps of Indian sailors and traders at least 2000 years ago, and is intimately associated with the growth of maritime trade and the development of Indian communities in Southeast Asia, through which the civilisations of India impacted on local societies. In later centuries, Islam, similarly, spread from the Middle East along shipping routes and through communities along the ancient maritime routes linking South and Southeast Asia. It took root in ports such as Aceh and Melaka astride the Straits of Melaka, and spread to the spice-rich islands of eastern Indonesia.

Maritime communities were junctions where different cultures came into contact and acted as filters through which these cultures permeated into the hinterlands. They were 'littoral societies', linking both land and sea, and were meeting points for a variety of peoples, cultures and ideas. Around the coast of India, ports were the entry points for Islam, and it was from Gujarat and the Malabar and Coromandel coasts that Indian converts to Islam spread the new faith to Lakshadweep and the Maldives, and further afield to insular Southeast Asia.

The growing internal complexity of maritime communities and the expansion of their external linkages in time created particular lifestyles. Such communities were frequently more cosmopolitan than land-based ones, and

The Nagore Durgah in Tamil Nadu—a shrine dedicated to the saint Shahul Hamid (1498–1558)—plays an important role in the religious life of many Tamil Muslim maritime traders.

Map 2.1 shows the leading trading ports of regions bordering the Indian Ocean. This network was important both in terms of its own regional trade and its link to the South China and Mediterranean seas.

An artist's impression of the ancient coastal port city of Dwarka in Kutch, Gujarat.

An 1874 sketch of Ceylon Pearl Fisheries, situated in the Gulf of Mannar. Ceylon formed an important link in the southern maritime trade zone that included the Coromandel and Malabar coasts, and the Lakshadweep and Maldives archipelagos.

they contained specialised groups (the fishermen, sailors, shipowners and traders) whose intimate links to the sea and its seasons created distinctive subcultures with sea-oriented religious beliefs and practices, such as the worship of particular Hindu deities and Muslim saints at dedicated coastal shrines. Indian sailors developed their own rich folklore, based on their religious persuasion—either Hindu or Muslim—and on their regular contact with the sea and foreign ports.

In addition to developing particular religious beliefs and practices within the corpuses of Hinduism and Islam, Indian sailors early on developed sophisticated navigational techniques based on the star compass and an intimate knowledge of sea currents and winds. Such knowledge made them masters of dangerous deep-sea voyages across the Bay of Bengal and the Arabian Sea at least 2000 years ago and led to the development of Indian shipping technology as craft were modified and developed to cope with new physical challenges. The millennia-long intermingling of Indian, Arab and Persian sailors led to a vigorous exchange and development of maritime technology and sailing skills, which were to leave Indian and Arab sailors unsurpassed as long-distance navigators until the upsurge of Chinese and European maritime skills in the 14th and 15th centuries.

Just as India is home to a complex and multifaceted network of civilisations, languages, social and religious practices, and economies, Indian sailors and traders before 1500 are equally complex characters to describe. Some were Hindu, others were Muslim; some were rich, many were poor; and some identified with fishing communities, while others had begun to evolve separate caste and group identities defined by their various maritime functions. The following case studies indicate the variety and complexity of Indian sailing and maritime life before 1800.

Gujaratis

At least 4000 years ago, sailors and merchants from Gujarat embarked on coast-hugging voyages that linked the Indus Valley and Gujarat with the earliest civilisations of the Persian Gulf and Mesopotamia. By 1500 AD, their descendants were pre-eminent Indian navigators and masters of the great export trade in cotton textiles out of northern India. This trade carried them westward to the Middle East and East Africa, and eastward to the Bay of Bengal and Southeast Asian ports such as Melaka and Aceh, where Gujaratis formed significant communities.

The sea route to Southeast Asia via the Malabar and Coromandel coasts was the most favoured by Gujaratis until the Portuguese disrupted it in the 16th century. At any one time during the sailing season, probably several

thousand Gujarati traders moved along this route in the company of tens of thousands of sailors. Some of these merchants and sailors were Hindus, but by 1500, many were local converts to Islam who played a significant role in the introduction of Islam to insular Southeast Asia.

The distinction between traders and sailors is difficult to define. There were some merchant magnates and guilds of traders who were set apart in lifestyle and social status from the majority of traders, but the difference between the mass of petty traders and sailors is less clear. Both were involved in petty trade, albeit in the case of sailors such trade was subsidiary to their main occupation and, to an extent, most sailors and petty traders shared a number of identities: some were simply sailors or petty merchants but many blended the two occupations, particularly when they were also owners or part-owners of sailing craft.

By 1500, the fortunes of Gujarati traders and sailors had apparently peaked. The arrival of the Portuguese in the Indian Ocean in 1498 and their subsequent occupation of Melaka, and the successful attempts of the Dutch and the British to dominate India's textile export trade, all but eliminated the Gujaratis from this eastern trade. Still, they proved resilient, and from the 17th century they reinforced their western networks, building up their links with ports in the Persian Gulf and the Red Sea and along the East African coast. Furthermore, they continued to work the coastal trade of western India and found niches as intermediaries for the Europeans in the ports stretching from the coast of Mozambique to Karachi.

Mappilas

The Malayalam-speaking Mappilas of modern Kerala (the ancient Malabar Coast) were, until the late 18th century, a major presence in the maritime trade of southern India. They are the descendants of early Arab and Persian traders and sailors who married locally and whose services gained them a niche in local society. Although numerically small, their skills as seamen and links to the markets and religion of the Middle East made them favoured intermediaries of local Hindu dynasties.

When the Portuguese arrived off the Malabar Coast in 1498, the external trade of the coast was mostly in the hands of the Mappilas. Other groups, such as the Gujarati, Jewish, Christian and Hindu Chettiar traders from the east coast were also involved in this trade but were not as dominant as the Mappilas, who, by the early 16th century, had carved out their own polity in the port of Kannanur (Cannanore).

The arrival of the anti-Muslim Portuguese in the Malabar Coast in the early 16th century heralded a period of bitter conflict between the European interlopers and

Traditional pearl divers. Control of the Gulf of Mannar was much in demand for the pearl fisheries it held.

the Mappila trading fleets as they battled for control of the pepper trade, the pearl fisheries of the Gulf of Mannar and trade with Ceylon. The Portuguese eventually drove the Mappilas from the pearl fisheries and the Ceylon trade, but they were unable to eliminate them from the pepper trade or trade with the Maldives for coir, which was a vital component in shipbuilding around the Arabian Sea.

Like the Gujaratis, the Mappilas were able to survive the Portuguese onslaught by reorienting their activities eastward; but, unlike the Gujaratis, they failed to find a niche in the maritime networks being constructed by the Europeans. By the end of the 18th century, following the depredations of Tipu Sultan and Haidar Ali and the British conquest of southern India, they were reduced to a small group of coastal merchants and petty shipowners.

For nearly 1000 years, the Mappilas were a source of traders and sailors who linked pepper- and timber-rich Malabar with the markets of the Middle East, northern India and the Lakshadweep and Maldives islands. Although devout Muslims, the Mappilas were well-integrated within Malayali society, having occupied a niche left vacant by the abhorrence of trade and mercantile activities by Malabar's Hindu upper castes. Indeed, the community's numbers were steadily augmented by the conversion of low-caste Hindu fishing communities such as the Tiyans and Mukkavans, who, by the 15th century, made up the majority of crews attached to Mappila merchant fleets.

Paravas

In the 13th century, Marco Polo noted the existence of a group known as the Paravas on the Tamil shore of the Gulf of Mannar—the 'Fisheries Coast'. The group mainly comprised poor sailors and fishermen, and was dominated by a few wealthy ship-owning families whose prosperity was founded on the pearl fisheries of the Gulf of Mannar and the Palk Strait—under warrant from local Hindu rulers—and from maritime trade with Ceylon and the Maldives.

By 1500, the fortunes of the Paravas had declined. Their control of the lucrative pearl fisheries and trade with Ceylon and the Maldives was contested by an alliance of local groups and the Mappilas. Locally, the Paravas came under pressure from other Tamil trading groups, such as the Chettiars and the Muslim Marakkayars. The Marakkayars, who had shared access to the pearl fisheries, were eager to gain control of these resources, and in alliance with their Mappila co-religionists, they gained the support of local Hindu rulers who, in return for higher rents and access to the Middle Eastern horses imported by the Mappilas, withdrew their warrants to the Paravas.

The Paravas were facing extinction. Some embraced Islam, others merged with more prosperous local Hindu groups. The majority turned to the Portuguese when they arrived on the coast in the early 1500s. In return for protection from their Muslim rivals, the Paravas converted to Christianity. When the Portuguese destroyed the Mappila fleets, the Paravas once more gained access to the pearl fisheries and their old markets in Ceylon and the Maldives.

A new, confident maritime community emerged after conversion to Christianity. Ironically, the Paravas now had a strong sense of caste identity and organisation, and in addition to once more taking to the high seas as sailors, pearl fishers and petty traders, they provided the Portuguese with a pool of expert sailors. When the Dutch ousted the Portuguese from the Fisheries Coast, the Paravas were quick to adjust to the new order, just as they did when the British ousted the Dutch in the late 18th century. By this time, the Paravas had consolidated their position and created a flourishing trading network which linked southern India to Ceylon and the Maldives, compensating for the decline in returns from the pearl fisheries. The small, fast and efficient Parava sailing ships found a ready niche in the new colonial economic order as carriers of small cargoes considered unprofitable by European shipowners.

Chulias and Chettiars

The origins of the Chulias are similar to those of the Mappilas. Both groups claim Arab and Persian ancestry, mixed with generations of local intermarriage. The mother tongue of the Chulias is Tamil, and over the centuries they have found a niche in the highly fragmented society of Tamil Nadu.

The community is not homogeneous and the name 'Chulia' is externally imposed. Tamil-speaking Muslims were divided into a number of caste-like groups based on occupation, wealth and religious orthodoxy. At the apex of Tamil Muslim society were the Marakkayars, whose main economic and religious centres were the ports of Nagapattinam, Kayalpattinam and Nagore. The prosperity of the Marakkayars was based entirely on maritime trade, shipping and the provision of skilled sailors. Next came the Labbais, another coastal-based group comprising sailors and agriculturalists, and below them communal boundaries blurred with a number of marginal groups straddling the Hindu-Muslim divide.

The Chettiars comprise a number of Hindu castes whose main activities focus on trade and moneylending. Tamil Chettiars were active across southern India, and on the east coast were involved in shipping along the coast and with Southeast Asia, as were the Marakkayars. Unlike the Marakkayars, the Chettiars were not sailors and they depended on other communities to man their craft.

Maritime trade and sailing underpinned the prosperity of most Tamil-speaking Muslims. Some, invariably Marakkayars, were rich traders and shipowners, but the majority were petty traders, shareholders in individual ships and/or sailors. The focus of Tamil Muslim maritime interest was primarily eastward across the Bay of Bengal. There was also a considerable Marakkayar presence on the east coast of Ceylon, where they were active in trade between the island and southern India.

On the route across the Bay of Bengal, the Chulias mixed with Gujaratis, Chettiars and many other maritime

A late 19th-century sketch of workers preparing pearl oysters for auction. The pearl fisheries in the Gulf of Mannar, both on the west coast of Ceylon and along the 'Fisheries Coast' of the Madras Presidency, were a government monopoly.

An Indian caravanserai in Bukhara, 1890s. After months of travel, Indian traders would remain for an extended period in a caravanserai, trading their wares.

intrusion of Europe into the economic world of the Indian Ocean region, traders and sailors were part of a complex and interlocked maritime community. This was not a homogeneous community but a collection of small communities defined by language, religion and geography. They were as multifaceted as Indian civilisation and society and were constantly evolving as economic, political, environmental and religious circumstances changed. However, as much as these communities changed over the millennia, the Indian sailor and trader remained an enduring, if anonymous, feature of Indian history and was central to both the economic life and the external links of the peoples of the subcontinent.

Kenneth McPherson

THE INDIAN CARAVAN TRADE

Since antiquity, the city of Multan (in modern Pakistan) was among India's most important northwestern commercial centres. In the 8th century, it was one of the easternmost outposts of the Umayyad caliphate and its inhabitants prospered by acting as middlemen in India's trade with the emerging Arab-Muslim empire to the west. In later centuries, Multan's significance as a commercial centre grew under the Turko-Afghan Delhi Sultanate (1206–1527). Opportunities in the region facilitated the development of a Multani commercial culture among some groups indigenous to the area, while other groups with a pre-existing propensity for commerce were drawn to Multan from other parts of the subcontinent. In the late 13th century, a court chronicler for the Delhi sultan, Jalal al-Din Firuz Shah Khalji (r. 1290–96), referred to the Indian merchant-moneylenders known as Multanis, who, at that time, were widely known both as an important source of credit for the Delhi Sultanate's nobility and as active traders in cotton textiles.

As the Multani firms prospered, they increased the number of agents at strategic locations in urban and rural markets across North India. Some agents were stationed in villages, where they advanced loans to farmers in exchange for a portion of the harvest. Other agents functioned as brokers, purchasing the remainder of the harvest for cash, supplying raw cotton to weavers in exchange for finished bolts of cloth, and moving the agricultural surplus and finished commodities from the countryside to urban or regional markets. Furthermore, a number of agents were known to operate as large-scale transregional traders in the subcontinent's major commercial centres. The Delhi sultans valued the Multanis as an important source of income from taxes, a convenient reserve of capital in times of need and, perhaps most importantly, as village moneylenders and dedicated operators of a rural credit system. Arguably, the Multanis' greatest service to the nobility was their introduction of a monetised economy to the Indian countryside, which greatly facilitated the Delhi sultans' efforts to collect taxes in cash rather than in kind.

The patronage of the sultans was clearly a significant factor in the rise of these firms; however, even more important was the increasing circulation of precious metals in the Indian economy. Scholars have long observed that India lacks significant reserves of gold and silver in its soil, and that pre-modern India's greatest wealth was its agricultural production. Since ancient times, the gold and silver that was minted into Indian coinage and circulated

groups from India. There was competition but the Chulias had a distinct advantage in insular Southeast Asia and the Malay Peninsula because they were Muslims, and so were welcomed by many local Muslim rulers. By 1500, the Chulias were prominent in the cotton textile export trade out of southern India and in the import of tin and tropical commodities from Southeast Asia. Many Chulias also served on Muslim and non-Muslim ships as sailors and skilled navigators, and were welcomed in the newly converted Muslim ports of Southeast Asia.

The arrival of the Portuguese in the early 1500s was as disruptive for the Chulias as it was for the Mappilas. The Portuguese drove the Chulias—but not their Hindu Chettiar compatriots—from Melaka and attempted to drive them from the Bay of Bengal. However, limited resources and practicality helped to shape a compromise, and by the end of the 16th century the Chulias were once more flourishing in trade with Southeast Asia, unofficially cooperating with the Portuguese and later the Danes, Dutch and British, for whom they provided sailing craft, merchant intermediaries and skilled sailors and navigators.

Both the Chulias and Chettiars survived the establishment of British rule in southern India in the 18th century. The consolidation of British control over the local textile industry and the growing domination of larger and more cost-effective European shipping led to a landward refocusing of Chettiar interests. Some, such as the Nattukottai Chettiars, moved into the financing of trade in collaboration with European interests and, in time, became one of the largest banking castes in India, with communities spread across Southeast Asia. Other Chettiar castes likewise focused on land-based commerce and moneylending, ending any direct involvement in maritime trade.

The Chulias were also forced by the arrival of the British to refocus their interests. Like the Paravas, they managed to find a particular niche within the new maritime economy, carrying small cargoes to Ceylon and Southeast Asia but, like the Chettiars, they also began to develop land-based interests, and from the early 1800s moved into general commerce and the leather industry.

OVERVIEW

These four cases illustrate the fact that the boundaries between fishermen, sailors and merchants were not as clear after 1800. Before 1800 and the advent of British rule across the subcontinent, and the overwhelming throughout the subcontinent was largely imported from abroad and exchanged in port cities and frontier towns for caravan-loads of Indian spices, cotton textiles, dyes and other agricultural goods. During the medieval and early modern eras, several historical processes conspired to advance India's monetisation and the prosperity of the Multani firms along with it. One such process was the deliberate effort of the Delhi sultans, which was continued under the Mughals, to encourage a general increase in trade across the northwest frontier.

Other factors contributed to this process of monetisation as well, the most important of which were the Spanish conquests in the New World and the almost single-minded fervour with which the conquistadors seized the rich gold and silver reserves of the former Aztec and Incan empires, melted down what was in use and established an elaborate network of mining settlements for further extraction. The average amount of Spanish silver exports from the New World between 1565 and 1685 was approximately 25,000–35,000 tons per year—an impressive sum which is believed to have doubled between 1685–1810. As ships loaded with gold and silver sailed from the New World, much of this wealth circulated around the globe and gradually found its way to the Indian Ocean, where it had a profound effect on Indian society.

As more wealth was injected into the Indian economy, the Multani firms benefited from a corresponding increase in opportunities to expand their commercial interests into new areas. Consequently, they enlisted more agents, dispatched them to more markets, and gradually grew more competitive. By the mid-16th century, some firms adapted to this climate of growing competition by diversifying their portfolios geographically and sending their agents abroad to pursue opportunities in the less competitive markets of Afghanistan, Central Asia and Iran. Thus, while sources from the second half of the 16th century observe Indian merchant communities in just a few major urban centres, such as Bukhara, Samarkand and Tashkent in Central Asia, and Qazvin and Kashan in Iran, over the course of the 17th century, some Indian diaspora communities grew larger, and many more emerged in dozens of smaller cities and villages across Afghanistan, Central Asia and Iran.

FEATURES OF MIGRATION

By the mid-16th century, the Multani firms had a well-developed system of enlisting agents and preparing them for work in distant locations. Agents were exclusively male and underwent rigorous training which encompassed complex accounting techniques; mathematical formulas for computing various types of interest; moneylending procedures; instructions for issuing and cashing *hundis* (bills of exchange); secret codes for recording commercial transactions; a variety of issues related to their own legal traditions and those of other legal systems; and a lengthy period of apprenticeship. This system of training was not unique in Indian business history, but the methods of the Indian diaspora differed from earlier practices in some important ways.

Before being dispatched abroad, Multani agents were lent a certain amount of capital, generally in the form of a commodity for export, most often cotton textiles, produced in abundance in India and one of the subcontinent's greatest export commodities since antiquity. As the Multani agents were long-established as creditors to cotton farmers and weavers, cotton textiles were available to

them in large quantities at prices below market value. Perhaps for this reason, while most observations of the Multanis focus on their moneylending activities, they are also not infrequently referred to as textile traders. In the 1660s, Raphaël du Mans described the totality of Multani merchants in Isfahan as 'cloth merchants' (*bazzaze*) and, as early as 1558, Anthony Jenkinson observed that Indian merchants in Bukhara were also traders in textiles.

Jenkinson's account is the earliest concrete reference to the Indian merchants in Central Asia and it provides some insight into the Indians' commercial operation. It is interesting, although somewhat misleading, that Jenkinson described Bukharan trade at that time as 'beggerly and poore' because he was astonished that it took the Indian merchants who came there two to three years to sell their merchandise before returning home, and they refused to bargain with him for his English wool. At first glance, Jenkinson's disappointment with the Bukharan market seems to suggest that the area's commercial climate was impoverished and devoid of opportunity. Reconsidering Jenkinson's conclusions in the context of the diaspora merchants' commercial techniques, it is apparent that the Indians he encountered were already operating in accordance with the standard model of the diaspora that was to become so familiar in later years.

The first order of business for Indian agents travelling to locations in Afghanistan, Central Asia and Iran was to arrange for their commodities to be transported by caravan across the inhospitable intermediary lands. This was an arduous journey and also an expensive one as, in addition to standard transportation expenses, they were required to pay customs duties at each political boundary. After several months of travel the caravan would arrive at its destination and Indian agents would take up residence in a caravanserai, commonly one owned and operated by their firm and placed under the direction of their firm's senior representative. This individual—known in Central Asia as the *aqsaqal* and in Iran as the *kalantar*—was responsible for supervising the local Indian community

The Indian community in Central Asia generally included a small number of Brahmans, who were enlisted to tend to the religious needs of the merchants while they lived abroad.

Map 2.2

CARAVAN TRADE ROUTES IN AFGHANISTAN, CENTRAL ASIA AND IRAN

Courtesy of Dr Scott Levi, Department of History, University of Louisville, US.

Indian caravan routes connected northwestern India to key trading centres in Afghanistan, Iran and Central Asia.

An Indian cremation ceremony in Bukhara in the 1880s. Public cremation ceremonies caused friction with local populations, who generally found the Indian tradition to be distasteful. Special approval from the state was needed to conduct the ceremony.

and mediating their relationship with the host state. At this point, the Indians would begin selling their merchandise. However, considering that every caravan that brought the merchants to distant markets also brought hundreds—or even thousands—of camel loads of cotton textiles, the Indians were inclined to sell only a small percentage of the total. They would hoard the rest for sale over an extended period of time in order to keep the market from saturating and driving down the price of their merchandise, and, by extension, the value of their capital wealth.

Thus, rather than demonstrating the destitute nature of the Bukharan market at the time of his visit, Jenkinson's inability to purchase Indian cloth at a discounted price seems more likely to have represented the Bukharan market's saturation with Indian textiles and the Indians' efforts to keep the price of their merchandise as high as possible. While Jenkinson was shocked that the Indians he encountered commonly spent two to three years in Bukhara before returning home, later observers report that it was typical for Indian merchants to spend several years working abroad before returning to India. On average, Indians stayed abroad for six to seven years, although some are known to have stayed in particularly lucrative posts for several decades.

Nature of trade

Indian communities were almost exclusively comprised of a rotating population of men. While these men were living in distant communities in control of considerable amounts of the firm's capital, the firm's directors back in Multan were responsible for watching over the agents' families. This arrangement served the dual purpose of reassuring the agents of their families' well-being in their absence, while simultaneously ensuring that the agents remained loyal and conducted themselves responsibly. Should an agent prove untrustworthy by absconding with the firm's capital, his reputation—and credit—would be ruined, and his family would ultimately be held responsible for any resulting losses. Such situations occurred, but rarely. During their extended periods abroad, the agents generally lived a monastic lifestyle as they actively participated in numerous commercial ventures, only one facet of which was the sale of their merchandise.

While the Multani merchants gradually sold off their textiles, they did not allow the cash they received to sit idle as they prepared for their return to India. Rather, they were trained to put their capital to work by reinvesting it in other more profitable commercial activities, most commonly in reasonably secure, interest-earning money-lending ventures. The Multanis in Afghanistan, Central Asia and Iran specialised in several types of loans, divisible into short-term cash loans on the one hand and agricultural loans on the other. As many farmers depended on

credit to get their crops planted, agricultural loans constituted an especially important and very lucrative venture for the Multanis. Before the planting season, even Indians who lived in cities ventured into the countryside, where they advanced loans to farmers, in cash or in kind, with the cumulative principal and interest collected at harvest time—it was a common arrangement for the Indian to receive half of the harvest. Although the risk involved in agricultural loans was greater than that of a loan against collateral, Indian moneylenders were attracted to rural markets as the interest earned was correspondingly higher and the term of an agricultural loan was usually six months or less, depending on the length of the growing season. To the Indians, this meant that the capital retrieved was available for other investments for the rest of the year.

Indian merchants, therefore, operated at a critical juncture between urban and rural markets, serving their host societies by providing investment capital to facilitate agricultural production even when local peoples could not afford the initial investment in seeds for planting or other necessary materials. It is tempting to attribute the Indians' success in these markets to the prohibition of *riba* (collecting interest from loans) in Islamic law. Muslim merchants across the Islamic world devised numerous techniques to circumvent this restriction; they were quite capable of providing credit for profit and they regularly did so. Instead, the Indians' dominance of the moneylending trade should be attributed to their access to their firms' vast reserves of capital wealth and their training, which emphasised moneylending for profit.

In addition to their role as rural credit agents, the Indians commonly purchased the remainder of the harvest for cash and arranged for its sale in urban markets. In this capacity, the Indians served their hosts by extending a monetised economy into the countryside, facilitating the collection of taxes in cash. They also served them by importing necessary goods, purchasing local products and arranging for their export, and supplying a considerable tax income for the treasury. The combination of these factors at least partly explains the motivation of Muslim administrators to protect the Indian merchants and ensure that they could conduct their business in a safe, predictable and reasonably agreeable social climate.

In some places, Indian merchants congregated in urban neighbourhoods, but the vast majority of references to Indians in Afghanistan, Central Asia and Iran are to Hindu merchants living in specifically 'Indian' caravanserais. These structures conformed to the standard architectural styles of the region and era, and the exteriors gave no indication of the inhabitants' cultural and religious uniqueness. The interior of the caravanserais, however, represented a Hindu microcosm within their Islamic host societies. Indian merchants were, of course, the primary residents of the Indian caravanserais, but these also housed Indian cooks, barbers, jewellers, tailors, servants and retail shops, where the Indians purchased many of the goods necessary for their daily lives, including religious paraphernalia, from other Indians. Within these caravanserais, Indians were exempt from many legal restrictions applicable to the general Muslim populace. For example, visitors to the Indian caravanserais of Bukhara commonly noted that whereas alcohol and tobacco were prohibited in the religiously conservative city, inside their caravanserais Indians smoked and drank alcohol freely.

Religious practice

Even in Central Asia's rather conservative religious climate, Hindus were generally permitted to celebrate their religious festivals: several 19th-century sources describe Hindu celebrations of Diwali, a festival in honour of the goddess Lakshmi, and another celebration that appears to have been Holi, a festival celebrating the approach of spring. According to one Russian observer of a Diwali celebration in Tashkent (in modern Uzbekistan) in 1895, the Hindus celebrated this holiday by abstaining from drinking alcohol, maintaining a strictly vegetarian diet of ceremonial Indian cuisine, illuminating the caravanserai with hundreds of oil lamps, and enlisting musicians, singers and dancers to perform devotional songs. This same visitor returned the following year for the celebration of Holi, which he referred to as a festival 'with alcohol'. This affair drew large numbers of indigenous spectators to the roof of the caravanserai, some of whom reportedly even joined the celebration.

The celebration of these festivals was not restricted to Russian colonial Central Asia. In Bukhara as well, the Muslim population had a tradition of allowing and even participating in Hindu religious celebrations. For example, before the commencement of some festival activities in Bukhara, farmers would bring their cows to Indian caravanserais so that the Hindus could sprinkle them with dry red dye and pray near them. In return, the Indians would feed the cows cottonseed, an unusual delicacy for the animals. Diwali was also celebrated in an Indian caravanserai in Bukhara, where the holiday was popularly referred to as Id-i Charaghan (Festival of Lights).

As individual Indian merchants generally spent a limited number of years abroad, there are only a few accounts of Indians who died there. When this did happen, it was a source of potential conflict due to the Hindu tradition of cremating the dead. While cremation ceremonies were common in India, Muslims in Afghanistan, Central Asia and Iran commonly considered it to be abhorrent. Nevertheless, since Hindus placed a great spiritual importance on this tradition, whenever a comrade died, the survivors went to great lengths to acquire permission from the relevant administration to conduct a ritual cremation. Permission was necessary largely in order to secure military protection for the duration of the ceremony, thereby discouraging any local troublemakers from disturbing the funeral pyre. Following cremation, the ashes of the deceased were returned to India.

The directors of the Multani firms sent Brahmins to supervise religious ceremonies and service the other spiritual needs of their agents. This was achieved by contracting Brahmins to live in a specific community for a stipulated period of time, following which they were replaced by other recruits. While the directors ensured the financial security of the Brahmins' families back in India, the Brahmins themselves were dependent upon the Indian merchants for their livelihood. There is no indication that they, at any time, participated in commercial activities.

Although Indians enjoyed great cultural autonomy within the confines of their caravanserais, Hindus (and other non-Muslim minorities) were required to obey certain social restrictions. They were generally forbidden from owning Muslim slaves and riding on horseback in towns, and they usually had to dress in a distinctive manner so that they could be distinguished easily from Muslims. For example, Hindus in 19th-century Central Asia were required to wear short, tight-fitting, single-coloured (usually black) *chapans* (a long, flowing outer robe) with minimal patterns and, although the fashion was to fasten one's *chapan* with a sash, Hindus and Jews were allowed to tie their clothes with only a hemp rope, probably to ensure that they did not carry concealed weapons in their sashes. Hindus were also instructed to wear distinctive square hats, tight *salwars* (pants) and leather shoes. They even had to have a distinctive hairstyle so that they could be distinguished from Muslim men who, at that time, generally shaved their heads.

Hindus were allowed to construct free-standing temples in only a few locations across the region. In Central Asia, Hindus used dedicated rooms in their caravanserais to function as religious libraries and places of worship. These rooms generally had a small altar surrounded by stone figures or, in later years, portrait images of Hindu deities. The temple room of a rather old Hindu caravanserai in Tashkent reportedly housed an icon of Kali that had been brought from Banaras, although the Indians who lived in that caravanserai in the late 19th century could not say when. (See Part VIII, 'Afghanistan, Central Asia and Iran'.)

Hindu communities in Iran were occasionally allowed to build temples outside of their caravanserais. At the end of the 17th century, John Fryer recorded the existence of two temples in the village of Naoband, a short distance northeast of Bandar 'Abbas, where the large number of Hindus living in that busy port city celebrated their festivals. There are also numerous accounts of a remarkable Hindu temple in Baku (in modern Azerbaijan), an important commercial centre on the Russo-Iranian trade routes traversing both the Caucasus Mountains and the Caspian Sea. This temple, situated some 25 km to the northeast of the city, was located in the vicinity of a wealth of naphtha deposits. Naphtha gases were used in the religious rituals of the Hindus. The temple was properly known by the Sanskrit name *jvala mukhi* (flame-mouthed), one of the less common names of the Hindu goddess Durga. In addition to servicing the needs of the Multani merchants, the *jvala mukhi* temple of Baku attracted countless other pilgrims from across India.

Scott Levi

Trading stalls in a Central Asian market area, 1880s. Indian merchants were widely known as wholesalers and large-scale importers of cotton textiles.

The sacred Ka'aba in Mecca, believed to be the first place created on earth and the point at which heavenly bliss and power touches the earth directly.

THE HAJ BEFORE 1800

The Muslim faith requires that all believers undertake the haj, or pilgrimage, to Mecca, where the Prophet Muhammad was born and where he first revealed parts of the Quran, at least once in a lifetime. Mecca attracts Muslims from all over the world—Africa, the Malay world, the Balkans, China and India.

INDIAN HAJIS

Indian Muslims had several options when travelling to Mecca. Some journeyed by land through Afghanistan and Iran to reach Arabia; others sailed from west coast ports, especially Surat, to the maritime gateway to Mecca, Jeddah, on the west coast of the Red Sea. Following their return, pilgrims were honoured as hajis. Some men, however, stayed overseas for longer periods, or indeed never returned to India. They studied in Mecca and Medina, where the Prophet is buried, undertaking the haj each year and, in the meantime, gaining knowledge of normative Islam from the famous *ulama* (religious scholars) of these two cities. Some even travelled further to other major Muslim cities of the early modern period, such as Cairo, Damascus or Baghdad. If they returned home to India after these travels, they were venerated and would often lead movements to purify Islam.

The number of people who went on the haj varied each year. We know little of the numbers from India before Islamic dynasties were established in the north from the 13th century. In the 7th century, Arab traders continued to visit western Indian ports after they converted to Islam, and soon, many local people joined the new faith. Some of them undertook the long sea passage across the Arabian Sea and up the Red Sea to Jeddah, then overland to Mecca to perform the haj. Their numbers depended on conditions in the Hijaz region, where the Holy Cities are located, and on the degree of support available from within the Muslim community in India. Political and economic conditions in India also affected the number of pilgrims able to travel.

The journey from India to Mecca was a long, difficult, dangerous and expensive one. Pilgrims on the overland route were subject to extortion from local tribal groups on the way, and the terrain, varying between mountains and desert, made travel arduous. The sea route was regulated by the monsoon winds, which circumscribed all sea travel at this time, and this lengthened the duration of the journey. The passage from Surat to Jeddah took less than a month, but ships had to wait for the correct monsoon to prevail for the return voyage. Ships on this route left Surat in March and returned in September. Apart from the dangers of sea travel at this time, the long delay in the Hijaz region meant increased costs for pilgrims. Sometimes they had to spend many months in the Hijaz waiting for the monsoon. The six months from March to September were the minimum time spent: as the monsoon is governed by a solar calendar and the haj follows a lunar calendar, the haj and the right time for sea travel did not coincide. If the haj was in November, a pilgrim would have to wait until the following September before his ship could catch the right wind to return to India.

Contemporaneous accounts in the 16th and 17th centuries describe huge ships, often owned by nobles or rulers, carrying 1000 or more pilgrims each. At least six of such ships usually made the voyage each year. Smaller ships carried less than 500 pilgrims each. A low estimate of the total number of pilgrims who travelled from India would be around 15,000 annually. The number of pilgrims declined sharply in the 18th century and the early decades of the 19th century.

Indian Muslim rulers often granted lavish funds so that pious but poor Indian Muslims could make the long and hazardous journey. In the early 16th century, Sultan Muzaffar of Gujarat provided a vessel and covered

Boats carrying pilgrims to the harbour of Al-Wajh.

all expenses for pilgrims to Mecca. The Mughals were especially generous when it came to the haj. For some years, Emperor Akbar (r. 1556–1605) appointed senior nobles to lead the annual pilgrimage caravan and paid large sums for the passage of poor people to Mecca and for their maintenance on the way.

NOTABLE HAJIS

From 1575 to 1582, Emperor Akbar's aunt, Gulbadan Begum, was part of a large party which spent some time at significant Muslim places in Iraq and Arabia. Four of these years were spent in Mecca. While the princess was in no hurry to return to India, members of her very large entourage were. They became an involuntary sojourning community in Mecca. The princess's long stay caused overcrowding and put pressure on the city's food supplies, and the Ottoman authorities finally took steps to move them on. Wealthy and pious nobles provided ships free of charge to the princess. This royal patronage declined in the 18th century as Muslim rulers in India faced the challenge of European attacks.

In the early 17th century, Abdulhaqq Dihlawi, a recognised authority on the Hadith (the sayings and actions of the Prophet) in Delhi, studied for many years in Mecca. His teacher was a student of one of the great Indian immigrants to Mecca, Ali al-Muttaqi, who came from Burhanpur and lived in Mecca from 1534 until his death in 1568.

Those *ulama* who did come home carried with them considerable prestige. Some tried to reform the religious practice of their fellow Muslims in India by using their knowledge of normative Islam as practised in the Holy Cities. One Indian sheikh had been profoundly influenced by Sufi (mystical) practice, to the extent of being considered unorthodox by some of his fellow *ulama*; then he went to Mecca to study 'the traditional sayings of Muhammad' and as a result gave up Sufi practice. 'Objecting to the ecstatic and vocal music [characteristic of Sufis] he followed the rule of the traditionalists and buried himself in outward piety, cleanliness, purification and devotion,' al Badaoni reported. He returned home and was influential at the court of Emperor Akbar. In 1580, his conservative ideas finally alienated the Emperor, who punished the sheikh by sending him on a haj. Nobles who fell out of favour with the Emperor were often given the 'privilege' of being sent off on a haj in order to get them out of the way.

Emperor Akbar's religious guide, Sheikh Salim Chisti, made two extended visits to the Holy Cities. On the first trip, he made a total of 14 hajs, and on the second, eight. Between these visits he travelled widely in the Muslim world. When he finally settled in India, he was a figure of enormous prestige. Sometimes the experience of Mecca made Indian visitors less orthodox. One scholar from Gujarat came back from Mecca convinced that he was the Mahdi (the Messiah), who had come to cleanse the world of sin.

SOCIAL IMPLICATIONS

Pilgrimage to Mecca had wide social implications. Even humble pilgrims became locally respected authorities with a measure of superior religious knowledge after performing the haj, for they had walked in the footsteps of the Prophet. This was especially so for the scholars who stayed and studied there for they acquired not only the respect due to all hajis, but also could claim knowledge of how things were done in the heartland of Islam—Mecca and Medina. Thus, they became exemplars of the normative practice of the religion. Yet, there was a wider significance still: people who went on the haj were very unusual in pre-19th century India simply because they had travelled outside the subcontinent. Apart from a few merchants, they were the only overseas travellers. They stood out from their fellow villagers because their horizons had been broadened by exposure to very different societies and cultures. Muslims from diverse backgrounds came together to perform the same rituals at the time of the haj. Indian Muslims thus had contact with fellow Muslims from most parts of the world. Upon their return, their skins showed the 'tanning of travel', that is, they had become aware of a macrocosm quite different from that of their home. Residents of port cities had experienced some of this, being by definition much more cosmopolitan than men from the inland but, among the general population of the interior, only hajis had this experience.

Michael Pearson

INDIAN SLAVERY, LABOUR MIGRATION AND THE EXPORT OF SKILLS

Slavery in India took many forms, ranging from the agrestic servitude which had a long tradition in the country, to the sporadic sale of their children and themselves by famine victims, to the streams of African labour which indigenous traders had been importing for centuries, and the relatively new trade in natives of India, exported via the coastal ports, and chiefly in the hands of European merchants.

INDIANS FOR SALE

War and famine were the chief producers of slaves in India. Dean Mahomed, who would later become the first Indian author in English, was sold as a boy after the 1769–70 famine in eastern India; he would never see his family again. In 1785, another crop failure led to hundreds more children being offered for sale. The Collector of Dacca reported seeing boats 'loaded with children of all ages'. Around the same time in Bombay, famine had brought so many indigent people into the city from the countryside that attempts were made to export them. However, here and in the Telugu districts, where a similar trade in the export of slaves was underway, the British attempted to legislate against the traffic and, in Calcutta in 1789, Lord Cornwallis famously wrote 'hardly a man or woman exists in a corner of this populous town who hath not at least one slave child...most of them were stolen from their parents or bought for perhaps a measure of rice, in time of scarcity.'

Many wealthy native and European households in India boasted African slaves. African child servants became a fashionable accessory of the nabobs in India as well as their counterparts at home, but their use as domestic servants was a luxury. Indian slaves cost less, particularly if procured at times of famine. Travelling through the North-Western Provinces (now Uttar Pradesh) in the 1830s, Fanny Eden described in graphic detail the famine victims she encountered and presented their purchase as an act of humanity: '...we have been surrounded by people dying of starvation...children who have

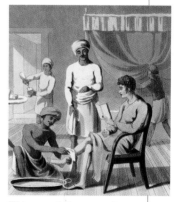

This aquatint was made from a drawing by Charles D'Oyly and published in The European in India, *by Charles D'Oyly and Thomas Williamson, 1813. It depicts a gentleman dressing, attended by his head bearer and other servants.*

41

Starving Indians beg for aid from a British official. In famine years, emaciated Indians flocked to the major port towns and many were exported as slaves from Portuguese, Dutch and French settlements.

A sketch of a street scene in Madras in the 19th century shows famine stricken Indians employed to carry sacks of rice onto carts. These starving people had a number painted on their chests and were allotted a rice ration for their day's work. Women, too weak to work, are shown picking up grains of rice which have escaped from the sacks.

not many hours of life left in them. Almost all our native servants have adopted either orphans or children they have bought for a rupee or two—a very common thing in these times of distress—and they generally keep them for the rest of their lives.' Starving Indians were also available for export as slaves, and while this was initially frowned upon by native rulers and later prohibited by the British, for much of the 17th and 18th centuries the export of Indian slaves was conducted through Portuguese, Dutch and French settlements in the region, and shipped by them, and also through British and Danish slavers.

The European factories, hungry for labour, used this hardship to procure workers for their ports and settlements, both in India and overseas. For example, after a severe famine in 1659–60, entire families offered themselves for sale in South India. The Dutch bought 2000 people for work in Ceylon. There was a ready market for Indian slaves in the Dutch settlements of Southeast Asia, and when available they would be shipped to Aceh or Tenasserim for sale. Where Mughal rulers held sway, European merchants had to be circumspect about slave exports. However, over the course of the 18th century, as central political authority over Indian ports declined, slave markets flourished around the European settlements.

DECEPTION AND KIDNAP

The number of involuntary labour migrants from India was swelled by the many victims of deception and kidnap. From the beginning of the 18th century, French settlers in the Mascarenes had begun sending ships to India to purchase Indian slaves. While labour could easily be procured at times of famine, demand-propelled migration inevitably fuelled abuses as individuals resorted to kidnapping in return for the financial benefits derived from the would-be exporters. In 1792, the British Resident at Calicut reported at length on the measures prevalent 'throughout the Malabar country' to supply the French exporters: '...it has long been a custom of the Moplahs [Mappila] to steal the children of the Nair and other Gentoo castes and carry them to the sea coast for sale...this shocking commerce has grown into great extent.' At that time, two French ships in the harbour held a cargo of around 300 slaves each. Among

them was the son of a local merchant, who was traced to one of the ships and released. At the Dutch settlement of Bimlipatam, a further 600 Indians awaiting export as slaves were released.

MERCHANTS AND THE TRADE IN PEOPLE

The clampdown on slave exports revealed that local merchants were heavily involved in their procurement. In 1793, the Town Major of Madras discovered a number of children in Black Town, waiting to be sold as slaves. They were from a wide socio-economic background—the goldsmith, merchant, labouring and fishermen castes among them—and most were aged between seven and 12. A group of 'Southern Chulia merchants' protested at the removal not only of these child slaves but also of their *tindals* (boatswain) and lascars. They explained the presence of the minors as follows:

...when we made a voyage to the northward lately in purpose of trade, several people of that part of the country having perished by the extremity of the famine, some of those who were victims offered their children, entreating us to be so merciful as to maintain them, so as to save them from the threatening destruction, some of us have been under the necessity of accepting them from motives of regard to the relief of their poverty, and with an intention of preserving them.

The governor of Madras disputed their claims on this occasion and ordered their ships and cargoes to be sold; the profit was to be applied to 'the maintenance of the children rescued from slavery, until they can be returned to their parents.'

In practice, the difficulty of re-assimilating Indian slaves released from the godowns and ship-holds was enormous. When more than 500 young Indians were freed at Bimlipatam, the council of Vizagapatnam ordered that they be redistributed among the local 'renter' class at Chicacole. The cultivators protested in March 1793, complaining of 'the heavy loss we suffered this year... by the effect of famine which had caused a failure of half the usual crop...it is well known we can reap no good by [these people], as we can get nothing done by them, but we will only be at great expenses in having them fed and clothed.' The council was not impressed, informing Michael Keating, the local Collector, that the renters' attitude was 'highly reprehensible...since we find they are solely intent on their own immediate interests, it becomes us to be equally attentive to our rights over them, and we accordingly desire you will instantly and peremptorily demand the payment of what is due from them on account of current kists [revenue demands].' The problem of the indigent rural population, whether kidnapped or sold into slavery by their families or on their own accord, was not easily remedied.

INDIAN SLAVES IN EUROPE

Some Indian domestic slaves travelled back and forth with their owners. Many ended up in Europe, where they faced mixed fortunes. An Italian visitor to Portugal in 1571 reported seeing female Indian slaves at the Duke of Bragança's palace treated like 'herds of horses'—forcibly impregnated so that their offspring could be sold. In 1688, a British newspaper carried an advertisement for a runaway Indian slave boy who could be identified by his neck collar, which was inscribed with the words, 'The Lady Bromfield's Black'.

INDIAN SLAVES IN THE INDIAN OCEAN TERRITORIES

Expeditions to collect slaves were made to Bengal and the Coromandel Coast by the Dutch governor of Batavia in the early 17th century, and many were also made to Ceylon. Christopher Fryke, who travelled in the region in the 1680s, recounted that his landlady in Colombo possessed 'twenty slaves from Bengal which she used very inhumanly', and he reported meeting a Dutch general of the 'East India forces' at the Cape of Good Hope who travelled with a fine retinue and 'a great many slaves from Bengal'. Indian slaves began to arrive at the Dutch settlement on the Cape from the mid-17th century. In 1677, 100 'Tuticorin' slaves were sent to the Cape, having sold themselves to escape starvation. In 1706, a Dutch political prisoner, Jacob van der Heiden, found himself in a cell at the Cape with an Indian slave, Ari, who told him that he had been kidnapped as a child while playing on the beach at Surat. He had been sold from one master to another before escaping to join fugitive slaves, living on stolen food until arrested. Robert Semple, who hired a slave guide at the Cape, heard a 'woeful tale...expressed vehemently in broken Dutch' from the Bengali man he had employed, who raged against his misfortune at having been enticed at the age of 13 onto a ship and brought against his will to South Africa to languish in slavery. More than half of all slaves arriving at the Cape in the 17th and 18th centuries were of Indian origin.

In the 17th century, the Dutch also had a small settlement on Mauritius, and they, and the French, who were established on the sister island of Réunion (then known as Bourbon), also imported Indian slave labour to help develop their embryonic colonies. On Mauritius, Indian slaves were often deportees from Batavia, Indonesia. They played a key role in an arson attack on the Dutch fort, which was a contributing factor to the eventual abandonment of the settlement. Indian slaves, shipped overseas, might be re-exported several times if they proved refractory. Catharine from Paliacatta, for example, had been a slave in Batavia before being sent as a convict to the Cape. Indians who transgressed Dutch laws in South Africa could also be banished to Mauritius and vice versa.

The first recorded slave on Réunion was a young Indian boy sold to a local colonist in 1687. By 1704, 45 Indian slaves had been brought to the island, and within a few years ships were being chartered specifically to bring slaves from the subcontinent. During the course of the 18th century, the French also settled on Mauritius and, from the 1760s, were actively recruiting Indian slaves for both islands. Negri, a 'Malabar' who embarked at Tranquebar in August 1784, later testified that economic

distress had forced him to go on board the *Beauté*, but claimed that he had expected to be employed as a crew member rather than sold on arrival, at a slave auction, to a free Indian already settled on Mauritius. By the turn of the 19th century, it is estimated that some 20,000 Indian slaves had been taken to the Mascarenes—around 13 per cent of the total servile population of the islands.

Indian slaves could rise to positions of great wealth. In the Indian Ocean colonies, where female European immigrants were scarce, it was not uncommon for Indian women to be freed in order to marry their male owners, subsequently amassing considerable property. Maria from Bengal, for example, married Jan Sacharias from Amsterdam in 1658, one of many Indian women to found families in the Cape and on the French islands. The descendants of 17th- and 18th-century French and Dutch settlers in the Indian Ocean owe much to their Indian forebears, recognised or not.

THE SLAVE MODEL AND EARLY INDENTURE

The organisation of early indentured migration in the succeeding century would adopt many of the features of 18th-century slave traffic. European agents at the principal ports acted as suppliers with the support of local intermediaries and 'recruiters'. These European private traders were quick to take advantage of adverse local conditions and sought to purchase slaves at low prices whenever a crop failure occurred. If ships arrived in years of crop surpluses, local political disputes could be stirred up; as a last resort, beggars would be rounded up in the port towns to make up the numbers. For example, in the late 18th century, high-caste beggars were forced onto two French slavers in the port at Yanam, prompting public demonstrations against the owners.

THE EXPORT OF SKILLS

The demand for labour in the developing European settlements of the Indian Ocean was not always or necessarily supplied by coercion. Contract labourers, soldiers and seamen were recruited for the Mascarenes from the 1720s. Indian workers were highly sought after in the Indian Ocean island colonies. They were judged to be less expensive to employ, easier to discipline and worked with greater care than the European artificers about whom frequent complaints of drunkenness and 'debauchery' were made. Indian masons, carpenters and blacksmiths signed contracts in Pondicherry and Cuddalore for service in Mauritius and Réunion, and lascars were recruited from ports across the subcontinent. After the expiry of their contracts, many stayed on. The skilled ones opened workshops, operating as tailors, cobblers and jewellers. Overseas Indian communities in the 18th century thus became slave and property owners themselves, forming an important middle class in the smaller island communities. Furthermore, wherever a group of Indians settled, service migrants followed, Indian doctors and priests among them. Even before the mass migration of indentured labourers in the 19th century, streams of voluntary migrants from India had already become established across the Indian Ocean. Freed Indian slaves added to their numbers, and, at the Cape and elsewhere, marriage and bequests made a number of female Indian migrants wealthy and respected. Few free Indian women migrated at this time, and Indian artisans and other settlers frequently married Indian women who had arrived as slaves.

Marina Carter

In the Isle of France (Mauritius) in the 18th century, a number of Indian slaves worked as palanquin bearers. The wealthier colonists employed four to six of these men for each vehicle, sometimes dressing them in elaborate livery.

Alongside most labour migration streams, a number of Indians arrived to perform a range of 'service' tasks. It was a common sight in the Mascarenes to see Muslim barbers attending to their clients in the streets.

THE AGE OF
COLONIAL CAPITAL

The expansion of British imperial control in India from the 16th to 18th centuries brought new imperatives for the movement of Indians. Early on, the colonial governments followed the British practice of using convict labour for their own interests.

More important in the long term for India was the creation from the 1830s of a system of indentured labour to provide a cheap workforce in the colonial plantation economies of the Caribbean, the Indian Ocean, South and Southeast Asia, Africa and the Pacific. This system was meant to replace slave labour in the local plantations, and it was these indentured workers who provided the foundation of the 'old' diaspora.

In South and Southeast Asia, variant forms of indenture—*kangani* and *maistry*, in which the recruiters became the overseers—were employed to better control the workers. In all forms, however, indenture was a harsh and exploitative system and, as we will see in the studies of the communities born of indenture, it scarred people for generations.

The 19th century also saw the beginning of free migration, mainly to British colonial territories for work and for trade. 'The Age of Colonial Capital' looks closely at Indian trading networks in Southeast Asia in this period to show the extent and value of trade and the importance of these opportunities for the development of the old diaspora.

CONVICT MIGRATION

A LITTLE KNOWN but important part of overseas Indian migration was the transportation of Indian convicts from South Asia to penal settlements across the Indian Ocean and Southeast Asia from the late 18th to mid-20th century.

THE PENAL SETTLEMENT

The East India Company (EIC) established its first penal settlement for Indian convicts in Bencoolen (1787–1825). Settlements in the Andaman Islands (1793–96 and 1858–1945), Penang (Prince of Wales Island, 1790–1860), Melaka and Singapore (1825–73), and the Burmese provinces of Arakan and Tenasserim (1828–62) swiftly followed. The British colony of Mauritius also hosted an Indian penal settlement between 1815 and 1853. After the Sepoy Mutiny of 1857–58, transportation to the Southeast Asian penal settlements was abandoned. Though the earlier attempt to settle the Andamans had failed, the islands were once again used as a penal colony and all Indian convicts were subsequently sent there. Transportation was supposed to be both a punishment and a deterrent to crime. In the eyes of many EIC officials the sea was central to how convicts experienced the punishment of transportation, for crossing the *kalapani* (black water) impacted on caste purity. Transportation was therefore believed to be a worse punishment than death. At the same time, it conveniently emptied overcrowded mainland prisons and supplied new EIC settlements with cheap, controllable and easily replaced labour. The convict workforce was vital to the development of early colonial infrastructure—clearing jungle, and constructing roads, lighthouses, fortifications, canals, bridges and buildings.

CONVICT TRAFFIC

As many as six transportation ships left from each of the Bengal, Bombay and Madras presidencies each year, though the number of convicts on board varied from less than a dozen to more than 200. However, given the lack of systematic records, it is difficult to quantify the total Indian Ocean convict traffic. Ship indents drawn up in the three presidencies suggest that the EIC shipped just over 2000 convicts to Bencoolen until 1825, at least 300 convicts to its first abortive Andaman Islands settlement and about 1500 to Mauritius. In 1825, the surviving Bencoolen convicts were transferred to Penang, which was by then also a penal settlement. Together, the Straits Settlements (Singapore, Melaka and Penang) probably received over 25,000 convicts, and the Burmese provinces received between 7000 and 10,000. A few thousand more

Indentured labourers who refused or were unable to perform the hard labour of sugar cane planting and processing were deemed 'incorrigible vagrants' and deported to India. To prevent them from re-embarking for Mauritius, their photographs were sent to the emigration agents at Indian ports, effectively 'blacklisting' them.

Exiled women formed only a small proportion of convicts in the Andamans, at most 10 per cent. They were not involved in hard labour but were engaged in domestic labour in the female factory.

from Ceylon were also transported to Southeast Asia. The total number of convicts transported to the Andaman Islands has never been calculated, though in the immediate aftermath of the 1857 mutiny 4000 were sent. With transportation continuing until World War II, the number of convicts sent there must at least have matched the Southeast Asian total.

Almost all the convicts were men; women never made up more than 10 per cent of the convict community. Most had been sentenced for serious crimes such as murder, robbery or dacoity and were serving life terms. Nearly all of the female convicts were transported for murder or infanticide. Others were transported for anti-British resistance or other 'political' crimes. Convicts came from all regions of India and Ceylon and were of various socio-economic backgrounds, but the largest proportion was from Bengal and the majority were poor Hindus.

CONVICT LABOUR

During the early part of the 19th century, convict labour was vital to the success of newly settled British territories. Indeed, it was not the Indian authorities but the penal settlements' demand for convicts that stimulated and controlled the supply. Upon arrival in the settlements, most convicts were put to work at hard labour. They cleared land, dug ditches, built roads and bridges, and constructed public buildings. Some remarkable structures built by convicts still stand, such as St. Andrew's Cathedral and the Istana, completed in 1862 and 1869 respectively in Singapore. Other convicts were engaged in skilled work like brick making, weaving, gardening and printing. In Mauritius, convicts worked in the nascent silk industry. Unlike the situation in most Indian jails, the penal authorities in these settlements were of the opinion that work should constitute both a punishment and a means of training and reformation. When F. J. Mouat, Inspector-General of Prisons Bengal, visited the Straits Settlements in 1861, he declared that the penal settlements there were the most remarkable example of successful industrial training for convicts in the world.

Organisational changes reflected the increasing preoccupation with reformative labour. Until the 1820s, discipline had been relatively slack. In 1824, the first set of convict regulations was produced when Sir Thomas Stamford Raffles devised the Bencoolen Regulations, a 'carrot and stick' management system which formed the basis of later convict regulations, notably the Penang Rules (1827) and the Butterworth Rules (1860). Convicts were divided into classes according to the length of their sentence, time served in the settlement and conduct. They were rewarded for good behaviour and punished for misdemeanours. The prospect of a ticket-of-leave (probation) was dangled to encourage them. In the meantime, convicts who displayed good conduct received monetary gratuities or were appointed as petty officers in charge of their fellow men. Convicts who broke prison regulations, on the other hand, were downgraded a class or punished with flogging or hard labour in iron fetters.

THE END OF TRANSPORTATION

Transportation to Mauritius ended in 1837 after India refused to bow to the colony's demand that no more serious offenders be sent. After the Indian revolt of 1857, European residents in Singapore began to regard convicts as a threat to security and refused to receive any of the so-called mutineers. With the establishment of the Andaman Islands as a penal colony, transportation to Southeast Asia ended by the 1860s. In 1873, the penal settlements in the Straits of Melaka were abandoned, though approximately 1800 convicts still remained. The authorities granted pardons to some surviving convicts, and ticket-of-leave holders disappeared into the general population. Convict transportation to Burma also ended at this time, when the authorities transferred those convicts still in the settlements to the Andamans. Before 1859, time-expired convicts were not provided with a return passage to India. As a result, most of them settled in Southeast Asia and married local women. In the Straits Settlements, many became part of the Jawi-Pekan (Indo-Malay) community. Their influence was particularly strong in Penang, which

Chetoo, an 'incorrigible' convict of the 5th class. He is dressed in the uniform and fetters reserved for the lowest 'class' of convicts who, because of their misconduct, were made to work in gangs employed in the harshest forms of hard labour.

was a mainly Jawi-Pekan settlement until the second half of the 19th century. In the Andamans, there was less inter-action between convicts and the islands' indigenous tribal inhabitants. Convicts, however, were eventually given 'self-supporter' status and their descendants now make up what is known as the 'local-born' community.

Clare Anderson

THE INDENTURE SYSTEM

Indian indentured emigration began as a direct response to the shortage of labour in the plantation 'King Sugar' colonies following the abolition of slavery in the British Empire in 1833, and the failure of the 'apprentice system', under which planters were able to obtain ex-slave labour until 1838. Conscious of their new-found freedom, dignity and access to the law, the apprentices refused to re-engage for any length of time. Their reluctance to do so led to the search for alternative sources of labour. In the end, the colonies would look to India, but many in the West Indies initially turned their attention to Europe and Africa. Between 1834 and 1837, some 3000 English, 1000 Scottish and German, and 100 Irish labourers were introduced into Jamaica, with smaller numbers going to St. Lucia, on three- to five-year contracts. The experiment failed, however, because of the high mortality rate among the workers due to 'insufficient sanitary precautions', the 'unsuitability of raw, unacclimatised Europeans for field work in the tropical sun, with the added temptation of unlimited drink', and general low morale. Trinidad tried to procure labour from neighbouring Grenada, St. Christopher and Nevis under a 'bounty' system, but this 'ill-contrived and injudiciously managed' system failed too, as did attempts to import workers from Sierra Leone, Gambia, the Kroo Coast of Liberia and, on the other side of the world, China. The Chinese tended to move out of

International traders and Indians jostle for space, bathing, cooking and collecting water, in the port of Calcutta, 1900.

Table 3.1

MAJOR COLONIES IMPORTING INDIAN INDENTURED LABOUR		
	Period of migration	No. of emigrants
Mauritius	1834–1900	453,063
British Guiana	1838–1916	238,909
Malaya	1844–1910	250,000
Trinidad	1845–1916	143,939
Jamaica	1845–1913	36,412
Grenada	1856–85	3200
St. Lucia	1858–95	4350
Natal	1860–1911	152,184
St. Kitts	1860–61	337
St. Vincents	1860–80	2472
Réunion	1861–83	26,507
Surinam	1873–1916	34,304
Fiji	1879–1916	60,965
East Africa	1896–1921	39,282
Seychelles	1904–16	6315

Source: Brij V. Lal, Girmitiyas: The Origins of the Fiji Indians, *1983.*

the plantations at the earliest possible opportunity to set out on their own as market gardeners and shopkeepers.

THE BEGINNINGS OF INDENTURE

The failure of these efforts shifted attention to India. Mauritius had been enjoying modest success with Indian labour since 1834, when 36 Dhangars were brought there on contract. The rudimentary contract bound the labourer to work for a planter 'or such other persons he may be transferred

to', and stipulated the duration of the contract (five years), remuneration (Rs. 10 per month), amount of food, clothing and medical facilities to be provided, and an optional free return passage to Calcutta at the end of the contract. The tentative venture proved successful. Between 1 August 1834 and the end of 1835, 14 ships were engaged to transport emigrants from Calcutta to Mauritius. By the end of 1839, over 25,000 emigrants were taken to the island. Other colonies followed suit, as Table 3.1 shows. By the time indentured emigration ceased, over 1 million indentured labourers from India had been transported to distant colonies across the globe.

For the better part of the 1830s, India left the recruitment and transportation of labourers to the laws of supply and demand. Many planters obtained their labourers through European firms based in Calcutta and neighbouring areas, but it was not long before recruitment irregularities came to the attention of the government. In 1837, the government of Bengal noted that the 'rude and ignorant' class of people who were being recruited either did not 'fully understand the terms of the contracts by which they bind themselves, or that they are really willing to proceed for long periods to a distance from their native country.'

Such doubts, coupled with reports of abuse and neglect of labourers on ill-equipped and poorly supervised ships, led the government of India to direct Indian law commissioners to draw up proposals to regulate indenture. These were incorporated in Act V of 1837. Among other things, Act V stipulated that the emigration of contract labourers be subject to orders from authorities in India; that the emigrant be required to appear before an official appointed by the provincial government; that the contract, in English and in the vernacular, must specify wages and the nature of the employment the emigrant would undertake in Mauritius; that a contract for over five years, and which did not provide for a return passage, not be approved; and that recruiters obtaining labourers through 'fraudulent means' be fined or imprisoned. Mere legislative enactment, however, did not stop abuses, which kept surfacing and led the government to temporarily halt emigration so that it could 'endeavour to devise adequate measures for the protection of such persons.'

On 22 August 1838, the government of India appointed a committee of six eminent persons—T. Dickens, Reverend James Charles, W. F. Dawson, Russomroy Dutt, J. P. Grant and Major E. Archer—to investigate and report on all aspects of indentured emigration. The committee examined witnesses from August 1838 to mid-January 1839 and submitted its final report in October 1840. Due to the massive and frequently contradictory nature of the evidence that came before it, the committee submitted two reports. The majority report made a scathing critique

of the indenture system: '...it distinctly proved beyond dispute that the Coolies and other natives exported to Mauritius and elsewhere were (generally speaking) induced to come to Calcutta by gross misrepresentation and deceit practiced upon them by native crimps, styled duffadars and *arkatis* and shippers who were mostly cognizant of these frauds, and who received a very considerable sum per head for each Coolie exported.' If the emigrants had been told where they were going, they would not have enlisted. The legislative measures to curtail abuse had failed; emigrants were threatened with legal action if they refused to emigrate after they had signed the contract; and they suffered social and economic disabilities in the colonies, whose laws and regulations had 'little practical utility in restraining illegal importations of

---

Sample contract for a labourer

Duffadar Bhuwanny.   No. 152.

I, PEROO, engage to proceed to Mauritius to serve E. Antard, père, or such other person as I may be transferred to (such transfer being made by mutual consent, to be declared before a public officer), as a khidmutgar, for the space of five years from the date of this agreement, on consideration of receiving a remuneration of Company's rupees ten (10) per month, and food and clothing as follows; viz.

14 chittacks rice,		1 blanket	
2 " dholl,	daily	2 dhooties	
- ½ " ghee		1 chintz mirjace	yearly
- ¼ " salt,		1 lascar's cap	
		1 wooden bowl	

also one lotah or brass cup between four persons, and medicine and medical attendance when required; also to be sent back to Calcutta at the expiration of my period of service, free of all expense to myself, should such be my wish, subject to the terms of my general agreement. Executed this   day of November 1837.

Peroo, his + mark.

নিখিতিও, শিক্ প্রেদমত্গার কস্ এক্বার প্রমিদ্ কার্যনধ্যাণে এই
এক্বার পাদের তারিখ অবধি পাঁচ বৎসরের মিয়াদ   অথবা
তিনি হাকিমের লোকের সাক্ষাতে উত্মার সন্মতি পূর্ব্বক জাহার নিক্টে
আমাকে শোপর্দ্দ করেণ মত্ুবগ্গিরি চাক্রি কবুল করিলাম মাহিনা কোম্পা-
নির   টাকার হিসাবে পাইব থোরাক পোশাক নিচের নিখিত
উপশীল মাসিক পাইব——

থোরাক প্রতি দিবস		পোশাক প্রতি বৎসর	
চাল ৭৯, চদ্দচ্ঠাক		কম্বল ১ এক	
ডাল ২০ দুইচ্ঠাক		ধুতি ২ দুই	
ঘৃত ২০ অর্দ্দচ্ঠাক		চিট্টবমৃত্রাই ১ এক	
লবন ৫ এক্কাচ্চা		কাপ্সের বাটী ১ এক	

চারি চারি জনে এক তাম্রা কিম্বা পীতল্লের লোটারী বাটী পাইব আর জখন
দরকার হয় চিকিৎসা এবং ঔষুধ পাইব আর চাক্রির মিয়াদ সম্পূর্ণ হইলে
জদি আমি বাসনা করি আমাকে পূনরায় কলিকাত্রায় আপনার থরচে
পোঁচাইতে হই বেক এই সাধারণ এক্বারনামার সর্তে মাসিক তাহাতে আমার
কিছু থরচ নাগি বেক না ইতি তারিখ
সন ১৮৩৭ সাল——

Height, 5 feet 3 inches; age, 28 years; colour, light; particular marks, none; caste, Mussulman.

I hereby certify, that this memorandum of contract has been inspected by me, and the contents thereof fully explained to the within named.

(signed)   F. W. Birch,
Calcutta, 20 November 1837.   Supt Calcutta Police.

Brij V. Lal, 'Leaves of the Banyan Tree: origins and background of Fiji's North Indian indentured migrants', 1980.

coolies.' To prevent 'great misery and distress', the committee recommended greater government control; formal conventions between India and the colonies; restriction of indentured emigration to specified well-supervised ports; the appointment of a chief superintendent and 'purveyors' (protectors) of emigrants in the colonies; fixing a specified proportion of women to accompany emigrating men; and government control of shipping.

J. P. Grant, in a minority report, dissented. He acknowledged irregularities in the system but urged against direct government intervention. The disadvantages, he argued, had to be clearly and dispassionately weighed against the 'incalculable' advantages to the emigrants themselves. It was to this view that the government itself was inclined, but considered it prudent to halt all emigration temporarily. The first round had been won by the 'humanitarians', who nevertheless continued their efforts to educate the British public about the evils of the 'coolie trade'; but the planters also began to canvass support, shifting their attention to Britain, which by then had emerged as the key battleground. While 'working hard with the Government and press', the planters showed 'unwanted anxiety to conciliate the abolitionists.'

REFORMS

More correspondence followed between the colonies, the Imperial government and the government of India, which indicated that the prohibition of emigration could not be continued for long. Reports from the colonies showed that while there certainly were problems and hardships, they were not as harsh as had been portrayed. Indeed, they offered evidence which pointed to material improvement in the conditions of the labourers. In January 1842, the Colonial Office passed an order, conditional upon the approval of the government of India, sanctioning emigration to Mauritius. Most of its principles were later incorporated into the government of India's Act XV of 1842, which was the first comprehensive measure to provide a semblance of government control and supervision.

Act XV provided for the appointment of an emigration agent on a fixed salary at the ports of embarkation in India and a protector of emigrants in Mauritius. The agent was required to personally examine each emigrant and ascertain that he (or she) fully understood the nature of the transaction. The agent was to give a comprehensive report of all the proceedings to the provincial government. All ships were henceforth to be licensed by the government and required to conform to certain prescribed conditions: dietary and medical supplies for the emigrants were to be set, as were accommodation facilities and the length of the voyage itself. Act XV was an improvement but it still had many defects. For a start, it dealt perfunctorily with the system of recruitment, but perhaps most important of all, there was no provision for the enforcement of the regulations. To no one's surprise, subsequent investigations continued to unearth problems.

Mauritius opened the way for emigration and it was not long after that the West Indian colonies renewed their request for Indian labour. In the past, the government of India had been reluctant to sanction emigration there. The islands were remote, there was the problem of inadequate communication, and the government feared the effects of the inevitable competition for recruits. It was the positive reports on the condition of the emigrants that changed the government's mind. Although 98 of the 414 emigrants taken to British Guiana in 1838 had died, many had done

well, with returning migrants bringing what the government thought were substantial sums of money. Hence, indentured emigration was allowed to British Guiana, Trinidad and Jamaica on the same terms and conditions as those applying to Mauritius. In the 1850s, indentured emigration was also sanctioned to some of the other smaller colonies in the Caribbean.

As the indenture system took root in the West Indies and elsewhere, and as its benefits became evident, the colonies tried to abolish the 'return passage' clause in the Emigration Act. Mauritius raised the question in 1851, followed two years later by British Guiana and Trinidad. In the case of Mauritius, the government of India agreed that repatriation should not be mandatory, provided the colonial government agreed to pay for the return passage of those unable, due to sickness or destitution, to pay their own way. Trinidad proposed to give free return tickets only to those who claimed the right of repatriation after 18 months of it being made available; others, even after 10 years of residence, should be required to contribute to the cost of the return voyage.

The government of India proceeded cautiously, as it had done in the case of Mauritius, but once it grasped the full implications of the proposal, it retreated from its earlier position. The Court of Directors stated in 1857 that it would 'view with great jealousy any proposals for depriving the natives of India of their absolute right to a return passage to their own country, unless such provisions could be framed as would perfectly secure them from the risk of undue influence when it was sought to obtain their consent to an arrangement for keeping them in the colony.' Lord Canning's government concurred: the labourers should be free to 'make their own bargain'.

Efforts to reform the system were genuine and partly successful but investigations in the late 1850s and 1860s continued to unearth evidence of irregularities and evasions. Some of these were brought to light by H. N. D. Beyts, who was sent from Mauritius to India to investigate matters related to immigration. He especially criticised the system of recruitment and the unscrupulous tactics employed by recruiters. Often, deception was practised 'in open defiance of the authority of the local laws', while the protector of emigrants was 'utterly powerless to prevent the abuses if not in all at least in nine-tenths of the cases in which offences were committed.' Recruits willing to go to one colony were regularly taken to another. Dr F. J. Mout, appointed by the government of Bengal to investigate problems relating to the shipping of emigrants, found

The ship Elbe, *brought many indentured labourers to Fiji.*

Migrant workers disembarking from a ship in Penang, c. 1905.

distressingly high rates of mortality on the voyages. The average mortality rate on the 12 ships which left for the West Indies during 1856–57 was 17.3 per cent, and on the *Merchantman* alone it hit 31.2 per cent. Mouat blamed the high mortality rate on the indifference shown to the health of labourers, poor diet and faulty screening, but the government put the blame squarely on inadequate facilities and conditions on the voyage.

Investigations such as Mouat's led to further changes, which were incorporated into Emigration Act XIII of 1864. For the first time, the duty of the protector of emigrants was defined precisely. Unlike the previous practice, when recruits were transferred directly to the port of embarkation from their district of origin, they now had to be interviewed by local magistrates, who had to be satisfied that the emigrants understood the terms and conditions of the contract. At the port of embarkation, the protector was required to personally interview each emigrant. The recruiters were granted licenses on an annual basis and had to wear badges to publicly reveal their identity.

Abuses in the indenture system were well aired, but the colonial emigration agents also complained of the obstructive attitude of local authorities who delayed correspondence and refused to grant recruiters' licenses, 'unless a respectable zamindar becomes a security for them.' The agent for Jamaica thought that the practice of daily police visits to the Emigration Depot was 'in truth sending wolves and vultures to look after and take care of lambs', a reference to widespread corruption in the police force. He complained that the impression abroad was that the government was opposed to emigration and that local authorities could impede recruitment at will.

LORD SALISBURY'S DISPATCH

The upshot of this and similar complaints was a letter from the secretary of state for the colonies, Lord Salisbury, to the government of India in 1875, enquiring whether under proper regulation and with due attention to the rights of the labourers, the government of India 'might not more directly encourage emigration and superintend the system under which it is conducted.' Emigration would be profitable for the migrants 'on grounds of humanity and with a view to promote the well-being of the poorer classes'; and it would also benefit the colonies which needed large supplies of cheap labour for economic development. If the government of India agreed, Salisbury promised, the emigrants would enjoy 'rights no whit inferior to those of any other class of Her Majesty's subjects resident in the colonies.' The government of India forwarded Salisbury's dispatch to the provincial governments for their response. All except Bengal declined to become involved. Bombay thought emigration would cause a loss of revenue because of labour scarcity. Madras thought its involvement could be misconstrued to imply that the government was intervening to protect the interests of the colonies at the expense of India. The matter was settled: the government of India preferred to see recruitment as a commercial transaction which did not require its intervention. It had little to gain from an involvement which might place it in the unenviable position of having to reconcile the interests of the colonies with those of the emigrants. But perhaps the real reason was political, based on the apprehension that if the government was too closely identified with the promotion of emigration, the responsibility for abuses in the system might be transferred to its shoulders.

Sample contract for a recruiter (Trinidad)

Allahabad, _____ 188.

1st. – I hereby agree to give you a contract for supplying intending emigrants for Trinidad during the season of 1880–81 from the districts and for supervising generally over their registration and other conveniences.

2nd. – When the coolies are gathered by you, not under 10 men, I will have a chalan and you shall give a chalan, and I will have amongst 100 men 40 women, and if women and men are not sent, the rates will be decreased and then you will have to agree upon it, and when your coolies arrive here at Allahabad and are on the station (in the train) and arrive at Calcutta, then whatever may be your rates according to that your money will be 'pakka.' If any coolies registered by the Doctor or by me run away or die or refuse at the time, the loss of which will be borne by you. Money you shall receive then when I will receive a letter from Calcutta saying all the coolies have arrived here safe: nothing will be paid for those under 10 years of age; over 12 you shall get half rate.

3rd. – Rates for out districts:-
Fatehpur, each man, Rs. 6; each woman, Rs. 8.
Bánda, Mirzapur, and Beylah Partabgarh, the same if you wish to work at Allahabad; out villages the rates will be each man Rs. 6 and each woman Rs. 7; you will receive nothing of those that are under 12 years of age.

4th. – All expenses for recruiting [sic], registration, food for coolies, and other expenses up to the time of arrival at the station must be paid by you.

5th. – Strong healthy field labourers are required and all such castes minor, whether male or female under 18 years of age, will not be taken unless accompanied by respectable relatives or (father or mother). No men will be taken of soft hands or weak. 'Panjábis' are altogether refused. Men should be recruited of those sort when they agree to be vaccinated and also eat on board of ship.

6th. – When you have taken the license of Trinidad and after which at any time without my license give the coolies elsewhere or have your license changed or send it by another man, and if made out there, whatever may be the rate of Calcutta I shall take from you: there will be no objection to it at all. Whatever this has been written if not done accordingly with License, and all, whatever may be the loss, it will all be taken from you and you will not hesitate at all.

Emigration Sub-Agent for Trinidad.

I agree to the terms and conditions of this agreement.

Recruiter for Trinidad.

Brij V. Lal, Girmitiyas: The Origins of the Fiji Indians, *1983.*

WOMEN

One source of complaint and controversy throughout had been the recruitment of women. The proportion of women to men in the emigrating population varied throughout the entire period of indentured emigration. In the very early years, few women were recruited as labourers. Between August 1834 and May 1837, of the 7000 indentured emigrants who went to Mauritius from Calcutta, fewer than 200 were women. The colonial planters wanted able-bodied men and instructed their agents to recruit men rather than women; but as reforms were made in the system and as social awareness grew of the problems caused by the paucity of women on the plantations, it became clear that more women should be recruited on the basis of a prescribed ratio. Some efforts were made in the 1840s and 1850s, but real advances came in the 1860s. In 1867, the Emigration Board advised the government of India to fix the proportion of female to male emigrants at 50:100. The government fixed the proportion at 33:100. The Colonial Office fixed the ratio at 40:100 and asked India to enforce it. The ratio remained in force throughout. Figure 3.1 shows that the

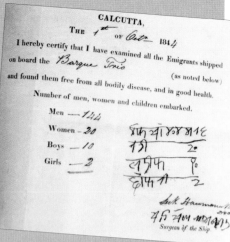

FROM LEFT: *A number of emigration depots were located on the banks of the Hooghly at Calcutta. Migrants thus had to face a long journey upriver before the sea voyage had even begun; from 1842 it was compulsory for a medical attendant to certify that emigrants were fit to embark before sailing. The surgeons employed on the 'coolie ships' were frequently native doctors. In this case, the Trio, which left for Mauritius in 1844, carried on board a Muslim medical attendant.*

CHALAN: THE JOURNEY

Once the recruiters had collected a few recruits, they took them to the sub-depot where they would stay for up to two weeks. The agency's travelling medical inspectors examined them. The ones considered unfit were rejected and they presumably found their way back to their villages. Those who passed were taken to the district civil surgeon for a medical examination before being presented to the sub-divisional magistrate for registration. By the time the recruits had passed through the sub-depot, 18 per cent of the original recruits were rejected, over half because they were unfit. Many also deserted and some were claimed by relatives.

Those who were registered then began their *chalan* (journey) to the port of embarkation, which could take up to two weeks. The recruiter accompanied the batch of emigrants, and he had to have a special certificate for this purpose. In Calcutta, the main emigration depot was at Garden Reach. Palms had to be greased along the way. In 1882, the police demanded 4 annas for each recruit and a rupee for the man in charge. At Howrah Bridge, constables had to be paid for recruits to cross it without harassment. In 1894, the police, angry at not being offered bribes, stood idly by as railway workers rushed the recruits, resulting in the loss of some 106 of them. At the emigration depot, a reception shed was set apart from the other buildings for the examination of freshly arrived recruits. Those who passed were then taken to the accommodation depot. Single males and females were kept apart and every effort was made to keep families together. Each agency had separate hospital sheds for treating ordinary diseases, observation sheds for suspected cases, and segregation sheds for the treatment of contagious diseases. There was also an inspection shed for mustering of emigrants for various purposes.

During their brief stay at Garden Reach, the emigrants were examined by the protector of emigrants. Further reductions took place. On average, a little more than three-quarters of the recruits who were admitted to the depot finally embarked for the colonies. If the number of those who migrated to all the colonies is compared to the numbers first brought to the depot up-country, the loss is staggering: in 1894, only 58.8 per cent of the original recruits finally boarded the ships; in 1895, 58.8 per cent; in 1896, 61.5 per cent; in 1899, 65.5 per cent; and in 1900, 61.4 per cent. The main reasons for this were the rejection of unfit recruits and desertion.

Once passed by the medical authorities and the protector of emigrants, the recruits spent a compulsory period of seven days at the depot before embarking. During this time, they did light work such as keeping the sheds clean and the garden and grounds in order. Games and amusements were encouraged to keep morale high. The prospect of a new life fostered a new sense of subaltern companionship and togetherness, cutting across the barriers of religion, caste and place of origin. Taboos about food, caste relationships or marriage that had been such an integral part of life in village India began to fracture and lose relevance, aided by the attitude of the authorities, who viewed the recruits not as people worthy of individual humanity and dignity, but as a mass of 'coolies', units of labour to be worked for profit. Nonetheless, fragmentation was one part of the equation. The other, equally important, was reconstitution, by which new ideas, values and associations were being forged along the way, more out of necessity rather than by choice, which would over time lay the foundations of a new, more egalitarian, more pragmatic, and less protocol-driven culture in the colonies. As the emigrants waited anxiously in the crowded depots for their ships to leave, they got a foretaste of things to come in the distant and strange lands for which they were destined, and from which most would never return.

The old Howrah pontoon bridge across the Hooghly at Calcutta, seen in 1905. Recruiters had to bribe the constables to allow emigrants to proceed across the bridge to the depot at Garden Reach. The pontoon bridge was replaced with a modern steel bridge in 1943.

Figure 3.1

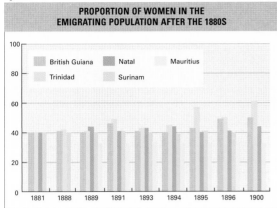

PROPORTION OF WOMEN IN THE
EMIGRATING POPULATION AFTER THE 1880S

British Guiana Natal Mauritius
Trinidad Surinam

Source: Brij V. Lal, Girmitiyas: The Origins of the Fiji Indians, *1983.*

Table 3.2

	Calcutta		Madras		Bombay/Karachi		French ports	
	No. (% of total during that period)							
1856–61	14,533	*(66.5)*	6479	*(29.6)*	860	*(3.9)*	N.A.	
1871–70	122,241	*(67.5)*	56,356	*(31.1)*	2479	*(1.4)*	N.A.	
1870–79	142,793	*(78.4)*	19,104	*(10.5)*	N.A.		20,269	*(11.1)*
1880–89	97,975	*(76.0)*	21,653	*(16.8)*	N.A.		9351	*(7.2)*
1891–1900	106,700	*(63.3)*	28,550	*(16.9)*	33,343	*(19.8)*	N.A.	
1907–16	66,839	*(62.3)*	32,369	*(30.2)*	8016	*(7.5)*	N.A.	

PORTS OF EMBARKATION OF INDIAN INDENTURED LABOURERS

Source: Brij V. Lal, Girmitiyas: The Origins of the Fiji Indians, *1983.*

quota was invariably met. In the case of Mauritius, the ratio was set at 33:100, and this too was met.

ADMINISTRATION AND RECRUITMENT

In 1882, the government of India passed an all-encompassing Emigration Act (XXII) which, with minor modifications in 1908, governed indentured emigration until its end in 1916. The act limited indentured embarkation to the ports of Calcutta, Madras and Bombay, and abolished it altogether from the French ports. Each colony was required to appoint an emigration agent, usually one of its officials, on a fixed salary, at the port of embarkation. As recruiting seasons varied for the different colonies, one emigration agent was able to represent a number of them. For much of the late 19th century, there were only two emigration agencies in Calcutta. One handled recruitment for British Guiana and Natal, and the other was shared between Trinidad, Mauritius, Fiji, Jamaica and, occasionally, the other smaller West Indian colonies of Grenada, St. Vincents and St. Lucia. Surinam, being a Dutch colony, had a separate agency.

The emigration agent himself recruited rarely, except in the vicinity of the depot. More commonly, he forwarded the requisitions from the colonies to the sub-agents up-country. In the United Provinces (UP), Major D. G. Pitcher found a number of them to be Jews, while in Bihar, according to George Grierson, many were former recruiters 'who had shown aptitude for the work.' In Allahabad in the 1870s, there were some Europeans who recruited as well. Some sub-agents, such as those for Trinidad, were paid a fixed salary supplemented by a commission to cover the expenses of recruitment. The British Guiana agency did not pay its sub-agents a fixed salary but gave them a higher commission, supplemented at the end of the season by a bonus for every 1000 emigrants who had embarked. The commission varied from place to place depending on the proximity of the location of recruitment to the port of embarkation, and it varied over time as well. Another factor impacting on the recruiter's salary was the availability of recruits. In 1886, rates for men and children varied from Rs. 17 to Rs. 23, while for women they ranged from Rs. 24 to Rs. 34. In Allahabad in 1882, the sub-agents were paid Rs. 28 for women and Rs. 18 for men; in 1905, the rates had increased to Rs. 40 for men and Rs. 55 for women, and they remained in that range until the end.

The sub-agents appointed and employed the recruiters, although in theory, the recruiters were directly responsible to the emigration agent. However, the recruiters were licensed by the protector of emigrants on the recommendation of the emigration agent. The licence was for a year (renewable) and had to be countersigned by the magistrate of the district where the recruiter intended to work. Their remuneration varied depending on which colony they worked for. The French colonies paid their recruiters a fixed salary, while British Guiana paid both a salary and commission. Ghura Khan, British Guiana's sub-agent at Buxar, paid his recruiters Rs. 5 to Rs. 8 a month, besides paying Rs. 5 for men and Rs. 8 for women. In Allahabad in the 1880s, recruiters received commissions only—Rs. 6 for men and Rs. 8 for women.

Recruiters came from varied social and caste backgrounds. In the Benares region between 1882 and 1892, of the 507 recruiters operating there, Muslims accounted for 205 or 40 per cent of the total, followed, at quite a distance, by the Banias (67), Kayasths (33), Halwais (18), Brahmins (17), Thakurs (16) and Chattris (13). Most of the recruiters were male and conducted their own business, but in many cases they also employed unlicensed recruiters called *arkatis*, who were employed where there were few recruiters or where the prospects for recruiting looked bleak. Little is known about these people. In the UP, Pitcher found the *arkatis* to be *chaukidars* (guards) and *patwaris* (record keepers) who welcomed the opportunity to make a few extra rupees by turning in 'troublesome characters'. In Bihar, George Grierson found that the *arkatis* came from all castes: some had been engaged in recruiting for a long time, while others were shopkeepers, peons, domestic servants, cloth sellers and even labourers.

REGIONAL ORIGINS

Indian indentured labourers emigrating to various parts of the world came from widely scattered regions of India.

A document certifying that an indentured labourer had completed his term of service and was a free man.

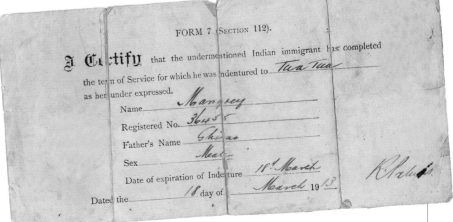

Table 3.3

SOUTH INDIAN INDENTURED EMIGRATION TO THE SUGAR COLONIES		
	No.	Percentage of total
Mauritius	144,342	31.9
Natal	103,261	67.9
British Guiana	15,065	6.3
Fiji	14,536	23.8
West Indies	12,975	N.A.
French West Indies	330	2.0
Réunion	2131	14.2

Source: Brij V. Lal, Girmitiyas: The Origins of the Fiji Indians, *1983.*

Table 3.4

DISTRICTS SUPPLYING OVER 1 PER CENT OF THE *WHITBY* AND *HESPRES* EMIGRANTS (1839)		
	No.	Percentage of total
Hazaribagh	72	17.8
Bankura	49	12.1
Ramgarh	36	8.9
Midnapur	27	6.7
Nagpur	20	4.9
Kasi	13	3.2
Cuttack	13	3.2
Muzaffarpur	11	2.7
Burdwan	10	2.5
Lucknow	10	2.5
Ayodhya	8	2.0
Ghazipur	8	2.0
Arrah	7	1.7
Bistopur	6	1.5
Chapra	5	1.2
Others	110	27.1

Source: Brij V. Lal, 'Leaves of the Banyan Tree: origins and background of Fiji's North Indian indentured migrants', 1980.

South India

South India has probably always been the most migration-prone region of the subcontinent. Systematic large-scale emigration from the region began with the development of European commercial enterprises in the 'Colonies of India System', that is, Burma, Ceylon and Malaya. As discussed elsewhere in this volume, the bulk of labour migration to these areas arrived under the *kangani* and *maistry* systems. In the case of Burma, 2,595,000 Indian migrants settled there permanently between 1852 and 1937, of whom a large number were South Indians; while in Ceylon, 1,529,000 stayed on in the country between 1834 and 1938; and in Malaya, between 1860 and 1938, the figure was 1,189,000. South India also contributed significant numbers of indentured labourers to the sugar colonies, as shown in Table 3.3.

Malaya and Ceylon drew most of their Indian labour from Tamil Nadu, while Burma drew a large part of its supplies from Vizagapatnam and Godavari in Andhra Pradesh, and to a lesser extent from Tanjore and Ramnad. Before 1842, large numbers of South Indian labourers came from Vizagapatnam, Coimbatore, Tanjore, Trichinopoly, Malabar and Chingleput. From 1842 to 1870, Godavari, Ganjam, Madras, Chingleput, Tanjore, South Arcot and Rajahmundry were the principal recruiting grounds, and from 1870 to 1899 North Arcot, Vizagapatnam, Trichinopoly, Chingleput and Madras gained primacy.

Western India

Western India was a minor region for recruitment because the provincial government there discouraged emigration. Furthermore, employment could be found at home in the textile mills and in road construction and irrigation work. Between 1842 and 1870, Bombay accounted for only 31,761 or 6 per cent of all indentured embarkations, all of them to Mauritius. The main districts of recruitment during this period were Poona, Satara, Ratnagiri, Nagpur and Sawantwadi. After the 1870s, some 43,221 embarked at Bombay and Karachi, of whom 85 per cent went to Mombasa, Kenya, to work in railway construction. Most of these migrants were from Punjab.

French India

Between 1842 and 1916, some 49,890 emigrants left for the French colonies, of whom 20,770 (41.6 per cent) left before the 1870s, the majority for the West Indies (16,011) and Réunion (4579). After the 1870s, over half of the emigrants went to the French West Indies, one-third to Réunion and the rest to French Guiana. The government of India was never keen to sanction indentured emigration to the French colonies, partly because of fears of rivalry and also because the French had a reputation for ill-treating their labourers. Embarkation from the French ports was prohibited after the promulgation of Emigration Act XXII, which restricted departures to Calcutta, Madras and Bombay.

North India

North India was the largest supplier of Indian indentured labour to the colonies. Although most emigrants left from the port of Calcutta, there were few Bengalis among the migrants. The majority were 'up-country' men. Before the 1870s, they came from the tribal and plains areas of Bihar, and from the 1870s onwards, from the depressed districts of eastern UP. In the 1830s, Dhangars from the

Chota Nagpur plateau were prominent. The list of those on two ships bound for British Guiana in 1839 gives some sense of the precise place of origin of the labourers (see Table 3.4).

In terms of their social background, 34 per cent of the emigrants were recorded as Dhangars and a further 15 per cent as tribal or quasi-tribal groups (Bauris, Bhuyias and Badgis), 8 per cent were Muslims, 8 per cent were Rajputs, 5 per cent were Kurmis and 3 per cent were Gowalas. The Dhangars were popular with their employers. Thomas Blythe and Sons of Mauritius said they were 'docile and industrious', while another planter, J. R. Mayo, remarked that 'they are temperate, and are particularly trustworthy where sobriety is absolutely necessary.' From the 1840s onwards, recruiting shifted to the more 'Hinduised' settled plains of Bihar, as Table 3.5 shows.

The shift from the tribal areas to more settled locations took place primarily because of the very high mortality rates among the tribal emigrants on the voyages out: cramped conditions on ill-fitted, perfunctorily supervised vessels must have taken a heavy toll on people used to life in the open air. But also, more employment opportunities were opening up in India itself. The largest employers of tribal labour in India were the Assam tea gardens, where systematic recruitment began in 1853. Throughout the entire period, the Chota Nagpur plateau remained by far the largest supplier. By the 1880s, the supply from Bihar also began to dwindle. The Biharis could find employment nearer home in the coal mines and on the indigo plantations, and in Calcutta, where they were in great demand as domestic servants and general labourers.

From the 1870s to the end of indentured emigration, the UP became the largest supplier of Indian indentured labour to the colonies. Within the province itself, the eastern districts furnished the largest numbers. These emigrants were poor; affected by natural calamities and famines which haunted the land with depressing frequency in the 19th century; left unhinged by the forces of change unleashed by British land policies and pernicious land revenue settlements; punished by the British for their role in the 1857 mutiny; and migration-prone. (Table 3.6 lists the largest recruitment districts for Fiji, but it is representative of late 19th century migration to all the colonies deriving their labour supply from North India.)

In all these districts, migration was an important aspect of life: in Azamgarh in the late 19th century, migration was 'known to be considerable'; in Allahabad, 'at all times an appreciable proportion of the population is absent in search of employment far afield'; in Gonda, migration 'was a natural way out of the difficulties with which the population did not know how to grapple'; in Sultanpur, migration was used as a strategy for 'restoring fallen fortunes or of easing off a redundant population which have long been familiar to the inhabitants of this district'; and in Ghazipur, it was 'hardly an exaggeration to say that there are few families in the district of which one member at least is not absent' in Bengal for the whole or part of the year. In Sultanpur, emigrants remitted Rs. 1,627,700 between October 1894 and September 1897. In Azamgarh, annual remittances in the 1890s amounted to Rs. 13 lakh, rising to Rs. 14.5 lakh in famine years. It was from this desperate, uprooted mass of humanity on the move, looking for better opportunities wherever they could find it, that the bulk of the indentured labourers came. The recruiters painted a rosy picture of bright prospects in the colonies and cajoled or coerced some into their nets, but the recruits clearly had their own reasons for leaving. They were simple people from humble backgrounds, but they were not the simpletons their critics thought them to be.

Brij V. Lal

THE *KANGANI* AND *MAISTRY* SYSTEMS

In addition to indenture, labour recruitment also took place under the *kangani* and *maistry* systems. Both terms are derived from the Tamil language: *kangani*, meaning 'headman', 'foreman' or 'overseer', and *maistry*, meaning 'supervisor'. The *kangani* system prevailed in the case of Malaya and Ceylon, while the *maistry* system was employed in Burma. Both systems had their own peculiarities, but they also shared similar features. Both used a network of middlemen and introduced a debt relationship to recruit labourers for the plantations in the colonies. Between 1840 and 1942, under the *kangani* and *maistry* systems, it is estimated that over 1.7 million Indians were recruited to work in Malaya (including Singapore), over 1.6 million to Burma and approximately 1 million to Ceylon.

KANGANI RECRUITMENT

The *kangani* system began in the coffee and tea plantations of Ceylon, before its introduction into Malaya in 1890. It involved the employment of an Indian immigrant as the *kangani*, to supervise the work of a gang of 25 to 30 persons on the plantation. In most plantations there was a chief or head *kangani* who was the principal link between management and the workforce. Under him were minor *kanganis* who were in charge of the gangs and reported directly to the head *kangani*. The subsidiary *kanganis* were known as *cinna kanganis* in Malaya and *silara kanganis* in Ceylon (*silara* and *cinna* are derived from Tamil, meaning 'minor' or 'deputy'). The subsidiary *kanganis* not only ensured the productivity of the gangs in the estate

but were normally dispatched to India to recruit more labourers. At other times, a reliable and trustworthy workman would be given the task of recruiting labourers with the expectation that he would become a *kangani* when he returned. It was also common, specifically in Ceylon, for a close relative of the estate *kangani* living in India to take up recruiting and become a *kangani*. Finally, there were also professional *kangani* recruiters who were engaged in full-time labour recruitment without having worked on the estates themselves.

The use of the *kangani* in its various manifestations ensured that it reached numerous and more remote parts within India. While the choice of who could be appointed a *kangani* was arbitrary, the system required, in principle at least, that the *kanganis* obtain a licence which authorised them to acquire potential recruits from their own district of origin. In the case of Malaya, for example, this is how a typical *kangani* licensing procedure unfolded: an employer requiring labour would approach the Labour Department and obtain a blank *kangani* licence form and enter the *kangani's* name, the maximum number of labourers to be recruited, the wage rate for the labourers, and the *kangani's* commission for each labourer recruited. The form would be given to the *kangani*, who would then proceed to Penang, the main port of disembarkation, and present it to the deputy controller of labour, who was tasked with registering the licence if it was found satisfactory. On arrival in India, the *kangani* would produce his licence to the Malayan emigration agent, who would endorse it and permit the *kangani* to engage the services of the agents of his employers, namely Messrs Binny & Co. in Madras, Messrs Adamson, McTaggart & Co., Ganapathi Pillai & Co., and the Madura Company (of Madura and Madras), who were the principal agents of the British India Steam Navigation Company.

The restrictions imposed through the licensing scheme were consistently ignored by the *kanganis* as this reduced their profit margins since they were paid on the basis of the number of recruits they brought across, and also because of the increased demand for labour brought about by the expansion of the tea industry in Ceylon in the 1870s and 1880s. Similarly, the *kangani* system was further boosted by the actions of the government of Malaya, which, from 1905, subsidised the shipping companies operating from South Indian ports, especially Negapatnam. Such measures in both colonies, coupled with recognition by the colonial government in India in 1910 of the advantages of the *kangani* system, ensured that this system of labour recruitment thrived for some time—until 1938 in Malaya and 1940 in Ceylon.

The *kangani* system, which technically recruited 'free' labour, established a hold over the labourers by creating a debt relationship that began even before the labourer departed from his village. The *kangani* created this debt by imposing on the recruit the cost of hosting a feast in the village before departing and money advanced to his relatives for labour services, as well as the cost of travel and food supplied throughout the journey. The advance required by the *kangani* was provided by the employers and the cost of recruiting was later entered into the estate's 'debt account' as a charge against the labourer. This debt tally was maintained by the *kangani*, who assessed it at his discretion. Every labourer thus began life in the estates with a debt account, which ceased at the end of the labour contract with the payment of wages less

This 19th-century sketch appears to depict a group of newly arrived immigrants as they are shown with identity papers tied around their necks and with the brass and other culinary utensils generally supplied to migrants for the voyage.

Female labourers in Ceylon plucking tea under the watchful eyes of an overseer (standing under an umbrella), c. 1880–90.

Control

Even though the *kangani* system remained essentially unchanged from 1837, there were shifts in the control of recruitment. The Indian Act XIV of 1839 penalised all contracts for labour and assistance with emigration performed outside the auspices of the EIC. The government of India lifted this ban with the promulgation of Act XIII in 1847. The only provision made by the government of India was that the government of Ceylon ensure that the colony did not become the point of departure for emigration to other colonies. The passing of Act XIII meant that the emigration of labour was re-established. A significant shift in the recruiting policy during this period saw labourers being encouraged to bring their wives and families with them. This ensured that the labourers became a permanent fixture on the planter's estate.

Between 1847 and 1861, the increased demand for labour witnessed much more vigorous recruitment. Governor-General Lord Elgin reinstated the significance of labour recruitment and emigration to the colonies for work, and supported the aggressive recruitment of labour, but at the same time called for a stringent observation of the provisions of Act XXV of 1859, to prevent the overcrowding of ships as a result of increased demand for labour. The Governor-General's dispatch also called for prompt checking and punishment, under the provisions of the Indian Penal Code, for any attempt at either compelling or inducing individuals and families to migrate against their will. Act XXV thus both reinforced the *kangani* system and put in place measures to protect potential labour recruits. However, the legislative protection failed to address the issue of protection of Indian labourers in the colony of Ceylon.

In 1861, the government of Ceylon proposed an ordinance calling for the inclusion of protective measures in the labourer's contract. This proposal was brought to the attention of the government of India in 1862 but was dismissed on grounds that the government was satisfied with the system of protection for Indian labourers. Two years later, at the instigation of the United Kingdom Parliamentary Committee, Ordinance XI of 1865 was passed, leading to the regulation of contracts for hire and services in the colony. The regulation, while protecting the labourer, also gave the employer the right to order a convicted labourer to return to work upon the expiry of his imprisonment to complete the term of service. These shifts, between 1847 and 1865, contributed to the development of the *kangani* system. During this period there was an unprecedented demand for labour and this saw a corresponding demand made by the *kanganis* for an increase in the advances given for recruiting labour. The plantation employers, however, hesitated advancing the money, fearing that the *kanganis* would appropriate it, while at the same time inducing the labourers to accept full responsibility for the advances.

Given this insecurity, the emergence of 'Coast Advances' in the late 19th century enabled the consolidation of the *kangani* system more fully. Coast Advances referred to a checking system put in place by the Ceylon Labour Federation (formed in 1898)—an employers' collective charged with checking the steady increase in advances—to ensure that the advances paid for the recruitment of labour were spent for those very purposes and not appropriated by the *kangani*. In 1902, the Labour Federation introduced the 'Tin Ticket' system, an adoption of the 'Value Payable by Post' system, where an

the outstanding debt. In principle, however, the labourer could not be compelled to repay the debt since the law permitted him to leave his work with 30 days notice, without any liability. However, there were few instances of labourers leaving their jobs and opting not to pay the debt because failure to settle the debt meant that the labourer would not be hired at another plantation.

Wages and debt

The debt relationship was further perpetuated by a wage system considerably unfavourable to the labourer. On the plantations, the head *kangani* was the central link between the planter and the labourers. He was in charge of supervising the labourers' work and paying them their wages, which came from a lump sum paid by the employer. For these services, the head *kangani* customarily received payments in various forms: he was paid for introducing recruits into the estates and received a commission of 2 cents per day for each resident labourer who showed up for work. This commission was called 'head money'. Occasionally, he was also paid a fixed wage by the estate owners to provide special services such as policing the labourers after work, ensuring that daily work quotas were met and that the labourers did not leave the gang. Furthermore, the *kangani* was also paid a commission of 3–4 cents per day by the estate for every labourer in his gang who worked. This was known as 'pence money'.

The wage system on the estates in Malaya differed from that in Ceylon in one crucial respect. In Malaya, the coffee and rubber planters and the government exerted personal control over the labouring community and paid the labourers' wages directly to them, thus removing the *kangani* from the wage distribution structure and considerably undermining his power and position without actually disrupting the relationship of bondage between recruited labourer and *kangani*. It was essential to maintain this relationship as employers relied on the influence of the *kangani* to keep the labourers on the estates and recover the travel expenses incurred. While the wage system in Malaya removed the deductions of the *kanganis*, it nevertheless still called upon the labourer to repay the expenses incurred by the employers. This issue was later addressed through the Indian Immigration Committee set up in 1907, which in 1909 outlawed the practice of recovering advances made in the course of emigration from the labourers' wages.

individual paid for an article delivered to them upon receipt of the article. The labourer's address was marked on a small tin disc punched with a letter to denote his district and two numbers, one denoting the number of the estate in the official register of the estates, and the other, a serial number to denote the particular number assigned to each labourer. The implementation of the Tin Ticket system kept the advances made to the *kanganis* down, thus expediting the immigration of labour and ensuring that labour was cheap and affordable. It also marked the start of increasing cooperation between the planting community and the government of Ceylon.

Labour recruitment was further regulated through the Coast Agency in 1904, a collective body of those from the planting community to finance and supervise the recruitment of labourers. The upshot was that there were three sets of *kanganis* operating within India: those who were controlled by the agency, those who were not, and the local recruiter in the colony. The centralisation of the recruitment process through the Coast Agency did not improve conditions for the labourer, who was still charged the expenses incurred on the journey to the estate. This culture of indebtedness, which was central to the *kangani* system, was accentuated by the increasing practice of the *tundu* system of advances, which was specific to Ceylon.

TUNDU

This system made provisions for an estate superintendent to issue a *tundu*—a written statement undertaking the discharge of a certain number of labourers on being paid the amount of outstanding advances—when the number of labourers on the estate exceeded work requirements. A *tundu* could be issued either before or at the end of the labourer's contract, and it meant that the *kangani* was permitted to scout for employment on other estates experiencing a labour shortage. On securing employment, for which the *kangani* received advances, he paid off the former estate superintendent, consolidated the remainder of the debt, and set up a new debt account to be settled at the end of the contract period in the new estate. The *tundu* system did no favours for the labourers because, in essence, the system simply transferred the labourer's debt and worked in favour of the *kangani*, who received higher advances, and the planting community, which could ensure an efficient workforce.

The issue of relieving the labourer's debt was addressed in 1911 by the Planters Labour Federation, which requested that the superintendent issuing a *tundu* specify the actual registered debt in his books; that all member estates refrain from paying more than the sum recorded in the *tundu*; that the initial debt at the time of recruitment be capped at Rs. 15 per head; and that all new labourers be brought to estates free of all charges related to travel and food. The labourers were nevertheless expected to write off the cash advance at the end of the first year if they remained employed in the estate. The attempt to stem the culture of indebtedness remained futile as a number of estates did not join the federation; there was internal disagreement about the rule which prohibited paying in excess of the sum specified on the *tundu*; and there were several planters who continued to invoke Section 24 of Ordinance XI of 1865, which sanctioned the courts to order a labourer to return to work to pay off his accumulated debt.

In response to reports of continuing abuse in Ceylon and Malaya, the Marjoriebanks-Marakkayar Commission was set up in 1917 to report on Indian labour emigration. The commission concluded that while wages were adequate, the *tundu* system increased the labourer's debt and was the compelling reason for his absconding from work, for which the labourer was later imprisoned. Subsequently, after the government of India affirmed the findings of the commission, Ordinance XLIII was passed in 1921. It prohibited debt-bondage of estate labourers, made debt contracts irrecoverable by law, and called for the wholesale abolition of the *tundu* system. Although the ordinance strove to alleviate the labourer's debt, it was bound to be unsuccessful unless the labourer was given the opportunity to begin his working life free of debt and opportunities for *kanganis* to pile illegal debts on labourers were closed. Responding to this, the government of India passed Act VII in May 1922 and established a 12-member Emigration Committee to put in place specific regulations with regard to labour emigration to Ceylon and Malaya. The passing of the 1922 Indian Emigration Act marked a defining moment in the *kangani* system of labour recruitment to Ceylon and Malaya and remained the template upon which subsequent emigration processes and practices in these colonies were framed.

Two specifications of Act VII that deserve mention are the stipulation that all emigrants must be aged 18 or over unless travelling as dependents with a parent or guardian, and Rule 23, which stated that the ratio of unaccompanied males must not exceed one in five of the emigrants (thus two out of every three male emigrants must be accompanied by their wives). Furthermore, there were rulings on hours of work; wages; welfare provisions (medical, sanitary and housing); the removal of penal sanctions for labour-related offences; the removal of liability for advances made to or on behalf of the labourer; the entitlement to free repatriation within one year of arrival; and the exclusion of the professional class of *kanganis* from recruiting labour. An agent of the government of India was appointed in both colonies to monitor the application of these rules. It was on these terms that *kangani*-assisted emigration to Malaya continued until 1932 and Ceylon until 1939, when it was banned by the Indian government because of the drastic reduction in wages following the slump in rubber prices and the Great Depression. The planting associations in the colonies, supported by their respective governments, contested the ban and convinced the government of India to reopen emigration. However, the reopening was rather short-lived as the government of India officially ended labour recruitment to the colony of Malaya on 15 June 1938, with the closure of the Emigration Depot at Negapatnam, and in December 1940 to the colony of Ceylon.

A kangani on a plantation.

Labourers standing outside a collection centre with their baskets of tea.

A head tindal maistry *of cart makers and wheelwrights.*

The British India Steam Navigation Company's liners at the quayside in the port of Rangoon, 1939.

MAISTRY

The main characteristics of the *maistry* system of labour recruitment to Burma were similar to the *kangani* system in that it employed a system of advances as an inducement for emigration, perpetuated a debt culture and continued to enslave the labourer to a middleman (the *maistry*, or supervisor). However, the two systems were also dissimilar. The gradation of middlemen-employers, the innumerable illegal deductions made by the middlemen-employers from the labourers' wages, and the regular pattern of underemployment differentiated the *maistry* system from the *kangani* system. The middlemen-employers collective followed a hierarchy: labour contractor, the head *maistry*, the charge *maistry*, and the gang *maistry*. A gang *maistry* was in charge of a small workforce of between 10 to 20 labourers, while a *maistry* who had control of several such gangs was known as a charge *maistry*. A *maistry* in charge of the entire labour organisation of a specific firm was known as the head *maistry*, while the labour contractor, who was at the apex of the hierarchy and who had a sound financial standing, was contracted to supply and maintain a labour force. The labour contractor entered into a contract with large operations such as rice mills, railways, ships, port trusts and public works to supply a stipulated number of labourers for a stated period, maintain the labour force and ensure that the labourers did their work. The corporations stipulated both the wage for each class of labour and the remuneration that the contractor received as a labour recruiter. To safeguard his contractual obligations, the contractor insisted that the labourer enter into an agreement which called for the labourer to place his thumb impression on stamped agreement forms or on blank stamped papers. This meant he had agreed

to serve the *maistry* for a specified period, and was an acknowledgement of the debt for the advances received. Because the terms of service and amount of debt were omitted when the labourer signed the agreement, the contractor could show any amount of debt and continue to call upon the services of the recruited labourer. In the *maistry* system, unlike the *kangani* system, the labourer worked as the servant of the *maistry*, who controlled the disbursement of wages and had the power to either hire or dismiss labourers (i.e. the organisation that demanded the labour force could not hire and fire labourers).

Migration to Burma was not subject to control as Burma was a province of British India until 1937. In fact, migration to Burma was encouraged because of the growing demand from the West for Burmese rice. The rice trade also promoted the emergence of paddy processing industries, mineral and oil refineries, saw mills and timber yards. Migration to Burma was undertaken mainly by Telugus and Circars from the northern coastal districts of Ganjam, Vizagapatnam, Godavari and Kistna. Labour migration to Burma was also more seasonal: labourers migrated to Burma between the months of October and December—the harvest period—and returned again between March and May.

Regulation of maistry

The passing of two acts, the Workmen's Breach of Contract Act of 1869 and the Labour Act of 1876, encouraged and established the *maistry* labour recruitment system in Burma. The former empowered a magistrate in Burma to sentence and imprison a worker for up to three months or impose a fine for the sum of money owed for refusing to fulfil his contract with the *maistry*. The latter provided for the appointment of a recruiting agent for labour in Madras. While the appointment of a recruiting agent meant that emigration could be regulated by the state, employers in Burma preferred recruiting Indian workers through the *maistries* as they found the *maistry*-recruited labour force much easier to manage. The passing of the two acts, coupled with the subsidies offered to shipping companies, saw a significant increase in the emigration of labour to Burma. In addition, British India Steam Navigation, which was the leading shipping company, with a vested interest in passenger traffic to Burma, employed large numbers of agents in the Madras Presidency to encourage potential labourers to emigrate. The main emigration route was the British India steamer circuit: Cocanada–Vizagapatnam–Gopalpur–Rangoon. Even with the passing of the two acts, the agents, who worked on a commission basis, continued to overcrowd the ships. This led to the passing of the Native Passenger Ship Commission of 1890, which recommended that all ships destined for Burma be staffed by a Hindu ship medical officer who was acquainted with the language of the labourers and so could act as a spokesperson for the passengers.

The commission's stipulations were enhanced by the All-India Deck Passengers Committee of 1912, which recommended the appointment of an inspector on every steamer to act as an intermediary and to protect the passengers against abuse. Furthermore, the committee recommended the appointment of an assistant protector of immigrants and emigrants, but these recommendations could not break the stranglehold of the British India Steam Navigation Company, which controlled passenger traffic between India and Burma. In 1925, the Workmen's

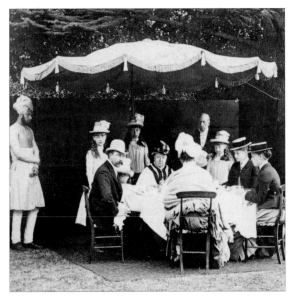

Breach of Contract Act of 1869 was repealed, but without the desired effect of nullifying the *maistry* system or providing freedom to the labourers, mainly because of the vigilance of the *maistries*, who continued to exploit labourers by entering into contracts with them. This contract had two main detrimental provisions: the first called on the labourer to agree to a service for a definite period at a wage below the rate fixed by the employer; while the second authorised the *maistry* to make weekly deductions from the labourers' wages to repay the interest-bearing advances received. The repeal of the 1869 act also did little to improve the conditions of the labourer in Burma. Some of the normal features of the *maistry* system that the labourer faced included the non-employment of the full number of men in a gang, illegal deductions from wages, the compulsory contribution of free services, and the provision of similar wages for both night and day labourers. This general structure and practice of the *maistry* system of labour recruitment to Burma continued until its abolition in 1937.

Vijay Devadas

FREE MIGRATION

The vast majority of migrants from India in the 19th century considered themselves 'temporary sojourners' and left to undertake a service or start entrepreneurial activities overseas for finite periods. Many servants and traders were habitual travellers: one ayah made the crossing to Britain from India more than 50 times. Lascars played a vital role in the maritime trade of India, and during the colonial period, like sepoys, were often caught up in the vacillating fortunes and internecine struggles of rival empire builders.

SEPOYS AND MIGRATION

Despite the British tendency to 'categorise' Indians in social and occupational groups, in practice there was a great deal of overlap. Many male and female servants ended up as indentured labourers, some of whom went on to further migrate as free or trade migrants, while lascars, awaiting return passages, could occasionally find themselves enslaved or forced to take on work as servants. Similarly, the sepoy often had a peasant or servant background, and once discharged, could also become an indentured or free migrant.

In the 18th and early 19th centuries, Anglo-French warfare saw the participation of increasing numbers of sepoys in overseas campaigns despite the aversion of some—particularly high-caste Hindus—to long sea journeys. Much trouble was taken to persuade a sepoy battalion to participate in a raid on a trading settlement at Bencoolen in 1789. Thereafter, sepoys helped the British to take the Moluccas in 1795, played an active role in the attack on Egypt in 1800–01, and served at Macao. Soon afterwards, several thousand sepoys were mobilised for the conquest of Mauritius (1810) and the expedition to Java (1811). The French and Portuguese territories in India also provided sepoys (called *topazes* in the 18th century) for their armies.

Some sepoys were already venturing further afield to become permanent overseas migrants. Dean Mahomed, from Patna in Bihar, served in the Bengal Army for 15 years before migrating to Ireland in the late 18th century. There, he married an Anglo-Irish woman and published an account of his travels. Less well known are the groups of *topaz* soldiers who began arriving in the French islands, where they mostly settled, from the 1730s onwards. Others found themselves in far-flung colonial outposts to which they had been taken as the 'spoils of war'—captured from enemy ships and subjected to months in detention while awaiting exchange. A few, like Sadayen from Pondicherry, found, to their disadvantage, that some colonists saw little distinction between military recruits and other labouring 'blacks'—he was tricked into embarking for overseas 'service' only to find himself sold as a slave. Fortunately for Sadayen, a chance meeting with a fellow Indian from Pondicherry who worked for a French officer in the local artillery regiment secured his release.

As the standing armies of India increased in the late 18th and early 19th centuries, a number of recruits were drawn from the growing class of impoverished rural cultivators or landless labourers and agrestic serfs. Over time, their home districts would become synonymous with migration as more and more of the destitute rural poor signed up. Thus, after a few men from Saran in Bihar joined Robert Clive's first sepoy battalion of Bengal in the 1770s, the district became an important recruiting ground: by the mid-19th century, more than 10,000 natives of Saran had served as sepoys. Regions with such traditions were then also likely to become key recruiting districts of indentured migrants. Similarly, in the Madras Presidency, many Pallan and Paraiyan labourers left to enlist as sepoys, and later, to migrate as indentured labourers. When indentured emigration began in the 1830s, the collector of Rajahmundry noticed that a significant number of the recruits were discharged sepoys or men who would have enlisted as sepoys had they not been 'undersized or prevented by some defect'. This was confirmed by enquiries made in the colonies. In Mauritius, numerous ex-sepoys from the Bengal and Madras armies were found among plantation labour recruits, along with men like Boodhoo Khan, formerly in the service of the Rajah of Morbaugh, and Rengasamy Naicken, a sepoy who had enlisted with the Danish government at Tranquebar.

The increasing pressure to serve overseas was opposed by some Indian soldiers. In 1852, an attempt to ship a regiment to Rangoon had to be abandoned when the majority of the sepoys refused to go. In general, however, as the

Queen Victoria (1819–1901) holds a garden party with members of her family at Osborn House on the Isle of Wight. An Indian servant waits on them.

Many natives from Bihar were recruited as sepoys in Robert Clive's (above) battalion in the 1770s. Indian sepoys were sent on overseas campaigns and many chose to settle in these areas as free migrants after they were discharged.

An illustration from the 1877 Christmas edition of The Illustrated London News. *It shows lascars at the Seaman's Hospital at Greenwich enjoying their Christmas dinner.*

19th century progressed, sepoys could be found wherever labour migration from India was set up. Also, more than a few sepoy rebels escaped the repercussions of their role in the mutiny of 1857 by emigrating to the sugar colonies. The less fortunate among them were sent as convicts to penal settlements such as the Andaman Islands, where some proved useful to the British as informants about the local inhabitants, viewed by colonial administrators as 'savage cannibals'. After 1857, the recruitment of sepoys by the British shifted increasingly to Punjab.

By the late 19th and early 20th centuries, sepoys were venturing to the colonies as free passenger emigrants. In British Guiana, Gul Mohamed Khan, an ex-sepoy, took a job as a police officer in 1877, while Harman Singh, formerly of the 96th Sikh Infantry Regiment, turned up in Mauritius in 1906 after his discharge, hoping to find suitable employment. Others were not so fortunate. Many overseas sepoys did not return from their tours of duty: all that was recovered of one hapless Indian on sentry duty in the lion-infested country along the Uganda Railway were bloodstained clothing and a torn limb. During World War I, more than 80,000 sepoys served in France, East Africa, Egypt and Mesopotamia. Their loyalty to the British did not go unnoticed and helped to dissipate the vestiges of mistrust prevailing after 1857.

THE LASCAR: RIDING THE IMPERIAL WAVE

Originally a word denoting a regimental servant, by the 19th century 'lascar' had become a familiar term for the seamen employed on EIC ships. Indian sailors had been embarking on voyages across the Indian Ocean since medieval times, but probably made their first appearance in Europe in the 16th century, when East Indians were

among the other seamen enumerated in Lisbon working on river craft. Their first contacts with Europeans were mostly unhappy experiences: lascars on Mughal ships, unlucky enough to encounter European pirates, would usually be forced to join the maritime outlaws and were put to hard labour on their vessels. Lascars were also caught up in state warfare and were taken prisoner when ships of rival nations were seized. Thus, in 1810, a group of lascars petitioned the governor of the Cape of Good Hope for compensation. Having been taken first by the French and then recaptured by the British, they had not received their wages in four months and had been 'compelled as a means of subsistence to embark in French vessels.' Even in times of peace, lascars encountered danger: in the early 1820s, the lascar crew aboard the trading brig *Mary Anne* were murdered off the Somali coast, reportedly at the behest of Arab rivals.

Lascars arriving in England were sometimes made to wait months for a return passage and, despite arrangements to provide them with lodgings, their plight was often desperate: ill-equipped for winter, poorly-fed and in many cases destitute. The mortality rate among the 3000 or so lascars who disembarked in London annually during the 19th century was as high as 10 per cent. Some took to begging and others to crime: in 1824, Sheik Brom from Surat was sentenced to transportation for an act of theft in London, one of several lascars who later arrived in Australia as convicts.

A number of lascars jumped ship and settled at various points around the Indian Ocean and in British port towns such as Liverpool and London's East End. Communities of lascars settled on French islands in the Indian Ocean from the early 18th century as well. Early Indian settlers in Australia included the crews of ships which arrived from India. When the British arrived at Penang in 1786, the first man ashore reportedly was a lascar, and Indian seamen were among early Muslim settlers in Hong Kong, initially living in dormitories on Lower Lascar Row. Some, like the founder of the influential Rumjahn family, married Chinese women and settled permanently in the colony. Today, many Muslim communities around the Indian Ocean have their roots in the lascar seafaring tradition, while more than a few Britons in the big port cities, if they study their genealogies, may find the trace of a long forgotten East Indian sailor ancestor.

INDIAN MERCHANT NETWORKS

Merchants from India were trading in the Gulf States from the 9th century. The earliest permanent commercial settlement was probably in Muscat around the 15th century. By the early 18th century, Indians were a dominant trading force in Yemen, and over the next few decades extended their influence as far as Zanzibar. Yet, as the 19th century began, the entire Indian merchant diaspora across the Red Sea and the Indian Ocean was no more than a few thousand strong. This would change dramatically over the course of the century—by its close the overseas Indian traders would number a quarter of a million.

A painting depicting a Hindu priest garlanding the flags of the 35th Bengal Light Infantry at a Presentation of Colours ceremony, c. 1850–54.

Yet this vast mercantile stream of out-migration, which chiefly occurred between 1880 and 1930, is largely absent from official records.

There are several reasons for this. Firstly, merchants departing India were not classified as emigrants before 1922. Secondly, a large number of them left India as labour or passenger migrants before shifting to trade, or as re-migrants, moving between Mauritius and South Africa—Thambi Naidoo, Mahatma Gandhi's right-hand man in South Africa, was a Telugu who had previously been an indentured migrant in Mauritius—or from South Africa to East Africa. South Indians sent to the Straits Settlements might later migrate to Hong Kong as sailors or traders. Other migrants, like the Gujaratis, could draw upon established family networks of trade stretching across generations and several destinations. Still others were people of various social and ethnic backgrounds who saw an opportunity to invest in new colonial ventures: Claude Markovits gives as an example the role of Parsis in the opium trade with China. Finally, there were the ethnic entrepreneurs: individuals who saw the benefits of marketing Oriental goods or perceived skills. In the 19th century, Indians made money as medical specialists, and the pedlar of Indian carpets and other such goods was a characteristic sight in Britain and elsewhere for many years. The diversity of the trade diaspora thus defies easy generalisation, and the migration trends did not make for settled, easily quantifiable communities. Rather, the phenomenon of Indian trade migration is one of circulation and dispersal, with the centre often being those family members left at home in India, to whom the migrants frequently returned.

Marina Carter

TRADING NETWORKS IN SOUTHEAST ASIA

Even before the advent of the Europeans in the 16th century there were important settlements of Indian traders in major Southeast Asian ports. However, though important individually, these merchants did not have a large overall presence in the societies in which they had settled until the late 19th century, when there was a dramatic increase in the number of trade migrants who came to Southeast Asia. Records show that the total number of 'non-labour' migrants from the Indian subcontinent to Malaya alone was 643,000 between 1844 and 1931. Burma and other Southeast Asian countries also saw a similar influx of Indian traders. Trading communities now came in much larger, organised waves and established their presence not only in the ports but also in the hinterlands. These migrants, continuing the traditional Indian overseas trade, played a catalytic role in creating the modern commercial world of Southeast Asia in the late 19th and 20th centuries.

The traders were different from other Indian migrants. Unlike the indentured labourers, they were free men, had close caste and regional networks and sources of information, and were endowed with some initial capital. More importantly, they could choose their destinations and flocked to areas which offered greater trading opportunities. However, such opportunities were uneven and certain regions, like Burma, were initially more attractive. Thus, by the mid-1930s an estimated 20 percent of all Indian migrants in Burma were traders: the Straits Settlements, with 14.3 per cent, and the Malay states, with about 5.6 per cent, were the other large settlements of Indian traders at this time.

MERCHANT COMMUNITIES

The trade diaspora was made up of specialist communities. Though they came from diverse trading castes from all over the Indian subcontinent, the bulk of the late 19th-century migrants were from the present-day states of Tamil Nadu and Kerala. Of these migrants, the most prominent were the Nattukottai Chettiars from the Ramnad district in the Pudukottai region, who migrated in waves from the 1830s onwards to Malaya, Burma and the Straits Settlements, and subsequently to Siam, Java, Indo-China and northern Sumatra. Then there were the Chulias and their important subsection, the Marakkayars, and the Mappila or Moplah merchants from Kerala. Among traders from other regions were the Muslim trading communities of the Dawoodi Bohras, who migrated from Surat to Bangkok in the 1850s, and the Khojas, who migrated from Kutch to the Straits Settlements in the late 19th century. Another important community, which arrived in smaller numbers in the late 19th century, were the Sindhis, who went first to Singapore and then moved on to the Dutch East Indies, Penang and Manila. However, Sindhi migration increased

Indian goldsmith and jewellery shops are common in many parts of Southeast Asia.

Jawaharlal Nehru at a meeting with Indian merchants in Singapore in 1937.

after the Partition of 1947, when Sind, their homeland, became a part of the newly established Dominion of Pakistan. The Sikhs, who first arrived as watchmen and part of the police force, later took to trading activities. It was only at the beginning of the 20th century that they found their economic niche in the textile and sporting goods trade and emerged in the business world, especially in Singapore, Malaya and Thailand. There were also other trading communities which migrated in smaller numbers, such as the Marwaris, Hindu merchants from present-day Rajasthan, who went primarily to Burma in the late 1850s.

Economic change

These migrations took place within the larger setting marked by critical changes in the world economy and the increased integration of the economies of Southeast Asia into the global capitalist system. European expansion in Southeast Asia in the 19th century was followed by increased commercial production of commodities such as rice, tea, coffee and rubber. The opening of the Suez Canal in 1869 and advances in transportation gave a further impetus to the process. As a consequence, Southeast Asian economies were transformed from entrepôts for Eastern commerce to primary producers which supplied food and raw materials to the industrialising world. The opening up of Southeast Asian economies offered enormous opportunities for the investment of capital to Indian traders.

Besides the new opportunities which Southeast Asia offered, migration was also propelled by changes taking place within the Indian economy. British ascendancy after the revolt of 1857 resulted in the shrinking of the trading activities of warring princely states and of trading overland along caravan routes. New trading posts and commercial centres were established by the British, who increasingly dominated trade. All this affected the fortunes of mercantile communities and propelled migration, both within and beyond the subcontinent. Some communities, like the Marwaris, moved within India to the port cities, where they were able to entrench themselves. Such communities migrated overseas in smaller numbers. Other communities, such as the Chettiars, found it more difficult to adjust to the new economic order. Circumstances propelled traders to take up the challenge of exploiting the new opportunities which were unfolding in Southeast Asia.

Settlement patterns

Once the 19th-century pioneers settled into their new environment and found the prosperity they were seeking, they acted as magnets, attracting their kinsmen. They nurtured links with the homeland and provided resources which allowed others to migrate. They established temples and community centres which served as a support base for the newcomers. In the long run, such institutions would play a critical role in fostering the ties of kinship and preserving traditional culture.

A Sikh man, c. 1890. The Sikhs were popular choices in security related roles, such as policemen and security guards.

The earliest pioneer trader in Singapore was Narayan Pillai, who accompanied Sir Thomas Stamford Raffles from Penang in 1819. Originally a clerk with the EIC, Pillai started his business career by setting up a brick kiln and became Singapore's first building contractor. Then he entered the textile business and his shop became reputedly one of the largest on the island. Once well established in his business, Pillai acquired land for Singapore's first Hindu temple, the Sri Mariamman Temple, in 1823. The Chettiars built magnificent temples in all the major cities in which they settled, including Saigon, Rangoon, Melaka and Singapore. These temples acted as meeting places, provided space for Chettiar chambers of commerce and were, of course, places of worship for Hindu devotees. The Chulias endowed mosques such as the Jamae Chulia Mosque in 1826 and the Al-Abrar Mosque, first built in 1827 and reconstructed in 1850, in Singapore.

Typically, newcomers started off as employees of those who were already well settled, and the enterprising ones later launched into economic activities on their own, often with the help of older, established trading houses. In Indo-China, the earliest Indian trading firms were those of two Chettiars from Karaikudi, who arrived soon after the French occupation in 1885, reportedly with a sum of Rs. 60,000. By the early 1930s, there were no less than 125 firms with investments exceeding Rs. 80 million. Exploiting the emerging business opportunities in the region, traders carved out distinct economic areas and became niche players within the new economies in which they were placed. Each community developed its own forte and Indian trading diasporas soon became indispensable in the growing commercialisation of the Southeast Asian economies.

Chettiars

The most important trading community between the late 19th and the mid-20th century was the Chettiar, who traditionally supplied rural credit and financed trade within the domestic economy of the Madras Presidency—a skill they leveraged in their new areas of settlement. As the commercial production of tin and rubber increased after the 1870s, the Chettiars moved in larger numbers to Malaya. They became a source of credit to local entrepreneurs, aiming to benefit from tin mining and the commercial cropping of rubber, and began to play an important role in the emerging plantation economy. Pioneer planter Tan Chayyan, who was the first to introduce rubber as a commercial crop in Malaya in 1895, could only launch his new enterprise with the aid of loans provided by Chettiar moneylenders. Chettiar support was especially valuable because European banks were very selective in giving out loans due to the need to maintain large amounts of liquid capital for exchange operations. Thus, Chinese tin miners, European planters and sometimes even Malay royalty had to rely on the Chettiars for credit. Among the prominent Chinese tin miners and rubber planters who started their enterprises with the help of Chettiar loans were Yap Ah Loy, Loke Yew, Khaw Sim Bee and Ng Boo Bee. Chettiars also lent money to Malay peasants and landowners in return for the mortgage of their property and the deposit of title deeds.

In Burma, too, the community found its niche in agricultural moneylending. Though the earliest Chettiar firms date back before 1850 in Moulmein, they migrated in larger numbers after the British annexation of Lower Burma. By the late 1880s there was 'a Chettiar within a day's journey of every cultivator' in Lower Burma. Until the 1870s, however, the Chettiars dealt primarily with indigenous moneylenders to whom they supplied credit and who, in turn, dealt with Burmese peasants. After the 1870s they enlarged their credit activities in a major way, following a dramatic increase in commercial rice production as a result of changes in landowning policy. Chettiars could now lend on the security of title deeds and began to directly finance Burmese cultivators. They moved into Upper Burma and towns in the hinterland such as Mandalay, Myingnan, Meitkila and Shwebo. Such was the expansion of their activities that by 1929 Chettiar firms had invested an estimated Rs. 750 million in Burma. Between the 1870s and 1930s the Chettiars were the most important financiers of commercial rice production in Burma and were the 'mainstay of agricultural finance' in Lower Burma. With them lies credit for the spread of rice cultivation. Sir Harcourt Butler, the governor of Burma, noted in 1927: 'Without the assistance of the Chettiar banking system Burma would never have achieved the wonderful advance of the last 25 to 30 years.'

It was agricultural moneylending that the community mastered in all areas of their settlement across Southeast Asia. In Indo-China, for example, they were involved in short-term agricultural lending which complemented the activities of the French banks. Though the Chettiars had business interests all over the region, statistics show that Burma was their main field of operation, with 1650 firms stationed there in the 1930s, compared to 1000 in Malaya and Singapore, 200 in Indo-China, 150 in other areas of East Asia, and 500 in Ceylon.

In all these areas, the Chettiars operated through firms and an agency system. Firms were set up in partnership with fellow caste members. The principal himself resided in the home district of Ramnad, where the firm was headquartered. Branch offices were managed by agents, caste men of moderate means who typically served for a period of three years. The proprietor himself would only visit the branches once or twice a year. One of the oldest and most prominent firms, established by Muthiah Chetty in the early 1900s, was headquartered in Kanadukatha in Chettinad, but had branches and agents in Ceylon, Burma, Malaya and French Indo-China. These agents were the family's 'own men, from their own neighbourhood' and some had been in their service for generations.

Besides participating in agricultural credit, Chettiar firms often engaged in the import and export trade, especially in the Indian Ocean region. The Burma Chettiars specialised in the rice and timber trade. P. A. Chocalingam Chetty, who inherited his grandfather's business in 1902, became an important exporter of timber. So large was his enterprise that consignments were shipped from Burma every week. His customers included the government of Madras, the states of Hyderabad and Mysore, and many private contractors in Madras.

Through their moneylending activities, the Chettiars accumulated enough capital and business experience to move into manufacturing in the 20th century. In Malaya they began to purchase rubber plantations: the well-known PKN Group, which had interests in Malaya, Burma, Ceylon and Indo-China, acquired the 69-hectare Nagappa Rubber Estate in Johor around 1926. In Burma, their extensive experience and networks made them insiders in the rice business. In 1916–17, out of a total of 318 rice mills, 16 were owned by Chettiars. They also set up saw and timber mills in Burma. At times, the mills fell into Chettiar ownership by default during periods of economic depression, when they were forced to foreclose properties upon the failure of loan repayments.

Another important niche carved out by the Chettiars and other larger Indian trading firms in the region was that of intermediaries for Western capital. They became the channel for credit from Western banks to the local community as European banks were often reluctant to deal with small and medium traders directly. Thus, local traders obtained their credit from the Indian moneylender against mortgages of crops or against promissory notes. The Indian trader, in turn, discounted these promissory notes—*hundis*—with the Western banks and obtained overdrafts on the security of bills or title deeds.

An Indian Chitty, 1900.

Singapore's Jamae Chulia Mosque, with its twin minarets, was built by the Chulias in 1826.

Marwaris

Though smaller in number, the Marwaris were also niche players and were particularly active in Burma. One of the most prominent early Marwari trading firms was that of Mirzamul Poddar, a powerful banker of Churu in Rajputana, who expanded his business to Burma in the 1830s. An estimated 260 Marwari firms belonging to the Agarwal subsection moved to Burma in the late 1850s from Calcutta and Assam. Shivbaksh Bagla was an important timber merchant in Calcutta in the 1870s and his firm was well known for its moneylending and rice trading interests in Burma. The primary activity of the community was discounting promissory notes, especially those related to the piece-goods trade from Bombay or Lancashire—a role they could perform because of close links with European banks. They were also involved with the financing of wholesale and retail trade, especially in timber and rice. Much like the Chettiars, they operated through firms which remained headquartered in Calcutta and Assam.

Muslim traders

Muslim traders from present-day Tamil Nadu and Kerala also played a significant role in the local economies of Southeast Asia. The Chulias and the Marakkayars were especially active in the Malay states, Burma and the Straits Settlements, and specialised in the retail trade. In Burma, Chulia shopkeepers could be found even in remote villages and some were well known as merchants of metal tools. There were an estimated 40,000 Marakkayars, mostly general merchants, in the Straits Settlements. In Thailand, Tamil Muslims were engaged in piece-goods, cloth and the trade of precious stones. Mappila merchants from Kerala were well entrenched in the restaurant business in Burma, Singapore and Sarawak.

The Gujarati Muslim merchants, Memons, Khojas and Bohras had a significant presence in almost all parts of Southeast Asia. They specialised in a range of businesses, including textiles, household appliances, rice and diamonds. Among the early Memon migrants was Adamjee Haji Dawood, who migrated to Prome in Burma at the age of 15 in 1885 to work with the Memon firm, Saleh Mohammed Ghaziani. In 1913 he set up Adamjee Haji Dawood and Co. Within 10 years he had amassed enough capital to start a match factory near Rangoon, considered at the time to be one of Asia's most modern factories. Dawood remained in Burma until World War II, after which he relocated to Calcutta and subsequently became one of the most prominent Muslim industrialists in the country. In both Burma and Indonesia, especially

in Jakarta, the Bohras dominated the export trade of sugar until the depression of the 1930s, after which they shifted to tea export and the Middle East. In Singapore, the community resided in Arab Street, where they were largely involved with the textile trade and some members had interests in the jewellery business.

Sindhis

Another trading community, smaller in number in the late 19th to mid-20th centuries, but which became prominent after the mid-20th century, was that of the Sindhis. Among the pioneering firms in the region was the one Wassiamul Assomull established in Singapore and Surabaya (Indonesia) around 1873. Many Sindhis came to work with Assomull, and after going through the trials and tribulations of newcomers, set up their own successful enterprises. Sindhis also moved to Penang and established firms such as Hassaram, set up around 1860. The Sindhis gained a reputation in the textile trade. Until the mid-20th century they were involved in importing textiles from Japan, China and India, and re-exporting them to Indonesia, Malaysia and Indo-China. In the mid-20th century, the community came to dominate the textile trade in many business centres, such as Jakarta.

Sikhs

By the early 20th century, a new trading community was emerging among the Sikhs, whose social base was not always rooted in trading castes. They mostly started off as pedlars or in small business endeavours. In the Philippines, Sikhs were engaged in the trade of textile and household appliances. They were, however, few in number and restricted their business activities to Manila and its surrounding areas until the mid-20th century. In Singapore and Indonesia, especially northern Sumatra, they entered the textile business in the years after World War I. In Jakarta, they were beginning to make their presence felt in the sporting goods business, which, from the mid-20th century, came to be their stronghold. It was only from this time that the community established a more conspicuous economic presence in the region.

As Southeast Asia became an important arena for World War II and the Japanese Occupation, Indian trading communities could not remain aloof from the events of the times. Like other trading groups, they suffered economic hardship in some regions, while in others they further entrenched themselves in the local economies.

CHANGES IN BURMA

In Burma, where the Indian trading diaspora was most deeply entrenched, Indians suffered the most. The closing of the rice frontier in the 1920s and the Great Depression of 1930 put land into the hands of moneylenders, as landlords and owner-cultivators increasingly defaulted on their loans. The consequent wave of anti-Indian sentiment in the 1930s often targeted moneylenders, blaming them for Burma's economic woes. By the late 1930s, the Chettiars controlled nearly 25 per cent of the cropped area in Lower Burma and 50 per cent of the land held by non-agriculturists. This undermined their economic moneylending function, which was hinged on a balance between liquid assets and investment in movable property. This strain was exacerbated by the disruption of the war years and the Japanese Occupation. Numerous Marwari, Gujarati and Chettiar traders were part of the war-induced mass exodus of Indians.

Osman, a Muslim trader in 19th-century Mascarenes. Mercantile families followed in the wake of indentured labourers and became important suppliers of foodstuffs and textiles for the overseas Indians.

Cars, such as the one pictured below, had become a status symbol for the wealthiest Indian merchants in the diaspora in the early decades of the 20th century.

RAJABALI JUMABHOY

Rajabali Jumabhoy (1898–2001) was a businessman, leader of the Indian community, founder of the Singapore Indian Chamber of Commerce (SICC), municipal commissioner, member of the Executive Council of Singapore, member of the Legislative Council and Legislative Assembly in Singapore, recipient of the Malayan Certificate of Honour and Commander of the British Empire, and patriarch of the most prominent Indian family in Singapore in the 20th century. He saw himself as much a part of the social world of his 'adopted home' as his original homeland. He arrived in Singapore in 1916 after completing his education and headed a transnational family business until his death in 2001, just before his 103rd birthday. With colonial authorities and rulers of the independent Republic of Singapore regarding him as a 'leader' of the Indian community, Jumabhoy took it upon himself to represent the community whenever the occasion arose. He moved comfortably in the top political circles of colonial and independent Singapore. His viewpoints were always those of an 'Indian in Singapore', but his public world was never restricted to the community.

When Jumabhoy arrived in Singapore, the family firm was a year old. The family belonged to the influential Kutchi Khoja trading community, closely linked with the Arabic trading world in the Middle East and Arab traders in Southeast Asia. Mobilising these links and those of the Bombay Khoja network, the firm dealt in cotton yarn and flour from Bombay, dates from the Persian Gulf and cloves from Zanzibar. A few years after his arrival, in 1922, Jumabhoy had a falling out with his brother and set up a separate company, R. Jumabhoy and Sons, as a commission agency dealing with a variety of goods such as coffee, sago flour, timber, firecrackers, hosiery, canned pineapples, rattan and tin ingot. As the business expanded, he set up offices in Hong Kong, Surabaya, Semarang and Bombay, and established agencies in the Middle East, Africa and England. In

the mid-1920s, Jumabhoy bought prime land on the island and made real estate the mainstay of his fortunes. This held him in good stead. In spite of the economic depression and post-war turbulence, he was able to move into new areas such as timber exports and shipping on the strength of his prudent investments. He enlarged his business to include the hospitality, food, retail management and beverage industries. The prominent symbols of Jumabhoy triumph were the S$200 million construction of Scotts Shopping Centre and The Ascott service apartments on Orchard Road. By the 1990s, the empire was worth S$300 million and spread across Malaysia, Singapore, Africa, and cities such as Mumbai and London.

Through the years, Jumabhoy operated in several different social spheres, maintaining close links with the Khoja community. As the first Kutchi Khoja investor in Singapore, he played an important part in fostering enterprise within the community. He typically sourced employees from the community and helped them nurture their own businesses over time. He also fortified links with the larger community of Gujarati merchants. In 1924, with 35 Gujarati exporters, he set up the Indian Merchants Association and served as its president for eight out of its 11 years of existence. When the need for a larger umbrella organisation of Indian traders asserted itself, Jumabhoy played a key part in the formation of the SICC in 1935, and as its founder president for nine years. Within a few years, in 1948, the Legislative Council granted the SICC a seat.

Apart from the traders' bodies, Jumabhoy was also instrumental in the establishment of several organisations catering to the larger Indian community. The most important was the Singapore Indian Association, set up in 1923 to network with regional Indian bodies and help harmonise the community's diverse elements. Later, in 1945, Jumabhoy helped to found the Singapore Indian Congress, modelled after and formed in solidarity with the Indian National Congress. Given his varied endeavours, the colonial

authorities perceived Jumabhoy as a leader of the Indian community.

Jumabhoy did not, however, restrict his networking to the community. In 1925, he joined the British-controlled Straits Settlements Singapore Association, 'the only political association which had great influence with the Government.' Due to his active intervention in the association, he was elected to its

Rajabali Jumabhoy was recognised as the leader of Singapore's Indian community.

executive committee four years later—the first Indian to be thus chosen. For his numerous public initiatives, he was awarded a number of honours and positions: justice of peace (1930), Malayan Certificate of Honour (1938) in recognition of his 'loyal and valuable service to the government of the Straits Settlement', and municipal commissioner (1938 and 1941).

During the war, the government assigned Jumabhoy the responsibility of overseeing the evacuation of the Indians. His requests to the viceroy and leaders like Gandhi helped to mobilise four ships for evacuation purposes. As conditions worsened, in February 1942 Jumabhoy led 992 Indians back to India on the last ship that the Japanese allowed to sail from Singapore. In India, he garnered support for the Indian evacuees from an array of leaders, including Gandhi, C. R. Rajagopalachari and Jawaharlal Nehru, and a plethora of forums, including chambers of commerce and public meetings. His efforts bore fruit, and at the end of the war, the British Military Advisory Council included him as a member. In 1951, Jumabhoy was nominated as a member of the Executive Council—the first Indian to be on the august body. Furthermore, as the president of the SICC, Jumabhoy served as a member of the Legislative Council from 1948 to 1955.

Jumabhoy's abiding concern was for the Indian community. Worried about its post-war status, he and other leaders invited India's first prime minister, Nehru, to lay the foundation stone for the Gandhi Memorial at Race Course Road. The Indian community, Jumabhoy being a main contributor, raised the entire cost of construction, which amounted to S$17,000.

Yet, through all those years, Jumabhoy never restricted his endeavours to the social world of the Indian community. He forged far-reaching linkages and developed close alliances with several public figures, such as David Marshall, and influential people from the world of business and trade. His philanthropy reflected his support for a range of causes. His 1955 victory as an independent candidate to the Legislative Assembly for the Chinese-majority ward of Telok Ayer bears testimony to his multicultural networks.

In 1962, Jumabhoy retired from public office but continued to maintain an interest in his business empire. When he died in 2001, his sons and grandsons took over the empire. Like several business patriarchs, Jumabhoy was unable to work out an amicable division of fortunes, and his later days were marked by acrimonious dealings between his sons' families.

Celebrated Indian poet Rabindranath Tagore (seated, left) was hosted to a tea reception at the home of the Indian Association's patron, M. A. Namazie, in July 1927. On the far left of the picture stands Mr Jumabhoy.

Labourers at work in a timber yard in Rangoon, c. 1890–99.

An Indian silver-smith with his wares, c. 1940.

Post-independence moves towards nationalism and indigenisation further marginalised trading communities. Legislative measures of the late 1940s—the Standard Tenancy Act, Tenancy Disposal Act, Agricultural Debt Relief Act, Land Nationalisation Act and Burma Foreigners Act—adversely affected moneylending and trading. The compensation offered for nationalisation was woefully inadequate. The Bank of Chettinad owned nearly 34,398 hectares of land but was recompensed a mere Rs. 150,000. Where compensation was available, remittance was problematic. The Chettiars, whose interests in Burma were valued at Rs. 900 million, were particularly affected. After decades of contributing greatly to Burma's prosperity, traders were forced to return to India.

Some communities, such as the Ismaili Khojas and the Chulias, stayed on in Burma, integrating themselves with the new economic regime by adopting Burmese names and accepting citizenship. The Chulias continued as petty businessmen and hawkers, several having set up repair shops selling used spare parts. With the closure of larger businesses in the 1950s, the economic dominance of Indian traders ceased. Trading interests were further marginalised after the coup d'état by General Ne Win in 1962 and the military takeover of private enterprises. Upon their return, larger groups, such as those of Raja Sir Annamalai Chetty and M. C. T. Chidambaram Chetty, moved into industry, especially cotton textiles. Others resumed trading, banking and speculative activities. In Burma, the Chettiars faced challenging legislation, but in other regions, such as Vietnam, and especially Saigon, they continued moneylending and investments in land well into the 1970s. Overall, in most other parts of Southeast Asia, with the increasing popularity of modern banking in the world economy, the younger generation was compelled to adopt new professions, moving away from the time-honoured activities of banking and moneylending.

CONDITIONS IN SOUTHEAST ASIA

The challenges for Indian traders in Burma were quite unique. Elsewhere in Southeast Asia, Indian traders flourished after the war. Trading groups became more deeply entrenched in their economic niches and rose in prominence. In Malaya, the Indian trading community swelled from an estimated 12 per cent of the total number of persons engaged in the commercial and financial sector in 1931, to 16 per cent in 1957. Large numbers moved into trade from other professions: in 1931, only 5.6 per cent of Indians were involved in commercial pursuits, but by 1957, as many as 13.4 per cent had taken to commerce. Indians had interests in retail trade, moneylending and insurance. In terms of overall presence, in 1970 Indian control of the industrial sector stood at 0.4 per cent in mining, manufacturing and construction, 3.5 per cent in wholesale and retail trade, and 3.2 per cent in transport. Malaysian Indian ownership of the corporate sector stood at 1 per cent in 1980, with investments at RM270 million. The growing confidence of the Indian trading diaspora after World War II was expressed through the founding of new chambers of commerce—the Bombay Merchants Association (Jakarta, 1949) and the Indian Chamber of Commerce (the Philippines, 1951), which later came to be known as the Indo-Filipino Chamber—and increasing membership in existing chambers. Membership of the Singapore Indian Chamber of Commerce, for example, rose from 202 in 1946 to 338 in 1965. Communities such as the Gujaratis, Sikhs and Sindhis reinforced traditional niches in textiles and the retail trade in the post-war years.

The Sindhi presence in business became prominent with increased migration following the Partition in 1947, when Sind became part of Pakistan. Hundreds of Sindhis reportedly came to Malaya, where the community already had a significant presence. These new members, predominantly traders, energised the community's textile niche. Many joined older businesses, while some set up smaller shops of their own. Soon, along with Sikh merchants,

A contemporary shop-keeper selling garlands.

Sindhis dominated the textile trade in Malaya. Textiles were imported from Japan, Korea, Taiwan and parts of China, such as Shanghai (with Singapore emerging as the centre for imports) and were re-exported to Indonesia, Indo-China, Ceylon, the Middle East, Yemen and America. The Korean War further boosted trade. Setbacks occurred in the 1950s after restrictions were imposed on imports by Indonesia, which had emerged as a significant textile market, and by legislation in the Philippines in the mid-1950s, restricting retail trade to the indigenous population. However, Sindhi businessmen maintained their presence in the textile sector by entering the import trade and wholesale textile/garment manufacturing in the 1960s. Traders took to producing popular American garment brands locally. By the mid-1980s, they controlled almost 10 per cent of annual garment exports. Further, they carved out a new niche in the field of electronics, importing from Taiwan and Japan and exporting to Nigeria, Ghana, the Middle East and parts of Asia and Europe. On the whole, the Indian mercantile community in the Philippines was engaged mainly in medium-scale trading and manufacturing, particularly of textiles. In Indonesia, some enterprising Sindhi firms moved into film imports and banking.

The Sikh trading community grew more visible too, with an increasing number of Sikhs quitting various professions to take up trade. The post-war (especially Korean War) boom catalysed the formation of new Indians firms as former employees grew enterprising. Often they entered moneylending and the retail, textile or electronic trades. In Singapore's textile sector, Punjabis outstripped the Sindhis. In Thailand too, they dominated textiles. In other countries, such as the Philippines, they remained largely in retail, moneylending and the vending of textiles and electrical equipment, though some entered manufacturing and exports. Their strongholds, however, were moneylending and textiles. In North Sumatra, especially Medan, and Jakarta and Surabaya, they took to sporting goods.

The Chulia, Mappila and Gujarati trading communities continued in sectors they were traditionally engaged in. The Chulias were prominent in the small restaurant business, textile trade and moneylending. In North Sumatra, Tamil Muslims who had long been involved in textile trading set up textile industries after the 1970s oil boom, but most stayed in the retail trade, wherein textiles were the dominant interest. Gujarati Muslim traders also kept to retail trade in most parts. The Marakkayars continued as general merchants and shopkeepers.

There was an infusion of new business specialities in the 1970s and 1980s, when large Indian corporates joined local Indian traders to set up industries. Aditya Birla of the Birla Group pioneered this move, being the first to enter Southeast Asia with local Indian support. In 1969, Birla entered Thailand by setting up Indo-Thai Synthetics Ltd; he followed this with Thai Rayon and then expanded into other countries across the region. Over the next few years, Birla launched over a dozen industries in Thailand, Malaysia, the Philippines and Indonesia with support coming largely from Indian investors. Some of these industries were Thai Acrylic Fibre, Century Textiles and Indo-Thai Carbon Black (Thailand); Indo-Phil Textiles, Indo-Phil Cotton Mills and Indo Phil Acrylic Mfg Co. (the Philippines); PT Indo Bharat Rayon, PT Elegant Textile Industry, PT Indo Liberty Textiles, and PT Sunrise Bumi Textiles (Indonesia); and Pan Century Edible Oils (Malaysia). Between 1970 and 1980, Birla promoted 10 companies in the region, their sales aggregating US$100 million. By 1990, the Birla interest in Southeast Asia, especially Thailand, Malaysia, Indonesia and the Philippines, had grown into an empire worth a whopping Rs. 12 billion. Locally based Indians and investors usually held 75 per cent of the equity in Birla ventures. Key investors in the Birla enterprises included established Indian traders in the region and elsewhere, such as Bangkok-based textile trader Amarnath Sachdev, Indonesia-based textile trader Haru Mehtani, and Antwerp-based diamond merchants Vijay Shah and Rashmi Mehta. Indeed, in the 1980s, Birla emerged as the largest Indian investor in Thailand and reportedly ranked among the largest holders of assets in the country.

Following Aditya Birla's lead, other groups have entered the region through similar collaborations with the local Indian community. These groups include the Kirloskars, Dalmias, Godrejs, Gaekwars and Lohias—the Lohias being owners of the massive Indo-Rama Group in Thailand. Prominent Indian businessman Sivnath Rai Bajaj collaborated with India-based Usha Company to set up Usha Siam, which produces steel wires and ropes in Thailand, and Sri Ambika Mills at Ahmedabad, which produces dye materials. Since the late 1980s, about 25 companies in textile manufacturing, some with Indian collaboration, have also been set up in Thailand. The report of the High Level Committee on Indian Diaspora in 2001 recognised this new era of symbiosis when it declared that Indian business investments in Thailand had 'contributed considerably to improving the image and prestige of the Indian community in local circles.' This new infusion of business continues the long-standing historical engagement of Indian trading communities with the commercial world of Southeast Asia.

Medha Kudaisya

The entrepreneurial spirit of the Indian community is manifested in the numerous shops they have opened all over the region.

THE AGE OF GLOBALISATION

The mid-20th century saw the beginning of a change in the pattern of Indian migration. For the first time, people moved not to the colonial periphery but to the metropolitan centres at the heart of the Empire-Commonwealth. Initially, this movement was to the UK, particularly to urban centres in England. The migrants came—some from India itself, some from colonial diasporic communities—to take advantage of labouring or service opportunities in Britain's post-war economy. Reaching a peak in the early to mid-1960s, the first movements were directed to Britain because Asian (and African) immigration into the white settler Dominions—Australia, Canada and New Zealand—was heavily restricted at that time. By the mid-1960s, restrictions were loosened and migration to the Dominions picked up, in part to ease the plight of Indians settled in East African colonies which had become independent and began to limit the position of Indian settlers.

In the last three decades of the 20th century, the character of Indian migration increasingly changed and a 'new diaspora' began to emerge. Spurred particularly by more flexible US policies for highly skilled migrants, Indian migration was increasingly dominated by professionals—academics, scientists, engineers, doctors and managers, many of whom showed considerable entrepreneurial flair. The US was the prime destination for those who became non-resident Indians (NRIs), but this new wave also moved into Britain and the Dominions. Many of these professionals have shown considerable entrepreneurial flair, establishing themselves as major players in global 'big business'.

The latter decades of the 20th century saw the return of a demand for contract labour in the oil-rich states of the Gulf and in the 'tiger' economies of Southeast and East Asia. Such labour became important to India because of the substantial 'remittances' made by the workers. These new contingents of labourers suffered many of the oppressive conditions of their 19th-century indentured forebears; but, unlike them, they were generally not allowed to settle in their host societies.

POST-WAR MIGRATION

WORLD WAR II marked a crucial watershed in the history of the Indian diaspora in the developed world. It was the beginning of the transformation of the Indian presence from one that was miniscule, transitory and peripheral, to one that became more substantial, permanent and central. The largest number of migrants in this period went to the UK, some because of old colonial links and others as a result of wartime experiences as soldiers and seamen. For communities from the Indian subcontinent, the combined experiences of war, the Partition and independence provided the initial motivation for the post-war exodus. This was subsequently strengthened by the nexus of kinship and friendship that enabled others to tap the economic opportunities that were becoming available in labour markets abroad.

An Air India ticket from Punjab to London in the early phase of post-war migration to the UK.

However, the official British mindset was traditionally against the permanent immigration of Asian (and black) communities to Britain. It is true that Asian and Indian immigration to Britain had failed to grow spontaneously in the inter-war period because of sluggish labour market conditions during and after the Great Depression of the 1930s, but the movement was also constrained by the various administrative measures applied by both London and New Delhi. After the war, even repatriation was mooted, and a number of restrictive measures were applied to stall the future immigration of Asians. This occurred during a period of full employment in Britain, when labour from Ireland and other parts of Europe was quickly absorbed, while job-seeking Indians and other Asians continued to be neglected.

The incessant deliberations at the British Cabinet, ministerial and other official levels between 1948 and 1961 were concerned with how best to limit Asian (and black) settlement in Britain without tarnishing the country's 'liberal' image. There was no reference to the war-related origins of these migrants or recognition of the extent to which the origins of 'the problem' were rooted in Indians meeting Britain's wartime needs. Viewed as opportune replacements for the considerable number of British merchant mariners conscripted into the enlarged wartime Royal Navy, the number of Indian sailors almost doubled between 1939 and 1943. A significant number of these Indian lascars were subsequently stranded by the loss of their vessels to German naval and aircraft attacks which torpedoed and bombed many Indian-crewed vessels off the British coast. A shortage of labour during the war ensured ample job opportunities in munitions and other factories for these stranded Indian sailors to earn a livelihood in Britain.

However, in spite of its liberal pretences, Britain was still far from being a multiracial society at the end of World War II; a situation that would change remarkably within a generation thereafter, when the country became multiracial and multicultural. Credit for this transformation can, in no small measure, be attributed to Indian immigrants who, alongside other 'coloured' people from Asia, Africa and the Caribbean, braved settlement in Britain in spite of political reservations and social disapproval at the time.

Although not all of them stayed on in Britain once their employment in war-related industries came to an end, some ex-sailors, like the Sylhetis, opened 'Indian food' outlets in London and gradually became residents. They were soon joined by others, many of whom were 'returnees' who were displaced as a result of the Partition in 1947. The Partition had the traumatic effect of dislocating people even in absentia—both Indians and Pakistanis—either from their places of residence or their ports of employment, or both. While they were away, their homes or places of origin had become part of a country which was no longer their own, or now belonged to two different countries: the families of Muslim sailors recruited in eastern Punjab had fled to Pakistan; Sylhet had become part of East Pakistan while Calcutta remained with India; and Mirpur formed part of Pakistani-ruled Azad Kashmir while Bombay became a 'distant' and 'alien' port in India. Two of the groups thus affected were those whose roots in Britain had grown stronger during World War II—the Muslim lascars from Punjab and Kashmir in the west, and those from Sylhet in the east—and who had been recruited for

many decades to crew the vessels sailing from the ports of Bombay and Calcutta respectively.

THE 'ANGLO-INDIANS'

Many Anglo-Indians—of British and Indian parentage—born in the subcontinent sought entry into the UK in the years immediately following India's independence. They were generally refused British passports. Initially, sympathetic officials at the British High Commission in India had helped small numbers of such Anglo-Indians gain passage to Britain with the issue of travel documents and even with small sums of money at the discretion of the high commissioner. However, by 1950 these officials were restricted from granting British passports to Anglo-Indians who were unable to produce documentary proof of their direct descent from an ancestor born in the UK. In practice, the High Commission also approached the Home Office in London for a police report when there were doubts about an application. In 1952, of the 545 cases referred, 294 (54 per cent) were deemed unfavourable and returned to India. In fact, the requirement for documentary proof was deliberately introduced since it was no secret that a large majority of the Anglo-Indians had no such proof to produce. In 1954, the High Commission was clearly directed 'to tighten up the qualifications for the grant of assistance and to severely reduce the funds available for this purpose' even though the Anglo-Indians 'may be technically our fellow citizens.' The concern behind this dictate was the belief of ministers that the influx of coloured persons into the country would bring in those more likely to become dependent upon British 'national assistance', Anglo-Indians being no exception.

The privileged position of Anglo-Indians in the railways and postal services under the Raj was coming under pressure in independent India. Therefore, they looked for alternative sources of employment in Britain, even as Indian citizens. British officials were not displeased that they also experienced difficulties in obtaining Indian travel documents. To the British authorities, it was preferable that the government of India maintain or even strengthen its procedures for granting passports to people who wished to settle in Britain. The Indian government itself was not quick to set up passport offices after independence. When it did, it accepted the British rationale for the need to insist on a financial guarantee or repatriation bond for anyone applying for a passport for the purpose of going to the UK. The Indian government agreed that if an Indian passport was to be issued, then emigration permission for travel to the UK should be endorsed by British passport authorities only after they were satisfied that the applicant had sufficient funds to support a reasonable standard of living in Britain.

THE VOLUNTARILY DOUBLE-DISPLACED

These restrictions led to the development of a 'cottage industry' for forged endorsements and passports on quite a large scale in India. According to rough estimates, up to 70 per cent of the 17,300 Indians who migrated between 1955 and 1957 are believed to have entered Britain on such documents. Travelling on forged documents naturally involved additional costs for the migrant in terms of

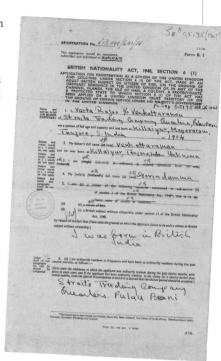

A document requesting the grant of British citizenship to an Indian migrant working for the Straits Trading Company in Singapore, 1954.

Lascars using the British navy's new 'mechanical sailors' to clean the decks of the SS Iberia, *c. 1931–50.*

Lord Louis Mountbatten, the last British viceroy of India.

large payments to middlemen, which certainly limited the number of people who could afford it. However, there were other loopholes, too, which made it difficult for the two governments to control the entry of Indians into Britain using the endorsement method of controlling exit from India. If one first travelled from the Indian subcontinent to a second country, and then from there to the UK, it was possible to bypass the hindrances. Particularly from the holy places of the haj, prospective immigrants could embark for the UK without fear of problems at either the airport of departure or arrival. While this loophole was used more by Pakistani Muslims visiting Mecca, Indian Sikhs used a second loophole involving a kind of voluntary 'double-displacement': under Section 6(1) of the British Nationality Act, a British subject was entitled to apply for a British passport after residing in a British colony for a period of at least 12 months. When Asa Singh, who travelled to Kenya on an Indian passport and stayed there for twelve months, applied for a British passport, the British High Commission in New Delhi reacted as follows:

…I do not see how we can prevent this person from joining his illiterate brethren in the UK…As persons from the Punjab think nothing of waiting two years before they can obtain a passport and scrape enough money to travel to the UK, it seems to me they will not hesitate to follow Asa Singh's example, solely to avoid the difficulties which they know exist in obtaining Indian passports.

THE INEFFECTIVENESS OF RESTRICTIONS IN THE UK

During the centuries of Imperial expansion and supremacy, Britain had made no distinction between the citizenship and nationality of the 'Monarch's subjects' residing in various corners of the Empire. This notion was disrupted after the end of World War II, when Canada in 1946, and India, Pakistan and Ceylon in 1947, introduced their own citizenship laws, prompting Britain to define for the first time its own citizenship. The British Nationality Act of 1948 introduced the unifying 'Citizenship of the United Kingdom and Colonies', which was available to all those who were deprived of citizenship in an independent Commonwealth country. However, it also reaffirmed Britain's faith in the unity of the Empire by recognising all citizens of territories that made up the Empire-Commonwealth—Britain, the colonies and the newly independent self-governing member states of the Commonwealth—as British subjects. As regards immigration and emigration throughout the Empire and the Commonwealth, the Nationality Act of 1948 only confirmed the situation that existed prior to it.

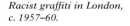

Racist graffiti in London, c. 1957–60.

Immediately after the end of World War II, employment opportunities in the UK became limited. The avenues of work that still existed were mainly in the clothing trade and large hotels, in the boiler rooms or as kitchen porters. The paucity of jobs along with opposition from employers and labour unions against the employment of 'coloured' people when white workers were available prompted many of the Indian seamen who had decided to stay on in Britain to try their luck as self-employed licensed pedlars.

Though all British subjects of the Empire and the Commonwealth were still free to enter the UK during the post-war decade of 1945 to 1955, the reality was that the immigration of Indians and other nationals of the subcontinent (Caribbean and African nationals too) was restricted by policy. Both the Labour regime of Clement Atlee (1945–50, 1950–51) and the Conservative regime of Winston Churchill (1951–1955) extensively debated legislation to restrict immigration during this period of full employment, when unemployment in Britain was below 2 per cent and unfilled vacancies fluctuated between a low of 1 per cent and a high of 2 per cent of the workforce. Attitudes at Whitehall were divided. At one point, encouraging migration from the colonies was even considered. However, others sought to prevent 'coloured' migration.

Indians did not start arriving in the UK in any significant numbers until the very end of the 1950s and the beginning of the 1960s. As immigration began to increase, the Commonwealth Immigration Act of 1962 was adopted, giving official legitimacy to British restrictions on the settlement of 'coloured' people from the colonies. The migration of South Asians, including Indians, was restricted to 'primary immigrants'. They were issued job vouchers in one of the three 'priority categories': those with a job offer in Britain; those with special skills that were scarce in Britain; or those eligible for an undifferentiated numerical quota based on the 'labour needs' of the British economy.

The restrictions of the 1962 Immigration Act were ineffective in controlling the entry of 'coloureds' until 1965. To uphold the 1964 election manifesto of the Labour Party, Lord Louis Mountbatten, the last British viceroy of India, undertook a tour of the Caribbean and India to persuade respective governments to self-regulate the movement of 'non-priority category' migrants to Britain. Fearing allegations of racial discrimination ingrained in the act, the Labour government attempted to shift responsibility to the governments of countries which were sending the migrants. However, Mountbatten's mission failed, leading to the adoption of a White Paper that became the basis of a restrictive bipartisan approach to immigration. It curbed the entry of semi-skilled and unskilled Indians who would not be eligible for the vouchers, which were meant mainly for the skilled 'primary immigrants'.

There was, however, a family reunification clause, which Indians were able to use to their advantage. The Sikhs, in particular, were more willing to bring their womenfolk and were economically more able to move their whole families from Jullundur and Hoshiarpur in Punjab to Britain under this clause. Other South Asian groups, such as the Mirpuris and Kashmiris from West Pakistan and the Sylhetis from East Pakistan, were less willing to do so.

Among the 'priority category' of immigrants entering Britain for the first time from 1965 onwards were professionals drawn from many parts of India, beyond Punjab and Gujarat. These professionals included doctors, dentists and research scientists from Kerala, Karnataka, West Bengal and Bihar.

Controversial British right-wing politician Enoch Powell.

THE 'TWICE-DISPLACED'

Highly skilled and professional Indians migrating from East Africa—the 'twice-displaced'—in the late 1960s and early 1970s added to the profile of the highly qualified Indian diaspora in the UK.

The East African Asians were British subjects who had settled in Kenya, Uganda and Tanganyika as merchants, traders, clerks and artisans. At the time of independence in East Africa, these Indians had the choice of either opting for local or British citizenship. Those who were uncertain of their fate under an African-majority regime opted for British passports issued by the UK and thereby escaped the requirements of the 1962 act. Those with British passports issued by the colonial governments or who had opted for local citizenship during the two-year probationary period after independence were subject to the act. Subsequently, under the Nationality Act of 1964, those with a UK-born father or grandfather had their British passports restored, even if they had renounced it to acquire the citizenship of another Commonwealth country.

When nationalisation and Africanisation intensified in post-independent East Africa, non-Africans left in large numbers. Kenya's Immigration and Trade Licensing acts of 1967 led to large-scale emigration later that year. In the last two weeks of February 1968, the number of East African Asians entering the UK stood at around 10,000, causing the British government to hastily enact the second Commonwealth Immigration Act in March 1968. Rushed through parliament in only three days, it subjected all such holders of British passports to immigration controls unless they, a parent or a grandparent had been born, adopted or naturalised in the UK. The legislation affected 200,000 people in all. Those allowed in under a voucher scheme, which was introduced to ameliorate hardships, nonetheless faced limitations on the employment of accompanying children and the elderly. This action was considered the 'most dishonourable conduct in the history of…immigration policy.' Simply put, it was a tool to deny civil rights to 'coloured' migrants from the colonies.

The British policy on East African Asian immigration was as indefensible as it was irrational. Collectively, the East African Indians were a well-educated and successful group comprising an extremely high proportion of entrepreneurs and professionally qualified people. Unwelcome in the UK, many of the twice-displaced, including some of the richest and best educated, went to Canada, the US, Australia and New Zealand. Paradoxically, on the domestic front, the 1968 act was criticised in Enoch Powell's 'Rivers of Blood' speech as being too generous to 'coloured' immigrants, including the Indians!

The exodus of Indians from Uganda followed the same broad pattern as in Kenya and Tanganyika. Idi Amin's announcement of the expulsion in August 1972 initially affected Ugandan residents of Asian descent who were either citizens of the UK or one of the countries of the Indian subcontinent. Subsequently, the expulsion was extended to all Ugandan citizens of Asian descent. Even exemptions that were officially in place for Ugandan government employees and professionals were widely ignored. As the crisis worsened, it became apparent that very few Indians would be allowed or willing to stay in Amin's Uganda. Edward Heath's government, though entitled under the 1968 act to limit even the entry of the large majority of those holding British passports, assumed responsibility for those whom no other country accepted. Heath's rallying of other prosperous countries resulted in about 23,000 Ugandan Asians, the majority of them Indians, finding homes, particularly in Canada. About 29,000 Ugandan Asians arrived in the UK.

Over time, however, the British voucher scheme became tighter and the number of permits was gradually reduced through the enforcement of new restrictions on nationality and immigration.

THE LIFTING OF RESTRICTIONS IN OTHER COUNTRIES

Prior to World War II, anti-Asian sentiment characterised immigration policy in North America. In Canada, the Order-in-Council P. C. 4849, passed on 24 December 1947, allowed non-immigrants who had served in the armed forces and who were honourably discharged to settle, provided they were not persons of Asiatic origin. However, the changing composition of the Commonwealth exerted its influence on the Canadian government. After Prime Minister Jawaharlal Nehru visited Canada in 1949, Indo-Canadians too were enfranchised. The explicitly racist provisions in the Immigration Act were changed to maintain Canada's image as a humane country. In 1962, new regulations to the act were introduced, prohibiting the use of race, colour and national origin as criteria for selecting immigrants. The points system that followed facilitated the increased immigration of skilled, educated and qualified Indians.

In the US, until World War II Indian immigration was dominated by labourers, such as those working in the Pacific Coast's lumber mills and docks. There were also a

Prime Minister Jawaharlal Nehru (centre) visited Canada in 1949. On his right is Louis St. Laurent, then the prime minister of Canada, and on his left is W. L. M. King, the former prime minister of Canada.

Nehru visited the Massachusetts Institute of Technology in October, 1949. This photograph shows Nehru being greeted by James R. Kalliair, the president of the school, as Indian students look on.

CALCUTTA'S VICTORIA INSTITUTION WAS ONE OF THE OLDEST GIRLS' SCHOOLS IN BENGAL, 1944. FEMALE INDIAN MIGRANTS ARE AMONG THE BEST-EDUCATED MINORITY GROUPS IN HOST SOCIETIES WORLDWIDE.

Figure 4.1

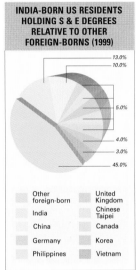

INDIA-BORN US RESIDENTS HOLDING S & E DEGREES RELATIVE TO OTHER FOREIGN-BORNS (1999)

13.0%
10.0%
5.0%
4.0%
3.0%
45.0%

Other foreign-born	United Kingdom
India	Chinese Taipei
China	Canada
Germany	Korea
Philippines	Vietnam

Figure 4.2

INDIA-BORN US RESIDENTS HOLDING S & E DOCTORATE DEGREES RELATIVE TO OTHER FOREIGN-BORNS (1999)

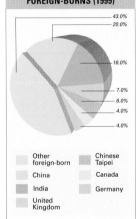

43.0%
20.0%
16.0%
7.0%
6.0%
4.0%
4.0%

Other foreign-born	Chinese Taipei
China	Canada
India	Germany
United Kingdom	

Source: National Science Foundation, Division of Science Resources Statistics (NSF/SRS), Scientists and Engineers Statistical Data System (SESTAT), 1999.

few educated Indians who were political refugees or students. Among the Indian students who were agitating for Indian independence were the son of the Maharaja of Baroda and the son of Rabindranath Tagore. In fact, Tagore had visited the US and praised the country for its international leadership, but he later denounced the Asian exclusions and refused to return to the US because of the 'utter lack of freedom' there. After the war, things changed. President Franklin D. Roosevelt had written to the chairman of the House Committee on Immigration and Naturalization in support of the withdrawal of barriers. He said, 'Statutory discrimination against Indians now serves no useful purpose and [is] incongruous and inconsistent with the dignity of both our peoples.' The bill resulted in amendments to the US Immigration Act in 1946. These ended almost 30 years of the exclusion of Indians by setting an annual quota of 100, following the lifting of barriers against Chinese immigrants in 1943. One objective of the change was perhaps to lessen the growing antagonism of Indians towards American troops who were still stationed in India after the end of World War II. The small step was consolidated further by Nehru's visit to the US in October 1949, which hastened the change in Indian immigration to the US from unskilled to highly skilled and professional migrants. This change resulted in further amendments to the Immigration Act in 1965.

While Britain aimed to avoid the racial problems persistent in the US, the US for its part welcomed diversity and learned to live with it. Indians soon came to be

counted among the highest educated, highest earning and most professional minority ethnic groups. In the 1960s, Australia too abandoned its 'White Australia policy' and followed Canada's path, attracting highly qualified Indians. The link that Indians had long maintained with Britain was thus severed. Canada and the US became the key destinations for Indian professionals through the 1960s and 1970s.

Binod Khadria

THE MIGRATION OF PROFESSIONALS

The migration of professionals from India increased noticeably from the late 1960s onwards. The brain drain involved doctors, engineers, scientists, teachers, nurses, architects and, in later years, IT professionals and entrepreneurs. By the end of the 20th century, Indian professionals had established themselves in the global arena. Moreover, within that period, the perception of professionals leaving India underwent dramatic change— from brain drain in the 1960s and 1970s to 'brain bank' in the 1980s and 1990s, and subsequently to 'brain gain' in the 21st century. This turnaround of perception in India is reflected in the ensuing euphoria whenever immigration quotas in developed host countries, mainly the US and Canada, the EU, Australia, New Zealand, Japan, Malaysia and Singapore are increased.

In 1999, there were 165,000 India-born US residents holding science, social science and engineering (S & E) degrees. This accounted for 13 per cent of all foreign-born residents with S & E degrees (see Figure 4.1), the highest share for any single diaspora group in the US.

As a sub-group of all S & E degree-holders, some 30,000 Indian professionals held S & E doctorates in 1999. This accounted for 16 per cent of all foreign-born American residents with S & E doctorates, second only to the Chinese diaspora in the US (see Figure 4.2).

Table 4.1 provides the occupational profile of all Indian immigrants entering the US between 1999 and 2001. It shows that a substantial majority of Indian immigrants with specified occupations were concentrated in the two top categories, i.e. 'professional and technical' and 'executive,

Table 4.1

CHANGING OCCUPATIONAL PROFILE OF INDIAN IMMIGRANTS ADMITTED INTO THE US (1999–2001)									
		1999			**2000**			**2001**	
	No. of Indian immigrants	% of all Indian immigrants	Indians as a % of immigrants from all countries	No. of Indian immigrants	% of all Indian immigrants	Indians as a % of immigrants from all countries	No. of Indian immigrants	% of all Indian immigrants	Indians as a % of immigrants from all countries
Professional and technical	3492	11.6	9.4	8632	20.6	14.7	19,935	28.4	23.8
Executive, administrative and managerial	1112	3.7	7.1	1644	3.9	7.9	3062	4.3	11.1
Clerical and administrative support	576	1.9	4.2	573	1.4	3.9	643	0.9	3.9
Sales	648	2.1	6.1	689	1.6	5.3	842	1.2	5.4
Service	559	1.9	3.2	798	1.9	2.6	1041	1.4	2.7
Farming, forestry and fishing	1328	4.4	11.7	1080	2.6	9.5	1161	1.7	12.8
Skilled workers	301	0.9	0.9	308	0.7	0.8	389	0.6	0.8
Total with occupation	8016	26.5	5.7	13,724	32.7	7.2	27,073	38.5	11.3
Occupation not specified	22,221	73.5	4.4	28,322	67.3	4.3	43,217	61.5	5.2
Total	30,237	100	4.7	42,046	100	4.9	70,290	100	6.6

Source: Statistical Yearbook of the Immigration and Naturalization Service 2001, 2003.

Table 4.2

INDIAN DIASPORA AMONG S & E FACULTIES IN THE US BY TEACHING FIELDS AND GENDER (1997)								
	Total	Indian diaspora	Indian diaspora as % of total	Indian diaspora as % of all diasporas	Indian diaspora as % of all Asian diasporas	Female % of Indian diaspora	Indian female diaspora as % of all female diasporas	Indian female diaspora as % of all Asian female diasporas
Physical sciences	37,020	688	1.9	9.3	19.4	16.7	18.8	9.9
Life sciences	53,055	1014	1.9	13.4	31.2	31.6	38.7	15.7
Maths and computer studies	44,375	2086	4.7	18.3	33.0	13.9	39.6	24.5
Social sciences	65,509	1491	2.3	15.5	32.2	6.3	10.7	5.1
Engineering	24,748	1597	6.5	17.8	27.4	0.9	23.3	6.3
Total in S & E	224,707	6876	3.1	15.3	23.2	12.1	26.8	12.9

Source: US National Science Foundation, 'Science and Engineering Indicators 2000'.

administrative and managerial'. Their proportion increased significantly during this period, demonstrating the strength of the highly skilled and knowledgeable Indian immigrant workforce in the US labour market.

Table 4.2 presents various indices of the Indian professional presence in S & E faculties in the US in 1997. It shows that in American S & E faculties, almost 7000 members of the teaching staff were of Indian origin, constituting 3 per cent of the teaching staff and 15 per cent of all diaspora staff in S & E faculties. The largest concentration of Indians has been in engineering, followed by mathematics and computer science, where they constituted about 7 per cent and 5 per cent respectively. Significantly, 32 per cent or about one-third of the Indian faculty in life sciences comprised Indian women.

The effects of such trends in India are increasingly evident in the growing shortage of teachers in technical schools. India's biggest global brand, the publicly subsidised Indian Institutes of Technology (IITs), is short of qualified teaching staff. By one estimate, some 380 critical vacancies at the seven IITs had no takers in 2005. According to surveys, the All India Institute of Medical Sciences (AIIMS) in New Delhi is at the top of the list of institutions from which more than half of their output of graduate doctors (56 per cent) from 1956 to 1980 had migrated. The magnitude of the brain drain from three IITs has also been substantial, with a large proportion of graduate engineers (between 20–30 per cent) having left, mostly for developed countries.

Until the end of the 1960s, the UK was the main recipient of Indian migrant professionals. This was mainly due to colonial ties between the two countries and the advantage which India gained from the British system of education with English as the medium of instruction, particularly at the higher professional and technical levels. During the 1970s, the UK was overtaken first by Canada and eventually by the US, which is still the most preferred destination for highly skilled professionals from India. Initially, the brain drain from India to the US was mainly associated with the exodus of high-profile Indian scientists, such as Nobel Laureates Har Gobind Khorana and Subramanyam Chandrasekhar. Indian professionals were among the best-educated and best-paid ethnic groups in medicine, engineering, law, architecture, teaching, IT, international finance, management, nursing, higher education, mainstream and ethnic journalism, English writing, film, and the TV and music industries. In the IT sector, several Indian IT graduates also emerged as important entrepreneurs in Silicon Valley.

The achievements of Indian migrant professionals are evident as well in other developed countries. In the EU as a whole, where the majority of Indians still reside in the UK, the Indian community is one of the highest-earning and best-educated groups, achieving eminence in business, IT, the health sector, and the media and entertainment industries. In Canada, where they constitute only 3 per cent of a population of 30 million, Indo-Canadians have recorded high achievements in medicine, academia, management and engineering. Their average annual income is nearly 20 per cent higher than the national average and their educational levels are also higher. New Zealand has also witnessed a rise in the entry of Indian immigrant professionals engaged in the domestic retail trade, medicine, hospitality, engineering and IT sectors. In India, this brain drain is now viewed not as a loss but as an opportunity, and therefore as advantageous.

HOST-COUNTRY PERCEPTIONS OF INDIAN PROFESSIONALS

The perception of Indian professionals in their host countries has also undergone a change. The UK has come a long way since the days of Enoch Powell. The change in values since 1971 has primarily been due to the immigrants themselves, who have defied expectations by rising to unforeseeable economic success. Today, the UK is a repository of success stories of Indian professional immigrants, such as Nobel Laureate Amartya Sen, Lord Swraj Paul and steel magnate Lakshmi Mittal.

By 1996, Indians accounted for 5–6 per cent of the overall immigration quota in the US, increasing to 7 per cent in the subsequent five years. In terms of the total number of immigrants in the US, India ranked seventh after Mexico, China, Philippines, Vietnam, the countries of the former Soviet Union and the Dominican Republic. However, if one considers only the number of 'principal' employment-based immigrant professionals and excluded spouses, children and other dependants, then India has ranked first since 1993.

Apart from being the first among those entering the US as permanent immigrant settlers, India also accounts for a large share of temporary foreign worker admissions into the US. In 1998, out of 372,000 'non-immigrants', as the temporary entrants are called under this category, India topped the list with 69,000, followed by Mexico's 51,000 (mostly unskilled), the UK's 39,000, and Canada's 20,000. Among professionals in the H-1B class, there were 62,544 admissions from India, followed by 38,190 from the UK, 10,000 each from Germany, France and Mexico, 9000 from Japan, 7800 from China, and 7600 from Canada. According to the last two US censuses, Indians are the most highly educated ethnic group of the Asian communities in the US, with 58 per cent of them having college and higher-education qualifications in 1990, rising further to 78 per cent by 2000.

The late Nobel Laureate Subramanyam Chandrasekhar has a NASA space station named after him—The Chandra Observatory.

Har Gobind Khorana was awarded the Nobel Prize in medicine (with Marshall Warren Nirenberg and Robert W. Holley) for work on the interpretation of the genetic code and its function in protein synthesis.

Figure 4.3

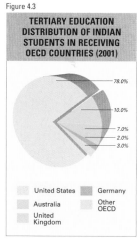

TERTIARY EDUCATION DISTRIBUTION OF INDIAN STUDENTS IN RECEIVING OECD COUNTRIES (2001)

- 78.0%
- 10.0%
- 7.0%
- 2.0%
- 3.0%

United States Germany
Australia Other OECD
United Kingdom

Source: OECD education database. Note: Excludes data for Canada, Greece, Luxembourg and Portugal.

An interesting shift has been the increased participation of Indian women in the American labour market. In the 1980 census, 87.2 per cent of foreign-born Indian female immigrants aged 25–34 years had completed high school—the highest rate among all Asian ethnic immigrants in the US, with the exception of Japanese women at 92.6 per cent. In terms of female median incomes, however, Indian women occupied an unchallenged top rank with full-time workers earning US$13,138 at that time.

In the UK, the number of British work permits issued to immigrants from India rose steadily from 1997 to 5663 between 1995 and 1999. In 1999, 51.4 per cent of the total work permits granted were for work in the computer industry. Approximately two-thirds of all software professionals entering Britain are from India. British government figures show that of the 18,257 foreign IT professionals working in Britain in 2000, 11,474 were from India. In 2000, the second highest number of IT professionals (2034) came from the US, and of these, many were of Indian origin. Of the 748 professionals who came from South Africa and the 708 who came from Australia, many were also reportedly of Indian origin. Among Asians, Indian professionals clearly gained a substantial lead in taking up IT jobs in Britain.

STUDENT MIGRANTS

The highly skilled migrants from India have come not only through the 'employment gate' but also through the 'academic gate' as students. Figures collated by the US Institute of International Education's 'Open Doors 2004' survey revealed that in 2003–04 India retained the top position in US university enrolments (followed by China, Korea, Japan, Canada and Taiwan) for the third year in a row. Indians accounted for 13.9 per cent of foreign students in the US. To sustain expensive higher education and meet short-term labour shortages, both the UK and the US now allow foreign university students to stay on and work rather than return to their countries of origin upon completion of their degrees. Further, the host countries gain political mileage as the foreign students become their long-term ambassadors in the international political arena. Growing competition among countries such as the US and UK, Canada, Australia, New Zealand and Ireland, and even non-English-speaking ones such as France, Germany and the Netherlands, are bringing even the Ivy League institutions to South Asia, particularly India, to look for the cream of students.

Many Indian immigrants who fuelled the growth of Silicon Valley were educated in the US at the postgraduate level after they emigrated with a first engineering degree (B.Tech./BE) from IITs, Regional Engineering Colleges and Banaras Hindu University, all of them institutions of excellence.

The Indian Institute of Information Technology, Allahabad. The newly established IIITs will build on the achievements of the IITs which have educated generations of highly skilled graduates who have made India so important in the IT world.

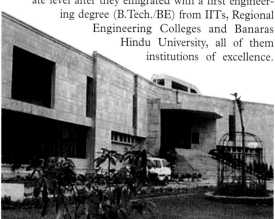

Figure 4.4

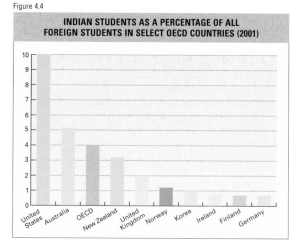

INDIAN STUDENTS AS A PERCENTAGE OF ALL FOREIGN STUDENTS IN SELECT OECD COUNTRIES (2001)

United States, Australia, OECD, New Zealand, United Kingdom, Norway, Korea, Ireland, Finland, Germany

Source: OECD education database. Note: Excludes data for Canada, Greece, Luxembourg and Portugal.

Similarly, scientists with Masters degrees in science and technology from universities such as Jawaharlal Nehru University or the University of Delhi; doctors with bachelors degrees in medicine and surgery (MBBS) from the AIIMS; and managers with postgraduate diplomas in business management from the Indian Institutes of Management (IIMs) have emigrated to pursue higher studies abroad, and then entered the labour market in their host societies.

Clearly, the US has been the most favoured destination for Indian students, attracting 47,000 in 2001, which accounted for 78 per cent of all Indian students enrolled in OECD (Organisation for Economic Co-operation and Development) countries (see Figure 4.3). They made up a substantial 4 per cent of all foreign students enrolled in tertiary education in OECD countries in 2001 (see Figure 4.4). In the US, they registered a far larger share of 10 per cent of all foreign students. By 2004, the Indian segment of all foreign students in the US had increased further to 14 per cent.

According to data from the National Science Foundation (NSF) on foreign-born Ph.D. students in US universities and those receiving degrees, the number of Indians in both categories is substantial. In 1996, of 1276 Indian recipients of US S & E doctoral degrees, the vast majority planned to stay in the US and many already had postdoctoral offers.

Apart from being considered the recruiting ground for fully trained and educated IT professionals, India continues to be a choice destination to shop for 'knowledge capital'. In October 2000, for example, four countries held 'education fairs' in Delhi and other Indian cities, and since then, such events have become regular. Most diplomatic missions have projected these fairs as a way of facilitating the search for foreign education by Indian students. However, in the process, these countries also compete for the generic Indian 'semi-finished' human capital, the Indian students, a body of professionals in the making.

INTERACTION WITH INDIA

Indian expatriate settlers have been interacting with their home country not merely to trace their roots but also to explore new avenues and sectors of mutual benefit, ranging from investment, to the transfer of technology and skills, and philanthropy and charitable works. This trend became more pronounced after the Indian economic reforms of the 1990s, which gave rise to a new range of opportunities for joint ventures between resident and non-resident Indians. However, with the exception of some high-profile names in the IT, business and entertainment sectors abroad, the Indian diaspora has remained largely out of public sight and awareness within India. The High Level Committee on Indian Diaspora was set up by the Indian government to recommend organisational frameworks, policy options, strategies and programmes to involve NRIs as well as 'persons of Indian origin' (PIOs) in accelerating the social, economic and technological development of India. The report, submitted to the prime minister in January 2002, produced strong evidence of deep and abiding ties with and commitment to India's welfare among the 20-million-strong Indian diaspora. The report also confirmed that the majority of Indians who had left did so because of economic reasons and not because of political, social or ethnic factors.

An important consequence of migration has been the remittance of foreign exchange to India, technically termed as 'private transfer payments' in India's balance of payments accounts. Although there was a rapid increase in remittances from skilled Indian migrants in the developed countries from the mid-1970s onwards, a significantly larger proportion came from semi-skilled and low-skilled labour migrants to the Middle East.

While remittances have contributed positively to the Indian economy, the volume of remittance has declined as families began to join the principal workers abroad, as has occurred in many parts of the state of Punjab, for example. The host country's immigration policy has had a great bearing on this. By prioritising 'family-reunification' over 'employment-based' immigration between the mid-1970s and mid-1980s, for example, US immigration law caused a decrease in the share of remittances arising from skilled migration to the country, especially when compared to those from Middle Eastern oil-exporting countries.

Following the expansion of the IT sector from the mid-1990s onwards, the priorities of the US and other developed countries have shifted from encouraging the migration of family and relatives to recruiting individual professional migrants from abroad to meet the economic needs of the labour markets in these countries. This had a positive impact on the amount of remittances coming from the younger generation of Indian H1-B visa holders in the US and work permit holders in the UK in the 21st century. However, an increasing proportion of such remittances has already begun to flow back to the developed countries in the form of overseas tuition fees paid by the growing number of Indian students who choose to migrate for education.

Apart from remittances, NRI professionals, especially those residing in developed countries and whose entire families have gradually migrated, have also found it attractive to put their surplus money in various 'non-resident' (NR) bank deposit schemes, particularly as repatriable deposits in India. These deposit schemes, floated by the Indian government in the 1990s, sought to draw foreign exchange to India by offering NRIs higher rates of interest

than what resident Indians would get on their deposits, apart from the flexibility of withdrawals in foreign exchange. Two special schemes, the India Resurgence Bonds (IRBs) of 1997 and the India Millennium Deposits (IMDs) of 2000, mobilised US$10 billion, thus doubling the bank deposit base of NRIs in India to about US$20 billion during the decade. However, both have been considered expensive for India as they have encouraged NRIs to borrow in Europe at lower rates of interest for investing in bank deposits in India, with the purpose of drawing the substantial interest differential. Furthermore, India's experience shows that the slightest instability in the country, whether political or economic, will witness the large-scale flight of these deposits.

On the technology front, the Indian software industry employed some 160,000 skilled people in 1996–97. This figure increased to 340,000 in 1999–2000 and is projected to grow in the future. India produces about 70,000 to 85,000 software engineers and about 45,000 other IT graduates annually. This growth determines the nation's capability to undertake research and to facilitate the absorption of international technology transferred to

The economic importance of the diaspora is underlined by the specialised transfer services offered by prestigious international financial institutions such as Citibank.

India's brain drain is of growing concern to the government.

'NRIs are India's biggest overseas lender, main source of foreign debt'

[Mumbai] Move over World Bank. The biggest source of India's foreign debt is now India's very own non-resident Indian (NRI). NRIs have emerged as the largest overseas lender to India, surpassing traditional sources such as multilateral and bilateral foreign agencies.

Throughout the 1990s and early part of this millennium, multilateral organisations such as the World Bank agencies formed a major chunk of India's outstanding external debt. Since then, however, NRI deposits in India have grown manifold and they now form the largest share of the country's stock of external debt.

And this is not a freak flash in the pan. While this trend of the NRIs being the largest overseas lenders started in 2003–04, it gathered momentum in 2005–06. In the quarter ended December last year, NRI deposits accounted for 28 per cent of India's outstanding external debt, while multilateral organisations formed 26.8 per cent of the total debt.

During April–February 05–06, there was a net inflow of US$1.9 billion against a net outflow of US$1 billion in the same period last year. Clearly, NRIs seem quite upbeat on the India story with the compound annual growth of NRI deposits being more than 20 per cent since 01–02, compared to a CAGR of 4 per cent of the outstanding external debt.

NRI deposits consist of rupee-denominated deposits, NR(E)RA, and foreign-currency-denominated deposits namely FCNR (B). Nearly 65 per cent of the deposits are now rupee-denominated as compared to just 30 per cent in 1990. This augers well for the stability of the inflows since in rupee-denominated deposits the exchange rate risk is borne by the individual depositor, unlike the FCNR deposits where the bank has to bear the risk.

During April–February 05–06, however, nearly 65 per cent of the inflows were in the FCNR account due to the recent volatility [of] the rupee. In spite of the recent hardening of rates globally, the interest rates offered to NRIs on rupee and forex deposits remain attractive.

And the recent hike in NRI deposit rates by RBI is likely to keep NRI money flowing into India. The ceiling on interest rates for NR(E)RA has been increased to 25 to 100 basis points above Libor (London inter-bank offered rate) for US dollar, for deposits of one to three years maturity.

FCNR(B) rates too have been increased to Libor rates compared to the previous cap of 25 basis points below Libor. At present the Libor rate in US dollars is at 5.4 per cent. It therefore makes more sense for NRIs to put their savings in high interest yielding deposits in India as compared to the low interest savings accounts in the country of their residence.

A number of steps have been taken to enhance the stability of NRI deposits: Rationalisation of interest rates of rupee-denominated deposits, linking the interest rates on forex deposits to the Libor and discontinuing with the short term NRI deposits.

The Business Times *(Singapore), Weekend Edition, June 3–4, 2006.*

India. Demand for IT graduates is projected to rise ten-fold by 2008, and to meet this, India will need about 2.2 million IT graduates. This figure excludes the overseas demand of 0.8 million, based on the announced intakes of the US, Germany and the UK only. India's present combined enrolment in all streams of higher education totals only a maximum of 0.4 million per year. Besides increasing the intake over the next couple of years, there are no tangible plans for meeting the increasing demand for IT professionals. The IITs are also under pressure to increase their intake but do not have the necessary physical infrastructure or human capital for this. New institutions like the Indian Institutes of Information Technology (IIITs) are now in place. The official patronage extended by the Ministry of Information Technology (MIT) in support of the flight of IT professionals to lucrative foreign destinations would, according to reports in the Indian media, spell disaster for Indian industry as it would lead to a shortage of quality professionals at home, restrict the growth of Indian companies and reduce Indian institutions like the IITs and future IIITs to hunting grounds for foreign companies.

Return migration, or the 'brain gain' that has been talked about as a panacea for brain drain, can only be assessed in terms of the engagement of returning migrants in India. The business media has given a lot of attention to MNC executives in the financial sector and young NRI professionals returning to India as 'angels' of venture capital. However, what is important is the continued return of NRIs to India and their engagement with ground level or 'alternative' development work rather than in promoting private capital interests. There are various initiatives, such as 'Action India', which is the brainchild of several Chicago-based Indians who are keen to pool their energies with resident Indians to hasten the development of India. Some of these are returned NRIs. One organisation formed by such individuals is the Returned NRIs Association (RNRIA) of India, based in Bangalore, with the motto, 'Back to Serve'.

There is another side to the return migration of professionals to India. While permanent settler admissions in developed countries have grown slowly, temporary worker entrants have grown more rapidly in the 21st century. This has been the fallout of a new trend emphasising return migration as part of 'effective migration management' policies in receiving countries in Europe and North America. In the case of legal migration, and particularly involving educated and qualified migrants, the British work permit, the German 'green card' and the American H1-B visa are all examples of policies to encourage the temporary migration of highly skilled professionals rather than permanent settlement.

OVERVIEW

Indian professionals have clearly established themselves in the global arena. In the US alone, the report of the High Level Committee on Indian Diaspora in 2000 estimated that 38 per cent of doctors, 12 per cent of scientists, 36 per cent of NASA employees, 36 per cent of Microsoft employees, 28 per cent of IBM employees, and 17 per cent of Intel employees were of Indian descent. However, while highly skilled Indians in any field of specialisation are given high professional positions, they are rarely appointed to top managerial positions, which are superior in terms of authority and control, in non-Indian owned organisations. In addition, while a few notable professionals have ventured into business, their figures are still small. In Silicon Valley, for example, only 7 per cent of all technology firms are run by Indians.

The success of Indian professionals in developed countries also affords an opportunity for mutually beneficial ties with the home country. Officials at the newly established Ministry of Overseas Indian Affairs feel that the real success of the India diaspora lies in building bridges with India. Of the 20-million-strong Indian diaspora, the NRIs and PIOs in the US alone number close to 2 million. Yet, this relationship is problematic given the diversity of the Indian diaspora, which is divided along subcultural, ethnic, religious, regional and linguistic lines. This sometimes makes it difficult for Indian professional migrants to take any uniform position on issues of concern to India. It also explains the number of professional and other associations and groups of NRI networks in the US itself. Efforts to unify these

To meet the ever-increasing demand for IT professionals, institutions such as the Indian Institutes of Information Technology have been set up.

groups or associations have not been successful, though what binds them together is a common 'Indian' cultural heritage. The Indian government is eager to establish strong cultural and emotional bonds with the diaspora that will assist their efforts to maintain and enrich cultural identity and foster better mutual understanding between the Indian networks. It is also concerned that certain sections of the wealthy and established professionals of Indian origin could become, if they are not already, supporters and sponsors of separatist activities in Punjab, Jammu and Kashmir, and the northeast.

Some policies encourage the return of professionals to India, either permanently or temporarily on specific assignments. Among the most well known of these is the 'Pool Officers Scheme', which offers temporary employment to permanent returnees; it was launched by the Council for Scientific and Industrial Research (CSIR) of the government of India. Another such scheme was the 'Transfer of Knowledge through Expatriate Nationals and Interface for NRI Scientists and Technologies' (TOKTEN-INRIST), which was aimed at temporarily returning scientists and launched by the CSIR in collaboration with the United Nations Development Programme (UNDP). Both schemes have been quite ineffective due to poor offers and poor implementation respectively. TOKTEN-INRIST had the scope for encouraging even private-sector industrial establishments by providing placements to the returning/visiting NRIs in their R & D units. The private firms were, however, frustrated with the bureaucratic handling of the TOKTEN-INRIST scheme by the CSIR. The University Grants Commission too had initiated the position of research scientist in the early 1980s primarily to attract Indians abroad with offers of placements in Indian universities and substantial research grants to supplement salaries. The scheme ran into rough weather due to the dilution of standards for accommodating unemployed degree holders from within India in all disciplines.

The overseas networks and associations of Indian professional migrants could play the catalyst's role in raising the average productivity of Indian workers at home by making long-term investments in education and healthcare the priority, rather than focusing on immediate profit-making ventures in India by their members. Networks of the professional Indian diaspora, such as the American Association of Physicians of Indian Origin (AAPI), Enterprising Pharmaceutical Professionals from the Indian Subcontinent (EPPIC), Network of Indian Professionals (NetIP), and The Indus Entrepreneurs (TiE), have shown the potential to make a contribution to India's economic and social development.

Binod Khadria

REMITTANCES

In 2005, the World Bank published the list of the top 10 developing countries with the highest volume of remittance flows for 2004. In the list, India was ranked at the top with US$23 billion, a position it has maintained for quite some time (see Figure 4.5).

Estimates by the World Bank show an upward trend in remittances to India from the 1970s onwards. This increase has accelerated significantly in the 21st century (see Figure 4.6). Accordingly, the proportion of remittances to the GNP (Gross National Product) has grown from a negligible 0.14 per cent in 1970 to about 2 per cent in 2000 and close to 5 per cent in recent years. These estimates of the flow of remittances are based on formal channels of transfer; informal channels of transfer, such as *hawala*, are not taken into account. The true level of remittances would be much higher than the official estimates if undocumented financial flows were included.

The exceptional volume of remittance flows in the 21st century has added to India's foreign exchange reserves, which are considerable. In addition, these remittances provide a potential source of additional savings, investment and capital formation and have a direct bearing on the balance of payments position of the country.

KERALA'S MIGRANTS

In India, Kerala leads, with the highest number of emigrants in the Middle East, from where most of the

Indian workers overseas are a source of significant income for India.

The Middle East is a popular destination for Kerala's migrants and the region accounts for a considerable portion of India's remittances.

Figure 4.5

WORKERS' REMITTANCES RECEIVED BY DEVELOPING COUNTRIES (2004)

US$ in billions

India	23.0
Mexico	17.0
Philippines	8.1
China	4.6
Pakistan	4.1
Morocco	3.6
Bangladesh	3.4
Colombia	3.1
Egypt	3.0
Brazil	2.8

Source: World Bank, Global Development Finance: Mobilizing Finance and Managing Vulnerability, *2005.*

Figure 4.6

TRENDS IN REMITTANCES TO INDIA (1998–2004)

US$ in billions

Sources: World Bank, Global Development Finance, *2000;* Global Development Finance, *2003; and* Global Development Finance: Mobilizing Finance and Managing Vulnerability, *2005.*

In Kerala, the effects of remittances can be seen in many aspects of life. Families with members who work abroad tend to have better homes with modern amenities.

Indian women at an e-learning centre in Kerala's Malappuram district browse the Internet and check their e-mail, 2004. The Indian government has declared Malappuram's 3-million-strong population e-literate as at least one member from each of the district's 650,000 households is computer literate.

Figure 4.7

TOTAL REMITTANCES TO KERALA (1989–2003)

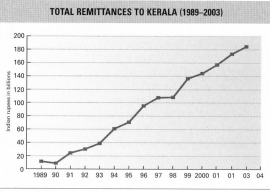

Source: K. C. Zachariah and S. Irudaya Rajan, Gulf Revisited (Thiruvananthapuram: CDS Working Paper No. 363), 2004.

remittances come. Almost all families in Kerala are affected by migration to the Gulf region in one way or another. Migration affects every facet of life in Kerala—economic, social, demographic, political and even religious. A recent study showed that 1.84 million Keralites were working abroad and among them, 89 per cent lived in the Middle East. The number of return migrants was 0.89 million. The number of 'non-resident Keralites' (NRKs), defined as the sum total of the number of emigrants and return migrants, was 2.73 million. There were about 40 NRKs per 100 households in 2004. In a study on migration in Kerala it was said that, 'Migration has provided the single most dynamic factor in the otherwise dismal scenario of Kerala in the last quarter of the 20th century. It is one of the positive outcomes of the Kerala Model of Development. Kerala is approaching the end of the millennium with a little cheer in many of its homes, thanks to migration and the economic returns that it brings. In Kerala, migration must have contributed more to poverty alleviation than any other factor including agrarian reforms, trade union activities and social welfare legislation.'

According to a recent estimate, total remittances to Kerala stood at about Rs. 185 billion in 2004—one-quarter of the State Domestic Product (see Figure 4.7). The infusion of Rs. 185 billion a year to Kerala via remittances has had a considerable impact on the Kerala economy. If that Rs. 185 billion was distributed equally among the 32.5-million-strong population of Kerala, it would give each person about Rs. 5680 per year or Rs. 473 per month, an amount sufficient to buy at least one kilogram of rice per day, per person.

THE EFFECTS OF REMITTANCES IN KERALA

The importance of remittances to Kerala's economy becomes more evident with the 2004 figures in mind: the remittances were 1.74 times the revenue receipts of the state; 1.8 times the annual expenditure of the Kerala government; and seven times the amount that the state received from the central government. The remittances were also sufficient to eliminate 60 per cent of the state's debt. The export of cashew kernels and marine products are two important earners of foreign exchange in Kerala:

remittances were 15 times the export earnings from cashew and 18 times that from marine products.

Expenditure on the education of children is a major item in the household budget, and emigration has had an impact on the amount that households spend on education: the average expenditure per NRK household was Rs. 7675, compared to Rs. 6080 in non-NRK households. Similarly, household expenditure on family health is an equally important item in the budget of Kerala households. In recent years, average expenditure on health per household has also increased to Rs. 3424. As expected, expenditure on health is also higher among the NRK families than non-NRK families.

One consequence of migration has been the large-scale increase in disposable funds at the household level. This increase has had a considerable impact on the consumption patterns of households in Kerala. After meeting the cost of emigration, remittances are used to acquire land, houses and consumer goods, including household amenities. Among those households with a migrant or returned migrant, the proportion with electrical connections was as high as 96.9 per cent, while the corresponding proportion among non-NRK households was only 81.9 per cent.

Nearly two-thirds of Kerala households use wood alone or in combination with other fuels for cooking. About 31 per cent of the state's households use LPG, while only about 4 per cent use kerosene. In 2004, about 42 per cent of NRK households used LPG, compared to only 26.5 per cent among the non-NRK households.

Migration seems to have had a very significant effect in the housing sector: 58.3 per cent of NRK houses in 2004 were considered either 'luxurious' or 'very good'. The corresponding figure among non-NRK households was only 17.1 per cent.

Between 1999 and 2004, the number of NRK households with telephones increased by 40.9 per cent, but only by 24.1 per cent among non-migrant households. During the same period, the number of NRK households with a television set increased by 31.4 per cent, compared to only 21.1 per cent among non-migrant households.

OCCUPATION AND EMPLOYMENT

A major motive behind migration is the improvement of economic conditions through occupational mobility. A comparison between the occupational composition of migrants prior to and after migration indicates that in fact, there was considerable upward occupational mobility due to migration. About 62 per cent of emigrants changed their occupations after migration and all of them switched to 'better' occupations. The proportion of former migrants without a regular occupation (e.g. the unemployed, students, unpaid family workers, etc.) has decreased by 19 per cent, while the proportion of former migrants in high-status occupations (e.g. government service, semi-government service, private sector and self-employment) has increased by 16 per cent.

Another major consequence of migration has been a reduction in unemployment. As a result of migration, the number of unemployed people has declined by 32 per cent and the unemployment rate has declined from 14 per cent to 11 per cent. The decrease in unemployment due to migration was greater among those with less than a secondary school education (37 per cent) than among those with a secondary school education or a degree (30 per cent).

Migration has also had a very significant impact on the proportion of the population living below the poverty line. The figure declined by over 3 per cent as a result of remittances received by Kerala households from their kith and kin abroad. This decline is especially significant among Muslim households, many of whom have migrant friends and family working in the Gulf states.

S. Irudaya Rajan

BUSINESS AND ENTREPRENEURSHIP

While the economic might of the Indian diaspora has become conspicuous only in the late 20th and early 21st century through the emergence of icons such as steel magnate Lakshmi Mittal, Indian commercial migrants have long played an influential role in the development of the diaspora. Their contributions have been evident not only in the economic sphere but also in their philanthropic activities, which have enabled the establishment of Indian social, cultural, religious and educational institutions abroad. However, overshadowed by studies of indenture and by contemporary interest in professional migrants, the history of commercial migrants and their networks has received little attention in the literature of the Indian diaspora—a situation unlike that of the overseas Chinese communities, where studies of their entrepreneurial networks have been prominent. Now, due to the substantial increase in the transnational flows of investment and trade

generated by the Indian business diaspora, it is important to take note of this key aspect of the diaspora.

A notable feature of Indian (and other) transnational entrepreneurial networks has been their effervescence during periods when there have been relatively few impediments to the flow of capital across boundaries. Merchant networks, financiers and trading communities, such as the Chettiars, Chulias, Gujaratis, Marwaris and Sindhis, were influential in the development of the diaspora in East Africa and Asia in the pre-colonial and colonial eras, when the institution of Empire allowed the relatively flexible movement of capital and goods across regions. The presence of these prominent business networks drawing from Asian traditions challenges Weberian ideas that the entrepreneurial impulse drew from an individual-centred puritan ethic. Furthermore, Asian business networks, with their emphasis on ties of kinship, enabled whole communities to act in an entrepreneurial spirit.

The rise of nationalism and the emergence of newly independent states in the second half of the 20th century regimented the flow of capital across national boundaries. Alongside economic policies informed by nationalist and socialist imperatives, this proved detrimental to some, such as the moneylending Chettiars in Southeast Asia. In South Asia, the Partition forced Sindhi bania traders and financiers to flee en masse to India and further afield, where they worked to rebuild their homes and businesses. In East Africa, the Indian commercial diaspora suffered from the propaganda of the emerging nationalist elite, who represented them as parasites with few loyalties to their 'host-land'. Africanisation policies not only severely curtailed the commercial interests of Indians; in the worst cases, as in Uganda, it led to their flight to the West.

In the later 20th century, newly independent states and the movement of Indians to the developed world provided opportunities for the emergence of a new class of entrepreneurs. In India, while government controls and restrictions constrained the capitalist impulse, the controlled domestic economy enabled profitable opportunities for incumbent groups while allowing fresh business groups to materialise at the national level. In the diaspora too, new entrepreneurs emerged, many of them Sindhi Hindus and Punjabi refugees of the Partition who may have abandoned their assets in the tragedy but brought with them their business acumen and a crisis-driven will to succeed. Most significantly, the movement from the 1960s of Indian professional and commercial migrants to the developed world would provide many, including the twice-displaced East African Gujaratis, with the opportunity to use their social and economic capital to develop businesses in the heartlands of capitalism.

The globalisation of economic activities since the late 20th century has witnessed the emergence of the Indian entrepreneurial diaspora as a key player on the world stage. Contemporary developments in transportation and information technologies have enabled these businessmen to operate virtually anywhere in the world. The liberalisation of state regulations and diminishing constraints on the flow of transnational capital has meant that many are now able to invest in places that can generate the highest returns. At the same time, in spite of their transnational locations, these expatriates are seen as important assets in India's drive towards becoming a major economic power. In addition to being an invaluable source of capital and foreign direct investment in the homeland, these entrepreneurs are seen as intermediaries, enabling understanding

Lakshmi Mittal is one of the Indian diaspora's most prominent businessmen.

Signs for computer companies on display in Bangalore, 1996. The city is considered India's IT capital and its very own 'Silicon Valley'.

DR SUDHIR GUPTA

A perceptive entrepreneur with the ability to discern opportunities in the diaspora, Dr Sudhir Gupta is the chairman of Amtel-Vredestein N. V., a leading international tyre manufacturing and trading conglomerate based in Russia and the Netherlands. Wide experience in Russia enabled Dr Gupta to identify potential business openings in Russia in the late 1980s and exceptional strategic skills enabled him to guide Amtel to international success.

Dr Gupta formed Amtel in Singapore in 1990, with a branch office in Moscow. It was initially concerned with trade in natural rubber, but through the 1990s it diversified with the acquisition of facilities for tyre and petrochemical production. In 2005, it acquired Vredestein Banden B. V., a leading European firm long established in the production of ultra-high and high performance tyres. The integration of Amtel and Vredestein created a pan-European tyre company that competes strongly in the global market.

Background and experience

Sudhir Gupta, born in 1958, has a strong academic background. As a science student in Delhi at age 17, he won a national scholarship to study at Moscow State University. He completed degrees in chemical technology and agrochemistry; his Ph.D. in chemistry was awarded in 1986. Subsequently, he studied finance and management at the Tokyo International Institute.

As the director (1986–90) of an Indian-owned store in Moscow, he gained the experience needed to start

Dr Gupta has been described as an 'inspired entrepreneur' for his achievements in Russia.

his own business. During this period he also travelled widely in Asia—some 15 visits in three years—to study the Asian market. Perceptively, he saw that the lack of Asian trade with the Soviet Union provided 'an

interesting challenge and a potentially lucrative opportunity.' This turned him from academic to entrepreneurial pursuits.

The situation in the USSR at this time paved the way for his entrepreneurial activities. He lived through enormous changes within the Soviet Union: the period of reform (Perestroika and Glasnost) under Mikhail Gorbachev; the collapse of communism; and the coming of 'a free-for-all capitalist economy'.

Amtel

Dr Gupta's research revealed that Russian manufacturers obtained expensive supplies of natural rubber from London rather than purchasing directly from producers. Amtel was formed as a trading house to capitalise on the opportunities which this offered. It effectively bypassed the London middlemen and purchased directly in Malaysia, Indonesia and Thailand, establishing a trade of 100,000 tonnes per annum, initially through Soviet government agencies. When the Soviet Union collapsed, Amtel went directly to the major consumers.

Diversification began in 1994: firstly, packaging, then petrochemical facilities related to tyre production, and in 1997, the acquisition of the Krasnoyarsk tyre plant. In 1999, Amtel acquired additional tyre plants in Kirov and Voronezh, along with petrochemical facilities for the production of Carbon Black and Nylon Tyre Cord. Further acquisitions were made in 2001 and 2002, leading to the establishment of Amtelshinprom (Amtel Tyre Industries), which created an integrated product supply and retail system. The establishment of the Amtel Holding Company followed in 2002 and the group invested in the upgrading of infrastructure and the unification of its technological base for higher quality production.

Dr Gupta touring one of his factories.

Research and development within the firm attracted researchers from the Moscow Tyre Research Institute and international manufacturers. To further ensure the supply of highly trained personnel, Amtel gave stipends to 350 students in the petrochemical field at institutes of higher education in Moscow and cities in which Amtel has its production centres, and also supported the development of a training programme.

Amtel-Vredestein

In 2005, Amtel acquired Vredestein Banden B. V. for 195.6 million in cash and created the integrated Amtel-Vredestein. This gave the group internationally significant 'brand' identification at the upper end of the market, which strengthened the firm's ability to compete. Amtel's global operations expanded in Europe, North America, Southeast Asia and the former USSR.

By 2006, Amtel-Vredestein had restructured its operations to provide a streamlined production base. It had three tyre plants—Enschede in the Netherlands, Kirov and Voronezh in Russia and a raw materials plant in Kemerovo, also in Russia. It is governed by a representative Supervisory Board, of which Dr Gupta is the chairman, and its top-management team synergises the strengths of its Russian and Netherlands units. Its total workforce stands at about 27,000.

From 2003–04 Amtel began to attract public investment. Templeton Strategic Emerging Markets Fund acquired a 3.75 per cent stake, which subsequently increased to 5.65 per cent. Amtel placed 10 per cent of its share capital among institutional investors through Troika Dialog Investment Bank, and Citicorp International Finance Corporation acquired a 4.1 per cent stake. The private placement of shares for Russian and foreign investors, valued at US$70 million, was undertaken through Alfa-Bank and Temasek Holdings. By June 2005, Amtel-Vredestein completed its public offer of shares on the London Stock Exchange.

Dr Gupta's achievements

In June 2005, *Indian International Rubber Journal* judged that the 'rise and rise' of Amtel was 'an astounding achievement for a company set up in far from ideal conditions a mere 15 years ago.' As an 'inspired entrepreneur', Dr Gupta had 'rewritten the history of the Russian tyre industry' and given a very impressive demonstration of Indian entrepreneurial skills in the global market place.

Amtel's headquarters in Moscow.

Peter Reeves

and facilitating the development of networks and connections abroad. Businessmen of the diaspora have also been crucial in encouraging other global corporations to invest or outsource in India. Links with the entrepreneurial diaspora have yielded considerable advantage to the Indian economy. An Evalueserve and World Bank Institute study quoted in *The Hindu Business Line* (October 2004) observed:

Indian offshore vendors and various captive centres of global corporations are...moving up the value chain and performing more complex and value-added activities for their clients. Apart from providing the required capital (through investments), the Indian diaspora is expected to increasingly play a crucial role in the gradual emergence of India's high-end knowledge services sector.

The ascendancy of an Indian transnational entrepreneurial elite has in turn led to efforts both in India and the diaspora to formalise the global commercial networks of NRIs and PIOs. One such initiative is the Memorandum of Understanding (MoU) signed by 15 business associations and chambers of commerce of the Indian diaspora in January 2004. Aimed at facilitating trade and investment flows among its members, the Federation of Indian Chambers of Commerce and Industry (FICCI) has been given the task of acting as the secretariat for this cooperative. The MoU reflects the extensive span of the Indian commercial diaspora, and include organisations from the Caribbean, North America, Europe, the Middle East and Southeast and East Asia. Other initiatives that have sought to facilitate such link-ups include The Indus Entrepreneurs (TiE), a global network of entrepreneurs and professionals founded in Silicon Valley in 1992.

While commercial groups of the diaspora may share many common characteristics in the 'Age of Globalisation', differences exist between groups, which can be analysed through the following categories:

- **Indian professionals turned entrepreneurs**
  This group is made up of Indian professionals who initially moved to the US as engineers and who went on to become venture capitalists and executives in medium- and large-sized companies by the 1990s. Many of these companies are based in Silicon Valley, where Indian IT professionals make up about one-quarter of the total workforce. Sabeer Bhatia, Vinod Dahm and Vinod Khosla remain icons in this field, where businesses operate at the cutting edge of technology. Many of these companies have gone on to invest in the development of India's high-end knowledge sector, providing both expertise and much needed capital.

- **The NRI business icons**
  More fragmented than the former in terms of industry, Lord Rajkumar Bagri, Dr Sudhir Gupta, Lakshmi Mittal and Lord Swraj Paul are some of the biggest names in this category. The NRI business icons share common characteristics: many were born in India and experienced a considerable period of apprenticeship before migrating. Futhermore, many of these entrepreneurs are based in the UK and other parts of the developed world. While they may have established their business empires abroad, they continue to maintain links with India whether, in terms of citizenship or in some cases by maintaining sizeable operations there.

- **The PIO business people**
  The most diverse category of the three, PIO business people represent the geographical spread of the diaspora, are found in a broad range of industries—at the cutting edge of technology as well as in more traditional enterprises—and have companies which may operate strictly at the local level or beyond the geographical boundaries of nation states. However, the common factor within this collective is that these prominent business people were brought up in the diaspora, and some of them are descendants of indentured labourers. PIO business people include notables such as Amar Gopal Bose, T. A. Krishnan, Hari Punja, Rita Sharma and Murli Kewalram Chanrai.

  Rajesh Rai

The annual TiE conference provides an opportunity for budding 'technopreneurs' to interact with venture capitalists, marketing gurus and policy-makers, such as the governor of the state of California, Arnold Schwarzenegger.

The Indus Entrepreneurs (TiE)

TiE was founded in 1992 in Silicon Valley as a non-profit organisation for entrepreneurs and professionals. In 2006, the organisation had over 8000 members with some 40 chapters worldwide. While membership is not limited to the Indian diaspora, its members are largely drawn from this group and its name signifies the South Asian or Indus roots of its founders. Sponsors for the organisation include some of the biggest names in venture capital, law, accounting and consulting, and the organisation seeks to encourage and cultivate entrepreneurship and free market economies. TiE Silicon Valley, one of the most active chapters of the organisation, holds meetings on a monthly basis, often featuring panel discussions with distinguished speakers, informing participants of emerging trends, technologies and corporate strategies. TiE's annual conference, famed for having a cast of notables as keynote speakers, provides budding entrepreneurs with the opportunity to network, seek the advise of marketing experts and gain new contacts among venture capitalists.

Based on www.tie.org.

The FICCI has been crucial in formalising global commercial networks for NRIs and PIOs. Pictured here are speakers at the India–Gulf Partnership Summit held in Dubai on 15–16 June 2006.

INDIAN PROFESSIONALS TURNED ENTREPRENEURS

Sabeer Bhatia

Sabeer Bhatia came into the limelight when he, along with his colleague Jack Smith, created the web-based e-mail, Hotmail, in 1995, and later sold it to software giant Microsoft for a staggering US$400 million in 1998. Bhatia's success has earned him widespread acclaim: venture capital firm Draper Fisher Jurvetson named him 'Entrepreneur of the Year 1997'; MIT named him as one of 100 young innovators who are expected to have the greatest impact on technology; *San Jose Mercury News* and *POV* magazine selected him as one of the 10 most successful entrepreneurs of 1998; and *Upside* magazine's list of top trendsetters in the New Economy named him as one of the 'Elite 100'.

Hotmail creator Sabeer Bhatia.

Born in Chandigarh in 1969, Bhatia was educated at Bishop's Cotton School at Pune and then at St. Joseph's College, Bangalore. For his Bachelor's degree he went to the Birla Institute of Technology (BITS), Pilani. In 1988, he received a scholarship from the California Institute of Technology. Later, he earned a Master's degree in electrical engineering from Stanford University. After graduation, he worked as a hardware engineer for Apple Computer for some time. It was there that Bhatia came up with idea of setting up Hotmail.

He is now working on at least five new projects: Navin.com, India's largest provider of voice mail services; InstaColl.com, a contextual collaboration solution; a project using Voice-Over-Internet-Protocol (VOIP); Hotseasons.com, a travel website that will focus on hotel ratings; and a project that turns your mobile phone into a personal organiser. Sabeer Bhatia continues to be an idol for all Indians who wish to make it big in Silicon Valley.

Vinod Dahm

Vinod Dahm, the creator of the Pentium chip, which runs almost 90 per cent of computers today, was born in Pune in 1950. He earned

Computer users can thank Vinod Dahm for the invention of the Pentium chip.

his Bachelor's degree in electrical engineering in 1971 from the Delhi College of Engineering. After working briefly in Delhi for Continental Devices, a semiconductor company, he went to the US to pursue a Master's degree in electrical engineering at the University of Cincinnati. Dahm joined the National Cash Register (NCR) at

Dayton, Ohio, in 1977, where he worked as a team member of the NCR's memory design group. While working at the NCR, he received many patents, and it was during one of his presentations in Monterrey, California, that Intel offered him a job. He went on to become Intel's microprocessor boss and later became vice-president of rival company AMD's Computation Products Group. He is now president and chief executive of Silicon Spice Inc., a telecommunications chip start-up based in Mountain View, California, which has been acquired by Broadcom.

Vinod Khosla

Vinod Khosla is one of the most influential people in Silicon Valley. He is in *Forbes* magazine's list of America's 400 richest people. Born in New Delhi, he earned a Bachelor of Technology degree from IIT, Delhi. He attempted to start his own company but the venture failed. He then went to the

One of the founders of Sun Microsystems, Vinod Khosla.

US and earned his Master's degree in biomedical sciences at Carnegie Mellon and later, a Master's in business administration from Stanford University. After graduating in 1979, Khosla rose to fame at the age of 27 when he, along with Scott McNealy, Andy Bechtolsheim and Bill Joy, founded Sun Microsystems. Khosla ran Sun Microsystems until 1985. He is currently a general partner of the venture capital firm Kleiner, Perkins, Caufield & Byers, which he joined in 1986. Khosla was among the first venture capitalists to realise that a combination of Internet technology and fibre optics would lower the cost of communication at higher speed while being easy to use. He played an important role in providing the start-up investment for numerous companies involved in the fields of multimedia, semiconductors, video games, Internet software and computer networking, such as Cerent Corp, Juniper Networks, Viant, Extreme Networks and Lightera. Vinod Khosla is also one of the founders of The Indus Entrepreneurs (TiE).

THE NRI BUSINESS ICONS

Lord Swraj Paul

A business magnate and a philanthropist based in the UK, Swraj Paul was born in 1931 in Jalandhar, India. Educated at Punjab University, he later obtained a Master's degree in mechanical engineering from MIT in the US. On his return to India, Lord Paul joined the Apeejay Surendra Group, which his

Lord Swaraj Paul has been bestowed with numerous honours.

father had founded as a small foundry for making steel buckets and farm equipment. A twist of fate led him to London to get his daughter cured of leukaemia. He started a business in Britain in 1968. After acquiring one steel unit in Britain, he went on to acquire more units and founded the Caparo group in 1978. His company developed into one of the leading producers of welded steel tubes and spiral welded pipes in the UK.

He was knighted by the Queen in 1978 and became the Lord Paul of Marylebone and a member of the House of Lords. He has since received various awards. Lord Paul was awarded the Padma Bhushan, one of India's prestigious civilian awards in 1983, and was bestowed with other prestigious honours, including the pro-chancellorship of Thames University (1998), chancellorship of Wolverhampton University and the Bharat Gaurav award by the Indian Merchant's Chamber. He is a member of the Foreign and Commonwealth Office's Foreign Policy Centre Advisory Council and MIT's Mechanical Engineering Visiting Committee. Despite being one of the richest persons in the UK, Lord Paul leads a very simple life. He stepped down from the management of the Caparo group in 1996, handing over his empire to his three sons. In his memoirs, *Beyond Boundaries*, Lord Swraj Paul details the main events of his life and business career, including his association with the famous and the mighty, including Indira Gandhi.

Lord Rajkumar Bagri

Rajkumar Bagri began his career in 1945 as an apprentice with the Binani Metals Group in Calcutta. Since then, his business life has largely revolved around metals. Between 1954 and 1959, he travelled to various mines, smelters, refineries and fabrication plants the world over and mastered the intricacies of metal trading. In 1959, Lord Bagri moved to London,

Lord Rajkumar Bagri is the first person of non-British origin to become chairman of the London Metal Exchange.

where he started his company, Metdist. In 1970, he became a member subscriber of the London Metal Exchange (LME), a highly successful and pre-eminent exchange in the world of non-ferrous metals. That, according to him, was a major step in furthering his business. Gradually, he took part in the governance of the premier metal exchange in the world and in 1993, he became chairman of the LME, the first person of non-British origin to be elected to the post. He has taken many path-breaking steps to keep LME a premier metal exchange in the world. In January 2003, he relinquished the chairmanship of the LME. The Metdist Group, led by Lord Bagri, has extensive trading and manufacturing interests in non-ferrous metals. The group has substantial investments in the manufacturing of rod and wire products. It also has a state-of-the-art integrated plant for the production of copper tubes for the air-conditioning industry. Currently, the Metdist Group's annual turnover is believed to be around £2 billion.

The Copper Club, Inc. named him as 2002's 'Copper Man of the Year', in recognition of his lifelong service to the international copper community. Acknowledging his services to the metals manufacturing industry and in furthering LME's position, Bagri was awarded the CBE (Commander of the Order of the British Empire) by the Queen. On 26 February 1997, Bagri was awarded a life peerage and took the title Baron Bagri of Regent's Park in the City of Westminster. He remains an active member of the Conservative Party of Great Britain.

Lakshmi Narayan Mitttal

Born in 1950 at Sadulpur in Churu, Rajasthan, steel tycoon Lakshmi Narayan Mitttal is a London-based industrialist and lives in the city's most expensive location, Kensington. With an estimated US$25 billion worth of assets, *Forbes* ranked him the third-richest person in the world in 2005, after Bill Gates (US$46 billion) and Warren Buffett (US$44 billion). He is obviously the richest Indian in the world and the richest person in Britain. His company, Mittal Steel, is among the world's largest producers of steel. Mittal holds steel assets which extend from Canada to Trinidad and Tobago, South Africa, Poland, Kazakhstan and Indonesia.

The foreign operations of the Calcutta-based family business were passed on to Mittal at an early age. Starting with Ispat Indo in Indonesia, Mittal has become the steel king of the world. With his vision and hard work, Mittal has expanded the moderate business of his family into a global steel giant spanning many countries. The companies of the LNM Ispat group include Ispat International NV, Ispat Karmet and Indo Ispat. From the core business of steel manufacturing, his group is now diversifying into shipping, coal, power and oil enterprises. The most fascinating aspect of his rise is said to have been his knack for buying obsolete steel companies at low cost and turning them into profitable ventures. His business interests, however, extend beyond failing installations, as evident in 2006 when he successfully launched a US$34.4 billion takeover bid for Arcelor, Europe's largest steel-maker.

Lakshmi Mittal has shown great skill in buying obsolete steel companies at low cost and making them profitable.

THE PIO BUSINESS PEOPLE

Amar Gopal Bose
Chairman and founder of Bose Corporation, Amar Gopal Bose was born in Philadelphia, Pennsylvania in 1929. His father, Nani Gopal Bose, was a Bengali revolutionary who fled Calcutta in order to avoid prosecution by the colonial police due to his anti-British activities.

An electrical engineer by education and training, Bose obtained a Ph.D. from MIT. During his early years as a professor of electrical engineering at MIT, Bose bought a high-end stereo speaker system in 1956 and was apparently not too happy with the

Music enthusiasts worldwide recognise the name Bose, a brand synonymous with speaker systems.

purchase. He was disappointed to find that speakers with impressive technical specifications failed to reproduce the realism of a 'live' performance. He aimed to design a speaker that would emulate the symphony hall experience at home. This eventually paved the way for his extensive research into speaker technology, concentrating on key weaknesses in the high-end speaker systems available during Bose's time, and focusing on psychoacoustics, which would eventually lead to his future company's success. Established in 1964, Bose Corporation currently employs around 8000 people and is a pioneering name in audio speaker technology. The name 'Bose' has become a symbol for quality and technical innovation in the world of audio systems.

Rita Sharma
Rita Sharma has emerged as the richest Asian woman in London, with a wealth of £95 million 20 years after she set up her own travel business in 1986. In 2001 she launched an online travel agency called www.bestatravel.co.uk. Today her company employs 100 people and has an annual turnover of £50 million. The website has thrived amid stiff competition and a downturn in the market.

Rita Sharma was honoured at the Eastern Eye Asian Business Awards, which celebrate the achievements of Asian businessmen and women, in April 2006.

Although born in Punjab, she was brought to Britain as a baby and grew up in the suburbs of Ilford. Her father manufactured women's garments for the department store C & A and her mother was a housewife. Sharma started working at the lowest level in a travel firm and was soon almost running it. At the age of 25, she decided to go into business herself and has never turned back.

Tatparanandam Ananda Krishnan
In 2005, Ananda Krishnan, TAK as he is called, was Malaysia's second (and the world's 138th) richest person, having a net worth estimated at US$4 billion. Born in 1938 in Brickfields, Kuala Lumpur's 'Little India', to a Tamil immigrant family from Ceylon, Krishnan studied at Vivekananda Tamil School in Kuala Lumpur. He went to the University of Melbourne for his undergraduate education before pursuing a Masters degree in business administration at Harvard University. Upon graduating in 1964, Krishnan's first entrepreneurial venture was in oil trading. Later, he moved into gambling (in Malaysia), stud farming (in Australia) and running a Hollywood cartoon studio. In the early 1990s, he began

Malaysia's iconic Twin Towers were funded by T. A. Krishnan.

diversifying in a big way in the multimedia arena. Currently, he has business interests in space, oil, power, shipping, telecommunications, entertainment, property and gaming. His companies operate in most parts of Southeast Asia. Krishnan also funded the building of the Petronas Twin Towers, the world's second-tallest building in 2005.

Hari Punja
A Fijian business tycoon of Indian origin, Hari Punja heads a Lautoka-based conglomerate of 15 companies, with investments in rice, flour mills, hotels, the media, printing, packaging and food processing. His companies have an annual turnover in excess of US$90 million. Punja also owns a stake in a

Hari Punja is one of Fiji's most prominent businessmen.

number of regional media organisations, particularly in commercial radio and television stations in Fiji and Papua New Guinea. He has held political office in Fiji, having served as a senator from 1996 to 1999.

Born in 1937, Punja, the fourth son of an Indian trader who emigrated to Fiji in 1914, was chairman and managing director of the Punja and Sons conglomerate founded by his father until 1998, when he broke away to form his own conglomerate, Hari Punja and Sons. He did this to give his sons a business to call their own, citing fears that potential disagreements between his sons and their cousins could lead to the collapse of the business. Now the business empire is run by the two branches of the family, who have an intense, but friendly, rivalry in the Fijian economy.

Murli Kewalram Chanrai
Murli Kewalram Chanrai, with an estimated net worth of US$720 million (2005), is the chairman of the Kewalram Chanrai (KC) Group. Founded in 1860, the KC Group has developed into a widely diversified conglomerate with interests in IT businesses, agricultural commodities, textile manufacturing, international trade and property development.

Chanrai's KC Group supplies raw materials to some of the world's leading food brands, including Nestlé.

Olam, a global supply chain leader of agricultural raw materials such as cocoa, coffee, cashew, rice and teak, with customers such as Nestlé, Sara Lee, Cadbury, Mars and Hershey, falls within the ambit of the KC Group.

Although Chanrai inherited the KC Group, his tenure saw a considerable expansion in its total wealth. By 2005, the conglomerate was operating in over 45 countries with more than 12,000 employees. Key values such as honouring commitments and being a good employer have generated loyalty from staff and customers. While the Chanrai extended family may have a prominent place in the organisation, it is subject to a 'family constitution' that governs their actions as shareholders. Chanrai has also stressed the need for higher management in the group to be direct stakeholders in the company. This had the effect of both increasing the motivation and accountability of managers, whether drawn from within or outside the family.

Binod Khadria

INDIAN LEADERSHIP
AND THE DIASPORA

Different political phases in India—the sensitivities of the nationalist struggle, the winning of independence, the trauma of Partition and the creation of the republican constitution of the Indian Union—engendered important changes in India's relations with the diaspora. A concern for the treatment of Indian migrant labourers during the nationalist phase was replaced by post-colonial disavowal after independence of any lingering responsibility for those who were now part of a separate nation 'overseas', and later, a tendency to view the skilled migrants who left India as a brain drain. However, by the last decade of the century, during the period of rapid economic liberalisation, the value of the diaspora was rediscovered, and Indian attitude came, as shown here in Part V, 'full-circle'. The new significance of the diaspora is manifested in Pravasi Bharatiya Divas (Overseas Indians Day) and the awards (*samman*) conferred by the government of India on high-profile members of the diaspora.

NATIONALIST INDIA: FORGING 'AN EMOTIONAL BOND'

INDIA'S NATIONALIST LEADERSHIP first turned its attention to the issue of Indians overseas as far back as the 1890s. Several founding figures of the Indian National Congress (INC) travelled abroad to study or work and many of them experienced first-hand the disadvantages that Indians faced overseas.

Racial discrimination and restrictive immigration policies in the colonies aided the forging of an emotional bond between Indians overseas and the emerging nationalist leadership. Both groups considered themselves engaged in opposing colonial regimes. As early as 1896, the INC in its Calcutta session recorded 'its most solemn protest against the disabilities imposed on Indian settlers in South Africa, and the invidious and humiliating distinctions made between them and the European settlers'; at the Ahmedabad session in 1902, it noted 'with regret' the 'Imperialistic spirit of the British colonies'; and at the Madras session in 1903, it viewed 'with grave concern and regret the hard lot of His Majesty's Indian subjects living in the British colonies in South Africa, Australia and elsewhere.' The INC also registered its outrage 'against the treatment of Indians by the Colonies as backward and uncivilized races.' 'In view of [the] great part the Indian settlers have played in the development of the Colonies', it called for 'all the rights and privileges of British Citizenship in common with the European subjects' to be granted to Indians. The Benares session in 1905 upheld 'the great constitutional importance of the principle of equal treatment of all citizens of the Empire anywhere in the King's dominions,' and called for a ban on indentured labour emigration; the Calcutta session in 1906 recorded 'deep regret and indignation' at Indians being 'subjected to harassing and degrading restrictions and denied the ordinary rights of British citizenship in His Majesty's Colonies'; and at the Allahabad session in 1910, the INC leadership admired 'the intense patriotism, courage

and self-sacrifice of the Indians in the Transvaal—Mohammedan and Hindu, Zoroastrian and Christian—who, heroically suffering persecution in the interests of their countrymen, are carrying on their peaceful and selfless struggle of elementary civil rights against heavy and overwhelming odds.'

Thus, the first decade of the 20th century marked the beginning of a vital ideological link between Indian political leadership and Indians overseas, a relationship that would only strengthen in ensuing decades. In its annual sessions in 1911 and 1912, the INC asserted its solidarity with Indian settlers in Africa. At Karachi in 1913, its leaders expressed 'warm and grateful appreciation of the heroic struggle' being waged by M. K. Gandhi and his co-workers, and called upon 'the people of this country of all classes and creeds to continue to supply them with funds.' Indians responded generously to the South African struggle: the donations included Rs. 25,000 by J. N. Tata. In 1915, at its Bombay session, the INC demanded the swift abolition of indentured emigration, condemning it as 'a form of slavery which, socially and politically, debases the labourers and is seriously detrimental to the economic

Gopal Krishna Gokhale was one of the leaders of India's independence movement and a senior member of the INC.

Mahatma Gandhi and Gokhale are pictured here in Durban, 1912, seated, fourth and fifth from the left respectively.

and moral interests of the country.' In 1916 at Lucknow, it expressed its 'ever-growing sense of dissatisfaction at the continued ill-treatment of Indian settlers.'

By then, sympathy for Gandhi's decade-long campaign for the cause of Indians in South Africa was spreading. Gandhi had attended the 1901 session of the INC as a delegate from South Africa. His personal contacts with Indian nationalist leaders, most prominently the veteran Gopal Krishna Gokhale, encouraged the INC to show solidarity with Indian communities not just in South Africa but also in Zanzibar, Fiji, Malaya, Burma and Ceylon. Gokhale contributed decisively by galvanising Indian public opinion in support of Gandhi's struggle, mobilising funds and directing Empire-wide publicity for Gandhi's activities. By touring South Africa, Gokhale signalled to the South African authorities that the weight of Indian political opinion was solidly behind Gandhi. This helped to bring Gandhi's South African campaign to fruition.

Gandhi's return to India on 9 January 1915 and his growing stature in Indian politics increased awareness of the anti-racist struggles Indians overseas were engaged in. The INC became more receptive to their plight and showed greater affinity with their cause. The work of Charles Freer Andrews and other activists brought into sharp focus the situation in various colonies. Between 1915 and 1920, strong public sentiment developed within India, leading to demands for the abolition of the indenture system in Fiji, followed by other British colonies. Abolishing indentured emigration would not have been possible without strong, sustained support from the INC leadership.

In the early 1920s, as the INC revamped itself into an effective mass nationalist organisation, it also formalised its links with Indians overseas. It affiliated with Indian organisations in other countries, enabling them to participate in and contribute to the deliberations at its annual sessions. Among its early beneficiaries were the British Indian Association of Johannesburg, the British Indian League of Cape Town and the Point Indian Association of Durban. By the late 1920s, several such groups enjoyed INC affiliation.

Soon, the consciousness of an organic link between Indians overseas and the anti-colonial struggle in India grew. In his presidential address to the 1926 Gauhati Congress, Srinivas Iyengar declared:

The lineaments of our great ancestry reveal themselves in us today...the adventurous spirit of early India which built up long ago a greater Bharat Varsha to the East and to the West, to the North and to the South is not extinct. It is now seen in the greater India which our brethren, in humble and laborious fashion, are building for us in far off lands against unparalleled odds. The status of Indians abroad, whether in South Africa or Kenya, in Fiji or Guinea [sic: Guyana], in Ceylon or Malaya, in America or Australia, depends inevitably upon the status of Indians in their own land; and the Swaraj for India depends in its turn upon the brave and unfaltering spirit of our kith and kin across the seas.

Iyengar noted with satisfaction that 'with patience and perseverance, our brethren are solving the question of racial equality all over the world. We can help them only by winning Swaraj for India.' He even suggested that the INC hold an annual session in South Africa to reinforce its solidarity.

For the INC leadership, the cause of Indians overseas was an extension of the anti-imperialist struggle in other parts of the Empire and presented an opportunity to highlight colonialism's underlying racist dimension. In 1929, the INC institutionalised this aspect by setting up an Overseas Department under Jawaharlal Nehru, who showed a special interest in international affairs. The department would stay 'vigilantly aware of all the legislations and enactments that adversely or otherwise affect Indian settlers abroad.'

Among the prominent leaders who undertook visits and study missions to report on the conditions of Indians overseas were 'Charlie' Andrews, a close associate of Gandhi, who visited South Africa and Fiji in 1916; Hridayanath Kunzru, who visited Fiji in 1923; Sarojini Naidu, who went on a mission to Kenya in 1923; V. S. Srinivasa Sastri, who visited Fiji and Australia in the 1930s; and Nehru, who visited Malaya, Ceylon and Burma in 1936 and 1939. Political leaders with non-INC ideologies also identified with the cause. In 1929, E. V. Ramaswami Naicker 'Periyar', founder of the Dravidar Kazhagam and the Self-Respect Movement in southern India, visited Malaya and Singapore to spread his message among Tamil migrants. Similarly, Communist leader A. K. Gopalan visited Malaya in 1939.

Though much of the nationalist leaders' concern was focused on migrant indentured labourers, miners and plantation workers, it also extended to merchant and trading communities who featured prominently in the diaspora. In the 1930s, when European interests discriminated against Indian clove traders in Zanzibar, INC leaders raised the issue in the Central Legislature and called for a boycott on cloves, forcing the authorities in Zanzibar to end discrimination. In the early 1940s, INC leadership took up the cause of the Chettiar and Marwari merchants when their substantial business interests in Burma were affected by discriminatory trade agreements in 1941. Gandhi himself took up the issue, compelling colonial authorities to retract the unfair proposals.

At the Round Table Conference on the Indian constitution in London, 1931, the INC's sole delegate was Gandhi.

The brilliant orator and Indian nationalist V. S. Srinivasa Sastri was deeply concerned with safeguarding the interests of Indians overseas.

In the 1940s, World War II and its adverse effects on Indian communities in Southeast Asia elicited widespread sympathy. Subhas Chandra Bose's formation of the Indian National Army (INA) and his call to Indians overseas to take up arms to liberate the motherland boosted the patriotic sentiments that Indians at home felt with regard to the overseas communities. After independence, B. Pattabhi Sitaramayya, a veteran INC leader and official party historian, observed, 'Indians abroad, it may look like a paradox to say so, paved the way really for Indian emancipation. It was the gospel of passive resistance that was conceived, developed and implemented in Transvaal in 1908...[that] paved the way for the development of non co-operation, passive resistance, civil disobedience and satyagraha...We therefore owe all that we are to the initiative, the originality, the daring and the sacrifice of the Indians abroad.'

DISENGAGING FROM THE DIASPORA

With independence, the close ties that the nationalist leadership had nurtured with overseas Indians became strained as the Indian leaders distanced themselves from the diaspora. The expectations that as a free nation India would support its expatriate communities, acknowledge the deep emotional bond with them, and even extend a helping hand when the need arose, were not realised.

An immediate question that arose after independence related to citizenship. A statement by Nehru prior to independence illustrates the change that came about. On 18 March 1946, Nehru arrived in Singapore for what was considered a historic visit. Addressing a crowd of over 10,000 Indians, he declared, 'India cannot forget her sons and daughters overseas. Although India cannot defend her children overseas today, the time is soon coming when her arms will be long enough to protect them.' Referring to the nationality issue, he promised, 'When India attains independence, she would immediately decide who her nationals were and Indians overseas would be Indian

nationals unless they choose to be otherwise.' Of course, Nehru and other leaders had not foreseen the Partition of 1947 and the large-scale uprooting of minorities and forced migration it would entail.

Before 1947, Nehru's view of citizenship hinged on a loose, undefined notion of the affinity of individuals to the motherland. Following the Partition, the Indian concept of citizenship was framed on the basis of territory. The 'country of birth' criterion could no longer be applied as millions had been uprooted from their birthplaces to become citizens of India or Pakistan, based primarily on religious identity. India's Constituent Assembly had to frame the nation's citizenship laws under such extraordinary and troubled times. Explaining the complexity of the issue to the Assembly on 8 March 1948, Nehru said:

Now these Indians abroad, what are they? Are they Indian citizens—are they going to be citizens of India or not? If they are not, then our interest in them becomes cultural, humanitarian and not political. That interest, of course, remains. For instance, take the Indians in Fiji or Mauritius. Are they going to retain their nationality, or will they become Fijian nationals or Mauritians? The same question arises in regard to Burma and Ceylon. It is a difficult question. This House gets mixed up. It wants to treat them as Indians, and with the same breath it wants a complete franchise for them in the countries where they are living.

With independent India's need to cultivate a more bounded sense of itself as a nation, the framing of citizenship became an issue. The Indian Constitution of 1950 merely laid down the principle that all those born in undivided India, or those with parents born there, could claim Indian citizenship; leaving to parliament the actual task of formulating citizenship laws, and in doing so, not ruling out the possibility of dual citizenship. However, citizenship laws in independent India could not be framed for the first eight years. Meanwhile, the government invited

Jawaharlal Nehru with employees of The Malayan Rubber Works in Klang, 1937. Nehru urged Indians in Malaya to form trade unions and agitate for better salaries and working conditions.

Andrews with his close associate, Rabindranath Tagore.

CHARLES FREER ('CHARLIE') ANDREWS (1871–1940)

In India's capital, New Delhi, the neighbourhood of Andrewsganj is dedicated to his memory. Yet, few Indians today can tell you who Charles Freer Andrews was or in what way he contributed to India and Indians overseas. Memories of him are faint and those who remember him do so because of the sepia-tinted frames of Richard Attenborough's film, *Gandhi*, which portrayed him, together with Mirabehn (Madeleine Slade), as two of the Mahatma's most faithful English disciples. However, no account of the Indian diaspora could be complete without a mention of the ceaseless campaign which Charlie Andrews carried on for decades to support Indians in South Africa, Kenya, Zanzibar, Fiji and other colonies in their struggle for racial equality. He will be remembered too for the sustained pressure he exercised, together with his colleagues in the Christian Church, upon colonial authorities to end the system of labour immigration under indenture.

Born on 12 February 1871 to middle-class English parents, Andrews had a strong Christian upbringing. A classical scholar at Pembroke College, Cambridge, he was drawn to India by the work of the Cambridge Mission to Delhi. Andrews landed in Mumbai on 20 March 1904, a few years after his ordination as a priest of the Church of England. He called this day his 'Indian Birthday', claiming to have been 'twice-born' and entering a new world of experience. From then on, the welfare of India and its children consumed his energies.

In India, Andrews was shocked to witness British racial discrimination against the 'natives'. He joined St. Stephen's College in Delhi to teach English and served as its vice-principal until 1914. His missionary work led to wide-ranging friendships with Englishmen and Indians alike. Deeply impressed by the spread of nationalism, Andrews decided not to restrict himself to missionary activities alone but to extend his help to Indians in their struggle for self-rule. In 1906, he attended the INC's session at Calcutta. He befriended many prominent Indian leaders, including Lala Lajpat Rai, the INC leader from Punjab; Swami Shradhanand of the Arya Samaj; and the poet, Rabindranath Tagore, who became a lifelong associate.

Andrews held a deep conviction that the Christian Church could offer a healing touch in the conflict between the different races and between capital and labour. He was irresistibly drawn to the cause of Indian indenture in the colonies as he could focus his energies and skills as a Christian clergyman to challenge racial discrimination and capitalist exploitation at the same time. Veteran INC leader Gopal Krishna Gokhale is credited with encouraging Andrews to proceed to South Africa to become a volunteer in the struggle of Indians against racism, which was gathering momentum under the leadership of Gandhi. Andrews arrived in Durban on 1 January 1914 and placed his services at Gandhi's disposal. He pointed out to Gandhi that the issue at hand was a question of Indian honour and that there could be no sacrifice of honour. They forged a lifelong friendship and became known as 'Mohan' and 'Charlie' to each other. Andrews's vigorous efforts at conciliation, his unequivocal advocacy of the moral strength of the Indian case, and his quiet appeal to the British sense of 'fair play' and the Christian principle of equality contributed significantly to the passage of the Indian Relief Act of 1914, bringing to fruition Gandhi's long campaign in South Africa and setting the stage for the Mahatma's return to the motherland.

Back in India, Andrews resolved to take up the issue of the degraded indenture system. He took over leadership of a campaign which Gokhale had initiated in the Central Legislative Assembly for abolishing indenture. Upon learning about the scandalous conditions of indentured Indians in Fiji, he undertook a long and arduous journey to the colonial outpost in the South Pacific. Indians who came to Fiji, he demanded, could only come under conditions that must be consistent with India's self respect. Andrews also argued that no labour contract could be contemplated which was not a free civil contract; there could be no recruiting except in family units; good homes with privacy must replace the

Andrews arrived in India on 20 March 1904, a day he called his 'Indian Birthday'.

filthy 'lines' where men and women were herded like cattle with no respect for the sanctity of family life; and the disgraceful 'coolie ships' must be replaced by a well-run public steamer service to keep Fiji and India in close contact. For several years, Andrews campaigned ceaselessly for ending the dreaded system of indenture. Finally, the colonial authorities in India and London yielded, and on 1 January 1920 the last indentured labourer was freed. The affection and gratitude which the Fiji Indians had for Andrews was expressed in the title which they bestowed on him, Dinabandhu, (Friend of the Poor).

Andrews then expanded his activities to include Ceylon, Malaya, Mauritius and the Caribbean, covering almost the entire universe where Indian labouring émigré had settled. He visited rubber and sugar plantations, mines and urban slums to study first-hand the wretched conditions under which Indians lived, to highlight the racial disabilities they faced and, above all, to give them hope. He looked upon himself as carrying on the struggle against racial discrimination which Gandhi had pioneered in South Africa. He remained a crusader for the rights of Indian immigrants in Kenya, Zanzibar and South Africa throughout the 1920s and 1930s.

Andrews died in Calcutta on 5 April 1940 at the age of 69. On his deathbed, he told the Mahatma, 'Mohan, I see Swaraj coming.' For 36 years, since making India his home, Andrews had given all his energies to upholding the principle of the dignity of India and its children overseas in their struggle against racial discrimination and colonial domination.

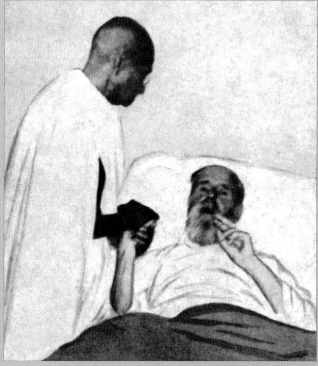

Gandhi and Andrews had a close relationship, referring to each other simply as 'Mohan' and 'Charlie'. The Mahatma was at his side upon his passing in 1940.

During a visit to Burma in 1955, Prime Minister Jawaharlal Nehru (right) and Prime Minister Colonel Gamal Abdel Nasser of Egypt (left), participated in a water festival ushering in the Burmese New Year. Burmese Prime Minister U Nu (centre) is shown in the act of throwing water on his Egyptian counterpart.

Indian poet and nationalist Sarojini Naidu (left) with G. D. Birla (centre) and Gandhi (right) on their way to the Round Table Conference in London, 1931.

Prime Minister Indira Gandhi's government continued to distance itself from the diaspora despite pleas for help from Indians in Kenya and Uganda in the early 1970s.

Indians overseas to register with their nearest missions, instructing the missions to register all Hindus and Muslims, whether born in Indian or Pakistani territory, as Indians if they expressed the desire. This left the legal status of Indians overseas undecided, causing much uncertainty and anxiety, as in the case of East Africa, where several Indians registered for citizenship with Indian missions. In the early 1950s, when they were offered British Commonwealth citizenship, they assumed that India would allow dual nationality. The Indian envoy in Nairobi reportedly assured them that they 'would not lose their Indian citizenship by acquiring that of the UK.' However, the Indian Citizenship Act of 1955 specified that anyone who had 'voluntarily acquired the citizenship of another country [should]...cease to be a citizen of India.' By disallowing dual citizenship, India had disappointed overseas Indian communities. In a single stroke, the Indian state cut itself loose from its diaspora.

Post-colonial India's policy towards the diaspora was deeply informed by Nehru as the country's prime minister and foreign minister. Convinced that it was in the best interest of overseas Indians to integrate into their host societies, he repeatedly argued for them to 'identify themselves with and integrate in the mainstream of social and political life of the country of their domicile.' There were many reasons for India's policy of disengagement and distancing. In the Cold War era, India's foreign policy was based on ideas of neutrality from the 'great power blocs' and solidarity with the 'Third World', in which friendship with newly liberated Africa and Asia was highly valued. Nehru's aspiration to propel India onto the world stage through its leadership of the Non-Aligned Movement depended on the goodwill of Afro-Asian countries, which hosted many Indian communities. Accordingly, India cultivated good relations with Asian and African states, though it meant neglecting the diaspora's interests. It did not adopt an interventionist policy on behalf of overseas Indians, lest India be seen as interfering in the domestic affairs of other states.

Furthermore, from 1950 onwards, under Nehru's influence India followed an economic model of planned development aimed at reducing income disparities, curbing the concentration of economic power, regulating private capital and encouraging reliance on the state. The

goal of national self-sufficiency led Indian policy-makers towards the framework of a closed economy, which did not value links with Indian mercantile communities overseas.

The evolution of Indian policy in the late 1940s and 1950s led to a sense of disappointment among Indians overseas, especially in countries where they faced harsh conditions, even victimisation. Indian trading communities in Burma, for example, faced discriminatory legislation which affected their interests adversely. Following decolonisation in the 1950s and 1960s, as the newly independent dominions of Africa actively pursued policies of Africanisation, conditions became rather unfavourable for Indian communities, sometimes forcing them to emigrate. Indeed, the situation in Kenya deteriorated to such an extent in the late 1960s that Indians migrated and sought asylum in large numbers. Yet, the government of India, under the prime ministership of Indira Gandhi, continued its policy of non-interference, taking no effective steps to help Indians in Kenya and insisting that they were legally the responsibility of either Kenya or Britain. In 1972, when Uganda's Idi Amin expelled Indians from the country, the Indian government continued its policy of non-involvement, not offering any effective help. This perceived apathy evoked widespread criticism within India.

COMING FULL CIRCLE

In 1977, when a non-Congress government led by the Janata Party assumed power, the first signs of an official rethink vis-à-vis the diaspora appeared. That official policies strike a balance between safeguarding India's foreign policy interests and show legitimate concern about Indians overseas was clearly a priority. This concern was pertinent as by this time Indian workers were employed in the Gulf region and their remittances brought in significant foreign exchange, especially for states such as Kerala. Indian parliamentarians raised questions about the welfare of Indian workers in the Gulf, obliging the government to adopt a more proactive policy towards the Gulf states so that it could effectively safeguard the interests of Indian communities there.

Remittances from the Gulf also made Indian policy-makers more aware of the economic potential of Indians

overseas and so they formulated a range of investment incentives for them, hoping to channel foreign exchange earnings into state-sponsored savings schemes. Limited banking reforms were introduced to facilitate foreign exchange inflow. In fact, it was in the early 1980s, when the volume of remittances grew, that the term 'non-resident Indian' (NRI) increasingly entered the official lexicon. Terms such as 'Indians abroad', 'person of Indian origin' (PIO), even 'expatriate Indians' also continued to be used, but were not clearly defined. However, the overall investment framework was still not entirely conducive to Indians overseas as Indian policy-makers were still hesitant about the role NRIs could play in the national economy. Even so, it was clear from the 1980s onwards that economic imperatives rather than ideological considerations would unmistakably shape the changing dynamics of the motherland and its diaspora.

When Rajiv Gandhi became the prime minister in 1984, definite signs showing the government's shift in direction foreshadowed an imminent, larger policy shift. The government built up its agencies for dealing with the diaspora. In 1985, it set up a Special Coordination Division in the Ministry of External Affairs as a nodal point to manage actions relating to Indians overseas. In 1986, it established a Consultative Committee for Non-Resident Indians, comprising representatives from different ministries, trade and industry, and a dozen NRIs from across the globe. It also attempted to develop a database on Indians overseas and formed an Indo-NRI Chamber of Commerce and Culture to promote investment and foster trade links in 1987.

That same year, when a political crisis erupted in Fiji, Indians were deeply interested in reports of ethnic discrimination against the Indian community there. India's official response this time was proactive, in marked contrast to the Ugandan crisis of 1972. In 1988, an Indian official delegation, led by Shanker Dayal Sharma, who was then the vice-president, visited Guyana to participate in celebrations marking the 150th anniversary of the arrival of Indians. The delegation also visited Surinam and Trinidad and Tobago to strengthen cultural and emotional ties with Indian communities there. The Indian government showed further support when the first Global Convention of Overseas Indians (New York, 1989) pioneered efforts to bring together people of Indian origin on a single platform, 'to discuss common problems and issues.' In 1990–91, when over 150,000 Indians were stranded in Kuwait and Iraq following the Gulf War, the Indian government promptly arranged for their evacuation. All these events were signs that 'India' was taking note of 'India Abroad'.

RE-ENGAGEMENT

India's re-engagement with the diaspora really took off only after 1991, when the Indian economy faced an unprecedented crisis arising from the bankruptcy of its foreign exchange reserves. As is well known, the crisis triggered a process of economic reforms as India prepared itself to exploit the opportunities and counter the threats arising from globalisation. There was now a deep realisation that India needed to reinvent itself economically for it badly needed investment in infrastructure, which neither the Indian state nor private business had the capacity to

mobilise. If India intended to develop economically and remain competitive in a swiftly globalising world, it had to aggressively pull in foreign direct investments and readily allow for the infusion of new technologies. It was in this new context of larger policy shifts that India re-engaged with its diaspora in the 1990s.

'NRI' became a buzzword in India in the 1990s as overseas Indians and their lifestyles captured popular imagination. However, though Indians at home became increasingly receptive towards the diaspora, domestic political instability decelerated the pace of official policy changes. In 1998, the government led by the Bharatiya Janata Party, with Atal Bihari Vajpayee at its helm, announced the introduction of a 'PIO Card' for Indians settled in specified countries, promising visa-free travel and privileges in matters of investment and education. In 2000, the government set up a High Level Committee on Indian Diaspora—chaired by L. M. Singhvi, a parliamentarian, jurist and former diplomat—responsible for assessing the issues concerning Indians overseas, suggesting new policy and organisational frameworks, and recommending a country-specific agenda to intensify India's engagement with its diaspora. In 2001, the Indian Prime Minister formally inaugurated the 6th Convention of the Global Organisation of People of Indian Origin (GOPIO) in New Delhi. On the recommendation of the Singhvi committee, the government implemented numerous novel policy initiatives, including the decision to celebrate the Pravasi Bharatiya Divas and institute the Pravasi Bharatiya Samman.

Perhaps the most significant initiative was the Indian government's announcement, at the inaugural Pravasi Bharatiya Divas held in January 2003, of sweeping changes to the country's 48-year-old Citizenship Act, granting Indians living in Britain, Canada, Australia, Finland, Ireland, Italy, the Netherlands and the US the privilege of claiming dual citizenship. The restriction of dual citizenship to only one constituency of the diaspora—the NRIs settled in affluent Western countries—led to

The former prime minister of Trinidad and Tobago and current Opposition leader, Basdeo Panday, presenting the GOPIO community service award to former Trinidad and Tobago law minister Ramesh Maharaj. FROM LEFT: *Vice-President of Surinam, Jules Rattankoemar Ajodhia; the former prime minister of Fiji, Mahendra Chaudhry; the chairman of the High Level Committee on Indian Diaspora, L. M. Singhvi; and the president of GOPIO International, Inder Singh.*

The introduction of the PIO card gave Indians settled in designated countries the benefit of visa-free travel and other advantages.

PRAVASI BHARATIYA DIVAS

The first Pravasi Bharatiya Divas, hosted by the government of India and the Federation of Indian Chambers of Commerce and Industry (FICCI), was held on 9 January 2003 in New Delhi. It opened with a *jugalbandi* between Ustad Bismillah Khan on the *shehnai* and Pandit Ravi Shankar on the sitar. Among the greatest living exponents of Indian classical music, both have been decorated with the Bharat Ratna, India's highest civilian award. That morning was unique for they performed together for the first time. Over 1200 Indian delegates from 55 countries were enthralled. The occasion marked a historic turning point in India's engagement with its diaspora. It was also laden with symbolism.

The first symbol was the *jugalbandi*, an Indian musical genre in which two artists with different instruments or vocal styles perform spontaneously in concert. The musical conversation of Khan and Shankar produced a harmonious synchronisation, wherein the two tuned into each other's aesthetic visions. *Jugalbandi* literally means 'tied together'. Indian leaders have often invoked this metaphor to describe the ongoing engagement between the motherland and the diaspora, between *Bharatvasis* (resident Indians) and *Bharatvanshis* (people of Indian lineage).

The second symbol was the date chosen for the event. On 9 January 1915, Gandhi, often called the first Pravasi Bharatiya, returned to India after two decades in South Africa to lead an epic struggle for freedom, initiating India's renaissance as a modern nation. The invocation of Gandhi's example was a powerful, symbolic appeal to Indians overseas to similarly become a part of the unfinished agenda of the 'freedom struggle' by helping India become a global power.

The origins of the Pravasi Bharatiya Divas lie in the recommendations of the High Level Committee on Indian Diaspora set up by the Indian government in 2000. The committee concluded that the goodwill existing among different segments of overseas Indians towards India and their 'deep emotional bonds' could be tapped through the right mix of policy reforms and initiatives. The Pravasi Bharatiya Divas, one such key initiative, aimed to provide a forum for understanding the sentiments and expectations of overseas Indians; create a framework for sustained interaction between the Indian government and the diaspora; acquaint Indians with the global achievements of Indians overseas; and help to create a network of communities spread across 110 countries. L. M.

Prime Minister Manmohan Singh releases a newsletter of the Ministry of Overseas Indian Affairs during the Pravasi Bharatiya Divas in Hyderabad, January 2006.

Singhvi, a parliamentarian and originator of the event, hoped that it would help 'maintain the hub and spoke relationship with India and create a new network of a web which embraces within its orbit all the concentric and multicentric convergences.' A US delegate labelled it a 'Herculean effort to network all Indians on Earth.'

A galaxy of prominent Indians from across the globe converged for the event, including Nobel Laureates Amartya Sen and V. S. Naipaul, Mauritian prime minister Anerood Jugnauth, international diplomat Shridath Ramphal, and Ujjal Dosanjh, the former premier of British Columbia (Canada). Many among these were honoured with the Pravasi Bharatiya Samman.

India's political establishment was in full attendance to laud the diaspora's achievements. In an emotionally charged address, Atal Bihari Vajpayee, who was then the prime minister, said, 'Many of you—or your forefathers—left India in search of fortune or a better livelihood. Today, India has itself become a land of opportunity. We want to share with our extended family our achievements, hopes, concerns, aspirations and goals.' He continued, 'We invite you, not only to share our vision of India in the new millennium, but also to help us shape its contours. We do not want only your investment. We also want your ideas. We do not want your riches. We want the richness of your experience.'

Several other speakers took up this motif of a shared destiny binding India with the diaspora. Singhvi spoke of 'the great potential of the human connectivity of the global Indian family.' Jaswant Singh, then the finance minister, invited the NRIs to 'join in this great adventure, which is the resurgent India on the move.' Overall, the attempt was to underscore the fact that the symbiotic relationship between India and the diaspora needed strengthening. This engagement was timely as India was rapidly emerging as a modern and dynamic economy on the world stage and the Indian diaspora could become a 'unique resource' and 'natural partner'. As a key Indian official stated, 'How many countries in the world have footprints all over the world? This huge human resource can play an important role in India's development and put our stand across to the global community.' The challenge for policy-makers in attendance was to script a common game plan with immense potential benefits to both India and the diaspora.

Such powerful exhortations from the Indian side drew strong responses from the diaspora. A. M. Ebrahim, a retired Supreme Court judge from Zimbabwe, acknowledged, 'We as PIOs can play a significant role in world peace and be the unifying force. As part of the global Indian family, we are a natural resource of India.' Lord Navnit Dholakia, a Liberal member of the British House of Lords, drew loud applause when he avowed that 'just as Hanuman, when asked to prove his loyalty to Ram, tore open his chest to reveal an image of Ram and Sita, NRIs, if asked to prove their loyalty to India, could open their hearts to reveal a map of India.'

Some other delegates were less enthusiastic about the proceedings. Many complained that the

President Abdul Kalam receives a memento from Jean Pierre Harrison, husband of the late India-born astronaut Kalpana Chawla—who was killed in the Columbia *shuttle disaster—during a gathering of NRIs at New Delhi's Presidential Palace in January 2004. The NRIs were in India to attend the Pravasi Bharatiya Divas.*

conference laid 'more emphasis on NRIs, not enough on PIOs.' The former Fijian prime minister Mahendra Chaudhry criticised the lack of concern shown towards PIOs suffering human rights violations. Bhikhu Parekh, an academic and British peer, sounded a note of caution: 'Lasting relationships are not built on "love and sentiments" but on a realistic assessment of expectations on both sides.' He called for an exchange between the people (not the government) of India and the diaspora so that it could be 'a dialogue among equals'. Nobel Laureate Naipaul cryptically remarked that the event had the 'element of a trade fair'.

Yet, many agreed that there had been tangible gains. According to Yashwant Sinha, who was then the minister for external affairs, the event showed unmistakably that 'India has completely shed whatever ambivalence it might have had towards its diaspora' and that significant policy announcements (such as the scheme for dual citizenship) had been made. Organisers claimed that the Pravasi Bharatiya Divas had 'created a consciousness of [a] Global Indian Family'; enabled India to recognise, through the Pravasi Bharatiya Samman, the achievements of Indians globally; generated a wave of positive sentiment within India about the diaspora; and, not the least, provided a platform for members of the diaspora to voice their views and concerns.

Continuing vigorous official efforts have sustained the momentum generated by the first Pravasi Bharatiya Divas. The annual event was held in New Delhi in 2004 and Mumbai in 2005. Each event sought to reinvigorate the idea of a 'Global Indian Family' and the ties that bind it to the motherland. As Prime Minister Manmohan Singh said to delegates in Mumbai on 9 January 2005, 'We speak different languages, we practise different religions, our cuisine is varied and so is our costume...yet, there is a unifying idea that binds us all together, which is the idea of Indianness.' Opening the event with a *jugalbandi* has now become a tradition, symbolic of the ongoing dialogue between India and its diaspora.

The 2004 Pravasi Bharatiya Divas began with a performance by Dr L. Subramaniam on the violin and Ustad Sultan Khan on the sarangi (Indian string instrument).

widespread criticism from other NRI segments, especially from the West Indies and countries such as Fiji, South Africa and Mauritius, where Indian communities are not well-endowed. In 2004, when an INC-led coalition spearheaded by Manmohan Singh assumed power, it adopted two significant measures: it established a separate Ministry of Overseas Indian Affairs; and at the Pravasi Bharatiya Divas held in January 2005, it declared that dual citizenship would be extended to all Indians overseas who migrated after the inauguration of the Indian Union on 26 January 1950, subject to the laws prevailing in their home countries, thus eliminating the basis of criticism of the earlier policy. However, dual citizenship would be granted without voting rights.

India's engagement with globalisation has been a cautious one. Triggered by an unexpected crisis, this engagement has been marked by anxiety and uncertainty in dealing with the dramatic forces that globalisation might and does unleash. Decades spent behind a closed economy, together with a deep sense of commitment to the idea of *swadeshi* and national self-sufficiency, have played major roles in shaping the mindset of Indian policymakers, making them look upon multinational corporations (MNCs) and foreign capital investors with distrust. There exists the fear that MNCs, once they invest in a big way in the Indian economy, may attempt to dictate the terms, undermine national sovereignty and negatively influence Indian culture. The Indian state's attempts to cultivate the diaspora must be seen within this context. It is widely perceived that Indians overseas are better endowed with investments, technological know-how, and entrepreneurial and managerial skills. It is also believed that they are capable of greater commitment to the cause of India's development. Furthermore, as the nation embraces globalisation, Indians at home have come to realise that Indians overseas are more compatible in cultural terms and more attuned to local sensitivities than they assumed.

The Indian political leadership's engagement with its diaspora has come full circle. In its nationalist, anti-colonial phase, the leadership showed genuine sympathy towards

Indians overseas. After 1947, post-colonial India developed a more bounded sense of itself as a nation state as it framed its citizenship laws. Its foreign and economic imperatives dictated a policy of disengagement from the diaspora. Now, as India reinvents itself as a global economic player, the state increasingly looks upon Indians overseas as assets. At the first Pravasi Bharatiya Divas, a leader from India Inc. said, 'The overseas Indians would scout opportunities, represent 'Brand India', network for Indian initiatives. They would be the flag bearers. They will help India shift from being a local player to being a global major.'

Gyanesh Kudaisya

Atal Bihari Vajpayee (fourth from the left), who was then the Indian prime minister, officiates at the second Pravasi Bharatiya Divas in New Delhi on 9 January 2004. On his left is L. K. Advani, the former deputy prime minister. Also present was the former Union minister for external affairs, Yashwant Sinha (second from the left).

Prime Minister Manmohan Singh lights a traditional oil lamp at the start of the Pravasi Bharatiya Divas in Hyderabad, January 2006.

Pravasi Bharatiya Samman winners

2003
- Sir Anerood Jugnauth (politics), *Mauritius*
- Lord Navnit Dholakia (business), *Tanzania*
- Rajat Gupta (business), *US*
- Professor Fatima Meer (human rights activism), *South Africa*
- Kanakshi Gokaldas Khimji (business, education), *Oman*
- Ujjal Dosanjh (politics, human rights activism), *Canada*
- Dato' Seri S. Samy Velu (politics), *Malaysia*
- Sir Shridath Ramphal (politics, academia), *Guyana* and *UK*
- Dr Manu Chandaria (business), *Kenya*
- Bob Naroomal Harilela (business), Hong Kong, *China*

2004
- Kalpana Chawla (aeronautical engineering), *US*
- Justice Ahmed Moosa Ebrahim (law, sports, art and culture), *Zimbabwe*
- Dr Mariam Chisti (medicine), *Kuwait*
- Sukhi Turner (politics), *New Zealand*
- H. E. Bharrat Jagdeo (politics), *Guyana*
- Fitz Remedios Santana De Souza (politics, law), *Kenya*
- Dr Narinder Singh Kapany (opto-electronics, philanthropy, art), *US*
- Professor Dipak Jain (academia, education), *US*
- Lord Meghnad Desai (economics, education), *UK*
- P. Mohamed Ali (business, public service, education), *Oman*
- Shashi Tharoor (diplomacy, journalism, literature), *US*

2005
- M. Arunachalam (business, the arts, promoter of India–China trade), Hong Kong, *China*
- Professor Jagdish Bhagwati (economics, academia, education), *US*
- Amina Cachalia (politics, human rights, women's activist and anti-apartheid crusader), *South Africa*
- Sir (Dr). J. K. Chande (business, chancellor of International Medical and Technological University, Dar es Salaam), *Tanzania*
- Professor Alokeranjan Dasgupta (literary arts and culture, German-Bengali poetry translator), *Germany*
- Ahmed Kathrada (politics, human rights), *South Africa*
- Professor Sunil Khilnani (political science), *US*
- Basdeo Panday (politics, former prime minister of Trinidad and Tobago), *Trinidad and Tobago*
- Lord Bhikhu Chhotalal Parekh (political studies, social activism), *UK*
- Dr Sam Pitroda (telecommunications, pioneer of the telecommunications revolution in India), *US*
- Vikram Seth (literature), *UK*
- Manoj Night Shyamalan (film), *US*
- Vijay Singh (international sports), *Fiji*
- Dr Sant Singh Virmani (agricultural science), *Philippines*
- Yusuffali M. A. (entrepreneur), *UAE*

LIFE IN THE DIASPORA

The Indian diaspora in the 21st century is the result of developments in both the 'old' and the 'new' diasporas. In the diaspora, Indians have worked very hard to preserve their identity, while showing skill and creativity in adjusting to the situation in which they find themselves in their new 'host societies'. The development of the Indian diaspora gives wide-ranging evidence of the sustainability of Indian languages, religious values and cultural norms. At the same time, it demonstrates flair and creative ability in developing popular culture (music, dance and cinema), skilful management in the promotion of Indian fashion and cuisine, and determined adaptability and prowess in a wide range of sports derived from other cultures. It is in these efforts to preserve as well as to adapt that the diaspora plays the important role of representing India as a major cultural force in the global village.

LANGUAGE

FOR THE PURPOSES of linguistic study it is helpful to demarcate three periods for the movement of people out of India. The first of these would be all movements prior to the 17th century, motivated by trade settlement or religious impulse. This relates to the 'Age of Merchants' in Part II of this volume. The second period sees forced or semi-forced movements under slavery and indenture to European colonies from the 17th century onwards, a process that reached its climax in the late 19th and the early 20th centuries. This is discussed in Part III, the 'Age of Colonial Capital'. The third, labelled the 'Age of Globalisation', consists of the voluntary movements of Indians in search of employment opportunities, mainly to Western countries, from the mid-20th century onwards. In this section, the focus is on the linguistic experience and heritage of the second and third diasporas.

SLAVERY, INDENTURE AND LANGUAGE

The relatively uniform socio-historical circumstances of the second diaspora have led to a significant body of research focusing on language adaptation, change, maintenance and decline. This is particularly true of the North Indian language varieties. The languages spoken by the indentured workers and their sources were as follows:

- In Mauritius and British Guiana, the earliest indentured workers to be recruited were called 'Dhangars', or hill coolies, from the tribal areas of Bengal, Bihar and the Chota Nagpur plateau. They would have been speakers of Austro-Asiatic languages like Santali, Munda and Ho. However, no trace of these languages or their speakers exist in the colonies, nor any appreciable influences on other Indian or creole languages of the territories. In Mauritius, however, some surnames like 'Dhongoor' and 'Dhingoor' attest to this early Dhangar segment of indentured immigrants.
- From South India, via the port of Madras, chiefly Tamil and Telugu, and in small numbers, Malayalam and Kannada were represented. The latter two languages did not have sufficiently large numbers of speakers to survive beyond a generation in most territories.
- From North India, via the port of Calcutta, travelled a variety of Indo-Aryan languages, including Bhojpuri, Awadhi, Magahi, Kanauji, Bengali, Rajasthani, Braj, Oriya and others. Also present was what Hugh Tinker called 'the lingua franca of the emigration traffic', Hindustani.
- From western and central India, via the port of Bombay, Marathi-speakers from the state of Maharashtra went mainly to Mauritius.
- A small number of Muslims among the indentured labourers would have spoken the village language of their area as well as variants of Urdu.
- Similarly, a small number of Christians would have spoken the language of their area of origin as well as English in many instances.

Smaller numbers of Indians with trading backgrounds usually followed the labourers to the colonies, paying their own passage and having the status of free rather than bonded individuals. In this way, languages such as Gujarati, Konkani (originally a variety of Marathi),

A Hindi language class at an Indian school in the Dutch colony of Surinam in 1933, where the Indian community developed a variant known as Surinam Hindustani, or Sarnami.

Memon, Bengali and Punjabi were also introduced in the colonies. In East Africa, the presence of Indian traders and clerks preceded the period of British rule, which saw the arrival of mainly Punjabi-speaking indentured immigrants to build the first railway line in Africa in the late 19th century. The majority of these immigrants returned to India after the expiry of their contracts. Punjabi-speaking Indians also went to Canada (c. 1900–14) as free immigrants in search of employment, an area where there had not been any prior indentured immigration.

The sociolinguistic milieu in which Indians found themselves was a particularly complex one. Not only did they frequently lack knowledge of the colonial languages (English, French and Dutch) and local languages, they also often could not converse among themselves. In particular, people from North India, speaking Indo-Aryan languages, would not have been able to understand people from South India, who spoke Dravidian languages. Gujarati-speaking merchants and Marathi-speakers would have been able to speak to indentured Indians from North India, often using a simplified version of Hindi known as 'Bombay Bazaar Hindustani', but they would not have been able to converse with speakers of Dravidian languages. A letter to the Protector of Indian immigrants in 1903 illustrates well the linguistic and social alienation among first-generation migrants, as was the case of a Telugu woman assigned to an estate in Natal: '...the lady is continuously crying and speaks a language [Telugu] and neither she can understand the rest of the labourers in the mills nor they her. The other coolies won't have anything to do with her. She cannot or won't work and she does not earn her ration.'

In such a situation, a pidgin language would be expected to thrive. In Fiji, for example, two pidgins developed for inter-ethnic contact in the colonial period: one based on Fijian, which arose before the introduction of Indians to the area; and another based on Hindi. In Natal, the existing Fanakalo pidgin (originally arising from contact between Europeans and the indigenous Zulu and Xhosa speakers) was taken up as a particularly useful language for communication not only with Europeans and Zulus, but between North and South Indians too. In other territories, Indians appear to have learnt the pre-existing creole language of the colony as a second language: Creole English in Jamaica, Guyana and Trinidad; Creole French in Mauritius, Seychelles and Réunion; and Sranan in Surinam (an English-based creole which later came under the influence of Dutch). In East Africa, the contact language learnt by Indians was Swahili, and in Malaya and Singapore, it was Malay.

For Indians in all of these territories, English would hold a high position as the language of learning despite the dominance of French and Dutch in some colonies. Indians in Surinam, for example, are multilingual in Sarnami (the local variant that developed out of the North Indian experience of indenture, also known as Surinam Hindustani), Sranan, Dutch, and for the educated classes, English as well. In Mauritius, the repertoire often includes Bhojpuri, Mauritian Creole, Hindi, French and English, the latter three usually introduced via the education system. Hindi was often less successful as a language of learning than English as its value was more cultural and symbolic. In

The Punjabi alphabet, like other Indo-European North Indian languages such as Hindi, Bengali and Gujarati, is derived from the Devanagari script.

certain territories, some North Indians learnt Tamil and some South Indians learnt a variety of Bhojpuri-Hindi. The terms 'Bhojpuri' or 'Bhojpuri-Hindi' in the immigrant context are convenient cover terms used by some linguists who have described the varieties; but they are not necessarily used by the communities themselves, nor does the term suggest there was a single language antecedent in India. Awadhi was in fact a major contributor in Natal, Surinam and Fiji. The term 'Overseas Bhojpuri-Hindi' (OBH) is again a useful label for the North Indian varieties that developed in the second diaspora.

Factors related to demography and prestige sometimes prevented an Indian language from being used as a common means of communication by Indians in most of the colonies. Instead, English or a form of creole eventually played that role. Fiji presents a notable exception as the local Fiji Hindi is used by all people of Indian descent. A similar situation occurred in Burma, where until World War II, Hindustani and not Burmese was the lingua franca of the Indian community in Rangoon, which included South Indians and Bengalis. In Surinam too, the Telugu community adopted Sarnami in time. The changes in language use also applies to the Tamil community of Surinam, though many aspects of South Indian culture remain strong. Although Tamil survives (tenuously) in Trinidad, at one

Seven **Grammars** of the Dialects and Subdialects of the BIHÁRI LANGUAGE

IN 3 VOLUMES SETS

Sir George Abraham Grierson

While holding government posts in Bengal, Sir George Grierson (1851–1941) carried out pioneering research work on Indian languages. Grierson's book (left) is the foundation on which linguistic adaptations which occurred in various locations can be assessed.

Enthusiastic responses from female pupils in a Gurmukhi (Punjabi) language class at a school in Bradford, northern England.

stage Bhojpuri did become an 'Indian', rather than just a 'North Indian', phenomenon.

Descriptions of Tamil, Telugu, Gujarati and Marathi in communities of the second diaspora are increasingly available, but as such research does not yet permit detailed comparisons, the linguistic adaptations of indentured North Indians will be briefly delineated. Fortunately, during the period of indentured immigration, Sir George Grierson was undertaking his monumental *Linguistic Survey of India*. Fieldwork for this project began in 1894 and the publication came to provide skeletal grammar and detailed samples of village languages throughout North India. Grierson's *Seven Grammars of the Dialects and Sub-Dialects of the Bihari Languages* preceded the survey and

was published between 1883 and 1887. These two sources serve as a baseline against which the linguistic adaptations that took place in the various territories can be assessed. The districts supplying the most immigrants were those from either side of what is now the Bihar/Uttar Pradesh (UP) border. Awadhi or Bhojpuri are generally the main vernacular languages of these districts, together with Hindi as a supra-regional language. There must have been considerable heterogeneity in the linguistic situation as people mingled together at the port depots, on board the ships, and later in the colonial plantations. Consequently, a 'common denominator' arose in each colony among North Indian immigrants. This process has been termed 'koiné-isation'—the development of a new dialect from existing dialects of a language and/or other closely related languages. The first detailed discussion on this process was offered by S. K. Gambhir on the Guyana-Bhojpuri koiné. He showed a blend of features from eastern and western varieties of Hindi, with Bhojpuri as the main contributor. He also noted the avoidance of forms that were peculiar to one North Indian variety, and some influences from English and creole.

In each colony the new koiné came to be considered a sub-standard version of Hindi and was strongly disparaged by those who had knowledge of the latter. In official lists and censuses it is stated as Hindi, though it is often colloquially known by other names: Kalkatiyā bāt (Natal), Puraniyā Hindi (Guyana), or just Hindustāni, Hindustaniyā or Hindi. The label 'Bhojpuri' is used in Mauritius but rarely elsewhere, where more localised descriptors occur, such as Sarnami, Naitali Hindi and Fiji bāt. Only in Surinam does OBH seem to have gained a measure of recognition as a variant in its own right, a legitimate possession of the Indian populace of the country. Although each colony developed its own koiné, strong parallels in terms of demographics, social change and linguistic processes resulted in their being, on the whole, more similar to each other than to any of their parent Indic varieties. Linguists have tended to identify these koinés as being closer structurally either to Bhojpuri or to eastern varieties of Hindi, such as Awadhi. To the former group belong Mauritius, Trinidad, Guyana and South Africa. To the second group belong Sarnami and Fiji Hindi. Three examples will explain these groupings:

- In Mauritius, Guyana, Trinidad, South Africa and Surinam, the present habitual is formed by the verb stem + *-la* + auxiliary: *ham dekhilā* ('I see'). In Fiji, the equivalent form is verb stem + *-tā* + auxiliary: *ham dekhtā hai* ('I see').
- For the future tense, first person, Mauritius, Guyana, Trinidad, South Africa and Surinam have *-b* (*ham dekhab* ['I will see']), while Fiji has *-egā* (*ham dekhegā* ['I will see']).
- For the third singular past tense, we have the following forms: *ū dekhlak* (Mauritius Bhojpuri); *ū dekhle* (Guyana Bhojpuri); *ū dekhal* (Trinidad Bhojpuri); and *ū dekhlak* (South African Bhojpuri), meaning 'he saw'. On the other hand, we have *ū dekhis* (Sarnami Hindi) and *ū dekhū /dekhis* (Fiji Hindi).

A number of such features can be accounted for purely in terms of demographic factors. Since recruiters started their operations in the more eastern parts of North India and gradually moved inland, colonies that

Fiji Hindi — a sample

These are the first paragraphs of a story told in Fiji Hindi, which capture the sounds and rhythms of the Fiji bāt discussed opposite.

Bhola aur us ke patni Sukhraji ek din sanjha ke kada gham se aaye ke aapan ek palia ghar ke poch men sustaat rahin jab un ke padosi, Nanka, aaye pahuncha. 'Ram Ram bhai,' Bhola se bolis aur ek lakdi ke baakas pe baith gaye. Sukhraji jaldi se kitchen men gaye chai banaye jab Bhola aur Nanka gaon ke chota mota baat kare ke suru karin. Jab Sukhraji teen piyaala chai laye ke lauti, to Nanka us ke taraf ghoom ke bolis, 'Bhauji hum ek baat poochi?' Sukhraji bolis, 'Bolo Babu.' Sukhraji gaon ke admi log ke naam laye ke kabhi nahin pukaare. E gaon ke aadat raha. Sab roj Babu ya Badkau bole. 'Tor Dewa ke saadi kare ke tem hoi gaye. Aur tum log ke umir bhi din ke din jaat haye. Tum bhi suno, Bhola.' Bhola chup-chaap sab sunat raha lekin kuch bolis nahin. 'Bhauji, toke Bhola ke alaawa chaahi koi aur dekh bhaal kare.' Nanka bada muhchutta, mehra aadmi raha. Okar muh men lagaam nahin raha.

'Tum log kaahye ke waaste ho,' Sukhraji jhut se jawab dihis. 'Tor bhi to larka hai Dewa.' E gaon ke rishta wala baat raha. 'Kahe nahin tum log bhi is ke baare men kuch karo. Humhi duno jane ke upar e jimmewari kaahe chorat ho.' Nanka bolis, 'Jon tum bole ho Bhauji waji to hum sune maan-gat raha.' Ek ghoont chai pee ke Nanka muskiaaye ke aage bolis, 'Lekin ek baat jaroor haye: samadhin se sab se pahile chaati humai millaib.' 'Arre tu jo kuch kare maangna karna,' Sukhraji hans ke jawaab dihis. 'Hamaar ladka ke ek accha ghar grihasti wali ladki khoj deo bas.'

Bhola and his wife Sukhraji were resting on the verandah of their lean-to house one hot afternoon when Nanka, their neighbour, dropped by. '*Ram Ram bhai,*' he said to Bhola—greetings brother— as he parked himself on a wooden crate. Sukhraji dashed to the kitchen to make tea as Bhola and Nanka engaged in small talk about village affairs. When Sukhraji returned with three enamel cups of black tea, Nanka turned towards her and asked, 'Can I say something *Bhauji*?' 'Yes, *Babu*.' Sukhraji never called village men by their name, she always called them *Babu* or *Badkau*, husband's younger or older brother, respectively. That was the village way. 'Dewa is ready for marriage,' Nanka said, adding mischievously, 'And you are not getting any younger either. Bhola *bhai*, you listen as well.' Bhola listened, but didn't say anything. 'You need someone besides Bhola *bhai* to look after you.' Nanka was what people in the village called a *muh-chutta*, a loudmouth, a harmless joker, an impotent flirt, not to be taken seriously.

'What are you people for?' Sukhraji replied instantaneously. 'He is your son, too.' This was village talk. 'Why don't you people do something about it instead of putting all the responsibility on just the two of us?' 'Was waiting for the word, *Bhauji*,' Nanka replied. 'All go now. But remember one thing, I will be the first to embrace the Samadhin [the bride's mother].' *Samdhin se chaati sab se pahile hum milaib.* 'You can do whatever you want with her,' Sukhraji replied smiling. 'Just find us a good homely girl for our boy.'

Brij V. Lal, 'Maarit', in Brij V. Lal (ed.), Bittersweet, 2004.

first imported Indian labourers have more of a Bhojpuri character, while those settled later by Indians have a more interior 'eastern Hindi/Awadhi' flavour.

LANGUAGE MAINTENANCE, CULTIVATION AND SHIFTS IN THE SECOND DIASPORA

It is noteworthy that OBHs have survived for over a century despite the original diversity of immigrants, the low status of the OBH koinés, and competition from local vernaculars and international languages. However, it is likely that three of the OBHs, in Guyana, Trinidad and South Africa, will not survive as colloquial languages since fluent speakers are to be found only among older groups. Although the use of Mauritius Bhojpuri is diminishing in cities and towns, it can still be heard in villages. The language is still recognised, as attested by the fact that the Mahatma Gandhi Institute in Moka hosted the second World Bhojpuri Conference in 2000. But despite this recognition, it is conspicuously absent in the education system. Sarnami, on the other hand, is alive and well, as is Fiji Hindi.

No single clear explanation exists for the different levels of success when it comes to language maintenance among OBHs. Length of time as an explanation is inadequate since the language survives better in Mauritius, the first colony of indentured Indian immigrants, than in Guyana, Trinidad or South Africa.

It has been suggested that OBHs fare better in the non-English-speaking former colonies. The 'English as killer language' view is not, however, without exception, since Fiji Hindi is not just alive in a former British colony, but has spread to non-OBH communities of South Indians. Another possible explanation is that of urbanisation and industrialisation, processes which developed more rapidly in Trinidad and South Africa than elsewhere. But this does not explain why Bhojpuri is obsolescent in Guyana, since it exists in a largely rural environment. Perhaps the fact that at the time indenture was operative, Indians were a slight majority in Surinam, Mauritius and Fiji is of significance. The factors behind language maintenance and shifts are complex and multifaceted. In the case of South Africa, the existence of two major Indian languages, Bhojpuri and Tamil (and other prestigious languages such as Gujarati, Urdu and Telugu), also explains why no Indian lingua franca emerged, and consequently, why Bhojpuri is in decline.

Though seldom the 'home' language of indentured workers, standard Hindi was (and remains) an important part of the cultural and educational life of Indians of the second diaspora. Its role was that of a diglossic complement to the OBH koinés, commanding prestige and making it the natural medium for formal speeches. Diglossia refers to the practice of using one language variety in informal domains such as the home or neighbourhood, but another variety in formal domains such as the school or for literary purposes. It was often introduced via education, mostly outside the official school curriculum (as in Natal) or as part of the mainstream curriculum (as in Fiji). Hindi films, the efforts of religious bodies and some popular Hindi books played a role too. But however great the prestige of Hindi, it must be conceded that it was not mastered

by the majority of the descendants of indentured immigrants. This is partly because education in Hindi was not sufficiently sustained and because of the competing need to master the dominant colonial codes such as French, English or Dutch (in addition to the local creole vernaculars). Finally, the classical language of Sanskrit has also been transported worldwide for religious use. In many countries, Hindu weddings are performed multilingually, with the sacred mantras of Sanskrit still being accorded a special place.

Indians in the diaspora have not been negligent in promoting their languages and culture via cultural societies, religious organisations and language academies. They have promoted written versions of their languages, often with considerable effort, given the special typewriters and printing press equipment needed. Early efforts pertained to journalism, with magazines and newspapers covering cultural, religious and political matters; creative writing accompanied these early efforts. The difficulty of reaching a widespread audience in one Indian language alone explains why most newspapers had to be multilingual, with English or other colonial languages featuring significantly. Moreover, many newspapers had a short lifespan. Diasporic writing would have been initiated by some of the earliest indentured immigrants themselves through their letters to families back home. These are still preserved in archival and institutional records in the colonies.

Of the colonies, Mauritius and Surinam seem to have the greatest tradition of writing in an Indian language. In Mauritius, a short-lived Tamil newspaper was started in 1868, *The Mercantile Advertiser*. It was followed by other short-lived Tamil newspapers and magazines (e.g. *Tamize Kalvi Kazagham*) in the 20th century. There was also a Telugu and French weekly periodical, *Jagapati*. Urdu, as elsewhere in the colonies, was well represented in poetic compositions presented at *mushairas* or *sham-e-gazal* performances. In Mauritius, Marathi was represented more in stage performances, though there was some religious and historical writing too, as in an account of Shivaji by Pandit Atmaram Vishwananth in the 1920s. As a result of demographics, Hindi is the Indian language best represented in writing in Mauritius, with a repertoire that includes journalism, poetry, short stories and historical works.

Siklon was a long poem by Janab Mohammed Miaji which spoke of a devastating cyclone in 1892. Manilal Maganlal Doctor launched the *Hindusthani*, a weekly and later a daily newspaper in Hindi and English, which ran between 1909 and 1913. The Arya Samaj, founded in Mauritius by Manilal in 1910, launched a fortnightly

The Indian Opinion, *founded by Mahatma Gandhi, carried articles in a number of languages.*

Subramani's Dauka Puraan *is a significant work in Fiji Hindi.*

Table 6.1

| MOST COMMON INDIAN LANGUAGES SPOKEN IN THE US | | | |
US rank	Language	Total in US	Area of highest concentration
14	Hindi	331,484	New Jersey
26	Gujarati	102,418	New Jersey
39	Punjabi	50,005	California
44	Bengali	38,101	New York
48	Malayalam	33,949	New York

Source: US Census Bureau, Census 1990.

journal, *Maurisas Arya Patrika*, which ran between 1911 and 1913. Though many journals were short-lived, the practice of journalism in Hindi has continued to the present in Mauritius. Other works of note include a history of the island, *Maurisas ka Itihas*.

Like Mauritius, Surinam has a lively history of vernacular writing, but the greater emphasis here has been on writing in the local vernacular, Sarnami Hindi, rather than standard Hindi. The first literary text in Sarnami appeared in 1968—*Bulahat* by M. H. Lutchman—and the first long piece of prose, in 1984—*Stifa* by Rabin S. Baldewsingh. The 1980s saw the emergence of an active Sarnami movement initiated by expatriates in Holland, which produced grammar and literature in the language.

In South Africa, the most noteworthy efforts in vernacular writing were those of Mahatma Gandhi's newspaper, *Indian Opinion*, which was mainly in Gujarati and English, and for a time also carried articles in Hindi and Tamil. Started by Gandhi in 1903, the newspaper continued after his death under the leadership of his son, Manilal, until 1960. As in other colonies, oral and musical traditions in various Indian languages continue till today, particularly through *terukuttu*, or 'six foot dance drama', performed in Tamil and showing a mixture of 'high' Tamil for religious matters and colloquial South African Tamil for comic scenes. Folk and popular music have been a means of promoting Indian diasporic culture and language worldwide, notably via the chutney music of Trinidad Bhojpuri and the bhangra of the Punjabi diaspora.

Fiji has also produced literary work in Hindi and the local variety, Fiji Hindi. Among the latter are the play *Adhuraa Sapna* by Raymond Pillai and the novel *Dauka Puraan* by Subramani, published in 2001.

LANGUAGE IN THE THIRD DIASPORA

Among Indian languages in the UK, Punjabi is the most widely spoken. Punjabi in the UK is, in fact, remarkable for

Hindu temples, such as this one in Mauritius, are colourful architectural expressions of deity worship.

the crossover appeal it has achieved. Young Britons of non-Indian origin have taken to aspects of Punjabi dance, music and even language. However, by the 1970s, younger Sikhs in Leeds found it increasingly difficult to maintain traditional forms of the Punjabi language, 'unadulterated' by 'code-switching' with English and other linguistic influences. 'Code-switching' is the practice of using two languages interchangeably in speech, perhaps even within the same sentence. While sometimes regarded by lay people as needless mixing, sociolinguists recognise code-switching as a skilled interweaving of two languages for special rhetorical and interactional effects. Bengali, especially its northeastern Sylheti variety, is the second most common South Asian language in the UK, with most speakers originating from Bangladesh. Gujarati-speakers are also numerous, with the majority coming from East Africa. It is remarkable that Gujarati has been maintained, surviving two transcontinental migrations. Like Bengali- and Punjabi-speakers, many older members of the Gujarati community switch to Hindi when communicating with other South Asians. However, as a 'mother tongue', Hindi is less well represented in the UK since its speakers hardly ever have a network of close relatives in Britain.

In the US, there has been a small community of Punjabi families in California since the early 19th century. Most immigration to the country took place largely from the 1960s onwards with the arrival of professionals who brought a knowledge of English and one or more Indian languages. They were followed by family members who were generally less educated, non-professional and employed in occupations ranging from manual work to managing motels. Data from the 1990 census shows five Indian languages among the 50 most-spoken languages in the country (see Table 6.1).

A study of a Kannada-speaking community (the Kannadigas in the New York area) has shown that although language loyalty is high among families, it is not easy for young people of the second generation to develop the social networks that would nurture the language. In this respect, Indians seem destined to follow a familiar three-generation pattern of language shifts among US immigrants. However, factors that do help in language maintenance are the presence of visiting family members from India, especially grandparents, as well as occasional trips to the motherland. South Asian languages are being used more by the younger generation in the UK than in the US; a difference that may be accounted for by the greater presence of extended family members in the UK. The wider geographical expanse of the US is probably also a contributory factor, making Indian social networks physically more scattered.

Rajend Mesthrie

RELIGIOUS TRADITIONS IN THE DIASPORA

A complex history of emigration has produced a diverse and dynamic religious tapestry in the Indian diaspora. The migrating communities have been defined by a strong sense of religious pluralism as well as ethnolinguistic and regional differences because they were drawn from across the Indian subcontinent. Almost all religions from India were carried to foreign shores by caste-based communities and labouring, non-labouring and professional groups. Practitioners and adherents of all of the major religious traditions from India—Hinduism, Jainism, Sikhism and a variety of religious reform movements—as well as Christianity, Islam and Zoroastrianism found them present early on in places where Indian emigrants settled. Both continuity with tradition as well as breaks from it, and thus innovation, can be identified for the various religious traditions now flourishing outside India, some for almost two centuries.

HINDUISM

Hinduism is the name given to the complex array of rituals, mythologies, festivals and customs recognised and practised by a majority of the inhabitants of India, and it has long historical roots there. This religion is defined by a variety of styles, philosophies and orientations. Its multidimensional nature is reflected in the daily acts of its practitioners. A series of calendrical and daily rituals and festivals, the strong presence of a theistic tradition and the predominance of *bhakti*, or devotional Hinduism, manifest themselves in Saivite, Vaisnavite and mother goddess worship as well as in the veneration of a range of village deities. These coexist with an array of India-based Hindu reform movements, from the Arya Samaj to the International Society for Krishna Consciousness (ISKCON) and Sathya Sai Baba, all of which come under the rubric of Hinduism. All of these elements are found in overseas Hindu communities.

About 84 per cent of Indian indentured migrants in the sugar plantation colonies in the Caribbean and elsewhere were Hindu, and included among them were Brahmins, who were present in smaller numbers (11–15 per cent). Peasants and low-caste groups constituted the bulk of these communities. Brahmins were essential to sustaining and directing the religious life of the people. This was markedly different from Malaya, where Brahmins did not work on the plantations. There, manual work was undertaken by lower non-Brahmin castes and Adi Dravida (untouchable) groups from Tamil Nadu who made up the bulk of the Indian community. Since many of the migrants stayed on in these colonies, thriving Hindu communities exist there today, constituting 34 per cent of the total population in Guyana; 25 per cent in Trinidad and Surinam; 38 per cent in Fiji; almost 50 per cent in Mauritius; 6 per cent in Malaysia; and about 4 percent in Singapore.

In the religious lives of North Indian Hindu labourers in the plantation colonies, the epic story of the Ramayana and the experiences of its central character, Rama, assumed particular significance. In places like Fiji, Guyana and Mauritius, indentured labourers and their immediate descendants saw links between their lives and the tale of Ram through the themes of exile and banishment. The eventual triumph of good over evil in the Ramayana held promise for the emigrants, who hoped for the end of their days of hardship and cruelty on the plantation.

The three principal religions of Mauritius are Hinduism, Islam and Christianity. About half of the Indian population is Hindu and their religious traditions are diverse, with representations of rituals and festivals provided by Hindi- and Bhojpuri-speaking North Indians as well as Marathis, Tamils and Telugus from the Deccan. Hinduism here is diverse, with components of Arya Samaj, Sanatan Dharma, theistic, devotional Hinduism and folk Hindu customs practised among North and South Indian Hindus. This religious tradition is marked by the presence of ceremonies such as fire walking, sword climbing and *kavadi* (piercing of body parts with metal rods) as well as animal sacrifices (during Kalimai Puja) and trance sessions where *ojhas* and *pujaris* act as spirit mediums and healers. Temples and *baitkas* abound: both are focal points for the observance of rituals and festivals, especially Maha Sivaratri, Holi, Diwali, Ram Jayanti and Krishna Jayanti, which are the most popular.

Hinduism in the plantation colonies displays a pluralism evident in the strong attachment to devotional Hinduism, the worship of a range of Vaisnavite, Saivite and village deities, and the observance of such festivals as Diwali, Dussehra, Holi, Kali Puja, Onam, Ponggal, Timithi and Tai Pucam. In some places, the ritual domain was directed and controlled by Brahmins, while in others, non-Brahmin ritual specialists and lay persons were in charge. At the turn of the 20th century, the Arya Samaj (formed in India by Swami Dayanand in 1875) sent missionaries overseas to bring Hindus back to the 'path'. Based on monotheistic Vedic precepts and preaching egalitarianism, the Arya Samaj rejected orthodoxy and the ritualism of the Brahmanical tradition and called for fundamental social reform. This struck at the very heart of the sort of Hinduism practised among overseas Hindu communities in the Caribbean and challenged the authority of the Brahmins and their brand of orthopraxy. Here, the Arya Samaj was successful in winning a significant number of converts from the upwardly mobile and educated sectors.

The success of the Arya Samaj propelled the previously fragmented community of Brahmins to collaborate, organise, formalise and fend off the challenge by presenting a more conventional Hindu religious tradition called Sanatan Dharma, the eternal religion. It eventually won over large numbers of Hindus, leaving the Arya Samajis in the minority. Despite specific shifts and contestations, the ritual complex surrounding the veneration of local, household and village deities—a strong feature of folk Hinduism—is the one stable element that continues. Village deities, or the *grama devata*, both male and female, were firmly placed and literally grounded—shrines and temples were built for them. Some village deities, such as Muneeswaran, have grown much 'bigger' and moved into Agamic temples, experiencing an upward social mobility that parallels the improved status of their devotees. This attachment to a village-based Hindu tradition demonstrates both the persistence and innovation of overseas Hindus.

From the early decades of the 20th century, there was a strong trend towards the Sanskritisation of Hinduism in the diaspora. The move towards a Brahmanic and Sanskritic strain of Hinduism resulted in the censure and critique of folk practices such as trance sessions, ecstatic ceremonies, self-mortification rituals and animal sacrifices. These shifts occurred in the rhetoric of social reform and modernity, which carried the idea that Hinduism had to refashion itself to be meaningful in the present. It needed to be relevant to urban, educated, rational and progressive Hindus, and not be an embarrassment by promoting a

Ritual practices, such as the carrying of kavadi, *abound in Hinduism.*

The Indian dance form, kathakali, is often performed during the Onam festival, which is popular with Malayalis both in India and the diaspora.

The worship of particular deities may vary from place to place. This massive Hanuman statue is found in Mauritius.

Although various diasporic Hindu communities celebrate Durga Puja, the festival is especially significant among migrant Bengali Hindus.

backward, superstitious, caste-based and ritualised construction of Hinduism. In the multi-religious, multi-ethnic and secular context of the diaspora, Hindu communities face additional pressure to organise, modernise and bureaucratise. Official constructions of Hinduism lean towards textual, philosophical and Brahmanic dimensions, sometimes leading to tensions within communities as folk Hindu practices still find strong support, and in some places even show signs of revival.

The second surge of migration saw different groups of Hindus leaving India; a post-colonial and post-World War II phenomenon which brought a large number of educated and professional migrants to North America, Europe, Australia and New Zealand. A majority of them were Hindus. Over time, as they settled and raised families, they began to mobilise the scattered community, form organisations and establish places of worship. From Indian cultural centres with a strong Hindu bent, temple societies were formed, leading to the building of Hindu temples, many of which were ecumenical in character. They brought together deities and rituals from separate (and sometimes conflicting) strands of Hinduism. Regional and linguistic variations remained significant, however, as Tamil, Telugu, Gujarati, Uttar Pradeshi, Hindu-Punjabi and other such groups marked their distinct identities and organised associations and places of worship along communal lines.

Sathya Sai Baba, founder of the eponymous Hindu reform movement.

In the 1970s, Hindus in North America and Europe were joined by their counterparts from the Caribbean, Fiji, Mauritius, Uganda, Kenya and Tanzania—the 'twice-displaced' who came armed with the experience of reproducing their religious and cultural traditions, having already done it once elsewhere.

Today, large Hindu temples exist in major urban centres in North America, the UK, Germany, the Netherlands, Australia, New Zealand, Singapore, Malaysia, Thailand, Vietnam, Philippines and Hong Kong, although worship within the home at the family altar remains at the core of Hindu religious practice. In South Indian Hindu practice, temple worship is central, whereas among North Indian Hindu communities, it is less predominant. Hindu temples have emerged not just as places of worship but as community spaces with an expanded set of functions. In all these places, varied constructions of Hinduism exist, as do contestations between its 'official' and 'popular' versions. The former tends to be

elite driven while the latter revolves around lay Hindus and every day forms of religious practice. In many places, popular Hinduism is defined by strong religious syncretism and hybridity. This entails a free and liberal use of deities, symbols and ritual practices associated with other religious traditions. In Singapore and Malaysia, this takes the form of liaisons with religious/folk Taoism, whereas in Trinidad convergences have occurred across Shango, Spiritual Baptist and Kali Mai traditions.

'India-derived' Hindu reform movements

In addition to the presence of theistic and devotional elements and folk Hindu practices, a range of 'India-derived' reform movements are also found in overseas Indian communities. Today, the Arya Samaj persists in all the major communities of the Indian diaspora, but its religious role has been reduced and it is redefining itself as a social and cultural movement which is concerned with religious education and other charitable activities.

Other India-based reform movements started to appear outside the subcontinent in the 1960s and 1970s. During this period, a number of movements led by living gurus made their mark overseas. These included the ISKCON, Sathya Sai Baba movement, Radha Soami Satsang, BK Raja Yoga Centre, Eckankar Satsang, Sri Ramakrishna Mission, Sri Aurobindo Society, Transcendental Mission, Divine Light Mission and Shirdi Sai Baba Sansthan. They travelled especially (but not only) to North America and found converts first among non-Indians. Eventually, some overseas Indians were also attracted to their teachings. These groups enjoyed widespread and increased popularity among Indians through the 1970s and 1980s. The initial excitement at and novelty of being self-consciously radical and different from 'institutionalised religions' seems to have now settled somewhat. Some of these groups have dwindled in size and popularity, and others have been embroiled in controversies and legal entanglements, ISKCON being one of them. Some, being more resilient, have become well-established and continue to attract new members from both the Indian and non-Indian communities. A case in point is the Sathya Sai Baba movement in Malaysia and Singapore, which now has 14 centres, all of which are well-supported by Chinese members to such an extent that Sathya Sai Baba *bhajans* (devotional songs) have been created in Mandarin.

While the Arya Samaj was successful in the sugar plantation colonies, it has drawn less support in countries such as Singapore and Malaysia, largely due to the predominance of South Indian Tamil-speaking communities. In Singapore, the movement continues to exist but its religious and spiritual aspects are marginal when compared to the various educational, cultural and social service functions it is increasingly performing. ISKCON also continues to have a presence in Southeast Asia although it has been 'de-registered' in places such as Indonesia and Singapore. Though lacking an organisational basis for legitimate existence, the group attracts individual members who find ways of reproducing their spirituality more informally. Members of Sindhi and Hindu-Punjabi communities support fellowship-based (*satsang*) meditation groups (such as the Radha Soami and Sadhu Vaswani) in the UK, North America and Southeast Asia. Sindhis also participate freely in the religious life of the Sikh community, often providing funding and other resources for building and sustaining gurdwaras. In Singapore and Malaysia, members of the Sindhi community frequent gurdwaras on Sundays and sometimes hold weddings there.

ISLAM

Indian Muslim communities in the diaspora are internally divided. The most prominent distinction is between the Sunni and the Shia, though there are also others like the Ahmadiyyas and Muhammadiyyas. In Malaya and Mauritius, aspects of folk Islam were brought by early North Indian Muslim migrants, as seen in the founding of *durgahs* and *keramats* (shrines). The category 'South Asian Muslim' encapsulates Muslims from Pakistan, Bangladesh and India, which makes it difficult to distinguish overseas Muslims of Indian origin (post-1947).

Historical data record the early migration of Gujarati Muslims (Dowdi Bohras) to East Africa and Tamil Muslims as traders and merchants to Malaya in the 18th century, and the migration of Muslims from Tamil Nadu, Andhra Pradesh, Bihar, Uttar Pradesh and Punjab as indentured labourers to British colonies from the mid-19th century. During the latter period, about 14 per cent of the indentured male labour recruited was Muslim.

In South Africa, an overwhelming number of Muslims came from India, brought there by the Dutch as slaves as early as the 17th century to work at the Cape of Good Hope. In the 19th century, the sugar cane plantations were worked by Indian indentured labour, of which about 10 per cent were Muslim. Additionally, large numbers of Muslims arrived as traders and merchants from India. The earliest mosques in South Africa date back to the 19th century: Juma Masjid, the largest mosque in South Africa, was built in 1884 in Durban, mainly by Memon traders. Gujarati Muslims established their own mosque nearby in 1885. A syncretic form of Islam developed in Natal through interaction with Hindu indentured labourers. There were also *madrasahs*, orphanages and mosques in Natal. A number of organisations and associations were also rapidly founded in South Africa through the initiatives of Indian Muslims and in response to the problems of apartheid there. Some prominent examples include the Hamidia Islamic Society, founded in 1906; the Central Islamic Trust, founded in 1952; and the Islamic Missionary Society, founded in 1958; all of which were concerned in one way or another with the propagation of Islam, the religious education of the young and the building of mosques and *madrasahs*. Between 1838 and 1917, about 80,000 Indian Muslims went to Guyana and Trinidad as indentured labourers, and smaller numbers went to Jamaica. Muslim communities continued to observe Ramadan and such festivals as Id-al-Fitr, Id-al-Adha, Milad-un-nabi and Muharram.

In Britain, there is a large South Asian Muslim population, the majority of whom come from Pakistan and Bangladesh. In Canada, Muslims from Hyderabad, Uttar Pradesh and Punjab started arriving between the 1950s and 1970s, largely as educated professionals. By 1996, there were some 60 Sunni mosques in all the major Canadian cities from Halifax to Vancouver. There are Shia mosques in Toronto and Montréal, and Ismaili Jamaat *khanas* (prayer houses) in urban centres. Muslims, like other migrant communities, have organised

themselves and set up places of worship and cultural centres. Two examples are the Islamic Society of North America and the Islamic Circle of North America, both of which are active in building mosques and Muslim schools, promoting missionary activities and holding conferences. The role of mosques expanded in these new settings. In addition to serving the traditional religious needs of their members, the mosques here (and also in the US and UK) serve as larger cultural centres which afford opportunities for social interaction among Muslims. This parallels the altered function of other religious institutions, such as Hindu temples and Sikh gurdwaras, which serve as multi-purpose centres and community spaces for Indians overseas.

Apart from the Sunni–Shia distinction, Islam is typified by a sense of universalism. Yet, Muslim communities in the diaspora continue to establish mosques and other cultural and ethnic-based associations and organisations which define them as Indian Muslims, Pakistani Muslims, Asian Muslims or Muslims from the Middle East, Turkey or Southeast Asia. The particularities of these mosques are apparent from such markers as the language used within, whether Urdu, Tamil, Hindi, Arabic or Malay, the origins of imams, the dress code, attitudes towards female members of the community, the cuisine and patterns of social interaction among the members.

SIKHISM

Sikhism was founded as a reform movement in the 16th century by Guru Nanak in Punjab. Sikhs now constitute a separate community with their own sacred book, the Sri Guru Granth Sahib, places and forms of worship, and succession of gurus, of which 10 are recognised. The five 'Ks' (*kesh* – uncut hair; *kara* – steel bracelet; *kanga* – wooden comb; *kaccha* – cotton underwear; and *khanda* – sword) in Sikhism are physical symbols worn by Sikhs who have been initiated into the Khalsa, thus identifying them and facilitating solidarity within the community. They date back to the creation of the Khalsa Panth by Guru Gobind Singh in 1699. Sikhism emphasises the equality of all and in principle rejects the caste system. Its male members are distinguished by uncut hair and beard. One of the central tenets of Sikhism is the idea of *seva* (service), to be given freely to all, regardless of race, religion, nationality, gender or age.

Durban's Juma Masjid is the largest mosque in South Africa.

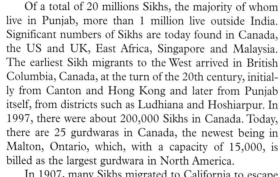

A gurdwara in Surrey, Canada, decorated for Baisakhi.

Guru Gobind Singh, the 10th Sikh guru.

Parades, such as this one in Canada, allow the Sikh community to share their cultural life with wider society.

Of a total of 20 millions Sikhs, the majority of whom live in Punjab, more than 1 million live outside India. Significant numbers of Sikhs are today found in Canada, the US and UK, East Africa, Singapore and Malaysia. The earliest Sikh migrants to the West arrived in British Columbia, Canada, at the turn of the 20th century, initially from Canton and Hong Kong and later from Punjab itself, from districts such as Ludhiana and Hoshiarpur. In 1997, there were about 200,000 Sikhs in Canada. Today, there are 25 gurdwaras in Canada, the newest being in Malton, Ontario, which, with a capacity of 15,000, is billed as the largest gurdwara in North America.

In 1907, many Sikhs migrated to California to escape the anti-Oriental riots in British Columbia. The first gurdwara in the US was founded in 1912 in Stockton. Restrictive immigration laws prevented the rapid expansion of the community in the first half of the 20th century, but the situation changed dramatically in the mid-1960s when these laws were liberalised, facilitating the inflow of larger numbers of Sikhs. This new group was, however, markedly different from the earlier groups in that they were younger and belonged to a professional class with a high level of formal education. In 2000, there were 80 gurdwaras in the US, of which 30 were in California.

A large Sikh community also exists in the UK, with most of its members arriving directly from the Doaba region in Punjab only in the 1950s and 1960s to fill shortages in labour following World War II. Significant numbers of Sikhs also entered the UK from East Africa and other former British colonies to escape the Africanisation policies of the 1970s. Between the 1950s and 1970s, more Sikhs arrived as migrant workers and settled in the industrial sectors of outer London and the West Midlands. Largely from rural backgrounds, these migrants were also divided by caste: the Jats (farmers) are present in large numbers in Southall, Birmingham, Wolverhampton and Huddersfield; while others, such as the Ramgarhias (craftsmen), Ramdasias (leather workers), Jhirs (water carriers) and Valmikis (sweepers) are found in smaller numbers in London and the West Midlands. They were joined in the 1970s by East African Sikhs. Their various migrant streams make for a highly differentiated Sikh community in the UK. Gurdwaras have become part of the religious and physical landscape of almost every major city in the UK.

The relationship of overseas Sikh communities to India was tested in 1984 when a conflict between the Indian government, led by Indira Gandhi, and the Indian Sikh community erupted. The storming of the most sacred of Sikh institutions—the Golden Temple of Amritsar—by the Indian army to expel armed militants shocked and angered Sikhs everywhere. In the diaspora, it alienated them from the Indian government and also galvanised them, creating a renewed sense of purpose and need for Sikh solidarity. Since then, greater efforts have been made to set up more gurdwaras and Sikh associations, with more attention paid to events affecting the Sikh community in India. However, the overseas Sikh community is divided in its concern with and focus on India, especially as the number of overseas-born Sikhs increases. The latter do not necessarily carry immigrant sensibilities or have an attachment to the 'homeland'. They have a different agenda; they are more concerned with problems and issues relating to their location and membership as citizens, albeit of Sikh-Punjabi ancestry.

Apart from daily prayers and the reading of the Sri Guru Granth Sahib in homes, Sikhs congregate in gurdwaras on Sundays for communal worship. The gurdwara is not just a place of worship for the Sikhs, but a core cultural institution; a centre for Punjabi language and culture. At its most basic, the gurdwara is home to the sacred book and enables communal worship. It has an attached community kitchen, or *langar*, where food is cooked and offered freely to everyone. This model has been replicated in the diaspora wherever Sikhs have settled in significant numbers. Apart from being a community space for interaction, gurdwaras in the diaspora also provide religious instruction to the young and teach the Punjabi language to facilitate reading of the holy book. Although Sikhism preaches universalism and brotherhood of all, internal distinctions are apparent, sometimes along caste lines and among the Khalsas and Sahajdharis of the community, on the basis of different perceptions of what it means to be a Sikh. These differences are often reflected in the separate gurdwaras and other Sikh associations that are founded by the communities in question.

Important events in the Sikh calendar include the observance of *gurpurbs* (anniversaries of the births and deaths of the various gurus, especially Guru Nanak and Guru Gobind Singh) and Baisakhi (the harvest festival). The Sikh community is part of a broader Punjabi culture and continues to participate in its rituals and customs. Whereas in the early years gurdwaras provided various kinds of support—sociocultural, legal, employment, immigration and welfare related—for newly arrived Sikhs, the function of the gurdwara in overseas Sikh communities today is confined largely to religious and cultural activities.

CHRISTIANITY

Indian Christianity comprises a number of different traditions: Syrian Christianity, Roman Catholicism, Protestant denominations, Pentecostal groups, the Church of South

India and the Church of North India. The late 19th century saw the migration of Methodist and Roman Catholic communities from southern India and Syrian Christians from Kerala to parts of Malaya. They have established churches all across the Malaysian peninsula and Singapore, around which the vibrant religious lives of these migrant groups are centred. According to the Singapore census of 2000, 12.1 per cent of resident Indians define themselves as Christian. The Tamil Methodist Church and several of its neighbourhood churches dot the island, together with the Mar Thoma Syrian Church and the St. Thomas Orthodox Syrian Cathedral.

In the 1970s, groups of Indian Christians emigrated to the UK and North America, and in smaller numbers to Australia and New Zealand. Indian Christians are a small minority in Hindu-dominated India but form a part of the majority population in the West, a situation quite unlike that of other Indian religious groups overseas. This group is distinct from other clusters of migrating Indians as it was dominated by women, largely from Kerala, as Christian families and institutions there produced a surplus of nurses who, in the 1970s, were needed in North America and the UK. Many migrated as families. Christians from Kerala always had priests and pastors to provide spiritual guidance to the community away from home.

A number of the migrants to North America were Syrian Christians who considered themselves upper caste. The largest Syro-Malabar parish in Canada, based in Toronto, has a membership of about 700 families. In the US, Chicago has a substantial population of Christians from Kerala. Here, a lay organisation called the Indian Catholic Association of America was established in 1979. In 1985, the Chicago Syro-Malabar Mission was founded and today it has 7000 members. In 2001, the first Syro-Malabar Catholic diocese outside India was established in the US following the appointment of a bishop. The parishes in these places have set up several organisations catering to the cultural and religious needs of the community. Indian Christian churches continue to have ties and affiliations with their counterparts in India, and church services and prayer sessions are offered in Malayalam (or other regional languages such as Tamil, Telugu, Gujarati and Hindi) and English. Overseas Indian Christians continue to use Indian languages and follow region- and ethnic-based customs, thus distinguishing themselves from the larger group of Christians in Canada, the US and the UK.

JAINISM

In the 6th century BC, the followers of Mahavira in India founded a highly ascetic tradition, Jainism, which is still practised by a small community. The twin principles of world renunciation and absolute non-violence constitute the group's core philosophy. The community is divided into two major ascetic orders, the Shvetambar and the Digambar, although there are several sub-sects within this larger division. It is difficult to define accurately the total number of Jains living outside India, though estimates range from 80,000 upwards. Part of the reason for this is the complex and amorphous nature of Jain religious identity, which has not always been singularly and exclusively defined. Within India, some Jains consider Jainism to be a part of Hinduism and thus do not distinguish themselves from Hindus. Overseas, Jains have worked with Hindus to build temples and found Hindu organisations, in addition to patronising such organisations. Recently, however, there has been greater self-consciousness about defining and maintaining strictly Jain institutions and organisations.

Jains have been migrating in small numbers to North America since the late 19th century. Early 20th-century Jain immigrants to East Africa were largely from Gujarat and of the Shvetambar tradition. In the late 1960s, members of this community moved to parts of Britain and North America. The Gujarati Jains are numerically dominant in both of these countries today. During the same period, significant numbers of Gujarati Jains arrived in North America directly from India, the UK, Burma, Southeast Asia and Hong Kong due to the easing of restrictions in immigration laws. In the 1950s, a group of Palinpuri Jains from Gujarat settled in Hong Kong, and today there are some 500 Jains there. When the community was small, the Jains did not build separate religious institutions but allied themselves with the Hindus and participated in building ecumenical Hindu temples, with space set aside for their own images within them.

Our Lady of Lourdes, a church popular with the Indian Catholic community in Singapore.

Mahavir Jayanti celebrations in a Jain temple in Kingsbury, London.

An imposing Jain temple in Leicester, the UK.

A Parsi family shrine with a framed illustration of the Prophet Zoroaster.

By the 1980s, with the growth of the community, increased financial and other resources, as well as pressure from the Jain leadership, Jains in Britain, Canada, the US and Hong Kong started to build their own places of worship and cultural institutions. There are some 57 Jain temples in North America today. The community in Toronto is the oldest in North America, its membership comprising 600 families. There has been greater organisational initiative since the 1980s, culminating in the formation of the Jain Study Circle later in the decade, which was entrusted with the religious education of younger members of the community, and also with publishing a quarterly journal. The Jain Association of North America was established in 1981. It brings together thousands of Jain participants at its biennial conference. A similar pattern is seen among Jains of Hong Kong, where the Shree Hong Kong Jain Sangh was founded in 1996 by Jains from various parts of India.

Jain communities in the diaspora concentrate their energies on building temples and establishing cultural societies concerned with preserving their traditions for future generations. As few religious specialists are found among overseas Jain communities, a great deal of the organisational work as well as leadership is in the hands of lay members of the community, a feature that is shared by several other religious groups in the diaspora.

ZOROASTRIANISM

In the 10th century, Parsis, the adherents of an old prophetic religion, Zoroastrianism, and originally residents of the province of Pars in modern Iran, migrated to Gujarat to escape persecution by Muslims in Persia. They lived for centuries in this Indian state but moved and settled in Bombay with the arrival of British traders. The Parsis found commercial success as traders and merchants and often acted as middlemen between the British and the Indians. By the 18th century, members of the community had become some of India's prominent merchants and were heavily involved in India's overseas trade. This took them to different parts of the British Empire, such as Yemen (especially Aden), East Africa and Hong Kong. A powerful group of Parsis also settled in Karachi, creating 'the first of the modern diasporas' among the Parsis. The

The sacred fire in the Inner Sanctum of the Zoroastrian Centre in London.

London's Zoroastrian Centre is a hub for the community's religious life.

second and more recent movement was a mid-20th century phenomenon which saw Parsis (like other South Asian communities) migrating to Britain, Canada, Hong Kong, the US, Australia and New Zealand.

In the 1960s and 1970s, because of Africanisation policies, Parsis from Kenya, Uganda and Tanzania began migrating to Britain, while the fall of the Shah of Iran saw Iranian Parsis joining their co-religionists in Britain and Canada. As with all diasporic communities, the reproduction of sociocultural and religious life for the Parsi community has been a challenge. In North America, many associations have been set up, starting with the founding of the Federation of Zoroastrian Associations of North America in 1986. The earliest associations were established in Toronto, Vancouver and Chicago, and Zoroastrian buildings were opened in New York, Chicago and Toronto. The associations bring members together, sponsor conferences and promote youth activities and religious education. The first Zoroastrian World Congress was held in California in 1993, and by 1999, eight such congresses had been organised. In Australia, the first Zoroastrian association was formed in Sydney in 1970, followed by one in Melbourne in 1978. Concerns regarding the future of the community have led to an intense and self-conscious attempt by Zoroastrian groups in North America to launch a massive religious education programme targeted at the youth.

An important question asked by members of the Parsi diaspora relates to the meaning of Zoroastrian identity. Though the community is small, attempts have been made to unify and create networks among members scattered across the globe. (In 2002, there were 194 Parsis in Hong Kong. The largest community is in Mumbai, with a total of 76,000, but even there their numbers are declining.) One such effort saw the founding of the World Zoroastrian Organisation in 1980 in London. Its work thus far has been concerned with providing assistance to needy members worldwide (including India), organising religious conferences and publishing. The Zoroastrian community overseas is far from homogeneous, having divergent historical and migratory experiences, languages, ethnicities, nationalities and religious sensibilities. Zoroastrian communities in Hong Kong, Britain and the US seem to be more concerned with asserting and maintaining a distinct cultural and religious identity than their co-religionists in Canada, given the latter's emphasis on multicultural policies. Among the issues facing Parsis are intermarriage with non-Zoroastrians and their initiation into the community, declining numbers, and difficulties in sustaining religious practices and in securing religious leaders. While some communities accept the authority of high priests from India, others do not. Two priestly councils now exist in North America—the Parsi North American Mobed Council (Toronto) and the Council of Iranian Mobeds (California). No Zoroastrian community in the diaspora has been able to build a 'fully consecrated temple where higher liturgies can be performed.' Some of the rituals are deemed too time-consuming, and the Gathas (hymns of the Prophet Zoroaster) and the Avesta (the holy book) are not accessible to those unfamiliar with Parsi, thus raising the question of possible translations into English. The distance between the religion as practised in the diaspora and in India is also becoming apparent. Indian Parsis are seen as practising a syncretist form of the religion, which includes elements of Hinduism, such as the patronage of gurus and holy men, and engaging in a more mystical and magical form of Hinduism. In contrast, diasporic versions of Zoroastrianism are self-consciously constructed to emphasise the theological, textual, rational and transcendental features of the religion.

OVERVIEW

The religious life of the Indian diaspora is vibrant, sustained by traditions drawn from home. After some 175 years of migration, Indians overseas have established places of worship, religious institutions and organisations which are not only central to the religious life of the community but also perform a broader role. They have also facilitated greater lay involvement in the organisation, direction and management of a religious domain, previously (and traditionally) the prerogative of religious specialists. In a familiar mode though, tensions between 'official' constructions of religion and 'popular' forms continue to define and divide communities. This is further complicated by ethnolinguistic, class, caste and regional distinctions. The persistence of folk Hindu traditions in the diaspora and the growing presence of healing and exorcist rituals in the cult of Babas in Britain is remarkable given the more Sanskritised, Brahmanic and literate traditions in these places. The tenacity of tradition, the ways of the ancestors, is evident even as this inheritance is interpreted in novel ways, leading to innovations in the religious domain. The growth of new solidarities among widely scattered religious communities is possible through new forms of technology and communication. The Internet is creatively appropriated by communities of the diaspora in the service of religion. This is as true for traditional religions as it is for new religious movements. Cyberspace allows individuals with similar religious sensibilities and sentiments, otherwise globally scattered, to find each other and build a renewed and often heightened religious consciousness and identity.

While India remains important, Indians overseas have added dimensions to an inherited tradition through hybridisation and syncretism, leading to the emergence of new and distinct religious movements, the identification of local gurus, new deities, festivals and rituals, and new forms of interaction and liaisons with other cultures and religions. Sustained, long-term interaction between diverse communities engenders change. The future contours of the religious domain between overseas Indian communities will be determined by a number of contextual and intersecting variables, and will be variously constructed and contested, but there is little doubt that the constituent religious traditions will continue to persist and thrive.

Vineeta Sinha

POPULAR CULTURE

Popular culture is an increasingly visible aspect of the Indian diaspora. Even though Indian communities all over the world have developed differently, they are connected, in part, through the consumption of various forms of popular culture such as film, television, music and fashion. These are now increasingly produced, distributed and enjoyed across the globe, wherever Indians have settled. Three specific examples are discussed here: popular Hindi cinema, cable and satellite television, and bhangra music.

COMMERCIAL HINDI CINEMA

Cinema is the most popular of India's daily art forms. The popular Hindi cinema industry in Mumbai produces approximately 1000 films each year. There are a number of other regional film centres making films in Assamese, Bengali, Bhojpuri, Gujarati, Kannada, Malayalam, Oriya, Punjabi, Tamil and Telugu. However, popular Hindi cinema has gained the national audience within India and an increasing audience worldwide. Its Hindi-Urdu vernacular makes it intelligible to most viewers throughout the subcontinent and the diaspora.

Since the mid-1990s, popular Hindi cinema has been increasingly referred to as 'Bollywood'. The exact origin of the term is unclear. Some claim that it was originally a derogatory term applied by the elite English-language press in India or by Western film commentators to popular Hindi cinema from Mumbai, which was seen as simply copying storylines and ideas from Hollywood. Whatever its origins, 'Bollywood' is now a widely accepted label for the mainstream Indian film industry. Its films are viewed in cinema auditoriums (both in mainstream multiplexes and in smaller Indian-owned cinemas), at home on video or DVD, and on cable and satellite television. In Bollywood 'star' shows, actors, playback singers and dancers all re-enact favourite scenes, songs and dialogues from Bollywood films. Millions of Bollywood music cassettes and CDs are sold the world over, providing a staple part of the programming of diasporic radio stations. Thousands of websites on the Internet are also dedicated to Bollywood cinema.

Since its inception in 1913 with the release of the first feature film, *Raja Harischandra* ('King Harischandra'), directed by D. G. Phalke, popular Hindi cinema has seen many developments and transformations, reflected in its three hours of storytelling. Some of these developments

Theatrical Bollywood stage spectaculars now tour the world, a testament to the wide spread of the Indian diaspora and the appeal of Bollywood.

Indian movies and music are easily available almost anywhere in the world.

An Indian couple check out the latest Indian movies outside a cinema in London, 1970s.

have been truly innovative, but many others have been run-of-the-mill, thus adding to the view of the films as being hurried and mass-produced for quick returns.

Popular Hindi films do not easily fit into simple categories or genres, unlike many Hollywood films. It is common for a commercial Hindi film to have elements of romance, song and dance, action, melodrama, mythology, comedy and suspense all in one. Nevertheless, a number of predominant genres have been identified, within which a corpus of films can be loosely classified. Important among these genres are the following: mythological or devotional films which recount or rework epic stories from the Ramayana or the Mahabharata as well as other religious traditions within the Indian subcontinent; historical films, which were particularly pertinent in the pre-1947 period, where the focus on actual Indian historical figures came laden with messages about British rule; social films, which are often evocative melodramas that engage with the hopes, ideals and broken promises of India as it emerged as an independent nation in the post-1947 period, and Muslim socials, which are best considered as a sub-genre of social films and were popular in the 1960s, inspired by stories from Urdu love poetry, whose appeal crossed religious boundaries; masala films, which are all-action films that often contain a variety of other genres (hence the label 'masala', or mixed) that capture the hopes and anxieties of every man and woman in a changing world; romantic films, depicting the universal boy-meets-girl love story, peppered with the numerous obstacles that they face along the way; and finally, non-resident Indian (NRI) films, which represent the relationship of the overseas Indian to the homeland through the particular lens of Bollywood cinema, and have been in the ascendancy since the mid-1990s.

DIASPORIC BOLLYWOOD CINEMA-GOING

The export of popular Hindi films, its music and star-studded shows overseas followed migrating Indians. The films have been used as entertainment and as a way of maintaining cultural and social links with the homeland. The 1960s and 1970s were of particular importance as Bollywood movies came to be exhibited in hired cinema halls all over the world, and since the mid-1990s, in mainstream multiplexes in cities with large Indian or South Asian populations.

The history of Bollywood film-viewing in Britain dates as far back as 1926, when King George V and Queen Mary held a royal 'command performance' of *Prem Sanyas* (also billed as 'Light of Asia') at Windsor Castle.

A film poster advertising Dharam Karam *at Liberty Cinema, Southall, in the UK, c. 1975–85. The reverse shows details for* Pyar Ka Sagar.

This film was produced in 1925 and was co-directed by the Indo-German team of Himansu Rai and Franz Osten. The stars of Bollywood visited England for the first Indian Film Festival in 1957. The legends of the 1950s—Guru Dutt, Mehboob Khan, Shammi Kapoor, Nargis, Nutan, Waheeda Rehman and others—all came, arousing excitement akin to going to see Elvis or The Beatles 'live' in concert.

Bollywood cinema-going became a regular feature of the popular culture activities of many overseas Indians. In the UK in particular, cinema-going was a sporadic activity during the late 1950s and throughout the 1970s. This gave way to the home video-viewing culture, but by the mid-1990s, cinema-going had made a comeback.

Mainstream cinemas in diasporic South Asian areas of settlement were hired on weekends throughout the late 1950s and into the 1970s for the screening of Bollywood movies. Attending such events became a family affair and fostered notions of leisure and interest in community politics. During the 1960s (before formal welfare and pressure groups came into being), people frequently came to Sunday matinees to speak with influential citizens about immigration problems or court cases. These weekend get-togethers were also moments for friends and family to meet and socialise after long weekday hours spent engaged in manual labour and contributing to the industrial drive sweeping across Britain.

British South Asian-run cinemas began to spring up nationwide in the 1970s, taking off where white British audiences were deserting the auditoriums. In major cities of South Asian settlement in the Midlands and the north of England in the 1970s, Birmingham had six cinemas, Leicester and Bradford had four and Derby had two. At the height of Bollywood cinema-going during this period, 120 cinemas in the UK showed Bollywood productions full- or part-time. There were at least four companies distributing popular Indian films, although now, two predominate (Eros Entertainment based in northwest London, and Yash Raj Films UK, also in London).

With the advent of video in the UK in 1977, Bollywood cinema-going ceased to exist, causing many cinemas to shut down. British South Asians, Indians in particular, were among the first households in the country to purchase their own VCRs (video cassette recorders). Whereas in the late 1970s a Bollywood cinema ticket cost £1 per person, imported Bollywood and other South Asian video cassettes were also hired at £1 each, allowing all households to view the latest films. Consequently, a thriving British South Asian video shop culture emerged

during the 1980s, responding to the lack of cultural and leisure facilities for Indians and other British South Asians. Up to 20 video shops existed in most British cities, and in Leicester alone there were 45 outlets during the 1980s. Meanwhile, Bollywood film production in Mumbai was suffering a malaise due to budget cuts and the onset of run-of-the-mill violent formulas. Video culture diminished Bollywood cinema-going in Britain, but video itself suffered a similar fate with the advent of non-terrestrial cable and satellite channels, such as Zee TV, in the early 1990s.

The resurrection of Bollywood cinema-going began in 1993 with a few late-night screenings developing into week-long screenings. This led to the reappearance of Indian-run cinemas, followed by the multiplexes. The return to big-screen cinema-going can be credited to the revival of big-budget spectaculars, with production costs soaring from £120,000 to £1 million by the mid-1990s, and also to the emergence of movies which appealed not only to Indian urbanites but also to diasporic South Asians in terms of themes and content. By returning to cinema-going more generally throughout the 1990s in the UK, overseas Indians and other British South Asians were taking part in the remaking of their areas of settlement by expanding their cultural and leisure facilities to include audio-visual entertainment, and by supporting the economies of nearby Indian restaurants as sites of pre- or post-screening activities.

The diaspora in Bollywood movies

One of the productions which proved popular with Bollywood movie-goers overseas in recent years, especially in Britain and North America, is *Dilwale Dulhaniya Le Jayenge* ('The Braveheart Will Take the Bride'; directed by Aditya Chopra; 1995), or DDLJ as it has come to be popularly known. In fact, this film marked the arrival of the diasporic or NRI character as a mainstay of popular Hindi cinema. As a result, the movie's main actor, Shahrukh Khan, began to regularly feature as the favourite diasporic and NRI hero in Hindi cinema from the mid-1990s. DDLJ tells the story of a rich and spoilt British Asian boy, Raj (Shahrukh Khan), who falls for a British Asian girl, Simran (Kajol), while on an inter-rail trek across Europe. Simran's father, Baldev Singh (played by the late Amrish Puri), finds out and relocates his entire family and livelihood to Punjab, where he plans to marry Simran off to his best friend's son. Raj follows Simran to India to win over her family and get them to accept a marriage between the two. DDLJ is the longest-running Bollywood film and is still showing in Indian cinemas in Mumbai—in June 2005 it entered its 500th successful week of exhibition. The movie is also one of the all-time favourites of contemporary Bollywood cinema in the Indian diaspora.

In *Pardes* ('Foreign Land'; directed by Subhash Ghai; 1997), Arjun (Shahrukh Khan) is the adopted son of a billionaire American NRI, Kishori Lal (Amrish Puri), who is sent to India to help arrange a marriage between a girl named Ganga (Mahima Chaudhary) and Lal's real son, Rajiv (Apurva Agnihotri). Rajiv is far from the perfect bridegroom for Ganga and through a series of star-crossed encounters spanning India and the US, Arjun and Ganga fall in love. *Pardes'* advertising by-line on album sleeves and movie posters reads 'American Dreams, Indian Soul'.

Aa Ab Laut Chalen ('Come Let Us Return'; directed by Rishi Kapoor; 1998), also set in the US, follows the dreams of a young lower-middle-class graduate, Rahul (Akshaye Khanna), who finds it hard getting a job in India and migrates to New York in search of a better life. There he finds crass materialism among the South Asian bourgeoisie, and love and simpleton ways, albeit in clichés, among the migrant working classes in New York's outer boroughs. To complicate matters, he finds his father (played by 1970s Bollywood superstar Rajesh Khanna), whom he thought was dead but was instead a wealthy American businessman who had also left India in search of a better life, and meets and falls in love with Pooja (Aishwarya Rai). The film ends by contemplating 'what is lost and found on the way to making riches and leaving the motherland behind.'

Contemporary Bollywood films with diasporic interests developed the theme of migration and settlement in Hindi cinema early on. Films of the 1970s invariably cast those who went abroad in supporting roles or as villains and depicted them as harbingers of the bad ways of the West, a corrupting influence or counter-reference to Indian values. As director Govind Nilhani, reflecting on the change in diasporic characters in an *India Today* interview, put it, 'The camera would start from those new shoes and tilt up, the trousers, the face with the cigarette hanging from the mouth. The foreign-returned had an affected manner, the girl had bobbed hair, a mini skirt. They had lost their Indianness and become alien.'

This image was perhaps best captured, and often quoted in other movies, in Manoj Kumar's version of *Purab Aur Pacchim* ('East and West'; 1970). In this film, Saira Banu plays the wild Western girl, with a blonde wig, who is tamed by the hero, played by Manoj Kumar, and becomes a Hindustani girl.

The 1980s continued this theme of 'the West as bad' amidst angry heroes who were fighting corruption and coming to terms with the social upheavals within India and overseas. In contrast, Bollywood movies of the 1990s represented the NRI as having a cosmopolitan mindset, speaking with an English or American accent, but with his/her heart and soul in the right place, respecting all things Indian. Film plots in the 1990s spanned cities across several continents, with diasporic characters taking centre stage. Film sets and costumes began to illustrate the look and feel of urban centres (openly displaying brand names such as Coca-Cola, Ralph Lauren and Nike) in which the characters could be in middle-class India or the urban diaspora of the West; this created affinities with audiences across the globe.

The Indian diaspora in the US figures prominently in Bollywood movies such as Pardes *(1997) and* Aa Ab Laut Chalen *(1999).*

Bhaji on the Beach *(1993) and* Bride and Prejudice *(2004) were directed by Gurinder Chadha. Born in Kenya and based in London, Chadha's movies are renowned for their engagement and representation of the lives of young Indians in the diaspora.*

Since the late 1990s, the cinema, once generally ridiculed as formulaic and trivial, has found its place on the international map of the cultural and media entertainment industries. The films *Dil Se* ('From the Heart'; directed by Mani Ratnam; 1998) and *Taal* ('Rhythm'; directed by Subhash Ghai; 2000) marked the start of regular top 10 and top 20 appearances on the UK and US box office charts respectively for popular Hindi films. *Lagaan* ('Tax'; directed by Ashutosh Gowariker; 2001) won the Audience Award at the 2001 Locarno Film Festival in Switzerland and was nominated for an Academy Award in 2001 for Best Foreign Film.

In 2002, the fascination with all things Bollywood seeped over into mainstream Western music (Bollywood songs and music remixed with pop and R & B), theatre (Andrew Lloyd Webber's musical *Bombay Dreams* was a West End success, with music by A. R. Rehman), television, fashion and the high-street department stores of the West (Selfridges and H & M's using Bollywood style to sell clothes and merchandise). The multiplexes, such as UCI and Warner cinemas, have also increasingly begun to show Bollywood films. These are predominantly attended by Indians overseas and other South Asians. The international exposure of Bollywood cinema was partly a result of Western cultural and entertainment industries 'discovering' Bollywood and using it primarily to sell goods, and partly to do with the ongoing efforts of Bollywood practitioners working across international borders and seeing their work gain global recognition at long last.

Traditional Bollywood film aesthetics have also been quoted, translated and parodied by diasporic Indian filmmakers. One such artist and film director is Gurinder Chadha, who, since her first feature film *Bhaji on the Beach* (1993), has regularly used Bollywood aesthetics to commentate on the lives of her diasporic characters. In fact, her 2004 film, *Bride and Prejudice*, was a fusion movie that drew heavily on Bollywood, Hollywood and black British film aesthetics in a reworking of the famous Jane Austen novel, *Pride and Prejudice*. The film also stars two popular Bollywood actors in main roles, Aishwarya Rai playing the female lead and Anupam Kher playing her father. Other Indian diasporic film-makers include Deepa Mehta and Mira Nair, based in North America.

With the growing popularity of Bollywood cinema, not least among its traditional overseas Indian audiences, the industry has become a mainstay in the programming of non-terrestrial television channels aimed at diasporic Indians and their South Asian counterparts.

SATELLITE TELEVISION

The increasing deregulation of the international audio and visual spheres since the early 1990s has seen the proliferation of cable, satellite and digital technology multimedia channels that cater to distinct ethnically and culturally grouped audiences across traditional geopolitical frontiers. These channels combine aspects of popular culture, entertainment, news and current affairs in

Meera Syal's best-selling novel, Life Isn't All Ha Ha Hee Hee *(1999), which explores the life of three young Asian women in Britain, was featured as a three-part series on BBC TV in 2005.*

Zee TV has brought ethnic programming to many Indian communities around the world.

pay-per-view packages. One such channel, Zee TV (UK-Europe), is the focus here. Headed by its founder and chief executive, Subhash Chandra, from India, it has a growing global team of employees. The channel simultaneously offers news and entertainment to overseas Indians as a distinct constituency and as part of a wider South Asian social collective.

Zee TV (UK-Europe) broadcasts from its studios in Northolt, Middlesex, in west London. Zee TV in India is much bigger in terms of its audience reach and corporate structure, which comprises its two sister channels Zee Cinema and Zee India. Together, the three channels are corporately known as Zee International. Since 1999, Zee TV has launched a variety of channels under the Zee Alpha label: Alpha Bangla, Alpha Gujarati, Alpha Marathi and Alpha Punjabi. These channels are marketed according to language and region within South Asia.

Zee TV (UK-Europe) is the most popular non-terrestrial channel in the European South Asian diaspora. Its emergence in 1992 and its development since taking over from the TV Asia channel in 1995 can be seen as a response to the historical marginalisation and misrepresentation of European South Asian audiences in mainstream audio and visual spheres. It can also be viewed as providing an outlet for diasporic South Asian audiences to engage with their local and global sense of selfhood.

The mainstream media of the EU states have often been criticised for disseminating and constructing problematic images of black and other ethnic minorities, thereby fuelling ideological images and perceptions of 'Euro-whiteness'. Television programmes on terrestrial channels that are aimed specifically at non-white groups tend to be constructed as 'minority' programming. In Britain, a number of such minority programmes are shown intermittently, in documentary series form and as film and drama imports from South Asia, as part of a season or series of programmes throughout the year. The composition of regular minority television in Britain currently includes BBC2's *Black Britain*, *Network East* and *East*. These programmes are presented as being produced by and for 'minorities', or 'others', and are not part of the mainstream of British broadcast programming and its concomitant identities.

Other programmes over the last five years, such as the BBC's comedy sketch show *Goodness Gracious Me* (2000) and the comedy chat show *The Kumars at No. 42* (2001), Channel 4's television series based on Zadie Smith's novel, *White Teeth* (2002) and BBC TV's three-part adaptation of Meera Syal's novel *Life Isn't All Ha Ha Hee Hee* (2005) have been interesting achievements in British television that have articulated a more complex sense of British cultural identity. However, such programmes have been possible as a result of ongoing struggles by black and South Asian media professionals for access to the means of production for more elaborate non-white representation. While the latter programmes are few and far between, on the whole there still appears to be little space available in the terrestrial British and European

The Internet has made it easier for the diaspora to stay connected to developments in the 'homeland', whether in fashion, entertainment, sports or politics.

broadcasting schedule for programmes which offer non-white British identities—hybrid or diasporic ways of thinking about identity—which can encompass both the British culture within which these audiences exist and the original homelands with which they wish to retain a sense of connectedness. It is in such a context that Zee TV (UK-Europe) appears.

Zee TV's schedule in Europe combines South Asian and Western programme formats. Its programming includes popular South Asian films from Bangladesh, Pakistan, Sri Lanka and Indian regional cinemas, in addition to its main feature films from Bollywood. Aside from film, the Zee TV schedule includes a range of news, current affairs and business programmes, religious, comedy, film review and health shows, and drama serials from India and Pakistan, as well as South Asian sports. The schedule is uniform across Europe, thus offering the possibility of an audio-visual pan-South Asian European identity. The Zee TV (UK-Europe) schedule is available on Zee Text (accessible on television sets throughout Europe, with teletext service provided by the non-terrestrial channels), in the British South Asian popular press in the UK, and some national and local mainstream newspapers throughout Europe. These listings also provide access to the channel's pan-South Asian European broadcasting for its viewers on the continent.

Zee TV (UK-Europe) is now in its 11th year. Since its initial European broadcast, the Zee network has now diversified into six main channels: Zee TV, Zee Music, Zee Cinema, Zee Alpha Punjabi, Zee Gujarati and South Asia World (SAW), which went on air in May 2005. The first three, in particular, continue to broadcast predominantly Hindi-language programming. The Zee Alpha Punjabi channel broadcasts its programmes primarily in Punjabi. This channel is part of the umbrella group of Zee's Alpha regional channels from South Asia. The Zee network is obviously keen to capitalise on the variety of linguistic and cultural traditions within India, the rest of South Asia and its associated diasporas.

Alongside the broadcasting of Zee TV in Europe and more globally (it also broadcasts in the US and Africa), a number of other channels have come and gone since 2000 as part of other media networks. Among those broadcasting in 2005 were: Sony TV (Sony TV Asia), the Bollywood 4 U network (B4U Movies and B4U Music), the Star TV channels (Star TV and Star Plus), ARY Digital, Ekushey TV, PTV Prime, Asian Television Network, Vectone TV (Vectone India, Vectone Urdu, Vectone Tamil), SAB TV, and the South For You channel.

Channels such as Channel East and the Reminiscent Television Network (RTV) had to withdraw their services after being on air for a year or two due to the lack of sustainable viewer subscriptions and competition from other channels. RTV, for example, broadcast a range of channels that were marketed for Bengali- (Bangla TV), Gujarati- (Gurjari), Punjabi- (Lashkara), Tamil- (CEEi TV) and Urdu-speaking (Anjuman) communities in 2001. Additionally, RTV also broadcast Asia 1 TV, which claimed to produce 'entertainment that highlights and creates understanding between Asians from varying religious and cultural backgrounds as a means of bringing together the British Asian population.'

Highlighting this fast-changing media-scape in relation to Zee TV underlines the intense competition between the different channels vying for similar overseas Indian and other diasporic South Asian audiences and advertising revenues. Such competition takes place, moreover, amidst the increasing liberalisation and deregulation of the international audio-visual spheres. What is noteworthy are the advertisements which are aired on these channels. Increasingly, cultural and social service providers (e.g. immigration and criminal law assistance, targeted specifically at non-white ethnic groups) and diasporic South Asian product vendors (e.g. subcontinental foods and stores, and retailers such as jewellers) are to be found advertising their goods. In part, this has to do with the competitive advertising rates offered by non-terrestrial channels, which are much lower than their mainstream counterparts. These channels are also viewed as an appropriate vehicle to relay messages to overseas Indian and other South Asian audiences through consumer service providers.

Non-terrestrial television, such as Zee TV, has managed to fill a niche due to openings caused by the international deregulation of the mass media. It has also attempted to provide overseas Indians with a sense of pride in their identity, while staying connected to other South Asian audience groups as well.

POPULAR MUSIC: BRITISH BHANGRA

The story of bhangra in Britain is of importance as it marks the arrival of Indian folk music in post-war Britain, a form that has developed into the genre that came to be known as 'British bhangra'. This new genre of popular urban music travels and influences bhangra music in other parts of the world. It also informs Punjabi folk bhangra back in India and has been taken up by Bollywood music composers. In turn, it has also been shaped again by these global exchanges. An overview of global bhangra music, therefore, needs to be set in context within select urban centres of the UK, primarily in Birmingham from the late 1990s, as it is in this city and the wider region that the music continues to thrive in a sustained manner.

Consider the following anecdote: glad rags abound, boys looking sharp and girls sharper still; vibrant colours and dress styles coalesce with the best of Western haute couture; a 'live' band plays the Indian drums—the *dhol*, tablas and *dholaks*—alongside a drum kit, keyboards and bass and electric guitars, with a lead singer at the microphone; a DJ throws in 'live' mixes and plays the MC for good measure, chatting in Punjabi and patois over break beats of hip hop, rap and garage; the lyrics of the songs, both from the band and over the DJ's decks, range from love stories to the travails of migration; the DJ sends a shout-out 'To the Birmingham massive!'; the crowd becomes ecstatic and dances with more glee, their bodies moving in ways that are part-South Asian,

This iconic figure of a Sikh wearing the Union Jack flag as a turban is closely associated with British bhangra.

Envy Roma Music is one of several British bhangra recording and distribution companies in Birmingham.

part-Western and more besides. This is a British bhangra night in Birmingham, UK.

The familiarity of scenes just like these justify Birmingham's status as the cultural capital of British bhangra. Over the last 15 years, the city has been home to some of the genre's biggest names: Achanak, Apna Group, B21, Bally Jagpal, DCS, Hard Kaur, Safri Boyz and XLNC. Birmingham houses several recording and distribution companies which have been responsible for the steady production of new albums over the last four decades. Among such companies are the Oriental Star Agency on Moseley Road, Nachural Records in Smethwick, Envy Roma Music in Handsworth and Movie Box Records in Small Heath. This collection of musical talent and expertise, coupled with a vibrant culture of 'live' performances at gigs, private parties and weddings, arguably makes Birmingham the centre of the British bhangra music industry.

In February 2006, the Birmingham Central Library hosted a photographic exhibition documenting the emergence of British bhangra.

> **From Soho Road To The Punjab**
> A Photographic Exhibition Tracing The History Of Birminghams Bhangra Music & Culture.

As a musical form for diasporic Indians and other South Asians in Britain, bhangra dates back to the late 1960s and follows the post-war arrival of migrant workers from the Indian subcontinent and East Africa. Many of them settled in large urban cities such as Birmingham, Bradford, Coventry, Leeds, London and Manchester, and began importing records alongside early Indian film music. One of the most popular genres was bhangra, sung in Punjabi. This traditional folk music is performed on festive occasions as a song and dance and is always accompanied by at least one *dhol* (a large, double-sided cylindrical drum). An *alghoza* (a twin flute) may also accompany the singing and dancing party, which consists mostly of male members. As they dance, the performers take turns singing, with the lyrics generally heroic in tone, often in praise of the motherland. These features fed the nostalgia of first-generation Indians in their new British surroundings, where they could reminisce about their cultures and countries of origin, especially in the context of their grim employment and housing conditions, and their encounters with racism from some sections of white British society.

Indian news, movies and music feature in UK-based newspapers and magazines.

A distinctively British bhangra took shape in the mid-1980s as an emerging second generation of Indian and other South Asian musicians began to experiment and improvise with technology, marking a direct engagement with notions of British and South Asian identity by locating their music in a British Asian framework. For example, the 1988 song *Soho Road Uteh* ('On Soho Road') by the Birmingham band Apna Sangeet (Our Music) was immensely popular for referencing the recognisable. The song tells the tale of two lovers who met in India, became separated and then attempted to find each other through a 'love quest-cum-song as journey'. Among the places travelled are Bradford, Coventry, Derby, London and Soho Road in Handsworth, Birmingham. Soho Road has global resonance with young Indians and other South Asians well beyond Birmingham, and is often deployed in British bhangra tracks. It invokes an easily identifiable social, cultural and political space made and developed by British South Asians, an iconic reference point.

With 'bhangra fever' gripping many South Asian youths across the country by the late 1980s, some bands attempted to cross over into the mainstream. Among these was Birmingham's DCS with their 1989 track *Rule Britannia*. The song was a call for national racial unity: 'We all live under the same sky, the same moon, so let's dance to the same old tune.' Such endeavours were unsuccessful primarily because of the cultural racism encountered by British bhangra artists from the mainstream music industry. Their albums sold in the thousands, mainly through South Asian music retail outlets, yet the returns from these smaller stores were not included or even acknowledged in the make-up of the British pop charts of the time.

Despite these problems, British bhangra remains an urban anthem for many British South Asians and incorporates their cultural politics. For British bhangra artistes and their audiences, the songs and music are as quintessentially British as Balti curries or the Royal Family. As a case in point, the Birmingham-based British bhangra band Achanak (literally translated as 'suddenly', referring to the band's rapid emergence on the British bhangra scene in the late 1980s with their track *Lak Noo Halade*, ('Move That Hip') continually used the word *nach* in all or part of the titles of their albums of the 1990s: Nach*urally*, *P*anach*e*, *Sig*nach*ure*, *S*nach, and *Top* Nach. *Nach* means dance, and the clever play and combination of this Hindi/Punjabi/Urdu meaning with a vernacular British vocabulary illustrates the band's eclectic vision for British popular music and its ensuing identities.

British bhangra no longer suffers from the invisibility of previous decades. The success of Birmingham's Bally Sagoo, who started his music career in the 1980s remixing British bhangra tracks, is fitting testimony to the enduring work of British Indian artistes. Sagoo now heads Ishq Records in Bordesley Green, an inner-city area of Birmingham, signing up-and-coming talent and distributing their work around the world. He encourages his artistes to be innovative and bring together different people to enjoy the music. As he states on his website, 'I am Asian, loud and proud, but I'm also British. I hope to have captured all those influences in our music, for people all around the world to relate to. For me, our music represents bringing different worlds together and uniting them as one.' British bhangra artists Malkit Singh and Balwinder Safri, from Birmingham but originally from Punjab, remain favourites, attracting large audiences and listeners among South Asians worldwide.

Uniquely, British bhangra has come to influence different styles of bhangra music, in North America for example, and even reconnects with traditional folk bhangra in Punjab. The bhangra beat has also been taken up by many Bollywood music composers throughout the 1990s and is featured in countless contemporary Hindi films. The music has also made inroads into mainstream popular culture through the fusion of different styles and aesthetics found in the work of, among others, musician Apache Indian, the Anglo-Asian fusion band Asian Dub Foundation, film-maker Gurinder Chadha, and BBC1 Xtra's Punjabi Hit Squad, who regularly feature and remix British bhangra on their radio show and in their music albums.

One of British bhangra's current trends is the mixture of R & B and garage with bhangra beats and lyrics. Here, a new generation of Indian and other British South Asian singers, dancers and music producers have emerged throughout the country, drawing inspiration from the early pioneering British bhangra artists. The RDB brothers from Yorkshire can be placed alongside the DIP boys, Dalvinder Singh and DJs Koka Krazy, Jet Jagpal, Dr Zeus and the Kray Twins, all from Birmingham.

Radio stations have always been crucial in disseminating Indian and other South Asian music in Britain, a position strengthened by the broadcasting of the BBC's Birmingham-produced Asian Network throughout Britain and beyond, globally via digital radio, satellite television and the Internet. Adil Ray's weeknight 10 pm show on the network, which was available on 1458 MW digital audio radio and online, and the 10 am slot on Saturday hosted by Polly on Birmingham's Radio XL 1296 MW, are examples, as are Radio 1's Bobby Friction and Nihal mid-week show.

Soho Music and Video, Envy and Roma Music Bank, also on Soho Road in Birmingham, provide the latest and back-catalogue British bhangra releases. News and features can be found in the regular South Asian magazines *Snoop* and *Desi*, and the weekly paper *Eastern Eye*. Alum Rock Road, Smethwick High Street and similar streets around South Asian areas of settlement in the region have equivalent stores. In fact, similar shops can be found in streets of diasporic settlement where Indians and other South Asians have relocated and made their homes around the world. It is also important to note that in the 21st century, larger mainstream chains such as HMV and Virgin have begun selling bhangra compilation albums as part of their World Music selections.

'Live' music gigs featuring the best of Birmingham-based and national British bhangra artistes have been held throughout the Indian diaspora. In the UK, 'live' gigs are often held during college and university terms to appeal to the youth. There you will find young British Asians and their friends from Birmingham, Bradford, Leicester, London and elsewhere, revelling in the beats of the drum and the *dhol*.

All this shows that British bhangra is here to stay, with Birmingham undoubtedly its focal point. The city's production and distribution companies continue to circulate the music around the world, and its artistes, old and new, perform locally and globally.

Rajinder Dudrah

Indian fashion in the diaspora

Initially an attempt to maintain traditional dressing abroad, Indian apparel now occupies a significant niche in the global fashion market. An array of Indian garments— the *sherwani* and *jodhpuri* for men, the sari, *salwar-kamiz* or *churidar kurta* and *ghagra-choli* or *lehenga-choli* for women— preserve a rich and colourful heritage. Women's garments are also complemented by accessories such as bangles and *bindis*, and cosmetics.

Indian fashion varies regionally both in dress and style. Women all over India wear the sari, although styles differ according to regions. The simple kurta and dhoti for men is also trans-regional but today the latter is often limited to semi-urban and rural areas. The *salwar-kamiz* or *churidar kurta* for women is more popular in Punjab, while the *ghagra-choli* or *lehenga-choli* is more popular in Rajasthan and Gujarat.

ABOVE: *Mumbai Se features creations by Indian designers.* BELOW: *On festive occasions, the traditional sari remains popular with Indian women in the diaspora.*

Indian fashion abroad had humble beginnings. In the old diaspora, migrant Indians wore their traditional garments as part of daily wear in their respective regional styles. Gujarati women tied their saris in such a way that the *pallu*, the end of the sari, would flow in front, while Madrasi women tied it so that the *pallu* flowed behind their shoulders. For working men, the shedding of traditional clothes became a matter of practicality. And so it was the women who held on longer to wearing traditional clothes.

In the 19th and early 20th centuries, however, it was not uncommon for Indian women to adopt forms of dress worn by local women. For example, photographs of Indian women from this period in Malaya and Singapore show that many had adopted Malay dress. This can be explained in part by the difficulty in getting access to Indian garments and the relatively small size of the diaspora. In areas where Indians made up a larger proportion of the population, Indian dress had a more sustained presence.

Over time, however, Indian dressing in the diaspora began to change. Traditional Indian clothes began to be worn primarily on festive occasions, such as Diwali and weddings. This was particularly the case for later generations, especially young adults, for whom Western casual wear, such as T-shirts and jeans, came to be favoured.

From the late 20th century onwards there has been a revival of interest in Indian fashion in the diaspora. The growth of the diaspora, easier access to Indian garments, the popularity of Bollywood, and the influence of Indian cable and satellite television have all contributed to this. Clothes worn by popular Bollywood celebrities in the latest movies tend to become fashionable, so it is not uncommon for Indian fashion outlets in the diaspora to stock replicas of designs worn by the stars of these movies. By purchasing replicas of clothes featured in a new movie, the diaspora stays in tune with fashion developments in the 'homeland'.

Beyond the diaspora, Indian garments have now become part of mainstream fashion, adopted by Indians and non-Indians alike around the globe. Indian clothes (such as the simple kurta) were popular in the 1960s and 1970s among minority groups in the UK and the US, who were often pejoratively labelled 'hippies'. The popularity of Indian dress among non-Indians, however, has grown considerably since the 1990s, alongside the popularity of traditional Indian cuisine, cosmetic art, spirituality and music. It is quite common now to see non-Indians in cosmopolitan cities wearing outfits comprising kurta tops with jeans, and dresses with pashmina shawls. Donning Indian clothes has also become fashionable with celebrities, such as Madonna and Nicole Kidman, who have been seen in Indian dress and accessories.

With the global popularity of Indian fashion, boutiques that specialise in upmarket Indian clothes have sprung up around the world, particularly where there is a significant Indian diaspora. Mumbai Se, located in the prestigious Palais Renaissance shopping arcade along Singapore's Orchard Road, is one such example that is popular with tourists as well as Indian and non-Indian Singaporeans.

Currently, nearly all of the top fashion moguls, from the renowned French designer Jean-Paul Gaultier to the Japanese designer Issey Miyake, look to Indian fashion for ideas and inspiration. Gaultier, for example, dressed his henna-tattooed models in saffron-coloured saris, while Issey Miyake created his entire collection using Indian fabrics and design. Indian fashion has even become increasingly popular in China, where Indian fashion was presented in Beijing in a 'Made in India Show'. In the past few years, moreover, top Indian designers have been exhibiting in fashion festivals globally. Some have been approached to work for world-renowned fashion houses such as the Paris-based Jean-Louis Scherrer, where Ritu Beri was named chief designer of the ready-to-wear division.

Wajihah Hamid

ABOVE: *Girls in a dance school in India learning bharatanatyam, a dance growing in popularity around the diaspora.*
BELOW LEFT: *Bharatanatyam performances are often organised in the diaspora to support charity efforts in South Asia.*

DANCE IN THE DIASPORA

Indian arts and fine arts in particular are gaining increasing popularity in the diaspora. The classical dance tradition of bharatanatyam, for example, has proven to be a resilient art form. Not only has it survived colonialism and cultural imperialism, it has also managed to thrive in a foreign environment. The vast number of Indian dance institutions and schools that have sprung up in the last few decades bear testimony to the tremendous popularity of this art form among the second, third and subsequent generations of the diaspora in North America, Europe, South Africa, Mauritius and the Asia-Pacific.

Bharatanatyam has become valuable cultural capital for middle-class Indian girls. The rejuvenation and revival of the dance form have to do, in large part, with nationalistic efforts undertaken in India in the 1930s and 1940s as part of the anti-colonial independence movement.

The myths perpetuated then linking bharatanatyam to an idealised 'pure' Indian past have, over the years, gained legitimacy. Fine arts in India were also associated with a profoundly transcendental view of art in Indian philosophy, which considered the material world to be an illusion. This perspective, however, seems to have been adopted by native practitioners as the 'authentic' historical context of the art. Today, many proponents of the art form, as well as connoisseurs, subscribe to this representation of an 'authentic' and untouched Indian cultural heritage.

The notion of learning a sacred art that used to be practised as a form of worship in Hindu temples is one that seems to be attractive to

members of the diaspora in particular, who may feel that engagement with bharatanatyam brings them closer to the more esoteric and spiritual elements of Hindu practice and life. For although bharatanatyam has become rather secularised in its evolution into a theatrical art form, it still retains strong influences from Hinduism. It draws on Hindu mythology and folklore in its depiction of gods and goddesses in many canonical performance pieces.

Classical Indian dance also fulfils a community function by providing Indian migrants with a positive sense of belonging, not only by symbolising a highly cultured heritage to which they can lay claim, but also by providing occasions at which they can meet in an Indian context, where a sense of community and identity can be participated in, constructed and affirmed.

The transnationalism of the practice of bharatanatyam is also apparent in the numbers of musicians and teachers who leave India and Sri Lanka in order to teach or perform abroad. Due to the presence of large Indian diasporas in Asia, Europe and North America, there is a sizable audience outside India who are receptive and eager spectators. The flow, however, is not one way; students as well, make frequent trips to India in order to learn new things, brush up on techniques or perform at dance festivals. Dance practitioners make a conscientious effort to keep abreast of developments in the dance scene in India. The style of costumes, accessories and choreography is still very much influenced by trends there. Dance performances outside the subcontinent are also frequently in aid of charity efforts in the South Asian region for orphanages, the urban poor or disaster relief. There is a continuous dynamic exchange of material as well as ideological products.

With the 'globalisation of ethnicity', wearing, singing and dancing 'Indian' has become fashionable. The widespread popularity of Bollywood and bhangra bears testament to that. Bharatanatyam too is being marketed and moulded in a modern form in order to appeal to younger generations of the Indian diaspora. The structural and semiotic transformations which Indian dance forms are going through could be seen, in part, as a result of this.

Artistes such as Akram Khan, Shobana Jeyasingh and Daksha Seth have attempted to fuse both ideological and structural elements of Indian dance forms, such as bharatanatyam and kathak, with more contemporary elements, drawing from contact improvisation and ballet, for example. This could be seen as a natural result of the growth and successful assimilation of South Asian diasporic communities into the West and as an articulation of new multicultural identities. It is significant that the most eminent choreographers of these hybrid pieces are themselves members of Indian diasporic communities.

The inclusion of Western elements into an Indian dance form, however, has also been critiqued for 'selling out' by trying to free itself from the stereotyped 'ethnic' label and make it more appealing to a mainstream non-Indian public. While hybrid dance performances seek to challenge stereotypical notions of the Indian 'other', the subversive quality of their work is compromised by the need to contain ideas of the 'other' within a dominant Western hegemonic structure. It seems to point to the existing perpetuation of an Orientalist perspective that the 'East' cannot be understood unless spoken for in 'Western' terms. Opponents of this fusion also insist that bharatanatyam should be preserved as a high art form in the interest of maintaining high standards in teaching and performance.

Choreographer Shobana Jeyasingh has merged traditional Indian dance forms with contemporary elements.

The performance and practice of bharatanatyam thus can act as a means through which the diasporic community reinforces its predominant concerns about the preservation of identity and cultural heritage. Its derivative hybrid forms, however, function to challenge entrenched notions of Indianness by transcending ethnic boundaries and creating mutable identities. This simultaneous reaffirmation and disruption of the solidarity based on ethnicity reflects the complex negotiations of Indian diasporic identities.

Laavanya Kathiravelu

Kathakali is another traditional Indian dance form which has grown in stature and recognition beyond the Indian diaspora.

CUISINE

At the beginning of the 21st century, Indian food has come to be widely appreciated in communities around the world, particularly where the Indian diaspora has a significant presence. The global popularity of Indian cuisine is manifest in the growing number of Indian restaurants, the sales of chilled or frozen meals and dishes, and the provision of ingredients for home cooking and consumption. Indian food and its preparation have also been the subject of a wide range of cookbooks and television features, the 'stars' of which, such as Madhur Jaffrey, have become celebrity teachers and interpreters of this subtle and very diverse cuisine. This was not always so.

FOOD IN THE OLD DIASPORA

In the late 18th and early 19th century, the dietary restrictions of high-caste Hindu sepoys on overseas duty were a matter of grave concern for colonial authorities. Lord Cornwallis, in a letter to the commanding officer at Fort Marlborough in 1789, emphasised that it was important 'to lessen and if possible to remove those prejudices which Hindus of every description entertain against going to sea. Due attention to these prejudices will be no less necessary on shore.' In Melaka, Munshi Abdullah, the eminent local writer, observing the dietary habits of Indian sepoys, noted that, 'some of the Hindoos...tied three strands of thread round their bellies and went on eating until the thread broke...There were those who could not eat fish or meat or anything containing blood but only vegetables.'

Unlike the sepoys, indentured labourers did not have such privileges. Their voyage across the *kalapani* was an exceptional and traumatic event that, among other transformations, ushered a change in dietary restrictions and, alongside that, changes in their cuisine. While the most steadfast, high-caste Brahmins may have continued eating dried fruits and nuts for some time (since eating food prepared by a non-Brahmin was taboo), most migrants were dependent on the cooked rations given to them on-board, of which 'salt fish' was an important component.

Indian migrants in the old diaspora carried with them regional foods, although, for indentured labourers faced with very meagre rations, there was little or no chance of cooking anything resembling the complete regional range. The rations given to indentured labourers were dependent upon the type of produce available in the plantation colonies. The lack of accessibility to some ingredients and easier access to certain 'new' ingredients reshaped Indian cuisine in the diaspora.

The typical ration of an Indian indentured worker in Trinidad in the 1860s comprised rice, ground maize, yam, vegetables, salted fish and meat, and coconut oil. Unlike in the homeland, where for many the consumption of meat and fish was either limited to special occasions or completely taboo, the accessibility of these items ensured a wider influence on their cuisine. In addition, the indentured worker could acquire from the market limited ingredients such as flour for *roti* or *chappati*, but these usually would not be of the same variety of flour found in India. Thus, at best, the migrants could hang on to some basic dishes and, to an extent, these dishes would become the basis of 'Indian food' as understood by the people of the host society.

In the context of Guyana, Vijay Mishra highlights *baigan-chokey* (roasted aubergine mixed with onions and condiments) and *dhal-puri* as standard 'indenture cuisine'.

Kumar Mahabir, in *Caribbean East Indian Recipes*, provides directions for the preparation of *paratha roti*, known in Trinidad as 'buss-up shut' because of its resemblance to a 'busted-up shirt'. He says this dish was widely available and eaten 'by Indian and non-Indian alike'. In a similar way, Madhur Jaffrey, in *Ultimate Curry Bible*, discusses how colonial Durban Africans could illegally buy Indian curry from small Gujarati-owned eateries, which they then christened 'Bunny (Bania) Chow'.

In the Straits Settlements (Penang, Melaka and Singapore), South Indians, who formed the majority of Indian migrants there, were better placed to maintain a more extensive regional range. These areas were, after all, in the heart of the 'spice islands' and thus, many of the raw ingredients and spices necessary for the preparation of South Indian cuisine were more readily available. Indian stalls and eateries were also more common with the development of Little India in Singapore. *Dosa* and *idli*, and the South Indian meal served on banana leaves were introduced quite early in this part of the world.

Despite the meagre rations, the availability of new ingredients and the interaction of migrant and local groups in the colonies provided a creative spur to the development of Indian cuisine. While 'fusion' cooking has often been used as a modern label for mixed cuisines, such hybridisation occurred early on in the plantation colonies and the Straits Settlements. Notable is the so-called 'Indian' *mee goreng* (fried noodles) in Malaysia, Singapore and Indonesia. *Mee goreng* is made from a variety of Indian, Chinese and Malay ingredients: noodles are fried with fresh tomatoes, potatoes, eggs, onions, cabbage, *belachan* (fermented shrimp paste) and canned green peas with a sprinkling of minced mutton. Similarly the 'Indian' *rojak*, literally and suitably translated as 'mixture', comprises boiled potatoes, fried dough, prawn fritters and hard-boiled eggs, served with a thick, spicy, peanut sauce. While it is unclear when the first *mee goreng* or *rojak*

Spices, essential ingredients in Indian cuisine.

The meals served during the long voyage across the kalapani *hinted at the changed diets migrants would encounter in their new homes.*

109

Mee goreng *(left) and* rojak *(right), two dishes with mixed culinary influences, which are popular in Malaysia, Singapore and Indonesia.*

were created, both dishes were common fare in the region by the mid-20th century.

Overall, however, before the mid-20th century, Indian cuisine in the diaspora had only tangential contact with, and influence on, the cuisine of the wider Empire and the host societies receiving Indian migrant labourers. This would change considerably over the second half of the 20th century.

CHANGE

While the foods and preparations which travelled to the plantation colonies moved naturally into the range of working-class ethnic cuisines, in the UK and white settler colonies of the Empire there were no signs of Indian cuisine being available or wanted. The first Indian restaurant to have an impact in Britain—but only at the elite level—was the posh Veeraswamy's in London's Regent Street in 1926. In 1948, at the end of Empire in South Asia, there were still only six Indian restaurants in the UK. This was also the case in the wider Commonwealth. Perth, the capital city of provincial Western Australia, had an Indian community from the 1890s but it did not have an Indian restaurant until the Dean family, who by then regarded themselves as 'Friends of Pakistan', opened The Khyber in the mid-1960s.

Home-cooked Indian food in these parts of the Empire was also very limited and, where it occurred, was often quite unauthentic. 'Curry powder' was a strange Anglicised version of the masala or spice mixture which it claimed to be. Moreover, despite some circulation of recipes and discussion of culinary techniques, the 'Indian' foods produced—kedgeree for *kichri* and English-style 'curry', which were often a vehicle for leftovers—were far from authentic.

CATALYST FOR CHANGE

The acceptance of Indian food in the UK, the settler colonies and other regions began with the arrival of growing numbers of Indian emigrants to these countries after World War II and the Partition. This produced changes which proved to be significant for Indian food and cooking, and the development of entrepreneurship within the Indian (and other South Asian) diasporic communities. The period also saw an increasing number of students

Veeraswamy's was founded in London in 1926.

Table 6.2

'INDIAN' RESTAURANTS IN UK, LONDON AND LEICESTER CITY (1950–2003)						
	1950	1960	1970	1980	1990	2000
UK	6	800	1200	3000	N.A.	8000
London	3	N.A.	N.A.	N.A.	N.A.	2000
Leicester	N.A.	N.A.	4	19	N.A.	80

Source: Panikos Panayi, 'The Spicing Up of English Provincial Life: The History of Curry in Leicester', in Anne Kersher (ed.), Food in the Migrant Experience, *2002.*

studying in Commonwealth, and especially British, universities; and there were many more officials in South Asian diplomatic missions and commercial establishments as well. Migration from the subcontinent was further reinforced in the 1970s by the coming of Indians forced out of East Africa.

Together, these factors resulted in the growth of communities from the subcontinent looking for Indian culinary provisions, utensils and prepared foods and meals. The emergence of such a market was an incentive for Indians to open shops or stalls to provide these goods and to establish restaurants and specialist shops for Indian sweets and takeaway foods such as samosas. Often, these were the most immediate areas in which migrants could make a start in business and manufacturing. The response of enterprising Indians and Pakistanis was evident from the 1960s onwards in the UK.

Opportunities also arose as the removal on restrictions on Indian migration to Australia, Canada and New Zealand in the 1960s began to take effect, and similar communities, often of professionals, began to form in other parts of the Commonwealth.

In the UK (not just in London), these developments had a second effect. The increasing availability of Indian foodstuff, preparations and eating places began to attract adventurous customers from the local population. This could be linked to both 'Raj nostalgia' and an interest in trying more exotic foods, or, as it has been argued, to escaping dreary English food! Whatever the reason, from the 1960s onwards there was an expansion in the number of restaurants, food preparation companies and the retailing of prepared food and cooking aids at the national and local levels in urban Britain.

The city of Leicester—which is said to be the second most densely 'curry-housed' city in Britain after Bradford—provides a good case study of the expansion of Indian restaurants after 1960. Leicester's Indian population grew from less than a thousand in 1951 to over 20,000 in 1971 and to 62,665 in 1983. However, it was not simply this growth in population which accounted for the increase in the number of Indian food outlets: 75 per cent of the clientele in Indian restaurants there were 'adventurous' English diners. Moreover, the increasing interest in Indian food was apparent in more than just restaurant clientele, it was also apparent in takeaways, groceries and greengroceries, and in the provision of Indian preparations and meals in supermarkets. The restaurants did increase in number in all areas of the city, including the Belgrave and Highfields areas, where many Indians lived, but there was growth in other areas as well.

Another important feature of the expansion was that over time, ownership of 'Indian' eating houses was more and more in the hands of Pakistanis and Bangladeshis, particularly the Sylhetis from Bangladesh. By the turn of the 21st century, 90 per cent of restaurants were said to be run by Sylhetis. Generally, however, these owners

have maintained the 'Indian' title, believing this is the well-accepted 'brand' name for the food served.

What also emerged from the expansion after 1960 was the formation of different sectors within the Indian food scene. The large expansion took place in what were curry houses. Beyond the curry house, however, there was also growth in upmarket restaurants in the big cities. These were extensions, in effect, of the earliest elite restaurants, like Veeraswamy's, which developed in the 1920s and 1930s. They placed a premium on both the setting and the type of cuisine served, and they had names to match their aspirations—Red Fort, Bombay Brasserie, Chutney Mary's, Viceroy of India and the like. A large number of these restaurants were in London, but increasingly in all the major cities—Edinburgh, Birmingham, Bradford and Coventry. In part, of course, this upmarket development drew on 'Raj nostalgia'. Pat Chapman's Curry Club and his cookbooks, with titles like *A Taste of the Raj*, appealed to the former connections and to those earlier 19th-century attempts to capture the flavours of Indian food (if somewhat more authentically this time around). An indication of the strength of this growth at the elite end was perhaps the appearance of the new Veeraswamy's in 1997.

The emergence of new elite restaurants was not the only change; another development took place, this time in British pubs, which began serving Indian food as part of pub fare and not merely as side dishes. Some pubs actually began to offer Indian food as their speciality.

In the US, the story was not as dramatic as in Britain. In part, this may have been because of a very competitive 'ethnic' food market in which Chinese, Italian and Mexican, in addition to French and Japanese cuisines, were extremely well-established by the time the Indian presence began to increase in the latter half of the 20th century. It was certainly not that Indian cuisine was absent, it was simply not as visible as other ethnic cuisines. What did become important were Indian grocery stores where, as one Bay Area owner explained to Purnima Mankekar, Indian expatriates came for 'Shopping India'.

INDIAN FOOD ENTREPRENEURSHIP IN THE UK

Many of the Indian food enterprises in the UK began as 'cottage' industries in the domestic kitchen, catering to stalls or small shops selling takeaway and/or sweets. In *Curry in the Crown*, Shrabani Basu describes the beginnings of these moves in Drummond Street near Euston Station in central London. Sweets were the first items to attract attention, and the two pioneering families were Jagdish Gupta from Bihar, who was linked to a well-known sweet shop in Calcutta, and Jayant Shah, who came as a migrant from Bombay but by way of transfer through Europe.

The Pathaks, who came to London in the mid-1950s from Kenya, where they had earlier migrated from Gujarat, began in similar fashion selling samosas and sweets before opening a shop in Drummond Street to sell fresh vegetables and ingredients for cooking. These early entrepreneurs were all expanding skills which they had developed in India and, in the Pathaks' case, had already deployed in a migrant setting in East Africa.

Somewhat later came G. K. Noon, who had gained business experience in Bombay, firstly in sweets at the Royal Sweet Shop, then in paper products and later in construction. He was quite successful in these ventures but was determined to enter the emerging market in London in the 1960s. This he did in Southall, where he began with a new Royal Sweet Shop.

There was another point of entry which was used by some migrant food entrepreneurs: they became the producers of or advisers on Indian food lines within shopping chains such as Marks and Spencers, which were serving food in their cafeterias and also selling their products to customers for home consumption. Several important moves were made in this way which had the dual effect of increasing the entrepreneurial pool and increasing the acceptability of Indian dishes.

Once established, these enterprises moved into the production of ingredients to assist in the preparation of dishes—not only the vegetables and condiments required but also powders and pastes for more authentic masala. Initially, these mixes were often sold by the producers. For a wider marketing reach, however, the producers needed to link up with retail outlets and distribution firms. The Pathaks, now using 'Patak's' as their brand name, were among the first to do this and to realise that they needed more factory space in which to produce their increasingly popular products.

A third stage was the production of chilled or frozen dishes, and even complete Indian meals, for consumption at home. This change came with the opening of supermarkets and their need for a much greater volume of production. The Pathaks and G. K. Noon made this move and they were joined by other new firms, one of the most successful of which was S & A, built up by Parween Warsi, the wife of a migrant doctor, who started production at home but took advantage of the new demands that came with the supermarket trade and the growing acceptance of Indian food.

Moreover, the development of major production facilities enabled entrepreneurs in the UK to gain strong positions in the export of Indian food mixes, dishes and meals to markets in Europe and further afield. Basu

The Pathaks have been highly successful in supplying Indian mixes to an increasingly cosmopolitan clientele.

Shrabani Basu's Curry in the Crown *traces the history of Indian food in the UK.*

G. K. Noon (right), one of the most successful Indian food entrepreneurs in the UK, with Prince Charles (left).

records Noon as having a substantial export trade with France, Germany, Switzerland and Italy, and S & A as being very active in France, Belgium and Holland. In the late 1990s, Patak's was exported to 52 other countries and it was estimated that 75 per cent of Indian food products sold in Australia were made by Patak's.

THE PLEASURE OF COOKING 'INDIAN'

In 'How to Make a National Cuisine in India: Cookbooks in Contemporary India', Arjun Appadurai shows how the 1960s saw moves in India aiming to define a distinctively 'Indian' cuisine. This was a novel move because despite the fact that there was significant preoccupation with food in India, there had never been a single national standard in the subcontinent. Rather, India had many strong regional and ethnic cuisines that were quite separate in style, technique and repertoire. Appadurai makes the point that in modern times 'Mughalai'-style cuisine gained a superficial reputation, in North Indian circles at least, as a certain standard for Indian food of that region, while 'colonial' practice also gave 'Indian' cuisine some notional form for outsiders. However, there was no authentic Indian style which subsumed the cuisines of different regions and ethnic groups.

The move towards a national cuisine in the 1960s was aimed at meeting the needs of the middle class. Many middle-class Indian women were confronted with a new situation in which public and shared dining began to be part of middle-class life. The process of constructing an Indian national cuisine was based on the publication of a wide range of cookbooks which gave recipes and directions for 'Indian cooking'. Many different formulas were tried: some combined regional and ethnic cuisines, and sometimes elevated the particular to 'national' status; some were wholly Indian in inspiration, while others were a fusion of different styles; some stressed 'modern' ideas with regard to nutrition and preparation; and others centred on particular ingredients or spices. In this process, some sense of 'Indian cuisine' began to appear for those who needed it. However, 'national cuisine' was never able to submerge the importance of regional cuisines. Rather, it developed by absorbing in different ways regional and ethnic cuisines and their culinary styles. In doing so, those styles were not displaced, but the fusion could be seen as 'Indian cuisine'.

This process was not only important in India, it was also important in the diaspora. In fact, authors of cookbooks often had diasporic backgrounds, where the sense of exile and the loss of the familiar was deeply felt. There was also a need for the display of culinary skills in the diaspora and a need, therefore, to remember, learn and practise cooking the food and the 'menus' of the homeland.

One remembers the Punjabi mother in Gurinder Chadha's *Bend It Like Beckham*, whose major worry was that she would not be able to teach her soccer-playing daughter how to prepare a 'full Punjabi meal—vegetarian and non-vegetarian!'

Contributing to the idea of Indian cooking from the diaspora is Madhur Jaffrey. Born into a well-to-do Delhi family, Jaffrey trained as an actress at London's Royal Academy of Dramatic Art and starred in a number of major Merchant Ivory films about colonial India. She has contributed greatly to the literature on Indian cuisine from the diaspora, moving freely as she does between the US and England and travelling very widely in Asia. Her first book, *An Invitation to Indian Cooking* (1973), was linked to an American television series which she presented. In 1982, she worked on a BBC television series on Indian cooking, the content of which was then published in a volume entitled *Madhur Jaffrey's Indian Cooking* (1983). *A Taste of India*, aptly subtitled *The Definitive Guide to Regional Cooking*, appeared in 1985. Her works are divided between those exclusively on Indian cuisine and some more comparative volumes such as *Madhur Jaffrey's World Vegetarian* (1999) and *Madhur Jaffrey's Ultimate Curry Bible* (2003). However, India, her experience of India and her ability to talk to the expatriate about India and Indian food is always present.

Parama Roy sums up her importance as follows:

> The fact that such a narrative as the one Jaffrey advances [in A Taste of India] resonates for a certain class-marked expatriate South Asian subject in the First World as well as for a more mainstream if upscale and culturally savvy, audience of non-South Asian Americans and Britons speaks volumes about the way in which these constituencies are articulated...and how both are—though with different degrees and varieties of affect—invested in The Wonder That Was India. How is it that Jaffrey's limpid prose and impeccable recipes can signify familiarity and comfort and exoticism and adventure as part of the same operation? A significant, if unquantifiable, proportion of the pleasure elicited by the star figure might be attributed, I think, to the specific trajectory of her diasporic voyaging.

This appeal to both Indian and non-Indian readers points to the wider significance of the cookbook-led movement for a national cuisine. The construction of a modern national 'Indian' cuisine by way of the cookbooks had one other effect: the production of these cookbooks paralleled the spread of Indian food through restaurants, food preparations and meals. The fact is that the popularity of Indian food, triggered as it was by the presence of larger Indian migrant populations, nonetheless depended on 'adventurous' diners from the local host society and 'adventurous' cooks looking to produce their own versions of 'Indian' dishes.

Peter Reeves

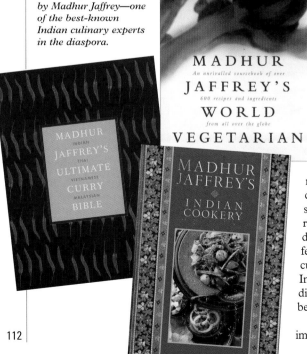

Patak's extensive range includes curry pastes, chutneys and snacks such as pappadums.

Three important works by Madhur Jaffrey—one of the best-known Indian culinary experts in the diaspora.

SPORT AROUND THE INDIAN DIASPORA

Sport follows various cultures to new locations, such as those which were opened up throughout the British Empire. The Indian diaspora, though, displayed a curious twist: games which followed the migrants to their new locations were essentially Anglo-Scot ones transported first to India, with traditional games and athletic activities (such as *kabaddi*) largely being revived much later. That pattern was driven by two conditions: the timing of migration from India and the cultural symbolism built into those British games within India. The precise forms which British sports displayed reflected those taken up predominantly in the 'home' location (such as the inexorable link between Sikhs and hockey). In understanding sports in the diaspora, it is useful to consider first what happened in India.

SPORTS IN COLONIAL INDIA

The timing of British rule in India after 1857 was important in positioning British games as a powerful symbolic force within the subcontinent. Later 19th-century British sports and games were invested with great 'civilising' significance, especially among males: cricket, rugby, golf, tennis, hockey and others sports were considered a means of training in life skills such as self-discipline, teamwork, obedience to rules both written and unwritten (the latter being a 'moral code'), consideration for others, and sportsmanship. (As these were regarded as necessary male traits, women faced a difficult challenge in taking up sports, and that pattern continued in the diaspora, as demonstrated in Gurinder Chadha's *Bend It Like Beckham*.) Wherever they went, the British took these games and the associated sense of the 'civilising mission'. In most colonies, the British attached great importance to the local communities they believed had taken up these games or codes most successfully and, conversely, attached less importance to those that did not. Within India, communities faced the difficult choice of whether or not to take up such games because, on the one hand, it might give them access to British lifestyles but, alternatively, cause them to abandon traditional practices and undercut their own culture. Those traditional forms included games such as *kabaddi* (in its many forms), wrestling and other forms of physical activity relating to hunting and warfare.

The Bengali story is instructive. During the late 19th century, a strong physical culture movement emerged to 'inform' the British that the 'effete Bengali' was a myth.

That movement failed but was replaced by two passions: football and cricket. In 1911, for example, the Mohun Bagan victory over the East York Regiment football team in the Indian Football Association's competition final was interpreted widely as a sign that Bengalis were the cultural and physical equals of the British. So powerful was sport's extended symbolism that Bengali art and literary triumphs, for example, stood for little against a football match. The forms of these games and their symbolic power extended far beyond the major city boundaries throughout India (cricket in South India, for example, was played well outside Madras limits by the turn of the 20th century), and this was important in creating the diaspora's sporting shape.

SPORTS AND INDENTURE

Where indentured labour was the primary reason for Indian migration, sport was used to initiate class/colour inequality. An interesting dichotomy lurked here: sport was to teach 'civilised' behaviours, yet its colonial organisation discriminated socially against the very groups supposedly being 'civilised'. This was complicated further by Indian labour—which was used to replace lost slave labour in the Caribbean—arriving in many locations just as organised sport was being instituted. The result was that they shared the discrimination with local black populations and ended up with two discriminations to combat rather than one.

SOUTH AFRICA

In 2004, the selection of Hashim Amla for the South African cricket team was a major milestone for the 'new' South Africa. Amla is the grandson of indentured labourers from Surat, and his long beard proclaimed his commitment to Islam, thus making his selection even more significant. He made his Kwazulu-Natal debut at the age of 18 and soon became a high-scoring batsman. Along with several other Indian players now appearing for Kwazulu-Natal, Amla's presence marked an important turnaround for the Indian sporting community there, which has struggled to make its presence felt, first during apartheid and then within the new South Africa, where the focus has been upon elevating 'African' players.

Throughout the apartheid era, Indian sport was contained within its own community, which stunted forms of development and interaction. Football, hockey, cricket

This image from The Illustrated London News, *1924, shows polo being played in the streets of Kashmir.*

Maharaja Ranjitsinhji made his debut for Sussex in 1895.

Kabaddi, *a popular village team sport which combines elements of wrestling with a 'tagging' contest, is usually played on a village field.*

Sewsunker 'Papwa' Sewgolum won the Natal Open golf championship in 1963.

E. S. Reddy, the former director of the United Nations Centre Against Apartheid.

The Kenya Kongoni cricket eleven shows that Punjabis were strongly represented in colonial cricket in Kenya.

and other sports struggled on with little recognition or support, some successes proving the injustice of the circumstances rather than any triumphal breakthrough. Predictably then, Indians figured prominently in the sports-based struggle against apartheid, especially after 1963, when Sewsunker 'Papwa' Sewgolum (whose main occupation in South Africa was as a caddy despite already having won the Dutch Open) won the Natal Open golf championship but was not allowed to receive his trophy inside the clubhouse. Instead, he stood outside in heavy rain. Although the incident was a catalyst, other sportsmen, including footballer George Singh, had already gained prominence with events such as the 1946–48 Indian passive resistance campaign. From 1963 onwards, Sam Ramasamy and others from the Indian community became prominent leaders against apartheid and creators of non-racial sporting organisations.

As E. S. Reddy (former director of the United Nations Centre Against Apartheid) pointed out, the international Indian diaspora network was at the heart of the anti-apartheid struggle. In 1963, Abdul Samad Minty of the British Anti-Apartheid Movement lobbied the International Olympic Committee on behalf of the South African non-racial sports movement. India itself took up the matter at governmental levels. These efforts were continued by people such as Jasmat Dhiraj and Bobby Naidoo in London, Hanif Bhamjee in Wales and Kader Ismail in Ireland. This was a clear demonstration of how powerful the diaspora might be in relation to important transnational matters involving Indians, irrespective of their location. In many respects, history determined that they had to be powerful.

KENYA

As in other Afro-Asian locations, the early days of Kenyan cricket, for example, were white-dominated. It was 1921 before the Asians Sports Association was formed and Asian cricket teams were created. In 1933, the first Europeans vs Asians match was played, and that fixture remained until 1966, when the first Asian exodus, mainly

to the UK, was under way. Jasmer Singh Grewal saw Kenyan cricket dominated by Indians—he was a good player but made his mark as an administrator and manager, becoming general manager of the Kenya Cricket Association.

Hockey started early among the Indians, and Kenya entered the Olympics first in 1956, becoming known as the '2nd Indian XI'. Indians dominated the game. Hardial Singh Kular came from Sansarpur village, near Jalandhar, an area famous for producing hockey players—at the 1968 Olympics there were eight players for different teams who came from there—and wooden hockey sticks, production of which it dominated. (A team bearing the Jalandhar name would win the first Indian national league title in 2005.) Kular went to Kenya and became a key figure in the Sikh Union Hockey Club, starting as a player and becoming the national president and head of the African Hockey Federation before he took on the vice-presidency of the Federation Internationale de Hockey (FIH).

Kenya was clearly stratified racially and the different Indian communities were clustered in specific occupations: the Punjabis were on the railways and in transport generally; and the Goans were clerks and civil servants. Such communal differences stuck and were reified through sports. One former customs official who had been transferred from India was reprimanded by his superiors for having played doubles tennis with an obviously Anglo-Indian (in colonial eyes, neither European nor Indian) friend who was a medical practitioner, despite the fact that the two had been at school together in England. The Sikhs and the Goans dominated hockey and their contests were fierce, frequently producing brawls involving spectators from the respective communities, indicating that sport among Indian communities was not automatically a unifying force—in some locations it was a clear divider, an ironic situation since Indians themselves were discriminated against.

MALAYSIA AND SINGAPORE

In Malaya, the story had a further twist. Labour was needed for the rubber plantations and, more specifically, for the development of the Malayan railway system (in Kenya the Sikhs had been prominent engineers and operatives on the railways too). There were two main sources of labour: Punjab and the Tamil-speaking south, but many of the southerners were, in fact, Sri Lankan Tamils. Although Indians from both communities were found throughout peninsular Malaya (and Singapore), they were concentrated mainly in centres like Kuala Lumpur, Ipoh and Penang, all of which had close connections with both major industries. Again, the main sports played within those communities were cricket, football and hockey, with golf becoming prominent later. The incongruous sight of a marvellous cricket ground in Ipoh is explained simply: Ipoh was a major centre for the railway network.

The Penang Cricket Club was in existence by 1863 and, in line with imperial practice, was mainly for Europeans, with the Recreation Club created for Eurasians. (The Indian Eurasian or Anglo-Indian diaspora is an important aspect of the story, as demonstrated in the Kenyan case. Many from these communities served in government departments throughout Africa and Asia,

and were instrumental in the development of many sports, notably hockey.) Among the leading figures in Penang was a Sri Lankan Tamil, M. (Sara) Saravanamuttu, an Oxford-educated journalist who became a leading cricket advocate in the local community. For many years, as in India, there was a competition between the communities—Indians, Sri Lankans, Chinese, Malays, Eurasians and Europeans. These matches continued until the racial riots of 1969, after which they were abolished. At club level, the Indian Association was a major force (throughout the 1950s and 1960s it had a strong mix of Tamils and Punjabis). Indians were constantly among cricket's administrative leaders.

Hockey is now a national game in Malaysia and the annual Sultan Azlan Shah tournament for the world's leading nations is a prominent international event. In 2003, India withdrew from the tournament in protest against Malaysian immigration authorities rounding up and deporting Indian IT professionals.

Malaysia and Singapore demonstrate another curious sports pattern. The modern form of badminton had its origins in India, and its organised rules were drawn up in late 19th-century England. It was a popular game that travelled with Indian migrants to new places, but was adopted quickly by Chinese migrant communities particularly, and they continue to dominate the game.

THE CARIBBEAN

In the Caribbean, Indians took to cricket early but faced considerable difficulties in gaining selection into colony or island sides as well as into the 'West Indian' team. It was 1950 before an Indian, the marvellous Sonny Ramadhin of Trinidad, was selected for the West Indies in test cricket. Yet, indentured labour migration to that island began as early as 1838, and by the turn of the 20th century, Indians dominated the population. Not surprisingly, Indian-based teams in Trinidad and Guyana existed from the late 19th century onwards, and in Guyana there were tournaments solely for Indian teams. Indian players thus faced a double jeopardy there over many years: they were segregated by the white elite, but the black population was also suspicious and so, towards the end of the colonial and into the early post-colonial period, even high-quality

players struggled to gain selection. That gave Ramadhin's selection even greater importance. His outstanding success in the West Indies' series win over England in England in 1950 was hugely significant because it showed that Indian players could not only be selected but could also be dominant.

Bowler Ramadhin was followed by the brilliant batsmen Rohan Kanhai and Alvin Kallicharan. Kanhai was born in 1935 in British Guiana's plantation country, his grandparents having arrived from Uttar Pradesh late in the 19th century. The inter-war years during which he was born saw Indians moving out of pure plantation work and into smallhold farming and trading. Kanhai was 14 when an Indian labour strike was put down by armed force, and so he witnessed the hard social and political struggles of his people.

One consequence of the agitation was an improvement of social conditions on the estates, including the establishment of excellent cricket grounds and the provision of coaches, the most famous of whom was Sir Clyde Walcott. A reorganisation of Guyanese cricket allowed 'country' players like Kanhai to shine from 1954 onwards. By 1956, Kanhai was playing for British Guiana, beginning an illustrious international career.

Fifty years on, Indians figure prominently in the West Indian side with players like Shivnarine Chanderpaul (a former captain) and Ramnaresh Sarwan (the team's former vice-captain) being world-class batsmen. Sarwan, in particular, believes cricket has made it possible for Indians to play an equal role in Guyanese life, even though the economic and political framework has been problematic. He was criticised for missing an 'Indians only' match organised by the Guyana Indian Heritage Association, suggesting that the facts of his birth continue to be extremely important to many people in Guyana. Although he missed the game because he was on holiday, Sarwan stated openly that cricket should not be used to divide the Guyanese. Between Kanhai and Sarwan came people like Inshan Ali, a marvellously talented player who, for many reasons (including his ethnic origins), probably played fewer games for the West Indies than he might have done had he arrived later.

NEW ZEALAND

In 1965–66, Narotam (Tom) Puna played three test matches for New Zealand. Like many others in the small New Zealand Indian population, he was born in Surat and travelled to New Zealand with his parents. Gujaratis had begun moving to New Zealand in the late 19th century and by 1920 there were about 2000 of them working mainly in market gardens and horticulture around

Rohan Kanhai (right) was an outstanding batsman for both Guyana and the West Indies.

The Sultan Azlan Shah Cup, an international hockey tournament, has been held in Malaysia for over a decade.

Shivnarine Chanderpaul, a fluent batsman and former captain of the West Indies.

Central Districts coach Dipak Patel (right) being congratulated after his side's victory over Canterbury in the Shell Cup final, 2001.

Auckland, where they faced considerable discrimination. After World War II, their numbers increased slowly, rising now to over 60,000. Among the new arrivals were Sikhs. Indo-Fijians became prominent after the coups in Fiji. Among other things, a strong cricket community emerged. Puna played for the Northern Districts side (mainly as a spin bowler) and was followed later by his sons, Ashok and Kirti. In 1966, though his test career was short, he was recognised as the 'Player of the Year', a landmark in a society then singularly white and conservative.

Many years later, Dipak Patel became a regular player for the New Zealand side too, but his story was more complex. He was born in Kenya in 1958 and reached England in 1968 as part of the early Indian exodus from that country. He played county cricket there, was a fringe player at national level, moved to New Zealand for personal reasons, fulfilled the necessary residential qualification requirements and became a prominent, if controversial, player. Among other things, he became the first spinner to open the bowling in a one-day international, at a time when the tactics of the game were still being formulated. Patel personified how varied the diaspora experience could be.

HONG KONG

As a British enclave from the moment of its annexation until its return to China in 1997, sport has always been a social staple for Indians in Hong Kong who worked in the service industry and the commercial sector, and more recently as professionals. The Hong Kong Cricket Club was formed in 1851, and in 1897 the Hong Kong Parsee Cricket Club was founded, followed in 1918 by the Indian Recreation Club (again showing how important

communal delineation was in all aspects of colonial social life). The creation of the Parsi club was particularly interesting because through the later years of the 19th century in India, Parsis were active in Bombay's cricket scene and they were just as instrumental in extending it to Hong Kong and elsewhere.

Hockey took longer to become established; the Hong Kong Hockey Association was created in 1933. The great Dhyan Chand recalled visiting Hong Kong on a world tour in the 1930s and noting large numbers of Sikhs in the police force supporting hockey. By the 1970s, Nav Bharat was the leading player, with Shaheen taking over from the 1980s. High-level international teams began visiting Hong Kong from the 1950s onwards, and in 1958 goalkeeper Slawee Kadir was the outstanding player in a loss to Pakistan.

CANADA

Canada reveals different patterns, with Sikhs being particularly prominent from the late 19th century. Manga S. Jagpal, for example, arrived in British Columbia in 1930 and became a gardener. Three years later, his employers placed him at the Jericho Golf and Country Club on Vancouver Island, where several Sikhs were employed and of whom he became the foreman in due course. Sport, in this sense, presented an economic opportunity in an environment not automatically welcoming, and Jagpal capitalised on this and purchased several farms. Half a century later, Kuldip Rai Sahi, said to be Canada's richest Indian, is also known as 'the king of golf' because he owns over 30 courses. In many places, golf has been used as a sign of Indian communities having 'made it', since the sport is regarded widely in socio-economic terms as an upper-level sport. That trend has been reinforced by Indo-Fijian Vijay Singh, whose enormous professional success has made him one of the world's top players. Singh struggled his way out of the Nadi caddy ranks following an introduction to golf by his aircraft technician father. In a country where political parity has been undercut severely, that social success has had significant resonance.

Andrew Singh Kooner represents the adaptive quality as well. He was born in Britain but arrived in Canada at three years of age and later became a boxer, winning the silver medal in his division at the 2002 Commonwealth Games. He reached the second round at the 2000 Sydney Olympics but lost to the eventual gold medallist. This Punjabi-speaker is open about representing his community as well as Canada, and carries a picture of Guru Nanak with him in every fight.

Yet more evidence of adaptation comes from the Punjab United lacrosse team. Some Punjabi boys growing up in Victoria on Vancouver Island in the 1950s discovered lacrosse, and a white neighbour put them on a team with some white boys. This was about the time when Canada had restrictive practices preventing Indians from full entry into social life. The team won a junior tournament in 1958 and became a sensation. A few years later, Nirmal and Ranj Dillon were in a team that travelled to Ontario to play off for a national title and suffered considerable abuse from spectators and curiosity from writers. They were later admitted to the Lacrosse Hall of Fame. Nirmal still coaches and has introduced other Indian boys to the game.

Sport in the diaspora has inevitably adopted a political hue in some places, including Canada. Daniel 'Toofan Singh' Igali won a gold for Canada in wrestling at the 2000 Olympics, but the Nigerian-born sportsman was best known as an innovative *kabaddi* player. Igali represented Nigeria in the 1994 Commonwealth Games, moved to Canada, and became interested in *kabaddi* while continuing his wrestling career. He was so important that the Toronto clubs for which he played flew him over from Vancouver on weekends to ensure his participation. When he was selected by the ruling Liberal Party in British Columbia to run for the 2005 provincial elections, it was seen as a clear bid for Indo-Canadian votes in the face of other Indo-Canadian candidates, even though he himself was not Indo-Canadian.

AUSTRALIA

Similar patterns appeared in Australia, with Indian associations using sport to mobilise the community and create links with other sections of society. The Sikhs now have an annual national competition involving several sports. This originated in the 1980s, when Sikh communities in South Australia met at hockey, leading to interstate fixtures and broadening to include other sports. By 2005 it was a three-day annual event held in different parts of Australia. The 2001 games also incorporated the World Cup of *kabaddi*, drawing teams from India, Canada, Pakistan, the US and UK, New Zealand and Australia (showing, incidentally, the late resurgence of that traditional sport in the diaspora). The Victorian Sikh Association is centred on sport; indeed, it began in 1988 as the Sikh Sports Association and broadened from there to include a wider cultural role. The association has teams playing regularly in state hockey competitions as well as in netball, golf, football and volleyball. In Victoria too, the Bengali, Tamil, Telugu and Maharashtrian associations also feature sports among their activities. The fact that these groups enter

teams as community ones has formed a major aspect of Australian multiculturalism and shows how sport has been used to both create a social identity and a connecting link to the wider community.

UNITED STATES OF AMERICA

The American pattern was different. While cricket, for example, has been in the US from very early days, it has struggled to survive since the Civil War, being restricted to a small number of players and, for the most part, reliant upon expatriates, Indians being a major force. Today, Indians and Asians generally dominate the game in California, where one interesting group is the Royal Bengal Cricket Club, a haven mainly for Bangladeshis. Most players are drawn from professional groups and include doctors, engineers and academics. In New York, clubs like the South Gujarat Cricket Club mix with university-based teams like Rutgers, which has an almost totally Indian side. Mainly because of player shortages, it is common for those with Indian and Pakistani affiliations to play on the same team, leading to the naive expectation in some quarters that the game might ease international tensions.

UNITED KINGDOM

Just as the Mohun Bagan victory in Calcutta in 1911 was interpreted as a cultural breakthrough, so too was the elevation of the Chennai-born Nasser Hussain to the captaincy of the England cricket team. Hussain was preceded as a national captain by Satinder Kehar in hockey, but hockey lacked the cachet of cricket, which is the imperial, as well as the English, game. Hussain displays the classic signs of a transplanted person, even though he reached England at a young age and showed promise early at a national level, spurred on by his father, who had played for

Winner of Canada's first Olympic gold medal in wrestling, Daniel 'Toofan Singh' Igali is also an expert in kabaddi.

The first round of the Masters Tournament, April 2006, at Augusta National, and Fiji's illustrious Vijay Singh hits to the second green on his way to a par 5.

K. S. Duleepsinjhi was a prominent test player for England.

India-born Nasser Hussain became the captain of the England cricket team in 1999.

Madras while working at the Madras Rubber Factory that would become so central to Indian cricket later. He 'always felt English', Hussain noted, even though he enjoyed returning to Chennai and felt comfortable in Indian surroundings. Ironically, he became controversial when urging England's Asian fans to support his team rather than India or Pakistan.

England has been the 'endgame' of the diaspora in many respects. While British imperial policy saw Indians move around the Empire to supply labour and service needs, it was only after Indian independence that Britain itself encountered large numbers of immigrants, supplemented later in particular by the exodus from East Africa. In sports, there was an earlier, spectacular Indian presence, especially in cricket. Prince Ranjitsinjhi of Nawanagar was a prominent England test player who toured Australia in the 1890s. He was followed by his descendant, Duleepsinjhi, who toured Australia in the infamous 'Bodyline' series of 1932–33 (where he was regaled with such wit as 'Hey Gandhi, where's your goat?') and later still by another descendant, 'Tiger' Pataudi. More is being discovered about the complex and enigmatic Ranji, but in some ways he was a forerunner of Hussain: considering himself more English than Indian, his service to Indian cricket was mixed.

Gradually, the post-war generations pushed through in British sport, but not easily. Anurag Singh, the Gonville and Caius-educated son of medical practitioners, for example, is a qualified lawyer who captained Cambridge. He has played for several counties and once played grade cricket in Sydney, where he reportedly endured considerable racial abuse. His brother was apparently the subject of a different form of discrimination: it was reported that despite having five 'A' levels, he was not admitted to Bristol University because he had attended a fee-paying school. As always, the 'image' as opposed to the 'reality' of this matter has been powerful.

In 1995 there were 432 domestic county cricketers in England, and of those just 18 were Asian, which one report saw as a healthy number when considered statistically, relative to population percentage. Others would argue that the British case has exhibited discrimination, reproducing at 'home' what was practised so strongly in the colonies. One report was adamant that UK cricket

faced a future crisis because it was still very 'white', with Asians, in particular, not represented anywhere near their statistical significance. Access to facilities and playing opportunities were excessively restricted. The Yorkshire County Cricket Club, in particular, has long been criticised for its selection policies being weighted against Asians even though, according to one parliamentarian, at least 60 per cent of players in the Bradford League are of South Asian descent. In 2002, the county had two first division players and several Asians in the development squad and bristled at the accusations, but statistically the number is still small.

While sport in the UK has been an introduction into wider society, for some in the diaspora it has also been a divider. It was this trend which caused the Sikh father from Kenya in *Bend It Like Beckham* to recall the discrimination he faced as a cricketer when he first arrived in England. Director Gurinder Chadha's own father found it hard to find employment in banking when he arrived from Kenya, and the film's use of sport to relay discrimination is telling. Such is the enthusiasm for cricket that by 2005 a new magazine was launched, pitched at British Asians, with a focus on the subcontinent. The editor saw the magazine as having a less Anglo-centric view of the game.

In British football, there is a decidedly low representation of Indians and Asians in league football. One 1994 report revealed a high degree of enthusiasm for football among young Asian males and a desire to play professionally, but there was also a strong perception that opportunities for football careers were closed to Asian players. Club officials argued that Asian communities displayed little interest, that Asian males were not physically suited to football, and that they had little natural talent. As a result, Asians play in Asian leagues, where the mainstream game does not recruit. Again, sport has divided rather than integrated Indians in Great Britain.

UK hockey, however, is represented massively by Indians, notably from the Sikh community. In 2001, Sunny Kanwal (captain of Coventry's Sikh Union side) noted that much of the game had gained impetus with the advent of East African Sikhs. With the arrival in Britain of displaced Indians from Kenya, Tanzania and Uganda during the 1960s and 1970s, younger players joined teams and clubs in schools, but found few outlets during the holidays. From the late 1960s onwards, the Sikh Union club, modelled on similar teams back in East Africa, began providing a focal point. Throughout the 1980s, the team affiliated with the Hockey Association and began playing in the league. This eventually led to similar teams emerging and intra-community competitions beginning. Tournaments involving Sikh teams were common as major cities had several Sikh teams, all with developing youth programmes.

THE GULF STATES

Perhaps the most recent and surprising diaspora contribution to sport has been the rise of cricket in the Middle East, with the International Cricket Conference shifting its administrative headquarters to Dubai. The creation of the ground and the tournament in Sharjah drew upon the

The stars of Bend It Like Beckham, *Parminder Nagra (second from left) and Keira Knightley (second from right), pose with players from the US women's football league.*

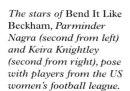

Though football is a popular sport with Indians, they have yet to be adequately represented in mainstream English teams.

extensive number of Indian expatriates working in the area. One negative has been the rise of illegal bookmaking related to cricket, orchestrated mainly out of the region and the cause of an Indian boycott of the tournament for some years.

CLOSING THE CIRCLE

Perhaps the most symbolic 'closing of the circle' has come with the role played by diasporic Indians or NRIs in sport in contemporary India. As part of the Indian government's attempt to attract NRI investment and support, it has emphasised sport as a major issue. When a major report on how India might capitalise on the intellectual capital of NRIs appeared, one significant recommendation was that cricket and/or hockey matches between Indian and diaspora representatives be organised, because members of the diaspora 'had distinguished themselves in...sporting events the world over.' Interestingly enough, among the first people honoured at the Pravasi Bharatiya Divas was Sukhi Turner, Punjab-born mayor of Dunedin and wife of the outstanding New Zealand cricketer, Glenn Turner.

Sports recognition for NRIs, though, was already being earned. Late in 2004, it was announced that three Punjabis (from Canada, the US and England) were joining forces to establish a sports academy of international standard near Chandigarh on land donated by the state government but with capital gathered abroad by NRIs. The organisers said that they wanted to free sport from the hands of the politicians who controlled it, a sentiment echoed by Mohinder Singh Gill, the great athlete for whom the academy would be named.

However, perhaps the circle really closes with those NRIs who, again in the Punjab, came together to support an annual fair which celebrated sports such as *kabaddi*, bullock-cart racing and other traditional sports alongside more modern ones. The aim was to promote traditional games such as the ones taken to numerous offshore sites by their forebears generations before.

The main point is that sport is becoming more, not less significant in shaping diasporic culture through two interlocking trends: the increasing significance of sport as a global business/media staple; and the growing complexity of the Indian presence overseas. Vijay Singh is a catalyst for emerging subcontinental golfers such as Jyoti Randhawa and Jeev Milka Singh, but their appearance is embedded in the story of golf as a social status marker, returning to India through the NRI experience. That developmental 'loop' is causing major structural impacts already. The relocation of the International Cricket Council's head office from London to Dubai can be attributed to the dominant position which the game now has in the creation of income in the world of international cricket. This began with the mediated, then direct, consumption of cricket by Indian labourers and skilled professionals in the Gulf. Sport for Indians overseas has transformed within 150 years from being a cultural preservation system to a tool for global power.

Brian Stoddart

Prince Ranjitsinjhi and his descendants left their mark on England's cricket scene.

A schoolboy cricket team at Woolgoolga in northern New South Wales, Australia, where many Sikh banana farmers live and work.

VOICES FROM THE DIASPORA

Diasporas are relatively exclusive minority communities all over the world whose identities are grounded in national or transnational networks and nostalgia for their (imaginary) home-lands. The Indian diaspora can be read as two relatively autonomous diasporas designated by the terms 'old' and 'new'. The use of 'old' and 'new' here is not meant to isolate communities: the old diaspora has become part of the new through re-migration (Fiji-Indians moving to Vancouver or Trinidadian-Indians to Toronto) and has also undergone transformations. The distinction between the two has to be kept in mind, however, so as to avoid merging two rather different diasporic experiences and to ensure that the global sweep and economic strengths of the new diaspora located in Western nations do not silence the lives of those diasporic Indians whose history is marked by the experience of indenture. The categories, therefore, have a strategic function: they recognise an earlier phase of migration, a reading of India based on a journey that was complete, one that was final. Collectively, the old and the new Indian diasporas designate a complex diasporic experience out of which have emerged literary voices of considerable sophistication.

THE OLD PLANTATION DIASPORA OF CLASSIC CAPITAL

FOR PEOPLE OF the old Indian diaspora, the departure from India was final. The idea of a lost homeland was more important than the notion of a new one, and the imaginary homeland provided them with many of the themes and idioms with which to create their lives afresh. Furthermore, people of the old diaspora came primarily as indentured migrants to colonies which already had large numbers of other colonised peoples, both indigenous and 'bound': the Malays and Chinese in Malaya/Singapore, descendants of slaves in the West Indies and Mauritius, and native peoples in places such as Fiji. They came to lands which already 'belonged' to someone else. This meant that legitimating their claims to the nation became more acute, as did their commitment to them. The length and intensity of their stay in these countries meant that they became indispensable to the national ethos itself. One cannot think of Fiji or Trinidad, for example, without its Indian diaspora.

With the exception of those in Malaysia, Singapore and parts of Africa, the people of the old Indian diaspora are linked to the production of one commodity—sugar. From Totaram Sanadhya and Bechu (indentured labour-ers whose lives have been documented) to David Dabydeen and Samuel Selvon, sugar functions as both commodity and metaphor. It sustained life but also sweet-ened the blood and led to diabetes: 'sugar-sweet blood' (*meetha khoon*) is the plantation culture's word for this debilitating condition. Selvon's *Cane is Bitter* (1957) and Dabydeen's fantasies of the cane-cutter (*Slave Song*; 1984) gain strength from the surplus value of 'sugar' as a symbol, the production of which was the cause of migration in the first instance. It locked them into the temporarily familiar, as V. S. Naipaul illustrates poignant-ly in *A House for Mr. Biswas* (1969).

In the arcade of Hanuman House...there was already the evening assembly of old men...pulling at clay cheelums that glowed red and smelled of ganja and burnt sacking...They could not speak English and were not interested in the land where they lived; it was a place where they had come for a short time and stayed longer than they expected. They continually talked of going back to India, but when the opportunity came, many refused, afraid of the unknown, afraid to leave the familiar temporariness.

Work on sugar plantations forged a new identity which was kept intact through the pretence that, in Naipaul's words, 'we had brought a kind of India with us, which we could, as it were, unroll like a carpet on the flat land.' In a poem by the Indo-Mauritian Somduth Buckhory, the same memory of India is reduced to a village in Bihar.

*Bharat
Sabse pahale
Ham Biharion Ka
Uttar Ka
Ek Chota Sa
Gaon hota...*

*Before all else,
India
To us Biharis
Is a small village
In the north...*

The Call of the Ganges, 1979

Some of the earliest voices arose from the experience of indenture, which began with the crossing of the 'dark waters' (*kalapani*) and the creation of new bonds of friendship across religions and castes in the hulls of ships

After the first journey, there is no other: migration and the (im)possible return are key themes in the literature of the Indian diaspora.

(jahaji bhai). That experience was carried through into plantation life, memories of which remained strong:

> one a de barrick have six room
> man dey one room
> oman dey one room
>
> who have wife
> dem livin different barrick
> who have cheren
> dem livin in one room
>
> only bar up in de center
> if you farting
> i could hear
> if you farting
> dem could hear

Noor Kumar Mahabir, The Still Cry, 1985

In Naipaul's *A House for Mr. Biswas*, it was Mr Biswas's experience in the barracks of Green Vale that triggered his desire to own a house.

As soon as he saw the barracks Mr. Biswas decided that the time had come for him to build his own house, by whatever means. The barracks gave one room to one family, and sheltered twelve families in one long room divided into twelve. This long room was built of wood and stood on low concrete pillars. The whitewash on the walls had turned to dust...The corrugated iron roof projected on one side to make a long gallery, divided by rough partitions into twelve kitchen spaces, so open that when it rained hard twelve cooks had to take twelve coal-pots to twelve rooms. The ten middle rooms each had a front door and a back window. The rooms at the end had a front door, a back window, and a side window. Mr. Biswas, as a driver, was given an end room.

A rare account or testament of life as an indentured migrant in Fiji is provided by Totaram Sanadhya, whose ship, the *Jumna*, reached Fiji on 23 May 1893. Sanadhya was to spend the next 21 years in Fiji, first as a bonded labourer, then as a farmer and priest. He married the daughter of a fellow migrant and returned to India with his wife and mother-in-law in 1914. His account of the years he spent in Fiji, *Bhut len ki katha* ('The Tale of the Haunted Lines'; 1994), begins with:

On the 28th of [May] 1893 I reached the Nausori plantation barracks as one of 141 indentured labourers of the Fiji Colonial Sugar Refining Company [CSR]. On the order of the Sector Manager, the English overseer [strictly 'English-speaking' as he was Australian] managed to allocate rooms to everyone else except me...he then tells me that I can only be accommodated in the haunted line...which I must now describe forthwith. Nausori coolie lines had 26 barracks. Each barrack had 24 rooms, 12 feet long and 8 feet wide [3.66 m x 2.44 m]. Three people lived in each room but if you were a couple you had the room to your selves. A mother with children would also be given just one room. In this way some 1500 men and women lived in the lines. Some six chains [120 m] away from the last barrack was the haunted line which had been inhabited at some time by indigenous Fijian workers of the CSR Company. When after an illness eight of them died, the others simply ran away. Since then this line has been called bhut len [haunted line] and no worker wants to live there. Nobody came close to it in the night...The overseer said, 'this will be your home for the next five years, should you leave it you won't get another, and at any rate it is a crime to abscond.'...This line had the usual 24 rooms...it was surrounded by thick, long grass...infested with mosquitoes and crickets...to one side of the line, some distance away, was the sugar mill whose engines made a dreadful noise all day. Some three chains [60 m] away was the [Rewa] river...Later all new coolies were given their weekly ration of food: 3 kilograms of flour, 1 kilogram of dhal, 250 grams of ghee, 125 grams of salt, and so on.

Born to East Indian parents in Trinidad in 1923, Samuel Selvon authored several novels, including Cane is Bitter, *published in 1957.*

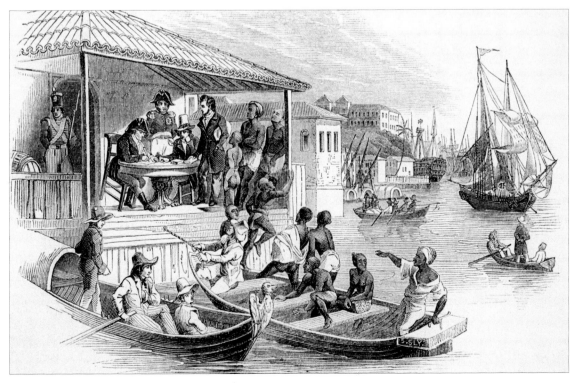

A sketch showing labourers landing in Mauritius c. 1842.

The experience of indenture survives with greater prophetic resonance in the memorially reconstructed oral texts, some replicating Indian dialects, others adapted to the local demotic. Fiji's finest poet, Sudesh Mishra, refers to the use of *bidesias* (monsoonal songs of love-longing) to overcome the sense of severance from the homeland:

ghir ghir badra, savanva ki hai rama
kauni nagariya me cahi re bidesia
gaiya behal more kothova pe bhuke roye
ankiyo se asuva bahai re bidesia
amuva ke daliya me kuhuke koyalia
manava me agiya lagaye re bidesia
hari hari patiya pe likh likh hari hari
kavani nagariya me cahi re bidesia

The monsoon clouds are gathered, O Rama,
But in which place dwells the stranger?
My cattle are tethered and weep from hunger,
Tears abound in the eyes of the stranger.
On a mango's branch the koel cries kuhuke,
He sets my heart on fire, the stranger.
Signing green leaves with the Lord's signature,
In what place abides the stranger?

The time is Out of Joint, 2002

The 'labour lines' were dreadful housing provided for indentured labourers and their families. They form the setting of Totaram Sanadhya's powerful Hindi memoir of living and working conditions in Fiji, Bhut len ki katha *('The Tale of the Haunted Lines').*

Sanadhya's recollections are the clearest contemporary account of an early Indian fragment. They also trace a number of key developments surrounding the old diaspora's experience of indenture as a whole. Of special value is Sanadhya's citation of the Tulsidasa Ramayana as a text which is read collectively by the early indentured labourers. The text, of course, has everything in it for the *girmit* (a synonym for indenture, a vernacularised form of the word 'agreement') experience: 14 years of banishment for the epic hero and God incarnate, Rama; trials and tribulations in the black forest of Dandak; the symbolic ravishment of his wife by the demon king Ravana; Rama's victory over Ravana; and his return to the utopian metropolis of Ayodhya. Years later, Mona Singh in Ramabai Espinet's *The Swinging Bridge* (2003) recalls:

I listened to music and a story, till then unknown to me, coming through the wailing voice of an old beggar woman, crying through the rain, breaking up the classical words of the Ramayana with her own tale of exile and banishment, and in broken chords and unexpected riffs telling the story of a race. Of racial and tribal grief, of banishment, of the test of purity.

Sanadhya also provides us with a very early example of a different approach to accommodation and adaptation. Once, Sanadhya accosts a decadent Indian guru and asks him why he eats meat, drinks alcohol and generally behaves 'like an animal'. The guru replies:

Yes it was because we were deemed animals in the first place that the recruiters sold us into indenture. We learnt animal ways right from the start. We lost all self-respect and coming to Fiji made us even more like animals. At least animals work according to certain fixed ways, certain principles, but we have neither social norms nor any one to tell us what these should be. So here we are, children of the great wandering sages of India now recast as the foremost gentleman animal, 'Mr Coolie Fiji'.

Noor Kumar Mahabir's Trinidadian collection of oral narratives capturing the indenture experience, *The Still Cry* (1985), may be placed alongside Sanadhya's *Bhut len ki katha*. Narrated by five people, Fazal, Moolian, Maharani, Bharath and Sankar, the stories replicate each other to a large extent and, in doing so, reinforce the uniform nature of the *girmit* experience. The passage and the barracks figure most prominently, but there are not unusual readings of India (glorious, healthy, where 'people no hungry'), of the *arkatis* ('feller fool me/bring me dis country') and of the drudgery of work ('I have to wuk/I have to slave trinidad'). Here is the voice of Maharani, a young Brahmin widow who runs away from home as she recalls a recruiter's chant:

cheenee chala
cheenee chalay
going tappu
tappu may
sara bara anna

Sifting sugar
Sifting sugar
To the island go
There in the island
Full twenty-five cents.

In Trinidad, Maharani's recollections touch on *jahaji bhai* relationships, work on the plantation, life in the barracks, sexual infidelities, alcohol dependency, murder and, generally, the struggle for survival; aspects which remain powerfully present in Harold Sonny Ladoo's uncompromisingly honest *No Pain Like This Body* (1972), a novel which Dionne Brand has called 'a Veda to the beginnings of Indian life in Trinidad.'

Years after Maharani, Rajkumari Singh, the first major female Indo-Caribbean poet, wrote a verse called 'Per Ajie' (Great Grandmother), which she dedicated to the first indentured immigrant woman:

Brij Lal's 2000 work, Chalo Jahaji *('Fare forward, fellow voyagers').*

This is a devastating speech, prescient, despairing and directed, suggestively, at Sanadhya himself, who, quite characteristically, misses the jibe. Even in its excessive self-deprecating style, the speech alludes to the kinds of creative social and religious accommodation that was possible only in this exchange, of which Sanadhya, finally, is more of an observer than a participant and actor.

Per Ajie
I can see
How in stature
Thou didst grow
Shoulders up
Head held high
The challenge
In thine eye.

Jeremy Poynting, 'You Want to be a Coolie Woman', 1990

For writers of the old diaspora (here our immediate examples are from the Indo-Fijian diaspora), plantation history (as in Raymond Pillai's 2001 play in Fiji Hindi, *Adhuraa Sapnaa*, or 'Shattered Dreams'), a lived memory of the passage (as in Brij Lal's *Chalo Jahaji*, or 'Fare forward, fellow voyagers', in 2000) and an 'ethical' relationship with indenture (in the works of Satendra Nandan and Mohit Prasad) remain defining features of their artistic endeavours. The latter is captured in a poem about mangoes by Mohit Prasad:

I caress an empty thought
as I clean out a brass plate
of thin dhal and broken rice bits,
I am carrying a mango seed
to plant at the end of this voyage.

Eating Mangoes, 2001

Occasionally the old Indian diaspora wrote in the vernacular, both standard and demotic, or in creolised English or patois French. Pillai's *Adhuraa Sapnaa*, Subramani's inimitable novel in Fiji Hindi, *Dauka Puraan* ('A Subaltern Tale'; 2001), the Guyanese David Dabydeen's poems and the Indo-Mauritian writer Abhimanyu Anat's *Lal Pasina* ('Bloody Sweat'; 1977) are examples of works written in these 'languages'. Pillai's character, Sambhu, comments on how the 'other' reads the indentured labourer as an unwanted aberration:

Hindustani log ke sab ke maage gaaR me laat lage.
lekin fir bhi nahii sudharegaa hamlog jahaa bhii jaay ke
bastaa, ham log bawaal karte rahtaa, aur laat khaate rah-
taa. daliddar kaam kare ke aadat hamlog ke khuun me hai.

We Indians need a good kick in the arse! But even then
we won't learn. No matter where we settle, we go on creat-
ing trouble. The habits of the wretched are in our blood.

Dauka Puraan is written in Fiji Hindi in the Devanagari script. Its author, Subramani, the bearer of a Tamil name, shows how the language transcended ethnic origins and became a signifier of the *girmit* ideology itself. Fiji Hindi is marked by self-mockery and irony; it reduces all speakers to the same level of linguistic competence. It is only in this language that Subramani's narrator, Fijilal (a name which takes us back to Sanadhya's 'Mr Coolie Fiji'), can relate a subaltern *puraan* which is part mock-heroic, picaresque, magic realist and historical. Here is a translation of a short passage from the novel:

So the Peace Corp fell for Josephine. Mrs Kallu said
no at first. She said, 'We are Thakurs, and a Kallu Karan
to boot.' Josephine walked around stomping her feet, declar-
ing, 'No way, boy! Who'll marry this stinking white man.'
For some days the village boys ran around singing, 'No
way, boy!' No sooner did Rabuka hit the coup, Kallu's
ready to marry off his daughter. What fun: on one side a
commotion about a coup, on the other wedding woes. When
they got the marriage permit, another wrangle began. The
Peace Corp bridegroom, Alistair, wanted to ride on a horse
to the wedding. Like a Rajput, swaying a shining sword.
Josephine stomped her feet from one room to the other,
'O no way, boy!' The village kids once again raise their
voice in unison, 'O no way, boy!' Mrs Kallu runs after
Josephine, 'Jo, listen to me, just listen.' Now Mrs Kallu says
Alistair this, Alistair that as if he was already part of the
clan. Finally, Alistair comes as a Rajput. All week they
covered his body with turmeric. He would lie down lazily
and ask the girls to cover his body with turmeric. As if
there was never enough of it. Only when Josephine yelled
at him did he stand up. On the day of the wedding he came
wearing a gaudy crown, sword in hand riding Saipu's
rickety horse. And within four months of the wedding,
Kallu's entire family disappeared. Alistair must have got
the right documents and overnight they left for overseas.
Leaving behind a relation by the name of Jamai. Looked
like absolute shit, beggarly. Kallu must have dragged him
out of some god forsaken place. I asked Pitambar, 'Why
don't we see Jamai?' You know what Pitambar said, 'What
will he do outside? He is enjoying the house, roaming
about, sleeping in one room today, in another tomorrow.
What is there for him outside?'

The vernacular, of course, had been used elsewhere too. *Lal Pasina*, a novel by the Indo-Mauritian Abhimanyu Anat, is a sprawling saga, part social critique, romance, and historical survey. Two moments in particular indicate the novel's strength. The first is the labourer Kisen Singh's account of a dream to his *jahaji* uncle Kundan. Kundan explains that dreams have no meaning, dreams are like sweat because sweat too has no meaning. Kisen is taken aback and answers that sweat is loaded with meaning. 'Look around us, the greenery, the crops, all these are related to sweat.' Kundan acknowledges that this is true, but the real beneficiaries of sweat are those who never shed a drop, those who benefit from the surplus value of labour. The second moment is Kisen's heroic act of getting between the planters and workers who do not wish to leave their allotted plots of land. A fracas ensues and the planters give the order to shoot. The narrator's voice intercedes, 'Kisen Singh's death was the death of history. And the death of history is apocalyptic.' Indenture as sacrifice is a theme pursued by another Mauritian writer, Deepchand Beharry, in *That Others Might Live* (1981), a novel which gains greater power in its Hindi translation *Taki ve ji sake*. In South Africa, the master–slave dialectic has led to writers using plantation narratives to write either about the legacy of indenture (Pat Poovalingam's *Anand* in 2004) or about liberation struggles in the country (K. Goonam's *A Coolie Doctor*). In the novels of Ahmed Essop, we get fragments of everyday life under South African apartheid rendered with irony and humour. So, whereas outwardly in *The Emperor* (1984) Essop has written a fable about a schoolmaster incapable of thinking beyond the boundaries of social regimentation, the real power of the novel lies in the coded references it makes to the wrongs of authoritarianism, along the lines of J. M. Coetzee's *Waiting for the Barbarians* (1980).

The Surinamese poet Cándani writes in Bhojpuri to capture a 'primal' wound arising out of the dislocation caused by indenture.

A bejewelled East Indian woman in Trinidad.

123

India-born South African novelist Ahmed Essop has written a variety of novels and short stories. His collection The Hajji and Other Stories *(1978) was awarded the Olive Schreiner Prize by the English Academy of Southern Africa.*

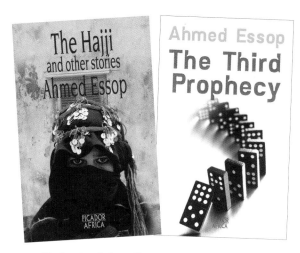

My lost youth I recall
A life spent in pain
And now days are asthmatic.

Remembering a farmer's life
Awaiting the hour's end
Eating with closed eyes.

Ghunghru tut gail, 1990

Jit Narain, another poet from Surinam but located in the Netherlands, also writes in Bhojpuri to express a longer narrative of indenture.

The recruiter makes indenture
The pain you suffered
Pain hidden behind the veil.

The body aches, the blood boils
This depot is alien
A stranger is recalled
The heart breaks.

And now in Dutch, an alien language
My mind roams.
What can I learn from your history?

I roll in white man's dirt
Holding my nose
Behind the same veil.

Jit Narain Ki Saranami Kavityen, 1988

The Indian Surinamese tend to maintain stronger cultural ties with India due to the presence of three large 'ancestral groupings' in the country: the descendants of African slaves, the Indians and the Javanese. There is also the historical legacy of being an isolated Dutch colony in an area that is English, French, Spanish or Portuguese. As a result, there is a more attenuated sense of otherness in Surinam, where many more CDs and cassette tapes of local Hindi music are produced. The Indian community also participates in cultural programmes with India and across diasporas, as evidenced in Hindi newsletters such as *Setubandh* ('The Bridge'), edited in its early years by Mahatam Singh.

In Guyana, however, there was one 'slave', Bechu by name, who represents an anomaly; an indentured labourer who slipped past the net, outwitted the recruiting agents and entered *girmit* as an extraordinarily articulate man in his mid-30s. He was exceptionally fluent in English, understood how capital had extracted labour from workers, and presented us with a fulsome testimony of resistance. Bechu, of middling Kurmi (agricultural) caste, Bengali in origin, and without a first name, reached British Guiana as an indentured labourer on the *Sheila* on 20 December 1894. He was 34, unusually slight for an indentured labourer, and unfit for work on Plantation Enmore, East Coast Demerara, to which he was indentured upon arrival. Within months he was given another task, that of assisting a 'creole driver', and then he moved to the manager's house as a domestic servant. These are unremarkable events and, like other 'incapables', Bechu should have been sent back to India upon the expiry of his initial five-year contract. He did go back, in 1901, but not before challenging many aspects of plantation power relations. What is unusual is the fluency with which Bechu wrote his critical accounts of overbearing and racist managers. Writing in impeccable English, Bechu used the discourse of the master against the master himself. Bechu's many letters mark the beginning of self-assertiveness, which was to transform itself into the politics of equal rights and fair pay for labour. Edited by Clem Seecharan in 1999, Bechu's letters may be placed alongside Totaram Sanadhya's as an early voice of indenture.

The legacy of Bechu survives in Guyanese writers Rooplall Monar and David Dabydeen, both of whom use creolised English as a primal cry, raw like a wound, to establish that 'the canecutter aspires to lyrical experience and expression but cannot escape his condition of squalor nor the crude diction that such a condition generates.' In Dabydeen's poem *The Canecutters' Song* (1986), this raw language turns lyrical as the white woman (of the master) becomes the object of desire of the canecutter (slave). Upon her the canecutter pours, almost as a religious tribute, sexual yearnings depleted by the conditions of indenture. The climax of such outpouring is framed in food, the *baigan-chokey* (roasted aubergine mixed with onions and condiments), which was the standard fare of indentured migrants. In *For Mala* (1986), the stark imagery of a womb squashed open, made hollow, and again transformed into a type of religious desecration ('Somebody juta Gaad holy fruit so man can't taste she sweetness no no!', where the Hindi word *juta* makes the puja offering itself unclean), carries the traumatic memory of the massacre at Wismar in 1964, where Afro-Guyanese went on a killing rampage that left many Indians dead, raped or mutilated within hours. The event is narrated even in the celebratory poem *For Rohan Babulal Kanhai* (1988):

And when darkness break and Blackman buss we heard
Wismar-side and bleed up we woman
And Burnham blow down we house and pen
Like fireball and hurricane
And riverboat pack with crying and dead
Like Old Days come back of lash and chain

David Dabydeen's poetry exemplifies the triumph of the hybrid as language and culture continue to change. It has been said that in the poetry of calypso, the West Indian comes into his/her own. The calypsonian Cephas Alexander, who styled himself 'The Mighty Killer', claimed to know some Bhojpuri and was famous for his Indo-Trinidadian calypsos. *Grinding Masala* is one of his best known calypsos in this genre:

This is really true
Ah decide this year to marry a Hindu

Aha! This is really true
Ah decide this year to marry a Hindu...

Things now getting sweet
They bring a set of dhal bhaat for me to eat
Lahd! Is pepper like fire
Ah cyan stan the bunnin I bawling fuh waataa
So big belly Ramlal
Come wid a coolie druman' a dhantal
Singing: Every time ah passin gal yuh grinin' massala...

Gordon Rohlehr, *Calypso Society in*
Pre-Independence Trinidad, 1990

In other cultural spheres, such as soca (soul calypso) and chutney music for example, the hybrids suggested above take more powerful forms. The word 'chutney' clearly refers to a kind of food, and it is food that helped to create both a relatively homogeneous indenture culture and a point of contact between Indians and Afro-Caribbeans. The food of indenture has remained unchanged across classes and gives many works of the old diaspora their unique semantic range. In Naipaul's early novels, each reference to lentils and rice or bhaji and *roti* repeats the standard cuisine of indenture: 'You ain't eat one whole roti?...You ain't eat bhaji?' Ma scolds her son Herbert in *The Suffrage of Elvira* (1958). In *A House for Mr. Biswas*, Mrs Tulsi scoops up 'some beans with a shovel of roti' and Seth dexterously worked 'with roti and beans' and made signs with his free hand to Mr Biswas. In her beautifully written first novel *The Swinging Bridge*, Ramabai Espinet notes how educated Indians in Trinidad would throw out 'almost everything Indian at first, and would slowly gather back into their lives only those relics that were essential for survival...[eating] sada roti, tomato chokha, wearing gold churias at weddings, drying mangoes for achar and kuchela, treating nara with a special massage, rubbing down the limbs of babies with coconut oil...'

Naipaul, too, in his Nobel Lecture (2001), signalled indenture cuisine out for specific comment and as a mark of difference: 'For example, we ate rice in the middle of the day, and wheat in the evenings. There were some extraordinary people who reversed the natural order and ate rice in the evenings. I thought of these people as strangers.'

Against the implied pull of fusion may be placed the evidence suggesting the urge to return. This is a key theme in *The Jumbie Bird*, a novel by the Indo-Trinidadian Ismith Khan. Published in 1961, the book traces the tensions in the small family of Kale Khan, comprising his son Rahim, his daughter-in-law Meena, his grandson Jamini and his estranged wife Binti. Kale Khan hates both India (from which he had fled) and Trinidad (the country to which he had come). His hatred for both countries is, however, not alike because while Trinidad can never be the homeland lost (and is therefore hated), India is the homeland that is responsible for the trauma of displacement. India then becomes the land responsible for Kale Khan's current condition and Trinidad is the space (symbolised by the novel's primary location around Woodford Square, named after Governor Woodford, an advocate of the indenture system) in which the loss works itself out. He had come as a free man and had participated in the anti-colonial Hosay uprising of 1884, and was not 'like the rest of these low-class coolies in bond'; but his first name, 'Kale', means 'black' and is an inflectional form of *kala*, as in *kalapani* (referring to the passage of indenture).

The figure of Maharani in Mahabir's collection of plantation narratives surfaces in the grandmother of Kamla in Lakshmi Persaud's *Butterfly in the Wind* (1990), another work in which ethnographic details act as anchoring points for the growth of the young Hindu girl, Kamla. The past, however, exists not as a traumatic memory (which it obviously did for Mahabir's subjects and for Kale Khan) but as inalienable features of the landscape. So in Persaud's work, there are references to the outdoor kitchen, the building of homes and the planting of hibiscus hedges, fruit trees and vegetables as signs of Indian presence. Sanadhya's observation of Christmas in Fiji is confirmed in Trinidad too: 'Christmas was the one festivity everybody in the village celebrated. Hindus, Moslems and Christians all planned what they were going to do for Christmas with equal fervour.'

Everyday life in the West Indies cannot be isolated from the powerful pull of creolisation. To understand something of that creolisation and the ambivalent position of the *girmit* ideology, the works of Samuel Selvon constitute a remarkable corpus. In Selvon, as in the writings of the linguistically creative Rooplall Monar of Guyana, is a certain celebration of the homogenising narrative of creolisation, even if the creolisation of the Indian is used to 'conceal [the Indian's] identity'. Although Selvon's first and perhaps most powerful novel, *A Brighter Sun* (1952), makes dialect 'the language of consciousness in West Indian fiction', the insistence on dialect and creolisation is nevertheless not without a certain ambivalence. The weight of the novel, however, is not carried by Tiger and Urmilla, people of Indian plantation culture, or even by the Creoles Joe and Rita Martin. That weight is carried by the drunkard and itinerant Sookdeo (he is not unlike the itinerant Sookiah in *The Jumbie Bird*), whose death comes soon after a modern road bisects his house and land, and his beloved mango tree is destroyed. Before Sookdeo dies he has a dream:

He dreamed in the night that a big 'dozer came up behind him while he was working in the ricefield, and when he turned round, the 'dozer scooped him up and flung him far into the swamp, over the coconut trees and the mangroves. Then, after that, he dreamed how he was in the canefields when his parents had brought him from India to work in Trinidad. He was in the cane fields and an

The Jumbie Bird, *Ismith Khan's first novel, was published in 1961.*

A mural in Port-of-Spain, Trinidad, depicting calypso: music that transcends class and ethnicity.

American came and said, 'Hey, you're Sookdeo?' And when he said yes, the American said, 'All right, we want you!'...and he ran into a patch of canes to hide.

The dream is structured to reflect Sookdeo's own life story but one of the centres remains sugar cane, a key motif in Selvon's work here and elsewhere. In a powerful short story, Selvon renders the motif of sugar cane with great ironic force. *Cane is Bitter* is a tightly written story about a young man's 'revolt' against timeless life on the estate: 'Nothing would change. They would plant the cane, and when it grew and filled with sweet juice cut it down for the factory. The children would waste away their lives working with their parents.' There is something in the nature of cane itself that generates the oxymoron: the cane's bitterness is a metaphor for the severity of plantation life, both socially and economically.

In Shiva Naipaul's *Fireflies* (1970), post-indenture culture, with its pettiness, sexual politics and spirit of material acquisitiveness, is rendered through the figure of Mrs Lutchman, who, with her husband dead and family gone, is left alone in the end, gazing at the chimneys of the sugar mill, a cruel reminder of her plantation past: '...sitting at the window, she would look out at the chimneys of the factory, listening to the faraway sounds of tractors and men's voices and the rumble of the trains on the railway that lay somewhere among the fields.'

The same exhaustion and futility is seen in the lives of Egbert Ramsaran and his son Wilbert in Shiva Naipaul's next novel, *The Chip-Chip Gatherers* (1973). Here, too, the road to riches from the old plantation Settlement (for this is what the locality is in fact called) continues to produce lives led on the edge of schizophrenia, mental fracture and unease. These lives find their metaphor in the labour of gathering chip-chip shells on the shore. The metaphor, however, remains undeclared until the final pages of the novel, where it appears as a tableau, through which the unproductive labour of post-indenture Indian culture is given ironic meaning.

Shiva Naipaul's second novel, The Chip Chip Gatherers *(left), was published in 1973. K. S. Maniam's,* The Return *(right), published in 1993, explores the Indian diasporic experience in Malaysia and the possibility of reconnection.*

...the wood...—metamorphosed—to the texture of living flesh...suggested totemic splendour; a sacrificial offering to the gods of fertility and plentiful harvests, divorced from its true time and place and function and condemned to rot slowly on this wind-swept, shimmering beach of swooping vultures, starving dogs, chip-chip gatherers and himself.

Outside the sugar cane-based old plantation diaspora, there is the old rubber plantation-based Malaysian Tamil diaspora. Here, the outstanding writer is K. S. Maniam. A key word in Maniam's works is the Malay *pendatang* (arrivals, illegals, boat people or, simply, unwanted immigrants). In Maniam's short story 'Arriving' (1995), Krishnan, a second- or third-generation Indian in Malaysia, finds Mat's perfunctory accusation ('You pendatang!')—even if amicably directed towards him—

unnerving, for, 'yes', he thought 'their great-grandfathers were pendatangs. Some of their grandfathers were pendatangs. Their fathers were not pendatangs. They're not pendatangs.' To be labelled forever as outsiders, as temporary sojourners, hurt. There was an arrival, a ship that was part of his historical memory, though not of his Malaysian identity. Krishnan recalls:

'The ship stank of human dung,' his father's words came to him, 'and we, the human cattle, floated above that odour, towards our new land.'

He tried hard to recall his father's memories of his voyage out to Malaysia but his memory was choked with some strange obstruction. Krishnan lay in that region between water and land trying to pull away from the matted, dark intrusion, but his determination seemed to fail. Yes, it had been his determination that had kept him innocent of his father's experiences. He had decided, when he became aware of his budding consciousness, not to be influenced by other people's memories and nostalgia. He clawed at familiarity. But he only floated, set adrift by this new uncertainty, towards an unfamiliar landfall.

The whiff of uncertainty, the denial of one's sense of belonging, the recognition that Malaysia had been part only of a 'familiar temporariness', transforms the familiar into the alien.

Krishnan's consciousness finds salvation through action, transforming the accusation of arrival itself into the redemptive condition of diaspora, a theme played out in Maniam's first semi-autobiographical novel *The Return* (1993), and in his short story 'Haunting the Tiger' (1996). Maniam has referred to two kinds of diasporic identification: the way of 'the tiger' and the way of 'the chameleon'. In his essay 'The New Diaspora' (1997), Maniam seemingly endorses both ways but casts his vote in favour of 'the chameleon' because, as he argues, the way of 'the tiger' means identifying with a nationalist consciousness, a move that replaces one ideology (the colonial) with another that replicates its totalising agenda. The chameleon, replacing an old skin with a new one, is the metaphor of the new diaspora—multiple, selective, hybrid and, in the end, free of nationalist jingoism. In *The Rice Mother* (2002), Malaysian Rani Manicka's impressive debut novel, the lives of Tamil migrants function as a kind of a *kolam* (ornamental figures drawn on the floor, wall or sacrificial pots with rice flour or chalk), the defining symbol of the Indian Tamil household, within which are buried both personal (traumatic) and nationalist (collective) histories.

V. S. Naipaul

The old plantation diaspora has produced many writers of note, but none more powerful or influential than V. S. Naipaul—Knight Bachelor and Nobel Laureate. The grandson of indentured labourers, Naipaul never loses sight of his indenture history. His works allow us to understand how 'life-worlds' (the everyday worlds in which

people live and work) in the old plantation diaspora are mediated in the literary archives and the kinds of labour needed to connect the aesthetic with felt experience. In reading his corpus, one gets not simply an account of facts that feed into art but how an examination of that interaction creates a fuller, larger cultural text. Such examination also requires thinking through historical processes hitherto silenced by (colonial) historicism. It is for this reason that Naipaul's works remain allegories of the diasporic writer and his relationship to colonisation. This may be addressed with reference to the structural inevitability of mimicry (a subversive imitation of sorts) in Naipaul's art, because for the colonised, mimicry was the only mode of self-legitimisation or self-transcendence apart from acts of violence. The origins of the counter-narrative go back in time to Naipaul's father, Seepersad Naipaul, about whom he writes, 'My father rejecting one world, came into contact with another. In him was played out the whole tragic drama of an ancient civilization coming into contact with a hideous colonial mimicry of another civilization.'

In 1976, Naipaul republished his father's collection, *The adventures of Gurudeva, and other stories* (first released in 1943). It tells us much about the genesis of the literature of the Indian diaspora since many of its themes were played out in the as-yet-to-be-fully-realised short stories of Seepersad Naipaul.

To return to questions of a diasporic allegory, the paradigmatic text is obviously *A House for Mr. Biswas*. There are earlier comedies—*Miguel Street* (1959), *The Mystic Masseur* (1957) and *The Suffrage of Elvira*—but *A House for Mr. Biswas* is exceptional. It is a mixed, sprawling, quasi-epic; sad and tragic, yet bursting with immensely comic moments. It is a text that displaces and then recreates India within the space of Hanuman House.

In *A House for Mr. Biswas*, Naipaul writes about the diaspora's 'familiar temporariness', the ambivalence of becoming part of the landscape and yet somehow beyond or beside it. The failure to find roots, the failure of Mr Biswas to actually build a house on solid foundations is part of the totality of the diasporic experience. The house, the sign that would have transformed the 'route' (the temporariness) into a 'root' (the familiar) is as unsteady as the sailing ships themselves. But the final house, with its ironic commentary (by Naipaul) on West Indian architecture, is also a statement about the extent to which even architecture echoes the layout of the barracks. The novel, therefore, begins and ends with death within the confines of a house that encapsulates the diasporic negotiation of space in terms of the history of indenture and its sites.

How terrible it would have been, at this time, to be without it: to have died among the Tulsis, amid the squalor of that large, disintegrating and indifferent family; to have left Shama and the children among them, in one room; worse, to have lived without even attempting to lay claim to one's portion of the earth; to have lived and died as one had been born, unnecessary and unaccommodated.

There is strong pathos here, but the pathos also mingles with the larger allegorical function of the space of a house: a space that one can own, an idea that has its basis, finally, in landless people suddenly gripped by the fear of living in a state of perpetual transience.

Beyond early plantation culture-oriented novels, Naipaul engaged with two other large ideas: that of an ancestral homeland, and the notion of religion and the nation state. His engagement with both ideas has produced difficult, uncomfortable books. With the idea of the homeland, an initial panic-ridden encounter was gradually replaced by a celebration of India's democratic spirit. The subject of religion led to an unwanted and sometimes misunderstood reading of Islam. The first book that came out of his visit to his ancestral homeland, *An Area of Darkness* (1964), remains the finest of his non-fiction works. The following passage from this book resonates with diasporic memory and homeland:

The letter finished, I went to sleep. Then there was a song, a duet, at first part of memory, it seemed, part of that recaptured mood. But I was not dreaming; I was lucid. The music was real.

Tumhin ne mujhko prem sikhaya,
Soté hué hirdaya ko jagaya.
Tumhin ho roop singar balam

It was morning. The songs came from a shop across the road. It was a song of the late thirties. I had ceased to hear it years before, and until this moment I had forgotten it. I did not even know the meaning of all the words; but then I never had. It was pure mood, and in that moment between waking and sleeping it had recreated a morning in another world, a recreation of this, which continued. And walking that day in the bazaar, I saw the harmoniums, one of which had lain broken and unused, part of the irrecoverable past, in my grandmother's house, the drums, the printing-blocks, the brass vessels.

Merchant Ivory's **The Mystic Masseur,** *with screenplay by Caryl Phillips, based on V. S. Naipaul's book of the same name.*

In 2001, Naipaul was honoured with the Nobel Prize in literature.

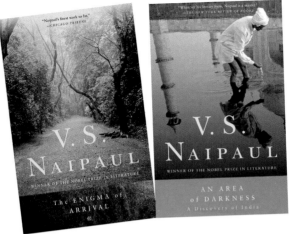
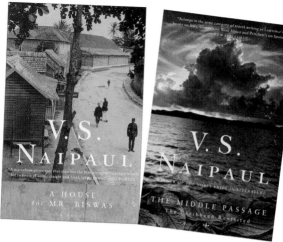

Illustrating the breadth of Naipaul's work. FROM LEFT: *the autobiographical novel,* The Enigma of Arrival *(1987); the record of the return to the 'homeland',* An Area of Darkness *(1964); and two influential novels,* A House for Mr. Biswas *(1961) and* The Middle Passage *(1962).*

The song is from the Hindi film *Manmohan* (1936), sung by Surendra and Bibbo. Naipaul cannot recall these details but he knows that it is a song of the late 1930s (the film may have reached Trinidad a few years after its release in India). Naipaul does not know the meaning of the words (he has it translated in a footnote) but he senses that the second line—*soté* (*soyé* in the original) *hué hirdaya ko jagaya* (the diacritics are Naipaul's), or 'you awoke my sleeping heart'—triggers a memory, recreates a history that takes him back to his grandmother's home, the home that is the centre of *A House for Mr. Biswas.*

Home and memory are concepts that remained relatively straightforward in the literature of the old diaspora, and they are rendered in a more complex manner in the literature of the new. Twenty-three years separate Naipaul's autobiographical novel *The Enigma of Arrival* (1987) from *An Area of Darkness.* The former is tragic; it is about absence, about journeys being final and unrepeatable. The diaspora now looks inward but without retreating into the language of the people who smoked *cheelum* on the verandah of Hanuman House and reminisced about India as home. In Salisbury, the heart of Druidic Stonehenge, Naipaul comes to terms with the English Romantic past (the movement that coincided with

Naipaul's novel takes its title from Giorgio de Chirico's surrealist painting The Enigma of Arrival.

the greatest period of British expansionism and with some of the worst excesses of slavery, which is also, in a strange way, part of his own history).

The Enigma of Arrival is also the name of one of Giorgio de Chirico's earlier surrealist paintings. But faced with de Chirico's painting, Naipaul wrote a realist history about his own departure from home and his own rootlessness. In the story that Naipaul composes around the de Chirico picture, he speaks of the man who arrives at a port, enters into the life of a bustling city, does his business, but then panics and wants to return. He is caught in a religious ritual of which he quickly becomes the intended victim. At the moment of death he finds himself mysteriously back on the quay:

He has been saved; the world is as he remembered it. Only one thing is missing now. Above the cut-out walls and buildings there is no mast, no sail. The antique ship has gone. The traveller has lived out his life.

Naipaul's indentured forebears discovered this in Trinidad; their ships had also disappeared and they were left stranded on an island off the coast of Venezuela. In Naipaul's case the ship always disappears upon each arrival as new spaces are transformed through a prior memory. For Naipaul, as for the diaspora itself, *The Enigma of Arrival,* de Chirico's version as well as his own meditation on the theme, is all about journeys and ships. It is about our first journeys, after which there is no other; and it is about later journeys parodying earlier ones:

…that journey back to England so mimicked and parodied the journey of nineteen years before, the journey of the young man, the boy almost who had journeyed to England to be a writer, in a country where the calling had some meaning…

The statement, with the period changed by one whole year, gets repeated later in this work: 'So that twenty years on I was making a journey that mimicked my first.' Behind this repetition is the primal journey of his people during indenture: after the first journey there is no other. For diasporic reconstruction, the past cannot be forgotten through an act of willed amnesia; but the ship has gone and the diasporic subject must now re-map the new space, master the landscape and engage with the nation's prior history. If there is humanist pathos in this, it is intentional, because Naipaul's final words in *The Enigma of Arrival* insinuate as much:

And that was when, faced with a real death, and with this new wonder about men, I laid aside my drafts and hesitations and began to write very fast about Jack and his garden.

And everything else he has written before and after remains exemplary, for V. S. Naipaul is the touchstone by which the literature of the old diaspora continues to be measured.

THE NEW INDIAN DIASPORA OF LATE CAPITAL

'Home', writes Salman Rushdie, 'has become such a scattered, damaged, various concept in our present travails' (*East, West*; 1994). 'Home' is the imaginary space of here and elsewhere, traversed by the people of the diaspora and, especially for Rushdie, the people of the new Indian diaspora. 'Home' has become a damaged concept as the idea of belonging forces us to face the issue of being 'hyphenated' individuals. For many in the new diaspora of late capital, the race to gain a hyphenated identity—Hindu-Americans, Indian-Americans, Indo-Americans, Muslim-Britons—signals the desire to enter into a kind of generic taxonomy and yet, at the same time, retain through the hyphen the sense of belonging 'here' and 'there'. For these hyphenated individuals located primarily in European or white settler nation states, diasporic space as a contradictory, often racist and contaminated space, now engenders the possibility of exploring hybrid, cross-cultural and inter-diasporic relationships. In the works of Bharati Mukherjee and Hanif Kureishi as well as in the film *My Father's Daughter* (2002) by a newcomer to the form such as Parul Bhatt, and in Monica Ali's *Brick Lane* (2004), the old plantation diaspora's break with India is replaced by the idea of a comforting homeland accessible to them via the Internet and modern technology, set against the seemingly threatening nation state in which their selves are located. The old diaspora broke off contact with the homeland—few descendants of indentured labourers know their distant cousins back in India—but the new diaspora incorporates 'India' into its bordered, deterritorialised experiences within Western nation states. The simplistic binaries of 'here' and 'there', 'dislocation' and 'yearning', and of an imagined homeland and its faked re-creation in another land give way to the realities of the here and now. To explore these further, we need to look at representative literature from the Indian diaspora of late capital.

CANADA: *KOMAGATA MARU* AND AFTER

The *Komagata Maru* was a Japanese ship that took 376 predominantly Sikh would-be migrants to Vancouver. It reached Vancouver Harbour on 23 May 1914 and stayed there for two months while the Canadian government decided what to do with it. In the end, the Indians were given provisions and told to leave. The incident brought to the forefront a number of racist phobias and highlighted the unease of a panic-driven racist Canada, which was bent on excluding darker-skinned colonial subjects. Upon their return to Calcutta on 26 September 1914, imperial India was equally ungenerous: 26 of the surviving passengers died in a confrontation with the police and many others were jailed.

The aftermath of the incident continues to haunt Indo-Canadian writers, reminding them of a period of racist exclusion. The observations of Indo-Canadian poet Sadhu Binning in *No More Watno Dur*, or 'No More the Distant Homeland' (1994), a poem with parallel Punjabi/English original texts, act as an important reminder of this difficult, often unspoken, history and also suggests the need for an ethical relationship to one's past in order to understand a diaspora's agony.

we forget the strawberry flats we picked
stooping and crawling on our knees
we forget the crowded windowless trucks
in which like chickens we were taken there
....
we forget the stares that burned through our skins
the shattered moments
that came with the shattered windows
we forget the pain of not speaking
Punjabi with our children
....
multiplying one with twenty-five
our pockets feel heavier
changing our entire selves
and by the time we get off the plane
we are members of another class.

The British Columbian poet Ajmer Rode, of Punjabi origin, speaks on behalf of all Canadians. In *Apology* (1990), a poem commemorating the 75th anniversary of the *Komagata Maru* incident, he writes:

That is why
today, on behalf of you and all
other good citizens, I bow my head and
profoundly apologize
for what we did to the Komagata Maru
passengers seventy five years ago.

The poet's voice here unites with that of the nation and, in doing so, presents the memory of the *Komagata Maru* as a national memory, not simply a diasporic one.

The short-lived magazine *Ankur* (1991–93) gives some insight into contemporary literary negotiations by the new wave of Indo-Canadian writers. In Jeevan Deol's poem 'Maru', (*Ankur*, April–June 1991) the diasporic public sphere continues to rework the metaphor of the *Komagata Maru*: 'My heart was on the Maru/...I am/Like the ship, /Forbidden to come ashore.' An essay in *Ankur's*

Indo-Canadian Sadhu Binning is one of the leading poets of the Indian diaspora.

No More Watno Dur (right) is a collection of Punjabi poems with English translations by Binning. A number of his works have also appeared in the journal Ankur (left).

Trinidad-born and Canada-based writer and poet Ramabai Espinet.

The writer, visual artist and video-maker Shani Mootoo was born in Ireland and grew up in Trinidad.

Ramabai Espinet's The Swinging Bridge *(left) was shortlisted for the Regional Commonwealth Writers Prize in 2004. Tanzania-born Yasmin Ladha's* Lion's Granddaughter *(right) is a collection of stories that celebrate the female spirit.*

fifth and sixth issues (Fall 1992 and Winter/Spring 1992) points to the difficulties of diasporic classifications. Ramabai Espinet uses the case of the Indo-Caribbeans to point out her own peculiar hybridity. She writes, 'We are not South Asian in the true sense of the word. We are a peculiar hybrid, our cultural world more pronounced than most other children of India outside its shores. We, for the most part, speak no language but a European tongue: English, French or Dutch, in its standard form as well as the peculiar version of our Creole.'

Ankur was primarily a literary magazine. Another influential South Asian magazine, the Vancouver-based *Rungh*, has a much wider brief and publishes essays on topics ranging from racism to 'queering the Indian diaspora' as well.

Unfixed selves: the 'twice-displaced'

There are members of the South Asian/East Indian diaspora in Canada who see themselves as twice-displaced. The literature of the writers discussed here—Ramabai Espinet, Shani Mootoo, Ian Iqbal Rashid, Yasmin Ladha, Neil Bissoondath, Cyril Dabydeen and M. G. Vassanji—is marked by both a different memory of the homeland and a different kind of accommodation within their new land. These writers also confirm the view of Michael Ondaatje (in 2001's *Anil's Ghost*, for example) that the failure to maintain the promise of poetry often leads to lives less rich and a lot more painful in multi-ethnic nations. In her poem *Rain Time* (1991), Ramabai Espinet speaks of the agonising condition of an erstwhile fixed self suddenly finding itself an 'unfixed self'. Espinet's unfixed self brings to the fore the element of diasporic or late modern 'hypermobility', as the poet herself came to Canada as an already established diasporic self—that of the Trinidadian East Indian with a complex 'indenture' history of her own. How does one write about these multiple identities; how does one negotiate living here and writing narratives invaded by earlier memories? As Mona Singh, narrator and protagonist of Espinet's debut novel, *The Swinging Bridge*, says, 'All that it took then in Trinidad was looking Indian; all it took now in Canada was skin colour.'

The point made by Espinet about the twice-displaced diaspora is richly portrayed in Shani Mootoo's short story 'Out on Main Street' (1993). The story telescopes the transition from the old to the new, from the life-worlds embedded in the plantation culture to the mobile, recent life-world of the new Indian diaspora. On Main Street, Vancouver, the Indianness captured in the specific names given to Indian sweets by the new diaspora also signal diasporic difference from within. In this hierarchy of the new and the old (the latter deemed to be culturally lower than the new), the Trinidadian-Indian confronts a past that had forever marked his/her life in ways very different from those of contemporary migrants. The story is replete with terms such as 'kitchen Indians', 'Indian-in-skin-colour-only', and 'bastardized Indian', about which the unnamed protagonist says:

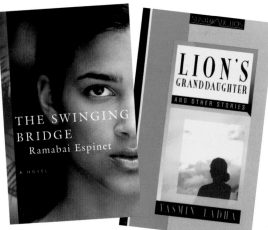

Cultural bastards, Janet, cultural bastards. Dat is what we is. Yuh know, one time a fella from India who living up here call me a bastardized Indian because I don't know Hindi. And now look at dis, nah! De thing is: all we in Trinidad is cultural bastards, Janet, all a we...I looking forward to de day I find out dat place inside me where I am nothing else but Trinidadian, whatever dat could turn out to be.

Those who are twice-displaced, those unfixed selves, signal a diasporic awareness that cannot be contained within theories of diaspora that neglect to specify historical moments, specific experiences and differences in historical conditioning. Twice-displaced migrants challenge theories of diaspora which fail to consider the different and uneven experiences of migration.

Ian Iqbal Rashid's unfixed self shares with Espinet and Mootoo a similar biography. He, too, can trace his ancestry back to India and, like Espinet and Mootoo, was born in an Indian diasporic community (Dar es Salaam) going back at least a hundred years. Rashid's poems speak about loss of a different kind. One of his collections, titled *The Heat Yesterday* (1995), is less about the memory of a homeland than it is about selves whose bodies problematise the whole idea of identity and self-hood. If Espinet's works forcefully remind us of the silent selves of women, Rashid's show us marginalised beings. In *Mango Boy* (1995), gay sexuality is illustrated through richly textured and lush metaphors.

*I eat mangoes, sliced
see the cayenne
sprinkled, machine-gunned through honey-coloured flesh*

Then I ride my lover high

Even as these themes of passion and desire get replayed, we are conscious of the poetry of the diaspora, and of making sense of our lives as transplanted, transcultural and uprooted communities.

Espinet, Mootoo and Rashid now speak not only of homelands and the agony of living as displaced individuals, but use their unfixed selves to weave magical poems that refashion selves and the idea of the citizen. They demonstrate how there is now a Canadian sensibility that transcends ethnic boundaries. The questions raised by these unfixed selves are taken up in Yasmin Ladha's interlinked series of stories on East African Indians. The unusual features of Ladha's collection *Lion's Granddaughter* (1992) are, however, a high degree of (post)modernist consciousness of the ficto-critical nature of writing and, not uncommon with this kind of writing, a continuous engagement with the reader. In a highly original and creative mood, she asks her (implied) reader (*readerji*) to be part of a narrative tapestry that captures both a lost place and the underlying sexual and political tensions of an Indian community in post-independent

East Africa. In the following passage, Ladha returns to the failure of binary thought (colonial/post-colonial; self/other) to explain the diasporic condition:

Readerji, is this binary inevitable? One is the colonizer, the other, the colonized. Then whoa, whoa Readerji. Now, please pick up speed and move! Chapa chapa, tout-suite (clap clap), fatafat, out of my text because I shy/sly from any confinement/circle/missionary position. Friction/fiction between mates facilitates ousting of hierarchical positions. I don't want to be the sturdy alphabet to set a novice at ease in Other literature—a vaccination prior to his/her flight into the Third World. But sometimes this has to be done, then I can't help it...

Two other important authors of the twice-displaced Indian diaspora are Neil Bissoondath and Cyril Dabydeen. As the author of the polemical and anti-multicultural *Selling Illusions* (1994), Bissoondath would appear to have very little diasporic sensibility. This is not the case, however, in his creative works, as in them he captures the very special trauma of the Caribbean Indian migrant. What we get in his short stories, such as 'Insecurity' (1986) and 'Security' (1991) is the sense of diasporic in-betweenness as one 'security' is simply replaced by another 'insecurity'.

The weekdays were long for him. He had not, even after many months, grown accustomed to the endless stretches of being alone. On the island, someone had always been there.
Neil Bissoondath, 'Security',
On the Eve of Uncertain Tomorrows, 1991

Like Espinet and Bissoondath, Cyril Dabydeen's poems also analyse the 'relocation' of one kind of 'labour' from one space (the West Indies) to another (Canada).

make the land intimately yours
one day you will tell your sons and daughters
you worked hard
then they'll begin to speak without an accent
and you will be proud to be truly Canadian.
Cyril Dabydeen, 'Refugee',
Islands Lovelier than a Vision, 1986

This is the voice of accommodation, without excessive anxiety or unease; it is a not untypical voice of the Indo-Caribbean migrant who, again in 'Patriot' (1986), concludes:

I am anxious to make Canada
meet in me
I make designs
all across
the snow.

'Labour', that harsh word which bonded the poet's grandparents to plantation life, continues to be part of the diaspora's work ethic in Canada, and in Dabydeen's work suggestively distinguishes the Indo-Caribbean diaspora in Canada from the South Asian generally, a point stressed yet again in his short story 'Jet Lag' (2000), where the 'cold and ice' of Canada in the narrator's 'veins' shadows his first visit to his ancestral homeland.

The most important Canadian writer of the twice-displaced diaspora is M. G. Vassanji. Here is someone who

Among the most important works by Kenya-born and Tanzania-raised writer M. G. Vassanji are The Book of Secrets *and* No New Land.

is part of a double migration: first from Gujarat to East Africa (where he was born) and then from there to Canada. Vassanji's past was always syncretic; he grew up speaking English, Swahili, Gujarati and Kutchi, and is always moved whenever he hears the Tanzanian and South African national anthems. In one of his earlier novels, *No New Land* (1991), the aesthetic becomes a site from which critical thinking can take place, and one of the ideological centrepieces of this critical thinking is the principle of recognition itself. Things do change:

Three years had passed since that blustery winter night when the Lalanis stood outside the Toronto airport, contemplating a mode of transportation. Much had happened in that period and there was, in a sense, no looking back. The children were well on their way, 'Canadians' now, or almost. There were many new faces in the buildings of Rosecliffe Park, and many others had disappeared, to Mississauga, Scarborough, and even as far away as Calgary. There were a few stories of success now...For many others, Nurdin among them, life simply 'went along'.

No New Land situates itself in the possibility of a heterogeneous, hybrid social and racial condition. Vassanji's world is thoroughly diasporic, incomplete, seeking to find new ground, a new consensus and a new point of view that would build on the successes of the Enlightenment ethos.

Vassanji's finest novel, *The Book of Secrets* (1994), is a remarkable story which deals with cross-cultural relations both within the diaspora and between diasporas and the colonial masters in East Africa. Its artistic strengths, however, are centred on the question of the value and nature of the idea of the book itself. It is a novel focused on the issue of how books hold secrets, how there are mysteries behind every book that require the skills of an imaginative archivist to impart their secrets, and how the location of the secret leads to the unfolding of the life of the researcher. To possess the book, own it and pore over it, was power. It is a book, the diary of Alfred Corbin, the assistant district commissioner, that the sultry beauty Mariamu must steal along with a Waterman fountain pen. The mystery of the book itself—the book as 'book', as its own materiality—is the centre of the text, and it is with this that Vassanji's text opens.

They called it the book of secrets, kitabu cha siri zetu. Of its writer they said: he steals our souls and locks them away; it is a magic bottle, this book, full of captured spirits; see how

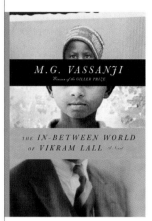

Vassanji's novel The In-Between World of Vikram Lall *won the Giller Prize in 2003.*

In Rohinton Mistry's Such a Long Journey *and* Tales from Firozsha Baag, *the migrant reconstructs memories of a past left behind.*

he keeps his eyes skinned, this mzungu, observing everything we do; look how meticulously this magician with a hat writes in it, attending to it more regularly then he does to nature, with more passion than he expends on a woman. He takes it with him into forest and on mountain, in war and in peace, hunting a lion or sitting on judgement, and when he sleeps he places one eye upon it, shuts the other. Yes, we should steal this book, if we could, take back our souls, our secrets from him. But the punishment for stealing this book is harsh—ai!—we have seen it.

In the end, the act of 'stitching', of writing a narrative around a diary, never completes the text, as Pius the narrator concludes:

It is, as she [Rita] put it, 'everything else', everything I have written and compiled in relation to the diary—what I have come to think of as a new book of secrets. A book as incomplete as the old one was, incomplete as any book must be. A book of half lives, partial truths...

And the novel ends with, 'But I must stop now, the man has arrived for the package,' before the name, date and city are revealed. It is a post-colonial text—a diasporic homage, in a strange unspoken sort of way, to the colonial world.

Vassanji addresses the diaspora as a multicultural nation in his novel *Amriika* (1999), a work which sadly lacks a centre and is neither able to develop the crisis of the individual (here, Ramji, coming to terms with life in America) nor expose the dynamics of the East African Indian life-world in a new country. In his more recent book *The In-Between World of Vikram Lall* (2004), there is much less of the political earnestness of *Amriika* and a lot more of the novelist as an accomplished storyteller. The story of Vikram Lall, an East Indian Kenyan, is told spiritedly with a strong emphasis on the racial dynamics of the country, especially the degree to which the Indian diaspora in Kenya created an exclusive world to which outside entry was impossible. One of Vassanji's key characters, Deepa, an Indian girl and Vikram Lall's sister, never ends her relationship with an African, Njoroge, and is finally rejected by her people.

Two issues emerge from these examples of the twice-displaced diaspora. First, the Indian diaspora in Canada cannot replicate the vibrancy of life in the West Indies and in East Africa; and second, there was, in the racial/sexual dynamics of life back 'home' an emotional substratum that can only be captured in art. For the diaspora, art becomes a way of explaining dislocation, memory and readjustment.

Recalling India

Traumatic memories of upheaval and the movement of people from the old to the new diaspora thus produced two types of literary recollections. A third, and the largest, type is produced by Indians who left their homeland barely a generation ago and who continue to leave for Western

democracies. Here, the loss of the abstract homeland and the psychology of melancholy and mourning are accented differently. Four writers—Rohinton Mistry, Ven Begamudrè, Anita Rau Badami and Shauna Singh Baldwin—stand out.

Rohinton Mistry is the best-known Indo-Canadian writer and among the finest in Canada generally. His first major work, *Such a Long Journey* (1991), belongs to that vibrant field of diasporic compositions where the migrant reconstructs, in fiction, memories of a past he/she has left behind. The productive space celebrated is the city of Bombay, seen from the point of view of the Parsis, descendants of people who left Persia to escape the massive conversions to Islam that had begun there in the 8th century. They brought with them Zoroastrianism and its cultural practices, many of which survive to this day. *Such a Long Journey* covers the period (primarily 1971) before Mistry's emigration to Canada and is rich in period detail. The novel centres on the life of Gustav Nobel, a struggling middle-class man who gets dragged into the affairs of the state and the city, from which he emerges, like some characters in classic realist texts, a stronger individual.

There is a wonderful tale in Mistry's collection of short stories, *Tales From Firozsha Baag* (1987), called 'Swimming Lessons', in which the diasporic writer's parents in India discuss their son's short stories. Since this is the final story of the book, one senses that the parents are in fact commenting on their son's works. What is said by them may be viewed as a useful introduction to Mistry's uniformly powerful books.

My hope is, Father said, that there will be some story based on his Canadian experience, that way we will know something about our son's life there, if not through his letters then in his stories; so far they are all about Parsis and Bombay...and Mother said that she would also enjoy some stories about Toronto and the people there; it puzzles me, she said, why he writes nothing about it, especially since you say writers use their experience to make stories out of it.

'Swimming Lessons' does say something about life in Canada, about the bleak life of immigrants living in low-rise flats in Don Mills, Toronto. It is an unhappy world—one of the Portuguese woman, the overbearing Berthe, a big Yugoslavian building superintendent with her own rebellious son and husband, the wheelchair-ridden old man in the foyer, and the Indian immigrant-narrator learning to swim and fantasising both about scantily clad Canadian women and the city he has left behind. As a diasporic narrative, it fits into the paradigm of coming to terms with the loneliness of displacement and the effort needed to master a new landscape, to map and read it as 'natives' do.

In his third work, *A Fine Balance* (1995), Mistry returns to Bombay yet again, but now the narrator refuses to name it, preferring to call it the 'city by the sea'. Although *A Fine Balance* covers the period from the 1930s to the 1980s, the bulk of the novel deals with

Mistry, the best known Indo-Canadian writer, is pictured here holding his novel, Family Matters.

1975–76. These were the years when India was ruled under a special emergency declared by Prime Minister Indira Gandhi. The 'State of Emergency', as the period came to be known, is the backdrop against which four characters—the Parsi widow Dina Dalal, the student Maneck Kohlah, and the tailors Ishvar and Om—play out their lives. Each has his/her own narrative through which, collectively, a much longer period of Indian social history is told as a kind of critical 'national allegory'. The critique is sustained, powerful, uncompromising, relentless and connected to lived experiences.

Mistry's fourth novel, *Family Matters* (2002), is a further 'meditation' on Bombay and its Parsi community. However, this novel also demonstrates a diasporic self-assurance. Nowhere is this more evident than in a self-reflexive reference to *A Fine Balance* that Mistry embeds in his work.

'Let me give you an example', said Vilas. 'A while back, I read a novel about the Emergency. A big book, full of horrors, real as life. But also full of life, and the laughter and dignity of ordinary people. One hundred percent honest—made me laugh and cry as I read it. But some reviewers said no, no, things were not that bad. Especially foreign critics.'

The reference here endorses levels of self-assurance now evident in writings from the Indian diaspora about the homeland. It is a statement as well about the legitimate 'objects' of art even as the writer is located, as in this instance, elsewhere (in Canada). There was a time, not too long ago, when the concept of sensibility itself was aligned to a European consciousness and a European world. The challenge of the (Indian) diasporic imagination has been to explode the self-evident primacy of this position.

Ven Begamudrè's *Van de Graaff Days* (1993) takes us back to the question of where one is at. In Canada, Krishna Rao and Rukmini, husband and wife, become divided selves, divided by language and space, and without the support of the usual extended Indian family. Like Shyam Selvadurai, a Sri Lankan Tamil writer in Canada and author of *Funny Boy* (1994), Begamudrè gives his narrative the point of view of the couple's child, Hari (Harischandra or G. Harris Chandra or HC as he is called at school). This point of view shifts the centre of the novel from a negotiated diasporic settlement within Canada to the gradual separation of Hari's parents. In this respect, Begamudrè explores a new kind of freedom that comes to the Indian diaspora. Gradually though, the aesthetic centre of the novel shifts to the father-son relationship, as the last word in the novel is '*Appa*', Telugu for 'father', a word hitherto not uttered by Hari. That relationship gets reestablished through the inter-generational transmission of the Van de Graaff electrostatic generator and through calendar art depicting the lovable elephant-headed god Ganesha. We are no longer getting overtly diasporic works, or diasporic works with a critical multicultural agenda. In its place we get an exploration of tensions within, and in *Van de Graaff Days* these tensions are within individual lives that are only tangentially linked to the larger narrative of migration and displacement.

Recalling homelands from a diasporic space is not uncommon. From the space of the new state, memory captures the experience of displacement as the migrant remembers a past or history, a sense of continuity from which he/she has been wrenched. The space of the diaspora heightens the imagination and sharpens one's recollections. A work that does this exceptionally well is Anita Rau Badami's *Tamarind Mem* (1996). The art of storytelling, fiction itself, is given legitimacy here. So, in a twice-told tale, stories are recounted by Kamini and Saroja, daughter and mother, about the same events and the same family, except the mother's story goes further back. The daughter reminisces alone in the confines of an apartment in Calgary; and the mother in a railway compartment, sharing her stories with a group of women who are travelling with her. In the end, 'Tamarind Mem', the term used by servants to describe Saroja's acid tongue, describes both mother and daughter as their narratives signify the silence of women, both at 'home' and in the diaspora.

Shauna Singh Baldwin's tales in *English Lessons and Other Stories* (1996) continue the strong trend in Indian diasporic writing towards representing female voices. Where Yasmin Ladha's narratives are the product of a twice-displaced diaspora, first in East Africa and then in Canada, Baldwin's stories are about initial displacement from India to North America. Her stories are largely about closed Indian communities, whether in North America or in India. Her richest stories though, such as 'Nothing Must Spoil the Visit', 'English Lessons' and 'Devika', speak of the collision of experience. Diasporic lives, represented in and through the literary, become complex sites marked by both discrepant memory and an awareness of their location in a multicultural polity.

THE UNITED STATES AND AUSTRALIA

The Indian diaspora in the US has had a bad press ever since the publication of Katherine Mayo's immensely popular *Mother India* (1927), a devastating critique of India and Indian casteism. A little before the publication of Mayo's book, Dhan Gopal Mukerji had written a spirited defence of his homeland as well as an account of his life in California in *Caste and Outcast* (1923). Mukerji's enthusiastic defence of India is palpable, as is his wish to write his own partial autobiography within the time-honoured Indian genre of hagiography. In the second part of the autobiography (called 'Outcast'), we get an early literary account of the (East) Indian in America who, a little prophetically, declares towards the end, 'So a Hindu, who wants to find a complete antithesis to his race and culture, had better avoid Europe and come straight to America.'

Bharati Mukherjee, arguably the best known Indo-American writer, seems to have heeded Mukerji's advice and went to America. In an essay in *The New York Times* (22 September 1996) entitled 'Two Ways to belong in America', Mukherjee surrenders herself to America: 'America spoke to me—I married it—I embraced the demotion from expatriate aristocrat to immigrant nobody, surrendering those thousands of years of "pure culture", the saris, the delightfully accented English.' But the price of self-transformation is never as clear-cut, as is evident from one of her more polemical novels about migration and displacement, *Jasmine* (1989), which deals with the 'alien', illegal migrant as one extreme type of diasporic body:

Anita Rau Badami's debut novel, Tamarind Mem, *was published in 1996.*

Montréal-born Shauna Singh Baldwin's (above) English Lessons and other Stories *received the Friends of American Writers Prize in 1996.*

Ven Begamudrè, writer of Van de Graaf Days, *was born in Bangalore and migrated to Canada with his family when he was six years old.*

But we are refugees and mercenaries and guest workers; you see us sleeping in airport lounges; you watch us unwrapping the last of our native foods, unrolling our prayer rugs, reading our holy books, taking out for the hundredth time an aerogram promising a job or a space to sleep, a newspaper in our language, a photo of happier times, a passport, a visa, a laissez-passer.

Dhan Gopal Mukerji's Caste and Outcast *is a spirited defence of his homeland and an account of his life in California.*

There are names mentioned, countries and airports: the Middle East, Sudan, Hamburg, Amsterdam, Paramaribo and Florida. There are unmarked jumbos, leaking trawlers, the modern and the Conradian in a journey out of one heart of darkness into another. In *Jasmine*, people of the Indian diaspora are part of a global odyssey as they renegotiate new topographies through travel. For women in particular, the collective horror of double oppression present in the old diaspora (from overseers on sugar plantations as well as their own men) is replaced by the constant abuse of their bodies as illegal migrants. Thus, even as Jasmine adopts the discourse of romance to smother over her fractured life—'I think maybe I am Jane with my very own Rochester...'—we cannot fail to recall the narrative of Mr Rochester's first wife, Bertha (*Jane Eyre*; 1847), the Creole imprisoned in the 'attic', as illustrated in Jean Rhys's post-colonial analyses of Bertha's madness as imperialist control of non-European sexual excess. Instead, the story of Jane and Mr Rochester is presented as the positive narrative of the hyphenated identity, which, in Mukherjee's words, should not be questioned too hard. Here, however, the celebration of the hyphen becomes an extraordinary dismissal of precisely the ways in which women in the diaspora have reacted to racism and sexism both from outside (the nation state) and inside (the diasporic patriarchal order within).

There is, quite possibly, too much enthusiasm here about the capacity of America to absorb outsiders, provided they do not press the hyphen too far. Susan Koshy ('The Geography of Female Subjectivity: Ethnicity, Gender and Diaspora'; 1994) makes the point that three oversimplifications mar the ideological side of Mukherjee's work. First, there is the presumption that the vastness of America allows triumphant feminism to emerge because American assimilation is so totally democratic that Jasmine's ethnicity is never an impediment to full participation. Second, there is a breakdown of differences between 'refugees like Du, illegal entrants like Jasmine, and the post-1965 wave of middle-class, highly educated professionals from Asia.' Finally, there is little attempt to engage with the diasporic subject as an active agent of change.

In the Tulsi household, Mr Biswas felt alienated, but the diaspora acted out its own history because this diaspora had become a defining feature of the island-state. In Mukherjee's *Jasmine*, the diaspora is precariously appended to the nation, as diasporic individuals can only retreat into their apartments or houses to act out the fantasies of living here and belonging elsewhere.

There was a time, a lot earlier, when movement and mobility were the order of the day. A novel that explores this earlier phase with exceptional artistic success is Amitav Ghosh's highly inventive *In An Antique Land*

Bharati Mukherjee is one of the best known Indo-American writers. Her early works include The Tiger's Daughter *and* Days and Nights in Calcutta, *published in 1972 and 1977 respectively.*

(1992), a book that combines ethnography with fictional discourse to trace events and genealogies back to their roots. This is the tale of the Jewish merchant Abraham Ben Yiju and his slave (the slave of the manuscript MS. H. 6, left behind in the Geniza, or chamber of a Cairo synagogue, by Ben Yiju). Although the book is fascinating as a text that recovers and reconstructs a medieval world of trade between the littoral states of the Arabian Sea, its real significance lies more in its examination of a world where identities were being formed and re-formed through contact and cultural adaptation. Ghosh's impetus for writing the book is located in the discipline of anthropology: a young doctoral student goes to Egypt to learn Arabic as part of his training; he masters it, returns to Oxford and writes his thesis. But that is not the text as given here. The anthropological enterprise gets transformed into a narrative of travel and translation. The native informant and the researcher fuse into one as the recovery of the narrative of the slave (finally named as Bomma) becomes an examination of two worlds: an earlier boundary-less world and a modern world of rigid boundaries and passports. Research becomes an 'entitlement', keeping a promise to recapture the memory of a life. The memory recovered—the history of the Indian slave from Mangalore—is, however, an occasion for nostalgia in as much as it gestures towards a time when the nomad or traveller was not an aberration to be rejected through protocols of immigration and exclusion, but a normative figure of celebration. Diaspora came with imperialism, which destroyed the old culture of accommodation of which Ben Yiju and his slave were a part. But just as the North African variety of Arabic (in the Hebrew script) used by Ben Yiju is an uncanny reminder of the Arabic that Ghosh himself learns at Lataifa and Nadshawy (in Egypt), so too does the narrative of travel and translation in medieval times connect with our own (post)modern logic of mobility, transition and translation.

All knowledge, however, need not be bound to the binary of 'here' and 'there', even if creatively. In the diaspora, that binary in recent times is no longer confined to writing constrained by the politics of identity formation, self-recognition or even homeland reconstruction. The binary is accented differently. Three writers—Jhumpa

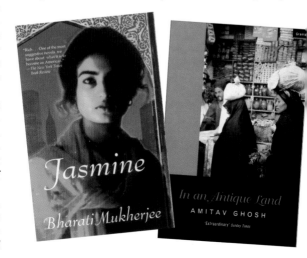

Mukherjee's Jasmine *(left) and Amitav Ghosh's* In An Antique Land *(right), were published in 1989 and 1992 respectively.*

Lahiri, Adib Khan and Shalini Akhil—may be mentioned here. We begin with Jhumpa Lahiri's collection of short stories, *Interpreter of Maladies* (1999). The point made by *The Wall Street Journal* about this collection—'Ms. Lahiri expertly captures the out-of-context lives of immigrants, expatriates and first-generation Americans of Indian descent'—is worth noting, for it captures the collection's decisive orientation towards the anxieties of the diaspora in the place where they are at, not where they came from. Reference to just two stories, 'A Temporary Matter' and 'Interpreter of Maladies', should make this clear. The first is the tale of a couple emotionally estranged from each other after the death at birth of their baby. There can be no continuity in their relationship; dialogue remained but the art of the dialogue had shifted. 'A Temporary Matter' touches so delicately on an emotional register often overlooked in theorisations about diasporas: the lived experiences of diasporic bodies as individuals, as people with very human dilemmas. In 'Interpreter of Maladies', a family's visit to a tourist spot, the Sun Temple of Konark in Orissa, is a template upon which is superimposed a relationship (that of Mr Raj and Mrs Mina Das) which had floundered and become irrecoverably damaged.

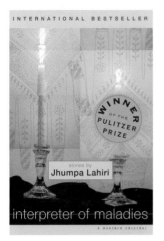

In 2003, Lahiri followed her successful short-story career with her first novel, *The Namesake*. This novel too is about movement and settlement in a new land; it is about re-creating another world in the new; about a fragment society lost in nostalgia for another world; and about children born elsewhere who cannot totally connect with the unchanging world-views of their parents. Ashoke and Ashima Ganguli, parents of Gogol and Sonia, believe that they have not changed; their worlds have remained intact. Yet the sense of 'inbetweenness' is located not in Ashoke and Ashima's American-born children Gogol and Sonia, but in themselves. For them, the hyphen makes them a 'resident everywhere and nowhere.'

Although the novel ends with Gogol reading Gogol (after whom Ashoke had named him: 'We all came out of Gogol's overcoat', the great Dostoevsky had said), we must not forget that the final chapter really begins with Gogol's mother, Ashima. On the day before Christmas 2000, Ashima prepares for a final party in the house she has shared with her husband and children for most of her life in America. The house has been sold and these are Ashima's final days there. Her son Gogol is on his way, her daughter Sonia and her future husband, Ben, are already there. She will fulfil a promise made or an undertaking given all those years ago to return to Calcutta. Now she will keep that promise: for six months of the year she will live in Calcutta at her brother's place. But this return to the past, a ghostly revenant, disembodies her, for she knows that 'she will be without borders, without a home of her own.' Ambivalence rather than certainty grips her, for she will return only part Indian on an American passport and with an American social security card. She will miss her job in the library, and the city, Calcutta, in which she will live for half the year, 'once home...is now in its own way foreign.'

Lahiri/Ashima's refrain morphs into a stronger metaphor when Iqbal Chaudhary in author Adib Khan's ground-breaking first novel, *Seasonal Adjustments* (1994), says at the end of a visit 'home' after many years in Australia, 'the womb was there all right, except I could not fit into it any more.' Eighteen years in Bangladeshi émigré society in Australia is not so much the end of a schizophrenic existence elsewhere, not so much a cure, as an encounter with a nation whose social and political system was under duress, where the horrors of the war of liberation against Pakistan left wounds so deep that the nation seems to have lost its will to live. Under these circumstances, Iqbal Chaudhary's return home with his daughter Nadine after his marriage to the Australian Michelle had broken down, ceases to be a journey of discovery and education (for his daughter); but instead triggers reflections on what it is to be a hyphenated individual and the ramifications for the person who no longer responds to the homeland without qualification. For the diaspora now engenders a 'being' of a different order; it reinforces the uncomfortable fact that 'life cannot be separated into their complex strands.'

The Bollywood Beauty (2005), the debut novel of the Indo-Fijian expatriate Shalini Akhil, is also about redefining selves, rethinking prejudices and working through the very idea of the diaspora. The novel, which is primarily filled with Indo-Fijian students in Melbourne, acknowledges the peculiar difficulties of the twice-displaced and of the struggle to hold together a body that outwardly looks Indian (and hence is reduced to a collective by the viewer) but is inwardly Indo-Fijian and Australian. Commenting on this fact, Kesh, the Australian-born Indo-Fijian, says: 'They were too far removed to be real Indians. They looked different. They ate different food. Hell, they even made up their own language.'

Jhumpa Lahiri's Interpreter of Maladies *(above, centre) won the Pulitzer Prize for fiction in 2000.*

The Sun Temple of Konark in Orissa is an important setting in Lahiri's Interpreter of Maladies.

A still from Hanif Kureishi's My Beautiful Laundrette.

THE UNITED KINGDOM

Diasporic negotiations have a fascinating history in the Indo-Pakistani (or South Asian) diaspora of Britain. This is not surprising given Britain's centuries-old links with the Indian subcontinent. Between the mid-1950s and the early 1970s, the Indian diaspora grew from a few thousand to over a million strong. It was a period during which European governments supported and even encouraged businesses and large corporations to seek cheap labour from abroad. The aim was to get people in as guest workers who, even after acquiring citizenship, would function very much like Abbè Sieyes's 'passive citizens', to be distinguished from 'active citizens'. The conflict between a presumed passive citizenry and an actively engaged diaspora is the context for many of the works of the Indian community, from Meera Syal's comedies and Hari Kunzru's imaginative reworking of the legacy of Rudyard Kipling in *The Impressionist* (2002) and the diaspora as a feature of the new Internet age in *Transmission* (2004), to Hanif Kureishi's heterogeneous corpus.

Hanif Kureishi

The nation, of course, sees the diaspora as 'passive citizens' who are not supposed to participate actively in the key affairs of the nation and are often thought of as subjects in need of some kind of diversity management. They exist as a homogeneous group defined through stereotypes of food, race, work habits and so on. Their world is seen as an exclusive world in ghettoised towns and suburbs, with their cultural interests revolving around religious halls and Bollywood cinema. Against such readings, the cinema of Hanif Kureishi and Gurinder Chadha represent the South Asian diaspora rather differently. In their films and books, the diaspora emerges as a diverse cultural group that requires high levels of critical engagement by the viewer and reader. Kureishi's films effectively began this

Kureishi's best-known works include My Beautiful Laundrette, Sammy and Rosie Get Laid, *and* The Buddha of Suburbia *(right).*

process of engagement, a process which also opened up the hitherto uncontested area of 'Englishness' itself.

Kureishi's staging of the narratives of the Indo-Pakistani diaspora takes on a form rather different from anything we have examined thus far. Unlike Indian diasporic works from Canada and the US, Kureishi's works raise questions that do not lend themselves to easy analysis. In the hands of Kureishi, matters are confounded because the Indo-Pakistani community in Britain reminds the 'English' of their own earlier imperial history and the inevitability of their presence in the metropolitan centre of the Empire after its collapse. Their presence also suggests the return of the repressed (as abject colonised bodies that existed, for the English, only in the power structure of imperialism) in a British nation state whose own history had been enacted elsewhere: 'The trouble with the Engenglish', stutters S. S. Sisodia ('whisky and soda', modelled on Ismail Merchant), 'is that their hiss hiss history happened overseas, so they dodo don't know what it means' (Salman Rushdie; *The Satanic Verses*; 1988). These 'repressed' diasporic bodies are now given a voice which redefines the nation and examines the anxieties of people uncomfortably located both 'here' and 'elsewhere'.

If Bharati Mukherjee distances herself from a radical engagement with the diasporic self (though it must be added that she never loses sight of issues related to it), in the works of Kureishi diasporic lives are not detached from the political agenda of the nation state. What we get is the construction of the despairing world of the migrant in the racist agenda of Thatcherite and post-Thatcherite Britain. Kureishi's *The Buddha of Suburbia* (1990) tellingly begins with, 'My name is Karim Amir, and I am an Englishman born and bred, almost.' The narrator continues, 'I am often considered to be a funny kind of Englishman, a new breed as it were, having emerged from two old histories.'

The new engagement is seen in Kureishi's early works, *My Beautiful Laundrette* (1985) and *Sammy and Rosie Get Laid* (1987), where post-colonial hybridity is celebrated through the exposure of the repressed diaspora. By lifting the lid on the community's own homophobic and exclusive rhetoric, by representing gay and lesbian diasporic selves and mingling the crisis of the working class with the anxieties of diaspora, Kureishi suggestively transforms the diaspora from 'passive citizens' to people who are full participants in the complex life of the nation. Indeed, in Kureishi's *My Son the Fanatic* (1997), it is the British-born son rather than the immigrant father who bares his growing allegiance to fundamentalist Islam and, in doing so, locates the latter in the failures of the immigrant dream.

The involvement of the diaspora in the affairs of the nation, its presence as 'active citizenry', is the key theme in all of Kureishi's books and films. When he presents complex sexual relations across cultures and races in *My Beautiful Laundrette* and *Sammy and Rosie Get Laid*, he does so to blast open the stereotypes of what Anna Marie Smith called the 'venomous homophobic representations' of the Afro-British and the Asian-British, especially in Thatcherite Britain. Furthermore, at a time when British television and film produced some of the most elaborate accounts of the British in

India (from *The Jewel in the Crown* to *A Passage to India*), Kureishi's works turned to contemporary Britain to examine the colonised subjects within, to show in fact what happens when the people of that bygone Empire become fully-fledged citizens of the erstwhile colonial power itself.

Salman Rushdie

If V. S. Naipaul established one kind of diasporic foundational narrative by using the life experiences of the old plantation diaspora to write realist texts, Salman Rushdie has created another, this time for the new Indian diaspora, writing of their experiences in the genre of magic realism. With Naipaul, the nostalgia for return remained strong, as was reflected in the old men on the verandah of the Tulsi shop, smoking their *cheelums* and ganja and reminiscing about their homeland. With Rushdie, the characters Gibreel and Chamcha debate the differences between being joined to the past and hence being, to a degree, 'continuous', and being a 'willing re-invention', a creature of 'selected discontinuities' (*The Satanic Verses*). What is celebrated is the challenge of the new and a rejection of the earlier distinction based on the purity of holding on to a memory. As Rushdie himself wrote in defence of *The Satanic Verses*: '...[it] celebrates hybridity, impurity, intermingling, the transformation that comes of new and unexpected combinations of human beings, cultures, ideas, politics, movies, songs.' But even when Rushdie touches on the old diaspora, as he does in *Fury* (2001), he transforms what is obviously Fiji into a magical world, part Swift, part E. T. A. Hoffmann, part Rabelais:

> Indian people of Lilliput-Blefescu have finally stood up for our right. Our culture is ancient and superior and will henceforth prevail...For one hundred years good-for-nothing Elbee cannibals drank grog—kava, glimigrim, flunec, Jack Daniel's and Coke, every kind of godless booze—and made us eat their shit.

The narrator in Rushdie's *The Ground Beneath Her Feet* (1999), Umeed Merchant (Rai), gives mobility a positive turn as he believes that in every generation, blessed or cursed, there are a few souls that are 'born not belonging'. These people 'come into the world semi-detached... without strong affiliation to family or location or nation or race.' Rushdie celebrates 'the non-belongers' and certainly the narrator feels that these people may well reflect the natural condition of humanity. So, in the domain of art we reinvent the figure of the 'tramp, the assassin, the rebel, the thief, the mutant, the outcast, the delinquent, the devil, the sinner, the traveler, the gangster, the runner, the mask' to fulfil our needs. Because these liminal figures belong to the borders of culture, they are forever on the margins. It is 'the fate of migrants', says Omar Khayyam Shakil, the narrator of *Shame* (1983) 'to be stripped of history, to stand naked amongst the scorn of strangers.' Shakil himself is a 'translated' man, with roots in India (place of birth), Pakistan (post-Partition Indian Muslim homeland) and England (where he 'lives'), which is why his narrative about Pakistan is peppered with diasporic anxieties, for Pakistan represents a certain kind of erased memory (its Indian past) that sits uncomfortably with the narrator's own diasporic condition in England.

In Rushdie's art, the centre therefore shifts to the margins and it is through marginal figures—from Saleem Sinai and Omar Khayyam Shakil to Saladin Chamcha, the Moor Zogoiby, Umeed Merchant and Malik Solanka—

that stories of those who do not belong are told. Two works, *Midnight's Children* (1981) and *The Moor's Last Sigh* (1995), illustrate this. *Midnight's Children* is an extraordinary work. It is, along with Naipaul's *A House for Mr. Biswas*, among the great novels in English of the second half of the 20th century. Its themes are not centrally diasporic, but its decisive position in the literary production of the diaspora must be stated without any qualification. Rewriting both the political and literary history of India (Saleem Sinai's grandfather, a doctor, is appropriately named Aadam Aziz, in a direct reference to that other Dr Aziz in E. M. Forster's *A Passage to India*), the Indian nation state is transformed into a magic realist narrative, for to represent the nation one must combine received colonial practices (both historiography and literature) with the nation's own felt life-world, the world of mystery and imagination, where genres are not kept apart but merge into one another, and where narratives are endless. In this respect, combining classical Indian and Sufi Indian narrative forms, *Midnight's Children* not so much creates an India of the imagination for the first time (as it has been said) but legitimates the nation's dazzlingly complex cultural forms. We sense this in the following passage, written as well in response to V. S. Naipaul's *An Area of Darkness*:

> On April 6th, 1919, the holy city of Amritsar smelled (gloriously, Padma, celestially!) of excrement. And perhaps the (beauteous!) reek did not offend the Nose of my grandfather's face—after all, Kashmiri peasants used it, as described above, for a kind of plaster. Even in Srinagar, hawkers with barrows of round dung-cakes were not an uncommon sight. But then the stuff was drying, muted, useful. Amritsar dung was fresh and (worse) redundant. Nor was it all bovine. It issued from the rumps of the horses between the shafts of the city's many tongas, ikkas, gharries; and mules and men and dogs attended nature's calls,

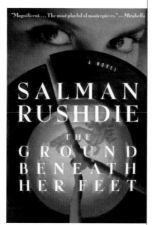

Salman Rushdie's The Ground Beneath Her Feet, *published in 2000. The Irish rock band U2 recorded a song with the same title in collaboration with Rushdie.*

A scene from a play by the Royal Shakespeare Company at the Barbican, based on Rushdie's novel Midnight's Children.

137

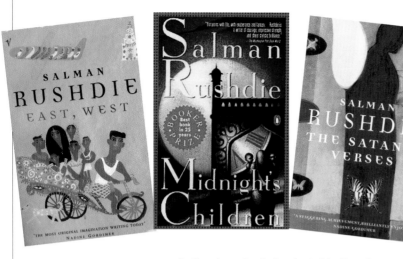

mingling in a brotherhood of shit. But there were cows, too; sacred kine roaming the dusty streets, each patrolling its own territory, staking its claims to excrement. And flies! Public Enemy Number One, buzzing gaily from turd to steaming turd, celebrated and cross-pollinated these freely-given offerings. The city swarmed about, too, mirroring the motion of the flies.

This is Saleem Sinai narrating to Padma, and as he narrates the text expands, becomes an allegory of the nation. The nation's history as well has to be 'chutney-fied', mixed and preserved as a history of smells and disbelieving; not a history of certainties, and certainly not a history of redemption but a history of mute silences, of bizarre coincidences as well as of irreconcilable differences; a history indeed of linguistic re-duplication, of 'writing-shiting'.

Rushdie's fiction invokes the value of the hyphen to write about ways in which disparate items are brought together. The Moor Zogoiby's life in *The Moor's Last Sigh* is the 'tragedy of multiplicity destroyed by singularity, the defeat of the Many by One.' But his life is also an allegory of the diaspora and of the author as well. This was Rushdie's first major post-fatwa novel. It was written from a position of exile, from the loss of multiplicity in the wake of a fundamentalist 'Oneness', both religious and secular. The Moor's tragedy is of course the tragedy of nations, like India, that most multifarious of all nations, threatened by a Hindutva of exclusiveness. This Moor's tale, 'complete with sound and fury', is located in the condition of diaspora. To celebrate it, Rushdie has to write a text about diasporic communities in India. He presents a family saga as a central template around which the history of India—its ironically presented European 'discovery' as the source of spice against its internal history as a 'sub-condiment' (not a 'subcontinent') of 30 jars of chutney with an as-yet-to-be-filled 31st jar which *is* 'Midnight's Children'—as its 'uncreated conscience' (after James Joyce's Stephen Dedalus), is given voice.

The Moor—as Scheherazade does in *The Book of 1001 Nights*—writes down his life-story to amuse Vasco Miranda. Yet his first reader—Aoi Uë,

'a miracle of vowels'—is frightened not by the narrator's appearance or deeds but by his words: 'She was frightened by my words, by what I set down on paper, by that daily, silent singing for my life.' What frightens is this power of writing that brings us close to Rushdie as a 'text' that circulates beyond the book, with effects not related to its reading. Rushdie's words are frightening because he comes 'already read', even by those who do not read him. He has become a sign of something else, around which a number of binaries are played out: freedom of speech versus censorship; liberalism versus fundamentalism; textual multiplicity versus textual singularity; the one versus the many; free thought versus bigotry; open versus close societies; universal law versus contingent law; contamination versus purity; diasporic difference versus assimilation; and many more. To think through these issues and to locate an aesthetics of diaspora in Rushdie, we need to comment on a text that was forcibly centred even when, like everything else Rushdie has written, it is a totally decentred, highly magical postmodern text—*The Satanic Verses*.

Few works of fiction have been the subject of debates as intense as those surrounding *The Satanic Verses* since its publication in 1988. Books were written on the 'Rushdie Affair', a film was made on the author's death (much deserved, as it turns out in the film) by the Pakistani film industry, and Tehran, for a considerable period, re-emphasised Ayatollah Khomeini's fatwa at any staged denunciation of the West. The author's life immediately following the fatwa became one of double exile. This book about migration, dispossession, cultural hybridity and the absence of centres in diasporic lives was the cause of Rushdie's second exile. To give these themes a narrative frame, they were hoisted on another moment in history, when 'newness' entered the world—the moment of Islam and its messenger, the Prophet Muhammad, or 'Mahound' as Dante and Rushdie's narrator both ill-advisedly call him. The entry of strange people into so many parts of the globe presents the older inhabitants with the threat of the new, not unlike the threat faced by desert peoples 1400 years ago from ideas no longer commensurable with their own. Thus, the central themes of *The Satanic Verses*—how 'newness' enters the world, how the many coexist with the one, and why love remains the only organising principle of our lives—are written in a hybrid discourse (true also of his other writings) that is borrowed from the Bombay film indus-

try, the idioms of Hobson-Jobson, the texts of a colonial English curriculum, the Katha-Sarit-Sagar, the vast Indian epic tradition, the Persian tale of the Simurg from Farid ud-Din Attar's *The Conference of the Birds*, as well as popular narratives from a range of sociolinguistic registers such as those of the female dacoit Phoolan Devi and Indian Penal Code 420 (Gibreel sings Raj Kapoor's well-known song from the film *Shree 420*), among others. *The Satanic Verses* situates itself in the midst of these heterogeneous discourses. It is from the space of hybridity and multiplicity that many of the characters speak. Mimi Mamoulian, for example, knows very well the meaning of the world as 'pastiche', a 'flattened world', and the author's own very postmodern intervention makes this clearer still:

> Gibreel...has wished to remain, to a large degree, continuous—that is, joined to and arising from his past...whereas Saladin Chamcha is a creature of selected discontinuities, a willing re-invention; his preferred revolt against history being what makes him, in our chosen idiom, 'false'? [Where Chamcha is therefore perceived as 'evil'] Gibreel, to follow the logic of our established terminology, is to be considered 'good' by virtue of wishing to remain, for all his vicissitudes, at bottom an untranslated man.
> ...But, and again but: this sounds, does it not, dangerously like an intentionalist fallacy?...Such distinctions, resting as they must on an idea of the self as being (ideally) homogeneous, non-hybrid, 'pure',...an utterly fantastic notion!...cannot, must not, suffice.'

Rushdie begins by offering the usual binaries of the continuous and discontinuous, tradition and modernity, and good and evil, only to undercut it with the intervention of the hybrid. Indeed, what this extended statement about the construction of the self indicates, in the context of diaspora, is that subjectivity is now formed through modes of translation and encoding, because in the world today erstwhile distinctions 'cannot, must not, suffice.' This last phrase, in fact, sums up the agenda of the book as a whole:

> If The Satanic Verses is anything, it is a migrant's-eye view of the world. It is written from the very experience of uprooting, disjuncture and metamorphosis...that is the migrant condition, and from which, I believe, can be derived a metaphor for all humanity.

Salman Rushdie, *Imaginary Homelands*, 1991

An arrest after young men broke away from a peaceful rally in Bradford calling for a change in blasphemy laws in the wake of the publication of Salman Rushdie's The Satanic Verses, *1991.*

Like Hanif Kureishi, Rushdie speaks of a 'post-diaspora community' in Britain which now becomes a site from where a critique of Britishness itself may be mounted. And with Rushdie, the literature of the Indian diaspora enters a phase of self-assuredness and artistic accomplishment from which it can only look forward to greater heights of artistic success.

A 'MINOR' LITERATURE

The literature of the Indian diaspora is an accomplishment worthy of being placed alongside all the other successes of this diaspora. Indeed, it may even be argued that it is one of its greater accomplishments, as the literature produced is among the best writing in English in the second half of the 20th century and after. Its special achievement, however, may be understood better, at least in theoretical terms, if we see it not so much as the literature of largely non-native speakers of English or of people who are not derived from Anglo-Celtic stock, but as literature written in a majority language by people of the diaspora. In this respect, Giles Deleuze and Félix Guattari's use of the term 'minor literature', which they employed to explain the work of Franz Kafka (a German-speaking Czech Jew) is very appropriate. The use of the term 'minor literature', therefore, signals a number of formal characteristics of the literature of the Indian diaspora: it removes the absolute link between peoples and mother tongues (somewhere Khushwant Singh said, 'English is my mother tongue but my mother doesn't speak a word of it.'); it places the writer in the midst of the greater concerns of the nation even when he or she may be seen as an outsider; and it voices, through a thoroughly nuanced use of English, something that belongs specifically to a diasporic group consciousness. The literature of the Indian diaspora as an example of a minor literature suggests that a minor literature does not come from a minor language but is something that a minority constructs in the majority language, in this case predominantly English. It is also a literature conscious of the larger political agenda of the people who constitute its subject matter, and as a consequence is often charged with the values of the diasporic community as a whole. As a minor literature reflecting these characteristics, the literature of the Indian diaspora is bold, imaginative and foundational.

Vijay Mishra

The 'minor' literature of the Indian diaspora fills the bookshelves at major bookstores, such as Kinokuniya in Singapore.

THE COMMUNITIES

THROUGH REGION AND country-based profiles of diasporic Indian communities around the world, Part VIII of the encyclopedia provides case studies which discuss the factors that led to movement and 'dispersal'; the nature of community-building in the diaspora; the political and economic outcomes for these Indian communities within their 'host' societies; and their continued connection with their country of origin.

Pictured here is a ship at Tanjong Pagar Dock, Singapore. Many Indian immigrants arrived in such vessels, which carried passengers to and from India. For the longer routes to the colonial plantation destinations in the Caribbean and the Indian and Pacific oceans, a class of 'coolie' ships was developed to carry indentured workers. Until the turn of the century, these were usually sailing 'clippers' but from c. 1906 steamers took over this trade.

REGIONS AND
COMMUNITIES

The modern Indian diaspora came into being over the 19th and 20th centuries. Different impulses and opportunities fuelled the migrations from which the diaspora grew. The background to this modern development was set in pre-colonial times, when trade provided an incentive for Indian merchants to circulate through Asia by land and sea and, in some cases, to lay the foundation of Indian communities. The 19th and early 20th centuries, however, saw much larger movements overseas of Indian labourers under schemes of varying degrees of 'contract', followed by the migration of a wider range of Indians through free migration to take advantage of the opportunities—service, business or labour—offered as the Empire expanded. By the mid-20th century there existed a widespread diaspora around the world. Unprecedented migration to the metropolitan centres of the disintegrating imperial state in the 1950s and 1960s was then further diversified as worldwide globalising pressures attracted professional and highly skilled migrants to move into advanced industrial regions, while labour and commercial migrants tapped economic opportunities in less developed areas that had begun to advance. From these movements came the Indian diasporic communities which this section of the encyclopedia details.

MAPPING THE DIASPORA

AS A STARTING point, we map the changes that took place in the population of the diaspora in the last three decades of the 20th century. The two maps on page 143 display, through proportional circles, the distribution of the Indian diaspora in 1971 (Map 8.1) and 2001 (Map 8.2). The maps achieve multiple objectives. The scale of the circles enables comparison of the size of the Indian diaspora in different countries at these two points in time. The colours of the circles used in these maps express different variables. For Map 8.1, the blue colour with a value variation (light blue to dark violet) expresses the proportion of the population of Indian origin as a percentage of the total population of the country, ranging from 0.01 per cent to 70 per cent. In Map 8.2, there are diverging hues to show the evolution of the population of Indian origin from 1971 to 2001. Blue indicates a decrease; yellow to orange indicate an increase; and red highlights new locations where there was no population of Indian origin in 1971.

THE SIGNIFICANCE OF 1971

The year 1971 was selected as an important marker in the history of the Indian diaspora for two reasons. The first was a change in migration policies in the West, which opened the gates for Asian immigration. The second was the growth of Africanisation policies in East Africa, which led to the re-migration of Indians from Uganda, Kenya and Tanzania. The maps show a clear shift in the spatial distribution of the population of Indian origin after 1971. Up to this date, colonialism remained the most important factor that had led to the formation of Indian communities in former colonies (including French and Dutch territories) and to some extent in the metropole. These changes affected migration to the US (Immigration and Naturalization Act 1965), Canada (White Paper on Migration 1966) and Australia (end of the Immigration Restriction Act 1966).

THE DIASPORA BY THE 21ST CENTURY

Map 8.2 highlights the different waves of migration that transformed the 'old' diaspora born out of colonial capital. The years between 1971 and 2001 saw a great dispersal of Indians, who can now be found in nearly every country that offers economic opportunities. The large-scale movement of professionals to North America, Australia and, to a lesser extent, Europe, is particularly notable. Large numbers of labourers have also moved to the Gulf countries, albeit mainly as temporary workers. Smaller numbers of Indians can be found in new locations such as the Baltic states and Eastern Europe, which were opened up by the end of the Cold War.

In the former colonies, the growth of the Indian diaspora between 1971 and 2001 has largely been the outcome of natural increase. In Fiji, Guyana and Surinam, political problems or better economic opportunities elsewhere have led to the re-migration of many Indians. Few of the East African 'twice-displaced' have returned to Uganda, but some have reclaimed their place in Kenya and Tanzania, although numbers remain considerably lower than in the 1960s.

SOURCES

The maps have been drawn from numerous sources for the purpose of providing realistic estimates. A. W. Helweg and U. M. Helweg's *An immigrant success story: East Indians in America* (1990) was particularly useful for estimates for 1971, while the report of the High Level Committee on Indian Diaspora, set up by the Indian government, aided in the assessment for 2001. This information was cross-checked with data from Hugh Tinker's *The Banyan Tree: Overseas emigrants from India, Pakistan, and Bangladesh* (1977) and various country-based census data.

Eric Leclerc

Map 8.1

TOTAL NUMBER OF PIO AND THEIR PERCENTAGE OF THE POPULATION IN HOST NATIONS (1971)

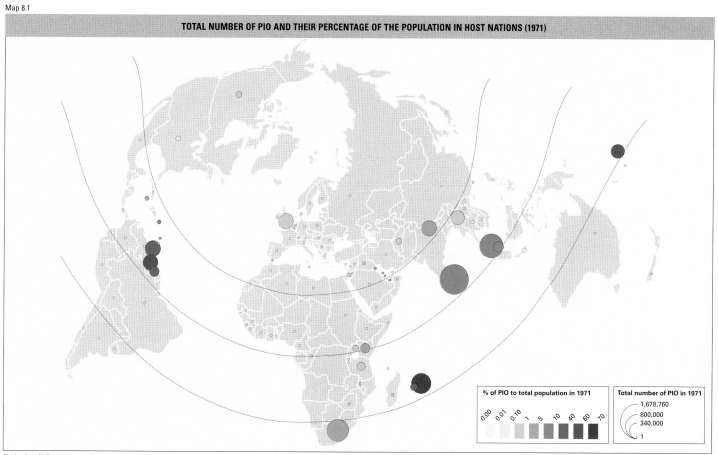

% of PIO to total population in 1971

0.00 0.01 0.10 1 5 10 40 60 70

Total number of PIO in 1971

1,678,760
800,000
340,000
1

Projection: J. Bertin, 1953. Source: Tinker 1977, Helweg 1990 (revised). Base map: FNSP/IEP Paris Cartography Laboratory, made with Philcarto (http://perso.club-internet.fr/philgeo).

Map 8.2

TOTAL NUMBER OF PIO AND GENERAL GROWTH (1971–2001)

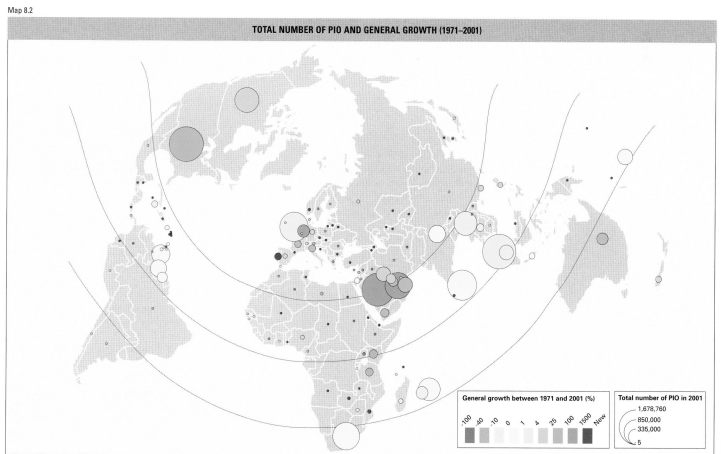

General growth between 1971 and 2001 (%)

-100 -40 -10 0 1 4 25 100 1500 New

Total number of PIO in 2001

1,678,760
850,000
335,000
5

Projection: J. Bertin, 1953. Source: report of the High Level Committee on Indian Diaspora, 2001 (revised). Base map: FNSP/IEP Paris Cartography Laboratory, made with Philcarto (http://perso.club-internet.fr/philgeo).

143

SRI LANKA

The majority of Indians recruited for work in the coffee and tea estates in Ceylon came from the southeastern districts of Tamil Nadu. For those who came via Mannar, the journey involved a long trek known as a 'death march' due to the large number who perished on the way to the plantations.

IT IS DIFFICULT to speak of 'overseas Indians' in Sri Lanka (known as Ceylon prior to 1972) before the advent of the British to the island. Sri Lanka was separated from the Indian subcontinent only at the end of the last glacial period, around 8000 BC. This is relatively late, particularly since the history of human habitation on the territory goes back to 30,000 BC. The early dwellers must have belonged to a wider South Asian megalithic culture, of which the Weddas—often called the island's 'original inhabitants'—are the last survivors. Hence, it is not entirely without justification that the Lanka Tamils today claim that the island (or at least parts of it) is part of the historical Tamilakam, the traditional South Indian homeland of the Tamils. The Sinhalese settlers who arrived on the island around the middle of the first millennium BC are of Indian origin too, as is borne out by their language, which belongs to the Indo-Aryan family of languages. Categories such as 'Sinhalese', 'Lanka Tamil' or 'Indian Tamil', therefore, do not correspond to ethnicity or, in the case of the two Tamil groups, language, but are political descriptions. Though the designation 'Indian Tamil' may have been in use during the 19th century, it was not until the 1911 census of Ceylon that the term gained official recognition. In that year, the category of 'estate' was also added to the existing categories of 'urban' and 'rural', a distinction that has been maintained in the census reports since.

INDIAN COMMUNITIES IN SRI LANKA OTHER THAN 'ESTATE TAMILS'

Indian Tamils migrated from South India to Ceylon mainly in the course of the 19th and 20th centuries. The

Map 8.3

LABOUR RECRUITING AREAS AND ROUTES TO CEYLON

Legend:
- Tea country
- Major labour recruiting districts
- Minor labour recruiting districts
- Rail route c. 1880s
- Sea routes
- Road routes

Source: S. Muthiah, The Indo-Lankans: Their 200-Year Saga, 2003.

vast majority of these migrants supplied much sought after labour to the plantations, especially the tea estates, of the island's central hill districts around Badulla, Ratnapura and Nuwara Eliya. The 2001 census classified 855,888 people as Indian Tamils, out of which 695,705 live on estates. These plantation workers were neither the only Indians nor the only Tamils who came to Ceylon. Other Tamil migrants were recruited in the late 19th century for the expansion of Colombo Harbour as well as for the construction of the island's roads and railways, finding employment in the dock companies or the railway and public works departments. Between 1891 and 1911, for instance, a little more than 5000 Indians worked regularly at Colombo Harbour. Their numbers reached 12,000 in 1931 but fell dramatically thereafter under the impact of the Great Depression. Today, 50,190 Indian Tamils are listed under 'urban', as reflected in the 2001 census. The remaining 109,993 Indian Tamils are part of the rural population outside the estates.

Indian dock workers transporting crates of Ceylon tea.

Table 8.1

BASIC DEMOGRAPHIC DATA								
	1901	1911	1946	1953	1963	1971	1981	2001
Lanka Tamils	c. 510,000 *(14.3%)*	528,024 *(12.8%)*	733,731 *(11.0%)*	844,703 *(10.4%)*	1,170,310 *(11.1%)*	1,415,567 *(11.1%)*	1,886,672 *(12.7%)*	736,484*
Indian Tamils	c. 441,000 *(12.3%)*	530,983 *(12.9%)*	780,589 *(11.7%)*	974,098 *(12%)*	1,122,850 *(10.6%)*	1,196,368 *(9.4%)*	818,656 *(5.5%)*	855,888 *(5%)*
Total population	3,565,984	4,106,350	6,652,339	8,097,895	10,590,060	12,711,143	14,864,750	16,864,544*

*Based on census reports from Ceylon/Sri Lanka. Note: *Due to the prevailing war, no complete census could be conducted in the northern province.*

Among the non-Tamil groups who settled in Ceylon since the beginning of the 19th century (and even before) are the Parsis (mainly from Bombay), Bohras and Memons (both Muslims from western India), and Bharatas, a Catholic community from Tuticorin. The oldest and, in terms of social and economic status, most important of these smaller groups were the Chettiars, a South Indian caste whose activities on the island date back to the 11th century. Though some of the Chettiar families today might claim their ancestry to that time, most of them arrived in Ceylon over the course of the 19th century, following the new business opportunities which the colonial government had created. Most significantly, they engaged in financial businesses, trading in government bills, investing in revenue farming throughout the island, and worked as moneylenders, an activity that made them the backbone of rural credit all over the British Empire in Asia. The Chettiars also ran agency houses that soon dominated the island's rice, wheat and cotton cloth import business. By the end of the 19th century, more than 100 Chettiar firms were registered in Colombo, a number which increased to almost 400 in 1914. Living in an exclusive area between the harbour and the business district (the Pettah), the Chettiar community was divided into two corporations (*nagaram*), each one attached to its own Hindu temple. The temple was not only used for religious purposes, it also served as the headquarters of the *nagaram*. According to the 2001 census, in which the Chettiars were listed as a separate ethnic group, there are now about 8800 Chettiars (0.05 per cent of the population), virtually all of whom live in Colombo or in the immediate vicinity of the city.

THE ADVENT OF THE INDIAN TAMILS

As the history of South Indian labour emigration during the colonial period has been dealt with in Part III of this volume ('The *Kangani* and *Maistry* Systems'), the case of plantation workers coming to Ceylon can be summarised rather briefly here.

The Colebrooke-Cameron reforms of 1833 abolished enforced labour, known as *rajakariya* on the island, redrew the administrative map and, most importantly, laid claim upon the former lands of the kings of Kandy in the interior of the island. As the climate and altitude of the hill districts proved ideal for the cultivation of coffee, a real estate boom set in, and by 1860, coffee plantations covered almost the whole of central Ceylon. With a sufficient supply of water and a reasonably stable temperature,

coffee plants provided a relatively rich and reliable yield without needing much care. Labour was needed to pluck, peel, wash and pack the coffee beans only during the harvest season between November and January. Sinhalese peasants were unwilling to undertake these tasks as they looked down on menial agricultural work. Hence, planters had to import labour from South India. After the ban on emigration was lifted in 1842, an increasing number of South Indians, mainly from the districts along the coast adjacent to the island (Tinnevelly, Ramnad, South Arcot, Madurai, Chinapoli and Pudukottai), were recruited for the plantations.

The recruitment of South Indian labourers was mainly in the hands of *kanganis* (foremen), who functioned as the headmen of the gangs they had recruited, and looked after the social and financial affairs of the workers in the estates. Headed by the *kanganis*, these groups embarked for either Colombo, if they came from the southern districts, or Mannar, if they came from further north. The route via Colombo was more convenient as motor vehicles were available. The route from Mannar, on the other hand, required long treks. These marches came to be known as 'death marches' because of the high number of immigrants who died from fever, malaria, dysentery or cholera on the way. After years of neglect, the colonial government gradually responded to the problem through legislation. An ordinance in 1865 made the provision of clean drinking water, sheds for shelter at night, and stations where basic medical care could be obtained, compulsory. In 1904, the Ceylon Labour Commission was founded, with recruitment offices set up all over South India aimed at checking the influence of the *kanganis*. In 1920, the Education Ordinance forced estate owners to provide primary education for the children of the workforce, and school attendance was made compulsory. Finally, minimum wages for estate workers were introduced in 1927.

In the late 1880s, the structure of plantation labour changed fundamentally as a result of a fungus that spread across the plantations and prevented any further cultivation of coffee. The tea plants that replaced coffee required different treatment and effected a threefold change in the labour force. First, since tea leaves were much lighter than coffee beans, female labourers could do most of the plucking. Consequently, the percentage of females among migrants rose significantly from about 10 per cent to nearly 50 per cent. Second, as tea leaves could be plucked all year round, there was an increase in the number of workers recruited. Year-long plucking also meant that labourers could not return to India and had to remain on the estates permanently. While the change on the plantations created a highly immobile Tamil labour force, it did not prevent movement entirely. Until the 1930s, recruitment in South India continued to be significant, in part to meet the shortfall created by labourers returning either permanently or for short visits to their villages. There

A passenger without proper inoculation papers spent between five to 10 days in camp before the necessary quarantine pass was issued.

Biologist and philosopher Ernst Haeckel described the coffee planter's bungalow as 'a one-storied house, built of stone, with a wide, projecting roof and verandah, surrounded by a lovely garden, and fitted with every English comfort adapted to the circumstances.'

145

On the plantation, men were involved in processing tea leaves and packing them into large chests that were carried to bullock carts bound for the harbour.

Tea plantations situated in the central highlands of Sri Lanka are home to the vast majority of the Indian Tamil populace.

Map 8.5

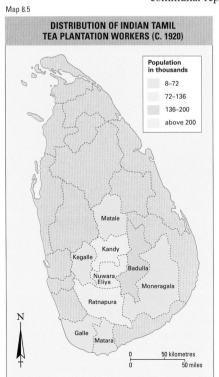

DISTRIBUTION OF INDIAN TAMIL TEA PLANTATION WORKERS (C. 1920)

Population in thousands

- 8–72
- 72–136
- 136–200
- above 200

Matale

Kandy

Kegalle

Nuwara Eliya

Badulla

Moneragala

Ratnapura

Galle

Matara

N

0   50 kilometres
0   50 miles

Source: V. Samarasinghe, 'Access of Female Plantation Workers in Sri Lanka to Basic-Needs Provision', in J. H. Momsen and V. Kinnaird (eds.), Different Places, Different Voices, 1993.

was also considerable mobility between estates depending on economic circumstances. *Kanganis* who wielded considerable influence over workers in the estates could, for example, lead whole groups to other plantations when they were dissatisfied with the current planter. A small number of Indian Tamils also entered the rural labour market outside the estates or took up jobs in the cities, especially in Colombo.

INDIAN TAMILS AND COMMUNAL POLITICS IN THE 1930S

During the 19th century, political representation of the people in Ceylon was largely symbolic. The three native members of the legislative council were hand-picked by the governor, who normally adhered to the principle of communal representation by selecting one Sinhalese, one Lanka Tamil and one Burgher (the Eurasian group). Among them, language or ethnicity did not play a major role as all three were drawn from the English-educated socio-economic elite. This situation changed after World War I. To reward the colonies for their contribution to the war effort, the British promised them 'responsible government'. Native politicians, elected from a limited suffrage based on wealth and education, were to form the majority in the legislative assembly of the colony and serve as ministers in its administration. The founding of the Ceylon National Congress (CNC) in 1919 was an attempt to create a political body that stood above communal interests or party politics. However, the first elections showed that the elitist alliance within the CNC was fragile, and that voters, the majority of whom where Sinhalese Buddhists, cast their votes along communal lines. In protest against the domination of the CNC by Sinhalese Buddhists, the Lanka Tamils formed a separate party, the Tamil Congress.

Further change came as a result of the work of a commission led by Lord Donoughmore, which had been sent to Ceylon in 1928 to evaluate the results of the franchise reform. It recommended that universal adult franchise be introduced. It was also stated that '40 to 50 per cent of the Indian Tamils on the tea estates should be considered as permanent residents,' and therefore be given the right to vote on the condition that they had been living on the island for a minimum of five years and intended to stay permanently. As a result of this far-reaching reform, Ceylon became a model colony. It was the only colony where universal franchise was introduced. In the single member constituencies set up, candidates of the ethnic majority in the constituency were elected. The dominance of Sinhalese Buddhists in the state council was inevitable.

The demographic situation in the thinly populated hill districts clearly favoured the Indian Tamils. However, because of the restrictions imposed on the Indian Tamils, few qualified for the first election in 1931, and even though the number of voters among them almost trebled by the 1936 elections, only two of their candidates were elected on both occasions. However, the prospect of winning more seats in the future was good as long as they voted (as they actually did) en bloc. Consequently, in the first elections after the war, six out of the seven up-country constituencies were won by Indian Tamils.

Although Sinhalese Buddhists of the CNC benefited from universal franchise, and the small group of non-CNC parliamentarians could not challenge their numerical superiority, they began to agitate against the enfranchisement of the Indian Tamils, whom they perceived as foreigners. One of their initial demands was a re-deliniation of the constituencies in the hill districts, which was intended to deprive the Indian Tamils of at least one of their seats in parliament. It became increasingly obvious that their ultimate aim was to exclude the estate workers altogether by repatriating them to India. During the 1930s, the idea of repatriation began to find supporters within the CNC, and leaders of the CNC announced their intention to repatriate the estate workers in 1944 and 1945 when they met with their counterparts from the Indian National Congress.

CREATING UNDESIRABLES

India, Ceylon and Burma were given full independence immediately after World War II, mainly due to the policy of the Labour government that had come to power in the summer of 1945. The new government agreed to a quick transfer of power, which, in the case of Ceylon, was concluded on 4 February 1948. The CNC, now renamed the United National Party (UNP), emerged victorious by a large margin from the first parliamentary elections held in 1948. In spite of the change in name, the party's political agenda remained unaltered, and it now began to push anti-Indian Tamil policies more strongly. Among the first policies enacted were the Ceylon Citizenship Act and the Indian and Pakistani Residents Act of 1948, and the Parliamentary Elections Amendment Act in 1949, which disenfranchised every person not holding Ceylonese citizenship. Residents on the island could obtain citizenship only if they produced evidence that they had been living on the island permanently and without interruption since 1936. This was a serious drawback as most of the estate workers had received only basic education, were largely illiterate and lived in an environment where not even standard records such as birth certificates were issued. In spite of the conditions, the new law required them to submit their application form for citizenship within one year.

The Tamils living in the estates were not the only group affected by the new citizenship laws. Those who had moved to Colombo to take up work in the harbour or in government departments, and entrepreneurs who had succeeded in opening small businesses such as shops or restaurants, clearly felt vulnerable and many decided to return to India before it was too late, although they were not immediately targeted by the repatriation scheme. By 1950, some 34,000 Indian Tamils had left Colombo and the west coast, taking their assets and belongings with them.

The Indian government under Jawaharlal Nehru, occupied with the integration of the millions of refugees who had come to India as a result of the partition of the subcontinent in 1947, did little to ameliorate the difficulties of the Indian Tamils in Ceylon. Nehru protested half-heartedly, intimating that his government did not concur with the view that they still held Indian citizenship. In the face of increasing pressure from the Ceylonese government, Nehru in principle accepted India's responsibility for the Indian Tamils on the island, but at the same time attempted to delay actual repatriation for as long as possible. On meeting Sinhalese Prime Minister Dudley Senanayake in London in 1953, Nehru agreed to allow 300,000 people to return to India, while 450,000 were to receive Ceylonese citizenship. The fate of the remaining 150,000 was not decided. For the time being, they were to be given the right to stay on

Repatriation

If judged by the official definition of repatriation as 'a return or restoration to native land', to call the transfer of Indian Tamils from Ceylon to South India 'repatriation' appears to be quite inappropriate, as the majority of the people returning had never been to India before, knowing it only as the land of their fathers and forefathers. The repatriation of Indian Tamils resulted from a deep-rooted fear among many Sinhalese of becoming a minority in what they believed to be their homeland. Unlike the Lanka Tamils, who had been living on the island for generations, the Indian Tamils, who came to the island during the 19th and first half of the 20th century in order to work in the tea plantations of the hill districts, could not claim Ceylon as their homeland, and thus leaders of the Sinhalese-dominated Ceylon National Congress began to demand that they be repatriated. Following their victory in parliamentary elections after independence, they increased pressure on Indian Tamils by enforcing laws that deprived these groups of their citizenship and franchise, placing them in a situation of statelessness. In 1964, India finally agreed to take back 525,000 people, while 300,000 were given the opportunity to apply for Ceylonese citizenship. These figures proved unrealistic as by the time repatriation was suspended because of the civil war, fewer than 340,000 Tamils had actually been relocated to India, while almost twice the originally envisaged number of Indian Tamils preferred to stay in Ceylon. In a pragmatic move, they were eventually given the citizenship of their choice in 1988.

Faced with the task of integrating hundreds of thousands of returning persons, the government of India cooperated with the state government of Tamil Nadu to design a rehabilitation programme, the main elements of which were transit camps, financial assistance and several settlement schemes, the best known of which is situated in the Nilgiri Hills. This mountainous area on the border of the states of Karnataka and Tamil Nadu had the advantage of being remote, thinly populated and, at over 1829 m, resembled the region where the settlers came from topographically and climatically. The resettlement scheme caused friction between the people of the Nilgiri Hills and the repatriated Indian Tamils. One positive impact, however, is that the area has become one of the key tea-producing centres in India.

the island. In effect, this meant statelessness for them. Further details were agreed upon a year later in a formal treaty, according to which Tamils who wanted to remain on the island had to show a 'sufficient knowledge of the language of the other area' (i.e. Sinhalese) and the Indian High Commissioner was entrusted with assisting those who wanted to return.

By 1956, as Buddhists were preparing to celebrate the 2500th anniversary of the Buddha's death, relations between the Sinhalese and the Tamils on the island had deteriorated considerably. S. W. R. D. Bandaranaike, who had left the UNP in order to found his own party—the Sri Lanka Freedom Party (SLFP)—promised in the 1956 election campaign to make Sinhalese the official language of the country with the slogan 'Sinhala only!' Demands to make Buddhism the state religion were also voiced. Supporters of the Federal Party, which represented the Lanka Tamils in parliament, responded with a non-violent protest, blocking the entrance to the parliament building. This led to anti-Tamil riots in Colombo and other cities of Ceylon.

Bandaranaike, elected as prime minister after the 1956 elections, agreed to let Tamil remain as one of the two official languages of the state. Though the pact between Bandaranaike and the leader of the Federal Party, J. V. Chelvanayakam, on the status of the two languages eased tensions momentarily, the Lanka Tamils had become estranged from the Colombo government, regardless of whether the UNP or SLFP was in power. At the same time, Bandaranaike's own supporters were infuriated by the compromise. The Prime Minister was assassinated by a Sinhalese Buddhist militant in 1959.

Realising that repatriation had progressed very slowly over the last decade—only 134,000 Indian Tamils had left the island, but natural increase had already made good their number—the Sri Lankan government put the repatriation question on the agenda again in the early 1960s. Prime Minister Sirimavo Bandaranaike (who

Jawaharlal Nehru at a gathering in Ceylon in 1956 commemorating the 2500th anniversary of the Buddha's death. His visit coincided with a time of tense relations between the Sinhalese and the Tamils, following the anti-Tamil riots in Colombo in 1956.

147

S. Thondaman (second from left) sending off representatives of the Ceylon Workers Congress to the International Conference of Free Trade Unions in the late 1940s.

followed her husband into office) pressed for a new treaty with Nehru's successor, Lal Bahadur Shastri, that raised the figure of Indian Tamil repatriation to 525,000, while only 300,000 were to receive Ceylonese citizenship. The treaty also stipulated a period of 15 years during which the transfer had to take place and pressed the Indian government to publish the number of returning Tamils annually so as to keep the process going. The fate of the remaining 150,000 was left undecided until a 1974 treaty between the two countries was signed. The treaty required half of this number to be repatriated to India and the other half to become citizens of the newly named Sri Lanka. By the time civil war broke out in 1983, rendering further transportation from the island impossible, an estimated 340,000 people had moved to South India.

Though the war involved Lanka Tamil radicals and the Sri Lankan government, Indian Tamils were affected as well. The estates became targets, subject to attacks by gangs of Sinhalese militants between 1977 and 1979, and between 1983 and 1985. The anti-Tamil pogroms of 1983 were particularly notorious for the systematic, island-wide destruction of Tamil property. For some time during this period, Indian Tamils were encouraged by Lanka Tamils to defend their rights jointly; however, by the late 1970s, the representatives of the Indian Tamils had come to the conclusion that their political aims would be better served by cooperation with the UNP.

NETWORKS AND ASSOCIATIONS

Initially, the organisation of the Indian Tamils had been shaped by their caste affiliation as well as by their dependence on the *kanganis*. The foremen yielded considerable power on the estates, where they not only acted as spokesmen on all questions concerning labour relations, but also managed a large part of the social life of the Tamil labourers. They issued documents and registration forms, arranged marriages, mediated disputes (about ownership rights and inheritance, for example) and frequently supervised the financial affairs of members of their group, which included the administration of wages, moneylending and supplying foodstuffs from their shops.

From the 1920s, however, the position of the *kangani* was somewhat challenged by communist agitators visiting

A Sunday religious class held in a temple on the outskirts of Colombo.

the estates, who forcefully reminded the Indian Tamils across the plantations of their common interest as workers and urged them to unite country-wide. The influence of these communists led to the formation of the Ceylon Indian Association in 1923, an organisation which fulfilled the roles of a trade union, political party and social club. The first true labour union, the All-Ceylon Estate Labour Federation, was formed in 1931; but given the persistent dislike of trade unions among the estate workers, along with the influence of the *kanganis*, this union did not survive the early phase of the Great Depression, which had a considerable impact on the plantation economy of the island. The next attempt to organise a workers' union was undertaken in 1939, mainly due to the instigation of Nehru, in the course of his visit to the island, promoted an organisation of overseas Indians as an instrument of self-help and self-reliance, in line with his view that Indians overseas should not rely on the Indian government but look after their affairs themselves. This led to the formation of two associations, the Ceylon Indian Congress, a party-like political organisation, and the Ceylon Indian Congress Labour Union, which served as a trade union. Of the two, the latter proved to be more consistent, surviving, albeit under the name Ceylon Workers Congress (CWC), from 1950 until today.

In the post-war years, the CWC was dominated by its long-time leader, Saumiyamoorthy Thondaman, who, by launching a hartal (public protest) in 1948 against the discriminatory laws affecting Indian Tamils had gained considerable recognition. In the following years, the CWC joined forces with the SLFP to oppose the politics of the UNP. The SLFP, however, was hardly any better in its approach towards the 'Tamil question', and the alliance was terminated in 1964 when Prime Minister Bandaranaike revealed her plans to register Indian Tamils in a separate electoral roll. The CWC's slow shift of support to the UNP after 1965 became public in 1977 when Thondaman openly backed J. R. Jayawardene in his quest to become president. This move increased the political weight of Thondaman considerably, and eventually he was able to press his advantage on the question of repatriation, citizenship and enfranchisement.

Thondaman not only became a Cabinet minister under Jayawardene, but also served in the committee that prepared the new constitution. At the insistence of Thondaman, fundamental citizenship rights were given to Indian Tamils in full; the category 'citizen by registration' (which Indian Tamils had rightly perceived as giving them the status of second-class citizens) was abolished; and their right to vote in local elections was reinstated. His final triumph came in 1988 when continued repatriation due to the civil war had become impossible and a pragmatic solution for the remaining Indian Tamils on the island had to be achieved. He managed to push through the Grant of Citizenship to Stateless Persons Act, whereby 'every person who is of Indian origin lawfully resident in Sri Lanka, who is neither a citizen of Sri Lanka nor India, and has not applied...for grant of Indian citizenship shall have the status of citizens of Sri Lanka and shall be entitled to all rights and benefits to which other citizens are entitled by law.'

The relationship between the two Tamil communities was less cordial and cooperative. Despite the fact that Sinhalese Buddhist militants made little distinction between Indian and Lanka Tamils in the course of the various anti-Tamil pogroms, each community tried to keep its distinct identity and emphasised differences rather than commonalities. Thus, in 1957, when Prime Minister Bandaranaike held talks with Federal Party leader Chelvanayakam on the future of the Tamil language in Sri Lanka, Thondaman insisted on talking to the Prime Minister separately. Similarly, when the Federal Party started to rally for support in the plantations, the CWC opposed this form of fraternisation as it threatened to undermine its own power base. Another principal difference in opinion became apparent in the mid-1970s as the Lanka Tamils increasingly drifted towards the demand for an independent state, whereas Thondaman saw the future of the Indian Tamils within the Sri Lankan state. The attitude of the latter was obviously due to the settlement pattern of Indian Tamils, who lived in well-defined pockets within the Sinhalese heartland. For that reason, the attempt to create an island-wide Tamil representation, the Tamil United Front (which later became the Tamil United Liberation Front) received only lukewarm support from Thondaman.

SOCIO-ECONOMIC PROFILE AND DEMOGRAPHIC TRENDS

The large majority of Indian Tamils belong to the low castes of South India. Approximately half of them are Adi Dravidas (untouchables) such as Pallar, Paraiyar or Chakkilyan, while Vellalar, Kallars, Ambalakkarars and other slightly higher (but non-Brahminical) groups constitute the majority of the other half. The caste system survived on the estates virtually intact and continues to affect marriage patterns and religious rituals. After Hinduism, which is practised by about 90 per cent of the Indian Tamils on the estates, Christianity (7.8 per cent, of whom 6.2 per cent are Catholics), and Buddhism are the most common religious orientations. Fewer than one per cent of Indian Tamils are Muslim.

The estates are almost completely autonomous and self-reliant microcosms, providing residents with all the necessities of daily life. The estates had always been private enterprises, but at a very early stage, state legislation had begun to shape the living conditions within: medical services, minimum wages, housing, schooling and childcare are all regulated by law. Ironically, though the plantations and their immigrant labour force were at the fore of the colonial welfare state in Sri Lanka, the Indian Tamils have been omitted from enjoying its benefits since independence. Instead, their welfare depended on the management of each plantation. This changed to a certain degree in 1975, when most of the estates were nationalised under a land reform programme and came under the administration of two government agencies, the State Plantation Corporation and the Janatha Estate Development Board.

DAILY LIFE AND WORKING CONDITIONS

Work on the tea plantation begins at 7am and ends at 5 pm, interrupted by a tea break in the morning and a lunch break at noon. During the main harvesting season (May–July), plucking goes on for seven days a week: Sundays and holidays draw double rates for the workers. Labour is clearly divided along gender lines: the actual

Saumiyamoorthy Thondaman (1913–99)

S. Thondaman (centre) pictured here with President R. Premadasa (right) and Mrs Premadasa (left).

The biography of Saumiyamoorthy Thondaman, the undisputed leader of Sri Lanka's Indian Tamils, is symptomatic of the ambiguous period of the early 20th century, when Indian Tamils were denounced as 'foreigners' by Sinhalese nationalists for keeping their Indianness alive through various links with India.

Thondaman's story begins with his father, Karuppiah, who had achieved social and economic success on both sides of the Palk Strait in an exemplary rags-to-riches story. Karuppiah left his home village of Munappudur (Ramnad district, Tamil Nadu) in 1873 at the age of 13, at the instigation of a *kangani*. First serving as an assistant in the boutique of a Tamil trader in the provincial town of Gampola, he later became a *kangani* himself, overseeing workers on a tea plantation. With the stable income of his official salary and payments which coolies made to him, Karuppiah returned to Munappudur to marry. He married again in 1903 in an elaborate ceremony that impressed the villagers after his first wife was rejected by caste members. The palatial home he built a year later at Munappudur was another symbol of his status. The basis for Karuppiah's economic advancement, however, lay in Ceylon, to which he returned in 1904, shortly after the birth of his first child. He purchased the Walvendon tea estate near Ramboda (Nuwara Eliya district) in 1909, becoming the first 'native' planter in that district, building a bungalow and buying a car. After acquiring the estate, he returned to Munappudur, where three more children, including Thondaman, were born between 1910 and 1914. Leaving his family in India, Karuppiah returned to Ceylon for seven years. Thondaman saw his father for the first time only in 1921, and his desire to be with his father paid off when he was finally allowed to go to Ceylon in 1923.

On the estate, Thondaman attended school while also training to follow in his father's footsteps as a planter. Being a bright student, Thondaman progressed to St. Andrews College at Gampola (1927–32) against all odds, taking special tutorials in English. During his final year at school, his marriage was arranged by his mother and sister in Tamil Nadu to a girl from a village near Munappudur.

Leaving his wife and son in India, Thondaman returned to look after the Walvendon Estate on behalf of his father, whose health was failing. It was during this period that the young planter was gradually drawn into politics, despite his father's disapproval. There is evidence that Mahatma Gandhi, in particular, stimulated Thondaman's interest in politics. Thondaman was witness to the anti-Indian agitation of Sinhalese nationalism, which emerged in the mid-1930s and culminated in the citizenship and electoral laws of the early post-war period. His formal entry to politics as the secretary of the Gampola branch of the Ceylon Indian Congress in 1939 was followed closely by his father's death in early 1940.

Thondaman's political career in independent Ceylon started with his entry to parliament as the member of parliament (MP) for Nuwara Eliya in 1947. Deprived of voting rights in the 1950s, no Indian Tamil candidate was elected during this period, but Thondaman returned to parliament through an appointment by Prime Minister Sirimavo Bandaranaike in 1960. Disappointed by her treatment of the Indian Tamils, he contributed to the defeat of her government in 1964 and was again appointed MP, this time by Prime Minister Senanayake of the UNP in 1965. Increasingly, as more Indian Tamils regained their citizenship and voting rights in the 1970s, their political influence returned as well. After a short spell at the helm of the Tamil United Front in 1971, from which he resigned due to the party's demand for an independent Tamil state, Thondaman was re-elected as MP for Nuwara Eliya in 1977, 30 years after his first entry to parliament. By then, he had thrown in his lot as well as that of the CWC with the UNP, and he consequently became the minister for rural development in the Jayawardene-led government.

Due to Thondaman's efforts, the degrading category of 'citizenship by registration' for Indian Tamils was removed from the 1978 constitution, and finally, in 1987, he persuaded President Jayawardene to grant citizenship to all Indian Tamils who were stateless. In the 1994 elections, the CWC campaigned alongside the UNP, and Thondaman re-entered parliament as a representative of the UNP-led government. When the SLFP-led coalition emerged victorious, he defected to become the Minister of Estate Infrastructure in the Cabinet of Chandrika Kumaratunga. He remained in this office until his death in October 1999.

Cottage-type houses for plantation workers, usually with more than one room per building and with better sanitation facilities, emerged in the 1970s.

plucking, which involves long walks in the plantations and shouldering an increasingly heavy load as the basket fills, is left entirely to women. Men are primarily involved in weighing and further processing the leaves (fermenting, drying, selecting and packing) in the factory. Gender division is also reflected in wages. Fixed by legislation since 1904 and agreed upon in a tripartite commission (including planters, workers and the state) from 1944, wages increased gradually until the time of nationalisation, roughly doubling between 1953 and 1974. Thereafter, wages increased considerably, doubling for a second time between 1974 and 1978, again until 1983, and have since continued to rise. Irrespective of this considerable increase, which has to be set against a high inflation rate all through the 1970s, the average income of plantation workers is still at the bottom of the national

income level and even trails behind the income of the rest of the rural population. Female plantation workers receive about 75 per cent of the wages paid to male workers.

The estate supplied housing for the workers and this usually consisted of single-room houses, known as the 'workers' lines'. Originally built for a migrant labour force and meant to be occupied only for a few months every year, the workers' lines was the main form of accommodation for workers until the 1970s. Since then, the situation has improved significantly and the number of buildings with more than one room has increased, while the average number of persons per room has increased from 2.6 in 1971 to 3.4 in 1981. The improvement in the housing situation is again a result of the government's takeover of the plantations and the subsequent replacement of the old lines with units providing at least two rooms. The 2001 census reveals that the number of single-room buildings has fallen to fewer than 10 per cent throughout the hill districts, although substantial differences still exist from estate to estate. Along with the reconstruction of buildings, sanitary conditions have improved. Practically all line buildings administrated by one of the two agencies now have access to tap water, which is also used in toilets. Hygiene standards have also improved with the construction of drains and sewage systems. Compared to the national average though, housing conditions on the estates continue to be at the lower end; however, the gap is less marked than it was 20 years ago.

In general, the supply of food on the estates can be considered satisfactory. Staples such as rice and flour are usually provided by the estate at a subsidised rate (which is deducted from the wage), as is firewood. Moreover, workers are usually given the opportunity to cultivate vegetables and garden fruit on small plots of land behind their houses. The estates usually also accommodate small shops, not infrequently run by former *kanganis*, from where a limited selection of additional foodstuffs can be obtained. Only the supply of meat and fish continues to be a problem, as the estates are not regularly included in the country-wide distribution networks, nor are they equipped with the necessary refrigeration facilities. Thus, the supply of protein poses a problem, even though

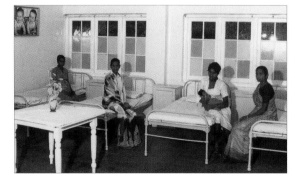

The maternity ward in an estate hospital. While health facilities in the estates have improved since the 1970s, there are still very few hospitals in central Sri Lanka.

Table 8.2

INCOME, EXPENDITURE AND FOOD CONSUMPTION (2002)							
	Income		Expenditure		Consumption		
	Mean household income (Rs. per month)	Mean per capita income (Rs. per month)	Mean household expenditure (Rs. per month)	Mean food expenditure (Rs. per month)	Rice (kg)	Flour (kg)	Bread (kg)
Urban	22,420	4997	22,196	7959	27.1	2.2	15.3
Rural	11,712	2835	12,063	5575	36.1	2.2	9.8
Estate	7303	1663	8786	5120	41.3	22.4	4.9
National	12,803	3056	13,147	5848	35.3	3.3	10.2

Source: Sri Lanka Department of Census and Statistics, 'Household Income and Expenditure Survey 2002', 2004.

vegetables are used as substitutes to meet the shortage in animal protein. An estate worker's average intake of calories is among the highest of any group in Sri Lanka, but chronic malnutrition has continued to affect almost 60 per cent of estate workers since the late 1980s. In 2000, the percentage of five-year-old children from the estates being underweight stood at 44.1, considerably higher than the figure for the national average of 29.4. Although this figure has been reduced, imbalanced nutrition is still widespread.

The generally poor health conditions of the estate workers highlight these findings. Although legislation requiring proper health care for the immigrants began as early as 1865, the health of workers on the plantations showed little improvement before the 1970s. Virtually all estates now have a dispensary from which a limited supply of medicine can be obtained, but not all dispensaries are under the management of an estate medical assistant as prescribed by law. In addition, the remoteness of many estates can create a problem in cases of emergency as there are few hospitals in central Sri Lanka and ambulance services are not always available. The upgrading of health facilities on the estates after the takeover by the state was supported by international aid programmes, mainly in the maternity and childcare sectors. As a result of these interventions, the number of one-year-old children possessing a health card, in which vaccinations and basic health checks are recorded, has risen from 53.5 per cent in 1993 to 78.3 per cent in 2003 (the national average is 88.6 per cent). A similar development can be discerned from the figures for full vaccination coverage, which have gone up from 82.3 per cent to 86.1 per cent during the same period, although still well below the national average of 93.5 per cent. Moreover, only 42 per cent of pregnant women on the estates were visited by a midwife in 2000, exactly half of the national average. In the past two decades, while the total fertility rate has declined from 3.1 to 1.9 at the national level, it remains at 2.4 on the estates. The basic health and life indicators show that despite slow improvements during the last two decades, Indian Tamils on the plantations continue to be worse off when compared to the rest of the Sri Lankan population, and among the Indian Tamils, women are more affected than men.

EDUCATION AND PROGRESS

Access to education on the estates has always been poor. During the colonial period, Indians were cheap labour for whom education was considered unnecessary, if not counter-productive. Accordingly, the plantations were slow to establish schools even after they were pressed to do so in 1920. In the 1970s, the number of schools increased to about 800 and were attended by a maximum of 77,000

Table 8.3

| | 1985–86 | | | 1991 | | |
	Male	Female	Average	Male	Female	Average
SRI LANKA LITERACY RATES (%)						
Lanka Tamil	89.4	84.3	86.6	N.A.	N.A.	N.A.
Indian Tamil	87.6	55.2	66.9	N.A.	N.A.	N.A.
Sinhalese	91.8	84.9	88.4	N.A.	N.A.	N.A.
Urban	92.4	86.1	89.1	94.0	84.3	92.3
Rural	88.5	80.7	84.6	89.9	84.3	87.1
Estate	74.5	45.9	59.4	79.0	52.8	66.1
All island	88.6	80.0	84.2	90.1	83.1	86.6

Source: Sri Lanka Department of Census and Statistics, 'Social Conditions' reports, 1985–91.

Table 8.4

NUMBER OF GOVERNMENT SCHOOLS									
	1972		1982		1987		1988	1992	2002
Badulla	283	(125)	342	(72)	534	(3)	543	560	570
Kandy	624	(133)	706	(51)	680		682	685	652
Kegalla	558	(41)	569	(39)	597	(7)	605	610	542
Matale	243	(25)	287	(18)	310	(1)	310	313	317
Moneragala	161	(5)	175	(12)	203		203	238	259
Nuwara Eliya	249	(322)	326	(144)	456		454	460	514
Ratnapura	494	(81)	546	(33)	587		586	589	593
Sri Lanka	8551	(785)	9243	(370)	9709	(11)	9741	10,042	9826

Source: Sri Lanka Department of Census and Statistics, 'Education' reports, 1972–2002. Note: Figures in brackets refer to estate schools.

pupils in 1972. With the closing of the estate schools following the nationalisation of the estates, both figures dropped continuously until 1987, when 1627 pupils attended the remaining 11 estate schools. The latest census figures are less informative, but if we take the 293 Tamil-medium schools which existed in the Nuwara Eliya district in 2001, this was approximately twice the number of estate schools that existed in 1982 (144). Analysing these figures, it should be noted that school attendance, though compulsory up to the age of 16, has been much lower on the estates, where children are expected to contribute to the family income through work. A survey in 1980–81 showed that around 40 per cent of children between five and nine years of age did not attend classes, twice that of the national average.

Hardly astonishing is the fact that Indian Tamils have the worst educational profile of all census groups. In 1981, only two-thirds of Indian Tamils qualified for the basic literacy standards, and if one is to account for the estate Tamils separately, the figure drops to below 60 per cent. Although there has been a slight improvement since the survey, there still exists a wide gap with the national average. The contrast to the national average becomes even more pronounced if gender differences are taken into account. In general, girls attend school less regularly and for a shorter duration than boys, working on the plantations or helping at home instead. The female literacy rate is therefore considerably lower than that of men, at 45 per cent compared to 75 per cent for males, in 1985. The figures for 1991 show a slight increase for both men and women, though unlike the national level, the gender gap has actually increased.

With education forming the key to social and economic progress, the low literacy and educational level of Indian Tamils will continue to prevent a substantial improvement of their situation in the foreseeable future.

Tilman Frasch

Although the number of schools on the estates has increased in the last three decades of the 20th century, school attendance remains considerably lower than in other parts of Sri Lanka due to the larger proportion of children who work to supplement family income.

Over 90 per cent of female workers on the estate are tea-leaf pluckers, the lowest position in the hierarchy of the plantation. They move up and down the hilly terrain several times a day, carrying baskets that get progressively heavier.

151

NEPAL

The 15th-century Royal Palace in Kathmandu, where the coronation ceremonies for Nepali kings take place.

THE DIASPORA IN Nepal is not merely a 19th- and 20th-century phenomenon. Given the contiguity of Nepal and northern India, and the very porous nature of the border, there has been a long history of migration from India to Nepal (as well as from Nepal to India). The dominant societies in both regions share important religious, cultural and social institutions: Hinduism is the dominant religion in Nepal and northern India; Nepali is closely related to Hindi, the dominant language of northern India; and Hindu society in both regions is caste based. An Indian element exists, therefore, within the foundations of Nepali society. Many Nepali Brahman and Rajput hill people (Parbatiya), who otherwise see their Nepali identity as being based precisely on not being from the plains (i.e. India), claim their high status from genealogies derived from Indian lines of descent originating from Indian groups who moved to the hills in medieval times.

THE INDIAN COMMUNITY IN NEPAL

Modern Indian migration was firstly associated with movement into the Terai, the low, alluvial plain along Nepal's southern border, which is an extension of the Gangetic plain of northern India. Here, the Madheshis (midlanders) include groups who are descended from Indian migrants who came to the Terai from the late 18th to the early 20th century, when Nepal had become a unified kingdom under the Shah dynasty and the Terai was increasingly cleared. These people are overwhelmingly Hindu and, from west to east along the Terai, used the Awadhi, Bhojpuri or Maithili dialects of Hindi, all of which are spoken in distinct regions of northern India.

Madheshis are often regarded as the 'Indian community' of Nepal. India's Ministry of External Affairs estimates that the community numbers around 4 million. Many in Nepal think that this claim is unwarranted since more than half of the group have taken Nepali citizenship. Claire Burkert captures the position of the people when she quotes a Maithili-speaking Kayastha as saying, 'First I am a Maithil, then Madheshi, and thirdly Nepali.'

Sometimes, the diaspora is said to comprise those who are India-born and migrated to Nepal from the 1920s

Table 8.5

INDIA-BORN POPULATION IN NEPAL (1961–2001)			
	No. of India-born persons	% of population	Population of Nepal
1961	324,158	6.6	4,912,996
1971	322,718	2.79	11,555,983
1981	222,278	1.48	15,022,837
1991	418,982*	2.2	18,491,097
2001	N.A.	N.A.	22,736,934

*Source: B. C. Upreti, Indians in Nepal, 2002. Notes: The population figure for 2001 is from the Nepal Population Census (NPC). The NPC does not provide 'India-born' figures. *Vidya Bir Singh Kansakar gives the following breakdown for the 1991 figures: 378,692 were in the Terai and constituted 4.4% of the Terai population; and of these Terai dwellers, 93,345 (24.7%) were male and 285,347 (75.3%) were female.*

mainly to the Terai (96 per cent) and the Kathmandu Valley (about 4 per cent). A variant sometimes cited takes only the figures for 'Indian citizens' in Nepal: 116,355 in 1981, 68,489 in 1991 and 102,468 in 2001.

MIGRATION TO THE TERAI

The Treaty of Sagauli (1816), which ended the Nepal War, required Nepal to surrender the entire Terai to the British, although the area from the Rapti to the Kosi rivers was almost immediately ceded back to Nepal in exchange for the commutation of pensions for leading members of the Nepal court. In 1860, the Far Western Terai was returned to Jung Bahadur Rana as an expression of gratitude for Nepal's assistance during the Sepoy Mutiny. Jung Bahadur turned the Far Western Terai into a family property and brought to it businessmen, traders and landlords. Nepal also legislated to allow foreigners to buy and sell land in the Terai. As a result of both the return to Nepal of the Eastern Terai in 1816 and the gift of the western lands in 1860, there was large-scale migration to the region, both from India and from the hills. In the late 19th and early 20th century, further clearing of the Terai encouraged Indian movement into the new lands opened up. During this period, Indian capital also moved into productive enterprises such as jute at Biratnagar, and the processing of matches, cigarettes, rice and vegetable oil.

Map 8.6 shows the main geographical regions of Nepal and the sections of the Terai along the southern border.

Map 8.6

GEOGRAPHICAL REGIONS

CHINA

Kathmandu Valley

East Inner Terai

NEPAL

Eastern Mountains

Western Mountains

Far Western Terai

West Inner Terai

INDIA

Midwestern Terai

Central Inner Terai

Eastern Terai

Source: Pradumna P. Karan, Nepal: A Cultural and Physical Geography, 1960.

Oxen feed on a haystack in the Terai plains.

The key period of 20th-century migration was ushered in by the Treaty of Peace and Friendship signed by Britain and Nepal in 1923. This formally recognised Nepal's independence and sovereignty, which brought new stimulus to migration until 1950, when Nepal was freed from Britain's 'protectorate'.

MIGRATION AFTER INDEPENDENCE: INDUSTRY, TRADE AND LABOUR

The period 1950–61 saw Indian migration hit its peak. This followed the new Treaty of Peace and Friendship signed between the independent states of India and Nepal in 1950. It allowed freedom of movement between the two countries and freedom to settle, with the same rights and provisions for security as the locals. Nepalis moved to India to work (and some to settle), while Indians were welcomed as migrants in Nepal. Indians moved into specialised roles in the growing urban economy, particularly in house construction, as carpenters, electricians and plasterers. They were also important as fruit and vegetable sellers, barbers, goldsmiths and as pavement watch repairers. By the mid-1970s, they were seen as dominant in many of these areas. Movement in quite large numbers continued into the Terai.

Indian businessmen also began to operate more fully from the 1950s in trade and industrial undertakings. Important among these businessmen were the Marwaris, many of whom were refugees from Burma. Some of them moved straight from Burma into Nepal, while others moved first to northern India and then to Nepal. The first factory in Nepal was established by a Marwari: the group came to have considerable power in Nepal's business life. Other Indian traders, some Indian citizens and other people who arrived from India set up operations to import third-country goods for re-export to India under special arrangements allowed to Nepali products. Others moved into the production of stainless steel and synthetic fabrics in factories established in Nepal near the border with India under the 1964 Bonus Voucher Scheme, which allowed exporters to retain 90 per cent of foreign exchange earned. Such exports to India undercut Indian production because of lower wage costs, and in 1969, India seized a large amount of such items as contraband.

Migrant labour was recruited mainly from the United Provinces, Bihar and West Bengal, although there were others from Rajasthan, Punjab and Haryana, and even some from western and southern India. The recruitment of labour for Indian factories was in effect a new version of the *maistry* system. The employer in Nepal appointed a 'master', who returned to his home village in northern India and recruited workers, whom he then took to Nepal.

In 1983, Indian entrepreneurs were attracted to the ready-made garment industry in Nepal because of the US decision to reduce quotas from India while retaining Nepal's quotas. This expanded Nepali production of garments by what were technically Indo-Nepali joint ventures. These garment producers often brought in Indian workers in quite large numbers. However, when the US imposed quotas on Nepali garments in 1985, many Indian producers left Nepal.

NEPALI CONCERNS

Early concerns about the impact of migration were centred on the question of Nepali citizenship. The requirements were first framed in 1953 and were considered difficult not only for people in the Terai but also for those in the

Map 8.7

Kathmandu Valley. It was clear that the regulations were seen as a means of restricting immigration. In 1962, the Panchayat government stated that the applicant had to read and write Nepali; have an occupation and reside in Nepal; must relinquish any earlier citizenship; and be a resident in Nepal for two years. In 1975, when the regulations were viewed as an important means of restricting migration, the residential requirement was increased to 15 years.

Despite these early attempts to limit immigration, many hill people, observing the inflow of Indian traders, industrialists and workers, began to question such developments. They saw Indians as 'foreigners', and 'Teraians' were often thought of as an Indian fifth column. In business, the Nepali middle class began to find it difficult to compete, making the dominant position of the Marwaris in commerce and industry especially unwelcome and leading to the growth of anti-Indian feelings. Moreover, in the 1970s and 1980s, this mood of anti-Indianism was used in official circles in Nepal to foster an aggressive Nepali nationalism, particularly during the period of strained relations between India and Nepal in the late 1980s.

By the 1980s, the situation was such that many hill people wanted greater regulation of the border and safeguards against Indian migration. In a report in August 1983, a task force of the National Commission on Population 'held Indian migrants responsible for numerous ill effects on the country' and recommended that a system of work permits be instituted. In 1987, the Panchayat government decreed, under the 'special arrangements' clause of the treaty of 1950, that Indians had to apply for work permits to work in three districts of the Kathmandu Valley. This was a period of difficult diplomatic relations between Nepal and India, and only the return to democratic government in 1990 brought about a more favourable climate for Indian migration—including the exemption of Indians from the work permits system.

OUTCOMES

Indian migration has changed the sociocultural and political context of the Terai and, perhaps to a lesser extent, Kathmandu. B. C. Upreti makes the point that there is 'something like Indianness which can be observed in Kathmandu in the cinema halls, newspapers and magazines, hotels, restaurants and dhabas [food stalls], market and business circles...' Indian migrants played an important role in the economic development of Nepal from the 1950s. Despite this, the Nepali middle class has been critical. They have found it hard to compete and Indian dominance is seen to weaken the position of Nepalis in their own country.

Peter Reeves

A street barber in Narayanghat in the Terai plains.

Indian food at Take Home Tandoori Chicken.

MALDIVES

The Maldivian buggalow was the mainstay of trade in the archipelago during the colonial period. It was an inter-island vessel that sailed as far as Ceylon.

THE MALDIVES ARE an archipelago of some 1200 islands which form 19 atolls, located southwest of the Indian subcontinent in the Indian Ocean. From the 12th century onwards, the islands were under the rule of an Islamic sultanate. In December 1887, however, when the archipelago became a protectorate of the British, Sultan Muinuddheen II signed an agreement recognising British suzerainty over the islands. The Maldives became independent on 26 July 1965 (although an air base on the southern atoll of Gan remained under British command until 1976).

SEAFARERS AND TRADERS

Lying on the major shipping route to the eastern Indian Ocean, the islands were visited by seafarers and occasionally by important travellers such as Ibn Battuta in the 14th century and François Pyrard de Laval in the 17th century. For most of their history, Maldivians did not encourage the settlement of outsiders, although traders from other South Asian regions did arrive and establish themselves, especially in the 19th century.

In the 1880s, C. C. Rosset reported that the bazaar in the capital, Malé, through which all foreign trade passed, was in the hands of merchants from Bombay. These merchants rented their shops from the Sultan, who personally owned all of such property in the capital. In 1935, Thomas W. Hockley reported that there were 46 firms (some of them more than a hundred years old) owning 52 businesses on the islands, and that the foreign merchant community comprised 250 Bohras (originating from western India, with a network spanning Ceylon), 50 Mappilas from Malabar and 50 Ceylon Moors. Between them, the merchants also owned 18 two-masted sailing vessels known as 'buggalows', which carried on a regular trade between Ceylon and the Maldives. Approximately 95 per cent of the trade was in the hands of foreign merchants.

A group of Bohra merchants who dominated trade in the Maldives in the 1930s.

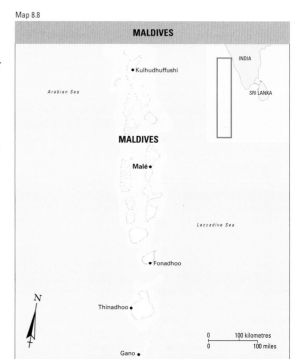

Map 8.8

ECONOMIC CHANGES

As an independent nation, the Maldives had to modernise its economy. The traditional fishing, fish processing and boat-building industries were augmented by shipping and some manufacturing and handicraft industries, but at least one-third of its current GDP and more than 70 per cent of its foreign exchange earnings come from tourism. Over 90 per cent of government tax revenues are derived from import duties and tourism-related taxes.

FOREIGN WORKERS

In 2000, there were approximately 9000 Indians out of a population of around 269,000. Since then, their numbers have increased to just under 17,000, making Indians the largest expatriate community in the Maldives. The community comprises accountants, doctors, teachers, engineers, managers and other professionals. From time to time, at the request of the Maldivian government, Indian professionals such as doctors, nurses, tutors, teachers and sports coaches have been sent to the islands from the subcontinent. Other skilled and unskilled Indians have also sought employment in the Maldives but, as in the case of other people who are not native to the island, gaining Maldivian citizenship remains difficult for them. Nevertheless, a large number of Indians in the Maldives are working on projects sponsored by India.

In 2001, the number of foreign workers serving the archipelago's tourism industry stood at about 29,000, mainly from South Asia. Most of them work in construction, business, hotels, restaurants and resorts. This figure

increased to 38,413 at the end of 2004. Likewise, the number of workers from India increased from 12,541 (including 1379 women) in 2001 to 16,657 (including 1865 women) in 2004. The employment pattern for Indian workers has remained fairly constant. Major concentrations of Indian workers are in education, health and social work.

Table 8.6 shows the main job categories for Indian workers in 2004 compared to the total number of foreign workers. It is clear that in nearly all of the categories listed, except for resorts, Indian workers form nearly half or more of the total expatriate workforce. In some sectors, such as education, health and social work, Indian workers fill nearly the entire quota of foreign workers.

There have been reports of some Indian job seekers, especially those from Tamil Nadu, being subjected to ill treatment by their employers and imprisoned after being promised attractive salaries. It has been reported that recruitment agencies in some South Asian countries charge a commission of as much as US$3000 per foreign worker seeking employment in the Maldives. This commission is usually divided evenly by the home country agent and the employment agency in the Maldives. As labourers often draw a meagre salary, they sometimes take as long as two to three years to repay their debts.

The considerable sex differential among Indians in the Maldives shows that the option of migrants bringing their families with them is limited to only a few Indian professionals. While Indian professionals have been known to live a relatively comfortable life in the Maldives, with the opportunity of travelling to India regularly, the labouring classes are usually only able to return to their families at the end of their contract. To prevent the abuse of Indian labourers, the Indian High Commission has attempted to protect the rights of Indian workers in the archipelago through stricter legal requirements, such as detailed employment contracts and payment for unfair dismissals.

Map 8.9

EARLY MALDIVIAN MARITIME TRADE

Courtesy of Peter Reeves, Head, South Asian Studies Programme, National University of Singapore.

Table 8.6

INDIAN WORKFORCE COMPARED TO TOTAL FOREIGN WORKFORCE IN SELECTED PROFESSIONS (2004)						
	Business	Construction	Education	Hotels and restaurants	Health and social work	Resorts
Indian workers	2471	4930	1954	1130	1132	2331
Other foreign workers	2215	4217	547	1329	210	7655
Total no. of foreign workers	4686	9147	2501	2459	1342	9986

Based on Maldives Ministry of Labour, 'Expatriate Employment by Industry and Nationality', 10 May 2001 and 31 December 2004. Note: This table does not include all job categories.

CONTEMPORARY DEVELOPMENTS

In 1994, the Maldives-India Friendship Association (MIFA) was formed. MIFA has organised cultural events and seminars under the patronage of the High Commission on several occasions. Since 1997, the India Club, under the auspices of the High Commission, has been organising annual community functions featuring Indian cultural shows. Thus, alongside the significant growth in the Indian expatriate population in the last decade, there has been an increase in cultural and community-based events.

In December 2004, the Maldives was affected by the Asian tsunami. Eighty-two people were killed and scores of others injured. Islands that catered to foreign tourists were badly affected. At least 12 of 80 resorts were damaged and the repair bill amounted to US$1.5 billion. India provided considerable aid to the Maldives following the tsunami. The Indian Coast Guard was the first international relief team to reach the islands. However, reconstruction efforts were hampered because most of the expatriate workers had left the country. In addition to construction, the teaching and health sectors, where large numbers of Indian expatriates were employed, came to a standstill.

Although some Indian workers have since returned, they view their stay as temporary, largely because traditional inhibitions against foreign permanent settlement persist. This is most notable in the contemporary restrictive immigration controls preventing foreigners from becoming citizens. The result has been that the Indian community in the Maldives remains a transient one.

Faizal Yahya and Peter Reeves

Map 8.9 shows the position of the Maldives in relation to the major maritime trading routes.

A late 19th-century engraving of the bazaar in which Bohra merchants traded.

A street in Malé's main shopping area for tourists. Many Indian workers on short-term contracts are in the tourism sector.

Dock hands loading cargo in Malé's harbour.

MALAYSIA

An Indian worker tapping rubber. Indian labourers played a crucial role in the development of the rubber plantation sector in Malaya.

IN THE 1940s, Indians made up about 14 per cent of Malaya's population. By 2000, numbering 1.8 million, they represented 7.7 per cent of the total Malaysian population of 21.89 million. Approximately nine-tenths of Indians may be classified as of South Indian origin, with the remaining one-tenth from North India.

Indian migration to Malaya was an important dimension of British colonial rule in Asia and coincided with the growth of the international economy in the second half of the 19th century. There were three main migration streams, each of which was associated with specific economic roles. The first and largest stream, the indentured workers, comprised mainly Tamils and Telugus who worked in the plantations, on the construction and maintenance of transportation lines (roads and railways), and at the ports. The second stream, the auxiliaries, consisted predominantly of North Indians who were recruited for the police force and security services, and Malayalis and Jaffna Tamils who were employed in clerical and subordinate civil service occupations. The third stream, the traders, comprised Indian merchants and the Chettiars, a money-lending caste from South India. North Indian migrants were far fewer compared to the other Indian migrant groups and constituted a distinct community. The occupational differentiation between the Indian migrants also had religious overtones and helped to create a distinctive diasporic consciousness among them.

The British colonial authorities governed Malaya following a 'divide and rule' policy and, in their attempts to articulate a 'Malay/Malayan' identity, they constructed an Indian (and Chinese) identity premised on 'otherness'. Indians were thus defined in relation to the Malays and Chinese in terms of their ethnicity and place of birth. Subsequently, the larger South Indian group asserted its 'Southern-ness', particularly 'Tamil-ness', as the dominant characteristic of Indian communal identity on issues of culture, religion and political representation. This division among Malaysian Indians persists despite attempts by some community leaders to make the term 'Indian' more inclusive.

Malaysian Indians have shown few gains where political and social mobility are concerned. The vast majority of labour migrants remain a disadvantaged group. This is largely due to their numerical standing vis-à-vis the Malays and Chinese. The historical, political and economic relationship between the Colonial Office in London, the India Office and Malaya before World War II was also an important contributory factor. There were fewer millionaires and traders among them, and their migration to Malaya was largely regulated by the colonial government, acting in concert with British planting interests. The more numerous Chinese, who did not constitute a predominantly labour-oriented diaspora, also had wider business and social networks, while the Malays benefited from state patronage.

There is also a distinction between the Indian middle class, which continues to do well, and the working class, which continues to underperform. Unlike the situation among the Malays and Chinese, there is little or no interaction between members of the Indian middle and working classes, possibly because of caste distinctions. The underperformance of the Indian working class may be attributed to the fact that Indian workers were drawn from the less favoured caste groups. Thus, they continue to be weighed down by the low self-esteem that usually characterises members of groups belonging to the lower castes and is worsened by the lack of interaction between the well-off and less well-off Indians. Furthermore, programmes aimed at improving the situation of working-class Indians and their children have yet to be put in place (e.g. for entry into residential schools with targeted education programmes). The marginalisation of working-class Indians is reflected in their poor performance in business, equity ownership and employment in professional sectors and the civil service. The disadvantaged position of the majority in the Indian community has contributed to a sense of dispossession and disadvantage among many Indians in Malaysia.

Map 8.10

THE HISTORY OF INDIAN MIGRATION TO MALAYA

Before the 16th century, Indian migration within Southeast Asia was on a relatively small scale and limited in geographic scope. There was significant mercantile or religious travel involving Indians in the region, which predated the arrival of European commercial interests. Indian traders were also prominent in Southeast Asia's leading regional entrepôts and, although trade was small in volume, it was a source for the transmission of ideas, new products and technologies. The consequent movement also resulted in migration from a country with a long history of manufacturing, a monetised economy, and sophisticated commerce. Gujarati and Chulia merchants had been trading with Southeast Asia, exchanging Indian-made textiles for Southeast Asian spices in a network that linked the ports of the Indian subcontinent with others on the eastern shore of the Bay of Bengal, in Burma, Thailand and the Malay states. Indian political institutions, specifically Hindu-Buddhist traditions of kingship, were introduced in Southeast Asia by the 7th century AD. Indian culture, in particular its Hindu-Buddhist religious-cultural systems, was the dominant external influence in the region.

Nineteenth-century Indian labour migration to Malaya laid the framework for the Indian community in the country. The fact that this migration had its origins in labour systems distinguishes it from previous movements of Indians into Malaya. This form of migration involved mass movements and the organisation of travel arrangements and employment opportunities in Malaya by private labour brokers, other intermediaries, state officials and, in some cases, employers themselves. Nevertheless, there were a minority of migrants who paid their own passage or relied on friends and relatives for their transportation costs. Migrant workers who were regarded as sojourners were managed by the Labour Department in the colonial administration and officials of the states, and repatriated to India during economic downturns. High levels of geographical and social exclusion in the plantations resulted in the establishment and retention of group ties based on language, religion and cultural norms, and a strong connection to the mother country.

The majority of migrants were poor and had been pushed into migration by factors in India such as pressure on land, natural calamities and exploitation by landlords. Pull factors in Malaya included growing economic opportunities, the opening up of the hinterland and the expansion of mineral and agricultural export production. An unrestricted migration policy, the absence of border controls, improvements in transportation technology and falling transport costs facilitated this migration. The bulk of the migrants were in no position to pay their travel and related costs, which were either met by labour recruiters or future employers.

The recruitment of Indian migrant workers was consistent with a rather elastic use of labour. The workers had many characteristics in common. They were young, predominantly unskilled adult males, comprising primarily illiterate peasants who had spent hardly any time away from their villages. They were involved mainly in the physical production of agricultural commodities, or in the construction and maintenance of transportation systems and public undertakings, and in the ports. After periods of employment, they usually, but not always, returned to their country of origin.

COLONIAL LABOUR POLICY

Three principles governed colonial labour policy: the acquisition of a plentiful, diversified and cheap supply of labour for colonial and capitalist enterprises; the (limited) assurance of the labourer's freedom of movement; and the provision of a limited amount of protection for workers. Crucially, a diversified recruitment policy meant that migrant labour could be manipulated easily and ensured that workers were not easily assimilated or readily accepted by the local inhabitants. The colonial government and employers collaborated to maintain low wage costs and sustain occupational differentiation based on ethnicity, resulting in vertical cleavages of ethnicity, kinship and religion, and facilitating the substitution of one worker group by another.

Indians were the preferred workforce for a number of reasons. Although the Chinese were hardworking and available in large numbers, their wage rates were higher than those of the Indians. The British also feared that a greater influx of Chinese migrants, who dominated the tin mining sector, might make them a potential social and political threat in Malaya. Moreover, Chinese workers could only be hired through contractors who organised the labour gangs. The Chinese also had a long tradition of group solidarity and social organisation, and were constantly bargaining for higher wages. As for the Javanese, recruiting them entailed fairly complex negotiations with the Dutch colonial government in Indonesia, and the Javanese were also needed for the Sumatran rubber plantations. As Kernial Sandhu puts it:

The South Indian labourer was preferred because he was malleable, worked well under supervision, and was easily manageable. He was not as ambitious as most of his northern Indian compatriots and certainly nothing like the Chinese...he was the most amenable to the comparatively lowly paid and rather regimented life of estates and government departments. He had fewer qualms or religious susceptibilities, such as aversion to crossing the dreaded kalapani and food taboos...and cost less in feeding and maintenance.

It was also easier to recruit South Indians because India was under the same imperial government, and its proximity to Malaya was an additional bonus. South Indian 'docility' fitted well into the dependent relationship between management and employee. A major drawback, however, was that South Indians lacked the funds for spontaneous mass migration. The recruitment of Indian plantation labour was both regulated and sponsored by the Malayan administration from the start.

A rubber estate with recently planted seedlings. Rubber trees take five to eight years to mature, after which they can be tapped for 20 to 30 years.

Women were an important part of the indenture system from the 1860s, although Malaya was often exempt from meeting the quota set by the Colonial Office.

157

Types of Migrant Labour

The main mechanism for recruiting Indian migrant labour in the second half of the 19th century and the first decade of the 20th century was the indenture system. Workers were contracted to a single employer for a period of one to three years and the contract was usually a written one. Wage workers were therefore not employees at will, but were often bound to their employment by enforceable labour agreements, which employers used where possible to manage their labour costs and supply. Breaches of written contracts were regarded as criminal offences, not civil. At the end of the contract, the worker had to repay his travel and associated costs (or these were repaid through deductions) before he was released from his contract. Since most workers earned very low wages and were too poor, they were re-indentured for a further period.

Another important mechanism for the recruitment of Indian labour was the *kangani* system, whereby planters sent established labourers to India to recruit other labourers from their villages or home districts. This system emerged around the late 1860s and became popular in the 1880s and 1890s. The *kangani* was paid a commission for each labourer recruited and acted as a plantation foreman for the labourers recruited by him. The contractual position of workers recruited through this mechanism was less harsh than that under indenture: the contract was usually a verbal one, the worker had the right to terminate his contract, and desertion was regarded as a civil offence rather than a criminal one. Nevertheless, this system had its abuses since the *kangani* usually had a vested interest in ensuring that the labourers did not abscond—he received 'head money' for every day worked by each labourer. To check the abuses, the colonial government introduced the licensing of *kanganis* in 1901.

Kangani-assisted recruitment peaked in the 1910s following the abolition of indenture. It began to decline in the late 1920s, a trend consistent with the global economic downturn; was suspended during the Great Depression; and was formally abolished in 1938.

A notable development in labour policy was the establishment of a centralised semi-official body, the Indian Immigration Committee (IIC), in 1907 to facilitate and supervise South Indian labour recruitment. The IIC's activities were strengthened in 1908 when, with the backing of employers, the Tamil Immigration Fund (which was renamed the Indian Immigration Fund in 1910) was set up to provide free passage for labourers to Malaya. All employers of Indian labour were charged a quarterly levy to cover travel and other related costs of free Indian labour migration to Malaya. This recruitment of voluntary workers was cheaper than the *kangani* system since intermediaries were bypassed. In addition, the hold of the *kangani* over workers declined. *Kangani*-assisted recruitment gave

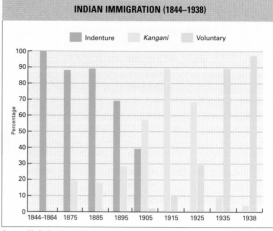

Figure 8.1

INDIAN IMMIGRATION (1844–1938)

Indenture   *Kangani*   Voluntary

Source: K. S. Sandhu, Indians in Malaya, *1969.*

way to free wage labour recruitment in the 1930s. The permanent settlement of Indians in Malaya also coincided with the emergence of 'freer' wage labour and the increased recruitment of female workers.

During the 1930s, government assistance for labour recruitment was regarded as inappropriate and the Indian Immigration Fund was utilised to repatriate unemployed workers. After the Great Depression, there was less pressure from planters for a centrally managed labour recruitment system since government-assisted migration was well publicised and most repatriated workers could finance their own return trips.

Thousands of Indian labour migrants arrived annually in Malaya under the two recruitment systems: between 1844 and 1910, about 250,000 indentured labourers came to Malaya. The peak of *kangani*-assisted recruitment occurred in the 1910s, when about 50,000 to 80,000 Indian workers arrived annually. From 1844 to 1938, *kangani*-assisted migration accounted for 62.2 per cent of total Indian labour migration compared to 13 per cent for indentured migration. In 1920, only 12 per cent of Indian workers were voluntary migrants, but this proportion had increased to over 91 per cent by the 1930s. The changing recruitment patterns and the breakdown of Indian immigrants by recruitment system are shown in Figure 8.1.

Until 1923, Indian immigration to Malaya was regulated first by the Indian government, and then by the Straits Settlements and the Federated Malay States (FMS) governments. In 1923, following the passage of the Indian Emigration Act a year earlier, the Indian government took over the regulation of Indian emigration to Malaya. A set of rules which defined hours of labour, working conditions and welfare provisions for Indian workers was put in place. More significantly, an agent of the government of India was appointed in Malaya to ensure compliance with the rules in the workplace. The agent also made recommendations to the Malayan government when there were perceived deficiencies. Indian leaders also visited Malaya to inspect workers' living and working conditions. In 1938, following the publication of the 'Sastri Report' (1937) on Indian labour in Malaya, the Indian government banned all assisted labour emigration to Malaya.

Working and Living Conditions

In the first four decades of the 20th century, Indians accounted for between 70 to 80 per cent of the FMS plantation labour force, as shown in Table 8.7.

The kangani *licence was introduced by the colonial government in 1901 to check abuses in the recruitment system. Only the holder of such a licence had the right to recruit labourers in India.*

Kanganis *on Sungei Wangie estate, c.1914. The* kangani *was a key intermediary between the plantation owner and Indian workers on the estate, and commanded considerable authority over the latter.*

Indeed, the rubber plantation sector could not have developed without the contribution of Indian labour. The plantation, however, was organised and operated for the benefit of the rubber companies, and workers were seen merely as costs in the equation. Moreover, since the Malayan government was itself a major employer of Indian labour, it suited the government's purpose to keep workers 'bound' and wage levels down.

In the late 19th century, the daily working hours of indentured labourers varied. The norm was eight hours, but some estates stipulated nine hours; others demanded ten hours. Conditions improved slightly in the 20th century, when the working day was limited to six consecutive hours and could not exceed more than nine hours a day. The labourer had to work six days a week, and if he worked for the full six days, he was eligible for a paid day off on the seventh. Overtime was paid at double the hourly rate. These conditions governing hours of work were retained in all subsequent statutes, including the Labour Code of 1923.

The Straits Settlements Ordinance of 1884 set the following rates for Indian labourers on three-year contracts: 12 cents a day for the first year and 14 cents a day for subsequent years for adult males; and 8 cents a day for the first year and 10 cents a day for subsequent years for females and males under 21 years of age. The higher rate, however, was not to be paid until the worker had paid off his/her debt to the employer (travel and other costs incurred on the journey to Malaya). Employers were also required to supply workers with food and groceries at wholesale prices since the sugar and coffee plantations were located in remote areas.

When indentured labour recruitment was abolished in 1910 (the final contracts ended in 1913), wages were freed of Indian government control. Nevertheless, the Malayan authorities aimed to ensure a cheap and abundant labour supply and they were frequently under pressure from the powerful planting sector to keep wages low. The practice of calculating wages on the basis of individual subsistence thus continued. The provision of compound accommodation was also used to justify the retention of low wage rates.

The impending passage of the Indian Emigration Act of 1922 was also propitious for future wage deliberations. In their negotiations on the terms for Indian emigration to Malaya, the Indian government recommended—and the Malayan authorities agreed to—the principle of a standard wage (as opposed to a minimum wage) and that this would be fixed by law. From 1922, a committee determined standard wage rates for Indian labour. With

the principle of a standard wage established, factors such as the locality and health conditions of estates became part of the equation for determining wages.

Malaya was divided into two regions: key areas and non-key areas. Key areas, mainly the Straits Settlements and FMS, included 'well-located' districts on the western half of the peninsula. These were relatively 'healthy' areas where the cost of living was comparatively low. Non-key areas included, for the most part, inaccessible areas in the interior, such as in the state of Pahang, and other districts on the eastern part of Malaya, where the cost of living was higher. Wages were calculated on a daily basis and on the basis of a standard budget that took into account the cost of foodstuff, clothing, festival preparations and household equipment.

The average daily wage of an adult Indian male (42 cents) was equivalent to 10.5 annas per day in South India. Moreover, agricultural work in South India was not available on a continuous basis, compared to 25 days per month in Malaya. Nevertheless, the cost of living was about 40 per cent higher in Malaya, thus the average monthly income of a plantation worker ranged between Rs. 12 and Rs. 15.

There were also differences based on gender, age and job classification. Plantation workers were generally categorised into three groups based on their job/skills classification—factory workers, rubber tappers and field

Until the second half of the 20th century, bullock carts with Indian drivers were widely used for the transportation of goods.

An early morning roll-call marked the start of a working day at the rubber estates. In 1884, male labourers in the Straits Settlements were paid 12–14 cents per day.

Table 8.7

RACIAL COMPOSITION OF FMS ESTATE WORKFORCE (1907–38)							
	Indians	(%)	Chinese	Javanese	Others	Total	No. of estates
1907	43,824	(75.5)	5348	6029	2872	58,073	287
1911	109,633	(66.0)	31,460	12,795	12,127	166,015	711
1915	126,347	(74.0)	27,446	8356	8592	170,741	719
1920	160,966	(74.3)	40,866	8918	5808	216,558	1105
1925	137,761	(74.7)	37,879	4165	4549	184,354	1206
1930	132,745	(78.2)	30,860	3665	2411	169,681	1757
1935	118,591	(77.4)	29,950	1941	2658	153,140	2345
1938	137,353	(80.4)	28,925	1762	2892	170,932	2388

Source: J. N. Parmer, Colonial Labour Policy and Administration: A History of Labour in the Rubber Plantation Industry in Malaya, *1960.*

Rubber plantation workers receiving their pay from estate officials.

Indian labourers often turned to wayside Indian medicine sellers despite the fact that colonial administrators considered their traditional remedies inadequate for curbing disease.

An estate hospital, the only medical facility for plantation workers.

workers. Of the three categories, tapping was regarded as skilled work while field work was considered unskilled. Thus, rubber tappers received higher wages compared to field workers. With regard to gender, female Indian workers earned less than male workers, normally between 70 per cent to 80 per cent of the wage for males. There were also differences based on age, with Indian child labourers earning between 30 per cent to 40 per cent of an adult male worker's wage. Wage rates were just sufficient to induce migration, despite claims by the Malayan authorities that conditions were better than in India. The absence of official figures for cost of living and wage indexes makes any precise appraisal of wages difficult.

Many plantations were in isolated frontier areas, far from towns and mining settlements. Often, there were no other settlements or signs of habitation nearby. The plantation was thus the 'boundary of existence' for workers. The estate consisted of a number of buildings with the following units: compound accommodation for the workers, the residences of the manager and other subordinate administrative and technical staff, a factory, office, shop, dispensary and a toddy (liquor) shop. Later additions included a crèche and a school. In larger estates, there was a hospital and recreational facilities. In the early years, however, workers were not provided with modern sanitation or even bucket latrines, nor was there any piped water. Drinking water had to be carried back from nearby rivers.

The death rates of indentured workers were high. A submission to a 1924 commission on the health of Indian plantation workers in Malaya stated that over 90 per cent of deaths among adult Indian workers were due to five diseases: malaria, dysentery, pneumonia, phthisis (pulmonary tuberculosis) and anaemia, which the Estates Health Commission Report argued was

'due mostly to malaria or ankylostomiasis.' Of these, malaria was the most devastating.

The working and living conditions of Indian labourers impacted on their death rates and disease profiles. From the perspective of disease profiles, plantation workers succumbed to malaria under the pioneering conditions of the estates. The nature of the relationship between Malaya and India was also important. Since Malaya was not a province of India, the Indian government insisted on the provision of health services to reduce mortality rates on plantations. Although some of these measures were not fully implemented, medical intervention in the form of quinine prophylaxis for malaria on the estates contributed to a reduction in mortality and morbidity rates among Indian workers in Malaya. Notwithstanding this, the stoppage of new planting and the opening of new estates were also beneficial factors.

INDIAN AUXILIARIES AND THE INDIAN PROFESSIONAL AND URBAN BUSINESS COMMUNITY

Apart from the rural (plantation) and urban labouring class, Indian auxiliaries in colonial employment and Indian commercial and professional migrants formed a distinct urban community in Malaya. They exercised considerable political, economic and social influence in the Malayan Indian community, which was disproportionate to their numbers.

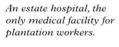

The auxiliaries predominantly comprised North Indians, particularly Sikhs, who were first hired as policemen in the Straits Settlements in the 1880s. They were also employed as a paramilitary force—the Malay States Guides, which was formed in 1896 following the creation of the FMS—and sought after as security guards, watchmen and caretakers by the colonial authorities and the private sector. Apart from being security personnel, Sikhs were 'free migrants', utilising their own or family resources to move. Sikh gurdwaras played a key role in aiding their migration and settlement in Malaya. The gurdwaras were guesthouses for travellers, places of worship and community centres, allowing Sikhs in Malaya to connect with other Sikhs in the community. The distinctiveness of this group was acknowledged by the appointment of specific Sikh community leaders, as opposed to Indian community leaders, in colonial society. Whether in the public or private sector, the majority of Sikhs migrated as single adult males and there was little family movement until after World War II. Other North Indians were predominantly merchants, traders, shopkeepers and pedlars.

Although no detailed separate records were kept of North Indian migration in either India or Malaya, a rough estimate of their numbers may be gauged from arrival and departure records, as shown in Table 8.8.

From 1921 onwards, Malayan Census Reports provided statistical information on the ethnolinguistic composition of North Indians in Malaya, as shown in Table 8.9.

The Indian mercantile, financial and commercial class represented a second major Indian urban group. Among traders, the Gujaratis were the most widespread and conducted international trade throughout Southeast Asia. Their trading network linked West Indian ports with those on the eastern shores of the Bay of Bengal, including the

Table 8.8

NORTH INDIANS IN MALAYA: MIGRATION STATISTICS (1927–36*)			
	Arrivals from overseas ports	Departures to overseas ports	Excess or deficit arrivals for overseas ports
1927	21,131	11,179	9951
1928	20,030	11,320	8710
1929	21,654	11,724	9930
1930	20,452	14,864	5588
1931	18,435	17,179	1256
1932	17,918	16,238	1680
1933	17,235	13,478	3757
1934	22,287	15,155	7132
1935	20,846	16,998	3848
1936	18,199	16,138	2061

*Source: Malayan Year Book 1937. Note: *For the years 1927–30 inclusive, figures represent arrivals, departures and movement via Straits Settlements ports only.*

Malay ports. They were specialist textile traders, distributing silk and cotton textiles from Ahmedabad and Baroda to the Southeast Asian region in exchange for rice and teak from Burma, pepper and tin from western Indonesia and Malaya, and spices gathered in the Straits of Melaka from neighbouring regions.

Like the Chettiars, the Gujaratis also developed a financial trading system throughout the region. They operated as bankers and merchant bankers, and their letters of credit (*hundi*) issued in one region could be cashed in another. In the 19th and 20th centuries, the Gujarati *shroffs* (bankers) became increasingly important as compradors to Western banks in Southeast Asia, securing credit for large urban textile firms or opium traders, with networks extending from Persia to China. The Gujaratis also provided short-term credit to the Chettiars. Their dominance in the Indian textile trade in the urban areas of Singapore, Malaysia, Indonesia and Thailand continues to this day.

Among the Indian financiers, the South Indian Chettiar moneylending caste played a major role as the regional supplier of credit in the expansion of export production in Malaya. The Chettiar financial networks were based on a complex structure of independent family firms that undertook moneylending and commodity-trading activities. In this flexible partnership structure, members of a particular family could have partnerships in many different firms. Each partnership operated through a system of overseas agents who were usually younger partners. The Chettiars also handled the remittances of overseas Indian communities through the Chettiar *hundial* shops in major urban centres. The Chettiars played an important role in financing Malay smallholder rubber production in Malaya. To prevent the large-scale transfer of land to the Chettiars, the British passed an amendment to the Malay Land Reservation Enactment in 1933 that prevented the Chettiars from gaining land in Malay reservations through default. During the inter-war period, the Chettiars made the transition from primarily short-term moneylenders to bankers, long-term creditors of trade and manufacturing, and land- and property-owners.

The third main urban Indian group comprised English-educated South Indians and Jaffna Tamils who were recruited as junior or subordinate administrative staff in the clerical and technical sectors and served as important intermediaries between colonial administrators and labourers. There were greater opportunities for this group in the Straits Settlements since the Malays were a small minority and the lack of treaty rights made it possible to employ Indians and Chinese in the junior administrative service. By 1947, about a third of Indians resided in the urban areas but the urban Indians were a fragmented group and were divided on linguistic, economic and class bases.

DEMOGRAPHIC CHANGE AND THE INDIAN COMMUNITY

The Indian plantation workforce comprised predominantly single adult males. Married men were discouraged from migrating because they could not afford to bring their families since wages were low, the norm of payment was a single-person wage, working conditions were harsh, and accommodation was available for single men only. In its 1864 legislation (Act XIII), the Indian government had stipulated that female recruits had to be included in all labour shipments following a ratio of 25 women to 100 men. However, Malaya was repeatedly exempted from this gender ratio provision. Nevertheless, a striking characteristic of the *kangani*-assisted recruitment system was the migration of families. Indeed, female migration, aimed at improving the gender ratio, was encouraged through a reduction on the levy paid on female workers.

Table 8.9

NORTH INDIANS IN MALAYA: ETHNOLINGUISTIC COMPOSITION (1921–47)			
	1921	1931	1947
Sikhs	9307	18,149[2]	10,132
Other Punjabis	6144	N.A.	20,460
Pathans	804	N.A.	3165
Bengalis	5072[1]	1827	3834
Gujaratis	403	N.A.	1301
Marathas	29	N.A.	556
Sindhis	N.A.	N.A.	728
Rajputs and Marwaris	N.A.	N.A.	1834
Parsis	N.A.	N.A.	98
Total	21,759	34,156[3]	42,108

Sources: M. V. del Tufo, Malaya: A Report on the 1947 Census of Population; and K. S. Sandhu, Indians in Malaya: Immigration and Settlement 1786–1957. Notes: [1] The figure for Bengalis in 1921 must be treated with caution since the term 'Bengalis' normally included all North Indians who embarked from Calcutta, the main port of disembarkation for North Indian migrants. [2] The figure for Sikhs in 1931 must also be treated with caution since it probably includes other Punjabis. [3] The discrepancy in the total for 1931 arises because other categories were used for North Indians (excluding Sikhs and Bengalis).

The Malay States Guides of Perak were recruited from India to restore peace following disturbances arising from feuds among Chinese clans.

Apart from playing a major role as regional suppliers of credit, Chettiar moneylenders also handled the remittances of overseas Indians.

By the 1930s, following increased female immigration, a growing number of Indian children were born and raised in Malaya.

The *kangani* also earned a higher commission for female migrant workers as well as for married couples. In late 1908, employers of new adult labour recruits were paid an allowance of 7 shillings each for males and 8 shillings 2 pence each for females recruited through a *kangani*, and 4 shillings 8 pence per adult recruited under the aegis of the Tamil Immigration Fund. Moreover, Rule 23 of the Indian Emigration Act (Act VII of 1922) stipulated that unaccompanied males were not to exceed one in five of the emigrants: thus, two out of every three male emigrants had to be accompanied by their spouses. Subsequent amendments to the Labour Code in Malaya further demanded the provision of rooms for married couples as well as childcare and educational facilities on plantations.

Census figures between 1901 and 1947 show an increase in female recruitment and the migration of families. The proportion of Indian women in these census years for every 1000 Indian men was: 171 in 1901; 308 in 1911; 406 in 1921; 482 in 1931; and 637 in 1947. These statistics also explain the increasing trend towards permanent settlement by Indian labourers by the 1930s. With increased female migration, more children also arrived in Malaya; by the 1920s, women accounted for 30 per cent of all arrivals. More children were also born in Malaya and raised locally, contributing to the transition towards permanent settlement and the availability of a pool of workers. Hence, job possibilities for women on plantations and elsewhere, the provisions of the 1922 Emigration Act, the 1923 Emigration Rules, and the establishment and reconstitution of families led to greater permanent Indian settlement in Malaya.

After World War II and independence, the character of the plantations began to change. Their alien origin, with little connection to indigenous economic structures in addition to expatriate ownership and control, resulted in plantation companies and management being taken over either by the national government or local companies. By the late 20th century, effective control of the largest plantation companies in Malaysia—Guthrie, Golden Hope, Highland and Lowland, KL Kepong and Sime Darby—was held by the ruling party, the United Malays National Organisation (UMNO), through the state-owned Permodalan Nasional Berhad and Amanah Saham Raya. The Malaysian government subsequently integrated the plantation system into the local economic environment by adapting it to land settlement schemes designed to redress landlessness among Malay peasants. A large number of rubber plantations were also converted into housing estates. This changeover resulted in many former Indian plantation workers being thrown out onto the streets, despite assurances by the state that the new owners would provide housing for them. These people then formed the poorest communities in urban squatter areas.

Female Indian workers carrying pails of tapped latex to the factory.

RACE, IMMIGRATION POLICY AND BORDER CONTROLS

Despite an earlier commitment to unrestricted immigration, colonial policy changed in the 1930s. New legislation restricted the entry of Chinese migrants, representing the first attempts by the colonial state to use border controls as a means of keeping out specific, unwanted migrants. The rationale for exclusion was economic and security-/politically-motivated, and coincided with depressed economic conditions worldwide and locally.

The first piece of restrictive legislation enacted in the Straits Settlements was the Immigration Restriction Ordinance (IRO) in 1928. In January 1933, the IRO was replaced by the Aliens Ordinance. This legislation was designed to 'regulate the admission of aliens in accordance with the political, social, and economic needs for the moment of the various administrations in Malaya' and 'to provide a means of registering and controlling aliens resident in Malaya.' The legislation was directed at the Chinese since Indians were classified as British subjects. Nevertheless, the British deported a number of 'undesirable' Indian labour activists in the latter half of the 1930s. In 1938, the Indian government banned all assisted Indian emigration to Malaya. In keeping with the export-oriented structure of the economy, a plural society in which ethnicity was clearly linked to economic function was in place by 1940.

Indians comprised 10 per cent to 14 per cent of the population between 1911 and 1947, as shown in Figure 8.2 and, together with the Chinese, had outnumbered other 'Malaysians' by 1940.

Compared to the Chinese, however, the Indians had a worse gender ratio and were slower to transform from a community of transients to one of permanent residents. In 1921, locally-born Chinese accounted for 22 per cent of the population, as opposed to 12 per cent for locally-born Indians. Since Indians were largely found on estates, they were classified as rural and agricultural. In the same year, the proportion of Indians residing in urban areas was 27.4 per cent against 52.8 per cent for the Chinese. Generally, therefore, Indians had a lesser impact on economic and communal structures in Malaya. About 90 per cent of them were unskilled workers and a very large number lived in isolated plantation communities. With the plantation as the boundary of their existence, they had fewer contacts with the indigenous Malays.

In the lead up to independence, the Aliens Ordinance was replaced by the Immigration Ordinance of 1953. This regulation resulted in even stricter border controls and laid down for the first time the specific composition of migrants to be allowed entry into Malaya. Unlike the earlier restrictions based on nationality and gender, the

Figure 8.2

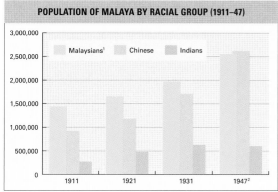

POPULATION OF MALAYA BY RACIAL GROUP (1911–47)

Malaysians[1] Chinese Indians

Source: Malaya Census Report, 1911–47. Notes: [1]'Malaysians' includes Malays and Indonesians; [2]1947 figure includes Pakistanis; the table excludes 'other' races.

Immigration Ordinance also specified nationality and occupation, and thus placed importance on the skills of the migrants. Permanent entry was restricted to, first, persons who could 'contribute to the expansion of commerce and industry'; second, to persons who could provide 'specialised services not available locally'; third, to 'families of local residents'; and fourth, to other persons on 'special compassionate grounds'. Clearly, this legislation was designed to appease Malay nationalists. New immigrants were also required to have a contract with a Malayan firm of at least two years and earn a salary of not less than M$400 a month. This legislation thus spelled the end of unskilled Indian labour migration to Malaya.

The end of the British Empire in Malaya briefly saw more restrictive legislation designed to curtail Chinese and Indian immigration. Immigration policy was largely dictated by economic and political considerations and the labour requirements of Western enterprises. Border controls, on the other hand, were shaped by economic and political considerations and were also designed to satisfy the aspirations of Malay nationalists. The British had ignored the potential conflicts and consequences arising from an unrestricted migration policy.

THE INDIAN DIASPORA: SOCIAL AND POLITICAL CHANGE

The British constructed the concept of Indian identity as a corollary to the articulation of a Malay/Malayan identity and Malay aspirations. This was consistent with their 'divide and rule' policy; their treatment of immigrant workers as transients; and was manifested in the population census reports that identified, differentiated and classified the diverse groups on the basis of ethnicity and place of origin. Identity was also reinforced through the education system. While English was the medium of instruction in schools in urban areas (attended primarily by children from urban, middle-class backgrounds), education for working-class children was provided in the vernacular and at the primary school level. Thus, plantation workers' children were schooled in Tamil only, which effectively ensured that they remained trapped in the plantation system without any avenue for upward educational and occupational mobility. This was despite the fact that by 1957 almost 65 per cent of the Indian population was locally born, a proportion that was bound to increase as immigration had virtually ceased.

Indian society in Malaya was divided along various lines. Linguistic and regional affiliations existed, but there were also religious divisions (e.g. Hindu, Muslim and Sikh) and the divisions caused by caste differences.

Nevertheless, while the Indian population represented some of the pluralism of the subcontinent, the character of the migration process, with its emphasis on recruitment from South India, gave this population a degree of homogeneity and cohesion. Approximately 80 per cent of Indians were Tamil and about 10 per cent were Malayalam, Kannada or Telugu speakers. Moreover, about 70 per cent were Hindu, though the Hindu faith did not provide cohesion in the belief structure and cultural/religious practices. Furthermore, the majority of Indians were from the labouring class, employed either on the plantations or in the construction and maintenance of public works and government undertakings (e.g. the railways) in urban areas. This provided them with a sort of unity based on economic activity or employment. Linguistic, religious and economic identity thus played an important role in shaping political activity and the construction of communal identity among Indians in Malaya.

LABOUR ORGANISATION AND LEADERSHIP

Before the 1930s, the direct employment of Indian labour by the colonial state and Western planting interests, reinforced by authoritarian and paternalistic structures, worked against the growth of class solidarity among Indian workers. Moreover, labour was in a weak position so long as the labour supply could be regulated through immigration controls. Two developments weakened this trend. The first was the emergence of free wage labour following the cessation of assisted labour migration. The second was the impact of the Great Depression on the plantation sector, which led to government restrictions on immigration and the emergence of a more stable labour force. While many workers took up offers of repatriation, a substantial number chose to remain behind and sought alternative ways to make a living on the land. An earlier provision for land allocation on estates for workers was enforced, and labourers were provided with small allotments. Some plantation owners even leased land to their workers. This process helped create a group of 'settled' labourers, reduced their dependence on the wage economy of the plantation structure and facilitated the permanent settlement of Indians in Malaya.

When economic conditions improved, labourers realised that they were not getting their fair share of the new prosperity and they became better organised and more militant. Vernacular newspapers, cultural associations and social action organisations mushroomed among

A temple next to the Kelly Castle plantation has the figure of the estate's owner among figures of the Hindu pantheon.

On the estates, Indian children were educated in Tamil-medium schools and taught by teachers brought in from India.

163

V. David: A champion of workers

V. David (1932–2005), a popular politician and leading trade unionist, is widely acknowledged as *makkal thondam*, or a champion of workers. He was born in Kuala Lumpur and educated there and in the US, where he obtained a doctorate in international relations in 1982.

David best exemplifies the political and trade union strand of Indian leadership in Malaysia. He was a founder member of the Selangor Mill Workers Union, which later became the Selangor Mill and Factory Workers Union. It subsequently became a national union—the National Union of Factory and General Workers. He served as its general secretary until the union was banned in 1958. He also held office as the general secretary of the Transport Workers Union, and in 1978 was elected secretary-general of the Malaysian Trades Union Congress.

David was a trade union leader and activist.

David was committed to improving labour rights and workers' lives. He was the founder and chairman of the Workers' Institute of Technology, which provided technical training for workers' children. He also lobbied for Tamil schools to improve the literacy rate among Tamil workers and for the promotion of the Tamil language.

In addition to trade union activism, David was a political activist and a prominent Opposition politician. He was a founding member of the Selangor Labour Party, which later merged with other state labour parties to form the Malayan Labour Party. He was also instrumental in the formation of the Gerakan Rakyat Malaysia and served as chairman of the Democratic Action Party (DAP), Damansara Branch. The DAP not only champions a 'democratic socialist pattern of society' but also adheres to an uncompromisingly non-communal stance, committed to advancing the rights of all Malaysians. He served as a member of parliament (MP) for five terms with the DAP (1978–95), until his retirement from politics in 1995. He also served in the Selangor and Penang state assemblies in 1959 and 1969 respectively. Due to his commitment to economic equality, social justice and political freedom, he was detained under the Emergency Regulations in 1958, and the Internal Security Act in 1965, 1969 and 1987–88 (under the Operation Lallang crackdown).

David was also active in the World Tamil Movement and served in international workers' bodies, including the International Labour Organisation governing body, the International Trades Federation and the International Trades Confederation.

This reflected not only modernisation and a growing trend in political awareness among the working class, but also showed a heightened ethnic consciousness linked to the redistribution of political and economic resources. Unfortunately, labour solidarity was weak and the government's policy of integrating the various state plantation workers' unions into a single union, enabling it to guide labour 'along a reasonable and non-political path', facilitated the amalgamation of the unions into the National Union of Plantation Workers (NUPW) in 1954. P. P. Narayanan, who had been crucial in the formation of the nucleus of the organisation in the late 1940s, led the NUPW for several decades. The NUPW stood, above all, for 'accommodation' and did not threaten the production system in the plantations. The urbanised union bureaucracy was largely divorced from the lives of the union members, and the leaders' connections with the colonial government and capital thus left workers in a state of dependency. Consequently, while the NUPW provided a vehicle for collective worker representation, it was weak and inhibited worker unity and militancy.

Compared to the labour leadership, the political leadership of the Indian community was more ideologically oriented. The influence of political events on the Indian subcontinent and the community's ascribed role in Malaya made it highly conscious of safeguarding its cultural identity. The leadership of Subhas Chandra Bose and local Indian leaders, such as Raghavan, led to a substantial number of Indians joining the Indian National Army (INA) and the Indian Independence League (IIL) during World War II (the IIL was established in Malaya and other major Southeast Asian centres during the Japanese Occupation to recruit men, collect funds and coordinate the Indian Independence Movement, which was spearheaded by the INA). An influential section of the Indian community was also closely associated with Tamil education, viewing it as central to the preservation and maintenance of Indian identity. Nevertheless, the Indian

the different ethnic groups. Urban labour organisations were formed and there were strikes in a number of workplaces and enterprises employing Indian labour separately and alongside Chinese workers, such as the railway workshops and the Batu Arang Colliery. The apparent boldness of semi-skilled and skilled workers stemmed from the fact that they enjoyed greater mobility and were willing to cooperate with the more militant Chinese in joint strikes to improve their working conditions.

These activities soon spread to the plantations, where leadership was initially provided from outside the plantation structure. Labour unions emerged, the workers made demands and subsequently backed up their demands with strike action, such as that by the Klang District Indian Union led by R. K. Nathan and N. Raghavan. The colonial government retaliated by deporting some of these leaders to India and enacting banishment ordinances. Thereafter, only organisations catering to religious activities were permitted, while working class-based and politically oriented groups were disallowed. After World War II, the tradition of militant leadership of plantation labour being provided from outside the plantation structure continued. The leaders appear to have originated from the groups that had retreated into the jungle during the war to fight the Japanese, or were disillusioned leaders from the Indian Independence League. These leaders worked with local leaders, among whom were *kanganis* and Tamil schoolteachers.

Subsequently, a group of leaders from within the labouring class of the plantations emerged. These leaders were young, literate in Tamil and influenced by the schoolteachers and *kanganis*. They participated in union activities at the grassroots level and rose to the membership of executive committees in regional general labour unions.

Sentul Works, the most important railway workshop, located on the outskirts of Kuala Lumpur. In the early 20th century, Indians comprised a large proportion of the total railway workforce in Malaya.

community did not have the economic clout of the Chinese community, nor its numerical strength or organisational ability, and so its influence was limited.

This political leadership originated in groups of professionals—lawyers, doctors and teachers—and businessmen in the larger urban centres and was predominantly North Indian. It established links with regional middle-class groups on the basis of Indian nationalist identity, forming the Malayan Indian Congress (MIC) in 1946. Early leaders of the organisation included John A. Thivy, Budh Singh, K. Ramanathan and K. L. Devaser. At the initial stage, the national level leadership of the Indian community had little in common with the labour leadership and, consequently, there was little inter-action between the two. The national leaders were also in a situation similar to plantation owners and, being employers of Indian labour themselves, they were opposed to the radicalisation of Indian labour.

Two factors further weakened the influence of this group. The first was a conflict over the reorientation of loyalty to Malaya rather than India, and the second stemmed from the ethnic and linguistic differences between the northerners and the southerners. During the early years of the Emergency, the MIC leadership became moribund. It revived gradually in the 1950s under V. T. Sambanthan's direction, when a division between the two groups emerged that culminated in the removal of the former, and the supremacy of the latter group. The change in leadership coincided with the redefinition of Indian identity as 'South Indian'. This resulted in an increased use of Tamil, the popularisation of traditional cultural practices, and an increased emphasis on Hinduism in its popular South Indian forms. As the MIC began to cater for the larger South Indian community, its base was broadened and India became a point of cultural and spiritual contact rather than a political link. In 1954, the MIC was incorporated into a political alliance with the other two communal parties in the country, UMNO and the Malayan Chinese Association (MCA), which forged an alliance in 1952 to contest the 1955 Federal elections under the banner of the Alliance, a united front.

V. T. SAMBANTHAN AND THE MIC

Sambanthan started a recruitment campaign among plantation workers, relying on the patronage of Hinduism in its popular southern Indian forms, the increased use and promotion of the Tamil language, and Tamil cultural practices. His gamble paid off and he was elected president of the MIC in 1955. He was also accepted by the Malay leadership because he downplayed Indian political—and to some extent, economic—rights in favour of cultural and language rights.

The MIC under Sambanthan's leadership thus failed to reconcile the needs of labour with the political aspira-tions of the middle class. The traditionalists and the lower middle class strengthened their hold within the party, while the upper-class professionals, business groups and intelligentsia moved away from it. Subsequently, two paths of leadership, political and trade union, emerged, with very little interaction between them. The Emergency Regulations in Malaya and new trade union legislation also led the leadership of the trade union movement to be passed from the Chinese to the urban Indians.

With Sambanthan as its leader, the MIC effectively became a Tamil party; it was also the weakest of the three political parties. It had a small electorate (7.4 per cent in

1959) and had very little support in the Indian community at large. Since the Indian community was geographically dispersed and divided, it comprised less than 25 per cent in any one constituency. Consequently, the MIC's over-riding concern was to remain in the Alliance government and obtain what concessions it could from the dominant UMNO. The diluting of the MIC's objectives and the deep divisions within the Indian community were to impact on Indian plantation workers and their current status in the Malaysian economy.

After Malaya achieved independence in 1957 the three major ethnic groups sought to increase their domi-nance in areas hitherto restricted to one group or another. In the case of the MIC, due to the smaller size of the

Nehru addressing the Indian community in Kuala Kangsar, Perak, in 1937. The Indian nationalist movement had considerable support from the local Indian community.

K. S. Maniam

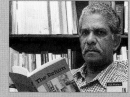

K. S. Maniam (Krishnan Subramaniam), author of numerous novels, plays and short stories, has established himself as one of the finest prose writers of his generation of Malaysians writing in English. Born in Bedong, Kedah, in 1942 to an Indian working-class family, Maniam spent his early years at the hospital compound where his father worked as a laundryman, and at the nearby rubber estate where his parents also worked as rubber tappers.

Maniam is one of Malaysia's leading Indian writers.

He enrolled at the Tamil-medium estate primary school where his parents worked but persuaded them to send him to an English-medium school at nearby Sungei Patani after the first year. Upon the completion of his secondary schooling, he had a brief spell as a medical student in India before leaving for the UK to study at the Malayan Teachers College in Wolverhampton. On his return to Malaysia, he taught at several rural schools before enrolling for an arts degree at the University of Malaya in 1970. He also completed a Masters degree in English at the university and was appointed a lecturer in 1979. He retired in 1997.

Despite his critically acclaimed literary achievements, Maniam is denied official recognition and public acclaim in his country of birth because he chooses to write in English rather than the national language, Malay. Yet, there are valid reasons for his choice of literary medium, reasons that are inherent in Malaysia's modern history as a former British colony and now independent state, to which immigrant communities have made a vital contribution. Nor does his use of English render him less authentic a Malaysian than his literary counterparts in the country.

Maniam looks at love and loyalty, tradition and modernity, and provides the reader with histori-cal insights into the Malaysian colonial and post-colonial human and physical world.

The following is an excerpt from his first novel, *The Return*:

My grandmother's life and her death, in 1958, made a vivid impression on me. She came, as the stories and anecdotes about her say, suddenly out of the horizon, like a camel, with nothing except some baggage and three boys in tow. And like that animal which survives the most barren of lands, she brooded, humped over her tin trunks, mats, silver lamps and pots, at the junction of the main road and the laterite trail. Later she went up the red, dusty path, into the trees and bushes, the most undeveloped part of Bedong. The people of this small town didn't know how she managed, but they saw her before a week passed, a settled look on her face, a firm gait in her walk.

K. S. Maniam, The Return, 1981

South Indian restaurants that serve food on banana leaves are common all over peninsular Malaysia.

Indian community relative to other communities and its scattered distribution, the ruling coalition ensured that the MIC received a quota of both federal and state seats as well as representation in the Federal Cabinet. In 1960, Sambanthan initiated the formation of a social cooperative, later known as the National Land and Finance Co-operative Society (NLFCS), to help plantation workers purchase plantation lands put up for sale.

For his part, however, Sambanthan ran the MIC largely as an informal party in deference to UMNO, rather than as a political party with a definite programme. In effect, the MIC became a vehicle for distributing privileges to supporters (i.e. senate and legislative votes, nominations for decorations and awards, licences etc.), furnishing the Indian vote and providing an instrument through which the leadership could entrench its role. This in turn spawned linguistic, cultural and religious tensions within the Indian community. The polarisation between the Indian political elite and the professional elite resulted in the latter distancing itself from the MIC, and the reduced political influence of the professionals in the country. It also saw increased participation in multiracial opposition parties and the formation of sub-regional communal parties.

Moreover, following the 13 May 1969 racial riots, many Indians realised that the MIC was not only the weakest link, but that it had sacrificed the greater good of Indians for the larger good of UMNO. Eventually, this rising dissatisfaction with Sambanthan led to a prolonged leadership crisis in the MIC. When Tun Abdul Razak succeeded Tunku Abdul Rahman as prime minister, the MIC was forced to become much more responsive to the dictates of UMNO. Sambanthan was forced to retire in favour of V. Manickavasagam in 1973.

Since 1969, Malaysian leaders have emphasised the forging of a truly united nation and the establishment of a national culture that would transcend separate ethnic identities. This policy emphasises that the national culture has to be based on the dominant Malay culture, with suitable elements included from other cultures. Islam is regarded as an important component in the moulding of a national culture. These considerations have been incorporated into the National Cultural Policy. This has affected non-Muslims in such matters as obtaining building permits for temples and churches. Islamisation is manifested in symbolic gestures: parliamentary prayers, the Islamic University and the Islamic Bank.

CHALLENGES

Although plantation crops make an important contribution to Malaysia's prosperity, the highest incidence of poverty in Malaysia is found among Malay smallholders planting rubber and Indian plantation workers on rubber and oil palm plantations. Concurrently, the continuance of the plantation 'system', with its emphasis on cheap labour, has resulted in falling real wages and the displacement of South Indian plantation workers by migrant Indonesian labour earning poverty-level wages. These migrant workers are recruited as guest workers on short-term contracts under the contractor system. Their willingness to accept low wages has resulted in Indian workers being excluded from a booming sector and has driven them from the plantations.

Two other factors have worked against the Indian plantation labour class. First, the emphasis on Tamil education in small and poorly managed estate schools has not equipped plantation workers' children for life in the competitive global economy. Second, the low emphasis placed on education (compared to the Chinese) has not enabled them to take advantage of limited opportunities in technical and tertiary education. *The Economist* summed up the situation in February 2003: '[Indians comprised] 14 per cent of juvenile delinquents, 20 per cent of…[Malaysia's] wife and child…[abusers] and 14 per cent of its beggars. They…[also comprised] less than 5 per cent of the successful university applicants.' Malaysia has not been the promised land for many Indian plantation workers.

The conversion of rubber plantations to housing estates and golf courses has also aggravated the situation. The reluctance of the rubber companies to provide alternative housing to retrenched workers and the lack of enforcement by the state has led to a drift to urban, inner city areas and the growth of urban Indian ghettos. Unlike the past, Indians no longer constitute the majority of plantation workers in Malaysia. Even as they have moved to urban areas in search of better paying jobs, they face a number of challenges, including a lack of economic opportunities, good housing and educational facilities.

In March 2005, the MIC held a forum on 'Malaysian Indians and the Ninth Malaysia Plan'. The forum was

Sikhs in Malaysia: New initiatives

Since the 1990s, Sikhs have fostered greater cohesion among themselves in terms of how they are perceived, and how they perceive each other. There are four main Sikh associations engaged in this task. The Malaysian Gurdwara Council is responsible for gurdwara affairs, including assistance with the recruitment of Sikh priests from India. The Khalsa Diwan Malaysia is entrusted with the responsibility of promoting Punjabi education and Sikh religious instruction. The Malaysian Sikh Youth Council oversees Sikh youth and their religious education, while the Malaysian Sikh Women's Awareness Network conducts capacity building sessions for the empowerment of Sikh women and promotes networking with other Indian groups. Its projects include health camps for Indian women from predominantly lower socio-economic groups. It has also included training and education sessions in a number of major cities to promote awareness of cancer as well as HIV/AIDS.

In the realm of politics, a large number of Sikhs are members of the Malayan Indian Congress (MIC) or the opposition parties. Karpal Singh, a prominent human rights activist and Sikh lawyer,

Karpal Singh, Sikh lawyer and human rights activist.

is an opposition MP. In 1986, the Sikhs and other Punjabis formed the Malaysian Punjabi Party (Parti Punjabi Malaysia), with the aim of lobbying for the effective political representation of Punjabis in Malaysia. This party is at best an interest group because it cannot compete with the MIC, the dominant Indian political party. In keeping with the smaller numerical strength of the Indians in Malaysia vis-à-vis the Malays and the Chinese, the share of the political pie for Indians is extremely small. The MIC encourages the Sikhs to join the party and strengthen it.

organised to debate issues on the Indian community and its access to economic and educational opportunities. The forum also sought to increase awareness of the Indian problems, with a view to calling for changes in the economic and social mix of the country.

GLOBALISATION IN MALAYSIA AND THE INDIAN DIASPORA

Malaysia made the transition to the status of a newly industrialised country in the last three decades of the 20th century. Despite rapid industrialisation and the petroleum boom, the country's prosperity is still heavily dependent on export earnings from rubber and palm oil. At the same time, services are increasingly driving Malaysia's economy, and the state's objective is to strengthen its position as a regional and global services hub and develop as a knowledge-based economy (KBE). The dual challenges of unskilled labour shortages in specific sectors on the one hand, and the need to provide knowledge workers on the other, has resulted in the return of an official policy on foreign labour recruitment. In the Malaysian state's drive towards a KBE, India has emerged as a major source of internationally competitive skilled professional workers, particularly for Malaysia's information technology sector. Concurrently, unskilled and semi-skilled workers, principally from Indonesia, have been recruited as contract workers for the construction, plantation, manufacturing and service (domestic work) sectors. This also includes Indian workers for the restaurant trade (in Indian restaurants). More significantly, in March 2005, the Indian and Malaysian governments took the first steps towards a formal Memorandum of Understanding on manpower recruitment on a contract basis from India. Malaysia is also pursuing investment opportunities in infrastructure development in India.

An Indian clothing store in Kuala Lumpur.

The Indian community has divided views on the Indian government's current policy of developing links with wealthy and successful overseas Indian communities and its celebration of Pravasi Bharatiya Divas. In 2003, MIC president Datuk Seri Samy Vellu was awarded the Indian Diaspora Award, but some Malaysian Indians feel that poorer overseas Indian communities have been neglected. Likewise, the Indian government's dual citizenship policy for non-resident Indians is sometimes seen as restrictive and confined largely to Indians residing in affluent Western countries.

There are suggestions, however, that the economic and technological rise of India will bring benefits to the Indian diaspora, especially those who have been neglected for a long time. The rise of India has provided powerful linkages for selected groups of Indians situated outside India. It remains to be seen how this new global diasporic exchange will benefit the community as a whole.

Amarjit Kaur

Thaipusam, one of the most popular Indian festivals in Malaysia, is celebrated on a large scale in Kuala Lumpur.

Tony Fernandes and AirAsia

Tony Fernandes (CEO, AirAsia) is one of Malaysia's most successful entrepreneurs of Indian origin. The 'Asian Branson', as he is often called, has revolutionised air travel in Asia and set a trend for low-cost air carriers in the region. Just as the mobile phone has provided communication links in the absence of land lines, Fernandes's low-cost carrier has united Asians and the Asian continent by providing affordable air travel.

Fernandes was born in Kuala Lumpur in 1964. He was sent to the UK by his parents to study medicine but switched to accounting. Upon graduating in 1987, he joined the Virgin Group in the UK before moving on to Warner Music International London. In 1992, Warner Music sent him to Malaysia to head Warner Music Malaysia, and he rose to become vice-president of Warner Music ASEAN. He left Warner Music nine years later to found Tune Air Sendirian Berhad, with the objective of making air travel more affordable for Malaysians, modelling it on trailblazers such as Dublin-based Ryanair and America's Southwest Airlines.

Fernandes turned AirAsia into a successful no-frills airline.

In September 2001, he and three partners bought AirAsia, a small Malaysian airline with just two aircraft (Boeing 737–300) for a symbolic RM1, and a RM40 million debt. He negotiated cheap landing rights at minor airports in Malaysia and introduced several cost-cutting measures, including the sale of tickets directly to travellers over the Internet, no in-flight meals, no frequent-flier programme and no business class. To keep costs down AirAsia uses only one type of aircraft, the Boeing 737–300, and does not use air bridges at terminals. Flight attendants help to clean the planes after passengers disembark.

AirAsia broke even a year later. The downturn in air travel after 11 September 2001 helped AirAsia by lowering the cost of buying and leasing planes. At the end of the financial year in 2003, AirAsia had earned RM30 million. The fleet was also expanded to 18 aircraft. No longer are its operations limited to Malaysia. AirAsia is now Southeast Asia's biggest low-cost carrier in terms of its fleet size and operates flights to destinations in Thailand, Indonesia and the Philippines; and from Bangkok to Singapore, China and Malaysia.

MYANMAR

MYANMAR (KNOWN AS Burma until the ruling military junta changed its name in 1989) has an association with India that goes back many centuries. In the Myanmar language, natives from the Indian subcontinent are known by the generic term *kala*, whose etymology is unknown. Some believe that it comes from the Pali word *kula*, signifying 'genealogy, lineage, or pedigree', while others have suggested that the word means 'foreigners'. Whatever its origin, most Burmans use the word to mean 'an alien'. Given that the overwhelming majority of Indians in Myanmar are either migrants or descendants of migrants from British India and pre-British India, the category 'Indians' includes migrants from the present-day nations of India, Pakistan and Bangladesh. Those of mixed parentage are excluded, even though many of those belonging to the so-called 'mixed races' (especially Muslims) have been demographically significant (the 1983 census identified over 233,000 Muslims of mixed race, most of whom could be of Indian descent) and have close ties to the Indian community rather than the indigenous in socio-cultural and religious aspects. It also does not include the so-called Bamar-Muslims, who are naturalised citizens with an ancestry that predates colonial migration.

The ancient Indian settlers in Burma had probably established distinct communities by the 2nd century AD. However, the earliest historical records of Muslim settlements in Rakhine (Arakan) and Bago (Pegu) date back to the 15th century AD. For many centuries, Indian communities lived in harmony with the natives in lower Burma and in the royal capitals of Shwebo, Inwa (Ava), Amarapura and Mandalay in central Burma. When Indian troops under British command defeated the royal army in the First Anglo-Burmese War of 1824, they probably sowed the seeds of Burma's prejudice and grievances against Indians and India, fuelling nationalist fervour in the 20th century.

INDIAN IMMIGRATION UNDER BRITISH RULE (1853–1942)

After the British annexed lower Burma during the Second Anglo-Burmese War (in early 1853), making it a province of British India, the Indian government encouraged the flow of Indian labour into what was known as British Burma. During the decade following 1876, the government subsidised the migration process undertaken by private agents in India. (Even after British Burma was formally separated from India in April 1937, the colonial government's unrestricted immigration policy continued.)

Following the final takeover of the entire country in 1885, migration continued unabated well into the 20th century, taking its cue from the laissez-faire economy of British Burma, which became rapidly integrated with the economy of British India and, subsequently, to the international economy. For example, the total value of imports into British Burma tripled between 1884 and 1911, and doubled again in the next 10 years. Similarly, the value of exports to India as a share of British Burma's total exports increased from 21 per cent to 52 per cent between 1884 and 1921, while the value of total exports increased more than six times. As the modern monetised economy developed, many Indians came to British Burma to work. Indian migrants played a significant part in transforming Burma's subsistence economy into a commercialised export economy.

Map 8.11

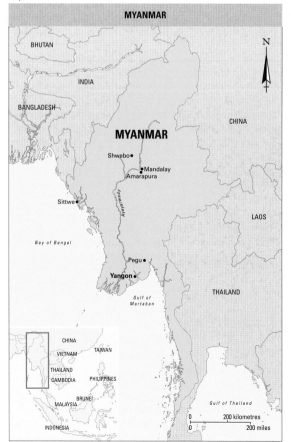

DEMOGRAPHY AND THE ROLE OF INDIANS

Table 8.10 shows that the Indian population in British Burma reached the half-million mark by the turn of the century, after a rapid increase over the preceding 24 years. The Indian presence was felt most, in terms of sheer numbers (see Table 8.11) as well as diversity of occupation, in Rangoon (Yangon), the capital city and the commercial centre, where the lingua franca was Hindustani. In fact, Rangoon resembled an Indian city until the Japanese invasion in 1942.

Many migrants were single males who were seasonal labourers and temporary residents. According to the 1931 census, there were on average only 19 females (ranging from three for Oriyas to 43 for Tamils) per 100 males in British Burma, excluding Rakhine. They came from various states in India (the majority from Bengal, Madras and Uttar Pradesh) and belonged to different language groups (in descending order of population numbers in 1931: Telugu, Hindustani, Tamil, Chittagonian, Oriya and Bengali, among others). Unfortunately, most labourers found themselves living and working under miserable conditions with little savings and were heavily indebted to the exploitative labour contractors known as *maistries*. Indigenous people often looked upon them with contempt.

Occupationally, the 1931 census enumerated that 51.5 per cent of the labourers were in industry, transport and trade; 30 per cent in raw material production (mainly agriculture); 9.5 per cent in miscellaneous activities (including domestic work); 6.5 per cent in public administration, arts and professional services; and 2.5 per cent in the exploitation of minerals. Ninety-six per cent of Indians employed in non-agricultural male occupations were sweepers and scavengers; 73 per cent were 'insufficiently described manufacturers, businessmen, contractors'; 49 per cent were unskilled and semi-skilled labourers; 48 per cent were clerical workers; 44 per cent were police and military personnel; 36 per cent were traders and shop assistants; 28 per cent were officers in organised industrial undertakings; and 27 per cent were craftsmen. The corresponding occupational representation of Indians in Rangoon exhibited a more accentuated but similar pattern: 99.9 per cent were sweepers and scavengers; 90 per cent were 'insufficiently described manufacturers, businessmen, contractors'; 89 per cent were skilled and semi-skilled labourers; 72 per cent were traders and shop assistants; 70 per cent were police and military personnel; 61 per cent were clerical workers; 59 per cent were craftsmen; 55 per cent were rentiers; 50 per cent were in the medical profession; 44 per cent were technical and professional personnel; 43 per cent were officers in organised industrial undertakings; and 40 per cent were general public service workers.

According to the Burma Trade Directory (1930), significant Indian representation could be found in urban business firms as well. For example, in 'small towns', 52 per cent of shopkeepers were Indians, as were 41 per cent of contractors, 38 per cent of merchants, and 31 per cent of service enterprises. However, in larger 'district towns' Indians represented 53 per cent of shopkeepers;

51 per cent of bankers and moneylenders as well as contractors; 40 per cent of importers/exporters; and 38 per cent of merchants. On the other hand, 83 per cent of bankers and moneylenders in Yangon were Indians, as were 58 per cent of merchants, 53 per cent of importers/exporters, 48 per cent of brokers and dealers, and 39 per cent of contractors. If the share of income/super tax payment is taken as a proxy for the relative strength of ethnic groups among the business class in the formal economy, Indians were second only to Europeans (at 70 per cent), contributing some 25 per cent (of which nearly 15 per cent was attributed to the Chettiars) of the overall tax payment in the financial year 1931/32. In contrast, the corresponding Chinese share was 3.5 per cent, while Burmans contributed only 0.5 per cent.

These figures seem to support the contention by both the elite and masses in British Burma that the Indians were monopolising jobs and dominating businesses. Through over-representation in terms of numbers across a wide spectrum of occupations in the modern economic sector, the Indian migrant community affected the daily life of the indigenous communities and the latter's dealings with the colonial administration. Their religious practices (especially Islam) and sociocultural customs, though tolerated by the mainly Buddhist majority, alienated many conservative Bamars, the main ethnic group. Negative perceptions and experiences created tensions between the two communities that were further accentuated by the socio-economic shocks brought about by the Great Depression of the 1930s.

The stage for the dramatic consequences of the Depression was set many decades before, when the Chettiar moneylenders from Madras began to penetrate the rural credit market in the 1880s. Their financial clout and efficiency managed to undercut the local moneylenders. Though reluctant to resort to foreclosure (they preferred cash repayment), they were compelled to take over land from a large number of insolvent Bamar cultivators hit hard by the huge drop in the price of rice in 1931—when it dropped by half—and were already reeling under the burden of a capitation tax. As the decade progressed, the continued slump of commodity prices led to further foreclosures. By 1936, the Chettiars owned some 25 per cent of agricultural land in the country (up from 6 per cent in 1930). The blame for rural impoverishment and land alienation in the Depression years was squarely placed on the Chettiars. The foreclosure issue and the increasing job competition between the urban poor and Indian labourers emerged during a period of deteriorating law and order

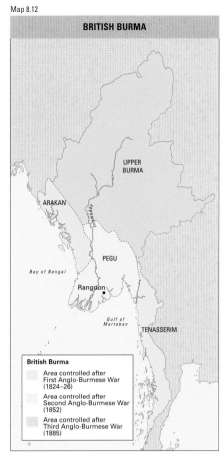

Map 8.12

Source: Patrick K. O'Brien (ed.), Atlas of World History, *1999.*

Burma was annexed by Britain between 1824 and 1885, and was administered as part of British India until 1937.

Table 8.10

INDIANS IN BRITISH BURMA		
	No. of Indians	%
1891	420,830	5.4
1901	564,263	5.4
1911	743,288	6.1
1921	887,077	6.7
1931	1,017,825	6.9

Source: W. S. Desai, India and Burma: A Study, *1954.*

Table 8.11

INDIANS IN RANGOON UNDER BRITISH BURMA		
	No. of Indians	%
1872	16,000	16
1881	66,000	44
1891	87,000	48
1901	119,000	48
1911	165,000	56
1921	187,000	55
1931	212,000	53
1941	280,000	56

Source: W. S. Desai, India and Burma: A Study, *1954.*

Indian refugees fleeing the capital, Rangoon, in early 1942 to escape the Japanese. An estimated 400,000 to 450,000 Indians trekked all the way to India over the western Rakhine range. Many perished on the journey.

A refugee carries his exhausted daughter.

exemplified by a peasant rebellion between 1930–32, which was crushed by Indian troops. This apparently led to a rising tide of resentment against the Chettiar community in particular and Indians in general during the 1930s. The issue of unregulated Indian immigration became increasingly publicised and politicised. Ironically, the new generation of nationalist politicians and activists drew some inspiration from the Indian National Congress and Indian Communist Party. Furthermore, several Indians could be found among influential cadres of the socialist and communist movements in British Burma.

Meanwhile, latent religious tensions between Buddhist Bamars and Muslim Indians were further intensified. There were growing calls to redress the disadvantageous position of Bamar females in mixed marriages from the increasingly nationalistic press and a new generation of nationalist politicians and activists who, unlike those of the older generation, were not influenced by the Indian business class. Heightened tensions between the two communities culminated in the bloody Indo-Burma riots of May 1930 among dockyard labourers, which soon spread to surrounding townships. Another round of anti-Indian rioting occurred in some towns in the Rangoon district during 1931. The last major anti-Indian riot (aimed mainly at Muslims) before World War II spread northwards from Rangoon to Mandalay in central Burma in the last week of July 1938. Another riot, though less severe, broke out in September in Rangoon.

In 1939, the colonial government belatedly appointed the Baxter Commission to look into the immigration of Indians. The commission's investigation revealed that no reliable statistics were available on the nature and extent of Indian immigration but that some 40 per cent of the total number of Indians in Burma in 1939 were born in the country. It also concluded that contrary to popular belief, Indian labour had been supplementing instead of displacing indigenous labour and that there was no evidence to indicate a serious excess of supply over demand, except in the capital city. Nevertheless, it recommended that proper immigration procedures and regulatory mechanisms be instituted for travel between the two countries and an immigration agreement be drawn up between the two governments. In 1941, the governments reached an agreement that in essence

would regulate the number and type of immigrants (based on occupation) through a two-tier permit system, restrict mixed marriages by migrants and classify Indians born in the country as domiciled. The agreement was vigorously opposed by Indian legislators and those with business interests, but with the outbreak of the Pacific War, events overtook the contentious debates over the agreement and laid them to rest.

Meanwhile, the Bamar-dominated legislature also passed—in spite of protests by the Indian community—other significant legislative measures that would affect the migrant community's social and economic relations with the hosts. One was the Buddhist Woman Special Marriage Succession Bill of 1939, aimed at deterring marriage between Indian males and Bamar females, and raising the status and enhancing the rights of Bamar spouses in mixed marriages (the 1931 census identified over 64,000 persons of Indo-Burman descent in urban areas alone). The Tenancy and Land Alienation acts of 1939 were also passed. The former was to ensure the security of tenure for the tenant and to standardise land rent in a fair manner. The latter's objective was to prevent the transfer of land to absentee landlords. All of these were rendered irrelevant by the Japanese invasion.

THE JAPANESE OCCUPATION, FLIGHT TO INDIA AND THE RETURN OF THE BRITISH (1942–47)

When the Japanese invaded Burma alongside the vanguard of the nationalist Burma Independence Army (BIA) led by General Aung San, a large number of Indians in the country fled to India. A vast majority trekked overland to the subcontinent through difficult terrain, encountering unprecedented misery and hardship, and suffering heavy casualties on the way. It was estimated that between 400,000 and 450,000 were a part of this arduous journey, of which some 5 to 10 per cent perished. Apart from isolated cases, there was no known communal violence during this traumatic exodus. As British Burma became a battlefield between the Allied forces and the Japanese, most Indians (and the indigenous people) lost their wealth and belongings through looting and war damage. Those who remained behind (around 300,000 to 400,000) were impoverished and suffered greatly under the harsh Japanese military rule; like others, many ended up in forced labour gangs run by the Japanese military.

On the other hand, the advent of the Azad Hind provisional government (c. 1943) led by Subhas Chandra (Netaji) Bose, which was supported by the Indian Independence League (IIL) and the Indian National Army (INA) in a bid to liberate India with Japanese assistance, created a difficult situation for the Indians in Japanese-occupied Burma. Compelled to pledge allegiance to the Azad Hind provisional government, they were taxed by both governments. But the IIL, which had around 100 offices throughout the country, did give them some protection. The headquarters of the Central Bank of Azad Hind and IIL were located in Rangoon. The Government of Independent Burma was led by Dr Ba Maw and the Azad Hind government by Netaji Bose, who moved his headquarters to Rangoon in January 1944. Operating under Japanese tutelage, the two enjoyed an amicable relationship.

When the indigenous resistance movement spearheaded by Aung San's troops turned against the Japanese in 1945, the INA forces, still allied with the Japanese

imperial army, stayed neutral and were not targeted. After the Japanese were defeated, many Indians returned to India. Around 246,000 arrived in the subcontinent, of which 142,000 returned to Burma within two years. The former were likely to be evacuees, while the bulk of the latter were from the pioneer labour units recruited by the Allied army to reinstated British Burma. An estimated 16,000 evacuees in India were brought back as labourers and skilled workers to aid the reconstruction and rehabilitation of physical infrastructure and services. The Muslim and Hindu divide in Burma's Indian community, which was bridged through shared adversity during the Japanese Occupation, resurfaced and became more pronounced following the formation of Pakistan in August 1947. On the other hand, the Indian elite who were in the forefront of the pre-war game of minority politics and had fled before the Japanese invasion, found themselves alienated because those who remained harboured resentment against these groups for leaving them in the lurch when the chips were down. They were displaced by a new generation of politicians and leaders who shared with the Bamar nationalists a vision of self-determination and resistance against the common enemy, the British colonialists. Having developed close camaraderie with Aung San's coterie of nationalist leaders, these Indians managed to marshal much-appreciated Indian support for the nationalists' civil disobedience and strike campaigns. Several of them rose to prominence in the nationalist political front known as the Anti-Fascist People's Freedom League (AFPFL) and were elected to the Constituent Assembly of the last colonial administration. Some,

mostly Muslims, became Cabinet ministers in the post-independence AFPFL government. Two Indians were also involved in the commission established to draft the new state constitution. When independence hero Aung San and some members of his Cabinet were assassinated on 19 July 1947, the Indian community lost its most valued friend among the country's top leadership.

In the three years before independence, several land acts were passed to reduce rent, settle land disputes and prohibit the transfer of immovable properties to non-citizens. All of these measures, though non-discriminatory in ethnic terms, hit the Indians hard as many of them were landlords and property owners. Furthermore, the spectre of Indian immigration once again haunted the nationalist politicians and, in June 1947, an emergency act imposing strict controls over immigration was instituted despite protests from India's Congress Party leaders.

THE INDIAN COMMUNITY IN THE PARLIAMENTARY ERA (1948–62)

No reliable data about the Indian population during the parliamentary era, in which the state was named the Union of Burma, can be found. Census taking was severely constrained by the civil war that broke out soon after independence and threatened the very existence of the central government during the first half of the 1950s. Estimates put the Indian population at around 600,000 in the early 1950s, of which some 132,000 were labourers comprising 14 per cent of the urban labour population. In Rangoon, Indians numbering some 126,000 still comprised 20.5 per cent of the city's population in 1952. Indians also constituted around 22.6 per cent of the total labour force in the city in 1953. However, their numbers fell steadily throughout the 1950s.

The government embraced nationalism and socialism as its guiding principles. Its nationalist socio-economic language and education policies, and indigenisation measures in the administrative and business fields led to further marginalisation and displacement of the majority of Indians who were non-citizens, causing the departure of tens of thousands in the few years following independence—some 50,000, including 12,000 who were destitute, returned to India by December 1949 and a similar number followed over the next two years.

In particular, the Disposal of Tenancies and the Land Nationalisation acts of 1948 virtually disenfranchised Indian landed interests. The Agricultural Debt Relief Act of 1948 severely affected the Chettiars, among others, by abrogating all debts incurred before 1 October 1946 and waiving interest on those incurred thereafter. These measures effectively ended the Chettiars' role in the economy. Strict controls imposed by the government on foreign exchange transactions curtailed the long-standing practice of remittances by Indian migrants. Opposition and petitions by Indian communities within and without the country, and India's official protests against these acts and regulations, came to naught.

The same aim of pushing the national interest was evident in the passing of the Union of Burma Citizenship Act of 1948, a significant legislation with profound implications for the Indian community. This act, together with the relevant provisions in the 1947 Union Constitution, clearly defined the parameters of acquiring citizenship for Indians and other resident foreigners. Not many Indians could meet the stringent eligibility criteria stipulated. Others who were eligible either opted out or failed

Burma's independence hero, General Aung San, delivering a speech in Rangoon at a public rally soon after the country was liberated from Japanese occupation in the second quarter of 1945. His assassination in July 1947 was a great loss to the Indian community in Burma.

INA leader Subhas Chandra Bose (left) in Rangoon with Dr Ba Maw, the adipadi *(head of state) of Japanese-occupied Burma in 1943.*

Medals belonging to a World War II Sikh army veteran, including the Burma Star and the 1939 and 1945 Indian Independence medals.

INA soldiers who surrendered to the British Indian forces of the 14th Army after they lost a fierce battle at Mount Popa in central Burma in early 1945.

171

A mosque in Mogul Street (now Shwe Bon Thar Street) in downtown Rangoon, famous for its gold merchants, c. 1890.

to register properly or on time for various reasons; the raging civil war that engulfed the entire country being one of them. No reliable figures are available for the number of Indians who managed to acquire citizenship during that brief window of opportunity, but one source suggests that it could be as few as 10,000 (out of several hundred thousand residents). Thus, the majority of Indians became 'aliens' under the purview of the Foreigners Registration Act, with its restrictive rules and regulations governing the behaviour of aliens in Burma. Subsequently, the constant threat of deportation looming over those classified as foreigners, in a land where they had virtually been permanent residents for generations, had engendered a sense of insecurity among those affected. As foreigners, they had no political rights, were shut out from many occupations and were denied certain educational and business opportunities.

However, Indians (including non-citizens) managed to find their economic niche in formal and informal private sectors as the economy recovered in the mid-1950s. This included working as general labour, domestic helpers, petty traders, retailers, shopkeepers, service providers, food sellers and brokers in the small business sector. Those with connections to the ruling party and access to capital were engaged in import/export, manufacturing, wholesale trade and extractive industries. Some non-citizens even managed to circumvent the indigenisation measures in foreign trade by using nationals as front persons. In fact, many Indian industrialists and traders managed to gain control of certain lines of business, such as foreign trade in rice, foodstuff, construction material and hardware, photographic equipment and supplies, books and stationery supplies, watches and textiles, as well as in real estate, cinemas, bazaars, brokerage, transport and construction. Indian, especially Muslim, enterprises were prominent in industries such as brassware, Indian cheroots, matches, textiles and knitwear, furniture and wood products, rope and coir, flour, soap, umbrellas and footwear.

Indian industrialists and businessmen during the parliamentary era were known to be quite influential, not only through their lobbying of the community's chambers of commerce—there were five in 1956—and various merchant associations, but also by being close to top politicians from the ruling party. They made campaign contributions to the ruling party and also garnered the goodwill of the ruling elite through contributions to the latter's favourite charities. Some prominent Muslims were even known to have made donations to Buddhist causes and many prominent Hindus regularly participated in Buddhist celebrations and ceremonies. Indian

Indian rice merchants in Rangoon. Rice trading was a prominent Indian business in 20th-century Burma.

ministers, who also served as patrons of Indian religious and community organisations, acted as useful intermediaries between the government and the community.

Although Buddhism was accorded a special position in the constitution, both Hindus and Muslims enjoyed freedom of worship under parliamentary rule. On the other hand, many Indians claimed to be Buddhists. Public religious activities were allowed so long as they did not infringe upon existing laws and regulations or compromise public order and safety. Deepavali and Id-al-Fitr were gazetted as public holidays and overseas pilgrimages for Hindus and the performance of the haj for Muslims were allowed within the bounds of existing rules on foreign travel and foreign exchange restrictions on citizens and resident foreigners. Religious organisations and trusteeships for Hindu temples, mosques and other religious buildings were allowed to operate under the supervision of the religious affairs ministry with some latitude, though building new places of worship was rarely allowed. There were also several religious schools operated by Hindu and Muslim organisations. Premier U Nu's amendment of the Union Constitution in 1961 to install Buddhism as the state religion created a storm of protest from Indian Muslims (as well as Christians), but there was virtually no practical impact on the Indian community as the constitution was abrogated when the government was toppled by a military coup within a year.

There were seven newspapers catering to Indians during the 1950s. The more prominent Indian organisations such as the All-Burma Tamil Muslim Association, All-Burma Pakistan Association (Bengalis), the General Council of Burma Muslim Associations (quasi-political), Arya Samaj (founded in 1897, religious), Sanatan Dharma Swayamsevak Sangh or Sangh (founded in 1950, socio-cultural), and the All-Burma Hindu Central Board (ABHCB, founded in 1953, covering all aspects of Hindu community life) were located in the capital, while those based on sectarian (such as the Shiite) or ethnolinguistic lines (such as the Chulias); or with fraternal associations linked to home (such as the Surtis); literary, social, cultural, educational or economic/business functions; and professional vocations, could also be found in the capital city as well as in other towns. The Gandhi Memorial Hall, the Ramakrishna Missionary Hospital and the Muslim Free Hospital were regarded as important icons of the Indian community in the 1950s.

Table 8.12

PERSONS FROM THE INDIAN SUBCONTINENT IN BURMA			
	1953[1] No. (%)	1973 No. (%)	1983 No. (%)
India	N.A.	N.A.	428,428 *(1.3)*
Pakistan	N.A.	N.A.	42,140 *(0.1)*
Bangladesh	N.A.	N.A.	567,985 *(1.7)*
Total	349,141 *(6.2)*	547,154 *(1.9)*	1,038,553 *(3.0)[2]*

Source: Government of Myanmar, census, various issues. Notes: [1]The 1953 census, done in two stages, in 1953 and 1954, covered only part of the country due to civil war; [2]difference due to rounding errors; Bangladesh did not exist before 1971; N.A. = not available.

In terms of social relationships, the Burma Muslim Dissolution of Marriages Act of 1953 allowed Muslim women the privilege of equal rights, as was enjoyed by Buddhist spouses, in matters such as initiating divorce and claims to property. Though many Indian women retained their traditional attire, Muslim women were rarely seen wearing veils. The majority of males took to Burmese dress or European attire. Tensions between Hindus and Muslims or between the Indians and the indigenous communities were not apparent during this period and no major communal violence occurred. Isolated incidents were promptly contained by community leaders and authorities. The long-standing communal rivalry and tension between the Indian Muslims and the Bamar Muslims were more pronounced and open in the parliamentary era than with either the Hindus or Bamars, but in the eyes of the Bamars, both groups were regarded as *kala*. Indian Muslims were known to be influential in Muslim organisations and were represented as 'the major force in the community life of the Muslims.'

INDIANS DURING THE REVOLUTIONARY PERIOD AND ONE-PARTY SOCIALIST ERA (1962–88)

The military staged a coup in March 1962 and ruled the country by decree for 12 years under the authority of the Revolutionary Council (RC), chaired by the armed forces chief, General Ne Win. Under its unique ideology, called the Burmese Way to Socialism, the RC launched a relentless programme of nationalisation and indigenisation that dispossessed capitalists, petit bourgeoisie and foreigners of their livelihood. Though non-discriminatory in ethnic terms, these measures hit the Indian community again as many had no alternative means of livelihood or support. It was reported that over 12,000 Indian businesses (mainly small retail shops) were nationalised in March 1964 and over 100,000 Indians were disenfranchised by the nationalisation drive. Reeling from the situation and the abrupt

termination of jobs, Indians were 'repatriated' in such large numbers that a special arrangement had to be made to transport them by air and sea. Over 117,000 left by sea between 1964 and 1966; an estimated 300,000 left the country during the 1960s.

Consequently, the number of Indians in Burma declined to just over 547,000 (1.9 per cent) of the total population in 1973, the year of the first comprehensive post-independence census (see Table 8.12). By 1983, the number had risen to over 1 million and the male to female ratio was far more balanced than ever before (see Table 8.13).

However, a comparison between the size of the Indian population in 1973 and 1983 (another census year) reveals an anomaly that indicates a hitherto undocumented immigration problem. The average annual population growth rate for Indians between 1973 and 1983 was an incredible 6.6 per cent. This figure far exceeds the natural increase and belies the fact that Burma was a closed state, where internal movement was tightly controlled, immigration not permitted, and long-term residence for foreigners well-nigh impossible. Again, as shown in Table 8.14, the number of Muslims in 1983 was 2.5 times (average growth rate of 9.9 per cent) that of a decade earlier, while the number of Hindus had increased by just 41 per cent. The latter was nearly twice that of the natural population growth rate for the entire country, estimated to be around 2 per cent. It is likely that the figure for the Indian Hindu population was inflated because the respondents (living under a military junta) had identified themselves as Buddhists in the 1973 census, while those in 1983 (living under a constitutional one-party state) correctly identified themselves as Hindus.

This conjecture is partly supported by the reduction in the Indian Buddhist population between the two census years. On the other hand, there is a distinct possibility that the huge overall increase in the number of Indians in general (Table 8.12), and Muslims (Table 8.14) in particular, was due to illegal immigration into Rakhine from Bangladesh. In fact, in 1983, Rakhine alone had over 497,000 Bangladeshis (24.3 per cent of the state population) out of a total Bangladeshi population in Burma of 568,000. In contrast, in 1983, there were only around 10,000 Bangladeshis in Rangoon out of just over 134,000 Indians, down from over 140,000 in 1953. The alternative explanation that a large number of Indians could have misrepresented themselves as belonging to some other indigenous ethnic group (like Rakhine) in the 1973 census is highly unlikely, given that the local enumerators could easily distinguish between Indians and others. Moreover, given the declining trend in the population of Indians with valid foreigner registration since 1961, as shown in Tables 8.15 and 8.16, the huge increment in the number of Indians between 1973 and 1983 could not have been officially registered as one of foreigners. It follows that since

A South Indian employee of a chicken biryani restaurant in Rangoon, c. 1980.

A famous Hindu temple dedicated to the goddess Kali, situated at the corner of Anawrahta Road and Kon Zay Dan Street in the central business district of Yangon. It is also reputedly one of the richest Hindu temples in Myanmar.

Table 8.13

PERSONS FROM THE INDIAN SUBCONTINENT IN BURMA (BY GENDER)									
	1953*			1973			1983		
	Male	Female	(M/F)	Male	Female	(M/F)	Male	Female	(M/F)
India	N.A.			N.A.			218,785	209,643	*(1.04)*
Pakistan	N.A.			N.A.			21,645	20,495	*(1.06)*
Bangladesh	N.A.			N.A.			284,629	283,356	*(1.00)*
Total	220,446	128,695	*(1.7)*	290,343	256,811	*(1.1)*	525,059	513,494	*(1.02)*

*Source: Government of Myanmar, census, various issues. Notes: *The 1953 census covered only part of the country due to civil war; M/F is the ratio of males to females in the population; Bangladesh did not exist before 1971.*

Table 8.14

RELIGIOUS BREAKDOWN OF PERSONS FROM THE INDIAN SUBCONTINENT IN BURMA ('000)											
	Buddhist		Animist		Christian		Hindu		Muslim		Other	
	1973	1983	1973	1983	1973	1983	1973	1983	1973	1983	1973	1983
India	N.A.	116	N.A.	4	N.A.	19	N.A.	143	N.A.	140	N.A.	5
Pakistan	N.A.	1	N.A.	—	N.A.	—	N.A.	1	N.A.	40	N.A.	—
Bangladesh	N.A.	2	N.A.	—	N.A.	—	N.A.	1	N.A.	564	N.A.	1
Total*	123	120	4	4	19	19	102	144	297	744	2	6

*Source: Government of Myanmar, census, various issues. Notes: *Total may not add up due to rounding (to the nearest thousand) errors; — = negligible.*

Sanatan Dharma Swayamsevak Sangh
50th Anniversary Souvenir
1950 - 2000

The cover of a special commemorative souvenir magazine marking the 50th anniversary (1950–2000) of the Sanatan Dharma Swayamsevak Sangh's establishment in Myanmar.

A refurbished mosque located on Maha Bandoola Road, a main thoroughfare in central Yangon, located a short distance from the landmark Sule Pagoda, which is regarded as the centre of the city.

citizenship criteria had been rather stringent since 1948, it is unlikely that the bulk of them could have become citizens either. The only plausible explanation could be that they were either stateless or were holding fake identification papers, claiming to be citizens.

In 1982, the government, led by the Burma Socialist Programme Party (BSPP, formed by the RC) instituted a new citizenship law which could settle the uncertain status of Indians and other foreigners in the country once and for all. The new law, which instituted three types of citizens (full, associate and naturalised), offered the opportunity for non-citizens in the country to become full citizens in three generations, provided they conformed to certain procedures. On the other hand, it has been pointed out that, 'for most...the legislation has made little difference' and 'either legal or illegal foreign residents are not concerned...as it does not change their status at all. Those excluded from full citizenship are aware that the decisions taken on their status are political.'

The political influence of Indians ended with the advent of the RC, which subsequently banned all political parties and activities. It also tightened the rules and regulations for all social, cultural and religious organisations, banned foreign media, imposed strict regulations and censorship on all publications and strictly controlled public gatherings and events. All these constrained the activities of the Indian community as well as the scope and performance of its organisations. The nationalisation drive and the autarkic economic policies depleted the financial resources of the Indian community and eroded its ability to support religious and community affairs. Indian hospitals were also nationalised. The RC's new educational policies that favoured citizens (both of whose parents must also be citizens) and instituted the use of the Burmese language as the instructional medium, as well as its nationalisation of private educational establishments in 1965, also affected the Indian community's efforts to educate and teach language skills to its youth. The isolationist orientation of the RC period (1962–73) also compromised the Indian community's links with the subcontinent. Indians resorted to keeping a low profile, though religious and sociocultural activities could still continue on a subdued communal basis, albeit within the constraints imposed by the security-conscious authorities. Despite the ruling elite's almost constant refrain on the evils associated with the role of the Chettiars and Indian immigrants during the colonial era, such harsh rhetoric did not lead to discrimination against the Indian community per se and there was little evidence of violence against it.

Towards the end of the BSPP era in 1987 and 1988, the increasingly agitated and discontented masses sometimes turned against Indians, especially Muslims. Those were just symptoms of the general malaise rather than actions driven by religious intolerance, racial hatred or bigotry. Unfortunately, the Indian community had become an easy and soft target for venting anger and frustration over the failed economy and political sclerosis.

In the economic sphere, the Indian community managed to find a niche in the formal (mainly for citizens) and the informal sector as small business operators, mainly in the service industry, and as traders and retailers as well as interlocutors in the interface between the emasculated official economy and the black market economy that grew out of the huge demand for scarce commodities.

In Rangoon, the pattern of distribution among the major occupational groups within the Indian community had not changed very much between 1953 and 1973. In the administrative and clerical field, the share was 15.8 per cent in 1973 compared to 16.2 per cent in 1953. Similarly, for trade and sales, the share was 24.5 per cent for 1973 against 25.2 per cent two decades before. Only in services did the share significantly drop to 6.7 per cent in 1973 from 13.2 per cent in 1953. The largest group, comprising crafts, industrial production and manual labour, saw their share increase from 35.6 per cent in 1953 to 39.7 per cent in 1973. However, in terms of the share of Indians in Rangoon's total labour force, there was a drastic decline from 24.6 per cent in 1953 to 4.8 per cent in 1973. When weighted by population, Indians were over-represented in trade, primary production and sales and services, and under-represented in administrative/clerical and professional/technical categories (probably due to indigenisation).

After the RC handed over power to elected officials in 1974, the environment for economic, religious and socio-cultural activities of Indians improved due to the general improvement in political governance brought about by constitutional rule. Nevertheless, the imperatives for assimilation with the indigenous majority continued to be strong, given the nature and orientation of the political regime and modalities of administrative governance of that era.

THE SITUATION OF INDIANS UNDER MILITARY RULE (1988–2004)

In the first few years of direct military rule under the junta, known as the State Law and Order Restoration Council (SLORC), the emphasis was on securing law and order after the tumultuous mass uprising that led to the military coup of 18 September 1988. Martial law was imposed and the Indian community, together with others in the newly christened Union of Myanmar, had little room to manoeuvre in daily life. Later, the regime opened up the political arena before the multi-party elections of May 1990. However, there was no evidence that the Indian community played an active political role in the heady atmosphere of the time leading to the elections.

Table 8.15

NUMBER OF REGISTERED FOREIGNERS FROM THE INDIAN SUBCONTINENT IN MYANMAR					
	1961	1970	1975	1991	2001
India	108,738	81,301	58,599	40,956	28,845
Pakistan	26,250	19,336	12,016	5414	226
Bangladesh	N.A.	N.A.	N.A.	1427	780
Total	134,988	100,637	70,615	47,797	29,851

Source: Government of Myanmar: Statistical Yearbook, various issues.
Notes: Bangladesh did not exist before 1971; N.A. = not available.

A Sikh temple along Thein Phyu Road in central Yangon.

When the junta refused to hand over power to the National League for Democracy (NLD) led by Aung San's daughter, Aung San Suu Kyi (who won the Nobel Peace Prize in 1991), a political stalemate set in and the promised transfer of power to civilian rule was deferred indefinitely. Subsequently, the SLORC was superseded by the State Peace and Development Council (SPDC) in November 1997, which reiterated the promise to return to civilian rule. However, at the end of 2004, the resolution to this political impasse, which had stalled the political reform process, was nowhere in sight. Under these circumstances, the Indian community prudently stayed away from involvement in anything political.

In the economic sphere, the SLORC abandoned the socialist command economy soon after its inception and carried out some economic reforms in line with a new market-oriented approach. Following increased efforts to attract foreign direct investment and encourage the expansion of private sector enterprises in trade, industry and services, the bias against non-citizens and foreigners has become less pronounced. This has benefited Indian commercial interests and entrepreneurs have been able to find new opportunities in the nascent private sector.

Today, Indians seem to be adapting well to the new economic and political environment. Despite allegations of religious persecution by expatriate dissidents and Muslim activists and the occasional outbreak of isolated violence against them, Indian Muslims appear to be in a better position to carry out their religious and sociocultural activities than during the socialist era. The practice of performing the haj and Hindu pilgrimages have continued with fewer impediments than before. Over 40 mosques in Yangon and several hundred all over the country appear to have been refurbished and rehabilitated. Similarly, some 30 or so prominent Hindu temples in Yangon and a few hundred around the country have been properly maintained. A few Hindu religious schools and over a dozen Muslim schools continue to operate in Yangon. Hindu institutions like the ABHCB, Sangh, Arya Samaj and All Myanmar Hindu Purohit Pujari Central Organisation are very much alive, albeit with a new generation of younger leaders. New and more development-oriented organisations such as the All Myanmar Tamil Hindu Foundation (AMTHF), founded at the turn of the century by young and dynamic Tamils, have appeared on the scene. The AMTHF, which operates as an NGO, has been engaged in imparting modern vocational skills to the Tamil youth, utilising information technology, with dozens of personal computers in Yangon and several in two other major cities. It also gives stipends to needy students, supports language teaching and looks after the old and infirm. Organisations such as the Islamic Religious Affairs Council and others for *muftis* (scholars learned in the Sharia) also cater to the religious needs of Indian Muslims.

The opening up of the economy since the early 1990s has resulted in the emergence of a new generation of Indian entrepreneurs of all faiths who have been able to exploit the opportunities offered by the government's support of the private sector. Many of them appear to be well off, with mobile phones, SUVs and air-conditioned offices. These groups have been found to be quite successful in trade, industry and services, and travel abroad holding business passports. This new generation of young and wealthy entrepreneurs, well connected to the authorities and with good organisational skills, has become quite influential in their respective communities.

Some of them have begun to aspire to community leadership, which puts the old guard on the defensive. In the Hindu community, the younger generation seems to be trying to overcome the traditional notion of the importance of caste and family in assuming leadership positions. The availability of satellite dishes and the growth of the MTV culture has also affected the Indian community, as it has other communities in Myanmar, with sections of the youth becoming more modern and fashion-oriented. The flood of consumer electronics has also modified the lifestyles of those who can afford them. In general, traditional customs and mores have come to be challenged by younger and more affluent members of the community, and there are some indications of an emerging generation gap. On the other hand, community leaders and religious and social organisations have also been trying to counterbalance this drift towards materialism through dialogue.

Population statistics have not been published since the last census of 1983. Rough estimates on the Indian population, based on past trends, suggest that Indians probably comprised about 3 per cent to 4 per cent of the total population in Myanmar in the mid-1990s. If this trend continued, the total number of Indians in Myanmar by the year 2000 could have been around 2 million.

Tin Maung Maung Than

A hawker selling Indian sweets at a railway station. People in Myanmar are generally fond of Indian sweets, and hawkers selling them are a common sight in downtown Yangon.

Table 8.16

NUMBER OF REGISTERED FOREIGNERS FROM THE INDIAN SUBCONTINENT IN MYANMAR ('000)											
	1987			1992			1997			2001		
	Male	Female	(M/F)	Male	Female	(M/F)	Male	Female	(M/F)	Male	Female	(M/F)
India	20.2	18.0	(1.1)	21.7	18.7	(1.2)	20.0	17.9	(1.1)	14.1	14.8	(0.95)
Pakistan	3.4	1.1	(3.1)	4.0	1.1	(3.6)	3.3	1.2	(2.8)	1.3	0.9	(1.4)
Bangladesh	1.0	0.2	(5.0)	1.1	0.2	(5.5)	1.3	0.5	(2.6)	0.5	0.3	(1.7)
Total	24.6	19.3	(1.3)	26.8	20.0	(1.3)	24.6	19.6	(1.3)	15.9	16.0	(0.99)

Source: Government of Myanmar: Statistical Yearbook, various issues. Notes: Data not available for years prior to 1987; M/F is the ratio of males to females in the population.

SINGAPORE

A Sikh traffic policeman. The first batch of 200 Sikh policemen arrived in Singapore in 1879. The local Chinese sometimes called them 'Mungkali kwai' (Bengali devils) because they struck fear among miscreants.

An early image of the Singapore River. The earliest Indian settlements were located on the west bank of the river. The area continued to be an important hub for the activities of Tamil merchants and traders throughout the 19th century.

Map 8.13

IN 2004, THE NUMBER OF Indians in Singapore was approximately 293,100 (8.4 per cent) out of a total resident population of 3.487 million. The figure reflects not only the total population of people of Indian origin who are Singapore citizens and residents, but also those who come from modern-day Sri Lanka, Pakistan, Bangladesh and Nepal. The labelling of all individuals of South Asian descent as 'Indian' can largely be explained by the way 'races' are classified in the Singapore census. Since census categories in post-independence Singapore recognise three main races—Chinese, Malay and Indian, alongside a fourth, termed 'Others', people from Sri Lanka, Pakistan, Bangladesh and Nepal have often been grouped together as 'Indian'. A further anomaly is that the census does not reflect individuals of mixed parentage, who are classified according to paternal descent.

The official census figure does not include non-resident workers in Singapore who hold temporary contracts. This group comprises professionals, mainly in the IT sector, labourers who service the construction industry, and domestic workers from various parts of South Asia. Official figures for workers on temporary contracts are difficult to obtain because the Ministry of Manpower in Singapore considers the information sensitive. However, independent surveys approximate the number of South Asians on work permits to be between 30–35 per cent of the total 'Indian' population in Singapore, or approximately 90,000–100,000.

A DIVERSE COMMUNITY

In Chinatown it is the ornate, carved spire of an Indian temple which dominates the view. In Serangoon Road a pall of incense and freshly-ground curry odours hover in the dense tropical air. Men in skirtlike dhotis and sandals sit in doorways carrying out their business. They measure tourists for suits, scoop peanuts into tightly-rolled newspaper cones or measure out dhal [lentils] on ancient brass scales.

Near the financial district along Market Street, the Nattukottai Chettiars from Tamil Nadu sit on straw mats carrying out their moneylending and banking activities with crude wooden boxes as safes. Behind City Hall along High Street, the Sindhis, Sikhs, and Gujeratis occupy shops well-stocked with carpets, jewellery and brassware. And outside the big hotels, fearsome turbaned and bearded Sikhs open car doors.

G. Swinstead and G. Haddon,
Singapore Stopover, 1981

Situated at the confluence of trade routes spanning the Indian Ocean, the Malay archipelago and the South China Sea, Singapore has witnessed the influx of people of diverse origins. The largest of these movements has been from southeastern China. Others have come from the neighbouring Malay peninsula, the outlying Indonesian islands and from the Indian subcontinent.

The Indian community forms a small minority of the total population but it has a significant influence on Singapore's development. Indians have, over time, carved a place for themselves in the country's political, social, economic and cultural life. After the establishment of a British presence, Indians were encouraged—in some cases manipulated and coerced—into migrating to the island. Indian migration produced a diverse community comprised of convicts, labourers, imperial auxiliaries, traders and businessmen. These days the primary migrants are professionals in the IT industry.

EARLY MIGRATION

Indian migration began in January 1819 with the arrival of Sir Thomas Stamford Raffles. Raffles's entourage included some 120 sepoys of the Bengal Native Infantry and a Bazaar Contingent, comprising dhobis (washermen), *doodh-wallahs* (milkmen), *chai-wallahs* (tea-makers) and domestic servants. Known locally as 'Bengalis' (possibly due to their association with the Bengal Native Infantry and their embarkation at Calcutta), the initial group of colonial militia and their camp followers came from what is now eastern Uttar Pradesh and northwest Bihar, then the principal recruiting ground for sepoys of the Bengal Native Infantry. While few of the early colonial militia remained in Singapore at the end of their tour, the persistence of a dhobi community from early times suggests that some members of the Bazaar Contingent left the garrison to assume the role of civilian immigrants in the new settlement.

Figure 8.3

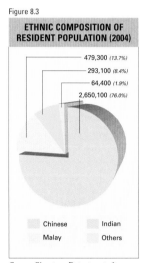

ETHNIC COMPOSITION OF RESIDENT POPULATION (2004)

479,300 *(13.7%)*
293,100 *(8.4%)*
64,400 *(1.9%)*
2,650,100 *(76.0%)*

Chinese   Indian
Malay   Others

Source: Singapore Department of Statistics, 'Population Trends', 2005.

The founding of modern Singapore

In the late 18th century, the British East India Company (EIC) saw the need for a base east of the Bay of Bengal that could safeguard its trading interests in India. Although the company had established trading posts in Bencoolen (1685) and Penang (1786), neither was ideal in facilitating and securing the burgeoning trade between India and China. The end of the Napoleonic War and the return of the Dutch to the East Indies in 1815 increased the feeling of insecurity of the British and intensified the search for a suitable port in the region. It was for these reasons that Singapore was acquired by the EIC as a trading outpost in 1819.

On his second visit to Singapore in June 1819, Raffles was joined by an associate from Penang, Naraina Pillai. Initially employed as a clerk in the colonial treasury, Pillai ventured into business, setting up a kiln producing bricks for the growing number of houses at the trading post. Following the arrival of a few carpenters, bricklayers and cloth merchants he recruited from Penang, Pillai began to build houses, set up a shop at the market place at Cross Street selling cotton piece-goods, and established himself as the most influential Indian merchant in early Singapore.

Established as a free port, Singapore began to attract traders from China and India. By 1824, the Indian community in Singapore numbered 756 out of a total population of 10,683. Muslims from Tamil Nadu, primarily Thanjavur and Ramnathapuram, were prominent among early Indians. Known as Chulias, these mobile traders had established an expansive network spanning Aceh, Burma, Johor, Kedah, Melaka, the Maldives and Ceylon, and were quick to move to Singapore following colonial settlement as shopkeepers and petty traders by the Singapore River.

Although most early Indians in Singapore arrived because of their association with the colonial militia or as 'free' commercial and labour migrants, 'forced' Indian migration followed soon after the Anglo-Dutch Treaty of 1824. The treaty, which secured the British position in Singapore, also resulted in the transfer of Bencoolen (present-day Bengkulu, Indonesia) to the Dutch in exchange for British control over Melaka. The closure of the British penal colony for Indian convicts in Bencoolen led to the establishment of an alternative detention facility in Singapore. In April 1825, the brig *Horatio* brought the first batch of 80 Indian convicts who had originally been transported from Madras to Bencoolen. This was followed by 122 convicts who arrived from Bengal a week later. The convicts represented a cross-section of Indian society, including Benares *brahmanas*, Sikh and Dogra Kshatriyas, Chettiar, Bengali and Parsi financiers and peasants, and untouchables from various parts of the subcontinent.

Housed in a walled compound at Bras Basah Road, Indian convict labour was used to clear jungles and construct roads, jetties, canals, bridges and buildings. Some of the finest architecture in Singapore in the 19th century was the product of convict labour, including St. Andrew's Cathedral (1862) and the Istana (1869). By 1860, the number of convicts on the island was 2275, of which few were known to have returned to India.

Large-scale Indian labour migration followed with the expansion of the port and the growth of the planta-tion sector in the second half of the 19th century. Commercial plantations produced gambier, cloves, nutmeg, pineapple, sugar cane and, towards the end of the century, rubber. Although Chinese farmers dominated the agricultural sector, European planters employed Indian labour; and in dairy farming and the laundry sector, Indians occupied key positions. Furthermore, the majority of workers employed in public projects, servicing the budding administrative, development, commercial and defence functions in the settlement, were drawn from India.

For much of the 19th century, Indian labour recruitment for the plantation sector was carried out through the indenture system. As elsewhere, indentured labour in Singapore was regulated through contracts. These contracts were for five years, at meagre wages, and

Indian convicts at the Singapore jail during the 19th century.

The Indian dhobi (washerman) settlement and convict colony (background).

Singapore under 'Indian' rule (1826–67)

In 1826, Singapore together with Penang and Melaka formed the Presidency of the Straits Settlements and was administered as the 'Eastern Presidency of the British-Indian Government'. The seat of government was retained at Penang, and Singapore was put under the charge of a Resident Councillor. This arrangement was to remain until June 1830 when, in an attempt to cut cost, the Directors of the EIC decided to abolish the Penang Presidency and reduced the Straits Settlements to the rank of a residency under the direct control of the Bengal Presidency. With the changes, the Governor of the Straits Settlements became a resident without executive and legislative powers. While he was empowered to make local regulations for the Straits Settlements, these would not have the force of law unless sanctioned by the Government of India. Consequently, all administrative decisions concerning Singapore, Penang and Malacca were made in Calcutta, and all legislation affecting the Straits Settlements was passed by the Legislative Council of India. In 1851, the Straits Settlements were transferred from the Bengal Presidency to the direct supervision of the Governor-General and the supreme government of India. Singapore was to remain administered by Indian hands, on behalf of the British crown (under the care of the India Office after it replaced the abolished EIC in 1858) until 1867 when the Straits Settlements were brought under the control of the British Colonial Office.

Singapore, for nearly half a century, was thus effectively a part of India. The island came under the legislative authority of the legislative council in India, and was nominally at least, under the jurisdiction of the Supreme Court of Calcutta. Not only was she administratively a part of India, but her civil service was regularly staffed with former members of the Bengal service as well as officers of the Madras Army whose Indian experience must have left an imprint on the Singapore they governed. The legacies of those years for the subsequent development of Singapore were indeed significant. Institutions which were developed by the British in India took root in Singapore. To a very large extent, Singapore's administrative and legal system—a centralized administration in which civil power was supreme—were based on British-India lineage. For instance, the Indian penal code, adopted in India in the 1860s and brought into effect in Singapore in 1871, still leaves its imprint on the country's legal system. Although Indian rule was terminated in 1867, the links between Singapore and India did not cease there; by the latter half of the 19th century, it had taken the form of immigrants from India who had been arriving in Singapore in large numbers, and making significant contribution to the development of the island colony.

Extract from Tan Tai Yong and Andrew Major, India and Indians in the Making of Singapore, *1995.*

included initial expenditures such as travel costs. During his sojourn, the labourer was subject to extreme demands made by employers. In 1876, following growing pressure to improve the plight of indentured labourers, the contract was shortened to three years. Nevertheless, through numerous liabilities which increased the labourers' debts, employers were often able to demand an extended period of indenture. From the 1870s, a parallel method called the *kangani* system was employed, whereby the *kangani*, a South Indian foreman, was paid by his employer to recruit labour from his home district or village.

The *kangani* system became the dominant mode of recruitment in the Malayan plantation sector following the abolition of indenture in 1910, but for governmental undertakings such as public works, municipal and harbour services, roads and railway construction, Indian coolies were often procured through direct recruitment by colonial authorities. Moreover, labour recruitment was not limited to assisted forms. There was a constant movement of free labour from the late 19th century, particularly after 1938, when all forms of assisted labour migration were abolished.

The vast majority of labour migrants came from South India, primarily Tamil Nadu. Famines and epidemics in the Madras Presidency, pressure on landholdings as a result of population growth, high unemployment and widespread poverty among lower castes compelled people to migrate. These conditions existed in other parts of the subcontinent as well, but the overwhelming representation of Tamil labour was due to the Indian government's refusal to sanction indentured emigration to Malaya and Singapore from any other part of India.

The mechanics of migration encouraged the recruitment of labourers from districts closest to the two authorised ports of departure at Negapatnam and Madras. Most of those who came to Singapore were from North Arcot, Tanjore and Trichinopoly. An unregulated illegal coolie trade from Karaikkal, Pondicherry, Cuddalore, Porto Novo and Nagore was also carried out by Indian-owned sailing ships before the government increased supervision in the 1870s.

Tamil labourers, particularly from the Adi Dravida (untouchable) castes, were preferred by colonial authorities not only because they were relatively inexpensive, but also because they were deemed 'docile', 'malleable', 'easy to manage', 'good for repetitive tasks' and, unlike Chinese labourers, were viewed as being accustomed to British rule. Moreover, a racial mix of labourers was encouraged as it underpinned the British policy of 'divide and rule' in Singapore and the Malayan peninsula. Employers were advised:

To secure your independence, work with Javanese and Tamils, and if you have sufficient experience, also with Malays and Chinese, you can always play the one against the other...In case of a strike, you will never be left without labour, and the coolies of one nationality will think twice before they make their terms, if they know that you are in a position that you can do without them.

The Selangor Journal, Volume 4, 1895

Although most of the Indian migrants to Singapore were labourers, the shortage of locally educated workers in the 19th and early 20th century resulted in growing demands from government and private employers for educated junior staff, teachers, doctors and administrators. To fill the vacuum, the government employed workers from Sri Lanka and South India. Prominent among these were educated Malayalis and Sri Lankan Tamils, who were attracted to Singapore by substantially higher wages. This latter group's ability to converse in Tamil was an added bonus in their role as intermediaries. While the Sri Lankan Tamils were dominant as junior staff during the period prior to the 1920s, the number of Malayalis increased considerably during the inter-war period, when many found employment due to the growing British naval and military presence in Singapore.

Though South Indians formed the majority of the Indian populace, there was a substantial increase in the number of North Indians following the arrival of the Sikhs in the 1870s. The successful exploits of the Sikh police, who were introduced in Hong Kong in 1867, created the perception that Sikhs were particularly useful in the police force. In 1879, Singapore received its first batch of 200 Sikh policemen. As word of their martial prowess spread, they came to be increasingly sought after as security personnel, which encouraged further migration. Sikhs preferred a position in the Straits Settlements Police Force, but those who could not find employment there were quickly absorbed into the private sector as caretakers, watchmen and guards. Over time, a number of Sikhs entered business, particularly moneylending, to supplement their income.

Singapore's rapid development as a free port led to an increase in the number and diversity of Indian commercial migrants in the second half of the 19th century. In addition to small traders, petty entrepreneurs, salesmen, pedlars and shopkeepers, the Indian community included a few merchants, financiers and contractors with substantial capital. In 1845, there were 17 Indian merchants in Singapore. The Nattukottai Chettiars were prominent commercial migrants. From their base in Ramnad and Pudukottai in Tamil Nadu, they established an extensive moneylending network spanning Ceylon, Burma, Malaya and Singapore. Their clientele included not only Indian traders but also European planters and Chinese businessmen. The Chettiars remained prominent

A Chinese tombstone guarded by statues of Indian bodyguards. Sikhs and 'Hindustanis' (migrants from Uttar Pradesh and Bihar) were the preferred security personnel in the city-state in the 19th and early 20th century.

The Sri Mariamman Temple, which is devoted to the goddess Mariamman, is the oldest Hindu temple in Singapore.

moneylenders in Singapore for over a century until the 1970s, when the growth of banks and other financial institutions dealt a major blow to their business.

Within the commercial sector, North Indians occupied a prominent position. The majority of North Indian commercial migrants in the 19th century were Parsis, Gujaratis, Marwaris and Bengalis. From the 1920s, particularly in the years before and after World War II, these groups were superseded by a large number of Sindhi and Sikh commercial migrants who established a prominent position in the textile industry, with a trading network that extended to Hong Kong, Kobe, Jakarta and Bombay.

INDIAN SETTLEMENTS IN THE 19TH AND EARLY 20TH CENTURY

From the 1820s, Indian settlements were found in the enclaves of the expanding town. Notwithstanding the military garrison, the earliest concentration of Indians was on the west bank of the Singapore River, close to 'China Town'. The area that came to be settled by Tamil Muslim traders was known first as Chulia Kampong, and later took the name Chulia Street. Nearby was Market Street, which had a concentration of Chettiar moneylenders. Testifying to the early prominence of Indians in the area, the oldest Indian places of worship can be found in the vicinity. As early as 1823, Naraina Pillai had been given a land grant to establish a Hindu temple at South Bridge Road, and in 1827, Singapore's first Hindu temple, Sri Mariamman Temple, was built on the site. Other early Indian places of worship in the area include Jamae Masjid Chulia (1826), Al-Abrar Mosque (Kochoo Pally, 1827) and Nagore Dargah (between 1828 and 1830), which underscore the early prominence of Muslim traders from the Coromandel Coast.

An important, albeit later, enclave for Indian commerce was High Street, popular among Sindhi, Sikh and Gujarati textile merchants, traders and financiers. By the late 19th and early 20th centuries, Tamil, Malayali and Telugu dock and railway workers could be found in the vicinity of the port and railway station at Tanjong Pagar. Malayalis also settled north of the island at Sembawang, where they were employed in the shipping industry and the naval base. Other Indian settlements included Kampong Glam, Arab Street and Jalan Besar, which had a concentration of Indian Muslim petty traders, and textile and jewellery merchants.

The most important area of Indian settlement was Serangoon Road. A popular Singapore travel guide declares, 'You can reach India three ways from Singapore: by air, by sea and by walking down Serangoon Road.' Known today as Little India, the area evolved from settlements of Indians engaged in cattle-related activities that serviced the convict prison. Built by convict labour, Serangoon Road was one of the main arterial roads that ran from the city in a northeasterly direction across the island. With the growing shortage of space in the city by the second half of the 19th century, Serangoon Road attracted Indian shopkeepers and traders who met the needs of the growing number of Indian migrants.

Serangoon Road had a spectrum of diverse Indian groups. Although the majority of Indians in Serangoon Road were Tamil, the presence of South and North Indian

associations and Hindu, Muslim and Christian places of worship there testifies to its heterogeneous mix. A caste dimension in settlement patterns was also evident prior to World War II, whereby the core Serangoon Road area was settled by caste Hindus, while municipal labour lines situated at the peripheries housed the Adi Dravidas. Although today Indians have resettled in many other parts of the island, the cultural landscape of Serangoon Road continues to be dominated by Indians.

From the second half of the 19th century, Serangoon Road became the most important Indian commercial and residential area.

SOCIAL AND POLITICAL LIFE PRIOR TO WORLD WAR II

By the end of the first decade of the 20th century, the Indian population in Singapore numbered approximately 28,000, or nearly 9 per cent of the total population. Still, for the majority of Indians, Singapore was simply an economic sojourn, a place to earn money before returning to their homeland. Between 1911 and 1921, for every 100 Indians arriving in the Malay peninsula, there were approximately 60 departing for India. Furthermore, testifying to the fact that few Indians settled with their families, children under the age of 15 accounted for less than 15 per cent of the total Indian population in 1921, a figure much lower than for any other community. The idea that Singapore was a temporary abode was a defining characteristic for the majority of Indians in Singapore until the advent of stringent migration controls in the second half of the 20th century.

There were many reasons for this pattern of migration. The arrival of the steamship in the mid-19th century and the improvement in communication links between the peninsula and India encouraged the movement of labour. Labourers tended to spend about three years in Singapore before returning to India for a period of three to six months. The stark difference in Indian male and female numbers in the colony also worked against permanent settlement. Attempts by Indian authorities to increase the number of female migrants were only partially successful because systems of labour migration that were subject to Indian ordinance primarily affected plantations and estates. In urban centres, Indian coolies and traders continued to be predominantly male. Even in the second decade of the 20th century, there were fewer than 200 women for every 1000 Indian men in Singapore.

N. R. Partha, the owner of Partha and Co. He was also the founder of the Orient, *a daily paper and the* Vijayan, *an Anglo-Tamil paper.*

Singapore Indian Association cricketers with their trophies in 1927. In its early years, the association's membership was overwhelmingly drawn from the higher echelons of Indian society.

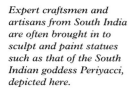

Expert craftsmen and artisans from South India are often brought in to sculpt and paint statues such as that of the South Indian goddess Periyacci, depicted here.

Uncertain of their position in the host country, where they were both numerically and politically marginal and with no economic incentive to relocate their families, few were willing to sever their ties with India, preferring instead to remit money to their spouses and families to alleviate debt, build a house or purchase land in their homeland. The view among Indians in the first half of the 20th century that Singapore was only a temporary home was magnified in times of economic and political uncertainty. During the Great Depression of the late 1920s and 1930s, not only was immigration from India restricted, but large numbers of Indians were repatriated as well. While the period after the Depression saw an increase in the number of Indians, the advent of World War II and the Japanese occupation of Singapore once again witnessed the departure of large numbers of Indians from the island.

In addition to transience, one of the key characteristics of the Indian population in Singapore was its heterogeneity. The community was divided along class, occupation, religious, ethnic and, prior to World War II, caste lines. The top echelons of Indian society in Singapore before the war included professionals, higher government officials and administrative staff, accounting for just over 0.5 per cent of the total Indian population. This group was characterised by wealth, higher education and a 'European' way of life. Mercantile groups, proprietors of businesses and moneylenders, who made up under one-tenth of the total Indian population, were generally excluded from this group and tended to be at a lower rung in the class hierarchy, with the exception of the most wealthy and educated. The middle class was composed of the lower ranks of government and army employees, teachers and police officers. They were characterised by their English education and white-collar work, which led them to embrace elements of Western culture and its social habits. This middle class in service-oriented occupations formed 5–7 per cent of the total Indian population. Those at the lowest rung of the hierarchy were largely uneducated. This group was made up of various types of coolies and labourers and comprised over 80 per cent of the total Indian population.

The heterogeneity of the Indian populace was also evident in religion. Although the majority of immigrants were Hindu, Hinduism as practised in Singapore was far too fragmented to provide cohesion. To some extent, differences were even strengthened: Tamil labourers, many of whom were Adi Dravidas, had shrines constructed for village deities and worship was led by non-Brahmin priests who followed the folk religions of South India. Neither did brahminical Hindu ceremonies among higher castes translate into unity, as South Indians were predominantly Saivite Hindus while North Indians were either Vaisnavite or followers of Hindu reform organisations such as the Ramakrishna Mission or the Arya Samaj. Moreover, Hindus were strongly divided by caste, particularly before World War II. Among Indian Muslims, linguistic and regional divisions undermined the possible unifying potential of religion. As mosques were built according to community needs, those frequented by North Indians held services in Urdu, while South Indian mosques held services in Tamil or Malayalam.

There was also a clear heterogeneity in terms of ethnicity. Although there was a Tamil majority, the many groups that comprised the Indian community included Punjabis, Malayalis, Hindustanis (migrants from Uttar Pradesh and Bihar), Bengalis, Telugus and Gujaratis. These differences were reflected in the myriad types of Indian organisations in Singapore in the first half of the 20th century. Most Indians were linked to organisations that catered specifically to their ethnic, sub-ethnic, linguistic, religious and caste sub-groupings.

In 1923, a section of the Indian elite, including administrators, professionals and merchants, joined to form the Singapore Indian Association. Its members came from the higher echelons of Indian society, but there was an attempt early on to represent the diverse provinces from which Indians came. The management of the association included 15 members, of whom at least three were drawn from the Madras Presidency, two each from the Bombay Presidency and Punjab Province, and one each from Bengal Province, the United Provinces, Sind and the Central Provinces. In 1936, the system of provincial representation was abolished, 'to prevent particular sections from dominating and to make the committee more representative of the general populace.'

Indian commercial groups have considerable influence in Singapore, and the Indian Merchants Association (renamed the Singapore Indian Chamber of Commerce in 1935) was founded in 1924 to promote the interests of the Indian mercantile community. Members of the chamber, who were some of the wealthiest Indian businessmen in Singapore, reportedly conducted as much as 70 per cent of Singapore's trade with India just prior to World War II. Although these organisations were pan-Indian in their affiliations, their elite composition meant that they largely excluded the vast majority of Indians.

The transient nature of the community and the tendency for Indians from all classes, especially merchants, to sustain links with India through short visits, encouraged the spread of 'homeland' political movements in the diaspora in the first half of the 20th century. Even when Indians were roused into political action by homeland concerns, the heterogeneous nature of the community mitigated attempts at cohesive Indian mobilisation until the advent of World War II.

The first political movement that influenced the Indian community was the Ghadar Party. Although the party aimed to overthrow the British Raj in India and had its base in North America, it was popular among Sikh and other Punjabi groups who had a substantial presence among sepoys and the police in Singapore. Growing disaffection and anger among Muslim soldiers at British actions in Turkey during World War I led to a violent revolt by Pathan, Sikh, Punjabi and Rajput soldiers against their British officers in February 1915. The immediate trigger for the outbreak was the rising concern among members of the native Indian Muslim infantry that they would be sent to Turkey to fight their co-religionists, and the spread of a rumour about the impending arrival of a German warship harbouring Indian mutineers. The rebellion, which is commonly known as the Sepoy Mutiny, was quickly crushed.

Of greater long-term consequence was the influence of the Tamil-oriented Self-Respect and Dravida Munnetra Kalagam (DMK) movements of Madras. The visit of E. V. Ramasamy Naicker, the leader of the Self-Respect movement, to Malaya in 1929 saw the proliferation of Tamil associations dedicated to moral, religious and social reform. Led mainly by journalists, schoolteachers and *kanganis*, these associations achieved some measure of success in propagating reforms within the Tamil community, such as eradicating the practice of self-immolation and popularising monogamous marriage. Towards the end of this period, the influences from Madras became increasingly political in character and began to penetrate the Indian labouring classes on the estates and in the public service. One such example is the serious outbreak of labour militancy at the Singapore Traction Company in 1938.

THE JAPANESE OCCUPATION AND THE INDIAN NATIONAL ARMY

The outbreak of World War II and the subsequent Japanese Occupation between 1942 and 1945 brought the fragile roots of the Indian community in Singapore to the fore. In 1941, the possibility of a Japanese invasion caused a number of Indian commercial groups and some professionals to return to India. As the threat of war shifted towards the Malay peninsula, migration among these groups increased. However, returning to India was not an option for the bulk of the Indian community. Financial limitations and the speed of the British surrender ensured that the majority remained on the island throughout the Japanese Occupation. Like other communities, they suffered from the economic hardship, scarcity of food, and health and sanitation problems that characterised the period.

A significant feature of the Japanese Occupation for the Indian community was the convergence of the 'homeland' nationalist aspirations of local Indians with the Japanese wartime ambition of removing the British presence in the East. This brought about a remarkable event in the history of Indians in Singapore, as the island became the focus of political and military activities for overseas Indians aiming to free their homeland from British rule.

Following the defeat of British forces in Singapore in February 1942, the Japanese organised conferences in Bangkok and Tokyo in June and August that year, where Indian leaders from Southeast and East Asia met to devise a strategy for Indian liberation from British rule. The Indian Independence League (IIL), the political wing of the movement, was formed. Rashbehari Bose, a long-time

Indian nationalist based in Japan, assumed leadership of the organisation. At the time of his arrival in Singapore in late 1942, the organisation had over 40 branches and 12,000 members. Alongside the league was the Indian National Army (INA), a military outfit that sought to recruit and train soldiers for direct engagement with British forces in India. Led by Captain Mohan Singh, a former officer in the British Indian army, the core of the INA was made up of British Indian army prisoners of war (POWs) in Singapore. By late 1942, the total strength of the army exceeded 16,000.

Attempts to unite Indian leaders under a pan-Indian umbrella resulted, at least temporarily, in an unprecedented unity among Indian groups. This was partly the result of the considerable efforts of prominent local Indian leaders such as S. C. Goho, K. P. K. Menon and M. V. Pillai. Support for these efforts, however, stemmed not only from a genuine feeling of Indian patriotism but also from pragmatic concerns. For many Indian POWs, joining the INA was preferable to life in a Japanese concentration camp. Likewise, the local Indian community's cooperation in Japanese initiatives was also linked to the hope that it would be spared the brunt of Japanese persecution.

The suspicion that the Japanese supported the movement to fulfil their own imperial objectives had a negative impact on the expansion of these organisations. Tensions between the IIL, the INA and the Japanese authorities over issues of autonomy and decision-making did not help, and neither did Rashbehari Bose's pro-Japanese sympathies. Consequently, the INA was temporarily disbanded at the end of 1942 and its first leader, Captain Singh, was arrested.

The situation improved considerably in July 1943, following the arrival of Subhas Chandra Bose. His leadership of the movement marked the peak of pan-Indian nationalism in Singapore. Soon after his arrival, Bose established the Provisional Government of Azad Hind (Free India) that was recognised by nine countries, including Japan and Germany. His charisma, oratorical skill and ability to persuade the Japanese to grant the IIL and the INA greater autonomy

A photograph of members of the Singapore Indian Chamber of Commerce, taken in the 1930s. At the time, most of Singapore's trade with India was carried out by its members.

The front cover of The War Illustrated *shows Indian troops arriving in the 1940s.*

Subhas Chandra Bose, leader of the INA.

DILLI CHALO! (ONWARDS TO DELHI!)

Soldiers of India's Army of Liberation!

Today is the proudest day of my life. Today it has pleased Providence to give me the unique privilege and honour of announcing to the whole world that India's Army of Liberation has come into being. This army has now been drawn up in military formation on the battlefield of Singapore, which was once the bulwark of the British Empire.

This is not only the Army that will emancipate India from the British yoke, it is also the Army that will hereafter create the future national army of Free India. Every Indian must feel proud that this Army, his own Army, has been organized entirely under Indian leadership and that when the historic moment arrives, under Indian leadership it will go to battle.

There are people who thought at one time that the Empire on which the sun did not set was an everlasting empire. No such thought ever troubled me. History had taught me that every empire has its inevitable decline and collapse. Moreover I had seen with my own eyes, cities and fortresses that were once the bulwarks but which became the graveyards of bygone empires. Standing today on the graveyard of the British empire, even a child is convinced that the almighty British empire is already a thing of the past.

When France declared war on Germany in 1939 and the campaign began, there was but one cry which rose from the lips of German soldiers—'To Paris, To Paris!' When the Brave soldiers of Nippon set out on their march in December 1941 there was but one cry which rose from their lips—'To Singapore, To Singapore!' Comrades! Soldiers! Let your battle-cry be—'To Delhi, To Delhi!' How many of us will individually survive this war of freedom, I do not know. But I do know this, that we shall ultimately win and our task will not end until our surviving heroes hold the victory parade on another graveyard of the British empire, the Lal Kila or Red Fortress of ancient Delhi.

Throughout my public career, I have always felt that though India is otherwise ripe for independence in every way, she has lacked one thing, namely an army of liberation. George Washington of America could fight and win freedom, because he had his army. Garibaldi could liberate Italy, because he had his armed volunteers behind him. It is your privilege and honour to be the first to come forward and organize India's national army. By doing so, you have removed the last obstacle in our path to freedom. Be happy and proud that you are the pioneers, the vanguard, in such a noble cause.

Let me remind you that you have a two-fold task to perform. With the force of arms and at the cost of your blood you will have to win liberty. Then, when India is free, you will have to organize the permanent army of Free India, whose task it will be to preserve our liberty for all time. We must build up our national defence on such an unshakable foundation that never again in our history shall we lose our freedom.

As soldiers, you will always have to cherish and live up to the three ideals of faithfulness, duty and sacrifice. Soldiers who always remain faithful to their nation, who are always prepared to sacrifice their lives, are invincible. If you, too, want to be invincible, engrave these three ideals in the innermost core of your hearts.

A true soldier needs both military and spiritual training. You must, all of you, so train yourselves and your comrades that every soldier will have unbounded confidence in himself, will be conscious of being immensely superior to the enemy, will be fearless of death, and will have sufficient initiative to act on his own in any critical situation should the need arise. During the course of the present war, you have seen with your own eyes what wonders scientific training, coupled with courage, fearlessness and dynamism, can achieve. Learn all that you can from this example, and build up for Mother India an absolutely first-class modern army.

To those of you who are officers, I should like to say that your responsibility is a heavy one. Though the responsibility of an officer in every army in this world is indeed great, it is far greater in your case. Because of our political enslavement, we have no tradition like that of Mukden, Port Arthur or Sedan to inspire us. We have to unlearn some of the things that the British taught us and we have to learn much that they did not teach. Nevertheless. I am confident that you will rise to the occasion and fulfill the task that your countrymen have thrown on your brave shoulders. Remember always that officers can make or unmake an army. Remember, too, that the British have suffered defeats on so many fronts largely because of worthless officers. And remember also that out of your ranks will be born the future General Staff of the Army of Free India.

To all of you I should like to say that in the course of this war you will have to acquire the experience and achieve the success which alone can build up a national tradition for our Army. An army that has no tradition of courage, fearlessness and invincibility cannot hold its own in a struggle with a powerful enemy.

Comrades! You have voluntarily accepted a mission that is the noblest that the human mind can conceive of. For the fulfilment of such a mission no sacrifice is too great, not even the sacrifice of one's life. You are today the custodians of India's national honour and the embodiment of India's hopes and aspirations. So conduct yourself that your countrymen may bless you and posterity may be proud of you.

I have said that today is the proudest day of my life. For an enslaved people, there can be no greater pride, no higher honour, than to be the first soldier in the army of liberation. But this honour carries with it a corresponding responsibility and I am deeply conscious of it. I assure you that I shall be with you in darkness and in sunshine, in sorrow and in joy, in suffering and in victory. For the present, I can offer you nothing except hunger, thirst, privation, forced marches and death. But if you follow me in life and in death, as I am confident you will, I shall lead you to victory and freedom. It does not matter who among us will live to see India free. It is enough that India shall be free and that we shall give our all to make her free. May God now bless our Army and grant us victory in the coming fight!

Inqualab Zindabad! Azad Hind Zindabad [sic]

Speech by Subhas Chandra Bose at the military review of the INA, The Padang, Singapore, July 1943, available at http://netaji.netfirms.com/netaji/speeches/todelhi.htm.

The INA was largely made up of local volunteers and former members of the British Indian army.

unified Indians and gained mass support for the movement. By 1944, the league had some 350,000 members. The increase in volunteer conscripts for the INA, which was renamed the Azad Hind Fauj (Free India Army), resulted in its numbers swelling to over 40,000.

With the slogan 'Dilli Chalo!' ('Onwards to Delhi!'), the INA began its military operations on the Burma front in early 1944. It launched the Imphal Operation between March and July, alongside three Japanese divisions, to capture the capital of Manipur in the hope of fomenting a general revolt against the British. The campaign proved disastrous. INA forces suffered from starvation and disease. By June 1944, most of the army had either surrendered to Allied forces or simply deserted the field. In August 1945, following the Japanese surrender, the INA was formally disbanded. The British Military Administration, that took charge of Singapore in September 1945, was clearly hostile to Indian nationalist aspirations and immediately demolished the INA memorial constructed by Bose. A number of Indian journalists and merchants were indicted for spreading Japanese propaganda and profiteering during the war, as were many officers of the INA who were court-martialled and sent to India to face charges of treason.

POST-WAR DEVELOPMENTS

The period of extraordinary pan-Indian unity during the Japanese Occupation disintegrated at the end of World War II. In addition to the re-emergence of the long-standing schism between North Indians and South Indians, the Partition had repercussions in the relations between North Indian Hindus and Muslims. Divisions were also evident in the South Indian community following the increased emphasis on linguistic identities in independent India and the concomitant reorganisation of the Madras Presidency into the linguistic provinces of Tamil Nadu, Kerala, Andhra Pradesh and Karnataka.

For Tamils in Singapore, the focus on linguistic identities fostered a unified Tamil identity that transcended caste and religion. The 1950s saw the flowering of Tamil literature, which included the works of the eminent playwright and poet Thiru N. Palanivelu. There were also considerable developments in the Tamil vernacular press, such as *Tamil Murasu*, under the leadership of G. Sarangapani, who had been influenced by the Dravidian movement of the pre-war period. The movement fostered the development of the Tamil Representative Council and the Tamils Reform Association, which brought together various Tamil organisations to propagate social reforms such as monogamy and to preserve Tamil linguistic purity and the Tamil language. While the movement was popular among the Tamil working and middle classes, the minority of English-educated Indian and Sri Lankan Tamils in the clerical and administrative sectors remained largely aloof.

The post-war period also witnessed the emergence of anti-colonial nationalism and the growth of labour militancy in Malaya and Singapore. Both of these movements drew support from sections of the Indian community politicised by their experience of the Japanese Occupation. Indian leaders such as C. V. Devan Nair figured prominently in the trade union movement in Malaya and Singapore, which demanded an increase in wages and better working conditions for labourers. Other notable leaders with socialist inclinations included S. Rajaratnam, who became one of the founders of the People's Action Party (PAP). The Tamil vernacular press, which was popular with working-class

Tamils, supported left-wing parties and published many articles aimed at spreading anti-colonial propaganda. Indian Muslims also extended their support for Malayan nationalism through pan-Malayan ethno-religious parties, such as the Progressive Party and the radical Labour Party.

In demographic terms, the aftermath of the Partition, which saw the displacement of Sikhs and Hindus, had repercussions in Singapore. *The Straits Times*, describing the substantial increase in the number of North Indian commercial migrants in 1948, noted:

Hundreds of Sindhis have arrived in Singapore in the last few months…Many have been helped to set up their own businesses….New Sindhi textile shops have sprung up in Changi, Nee Soon, R. A. F. Seletar, Naval Base, Middle Road, Arab Street, and in the centre of town…Besides Sindhis, Sikhs have also been arriving in large numbers, some of these Sikhs, well established businessmen in Bangkok, have opened up branches in Singapore…Other Sikhs are from West Punjab.

Migration, however, was not limited to these groups. The prolonged period of economic development in Singapore following the Korean War resulted in an increase of commercial migrants from various parts of India. There was also a substantial escalation in the number of Indians moving from Malaya to Singapore due to safer conditions and better prospects. Malaya was under a prolonged period of Emergency rule, which was aimed at stemming the growth of communist groups and labour militancy. Some 40,000 Indians emigrated from Malaya to Singapore between 1947 and 1957, accounting in part for the substantial increase in the number of Indians in Singapore in that decade.

Immigration acts in 1952 and 1959, however, constrained Indian movement to the island. The 1959 ordinance was particularly harsh, requiring those seeking an employment pass to have a monthly salary of no less than S$1200, and otherwise restricting admission only to wives and children of Singaporean citizens. By the 1960s, Indian migration to Singapore was severely constrained and, of the few who arrived, the vast majority were the wives and children of Singaporean citizens.

INDIANS IN INDEPENDENT SINGAPORE

Singapore became independent on 9 August 1965 following a failed merger with the Malayan Federation. While the Indian experience in Singapore and Malaya before

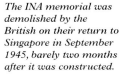

The INA memorial was demolished by the British on their return to Singapore in September 1945, barely two months after it was constructed.

G. Sarangapani, editor of Tamil Murasu *and one of the founders of the Tamils Reform Association in Singapore, speaking at a Tamil celebration in Lorong Lalat, 1966. The guest of honour at the event was the former prime minister, Lee Kuan Yew (seated, right).*

INDIAN POLITICIANS IN SINGAPORE

S. Rajaratnam

On my identity card, it says my race is Indian. But I don't care if you call me an Indian or an Eskimo. What is important is whether you consider me a good man.

S. Rajaratnam was born in 1915 in Jaffna, Ceylon, and raised in Malaya, where his father was a supervisor of rubber estates. A nationalist who worked tirelessly for Singapore, Rajaratnam shaped the values of a new nation and helped to establish Singapore's credentials around the world.

In 1937, Rajaratnam went to England to pursue a degree in law. The advent of World War II and an emerging interest in socialism and anti-colonialism, however, disrupted his studies and led to a move towards politics. Upon his return to Singapore in 1948, Rajaratnam worked as a journalist and gained a reputation for being a critic of colonial rule. In 1950, he was appointed associate editor of the *Singapore Standard*, and later worked for *The Straits Times*. In 1959, he resigned from his post at *The Straits Times* and stood for elections in the Kampong Glam constituency. He would remain a member of parliament (MP) for the constituency for 29 years.

Along with Lee Kuan Yew, Goh Keng Swee and Toh Chin Chye, Rajaratnam was one of the founder members of the People's Action Party (PAP). An idealist and a visionary, he believed profoundly in a multiracial, multi-religious society, principles he enshrined in Singapore's pledge. As independent Singapore's first minister of foreign affairs, his efforts went a long way in strengthening the country's international reputation. His political skills were best demonstrated when he led a diplomatic offensive against Vietnam's invasion of Cambodia in 1978–79. He remained foreign minister until 1980. From 1980 to 1984, he was the second deputy prime minister (Foreign Affairs) and became a senior minister in the Prime Minister's Office in 1984, a post he held until his retirement from politics in 1988.

Rajaratnam (second from left), then the minister for culture, seen here at the 4th Malaysian Ceylonese Games and Cultural Festival in 1964.

We, the citizens of Singapore,
pledge ourselves as one united people,
regardless of race, language or religion,
to build a democratic society
based on justice and equality
so as to achieve happiness, prosperity and
progress for our nation.

The Singapore pledge, penned by S. Rajaratnam in 1966.

C. V. Devan Nair

Born in Malaya in 1923, Devan Nair—the third president of Singapore—is remembered most for fighting British colonial rule and for his work as a trade unionist. The one-time communist sympathiser was detained between 1951 and 1953 for being a member of the Anti-British League. Nair was instrumental in the formation of Singapore's National Trades Union Congress in 1961 and fostered a cooperative tripartite relationship between workers, the government and employers. The only leader of Singapore's ruling PAP elected to the Malaysian parliament following the brief merger of the two countries in the 1960s, Nair also founded Malaysia's biggest opposition party, the Democratic Action Party. He stayed on in Malaysia after the two countries separated in 1965 and returned to Singapore in 1969. In 1979 he was elected to the Singapore parliament but relinquished the post in 1981 to become the president. Four years later, he resigned amidst allegations that he was an alcoholic—charges he later strongly denied. Following the controversy, Nair left Singapore for the US and later moved to Canada, where he passed away in December 2005.

C. V. Devan Nair (1923–2005), was the third president of Singapore.

S. Dhanabalan

S. Dhanabalan has had a distinguished career both in politics and business. Born in 1937, he received his early education at Victoria School and pursued an economics degree from the University of Malaya. Upon graduating, Dhanabalan joined the Administrative Service with stints at the Ministry of Finance and the Economic Development Board before joining the private sector as vice-president of the Development Bank of Singapore (DBS).

In 1978, Dhanabalan began his political career as an MP for Kallang. In a high-profile political career that spanned the 1980s and early 1990s, he held various Cabinet minister portfolios including foreign affairs, culture, community development, national development, and trade and industry. Retiring from politics in 1996, Dhanabalan was appointed chairman of Temasek Holdings, the government's investment vehicle. With a portfolio in excess of S$100 billion, Temasek has stakes in major Singapore companies such as Singapore Telecommunications, Singapore Airlines, DBS Bank and Neptune Orient Lines, and is a key investor in several Asian and OECD companies. In addition to his political and business pursuits, Dhanabalan was also a founder member of the Singapore International Foundation and president of the Singapore Indian Development Association (SINDA) from 1996 to 2002, of which he remains a life trustee.

Dhanabalan held various Cabinet positions in the 1980s and 1990s.

S. Jayakumar

Few parliamentarians in Singapore have had a more distinguished political career than S. Jayakumar. An MP since 1980, he has held numerous portfolios in the Cabinet, including labour, home affairs, law and foreign affairs. Jayakumar was appointed deputy prime minister in Prime Minister Lee Hsien Loong's Cabinet in August 2004 and, in September 2005, he assumed the role of coordinating minister for national security.

Born in 1939, Jayakumar received his early schooling at the renowned Raffles Institution. After graduating with a law degree from the University of Singapore, he was admitted to the Bar in 1964. Choosing instead to pursue a career in academia, he taught at the Faculty of Law in the National University of Singapore from 1964, during which time he also received a Master of Law degree from Yale (1966), and wrote three books and 32 articles on constitutional law, international law and legal education. Seconded to the Ministry of Foreign Affairs in 1971 to serve as Singapore's permanent representative to the UN, he was also a member of Singapore's delegation to the UN Law of the Sea Conference in 1974. In the same year, Jayakumar was appointed dean of the Faculty of Law—a position he held until 1981.

S. Jayakumar, the deputy prime minister of Singapore.

Based on Melanie Chew, Leaders of Singapore, 1996; Clement Mesenas, 'The Passing of a Titan', Today Online, 22 February 2006; www.singapore-window.org/sw02/020524af.htm; and http://en.wikipedia.org/wiki/S_Jayakumar.

Rajaratnam holds a press conference at the Singapore airport during his term as the minister for foreign affairs in November 1965.

independence showed many similarities, the period after separation was marked by considerable differences in the development trajectories of the two Indian communities. Since independence, the PAP has dominated the political scene. The 40 years of independence have witnessed a period of unparalleled political stability, dramatic economic growth and diversification, extensive urban renewal and the implementation of a significant social welfare programme. These changes have affected all communities living in Singapore.

It is possible to identify two phases in the development of the Indian community in Singapore. The first occurred between 1965 and the early 1990s, a period which saw the development of a settled Indian community subject to the state-building concerns of the newly independent nation. The second covers developments from the mid-1990s onwards, in which Singapore witnessed the arrival of new professional migrants from India, adding a significant dimension to the nature and development of the local Indian community.

One of the primary concerns of the government in the post-independence period was the need to inculcate a sense of loyalty among its citizens, a matter of particular concern given the multiracial composition and transient nature of large sections of the populace. To achieve this, the state, through the use of national symbols in schools and other public institutions, campaigns and compulsory male conscription to the military, instilled a sense of national identification among its citizens. While the government has maintained a vigil on communal, racial, religious and linguistic concerns that threaten to polarise groups, the attempt to construct an integrated Singaporean identity was not entirely divorced from the racial and, accordingly, linguistic and religious, backgrounds of the people. Racial affiliations, at least for the three main races—the Chinese, Malays and Indians—have been acknowledged, and even recognised, as the essential building blocks of a Singaporean identity. Consequently, the identity of individuals in Singapore has nearly always been recognised in a hyphenated form: Chinese-Singaporean, Malay-Singaporean and Indian-Singaporean (or vice-versa). The acknowledgement of three main races, however, may pose a problem for minorities who do not fall into these categories. The simplification of the racial matrix into three groups has meant that South Asians, regardless of their particular origins, have largely been labelled 'Indians'. Where this has generated protest, as in the case of a number of Sikhs following the growth of the Khalistan movement in the 1980s, individuals can classify themselves in a fourth category, labelled 'Other'.

The cultivation of a Singaporean identity has been largely successful in converting Indian migrants into Indian-Singaporeans. Unlike in the past, when most Indians saw Singapore only as an economic sojourn and owed primary political allegiance to India, a product of the post-independence socialisation process has been the development of a more settled Indian population with diminishing contact with India and the establishment of roots in Singapore. While some first-generation migrants remain nostalgic for the 'homeland' and may harbour aspirations of an eventual return, the younger generations, socialised in post-independence Singapore, largely hold an ambivalent attitude towards India. They are sympathetic to the land of their forebears and possibly even celebrate Indian culture, but they show no desire to return.

The period from 1957 to 1990 saw a decline in the number of Indians from under 9 per cent to 7.1 per cent of the total population. The closure of British military bases after independence resulted in the voluntary repatriation of many Indian workers. Malayalis, who formed a large proportion of the total workforce at the British naval base, were especially affected, as reflected in the decline of their numbers from 16.8 per cent of the total Indian population in 1957 to only 8.1 per cent in 1980. There was also a generic, albeit limited, return of male working-class migrants, who rejoined their families in India after retirement.

Restrictions on migration following independence limited new immigration, and by the late 1980s there was also evidence of re-migration of a small number of Indian-Singaporean professionals to Australia, Canada and the US. However, the Indian population saw consistent growth in terms of absolute numbers in the period after independence, nearly all of which was accounted for by natural increase. Testifying to the settled character of the Indian population, the period saw the proportion of Indian men to women fall from 226 to 100 in 1957, to 118 to 100 by 1990.

Politically, Indians have been well-represented in government. Over the 40 years of independence, the republic has had two presidents and numerous Cabinet ministers and members of parliament (MPs) drawn from the Indian community. Indians in Singapore also participated in and benefited from the extraordinary economic growth of the 1970s and 1980s. By 1990, the average annual income of Indians had grown to over US$10,000 (at current rates). In addition, the post-independence period witnessed considerable upward social mobility among Indians. No longer consigned to the labouring classes, a growing number of Indians were either in professional, technical, clerical and managerial positions, or in the sales and service industries by 1990. The Indian community has also made a considerable mark in sectors such as law. Taking advantage of the strong emphasis on English education in the community, Singapore's strict adherence to meritocracy and the emphasis on English as the administrative language in the public sector, Indians joined the civil service, where they continue to be well-represented at all levels. What has been notable in the economic development of the Indian community in Singapore was the considerable addition of Indian women to the workforce. While Indian women comprised less than 3 per cent of the total Indian labour force in 1957, more than half of all Indian women participated in the formal economy by 1990.

One of the key issues affecting the Indian community in the post-independence period was the development of Indian languages. The government, in an attempt to represent the multiracial composition of the population, designated Tamil as one of the four official languages of Singapore, alongside English, Mandarin and Malay. Although the post-independence period saw the closure of numerous Tamil-medium schools as Indian students flocked to public schools, the Tamil language has benefited considerably from official recognition. The policy of bilingualism in public schools, requiring students to study

Map 8.14

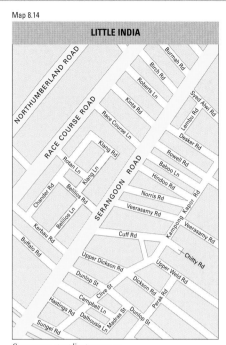

LITTLE INDIA

Source: www.streetdirectory.com.sg.

Street names in Little India bear testimony to the area's history. Cattle farms used to be located on what is now Buffalo Road, while Veerasamy Road is named after Dr N. Veerasamy, the medical practitioner who was a leading member of the Indian community in the first half of the 20th century.

Indian girls at the Holi festival organised by the Bhojpuri Society in March 2006.

185

S. R. Nathan

*I do the very best I know how—the very best I can;
and I mean to keep doing so until the end.
If the end brings me out alright,
what's said against me won't amount to anything.
If the end brings me out wrong,
ten angels swearing I was right would make no difference.*

A tablet containing the above lines, penned by Abraham Lincoln, occupies a prominent place in the office of Sellappan Rama Nathan, the sixth president of Singapore. His life has been guided by its tenets.

President S. R. Nathan, the 'People's President'.

S. R. Nathan was born in 1924 in Singapore. Prior to becoming president, he held senior government positions in various ministries, including foreign affairs, home affairs and defence. A popular high commissioner to Malaysia (1988–90) and a successful ambassador to the US (1990–96), he was also chairman of the Singapore Hindu Endowments Board (1983–88) and a founder member of SINDA in 1991. In addition, he was the executive chairman of the Straits Times Press Ltd, and held directorships in various companies, organisations and institutes, including the Institute of Defence and Strategic Studies.

Yet his impressive portfolio belies a humble beginning. His is a story of a man rising in trying circumstances; a path charted not by academic qualifications but by wisdom gained through experience. In his early years, he witnessed the decline of his family's fortune when his father, a law clerk in a firm that serviced rubber plantations, accrued debts following the rubber slump of the 1930s. Soon after, unable to cope with the hardship, his father killed himself. Nathan began working long before he completed his schooling. In his teens, he was employed as an office boy with Arbenz and Co., a Swiss firm, and later worked as a clerk in Muar, Malaya. During World War II, he mastered the Japanese language to such an extent that he was employed as a translator and soon found himself attached to the top official of the Japanese civilian police force. After the war, he continued to work and study concurrently and graduated (with distinction) from the University of Malaya in 1954 with a diploma in social studies. He joined the Singapore Civil Service as a medical social worker in 1955 and was appointed Seamen's Welfare Officer the following year. In 1962, he was seconded to the Labour Research Unit of the Labour Movement, first as assistant director and later, director. The early experiences as a social worker and in the labour movement were vital. They provided him with the opportunity to learn on the job, to harness his interpersonal skills and to cultivate an ability to understand others.

Throughout his career, even as he rose through the ranks of the civil service, Nathan remained unassuming and stayed away from public attention. He was often more willing to 'lead from the back', leaving the limelight to others. During times of crisis, however, he established himself as a man of action. During the *Laju* affair of 1974, he was in the team that negotiated for the release of crewmen following the hijacking of the *Laju* ferry. He later led the delegation that accompanied the hijackers on their flight to Kuwait. As president, Nathan has endeared himself as the 'People's President'. He is known for his humility and ability to reach out to the common man. Even as he holds the highest office in Singapore, the austere words of his late mother, 'duty and not the reward', continue to guide his conduct.

Based on 'In Conversation: S. R. Nathan', Television Corporation of Singapore, 1996; and www.istana.gov.sg/PresidentSRNathan/index.htm.

English and one other official language, ensured the inclusion of Tamil in the national curriculum. In the mid-1970s, there was a concerted campaign led by leaders such as C. V. Devan Nair, who was then the secretary-general of the National Trades Union Congress, to foster a Tamil renaissance. These efforts were successful in increasing Tamil literacy from 54 per cent of all Indians (aged 10 and above) to nearly 60 per cent in 1980. By 1994, Tamil was offered in well over 200 public schools. Furthermore, government assistance also enabled the establishment of a Tamil television and radio channel.

Socialisation in public schools and the ambivalence of the new generation of Indian-Singaporeans towards India resulted in a growing disinterest in Indian social organisations. However, the inclusion of the Tamil language did usher in the development of Tamil-language cultural societies and Indian cultural societies (whose core members are usually composed of Tamil-speaking pupils) in public schools and at the tertiary level. While these groups have continued the propagation of Tamil culture as well as

'Indian' culture in general through dance, drama, debates and other activities, they differ from Tamil organisations during the pre-independence period in their general lack of concern for socio-political developments in Tamil Nadu.

The adoption of Tamil as the prescribed second language for Indians strengthened divisions within the Indian community. Most North Indians, whose mother tongue was distinct from Tamil, took up the study of Malay instead, given the perception that Malay was easier to learn and more useful for inter-ethnic communication. Moreover, the requirement for North Indians to study two foreign languages in the curriculum had a detrimental impact on their own mother tongue and, by the 1980s, the percentage of Indians proficient in non-Tamil Indian languages had declined from 5.2 per cent in 1970 to under 1.7 per cent in 1980.

Another issue affecting the Indian community up to the early 1990s was the decline in Indian students' preference for and performance in technical subjects. Although Indians were well-represented in the arts and law at the tertiary level, few were taking up engineering and science, and there was a general deterioration in the performance of Indian students in mathematics and science at secondary and pre-university levels. The growing concern in the community about this decline resulted in the formation of the Singapore Indian Development Association (SINDA) in 1991. Through government funding and voluntary contributions from the salaries of employed Indians, SINDA has undertaken numerous educational and welfare programmes that have been fairly successful in alleviating some of the socio-economic and educational problems confronting the local Indian community.

CONTEMPORARY TRANSFORMATIONS

By the late 1980s, Singapore faced a crisis of sorts that led to a rethinking of its earlier restrictive immigration policies. A considerable decline in the birth rate resulted in growing fears of a rapidly ageing population. Moreover, there was a need to deal with the shortfall in the number of professionals for Singapore to sustain its competitive edge in leading industries and to meet the requirements of economic restructuring. Together, these imperatives led to the recruitment of professionals, mainly from China and India, many of whom have been encouraged to settle permanently.

Since the 1990s, the most prominent development in the Indian community has been the substantial increase in the number of Indian professional migrants arriving in Singapore, which has had repercussions both in the

A traditional Hindu wedding ceremony.

community and at the national level. The number of Indians grew from 194,000 in 1990 to 293,100 in 2004, reflecting an increase from 7.1 per cent to 8.4 per cent of the total population. Given that their fertility rate hovered at a consistently low level during the same period (1.89 in 1990 and 1.36 in 2003), the increase is largely due to professional migrants who have taken up citizenship or permanent resident status. Nonetheless, it is unclear how many professional migrants actually intend to settle permanently.

The arrival of professional migrants has had a positive impact on the educational and income profile of the Indian community. The average annual income of Indians between 1990 and 2000 grew from approximately US$10,000 to US$22,600 (at current rates). During the same period, the percentage of Indians with tertiary education increased from 4.1 per cent to 16.5 per cent. Although these changes can be partly explained by the general rise in income and education level among all groups, the increase in both these indicators has been more substantial among Indians than any other major ethnic community.

Official statistics paint a rosy picture of the position of Indians in Singapore, but they do not account for the sizeable number of labourers and domestic workers from South Asia (mainly South India, Bangladesh and Sri Lanka), whose numbers have increased considerably from the 1990s onwards. Not unlike indentured workers in the past, contemporary South Asian labourers and domestic workers are bound by a demanding contract, usually for a period of two years, during which time they are expected to work long hours under difficult conditions, with few benefits or holidays, and at very low wages. Though essential as a source of cheap labour in the construction and domestic services sector, strict regulations ensure that Indians in these groups, unlike their professional counterparts, are excluded from the possibility of gaining Singapore citizenship or permanent resident status. They have been kept out of the public eye, but are subject to constant monitoring by the authorities to ensure their return at the end of their contracts.

The arrival of professional migrants, temporary labourers and domestic workers has made the Indian community more heterogeneous than before. In addition to perennial differences based on ethnicity, language and religion, new divisions have emerged between the old diaspora, the new diaspora of professional migrants, and the sojourning groups of temporary labourers and domestic workers. Recent sociological research on the complex ways in which these groups relate to each other show resentment among members of the old diaspora against the new professional migrants, who are seen as snobbish, cliquish, arrogant and selfish economic migrants with little loyalty to Singapore. Unsurprisingly, the new professional migrants seem to share similar sentiments towards members of the old diaspora, whom they view as jealous of their success, arrogant and uncongenial. On the other hand, although both these groups may sympathise with their labouring South Asian counterparts, few, if any, maintain significant social interaction with these groups.

In spite of the divisions that exist between these groups, the arrival of professional migrants has proven to be advantageous to certain sections of the old diaspora, particularly from the minority non-Tamil South Asian language communities. The initial exclusion of these languages

A wide variety of Tamil magazines can be found in street-corner stalls along Serangoon Road.

from the national curriculum resulted in a significant decline in proficiency in these languages, but this has changed considerably since the 1990s. Initially, the influx of new professional migrants, many of whom were non-Tamil, provided important regenerative contact for these languages. More significantly, in 1990, the government allowed the inclusion of Hindi, Punjabi, Bengali, Urdu and Gujarati in the curriculum in an attempt to counter the distress of non-Tamil Indian students who were having difficulty coping with the study of Tamil, Chinese or Malay as a second language. This was done with the condition that education in these languages would depend on the initiative of the respective communities.

Many of these minority South Asian languages had less than 20 students before gaining recognition in 1990. However, their numbers have grown tremendously over the last 15 years. In 2004, approximately 6000 students took up the study of either Hindi, Punjabi, Bengali, Urdu or Gujarati as a second language from kindergarten to the pre-university level. Although student numbers have grown for all groups, the study of Hindi has rapidly increased. With some 3400 students in 2004, Hindi outnumbers all the other non-Tamil South Asian languages combined. Although a significant number of new professional migrants may not be from the Hindi-speaking states of India, their choice of Hindi as a second language for their children reflects their transient position. Since many new migrants see Singapore as a transitory location and

J.Y. Pillay, the former chairman of Singapore Airlines (1972–96), with Ong Teng Cheong, who was then the deputy prime minister. Pillay is best known as the man who led the national carrier from being a small start-up to a global industry leader.

Sat Pal Khattar

Sat Pal Khattar is an eminent lawyer and businessman with extensive investments in Singapore, India, Mauritius, the UK and other countries. A former senior legal officer with the Inland Revenue Department, Khattar, along with Dr David Wong, founded Khattar Wong and Partners in 1974. The firm grew to become one of the largest law firms in Singapore. While he remains a senior consultant in the firm, his energies have, especially following the liberalisation of the Indian economy in the 1990s, been channelled towards fostering business and economic cooperation between Singapore and India. An acclaimed philanthropist, he is a life trustee of SINDA, a self-help group formed to address the pressing educational and socio-economic issues facing the Indian community in Singapore.

Lawyer and philanthropist Sat Pal Khattar.

Table 8.17

	1931	1947	1957	1970	1980	1990	2000	2004
TOTAL POPULATION AND THE TOTAL NUMBER OF INDIANS ('000)								
Indians (%)	52.5 *(9.4)*	71.9 *(7.7)*	129.5 *(9.0)*	145.1 *(7.0)*	154.6 *(6.4)*	194 *(7.1)*	257.3 *(7.9)*	293.1 *(8.4)*
Total	557.7	938.1	1445.9	2074.5	2413.9	2735.9	3263.2	3486.9

Sources: C. A. Vlieland, 'British Malaya: A Report on the 1931 Census', 1932; M. V. Del Tufo, 'Malaya: A Report on the 1947 Census', 1949; and various census reports from Singapore, 1957–2004.

The opening of Indian Culture Month in Singapore, 25 March 1990.

Singapore resident Meira Chand is the author of seven novels, her most recent being A Far Horizon *(2002).* House of the Sun *(1989), written during her time in Japan, was adapted for the stage in London.*

may harbour thoughts of returning to India, their choice of language is influenced by language policies in India, where Hindi holds a dominant position. A further testimony to the transient nature of many of the new professional migrants is the growth of Indian international schools in Singapore, which offer curricula based on either the Indian Central Board of Secondary Education (CBSE) or the Indian Certificate of Secondary Education (ICSE).

Another important transformation in recent years relates to the growing communication linkages between South Asia and Singapore. The Internet now enables Indians in Singapore to keep a close watch on developments in South Asia. Indian cable channels on Singapore television—Sony, Star Plus, Sun and Zee-TV—have become standard fare for many, and it is not uncommon to find Indians in Singapore, both new professional migrants and from the old diaspora, spending much of their leisure hours watching serials or Bollywood (Bombay cinema) and Kollywood (Tamil cinema) movies on these channels. While they have become key components of entertainment in Indian daily life, the significance of these channels on the nature and identity of Indian communities in Singapore remains unclear.

The late 1990s also witnessed growing government interest in South Asia, particularly India, as an economic partner. Singapore has, since the Indian economic reforms of 1991–92, sought to establish a free trade agreement with India alongside numerous educational and economic initiatives focused on the subcontinent. Of particular note in education was the formation of a South Asian Studies Programme at the National University of Singapore in 1999, and the Institute of South Asian Studies in 2004. The former is concerned with the academic study of South Asia as a region, while the latter seeks to promote public awareness of South Asia, undertake research on key South Asian economic and political issues, and act as a think-tank for government and commercial interests in the region.

CONCLUSION

Although the Indian diaspora in Singapore was born out of the imperial enterprise, its development has been unlike that of the former colonies with sizeable Indian populations, such as those in the Caribbean, Africa and Fiji. An urban setting that facilitated the spread of information and the existence of constant and considerable trade, communication and transportation linkages between India and Singapore since the beginning has ensured that the Indian experience in Singapore was infused with the cultural currents of South Asia. It also ensured a greater degree of mobility among migrants, best understood as a circulation of labour, at least until the advent of nationalism in Singapore resulted in growing restrictions on migration in the post-war period. Since independence, Singapore's adherence to meritocracy has enabled Indians to prosper from its extraordinary economic growth. At the same time, the nation's unique blend of multicultural policies has facilitated the preservation and development of their ethnic identities.

The journey of Indians to Singapore cannot be explained by a single dominant trajectory or system of migration. Rather, the community itself has been made up of numerous movements, diverse in chronology, composition and character, which have added significantly to its heterogeneity. This heterogeneity and divergence, along with the continuation of migration from the 1990s, has added to its dynamic nature and produced an Indian diaspora that is distinctive.

Rajesh Rai

Singapore's Little India bustles with activity, especially on Sundays, when Indian contract workers are given the day off.

THAILAND

THE RICH PROSPECT and commercially viable location of Thailand (known as Siam until 1949) has drawn the attention of Indians since time immemorial. Defined as a meeting point of cultures, the country has constantly been popular with enterprising Indians.

While there may be differing opinions on the exact location of Suvarnabhumi, it is largely believed by scholars that more than half of today's Thailand formed a part of this legendary geographical location. It was the Arthasastra of Kautilya which first used the term 'Suvarnabhumi' and suggested its coastal route for the Indians, a route which was bound to touch the port towns in southern Thailand. Later, the Buddhist delegation of Ashoka Maurya, under the command of Sona and Uttara in the 3rd century BC (described extensively in the Dipavamsa-Mahavamsa), arrived at a point known even now as Nakhon Pathom (*nagara prathama*, or 'the first

Map 8.15

city'), 30 km north of the coast in central Thailand. A series of archaeological finds featuring early Buddhist motifs, such as the Wheel and the Deer, in and around the Nakhon Pathom Chedi (*prathama chaitya*) lead us to believe that Sona and Uttara, the two Buddhist monks from Pataliputra, were the first recorded Indians to arrive and settle in Thailand. They landed at the Isthmus of Kra, an important trading area.

The distance between the two seas at the Isthmus is around 200 km, so there is a reduction of 1500 km when one makes a journey between the Straits of Melaka and the Gulf of Thailand. There are many rivers feeding the Isthmus, thus facilitating the trans-peninsular crossing of merchandise. With adequate facilities for the early Indian settlers and the monsoon seasons making them stay for at least six months, the Isthmus was a natural location for the growth of city-states. It is no wonder Sona and Uttara took this voyage, having heard of the possibility of the spontaneous acceptance of Buddhist ways of life in the region, which was already dotted with and known by Indian merchants criss-crossing with the easterly and westerly winds.

EARLY CONTACTS

Indian contact with Thailand continued throughout history, as attested by numerous references in Chinese annals from the 4th and 5th century onwards. Falsifying the notion of crossing seas being taboo, the Indian *brahmanas* began arriving in various locations in Thailand from the 3rd century AD. The earliest references to *brahmanas* in Thailand come from the peninsula. The *Nan-chou I-wu Chih*, a source from the 3rd century, states that the people of Tun-sun (southern Thailand) practised Brahmanism as propounded by the immigrant *brahmanas*. The people also studied the sacred texts. The *T'ai-ping Yu Lan*, which recorded events before the 9th and 10th centuries, reported that the natives of the region even gave away their daughters in marriage, thus helping them retain the facilities of the *brahmanas*. This was also a way of making the *brahmanas* settle permanently in the region, says the *T'ai-ping Yu Lan*. According to the *Wen-hsieh T'ung K'ao*, the kingdom of P'an-p'an in isthmian Thailand had 10,000 Indian *brahmanas*. Langkasuka was another city-state in coastal Thailand with many *brahmanas*, as was Ch'ih-t'u. These kingdoms have been erratically located in the Chao Phraya basin and the Isthmus of Kra.

The Indian *brahmanas* helped in the administrative work of the royalty in pre-modern Thailand. A vivid description of the Ch'ih-t'u court shows 'several hundred *brahmanas* sitting in rows facing each other, and the king in the center.' Another Chinese source described how scores of *brahmanas* from India approached the king for support in the kingdom of B'uan-b'uan, identified by archaeologists to

The Buddha's humble downcast expression is characteristic of the Dvarvati School (Mon Kingdom), which spanned the 7th to 11th centuries and was influenced by the Indian sculpture of the post-Gupta era.

Prayers being said at a Brahman temple in Bangkok.

Nakhon Pathom Chedi located 56 km west of Bangkok. It is believed that it was here that Indian Buddhist monks sent by Emperor Ashoka first introduced Buddhism to the country now known as Thailand.

be near modern-day Pattani. In the early 7th century, Chinese envoys to another state in peninsular Thailand described the important ceremonial functions performed by corps of several hundred *brahmanas*. These royal advisers commanded greater respect than the Buddhist monks in the kingdom.

The followers of Indian *brahmanas* in isthmian Thailand were generally smaller in number, but there is no doubt that their services were offered to both the ruler and the ruled. From the outset, the *brahmanas* confirmed their importance to the ruling class with the elaborate ceremony of consecration, a prerequisite for kingship following the Indian pattern, and 'a jealously guarded prerogative of the *brahmanas*.' This exalted their status and royal connection automatically, and led the common people to ask the *brahmanas* to bless them with prayers and lead them in chanting for good luck, prosperity and health—a practice still in vogue in Thailand, though only nine such Indian *brahmana* families are left.

Indian cultural influence recurs in the history of Thailand. The resemblance of Dvaravati art (7th–8th century) to Indian Amaravati art is ascribed to the arrival of Indian artists and sculptors. Later on, Sukhothai epigraphic records (13th–15th century), the few remaining pages of the Ayutthayan chronicles (16th–18th century) and European (in particular Dutch) accounts refer to Indians arriving at the court of Ayutthaya. It is very difficult to say who was the first to settle down in more recent times. The ancient tradition of the South Indian *brahmanas* coming to the small city-states in southern Thailand and the discovery of a 10th-century Tamil inscription at Takua Pa in southern Thailand suggest that Tamil settlements might have continued for some time.

THE 19TH CENTURY

The presence of Indians in modern Thailand can be traced back more than a century. Tamils from Penang are reported to have settled in Phuket in southern Thailand as early as the 1860s. King Chulalongkorn's visit to India in 1871 created an opportunity for Indians to trade in the capital city of Bangkok. Those Tamils living in southern Thailand developed an expertise in the cattle trade and the mining of precious stones. Service groups, such as the Chettiars, began moving to Bangkok from Phuket, Penang and Singapore. This was when the Thai royalty offered a specially designated area for both Indian and Chinese traders. Not far from the Grand Palace and the Chinese settlement of Yaworat, an Indian market area known as Phahurat (Bahu-ratha in Sanskrit) was developed. It is still the only market where Indians own or run most of the

Sukhothai's Wat Sri Sawai centres on three laterite prang towers dating from the 13th century. Bayon-era Khmers built it as a Hindu sanctuary, which the Siamese later used for Buddhist rituals.

shops. In 1879, King Chulalongkorn granted land to a group of South Indian businessmen living in Bangkok, on which the Sri Maha Mariamman Temple was built. By the early 20th century, the Bohras and Tamil Muslim merchants from Pondicherry and Karaikkal were the only important Indian businessmen in Thailand.

Though Thailand was able to avoid European colonial control, several European companies played a dominant role in the country. The contracts of several development projects were awarded to British companies operating there. By the beginning of the 20th century, many British citizens were holding senior positions in various government departments.

As a result, British Indian labourers from Malaya and Singapore arrived in Thailand to work on projects such as the railway link from Malaya to Bangkok. The labourers came from the Madras Presidency, the clerks were mostly Parsi and the watchmen were generally from the United Provinces (UP) and Punjab. Some Bengalis also came directly from Calcutta. After the influx of recruited labour, many Indians began to come on their own accord and entered either through northwest Burma or from the borders with Malaya. Punjabis also migrated during the late 19th century, via Burma, from the districts of Sialkot, Gujranwala and Sheikhupura.

BEFORE WORLD WAR II

In 1920, there were already several Sindhi firms operating in Bangkok. The Bombay Store and the Karachi Store were among the most famous. The population of the Indian community in Bangkok in the 1920s was between 6000 and 8000. Indian wholesale dealers were located in Rajawongse Road in Bangkok. The major companies in the Rajawongse area in 1920s, as recalled by the late Shri Ramlal Sachdev, were: A. T. E Maskati, A. K. H. Wassi, M. A. Moghul, S. A. Malbari and A. E. Nana. These companies were all owned by the Bohra community. The Punjabi firms included Mukandlal Gurudas, Thakur Singh, Ladha Singh, Ram Singh Hari Singh, Labhsingh, Nadhansingh, Nand Singh Gian Singh, Boorsingh Indersingh, K. R. Indersingh and Ladhasingh Bhagwansingh. These were followed by M. D. Ramchand & Co. of Baboo Mangaldas Sachdev, which set up an office in 1924 and had business establishments both in Nakhon Sri Thammarat and Bangkok. The Indian business community imported many items from Calcutta for their compatriots in Thailand, including ghee, *ata*, dhal and *badam*, and text such as the Ramayana and Tota Mainai Ka Kissa. Shri Gilitwala imported Ayurvedic medicine as early as 1920.

Qayumbai Tohfa Farosh, a leading Bohra born in Bangkok in 1912, said that in the 1920s and 1930s, the wages of an Indian watchman for the European companies amounted to about 20 baht a month. Most of these watchmen were from the eastern UP. They also worked in the rice mills and sawmills along the banks of the Chao Phraya. Their sincerity, honesty and hard work helped many of them to get government jobs with the railway department, post office and police department.

The Gujaratis dealt mainly in precious stones and the export of Thai rice to India, while other groups traded in textiles. Indian businessmen showed courage and vigour, earning them much prestige and wealth in Thailand. Their working day would often begin at dawn and finish late. Indian vendors walked the streets of Bangkok in all kinds of weather with the weight of their merchandise on their backs.

Gradually, the Indians prospered, and among the wholesalers, two merchants, A. E. Nana and Ladhasingh Bhagwansingh, quickly branched out into the real estate business with great success. A few Bohra companies were also popular for their stationery businesses, particularly A. R. Salaibhai, D. H. Siamwallah and Abas D. Vast. In Chareon Krung Road there were two Punjabi shops dealing in sporting goods. Some textile retailers—mostly Punjabi—did venture out of Bangkok and were soon represented in every province of the country.

Onkar Singh and Jagdish Singh were two doctors of medicine who opened clinics in Bangkok. Two Indian primary schools were also established. The Sikh Vidyalaya was run by Shri Guru Singh Sabha and was located in Phahurat on Soi Italian (later known as Gurudwara Gali), and the Namdhari Gurudwara School, on Yaworat Road, was run by Gurudwara Namdhari Sangat. Most of the students attending these schools were Punjabi, as the Indians from the UP had left their families in India. These schools had 200 pupils between them. In the difficult days after World War I, the overseas Indian community tried hard to cope with the situation in the country.

There were six Indian associations in Thailand by 1925. These were the Vishnu Mandir, Arya Samaj, Shri Maha Mariamman Temple, Sri Guru Singh Sabha, Gurdwara Sangat and Jamaiat ul Islam. These associations and schools enriched the Indian community. In 1925, the Hindu Sabha was established, and in 1926, representatives of all the Indian societies in Thailand visited the palace to offer their respects and congratulatory messages to the newly crowned King Prajadhipok (Rama VII). The Hindu Sabha was among them, and their message was prepared and delivered by a visiting Indian scholar named Diwan Mangal Sen. It was a very impressive message which was gold embossed on blue satin, encased in a beautiful frame. The following year, the Indian Association

Phahurat, Bangkok's 'Little India'. The busy shopping area affords locals and tourists the opportunity to purchase Indian food, clothes, textiles and movies.

was formed. A. E. Nana, who had branched successfully into real estate, donated a parcel of land for this purpose. Nana was elected as the association's Life President. The association was later renamed the Indian Thai Chamber of Commerce.

In 1929, Swami Satyananda Puri arrived in Thailand at the suggestion of Rabindranath Tagore. A former revolutionary in Bengal who had taught Oriental philosophy at Calcutta University and also at Santiniketan, the Swami's influence imbued the Indian community in Thailand with patriotic thoughts for their motherland. Initially, the Swami stayed at the Hindu Sabha. He lived in this modest abode without the slightest complaint for two years. He then opened a small ashram by the Chao Phraya. The Swami learnt to read and write the Thai language remarkably well in only a few months. From the ashram he started publishing a newsletter in Thai, which drew the attention of the Thai elite, including the royal family.

The Sri Mariamman Temple on Silom Road is one of the largest Hindu temples in Bangkok.

A poster of the INA's Rani of Jhansi regiment.

From 1930 to 1933, several events occurred which had enormous consequences for Indians living in Thailand. The Great Depression affected all Indian merchants and many businesses had to close down. This was followed by the revolution of June 1932, which brought about the end of absolute monarchy in Thailand. The uncertain circumstances did not last long, however. In 1933, the economic situation began to improve, although the main source of textiles was now Japan as supplies from Britain had dwindled considerably. Slowly, several Indian firms began to move from Phahurat to the Rajawongse and Sampeng areas, where they would prosper.

At that time, a great Indian personality from Sialkot, Pandit Raghunath Sharma, served the community in numerous ways. He encouraged young Hindus to join the movement to free India from British rule. He inspired the Indian youth to become more organised. His brainchild, the Hindu Yuvak Sabha, established in 1929, became the prime youth group for the Indian community. Every week, about 35 youths would meet to plan their activities. Pandit Raghunath Sharma believed in inculcating moral values among young Hindu minds. Initially, he started Ramayana Katha in a private house in Trok Italian every Wednesday after 8 pm. This marked a turning point for the community.

Notable Indian religious and cultural institutions in Thailand

Arya Samaj
The Vaidik Dharma Pracharini Sabha was started in May 1920. In March 1923, the third annual conference was celebrated in the new Arya Samaj temple with great enthusiasm, and in May that same year, the Bangkok chapter of the Arya Samaj was officially affiliated with the main organisation in India. Shri Ganga Prasad Upadhyaya, who came to Bangkok in the 1930s, had a profound impact on Indians in Thailand and announced an annual scholarship of 1000 baht for the student securing the highest grade for Sanskrit. In 1934, the Arya Samaj set up a separate committee to organise assistance for the earthquake victims in Bihar. About 380 members of the Arya Samaj in Thailand were actively engaged in the provisional government of the Indian National Army (INA). During the war, the Arya Samaj Mandir was converted into an INA training camp.

Hindu Dharma Sabha
From a modest beginning in 1915, the Hindu Dharma Sabha has grown into a respected institution through the selfless, untiring and relentless efforts of its founding fathers, namely Uma Shankar Chaubey, Sunder Dass Pawa and Ram Deo Ojha. In 1920, the Dharma Sabha laid the foundation of the Vishnu Mandir. In due course the *mandir* added a library, school, cremation ground and a *dharmshala*. Temples dedicated to Shiva, Hanuman and Durga were also built, and for many years now the Hindu Sabha has been celebrating Hindu and Buddhist festivals with élan. It has also continued to participate in an array of local charities with enthusiasm and fervour.

Thai-Bharat Culture Lodge
Founded by Swami Satyananda Puri, the Thai-Bharat Culture Lodge evolved from an earlier organisation, which he began in 1932 with the aim of propagating Oriental culture. The Thai-Bharat Culture Lodge was started in October 1940 with the aim of encouraging the comparative study of Indian and Thai cultures, thus increasing awareness among both Thais and Indians of their historical links. Until 24 March 1942, when he left for that fateful journey to Tokyo, the organisation was under the active leadership of the Swami.

The Thai-Bharat Culture Lodge was the centre for the Indian National Council during the war and was central to the efforts of the INA in Thailand. The Swami had gained permission from the Thai government to make news broadcasts and commentaries in Hindustani through the Publicity Department of the national Thai radio station. His first message was to Mahatma Gandhi, and it was repeated over the air for many days. It was a respectful but powerful plea for the honest aims of the Mahatma to 'get to the right target of war.' Next, due to the frequent Allied bombing of Bangkok just after the invasion, the Swami established a free hospital on Siphaya Road in a bungalow belonging to an Indian, Mr Salebhai, whose family members still live in Bangkok. He willingly vacated his premises for this purpose. Indian doctors who offered their services included Dr Onkar Singh, Dr Jagdish Singh, Dr C. Roy and many more. It was opened by the Thai Minister of Health, who donated a fully equipped ambulance through the local Red Cross. Another ambulance was purchased with the donations of local Indians.

In 1945, the organisation was closed by the Allied Field Security Department. Later, Pandit Raghunath Sharma was permitted to reopen the Thai-Bharat Culture Lodge on 29 July 1946.

For the first time, the feeling of a distinct identity began to emerge among the people. The Hindu Yuvak Sabha organised Bangkok's first Indian stage dramas, *Draupadi Cheer Haran* in 1933 and *Danveer Karna* in 1934. Both were staged at the Bon Moh Theatre. The plays are still remembered by older members of the Indian community. The Hindu Yuvak Sabha was also put in charge of controlling the surging crowd of overseas Indians when Jawaharlal Nehru made a stopover at Don Muang Airport when returning from Indonesia in 1935.

By 1939, with the growing prospect of war in Southeast Asia, a sense of uneasiness emerged in the Indian community. Apprehensive Indians began to transfer part of their holdings back to the subcontinent as a precaution. Family members, usually women and children, were also sent back.

During the war, the Japanese made Thailand their military base for strikes against Burma and, through Malaya, Singapore and the Netherlands East Indies. When restrictions were put in place to prevent the movement of Indians in Thailand, the community turned to Swami Satyananda Puri for advice. Following the opening of the Thai-Bharat Culture Lodge in October 1940, the Swami's influence over senior Thai officials and members of the royal family had increased due to his integrity and honour. The Swami held a meeting with Prime Minister Phibul Songkhram and asked him to clarify the position of Indians in the event of war. The Prime Minister assured the Swami that Indians would face no difficulties or problems as far as the Thai government was concerned. He was also assured that the Japanese intended no harm, provided the Indians did not interfere with their 'work'. As far as permission for domestic travel was concerned, any Indian who obtained a permit from the Thai-Bharat Cultural Lodge could travel freely within the borders of Thailand. The Swami was given full authority to issue the necessary permit, thus providing great relief to the Indian community. He then changed the name of the lodge to the Indian National Council. The building was the same but its role had shifted from a cultural one to a political one. The Japanese then officially announced their commitment to assisting the Indian people in their struggle for independence from Britain. The council was inaugurated in the grand hall of the Silpakorn Theatre by the Thai Foreign Minister on 23 December 1941.

In fact, the Japanese had been secretly dealing with the Indians in Thailand for some time. Hikari Kikan, the Japanese-Indian liaison group under Colonel Yamamoto, used undercover agents posing as businessmen to infiltrate the Indian community and sound out the possibility of collaboration, disguised as a matter of mutual interest.

A Sikh enclave in Pattani, which was under the influence of Hikari Kikan, and its leader, Bhai Shandar Singh, sought help from the Japanese in the Indian struggle for freedom. The Japanese insisted on the acceptance of Rashbehari Bose, then living in Japan, as head of the Indian independence movement in Southeast Asia. Rashbehari Bose formed the Indian Independence League in May 1942, chose Bangkok as its headquarters, and held the first conference of the league under his presidency. A number of Indians living in Thailand attended the conference, along with delegates from Malaya and Burma. Captain Mohan Singh deserves special mention as he was responsible for the formation of the Indian National Army (INA), which was made up of Indian recruits from the region.

However, for the Indians in Bangkok, the situation in India held far more interest than the intentions of the Japanese. Disillusioned with Rashbehari Bose's leadership, many Indians in Thailand wanted the movement to be handed over to Subhas Chandra (Netaji) Bose, who had left India in 1941 to work from Germany. It is worth noting that Bangkok was the place where the ideas of the Indian Independence League (IIL) had taken shape even before the arrival of Netaji in Southeast Asia.

Among the revolutionaries living in Thailand in 1941 were two remarkable people: Giani Pritam Singh, a devout Sikh who arrived in Bangkok in 1933 after the suppression of the Civil Disobedience movement in India; and with him, Baba Amar Singh, another Indian freedom fighter, who had been in detention for 22 years in the dreaded Andaman Jail. According to British intelligence records, Pritam Singh had contacted the Japanese embassy in Bangkok in June 1941. Later on, he—along with Bhagwan Singh and 15 supporters—was sent to the Thai-Malaya border and given the duty of broadcasting Japanese propaganda through loudspeakers to the front lines of the British Indian troops. Sardar Kishan Singh, Babu Sudershan Singh and Bhagwan Singh were asked to cross into Malaya to reach the Indian soldiers serving in the British Indian Army.

THE POLITICS OF THE INA IN THAILAND

In February 1942, Swami Satyananda Puri tried to contact Netaji in Germany. Netaji's voice on the Azad Hind radio station from Berlin had made his name a legend among many Indians in Thailand. The Swami was quite sure that Netaji would inspire and build confidence among members of the Indian National Council.

The Japanese clearly disliked the Swami's promotion of Netaji over Rashbehari Bose, and the Swami's Indian National Council and the IIL were now at loggerheads. Naturally enough, when the plane carrying Swami Satyananda Puri, Giani Pritam Singh, Baba Amar Singh and Captain Mohammad Akram to the Tokyo Convention crashed in Taiwan on 24 March 1942, killing all of them, a permanent suspicion of the Japanese crept into the minds of the Indians in Thailand, especially since no enquiry was announced and none of the bodies were ever found.

The Japanese, however, suffered a setback as Rashbehari's IIL failed to enthuse the Indians to join the war on the side of the Japanese. Finally, Netaji was called in to take over responsibility from Rashbehari Bose on 4 July 1943.

By the time Netaji visited Thailand in late 1943, nationalist feelings in the Indian community were running high. On 27 July, he left Singapore for a 17-day tour of East Asian and Southeast Asian countries, with the prime objective of enlisting moral and monetary support for his movement. He was given a rousing reception in Bangkok on 4 August and met the Thai prime minister: he won the support of the Thai government. At a meeting in a Chinese hall in Sruiwong Road, a crowd of over 3000 Indians gave him a stirring ovation. Netaji stirred people to pledge money and materials for the INA. Darshan Singh Bajaj, who personally gave Netaji 95,000 tael in the hall, and who had a long association with the man as the supply officer of the INA, recalled: 'I was only a small donor compared to the others.' Netaji himself donated money to a hospital and Chulalongkorn University. This act of goodwill won the hearts of the Thais, which not only

led to the Thai government's full support for the Indian struggle for freedom, but also created an atmosphere of mutual trust and friendship with the Indians in Thailand for years to come.

Netaji's visit to Bangkok in November and his memorable speech before Indians in the packed University Hall at Chulalongkorn University is still fresh in the minds of the older generation of Indians. His call for unity among the Indians for the cause of the motherland and his famous slogans of 'Jai Hind' and 'Dilli Chalo' had an extraordinary impact. Netaji united Indians with his genuine passion and for a while they forgot their differences and donated time, effort and money generously. Young Indian men joined the INA while young Indian women were recruited into the Rani of Jhansi Regiment.

Netaji then called for a meeting of the senior members of the Indian National Council and the remnants of the Hikari Kikan-influenced league. He was well aware of the damaging split and the last thing he needed was discord in the ranks of the Indian community in Thailand. There were approximately 4500 members of the Indian National Council in Bangkok at the time of his arrival. At the meeting, Netaji listened to the different views of the council and the league. He then called upon the two factions to reconcile and work towards their greater duty of winning India's independence: the two groups agreed. Netaji established a new structure for the organisation and announced that Isher Singh, formerly of the Rashbehari Bose group, would be the chairman of the IIL in Bangkok. He also nominated Singh as the official representative of the provisional government of India in Thailand. Pandit Raghunath Sharma was named the territorial secretary of Thailand.

In Thailand, there were 2000 Indians working directly for the INA. A military training camp was situated in Chonburi, near Bangkok, where the Japanese taught 250 men to operate anti-aircraft guns. There were also 50 women of the Rani of Jhansi Regiment from the Bangkok area. The news of recruitment in the INA had a deep impact among the Indian youth in Bangkok: almost every household supplied one soldier. Teenagers were upset at not being able to join the INA. Krishan Lal Matta, then only 13, argued with Netaji in a public gathering in

Balak Sena, also known as the Young People's Force, where 30 boys trained with the INA.

George Singh, a Thailand-born Indian tailor. It is common to see Indian tailors on the streets of Sukhumvit.

support of an 'army' of his age group: '*Humara kya kasoor hai ki humlog deshki seva nahin kar sakte?*' ('What is our fault that forbids us from serving the motherland?') Netaji approvingly ordered the creation of the Balak Sena (Young People's Force) and about 30 boys were trained along with other recruits of the INA. Shri Matta became known not only as a successful merchant but as a proud creator of the Balak Sena.

NETAJI'S LAST DAYS

Netaji's final visit to Bangkok was from 14–17 May 1945. He stayed in a house belonging to Sewakram Mahtani, the IIL's finance secretary. At Pandit Raghunath Sharma's house, there was a stream of visitors—INA officials, league workers and merchants wanting to know Netaji's plans. At dawn on 17 May, Netaji bade farewell to his supporters. He would never return.

On 3 September 1945, British forces arrived in Bangkok and, once more, Indians living in Thailand were placed in a dangerous situation. The officers of the IIL were immediately targeted. The British raided the Indian National Council and confiscated all its documents. They arrested key members of the movement, including the league's chairman, Isher Singh, Pandit Raghunath Sharma and Babu Maghar Singh of the Publicity Department. They were taken to Singapore for further interrogation. Later, the British undertook a further enquiry in Bangkok of all those who had either participated in or supported the league.

Indian fast food outlets and restaurants are popular among locals and tourists in Bangkok.

HOT CURRY
INDIAN FAST FOOD
OPEN: 11.00 AM. TO MIDNIGHT
FREE HOME DELIVERY
PLEASE CALL AT: 02-2294984

POST-WORLD WAR II DEVELOPMENTS

After World War II, Indians wanted to be reunited with their loved ones in India. The human traffic flowed both ways. In the post-war decades of the 1950s and 1960s, the steep rise in prices and the shortage of goods benefited the Indian business community. Those from the textile sector established the first textile producing units in the country. Thonburi Textiles and the Century Textiles Co. were two of the pioneering companies. Diwanchand Kundanlal created a large textile project in a joint venture with a Japanese company. Some textile retailers, most of whom were Punjabi, ventured out of Bangkok and were soon represented in every province of the kingdom.

The economic boom and the emphasis on tourism following the advent of the Vietnam War brought a new range of business opportunities to the Indian community in Thailand. As more tourists began to visit, tailor shops dominated by Indians sprang up. The best tailors in Thailand today are Indian, and the most sought-after local brand in apparel, Jaspal, is owned by an Indian family. Members

A shrine built for Vishnu in Bangkok.

of the Sindhi community branched out into antique shops along Sukhumvit Road.

The presence of a large number of Indians in various international and UN organisations, multinational companies, banks, financial institutions, and the progress that India has made in the field of information and communication technologies have helped in giving India and Indians in Thailand a progressive, modern and forward-looking image. The community is held in high esteem in official and political circles as well as among the common people of Thailand. Addressed as *khaek* (guest), all Indians are generally treated with respect. The setting up of Aditya Birla Group of Industries (1970), Indo-Rama Group (1990) and Thai Baroda Industries (1995) has contributed considerably to improving the image and prestige of the Indian community in local circles as well. The involvement of Indian social and cultural organisations in charitable and philanthropic activities has also played a significant role in this. The creation of the India Studies Centre at the Thammasat University in Bangkok, with a 10 million baht endowment fund, was possible only due to the generosity of the Indian businessmen in Thailand on the eve of the visit of the former Indian prime minister, Narasimha Rao, in 1993. Some of the members of the community have also been decorated with honours and awards by the Thai government.

Almost all Indians in Thailand—about 80,000—are found in urban centres. About 75 per cent live in Bangkok. Other cities with sizeable numbers of Indians are Chiang Mai, Chiang Rai and Lampang—all in northern Thailand. Sikhs comprise the largest component of the Indian community, numbering around 35,000, followed by Hindus from Punjab, numbering about 20,000. There are about 2000 Indians from Gorakhpur-Ballia-Azamgarh (eastern Uttar Pradesh), followed by a sizeable number of Bohras, Gujaratis, Marwaris, Maharashtrians, Sindhis and South Indians. In recent times, many Marwaris from Rajasthan have established themselves in the gems and jewellery business. Many Indians are playing an active role in the economic development of Thailand through at least 60 sectors of trade and commerce, as reflected in the records of the Bharat Overseas Bank (established in 1973) in Bangkok, then the only private bank allowed by the Reserve Bank of India to operate abroad. No field has been left untouched by Indians: education, travel, banking, gems and jewellery, hotels, restaurants and fruit and vegetable exports.

Amarjiva Lochan

INDONESIA

EARLY CIVILISATION IN both Java and Sumatra showed considerable Indian influence from the 1st century AD. Indian scripts and Hinduism were influential in the development of language and religion in Java. By the 5th century AD, Buddhism was believed to have reached Sumatra. The continued popularity of the epics, the Ramayana and Mahabharata, the magnificent stupas of Borobudur, the Prambanan Temple in Yogyakarta, and the persistence of Hinduism in Bali, are testimony to the connection with India. Evidence of the earliest settlements of Indian traders and missionaries is negligible. The later immigrant groups were Tamil Muslim traders in the archipelago from the 16th century onwards. Indian missionaries in Southeast Asia were integral to the spread of Islam.

From the end of the 19th century, indentured labourers from Tamil Nadu came to work in the rubber and tobacco plantations. A small minority became barbers and businessmen. Sikhs were employed as security personnel and watchmen. By the early 20th century, some Sikhs had set up dairy farms, while others had become moneylenders. Economic opportunities in Medan in the early 1900s also attracted the Nattukottai Chettiars, who drew upon the lack of rural credit to establish a moneylending trade. Similarly, the Sindhis established their presence in port cities such as Surabaya and Semarang in the 20th century. Their numbers increased after the Partition, which displaced most Hindu Sindhis from Sind.

In 1930, the census showed that there were 30,000 Indians in Indonesia; but the issue of who was an Indian was a tricky one. Given the Dutch system of indenture, the actual numbers of Indian contract workers and other supposed 'free' labourers are difficult to determine accurately. Similar demographic complications exist today due to the assimilation of Indonesian-Indians, which has led to a significant number of Indonesians of Indian descent

asserting an Indonesian identity instead of an Indonesian Indian one, and in the case of some, even being unaware of any Indian descent. Some individuals in Pasar Baru, Jakarta, who are of Indian descent, recently reacted strongly to the 'home' community identifying them as Indians. This problem of identifying Indians was aggravated by assertions of Indonesianness over Indianness by a significant number of Indonesians of Indian descent in the post-independence era. The Indian government's official estimate of persons of Indian origin (PIOs) in Indonesia was 55,000 in 2000. In 2002, some 2000 Indian families were registered as living in Jakarta alone.

POST-WAR SETTLEMENTS

The settlement of Indians in Indonesia was largely a post-World War II phenomenon. One significant aspect of this period was the resettlement of many Tamils and Sikhs, who had settled in rural locations in the pre-war era, in urban areas. The post-war Indian diaspora is concentrated in urban settings such as Medan, Surabaya and Jakarta. There are also sizeable numbers of Indians in areas such as Banda Aceh (Sumatra), Jayapura (Irian Jaya) and Manado (Sulawesi). The spread of the community to far-reaching locations was made easier by the natives, who regarded the Indians as a non-threatening minority and thus welcomed them. The ability of the Indians to assimilate into Indonesian culture by learning the dialects and through intermarriage further cemented their place as a favoured community to be associated with.

The Indian diaspora is particularly apparent in these Indian enclaves or areas of convergence across Indonesia. Indianness in Indonesia is manifest in Indian attempts at communal existence in areas such as Kampong Keling in Medan, and Pasar Baru, Pintu Air, Chempaka Putih and Tanjung Priok in Jakarta. One marked space of Indian assertion is Pasar Baru—one of the oldest Indonesian

A stone stele depicting Shiva and Parvati; Klaten, Central Java, 8th–9th century AD, from the Museum Nasional (No. Inv. 6091).

Map 8.16

Borobudur, the largest Buddhist monument in the world, is evidence of Indian influence in Indonesia's early civilisation.

markets for textiles, curtains and sports equipment, otherwise referred to as the 'Little India' of Jakarta due to the high number of Indian businesses located there. Little India, however, has recently become less Indian due to the rising price of land in Pasar Baru, which has led Indians to relocate their businesses and homes to outskirts such as Chempaka Putih and Tanjung Priok.

ECONOMIC ROLES

Indian trading groups have played important roles at various stages of Indonesia's history. The founding of the first Sindhi firm, Wassiamul Assomull & Co., in Java by the end of the 1870s set the stage for the establishment of other Sindhi businesses later in Jakarta. A traditional merchant community, the Sindhis travelled far and wide in Asia and Africa: even after choosing a new country as their home, they were known to uproot and move on. Political turmoil in Vietnam, for example, made some Sindhis seek a home elsewhere, and Jakarta became an important destination. They were joined by other Sindhis after the Partition. Sindhis who came to Indonesia stayed in the wholesale business. Another traditional 'trading diaspora', the Gujaratis, reached the Indonesian archipelago by the 19th century to trade in commodities such as sugar and tea, though on a smaller scale than the Sindhis. Like the other Indian sub-communities, the Gujarati migration followed a colonial network of migration.

Similarly, the Sikhs have been crucial players in the Indonesian economy, largely through operations in the Tanjung Priok area of Jakarta. By the first quarter of the 19th century, there was a sizeable Sikh population in this area. Indonesian Sikhs embraced many professions and were anything from watchmen to moneylenders and taxi renters. Sikh entrepreneurs arose largely during the Dutch colonial period, when the Dutch need for sporting goods led a considerable number of Sikh businessmen to pursue sporting goods ventures. Two prominent examples that were established to meet this colonial demand are Bir and Co. and Bose and Co. M. S. Gill, an Indian success story, inherited a sporting goods business established by his father in the 1930s and expanded it as a franchise with several branches throughout Southeast Asia. The Indian community in Indonesia, as characterised by Gill, has been entrepreneurial.

Beyond the business sector, the entertainment industry has witnessed the rise of firms owned by Indonesian Indians, such as Rapi Film Co., Parkeet Films and Nusantara Films. As a result of the boom in this industry, several Cinetrons, especially in the Medan area, are run by the Punjabi community.

Hindu temple architecture in Bali features walled courtyards filled with shrines and pavilions that are open to the sky.

Another diasporic success story is that of steel tycoon Lakshmi Mittal, who owns Ispat Indo, which started its operations in West Java in 1976. Mittal, currently based in London, moved from India to Indonesia for a short period to set up the company, which has evolved into Indonesia's largest privately owned steel company. Mittal, and others like him, have had much to do with the rapid global expansion of the steel industry, which, until then, had been almost entirely state-controlled.

In politics, the emergence of H. S. Dhillon has been pivotal. Educated at Cornell University, Dhillon has played an active role in Indonesian politics and is also an active member of the Indonesian Human Rights Commission.

Although small in number relative to the native population, Indians in Indonesia have also played a critical role in developing essential aspects of the Indonesian religious, cultural and economic landscape. The gurdwara in the Tanjung Priok area, the Shiv Mandir and the temples in Medan and Yogyakarta are important places of worship for members of the Indian community. These religious sites have increasingly become avenues of Sikh and Hindu expression. While the gurdwara functions as an important site for Indian unitary expression, drawing individuals from the Sikh, Sindhi Hindu and even Punjabi Muslim communities, increasing polarisation has marked the religious practices of the communities. A number of Sindhi Hindus have begun to assert a Hindu identity in the Shiv Mandir at Pluit. Similarly, the three Tamil Hindu temples in Medan, especially the Sri Mariamman temple built in 1930 in the Binjai area, have functioned as important sites of asserting Tamil Hindu identity.

In the 1930s and 1940s, a group of affluent Indians, reacting to the discriminatory membership of foreign clubs in Indonesia, decided to establish the Bombay Merchants Association. Initially dominated by Sindhis, the association promoted Sindhi interests. However, influenced by Indian nationalism, it was renamed the Gandhi Seva Loka and now represents pan-Indian interests. Similarly, an Indian Women's Association was set up to represent the interests of Indian women. One of the premier institutional manifestations of Indianness remains the Gandhi Memorial School, established in 1953, which celebrates a certain notion of Indianness within the diaspora. Similarly, the Jawaharlal Nehru Institute Cultural Centre is concerned with Indian cultural activities and the promotion of Indianness. Through their flexibility, Indian communities have integrated well into Indonesian society. This has enabled their success not just in business but in maintaining their cultural heritage.

Bilveer Singh

BALI: A DIASPORA IN THE MAKING?

Vajpayee has been in Bali for a day but the memory of his visit will live with the Balinese for many years. They are virtually treating his coming as a blessing of God: all because he has brought them the water from the Holy Ganga, which he presented to the Governor and also poured into the Indian Ocean.

Indian Express, 15 January 2001

To describe the Balinese Hindus as a diasporic community is certain to raise a few eyebrows among scholars and laymen alike. Clearly, they do not correspond to many of the normal characteristics of a diasporic community in terms of the migration process, the historical experience of displacement, and the maintenance of long-term connections with the homeland. Nevertheless, a brief account of recent historical and social developments in Bali will challenge us to rethink some of our preconceived notions of what constitutes a diasporic consciousness in the age of globalisation.

The roots of Hinduism in Bali are often traced back to the 14th century and the Hindu Javanese empire of Majapahit. This historical legacy left a powerful imprint on contemporary Balinese society and religion. Indeed, Balinese Hinduism contains many features familiar to Hinduism as practised on the subcontinent, including a Sanskrit liturgy, a hierarchical caste-like system and the worship of Hindu deities. Nevertheless, Balinese Hinduism also exhibits marked differences unique to Bali itself, such as inter-caste marriage, ancestral worship, the consumption and sacrifice of animals, and a host of other elaborate ritual practices and ceremonies. It was not until the onset of colonial rule and the rise of a Balinese intelligentsia that the so-called great tradition associated with India began to hold sway over local practices.

Following the advent of Dutch colonial rule in the Indonesian archipelago, the Balinese became increasingly aware of their identification with the Hindu religion and connections to India. The Dutch orientalist view of Bali as a Hindu stronghold emphasised both differences (from Islam) and continuity with Hinduism. Along with administrative practices that sought to standardise the Balinese religion with the Hindu tradition, the Dutch also encouraged the nascent Balinese intelligentsia to forge links with India. Significantly, the establishment of such connections coincided with a

Finely dressed Hindus head to the temple in a procession. They hold elaborate rituals and ceremonies that are unique to the practice of Hinduism in Bali.

period of Hindu revivalism on the subcontinent during the late 19th and early 20th century.

Reference to India as the source of the Balinese religion and its authority received further stimulus under the post-colonial regime. Sukarno's national integration policy gave official recognition and state support to what it considered to be world religions (*agama*), including Islam, Christianity and Buddhism. The Balinese religion was, however, excluded from the fold and dubbed as animistic and inferior. To gain official recognition, the Balinese intelligentsia attempted to sanitise the Balinese religion of its ritual practices (*adat*), highlighting the ancient Hindu religion and Indian civilisation as the original source of the Balinese religion and cultural practices. In order to promote this view, key Hindu texts such as the Bhagavat Gita were translated into Bahasa Indonesia, while Indian scholars were invited to Bali to teach religion, and a few Balinese youth were awarded scholarships to study in India. Eventually, in 1965 the Balinese religion was recognised and declared a world religion (*agama* Hindu). Thus, the Hindu religion became an essential marker of Balinese culture. The emphasis on religion and traditional Hindu values was reinforced further during the 1980s by the governor of Bali, who advocated 'a return to roots' view, as well as the burgeoning tourist industry, which promoted Bali and the Balinese as 'more Hindu than the Indian Hindus'. This expression of difference, represented in religious and ethnic terms, influenced the Balinese people's own perception of their culture, art and ethnic identity.

The process that led to the formation of a Balinese Hindu identity was also informed by broader political developments taking place at the state level. The growing sense of being a minority and victims of state prejudice was compounded by the bloody events following former president Suharto's rise to power. Under the 'New Order' regime, the Balinese sense of exploitation intensified as many felt the

government and rich Muslim Javanese were capitalising on the island's thriving tourist industry. Moreover, the animosity between the Balinese and Muslims was exacerbated due to the flow of cheap Javanese labour arriving on the island, and more recently, as a result of the Bali bombing and the rise of Islamic fundamentalism.

On the Indian side, Bali is becoming increasingly known, not least because of the recent terrorist attacks. Over the last three years, the former prime minister of India, Atal Bihari Vajpayee, visited the island three times—most recently when attending the ASEAN Summit in 2003. On this occasion, a web-based newspaper reported the strong dismay expressed by the secretary of the right-wing Vishwa Hindu Parishad at Vajpayee's reluctance to promote Hindu culture on the island. The secretary accused the Prime Minister of 'sacrificing the global religious interest of nearly a billion Hindus.'

The resurgence of Hindu nationalism also meant that certain institutions have become increasingly interested in endorsing the Bali–India connection. The popular international magazine, *Hinduism Today*, describes Bali as a lush Hindu enclave fighting to preserve its culture in the face of contemporary changes. Other newspaper reports emphasise the need to revive ancient links with the support of the Indian government and promote cultural activities, the building of temples and mutual pilgrimages.

In the age of globalisation, with the increasing availability of information and electronic media, lower costs of travel and the expansion of transnational communication networks, the need to consider the diaspora as having a kind of consciousness as well is central to our understanding of the experiences, attitudes and cultural maps that certain groups share historically. This is especially evident in a place such as Bali, where religious identities are constantly intermingling with local ideas, and the economies of the host societies are influenced by the broader forces of globalisation.

Assa Doron

Ink drawings of the Ramayana were made in Bali in the early 19th century. This drawing depicts heavenly musicians, which are seen as necessary attributes of the abode of the gods.

Publications produced in Bali which reflect the strong influence of Hinduism.

THE PHILIPPINES

THE INDIAN COMMUNITY in the Philippines is fairly small and diverse. In the early 21st century the figure stands at about 28,000, which is a significant jump from the 1970s when there were about 2000 Indians. Of these, about 3000 people of Indian origin have acquired Philippine citizenship.

The Indian diaspora, encompassing the dominant Punjabi and Sindhi communities, gained visibility in the Philippines only after the partition of India in 1947. However, the Indic influences apparent in surviving archaeological artefacts, the findings of anthropologists and the prevailing influence of Sanskrit on Filipino languages and literature point to an era of contact as early as 300 BC to 200 BC.

The tenuous linguistic connection was first brought to light in the late 19th century, when a scholar identified 200 words in Tagalog derived from Sanskrit. Lingering traces of Indian influence are also apparent in Filipino folktales. Whatever little Indian influence could be discerned in ancient Philippines was of an indirect kind, possibly from the Hinduised kingdoms of Southeast Asia. There is no evidence of any direct relations between India and the Philippines before the arrival of the Spanish.

A naval expedition against Manila in 1762, which comprised a contingent of 600 British Indian sepoys and labourers, left their legacy after the conclusion of the Seven Years' War in 1764. Settling in a *barangay* (village) called Dayap in Cainta, these Indians were listed in church records as a distinguishable racial category—*morenos* (the dark-skinned).

The clandestine 'Manilha Trade' between 1644 and 1765, where the British East India Company engaged in subterfuge, and the conquest of Sind and Punjab in 1843 and 1849 respectively, were two of many factors that led to the Sindhi and Punjabi presence in Manila. The first Sindhi traders appeared after the American occupation of the Philippines in 1898, which resulted in the penetration of the Manila market by British merchants. The early Sindhi presence was marked by the establishment of the Pohumal Brothers Company: many third-generation Filipino Sindhis are descendants of the company's employees and of other early Southeast Asian firms. Similarly, some old trading houses like G. Assanmal and Co. (1925) and Crown Silk Store (1932, re-established in 1947 as Gurnamal Sons) exist as markers of the early Sindhi presence.

Indian president Abdul Kalam exchanges a toast with Philippine president Gloria Arroyo during a visit in 2006.

SINDHIS AND PUNJABIS

Some Sindhi businesses moved into Manila before the partition of the subcontinent. As heirs to a traditional seafaring merchant community, Sindhis travelled far and wide in Asia and Africa. Sometimes, even after choosing a new country as their home, they would uproot themselves and move on. Manila became an important

Map 8.17

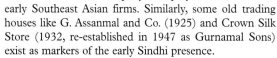

THE PHILIPPINES

destination, particularly with the onset of political turmoil in Vietnam. Many Sindhis also left Sind after the Partition and ended up in Manila. The Sindhis who landed in the Philippines stayed in the wholesale business, and continue to do so. There is another group of Sindhis, however, who operate within the retail sector and reside in the provinces. Even though business connections between the two groups are robust, a certain amount of social distance exists between them.

The Sindhis in Manila are wealthy, but not wealthy enough to provoke resentment. Since they are not as dominant as the Chinese, they have not drawn comparable adverse attention. The Sindhis have also been quite insular, preferring to marry within their community.

On the other hand, the Punjabis, who arrived in Manila around 1902 have freely assimilated with the local population. The first group of Punjabi migrants, comprising Ghummars from Sangatpur (a rural village in Jullundur, East Punjab), were recruited by the British to work for the military, building fortifications and military cantonments. As Sir Henry Johnson noted, a number of the Punjabis were 'reserve soldiers of the Indian army who [have] served with the Malay police or Hong Kong police…[and] in the spirit of adventure drifted across to the Philippine Islands and engaged themselves in the services of the Americans...'

The contemporary Filipino-Indian is referred to as 'Bumbai'. The term can be traced back to Indian ships arriving from Bombay in the 20th century, and most Sindhi shops bearing names such as 'Bombay Merchants' and 'Bombay Store'. Its contemporary derogatory connotation is a result of colonial and missionary stereotypes of the 'Bumbais of Cainta', and the stereotypes attached to the physical appearance and occupations of the Sikh immigrants. Filipino children used to be warned about the 'Bumbai' who would come on a motorcycle and take them away.

In terms of numbers, Punjabis dominate the Filipino-Indian community. Despite their number and their assimilationist proclivities, Filipino Punjabis are sometimes pejoratively called 'five-six Indians'. The Philippine president, Gloria Macapagal-Arroyo, recently displayed the prevalence of this stereotype with the comment, 'Who does not know the five-six Indians?' This 'five-six' appellation developed from the occupations of the Filipino Sikhs in the early part of the 20th century, namely from moneylending without any collateral but on usurious terms. The 'five-six' Sikhs went into moneylending because there was no rural credit system in the Philippines. The system was simple: it involved no paperwork and the Sikhs travelled to their customers in the countryside on motorcycles.

It is unfortunate that there is no reliable estimate of the size of the Indian community in the Philippines. The notion of 'five-six Indians' indulging in illegal work complicates the picture. Even Indian commentators have written off the Filipino Punjabis as a people who have 'mastered [the] art of the fake visa.'

Filipino Sindhis have sometimes distanced themselves from other Filipino Indians in order to assert an exclusive Indian identity. They often equate themselves as the Indian counterpart of the diasporic Chinese community, with centuries of mercantile specialisation. To emphasise their distinctiveness, they have adopted English as their mother tongue. This distinguishes them from other Sindhi diasporas which have integrated with other Indian ethnic groups through language, such as Hindi and Urdu. The Sindhis have also been keen to preserve their linguistic tradition by organising Sindhi classes for the younger generation at various times; but these efforts were not successful as the community could not sustain their interest. Religious, philosophical and cultural activities have fared better.

Filipino Sindhis have at times asserted an 'Indian' cultural superiority towards other groups, such as the Punjabis, who have assimilated into Filipino society. Even Sindhi individuals assimilated into Manila's 'permissive society' are referred to as *jattu* (a derogatory term denoting social backwardness in contemporary Filipino Sindhi discourse). The children of Punjabi and Filipino intermarriages are often labelled as 'Bombay mestizos'. One interesting example of such an intermarriage was Ramon Mangatsingh, a former mayor of the city of Manila.

More recently, a significant third group of Indians have entered Filipino society. This group of about 300 consists of Indian expatriates from different parts of India, made up of embassy staff and professionals employed in international organisations such as the Asian Development Bank and the International Rice Research Institute, and transnational corporations. This group will draw and deserve more attention over the next few years due to the Philippine government's growing economic interests in India and President Arroyo's expressed desire to make Manila a 'Little Bangalore'.

Community divisions are also apparent in the institutions that represent business, religious or cultural interests. For example, a group of affluent Sindhis reacting to the discriminatory membership of foreign clubs in the Philippines decided to establish the Bombay Merchants Association in 1937. Although the association was created to cater to 'Indian' needs, it excluded Filipino Punjabis.

Led by nationalistic sentiments, certain Sindhi individuals started looking for an institution which would articulate a more integrative Indian identity. During World War II, nationalistic Indianness was evident in the enthusiastic support of sections of the Indian community for the Indian Independence League led by Subhas Chandra Bose, particularly after Bose's arrival and the Philippines' recognition of the Azad Hind government. The nationalist impetus led to the establishment of the Indian Chamber of Commerce in 1951, which eventually changed its name to the Filipino-Indian Chamber of Commerce (FICC). In the Philippines, commercial associations are usually organised on ethnic lines. The FICC is dominated by Sindhis, who constitute about 95 per cent of its membership.

The religious dimension of community life has been more successfully organised. The Khalsa Diwan and the Hindu Temple are two very important places of worship for members of the Indian community. The establishment of the gurdwara in 1929 was an important expression of Filipino Sikh identity. It provided an opportunity for Sindhi Hindus and Punjabi Sikhs to work together in its maintenance.

Sikhs in Manila celebrate the 535th birthday of their religious founder, Guru Nanak Dev, at the Khalsa Diwan in 2004.

THE MUSLIM COMMUNITY

There is also a small South Asian Muslim community in the Philippines comprising Punjabis, Sindhis and Gujaratis (Bohras). A significant change occurred following the partition of the subcontinent. This was manifest in the way some Muslims asserted a Pakistani identity as different from an Indian one. The repercussions of the Partition were also manifest in the gurdwara, where the Sikh and Sindhi Hindu congregation became increasingly polarised from Muslims patronising the premises. Similarly, the Partition's religious polarisation contributed to a marginalised Sindhi Hindu congregation forming a *mandir* in 1960.

Among the Hindus, Sikhs and Muslims living in the Philippines are a few Indian priests and nuns. Manila has been one of the destinations for education and theological training of the Indian Catholic clergy. A significant facet of the Indian diaspora in the Philippines are the Born Again Christians, converts to Christianity. The Sindhi church in the only predominantly Catholic Asian nation is the first of its kind and is a major landmark in the history of Sindhi Christianity.

Kripa Sridharan and Terenjit S. Sevea

The Khalsa Diwan Sikh temple at U. N. Avenue, Manila, an area where Indians often gather.

INDO-CHINA: VIETNAM, LAOS AND CAMBODIA

The South Indian textile shop was ubiquitous in the towns and cities of colonial Indo-China. This one was in the port town of Cap St. Jacques (Vung Taa).

THREE HINDU KINGDOMS (Funan, Champa and Kambuja) ruled large areas of modern-day Vietnam and Cambodia from the 1st century to the 13th century AD, drawing on cultural and religious influences already established by long-distance traders from India. A modest maritime trade with Indian ports continued beyond the eclipse of these civilisations: Tamil-speaking Muslims were among the merchants involved in the period of vibrant trade in the Mekong Delta from the mid-18th century to the mid-19th century.

MOVEMENTS IN THE COLONIAL ERA (1859–1954)

Indian migration became significant again during the French occupation of Indo-China. The French-held ports of Pondicherry and Karaikkal on the southeast coast of India served as supply points during French manoeuvres to gain control of the trade centre of Saigon (1859) and subsequently to claim Cochin China as a colony for France (1867). Accompanying the French ships were Tamil soldiers who took part in the conquest

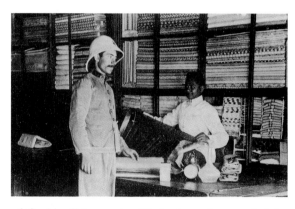

of Cochin China, and cattle herders who supplied the troops with milk and transport. Many Tamils stayed on to supply milk to a growing European population and to fill service contracts for the French in Saigon and its adjacent Chinese market town, Cholon. Several of these early arrivals—mainly Hindus of humble origin—prospered, amassing sufficient wealth in the early decades of the colonial presence to construct a Mariamman temple in central Saigon.

The French presence in Cochin China served as a vehicle for several other types of free migration to the countries of Indo-China. French-educated Indians from Pondicherry and Karaikkal took up subordinate posts in the Cochin Chinese administration, working as clerks, interpreters, accountants, tax collectors, legal clerks and customs officers. Many postmen, policemen, prison guards and lighthouse watchmen were also from French India. Later, magistrates and doctors from French India also worked in Indo-China. Most of them were Catholic converts and French citizens. From 1909, French Indian soldiers were called upon in Cochin China. After their release from duty, these soldiers often stayed on to seek employment in the administration. Once other areas of the Indo-Chinese union were brought under French protection (from 1887), some French Indians found administrative work in the main urban centres of Hanoi, Haiphong and Phnom Penh. In addition, subordinate posts in private French firms in Indo-China were frequently filled by French Indians.

South Indian Muslim merchants were active in colonial Indo-China in the import of textiles and jewellery, money-changing and petty trade. A few became powerful property owners. Marakkayar Muslim traders from Karaikkal and the Tanjore district in British India were mostly settled in Cochin China and Cambodia, while Pondicherry Muslims dominated trade in Tonkin. South Indian Muslims also took up tax farming contracts with the French authorities, collecting tax on market stalls and ferry crossings.

The moneylending caste of Nattukottai Chettiars from Chettinad in Tamil Nadu began operations in Cochin China from the 1870s. Their clients were mainly landowners

Map 8.18

MODERN STATES OF INDO-CHINA

CHINA

N

VIETNAM

• Hanoi

Haiphong

LAOS

Gulf of Tonkin

• Vientiane

THAILAND

• Da Nang

Mekong

Xekong

• Siem Reap

Tonle Sap

CAMBODIA

Phnom Penh •

Gulf of Thailand

• Ho Chi Minh City

CHINA

INDIA

MYANMAR

Mekong Delta

PHILIPPINES

MALAYSIA

INDONESIA

0   150 kilometres

0   150 miles

in the rice-growing areas of the Mekong Delta, small businessmen and government employees in towns throughout Cochin China, but they took little interest in other parts of the Indo-Chinese union. Their strength lay in their willingness to lend with low security and they owned considerable urban property in Cochin China, to which, during the economic depression of the 1930s, they added large tracts of agricultural land gained from foreclosures. Despite the role played by Chettiar financing in the development of rice cultivation in the Mekong Delta, they earned the label of 'black vultures' from the Vietnamese because of the high interest rates they demanded and their failure to reinvest profits in Cochin China.

A small number of Sindhi and Gujarati merchants, referred to as 'Bombay', operated in Indo-China in the colonial period. Gujarati merchants were active in rice exports and shipping along the inland waterways of the Mekong Delta. From the 1890s, several major Sindhi firms opened retail operations in Saigon and Phnom Penh, where they came to dominate the trade in Asian silks and exotic novelty goods. Among the poorest of the Indian migrants to Indo-China in the colonial period were the Pathans and Sikhs, who worked as watchmen, policemen, drivers and milkmen. In Cambodia, the Pathans were also frequently employed as butchers.

STATUS AND POPULATION

Indians in colonial Indo-China were classified as either French citizens, French Indian subjects or British Indian subjects. As 'foreign Asians' on French colonial soil, British Indian subjects were organised into *congrégations*, following a long-standing system for the overseas Chinese. Indian *congrégations* were organised according to religion, and an elected *chef de congrégation* was held responsible for ensuring that all members paid their taxes prior to leaving the country. All Indians, regardless of their status, were subject to French law in Indo-China. This was of particular benefit to the Chettiars, who were able to use the French courts to seize assets from debtors who defaulted on loans.

The Chinese migrant population in Indo-China, which, in 1921 stood at 156, 000 in Cochin China alone, dwarfed that of the Indian migrants, which never exceeded 7000 prior to 1954. Tamils and South Indian Muslims made up the vast majority of Indian migrants throughout Indo-China in the colonial period. Cochin China was the

territory with the largest Indian migrant population, with Saigon-Cholon accounting for over one-third of the total Indian population in Indo-China. Elsewhere, the cities of Phnom Penh, Hanoi and Haiphong had sizeable Indian populations. Before 1954, the Indian population in Laos was negligible.

GENDER, FAMILY AND COMMUNITY

The migrant Indian population was mostly male, but the gender imbalance was narrowed by the number of French Indians working in the administration, who were entitled to free passage for their families and thus brought their wives to Cochin China. By the late 19th century, Catholic Tamil families were settled in Saigon. Muslim migrants tended to leave their wives in India, but sometimes had legitimate second marriages in Indo-China, and the children of both unions moved between India and Indo-China for education and work. Chettiar migration followed a fixed pattern of three-year stints overseas, after which men returned home to Chettinad to visit their wives and children. Chettiar women began to reside in Indo-China in small numbers from the 1930s. There were also instances of unions (often unrecognised) between Indian migrants and local women that resulted in many children of mixed origin, often Indo-Vietnamese or Indo-Khmer.

The preponderance of Tamil speakers among the migrants led to the development of a modest but thriving Tamil community in Saigon from the turn of the 20th century, and a 'Tamil quarter' comprising several streets soon developed. French Indians working in the administration resided in rue Lagrandière; Indian Muslim businesses dominated Vannier, Vienot and Catinat streets; and rue Ohier was the seat of the Chettiars. Indian migrants financed the construction of four Hindu temples and two mosques in Saigon-Cholon. Two schools were established in Saigon to allow young children to have a rudimentary education in Tamil. Indian merchants supplied the community with a variety of products from home, including spices, arrack and sesame oil. From 1926 to 1941, the newspaper *Saigon-Dimanche* (later *Indochine-Inde*) was the organ of the various Indian communities in Saigon and throughout Indo-China.

PRE-INDEPENDENCE POLITICAL INVOLVEMENT

Before World War I, Indians in Indo-China were largely uninvolved in politics related to the British occupation of India. French Indians in Indo-China, however, engaged in an active struggle for equal rights in French India. From the 1930s, there was a general move for social reform among overseas Indians: caste, dress and the role of women were among the issues raised in meetings of the numerous Indian associations in Saigon during this period.

World War II gave rise to a complex situation in Indo-China for Indians. When the French governor of Pondicherry, M. Bonvin, came out in favour of Resistance leader Charles de Gaulle, French Indians in pro-Vichy Indo-China were suspect. Those working in the administration were relegated to the position of

Map 8.19

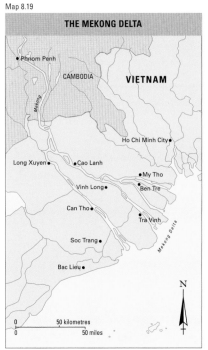

THE MEKONG DELTA

Source: GEOATLAS Asia Vector by Graphi-Ogre.

A ration card for sugar and matches belonging to Mr Lokoosingh of the Sindhi firm, Pohumull Brothers. Indian requests for European rations following Indo-China's French re-occupation (September 1945) were declined.

A 1930 photograph of Saigon's Ohier Street, the hub of Chettiar life in Cochin China. Money-lending businesses, a Chettiar Association (left), dormitory (centre), and temple were all located here.

in Indo-China, took out their frustration on the local Indian population, who were specifically targeted in looting and attacks in Saigon in September 1945.

HISTORICAL EXPERIENCE IN THE INDEPENDENT STATES OF VIETNAM, LAOS AND CAMBODIA

French rule in Vietnam ended with the defeat at Dien Bien Phu in 1954; Laos and Cambodia gained independence soon afterwards. Indians closely associated with the French administration left Indo-China for India or France, although some stayed on to work in the private sector or in French technical assistance programmes. Despite Indian prime minister Jawaharlal Nehru's cordial relations with Ho Chi Minh's government, Indian businessmen in North Vietnam found conditions difficult under the new communist regime. Some 400 of them moved to South Vietnam and Laos, or returned to India.

In South Vietnam, however, Indian businessmen and their employees benefited, like others, from the greater trading opportunities offered by the growing American presence. Such opportunities included the expansion of import-export trade, foreign currency deals and contracts from the American military. Some South Indian Muslims who had begun to open cinemas in Indo-Chinese cities and distribute Indian films from the 1930s, saw their businesses flourish in the

newly independent South Vietnam. From the 1950s, in spite of the departure of many French Indians, there was an increase in the expatriate Indian population in South Vietnam. Moreover, despite growing unrest, Indian businessmen in Laos and Cambodia (mainly Tamil Muslim importers and petty traders), like their counterparts in South Vietnam, also continued to do well in the post-independence period.

A postcard of the central mosque in Saigon. It is now used by ethnic Cham and is frequented by a new wave of overseas Indians and other expatriate Muslims.

The identity card of an Indian with French nationality, dated 1956.

India's involvement in negotiations for Vietnam's independence cemented ties between Jawaharlal Nehru and Ho Chi Minh. This 1958 photograph shows the friendly relations the two men enjoyed.

'Asiatic cadre' and lost their citizenship rights. Furthermore, communications and remittances from Indo-China were cut off for the duration of the war. Akin to other parts of Southeast Asia, Subhas Chandra Bose's Indian Independence League, with the assistance of the Japanese occupying forces, attempted to raise funds from overseas Indians with the aim of removing British rule in India. While some Saigon-based Indians sided with Bose, many Indian businessmen objected to the coercion used to solicit contributions. French Indians in the colonial administration largely opposed the movement as they were loyal to de Gaulle.

In September 1945, when General Douglas Gracey arrived in Saigon as the head of an Indian division of the British army to accept the Japanese surrender, resentment of Indian wealth and privilege in Indo-China rose to the fore. Vietnamese revolutionary forces, convinced that Indian soldiers sought to aid the French return to power

THE FATE OF INDIAN COMMUNITIES FROM 1975

In 1975, victory for the communist forces in all three states of the former Indo-China marked a watershed for overseas Indians who remained in these states. The initial change of power in Cambodia was the most traumatic. On 17 April 1975, when Khmer Rouge forces took over Phnom Penh, 33 Indians took refuge with other foreign nationals in the French embassy. Others from the provinces left by convoy to Thailand in May of the same year. Their abrupt departure resulted in the loss of

All over the world an evolution is in progress. More and more, people have the tendency to blend their customs of dress with the ethic of Western Civilisation.

The first to do this, the Japanese, seem to have understood that the necessities of modern life were incompatible with certain ways of dressing which, although they may have followed respectable customs, were clearly out of date...It was because of this heroic decision that they managed to maintain and extend their privileged position equal to foreign powers, simply because they adopted their methods while conserving their national character...What holds for the Japanese...holds equally for the Hindus. Too many expatriate compatriots who could wear European clothing continue to dress in incommodious national dress. We hope that those to whom we address ourselves here are not upset if we permit ourselves to give them some advice. It is in their interest, and in the general interest of everyone.

It should be noted, however, that among the detractors of European costume, many if not all of them willingly borrow an accessory of western dress, be it a vest, a waistcoat, shoes, socks, a shirt etc. None refuses to ride in a automobile if he can, nor to profit from the advantages of modern life; electricity, the telephone.

This is no doubt legitimate but suggests that those who claim to protect the ancestral customs and habits by insisting on wearing national dress are fooling themselves. It is in the heart that one can keep the sense of the things of one's country, and not in dress...in Tonkin, all the Indians, whether they be Muslim or Chettiar, wear European dress, wearing only a fez or cap. Why should it be different in Cochinchina? While a good number have decided to adopt European costume, numerous others would like to do so but they are waiting for a movement to be launched, as they do not want to act alone...it must be hoped that this movement will intensify and that before the end of the year Indians with an anachronistic silhouette, with draping loincloths and chignons will no longer be seen. Something of the picturesque will be lost, but the dignity of backward Indians will be gained...

Extract from 'A Clothing Crusade for Indians residing in Indochina' (Une croisade vestimentaire pour les Indiens résident en Indochine), Saigon-Dimanche, 3 March 1933.

livelihoods, belongings and their adopted home, although those who did manage to leave could consider themselves fortunate. Fourteen Indians are known to have perished at the hands of the Khmer Rouge. Indians of mixed origin could not leave if they were unable to prove their foreign nationality. The fate of many of these people, like that of so many Cambodians, remains unknown.

Communist forces took Saigon on 30 April 1975. The closure of businesses and currency restrictions soon made it clear that there would be no place for business-men in the new Vietnam. Cordial relations between New Delhi and Hanoi made the departure easier for Indians than it was for other foreigners. By 1977, most Indians and people of mixed Indian origin had left Vietnam for India or France. Very few remained and only some 200 persons of Indian origin were estimated to be in Vietnam in 1980.

The rupture in Indian business was less severe in Laos than the two other states of Indo-China. When the communist government in Laos came to power in December 1975, the new regime did not clamp down immediately on private trade. Consequently, a relatively large number of foreign businessmen remained in Laos, and although they had to accept some restrictions, they were allowed to continue operating their business. In July 1980, there were 35 licensed Indian businesses in the Laotian capital, Vientiane.

Overseas Indians in Indo-China's 'Open Door' States from the 1990s

The demise of the Soviet Union affected all three states of the former Indo-China and, from the early 1990s, led them to introduce open-door, free market policies. This has had an impact on the people of Indian origin who remained in these countries, and has also led to the forma-tion of new Indian expatriate communities.

The *renonçants*: French Indian citizens in Indo-China

The 1881 Renunciation of Personal Status law allowed natives of the French possessions in India to voluntarily renounce their 'caste and customs' and consent to be subject to the French civil code. These *renonçants*, who were required to adopt surnames as a sign of their transformation, held the same rights as French citizens from the metropole. Renunciation grew out of the efforts of one influential caste in Pondicherry to gain equal standing with the French colonisers. While it never became widespread in French India—many were put off by the prospect of having to give up long-held customs and values—it appealed to French Indians seeking work within the administration in Indo-China as it secured them the privilege of work on the same terms as their metropolitan counterparts. The introduction of the renunciation law in India led to a scramble to renounce 'caste and custom' among the considerable number of French Indians already present in Cochin China, and a wave of newly 'renounced' migrants soon followed.

Though few in number (600 in the 1890s; 2000 by 1937), the *renonçants* were a powerful force in Cochin China. Prior to World War I, local authorities in Saigon attempted to undermine their citizenship rights. The expatriate *renonçants* appealed successfully to higher authorities in France to uphold their status; a triumph in the French Empire for the notion of citizenship free of racial distinction. *Renonçants* also played an important role in colonial elec-tions in Indo-China: as French citizens, they were among a small elite of naturalised Vietnamese and French who had the right to vote for the Cochin Chinese representative in the French National Assembly.

A milestone in the plight of people of Indian origin remaining in Vietnam after 1975 was the state visit of Vice-President K. R. Narayanan in 1993. Thereafter, most Indian places of worship in Vietnam which were closed since 1975 had been reopened. Many Indians of mixed origin who had left Vietnam following the com-munist takeover returned to re-establish contact with relatives in the country and, in some cases, to start up businesses again. From the early 1990s, Vietnam began to attract a new group of Indians working as professionals, businessmen or employees of Indian and international companies. The expatriate Indian community in Vietnam now consists of some 400 persons, settled mainly in Hanoi and Ho Chi Minh City (formerly Saigon-Cholon). Approximately 100 of these are persons of Indian origin who had remained in Vietnam after 1975 and retain Indian citizenship. In the contemporary period, Indians of mixed origin, although they often know little about their Indian heritage and speak no Indian language, have become more visible in Ho Chi Minh City. Indian places of worship have also become more active and new restaurants have been established to cater to a growing Indian clientele.

Similarly, in Cambodia there has been an influx of Indian expatriates from the early 1990s. In 2002, there were 150 non-resident Indians and 150 people of Indian origin in the country, and an Indian Association had been established.

In Laos, where there was less of a rupture with the past as was experienced in Vietnam and Cambodia, the Indian community, located primarily in Vientiane and Xekong, numbered about 125 in 2002.

Natasha Pairaudeau

Vietnamese worshippers pray to Ba Den (the Black Lady) at the Mariamman temple in Saigon.

BRUNEI DARUSSALAM

A LTHOUGH THE INDIAN presence in Brunei has always been small and transient, Indian influences on Bruneian culture have been strong and go back to its origins. Brunei first appeared in Chinese historical sources some 1000 years ago as a Hindu-Buddhist kingdom. Like other kingdoms in Southeast Asia, it was linked to an extensive trading network that connected the region to India and China. Indian influences are evident in some of what is today defined as 'traditional' Bruneian culture, such as certain royal and family rituals, mythology, social hierarchies and the symbolism and terminology associated with all of these.

The early Indian influences on Brunei did not directly come from India. They were transmitted to Brunei via the main centres of Hindu-Buddhist civilisation in Southeast Asia, such as Srivijaya and Majapahit; but Indian influence is also apparent in more recent borrowings from other Malay sultanates as part of a nationalist reconstruction of the Brunei-Malay tradition. Indian influences on Bruneian culture go back so far and are so deep that they are hardly identified as Indian anymore, particularly since some of these influences have, in recent years, been cleansed of their more obvious Hindu elements for religious reasons. There is no evidence of the presence of a permanent Indian community in Brunei in pre-colonial times, apart from visits by Indian merchants.

THE COLONIAL PERIOD:
THE ARRIVAL OF THE FIRST INDIANS

An Indian community began to develop in Brunei following the establishment of the British Residency in 1906. The British relied on personnel recruited mainly

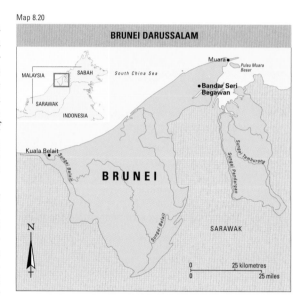

Map 8.20

in Malaya (including persons of Indian origin), and to a lesser extent in India, to staff the new administrative institutions and commercial enterprises they established in Brunei. The first Indians in Brunei were Punjabi and Sikh policemen, some of whom had previously worked for the British North Borneo Company in neighbouring Sabah. Indians were also recruited in the plantation and petroleum industries.

World War II interrupted the political and economic development of Brunei. However, following the war there was a sharp increase in the number of immigrant workers, particularly Chinese, and to a much lesser extent Indians. Malayalis, who had previously worked in the Middle East, formed most of the drilling crews in the oil fields. Rising oil revenue in the post-war period made a rapid expansion of state institutions possible, allowing the recruitment of qualified expatriate staff, including many Indians. Engineers from South Asia, particularly from Ceylon, played an important role in the construction of the physical infrastructure under the Public Works Department. Many Indians were employed in the education sector as teachers and in the health sector as doctors, nurses and technicians. Indian lawyers, particularly from Malaysia, began practising in Brunei, where civil and criminal law is still based on British Indian law. In 1962, Brunei experienced a rebellion that was put down with the help of British Gurkha troops. Since then, Gurkha soldiers have continued to play an important role in Brunei's security, both in the British Gurkha regiment guarding the oil installations and in the Gurkha Reserve Unit employed directly by the government to protect state institutions.

DEVELOPMENTS FOLLOWING INDEPENDENCE

Following independence in 1984, the government adopted a policy of localisation with regard to the public sector workforce. Brunei's economy depends primarily on oil

In the period after World War II, Malayalis were heavily employed in Brunei's petroleum industry. Their numbers declined considerably when the government adopted a policy of localisation after independence in 1984.

Indian-run businesses in Brunei have been successful in recent years for two reasons. The first reason lies in their tightly-knit social networks. The various economic niches in which Indians operate in Brunei tend to be dominated by particular communities which are defined by caste or religious and geographical origin. These networks tend to form as kinsmen from the same place in India help each other to migrate. Business, family and community intersect to link individuals and other businesses into large networks with access to bureaucracy and capable of mobilising labour and capital.

Transcending caste, religious or regional identities are a number of organisations, such as the Indian Association of Brunei-Muara (one of the oldest community organisations in Brunei), the Indian Association of Kuala Belait, and the Indian Chamber of Commerce, which serve as focal points of the Indian community, but are not really in a position to represent their interests vis-à-vis outsiders.

The second reason for the success of Indian enterprises in Brunei is the fact that these businesses rely almost entirely on male migrant labour from India, which keeps the cost of labour—in terms of accommodation, food and social services—low. Their families remain in India and depend on their remittances. Due to the marked imbalance in the gender ratio, the Indian community hardly grows, a situation exacerbated by the high turnover of migrants.

In some ways, Indian migration to Brunei follows the same pattern as that of other countries in Southeast Asia. The migrants come from the same communities and places, and inhabit the same economic niches as Indians in Malaysia, for example. Indeed, some of them have come to Brunei via Malaysia. In other aspects, however, the Indians in Brunei are very different from Indian communities elsewhere in the region. They are almost exclusively a transient community and nearly all of them will eventually leave Brunei to return to their place of origin. Only a tiny number of Indians have been granted permanent resident status, and even fewer the status of citizens, usually as a result of intermarriage with Bruneians, which in some cases has led to the beginning of a process of 'de-Indianisation' and assimilation into the dominant Malay community.

Frank Fanselow

revenue and the state can afford to employ some 70 per cent of the local (mostly Malay) workforce under conditions considerably more favourable than the Chinese-dominated private sector. As a result of this localisation policy, there has been a marked decline in the number of Indians working in government jobs, such as teachers and engineers. Today, Indians in government employment only remain in highly specialised positions, for which there is still a shortage of qualified local manpower, such as in the health and tertiary education sectors.

While there has been a sharp decline in the number of Indians in the public sector, their numbers have dramatically increased in lower-skilled jobs in the private sector, into which it is difficult to recruit locals as they prefer better-paid government jobs. The post-independence construction boom attracted many Indian and Bangladeshi workers. A few decades earlier, unskilled local workers had worked under the direction of engineers from South Asia, but these days, manual workers from South Asia work under local engineers.

The boom in the construction industry has largely passed, and so many Indian workers from the industry have left; but in the last decade, Indians have nearly monopolised certain niches of the retail and service sectors. These Indians are predominantly from South India and are mostly Tamils, many of them Muslims. They often operate in economic niches that have long been characteristic of their respective communities in India itself and among Indians in Southeast Asia. Examples of these are the many barber shops (*kedai gunting*) which are run by members of the Tamil Maruttuvar caste, laundry shops (*dhobi*) run by the Vannan from Tamil Nadu, and textile and tailoring shops (*kedai jahit*) run by members of various weaving groups from North and South India as well as Bangladesh. Almost the entire urban sector of grocery stores (*kedai runcit*), previously dominated by the Chinese, has in the last decade been taken over by Tamils, mostly Marakkayar Muslims from centres along the Coromandel Coast, such as Negapatnam and Nagercoil. Some of these shops evolve into coffee shops (*kedai kopi*) selling Indian Muslim food. Recently, the most successful Indian businessmen have developed these small-scale street-corner businesses into larger modern enterprises, such as department stores, chains of shops and restaurants and wholesale import companies. In these areas too, they have successfully competed with the Chinese, who had traditionally dominated the private retail and wholesale sectors of the economy.

Nazmi Textile Mall is named after its Indian Muslim owner, who came to Brunei as a trader, and built the largest chain of textile stores in the kingdom.

A shop belonging to the C. A. Mohamed family, one of the prominent families of Indian origin in Brunei. Mohamed came to Brunei in 1929 to work in the oil fields. He later opened a canteen for Indian oil workers and set up a spice shop. Today, the family owns several shops and restaurants serving Indo-Malay food.

HONG KONG

INDIANS STARTED SETTLING in Hong Kong in 1841, when the British army gained control over the territory. The army had recruited many of its soldiers in India for the expansion of the Empire to the Far East. Indian soldiers contributed to Britain's victory over China in the First Opium War (1839–42). As a result, Hong Kong became a British colony and China had to open a number of its ports, called the 'Treaty Ports', to foreign trade. Their growing economies motivated the immigration of many Chinese and non-Chinese, including traders, employees, police constables, soldiers and government clerks from India.

Until the middle of the 20th century, soldiers, police constables and traders were the largest groups of Indian immigrants. From the second half of the 20th century, when Hong Kong's economy expanded, the immigration of Indians accelerated in both higher-skilled and lower-skilled occupations. The largest group of Indian migrants were those engaged in trade. The return of Hong Kong to China in 1997 did not result in a drop in the number of Indian residents because China maintained Hong Kong's free trade policies. At the beginning of the 21st century, Indians in Hong Kong included academics, bankers, doctors, investors, journalists, office workers, traders, restaurant owners, security guards and tailors. Table 8.18 shows the official estimates of the number of Indian residents, excluding soldiers. For the years before 1947, the estimates include individuals with passports issued in India, and with origins in India or Ceylon. The estimates for 1961 and 1966, however, do not count Indian residents separately, but include them in the category of non-Chinese 'East Asians'. Those for 1991 and 1996 refer to Indian, Pakistani and Sri Lankan residents.

Even before Hong Kong became a British colony, Muslims, Sephardic Jews and Parsis from India lived in the nearby southern Chinese city of Canton (Guangzhou), which was the only place in China where foreign merchants were allowed to trade. Their main activity was the import of opium and cotton from India and the export of silver, tea and spices from China. There were 41 Parsi and 32 British merchants living in Canton in 1831. When Hong Kong became a colony, many of the foreign traders in Canton moved their offices to Hong Kong because of greater political stability. Ebrahim Noordin, a Bohra Muslim, was one of the first traders from India to open offices in Hong Kong. Some of his descendants were still in the territory at the beginning of the 21st century. Selling provisions to the British garrison or working for the colonial administration also brought Indians to Hong Kong, in addition to the Muslims and Sikhs whom the Royal Hong Kong Police had recruited in Punjab. The police force recruited Indian constables because its earlier attempts at setting up a group composed exclusively of Chinese constables had failed. Indians were perceived as more loyal to the British. In 1898, for example, the Royal Hong Kong Police employed 296 Chinese, 226 Indians and 112 Europeans. Unlike the Chinese constables, the Indian policemen were given firearms.

CHANGES IN THE 20TH CENTURY

With the decline of trade between India and China in the early 20th century, a number of Indian merchants left Hong Kong, and many of those who stayed started stock-broking firms or invested in property. Changes also took place among the soldiers in the British garrison. With the independence of India from Britain in 1947, most Indian soldiers returned to India and Pakistan. They were replaced with Gurkhas from Nepal. The number of Indian police constables in Hong Kong also gradually declined after the 1950s because the police force started to replace them with Chinese recruits. After leaving the army and the police force, a smaller number of Indians remained in Hong Kong to work as watchmen, open restaurants or start small businesses. Although Hong Kong's economy had come to a standstill during the Japanese Occupation (1941–45), it expanded rapidly after the 1950s, which increased the migration of Indians to Hong Kong in the second half of the 20th century. This expansion was due,

Indians, particularly Sindhis, opened numerous tailor shops in the Tsim Sha Tsui area in the second half of the 20th century.

Table 8.18

NUMBER OF INDIAN RESIDENTS IN HONG KONG (1845–2001)				
	Total	Male	Female	Children
1845	362	346	12	4
1855	391	213	79	99
1861	784	701	54	29
1870	1435	1394	18	23
1876	639	613	15	11
1901	1453	1108	345	N.A.
1911	2012	1548	464	N.A.
1931	4745	3989	756	N.A.
1941	7379	N.A.	N.A.	N.A.
1961	20,286	N.A.	N.A.	N.A.
1966	17,530–22,100	N.A.	N.A.	N.A.
1991	14,329	N.A.	N.A.	N.A.
1996	20,955	N.A.	N.A.	N.A.
2001	16,481	N.A.	N.A.	N.A.

Sources: K. N. Vaid, The Overseas Indian Community in Hong Kong, 1972 (for 1845 to 1966); and Hong Kong Special Administrative Region, Census 2001 (for 1991, 1996 and 2001).

Map 8.21

HONG KONG

GUANGDONG PROVINCE

Deep Bay

Mirs Bay

N

HONG KONG SPECIAL ADMINISTRATIVE REGION

NEW TERRITORIES

Kowloon

Hong Kong Island

Lantau Island

Lamma Island

SOUTH KOREA

JAPAN

CHINA

South China Sea

TAIWAN

0   10 kilometres
0   10 miles

at least in part, to the large number of refugees who had fled the civil war in China, significantly increasing Hong Kong's labour force. Many of the newer immigrants from India were traders who made use of their diasporic networks, exchanging a wide variety of goods. The 1947 partition of the subcontinent motivated many Sindhis to move to Hong Kong and they became the largest group of Indians in the territory, although a few prominent Sindhi families, such as the Gidumals and the Harilelas, had already settled in Hong Kong in the early 20th century. Sindhis made significant contributions to Hong Kong's export economy, especially to the Middle East and Africa. By the turn of the 21st century, Gujarati traders came to rival the number of Sindhis in Hong Kong.

Globalisation, with its acceleration of transnational movements of individuals and capital, explains why Indians in Hong Kong became engaged in a wide variety of economic activities towards the end of the 20th century, although trade remained prominent. With a few exceptions, the distinguishing factor between these Indians and those who had been in Hong Kong in the second half of the 19th century and the early 20th century was that the latter group placed less importance on having networks with individuals in Hong Kong to help with their integration. In 2001, there were 16,500 Indians living in Hong Kong (although non-official estimates of their number are higher), and they are responsible for nearly 10 per cent of Hong Kong's exports. With the territory's population approaching 7 million in 2005, their contributions to trade are disproportionate to their number.

CULTURAL AND SOCIAL TRANSFORMATIONS

While there is no single pattern that describes how the different cultural and social characteristics of Indians in Hong Kong changed, distinct transformations can be discerned according to how groups of Indians maintained links with Indians living elsewhere and constructed their own ethnic communities in Hong Kong. Throughout their settlement history, Bohra Muslims remained a tightly-knit community with strong links to Bohra communities in India and elsewhere. In the second half of the 19th century, maintaining shared traditions supported the economic activities of the community in Hong Kong, who traded almost exclusively through Bohra networks. Bohra offices in Hong Kong, such as Kaymally and Co., served as their meeting places and provided religious facilities. Twentieth-century Bohras in Hong Kong, most of whom were not descendants of those who settled in the territory earlier, no longer exclusively employed co-religionists in their offices. However, this change in business practices did not alter the fact that maintaining cultural links with co-religionists in India remained the defining characteristic of the Bohras' identity in Hong Kong. They traditionally follow the guidance of their successive religious leaders, called *dais*, who live in Mumbai. Adhering to this centralised religious leadership favoured strong traditions and largely prevented exogamy. Given that Bohras in Hong Kong were a small community consisting of approximately 180 individuals in 2000, the turnover of its members, and especially the immigration of Bohras from India, also counteracted partial assimilation with Western and Chinese culture.

The settlement of Parsis from Bombay and Gujarat in Hong Kong included an extended period of Anglicisation, lasting well into the middle of the 20th century. The Westernisation of Parsis has its roots in the restrictions

that were placed on them when they settled in India centuries ago. During the 17th century, Parsis in India adopted elements of Western culture to promote their work as middlemen for British and other European traders who opened offices in the subcontinent. This cooperation made many Parsis prosperous, and a number of them built dockyards to engage in long-distance trade. Some of those trading with the Far East opened offices in Hong Kong in the second half of the 19th century. Parsi resources and trading skills were valued by Britain, which bestowed a number of privileges upon them, including the licence to sell liquor in its territories in the East.

This was important in launching the career of Hormusjee Ruttonjee in Hong Kong at the turn of the 20th century. He and other prosperous Parsi merchants in Hong Kong, such as Hormusjee Mody, were also

Indian and Chinese constables of the Royal Hong Kong Police standing for inspection in 1906. Unlike their Indian counterparts, Chinese constables were not given firearms. Sikhs filled most of the positions in the Armed Constabulary Section by 1870.

Dr Hari N. Harilela

Members of the Harilela family, and Dr Hari N. Harilela in particular, play a leading role in supporting the social and economic interests of the Indian communities in Hong Kong. They are the descendants of Naroomal Mirchandani from Hyderabad, Sind, who settled in Canton as a trader at the turn of the 20th century. During the recession in America in the 1930s, he lost his entire fortune and moved with his family to Hong Kong. Dr Harilela, who was born in 1922, recalls that he had to give up his schooling to hawk goods to the soldiers of the British garrison. There, he befriended Indian Muslims who were commissioned to tailor jodhpurs and he learned their skills. This eventually launched the Harilelas into mail-order tailoring, with 600 tailors under their employ. They continued to prosper by investing in numerous other ventures, including hotels. Dr Harilela, who speaks fluent Cantonese, holds key positions in many Indian organisations in the territory, among them, permanent honorary president of the Indian Chamber of Commerce. He is also a justice of the peace, serves the Hong Kong General Chamber of Commerce, and is a Hong Kong Affairs Adviser to the People's Republic of China. He has received honours from numerous organisations, among them, the Gold Bauhinia Star from the government of the Hong Kong Special Administrative Region and the Pravasi Bharatiya Samman (the non-resident Indian award) from the Ministry of Overseas Indians for his services to India and its diaspora. What is distinctive about the Harilelas is that many members of their extended family live together in a large Mughal-style mansion which they built in Hong Kong. This house may accommodate up to 100 individuals, including servants. The Harilelas explain that they adhere to this lifestyle because they gain strength from family cohesion.

Dr Harilela (centre) and his wife welcome Jawaharlal Nehru (left) during his visit to Hong Kong in 1957.

The main building of the University of Hong Kong was built thanks to a donation from Hormusjee Mody, a prominent Parsi trader and philanthropist.

Sikhs work as security guards in modern-day Hong Kong.

Muslims praying in Jamaia Masjid, Hong Kong's oldest mosque, in Shelly Street. It was built in 1915 by a Muslim merchant from India.

renowned philanthropists. In 1912, Mody took the initiative to establish Hong Kong's first university, the University of Hong Kong. In 1948, Ruttonjee established the Ruttonjee Tuberculosis Sanatorium. Despite Anglicisation, Parsis never accepted exogamy, and as of early 2005 they still excluded individuals with non-Zoroastrian fathers from their religious activities, the core of Parsi community life. Nonetheless, a few Parsi men married Chinese women in the late 19th and 20th century, and intermarriages with Westerners were in place by the late 20th century. However, the large majority of Parsis continued to look for spouses from the much larger Parsi community in Bombay and in Zoroastrian communities in other parts of the world. This explains why, at the start of the 21st century, Parsis in Hong Kong asserted that they were first and foremost Indians.

Throughout their settlement history, the descendants of Sunni Muslims from India who had married Chinese women integrated strongly into Chinese culture. The fact that the Sunnis in Hong Kong were culturally a heterogeneous group supported this practice. They had migrated from different regions in India, so they did not necessarily share languages, kinship structures, diasporic networks or lifestyles. This hindered the establishment of a social network in the territory that could have easily integrated female immigrants with women from similar regions of origin. A number of Sunnis from India married Chinese women who converted to Islam. The relative prosperity of the Sunnis made such marriages more acceptable among segments of Hong Kong's Chinese population. The children from these cross-cultural marriages usually remained Muslims but rarely maintained links with India or spoke any language other than Cantonese and English. It was not uncommon for daughters to remain celibate and to work.

Less integrated into Chinese culture were Muslims and Sikhs who worked in the police force and the army. For an extended period of time, these police constables were not allowed to marry Chinese women. They were employed on temporary contracts and many were not allowed to bring their families from India to Hong Kong. Like the soldiers from India, they saw themselves as sojourners. Believing that they would eventually leave the territory, they had little incentive to make significant changes to their cultural identities. Despite other disadvantages in relation to their British colleagues, such as lower salaries and more limited career prospects, police constables and soldiers from India were mostly loyal to their British employers. When Hong Kong was attacked by the Japanese in 1940, more than 1000 Indian soldiers lost their lives in its defence. The Muslims' and Sikhs' good reputation for protective services in the colony made them popular as private guards for the factories and offices of Chinese and Western residents. The opportunities for private employment led some of them to resign from the police and the army, and motivated prospective immigrants from India. To support their endeavours in Hong Kong, both Muslims and Sikhs established communal male dormitories, which offered them an inexpensive place to live in as well as access to an informal job market. These dormitories also supported links with relatives in India, facilitating an eventual return.

Sindhi immigrants also continued to define their cultural identities primarily in relation to their home province, but many of them assimilated with Chinese culture to some extent by learning to speak Cantonese. They felt it necessary to do so because unlike many merchants from India who had settled in Hong Kong in the second half of the 19th century, Sindhi traders were rarely able to employ middlemen to negotiate their transactions with the Chinese. Yet as members of a larger ethnic community in Hong Kong with a fairly homogeneous cultural identity, Sindhis—and Gujaratis—did not experience great difficulty in relying on their transnational networks and ethnic communities in Hong Kong to support their distinct traditions. However, those living in Hong Kong for an extended period of time, especially during its colonial period, intertwined their traditions

with aspects of Western culture. Their prominence explains why Sindhis took leading roles in advocating the trading interests of the wider Indian community in Hong Kong. Sindhis were instrumental in founding the Indian Chamber of Commerce in 1952, which obtained permission from the government to issue certificates of origin for exported goods produced in Hong Kong.

A very strong sense of ethnicity is maintained among Jain diamond traders. Most of them moved to Hong Kong after the 1970s, working in branches of Indian-based family businesses which employ relatives and individuals from the same place of origin in senior positions. Jains closely intertwine family, business and religion to assure secrecy and trust, which they deem crucial for their trade. Their leading role in trading diamonds from India further explains why they have little motivation to alter their identities, although many of their clients are Chinese. Rather, Jains maintain the characteristics of an ethnic enclave, socialising with co-religionists and other individuals from Gujarat and Rajasthan.

From the mid-20th century, it became more common for entire immediate families, instead of just men, to move to Hong Kong, and this had significant implications for the organisation of Indian communities in the territory. The quest to maintain distinct traditions became more pronounced because entire families now had to address the fact that they were a minority culture in Hong Kong. To increase the pride of young people in their cultural heritage and involve women in more social activities, several new cultural associations were founded. Such associations offered a wider range of social activities than those offered by the Indians' existing religious associations. The first two of these organisations were the India Club, founded in 1941, and the India Association, established in 1948. They promoted social events, sports and Indian art and culture. In subsequent years, associations based on regions of origin were established to celebrate the diversity of Indian customs in Hong Kong.

POLITICAL CHANGES

Before the 1960s, there were no restrictions against migration from Hong Kong to Britain. However, with Britain's gradual withdrawal from its colonies, it wished to prevent large-scale immigration from these territories. Uncertainty over the territory's political future motivated Indians to found the Council of Hong Kong Indian Associations in 1973. The council's aim was to persuade Britain to grant British citizenship to Indians in Hong Kong. Unfortunately, its efforts towards this goal were unsuccessful. In 1981, Britain introduced the status of British Dependent Territories Citizens for the residents of its colonies, which disqualified them from obtaining British citizenship. This was given to only a few hundred Indians before Hong Kong's return to Chinese sovereignty in 1997. At that time, Indians could not become Chinese citizens and they were concerned that their descendants in Hong Kong would become stateless.

Many long-term Indian residents consider themselves 'Hong Kongers'. They are proud to maintain their distinct cultures, yet they feel that Hong Kong is their home, especially because many of them have

made it the base for their economic activities. In fact, since 2002, non-Chinese permanent residents in Hong Kong have been able to apply for Hong Kong Special Administrative Region passports (i.e. for Chinese citizenship), and this is evidence of their identification with the territory. However, as of early 2005, only very few such passports have been issued to non-ethnic Chinese individuals.

The beginning of the 21st century marked the beginning of two more political developments with a significant bearing on the lives of many Indian residents. One was the debate over whether anti-racial discrimination policies should be introduced and how these will be implemented. The death of a woman of Indian origin in the Ruttonjee Hospital in 2000 sparked a public reaction against racism. Individuals and NGOs urged the government to introduce anti-racial discrimination legislation. The second development was the public attention given to the difficulties children of ethnic minorities encounter when studying in Hong Kong's public schools. After 1997, most schools changed their medium of instruction from English to Chinese. By 2004, Hong Kong's Education and Manpower Bureau had started to pay attention to the problems that these children face in finding places in public schools, and in pursuing their studies in Chinese. Improvements in these areas are likely to increase the integration of Indians into the Hong Kong Special Administrative Region.

Caroline Pluss

Indians playfully celebrate the festival of Holi.

Gurda Singh shows support for China's claim on the Diaoyu Islands, September 1996.

The Council of Hong Kong Indian Associations, an apex body formed by a number of Indian organisations in Hong Kong, has been actively lobbying the British Government to re-consider the status being provided for the non-Chinese ethnic minority population of Hong Kong who are British Dependent Territory Citizens [BDTC]. ...BDTC status for people from Hong Kong will cease in 1997 and all BDTC will be able to acquire the newly-created title of BNO (British Nationals Overseas) from 1st July 1987. Since this status cannot be transmitted to future generations born after 1997...the children and grandchildren of the minorities [in Hong Kong] are being provided with another form of nationality—that of BOC (British Overseas Citizens). However, the third generation will be born stateless. It is understandable why the minorities are unhappy with the above arrangement as the BNO [status] will not provide them with effective citizenship.

Extract from K. Sital, A Place Under the Sun: 1997 and the Hong Kong Indians, 1986.

A diamond trader in Hong Kong.

CHINA

Buddhist art in the renowned cave temples of Dunhuang, at the edge of the Gobi Desert, in north-western China. Dunhuang was on the Silk Road and was an important centre in terms of China's contact with Buddhist India.

AS EARLY AS the 1st century AD, Indian traders settled in the present-day province of Yunnan in southern China, bordering India. Negotiating the difficult territories of the southern silk routes through northeast India and northern Burma, Indians traded in textiles, handicrafts, crystals, herbs and pearls. The Chinese patronage of Buddhism also led to the search for learned Buddhist monks from India, the first of whom were Kasyapa Matanga and Dharmaratna, who arrived in the Chinese capital during the reign of Emperor Ming between 58–75 AD. Kumarajiva was the next Indian known to have settled in the Chinese capital in the 4th century AD: he was honoured as the 'Imperial Guru'. A great many Indian monks migrated to China and other countries between the 6th and 13th centuries.

Indians made a special contribution in the field of astronomy. Among the best known astronomers was Gautama Zhuan (712–776 AD), who was the director of the Bureau of Astronomy at the Tang court. Indian artisans, painters, sculptors and musicians travelled to China during the golden age of the Tang dynasty (618–907 AD). The three great Buddhist centres of Dunhuang, Longmen and Yunkang, located along the Silk Road in northwestern China, show the profound influence Indians had on Chinese painting, sculpture and architecture.

At the close of the 12th century, Chinese shipping had developed considerably. In South India, the rise of Chola power saw an increase in its naval strength. The growing importance of Chinese trade drew the attention of the Chola king, marking the beginning of maritime trade between China and South India. From the 11th to the 15th centuries, Indian—especially Tamil—merchants and sailors settled all over Southeast Asia and southern and southeastern China. A parallel migration saw the arrival of maritime merchants from Fujian province moving from coastal southern China to Calcutta.

From the late 15th century, Indian traders continued to be active in the Indian Ocean and traded goods with their Chinese counterparts. Their meeting points were not at the Chinese ports but in Melaka, which had become the principal entrepôt in the Malay archipelago from the late 15th century. By this time, Cambay and Surat had superseded Calicut and the Gujarati traders gradually took over. The Portuguese occupation of Melaka in 1511 did not displace the Indian traders. There was a brief revival of Indian trade with Southeast Asia and China at the end of the 17th century, but Indian shipping and trade was declining during the first part of 18th century.

During the second half of the 18th century, there was a revival of Indian trade with China following the extension of the British-sponsored and Bombay-based China trade. Parsi traders went out on their own in search of profitable businesses. Still, the dominant section of them acted as agents of British commercial establishments. Unlike the traditional trade between India and China, 18th- and 19th-century Chinese trade was mainly an offshoot of British trade, which consisted of bulk raw cotton and, later, the opium trade. The East India Company, finding it increasingly difficult to procure the required amount of bullion to pay for Chinese goods, such as tea and silk, began to export raw Indian cotton, textiles and opium.

Map 8.22

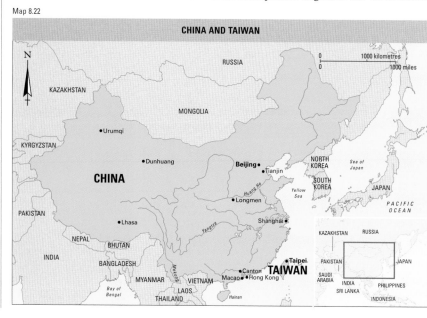

CHINA AND TAIWAN

It was in this context that Indian traders started arriving in China. They arrived in small numbers from Bombay in the ports of Macao and Canton on the southern China coast. With the increase in the cotton and opium trade, and with opportunities for trade with China in the 'Treaty Ports' and the newly acquired British colony of Hong Kong after the first Opium War in 1840, the number of Indian traders and businessmen in China increased.

SETTLEMENTS AFTER THE OPIUM WAR

From the middle of the 19th century, the size of the Indian community in China further expanded with the arrival of successive contingents of soldiers, policemen and watchmen from India. Indians in the security services played a major role in Britain's military contingents and were stationed in numerous garrisons in eastern China, including Hong Kong, Shanghai, Canton and Tianjin.

At Xinjiang in the western region of China, the Indian community comprised traders and moneylenders from Punjab, Sind and Kashmir who trekked over the mountain ranges dividing India and China. They became familiar faces in the bazaars of southern Xinjiang. A number of them settled permanently in this region. By the early 1930s, the tentative estimate of the total number of Indians was about 10,000, of which approximately 5000 were in Hong Kong, 3000–4000 in Shanghai and the other cities and towns of eastern China, and about 1000 in Xinjiang.

However, Indians were uprooted during the turbulent period of war and revolution in China in the 1930s and 1940s. Barring the Indians in Hong Kong, who continued to thrive, almost nothing was left of the community on the Chinese mainland after 1949.

After attaining independence from British colonial rule in 1947, India maintained cordial relations with China. The two jointly initiated Pancha Shila (Five Principles of Peaceful Co-existence) in the 1950s, and cordial relations continued until the Chinese attack on the northern border of India in 1962. That border dispute has not been fully resolved and has severely strained the relationship between the two countries. However, there has been some improvement with the signing of the 'Agreement on the Maintenance, Peace and Tranquillity along the Line of Actual Control in the India-China Border Areas' in 1993. The turn of the century saw an increase in the number of tourists and other types of visitors to China, but the number of Indians residing there remains small.

TAIWAN

Until recently, with the exception of the influx from mainland China in the mid-20th century, there has been relatively little immigration to Taiwan. From the 1980s, the island faced severe labour shortages, partly due to a declining birth rate. Between 1952 and 1988, Taiwan went through a demographic transition and the annual rate of natural increase in its population fell from 3.7 per cent to 1.2 per cent. This shortage is particularly evident in blue-collar industries because Taiwan's educated population has higher job expectations.

Continued economic growth at more than 8 per cent exacerbated the problem of labour shortages. For many years the government opposed the introduction of unskilled labour from foreign countries. This resulted in the flow of illegal migrant workers from other Asian countries, estimated at 45,000 in 1991. Until 1992, instead of recruiting workers from China, Taiwanese entrepreneurs were outsourcing work to the mainland. In 1992, Taiwan approved a law which lifted a ban on the migration of Chinese workers.

In 2001, the total number of persons of Indian origin in Taiwan was about 1800. Despite their relatively small number, the Indian community is the eighth largest expatriate community in Taiwan, after Thailand, the Philippines, Vietnam, Indonesia, the US, Japan and Malaysia. The community can be categorised by the professions of its members.

The first category comprises businessmen of Sindhi origin. At their peak in 1982–83, there were about 250 families of about 1200 individuals. In 2004, there were only about 80 in Taiwan. The average net worth of each family is about US$1 million; there are about four or five families with a net worth in excess of US$5 million. Almost all of them are engaged in the import/export trade, though not with India. With Taiwan's economy slowing down and mainland China offering increasingly attractive prospects, the Indian population has been declining, with some relocating to mainland China instead.

The second category consists of diamond merchants from Gujarat. There were about 50 families in this category, most of whom arrived between 2000–05. They are well off and their numbers have increased since diamonds became an increasingly important Indian export to Taiwan.

There are about 150 Indians engaged in scientific work, generally on two-year contracts. Although they maintain a low profile, they are highly regarded. There are also some 80–100 software engineers and professionals from India, most of whom are single. Some are married, but their wives and children remain in India. The number of individuals in this group is expected to increase. India-based companies, such as Tata Consultancy Services and WIPRO, have small offices in Taiwan. There are also 10–15 other Indian professionals working for MNCs and banks, and approximately 200 others who are self-employed or engaged in a variety of businesses, including restaurants, real estate agencies and travel agencies.

Businessmen of Sindhi origin were the earliest to migrate to Taiwan. Their peak migration period was the early 1980s. Almost all of them are engaged in the import/export trade. During the 1990s, the first Gujarati diamond merchants arrived. The later group of migrants were scientists, software engineers and other professionals, who arrived during the second half of 1990s. The Indian community maintains a very low profile in Taiwan and has very little organised interaction with other communities.

B. A. Prakash

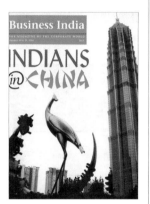

An issue of Business India *magazine, which featured an article on increasing Indian business activity in China.*

A Chinese military delegation crosses the India–China border on 15 August 2004 to take part in India's 58th Independence Day celebrations in Bomdila, the headquarters of the West Kameng district in Arunachal Pradesh.

JAPAN

THE RELATIONSHIP BETWEEN India and Japan has a long history and is rooted in shared spiritual values. This relationship began eight centuries ago, when Buddhism found its way through the trade routes of China to Japan. Direct contact between the people of the two countries gained momentum only after the mid-19th century. In the 1860s, a few Indian scholars, mainly from Maharashtra, arrived in Tokyo to pursue higher education. They were soon joined by commercial migrants from India. Treaties signed between the US and Japan in 1854 and 1858 resulted in the expansion of Japanese commercial and trade relations with other countries. This marked the beginning of commercial ties between India and Japan, albeit on a small scale.

Around the 1870s, Indian businessmen began to travel to Yokohama and Kobe to buy Japanese produce, particularly silk. Japanese–Indian trade linkages encouraged the gradual migration of traders and businessmen to Japan. This movement, initially to Yokohama, was the focal point of the silk trade in Japan, although later, a large number of Indian migrants moved to Kobe as it became prominent as a trading centre for Asian countries. The movement of commercial migrants intensified in the last two decades of the 19th century. Trade between the two countries expanded following the opening of shipping routes to Calcutta in 1910 and Madras in 1936.

By the beginning of the 20th century, Indians in Japan had founded their own social organisations. In 1902, Indian students in Tokyo established the Hindustan Association and, in Kobe, the Oriental Young Men's Club. That same year, some Japanese interested in Indian culture and seeking to foster Indo-Japanese relations founded the Japan-India Club with the support of Indian residents in Tokyo. This marked the beginning of the

Map 8.23

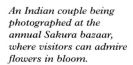

A Japanese bride and an Indian bridegroom getting married in a traditional Indian ceremony.

An Indian couple being photographed at the annual Sakura bazaar, where visitors can admire flowers in bloom.

Indo-Japanese Association. The Indian Merchants' Association was established in Yokohama in 1921.

In 1923, 36 Indians were reported to have died in Yokohama following the Great Kanto Earthquake. At the time, there were some 50 Indian trading firms in Yokohama. The tragedy led Indians to move from Yokohama to Kobe, where they were provided with relief by Indian social organisations based there. In the aftermath of the quake, a number of the remaining Indian businesses regrouped to form the Yokohama Silk Trade Reconstructive Association, which gave incentives to attract Indian trading companies to return to the city. Nearly 10 Indian firms returned to Yokohama, but Kobe would become the main social and commercial centre of Indian businessmen until the 1970s.

The first half of the 20th century saw a constant increase in the number of Indian commercial migrants and trading firms in Japan. This occurred in spite of the adverse effects of the Indo-Japanese Trade Treaty of 1934, which imposed import controls on general textiles and raised import duties on general merchandise. Between 1923 and 1939, the number of Indian trading firms increased from approximately 120 to 200. By 1939, the total number of Indians in Kobe alone was estimated at 600.

DEVELOPMENTS DURING WORLD WAR II

The war of 1939–45 witnessed the deterioration of trade and commercial linkages between India and Japan. This had a critical impact on Indian firms based in Japan. A large number of Indian firms were forced to close, and many Indian commercial migrants relocated to Bangkok, Singapore and Rangoon. In Kobe alone, where the Indian population stood at 632 in early 1939, their numbers had declined to 40 by the year's end.

When Japan joined the war on 8 December 1941, Indians in the country were treated with hostility and were incarcerated in a detention centre for foreigners. However, the situation underwent radical change with the arrival of Subhas Chandra Bose, who formed the Azad Hind Army and sought the help of the Japanese government in his fight against British rule in India. This brought about a change in the attitude of the Japanese towards Indian nationals. The Japanese government supported the Azad Hind Army of Bose and the Indian independence movement led by him. Many Indians arrived in Tokyo for military training during that period.

When the war began, the total number of Indians living in Japan was approximately 1000. During the war, over 600 left for India, although many returned soon after the war ended. The post-war period was characterised by the revival of Indian migration to Japan. One of the reasons for the increase in the movement of Indian businessmen during this period was the boom in the textile trade. During the 1950s, Indian businessmen were also involved in the pearl trade and a number of them opened garment shops that catered to US military personnel and their families. The 1960s and 1970s saw a continued increase in the number of Indians in Japan, although as a percentage of the total population, it remained relatively insignificant.

THE CONTEMPORARY SITUATION

The recent movement of Indians to Japan is different from the earlier patterns of migration. The 1980s and 1990s saw an increase in the number of both labour and professional migrants settled in various locations. In 1984, 41 per cent of the total number of Indians lived in Hiyogo prefecture, and 26.1 per cent in Tokyo. By 1997, Tokyo had the highest number of Indians, showing an increase of 3.8 per cent, and exceeded Hiyogo in importance. There was a decline in the number of Indians in Okinawa and Yamaguchi, while numbers in Saitama, Chiba and Ibaragi, in addition to Tokyo, increased.

The new migrants have largely remained aloof from Indian social organisations in Japan. Many deviated from what were regarded as traditional 'Indian occupations'. A number were workers with low wages, some of whom were employed as cooks in restaurants. Following the liberalisation of the Indian economy in 1991, many Japanese firms have invested in India, building factories for the production of automobiles and other industrial products. The development of these industrial units resulted in a number of Indians going to Japan to undergo training.

In 2001, there were about 10,000 Indians in Japan, consisting of 9000 non-resident Indians and 1000 persons of Indian origin. Most of them are concentrated in the Tokyo-Yokohama and Osaka-Kobe regions. Others are spread out in Nagoya, Okinawa, Sapporo, Sendai and Niigata.

The Indian trading community in Japan is financially well off and engaged mostly in the export of electronic goods, textiles, automobile parts and jewellery, as well as in the import of handicrafts, garments, precious stones and marine products from India. The non-trading community consists of students, engineers, exchange students and yoga practitioners, besides officials of the Indian government and public sector undertakings. The number of Indian engineers—particularly computer software engineers—increased substantially from 120 in 1993 to over 800 in 2000. There are approximately 60 academics and translators working in various universities. About 870 Indian cooks work in Indian restaurants, which are very popular in Japan. There are over 120 of these restaurants in Tokyo alone, most of which are owned and managed by Japanese. There is also a small Sindhi community in Okinawa that provides mainly tailoring services to the American army.

In the second half of the 1990s, Indians in areas of Tokyo formed an association of their own called the Indian Community Activities Tokyo (ICAT), which organises cultural functions, the main ones being the Holi Musical Evening, Deepavali Get Together and Sakura Ladies Charity Bazaar. The Deepavali function is the most popular and is attended by over 2500 persons of Indian origin in and around Tokyo. The three active associations of the Indian community in the Osaka-Kobe area are the Indian Social Society, the Indian Club and the Indian Chamber of Commerce and Industry. A few Indian religious organisations can also be found in Japan, such as the Ramakrishna Mission, which has a branch in the Osaka-Kobe area. There is also a gurdwara on the premises of Namaskar Indian Restaurant in Tokyo, where Sikh devotees meet twice a month. The Bengali and Marathi communities have also set up their own cultural organisations. Many of them perform classical, folk and film-based musical and dance items which are often exhibited at community functions and get-togethers.

Among the prominent commercial organisations in Japan are the Indian Merchants Association of Yokohama, the Indian Chamber of Commerce and Industry, the Japan-India Business Cooperation Committee and the Standing Committee of the Japan-India Business Cooperation.

Indians have adapted themselves fairly well in Japan and inter-community marriages are on the rise. It is apparent, however, that only a small number of Indians are Japanese citizens. Rules and regulations for acquiring Japanese citizenship remain very stringent, although these requirements are generic and not directed solely at Indians.

B. A. Prakash

Japanese performers at a cultural show playing classical Indian musical instruments, the tabla (left) and the sitar (right).

The Vedanta Kyokai, *a monthly newsletter of the* Vedanta Society of Japan, *which was founded in 1959.*

AFGHANISTAN, CENTRAL ASIA AND IRAN

LONG BEFORE THE Portuguese arrived via the Indian Ocean in 1498, vast networks of caste-based Indian family firms already dominated the commercial economy of India. The directors of these firms enlisted thousands of agents and trained them to engage in a huge variety of commercial activities. These included diverse money-lending operations in both urban and rural settings, brokering, money changing and large-scale transregional trade. During the period of European expansion in the Indian Ocean in the 16th and 17th centuries, some Indian family firms began aggressively expanding their own commercial interests by dispatching agents to distant markets beyond the boundaries of the subcontinent.

From the mid-16th century, Indian communities began to appear in port cities, urban centres and villages dotting the countryside across Afghanistan, Central Asia and Iran. In the 17th century, Indian merchants gradually moved northwards through the Caucasus and up the Volga river, reaching Moscow and St. Petersburg. The Indian merchants who travelled to these regions established communities of several hundred to several thousand Indians. The most important 'nodes' were found in the cities of Kabul and Qandahar (Kandahar) in Afghanistan, Bukhara (in modern Uzbekistan) in Central Asia, Bandar 'Abbas and Isfahan in Iran, and Astrakhan in Russia. Iran's central position in the Eurasian caravan trade made it a particularly attractive location for Indian merchants who flocked to the region in large numbers. By the mid-17th century, the Indian community of Isfahan, the capital of Safavid Iran, had as many as 15,000 Indian merchants. One contemporary European observer has suggested that there were more than 20,000 Indian

Indians in a caravanserai in Bukhara, c. 1890. Many observers reported that although smoking was outlawed, Indians were permitted to smoke freely in their caravanserais.

The Samarkand market area in the 1890s.

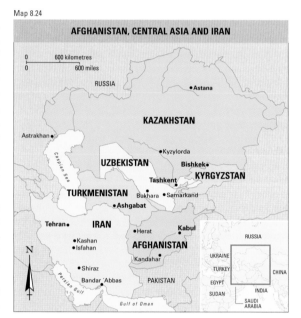

Map 8.24

AFGHANISTAN, CENTRAL ASIA AND IRAN

merchants living in Safavid Iran. At the time, Central Asia was home to an estimated 8000 Indian merchants, and a similar number are likely to have lived and worked in the urban and rural markets of Afghanistan.

TRADING COMMUNITIES

These Indian communities were predominantly populated by individuals referred to in the 16th and 17th centuries as 'Multanis', a designation that identifies them as agents (*gumashta*) of any of a number of heavily capitalised, caste-based family firms centred in the city of Multan in present-day Pakistan. While the associates of each individual Multani firm were restricted to a single caste, the term 'Multani' was more generally applied to the diverse conglomeration of Indian merchants who participated in commerce as agents of any one of those numerous firms. The vast majority of such individuals belonged to a variety of Hindu commercial castes, including the Khattris, Bohras, Bhatias, Lohanis and others. The diaspora was also religiously diverse: it had a significant minority of Muslim Multanis and smaller populations of Marwari Jain and, later, Sikh merchants.

The rise of Sikh communities was a result of the growing number of individuals and families in Northwest India who had abandoned the Hindu Khattri caste for the similarly commercial Sikh Khalsa. Since a significant number of Multani merchants were Khattris, it is probable that many, if not most, of the Sikh merchant families that came from Amritsar and who went on to establish communities in Afghanistan, Central Asia and Iran during the 18th and 19th centuries had ancestors who were fully engaged in similar commercial activities as Hindu Multanis.

The presence of significant numbers of Hindu (as well as Jain and Sikh) Indians in Muslim states—individuals

technically unprotected by the Islamic legal traditions generally honoured by the rulers of their host societies—makes the Indians' ubiquitous nature in these societies all the more remarkable. Despite their inferior status, the tens of thousands of Indians inhabiting this merchant community functioned in a unique economic position that the Muslim ruling elite regarded as crucial to the well-being of their society. These Indians were large-scale transregional traders who provided their host societies with necessary commodities and a market for their own products. Even more important, however, was the large amount of investment capital that these Indians brought to their host societies and their expertise in using this wealth as moneylenders in both urban and rural markets. It was for these reasons that the predominantly Hindu Indian merchant communities were nearly always welcomed and protected by the Afghan, Central Asian and Iranian states even in the 20th century.

AFGHANISTAN

Throughout much of the early modern era, the territory that is today Afghanistan was carved by three different governing powers: the Mughal Empire to the east, the Safavid Empire to the west and the Bukharan Khanate (or, from 1785, the Bukharan Amirate) to the north. The boundaries between these states fluctuated frequently and sometimes erratically: the city of Qandahar changed hands between the Mughals and the Safavids on a dozen occasions and, for a brief 18-month period under Shah Jahan (r. 1628–58), a Mughal army crossed the Hindu Kush and occupied Balkh, just 70 km south of the Amu Darya.

In the early decades of the 18th century, both the Mughal and Safavid empires began to decentralise, and as their spheres of authority retreated from the frontier zones, the pastoral tribes grew in strength. In 1722, a Ghilzai tribal confederation invaded Safavid territory, sacked the capital of Isfahan, and fatally weakened the Iranian state of Shah Tahmasp II (r. 1722–32). One Safavid commander, known at the time as Tahmasp Quli Khan, was able to eject the Ghilzai invaders from Iran and usurp government control for himself, tyrannically ruling as Nadir Shah from 1736 until he was assassinated in 1747. Following Nadir Shah's death, command of his eastern territories fell to a particularly skilled and loyal commander, Ahmad Khan of the Abdali tribe, and it is here that the initial stages of state formation in modern Afghanistan can be traced.

> *I feasted my eyes with the beauty of the bazar at Shikarpur. After passing through lanes closely peopled, I stepped into the large bazar, and found it full. There was no shop in which I did not observe half a dozen Khatri merchants, who appeared to me to have no time to speak to the purchasers. Such was the briskness of trade going on in the bazar...It occurred to me that the reason why Shikarpur surpasses Amritsar in wealth is, that its inhabitants, who are for the most part Khatris, have spread themselves in almost all the regions of Central Asia, whence they return loaded with gains to their families at Shikarpur. There is not so much commerce carried on at Shikarpur, I believe, as in Multan and Amritsar, but you will see all the shopkeepers writing Hoondees, or bills of exchange, which you can take in the name of their agents at Bombay, Sindh, the Panjab, Khorasan, Afghanistan, part of Persia, and Russia.*
>
> Mohan Lal, Travels in the Punjab, Afghanistan, Turkestan to Balk, Bukhara and Herat, *1846.*

Upon ascending to the throne at the age of 25, Ahmad Khan was renamed Ahmad Shah Durrani; 'Durrani' being a shortened form of *Durr-i Durran*, or 'Pearl of Pearls', a possible reference to his tendency to wear a pearl earring. Ahmad Shah declared the sovereign independence of his territory, Afghanistan, and he established his capital in the city of Qandahar. Looking eastward, towards the realm that he saw as his inheritance from Nadir Shah, Ahmad Shah and his tribal coalition clashed with the armies of the Mughals, Marathas and Sikhs. He extended his territory deep into Baluchistan and Sind, and similarly conquered much of Punjab and Kashmir.

Indian merchants had, by this time, long been present in cities and villages across the territory of Afghanistan, but their commercial presence took on a new importance with the rise of the Durrani Afghan state. While the Ghilzai Afghans and Nadir Shah had formerly used the 'unprotected' status of the Hindu Multanis as an excuse to confiscate their wealth, Ahmad Shah reversed these short-sighted and predatory policies. Instead, he protected the commercial interests of Indian merchants and encouraged them to establish communities throughout his territory, which they did in large numbers. During the course of his 25-year reign (1747–72), Ahmad Shah was able to use the commercial connections and investment capital of the Indians to add a considerable tax base to the economy of his largely pastoral-nomadic frontier region.

Developments from the late 18th century

By the end of the 18th century, following Mughal decentralisation, the city of Multan had suffered repeated invasions and turmoil which led many of the Multani firms to relocate to Shikarpur, a smaller city in the neighbouring province of Sind, which had been annexed by Ahmad Shah early in his reign. Compared to Multan, Shikarpur was a young urban centre of minor importance—it was

A lithograph of the city of Kandahar in the 1840s.

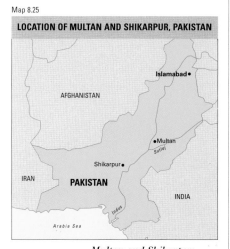

Map 8.25

LOCATION OF MULTAN AND SHIKARPUR, PAKISTAN

Multan and Shikarpur were at different times the central locations of Indian firms that sent agents to work in Afghanistan, Central Asia and Iran.

A lithograph of the king of Kabul with one of his sons, c. 1848.

founded in c. 1616 as a hunting retreat. However, the Multani merchant households found the city's location agreeable. It was firmly situated in Durrani territory and its proximity to the Indus offered access to ports along the Indian Ocean as well as the Bolan Pass route to Qandahar, Ahmad Shah's capital city, an important commercial centre and a diaspora node.

Thus, from the end of the 18th century, sources began to refer to significant numbers of 'Shikarpuris' (or 'Shikarpuri-Multanis') engaged in various commercial activities across urban and rural Afghanistan. Probably the largest Indian community in Afghanistan was in Kabul. In the 1840s, nearly 2000 of Kabul's total population of some 60,000 were Hindus. Alexander Burnes observed in Kabul no fewer than eight 'great houses of agency' (family firms) that were operated by some 300 families, and he himself took advantage of the Shikarpuris' financial services. While in Kabul, he reportedly cashed a *hundi* for Rs. 5000, for which the agents offered to issue additional *hundis* cashable at their offices in Nizhny Novgorod, Astrakhan or Bukhara, the latter of which Burnes readily accepted.

In the early modern era, Qandahar enjoyed a central position in the caravan trade of Mughal India, Safavid Iran and Uzbek Central Asia. Angus Hamilton mentions that Qandahar continued in this role even into the 20th century, at which time it was still home to some 300 Hindu families living in their own quarter of the town. Another large Indian node in Afghan-controlled territory was Qalat, Baluchistan; an important city on the trade routes connecting Qandahar with Multan, Shikarpur and the Indian ports to the south. Other sources note the commercial dominance of Hindu merchants in Faizabad, Taliqan, Khanabad and Tashkurgan (Khulum), as well as their activities in Jalalabad, Maimana, Ghazni, Lalpura and, in the 19th century, Mazar-i Sharif. The wealth of these communities and their relationship with the state are illustrated by the report that, in the mid-1830s, the Durrani Amir in Kabul, Dost Muhammad (r. 1826–39, 1843–63), raised nearly Rs. 500,000 for his military with loans from Hindu and Muslim merchants and

by collecting the *jizya* (a tax that is levied specifically on non-Muslims in an Islamic state) from Hindus in Kabul, Ghazni and Jalalabad.

Herat was another important centre of Hindu commercial activity in Afghanistan. Near the end of the 18th century, George Forster reported that there were roughly 100 Hindu Multanis in Herat, occupying two caravanserais and conducting 'a brisk commerce, and extending a long chain of credit.' Just a few years later, in 1810, the British Captain Charles Christie observed some 600 'highly respected' Hindu merchants there. In the 1840s, the French soldier and traveller J. P. Ferrier observed an 'immensely rich' community of Shikarpuri Hindus. He reported that, in addition to their trade, these Hindus enjoyed a privileged position in the government of Yar Muhammad and were even granted the right to farm nearly all the taxes in the district. Christie attributed the Hindus' privileged status to the government administrators' appreciation of their role as the primary suppliers of investment capital for the region and concluded that because of this, 'the government is sensible of their value, and they have in consequence much influence. They live in the best Suraés, and have gardens outside, but do not venture to bring their families with them to this city.'

Herat was not the only location in Afghanistan where Hindu merchant-moneylenders were active in government administration. During the reign of the Durrani ruler Timur Shah (r. 1773–93), son and successor of Ahmad Shah, Indian merchants were reported to have played an active role in the financial administration of the state. The Durrani ruling elite made it a policy to farm out tax revenue collecting privileges throughout their realm, and the tax-farmers were often Shikarpuri merchant-moneylenders. The Shikarpuris were also known to extend large loans to the Afghan nobility against future tax revenues, and even to finance the state's military campaigns.

This symbiotic relationship continued to develop throughout the 19th century. In the early 1820s, William Moorcroft and George Trebek observed and described the activities of two Hindu merchants, Atma Ram, a native of Peshawar who was appointed to the position of *diwanbegi* (finance minister) under the Afghan ruler Mir Murad Beg; and Atma Ram's deputy, a Hindu customs officer named Bysakhi Ram. According to Moorcroft, while travelling from Ghazni to Khulum, his company had the ill-fortune to meet Bysakhi Ram, who blatantly abused his position by attempting to extort a bribe from the company and forcing them to sell their goods at Tashkurgan 'in order that the Hindus might reap the profit of a resale at Bokhara.' Several years later, Atma Ram bought the privilege to collect transit taxes on the Kabul-Bukhara caravan route for an annual payment of Rs. 25,000. By the late 1830s, caravan traffic was apparently deemed to be more valuable and the price of this privilege was raised to Rs. 40,000. In addition to dominating the taxation of the Indo-Central Asian transit trade through Afghanistan, and nearly monopolising Afghanistan's trade with Yarkand in Chinese Turkestan, Atma Ram is also a rare example of a Hindu official in an Islamic administration whose influence was so great that he was even allowed to own a considerable retinue of Muslim slaves.

The market area in old Tashkent during the late 19th century. In the 18th and 19th centuries, Tashkent grew in size and commercial importance due to its strategic location along trade routes leading to Russian markets in the north.

A busy market area in front of the Arq (fortress) of the Bukharan amir in the 1890s.

Shikarpuri-Multani firms orchestrated transregional trade between India and Afghanistan well into the 20th century. According to a report of the Banking Enquiry Committee for the Centrally Administered Areas dating back to 1929–30, India's trans-Khyber trade at that time was dominated by some 50 Shikarpuri families in Peshawar, all of which were affiliated with the Multani firm of Naraindas Chelaram. This influential firm was established in Peshawar in the late 18th century, when the Durrani ruler Timur Shah made Peshawar his winter capital, and continued to provide important financial services to the Durrani state even until the mid-20th century. However, the partition of the subcontinent in 1947 saw the withdrawal of Hindu merchants from Pakistan, thus denying Afghanistan the financial skills and investment capital of the Indian firms that were so integral to the centralisation of the Durrani Afghan state.

CENTRAL ASIA

By the middle of the 16th century, Bukhara was home to the largest number of Indians in Central Asia. Throughout approximately 350 years of Indian settlement, Bukhara functioned as the centre of Indian commercial activity in the region. It is unfortunate that there are few accounts of early modern Central Asian society to which we might turn in an effort to determine the precise size of these communities. However, as Russian and British strategic and economic interests in Central Asia increased during the 19th century, so too did the number of travellers visiting this region. Their travel accounts offer a more detailed analysis of the Indian communities in the region, and several provide estimates of the number of Indians in 19th-century Central Asia.

The Indian community in 19th-century Bukhara occupied many, if not most, of the caravanserais in that city. The total number of Indian merchants in the city was between 400 and 600. Indian dispersion in cities and villages throughout sedentary Central Asia appears to

have been extensive. In the late 19th-century Bukharan Amirate, Indians could be found in Ghijduvan, Vangazi, Babkent, Qarshi, Guzar, Yakkabag, Chirakchi, Kerki, Baisun, Kitab, Kermin, Tashkupruk, Khatirchi, Nurata, Ziauddin, Shahrisabz and Karakul, as well as in numerous other cities and villages. In the neighbouring Russian Turkestan, Indian communities were likewise present in cities and villages throughout the Samarkand, Syr Darya and Farghana oblasts (administrative districts). In the Samarkand Oblast, Russian colonial documents mention Indians living in the cities of Samarkand, Kattakurgan, Jizzak and Khojent, as well as in such small villages as Paishambe and Uzensakan. In the Syr Darya Oblast, Indians lived in Tashkent, Auleata and Chimkent, as well as in the villages of Telau, Ablik, Toitepa, Zengiata, Chinaz, and Merk. In Farghana, Indians are known to have lived in the urban centres of Old Margilan, Skobelev, Khoqand, Andijan, Osh, Namangan and Chust, as well as in a considerable number of villages, including Rishtan, Yengi Kurgan, Ichkurgan, Kuba, Aul, Bulakoshi, Khojevat, Chimion, Khoqan and Kishlak. In the 19th century, Hindus were even known to have spread to the

The living quarters of Indians in Bukhara during the 1880s.

The Bibi Khanum Masjid complex (background) in Samarkand was built between 1398 and 1405. It was constructed by many of the Indians that Timur Shah captured during his infamous sack of Delhi in 1398.

As the debtor, and the vast majority of the rest of the population, including the dispatcher, were unable to read the order, he typically had little or no means of finding out what the letter was about and, failing to appear, lost all rights to the property designated as collateral. Even when the debtor appeared before the judge as required, the Indians were widely reputed to have bribed judges in order to secure a favourable verdict, and Bukharan administrators went out of their way to protect the commercial interests of Indian moneylenders.

Conversely, at least in Central Asia, debtors also earned a reputation for being rather adept at cheating their Indian creditors. The most common method was for debtors to take loans without any intention of repaying. More interesting, however, was a technique by which debtors 'washed out' the figures on their loan contracts and rewrote them as more advantageous to themselves, a practice at which debtors in Tashkent were said to have been very skilled.

For the most part, Indians and their debtors operated in a predictable manner and Indians remained the dominant financial community in Central Asia until the end of the 19th century. Even conducting an honest moneylending business was very lucrative as, within two or three years, agents could more than quadruple their initial capital. Of course, the vast majority of the agents' earnings went to the firms which had, after all, trained the agents, provided the initial investment and financial services, assumed the greater part of the financial risk, and in some cases advanced funds to the agents' families in their absence. Still, the Indians were able to accumulate a considerable amount of wealth rather quickly, and this motivated many Indian merchants to stay in these particularly advantageous locations for longer periods of time, or to make repeated ventures into the region.

Given the political rivalry between Russia and Great Britain in the 19th century, one might expect to find the Russian colonial authorities troubled by the several thousand Indian merchants—British subjects and potential spies—widely dispersed throughout Russian colonial territories. The British did, in fact, enlist some Indians as spies, and on occasion some of these spies were known to have posed as merchants in order to gain entry to Russian Turkestan. But, at least in terms of the policies directed towards the Indian merchant communities in his territory, the Russian governor general of Turkestan, Konstantin von Kaufman, was not overly concerned with

Semirechinski and Zakaspiiski oblasts (in modern Kazakhstan and Turkmenistan) and to have lived in Vernyi (modern Alma-Ata), Tokmak and Kopal in the territory on the border of Chinese Turkestan (in modern Kyrghyzstan). This is by no means an exhaustive list of the Central Asian cities and villages where Indian merchants visited and settled.

Archival records of the 19th century suggest that the population of Indians in the Bukharan Amirate was approximately 5000, with an additional 3000 Indians, almost exclusively Hindus (with some Sikhs and Jains), residing in Russian Turkestan. Several hundred more lived across the Tien Shan mountain range in Kashghar, Yarkand and other cities of Chinese Turkestan.

The people who most frequently took advantage of the moneylending services offered by the Indians in Central Asia included farmers, handicraft producers and those without alternative sources of credit, commonly soldiers. From the perspective of Indian moneylenders, even signature-based loans to soldiers were reasonably secure as these clients had a regular income. Indians also encouraged the debtors' ability to repay their debts by restricting the loans to reasonably small amounts. Nevertheless, the Indians granted a large number of such loans. Reports suggest that loans granted against only a signature were advanced at an extraordinarily high interest rate. Loans made against collateral were, of course, much more reasonable.

Exploitative usurers

Popular traditions portrayed the Indians as exploitative usurers, and it is perhaps only natural that dishonest business practices occasionally found their way into the Indian moneylenders' relations with their clients. The comparatively well-educated moneylenders occasionally took advantage of the illiteracy of the majority of their clients. One method by which they achieved this was by claiming that payments on a loan made against collateral had not been received. The moneylender could then appeal to a *qadi* (judge), who would issue a judgment demanding that the debtor appear before the judge prior to a certain date.

A 17th-century mandate issued by a Bukharan Khan:

We are thinking about the condition of the greater community of people. Those of other religions obey the farmans that we make and help us very much; for this reason we will weaken the grip of those who try to oppress them. The goods and property of these people should not become ruined; they are protected. Their protection will come from here and their aspirations should be directed to Bukhara. And regarding the Hindus who live in the territories of Bukhara, Balkh, Badakhshan, Qunduz, Taliqan, Aibek, Ghuri, Baghlan, Shabarghan, Termiz, Samarqand, Nesf [Qarshi], Kish, Shahrisabz, and wherever else they may live: whoever knows the aqsaqal [the community elder, lit. 'White Beard'] must obey and respect him as he is working for their best interest.

Oriental Studies Institute of the Academy of Science of the Republic of Uzbekistan, Maktubat munsh'at manshurat, Ms. No. 289, fols. 185b-186a.

British espionage. He even rejected numerous proposals advanced by his subordinates suggesting that the Russians evict the Indians from their territory.

Although Kaufman did consider Indian moneylending to be exploitative and contrary to the interest of his colonial subjects, he was particularly concerned with Indian ownership of an increasing amount of agricultural land—farmland that had been used as collateral for loans that had defaulted. For Kaufman, the threat of a British invasion of Central Asia must have seemed much less pressing than the Indian moneylending operations, which were effectively transferring ownership of large portions of Russian colonial territory into Indian hands one plot at a time. Still, Kaufman was sensitive to the Indian contribution to the Central Asian economy, and he recognised that their extension of rural credit was crucial to the well-being of his subjects. The abrupt removal of the Indians from Central Asia was therefore not desirable. To do so without first establishing institutions that could take their place would wreak havoc upon the region's agrarian economy and ultimately lead to economic collapse and famine.

Rather than evict the Indians, Kaufman published a circular in 1877 that outlined a series of policies designed to undermine the moneylending operations of the Indians. The most important of these was the prohibition on Indians foreclosing on loans that had been made using agricultural property as collateral. The publication of this circular shocked the Indian communities as Central Asian farmers refused to repay even the principal of their debts, and the Russian administration refused to respond to Indian complaints. Furthermore, the long-term commercial prospects of Indians in Central Asia were terminated by Kaufman's concomitant implementation of a state-sponsored Russian colonial banking system that rapidly expanded throughout the region. This measure effectively ended the ability of the Indians to continue in their unique role as Central Asia's premier financiers and removed the moneylenders from their intermediary position between agricultural producers and the market. Ultimately, Kaufman's policies brought about the rapid withdrawal of Indians from Central Asia in favour of emerging opportunities elsewhere.

IRAN

Indian family firms began placing agents in Iran at roughly the same time as they did in Central Asia. In 1562, Anthony Jenkinson wrote about meeting Indian merchants in Qazvin, the capital of Safavid Iran from 1555 until 1598, when Shah 'Abbas I moved the capital to Isfahan. Just a few years after Jenkinson's visit, Thomas Bannister and Jeffrey Ducket travelled to Iran (1568–74) and passed through Russia, visiting Astrakhan and other cities later known to host Indian communities. However, their account mentions nothing of Indians until they reached the northern Iranian city of Kashan, which they described as a major entrepôt boasting a significant population of Indian merchants. Later travellers to Kashan observed that the city thrived as a commercial centre and continued to host a vibrant Indian community up to the end of the 18th century.

A group of Shikarpuri merchants and their servants in Central Asia. The Shikarpuris came from Sind. This photograph is from the late 19th century and is preserved in a large personal album compiled between the 1870s and 1890s. It belonged to a colonial Russian family in Central Asia.

During the 17th century, the Safavid capital of Isfahan played a central role in Indian commercial activity abroad. The earliest available observation suggesting the presence of an Indian merchant community in Isfahan was made in December 1617 by Pietro Della Valle, who identified Indians as the most important of the foreign trading communities in Iran at the time. Two decades later, in November 1637, Adam Olearius visited Isfahan and reported that there were roughly 12,000 Indians living there at any given time. The presence of such a large number of Indian merchants in 17th-century Isfahan is supported by Jean de Thevenot, who estimated there were more than 15,000 Indian merchants during the 1660s, and also by Englebert Kaempfer, who, 20 years later, suggested that Isfahan's Indian merchant population should be placed at the lower—although still remarkable—figure of 10,000. These very impressive figures are corroborated by the reports of Indian merchants themselves. In 1647, an Indian merchant identified only as Sutur, who lived in the Russian port of Astrakhan, reported to his Russian hosts that there were some 10,000 Indian merchants who lived in Iran at that time. Sutur's care in expressing that these Indians lived in Iran suggests that others, such as peripatetic caravan traders, went unaccounted for in his estimation. Considering these estimates, it seems reasonable to accept Jean Chardin's assertion that in the 1660s, the total population of Multanis residing in the Shah's territory was in excess of 20,000.

The impressive number of Indians in 17th-century Isfahan was partly due to its location at the crossroads of caravan routes traversing Iran, and to the precedent set by the early patronage of Shah 'Abbas I (r. 1587–1629). Commodities passed through Isfahan as caravans moved goods from India to the Mediterranean coast, from where they were transported to North Africa and Europe, and between the Indian Ocean and Caspian Sea, from where they were taken to Ukraine and Russia, largely via Astrakhan. The Iranians endeavoured to maintain control of the Caspian Sea route to facilitate their trade with Russia and circumvent Ottoman territory during the frequent periods of Safavid-Ottoman or Ottoman-Russian hostility. This added commercial importance to the

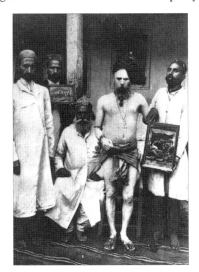

In another late 19th-century photograph from the album mentioned above, religious images from the temple room of a caravanserai are displayed, demonstrating the importance of religious observance to Indian merchants away from the homeland.

A view of Isfahan, 1703–04, drawn by Cornelius de Bruyn. During the 17th century, Isfahan was the capital of Safavid Iran and home to 10,000–15,000 Multani merchants.

Iranian cities between Isfahan and the Caspian coast, especially in the Gilan and Shirwan provinces, the location of a number of Indian diasporic communities since the years immediately following the Safavids' re-conquest of these provinces from the Ottomans under Shah 'Abbas I.

In the early 17th century, Indian merchants trying to mediate Russia's growing trade with the East began to spread northwards from their Iranian centres to the Gilan coastline in northwestern Iran and into the Safavid-controlled Caucasus, largely concentrating in ports along the Caspian Sea. Information from 17th-century Astrakhan demonstrates the regular movement of Indian merchants from Astrakhan to Qazvin, Tabriz and numerous coastal cities in Gilan and Shirwan provinces. In 1671, John Struys visited Shemakhi, the old capital of Shirwan province, where he came across a community consisting of roughly 100 Hindu merchants. During his travels through the Caucasus, Struys also recorded visiting Indian communities in Baku, Ardebil and Derbent, the capital of Daghestan, on the northwest coast of the Caspian Sea. At that time, Baku was an important commercial centre for merchants involved in trans-Caspian commerce, much of which was mediated by Hindu and Armenian merchants. Most of those Indian merchants who travelled to the Caucasus did so via the Indian Ocean maritime routes, embarking at the Sindhi port of Thatta, travelling by sea to Bandar 'Abbas or Basra, and continuing northwards across Iran by caravan.

> *Only a few Indians were left in the town; these people had advanced money to the Muhammadans against promissory notes (sanad) and jewels, gold, silver and house ornaments (zinat). Mahmud took all these valuables from them without payment, not even regarding them as forming part of their indemnity. The shops of those Multanis who had died or had fled were consequently closed, but Mahmud had them opened and seized all their contents.*
>
> Petros di Sarkis Gilanentz and Caro Owen Minasian,
> The chronicle of Petros di Sarkis Gilanentz
> concerning the Afghan invasion of Persia in 1722,
> the siege of Isfahan and the repercussions in northern Persia,
> Russia and Turkey, *1959*.

While in Iran in the 1620s, Thomas Herbert observed Indian merchant communities in Bandar 'Abbas, Isfahan and Amol, the latter being one of the principal towns of Mazandaran province, located on the southern shore of the Caspian Sea. In 1645, the British established a commercial 'factory' in Basra and, shortly thereafter, the city's improved commercial potential attracted Indian merchants. According to Jean-Baptiste Tavernier, although Indian moneylenders had offices in the ports of Bandar 'Abbas and Bandar Kung, an important port city at the time located some 150 km west of Bandar 'Abbas, their central offices were inland, in Lar, Isfahan and Shiraz, the capital of Fars province, where, according to John Chardin, Indians owned one of the finest bazaars in the city. Writing just a few years after Chardin, John Fryer claimed that there were Indian merchants 'in all the cities of Persia'.

Religious difficulties

A picture emerges of Indian merchants dispersed throughout much of Iran and involved in all levels of trade there, even—as was the case in Afghanistan—in the financial affairs of government administration. Being so intertwined with Iranian society, it is not surprising that the fate of Indian communities in Iran followed the vicissitudes of their host society. The Indian merchant communities in Iran suffered severely during the 1722 Ghilzai Afghan invasion of Isfahan and the occupation of much of Iran. According to the chronicle of one Armenian observer, the invading Afghan forces decimated the Hindu community of Isfahan. The Afghans reportedly demanded a considerable sum of 25,000 tomans from the Hindus as 'indemnity'. However, because their capital was engaged in investments, they were able to raise only 20,000 tomans on such short notice. The Afghans responded violently and, fearing for their lives, many Hindus fled to safer places or returned home, while others were so distraught at their financial ruin that they drank poison or simply died of grief.

Anti-Hindu activities continued in the wake of the Afghans' ejection from Iran by Nadir Shah Afshar (r. 1736–47). Reports from the Indian communities in later years suggest that Nadir Shah used their unprotected status (by Islamic law, Hindus, unlike Jews or Christians, were not considered *dhimmis*, or 'people of the book', and were therefore not required to be protected) as a pretence for confiscating much of their wealth and property. This traumatic experience remained in the Hindus' collective memory even as late as 1824, when the community of Indian merchants in Baku reported to George Keppel that although they had no complaints about their treatment in Iran at that time, Nadir Shah had treated their predecessors with great cruelty—impaling them, and putting them through several kinds of tortures.

Prosperity returned to Indian merchants in Iran in the decades following Nadir Shah's assassination in 1747. The founder of the Zand dynasty, Muhammad Karim Khan (r. 1751–79), effectively seized power in southern Iran and brought an era of prosperity to much of the country. This was accompanied by the Zand administration's policy of tolerance towards foreign merchant communities. This was especially evident in the encouragement of British commercial activity in the Persian Gulf port of Bushahr and in the return of significant numbers of Indian merchants to Iranian markets. Government-sponsored anti-Hindu activity in Iran had ended by 1802, when Edward Waring reported that in Bushahr, 'the Hindoos live unmolested by the Persians, and are neither insulted nor oppressed by the government.' The Hindus' return to Iranian markets was likewise observed by George Forster, who, in the late 18th century, encountered nearly 100 Indian families living in their own private quarter in the eastern Iranian town of Tarshish, where 'they conducted business without molestation or insult.' Forster also noted significant Hindu merchant communities in the Iranian towns of Meshed, Yazd, Kashan and Qazvin. He reported that although there were a number of Indian communities active in Iranian towns on the shores of the Caspian Sea, there were larger Indian communities in the numerous Iranian ports along the Persian Gulf engaged in maritime commerce. Indian firms, especially Shikarpuris and Sikhs, continued to send agents to Iran throughout the 19th and 20th centuries, and they showed an impressive ability to adapt to changing circumstances by engaging in a wide variety of commercial activities.

INDIAN MERCHANTS: THEIR SIGNIFICANCE

At first glance, the ability of Indian merchants to maintain thriving communities in Afghanistan, Central Asia and Iran appears to be a historical aberration, as they represented a significant Hindu population in Muslim states, where they were technically unprotected by Islamic law. However, with a few notable exceptions, Indian merchants enjoyed the steadfast protection of their Muslim hosts. This can be attributed to several factors. These Indians were widely respected as large-scale transregional traders whose fortitude, technical knowledge and commercial connections were valuable resources for the state. They supplied their host societies with necessary commodities, a commercial outlet for their own products, and were an important source of tax income for the state treasury. More important than their transregional trade, however, was their penchant for interest-oriented moneylending ventures, including the operation of elaborate rural credit systems. This promoted the expansion of their host states' agricultural tax base and, by extending a monetised economy into the countryside, also facilitated the states' collection of tax revenue in cash. In this way, the Indians in Afghanistan, Central Asia and Iran connected the economies of their host societies with the vast resources of

India's agrarian economy, which they expertly employed as an engine for investment in foreign markets.

In Afghanistan and Iran, and perhaps also in Central Asia, Indian merchants assisted efforts to transcend divisive tribal loyalties and maintain a centralised bureaucracy by offering numerous other financial services to the state. These included revenue collection, extending credit to the nobility, financing military campaigns, managing trade routes, and even serving in high posts within the states' financial administrations. The combination of these factors motivated their Muslim hosts to welcome Hindu merchants into their territory and protect their interests, despite popular traditions portraying the Indian merchants as exploitative usurers.

In the 1870s, Konstantin von Kaufman, the governor general of the Central Asian Russian colonies, implemented a series of revolutionary policies that targeted the Indian merchants in his territory, undermined their business interests and, by the end of the 19th century, effectively brought an end to the Indian communities in Central Asia. In Afghanistan, Indians maintained an active commercial presence right up to 1947. In Iran, their commercial activities have extended even into the 21st century. Indeed, the celebrated Hinduja family, operators of one of the wealthiest commercial firms in the world, began as a modest Shikarpuri firm in 20th-century Iran.

In the end, the socio-political trauma associated with the Partition provoked the mass migration of the Shikarpuri-Multani firms from Pakistan largely to Bombay. From this new centre, the Indian firms directed their attention away from Afghanistan and Central Asia and focused on emerging commercial opportunities literally across the globe. By the beginning of the 21st century, large numbers of Shikarpuri-Multani merchants had established a vast network of communities that stretched from Hong Kong to Manila and Singapore in the east, and across much of Africa and Europe to the Caribbean islands, Central America, Canada and the US in the west.

Scott Levi

A view of Bandar ʿAbbas, c. 1704, drawn by Cornelius de Bruyn. The rather large Indian population of this vibrant Persian Gulf port city maintained two free-standing Hindu temples northeast of the city.

A caravanserai in Isfahan, drawn by Cornelius de Bruyn. Indians in Iran lived in caravanserais similar to this one.

SAUDI ARABIA, OMAN AND THE GULF STATES

Indian workers often use bicycles to commute. Seen here are dry dock workers in Dubai cycling home at the end of the day.

An Indian camel rider in Oman.

I N 2001, the number of Indians in the Gulf Cooperation Council (GCC) countries of Saudi Arabia, Oman, Kuwait, Bahrain, Qatar and the United Arab Emirates (UAE) exceeded 3.3 million. According to 2002 estimates, the Indian population in the GCC countries constitute about 11 per cent of the total population (national plus non-national), the vast majority of whom reside in Saudi Arabia (46 per cent) and the UAE (27 per cent). Their numbers as a proportion of the population vary from just under 7 per cent in Saudi Arabia to almost 33 per cent in the UAE. In 2002, Indians alone constituted 28 per cent of the total expatriate population in the GCC countries.

Although the Indian presence in the countries of the Middle East has a long history spanning several centuries, their numbers remained small and largely confined to Indian traders travelling between Mesopotamia and the port cities of western India until the 1930s. Some of these merchants were also known to have settled in the neighbouring Gulf States, where Dubai was the main entrepôt for the trade of Indian goods throughout the Arab region. Trade linkages between Bahrain, Oman and India expanded during the period of British rule, when these countries were British protectorates under the jurisdiction of the Bombay Presidency.

THE DISCOVERY OF OIL RESERVES

Indians began to emigrate in sizeable numbers during the 1930s following the discovery of oil reserves in the region and the development of the Bahrain Petroleum Company. They constituted about 94 per cent of the total clerical and technical employees, and nearly 91 per cent of the

total number of artisans employed by the company. In 1949, Indian expatriates also made up 86 per cent of the ministerial and technical staff in the Kuwait Oil Company. Furthermore, in several other companies in the Gulf States, Indians were employed in large numbers as clerks, technicians and artisans, and many also functioned as skilled and professional workers. However, the majority of Indian workers in the Arab region at the time were employed in unskilled and semi-skilled work in construction sites and the household sector.

In spite of the increase from the 1930s, the overall number of Indians in the Middle Eastern countries at the end of World War II remained minute. Even among the states with the largest concentration of Indians—Bahrain, Kuwait and Oman—none had an Indian populace in excess of 1300 in 1948. In Qatar and Saudi Arabia, the Indian presence was almost negligible. However, between 1948 and the early 1970s, their numbers increased consistently from under 14,000 to nearly 40,000. Following the increase in oil prices in 1973, which marked the beginning of massive development in the region, the number of Indian migrants in the Gulf increased at a rapid rate.

During the first few years of the 1970s, the manpower needs of massive developments in infrastructure, agriculture, industry, transport and communications in GCC countries were met primarily by immigrant labour from other Arab nations, such as Egypt, Jordan, Palestine and Yemen. Nevertheless, the number of Asian (non-Arab) expatriates also showed a rapid increase from 1970 onwards. For instance, while non-national Arab workers in Bahrain, Kuwait, Qatar and the UAE increased by 36.5 per cent during 1970–75, the corresponding increase in Asian (non-Arab) expatriate workers (mainly Indian and Pakistani) was 195.2 per cent. In 1975, Indians constituted 39.1 per cent, Pakistanis 58.1 per cent and other Asians 2.8 per cent of the total Asian (non-Arab) expatriates in the Middle East.

Since 1975, the increase in Indian inhabitants in the GCC region has far outstripped that of Pakistanis and other Asians. Moreover, until 1990–91, when the Gulf War broke out, there existed large numbers of non-national Arabs working in the Gulf countries, including Palestinians,

Map 8.26

SAUDI ARABIA, OMAN AND THE GULF STATES

KAZAKHSTAN

IRAQ   IRAN   TURKEY   CHINA
IRAN   AFGHANISTAN
EGYPT   PAKISTAN
SUDAN   INDIA
ETHIOPIA

IRAQ   IRAN

KUWAIT
•Kuwait City

Persian Gulf

SAUDI ARABIA

BAHRAIN
Manama•   Ras Al Khaimah
•Doha   Umm Al Qaiwan•
QATAR   Sharjah•   •Ajman
Riyadh•   Abu Dhabi   Dubai   •Al Fujirah   *Gulf of Oman*
•Medina   UAE   •Muscat

Red Sea

OMAN

Jeddah•   •Mecca

Arabian Sea

SUDAN

0   300 kilometres
ERITREA   YEMEN   0   300 miles

Jordanians, Yemenis and Egyptians. Since the war, workers from South Asia, primarily India, as well as from Southeast Asian countries, have come to replace them. The Indian expatriate population in the region has shown an increase from fewer than 258,000 in 1975 to 3.318 million in 2001 (see Table 8.19).

Although admission to GCC countries for work or residence was relatively easy before the mid-1970s, the governments of these countries have since introduced restrictions on entry to non-national populations due to concerns over the alarming growth in their numbers. It is almost impossible, therefore, even for non-national Arab persons born in GCC countries to obtain naturalisation, and it has become increasingly difficult for non-nationals to bring their families with them. Indian workers in these countries have been subject to the growing restrictions. As foreign nationals, they are not permitted to own any business or landed property, and are required to have a local citizen or agency as a major partner in their enterprises.

In all the Gulf countries, Islam is the state religion, the Sharia is the basic law and Arabic is the only official language. The entire region is sparsely populated: Saudi Arabia has a population of 22.5 million, while the others have populations that ranged from 0.5 million to 2.6 million in 2003.

LABOUR NEEDS OF THE GULF STATES

Shortage of manpower has been endemic in all of these countries and for all categories of work—from professionals such as doctors, engineers, architects, financiers and accountants, to semi-skilled workers such as craftsmen, artisans, drivers and technical personnel, to unskilled workers needed in construction sites, farms, livestock ranches, shops and households.

Accordingly, Indian workers in the GCC countries fall into these various categories. The number of Indian expatriate workers in white-collar jobs has increased considerably in all the Middle Eastern countries, where they assist well-paid nationals in government departments and public sector undertakings. Indian white-collar workers and professionals constitute about 30 per cent of the total number of Indian workers in these countries. Professionals who are highly skilled and technically trained remain in great demand and are offered high salaries. They are allowed to bring their families with them to their country of work, but are restricted from keeping their children in the country once their high school education has been completed. Moreover, expatriates are not allowed citizenship in any of the GCC countries except Oman, where such rights are granted only after 20 years of residence in the country. Some other exceptions exist, but not very many, and those are limited to ethnic Arabs from other Gulf countries.

In general, life is comfortable for professionals and white-collar workers. They are often able to maintain social contacts with similarly placed compatriots and nationals, and are active participants in the sociocultural activities of various associations. These associations are set up among Indians based on place of origin, religion, language and profession. Hundreds of such associations can be found in the various GCC countries, but most of them exist in the UAE and Kuwait. Such associations are much less common in Oman and Saudi Arabia. Professionals and white-collar workers in the GCC countries have also established a large number of schools throughout the region which follow the Indian curriculum. Indian

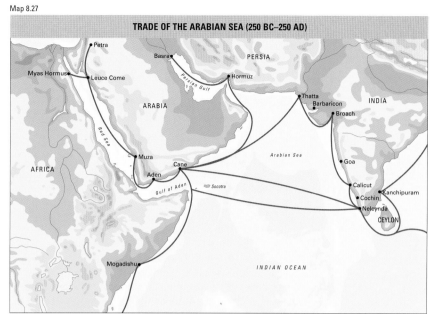

Map 8.27

TRADE OF THE ARABIAN SEA (250 BC–250 AD)

Based on information drawn from 'The Red Sea Trade Route, 250 BC to 250 AD', available at http://nabatea.net/redsea.html.

expatriate communities in the Gulf countries run 59 schools: three in Bahrain, nine in Kuwait, 10 in Oman, three in Qatar, three in Saudi Arabia and 31 in the UAE.

Semi-skilled and unskilled workers constitute about 70 per cent of the total number of Indian migrants in the Gulf countries. The demand for low-skilled workers, such as housemaids, cooks, porters and gardeners remains considerable. These workers are not protected by any local labour law. In some of the Gulf countries, female employees working in households as housemaids or governesses are treated with contempt and derision, and are sometimes exploited sexually. Unskilled and semi-skilled workers in general, who work in infrastructural and other development projects, live under miserable conditions and are accommodated in crowded small rooms in labour camps. Their toilet and kitchen facilities are inadequate. Working conditions are also pitiable. Such difficult circumstances, in addition to inclement weather, inability to participate in social and cultural activities, long periods of separation from their families and relatives, and emotional deprivation have been known to wreck the lives of hundreds of low-skilled workers in the Gulf region.

Unskilled and semi-skilled workers have a high rate of turnover as they work only for short periods on temporary contracts. Those who complete their contracts have to return home; however, a large proportion do manage to return under new work contracts after a period of not less than one year. There have also been several cases of recruiting agents duping illiterate jobseekers, often in

Indian merchants have a long history of trade relations with maritime ports in the Persian Gulf, the Gulf of Aden and the Red Sea.

Table 8.19

INDIAN EXPATRIATE POPULATION IN THE MIDDLE EAST (1975–2001)						
	1975	**1979**	**1983**	**1987**	**1991**	**2001**
UAE	107,500	152,000	250,000	225,000	400,000	950,000
Bahrain	17,250	26,000	30,000	77,000	100,000	130,000
Qatar	27,800	30,000	40,000	50,000	75,000	131,000
Kuwait	32,105	65,000	115,000	100,000	88,000	295,000
Oman	38,500	60,000	100,000	184,000	220,000	312,000
Saudi Arabia	34,500	100,000	270,000	380,000	600,000	1,500,000
Total	257,655	433,000	805,000	1,016,000	1,483,000	3,318,000

Sources: Rahman Anisur, Indian Labour Migration to West Asia: Trends and Effects, 1999; and S. Irudaya Rajan, From Kerala to the Gulf: Impacts of Labour Migration, 2004.

An Indian family strolling in Karama, Dubai. Indian professionals in the Gulf are allowed to bring their families with them. Lower-skilled workers, however, do not enjoy this privilege.

collusion with prospective employers. The employee is required to hand over his travel documents to the prospective employer, who keeps it in his custody and is able to exercise undue control over the employee, often ignoring the terms of employment. There have also been reports of bogus employers in the Gulf countries who import labour just to hawk them to others for an attractive commission.

Indian expatriates, particularly the uneducated and unskilled, are thus often subjected to several forms of exploitation by recruiting agents and prospective employers: refusal to give employment; non-payment of wages; deduction of permit and other fees from their meagre wages; non-payment of overtime fees; uncomfortable transport arrangements; inadequate medical facilities; negation of legal rights to seek remedy for complaints; making migrants ignorant carriers of smuggled goods; and victimisation and harassment of women recruited for the jobs of housemaid, cook and ayah. Moreover, 'Gulf marriages', where poor girls are given in marriage to elderly Arabs on a visit to India, or even to persons unknown to the girls and their families, for paltry prices are not infrequent.

Generally, non-resident Indians in the Gulf countries, highly skilled or otherwise, keep in close contact with their families in India and go home for visits whenever possible. They also keep abreast of socio-political and economic developments back home through radio and TV channels. They have made impressive and ready contributions in times of natural disaster in different parts of India, and contributed to India's deposit mobilisation drives through the issuance of bonds. Though all categories of Indian expatriates in the Gulf countries endeavour to save from their earnings as much as possible, the bulk of the foreign remittances by private transfers accrue from the unskilled and the semi-skilled workers.

THE UNITED ARAB EMIRATES

During the 19th century, the UK established control over the defence of the Trucial States along the coast of the Persian Gulf. The federation of the United Arab Emirates was formed in December 1971, comprising the seven Trucial States of Abu Dhabi, Dubai, Sharjah, Ras Al Khaima, Al Fujirah, Ajman and Umm Al Qaiwan. The population of these states, which numbered approximately 100,000 in 1960, grew rapidly to nearly 200,000 in

Table 8.20

MAJOR EXPATRIATE COMMUNITIES IN THE UAE (2002)		
	Expatriate population ('000)	% of total expatriate population
Indian	1000	46.6
Pakistani	450	21.0
Bangladeshi	100	4.7
Sri Lankan	160	7.5
Filipino	120	5.6
Others (Middle East)	315	14.6
Total	2145	100

Source: Giovanna Tattolo, 'Arab Labor Migration to the GCC States', available at http://jmobservatory.eco.uniromal.it.

1975. That year, the expatriate population made up roughly 63 per cent of the total population of 525,000. Not only has the total population continued to increase rapidly since then (from 525,000 in 1975 to 2.3 million in 2001), the proportion of the expatriate population has also grown from 63 per cent to 80 per cent. Among expatriates, Indians are the largest group, accounting for some 47 per cent of the total expatriate population (see Table 8.20).

From the early 19th century, Indian traders were known to import pearls and dates from the UAE region in exchange for Indian textiles. After World War II, the number of Indians in the region began to increase exponentially. Three-quarters of Indian workers in the UAE were unskilled labourers, a large majority of whom were from the South Indian states, particularly from Kerala. Indians in the UAE have developed social and cultural activities on a large scale, based on linguistic and religious identities, and they project their Indian cultural background to the UAE population. They have established 31 Indian schools, built temples, churches and gurdwaras. Indians have also been allowed to set up cremation grounds for the benefit of their community, as Hindus and Sikhs are not permitted by religion to bury their dead. Indians in the UAE have made substantial financial contributions at times of national calamities and crises in India. The large presence of Indians in the region is causing alarm in the Emirates, which have begun a policy of 'Emiratisation', aimed at raising the proportion of native workers in the workforce to about 40 per cent by 2015.

Dubai

India has a long history with Dubai, which acted as an Arab entrepôt for South Asian goods transported mostly in Indian-owned Arab dhows, for trans-shipment to other parts of the Gulf region and throughout the Arab world. There also existed a flourishing illegal trade conducted through the collusion of Indian merchants and their Arab partners, which involved the export from Dubai of goods restricted by the Indian government, such as gold, watches, tape recorders and transistors.

In 1941, Indian merchants in Dubai formed the Indian Association. It ran a clubhouse which had a bar, screened Indian movies, organised dances and other functions, and

An Indian baker in a guest workers' shanty town in Abu Dhabi.

population of 30,000; and Ras al-Khaimah, with a population of 45,000. The socio-economic characteristics of Indians living in these areas are broadly similar to those of their counterparts elsewhere in the UAE.

The UAE follows a policy of recruiting foreign labour through work contracts based on licences issued by the ministry of labour to agents who recruit labour. One of the reasons for the recruitment of a large number of Indians for labour in the UAE is their willingness to accept salaries at far lower rates than those given to workers from the West or even Arab immigrants from countries such as Egypt, Lebanon and Jordan. The remuneration of Indian workers is often kept below the market rate and they are sometimes pressed into accepting wages even lower than that stated in their work contracts.

Accommodation and health facilities at worksites that house these Indian workers are poor or inadequate. Moreover, there have been numerous instances of abuse, particularly with regard to the length of the working day. Indian workers have been unable to do much about their difficult conditions given the strong buyer's market and the fact that unionisation, wage bargaining and strikes are illegal. Unskilled workers are denied the protection of labour laws and employers have often kept the passports of the emigrants and their families.

In the late 1990s, the demand for expatriates fell in the UAE following the recession and a glut of foreign workers in the labour market. Consequently, the UAE government changed its immigration policy in order to rectify the demographic imbalance. The policy measures that were adopted included denying visas for unskilled labourers from India, Pakistan and Bangladesh; repatriation of unskilled foreigners already in the UAE; and increasing the cost of recruiting unskilled expatriate labour.

Immigration policies and procedures introduced in 1999 created great hardships for migrant workers from India, in particular the policies regarding the recruitment of contract labour, the laws controlling work contracts, and the lack of checks on contract violations and the non-fulfilment of conditions of contract by employers. In 2002, 40 per cent of the cases filed by Indian migrant workers against their employers alleged that the latter were violating the terms of contract. As the migrants had reached the UAE after incurring considerable expenses, they had little option other than to accept the terms and conditions imposed on them by the employers. Denial of

Indian construction workers in the UAE. Low-skilled workers in these industries are often faced with inadequate housing and medical facilities. Although stricter regulations have been introduced to improve their plight, many employers continue to ignore these rules.

ran its own restaurant. A school was founded by the association in 1962, and that same year, the merchants also built a Hindu temple. As the UAE's oil exports from Dubai began in 1963, Indians also came to be employed in petroleum companies as technicians, managers and support staff on three-year work permits issued by the government, which could be easily renewed. Through its trade expertise, manpower skills and loyal support of the rulers of Dubai, the Indian community thus managed to obtain protection for its temples, churches and cremation grounds, as well as support for its business interests.

By the end of the 1970s, Indians had become the most settled expatriate community in Dubai. Since they constituted a large proportion of the manpower in trade and commerce, Hindi was widely used in the market place. Indians occupied supervisory and technical positions in the electrical power plants, provided medical personnel for hospitals and constituted the largest pool of office workers. Cinemas screening Malayalam and Hindi films have become common in Dubai. Numerous small Indian eateries and restaurants have emerged as well.

Abu Dhabi

Abu Dhabi is the federal capital and the largest city of the UAE. In 1992, its population was estimated at 475,000. Abu Dhabi is the Emirate which has drawn the largest number of Indians in the Gulf region. The diaspora in Abu Dhabi consists of unskilled and semi-skilled construction workers; professionals such as engineers, managers and doctors; middle-level employees such as paramedical personnel; and office workers, who are present in large numbers. By the early 1980s, the Indian community in Abu Dhabi had formed a network of local community organisations such as the Indian Centre, Malayalee Samajam, Kerala Art Centre, Indian Ladies Association, Indian Islamic Centre and St. Joseph's Club. The Indian Association also runs two schools.

Sharjah, Ajman and Ras al-Khaima

A large concentration of Indian workers can also be found in Sharjah, with a population of 130,000; Ajman, with a

The Damodardas Jethanand & Sons store in the Old Souk market, an area which has numerous shops selling Indian textiles and snacks.

A line of Indian expatriates await the bus to Sharjah.

transfer their sponsorship after two years of service with their current employer. Firms which intend to recruit workers should get the contracts signed by jobseekers while they are still in India, to ensure that the workers have a salary and contract that is agreeable to them before they arrive in the UAE. Measures for a new work permit model, with full details regarding basic salaries, are now in place.

non-wage benefits, prescribed by UAE law, to expatriate workers of all categories (unskilled, semi-skilled and skilled) is quite common. Unfortunately, Indian workers in the UAE have little recourse for such violations, nor does the UAE have labour courts in which aggrieved workers may seek redress. Furthermore, according to UAE rules, only expatriate workers earning a monthly salary of 3000 dhirhams and who are holding accommodation rights are entitled to bring their families. Consequently, 75 per cent of Indian migrants do not have families with them.

The labour policy of the UAE government has resulted in the segregation of expatriate workers, particularly those in the unskilled and semi-skilled categories, from the national population and workforce. They are kept in labour camps at sites away from cities and towns. Necessities such as electricity, air-conditioning and water, and amenities such as cooking facilities, are not available in about a quarter of the labour camps. Overcrowding is also a problem. As a result of the fall in the number of migrant Indian workers and the reduction in their wage levels, the amount of savings of Indian expatriates has fallen drastically.

Recently, new rules and regulations for expatriate employers have been introduced. A number are being considered in the UAE (and Qatar) which will favour legally employed Indian expatriates, while punishing defaulters, illegal workers and others who flout immigration and labour laws. The new rules allow expatriates to

The UAE government is also considering introducing optional exit permits for expatriates going on holiday in order to do away with the current practice of employers holding employees' passports. To prevent the exploitation of Gulf jobseekers by touts in India acting as recruiting agents, the UAE government plans to set up a holding company to supply the manpower for bringing skilled personnel to the country. The UAE is also taking pains to ensure that no favouritism is practised in the recruitment of workers. Additionally, workers who default, leave their sponsors and take up other employment in the country will be convicted, jailed and later deported. A federal law allowing the creation of workers' organisations and unions in the UAE is also being considered. This would be a watershed in the history of the GCC countries.

In spite of stricter regulations both in the UAE and India, malpractice abounds. Reports of female workers found abandoned and clandestine clearance rackets flourishing in India appear regularly in the media. Indian women are recruited ostensibly for babysitting positions, but are left on the streets upon arrival in the UAE. Most of them end up in jail after a period of prostitution. Networks of middlemen illegally recruit women for employment as housemaids. In 2003, the government of India prohibited the recruitment of women below 30 years of age for employment in the Gulf countries. Emigration in the case of women above 30 years of age was open only to those who had their contract, sponsor's declaration and work visa certified by the Indian embassy in the country of employment. Despite such stringent rules, scores of women emigrate with forged documents, each woman paying not less than Rs. 20,000 to touts and others who claim to be authorised agents.

BAHRAIN

Bahrain is a small country with minimal oil reserves. However, its central location among the countries of the Persian Gulf has enabled it to develop into a prominent centre for petroleum processing and refining. It has also grown into an international banking centre. By the end of the 1970s, expatriates formed 40 per cent of the labour force in Bahrain, with a local population then of 225,000. The proportion of expatriates was maintained at about 40 per cent until around 2002, though the total population registered a sharp increase from 262,000 in 1975 to 690,000 in 2001. Bahrain's Indian population in 2002 numbered approximately 130,000, most of whom originated from Kerala and other South Indian states.

Indian High School – Dubai

Founded in 1961 and run by a Board of Trustees, the Indian High School in Dubai is recognised by the Central Board of Secondary Education of the government of India. It prepares students for grade 10 and grade 12 examinations. The first batch of grade 10 students graduated in 1977 and the first batch of grade 12 students in 1979. The school has two campuses, with the branch school accommodating girls in grades 1 to 4. The school runs two shifts, the morning shift for girls and the afternoon shift for boys.

A volleyball match at the Indian High School in Dubai.

The school has a fleet of 71 air-conditioned buses to transport staff and students to school and back. It has three libraries, three computer laboratories, three science laboratories and a home science laboratory. Three counselling centres under the leadership of expert counsellors also function in the school. In addition, the school has full-time medical officers and nurses. The splendid Sheik Rashid Auditorium, which has a seating capacity of 1800, was inaugurated in January 1994.

The Indian High School is one of the leading institutions in the Gulf countries under the control and guidance of Indian expatriates.

Based on www.indianhighschooldubai.org/aboutschool.html.

In the first half of the 20th century, Indian merchants established import businesses in rice, tea, sugar and shoes, subsidised Arab smugglers of gold and pearls, and managed the trade in hashish and opium from Kabul to Bombay, the Gulf and elsewhere in the Middle East. With the development of the Bahrain Petroleum Company in the 1930s and the establishment of refineries, Indians were recruited for work in Bahrain as ministerial staff and technicians. The number of merchants from Gujarat and Sind and the number of nurses from Kerala who arrived in Bahrain also rose. The large influx began after 1973, following the hike in the price of oil. This period also coincided with other favourable developments, such as independence in 1971 and the beginning of large-scale construction work in aluminium plants, shipping yards, banking institutions and petrochemical complexes. Employment opportunities for Bahrainis increased by 10 per cent per year during the latter half of the 1970s, but the best jobs in offshore banking, dockyards and communications went to expatriates. Indians had a particular advantage due to their familiarity with the English language and their relatively high levels of education and work experience. They were also prepared to work for wages much lower than those given to Europeans, Americans and Arabs. There were reportedly 9000 Indian workers in Bahrain by the mid-1970s.

The Indians are Bahrain's largest expatriate community even today, and account for about 30 per cent of its total workforce. Indian workers who are employed as skilled and semi-skilled labourers in the construction, maintenance and service sectors account for about 70 per cent of the Indian diaspora in Bahrain. In general, they have earned a good reputation in terms of their conduct, loyalty, productivity and non-involvement in local affairs. However, Indian housemaids, who number about 10,000 in Bahrain, occasionally face problems of maltreatment. A sizeable number of Indians also trade in provisions, jewellery and electronic goods, on both a wholesale and retail basis. Others work as carpenters or barbers and in other artisanal positions.

The Indian community has established schools and several sociocultural associations. There are 43 such organisations, including Keraleeya Samajam. These associations function under an umbrella organisation, the Coordination Committee of Indian Associations (CCIA). The Indian associations actively promote Indian culture. They also run specialised institutions, such as clinics for the mentally disabled and geriatric wards, and they offer donations for relief efforts at times of national disaster and to philanthropic organisations. Bahrain's liberal attitude to non-Muslim religious practices has enabled Indians to build churches, temples and gurdwaras in the country.

QATAR

Qatar had a local population of about 68,000 at the end of the 1970s. The expatriate population of the state in 1970 numbered 66,074, of which some 3600 (5.5 per cent) were Indians; however, by 1975 this figure had risen to 27,800. The increase has been quite rapid since then, rising to 75,000 in 1991 and 131,000 in 2001. In 2004, the figure hit 170,000, almost one-third of the total number of residents. Indians are highly respected in Qatar for their sincerity, hard work, technical expertise and law-abiding nature. Indians are employed in almost every local establishment, governmental or private, in various capacities.

A large proportion of the Indian community is engaged in unskilled and semi-skilled work and, therefore, belong to the low or lower-middle income groups. Only a small number, approximately one-tenth of the community, are engaged in professional jobs as doctors, engineers, accountants and bankers. The number of Indians who have established themselves as entrepreneurs is quite small. Nevertheless, they are affluent. The annual remittances from Qatar to India are estimated to be about Rs. 12 billion.

The Indian community has established four schools in Qatar—two of them started at least a decade ago—affiliated to the Indian Central Board of Secondary Education (CBSE) and the Kerala State Education Board syllabuses. An Indian cultural centre functions under the aegis of the Indian embassy and is the centre of the community's cultural activities. It oversees the activities of nearly 50 sociocultural organisations affiliated to it. These activities have attracted the attention and appreciation of other expatriate groups and even the local population.

KUWAIT

In 1976, Kuwait was the richest of the Arab states, with a per capita GNP of US$15,840. The total population of

Employees of the Bahrain Petroleum Company leaving the mosque of Manama after their prayers.

Dubai Municipality Roads Department engineers surveying Hatta Road. Indian professionals, who account for one-tenth of the total Indian population in the Gulf States, are respected for their technical expertise, sincerity and hard work.

Jamal Al Hai (left), a director with Dubai's department of civil aviation, presenting a memento to V. P. Arora (right), the deputy managing director of Indian Airlines, to mark the arrival of the carrier's inaugural flight from Jaipur via Delhi at Dubai International Airport in February 2002.

227

The Indian community gathers to celebrate Republic Day at the Indian embassy in Bahrain on 26 January 2006.

Kuwait in 2000 was estimated at between 1.32 million and 2.2 million. The Indian community is the largest expatriate community.

The Indian connection with Kuwait has a long history. Even during the early days, when Kuwait was just a small fishing and pearl-diving harbour town, trade flourished because of the dhows sailing between Mesopotamia, Sind and western India. Arab traders came to India, some of whom settled in Calicut and married local women, while Indians worked as pearl-divers in Kuwait. Indian merchants shipped rope and tea from Kerala in exchange for dates brought to Kuwait from Basra. The Indian presence became stronger after British intervention in the region. Indian officials began living and working in Kuwait, and the Indian rupee became its official currency. It was only in 1962 that Kuwait gained independence from the British.

Oil was discovered in Kuwait in 1930 and crude oil exports began in 1946. By the early 1950s, development projects were being initiated. The expansion of social services and construction activities led to a massive inflow of expatriates. By the mid-1970s, the imported labour force had become twice as large as the native labour force, though in those days the bulk of immigrant workers came from other Arab countries. In the early 1970s, the number of Indian workers reportedly stood at around 21,000, increased to 32,000 in 1975, and to 65,000 by 1979. More than half of this number were unskilled workers employed in the construction industry or as domestic help. Indian migrants, particularly those from Kerala, also worked in health services as doctors and paramedics. Keralites, who formed the largest ethnic group among Indians in Kuwait, had a high proportion of Catholics among them. However, Muslims and Hindus were also a significant proportion of the expatriates from Kerala. As in the many other Arab countries in the Gulf region, Indian expatriates established schools and social clubs in the country. Hindu shrines and Sikh gurdwaras were also set up.

The influx of Indians in large numbers followed the expansion of development activities in the late 1960s and the early 1970s. They settled comfortably in Kuwait and sent their children to non-Arab schools. They also set up social clubs and art circles. Indians were conspicuous in the Kuwaiti hotel industry, domestic services and medical jobs, but there was also a group who sought illegal jobs.

The Iraqi invasion of Kuwait in 1990 had a serious and dramatic impact on the non-national populations in all GCC countries. A huge proportion of the non-national population fled Kuwait. Before the Iraqi invasion, Kuwait had about 170,000 Indians. Only a small number remained following the start of the war.

However, since the end of the war, the size of the Indian diaspora in Kuwait has grown to 294,000. Indian businessmen in Kuwait, engaged in trading foodstuff, jewellery, garments and motor parts, have done quite well. A section of Indian expatriates is made up of professionals, such as engineers, doctors, accountants, scientists, software experts, management consultants and architects. Another is made up of skilled personnel, such as technical staff and nurses. But the majority are unskilled workers, mostly housemaids and ayahs working in Kuwaiti households.

The Indians in Kuwait have various cultural organisations founded on factors such as place of origin, language and religion. They hold occasional functions in the Indian Arts Circle Auditorium or the Indian embassy. At present, there are nine Indian schools in Kuwait with affiliations to the CBSE of India.

OMAN

The Indian connection with Oman in the modern era began in 1856, when the British became involved in Omani affairs soon after the death of the sultan. The imperial influence in Muscat grew between 1891 and the early 1930s through the prohibition of the transfer of Omani territory without British permission; Britain's guarantee of protecting the Muscat/Matrah conurbation from tribal onslaughts; the ultimatum issued by the British to the sultan against granting coaling facilities to the French; and the dispatch of Indian Army troops to Muscat to defend British residents against attack by Imamate forces.

In the 19th century, Indian merchants had a dominant position in the economy of Oman. They handled the traditional trade of rice, coffee, tea and cotton goods in exchange for dates, dried fish and pomegranates from Oman. In addition, many Indians were the import and export agents of Western companies in Oman. They managed both wholesale and retail trade, and functioned as bankers. By 1856, few products were exchanged in the Omani empire without an Indian merchant being involved in some way. The Indian merchants included Muslims from Sind and Hindu merchants from Gujarat. While the Muslim merchants became Omani citizens, Hindu merchants were not allowed citizenship, although

A waterfront house in Muttrah, Oman. Muttrah is home to one of Oman's oldest trading ports. A number of the older buildings show the influence of Indian architectural styles.

Sindhi and Gujarati merchants in Oman

Indian merchant activity in Oman has a long history. By the 15th century, there was clear evidence of Indian merchants settled in Muscat, the principal city and port of Oman. Indian merchants were important in the 16th and early 17th centuries due to their linkage with the Portuguese as they endeavoured to establish a monopoly over the Indian Ocean and the Gulf trade. By the mid-17th century, however, Indian merchants in Oman moved to link themselves with local political forces and helped those forces to push the Portuguese out of Oman. This began a period of growing importance for the Indian merchant communities in Oman, which lasted until the late 19th century.

The period from the late 17th to 19th century saw considerable change in the merchant communities in Oman and major changes in the conditions under which they operated. The earliest of these merchant groups were the Sindhi Bhattias, whose operations were based in manufacturing and the trading position of Thattha. These groups made themselves an important element of economic life in Oman and were so fully accepted that they were able to build temples and practise their religion. By the 18th century, there were as many as 1200 Sindhi Bhattias settled in Muscat. Their assistance in actions against the Portuguese put them in good stead, and a contemporary account notes that they were 'permitted to live agreeably with their own rules, to bring their women hither, to set up idols in their chambers, and to bury their dead.' There were two temples at this time in Muscat.

From the 1780s to the 1820s, however, the Sindhi Bhattia presence declined in importance. The economy of Thattha collapsed because of changes in the course of the Indus, which left the city stranded. Commercial patterns in Oman changed as the rulers began to assert an even greater role in trading, with the result that Indian merchants had to take careful measures not to trespass on the rulers' trading prerogatives. As these changes were taking place, the economic power of the Kutchi Bhattias was growing and they were able to establish themselves in Oman from the late 18th century into the 19th century. By 1836, they were recognised as the 'principal merchants' in Muscat and their influence increased when the sultan of Oman shifted his capital to Zanzibar and played a much smaller role in commercial affairs in Muscat. By 1840, the Kutchi Bhattias numbered more than 2000.

In the late 19th century, conditions began to change yet again as the regime became more fundamentalist and the Bhattias found themselves under pressure. They began to leave Oman and, by 1870, there were only 250 Bhattias left. The Indian Khojas from Sind and Gujarat then became the economically powerful group. The Khojas had strong modern shipping interests and good connections along the west coast of India, through the Gulf and to the east coast of Africa. These connections worked very much to their advantage in the new, more international economic climate in which Oman found itself.

Peter Reeves

they held a secure place in the economy. Indian merchants worked closely with government officials, provincial governors and the ruling family.

Compared to its neighbours, Oman has found it easier to accept non-Arab and non-Muslim expatriates who arrived after the 1973 hike in oil prices. In 1975, there were nearly 71,000 expatriate workers in Oman, of whom 26,000 (approximately 37 per cent) were from India. Indians worked in building sites in towns and as tailors, plumbers, welders and petrol pump attendants in rural areas. Some Indians were directly employed by Arab households as ayahs, cooks, sweepers and gardeners. By 2001, the Indian population numbered some 311,000 out of a total population of 2.3 million. Indians accounted for 14 per cent of the total population, but they formed 58 per cent of the expatriate population in Oman.

Oman is perhaps the only Arab country that grants citizenship to foreigners. Any person, irrespective of religion, who has lived in Oman for a minimum of 20 years, can apply for citizenship. About 1000 Indians had acquired Omani citizenship by 2001.

Social life among the various communities in Oman is highly segmented. The Indian middle class maintains some social contacts with English-speaking Arabs other than Omanis. In 1974, the sultan granted the Indian community land to build a social centre. In 1996, Oman declared that its residents had the freedom to follow any form of worship and religious practice. Muscat has two Hindu temples, one of which has existed for over a century. Two Sikh gurdwaras have recently been established in the labour camps. There are also seven churches in Oman which serve various denominations of Christians.

The Indians are a heterogeneous group. They consist of unskilled, semi-skilled and skilled workers, who make up 25 per cent, 30 per cent and 35 per cent of Indian personnel respectively. The remaining 10 per cent comprise engineers, bankers, financial experts and professional managers. In 2001, there were nearly 2000 Indian doctors. Several Indians hold senior management positions in the corporate sector and positions in ministries, government departments and public sector undertakings. Indians are also employed in newspapers, mostly in the English-language press.

Culturally, Indians in Oman are proud of their heritage and maintain strong links with India. They organise a large number of cultural events, often with the participation of artists from India. As many as 14 Indian schools function in Oman, 13 following the CBSE syllabus and the syllabus of the Kerala State Education Board. Several cinema halls in Muscat screen only Hindi and Malayali films. More than 25 Indian associations formed on the

basis of linguistic, regional and other affiliations function in Oman. However, the Indian Social Club is currently the only authorised representative of Indians in Oman. The community has always contributed generously in cash and in kind to international relief efforts for national disasters.

SAUDI ARABIA

Saudi Arabia is the largest member of the GCC states, with a land area of about 2,240,000 sq km. Much of the country remains uninhabited, being harsh, sandy and dry desert with temperature extremes. It has permanent pastures in about 56 per cent of the land in use, with arable land constituting as little as 1 per cent and forested land constituting another 1 per cent. The absence of perennial rivers or permanent bodies of water has deprived Saudi Arabia of freshwater resources. Sea water desalination plants are used extensively.

Even though the 'Indian connection' was the most significant political, economic and cultural link that Saudi Arabia had with the outside world until the late 1960s, the presence of Indian workers among the expatriates was small at the time. Before 1973, the Indian connection was limited to trade in Indian goods by Indian merchants, while Saudi businessmen traded Arabian goods in Indian cities such as Hyderabad and Bombay. Even after the hike in oil prices, there were only about 34,500 Indians in Saudi Arabia in 1975, with a total population of nearly 773,400. The departure of about 1 million Yemenis from Saudi Arabia following the Gulf War of 1990 provided a golden opportunity for expatriates from India to secure

An Indian gold merchant counts gold rings from India in Muscat's Mutrah Souk. Gold jewellery is often given as part of the dowry for brides in Arab societies.

The Indian Muslim presence in Hijaz

In January 2006, the Saudi authorities increased the quota for Indians making the haj by 10,000 pilgrims. An increase of Indian Muslim hajis from the annual 10,000 pilgrims in the Mughal era to 53,000 at present makes the haj the biggest regular diasporic movement of Indian Muslims. Historically, travelling to Hijaz has not merely been an expression of 'return' to a *ruhani watn* (spiritual homeland) for Indian Muslims, who also claimed to be *khadms* (protectors/servers) of Mecca and Medina. The Indian Sufi Shaikh Ali Muttaqi declared himself a Mahdi (messiah) in a state of ecstasy, with popular consensus at Mecca; the Begum of Bhopal urged the Turks to leave the running of Mecca and Medina to her; and the Lucknow-based Muslim Hijaz Committee passed a resolution to 'liberate' and protect sites of Indian pilgrimage, such as tombs, from Saudi authorities.

There is a historical tradition of Indian Muslim writing on travels to Hijaz in the form of trave-logues, letters and guides from major religious thinkers such as Maulana Abul Kalam Azad and Maulana Siddiq Hassan Khan Bhopali. Following the first generally accepted account of haj writing by Maulana Rafi'u'd-din Murarabadi in the late 18th century, literary figures such as Shefa, Abdul-Majid Daryabadi and Shorish Kashmiri; leaders such as the Begum of Bhopal, the Nawab of Rampur and Muhammad Zafrullah Khan; and Anglo-Indian Orientalists such as John F. Keane, have documented their travels to Hijaz.

Indian Muslim records of Mecca and Medina began in the late 16th century. Shaikh Abdul-Haqq bin Saifu' Din charted the Indian religious and intellectual movements between India and Hijaz, and Shah Walliullah Dihlawi's biography details 17th- and 18th-century Indian Muslim Sufis in Mecca and Medina. Mirza Irfan Ali Beg's information for the *Anjuman-i Islamiyah* was pivotal here as he looked for Indian Muslims in circumambulations, barefoot journeys to Medina, and hospice, garden and mosque endowments. Nineteenth-century Mecca, according to observer Sadiq Bay, was a 'melting pot' of mobile groups, of which Indians were a part. The Indian diaspora in Hijaz even included Sufis seeking Ottoman asylum after being exiled by Mughal rulers. In spite of con-temporary quotas, the diaspora makes Mecca one of the most cosmopolitan areas in the world.

Indian Muslim travels to Hijaz form an important historical chapter of the Indian diaspora. Free from an age of quotas and visas, the Punjabi Sufi Naushah Ganj Baksh's father made seven hajs (a presumably traditional number). Kashmiri *qalandars* from the 1650s moved permanently to Hijaz, and Manikpur's Haji Ibrahim Muhaddis Qadiri spent 24 years in Mecca learning the Hadith (the sayings of the Prophet Muhammed). Some Indian Muslims travelled in large groups: Shaikh Muhammad Ma'sum went to Mecca with 100 dervishes (1656–57); and Shah Abdul Aziz departed for the haj with 800 passengers (1821–22) during political upheavals.

The development of Portuguese and Dutch ships between the 16th and 18th centuries facilitated the move-ment of Indian Muslim scholars to Hijaz, who started schools. The Indian Muslim Sufi Shaikh Ali Muttaqi acquired rare Arab books for copying and transmitting. Another Sufi, Shaikh Muhammad bin Fazlu'llah, respected by Hijazi *ulama* and Sufis, divided the *futuh* between the needy in India and Medina. Shaikh Abdul-Wahhab, whose *khanqah* (abode of Sufis or dervishes) became a haven for Indian pilgrims to Mecca and who supported their travel to Medina, also earned prestigious titles in Hijaz.

Pilgrims at Arafat.

The *Maarijul-Wilayat* records that the Indian Chistiyya *silsila* (order) was popular in Hijaz from the time of Fuzayl bin Iyaz. Indian Sufis in Hijaz, including Mir Saiyid Sibghatullah bin Ruhulla, spread their teachings to the rest of the 'Muslim world'. The famous Indian Chisti, Shaikh Salim Chisti, began a 13-year pilgrimage to Hijaz in 1524–25, visiting modern-day Iraq, Syria, Turkey and Iran. Nanak (the first Sikh Guru), a 16th-century pilgrim, was given the title of *muwahhid* in a tradition similar to his Sufi predecessors. Indians of the diaspora were initiated into Chistiyya, Qadiriyya and Naqshbandiyya Sufi orders in Hijaz. In 1656, Indian Muslim Naqshbandis, such as Shaikh Adam Banuri, and other pilgrims asserted an Indian Muslim presence through direct conflict with the Hijazi *ulama* and Sufis over differing mystical claims.

Travelling to Hijaz revived Islam in the diaspora. Shah Walliullah returned to India in 1732 to revive Islamic discourse in India; and Shah Abdul Aziz returned from witnessing Muhammad bin Abdul-Wahhab's puritanical movement in 1822 with the aim of establishing a similar Sunni govern-ment from Peshawar to Calcutta. While the author of 18th-century Sufi masterpieces such as *Kashkul* returned from Hijaz to gain Indian Chistiyya respect, the 19th-century Haji Shariati returned from Hijaz to form the anti-colonial Faraizi Movement. In the 20th century, scholars from an Indian Muslim body, Ahl-i Hadith, travelled to meet Ibn Saud in Hijaz and attend the Hijaz Conference. The Ahl-i Hadith is an interesting aspect of the diaspora as Hijaz returnees identify themselves as *salafi* and publish Urdu, Hindi and English translations of fatwas by the Saudi *ulama*. Due to Saudi mone-tary assistance for Indian Islamic institutions and publishing houses, the diaspora encompasses *madrasah* students in Saudi Arabian Islamic universities (educated to return as Indian *madrasah* teachers) to *salafis* employed in the Saudi public and private sectors. Recent pressure on the Indian government by Indian Muslim organisations for increasing haj quotas promises an even more visible Indian Muslim presence in Saudi Arabia.

Terenjit S. Sevea

jobs in Saudi Arabia. Since then, the Indian population has increased to 1.4 million in 2002.

There are three categories of Indian workers in Saudi Arabia. The first group comprises doctors, engineers, accountants and managers, most of whom are employed in the government and private sector on term contracts. This category accounts for more than 5 per cent of the Indian community. Nearly 10 per cent are employed as clerks, secretaries, account clerks and storekeepers. The rest, accounting for nearly 85 per cent of the Indian diaspora in Saudi Arabia, work in project sites and indus-trial establishments as operations and maintenance staff. In addition, there is a group of illegal immigrants who either work in the country without sponsors, or who have come to the kingdom on haj visas, and then stayed on to take up work.

Indians are held in high esteem in the country and are considered indispensable to Saudi Arabia's infrastructural, agricultural and industrial growth. They are seen as peace-ful, loyal, disciplined and devoted workers. The Indian community has adjusted well to the environment and has established several cultural and social organisations. International Indian schools have been established in several towns of Saudi Arabia, in which about 32,000 Indian children are enrolled under the CBSE pattern up to the 12th standard. Social and cultural events are organ-ised regularly by the community and parents participate actively in school activities. However, Saudi Arabia does not allow expatriates to have any political roles.

In recent years, Indians in Saudi Arabia have been remitting about US$4 billion to India annually, the largest amount from any single country. The Indian dias-pora in Saudi Arabia invested heavily in the 'Resurgent India Bonds' in 1998 and the 'Millennium Deposit Bonds' in 2000, which have contributed to India's foreign exchange reserves. They have also responded generously to calls for disaster relief.

In recent years, the Saudi system has shown some signs of modernisation and employers are now much more sensitive to the needs of their workers. Still, living conditions in Saudi Arabia continue to be onerous and irksome to some.

Recently, the Saudi perception that foreigners are a security threat has led to a move towards 'Saudiisation'. It is expected that about 3 million expatriates will have to leave Saudi Arabia to increase the percentage of Saudis in the workforce to 80 per cent by 2013. If brought to fruition, Indians would have to bear the brunt of this policy, given that they remain the largest expatriate community in the kingdom.

SOCIO-ECONOMIC PROFILE

The Indian population in the Gulf region has shown a positive shift in its socio-economic profile since the late 1980s. There has been an increase in absolute numbers and in the proportion of professionals and white-collar workers. The professionals and white-collar workers employed in these countries live relatively isolated lives: their contact and interaction with the native population are mostly formal and impersonal. The most important and perhaps the only attraction in these countries is the high remuneration that their services can fetch. Nonetheless, they maintain lively contacts with other Indians in the region, the extent of which is influenced by shared religion, language, place of origin and profession. Only highly paid professionals and white-collar workers

A senior Indian economist in Saudi Arabia

Dr Prajapati Trivedi, a senior economist of the World Bank, is on secondment as economic advisor to the ministry of economy and planning in Saudi Arabia. He is responsible for public policy advice on a wide range of national long-term strategies for the kingdom. He authored a key paper on public sector efficiency for the Vision Symposium, which was jointly organised by the World Bank and the ministry of economy and planning. Dr Trivedi is also the guiding hand behind public sector reform issues within the ministry.

Dr Trivedi is recognised as the most qualified and one of the highest-ranking Indian expatriates in Saudi Arabia

Based on www.yahind.com/articles/interviews/prajapati_trivedi.shtml.

are allowed to bring their families with them. Their children are enrolled in Indian schools, which generally follow the CBSE syllabus; there are also a few schools which follow the Kerala State Education Board syllabus.

Indians in the Gulf countries make frequent visits home and maintain regular contact with friends and relatives. With improvements in the channels and methods of communication, Indian expatriates have kept abreast of the socio-political, cultural and economic development trends in India. They participate actively in relief and rehabilitation following natural disasters. They send almost all their hard-earned savings back home to India, mostly by way of remittance and also by way of FCNR (Foreign Currency Non-Resident) deposits in Indian banks. The bulk of such remittances, however, come primarily from the unskilled and semi-skilled workers who form the vast majority of Indians in the Gulf region.

LABOUR IN THE GULF STATES

Labour force participation rates among the national populations of the GCC countries have historically been very low. High birth rates have resulted in populations with more than 50 per cent under 15 years of age. In addition, the GCC countries have, in general, highly conservative Muslim populations where the female labour force participation rates are notoriously low. Adult male labour participation rates also remain low due to domestic economic policies, highly subsidised rates for housing and public utilities, free and high-quality education and healthcare facilities, generous pension provisions and liberal family allowances. These policies have tended to make the national populations indolent and averse to participating in work, physical or otherwise, even during the prime years of their adulthood. The few who do participate have proven themselves to be inefficient, thanks to the excess of incentives bestowed upon them. It is the public sector which has provided the nationals with employment, primarily to ensure their loyalty to the state. They prefer to join the public service as they are attracted by the high rates of remuneration.

Nationals are not likely to be able to fulfil the manpower requirements in any of these countries in the foreseeable future. A surprising result of the excessive and perverse incentives given to national populations in education and training has been the unbalanced occupational turnout of the education system. Students have almost exclusively opted for studies in arts and law, allowing them to enter more agreeable areas of the public sector. The proportion of students specialising in natural sciences, engineering, medicine, information technology and agriculture has been very low. Few GCC nationals

participate in vocational training courses. As and when public sector employment ceases to be available at a stage not far off in the future, GCC nationals will find it difficult to obtain private sector employment where high-level skills and vocational training are required. National unemployment has already emerged as a problem in these countries, and it is likely to become increasingly serious in years to come.

Non-national labour is undoubtedly much less costly than national labour and is available in high numbers from Asian countries, particularly India and Pakistan. However, GCC countries are conscious of the non-monetary costs involved when huge non-national populations are present in their countries, including threats to national security and national culture. It is because of this that the GCC governments are calling on private sector employers to curb the employment of non-nationals and to turn increasingly to nationals. Until now, such requests have remained, by and large, unheeded.

ARABISATION

All the GCC countries have thus launched policies of 'Arabisation' of their workforce. Perturbed by the presence of expatriate labour across all occupations and skill levels, which constitute around two-thirds of the total workforce and 95 per cent of labour in the private sector, Saudi Arabia followed a policy aimed at increasing the employment of Saudi nationals across all sectors of the national economy and at arresting the outflow of Saudi income in the form of remittances to countries abroad in the 1990s and early 21st century. Between 1993 and 2002, expatriates remitted US$156.1 billion from the kingdom, which accounted for more than 5 per cent of its

The International Indian magazine focuses on Indian expatriate communities in the Middle East.

Indian financial analysts working in Standard Chartered bank in Dubai.

Indian workers up early in the morning to buy fruit from an all-night grocery store in Sharjah.

K. S. Rajan

K. S. Rajan was born in Tellichery, Kerala, in July 1945 to the Chandramana Namboothiri family of Ezhimala. He holds degrees in economics, English literature and business administration.

Rajan is a prominent member of the Indian community in Riyadh and is also a well-known champion snooker player. He was the general secretary of the Malabar Airport Development Committee, president of the Kohinoor Toastmasters Club and joint secretary of the Embassy of India Club in Riyadh. He was also the election commissioner for the first election of the International Indian School. He organised and participated actively in two national seminars held in India on 'Development of Human Resources for Industrial Growth' and the 'Role of Instrumentation in National Development', and received an award from India's president for the latter.

In 1975, Rajan joined Saudi Catering and Contracting, one of the top 100 companies in the kingdom, as a marketing officer. He is comfortably settled in Riyadh with his family. His article 'Courageous Decision Made This Kingdom' appeared recently in a book released by the Saudi ministry of information entitled *Encounters with Saudi Arabia*. Rajan's counsel to his fellow men is 'Work sincerely and efficiently and respect the laws of the country to be happy.'

Based on www.yahind.com/articles/interviews/ks_rajan.shtml.

GDP. The attempt at indigenisation of the workforce is not confined to Saudi Arabia. All other GCC countries have launched similar policies.

In 2003, the Saudi manpower council decreed that the number of expatriates in the kingdom should not exceed 20 per cent of the total population by 2013, and that the population from any single foreign nation should not exceed 10 per cent of the total. If the projected statistics are ever to be realised, about 3 million expatriates would have to leave Saudi Arabia. More recently, the kingdom, through its ministry of labour, has increased the pressure on small- and medium-sized businesses to employ more Saudi citizens, a measure that will be difficult to enforce due to problems of regulating and overseeing their performance and the difficulty on the part of these businesses to employ Saudi citizens at their privileged terms of service and high rates of remuneration. In 2001, the 120-member consultative committee to the Council of Ministers, the Shoura, began applying the indigenisation measures to large public sector conglomerates, such as Saudi Aramco.

Arabisation efforts in certain professions, such as medical and paramedical personnel, are bound to have only limited success. Arabisation would not be achieved substantially in the profession of nursing, for example, due to the specialised training required, the need for English-speaking nurses, and the religious taboos and general reluctance on the part of women in the kingdom to take up the profession.

As part of the policy of Arabisation, GCC countries have imposed serious restrictions on non-national workers bringing their families with them. Kuwait has, for example, ruled that dependants will not be allowed to enter the country if the worker earns less than US$1500 per month in the public sector and US$2200 in the private sector. The corresponding figure in the UAE is US$1089.

If the policies of the GCC countries remain unchanged, it is unlikely that any significant decline in the size and proportion of the non-national population will take place. Since the current structure of incentives for national workers is likely to continue, private sector employers will continue to hire expatriates. If the current educational and training preferences of the national populations continues, nationals will also continue to acquire qualifications and training in occupations which are not of great value in the labour market. Even if employers prefer appointing nationals, they will have difficulty finding nationals who have the appropriate mix of skills.

Indian workers commute from one bank of the Dubai Creek to the other.

Signs of India's growing involvement with the diaspora can be seen in this session of the India-Gulf Partnership Summit held in the Dubai Chamber of Commerce and Industry, 15–16 June 2006.

Fears about the stability and level of oil prices have led to a decrease in public expenditure by most of the GCC countries. In their bid to reduce public expenditure and eliminate fiscal deficits, the GCC governments have also been trying to shift several public sector enterprises and activities to the private sector. Attempts are also being made to increase non-oil revenue. The governments are also engaged in an ongoing attempt to cut subsidies in areas such as wheat production, fuel and communications. They are considering reducing the pension burden by cutting back on rates and benefits.

EXPECTATIONS

In the 21st century, Indian contract workers in the Gulf States, whether they are labourers, skilled workers or professionals, provide India with a very important source of foreign exchange. Remittances to India constitute a source of capital for development purposes greater than any other single form of 'development aid'. In 2003, remittances, which formed 27 per cent of India's exports, amounted to almost eight times the Overseas Development Aid and five times the Foreign Direct Investment which India received from international sources. Commentators now talk of remittances in terms of Personal Development Assistance.

Although 21st-century contract workers are much more important as contributors to the economy of the homeland than earlier migrants, such as indentured workers, the oppressive living and working conditions they face still have much in common with the earlier periods of labour movements. Modern contract workers, however, are more aware of their value and therefore have expectations that the government of India will bring about improvements in their conditions. They expect the ministry of labour, for example, to prevent malpractice by recruiting agents in India, who often exploit gullible emigrants and swindle hefty amounts from them as fees for visas and work passes.

Workers expect state governments in India to set up appropriate agencies to advise prospective emigrants about their rights and obligations and the conditions they can expect in the host countries. They want the state governments to devise the means to save them from all forms of exploitation by agents in India and employers abroad. The government of India, therefore, needs to be able to guarantee the authenticity of jobs offered to recruits and the reliability of the parties offering such jobs. The government is expected to prepare a Standard Labour Export Agreement with the concurrence of the Gulf countries, which would cover areas such as minimum wage, free housing, weekly holidays, length of the working day, overtime allowances, return air tickets and compensation for on-the-job training and injury.

One of the major expectations is that the government of India should take the steps necessary to put a stop to the practice of employers who take the passports and travel documents of their employees upon arrival. It is also hoped that the Indian diplomatic missions and consulates in the Gulf countries will take a more active interest in understanding and finding solutions to problems faced by workers when living and working in foreign companies. Another hope is that the government of India will take steps to refund workers' deposits with the Protector of Emigrants and put it towards the expected costs of repatriation to India.

Indians abroad also want to see the government taking steps to reduce the exploitation and harassment of returning workers by customs officials in airports and to reduce the cost of air travel between the Gulf countries and India. They also seek relief from the unjustified 'airport users' fee' levied by certain airports. In addition, it is hoped that the government will provide protection to female Indian workers—in particular women recruited as cooks, housemaids and governesses, categories to which local laws in the GCC countries do not apply—from physical violence, molestation and sexual abuse.

On a quite different level, there are now a number of areas in which those who regard themselves as non-resident Indians (NRIs) would like to see recognition of their economic importance. Generally, they would like to see consular work simplified and computerised to make it efficient and expeditious. Some also have economic expectations regarding the issuance of bonds for the implementation of capital-intensive projects with workers' funds and participation, and the prevention of bank fraud in dealing with accounts. Others seek preferential treatment for NRIs in importing machinery and equipment for setting up industrial units in India, and for trading in equities such as shares and debentures. They would also like to be granted permission to exercise their franchise in Indian elections to the parliament, state legislatures and local government bodies. In addition, some would like to see seats reserved for them in the Rajya Sabha. Some of these ideas are currently being explored.

S. Irudaya Rajan and P. R. Gopinathan Nair

Schoolchildren singing patriotic songs at the Indian embassy in Bahrain to celebrate Indian Independence Day on 15 August 2005.

233

YEMEN

THERE IS A LONG history of Indians and Indian settlements in the southern littoral states of the Arabian peninsula. Indian merchants and middlemen based in Yemen were historically active in the Red Sea trade, while others based in Oman were involved in trade in the Gulf and the wider Indian Ocean networks. We can picture these connections using accounts of three situations: Ashin Das Gupta's account of Gujaratis in the Red Sea trade; R. J. Gavin's account of merchants, professionals, soldiers and workers in Aden between the 1840s and 1930s; and the post-colonial situation in Yemen.

GUJARATIS AND THE RED SEA TRADE

In the 17th and early 18th centuries, Gujarati merchants, principally from Surat but also from Cambay, Diu and Ahmedabad, were highly important in trading activities centred in Yemen but also stretching along the Hadhramaut and through the Red Sea area. The prime trade from the Gujarati side was in textiles; it is estimated that at its peak, this trade was worth Rs. 4 million per year. A fleet of 20 Gujarati vessels—'the fleet of Hindustan'—made the journey each year to Mocha particularly to service the great haj markets at Jeddah and Mecca to the north and also the local trade in textiles.

Many Gujarati merchants in this period were settled in Yemeni cities such as Mocha and also in the port towns of the Habash and Hadhramaut. Major Gujarati Muslim merchants from Surat and a wealthy Bohra community from Ahmedabad were the most notable of this group and were the owners of warehouses and mansions in Mocha. The wealthiest of these merchants tended to come and go each year with 'the fleet of Hindustan'.

Still larger in number were the communities of banias from Kathiawar, many of whom were settled more permanently in Yemen. These merchants played vital roles in the economic life of Yemen but, unlike the Muslim merchants, they were treated harshly and regarded as social inferiors because of their religion. They were not allowed any public practice of their religion: any bania who died in Yemen

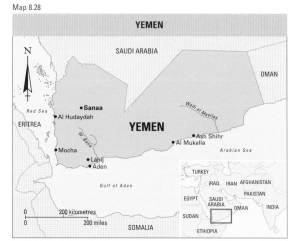

Map 8.28

Amerya school and mosque in the city of Radaa, 160 km east of Sanaa. Built by Yemen's Bani Taher royal family in 1504, Amerya is one of the country's most famous historic buildings.

was buried, not cremated. Neither were they allowed to bring their womenfolk to Yemen nor permitted to have relations with Arab women. In the late 17th and early 18th centuries, they persevered despite these handicaps. However, by the 1720s, changes in trading patterns due to greater competition from European trade, along with the rise of Islamist movements that led to the persecution of the banias, brought an end to the exodus of the Gujaratis and settled Indian communities.

COLONIAL ADEN

Indian merchants began to operate freely in Yemen again in the early 19th century under British auspices as British imperialism sought to exert dominance in the littoral states of the Indian Ocean. That influence increased with the British acquisition of Aden in southern Yemen in 1839. Aden and its hinterland were now open to direct British control. Moreover, as a port, Aden was important not only for the Red Sea and the Indian Ocean's commerce and passenger traffic but also for its natural harbour, which aided the development of a naval base for the imperial defence. The port of Aden and the coastal area of the Hadhramaut, running eastward as far as the Omani territory of Dhofar, was under the Bombay administration from 1839 until just before the outbreak of war in 1939.

As the territory was under the Bombay administration, a considerable influx of Indians to Aden occurred, resulting in the existence of a strong Indian community.

Indians coming to Aden covered a wide spectrum.

A view of Aden in 1864.

Table 8.21

	Arabs	Somalis	Jews	Indians	Europeans	Others	Total
POPULATION OF ADEN BY COMMUNITY (1839–1955)							
1839	617	63	574	35	N.A.	N.A.	1289
1849	4845	2877	1150	7605	778	1860	19,115
1856	4812	2896	1224	8568	791	2452	20,743
1881	13,285	9150	2121	7265	2101	789	34,711
1901	N.A.	N.A.	N.A.	N.A.	N.A.	N.A.	39,986
1921	N.A.	N.A.	N.A.	N.A.	N.A.	N.A.	57,571
1931	29,820	3935	4120	7387	1145	331	46,738
1955	103,879	10,611	831	15,857	4484	2608	138,270

Based on R. J. Gavin, Aden Under British Rule, 1837–67, 1975.

At the labouring level, there were contract workers who were employed to build new fortifications needed for the naval base, which took some 15 years to complete. Then there was the garrison itself, which, with its need for provisions and services, was a major sector of the economy of the city. Many Indians were engaged in various services for the garrison. There were also those who found employment in the administration itself. By the 1850s, there was an almost complete turnaround in the subordinate clerical services of the administration: the Arabs and Jews who had formerly managed this work were completely replaced by Indians.

Perhaps the most notable group were the Bombay and Gujarati merchants who, building on their connections with the garrison, gradually moved into wider trading activities, brokerage and newer forms of investment, such as hotels. As they grew increasingly wealthy, they became leading figures in the Indian community. Especially important among this group were Parsi merchants from Bombay, such as Sorabji Cowasji, Edulji Manockji, Cowasji Dinshaw and others who were well-connected to the administration—a Manockji was the head accountant and treasurer from 1856—and wielded considerable influence both in Aden and Bombay, from where the administration was directed. They maintained their importance in the competitive trading milieu that developed, in which there were American, French, German and Italian firms vying with them; and they used, as did other foreigners, their connections in Europe, the US and (especially) Bombay to further their aims. Below them in position and wealth were 'rank and file' Indian firms, which also prospered as members of the Aden Chamber of Commerce in servicing the garrison, passenger liners and bunkering activities, as well as local trading activity.

Indian merchants were not confined to Aden itself. They moved widely through the Hadhramaut and became important in the smaller port towns there. Gavin records that 'the port of Mukalla had an Indian flavour about it, the Parsi traders had the ear of the authorities and much Hindustani was spoken in the streets.'

POST-COLONIAL YEMEN

In the immediate post-war period, Aden's economic activity expanded greatly due to the general upsurge in world trade. The expansion of Aden's port was stimulated by increased tanker traffic to and from the oil fields of the Gulf. Except for the periods when the Suez Canal was closed, the port of Aden continued to expand throughout the 1950s, and in 1958 it was the busiest harbour in the world after New York. Moreover, as the only sovereign British base in the Middle East, the colony offered security to foreign investors. Local trading agencies made profits out of the shipping boom and the increase in port traffic, and most expanded their businesses in new directions. The Aden government, and especially the British armed forces, added to the boom by building hospitals, schools, barracks, housing and shopping facilities for the military personnel. An estimated 40,000 labourers, mostly Indian, were attracted to the colony to execute these projects.

After the departure of the British from Aden and the proclamation of the People's Democratic Republic of Yemen on 14 October 1967, the Indian community numbered more than 100,000, about 1.41 per cent of the population. When the two parts of Yemen united and the Republic of Yemen was proclaimed on 22 May 1990, the number of Indians remained at around 100,000. These people of Indian origin are concentrated in the southern part of the country, around Aden, Al Mukalla, Ash Shihr, the Lahij province and the ports of Mocha and Al Hudaydah. The community poses no problems and has acquired local citizenship.

Other Indian expatriates in Yemen are mainly hospital personnel, professionals, academics, and skilled and semi-skilled workers. Estimated at around 9000 in 2004, about half of them are from Kerala, and the rest are from Andhra Pradesh, Tamil Nadu and Goa.

Peter Reeves and Irena Knehtl

British troops marching through the streets of Aden. After Aden became part of the Bombay Presidency in 1839, a large number of Indians, including administrators, merchants and labourers, arrived.

Mohammed Jumaa Khan (1903–64)

Mohammed Jumaa Khan is considered one of Yemen's greatest singers. He enriched the country with countless songs that are still sung today not only in Yemen but in the whole region. He was born in Qarn Majid in Wadi Dawan, Hadhramaut, to a Yemeni mother and an Indian father, a soldier whose army had been recruited by Sultan Al Quaiti to establish power in the Hadhramaut region.

Hadhramaut is the coastal region of southern Arabia, extending from the Gulf of Aden in the Arabian Sea, eastward along the Yemeni coast, to the Dhofar region of Oman. Historically, the name refers to the Hadhramaut sultanates, a collective term for the Quaiti and Kathiri sultanates which were loosely under the British protectorate of South Arabia, guided by a British resident at Aden until 1967. The northern edge of the Hadhramaut slopes down to the desert of Al Rub al Khali, the 'Empty Quarter'. Hadhramis harvest crops of wheat and millet, tend to date and coconut groves, and grow coffee.

Young Khan loved music and singing since his childhood. He was appointed a member of the sultan's music band and later became its leader. After his retirement, he moved from place to place in Hadhramaut, singing his songs to the people. He recorded many of his songs and is credited with the revival of traditional Hadhrami songs and ballads. His music and texts derive from the local rhymes of daily life and dances.

Khan, a Yemeni singer.

ISRAEL

The cornerstone from Kochi's oldest synagogue.

Map 8.29

THERE ARE MANY parallels between the creation of the modern states of India and Israel. Both are former British colonies: India became independent in 1947 and Israel one year later. Both states were partitioned out of larger colonies along religious and demographic lines: India was carved out of the larger section of British India, where the majority of the population was Hindu; and Israel was created on about 22 per cent of British Mandatory Palestine, in areas where Jews were the majority. In both cases, the Muslim population was contained within neighbouring states, Pakistan and Jordan respectively. In addition, huge and disputatious population transfers followed upon the creation of these new states, leaving a legacy of strife.

At the time of India's independence, there were approximately 35,000 Jews among the population of 330 million. Indian Jews are essentially of three groups. The oldest Jewish community in India is found in and around Kochi (formerly known as Cochin), a port city on India's southwest coast in the state of Kerala. Arguably the oldest Jewish community east of Iran, Kochi Jews claim that their ancestors arrived at nearby Cranganore in 70 AD, at the time of the Roman conquest of ancient Israel and the sacking of Jerusalem. Historical evidence cannot explicitly confirm this claim, but it does demonstrate its plausibility. Jews in Kochi acculturated well into local society without losing their distinct identity. They held high positions in government and the military, and prospered as agriculturalists, shipbuilders, international spice merchants and petty traders. They were divided into Malabaris, descendants of the original refugees, and Pardesis (foreigners), who were mostly Sephardic Jews of Eastern origin (including North Africa and the Arab countries) who arrived in the early 16th century. Their population peaked at around 2500.

The second group, the Bene Israel Jews of the Konkan Coast near Mumbai, are of unknown origin. They claim to be the descendants of shipwrecked individuals who managed to find a niche in local society as oil-pressers. Eventually, they encountered Jews from Kochi, Christian missionaries, the so-called Baghdadi Jews of Mumbai, and other significant reference groups, all of whom led them on an unlikely journey to finding their identity. Bene Israel Jews migrated from Konkani villages to Bombay to work in British India's civil

service, railroads, military and banks, and eventually became active in politics, education, law and a number of professions. Satellite communities sprang up in Ahmedabad, Pune and New Delhi. Their population was between 25,000 and 30,000 at the time of independence.

Finally, Arabic-speaking Jews from the Middle East, known in India as 'Baghdadis', were attracted to Indian port cities just as the British were establishing themselves in the region. Jews from Iraq, Syria, Turkey, Iran and elsewhere settled in Surat, Bombay, Calcutta, Madras and Rangoon in pursuit of both opportunity and freedom. The Baghdadi community included a number of celebrated business magnates, especially in textiles, trade and real estate. They established a trading network across Asia, with leading families setting up branches in Malaya, Singapore, China and Japan. Others in the community pursued medicine, law, education and business, and played a key role in India's fledgling film industry. India's Baghdadis numbered around 6000 at the time of independence.

After independence, most of India's Jews migrated to Israel, but a number of them from the Baghdadi community in particular opted for life in other areas of the British Commonwealth. Their migration was so complete that today there may be only 6000 Jews in India, while there are as many as 60,000 'Israelis of Indian origin'.

THE CONDITIONS AND SPECIFIC FEATURES OF THE MIGRATION PROCESS

Each of India's three Jewish communities—Kochi, Bene Israel and Baghdadi—has its own migration history.

Kochi Jews

The dismantling of Kochi's Jewish community began in the 19th century under British rule. Lured by social and economic prospects, a number of families moved north to Bombay, Calcutta and Rangoon, where they assimilated into the Baghdadi Jewish communities that had been established there. While their migration did not significantly deplete the community's population, it did drain some of its vitality.

Much more devastating to Kochi's Jewish numbers was the creation of the State of Israel in 1948. Emigration to Israel, which began with a few families in 1948 and accelerated during the 1950s, took its toll. Of the 1935 Kochi Jews reported in 1941, only a few hundred remained 20 years later. A second mass exodus in the 1970s and early 1980s was so great that it left a void. In the early 21st century, there may be no more than two dozen Jews remaining in Kochi and neighbouring towns.

A number of factors led to the migration of Kochi's Jews. First among them is the biblical prophecy to return to the 'Land of Israel' (Eretz Yisrael) to help build a Jewish homeland. Zionist groups began to emerge in villages and cities all over India, including Kochi, around the turn of the 20th century. Many Kochi

Jews had an undaunted commitment to make *aliyah* (going up)—the process of immigration to Israel—to the Promised Land. A group of Malabaris in the 1950s declared, 'When we heard of the establishment of the State of Israel, we decided to go up and rebuild the land of our forefathers. Many have already gone, and the others are waiting for their turn.'

A not so lofty but no less compelling reason for emigration was better economic opportunities. In general, there were two groups which fell into this category of migrants: the poor, who had little to lose, and those who were once wealthy, who had already lost a great deal. Among the latter group were those who had made their fortunes through import trade ventures only to see their businesses fold when the national government clamped down on the import of luxury goods. It was also during this period that the local government took over the regional ferry service, which had been a privately-run Jewish concern. Beginning in 1957, vast tracts of land owned by Jewish families were seized and redistributed—the outcome of land reform policies rather than anti-Jewish sentiments—among the general population by Kerala's freely elected Communist government. This was followed in 1979 by the nationalisation of the Jewish-run electricity company. Fortunes fell and generations-old family businesses disappeared. With their key means of livelihood gone, Jews who owned or were employed by these companies sought new economic opportunities elsewhere.

Others left India due to the changing political climate. There were no pogroms to threaten them, like the systematic tyranny that plagued European Jews at times of political upheaval; nor did they face sectarian violence, a common occurrence among religious and ethnic groups today. It was more a case of the Kochi Jews becoming inconspicuous, losing certain privileges, and feeling a sense of a disenfranchisement, as did all the minority groups, even privileged ones, when India became a majority-ruled democratic nation.

Another segment sought the excitement of a new life. In India, Jews, like their countrymen, could carry on the traditions and livelihoods of their elders under secure and perhaps monotonous circumstances. Israel was an unknown world where they could start anew, an idea that was particularly appealing to a number of young people with a pioneering spirit. On a more mundane but no less ardent level were the myriad personal reasons that Jews had for leaving. The respectability of immigrating to Israel masked what could actually have been an escape from family squabbles, a business fallen on hard times or the lack of eligible marriage partners.

Bene Israel Jews

During the first half of the 20th century, the Bene Israel were caught between two strong nationalistic movements: the Swaraj movement for Indian independence from Britain, and Zionism, the movement that led to the establishment of the State of Israel. All three of their reference groups—the Indians, British and other Jews—were involved in conflict. The Bene Israel loved and admired both their Indian neighbours and their British patrons. Nevertheless, by this time their transformation into members of the international community of Jews was irrevocable despite harsh treatment from the Baghdadis, who had discriminated against them for a hundred years.

The marginal position of the Bene Israel, indeed of all Indian Jewry, became clear in 1938 when a Jewish delegation met with Mohandas Karamchand Gandhi. When they asked the Mahatma what their role should be in the Indian-British struggle, he replied, 'Although I would welcome your help in our freedom struggle, I would advise you not to take part as a community since you are so small you would be crushed by three mighty conflicting forces of British imperialism, Congress nationalism, and Muslim separatism.'

Yet the Bene Israel were initially ambivalent about Zionism. They mistrusted 'foreign' Jews because of their unhappy experiences with the Baghdadis. Many adopted the prevailing Indian view of Zionism as a British incursion into Arab territory; however, the fact that fringe elements in the Swaraj movement embraced Hitler's cause helped propel the Bene Israel towards the British and Zionism. Ultimately, the vast majority of the community opted for life in Israel.

Baghdadi Jews

Arabic-speaking Jews migrated to Indian port cities around the time when the British were consolidating their rule in India. Known as Baghdadis, their communities were headed by leading industrialists and the community as a whole tended to identify more with the British and other Europeans than with Indians. Indeed, in many Baghdadi households the first spoken languages were Arabic or English, with Hindustani or Bengali reserved for instructing the servants or bartering in the market. For a century, the Baghdadis considered themselves

The Cochin Synagogue clock tower, which was built in 1768. Its three faces bear Hebrew, Indian Devanagiri and Roman numerals.

A Jewish woman touches a mezuzah on her doorpost.

Lokam irubhagannalil ('Our Ancient Hope')

Dwelling in both sides of the world is the national spirit of the Jews.
When it revives and turns toward God, Zion will be protected.

The hope we've had since ancient times has not faded from our hearts—
Our hope to return to the land given us by the One God.

Beloved relations in many lands, hear the song of our future.
As long as Jews remain alive, our hope will endure.

The city of Jerusalem is like the eagle. It will be made new again.
The kingdom will live and endure, filled with splendor and praise.

The House of Jacob again will reside there, through God's sacred love.
By God's grace the King messiah—Mashiah Raja—will rule over her.

The hope that You have given to us, may You be pleased to fulfill,
And may You protect those who sing in praise of You, Oh Lord.

The hope we've had since ancient times has not faded from our hearts—
Our hope to return to the land given us by the One God.

Song translated from Malayalam, from Scaria Zacharia and Barbara C. Johnson, Oh, Lovely Parrot! Jewish Women's Songs from Kerala, *2004.*

The Cochin Synagogue's brass bimah, *or pulpit, sits in the centre of the main sanctuary. A unique feature of Kerala's synagogue architecture is the two* bimahs *in each synagogue—one located downstairs and the other, upstairs.*

European and sought to have their identity confirmed by gaining privileges reserved for the ruling elite. Their goal of achieving a 'European' classification from the British was never attained.

By the middle of the 20th century, two events made the desire for 'European' classification an obsolete issue for the Baghdadi Jews. First, Indian independence was in the offing and the classification 'European' would no longer be an advantage. Second, when several thousand Ashkenazi (Jews from northern and eastern Europe) refugees fleeing Nazism arrived in India, the debate came to an abrupt end. Even the most pretentious Baghdadi got the message that the Holocaust made clear: distinctions among Jews were meaningless, a point of view that gave a certain clarity to the Zionist ideology as well.

EXPERIENCES IN ISRAEL

At the end of World War II, it became obvious that Britain would soon grant independence to India. At the same time, Indian Jews were acutely aware of the Zionist struggle. These two forces offered competing

Palestine Is Our Only Destination

It is our sincere ambition,
To be freed from foreign domination.
Palestine is our inspiration,
To build our home, a Jewish nation.

For God is always on our side,
He is our sincere guide,
Then who should we fear,
When we have Him near,
In days of sorrow and darkness?

We have passed through darker situations,
And won for us thrilling admiration.
Jerusalem is our destination,
The home and hope of our salvation.

Now we make an open declaration
To every anti-Jewish nation,
All their baseless, ruthless persecution
Will never bring our ruination.

Song written in English by Cecil Koder of Kochi, 1930s, sung to the tune of Hatiqvah, *from Nathan Katz and Ellen Goldberg,* The Last Jews of Cochin: Jewish Identity in Hindu India, *1993.*

identities to all of India's Jews, the Kochi Jews, the Bene Israel and the Baghdadis: they must become Indians or make aliyah as Jews. While the two identities had existed somewhat harmoniously in the past, the modern period bifurcated them.

Kochi Jews

Upon making *aliyah* to Eretz Yisrael, the Kochi Jews encountered an Ashkenazi-dominated country whose Zionism was primarily expressed in social and humanistic terms. This was an ethos far different from their own, which was messianic and religious, as it generally is for the Sephardim.

Ironically, most Kochi Jews in Israel feel they could have been more observant of their religious practice in India than in Israel. There is still a sense of religious continuity when Kochi Jews gather for festivals or when women come together to share and perform their unique songs in Malayalam. Many confess disillusionment with secularism in Israel, but at the same time do not identify with the practices of many Ashkenazim, which separate them from the larger world. In general, Sephardic terms are quite applicable to the Kochi Jews. Full participation in Judaic religious life does not require a distancing from other groups, whether Gentiles or less observant Jews. Indeed, Kochi Jews sometimes consider their Ashkenazi co-religionists 'fanatics', not because they observe the religion more strictly, but because of their isolation from those who think differently.

The Kochi Jews soon discovered that it was not simply philosophical differences of opinion that explained why Israelis do not always observe religious and life-cycle rituals as fully as they themselves once did in India: there was simply not enough time for festivals and special occasions to be enjoyed in a leisurely fashion. For Kochi Jews who had made *aliyah* for religious purposes, the preclusion or limitation of ritual observance is, at times, resented. Limited time for the celebration of festivals and other events and the fast pace of Israeli life have also affected social cohesion and community solidarity. Other factors include, as Gilbert Kushner wrote, 'the influence of an Israeli (especially Ashkenazi) emphasis on individualism and the nuclear family at the expense of Indian...values which stress the extended family and the wider ethnic community.' Kochi Jews in Israel miss the social cohesion they enjoyed in India.

Bene Israel Jews

When the Bene Israel Jews arrived in Israel, one of their worst fears was realised. In India, they had endured aspersions from their Baghdadi neighbours for a century. The chief Sephardic rabbi in Israel at the time, Itzhak Nissim, who was himself from Baghdad, was all too aware of the Baghdadi doubt regarding the 'Jewishness' of the Bene Israel, and he was inclined to believe the gossip emanating from Bombay and Baghdad. The controversy involved the two related but distinct questions of the community's origins and lineage.

The origins of the Bene Israel simply cannot be known for sure because of the lack of historical information. The second issue, pertaining to lineage, is a complex one because Judaic law, or Halacha, governs marriage and divorce. When a marriage is not ended according to Halacha but the woman remarries anyway, the offspring of the second marriage are tainted with *mamzerut* (illegitimate status), since the woman is technically still married to the first husband. Jewish communities that are beyond the reach of the rabbinate—such as the anti-rabbinic Karaites, and possibly the Beta Yisrael of Ethiopia and the Bene Israel—run the risk of rampant *mamzerut*, a flaw (*pagam*) that disqualifies them and their offspring from marriage with other Jews. This issue caused the greatest Halachic difficulty.

The controversy spread beyond rabbinic circles and into the political realm. At one point, to protest being labelled as 'bastards', the Bene Israel, who are called *Hod'im* (Indians) in Israel, conducted satyagraha, or civil disobedience, on the steps of the Knesset (the Israeli parliament). Despite his predilections and much to his credit, Rabbi Nissim conducted a thorough inquiry. His report, which had all the relevant rabbinic documents, travellers' accounts and scholarly writing, concluded in essence, 'that (1) the Bene Israel were Jews, and (2) that there was no evidence that could cast doubts on their family status and divorce procedures.' Curiously, it was the Bene Israels' fidelity to a Hindu custom that had kept them within the structures of Judaic law. Divorce and remarriage are prohibited in Hinduism. As a result of Sanskritisation, the Bene Israel emulated their Hindu neighbours in abjuring both, so the problem of irregular divorce and subsequent remarriage has not arisen in their case. This coincidence relieved them of the burden of presumptive *mamzerut*.

The matter was thus settled, or so it seemed. In 1997, an Ashkenazi rabbi in Petah Tiqveh refused to register a marriage between a Bene Israel *sabra*, or native Israeli, and her Ashkenazi groom. The matter caused controversy, but worldwide rabbinic opinion was virtually universal in support of the young woman. The hard-line rabbi was suitably castigated and the marriage was celebrated.

Despite occasional encounters with ignorance or bigotry, the Bene Israel have flourished in their new home. Today, their population in Israel is 10 times greater than India's, with 50,000 compared to the subcontinent's 5000. Despite their growth in numbers, however, the Bene Israel still struggle with an outsider status. For generations, the Bene Israel were Jews in India. Now they are Indians in Israel.

Baghdadis

In pre-independence India, the Baghdadis had two options when it came to identity: struggle to be classified as 'European' or embrace being Jews and participate in the *aliyah* to the soon-to-be-established Israel. After independence, a third option became available to some Baghdadis: they could choose to be British. Most Baghdadis found this possibility attractive. For years, leading Baghdadi families travelled to England frequently; some even maintained residences there. Most Baghdadi families in Bombay, Calcutta or Rangoon had relatives in London. After the fall of the Ottoman Empire and the establishment of British rule in Iraq (1921–33), life for Jews in Iraq, the home country, temporarily improved. (Iraq sympathised with Nazi Germany and after the war helped to lead the Arab rejection of coexistence with Israel.) India's Baghdadis simultaneously increased their business dealings with relatives both in Iraq and England, and developed an even greater attachment to the British. By the mid-20th century, they were fluent in English and accustomed to British culture, clothing and even cuisine; a half century of Anglicisation in India made Britain a natural home. Many moved

> *The Zionist idea has made its victorious entrance also into Cochin. We have already many enthusiastic friends in the Jews Town of Cochin, in Bombay, in Calcutta, in Rangoon, in Mala, on the Malabar Coast, in Ernakulam, in Shenomangalam, etc. I hope in a very short time to be able to submit to you...a report about the formal establishment of Zionist branches in the above mentioned and other cities as well as about the consolidation of these branches into a Sub-Federation of the 'English Zionist Federation'.*
>
> Letter by Naphtali E. Roby of Kochi to Die Welt, the Zionist newspaper published by Theodor Herzl, 1903.

there in anticipation of Indian independence in 1947, or did so soon thereafter. Many other Baghdadis settled elsewhere in the English-speaking world. Those who moved to Israel became Israeli. They participated easily in that nation's economic, social and cultural life, and seem pleased to be in the Middle East again, where they have merged with the Iraqi community rather than the Indian community.

MAJOR ISSUES TODAY

Israelis of Indian origin face one overriding issue today: preserving their unique culture. The Kochi Jews are spread around the country and have no major population centres. The largest concentration is found at Moshav Nevatim, near Beer Sheva in the south. There, a Kochi-style synagogue has been constructed and, recently, a modest museum was opened. As the community is quite small, numbering perhaps 5000, members keep in contact informally by telephone and often gather for holidays and life-cycle celebrations. Kochi women have started to congregate on a monthly basis to chant their unique Malayalam songs.

A focal point for the community is the permanent exhibition of the interior of a Kochi synagogue in the Israel Museum in Jerusalem. It was quite controversial in the beginning, but it has become a mark of the community's identity, instilling cultural pride and sharing Kochi Jewish culture with a wider audience in Israel.

Kochi Jews also play a key role as mediator between the governments of Israel and Kerala. A number of bilateral agreements to promote agriculture, information technology and tourism have been brokered by Kochi Jews in Israel.

The Bene Israel are a much larger community and are more visible in Israel. One of their unique religious observances in India is the *malida* rite, a propitiation of Prophet Elijah, who is believed to have visited India. There is a shrine dedicated to him at Khandala, a Konkani village. The Bene Israel have transported the *malida* rite to Israel seamlessly, relocating it from Khandala to the Cave of Elijah the Prophet on Mount Carmel in Haifa. Participation in a *malida* there has become an important identifying feature for them.

The Bene Israel are also involved in the burgeoning economic, cultural and tourism-related relationship between India and Israel. The Indian embassy in Tel Aviv recently hosted a Marathi festival to celebrate the language and culture of the their home state.

Despite some initial difficulties in adjusting to a new, modern, stressful life in Israel, Indians have made a comfortable home for themselves. Enhanced bilateral relations between India and Israel reinforce their sense of security in both countries.

Nathan Katz

Torah scrolls from India at the Cochin-style synagogue in Moshav Nevatim.

TURKEY

The Blue Mosque, which was built between 1609 and 1616, is one of the most prominent land-marks in Istanbul.

At the height of its power under Darius I (521 BC–485 BC), the Achaemenid Empire included the northwestern regions of the Indian subcontinent.

Map 8.30

TURKEY AND ITS predecessor states in Asia Minor have had a long history of contact with South Asia. During the Mohenjo Daro period of Indian history (3rd–2nd millennium BC), it is likely that merchants from the Indus Valley visited modern-day southeast Turkey, which is historically part of Mesopotamia. The empire of Mitanni in Anatolia (2nd millennium BC) had an Indo-Aryan ruling nobility with typical Indian names such as Mitra and Varuna. These Indo-Aryans, however, did not come to Mitanni from South Asia, but most probably were relations of those Aryans who left the Transcaucasus and stayed in the Middle East while the majority left for Iran and India.

The Achaemenid or Old Persian Empire included both Northwest India and the territory of present-day Turkey. During the Achaemenid era, Indians not only visited Asia Minor but also participated in the military actions of the Persians, including the Persian-Greek Wars. The ancient Greeks who inhabited the coast of Asia Minor travelled eastward as far as parts of western India. Around 331 BC, Alexander the Great defeated the Achaemenid Empire and added a significant part of India to his state. His empire did not last long. During the Hellenistic period (c. 320–30 BC), Asia Minor had contacts with Indo-Greek countries, and in the Roman period, Asia Minor was the main trading route between India and Italy.

The Romans and Byzantines were familiar with famous Indian spices, precious stones and iron. The 4th-century Latin manuscript *Expositio totius mundi et gentium* ('Total Description of the World') informs that Indian goods were a significant part of trade in Constantinople, Antioch (modern-day Antakya) and Ephesus. Another text, the *Institutiones Digesta* (3rd century AD), speaks of *capilli Indici* (diamonds), *opia Indica* (rubies and other precious stones), *spadones Indici* (pepper and coriander) and other Indian goods.

With the acquisition of Arabia in the 16th century, the Ottoman Empire witnessed huge numbers of Indian

Muslims travelling to Mecca and Medina, sacred cities of Islam which were protected by the Turks. The Ottoman Turks and Indians cooperated in trade and military action as well as in areas related to religion and culture. The Ottoman sultan, Selim the Grim (1512–20), entered into negotiations with Muzaffar Shah of Gujarat about possible joint strikes against the Portuguese in Goa. Following these negotiations, Turks were not uncommon guests in Indian ports, while Indians often frequented Ottoman cities. From the 1550s, trade between the Ottoman Empire and the Indian states expanded to unprecedented levels and travel between the two regions became common. At the same time, however, the influential Armenian, Greek and Jewish merchants who had dominated the Ottoman market for centuries prevented the intrusion of Indians in the local market.

Indian Muslim rulers maintained contact with the Ottoman Empire until the completion of the British conquest of India in the mid-19th century, but informal visits of Indian emissaries to Istanbul continued even after that date. As part of the British military corps, Indian sepoys would later visit Turkish seaports as well. By the end of the 19th century, Turkey was one of the few independent Muslim states in Asia. It received Indian Muslim adventurers who sought to live in the country of the Khalif, the designated head of the Sunni Muslims, a title assumed by the Ottoman sultans. Prior to the dissolution of Mughal rule in India, Ottoman assertions did not find much Indian support, but following its formal end in 1858, Indian Muslims increasingly turned to Istanbul in search of spiritual leaders.

WORLD WAR I AND THE KHILAFAT

During World War I, thousands of Indian troops, mostly Sikhs, were stationed in British-occupied areas of Turkey. Few of them, however, remained after the British forces left the country. The importance of Turkey for millions of Indian Muslims grew soon after the war, during the Khilafat Movement. Although ostensibly initiated as an attempt to save the Ottoman Empire from falling apart and to preserve the position of the Ottoman sultan as the Khalif, the movement also became a part of the Indian nationalist cause. The leadership of the Khilafat Movement consisted of Indian Muslim intellectuals such as Dr Ansari, Hakim Ajmal Khan, Ulama Abdul Bari and Maulana Abul Kalam Azad; journalists such as the Ali brothers and Hasrat Mohani; and lawyers such as T. A. K. Sherwani and Syed Zahur Ahmad.

The first formal protest against Indian military help in Britain's fight against Turkey was launched in December 1915 at the annual meeting of the Muslim League in Delhi. The objective was to highlight Muslim sentiment for the caliphate and to send a clear message to the Allied powers at the peace conference that they wanted the Khalif to retain his authority over Muslims. Pressure was exerted on the British government and Allied forces by way of petitions, deputations and non-cooperation with the government.

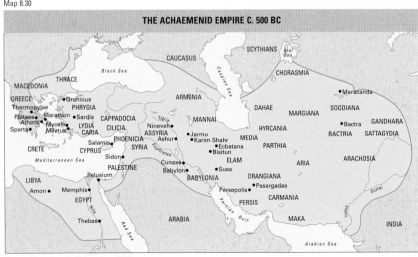

THE ACHAEMENID EMPIRE C. 500 BC

Source: Encyclopedia Britannica, 1994.

Map 8.31

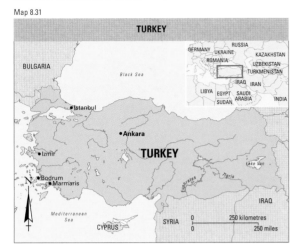

As a result, during the Khilafat Movement, tens of thousands of Indian Muslims attempted to migrate to Turkey. This went on for about six years until events in the Middle East—the Treaty of Lausanne in July 1923 and the abolition of the caliphate by Mustafa Kemal in March 1924, in particular—caused a considerable decline. When the terms of the proposed treaty were published in India in May 1920, angry Indian Muslims, encouraged by a fatwa from Maulana Azad, opted for *hijrat* to neighbouring Afghanistan and distant Turkey. However, the majority of Indian emigrants, or *muhajirs*, did not reach Turkey; most of them settled in Afghanistan. Others were stopped in Russian Turkestan, where some of them were recruited for military training and anti-British agitation.

The rise of nationalism in Turkey under Mustafa Kemal (also known as Atatürk), who emphasised secular reform, closed the Khilafat issue but did not stop the movement in India. Khilafatists in India continued the struggle, claiming the independence of the Jaziratul-Islam. In Turkey, nationalist Muslims transferred their allegiance from the puppet Sultan Wahiuddin to the independent Mustafa Kemal. The prominent Indian nationalist Obeidulla Sindhi visited Turkey, where he held discussions with the *muhajirs* and drafted a programme for Indian national revolutionaries called, 'The Constitution of the United Republic of India'. Around the same time, several revolutionaries in Bukhara, who were stopped by the Soviets in Russian Turkestan, expressed their dissatisfaction with Soviet military and ideological training. With the growing disillusionment of the Soviet-Muslim Alliance, more conservative members of the *muhajir* movement sought to leave Bukhara for Kemalist Turkey.

Turkey also became the destination for Indian revolutionaries who were not directly associated with the Khilafat Movement. One such revolutionary, Abdurrabb Barg, began his career as an official of the British Foreign Political Department and worked in British diplomatic missions in Baghdad and Istanbul. He joined the revolutionary movement in the 1890s and during World War I, gave up British service to join the Turkish army. He conducted revolutionary propaganda work among Indian prisoners of war (POWs) in Turkey. Towards the end of the war, Abdurrabb left for Germany and joined the Berlin Committee of Indian revolutionaries.

A close associate of Abdurrrabb, Mandiyam Prativadi Bhayankar Acharya (1888–1946), became a revolutionary while studying in England in 1907–08. Later, he cooperated with the leaders of the Indian revolutionary émigré group in Paris. During World War I, he was sent by the Berlin Committee to Turkey, where he spread revolutionary propaganda among Indian soldiers of the Anglo-Turkish front. The Ghadar Party also expressed interest in working with Indian POWs in Turkey. From 1923 onwards, leaders of the party, including Rattan Singh and Dalip Singh, shuttled between San Francisco, Moscow, Istanbul and Kabul to arrange a united Indian revolutionary army.

The post-1930s were a period during which Indians in Turkey became less visible. For Muslims, the idea of the *hijrat* suggested assimilation in the Muslim country and not the retention of a distinct ethnic identity. In addition, the number of successful *muhajirs* from India to Turkey was so miniscule that Indians remained largely obscure in the public arena until the late 20th century.

Since the mid-1990s, economic globalisation has brought many Indian transnational businessmen, as well as Indian, Pakistani and Bangladeshi refugees and illegal migrants to Turkey. The most recent development in the history of Indian contact with Turkey is the settlement of expatriate Indians, especially those from the UK, in Turkish seaside resorts, particularly in Marmaris and Bodrum. This has led to the opening of a number of Indian restaurants in Turkey. One of them, the Taj Mahal, claims to have an Indian from Bradford as its chef.

MODERN BUSINESS PRESENCE

Indian businesses are not limited to restaurants alone. A number of traders import and export goods between Turkey and India. Among the Indian exports to Turkey are computer software, ferrites, TV picture tubes, automobile parts, electronic components, agricultural machinery, processed food, building materials, drugs and pharmaceuticals, jute, rice and handicrafts. Turkish goods exported to India include non-alcoholic beverages, leguminous vegetables such as lentils and chickpeas, TV sets, cables, food-processing machinery, glass and glassware. The volume of trade between the two countries grew to about US$1.2 billion in 2004, with the balance of trade favouring India.

Indian jewellers are particularly interested in the Turkish market, as are Indian fashion designers. Indian clothes with gilded and embroidered materials or mirrors and beads are featured in the collections of almost every popular Turkish fashion brand. One of India's home and accessories brands, Pondicherry, opened its first branch in Turkey in 2004.

Indian expatriates are settled mostly in Istanbul, Izmir, Bodrum and Marmaris. The growing needs of businessmen travelling between India and Turkey led to the introduction of direct flights between Istanbul and New Delhi in September 2003.

The emergence of Turkey as a key transit area for South Asians entering Europe and the possibility of Turkey being included in the European Union have made it an important stepping stone for Indians, Pakistanis and Bangladeshis who seek refuge or are simply trying to find better lives in Europe. On 10 May 2002, the English-language daily *The Turkish Times* reported that 116 Indian asylum-seekers had been deported by the Greek government to Edirne in western Turkey, from where they had tried to enter the European Union. The same newspaper has reported instances of illegal Pakistani immigrants in Izmir trying to cross the Aegean Sea to Greece. Despite its long history of tolerance towards immigrants, including Jews, Poles, Chechens and Russians, Turkey is unlikely to allow the continued flow and settlement of Indians as this could have a negative impact on Turkey's chances of joining the European Union.

Igor Kotin

Volunteers of the Khilafat movement, c. 1919. Thousands of Indian Muslims sought to move to Turkey in an attempt to defend the position of the Khalif and prevent the disintegration of the Ottoman Empire.

The Taj Mahal Restaurant in the Turkish resort town of Marmaris.

241

SOUTH AFRICA

Indentured Indians from Madras and Calcutta were brought in small boats to the Durban shore. After undergoing a medical examination, they were housed in barracks until assigned to employers.

THERE ARE APPROXIMATELY 1.2 million people of Indian origin in South Africa. While they comprise a mere 2.6 per cent of South Africa's population of 45 million, they have a very visible public profile in KwaZulu-Natal (KZN), where 72 per cent of Indians live and where they constitute 10 per cent of the population, and to a lesser extent in Gauteng, home to 20 per cent of the Indian population. Mosques, temples, Indian traders, Hindi movies and even Indian cuisine, festivals and rituals are visible in most parts of these provinces. Freedom of movement from the mid-1980s has seen Indians increasingly settle in other parts of the country. Apartheid saw the establishment of large townships like Chatsworth, Phoenix and Lenasia, where thousands of Indians still live in an all-Indian milieu. The majority of Indians are descendants of indentured labourers who arrived between 1860 and 1911. Their ancestors arrived long before the subcontinent was partitioned, and they have deep roots in South Africa, where they have been living for five generations.

ARRIVAL AND SETTLEMENT

The first Indians in South Africa were slaves imported by the Dutch East India Company in the 17th century from Bengal and South India. They were few in number and came to be absorbed into the Cape Malay population. The majority, however, are descendants of the 152,184 indentured labourers introduced into Natal (now KwaZulu-Natal) between 1860 and 1911 to work on sugar plantations, as the indigenous Zulu, who had access to land on colonial locations and Christian missions, resisted absorption into the capitalist economy. Indian migrants were highly stratified: 62 per cent were men, 25 per cent were women, and 13 per cent were children; 60 per cent were Tamil and Telugu speakers from Tamil Nadu and Andhra Pradesh in southern India, while the

rest were from Bihar and Uttar Pradesh in the north; over 80 per cent were Hindu, about 15 per cent Muslim, and there was a small number of Christians. Indian migrants comprised several hundred castes ranging from Brahmins to Pariahs. Madras was the point of departure from the south and Calcutta from the north.

Entrepreneurs from Gujarat, on the west coast of India, followed from the early 1870s. They were termed 'passengers' because they came at their own expense and were subject to the ordinary laws of the colony. The Whites incorrectly called them Arabs because the majority were Muslim. Passengers played a significant role in shaping Indian society. They dominated Indian trade, competed with the Whites, provided credit and job opportunities for Indians, and took the lead in establishing religious and educational institutions. Passengers were able to keep their social distance from other Indians. They saw migration as temporary and maintained links with their homeland through visits, marriage in India, and by remitting money to build wells and schools in their villages of origin. Gujarati Hindus and Muslims also had more in common with each other than with their co-religionists among the indentured migrants.

Indenture made it difficult to preserve caste distinctions. Migrants were recruited as individuals and found it difficult to maintain caste separation during the cramped journey overseas. The breakdown of caste accelerated on plantations, where the migrants did the same work at the same rate, irrespective of caste status and taboos. They were also housed together in barracks and subject to communal bathing. Ramadeen, an indentured labourer, told the Wragg Commission of 1885 that in Natal he had 'eaten with different people and broken my caste, my friends in India will not even eat with me. No fine could bring me back my caste.' The broadest regional distinction was between 'Madrassee' and 'Calcuttya'. The Protector's files contain many examples of labourers from South India refusing to work with those from North India and vice versa.

Indenture spawned harsh laws that governed every aspect of the migrants' lives. They had to work for five years for the employer to whom they were assigned. Overwork, malnourishment and squalid living conditions formed the pattern of daily life for most agricultural

Map 8.32

SOUTH AFRICA

0   300 kilometres
0   300 miles

N

ZIMBABWE

BOTSWANA

NAMIBIA

LIMPOPO

MOZAMBIQUE

Pretoria   MPUMALANGA
GAUTENG
Johannesburg

NORTHWEST
PROVINCE

SWAZILAND

INDIAN OCEAN

Alexander Bay

Orange

Kimberley
Bloemfontein

FREE STATE

LESOTHO

KWAZULU-
NATAL

Durban

SPAIN   TURKEY
IRAQ IRAN
ALGERIA LIBYA EGYPT SAUDI
ARABIA
MALI NIGER   SUDAN
NIGERIA   ETHIOPIA
DEM. REP. KENYA
OF THE
CONGO TANZANIA
ANGOLA
MADAGASCAR

NORTHERN
CAPE

ATLANTIC OCEAN

EASTERN
CAPE

East London

Cape Town

WESTERN
CAPE

Port Elisabeth

Cape of Good Hope

workers; indentured Indians had few ways of resisting. Rigid controls included draconian laws which viewed all contractual offences as criminal acts and sanctioned legal action against Indians for laziness and desertion. Indians could not go more than 3.2 km from the estate without their employer's written permission. They could not live off the estate, refuse work, demand higher wages or change employer. Tripartite stratification, made up of White employers and management, an intermediate class of sirdars (labour supervisors), and the mass of indentured workers, coupled with the coercive apparatus of the state, particularly the legal system, which favoured planters, ensured that the leverage of employers was largely, though not entirely, unchallenged. Complaints to the Protector about excessive working hours, poor housing, non-payment of wages and corporal punishment were mostly in vain as the skilled testimony and race of the employer invariably won the day. Resistance was mostly indirect and included flight, arson, stealing, absenteeism, suicide, feigning illness and destruction of property.

Passenger migrants settled throughout Natal and the Transvaal (now Gauteng, the Northwest Province, Limpopo and Mpumalanga), with small numbers in the Cape as well. The discovery of gold on the Witwatersrand (1886) and diamonds in Kimberley (1869) gave impetus to railway construction and harbour development in Natal. Some Indian traders followed the railway line to the Transvaal, settling in towns such as Ladysmith and Charlestown, while others established themselves in Dundee and Newcastle in the coal-mining interior of northern Natal, in sugar-producing areas along the Natal coast, as well as in the tea-, maize- and wattle-growing midlands in villages such as Ixopo, Richmond and Estcourt. Passenger migrants were joined by free Indians as well as indentured Indians who had fled their employers. There were 149,791 Indians in South Africa in 1911. Of these, around 30,000, or 20 per cent, were of passenger origin, while just over 130,000 lived in Natal. Free Indians were among those scattered throughout South Africa, though restrictions on inter-provincial movement limited their numbers.

ECONOMIC COMPETITION AND WHITE OPPOSITION

Economic competition from Indians provoked strong opposition from the Whites. While indentured immigrants were free to return to India after 10 years, over half of them remained in Natal. Some stayed because of the difficulty of reintegrating into Indian society, while others had started families and probably felt that they could make something of their lives in Natal. Most free Indians grew fruits and vegetables for the local market on land rented from absentee landlords and land companies. There were 2000 market gardeners in Durban by 1885. Indians branched out into other vocations as well. The 1904 census listed Indian accountants, shoemakers, cigarette makers, clerks, cooks, domestics, laundry workers, plumbers, fishermen and tailors. The permanent settlement of free Indians and the growing passenger presence stirred White hostility.

Indian merchants imported rice, spices and apparel for their compatriots. They were linked to one another and to smaller traders by an extensive network of trade and credit since White-owned formal banks initially shunned 'Indian, Arab or Banyan' traders. Passenger migrants rapidly dominated trade in the relatively open ethnic economy at the expense of free Indians, and also

Map 8.33

RAILWAY LINES

— Passenger routes
— The Blue Train

BOTSWANA

NAMIBIA

Messina
Gaborone
Lobatse
Mafeking
Pretoria
Komatipoort
Johannesburg
Maputo
Ladysmith
Kimberley
Bloemfontein
Pietermaritzburg
Durban
De Aar
Beaufort West
East London
Cape Town
Port Elisabeth

The railway lines show the routes taken by Indians to the diamond and coal mining regions. The Blue Train, now a luxury service, was once involved in the discovery of gold and diamonds.

Source: 'Train travel in South Africa', available at www.seat61.com/SouthAfrica.

competed with Whites. The Wragg Commission noted in 1885 that Indian traders were the cause of 'much of the irritation existing in the minds of European Colonists.' The Whites testified that Indians were 'dishonest', undercut them, supplied illegal liquor to Africans and were addicted to drinking.

By 1894, the Natal Indian population of 46,000 exceeded the White population of 45,000. Natal was unique in that the Whites and Indians were alike in numerical and class terms. White traders lobbied for trade protection, while White workers sought to monopolise better-paying jobs. Once Natal achieved self-government in 1893, laws were promulgated to limit Indian franchise, curb immigration, restrict trade and impose burdensome taxation. Act 17 of 1895, which levied a £3 annual tax on indentured Indians who chose not to renew their contracts, was intended to keep them locked into the system or force them to return to India. The law created terrible hardship. The percentage of Indians who re-indentured or returned to India after 10 years in the colony increased from approximately 20 per cent per annum to 80 per cent between 1907 and 1913. Between 1898 and 1910, immigration laws were used to prohibit

Indians outside a diamond merchant's store in Kimberley. After completing their contracts, Indians were free to engage in any activity of their choice. Many 'free' Indians made their way to Kimberley, which was booming economically following the diamond discoveries of the 1860s.

The Victoria Street Early Morning Squatters' Market (1910–34) in Durban gave Indian market gardeners an opportunity to sell their fruits and vegetables between 4 am and 9 am.

34,872 Indians from entering Natal, while Indian traders were barred from prime trading areas. Racist legislation categorised Indians, Africans and Whites as distinct races and laid the foundation for White political, economic and social dominance.

Anti-Indian legislation was introduced throughout South Africa. Law 3 of 1885 provided for separate residential and trading areas for Indians and 'Arabs' in the Transvaal; the Orange Free State (OFS) prohibited Indian settlement from 1891; and the Cape introduced immigration restrictions from 1903. At a Customs Conference in 1903, Natal, the OFS, the Cape and the Transvaal resolved that the 'permanent settlement of Asiatic Races would be injurious and should not be permitted.' In April 1903, the Transvaal issued a notice to establish segregation. It passed a law in 1907 requiring Indians to register and tightened immigration laws. As South Africa moved towards the formation of the Union in 1910, Indians made representations to imperial authorities in Britain for protection, but to no avail. They, like Africans, were sacrificed in the interest of reconciliation between the Afrikaners and the British.

GANDHIAN POLITICS AND THE MAKING OF 'INDIANNESS'

Organised political activity began in 1894 with the founding of the Natal Indian Congress (NIC), in response to the Indian Disenfranchisement Bill. Mohandas K. Gandhi, who had been brought to Natal in 1893 by Dada Abdoolla, a well-established Gujarati businessman, to assist in a personal matter, was its first secretary. The NIC's strategy was primarily constitutional and comprised petitions and memoranda to private persons and government officials. 'Indianness' became clearly defined in Natal from the 1890s as part of the political vocabulary. Gandhi gave Indianness form and direction within an imperial context, but its origins were broader. He saw Indian immigrants as an extension of the diverse strands of those in India, but in Natal, he and other Indians recognised the advantage of considering themselves 'Indian', rather than as disparate groups divided by caste, class, religion or language. Gandhi promoted unity and encouraged Indians to focus on the larger issues that united them, but he also respected the diversity among Indians and did not seek to diminish it. When he first used the term in 1894, Indianness implied a geographic unity. Later, he stressed the cultural and religious diversity of India. In *Hind Swaraj* (1909), he argued that the people of

the subcontinent had always constituted a *praja* (nation). The capacity of Indians to assimilate meant that the nation was a unified whole in spite of its many different parts. Gandhi defined India as a civilisation and a territory. If people on the subcontinent could be called 'Indians', so too could those who had migrated.

Among the free Indians in Natal, an educated elite gradually emerged as a result of the early opportunities provided by mission schools. Most were reasonably well off until the post-1903 depression. They formed the Natal Indian Patriotic Union in 1908 to highlight the burden of the poll tax. Poor organisation and lack of finance, however, caused its collapse within a year. The Colonial Born Indian Association was formed in March 1911 to protest against restrictions on inter-provincial migration because educated Indians hoped to find jobs in the Transvaal and the Cape due to shrinking opportunities in Natal.

While Indians in Natal laboured under the poll tax between 1906 and 1910, Gandhi was preoccupied with passive resistance against registration in the Transvaal. He introduced satyagraha (truth force) as a new weapon against oppression. While Gandhi (and many of his supporters) was imprisoned in 1913, he underwent a fundamental transformation that influenced the strategies of mass resistance which he employed in 1913 and 1914. When Gandhi visited London in 1906, he met militants such as V. D. Savarkar (1883–1966) and read William Mackintire Salter's *Ethical Religion*, which deeply influenced him. By the time he visited London again in 1909, Gandhi had little faith in the imperial government and questioned the value of 'modern civilisation'. He developed a strong bio-moral dimension to his thinking, which he expressed in the *Indian Opinion* through a series of articles in 1912, emphasising that only those who were chaste, in control of their bodies and could overcome the fear of death could be their own masters.

The Act of Union in 1910 strengthened existing anti-Indian legislation in South Africa. The passive resistance movement that Gandhi had initiated in the Transvaal consisted mainly of negotiations between him and the government between 1909 and 1913. When Gopal K. Gokhale, a member of the Imperial Legislative Council of India, visited South Africa in 1912, the poll tax was at the forefront of Indian grievances. Gokhale discussed the tax with the Union government and left behind the

M. K. Gandhi (seated, centre) spent 21 years in South Africa (1893–1914). Here, he is seen outside his law office in Johannesburg with Henry Polak (seated, left) and Sonja Schlesin (seated, right).

impression that it would be repealed. When the South African government denied this, Gandhi sought its repeal. The tax was one of several demands listed by Gandhi; others included equitable licensing laws and the validity of Indian marriages. When the government rejected these demands, Gandhi initiated a strike by 4000 Indians on 16 October 1913 at the coal mines in northern Natal. He illegally crossed into the Transvaal on 23 October with 2000 protesters, thus courting mass arrest. The success of the strike was assured when 15,000 Indians on coastal sugar estates joined at the end of October.

In India and England, violence associated with the strike, police brutality, the arrest of thousands of Indians and the use of mine compounds as prisons led to widespread negative coverage. Shortly after the strike ended, Gandhi corresponded with Jan Christian Smuts, who was the Interior Minister of the Union of South Africa. The result was the Indian Relief Act of 1914, which abolished the tax, facilitated the entry of wives and children of Indians living in South Africa, recognised marriages contracted according to Indian religions, and provided for free passage to India for those who gave up their right to live in South Africa. Indians were still banned from the OFS, and only Indians born in South Africa before August 1913 were allowed to enter the Cape. Restrictions against Indian immigration remained. While the Act 'constituted a complete and final settlement of the controversy' for Smuts, Gandhi considered it the Magna Carta for Indians, providing them with breathing space until they resolved their outstanding grievances.

The mobilisation of Indians on the basis of race and their dependence on India during critical moments of resistance were crucial in shaping Indianness. The privileged economic position of Indian merchants was neutralised by the policies of the government, which divided the population into distinct 'races', and accorded each race specific rights and privileges. This forced the creation of a 'made-in-Natal' Indian consciousness. The formation of a racial and ethnic organisation, the NIC, masked class cleavages and fostered a separate racial and ethnic political identity. Gandhi argued that Indians were entitled to full British citizenship. He and the leadership that followed him turned to India each time their rights were threatened. This was important psychologically for Indians, but it also formally isolated their political resistance from that of other disenfranchised Blacks. Gandhi argued that because of their illustrious past, Indians deserved greater affinity with Whites, and that it was unfair to lump them with Africans. Gandhian politics helped to embed Indianness into the racialised ethos of emergent White supremacy in South Africa. Racial tension between Indians and Africans was exacerbated by transformations in the political economy. Although Whites created the racial hierarchy, the subordinated Africans' antipathy was increasingly directed against Indians, who were blamed for their economic subordination.

Indianness was evident in the daily lives of migrants. Concern for those in India showed in times of natural disaster. When famine struck northern and western India in 1900, the Indian Famine Relief Fund in Natal collected £5000. South Africa's Indians identified with movements in India, such as the Swadeshi movement against foreign goods, led by P. A. Moodaly. Prominent individuals addressed the issue publicly and crowds sang *Vande Mataram*. Indians also remitted money to India through the office of the Protector and the post office.

While migrants were strongly tied to their ancestral land, they also established their lives and homes in South Africa. They began investing money in the Natal Government Bank. Sport was another indicator of adaptation. Athletic bodies for cricket, football, cycling, boxing and other sports were formed by Indians for Indians. The Sam China Cup was an inter-provincial football tournament started in 1904 for Indians from different provinces. In a letter to the *Indian Opinion* on 1 June 1912, 'Indo-Junius' explained that the 'far-reaching and beneficial result of the Tournament is the bringing together of Indians from all parts of the Union and better understanding between them—which would but prepare the way for South African Indians acting as one body.'

Religion, however, was the base around which migrants organised their lives. Mosques and temples were crucial in reconstructing religious life in South Africa. From the time of their arrival, Indians erected tiny wattle-daub-and-thatch shrines and temples on sugar estates. The first wood-and-iron temple was built in Rossburgh in 1869. Temples dotted the Natal coastline. It was at temples that communal worship was experienced, birth, marriage and death ceremonies observed, and numerous festivals celebrated, including Thaipusam, Diwali, Parattasi, Holi and Krishna Jayanti. Visiting Indian missionaries set up bodies to unite Hindus, establish vernacular education and offer religious training. Professor Parmanand, who arrived in Durban on 5 August 1905, formed the Hindu Young Men's Society, which encouraged members to study Tamil, engage in missionary work and visit India to understand their heritage. He was followed by Swami Shankeranand, who, shortly after his arrival in 1908, established Hindu societies all over Natal and convened a national conference in 1912, where the Hindu Maha Sabha was formed.

The mosque was the heart of the Muslim community. The first mosque in Durban was built on Grey Street in 1881 by passenger Indians—Aboobaker Amod and Hajee Mahomed. It remains the largest mosque in the southern hemisphere. Mahomed Soofie, a mystic who arrived in Durban in 1895, built 13 mosques and *madrasahs* by the time of his death in 1910. Most Muslims observed

The Vishnu Temple, built in 1880 by Tamil and Telugu indentured labourers, was rebuilt in 1924 by Kothanar Ramsamy Pillay. He built nine temples in South Africa between 1893 and 1924. The apartheid government expropriated the land in 1967 without paying compensation and demolished the temple.

Religion and culture were an important base around which Indians organised their lives. This picture shows a rath (chariot) *used by Hindus during a religious festival, such as Krishna Jayanti.*

the festivals of Muharram and Id, visited tombs and participated in devotional music known in the Sufi tradition as *qawwali*. Muharram helped to forge a pan-Indian identity because Hindus and Muslims participated in this festival together. Anglican and Catholic organisations were also active. They used networks of relationships with Madras to import educated Christian Indians from southern India to teach in state and church schools.

The media was vital in promoting Indianness. Gandhi started the *Indian Opinion* in 1903. At its height between 1906 and 1908 it had 3500 subscribers, but many more readers. The *Indian Opinion* reported widely on religious, social and political activities in India and South Africa.

Swami Shankeranand of the Divine Life Society at the Mitra Hall in Mowbray, Cape Town.

Another leading newspaper, the *African Chronicle*, was started in 1908 by P. S. Aiyar, a journalist from South India. Published in Tamil and English, the *African Chronicle* focused on events related to Tamil-speaking immigrants. It promoted the study of Tamil, emphasised the value of education and religious festivals, and exposed the conditions of indenture. Unlike Gandhi, Aiyar gave space to Indian activists who challenged the conservatism of the Indian National Congress (INC). The *Indian Views*, started in 1914 by M. C. Anglia, covered similar issues but from a Muslim perspective.

DEVELOPMENTS BETWEEN THE 1920S AND THE 1940S

Indians were transformed into an urban-based proletariat in the three decades following World War I. The decision of the Indian Legislative Council to ban indentured emigration to Natal from 1 July 1911 did not affect White employers due to the availability of African migrant labour; this followed legislation by the South African government which denied Africans access to land. African labour was cheaper for employers because families did not have to be accommodated, they did not have to import staples such as rice, and they could employ Africans seasonally. The percentage of economically active Indian workers in agriculture fell from 26 per cent to 3 per cent between 1921 and 1950, while in industrial employment their numbers increased from 14 per cent to 33 per cent.

Although Indians engaged in passive resistance in 1913, they remained loyal to the British Empire. They were confident, according to the *Indian Opinion*, that 'in future years to come, better prospects are awaiting us, under the aegis of the same Empire when it has emerged triumphantly from the present ordeal.' Seven hundred Indians served as stretcher-bearers in East Africa during the war. The expectation that this would result in more equitable treatment was shattered by the revival of anti-Indian agitation after the war. The South African League, formed in 1919, declared that Indians were a 'serious moral, economic and political menace', and demanded their repatriation 'as speedily as possible.' Anti-Indian sentiments were particularly strong during economic depressions and elections, when White candidates would disparage Indians in order to earn votes. H. H. Kemp, the Durban municipal councillor, told a meeting in 1919 that 'the only cure for the Asiatic is the surgeon's knife and a silver bullet.'

The Asiatic Inquiry Commission, set up in 1920 to investigate complaints by Whites, found that the 'Asiatic

menace' was a myth and recommended voluntary trade and residential segregation, and stricter enforcement of immigration laws. A law passed in 1922 restricted Indian trade and land ownership in Durban, and in 1924, Indians were deprived of the municipal franchise. Legislation was also passed in the Transvaal to close loopholes that allowed Indians to purchase property beyond the region.

The revival of anti-Indianism served to stimulate national unity among Indians. A conference of South African Indians in August 1919 stressed moderation and closer links with India. The chairman of the Transvaal, E. I. Patel, argued for constitutional protest because the sparse White population 'has a natural objection to being swamped by Indian immigrants in addition to being outnumbered by its aboriginal peoples.' Swami Bhavani Dayal represented South African Indians at the annual meeting of the INC at Amritsar in December 1919. From 1922, South Africa sent 10 delegates to the annual meeting. A follow-up conference in Durban in May 1923 led to the formation of a South African Indian Congress. Sarojini Naidu (1879–1949) was elected as its president during her visit to South Africa in February 1924.

The Areas Reservation Bill of 1925, which made segregation compulsory, struck directly at the material interests of traders, who called for a round-table conference with the imperial and Indian governments. The conference took place in Cape Town in December 1926. South Africa hoped to solicit India's help in repatriating Indians, while the Indian government took part in order to placate the public in India, who were agitated by discrimination against Indians in the Empire. Under the Cape Town Agreement, the Reservation Bill was scrapped, India agreed to a scheme which would see the voluntary repatriation of Indians, and South Africa pledged to 'uplift' the living standards of Indians through education and welfare. An Indian agent was appointed to monitor the agreement and facilitate relations between Indians and the Union government. V. S. Srinivasa Sastri (1869–1946), the first Indian agent, warned that if Indians united with Africans, India would not intervene on their behalf, and Whites would be 'antagonised'. He advised Indians to 'fight our own battle, for their [African] status is greatly inferior to ours and by making common cause with them, our community will only be disabling themselves in the very severe combat that has fallen their lot.' Srinivasa Sastri was also a moderating influence; he formed the Durban Indo-European Council in 1928, an alliance of Indian merchants and White liberals that focused on social services, education and child welfare. He also encouraged Indian merchants to entertain Whites lavishly. Extravagant lunches were served at the Orient Club in Isipingo, built by traders in 1924. Among the White guests were

Gandhi (seated, centre) organised a volunteer ambulance corps during the South African War (1899–1902) to demonstrate loyalty to the British Empire and show that Indians were deserving of full rights. Instead, segregation was intensified.

the Governor-General of South Africa (1930) and the Chief Magistrate of Durban (1936).

Younger Indians, however, criticised Srinivasa Sastri. Dr Yusuf M. Dadoo (1909–1983) complained in the 1930s that the agency, 'being muzzled by the dictates of Whitehall, has become a very useful medium of holding back any form of radical and progressive leadership...It has become the spearhead of compromise and defeatism.' All sides were disappointed with the agreement. Indians were disappointed that the 'uplift' clause did not lead to full citizenship, while the South African government was frustrated that very few Indians were repatriated. In fact, between 1926 and 1930, the Indian population actually increased by 12 per cent.

Indian society became firmly rooted in South Africa during these decades. This is reflected in developments in education, welfare and sport. Government neglect resulted in welfare work being carried out by private Indian organisations. One of the earliest was the Aryan Benevolent Home (ABH), opened in 1921 by the Arya Yuvuk Sabha (AYS), a religious group established in 1914 to preserve Vedic culture. Muslims, led by A. I. Kajee, formed the Muslim Darul Yatama Wal Masakeen (Muslim Home for Orphans and Destitutes) in 1934 to feed and educate orphans. The R. K. Khan Hospital and Dispensary Trust, funded by Gandhi's contemporary, the advocate R. K. Khan (1874–1932), started clinics at Somtseu Road, Clairwood and Sea Cow Lake from the mid-1930s, which offered free medical treatment to the poor. The Durban Indian Child Welfare Society was formed in 1927 by middle-class women to deal with poverty, neglect and mental deficiencies among children. By 1950, 44 Indian organisations were registered under the Welfare Organisations Act.

The same applied to education. Early education was provided by Christian missions rather than the government. The 1909 Education Commission noted that the government was lagging behind in providing schools for Indians, whose 'contributions to the revenue entitle them as our fellow subjects to elementary education at least.' In August 1911, the Durban Indian Educational Institute was formed by a teacher, H. L. Paul (1879–1935), and merchants, such as Abdul Kadir and Ismail Gora. It was expanded into the Durban and District Indian Educational Committee in 1918. The aim was to 'secure education for Indians in the Province not inferior to that provided for other sections.' Indian traders funded the construction of buildings, provided furniture and books, and started feeding schemes at many schools. In 1926, only nine of the 52 schools were built by the government, the rest were community initiatives. These schools were only able to accommodate 30 per cent of Indian children of school-going age. The pride of Indians was Sastri College, the first high school for Indians in South Africa, opened in Durban in October 1929.

Indian traders were also concerned about raising the skills of workers. In August 1929, the Natal Indian Workers Congress and Indian Teachers Society formed an Indian Technical Education Committee and started 'Workers' Continuation Classes' to upgrade the knowledge of those in employment and prepare the young for work. Important progress was made when M. L. Sultan (1873–1953), who was born in Malabar, South India, and had come to Natal as an indentured worker in 1890, donated £50,000 for Indian higher education in January 1942. The contribution of Sultan, who had made his

Indians valued formal education and invested their own resources in building schools because the state made little provision. Lessons were often held outdoors due to the shortage of classrooms.

fortune in farming, led to the establishment of the M. L. Sultan Technical College, which evolved into one of the largest providers of technical education in South Africa.

THE RADICALISATION OF INDIAN LABOUR

Urbanisation and desperate economic conditions during the depression of 1929–33 spawned dynamic young leaders like H. A. Naidoo (1915–70) and George Poonen (b. 1913) who challenged the political leadership of Indian traders from the mid-1930s. Many of the new leaders had experienced the harshness of working-class life and were members of the Communist Party. They took up workers' issues and tried to forge cross-race partnerships with Africans. Poonen was forced by family poverty to leave school at the age of nine. He held several menial jobs and attended night school. In 1934, he and Naidoo both worked at a clothing company, where they organised a protest strike and were fired. Shortly thereafter, they were recruited to the Communist Party by Eddie Roux. Naidoo was elected as its secretary and Poonen as the party organiser of the Durban branch in 1935. Poonen became the chairman in 1938. He worked hard to organise Indian workers. Between 1934 and 1945, 43 unions with Indian membership were registered in Durban. By 1943, 16,617 Indians were unionised. Indian workers were involved in 46 strikes in Durban between 1937 and 1942.

These strikes had important ramifications. Employers replaced Indians with African scab labour because the Indians were more militant than the Africans. The *Indian Views* warned on 6 February 1943 that 'the potential danger of scabs among Africans must not be lost sight of. In the unskilled field the Indian is not indispensable.' Indian union organisers approached Indian capitalists, who raised funds throughout South Africa to provide food and shelter for dismissed Indian workers. While this reinforced Indianness, dismissals resulted in many Indians becoming disenchanted with unions and strike action. They became conservative and concerned about protecting their jobs.

A radical professional class began to emerge at roughly the same time as trade unionists. Dr G. M. 'Monty' Naicker (1910–78) and Dr Kesavaloo Goonam (1906–98), whose grandparents had come as indentured workers, and Dr Yusof M. Dadoo of Johannesburg, belonged to this group. All three qualified in Edinburgh in the 1930s. Influenced by students from India who were highly critical of the British, they became politicised through their involvement as committee members of

The Natal Indian Congress began its activist phase in the mid-1940s, when more radical leaders came to the fore. Here, Indians march for free and compulsory education.

the Edinburgh Indian Association. When they returned to South Africa, Dadoo to the Transvaal, and Goonam and Naicker to Natal, they became involved in Indian politics. The new leaders were also prominent in the Non-European United Front, which had been initiated by the Coloured petty bourgeoisie in the Cape. The election of Dadoo and Naidoo to the National Council in April 1939 marked the first attempt by Indians to forge a common 'Non-European' identity. Moderates and successive Indian agents continued to oppose alliances with non-Indians, except with White liberals.

Moderate Indians cooperated with the Lawrence Committee, which had been appointed in February 1940 to examine Indian 'penetration' into predominantly White areas. They attempted to stop Indians from purchasing land so as to preserve segregation. Agitation on the part of the Whites, who felt that the committee did not go far enough, resulted in the Pegging Act of April 1943, which banned property transactions between Whites and Indians in Durban for three years. Moderate Indians lobbied the government, resulting in the Pretoria Agreement of April 1944, which led to the suspension of the Pegging Act. In return, moderates formed a body to monitor voluntary segregation. This formally split Indian politics between 'moderates' and 'radicals'. Radicals formed the Anti-Segregation Council in April 1944 to mobilise the masses through meetings all over Natal. The NIC's registered membership increased from 3000 to 22,000 within a year. The annual election of the NIC on 21 October 1945 was attended by 7000 Indians, who elected all 46 nominees of the radicals to the executive. Twelve were members of the Communist Party.

PASSIVE RESISTANCE (1946–48)

The NIC launched a passive resistance campaign against the Asiatic Land Tenure and Indian Representation Bill of 1946, which Indians referred to as the 'Ghetto Act' because it was the first law providing for the compulsory segregation of Indians in Natal. The themes used by

leaders to rally Indians harked to the past and emphasised Indianness. The rhetoric was couched in racial and national terms and much faith was placed in India. Dr Naicker called for a round-table conference, and a delegation was sent to India to conduct a propaganda campaign. The *Manifesto of the Indian Community* appealed to Indians to 'render all support, financial, moral and otherwise, to our struggle of resistance. Ours is a common struggle!' As a mark of protest, India severed trade links with South Africa, withdrew its Indian agent, Ramrao Deshmukh, and raised the issue at the United Nations (UN) in December 1946. The UN called upon the South African government to treat Indians in accordance with the provisions of its charter.

The campaign began on 13 June 1946. By the time it was halted in June 1948, over 2000 arrests had been made. Factory workers, housewives, laundry workers, municipal workers, shopkeepers, tailors, waiters and bus conductors volunteered for arrest, even though the law mainly affected merchants as it closed an important avenue of investment. Volunteers who forwarded their names to the Passive Resistance Council were put into groups ranging from five to 20, which then offered themselves for arrest. A farewell reception was held at 'Red Square' in Commercial Road, where leaders reiterated the history of the struggle and the implications of the bill, and provided advice on coping with prison life. The volunteers were then garlanded. Upon their release, thousands welcomed them back at Red Square. A Resisters' Volunteer Corps procured donations from Indians throughout South Africa and India to see to the welfare of resisters.

Indianness was at its height during this campaign. The passion and fervour was increased by Indian independence celebrations on 15 August 1947. A meeting at Albert Park was attended by 15,000. The flags of India and Pakistan were unfurled side by side, and pictures of national leaders were hung on the stage. The NIC relied on Indian support; when Dadoo and Naicker returned from the All-Asia Conference in March 1947, Naicker told an NIC conference that 'India recognised that we in South Africa were not only fighting for our just rights but also to preserve the national honour and dignity of all Indians.' Soon after Gandhi was assassinated, Dadoo told a gathering of resisters on 29 February 1948 that they 'were fortunate in having a worthy successor in Pandit Jawarharlal Nehru whom we have accepted in the Resistance Movement as our undisputed leader and adviser.' After a two-year struggle, passive resistance ended suddenly in June 1948 when the National Party defeated Smuts in the general election.

Smuts's refusal to hold a round-table conference and India's withdrawal of its agent severed the political link with the subcontinent. The sense of an international 'Indianism' gradually dissipated as working-class Indians became absorbed in building permanent homes in South Africa, and radicals were keen to stress their South African roots too. They began to talk less of 'the glory of the Indian nation'. The campaign reinforced the need for Indians to find allies among Africans, and they opted for a multi-racial strategy. They gave practical impetus to this in March 1947 when Dr Dadoo of the Transvaal Indian Congress, Dr Naicker of the NIC, and Dr A. B. Xuma, president-general of the African National Congress (ANC), signed the 'Doctor's Pact', pledging 'the fullest cooperation between the African and Indian peoples.' However, non-racial unity was confined largely to the leadership, and the spectre of racial tension reared its ugly head when the Afro-Indian riots of 1949 brought the relationship between Indians and Africans into sharp focus.

Simmering tension between Indians and Africans gave way to four days of violence in January 1949, resulting in 142 deaths and the destruction of thousands of stores and dwellings. Months after the riots, hundreds of refugees were still living in emergency camps. The conflict started late in the afternoon on Thursday, 13 January, when an Indian storekeeper in a crowded Indian market assaulted an African youth. An altercation involving Indians and Africans followed in the vicinity of the market. By midday on Friday, African migrant workers had congregated at the docks and marched in formation towards Indian areas, with police collusion. Terror was unleashed on the largely impoverished Indian working-class population. Arson, looting and killing continued over the weekend. The situation only subsided when the navy intervened on Monday afternoon.

Sociologist Fatima Meer has suggested that the pronouncements of Whites triggered the attack by fuelling anti-Indianism. A typical example was a candidate for the United Party telling a meeting in Durban in 1948 that 'personally, I would like to solve the problem by shooting them, but I can't lay myself open to the charge of murder.' However, this fails to explain widespread African support. Racial mobilisation was not foisted upon Africans by Whites. Such feelings were the result of friction between the two communities. The all-White commission investigating the riot concluded that the Indians had brought the violence upon themselves as a result of the 'bad precepts and examples' they set by 'engaging in passive resistance and had not scrupled to invoke overseas assistance.' The report concluded that riots were inevitable because racial groups were inherently antagonistic. This ignores why the attacks were directed at Indians rather than Whites, and why they occurred when they did.

The root of the violence was the competition for jobs, social space and services in Durban, whose population more than doubled between 1936 and 1951. There were 123,165 Indians, 109,543 Africans and 129,683 Whites in Durban in 1951. Indians, who were incorporated into the local economy before the Africans, established a niche as semi-skilled and unskilled industrial operatives, positions to which Africans aspired. Indian bus owners controlled routes to non-European areas, Indian traders dominated retail trade in these areas and were landlords to African shack dwellers in Cato Manor. Relations between Indian landlords and African tenants, shopkeepers and their customers, and bus owners and their passengers, were fraught with tension as inflation cut the level of real wage levels for Africans in the 1940s. These complaints emerged

Indians undertook a campaign of passive resistance between 1946 and 1948 against the 1946 'Ghetto Act', which demarcated areas in Natal where land transfers across racial lines were forbidden. During the campaign, mass meetings were held in Pine Street—in what was known as Red Square—to pay homage to resisters.

strongly in the evidence given by African witnesses to the Riots Commission. The situation was exacerbated by residential segregation between Indians, Africans and Whites. The 1951 census showed, however, that in Durban the economic gap between Indians and Africans was marginal. The per capita income was £40.02 for Africans, £45 for Indians and £282.74 for Whites. This confirms the many reports that the masses of Indians lived in poverty.

Indians denied the African allegations. The conservative Natal Indian Organisation submitted a statement that Indians were not the cause of African disabilities: '[Africans] knew that their oppressor was the European, but he also knew the might of the European...He was afraid to show his hostility to the European. He found in the Indian a convenient scapegoat.' The commission failed to examine underlying causes. The riots had a significant impact on the consciousness of Indians. R. S. Nowbath, editor of the *Leader*, wrote on 29 January 1949:

...[those Indians] who have seen their homes destroyed in front of their eyes, those who have seen a lifetime's savings go up in smoke, those who have seen their children hacked in front of them, and those who helplessly watched their daughters raped, will not, they cannot, forget. The generation that lived through that night of terror, January 14–15, will never forgive the African. For two generations at least the embers of hate will smoulder.

BLACK POLITICS IN THE APARTHEID YEARS (1948–94)

The riot was politically significant in that it ended the racial politics of the previous decades. Indian leadership hoped to correct this by appealing to a new dynamic built around freedom's indivisibility. The riots heralded a decade of passive resistance by a multiracial forum, of which progressive Indian organisations became an integral part, with the ANC, henceforth, the more important player. Around 8000 people were arrested during the Defiance of Unjust Laws in 1952. However, there were only 246 arrests in Durban, and little Indian-African cooperation. In June 1955, the Congress of Democrats, which included the South African Indian Congress, adopted the Freedom Charter, which embraced a multiracial identity. The Treason Trial that followed the arrest of leaders included many Indians and served to strengthen unity. The year 1960 saw the banning of the ANC, the South African Communist Party and the Pan-Africanist Congress following the killing of 67 anti-apartheid protesters at Sharpeville on 21 March 1960. Although the NIC was not banned, its leaders were served restrictive orders and the organisation was effectively silenced. This

A White policeman facing a group of Indian youths during the riots. The 1949 Durban riots reflected bitter racial tensions between Africans and Indians as 142 people died, and homes and businesses were destroyed.

Indians were forcibly
moved from their homes to
racially segregated town-
ships such as Chatsworth
and Phoenix. Westville
and La Mercy were made
available for Indian
middle-class housing.

Map 8.34

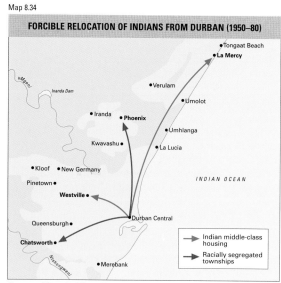

FORCIBLE RELOCATION OF INDIANS FROM DURBAN (1950–80)

Indian middle-class housing

Racially segregated townships

Courtesy of Surendra Bhana, Professor of History, University of Kansas, US; and Goolam Vahed, Associate Professor, Department of History, University of KwaZulu-Natal, South Africa.

The Group Areas Act of 1950 forcibly relocated thousands of people into racially defined areas. Here, an Indian family prepares to move.

Africans, Indians, Coloureds and Progressive Whites joined hands to engage in passive resistance in the 1950s. The high point was the adoption of the Freedom Charter in 1955.

250

ended an important link between Indians and Africans, albeit a tenuous one since the alliance between the NIC and ANC failed to effect a transition to non-racial politics at a mass level.

As apartheid became entrenched, racial boundaries became firmer. Apartheid had ambiguous consequences for Indians and many suffered under it. Between 1950 and 1980, around 140,000 Indians were forcibly relocated in Durban from their original homes to new residential areas under the Groups Areas Act of 1950. For most, it meant relocation from shacks and wood-and-iron homes to racially segregated townships like Chatsworth and Phoenix, where living conditions were relatively better. However, they were moved far from their places of employment, resulting in higher transportation costs, the break-up of extended families and great adversity for the elderly. This disruption of family and community life resulted in the loss of dignity, feelings of helplessness and depression among many Indians. Social change and relocation increased alcoholism, crime and divorce rates. Areas such as Reservoir Hills, La Mercy and Westville were simultaneously made available for segregated Indian middle-class housing (see Map 8.34).

A BROADER MEANING OF 'INDIANNESS'

The restructuring of urban space redefined Indianness. By 1960, most Indians were South African-born, and Indianness had a broader meaning. The notion of Indianness was not linked to or dependent on India for support, but was centred on South Africa. It was on these terms that Indians were able to engage with other South Africans in protest against the apartheid government. Much of what defined Indians was still rooted in their culture and religion. In fact, apartheid, by further racialising citizenship and heightening a sense of ethnic separateness, strengthened cultural and religious practices among succeeding generations of Indians in South Africa. Most Indians were comfortable with this redefined Indianness, which allowed them to participate in multiracial arrangements of the liberation movements that eventually led to the overthrow of apartheid.

Apartheid promoted racially segmented politics. Progressive Indian groups resisted government policies under very difficult circumstances, but there were many

who collaborated. The legal position of Indians changed in 1961 when they were granted the status of permanent residents. A Department of Indian Affairs was established as the government tried to administrate them as a fixed category under the apartheid system. Indian advisory bodies were created to separate them from Africans and Coloureds. The South African Indian Council, which comprised nominated members, was inaugurated in 1968. Local Affairs Committees were also established to advise local authorities on matters affecting Indians. Conservative elements who had been displaced from the NIC in the 1940s found a home in these bodies. Economic mobility after 1960 was due in large measure to the expansion in education, which came under the control of the Department of Indian Affairs in 1965. The building of schools, and free and compulsory education resulted in greater access to education. According to the 2001 census, only 13 per cent of Indians over the age of 20 had not been to secondary school. In contrast, 48 per cent of Africans had never been to secondary school. The expansion of the M. L. Sultan Technical College, the establishment of the Springfield College of Education for training teachers and the University of Durban-Westville in the 1960s increased the number of Indian professionals and artisans.

Working classes benefited from the emergence of Indian industrialists. Large companies like Lockat Bros. and Kingsgate Clothing Group were prominent in the manufacture of clothing. Indians dominated semi-skilled positions in the clothing and textile industries. Family income was augmented by large numbers of women entering wage employment from the 1960s. Trade unions with Indian membership focused less on politics and more on improving the economic position of employees. There was a relative advantage in being Indian as restrictions on residence and movement, such as the pass laws and influx control only applied to Africans. Indians were better placed economically in comparison to Africans. Of the economically active population, 69 per cent of Africans, but only 27 per cent of Indians and 12 per cent of Whites, earned less than R1600 per month in 2001. Further, only 9 per cent of Africans, but 25 per cent of Indians and 28 per cent of Whites earned a 'middle-class' wage of between R3200 and R6400.

Moderate politics was challenged from the mid-1970s by extra-parliamentary opposition bodies on several fronts. Steve Biko's Black Consciousness Movement challenged existing racial identities by seeking to construct a new political identity, 'Black', which included Indians, Africans and Coloureds. Young Indians, such as Saths Cooper and

Strini Moodley, found this philosophy appealing and challenged the racialised politics of older leaders. The effect on Black consciousness was considerable and wide-ranging, and was accompanied by a resurgence of worker action. The Durban strikes of 1973, essentially by Africans, heralded mass worker action. The Federation of South African Trade Unions, formed in April 1979, had a membership of 320,000 by 1983. Political resurgence made mass confrontation inevitable: it started in Soweto on 16 June 1976. In 1983, the tricameral parliament gave ineffective representation to Indians and Coloureds, and ignored Africans. The NIC's vigorous anti-election programme, which included mass rallies and house-to-house visits, resulted in a voter turnout of around 10 per cent as Indians emphatically rejected the reforms.

Though small numbers of Indians embraced the politics of Black consciousness, the masses of Indians participated in the multiracial anti-apartheid congress movement. The revived Natal and Transvaal Indian congresses formed strong components of the United Democratic Front, which was launched on 20 August 1983 to protest against the tricameral dispensation. It included trade unions, religious bodies, student organisations and civic associations. Based on the Freedom Charter, the Democratic Front attempted to reinstate the heritage of non-racialism. Another workers' organisation, the Congress of South African Trade Unions, became a powerful player in the mid-1980s—Jay Naidoo became one of its highest-ranking officials. Further arrests were made and a second trial for treason followed in the 1980s, in which Indians stood accused alongside their fellow disenfranchised South Africans. Mass campaigns heralded a cycle of protest around townships, schools and factories. African youth seized the political initiative and made townships literally ungovernable. This, together with Western sanctions, which induced an economic crisis because of the shortage of skills and capital, forced the nationalist government into reform. This led to the release of Nelson Mandela in February 1990, the removal of bans on political organisations, multi-party negotiations and, ultimately, to South Africa's first democratically elected government on 27 April 1994.

Politics was once again ahead of popular sentiments. Many Indians took part in multiracial campaigns against apartheid but were afraid of majority rule that would inevitably lead to African rule. Indians had participated with their fellow disenfranchised South Africans to stamp out racial discrimination. Many suffered imprisonment, torture and exile, and some paid the ultimate price. Suliman Saloojee (1964), Ahmed Timol (1971) and Dr Hoosen Mia Haffejee (1977), for example, were political

prisoners who were murdered by security forces while in detention. And yet, there was consternation among many Indians as South Africa moved towards non-racial democracy. An April 1987 study by Markinor found that 53 per cent of Indians worried 'really often' or 'quite often', and 27 per cent 'sometimes', that Africans would again attack Indians; and 53 per cent 'strongly disagreed' that Indians would be safe under African rule.

The unease of Indians was due to the fact that the apartheid regime had made higher per capita allocations for Indian education, housing and welfare. Natal was also unofficially an Indian professional employment region, and the working classes monopolised unskilled positions in industry and the municipality too. This was part of the strategy employed by the apartheid regime to foster divisions on the basis of economic privileges. Indians realised that affirmative action and the equalisation of benefits would reduce per capita expenditure on them and curtail their employment opportunities. In these circumstances, the apartheid past suddenly appeared rosier. Working-class Indians feared African rule the most. They were worried that while apartheid denied them opportunities because they were 'too black', majority rule would marginalise them for not being black enough.

Approximately 70 per cent of Indians, mostly working-class, voted for the apartheid-regime Nationalist Party in 1994. Support for the ANC came from professionals and students. At a provincial level, there was massive support for the racially exclusive Minority Front Party led

At least 156 people, including 21 Indians, were charged for treason in 1956. Here, a group of activists are camped outside a police station in support of the prisoners.

Jay Naidoo became a member of South Africa's first non-racial Cabinet in 1994. He is seen here with his Canadian wife, Luie Page.

The United Democratic Front (UDF) emerged in the early 1980s to defy the apartheid state. The NIC was an important member of the UDF. Zac Yacoob (second from left) and Mewa Ramgobin (second from right) feature in this photograph.

The Congress Alliance of the 1950s

Conservative Indian leadership had shied away from seeking political alliances with Africans or confronting the government. This leadership was ousted in the 1940s, regionally and nationally, by the likes of Dr G. M. Naicker and Dr Yusof M. Dadoo, who were bold in their approach. As South Africans, they insisted on equal rights and actively sought to work with the African majority. They forged an alliance with the African National Congress (ANC), which spearheaded the liberation movement. It set the stage for a decade of defiance and passive resistance in the 1950s. Together with Africans, progressive Indians became a part of the non-racial vision, as articulated in the 1955 Freedom Charter.

Dadoo was the most prominent leader of this era. He was heavily influenced by Gandhi but also read Marxist literature in Edinburgh, where he studied in the 1930s, and joined the Communist Party when he returned to South Africa. A square in the African township of Orlando was named Dadoo Square in his honour in 1940. He was also one of only three South Africans, along with Chief Albert Luthuli and Father Trevor Huddleston, to be conferred the Isitwalandwe at the Congress of the People in 1955, in recognition of his contribution to the freedom struggle. In exile, Dadoo became the leader of the Communist Party of South Africa and was a tower of strength to Oliver Tambo and the ANC. He was vice-chairman of the Revolutionary Council of the ANC from 1969.

Participation in the Congress Alliance put Indians squarely within the liberation movement. This set the stage for the tradition of resistance to apartheid for the next four decades and paved the way for a later generation of progressives, such as Mac Maharaj, Mewa Ramgobin and Jay Naidoo, to participate in the ANC. It also ensured substantial Indian participation in the creation of democratic structures in the new South Africa.

Indian Muslims are seen praying on the roof of the oldest mosque in Natal, the Grey Street mosque, built in 1881. It is an important tourist attraction.

Table 8.22

	Gauteng	KwaZulu-Natal	South Africa
POPULATION OF SOUTH AFRICA AND THE PROVINCES OF GAUTENG AND KWAZULU-NATAL BY COMMUNITY (2001)			
Black African	6,522,792	8,002,407	35,416,166
Coloured	337,974	141,887	3,994,505
Indian or Asian	218,015	798,275	1,115,467
White	1,758,398	483,448	4,293,640
Total	8,837,179	9,426,017	44,819,778

Based on Statistics South Africa, Census 2001.

by Armichand Rajbansi. Profound differences remained between Indians and Africans. As Fatima Meer pointed out, while Indians are outwardly 'a modern sophisticated people presenting themselves in the western mode as a result of their dress and English language, inwardly family ties and religion keep them firmly moored to traditions that are intrinsically Hindu and Muslim and that distinguish them from other South Africans. Non-Indian South Africans are deeply sensitive to this boundary line and are rarely able to penetrate it beyond enjoying Indian cuisine.'

THE POST-APARTHEID ERA

Indians are facing new challenges in post-apartheid South Africa which are reshaping their identities in fundamental ways. South Africa's first democratic election of April 1994 gave birth to the 'rainbow children of God'. Indians participated in drawing up the constitution and are full-fledged citizens of the country. According to the 2001 census, 98 per cent were born in South Africa and 94 per cent regard English as their first language. Apartheid cast a long shadow by legally separating people on the basis of race. The colour of one's skin continues to be salient in post-apartheid South Africa, where people are classified as 'White', 'Coloured', 'Indian or Asian', 'Black African' and 'Other' for official purposes. While the government deems this essential to achieve affirmative action objectives, racial classification is perpetuating identity politics.

The situation is compounded by South Africa's neoliberal economic transition. Though a left-wing alliance, the ANC government is a right-of-centre government whose support comes from White capital and an aspiring African elite. The burden of the poor, meanwhile, has increased through a shift from subsidised to commodified services. This has resulted in price increases in such basic services as water, electricity and transport, and the imposition of cost-recovery mechanisms such as disconnecting services and repossessing property when the poor cannot pay. Unemployment hovers around 40 per cent, casual labour is increasing and the gulf between unionised and non-unionised workers is widening. This is exacerbated by pension decreases in real terms, the absence of a social wage and 'user fees' for school, health care and other services. Between 1995 and 2000, the richest 10 per cent of Blacks received an average income increase of 17 per cent,

while the poorest 40 per cent suffered a 21 per cent decrease. Political pressures are mounting as a result of poverty, landlessness and discontent among the poor.

Indians fear that frustrated African aspirations may be vented on them, a concern underscored by the controversy sparked by playwright Mbongeni Ngema in 2002. His song, *AmaNdiya*, meaning 'Indian' in Zulu, attacked Indians for their alleged unwillingness to accept Africans as equals and for remaining exploitative. It also protested that post-1994 migrants from India and Pakistan were flourishing in small retail trade in urban and rural areas. Ngema urged 'strong men' of the Zulu nation to stand up to Indians. When Indians protested that the song was 'hate-speech', Ngema responded that his song reflected 'the views of Black Africans throughout the country, from taxi stands to soccer matches.' The aspiring African bourgeoisie is peeved that business areas remain out of their grasp. Although the majority of Indians are descendants of indentured labourers, Ngema and others like him continue to caricature Indians as prosperous traders and pseudo-citizens whose loyalty to the nation state is questionable. Saths Cooper, the former vice-chancellor of the University of Durban-Westville, described the relationship between Indians and Africans, 10 years into non-racial democracy, as one of 'passive aggression'.

There have been winners and losers among Indians in post-apartheid South Africa. Indians who are victims of affirmative action or have failed to adapt to changing conditions resulting from the liberalisation of the economy, students denied places at university because of racial quotas, and others who have suffered materially from change, are peeved. Other Indians have benefited enormously by aligning themselves with Black political power, old White capital, new Asian capital from Malaysia, or by establishing links with the diaspora. This emerging diasporic identification is not a remnant of dormant apartheid racial identities, but a creation of the new globalised world order. It has not diminished their attachment to the nation state. Most Indians who complain about being marginalised have nowhere to go because they lack the appropriate skills and capital. Secondary migration to Canada, Australia and the US, mainly among professionals, has been negligible. The link to India is tenuous at best. Despite feelings of anxiety and frustration, most Indians remain firmly rooted in South Africa.

South Africa's Indians have always exercised the right to be culturally diverse. They continue to exercise this right in post-apartheid South Africa, but as part of the political process. They are taking advantage of the new constitution and new freedoms of the post-apartheid state to redefine the kind of Indians they want to be. The sense of an Indian community was always a loose one, and Indian identities are increasingly revolving around specific Tamil, Muslim or Hindu heritage. South Indians, for example, are attempting to reverse the decline in their

Krishna devotees during the annual Rath Yatra festival to honour Lord Vishnu.

vernaculars. The South African Tamil Teachers' Federation has initiated vernacular classes for adults and children which use religion-oriented texts so that culture and religion are imparted. Children also engage with Tamil culture by singing at religious events, and the *Tamil Guardian International*, published monthly in Chatsworth, features local and international news about Tamils. A weekly television programme, *Eastern Mosaic*, has contributed to the revival of Hindu culture by showing film adaptations of, for example, the Ramayana and Mahabharata. Hindi films have been screened on national television since 2004. Tamil-speakers have protested the absence of Tamil-language films, since Tamils and Telugus comprise 63 per cent of Indians. The South African Tamil Federation even organised a petition and submitted a list of 'appropriate' films to the national broadcaster in July 2004: their struggle continues.

There has been a revival among all four streams of Hinduism prominent in South Africa—Sanatanism as well as the reformist movements Arya Samaj, Neo-Vedanta and Hare Krishna. The Arya Samaj movement was established following the visits of Vedic missionaries, Professor Parmanand in 1906 and Swami Shankeranand from 1908 to 1912. Neo-Vedanta was consolidated in the 1940s after the visit of an envoy of the Ramakrishna Mission in India, Swami Adhyanand. The Ramakrishna Centre of South Africa was founded in Durban in 1946 by D. Naidoo, who took monastic vows in India and returned as Swami Nischalananda in 1953. The Hare Krishna movement, founded in America in 1966 by Swami Prabhupada, took root in the 1980s. Its headquarters are at the Shri Radha-Radhanath Temple in Chatsworth. There has been a resurgence in Hindu participation in festivals. The most spectacular is Ratha Yatra, a five-day Hare Krishna festival of chariots in honour of Lord Jugannath (Vishnu), 'Lord of the Universe', observed annually on the beachfront in December. The procession, with its huge red chariot containing images of relevant deities and the founder, is pulled by devotees along the beachfront and ends on the lawn of an amphitheatre, where there are souvenir stalls, book displays, food stalls, dancing and music, and various exhibitions. Interviews with participants suggest that increased interest in festivals is due to the fear of diseases, especially measles and AIDS, increasing scepticism of Western medicine, insecurity resulting from crime and violence, and feelings of discrimination in post-apartheid South Africa.

There has been a high level of conversion to Christianity among Hindus as a result of inroads made by Christian evangelists, in particular Pentecostals. In 1996, 18 per cent of the Indians were Christian; by 2001 this had increased to 24.4 per cent. While almost 90 per cent of indentured migrants were Hindu, they made up just 47.3 per cent of Indians in 2001. The Muslim proportion of the Indian population remains constant at around 25 per cent. Muslims, too, are undergoing important changes: more women veil their face; there is greater concern with observing dietary regulations; the number of Muslims going annually to Saudi Arabia on pilgrimages has increased considerably; and there has been a return to authentic Islamic dress. Islamic finance and insurance are growing among the community and many Islamic schools have opened as well.

Indians have featured strongly in representative institutions since 1994. Members of parliament have included Kader Asmal, Vally Moosa and Dullah Omar; Dr R. A. M. Saloojee and the late Ismail Meer featured at provincial levels; the late Justice Ismail Mohammed occupied the most senior legal position in the country; Gadija Khan was the head of all magistrates in the Western Cape; and Essop Pahad is a key member of President Thabo Mbeki's office. This success was not matched by Indian support for the ANC. Most Indians from lower income groups voted for the National Party in 1994 and the Democratic Alliance in 1999 because of fears of affirmative action and escalating crime. The ANC failed to win elections in KZN and the Western Cape, provinces with significant numbers of Indians and Coloureds respectively. This changed in 2004 when large numbers of Indians voted for the ANC. This was due to the political stability of the past decade, a perception that crime was decreasing, ANC leaders reaching out to minorities, and the economic prosperity of the middle and upper strata. Muslim voters turned to the ANC because of its support for the Palestinians, criticism of the invasion of Iraq by the US in 2003, and the protection of religious freedom. Newspaper columnist and community activist Ashwin Desai has also shown that in many townships, the Indian, African and Coloured poor are joining forces across racial lines to confront local municipalities over commodified services.

The tensions between Indians and Africans are not permanent. The causes of the hostility were sown by the politico-economic system that White rulers created. They assumed that ethnic divisions were natural and imposed them on the population in order to divide and fragment Indians, Africans and Whites. But ethnic particularism is neither primordial nor timeless. It is contingent, flexible and contested. The opportunity to rise above the hostility exists in the new South Africa. Indians have a widespread sense of belonging to South Africa. They have historically adjusted to changes in rulers and policies, and they will adapt to new circumstances. Many are already doing so. They must accept, however, that the masses of the impoverished, who are Africans, will have to be helped by the system and that they must participate in that endeavour.

Surendra Bhana and Goolam Vahed

Gandhi Square in Johannesburg's city centre. In October 2003, a 2.5-m-high bronze statue of Gandhi (in the background) was unveiled at the square.

EAST AFRICA

Indian traders were prominent in the valuable ivory trade from East Africa, which was a major supplier of this sought-after commodity.

INDIANS IN UGANDA, Kenya and Tanzania share a history in which cultural encounters, collaborations and conflicts became the backbone of Indian-African relations. Indians traded along the East African coast long before the arrival of the Europeans. Nevertheless, their numbers and socio-economic importance grew steadily only with the establishment of the European colonies in East Africa in the late 19th and early 20th centuries. In spite of an increase in numbers following the advent of colonialism, they remained a small community, never accounting for more than 2 per cent of the total population. However, they played a significant role in the economic and political history of East Africa. Indians built the Uganda Railway from Mombasa to Kampala, acted as middlemen between the African farmers and European traders, and published the first newspapers. Some of them were active in the local African independence movements as well.

Still, many Indians were not recognised for their contributions to African society. In the late 1950s, on the eve of the independence of East African nations, many Africans saw Indians as ruthless and arrogant foreign exploiters. These racist beliefs were used as justification for European, and later African, politicians to pursue the Africanisation of the local economy. This included the nationalisation of buildings and industries in Tanzania and to a lesser extent Kenya, and the expulsion of all Asians (70,000) from Uganda by General Idi Amin in 1972. In Tanzania and Kenya, the historical experience was less dramatic but there, too, between 40–50 per cent of

Indians migrated to the UK, US and Canada for a more secure political and economic environment. Since the 1980s, Indians have reclaimed their place in these East African nations. In Kenya and Tanzania, many Indians have also regained their trading licences. Though Indians are still not well integrated into East African society, they have found a place for themselves there. Since the late 1980s, some Indian families have even returned to Uganda despite their earlier traumatic experiences.

EARLY ENCOUNTERS

Map 8.35 of the Indian Ocean shows why there has existed a long history of trade and the exchange of ideas, crafts and human traffic between western India, the Arab countries and East Africa. Direct trade between the regions was subject to the monsoons. From November to March, the beautiful dhows sailed from western India to East Africa, and from April to September the return journey was made. The trade in cotton textiles, ivory and spices was profitable but dangerous. Many traders did not return home. The rough sea, pirates and various diseases claimed the lives of many traders and early adventurers.

Early contact between Indians and East Africans goes back at least 2000 years. The first written evidence of these early encounters is the *Periplus of the Erythraean Sea*, written by a Greek pilot in the 1st century AD. Around that time, the first sizeable trading posts, such as Kilwa, Malindi and Mogadishu, emerged along the East African coast. When Vasco da Gama arrived in Mozambique, Mombasa and Lindi in 1497, he was surprised at the number of Arabs and Indians he found there.

Trading activity between India and East Africa was strengthened when the Arab ruler Seyyid Said moved his capital from Oman to Zanzibar in 1832. The Sultan appointed Jairam Shivaji, an Indian, as the customs collector. Fellow community members flourished in the shade of Shivaji's position and many Indian residents in Oman followed him to Zanzibar. A commercial treaty in 1839

Dhows, traditional lateen-rigged sailing vessels, are common to the Indian Ocean. A large dhow typically contains a crew of approximately 30, while smaller ones usually have a crew of 12.

Map 8.35

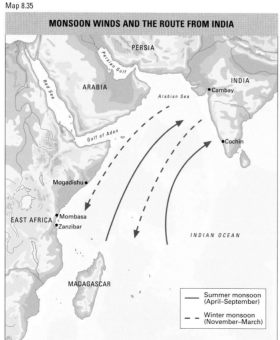

MONSOON WINDS AND THE ROUTE FROM INDIA

PERSIA

Persian Gulf

Red Sea

ARABIA

INDIA

Arabian Sea

Cambay

Gulf of Aden

Cochin

Mogadishu

EAST AFRICA
Mombasa
Zanzibar

INDIAN OCEAN

MADAGASCAR

—— Summer monsoon (April–September)

- - - Winter monsoon (November–March)

Source: Gijsbert Oonk, Asians in East Africa: Images, Histories and Portraits, *2004.*

Monsoon winds in the Indian Ocean played a critical role in determining early maritime trading patterns.

between Said and Britain guaranteed British subjects the freedom to enter Zanzibar and to reside and trade within the Sultan's dominion. The establishment of a British consulate in Zanzibar further encouraged Indians to settle because of the sense of security and the expectation of protection in their dealings with the Arab aristocracy. The number of Indian traders in Zanzibar grew steadily from 2500 in 1870 to 6000 in the early 1900s. These traders were mainly Muslim, but there was a small Hindu community. (The Muslims—especially the Khojas and Ithnasheries—settled earlier with their families than the Hindus—the Lohanas, Shahs and Patels, among others—due to the Hindu taboo on overseas travel.)

In 1873, Sir Bartle Frere, who investigated East Africa's slave trade, wrote admiringly of Indians in Zanzibar:

Arriving at his future scene of business with little beyond the credentials of his fellow caste men, after perhaps a brief apprenticeship in some older firms he the Indian trader starts a shop of his own with goods advanced on credit by some large house, and after a few years, when he has made a little money, generally returned home to marry, to make fresh business connections, and then comes back to Africa to repeat, on a large scale.

This was the general pattern followed by many Indian traders. It was exceptional for the family's eldest son to make the exploratory trip to Africa. More often, the second or third son was chosen to take this first step. This pattern allowed those who could not find a job in East Africa or were not successful in business to return to India or to travel to South Africa to try their luck elsewhere. India served as a reservoir of new recruits for Africa as well as a safety net for those who were not successful abroad.

Until the 1890s, there was very little Indian movement to the interior. Generally, the Indians remained in Zanzibar or the coastal port cities. They left perilous travel to the interior to the more experienced Arab and Swahili traders. Among the Indians, the Muslims were probably the first to 'discover' the interior. The first Indian known to have settled up-country was Musa Msuri, a Khoja from Surat. In 1825, he and his brother Sayyan set out on an expedition from Zanzibar and were probably the first non-Africans to reach Unyamwezi territory in western Tanzania, where they traded cloth and beads for ivory, turning a handsome profit. On his return, Sayyam died. Musa continued conducting caravans for another 30 years, reaching as far inland as Maragwe and Buganda in Uganda. Allidina Visram was the leading merchant in East Africa and reached Uganda before the railway did.

Ivory was the major trade of Indians in East Africa—it was first sent to Bombay, partly for re-export to China and the West. Many Indian merchants were also involved in the trade of spices, goat skin, dried fish and other agricultural cargo. A number of established Indians, such as Visram and Parroo, were involved in financing the East African slave trade. Some also traded slaves directly, although on a small scale, partly due to British pressure to abolish the trade. On the other hand, there were Indians such as Tharia Topan, who was knighted by the British in 1890 for services rendered in suppressing the slave trade.

MIGRATION PATTERNS (1890–1970)

The largest number of Indians in East Africa, particularly those who were free migrants, came from Northwest India, primarily Gujarat, Saurasthra, Kutch, Sind and, to a lesser extent, Maharasthra. Even today, Kutchi and Gujarati remain the predominant Indian languages spoken among Indian migrants in East Africa. In addition, Punjab supplied nearly all of the indentured labourers who worked on the Uganda Railway, and the former Portuguese settlement of Goa was the origin of many higher-level civil servants in British East African territories.

The year 1890 marked the end of the Arab ascendancy in East Africa and the region was partitioned among the European powers. By then, over 6000 Indians lived in Zanzibar and along the East African coast. Between 1890 and 1914, this relatively small number was augmented by almost 38,000 indentured labourers (mainly males) who worked on the construction of the Uganda Railway. These railway workers generally came from Punjab on a contract of between three and five years. Almost 80 per cent of them left East Africa at the end of their contracts. Roughly 7000, however, remained in East Africa at the end of their contracts. Upon its completion, the railway was manned for several decades by Indian drivers, foremen, stationmasters, linesmen, telegraphers, mechanics, gangers, repairmen, upholsterers, carpenters and other artisans. Others settled as *dukka wallas*, or petty traders, along the railway line and in the interior, selling salt, sugar,

Map 8.36

An Indian man in Zanzibar is photographed with his bicycle, which was considered an important status symbol in the early 20th century.

East African currencies

In the 19th century, a number of currencies were in use in East Africa. The most well known were the Maria Theresean dollar and cowries (shells) from the Maldives. Nevertheless, because of steadily increasing trade with India, these were replaced with the Indian rupee. In 1890, the DOA (German East African Company) affirmed its importance by requesting the German government to produce German silver rupees. Through a number of financial reforms, this eventually led to the production of German rupee notes in 1905. This, no doubt, was an official recognition of the importance of the Indian rupee, and therefore the Indian business community. After 1920, the British East African Currency Board produced shilling notes, on which English, Arabic and Gujarati languages featured on the front. Note that at that time there was no reference to Swahili yet.

Extract from www.asiansinafrica.com.

The German 'One Rupee' note (above) and the East African Currency Board's 'Five Shillings' note (right).

The Mazeras bridge on the Uganda Railway. The railway was built by Indian workers and linked the port city of Mombasa to the Ugandan and Kenyan interior.

soap and various local produce in areas around railway stations. These traders represented the most conspicuous image of Indian existence in East Africa. For many Africans, these shops and their products were among their first encounters with a larger world. Many of the early small shopkeepers worked 14- to 18-hour days behind counters, running errands, cleaning and organising their shops. Most of them started to work in a *dukka* in the city with a brother or relative. After some time, they would open their own shop up-country with goods purchased wholesale or taken on credit from their former employers. As a result, the initial shop became both a retailer and wholesaler. These traders lived a frugal exis-

tence, spending their profits only on the barest necessities. Many even slept in a separate space in the shop, in the interest of accumulating capital to expand their business.

The next wave of migration was linked to the growth of British colonial power in East Africa. After World War I, in addition to Kenya and Uganda, the British secured control of the former German East African colony, Tanganyika. A growing number of Indians found jobs in the civil service. By now, many traders, businessmen, artisans and employees had made Africa their home. They, especially the Hindus, invited their women, children, parents and in-laws to settle with them. Between the two world wars, the total number of Indians in East Africa doubled from approximately 55,000 in 1921 up to 105,000 in 1939.

The largest increase in the Indian population in East Africa occurred after World War II. In 1969, around 300,000 Indians lived in East Africa. Approximately half of this growth can be attributed to economic expansion in the East African region, particularly in Kenya. However, unlike the preceding periods, the other half of the growth in population can be attributed to natural increase. Although the number of migrants arriving in East Africa continued to increase every year, the percentage of migrants as a proportion of Indian residents gradually diminished.

The Uganda Railway

The need for a railway to promote the economic development of East Africa had been emphasised by the Imperial British East Africa Company. The construction of the railway began in Mombasa in December 1895. The first locomotive reached Kisumu on Lake Victoria in December 1901 and the line was completed in 1903. The railway was built under the guidance of British engineers with the help of more than 35,000 indentured labourers, mainly from Punjab. In the first six years, these labourers and artisans constructed the railway and bridges through difficult terrain and under extreme circumstances. In the years before 1902, around 2500 Indian contract workers died and 6500 became invalid. Some were attacked by wild animals, as represented in the film *The Man-eaters of Tsavo*. It is ironic that the first comprehensive history of the Uganda Railway, by M. F. Hill, *Permanent Way: The Story of the Kenya and Uganda Railway*, being the official history of the development of the transport system in Kenya and Uganda, does not mention the use of Indian labour at all. Instead, the construction of the railway is celebrated as a British achievement.

Called the 'Lunatic Line' by its detractors, the railway became strategically and economically vital for both Uganda and Kenya. It was used in the suppression of slavery and became an impor-

Indian workers on the Uganda Railway.

tant instrument against German East Africa in World War I. The railway allowed heavy equipment to be transported far inland with relative ease, and it was important for the export of colonial products such as coffee, tea and cotton.

The railway still operates as an economic lifeline for East African countries. Yet, in spite of its importance, since the 1980s and 1990s, there has been a growing lack of concern for safety, which has resulted in an increasing number of accidents reported despite the fact that the maximum speed of the trains on the railway is only 45 km per hour.

Table 8.23

NUMBER OF INDIANS IN EAST AFRICA (1921–2000)			
	Kenya	**Uganda**	**Tanzania**
1921	25,253	5200	10,209 + 13,772 in Zanzibar
1931	43,623	14,150	25,144 + 15,247 in Zanzibar
1939	46,897	17,300	25,000 + 15,500 in Zanzibar
1962	175,000	77,500	92,000 + 20,000 in Zanzibar
1969	140,000	75,000	85,000
1972	105,000	1000	52,000
1984	50,000	1000	30,000
1995/2000	100,000	12,000	90,000

Source: R. Gregory, South Asians in East Africa, 1890–1980, 1993. Notes: Figures for 1969, 1972 and 1984 are estimates. Figures for 1995/2000 are based on a report by the High Level Committee on Indian Diaspora. Their numbers for Tanzania and Kenya are highly overestimated. A more realistic estimate would be 45,000 and 70,000 respectively.

THE COLONIAL EXPERIENCE

Germany and Britain were the main contenders in the scramble for East Africa. Both countries had a long history of sending missionaries, explorers and adventurers to the region's interior. By 1900, Britain had a sphere of influence that spanned much of Kenya and Uganda, while the Germans had gained control of Tanganyika. Zanzibar became a British protectorate in 1890. In 1920, when the Germans had lost World War I, Tanganyika became a British protectorate too.

The establishment of British and German rule in East Africa offered new economic opportunities for Indians there. This involved not only the building of the Uganda Railway, which opened up the interior, but also the growing trade of cash crops such as cotton, which the British authorities promoted in order to feed the factories in Lancashire and Manchester. Some Indians also owned ginneries. During this period, Europeans and Indians owned almost all the means of production and distribution. Africans were openly discriminated against in the provision of basic business services, such as bank loans and the issuing of trading licences. Unlike the Indians, the difficulties of the Africans were exacerbated by their lack of familiarity with the monetary economy. Furthermore, a number of Indian migrants who could speak English were often able to negotiate with the colonial government, unlike the Africans.

Both the Africans and colonial officials regarded the Indians in East Africa as a single group. The Indians themselves often acted as a united force despite their communal differences. From the early 1900s, they established numerous political organisations in order to speak with one voice. In 1909, the Committee of Indians was formed in Zanzibar; it was later renamed the Indian National Association. In 1914, Indians founded the East African Indian National Congress (EAINC), which was modelled after the Indian National Congress (INC) in India, and sought to unite its countrymen in East Africa. Although the East African branch was successful in achieving its aim, it would, over time, find itself divided over political issues. In the 1950s, Tanganyikan Indians established their own territorial organisation, the Asian Association, and the EAINC was renamed the Kenya Indian Congress.

These political organisations were predominantly engaged in fighting discrimination. They protested against the number of seats reserved for Asians in the legislative council in Tanganyika, established in 1926. There were 13 official seats and 10 non-official members, the composition of which was clearly biased, the Asians having only

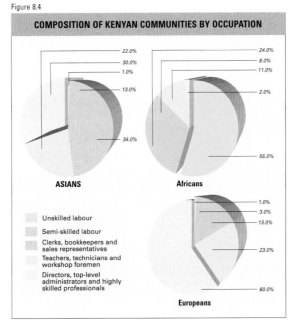

Figure 8.4

COMPOSITION OF KENYAN COMMUNITIES BY OCCUPATION

ASIANS — 22.0%, 30.0%, 1.0%, 13.0%, 34.0%

Africans — 24.0%, 8.0%, 11.0%, 2.0%, 55.0%

Europeans — 1.0%, 3.0%, 13.0%, 23.0%, 60.0%

Unskilled labour
Semi-skilled labour
Clerks, bookkeepers and sales representatives
Teachers, technicians and workshop foremen
Directors, top-level administrators and highly skilled professionals

Source: Republic of Kenya, 'Employment and Earnings in the Modern Sector, 1968–1970', 1972.

three non-official seats and the Africans none. Most of the medical and educational services available for Asians were also inferior to those for Europeans. In addition, as in India, Asians were not appointed to higher posts in the civil service. But despite such bias, Indians were still in a privileged position compared to Africans.

In Kenya, white settlers were even more focused on their own economic prosperity and their influence raised the so-called 'Indian issue', that of whether it was legally and morally right to reserve the best agricultural land for whites only. In 1908, the exclusion of non-whites from the 'White Highlands' became an official policy despite massive protests. In 1923, the Devonshire Declaration attempted to resolve the conflict by asserting the paramountcy of African interest, and yet continued to reserve the highlands for white settlement. The INC in India passed several resolutions to boycott British goods, but with little result.

In other areas, however, Asians in Africa gained important political and economic success. In 1934, the government of Zanzibar introduced legislation to protect the interests of Arab clove traders and planters. The new measures placed a moratorium on mortgage debts and prohibited the transfer of Arab- and African-owned agricultural land to non-Arabs and non-Africans without the sanction of the British administration. The legislation followed the loss of the Arab monopoly on clove plantations and trade to Indian moneylenders. Indians in Zanzibar, with the support of the India Office in London and the British Indian government, protested strongly against the measures. Nevertheless, since the legislation was not withdrawn, the EAINC arranged a clove boycott, which resulted in a compromise between the government of Zanzibar and the Indian community, not least because India was the most important export destination for cloves.

The National Bank of India in Dar es Salaam.

Indians reaching out for immigration forms outside the offices of the British High Commission in Kampala, Uganda, on 14 August 1972. They sought vouchers to permit their entry into England following General Idi Amin's expulsion orders.

These early colonial experiences show the development of a highly hierarchical society, often described as an 'upside down pyramid': at the top was a very small European colonial elite; below them were the Indian migrants; and at the bottom were the majority of Africans. Social stratification following this pyramidal model remained a feature throughout the colonial period. The correspondence between class and colour can be easily seen in many censuses. The occupational structure of Kenya in the 1960s, represented in Figure 8.4, provides an excellent example of these hierarchically structured societies. Two observations are important here: first, that the general stereotype of the Indian migrants in East Africa being traders and moneylenders belies the fact that a significant portion of the community contributed to East African society as teachers, administrators, lawyers, doctors and clerks; and second, by the 1960s, the Africanisation project initiated by the colonial government (and continued by the independent African countries) to improve the participation of Africans in the general economy had taken longer than many government officials anticipated. Indians and Europeans remained the predominant economic force in spite of the fact that Europeans accounted for only about 1 per cent of the total population, while Indians accounted for only 2 per cent.

THE INDEPENDENT EAST AFRICAN STATES AND INDIANS

The independence of the East African states in the early 1960s raised questions about the nature of the Indian settlements. Were Indians to be seen as settled 'Asian Africans' or were they temporary migrants? By the late 1960s, the East African economy had declined and the uncertainties and consequences following the independence of the East African states were to have an adverse impact on the Indian community.

The constitutions of the newly independent East African states gave those Indians who were not automatically citizens by virtue of their birth (one of the parents as well as the applicant had to be born locally) an option to register as citizens within a grace period of two years. Most Indians preferred to keep their options open until the last few months of the grace period. While legally they had a right to do this, East African governments took their procrastination as an expression of a lack of faith in these states. Hence, they introduced periodic embargoes. In the case of the Ismailis and other Muslim communities in East Africa, the leadership actively encouraged local citizenship. Others maintained their British citizenship as a precaution. The absence of the need to make a concerted choice had a long-term significance with regard to the manner in which Asians were to identify and align themselves with East Africa.

The push towards rapid Africanisation resulted in the adoption of various discriminatory schemes in the East African countries. Tanzania introduced a system of work permits and only allowed foreigners to take up jobs which could not be fulfilled by locals. These measures were quickly followed, after the Arusha Declaration of 1967, with the nationalisation of industries and the main economic institutions, such as banking and insurance, along with measures affecting the acquisition of buildings. Such legislation affected the Asian community in particular. As a result, by 1971, more than 30,000 had left the country, and in 1972 only 52,000 Indians remained in Tanzania.

In Kenya, the overall approach taken by the government was to build a strong indigenous class of traders, bankers and industrialists. Though nationalisation did indeed take place, the majority of Indians who suffered from various Africanisation policies were small traders and people working in lower clerical and semi-skilled jobs. It became increasingly difficult for Indians to find employment or get licences in these areas. Since most licences and permits were granted only for one or two years, this increased the economic insecurities of many Indians from lower economic strata. In Kenya, more than 40,000 Indians left the country before 1972.

In Uganda, the Africanisation programme began following the Kenyan pattern but changed from the early 1970s to follow the Tanzanian pattern. The 1969 Immigration and Trade Licensing acts were modelled after the Kenyan acts, and they had the same objective, with the exception that all categories of occupation required work permits. In May 1970, the Ugandan government announced partial nationalisation. In 1969, of the 78,000 (1961) Indians in the population, 25,000 of whom were recorded as citizens, only 5000–10,000 had left before the expulsion by General Idi Amin.

THE EXODUS

From the late 1960s, the future of Asians in East Africa became uncertain. They knew that they would have to leave one day, and yet held on to the hope that this would not be the case. Their most pressing concern, and therefore the most important subject of their conversations, was how much time they had and what stage they had reached in securing a British visa or a local work permit. Following the nationalisation projects across the region, they did their best to secure economic and social capital. Information on who was reliable (or corrupt) in the immigration office, the export department or the foreign exchange section became increasingly valuable. However, not all Indians had the means and/or the right network to access these channels of information.

On 5 August 1972, General Idi Amin delivered his ironically labelled 'Asian farewell speech'. He gave Asians 90 days to pack up and leave Uganda, making no distinction between citizens and non-citizens. His main argument was that the Indians had come to build the railway and since the construction of the railway was complete, there was no reason for their continued presence in the country. In this speech, as well as earlier ones, he accused Asians of the 'economic sabotage' of the country through their unwillingness to invest in Uganda, and of exploiting and draining resources. The problem with these accusations was that they were neither fully true nor false. The construction of the railway was complete, but many who had come for that purpose had stayed on as traders and artisans. Many also came to work in the colonial civil service. While a few Indians may have been involved in the 'economic sabotage' of the country, especially in the later stage of uncertain political rule, the way to deal with this was through the courts.

Following the General's expulsion orders, not only were the houses, shops and other properties of Indians in danger, so was their physical and emotional well-being. Their precarious position was reinforced by Amin's use of terror and destruction to achieve his aims. Within a few weeks following the ultimatum, some 50,000 Asians left, with just the baggage in their hands. They were allowed to carry only £55 in cash with them. In 1973, a mere 1000 Indians remained in Uganda. Despite the fact that neither Kenya nor Tanzania followed the Uganda pattern, insecurity in these countries also caused massive migration.

WHERE DID THEY GO?

During the negotiations for independence, the British succeeded in securing fairly generous citizenship laws for Asians. In addition, Asian minorities were given the right to a British passport, and with that the right to enter Britain. Due to the policy of Africanisation, a growing number of East African Asians began to migrate to the UK from 1965 onwards. Simultaneously, Britain saw a growing influx of Indian migrants from South Asia and the Caribbean. By 1967, there was increasing speculation that Britain might consider closing its doors to Indian migrants. Rumours of such a possibility increased the number of Indian migrants from East Africa. Finally, in the 'restriction act' of 1968, the British did close their doors to British citizens overseas who had 'no close connection' with Britain, i.e. where neither they nor their father or grandfather were born in Britain. When the time came to honour the African-Asian British passport-holder's right to entry, these migrants faced extreme difficulties. As a compromise, a quota system allowed 1500 families to enter Britain every year. British immigration policy from 1969–72 can be best characterised as 'forced generosity', as most immigration policies were the result of strong national and international political pressures and were never spontaneous. The measures taken by the British government caused considerable hardship to the African-Asian community.

The British were not the only ones who preferred short-term policies in their own interest instead of affirming the right of citizenship and minority rights. The Indian government, in general, gave priority to its relations with host governments instead of the well-being of Indians. In 1954, Jawaharlal Nehru advised Indians in East Africa to cooperate with Africans, adding that they could not expect protection from the Indian government, that they were

guests in the African countries, and if Africans did not want them, they should leave. He was quick to add as well that India had her own problems to solve before thinking about others. Yet, beyond the Indian government's lack of sympathy for their situation, the decision by East African Indians not to 'return' to India was primarily economic. For many, it was a choice of migrating to the UK or returning to India, which, while secure in a political sense, offered few economic opportunities. Most East African Indians chose the former, although some, especially the older members of the community, chose the nostalgic option of spending the last years of their lives in their homeland.

After Britain, Canada and the US were the main destinations of East African Indian migrants. An important reason for their openness to the immigration of these refugees was the presence of highly skilled professionals as well as potential investors. Since few Goans had British passports, the majority of them found their way to the US. In addition, the leader of the Ismaili community, the Aga Khan, arranged a deal with the Canadian government following the nationalisation of buildings in Tanzania, that resulted in Canada becoming a major destination for many Ismailis from East Africa.

ASIANS IN EAST AFRICA (1980–2000)

The 1980s and early 1990s saw considerable improvements in race relations between Africans and Indians in East Africa. Public debate shifted from Africanisation in the colonial period to socialism (independent Tanzania) and capitalism (independent Kenya and Uganda), and to the 'indigenisation of South Asians' in the 1980s and 1990s. An important reason for this shift was the declining economic situation in Uganda, Kenya and Tanzania, which made it necessary to re-establish the economic and social roles of Asians in East Africa. In the late 1970s and early 1980s, the decline in agricultural production and severe deficits in the national balance of payments led to immense food shortages and inflation. The crises deepened as a result of the increase in oil prices, the Tanzania-Uganda War in Kagera (1978–79) and the fall in the production of export crops. Consequently, these states had to accept the rehabilitation plans of the International Monetary Fund (IMF) and the World Bank, which included the liberalisation of markets and the acceptance of a multi-party democracy.

The most profound example of these changes in East Africa was the rehabilitation of the Ugandan Asians. When President Yoweri Museveni gained power in 1986 in Uganda, he ended years of civil war and promoted

An elderly Indian woman arriving in the UK from East Africa is helped off a plane at London's Gatwick Airport, February 1968.

Considerable violence followed the failed coup to overthrow the Kenyan government in 1982. Pictured here are a looted shop and a body lying on the pavement of a Nairobi street.

Figure 8.5

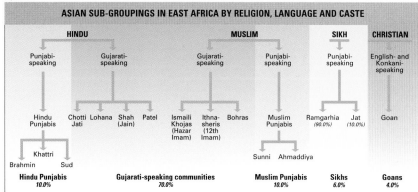

ASIAN SUB-GROUPINGS IN EAST AFRICA BY RELIGION, LANGUAGE AND CASTE

| HINDU | | MUSLIM | | SIKH | CHRISTIAN |

Punjabi-speaking / Gujarati-speaking — Gujarati-speaking / Punjabi-speaking — Punjabi-speaking — English- and Konkani-speaking

Hindu Punjabis / Chotti Jati / Lohana / Shah (Jain) / Patel — Ismaili Khojas (Hazar Imam) / Ithna-sheris (12th Imam) / Bohras — Muslim Punjabis — Ramgarhia (90.0%) / Jat (10.0%) — Goan

Khattri
Brahmin   Sud

Sunni   Ahmaddiya

| **Hindu Punjabis** 10.0% | **Gujarati-speaking communities** 70.0% | **Muslim Punjabis** 10.0% | **Sikhs** 6.0% | **Goans** 4.0% |

Source: Yash Tandon and Arnold Raphael, 'The New Position of East Africa's Asians: Problems of a Displaced Minority', Minority Rights Group Report, 1984.

Uganda as a secular state. In part due to pressure from the World Bank, he encouraged Asians to invest in Uganda again. A key measure adopted in Uganda involved the return of confiscated properties and businesses to Indians. As a result, over 5000 properties, including Hindu temples, have since been reclaimed. According to official government sources, following these measures, unclaimed properties amounted to only 20 per cent of the total land confiscated earlier. However, Ugandan Asian sources in the UK claim that more than 50 per cent of the properties confiscated, especially those belonging to the lower and lower-middle classes, have yet to be returned.

During the same period, public debate in Tanzania saw a shift in rhetoric. In the economically difficult years of the early 1980s, Tanzanian Asians were seen as smugglers, quick money-makers and 'evil barons', but following

An Indian colony in East Africa?

After World War I, the question of the future of German East Africa raised interesting options. The possibility that the conquered territory would be reserved for Indian colonisation and be administered directly by the government of India generated much enthusiasm in India, Africa and Britain. India's monetary donation to the Allies and the contributions of Indian troops in East Africa strengthened this possibility.

The leader of the Ismaili community, the Aga Khan, was one of the proponents of this idea. In 1917, he created a sensation by releasing the will of the Indian politician Gopal Krishna Gokhale, who died in 1915. In his will, Gokhale stated: 'German East Africa, when conquered from the Germans, should be reserved for Indian colonisation and be handed over to the Government of India.' The Aga Khan repeated this idea in his book, *India in Transition*, in 1918. In addition, he wrote papers and memoranda to the Imperial War Cabinet. Lieutenant-Colonel Theodore Morison, who published an article in *The Nineteenth Century* called 'A Colony for India', backed him up.

The idea of an Indian mandate in German East Africa was, however, controversial. Firstly, the importance of the role of Indian troops in East Africa was disputed. In addition, Indian Congress leaders such as Gandhi, his right-hand man for East Africa, C. F. Andrews and, later, Jawaharlal Nehru, were promoting Indian humanitarianism on African questions. Andrews especially supported the Indian right to equal treatment in East Africa but was opposed to Indian imperial influence and therefore advocated the paramount interest of Africans. The movement for an Indian colony was also opposed by other organisations and individuals in Britain. Finally, the European community wanted former German East Africa to develop into a Crown colony and, ultimately, a dominion. After 1920, the idea of an Indian colony in East Africa faded. Nevertheless, the consideration of such a possibility can be seen as a rather late European recognition of the importance of India and the Indians in East Africa.

The Aga Khan with his wife, Andrée Joséphine Carron.

the implementation of the IMF programme, they were seen as the 'saviours' of the economy. A new era of social, political and economic change followed the inauguration of Ali Hassan Mwiny as the nation's president in 1985. Economic policies moved from emphasising small-scale communal production in agriculture to the support of large-scale farms. Former coffee and sisal estates were denationalised and the Building Acquisition Act of 1971 was loosened. While these efforts improved the lot of many Indians, they continued to suffer formal discrimination from the state, which, until the 1990s, did not allow citizens of South Asian background into the ranks of the civil service. Informal discrimination against South Asians also continues in daily life.

Throughout the 1980s and 1990s in Kenya, President Daniel arap Moi consolidated power in the presidency and remained faithful to the capitalist path. During this period, the position of Asians improved, although in exceptional cases they were subject to attacks, such as during the unsuccessful coup attempt of 1982, when Asian homes and shops were looted. To some extent, negative sentiments towards Asians continue to exist in part because they are closely identified with the corruption that has tainted the Moi government. The most profound example of this corruption was the 'Goldenburg Saga' of the 1990s, which involved the finance minister and several African and Asian businessmen who received US$455 million under a scheme to encourage exports, when in fact little or no export actually took place. Yet, in spite of rumours of possible collusion between some Asian businessmen and the Moi government, the opposition refused to play the race card and instead held the Moi government responsible for the irregularities. This movement away from racial politics represents the mature nature of responsible local political leaders, many of whom acknowledge the economic importance of the Asian community and their place in Kenya.

The dilemma that Asians in East Africa find themselves in currently is that they have neither the political nor the institutional capacity to counter anti-Asian sentiments. In spite of their generous contributions to building hospitals and schools, and the provision of social services, their role has been underplayed because of the lack of Asian representation in the media and politics. In addition, there is a clear need for Asians to articulate a new identity for themselves in East Africa. Two options exist: the old option, favoured by many South Asian traders and businessmen, emphasises the need to maintain a low profile through 'silent diplomacy', i.e. by not participating in public debate, living a sober life and not showing their wealth; and the second option, favoured by many middle-class professionals, writers and artists is the celebration of an 'African Asian' identity in which they emphasise their loyalty to their home, Africa. This option was highlighted during the popular Asian heritage exhibition in Nairobi, at the National Museum of Kenya. Reflecting the changing times, the exhibition sought to challenge stereotypes about the Asian community while acknowledging that the community is as much a part of modern Africa as any other group.

INDIAN COMMUNITIES IN EAST AFRICA

Indians in East Africa are an extremely diverse community. The most well known division is that between the Hindus and Muslims. Two other key religious groups include the Sikhs, many of whose forebears worked on

The opening of an
Ithnasheri guest house in
Mombasa, 1926.

together despite their differences. Due to their small numbers, Jains often attend Hindu functions, especially those that relate to the Vania caste. In general, however, Jains maintain stricter regulations on diet and most of them remain vegetarian. Caste is much less significant among Punjabi Hindus, and they form a single community in East Africa. As most Punjabi Hindus were employed by the colonial administration, they were particularly hard-hit by the Africanisation projects of the late 1960s and early 1970s.

Muslims

The major division in the Muslim community is between the Sunnis and the Shias, who split over the successor of the Prophet Muhammed. The Shias further divided over the succession of the sixth imam in the 8th century, resulting in the Ismaili Khojas separating from the main Shia group. The majority followed Musa al-Qasim and another five imams. This group is known as the 'Twelvers', or Ithnasheris. Many Ithnasheris in East Africa live on the east coast. They are the largest Muslim community and the most integrated in East African society in terms of their knowledge of Swahili and intermarriages with Swahilis.

The Sunnis are much smaller and even more divided. They came from Sind, Kutch and Gujarat and many of them have preserved elements of the Indian caste system. They are conservative and seldom marry beyond the extended family.

The Ismaili Khojas are the most influential group among Muslims. In the late 19th century, they accepted the Aga Khan as a direct descendant of the Prophet Muhammed. Because they had a living guide, they appear to have been more flexible in adjusting to changing conditions in East Africa. In 1952, the Aga Khan advised his followers to regard East Africa as their permanent home, to replace Gujarati with English as the medium of instruction, and encouraged women to wear Western dress and get jobs. The Ismailis are well known for their contribution to education, building hospitals and forming societies which enabled their members to build their own houses.

Sikhs

Most Sikhs in East Africa came as indentured labourers to work on the Uganda Railway. Others were employed in various positions within the colonial administration. Whereas in Punjab the landowner and farmer castes form the largest Sikh subdivisions, 90 per cent of the Sikhs in East Africa belong to the lower-ranking Ramgarhia caste. Like the other communities, they show a strong preference for endogamous marriage within the community, although intermarriage with Hindu Punjabis is not uncommon.

Goans

Goans, from the former Portuguese colony of Goa, are Roman Catholics. They have preserved their Portuguese names, speak English at home and observe the Sabbath. Many were employed in the British colonial administration as civil servants and as clerks in banks. Like the Punjabi Hindus, they were among the first to loose their jobs as a result of the Africanisation project. Of those who have remained in East Africa, many work as teachers, doctors and professionals. In contrast to the Hindu and Muslim communities, love marriages (mostly within the community) are much more common among Goans than arranged marriages.

Gijsbert Oonk

the Uganda Railway, and the Christian Goans, who served in the colonial administration and were employed as clerks in the larger Indian firms. Around 70 per cent of Indian Africans speak Gujarati (and Kutchi), and this includes both Hindus and Muslims. Over the course of time, the importance of caste and sub-caste within these communities has declined. Being a minority community in an often hostile environment, the Indians have a shared history of deprivation and discrimination. Nevertheless, in spite of such shared experiences, marriages between Hindus and Muslims remain rare.

Hindus

Hindus have three different types of worship: worship of deities, recitation of sacred texts and pilgrimage. In East Africa, no places of Hindu pilgrimage exist. In the past, pilgrimage to India was rare, although there has been an increase since the 1990s. The composition of Hindu castes in East Africa has largely been influenced by regional and occupational patterns. Brahmins arrived in East Africa to serve the community in religious ceremonies. Many Brahmins opened restaurants and sweetshops that reflected typical Hindu traditions, influenced by a strong notion of purity and impurity in relation to food and the acceptance of food from others.

The trading castes are represented by Bhatias, Vanias and the Lohanas, who came as merchants, traders and brokers from Kutch in Gujarat. The Patels came from central Gujarat, most from an agricultural background. From the 19th century onwards, some Patels shifted from agriculture to rural trade. The remaining Gujarati Hindus belong mainly to the artisan castes. Jains and Gujarati Hindus in East Africa have largely congregated

*A Sikh grandfather
with his young
grandson in
Moshi, Tanzania.*

261

Descendants of Sunderji Damodar, a leader of the Indian community in Mombasa.

LEADING INDIANS IN EAST AFRICA

Sunderji Damodar: The 'old man' of Mombasa

Sunderjibhai (1906–2004) was known in the family as 'uncle' or respectfully as 'the old man'. Towards the later part of his life, he was partially blind, had difficulty walking and his voice was low. Nevertheless, at the age of 98 he still made daily visits to his office (now run by one of his sons) six days a week.

In 1916, at the age of 10, he arrived with his father, Nanjibhai Damodar, in Zanzibar. They were asked to look after the shop of a relative, Kesawji Dewanji, whose sons did not want to settle in East Africa and had returned to India. The business flourished as they made use of the advantages of having a family business. Not only did they use their family network in Zanzibar and India, they were also able to circumvent restrictions put in place by colonial law. Since the law restricted a person from being both a broker and a trader, Nanjibhai applied for the broker's licence while his son acquired the trading licence. In this way, the family was able to provide both these services to their clients.

Sunderjibhai lived with his two sons and their families in a house typical of extended families in Mombasa. He wore traditional Indian dress—white *khadi*, dhoti and pyjama. His house comprised a large living room with colonial furniture and a traditional Gujarati rocking couch (which we still see in many Gujarati houses in East Africa). The portraits of his parents occupied a prominent place and were decorated with fresh flowers. Except for some small traditional African crafts, the living room exuded a Gujarati atmosphere.

The house of Sunderjibhai was a typical 'one kitchen house'. Though three married couples lived in the house (Sunderjibhai and two married sons with their children), they shared one kitchen. Since there was no table in the kitchen, women sat on the floor

while cleaning the vegetables, cutting the fruits and preparing the meals. In their tasks they were assisted by a Gujarati Brahmin (female) cook. Next to the kitchen was the dining room with a big family table where the meals were shared. Shoes had to be removed before entering the dining room, and men and women ate separately. Neither liquor nor meat could be found in the house and the family maintained their Gujarati (Vaishnava) tradition of being vegetarian teetotallers.

Based on Gijsbert Oonk, Asians in East Africa: Images, Histories and Portraits, 2004; and www.asiansinafrica.com.

A. M. Jeevanjee: 'The Grand Old Man of Kenya'

A. M. Jeevanjee (1856–1936) was the eldest son of a Bohra Muslim family in Karachi. He left the family business in 1886 for Australia, before arriving in Mombasa in 1890. He started trading by provisioning ships in Mombasa, went on to help in the construction of the Uganda Railway, and founded the newspaper the *African Standard*, later known as the *East African Standard*. In time, his firm constructed government offices, staff quarters, post offices and railway stations. At the turn of the 19th century he was probably the leading property owner in Nairobi and Mombasa. Although he became very wealthy, as an Asian he was also discriminated against in colonial East Africa. The seeds of his political aspirations were sown in the early 1900s, when Europeans claimed selected agricultural lands

A. M. Jeevanjee in the robe presented to him by the Aga Khan.

for their own use only. These so called 'highlands' were disputed from the very beginning. Jeevanjee, then president of the Mombasa Indian Association, at a meeting organised by the association in 1906, declared: '...we have been in this country for over two hundred years...whereas the majority of the Europeans have only been in this country a year or two. We do not ask for preferential rights, we only ask that no distinction be made between the European and Indian Settler.' This dispute was not settled until the 1930s.

In 1905, Acting Governor Frederic Jackson put forward Jevanjee's name as the best-qualified Indian representative for the Legislative Council. Nevertheless, others opposed the nomination on the grounds that it would lead to similar demands on the part of the Arab and Swahili communities as well. This quintessential British argument to exclude 'all others' by arguing that they could not include 'everyone', was a typical example of how they defended their own interests in the short term. Eventually, Jeevanjee was appointed in 1910 as an 'individual' and not as an Indian. Nevertheless, he made it clear from the outset that he considered himself an Indian representative.

In 1914, Jeevanjee was one of the founding members of the East African Indian National Congress (EAINC), which incorporated all of the Indian associations in East Africa. The new organisation was modelled on the Indian National Congress (formed in 1885). Among its first demands was that

election to both the legislative and municipal councils be on a common roll—a demand it maintained consistently for almost half a century before it pulled out of the political arena in 1962. An often used one-liner by the EAINC was 'no taxation without representation'.

World War I encouraged a more modest approach towards the British. The EAINC as well as the Indian National Congress supported the British War Office. From the 1920s onwards, as Indians and Africans shared certain common interests, African leader Harry Thuku authorised Jeevanjee to present the African case in London. Though African and Indian leaders had cooperated before, the Europeans were very much concerned about this 'new collaboration'. On 16 April 1923, when the long feud between East African Indians and Europeans had reached a critical stage, representatives of European settlers, Indian East Africans—including Jeevanjee—and Indian representatives from India and the British government came together in London. The outcome of the meeting was the Devonshire Declaration. It stated that Kenya was an African country, the highlands were to remain 'white' and the Legislative Council should consist of 11 elected Europeans, five elected Indians, two Arabs and a missionary, to be appointed to represent African interests. The EAINC reaction was to stop paying taxes wherever possible. Again the congress would repeat its original aim to protect Indian interests through their own representation. In the years that followed, the highlands remained high on the political agenda. Nevertheless, Jeevanjee slowly retired from political involvement as his business faced financial problems. He died on 2 May 1936 in Nairobi. By then he was known as 'The Grand Old Man of Kenya'.

Based on Zarina Patel, Challenge to Colonialism: The Struggle of Alibhai Mulla Jeevanjee for Equal Rights in Kenya, 1997.

General Jan Christian Smuts (left) visiting Jeevanjee (right) in Nairobi, 1933.

MAURITIUS

MAURITIUS WAS UNINHABITED until the arrival of European settlers in the 17th century. The Dutch brought slaves and convicts from their settlements in India and Southeast Asia but left after a few unhappy years as they were threatened by pirates and the island was overrun by rats. The French colonial period, which lasted from 1721 until 1810, saw the establishment of the island as a strategic entrepôt on the Indian Ocean trade route. During this period Indians played a key role in the development of the colony as workers, companions, servants and slaves. After the British takeover, Mauritius was transformed from a port of call into a thriving sugar exporter, and recourse to Indian labour was greater than ever before. By the last quarter of the 19th century, the island had become Britain's premier exporter of sugar, and Indians were the dominant ethnic group. Since independence, the socio-political life of Mauritius has in large measure been determined by its citizens of Indian origin, who retain a strong sense of cultural identity with their immigrant forebears.

In few other former colonial lands have Indian immigrants been so crucial to the creation and development of the host state. While settlements like Ceylon and Malaya played host to much larger numbers of Tamil workers in the colonial period, the crucial distinction between immigrant Indians and other ethnic groups which claimed a separate and superior status on the basis of their indigenous origins delimited and circumscribed the economic and cultural impact of the Indian community. The relatively late peopling of Mauritius, by contrast, meant that immigrants from French and British India were among the first colonists and quickly became the most numerous. The importance and diversity of the Indian presence is consequently a striking feature of its social history. The rich and varied experiences of Indian immigrants on the island have made Mauritius a microcosm of the historical Indian diaspora.

THE INDIAN PRESENCE IN THE ISLE OF FRANCE

Soon after the French took possession of the island in 1721, naming it the Isle of France, free artisans, slaves and soldiers were brought from the French *comptoirs* (trading posts) in India, providing the first link in a chain of Indian migrants which has embraced the entire history of its settlement. Some were awarded land grants and became employers of slaves and respected members of the coloured elite. Contractors, traders and colonial administrators emerged from their ranks, grasping fully the opportunities offered by a frontier society and striving to retain their influence as the island grew and developed into the 'Paris' of the Indian Ocean and the most important colonial possession of the French in the region.

Indians were among the many ethnic groups sold or involuntarily conscripted into the economic and military service of the French East India Company. Direct slave importation from the French settlements in India, notably Pondicherry, were recorded from the 1720s. Around the same time, batches of 50 or more soldiers were being brought over from the same regions. Other Indians were enslaved as the spoils of war, captured from British ships where they had been working as crew members. Others were forced to sell themselves as slaves to escape famine. It was no coincidence that heightened activity in the slave trade along the Indian coast reflected the increasing scarcity of food and the prevalence of epidemic diseases on the subcontinent. In all, it has been estimated that more than 20,000 slaves of Indian origin were transported to the Mascarenes over the course of the 18th century, chiefly from French-controlled ports in southern India and from the French settlement in Bengal. At the beginning of the 19th century, shortly before the British takeover, 6000 Indian slaves remained on the island, representing one-tenth of the total servile workforce. Increasingly, most slaves were Creole, or born locally. The remainder were from Madagascar and East Africa; and a few were Malays from Southeast Asia.

The Isle of France functioned principally as an entrepôt, where ships could be repaired and resupplied en route to or from the Indies. It was not yet a plantation colony and, with its subordinate sister island of Bourbon taking on a primarily agricultural role as the granary of the Mascarenes, most slaves on the Isle of France worked as domestics, artisans and general hired hands. Labour in the early years was at a premium. Skilled workers were urgently needed to develop infrastructure—the harbour, homes, storehouses, administrative buildings, defence works, roads to transport goods and canals or aqueducts to carry water. A naval and military force was recruited from France and from its settlements in India, and free

An illustration of an Indian artisan at work in 18th-century French India. Many master craftsmen migrated to Mauritius from Pondicherry to build the infrastructure of the newly acquired French colony.

Map 8.37

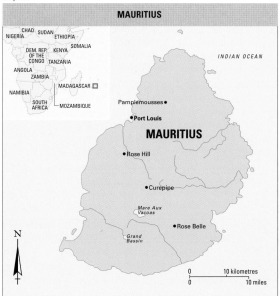

MAURITIUS

CHAD SUDAN ETHIOPIA
NIGERIA
SOMALIA
DEM. REP. KENYA
OF THE
CONGO TANZANIA
ANGOLA
ZAMBIA
MADAGASCAR
NAMIBIA
SOUTH
AFRICA MOZAMBIQUE

INDIAN OCEAN

Pamplemousses

Port Louis

MAURITIUS

Rose Hill

Curepipe

Mare Aux Vacoas

Rose Belle

Grand Bassin

N

0   10 kilometres
0   10 miles

and slave settlers on the island itself were trained to man the coastal fortifications, participate in the local militia and engage in marine combat. Free and enslaved Indians also participated in French naval and military manoeuvres against the British.

Masons, carpenters, dockers and sailors were also needed, but the prohibitive cost of bringing skilled workers from Europe led the colonial administrators to recruit many artisans from Pondicherry and Karaikkal on three-year contracts from 1729 onwards. Jewellers, shoemakers, tailors and seamen were also recruited from India. The 'Malabar' workers, as they were called, were frequently compared favourably with European artisans and worked alongside them in the ateliers of the French East India Company, but differential salary scales protected the status of white craftsmen, and the various ethnic groups occupied separate areas of the capital. In this manner, the distinctive Camp des Malabars and Camp des Lascars came into being. The Indian community became increasingly economically diversified as workers were sought for roles as varied as office messengers and maroon-slave hunters. Surviving work contracts from this period prefigure those which would be assigned to indentured labourers in the 19th century and reveal similar difficulties. In 1783, 16 engagements were drawn up between Laurent Lacoste and a group of workers from Cuddalore, offering free passage, monetary wages and food rations in exchange for assistance in the manufacture of cotton on the island. In this case, the venture did not succeed and one of the workers, Routrouchety Sadavendannay, headed a legal campaign for redress.

GENDER RELATIONS

Like most frontier societies, the Isle of France in the early years was characterised by a preponderance of men. The immigration of free Indian women was encouraged, and many men purchased female slaves from India, often to serve the dual role of companion and servant. The offspring of these slave women with their European, Indian and African owners became the foundation of the coloured community. In the Isle of France, relations between whites, free coloureds and slaves were quite fluid, not least because it was relatively common for slave owners (for example, free Indian men) to share the same ethnic origin as some of their slaves. The presence of a free

Indian community alongside the enslaved helped to provide avenues for redress and expression for the latter, which could do much to mitigate the terms and conditions of their servile status. The role of the free Indian population in the manumission of enslaved compatriots, particularly following the liberalisation of enfranchisement laws in the Revolutionary period (1793–97), provides the best example of such links. Some liberated their slaves in order to marry them, as in the case of Cheik Ally, who freed his slave Amina in 1738. Often, such marriages formalised a long-standing partnership. Many marriages occurred during the years of the French Revolution, when laws forbidding relationships between different social classes were relaxed. The preponderance of males among the free Indian workers explains the many marriages to female slaves. Owners frequently gave up their female slaves in order to formalise the relationship contracted with outsiders. Thus, Marie, the Bengali slave of a European merchant, was entrusted to Felicien Jerome, a free Indian from Karaikkal, for marriage.

The problems of identifying the regional origins and antecedent history of slaves are legion. However, later British slave returns provide much information about those Indian slaves still alive in 1817, when registrations were first compiled. The names of some reflected their occupations: one Indian cook was called Azor La Sauce. In other cases the surname suggested an actual or ascribed regional origin: Jean Bengali, Silvain Talinga, Francois Malabar and Nancy Patna are some examples. Caste status or religion could be similarly incorporated in a name chosen by the owner: Hector Bramine, Adesh Musulman, Lindor Chetty and Catherine Pillay were all listed as slaves.

The scale and timing of immigration by free Indian women is not well known, but the available evidence suggests that female and family immigration was not discouraged by the French administration, enabling some Malabar workers to settle with their kin on the island. In certain cases, the migration of a spouse was prevented by members of the extended family in India; and in others, economic reasons, such as the inability to pay for travel costs, resulted in the return of male migrants to rejoin their spouses in India. Many workers sent a stipulated share of their income to family members in Pondicherry through the authorities. Nevertheless, from the 1730s, marriages between free Indians were being celebrated, demonstrating that some free single women did travel to the island from India. Some arrived as the companions of European men or entered into relationships with them on the Isle of France. Such relationships were also formalised during the Revolutionary and Napoleonic eras. For example, Justine of Coringha married Jean Martin, born in Toulouse, in 1803.

Over the course of the 18th century, many such women, free immigrants and former slaves alike, became independent property owners, often following liaisons with colonists who bequeathed goods and slaves to them. Marie Rozette, for example, a freed female slave of Indian origin, had a huge fortune and owned a large landed property and 12 slaves by 1790. She had increased her capital through moneylending and buying and selling land, and was one of the wealthiest women on the island. Increasingly, marriages of free Indian settlers were arranged with the Creole daughters of such women or of Indian families settled in the colony. Marriages with women freed from slavery were evidently not considered

Illustrated here is an emaciated Dhangur, a tribal or 'hill coolie' migrant. Dhangurs were among the first migrants to Mauritius.

A lascar crew on the deck of a ship carrying indentured migrants.

socially demeaning. Even in the late 18th century such unions were attended by community leaders: when Pierre Capiron, a South Indian clerk, married the daughter of a Bengali slave, the Chef des Malabars, Denis Pitchen, attended the celebration. The witnesses at such weddings were a roll call of influential figures in the community: Jean Baptiste Arlanda, a merchant, and Kistnen, a doctor, were frequently called upon to be witnesses at such functions; their Tamil signatures suggesting that their presence also acted as the cultural affirmation of a South Indian identity. Matrimonial alliances between propertied parties were negotiated with great care and often served to strengthen the status of those involved. The average age at marriage was 14 for women and 20 for men.

THE ROLE OF RELIGION

The relationship between Christian Indians from the French settlements and South Indian Hindu traders is an interesting one. The wealth and influence of both groups, together with a shared ethnicity, increased the desirability of intermarriage: Sinnatamby Marimoutou Chety, for example, married a Creole Christian in 1808. On the other hand, Hindu and Catholic factions vied for control of the community and for the leadership post of Chef des Malabars. The appointment of Denis Pitchen as head of the Malabars in 1784 was an attempt by the state to subvert the power of the Hindu faction with the appointment of an Indo-Catholic. The Catholic fervour of some Malabars—they petitioned for a chapel to be built in the Camp des Malabars—may have aggravated tensions between the two groups. However, evidence suggests that the Indo-Christians themselves retained many Tamil rites and traditions: Indian dress (turbans and saris) continued to be worn, while some of those who took Christian names continued to observe Hindu practices in private.

Among the 18th-century settlers, southern Indians, and in particular the Tamils of Pondicherry, played a major role. A significant number of owners of Indian slaves in the Isle of France during the 18th century were themselves from this free South Indian Malabar community and, therefore, more likely to register their slaves according to their original Hindu or Muslim names. That they were allowed to do so suggests a certain freedom of religious expression. The lascar community successfully petitioned to construct a mosque in 1802 and began its construction in 1804. The increasing wealth of the Malabar community at the close of French rule was both a measure of their acceptance in the upper echelons of Creole society and testimony to the value placed upon their skills by the French administration. Alongside the commercial activities of South Indian merchants, Malabars realised large profits from the hiring out of slaves and buildings, construction and moneylending. Some Malabars, like the Nalletamby family, who owned a colonial manor in the capital, lived in grand style. Indian slave owners, such as the merchant who was prosecuted for cruelty in 1788, were as exploitative of servile labour as the white colonists. In general, however, free Indians performed a crucial intermediary role between whites and slaves, working as hunters of runaway slaves and as couriers for the slave trade, but also as interpreters and manumitters of slaves. Although the colonial state sought to entrench divisions between the free and enslaved through legislation, common ethnicity frequently broke down the legal barriers which separated them. The Revolutionary period, which liberalised enfranchisement laws, also increased the numerical strength and political voice of the free Indian population. They would play an important role in the introduction and settlement of the great waves of Indian immigrants in 19th-century Mauritius.

CONVICTS, INDENTURED WORKERS AND TRADERS IN BRITISH MAURITIUS

The British conquest of Rodrigues in 1809 and the Isle of France (which they renamed Mauritius) in 1810 would bring many more Indians to the conquered territory in the guise of convicts, coolies, traders and sepoys. Both in cultural and economic terms, the links between the small group of free Indian elite and the large numbers of labourers were of immeasurable importance in defining and regulating the pattern and scale of Indian settlement in Mauritius.

When the British arrived, they brought with them a large force of European and Indian troops, together with a number of officials and assistants destined to form the civil government in the event of a successful conquest. Many of the troops returned to India and the Cape of Good Hope within a few weeks or months of the takeover, but Indians were among the trusted staff who accompanied the conquering forces, or were called upon soon after to help run the island. In this way, Veliavel Annasamy came from India to take up a position as a clerk in the British administration. He quickly established profitable relationships with the British colonial elite and became a part-owner with Charles Telfair (an ex-naval surgeon and member of the British governor's inner circle) of a sugar estate in 1822. By 1827, he had over 80 slaves working for him. Another Tamil merchant, Rama Tiroumoudy, also became a part-owner of the estate Bon Espoir. Men like Annasamy were able to take up important positions in the new administration because the British could neither communicate with nor trust the Francophone Creole inhabitants. Members of the existing Indian community also quickly signed an oath of allegiance to the British and took jobs in the new government. Visitors to the island were surprised by the profusion of Indian faces among the civil servants.

Ratungee Bickagee, a Parsi merchant arriving soon after the takeover, also recognised the opportunities offered by the new British colony. By the 1820s he was well-established—even residing in the European quarter

A portrait of a successful Tamil trader in 19th-century Mauritius. Following the British takeover of Mauritius, there was an increase in the number of Indian merchants arriving on the isle.

Indian sepoys in the service of the British Raj.

of the capital—and engaged in the lucrative business of importing goods from India, occasionally also acting as a shipping agent and investing his profits in land and the burgeoning sugar industry. Tamil professionals also began to settle: Dr Sinapoulay Maleapa returned to India from Mauritius in 1825 to get members of his family to marry 'persons of their caste' back on the island. A chain migration of Indians was already underway.

The British faced a challenge in their new colony. They immediately saw the potential for economic development in Mauritius: the island possessed fertile, virgin soil, but had a poor road system, and much of the land was forested. Furthermore, obtaining the large workforce needed to create the necessary conditions for growth was hampered by a policy that the British had themselves introduced: the abolition of the slave trade. By the early 19th century, the slave population of Mauritius was in terminal decline. Continued slave trading brought a few clandestine African and Asian captives to the island, but the number of new Indian slaves reaching the Mascarenes was much smaller than decreases brought about by death and manumission. By 1830, there were only an estimated 3500 Indian slaves in Mauritius out of a total slave population of 68,000.

To meet these challenges, the first governor of Mauritius recruited convicts from India, who were distributed to favoured individuals—like Toussaint Antoine de Chazal, who was attempting to develop a silk industry project—or sent to work for the Roads and Bridges Department. The several hundred convicts (of whom only a handful were women) who arrived from India between 1815 and 1853 became a common sight in the colony, working in chain gangs. Charles Darwin, visiting Mauritius in 1836 during his famous voyage with the *Beagle*, reflected:

> *Before seeing these people I had no idea that the inhabitants of India were such noble looking men: their skin is extremely dark, and many of the older men had large moustachios and beards of a snow white colour; this, together with the fire of their expressions, gave to them an aspect quite imposing.*

The regime of hard labour, discipline and segregation prescribed for convicts was not strictly observed in practice. Indeed, the group actively resisted such impositions, and while a few escaped convict life through desertion and suicide, most proved remarkably adaptable, side-stepping the authorities even when continuing to engage in petty

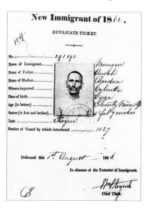

and serious crime, picking up Creole (the lingua franca of the island), forging relationships and successfully integrating into Mauritian society through marriage and the acquisition of property. Working in various locations around the island, convicts witnessed the illegal landing of slaves and used their knowledge to advantage whenever possible, sometimes denouncing the importers to the authorities, and at other times collaborating with law-breakers and runaways. During the tumultuous years between 1839 and 1842, when apprentices had been liberated but indentured workers had not yet arrived in large numbers, convict labour was at a premium as wages soared and those with the necessary skills were able to profit from the opportunities offered. After 1837, no more convicts were transported to Mauritius, and by 1853 all survivors had been liberated.

INDENTURE

Meanwhile, a combination of economic opportunity and labour shortage was paving the way for an experiment in Indian indentured immigration which was to prove momentous for the plantation colonies of the British Empire. In 1825, Mauritian sugar was granted tariff equity with West Indian produce entering the British market. The stage was now set for the emergence of Mauritius as a rival to the Caribbean sugar colonies. To meet this new challenge, attempts were made to import Asian workers, and as it became obvious that slavery was soon to be abolished (in 1834–35 slaves were converted into apprentices, to be fully free in 1839), steps were taken to lobby for a government-regulated indenture system which would guarantee the low-cost labour of 'free' immigrants for a fixed term.

The presence of a flourishing Indian community, and in particular estate-owners such as Annasamy and Tiroumoudy, played an important part in the decision to import indentured workers from the subcontinent. Both were among the first importers of Indian labour during the mid-1830s and their opinions were sought when the mode of recruitment was being discussed in the first years of the system's operation. Their insistence on the beneficial effects of family migration helped to influence subsequent policy towards indentured Indians at a time when colonial employers elsewhere in the Empire were turning away recruits who wished to bring their families. The historic link with Pondicherry and the French Indian settlements was renewed with the importation of labourers from the those settlements and of foodstuffs and clothing for this new immigrant stream. During the 1837–38 season alone, more than 4000 immigrants travelled from Pondicherry to Mauritius. At the same time, links with British and Indian merchants at the ports of Calcutta and Bombay were developed and several thousand labourers were recruited. But merchant-sponsored migration was flawed in many respects. Insufficient attention was paid to the suitability of recruits for the agricultural labour expected of them and many dissatisfied migrants had to be repatriated. Objections to the nature and manner of labour mobilisation were expressed by reformists in India and by the Anti-Slavery Society in Britain; and amidst mounting denunciations of indenture as the 'new slave trade', labour emigration was prohibited in 1839. However, recognising the importance of furnishing the sugar colonies with a new source of labour, and remembering the proximity of Mauritius to India and the likelihood of its success in that colony, the British secretary of state announced the resumption of Indian migration to the island in 1842 under new government controls. Mauritius was thus selected as the site of what was termed a 'great experiment' in the production of sugar by free labour.

Emigration depots were set up at the three presidency ports of Calcutta, Madras and Bombay, with a staff of officials appointed to oversee the exodus, and Indian immigrants began to arrive en masse in Mauritius from early 1843. Through Calcutta came the Bengalis and up-country migrants from the United Provinces and Bihar. From Bombay came the Marathas, chiefly from coastal districts such as Ratnagiri, and from Madras came Tamil and Telugu migrants. Indentured immigration was briefly suspended in 1856 after stringent quarantine laws led to the deaths of hundreds of Indians housed in flimsy tents on an offshore islet during a cyclone, and declined from the 1870s, although smaller annual intakes continued to be received into the early 20th century. Nevertheless, over a 40-year period, immigrants from India had transformed the demographic make-up of Mauritius and had become the dominant population group. Half a million migrants arrived over the course of the 19th century, of whom around one-third returned to India.

The first shiploads of immigrants were overwhelmingly male, and the colonial administration quickly realised that inducements to family settlement should be made. Bounties were offered to men migrating with their wives and female relatives, and rules put in place to restrict ships leaving without an adequate proportion of women (this was eventually set at one-third of the total). Female immigrants were exempted from the onerous clauses of the indenture contract in order to facilitate their settlement, with the result that many were in effect chain or marriage migrants, arriving to join spouses or expecting to marry male immigrant labourers soon after their arrival.

An immigration depot was established on the island to receive newly arriving immigrants and to enable employers to negotiate for their services before contracts were entered into by both parties. A Protector of Immigrants was employed to oversee the system and intercede in labour disputes. In practice, the labourers were often imposed upon by intermediaries, or prevented from exercising their right to freely choose an employer through legal impediments. However, while much discomfort and disaffection was experienced in the early years as both labourers and employers struggled with the new arrangements, Indian migrants were soon able to take advantage of opportunities offered in the expanding sugar colony.

The appointment of sirdars, or labour supervisors, was one avenue of socio-economic mobility. The sirdars earned higher wages than ordinary labourers and were able to supplement their income through shopkeeping and moneylending. As an intermediary between European planters and the Indian workforce, other profitable sidelines soon emerged. The sirdar was instrumental in recruiting new arrivals and time-expired labourers to the estate, overseeing re-engagements, and brokering labour disputes and agreements. Both sirdars and ex-indentured labourers were also able to make money by returning to India to recruit new labourers, generally from among their kin and fellow villagers. Recruiting returnees eliminated the costly and often deceitful methods of commercial contractors—the *arkatis* and *maistries*—and ensured that new migrants would be going to an estate where members of their own ethnic group were already residing. Abuses were possible and committed, but by and large the method was preferable for both employers and migrants alike, and contributed greatly to the popularity of Mauritius as a destination for indentured labourers long after the decline of wage rates and economic prosperity there. This chain or circular migration operated with difficulty within the official indenture scheme, and it was only by paying one's passage, as increasing numbers of migrants did, that a trouble-free journey from village to plantation of choice could be assured.

As time-expired Indians moved off the estates and into the Indian villages which developed around them, their continuing availability for plantation labour was ensured and regulated by job contractors. Increasingly, such men became the employers of the Indians, rather than the plantation owners. It was the job contractors who received a lump sum for the labour and who distributed wages to the workers. Their own remuneration could be significant as they were able to avoid many of the overheads previously borne by the estate owners. The elite sirdars and contractors who emerged from the ranks of the indentured labourers were further enriched by the major land transactions which took place in the last quarter of the 19th century in Mauritius.

Known as the *grand morcellement*, or parcelling of lands, the acquisition of major tracts of scrub and marginal cane fields by Indian immigrants was facilitated by the worldwide depression in sugar prices during this period, which forced many estate owners to sell off or subdivide

A 19th-century painting captures the embarkation of Indians from the port at Calcutta.

The Vishnu Kchetre Mandir in Mauritius, built in 1931.

their property. With the assistance of wealthy Indian merchants settled in Mauritius, enterprising sirdars and contractors with some capital of their own to invest joined forces to make collective land purchases, which were then divided into smaller strips and sold to ex-indentured labourers. Some Indian immigrants became sugar estate owners in their own right. Ramtohul, who purchased the plantation of Mon Choix for Sp.$49,000 in June 1870 with a Sp.$10,000 cash down payment, was one of the first ex-indentured Indians to reach this elevated position.

THE ECONOMIC RISE OF THE INDO-MAURITIANS

By becoming estate owners, the migrants were following in the footsteps of South Indian traders who had begun to move into agriculture as large landowners: in 1845 the Sinnatambous controlled the Mauricia estate, and by 1852 Tiroumoudy had taken over Bon Espoir plantation,

and the estate of Clemencia was owned by the Arlanda family. Established Tamil and Parsi merchants like Tiroumoudy and Bickajee encouraged their co-religionists to settle, and by the 1840s the economic advancement of Mauritius on the back of indentured labour was also attracting the attention of Gujarati traders. Esmaljee Mamodjee was one of the first Surati merchants to open a shop in the capital in the mid-1840s. Muslim merchants followed a practice prevalent in India and settled in specific areas of the capital. Thus, a Memane Bazaar developed around Reine and Royale streets, and a Surtee Bazaar began on Rue de la Corderie. Gujarati merchants established significant business interests in the transport of Indian migrants, food and textile imports, and in moneylending and real estate. The facilitation of credit to indentured labourers is important in understanding their successful move into landownership. Gujarati merchants also became interested in agriculture, placing their liquid assets in sugar cane cultivation, particularly after 1865, when sugar began to be exported to India. Sugar exports to India peaked in 1910, and since the price of sugar began falling from 1880 and numerous estates were available for purchase, Gujaratis moved into this sector at that time. Many Tamil merchants, however, began to leave the colony, a number of them heading for South Africa, where indentured Indian immigration to Natal had just begun.

For the Indian community, whether ex-indentured labourer or merchant, the acquisition of wealth and land brought prestige and social status, which was increasingly translated into acts of religious and cultural philanthropy. After the Tamil sirdar Songor Itty married Doya Kishto, a prosperous Bengali widow, both of whom owned plots of land near the estate of Clemencia, they donated part of their wealth to their Hindu co-religionists, building a temple on their land. In this they were assisted by Sinnatambou and Soobramania Pyneeandee in Port Louis, who supplied bronze statues for the interior. In 1867, Itty, by then a shopkeeper in Riviere Seche, and his wife donated the temple to the Hindu community. Sinnatambou himself played an important role in the sociocultural life of the Indian community: the Shri Krishnamoorthy Draubadai Ammen temple at Terre Rouge was built by Tamil merchants on land purchased by the Sinnatambou brothers in October 1845 and was opened for worship in 1850. Visitors to Mauritius describe *timithi*, or fire-walking ceremonies, and *kavadi* processions there in the 1860s which attracted crowds of 30,000 or more. Such events naturally brought great prestige to the organiser, and rival temples and organisations were soon founded. As landownership led to the creation of Indian villages, other Tamil and North Indian temples were constructed, resulting in the arrival of priests from India, along with service migrants such as barbers, launderers and jewellers. By the beginning of the 20th century, only 15 per cent of Indians still lived on estates.

Dookhee Gunga, born in Mauritius in 1867, the son of an indentured labourer who arrived from Calcutta in 1854, is another example of the role of wealthy individuals in the construction of a community. Successful land deals made him a millionaire by 1920 and he donated large sums of money for the construction of Hindu temples and cremation grounds throughout the island. He also founded the Gita Mandal, in association with other wealthy Indians (including the Ramtohul family), which was set up to administer a number of Hindi schools in Mauritius. Gunga financed the first Hindi publications to

---

The myth of Ganga Talao and the origins of the Maha Shivaratri pilgrimage to Grand Bassin

The serene volcanic crater lake of Grand Bassin, nestled amidst the tall slopes of southern Mauritius, and fed by no visible tributaries, soon gave rise to a belief in its magical qualities. Its alternate name, the Lake of the Ganges (Ganga Talao), and the institution of an annual pilgrimage to Grand Bassin is indicative of the hunger for sacred sites in late 19th-century Mauritius and the means by which popular imagination could create a meaningful and later mass movement, which today attracts pilgrims to join in the Maha Shivaratri festivities from all over the Indian Ocean region.

The transformation of this upland lake into Ganga Talao is usually credited to an enterprising Hindu priest, Jhumun Seesahye. In 1897, he reportedly dreamt of holy Ganges water springing from Grand Bassin. Leading his followers to the spot, he set in motion what would become an annual pilgrimage.

This story has itself become part of Mauritian folklore. In Ramesh Ramdoyal's book *More Tales from Mauritius*, the priest Jhummungeer's dream is recounted as follows: 'He dreamt he was bathing in the river Ganges. Suddenly a mighty current pulled him down and swept him for days on end through a channel under the sea. When he came to the surface he found he was in an enchanted lake inhabited by heavenly fairies...The fairies told him "You and your people can quench your spiritual thirst in this very lake. You need no longer miss the holy Ganges that you have left behind."' In this short story the site is called Pari Talao, or Lake of the Fairies.

An offering at the 'Ganges' of Mauritius, Grand Bassin.

be printed on the island and, after his death in 1944, a government school was named in his honour.

Muslim merchants were also active in establishing community organisations and places of worship which corresponded to their various sects. A Kutchi Memon society was set up in 1850 and ran the Jummah Mosque, built in 1852. In 1863 two more mosques were built at Rose Hill and Rose Belle. The Soonee Surtee Mussalman Society was founded in 1892 and, some years later, the Bohra Muslims erected their own mosque and established a cemetery. A commemoration of the Shia Muslims—known as the Yamsey, or Ghoun, a local variant of Muharram—acquired great significance for the Indian community in the 19th century. Held in Mauritius since the late 18th century, it bears some resemblance to the Muharram of the Konkan Muslims in Bombay. Originally confined to Port Louis, the event was adopted by Indian workers across the island in the 19th century and became one of the most important cultural events for Indo-Mauritians up to the early 20th century, when Sunni leaders began to declaim against the participation of their adherents, and Hindus ceased their involvement. Then, once again Muharram was confined to Port Louis.

Hindus, instead, began to adopt annual rites and rituals of their own. Water, and particularly the sacred river Ganges, played, and continues to play a large part in the spiritual world of the Hindus, and Indo-Mauritians made use of rivers, lakes and the sea to recreate the religious festivals of their homeland. In 1895, a temple, or *ashthan*, was erected on the banks of the Grand Bassin, in the island's south, and soon found itself the centre of an argument by rival priests Jhumun and Teeluckdharry, as the site became increasingly popular with Hindu pilgrims.

FROM ESTATE CAMP TO PARLIAMENT: THE POLITICAL RISE OF INDO-MAURITIANS

While the first generation of Indian immigrants sought to establish themselves in positions of authority on the plantations, and to become wealthy landowners and religious and cultural patrons in the Indian villages which grew out of the *grand morcellement* of the late 19th century, their children had different aspirations and would become an educated and politicised elite. However, it was the merchant communities who were the first of the Indo-Mauritians to be appointed to political office by the colonial administrators.

Annasamy had been a member of the—unofficial—Colonial Committee as early as 1827, and by the mid-19th century prominent members of the Tamil community such as Sinnatambou Chettiar and Moonisamy

Mudaliar had been appointed to District Committees. The wealth of the Pitchen, Pragassa, Rayapa and Sandapa families had, by 1850, qualified them to be on the electoral lists. Gyanadicrayen Arlanda was nominated to the Council of Government in 1886, as were a number of Muslim members by Governor Pope Hennessy in the 1880s. A 'Calcuttya' (this term is used to denote the Muslim descendants of indentured labourers, not necessarily from North India, but dominated by Bhojpuri-speaking Biharis) Muslim, Abdoula Goolam Dustagheer, became the first Indo-Mauritian to stand for election in 1896 and 1901. Then, only around 400 Indo-Mauritians qualified for the franchise. Dustagheer was not elected but received some votes from outside his community. A Muslim from the lascar community, Dr Hassen Sakir, was successfully elected as a municipal councillor in Port Louis in 1900.

Mahatma Gandhi visited Mauritius briefly in 1901 and sent an envoy, Manilal Doctor, to the island in 1907 to foster the political organisation of the community. Doctor launched the *Hindustani* newspaper and represented Indians in a number of court cases until his departure in 1911. By the 1920s, a number of Hindu intellectuals who had risen from the ranks of indentured labourers began to make their voices heard. Ramkelawon Boodhun, the son of an immigrant railway worker, and a barrister educated in Britain, stood in the general elections of 1921, and despite failing to win a seat, was nominated by the governor to represent Indo-Mauritians, along with Dr Hassen Sakir, between 1921 and 1926. Boodhun Lallah, the son of Indian immigrants, also dabbled in politics, standing and losing to a white candidate in the general elections of 1911. Indians campaigned against the Retrocessionist movement, which sought to achieve a renewed attachment to France, but were weakened by caste differences. In the 1926 general election, Rajcoomar Gujadhar, of Bihari origin, and Lallah, were both elected under the banner of l'Union Mauricienne.

Around this time, important steps towards the political mobilisation of the Muslim and Hindu communities were taken by visiting clerics from India and local pandits.

A Port Louis street during Ghoun, or the festival of Muharram. Elsewhere in the colonial empire it is known as Hossay or Tazia.

Indira Gandhi, visiting Mauritius greets Prime Minister Ramgoolam and his wife.

Excerpts from speeches by Seewoosagur Ramgoolam on Independence Day

I am deeply grateful to the people of Mauritius who have made it possible for our country to take its rightful place in the comity of nations as a sovereign democratic state...My wish today is that of all true patriots who believe in the future of Mauritius. Let us all work together, for the country belongs to all of us; and let us contribute our share in the building of a strong, free and happy Mauritius...I know that I am echoing your own thoughts when I say that all of us, in a spirit of unity and solidarity, are determined to go forward and work together for the welfare and happiness of our people.

12th March 1968

We, in Mauritius, are dedicated to the ideals of a society based on justice and equality, and our primary duty should be to strive for the improvement in human conditions by reducing human suffering through the eradication of poverty and other social evils.

12th March 1969

...[It] is the labourers and workers of Mauritius with their sickles and hoes who have built and transformed this country from a remote and barren outpost in the middle of the Indian Ocean into a dynamic, progressive and independent sovereign state.

12th March 1973

Ramgoolam, seen here with the last British governor of Mauritius, on Independence Day, 1968.

President Anerood Jugnauth (left) and Prime Minister Navin Ramgoolam (right) listen to the national anthem during Independence Day celebrations in Port Louis, 2006.

Indian women carrying placards demanding independence from colonial rule.

The economic depression of the 1930s helped to radicalise the working classes: trade unions were formed and a labour party founded in 1936 by Dr Maurice Curé. Celebrations for the centenary of the arrival of indentured labourers in 1935 served to invigorate the Indian community. In the 1940s, Basdeo Bissoondoyal launched a movement to mobilise Hindus and to raise the number of voters following the promulgation of a new constitution in 1947, which enfranchised men and women who could pass a literacy test. The number of electors rose from fewer than 10,000 to more than 70,000. Elections to the Legislative Council in 1948 saw the first important mobilisation of Indo-Mauritians, but while the Hindus gained a number of seats in rural districts where they constituted a majority, the Muslim candidates were all defeated, demonstrating their minority status.

In 1959, the Comité d'Action Musulman (CAM) formed an alliance with the Labour Party, headed by a British-trained Indo-Mauritian doctor, Seewoosagur Ramgoolam, and went into the elections as a pro-independence alliance. The Independent Forward Bloc (IFB) of Sookdeo Bissoondoyal also contested the election. The Parti Mauricien opposed independence. Labour won a decisive victory and their leader became the chief minister in 1961. Three years later, a ministerial system was introduced and Ramgoolam was appointed prime minister. The 1960s saw the rise of the Parti Mauricien Social Démocrate (PMSD) with Gaetan Duval as its head—he ran an ethnic campaign, garnering the support of the Creole community and raising fears of political domination by Hindus. He supported a continuation of the link with Britain. The elections of 1963 were marked by violence and a heightened sense of communalism.

During this period, a number of constitutional conferences were held in London against a backdrop of mounting ethnic tension at home, and delegates clamoured for an electoral system which would provide adequate minority representation. At the final constitutional conference in 1965, a 'Best Loser' system was adopted, guaranteeing seats for minorities. At this time, secret negotiations were also conducted with the British

for the creation of the British Indian Ocean Territory (BIOT) around the Chagos archipelago. The island of Diego Garcia would later be leased by the British to the Americans for use as a military base. The 1967 elections became, effectively, a referendum on independence. The Muslim vote was split, with some members supporting the pro-independence alliance, and others the PMSD and IFB. The independence party won, acquiring an absolute majority. However, in January 1968 racial violence erupted in Port Louis and spread to other parts of the island. Members of minority groups emigrated to Australia, Europe, South Africa and Canada amidst rabble-rousing rumours—circulated chiefly by Duval's PMSD—that a *bateau langouti* was en route to the island, implying that Mauritians would be forced to adopt Indian dress. The Indo-Mauritians had won, but the road ahead would not be easy, exacerbated by a constitution which institutionalised communalism through the 'Best Loser' system and the obligatory ethnic identification of candidates.

MANAGING MINORITIES: POLITICS IN INDEPENDENT MAURITIUS

On 12 March 1968, Mauritius became a sovereign independent state within the Commonwealth, with the Queen as its head of state. Ramgoolam ushered in Fabian-style socialism, which championed the creation of a welfare state and free education. However, in order to appease the various constituents of the multi-ethnic society, he was obliged to pander to diverse interests and include in his Cabinet individuals who would soon acquire unsavoury reputations for graft. The championing of ethnicity over meritocracy remains a major obstacle to effectiveness in Mauritian governance.

Against a background of increasing dissatisfaction with ethnic-based politicking and corruption, a Club des Etudiants Militants was formed in Mauritius on an avowedly anti-communal platform, which would lead to the creation soon afterwards of the Mouvement Militant Mauricien (MMM), with a young Franco-Mauritian graduate, Paul Raymond Berenger, at its head. The working class and the young rallied to the new radical ideas of the MMM, which began to work with the trade unions and provoked a general strike in 1971. At this time, the Mauritian economy was progressing with the creation of the Export Processing Zone (EPZ) and diversification into sectors such as tourism. Nevertheless, in the 1976 elections, minorities voted overwhelmingly for the MMM, showing that the nationalist message was appealing to

Thaipusam celebrated in the sugar cane fields.

many voters. However, the MMM itself had fielded candidates according to the ethnic make-up of constituencies, thus helping to consolidate the politics of patronage which had predominated since independence. In the 1980s, an economic crisis loomed as unemployment rose and the devaluation of the rupee weakened the purchasing power of Mauritians.

In the 1982 elections, the MMM—in alliance with a breakaway Hindu faction grouped under the Parti Socialiste Mauricien (PSM) banner—won an overwhelming 60–0 victory, with Anerood Jugnauth becoming prime minister and Berenger taking the post of minister of finance. Rapidly, however, conflict between Berenger and the PSM, under Harish Boodhoo, surfaced along with disagreements within the MMM over policy, leading to a split and the dissolution of government in 1983. Muslims and Creoles followed Berenger, while Hindus largely supported the breakaway faction led by Jugnauth, who founded the Mouvement Socialiste Mauricien (MSM) and went into a coalition with Labour and the PMSD. The MMM, with Berenger as its head, lost the election to Jugnauth. In 1987, the MSM alliance was re-elected, but minority dissatisfaction was expressed through violence at football matches (the teams have an ethnic affiliation) following a rupture with the largely Creole PMSD party. Needing better minority representation, Jugnauth turned to his old party and won the 1991 elections in a coalition with the MMM. On 12 March 1991, Mauritius became a republic, with a Tamil and former labour politician, Sir Veerasamy Ringadoo, serving as its first president. In 1992, a Muslim MMM politician, Cassam Uteem, would succeed him in this largely symbolic role. Around the same time, an Islamist party, the Hizbullah, was founded, which would win its first ('Best Loser') seat in the legislative assembly in 1995, at the same time that the MMM/Labour alliance recorded a second 60–0 victory against Jugnauth's MSM, which had then been in power for 13 years. The leader of the Labour Party, Navin Ramgoolam, became prime minister, but an alliance in which Berenger played second fiddle was not destined to last, and he returned to the ranks of the Opposition.

In February 1999, serious riots erupted after the death of the popular Rastafarian singer Kaya—who was imprisoned for possessing marijuana—in police custody. The police were unable to deal with the situation and looting was widespread over succeeding days. With the authorities seemingly paralysed, young Hindu thugs took revenge for what was seen as a Creole-inspired revolt by attacking and burning homes belonging to Creoles in Hindu-dominated towns and villages. An atmosphere of insecurity prevailed and amidst general disillusionment, a new alliance of the MSM and MMM, which proposed a power sharing formula between Jugnauth and Berenger, gained the support of the electorate in the 2000 elections. Voters found the notion of a non-Hindu becoming prime minister appealing as a means of breaking an ethnic deadlock over political appointments and ushering in a new era of meritocracy. Since then, however, Jugnauth has retired from the MSM to become president, leaving his less well-known son in charge of the party, while the hoped-for meritocracy has not been realised. Instead, the communalisation of political and sociocultural organisations has continued apace, leading a resurgent Labour Party to begin its campaign for the 2005 elections by adopting an anti-communal platform.

CONTEMPORARY MAURITIUS

The total population of Mauritius now numbers some 1.2 million, of whom Christians—Chinese, Creoles and Franco-Mauritians—constitute 33 per cent. The remaining 67 per cent is of Indian origin. Among this community, Hindus make up the largest group at 50 per cent, and Muslims at 17 per cent. More than 30 years after independence, Mauritius remains a nation in name only: in reality it is a very complex society of micro-entities, in which colour, creed and manner of immigration constitute important differentiating factors.

The Indo-Mauritians are not a homogeneous group, but are divided along regional, caste and religious lines. The largest North Indian (chiefly Bihari) Hindu component is split into caste-based divisions known as Maraz, Babujee, Vaish and Ravived, and there are also Tamil, Telugu and Marathi minorities. The Bihari Hindus hold the trump card in terms of numbers and play a key role in politics—every prime minister since independence has been a Vaish Hindu except for the Franco-Mauritian

A Creole woman in line with Indian worshippers at Thaipusam.

Table 8.24

	1990		2000	
	No.	%	No.	%
Bhojpuri only	201,600	19.1	142,400	12.1
Chinese languages only	3700	0.4	8700	0.7
Creole only	652,200	61.7	826,200	70.1
English only	2200	0.2	3500	0.3
French only	34,500	3.3	40,000	3.4
Hindi only	12,800	1.2	7300	0.6
Marathi only	7500	0.7	1900	0.2
Tamil only	8000	0.8	3600	0.3
Telugu only	6400	0.6	2200	0.2
Urdu only	6800	0.6	1800	0.1
Other (including combination of languages)	121,000	11.5	141,300	12.0
Total	1,056,700	100*	1,178,900	100

LANGUAGE USUALLY OR MOST SPOKEN AT HOME BY THE RESIDENT POPULATION

Source: *Republic of Mauritius, Housing and Population Census 2000. Note: *Difference in the total due to rounding errors.*

The Jummah Mosque in Port Louis.

A stone plaque commemorating an indentured immigrant, Ramyead, on the family tombstone.

In Loving Memory of

RAMYEAD, Immigrant No. 222317
1829 (Bihar) - 1896 (Camp Banane, Savanne)
Resting Peacefully
With several of his grandchildren.
He arrived in Mauritius with his wife
on Tuesday 25th January 1859.
God Bless them and all their
Immigrant Comrades

Berenger, who, however, has only acceded to the top job on a power-sharing basis.

The Muslim component of the Indo-Mauritian majority is divided into Calcuttyas and smaller minorities known as Surtees, Memons, Bohras, Khojas, Coknis and Anjouanes. All are from Gujarat, apart from the Coknis, a community of seafarers from the Konkan, believed to originate from Afghanistan and the Middle East, and the Anjouanes, descended from followers and family members of Sultan Seid Ally, a political exile from the Comores. These groups are further divided into Sunni and Shia, although it is the Sunnis who predominate. A small group of Ahmadiyyas can also be found in Mauritius. Around 3000 Mauritian Muslims participate each year in the haj. An urbanised community, Muslims in Mauritius, like all other groups, have adopted many Western customs and Muslim women dress in Indian and European styles.

The lingua franca of all Mauritians is Creole, with the middle classes also fluent in English and French, and the Gujaratis continuing to use their mother tongue in the home. The ancestral language of the Calcuttya Muslims, like their North Indian Hindu cousins, is Bhojpuri, though this is now a dying tradition as it is only spoken by the older generation. However, ancestral languages are undergoing a revival for those of Asian origin and are taught in schools and given air-time by the media (Mandarin for the Chinese, Urdu, Hindi, Tamil, Telugu and Marathi for Indo-Mauritians), although these are not generally spoken at home. In the mosques, Urdu is commonly used and translations of the Quran in that language are available. Indians and Pakistanis are often brought in to officiate in mosques and temples. Increasingly, however, Muslims identify with the Arabic language, and in the 1983 election, 40 per cent of Muslims stated this as their 'ancestral language'. The written language of education and government remains English, but verbal communication is generally in Creole or French, and the media is overwhelmingly French.

In Mauritius, the preponderance of people of Indian origin means that cinemas are as likely to show Hindi as they are French films, the sari and the *salwar kamiz* are common forms of dress, and Bhojpuri bands compete with *sega* and European music for the hearts and minds of the island's youth. The ubiquitous red flags, or *jhandi*, which can be seen in front of houses throughout the island signify that the occupants are Sanatanist or orthodox Hindus—an eloquent symbol of the cultural dominance of this community in modern Mauritius. While the ethnic compartmentalisation of Mauritian society persists, with most Indo-Mauritians viewing marriage with a foreigner as a preferable option to an alliance with a Mauritian of another ethnic, and especially religious, group, intermarriage is not unusual, and is increasingly the norm for the smaller minorities.

Recent economic opportunities provided, for example, by the creation of the EPZ have produced a small but important new immigration stream from India: Indian factories have taken advantage of the EPZ to set up in Mauritius and are employing Indian and Sri Lankan workers. Ali Parkar, head of the Star Knitwear Group, interviewed in 2005, reported that 800 of the 2500 workers in his Mauritius-based textile business were from India and Sri Lanka. He explained, 'as an Indian national, when I had to recruit foreign workers in 1986, I turned to those with whom I felt closest. I also think that Indians can fit in more easily in Mauritius; those whom I employ at Riviere du Rempart and Centre de Flacq feel at home. In Mauritius they celebrate the same festivals as us—Diwali, Id or Maha Shivratree—and this contributes to their integration.'

As a country in which the descendants of Indian immigrants have been and will continue to be politically dominant, Mauritius has benefited from close ties with India, which has financed a number of tertiary institutions and regularly sends VIPs to meet with local politicians. In March 2005, the Indian prime minister Dr Manmohan Singh paid a visit to the island, affirming continuing financial support, which in recent years has seen significant Indian aid in the computer, medical, engineering and artisanal sectors of the economy. The growth of an offshore finance sector on the island has also prompted the signing of double taxation treaties with India. However, there has been a worrying trend in Mauritius, as seen in other overseas Indian communities, to subscribe too closely to the agenda of right-wing Hindu organisations and parties. The increasing communalisation of culture is a significant indicator of this trend, exemplified by the recent proliferation of ethnic-based centres and single-issue foundations. It remains to be seen whether future governments in Mauritius will rise to meet the challenge of fostering genuine nationhood based on shared history and heritage, as is desired and demanded by its tolerant and open-minded inhabitants.

Marina Carter

THE MASCARENES, SEYCHELLES AND CHAGOS ISLANDS

THE SOCIETIES OF the Mascarene islands (which consist of Mauritius, Réunion and Rodrigues), and their dependencies in Seychelles and Chagos, were created during the period of European colonisation of the Indian Ocean. The residents of these islands, uninhabited before the 17th century, are all descended from immigrants. These small colonial outposts were initially settled in piecemeal fashion: passing ships would offload a few hopeful settlers or reluctant slaves picked up along the trade route on the coast of Africa or the Indies, and the polyglot populations that resulted became a source of wonder for later travellers. Charles Darwin, visiting the region aboard the *Beagle* in 1836 noted that 'the various races of men walking in the streets afford the most interesting spectacle.'

Indians played an important part in the creation of Mascarene society from the outset. Asians from the European 'factories' were imported alongside Africans and Malagasies to serve as slave labour. A number of skilled free immigrants also arrived from India as they were cheaper to employ than Europeans, and agreements signed with Pondicherry artisans led to the establishment of a wealthy, free, Malabar class in the islands by the late 18th century. The crews of sailing ships, known as lascars, were also frequently sourced from Asia—most were Muslims. To this day, the terms 'Malabar' and 'lascar' are local slang for Hindus and Muslims respectively. The conversion of Mauritius and Réunion into plantation societies in the late 18th and early 19th centuries led to the large-scale introduction of agricultural workers, chiefly from India. Mauritius recruited indentured labour from several states: Biharis and Tamils were the largest group; and Marathis and Telugus arrived in smaller numbers. Réunion imported mostly Tamils, principally Hindus; many Muslims and a few Christian Indians were also indentured. Merchants and service migrants from India followed in their wake. Today, the descendants of Indian immigrants continue to play a vital part in the cultural, economic and political spheres of the Mascarene islands.

SEYCHELLES AND CHAGOS ISLANDS

The Seychelles, first settled in 1770 with 28 colonists from the Isle of France, including five Indians, only had a population of 2000 at the beginning of the 19th century. By the end of World War II, the Seychelles population had grown to 36,000, swelled by Indian immigrants, Chinese traders and liberated Africans. A dependency of Mauritius during British rule, the Seychelles gained independence in 1976 and has since gone its own way. Unlike Mauritius and Réunion, socialist influence has given Creole the status of an official language there. Today, the Seychelles is culturally more similar to Rodrigues—another former island dependency, which remains part of the Republic of Mauritius—in that its majority Creole population of mixed origin is largely Roman Catholic. While the descendants of Indian slaves and indentured labourers have by

and large merged with the Creole group, a few mercantile families conserve their distinct status and traditions. On Rodrigues, for example, 70-year-old Golah Mackoojee represents the third generation of an Indian family who has owned a clothing and fabric store in the capital, Port Mathurin, since 1901. The Chagos islands, which were peopled by slaves and indentured labourers of Asian and African origin, were ceded in 1968 to form the British Indian Ocean Territory and their populations dispersed to the Seychelles and Mauritius.

RÉUNION

Bourbon island (as it was then known), the first of the Mascarene islands to be permanently settled beginning in 1663, received its first contingent of Indians nine years later, when 15 Indian prisoners were sent there from San Thomé. As the embryonic colony needed female settlers, 12 Indo-Portuguese women and two young girls arrived from Daman in 1678. These early arrivals were not slaves as such; indeed, so small was the settlement that every inhabitant was valued. The administrators were even prepared to accept pirates, some of whom married the Indian women and founded families.

Over the course of the 18th century, with the development of cash-crop cultivation, principally coffee, and large-scale slave importation, Bourbon rapidly became a society where 'blacks' outnumbered 'whites' and hierarchical demarcations of slave labour and free labour were asserted. The composition of the labouring population also underwent significant changes. In 1709, a quarter of the slave population on Bourbon was of Indian origin, coming from Bengal, the Malabar coast and Surat.

A mid-19th-century sketch of a Tamil doctor in Réunion.

Map 8.38

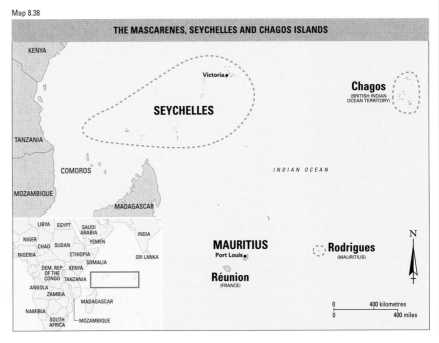

A mid-19th-century street scene in Saint-Denis, Réunion, showing diverse members of the population, including Indians.

Ismael Mamodjee Omarjee (left), an Indian Muslim trader who settled in Réunion, with his son.

This number decreased as organised slaving voyages to Madagascar and the East African coast got underway. By 1765, Indians constituted only 5 per cent of slaves on the island. During the same period, increasing numbers of free immigrants arrived from Pondicherry, chiefly masons and carpenters. Contract labourers went overseas to work for French agriculturalists more than a century before the onset of indentured migration from British India. By the time of the French Revolution, a dynamic class of free 'coloureds', known as *libres*, including many persons born in India or of Indian origin, existed side by side with a slave population, which also had a significant Indian minority, between whom intermarriage was common, temporarily facilitated by more liberal legislation. Despite such challenges to old attitudes during the revolutionary years, slavery was never seriously threatened in the French Indian Ocean islands. The institution of slavery was maintained until 1848, surviving the British conquest of Bourbon in 1809 and the subsequent restoration of French rule in 1815.

During the 19th century, new waves of Indian migration took place, coinciding with the development of the sugar industry on the island, renamed Réunion after the final collapse of Bourbon rule. Little sugar had been grown there until the Anglophile son of the prominent Desbassayns family introduced the latest machinery and began large-scale production on his estate. With the British now engaged in an anti-slave trade crusade along the East African coast, local planters began to source Indian contract workers to serve as new labour from 1828. After the abolition of slavery on Réunion in 1848, Indian labour immigration was considered crucial to continued economic growth, and in 1860 an accord was signed with Britain—then the effective controller of India—to facilitate the importation of British Indian labour. Within a few years, however, complaints of ill-treatment led to a commission of enquiry in 1877. Among the unhappy labourers was Jules Doressamy, the son of an Indian woman, who complained to the commission that because he could not find an employer, he had been sentenced to break stones. The litany of allegations, many well-founded, provoked the suspension of Indian migration to the island in 1882. Negotiations to restart immigration floundered amid continuing reports of abuse, and in 1891, a further investigation into the conditions and treatment of Indians on Réunion was carried out.

Merchants and other service migrants followed this ebb and flow of population growth. Gujaratis, in particular, established themselves in wholesale and retail trade from the mid-19th century onwards, including some families who moved to the island from Mauritius. Female immigration progressed more slowly. In 1911, there were only 90 women among a population of 584 Indo-Muslims on Réunion.

In 1946, Réunion became a *département d'outre-mer* (overseas department) of France, albeit in the distant waters of the Indian Ocean. Though long neglected, with high infant mortality, rampant malaria and poor infrastructure, rapid modernisation fuelled by generous capital inflow from the metropolis has brought better health care and the eradication of epidemic diseases, leading to a demographic explosion, even though many Réunionnais were also free to settle in France. Telecommunications and consumer revolutions followed, and the island is now the most advanced in the region, though still heavily dependent on French social security handouts.

European pirates and Indian wives

Monique Vincendo, the daughter of a female Indian settler, married a French pirate on Bourbon when she was only 13 years old. He had disembarked from a notorious pirate ship commanded by Avery, fresh from capturing the Surat-owned ship *Ganj-I-Sawai* and torturing those on board. Her husband disappeared in the forests of Bourbon one day. Monique, who was suspected of having an affair with another pirate settler, was arrested together with her lover. They were imprisoned for three months and interrogated several times, but no body was discovered and the couple were released. Monique married her second pirate in 1726.

The pirate Avery, depicted here bursting into the cabin of female passengers on the Ganj-I-Sawai.

The integrationist French policy in Réunion, which ensured that generations of residents of Indian origin took Christian first names, has now been relaxed, and a rediscovery of cultural identities, aided by the dominant Indian population of its closest neighbour, Mauritius, is ongoing. *Metissage* (the mixing of races/cultures) still defines the culture and people of Réunion, for this is the classic 'melting pot' society of the region, where more than three-quarters of the population define themselves as of mixed origin, and the overriding importance of the French language and culture is not likely to be supplanted by burgeoning and competing religious and ethnic claims. Instead, the Réunionnais seem happy to juggle multiple identities in a society increasingly comfortable with manifestations of non-Western cultural and religious traits. More recent arrivals are clearly distinguished: metropolitan French are known as Zoreilles (an allusion to the large ears of Europeans) and the offspring of the Indo-Muslim traders are called Z'Arabes.

RELIGION AND ETHNIC IDENTITY

The first mosque on Réunion, in the capital Saint-Denis, dates back to 1905. Today there are several more on the island, funded by the community who pay *zakat*. Ramadan and Friday prayers, and the various Id celebrations, are kept up by Muslims. Although a few women have now taken to wearing the veil, most of them dress in Western attire. The Muslim population numbers around 6000 and includes within its ranks important entrepreneurial families. Moussa Locate arrived on Réunion around 1870 from a Surat suburb with his three sons: one went to Mauritius and two stayed in Réunion. Of the latter two, one set up a successful business in Saint-Paul but was assassinated in 1900, after which Locate left and established a business in Rangoon. One son remained and today his descendants head a group of companies with important interests in the fields of medicine, consumer goods and appliances. Ismael Mamodjee Omarjee, a relative of the Locates, arrived in Réunion in 1875 and set up shop on Rue des Bons Enfants at Saint-Pierre, where the huge family business is still headquartered. Remembered for his charitable work, including distributing food and drink to families during the Spanish flu epidemic of 1919, Omarjee's picture still adorns the family store. Another well-established Muslim business family, the Ravates, settled in Réunion in the late 19th century, establishing a clothes and textile shop in Saint-Denis. Adam Ravates, the founder's son, expanded the family business until the store became well-known for its huge range of household goods—its famous advertising slogan was 'Everything at Ravate'.

Today, a quarter of the population of Réunion is of Tamil descent. Many immigrants from French India, notably Pondicherry, were Catholics, and a small church at Saint-Denis, now somewhat neglected, Saint-Thomas des Indiens, symbolises their religious faith. Most Tamils in Réunion today are Hindus. They began to build their small temples, known as *koylous* locally, from the mid-19th century—the first is believed to date back to 1858 and is located at Chaudron. At this time, the principal annual festival of the Hindus was Pongal (the harvest festival in India), held at the beginning of January in Réunion. Fire-walking ceremonies and dances involving a monkey-like figure known locally as *jacquot mayaco* were also recorded. Several Hindu traditions of Réunion have been subsumed within Catholic celebrations. Thus, the cult of Mariamman has assimilated with worship of the Virgin Mary, while the birthday of Krishna is associated with that of Jesus Christ. Saint Expedit, venerated locally, although not recognised in Rome, was identified by Hindus as a manifestation of Kali. Visits to the Black Virgin at Nôtre Dame de la Salette to honour a promise made in exchange for a request exacted are still conducted in a style similar to that of a Hindu puja ceremony and suggest the syncretism prevalent in these small polyglot societies. Certainly, many of the folk beliefs of immigrants have survived: prayers are made to deities to cure diseases, and the local term for a sorcerer, *pusari*, suggests the assimilation by Creoles of magical practices identified with Hindu priests, known as *pujaris*.

The goddesses Draupadi, Mariamman and Kalimai are celebrated in annual festivals held at several Hindu temples on Réunion. *Samblani*, or traditional funeral ceremonies, are performed along with other rites of passage, such as the shaving of a child's head. The *pandyale*, the ritual body-piercing and fire-walking associated with Tamil *kavadi* processions, takes place in early January. Mariamman is honoured in May every year, and Kali in August, when animal sacrifices continue to be made.

Marina Carter

A Tamil temple. While early Tamil migrants in Réunion were strongly discouraged from practising Hinduism overtly, there has been a revival of Hindu festivals since the 1990s.

SOUTHWEST INDIAN OCEAN

MEDIEVAL ARAB SOURCES speak of colonies of South Asian merchants that flourished along the Indian Ocean littoral. From the 9th century onwards, traders from India frequented the coasts of Oman, Socotra and Aden. The southwest Indian Ocean islands were also mentioned by 11th-century writers such as Al-Biruni under names like Al-Wakwak and Kumair, but how and when the first Hindu and Muslim traders from India arrived off these shores is unclear. Travel accounts from the 1600s note the existence of commercial contacts between western Indian ports and Madagascar, and recent archaeological excavations have uncovered jewels and pearls believed to have originated from Cambay in Gujarat. Pirate captures of Mughal shipping led to the dissemination of Indian treasures and the offloading of Indian shiphands at their various island ports of call, but it is with the colonisation of the region by European settlers from the 17th century onwards that the first recorded migration of Indian labour to the southwest Indian Ocean occurs. From then on, slave and free, skilled and unskilled, male and female Indians would be key to the development of plantations in the Mascarenes, and play a role, albeit less significant, in the peopling of the Seychelles, Comoros and Chagos island groups. In their wake, small communities of Indian merchants and other service migrants settled. Today, persons of Indian origin predominate in Mauritius, are important in Réunion, and constitute small but economically significant minorities on the islands of Madagascar, Seychelles, Rodrigues and the Comoros.

Indian workers in a Madagascar cotton field, late 19th century.

Map 8.39

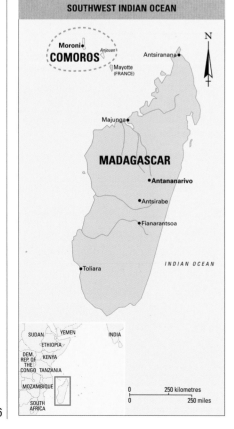

MADAGASCAR AND THE COMOROS

Unlike the Mascarene and Seychelles island groups, where most Indians arrived as slaves or indentured labourers, the Indian presence in modern Madagascar and the Comoros is predominantly the result of free immigration. Many came as artisans or skilled workers and shifted to trade after reaching their destination. A significant number were migrants who had already spent time in the Mascarenes or elsewhere in the region. This was migration driven by the search for opportunities, rather than forced mobilisation or an escape from desperate socio-economic conditions. These small agglomerations of individual adventurers escaped the official record until well into the 20th century. Although they are tiny minorities on their respective islands of settlement, the overseas Indians of Madagascar and the Comoros islands have an economic influence which far outweighs their numbers.

French accounts of Madagascar and Anjouan reveal that small trading communities were already present on these islands by the late 18th century. In 1775, Mayeur noted that Indians of Surat traded with northwestern Madagascar and also with Imerina (Fianarantsoa). Dumaine found a well-established settlement of Indians in Majunga, with their own mosque, when he visited in 1792. He asserted that Surat merchants sent two large ships loaded with textiles to Madagascar each year, which they traded for tortoiseshell, silver, slaves and other goods. Other sources cite the organisation of caravans by Indian merchants to trade with Tananarive, within Madagascar itself.

By the mid-19th century, British and American traders were taking advantage of the presence of resident Indian merchants to establish profitable commercial voyages themselves. One of the best sources for this period is the account of an English merchant, J. S. Leigh, who spent several months in Majunga between 1837–39 and described his social and business interactions with Muslim and Hindu merchants, known respectively as Karana and Banians. In 1870 there were around 50 Indians residing at Majunga and a similar number at Mayotte (formerly part of the Comoros). The establishment of sugar plantations on the latter island from the 1850s suggests that a large proportion of these Indians were employed in sugar production rather than in commercial activities.

By the end of the 19th century, some 300 Indians had settled along the northern, eastern and western coasts of Madagascar and controlled the retail trade in several towns. Economic developments had brought in Indian Sunni Muslims and a few Tamils from neighbouring Mauritius. Not all of the new arrivals were wealthy or in trade. In 1899, Moonsamy, a Tamil immigrant from Mauritius, asked for assistance to leave Madagascar and return to India, and around the same time a request was made to the British Consul at Tamatave to send the destitute Bibi Nageea—born on Mauritius to Indian parents—and her children back to Mauritius as deck passengers. With the arrival of French colonisers, cotton and other

An Indian Ocean family: the Currimjees

On 4 March 1881, Currimjee Jeewanjee arrived at Mauritius aboard the French ship *Nenuphar*. He had left his family, who ran a hardware store in Mandvi, at the age of 20 to work for some friends of his father. The following year, his brother Noorbhoy, aged 20, followed him to Mauritius. In 1890 they founded a company together. Succeeding rapidly in business, which, like most of the Gujaratis who settled in the southwest Indian Ocean region, was concerned with the wholesale rice and lentil trade from India and the return cargoes of sugar, the Currimjee brothers, with the help of a third brother residing in Bombay, opened branches in India and Réunion. Over time, the family business spread to the East African coast and Madagascar, where, in 1936, Abdulla Currimjee bought a cement business. Today, the Currimjee family runs a diversified and highly successful network of companies, with interests as diverse as soft drinks and mobile telephones, which is one of the largest commercial-industrial conglomerates of the region.

Currimjee Jeewanjee, doyen of the family.

agricultural industries required labour, but most of the new intake of Indian workers left when their contracts ended. The French viewed the Indians with some suspicion. Their links with British India led General Joseph Simon Gallieni to attribute the insurrection of 1898–99 in the northwest to the Indians, Comorians and other Muslims, perhaps acting with support from England.

Nevertheless, the Indian community continued to grow and prosper, and became increasingly urbanised in the 20th century. At Diego Suarez (Antsiranana), the Sunni Surtees established a mosque in 1905, and Gujarati teachers were brought from India in the 1920s, with a number of Indian schools being set up in the 1930s and 1940s for the offspring of Muslim and Hindu traders. By the 1970s, people of Indian origin numbered nearly 10,000 and were concentrated in the towns of Majunga, Diego and Tulear. However, from the mid-20th century onwards, local political instability pushed a number of families to relocate to the nearby Mascarene islands, or further afield, principally to France and Canada. In 1977 and 1979, pillaging of Indian-owned shops occurred, and this was followed by more serious trouble in several towns on Madagascar in 1987, when shops were looted and homes burnt. A number of families were ruined and outmigration intensified. On 27 January 1994, anti-Indian riots again erupted, this time in Antsirabe, and several families fled to Tananarive.

The visibly well-off Indian community is an obvious target in an impoverished country and, as such, has adopted a number of strategies to deal with the situation: some families have acquired Malagasy nationality (a large number remain stateless); in 1983, the Association des Communautés Indo-Malgaches (ACIM) was formed, under a Hindu president, to provide greater protection to the Indo-Malagaches; and a number of urban Indian groups have set up neighbourhood-watch organisations to coordinate help in case of further violence. Several Indian Muslim families have taken Pakistani nationality and some Hindus have become Indian nationals, while others have family ties on Mauritius and Réunion, and still others are using economic assets as leverage to gain French nationality and legal status abroad. As Sophie Blanchy has written: 'like Sinbad the sailor, they wander the Indian Ocean, in quest of an unlikely treasure, a nationality, a document, which they are often prepared to purchase, with money laboriously earnt in the family business.'

The multiple identities of the Indians in Madagascar and the Comoros are both an asset and a complication. The legacy of the colonial era has given the older generation a sense of being French. To the local peoples they are the Karana and the Banian, symbols of foreign wealth, seen as exploiters, endowed with imaginary fortunes—a controversial minority in short. They are also multilingual, having grown up speaking Malagasy and Gujarati, and acquiring knowledge of French and English at school and in their business lives. A few also speak Hindi, Urdu and Swahili. Within their community, they are divided along ethnic and religious lines. While most Muslim families originally came from Kathiawar and Gujarat, they belong to diverse Shiite and Sunni groupings. The Hindus represent several castes. The 20,000-strong community is, above all, a crucial element of the Malagasy economy and, following the return of political stability, albeit precarious, their contribution is likely to continue and, with increasing numbers of converts to the Mission Islamique Chiite, even to grow.

Marina Carter

A contemporary fruit and vegetable market in Madagascar.

TRINIDAD AND TOBAGO

THE HISTORICAL EXPERIENCE of the Indians in Trinidad in many respects parallels that of their counterparts in other countries that formed the 19th-century Indian plantation diaspora, but there are some striking divergences. Unlike Fiji, there was no indigenous population when the Indians first arrived in 1845; and unlike Mauritius, the non-Indian groups at that time were relatively small. Within just over three decades of migration, the Indians constituted a third of the population of Trinidad. Today, with a community of about half a million, Indians are the largest single ethnic group in Trinidad. Oil and hydrocarbon resources dominate the economy and pushed Indians out of agriculture at a faster pace here than elsewhere. Here too, because of the island's geographical location, cultural and other influences from North America arrived sooner and were more pronounced in impact. Indians in Trinidad were also influenced by historical currents at work in the Caribbean. These included movements towards self-determination and the forging of a pan-Caribbean identity, especially in the second half of the 20th century. The upshot is a unique quality which not only distinguishes Trinidad from other countries with sizeable Indian populations, but also from its neighbours in the Caribbean, though admittedly there are some strong similarities with Guyana and Surinam.

ORIGINS

Between 1845 and 1917, a total of 143,939 immigrants from India were taken to Trinidad under the system of indenture to work on sugar plantations. They were generally from the same catchments as immigrants to other British colonies where the indenture system was in effect. The first entry on the log of the first vessel to Trinidad is 'Bhuruth, male age 20' and he came from the main source of recruits, the aboriginal borderland of Chota Nagpur. Before long, the Calcutta hinterlands emerged as the prime recruiting ground. After 1870, the net was cast more widely, and thereafter, the eastern part of the North-Western Provinces and the extreme west of the Bengal Presidency, comprising modern-day Uttar Pradesh and Bihar respectively, supplied the majority of migrants. Smaller numbers came from Madras, but they developed a reputation for being more prone to sickness and less satisfactory as labourers. Madras thus became a supplementary source of immigrants in times of severe scarcity from other areas, but in the last decade of indenture, several ships would sail from there to Trinidad as well.

The bulk of migration was from the Bhojpuri-speaking region of North India, which had a folk tradition centred on the *bidesia*, a term applied to migrants

Map 8.40

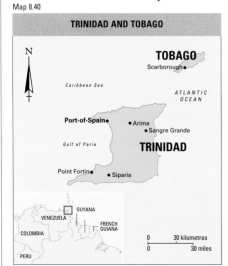

by loved ones whom they had left behind. Both in the homeland and in new destinations, this tradition, expressed mainly in stories, songs, theatre and dance, developed from the emotional turmoil, the sense of longing and displacement, and the pain of separation associated with migration. The dilution of that tradition in Trinidad, slowly over the period of indenture but with greater pace in the 20th century, and its disintegration into a tourist-like visit to the ancestral homeland, from which the traveller returns with feelings of ambivalence, are themselves markers of arrival and attachment to a new homeland.

There are several key factors which contributed to Indian indentured migration. The foremost of these was the problem of food shortages, which increased in North India during the 19th century. The commercialisation of the Indian economy generated by British economic policies contributed to the ebb and flow of food supplies in India. The drain of Indian raw material and the influx of British manufactured goods further undermined the domestic handicraft industry and put village artisans out of business. British land taxation policies created a web of landlordism, indebtedness and exorbitant land rents. These conditions, in turn, led to the rise of landless labour. Given the circumstances, it is easy to see why many fell prey to the blandishment of labour recruiters. Others migrated because of quarrels with their families or fellow villagers, or because they could not find work. Some, including those involved in the 1857 uprising, were fleeing from the police. Female migrants included widows who sought to escape the array of social disabilities imposed on them.

Of the total number of Indian migrants to Trinidad between 1874/5 and 1917, 85.03 per cent were Hindu, 14 per cent were Muslim and 0.07 per cent were Christian. Migrants to Trinidad were drawn from a large number of castes. About one-third of the Hindus among them came from castes which were accustomed to some form of agricultural work, roughly one-tenth came from the higher castes, and another tenth could be termed artisans; many others were simply general labourers.

Map 8.41

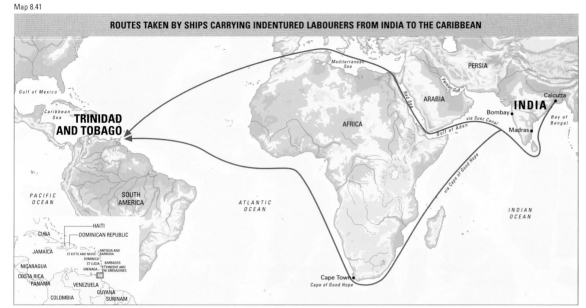

ROUTES TAKEN BY SHIPS CARRYING INDENTURED LABOURERS FROM INDIA TO THE CARIBBEAN

Courtesy of Peter Reeves, Head, South Asian Studies Programme, National University of Singapore.

It took sailing ships on the earlier route around the Cape of Good Hope approximately 90 days to reach their destination. However, following the advent of the steamship and the opening of the Suez Canal in 1869, the time-span for the voyage was shortened to between 30 and 50 days.

An Indian worker in a sugar cane field: 143,939 indentured Indians were taken to Trinidad to work on sugar cane plantations.

MIGRATION

Initially, Indian migration developed largely through a series of ad hoc decisions and bargains made between the Indian government and various colonies; but by the 1860s, attempts were being made to consolidate the laws and regulations embodied in the various immigration ordinances. Yet differences remained between the colonies. The first set of rules was printed in the 'Annual Report of the Emigration Commissioners 1845' and included regulations regarding the provision of warm clothing and adequate space on the journey to the Caribbean. In 1855, a handbook of instructions was issued for surgeons on vessels engaged in transporting indentured Indians between India and the West Indies. This covered rules related to vaccination, the selection of cooks and the provision of rations and separate quarters for the sick. From the 1870s, the rules aboard immigrant ships were more comprehensive and more effectively enforced.

Notwithstanding the social and economic push factors of Indian emigration, it was still necessary to paint an appealing picture of the destinations to which the Indians were headed. This task fell to the recruiters and their unlicensed agents, called *arkatis*, who operated in the districts and villages. The main objective of the recruiter was to get his catch approved by the local magistrate, a task generally accomplished in the briefest of encounters between the magistrate and the prospective migrant, in which no real attempt was made to discover whether the latter understood what he was embarking on. Where it was suspected that the recruit would prove troublesome, a more amenable substitute was often procured. Following the magistrate's approval, the recruits were taken to the main port on the coast. In the early years, when the journey was by foot, it took between 30 to 40 days to reach the port; later, by railway, it took about two days.

Upon arrival at Calcutta, the migrants to Trinidad were housed at the depot at Old Road, Garden Reach, and after 1875, at No. 9 Garden Reach, where they stayed for one to three weeks. If no ships were available, the time spent at the depot could extend up to three months. The migrants were medically examined to assess their suitability as agricultural workers. This examination often proved ineffectual. All were issued with clothing that bore

no resemblance to what they usually wore. Social restrictions and taboos began to dissolve. The migrant found himself in the midst of strangers of different castes whose appearance, language and social habits often seemed foreign and wrong. The physical conditions at the depot often bred debilitating diseases such as cholera and dysentery. Yet unsurprisingly, and notwithstanding the segregation of single men and single women at the depot, many relationships and 'depot marriages' were established.

In the early years of Indian emigration, wooden sailing vessels of teak were employed. These were specially built for the bulk carriage of human cargo, with an emphasis on stability rather than speed or style, and were relatively small in size. By the 1850s, a larger class of ships, some able to carry over 300 individuals, began appearing. In 1861, the Nourse line of even larger ships became the principal immigrant carrier, especially to the Caribbean. The next decade saw the emergence of steamships. These new vessels enabled year-round immigration rather than sailing only in favourable weather; they also shortened the voyage to the Caribbean from 90 to 50 days, and in the process, helped to reduce morbidity and mortality during the trip.

On the ships, the surgeon superintendent was in charge of health and safety. He was paid according to the

A group of Indians shelling cocoa pods. In addition to the sugar industry, thousands of Indians were also employed on the cocoa plantations in Trinidad.

A group of Indian men anxiously awaiting the pay master. The picture shows the presence of young and old among the Indian labourers.

number of Indians who landed alive, and therefore had an incentive to look after their welfare. He usually had two assistants, each charged with specific duties. A number of sweepers were engaged for the voyage, and cooks were selected from among the migrants, usually from the highest caste. 'Second-time' migrants were selected as sirdars, or headmen. On board the ship, sleeping quarters were strictly segregated, with single women occupying the rear section, families in the middle, and single men at the front of the ship. Daily life on-board the ship followed a specific routine. At least half the migrants were expected to be on deck at all times during the day and were encouraged to pass their time playing their musical instruments, getting some form of physical exercise, or engaging in other diversions. However, homesickness, seasickness, depression and diarrhoea were common. High mortality rates, quite often the result of cholera outbreaks, were not unusual. During the period 1869–1901, the average mortality rate on the voyage from Calcutta to Trinidad was 1.8 per cent annually. Between 1901 and 1917, this fell to 0.94 per cent per year. The overall average mortality rate between the years 1869 and 1917 was 1.5 per cent: the highest was 4.22 per cent in 1894 (111 deaths); and the second highest was 3.33 per cent in 1877/8 (73 deaths). The high seas and icy winds around the Cape of Good Hope proved to be the most trying period of the voyage. The opening of the Suez Canal in 1869, however, alleviated the situation.

On arrival at Trinidad, the migrants were lodged on Nelson Island, just off the Port-of-Spain harbour, for a medical examination and recuperation. This was followed by a period spent in the local depot, which varied from 48 hours to as long as six weeks depending on demand from the planters.

Between 1850 and 1917, a total of 30,002 immigrants returned to India. The provision of return passage to India was a part of their contract. Except for the earliest return voyages, their mortality and sickness records were generally better than those for incoming migrants. Those who left after 1895 had to meet part of the travel cost. Migrants who left were usually disappointed with what awaited them upon their return to India and some re-emigrated. Those who managed to return to their villages faced ostracism for losing their caste from crossing the *kalapani* or 'black waters'. Some returning migrants did not immediately proceed to their villages; others lost their earnings through robbery and gambling. Many of them ended up in the slums of Calcutta and frequently around Garden Reach, where they had first started their journey. Some, however, did manage to surmount the obstacles and settled down to a relatively prosperous life.

LOCAL EXPERIENCE

The first years of indenture in Trinidad were a period of experiment and, without settled conditions or rules, the

An elaborately dressed Indian woman. Jewellery, gold or silver, was a common means of both securing and displaying the wealth of the family.

experiences of the earliest arrivals were harsh, a situation which in fact led to the suspension of immigration for four years. The immigration laws were revised from time to time but the central feature of the migration process—a long contract with a single employer, with penal sanctions for breach of contract—remained. Thus, a more useful division into time frames rather than periods marked simply by the passage of new laws would offer the following: the years leading up to the 1870s, when barracks life on the plantations was dominant; the 1870s to the 1920s, when village settlements were more pronounced, albeit on the periphery of the plantations; the period between the 1920s and the 1940s, when many Indians moved to non-agricultural and urban or semi-urban environments; and the post-1940s, when the exodus from agriculture and the countryside was heightened. Throughout, two processes are evident: changes within the Indian community itself, and in the relationship between Indians and other groups. Though these occurred in different spheres, they were nevertheless intimately connected.

Life on the plantations was theoretically conditioned by immigration contracts, but in reality by the power of the planters. Customs and procedures at the workplace remained fashioned by the legacy of slavery in the Caribbean, by pressures from climatic factors which determined the growing and harvest periods for sugar cane, and by the requirements of social distance. The basic wage laid down by regulation was 25 cents for a seven-hour day, over a 45-hour week, but both the wage rate and the duration of the working week were subject to fluctuations. At harvest time, some Indians were required to work 15 hours a day. In the fields, the bulk of the work was organised by the task involved, which was theoretically measured by what an able-bodied adult male could accomplish in seven hours. However, there was no standard task and the flexibility which this gave rise to was exploited by planters. In times of falling sugar prices, the size of the task was simply lengthened. Most of the protests in the fields were related to disagreements over task work.

Disputes over the real meaning of the terms of the indenture contract were also inevitable. The Indians had their own expectations, based not so much on the written contract, which in any case they could not read, but on the promises and inducements they had received. Their employers in Trinidad, on the other hand, knew only one way to do business, and this was to keep their workers under the strictest control. In this they were aided by their close ties to the judicial authorities who presided over breach-of-contract cases. Not everything went to court though. Some employers were able to get away with punitive actions, including floggings, arbitrary fines and the notorious 'trust week', whereby the wage for one week was withheld as a guarantee of satisfactory performance the following week. Workers who were not cowed by these devices were sometimes co-opted into the system of control and appointed as 'drivers', or leaders of work gangs, or neutralised by the threat of banishment to other plantations, where they had no contacts.

Fifty years after the start of indenture, Indians accounted for 31 per cent of Trinidad's population. The community included the following: those born in India and those born in the colony; those who were indentured and those who had completed their contracts; and among the latter, those who had not yet completed the mandatory 10-year period of 'industrial residence' in the colony to qualify as a free Indian and those who were so qualified; and those living on sugar plantations and in emerging village settlements. Various permutations were possible but two types were most common: those born in India, indentured and resident on a plantation; and those locally-born or not, living in a village and free. In time, the size of the latter category would grow, and so too would the locally-born component of it. Earning a livelihood in the sugar industry remained the rule rather than the exception, though in time the exception would be more frequently visible. Outside their community, the Indians would encounter various plantation officials as well as agents of the local administration. They had already met Christian missionaries from the 1870s onwards. In all these encounters, Indians were regarded as subjects.

This occurred against a background of increasing dependency arising from the normal cycle of family development. Before the 1870s, the predominance of males over females had ensured that many males remained unattached. In the later decades of the 19th century, there were more females available due to changes to the recruitment policy, local births and declining infant mortality. In the free Indian population, the number of families was growing. The search for additional income became more compelling and plantation authorities tried to direct it by encouraging more and more settlement on lands near their holdings. This led to the rise of cane farming, which the authorities encouraged and controlled to ensure that it complemented their interests.

For the sugar mill owners, cane farming provided a source of cane that was cheaper than cultivating cane on their own estates, a result of the pricing system. The returns which the cane farmer obtained were often unpredictable due to the influence of many factors, including the nature of his landholding, whether freehold or tenanted, and sometimes the condition of the cane supplied. This last point, like judging the performance of a task in field labour, was often arbitrary. Complaints about the pricing system led to the introduction of a sliding scale in 1895, under which the return to growers was supposed to be based on the London price for muscovado sugar (unrefined sugar with high molasses content); but the scale showed more of a tendency to slide down rather than up, and payment for cane remained a sore issue for a long time.

Nevertheless, the attraction of cane farming for Indians in Trinidad who had completed their indenture contracts continued to grow for several reasons. Though never happy about the price paid by the mill owners, the Indian cane farmer recognised that the ready cash which he obtained represented more than the pure monetary value of the payment. It was tied to a cycle in which debts were incurred during the growing season and discharged when the cane payments were received. If the plantations wanted to lease land to ensure a supply of cane, the farmer knew that whatever the terms of the lease, he could exploit the land to the fullest. In time, an efficient system of intercropping emerged, which provided food crops for domestic use and for sale. Considerations of status were not to be discounted either. In the Indian community, the cane farmer enjoyed a higher social standing than the ordinary labourer. By the 1920s, cane farmers were providing the mills with a third of their cane supply, and cane farming itself had become an important avenue by which Indians would achieve a measure of economic mobility.

SETTLEMENT

Cane farmers (and rice growers in neighbouring Guyana) were part of an increasing segment of the Indian population who had decided to forego a return passage to India and chose to remain in the Caribbean. This was a decisive move in terms of settlement. Exactly how abrupt it was for the individual concerned is a matter of conjecture. The possibility that hard-headed calculations were involved with regard to the prospect of a better life in the Caribbean than what the individual thought was available to him in India cannot be discounted. The memory of what he left behind and what had induced him to leave in the first place must also have been a consideration. Certainly, both official spokesmen and planters were keen to say that Indians had improved their lot in the Caribbean, and pointed references were often made to the amount of money they had registered as savings or had remitted back to India.

The notion of a space which could be regarded as home was crucial in the decision to settle in Trinidad. Home was where the family—both natural and ascribed, and including those with whom a bond had been formed as shipmates—was located. Moreover, it was a space which had acquired, for Hindu Indians, a kind of sacred

An Indian woman next to a standpipe. The house in the background reflects a blend of the old and the new: mud walls and a galvanised iron roof.

An Indian village scene. Until the latter half of the 20th century, most of the dwellings were usually of the type shown: constructed of tree branches and a mixture of dirt and cow dung with a thatched roof.

halo associated with *bhumi*, or the earth. This was also connected to the performance of religious rituals which involved the consecration of space, or with the redesigning of the landscape through the planting of sacred trees and other vegetation. In addition to this, there were the normal activities carried out by settlers: the building of ponds, the diversion of watercourses, the clearing of land, the rearing of animals, and the naming or renaming of places. By 1900, substantial numbers of Indians had begun to think of Trinidad as their homeland, a sentiment which the general population was unwilling, for a long while, to associate with Indians.

The decision to stay in the Caribbean was usually coupled with the acquisition of property, firstly through the commutation of return passages to India, and more generally, after the 1880s, through land purchase. Commutation was not an easy process: complications arose during the surveying and allotment exercise; the quality of the land and its location were often unsuitable; and in some cases no proper title could be produced. The buying of land presented difficulties of its own, not the least of which was the insistence of the sugar planters that their workforce not be depleted by competing demands for labour and by concerns among the general population that Indians were buying too much land. Nevertheless, the number of Indian landholders continued to increase.

The acquisition of property altered the nature of interactions between Indians and officialdom. Landholding gave Indians an opportunity to approach those in authority with more confidence than they did during indenture. Indians were joining the Caribbean mainstream, where property and status as a ratepayer were the foundation for making demands, staking claims, and eventually for taking political action. Up to the 1920s, however, Indians, especially in places where village settlements developed, were caught up in reordering their lives. All the same, from the 1870s onwards, tangible markers of attachment to Trinidad were emerging, ranging from the physical to the less concrete, from structures and buildings to behaviour, beliefs, celebrations, rituals, ideas and discourse. Taken altogether, they identified both a degree of resilience and a creative adaptation to emerging circumstances.

SOCIAL AND CULTURAL CHANGE

The diverse backgrounds of Trinidad's indentured population were moulded over time into a more uniform culture, one which had a more general notion of being 'Indian', but also one which was clearly marked by the dominance of the Bhojpuris.

The rhythm of life in Indian villages in Trinidad was attuned to Bhojpur traditions and, in particular, the devotional aspect of Hinduism, which was one of its hallmarks. The seasonal nature of sugar cane growing was matched by ritual observances, festivals and celebrations. Indeed, the tempo and languor of some of the observances could hardly be accommodated outside a peasant environment. Devotional Hinduism was particularly appropriate to a community, if not in exile, at least away from its ancestral moorings. Though it was characterised by submission to a loving and personal god, it also carried a sense of democracy, subversive of priestly authority and conducive to more liberal discourse. This was why in village settlements the full force of high-caste pretensions was altered. The institution of caste itself could not be resurrected, but the idea of differences in ritual purity, endowed by birth, remained strong. By the 1920s, further refinement would lead to a situation in which, for many people, the intricacies of caste were simplified into a notion of the high, the respectable and the low castes. In the reconstitution of Indian tradition in Trinidad, the role of caste and by the 1920s, the status of women, would emerge as marks of distinction as compared to the situation in rural India.

The focal point of most village settlements quickly became religious structures and, given the preponderance of Hindus over Muslims among the Indian population, the centre of gravity was more often a temple than a mosque. The endowment of temples was a long-standing Hindu tradition in India, meant to confer both blessings and status and, like many Hindu rituals, was almost part of an exchange between the supplicant and the gods. Even under less than ideal circumstances, the erection of a temple was, for Hindus in Trinidad, almost a compulsion. By 1920, it was rare to find an Indian village settlement on the island without a temple. Though it was possible to identify a main god presiding over the temple, such as Shiva or Vishnu, the strict sectarian attachments of India were not replicated. The earliest structures were no more than a humble receptacle for the gods, but the iconography of the design suggested an encompassing of the whole universe. In the small, modest space, ritual performances of an individual nature were the most common activity and were almost like a pilgrimage. When group or community activity was required, there could have been no more natural spot than the temple surroundings. Thus, before long, a crude tent or shed was attached to the original structure to cater to such occasions.

Here too, village assemblies like the panchayat, which functioned as a forum for exchanging opinion, though more frequently as an informal tribunal, would meet. In Trinidad, the normal markers of authority to sit in the panchayat were broadened to include new attributes. Thus, the power of high caste status or suitable age was moderated by factors such as having resided in the colony for a long time and familiarity with local circumstances, and especially knowledge of the English language. There was a special regard for individuals capable of acting as go-betweens. In the cane fields, this was the driver or head of the work gang. In the village settlement, this could be

A sadhu in the inner sanctum of a Hindu temple. Until the 1970s, the sadhu would often reside at the temple, taking care of both its physical amenities and the religious needs of the community.

A sadhu outside a mid-19th century temple. The temples and mosques built during this period were essentially collective efforts at strengthening community life.

the shopkeeper who had outside connections. Increasingly, in the first decades of the 20th century, literacy grew in importance. Paradoxically, the spread of Western legal and other influences at the same time would undermine the reach and power of village tribunals.

Dispute and discourse about the boundaries of proper behaviour featured in the process of reconfiguration. Conversation within the Indian community was facilitated by general knowledge of Puranic myth and stories, and especially by familiarity with the Hindi version of the Ramayana. At once poetry and scripture, the Ramayana was also an encyclopedia, giving the reciter and his audience a broad canvas on which to practise the art of embellishment. The looseness with which Hindu orthodoxy was defined and the operation of an unspoken formula permitted variation and departure, but not too far from the core principles, and certainly, given the awareness of a larger, sometimes unwelcoming society, not in a way that would go against the common good of the community.

The general pattern of Indian settlement included rural residence, plantation and peasant agriculture, and the heavy influence of Indian ideas and organisational forms. Where numbers permitted, settlements tended to acquire a certain character, either of their own or in association with neighbouring villages. This was made possible by the composition of the Indian population, drawn as it was from diverse castes, and by the opportunity presented after indenture to resurrect caste-based artisan and other skills. Some activities, such as those connected with agriculture or efforts to make low-lying and swampy land habitable transcended all castes; but specialists soon emerged to provide a range of services. These included ritual specialists and those skilled in making religious paraphernalia; people with a rudimentary knowledge of medicine, including massage therapy; entertainers; decorators, including tattoo artists; jewellers; potters; barbers; and midwives. As the villages grew and an aversion to intra-village marriages began to take hold—a resurrection of an Indian idea, the roles of messenger and matchmaker, emerged as well. The villages which Indians created in Trinidad had the possibility of being self-sufficient. This alone elicited the observation that they had intended to insulate and isolate themselves. The situation was clearly misconstrued.

URBANISATION AND PROGRESS

By the 1920s, some Indians had drifted to the towns and were engaged in a variety of occupations. At the top end were a small group of businessmen who, on the returns from landholding or small-scale retail, had ventured into commercial activity. At the lowest level, some Indians provided menial services as porters or scavengers. In the middle were retailers of milk or coal, pedlars and a few

clerks. Rapid strides into professional occupations were made in the 1930s. This was brought about by the exploitation of educational opportunities, many provided by Christian missionaries who enabled the Indians to participate more broadly in society.

After the 1920s, Indian educational, cultural and social life underwent tremendous transformations. At an elementary level, there was a tussle between retaining what could loosely be termed the 'traditional' and the need for modification. The sometimes overriding tendency to retain the traditional and familiar was rooted in the community's deep concern with, or even fear of losing, those elements which defined their very existence in Trinidad. On the other hand, the modification of elements of tradition and custom was generated largely by the changing economic, social and political milieus.

The approach to religion illustrates the hesitant tendencies. Until the late 1970s, Indian religious thought and attitudes were steeped in tradition, unquestioning faith and, in the case of Hinduism, rites and rituals. A flurry of activity inspired by the Arya Samaj in the 1930s, though influential in some quarters, did not alter this picture. After the 1970s, economic and educational achievements among Indians, together with influences from the wider community, led to more probing into religious matters. Emphasis was now placed on philosophical teachings. Hindu pandits and Muslim imams had to change their approach to preaching to cater to these new demands. Major Indian life-cycle rituals also changed. Transformations in the form, scale and function of socio-religious observances, such as the Hindu festivals of Ramlila and Diwali, and among Indian Muslims, Id-al-Fitr and Muharram, indicated the delicate balance between the processes of continuity and change. New elements were added to Indian culture, many of which served to localise both Hinduism and Islam. Yet, the fundamental principles of these religions remained relatively intact. All the same, the fear of the dilution of Indian sociocultural institutions drove many socio-religious leaders and organisations in the 1980s to intensify efforts to promote what was conceived of as 'pure' Hinduism or 'pure' Islam.

Another example of the tension between tradition and change can be drawn from family life. By the late 1920s, with the gradual balancing of the age and sex ratio, a stable, though not rigidly standard, pattern of family life had been established among Indians, drawing heavily on the traditional features of the family in India. These included

The market place served as possibly the earliest point of community interaction between Indians and other ethnic groups in Trinidad.

Itinerant musicians played a crucial role in the development and dissemination of various Indian art forms in Trinidad.

One of the first big public things I was taken to was the Ramlila, the pageant-play based on the Ramayana, the epic about the banishment and later triumph of Rama, the Hindu hero-divinity. It was done in an open field in the middle of sugar-cane, on the edge of our small country town. The male performers were barebacked and some carried long bows; they walked in a slow, stylized, rhythmic way, on their toes, and with high, quivering steps; and when they made an exit...they walked down a ramp that had been dug in the earth...Everything in that Ramlila had been transported from India in the memories of people. And although as theatre it was crude, and there was much that I would have missed in the story, I believe I understood more and felt more than I had done during The Prince and the Pauper...at the local cinema...The Ramayana was the essential Hindu story. It was the more approachable of our two epics, and it lived among us the way epics lived. It had a strong and fast and rich narrative and, even with the divine machinery, the matter was very human. The characters and their motives could always be discussed; the epic was like a moral education for us all...I didn't have to be taught it: the story of Rama's unjust banishment to the dangerous forest was like something I had always known. It lay below the writing I was to get to know later in the city, the Anderson and Aesop I was to read on my own, and the things my father was to read to me.

Extract from V. S. Naipaul, Reading and Writing: A Personal Account, 2000.

the interplay between patrifocality and matrifocality, authority based on age and gender, focus on the family as a group rather than on the individual, and deference to elders. The extended family structure prevailed and authority was based on seniority and gender. The oldest male was usually the figure of authority, and the female members of the family were usually under the control of the eldest female. Arranged marriages remained the prevalent practice and this allowed the family to function as the strongest propagating agent of caste and other sensibilities. Indian parent-child relationships were characterised by a high level of respect, duty, obedience and even fear on the part of the child.

From the early 1970s, however, there was a shift away from the traditional extended family to the nuclear system. This was accompanied by a gradual transformation in values and ideology; yet the emergent nuclear family form took with it aspects of the extended family system, such as patriarchal values, hierarchy and deep-seated filial bonds. Authority was based on an amalgam of age, education and socio-economic status. The practice of arranged marriages took into account the consent of those to be wed. Formal education in English and the ensuing transformations in occupation and economic status determined both the degree and nature of the changes within Indian families.

Until the 1950s, the use of the Bhojpuri dialect dominated the more intimate settings of the home, village and workplace. However, the English language had already begun filtering in through the efforts of Canadian mission schools and through the community's increasing interaction with the English-speaking population. By the 1940s, the local English-based dialect was evident in Indian homes and in community interaction, to the extent that a sort of 'bilingualism of multiple orientation'—two languages interacting and spoken in varying blends—characterised the linguistic situation. By the 1970s, English had replaced Bhojpuri as the primary mode of communication. Hindi, Urdu and Bhojpuri were restricted to particular contexts, and this was to decrease steadily over the ensuing decades.

Both the concept of community and village life itself underwent substantial transformation. Until the 1940s, the structure, social systems, relationships, values and communal activities in predominantly Indian villages echoed the values and constructs of villages in India. Later, Indians became increasingly convinced that some degree of integration was necessary if they were to get ahead in Trinidad. Thus, each progressive generation brought with it a higher degree of affiliation and more comfortable interaction with the larger Trinidad community. The changing structure of community was evident in a number of developments: in the rapid replacement of the fictive kin ideology and terminology with the concept of 'neighbour', devoid of any feeling of kinship; and in the dilution and eventual demise of traditional social systems such as the panchayat and forms of cooperative brotherhoods, and communal institutions such as Hindu and Islamic village schools.

Until the 1930s, Hindu and Muslim efforts in education were aimed almost exclusively at teaching Indian languages and matters of religious and cultural importance. However, the growing awareness of the importance of English education was evident in the establishment of the first Indian secondary school in 1930. Before this, Indian contact with English education had been through the Canadian Presbyterian Mission, which was always

suspected of using education to convert Indians to Christianity. Large-scale formal education of non-Christian Indians occurred only during the 1950s through primary schools established by Hindu and Muslim organisations. These schools were marked by continuous debate over such issues as the inclusion of Hindi and Arabic in the formal syllabus and the teaching of Hinduism and Islam at both the primary and secondary levels. By the 1950s, other debates, such as those surrounding the grant of adult franchise to Indians, the recognition of Indian marriages, the controversy over divorce and the campaign against the refusal of government grants to Indian schools reinforced the need for schooling in English.

POLITICAL AND ECONOMIC DEVELOPMENTS

The sugar cane fields and surrounding villages provided ample opportunity for Indians to experience first-hand power relations in Trinidad. There were some spectacular occurrences, such as the disturbances related to the Muharram procession of 1884, when Indians on plantations in southern Trinidad, defying new regulations, attempted to take their celebrations into urban areas. Fifty years later, Indians on plantations in central Trinidad staged widespread protests over wage reductions—in retrospect, their efforts can be seen as the forerunner to general labour disturbances in the Caribbean in the late 1930s, which were a watershed in the history of the region. Generally, Indians resorted to protest to protect some accustomed right or privilege, and hardly ever in defence of any new claims. The bulk of the rural Indian population remained outside mainstream politics until their value as a bank of voters became undeniable, first in partial elections in the 1920s and then more obviously with the advent of adult franchise in 1945. Before this, the general attitude of the colonial government was to restrict political participation to people who had a sufficient stake in society and who shared the values approved by the validating elites. Indians were found wanting on both grounds. There was also always the fear that if not controlled or divided, they would one day 'take over' the country.

The first forays into mainstream politics were made at the municipal level by middle-class individuals, who were often the product of education in missionary schools, and in one or two cases, of professional training in law. They could not help becoming involved in general issues affecting their community, such as proposals in 1897 aimed at abolishing free return passages to India. However, they were divided on one issue of major importance which demanded a resolution in the 1920s, namely, how elective government was to be organised. The division mirrored a debate over the appropriate response to living in a multicultural society, an issue by no means fully resolved.

Some, perhaps following the example of constitutional development in India, advocated communal representation, while others argued for a general electorate. The Indian independence movement had an even greater impact, however, in arousing Indian assertiveness and pride, which the political leaders were not slow to exploit, as they did in major celebrations to mark the 100th anniversary of Indian immigration in 1945.

Political parties

In Trinidad, it was perhaps inevitable that electoral politics would throw up ethnically based parties, however much the leaders wished to claim that their organisations were non-communal. In the case of the major Indian-based parties, labour issues related to sugar workers merged with cultural and religious issues affecting the Indian population as a whole, including those Indians who, in other circumstances, might have remained apart.

Against this background, the People's Democratic Party emerged in 1953. Its leader, Bhadase Sagan Maraj, held office simultaneously as president of the sugar workers' union and as head of the Sanatan Dharma Maha Sabha. The awareness that such a base would only keep the party in the Opposition stimulated bridge-building strategies, which led to the formation of the Democratic Labour Party in 1957. A similar trend was observed in the 1970s and 1980s when the United Labour Front, whose base was Indian sugar workers, allied itself with parties having broader ethnic support, and under that umbrella managed to rule for a while. Political and other divisions led to a fallout in the 1980s, however, and an Indian-based faction successfully acquired some crossover support to win the general elections of 1995 as the United National Congress. With the support of a smaller party, it formed a government under the leadership of Basdeo Panday, the first person of Indian origin to become the prime minister of Trinidad and Tobago. He was also the head of the sugar workers' union. The United National Congress narrowly won the general elections of 2000, but within a year, internal divisions in the government over allegations of corruption forced a re-election. This produced a deadlock and the president, exercising his own powers but making pointed references to 'spiritual and moral values', decided to appoint the leader of the rival party as prime minister. The parliament elected in 2001 proved unworkable and new elections were held in 2002, which the United National Congress narrowly lost.

Political developments in the last decade of the 20th century rekindled some of the debates which have been present since Indians first arrived in Trinidad. While Indians regard themselves as full citizens of the state of Trinidad and Tobago, their attachment to ancestral traditions, however transformed and localised, has led some to question their patriotism. This is especially directed at those who participate sparingly in the mainstream Creole culture of the Caribbean. Both sides misunderstand the degree to which Indian institutions and values have been affected by the Caribbean environment, as well as the degree to which the Indians themselves have contributed to shaping not only the culture, lifestyle, food and music, but also the ethos and sensibilities of Trinidad, and perhaps of the wider Caribbean.

The jostling for political office has been heightened by anxiety over the control of Trinidad's hydrocarbon riches. This has increased competition for state employment and contracts, and raised serious questions about the promise

in the national anthem that 'here every creed and race finds an equal place.' Controversy over that sentence was once centred on whether or not it was grammatically correct; in recent times, it has shifted to whether it is substantially accurate. This has prompted a closer examination of the practices of state and quasi-state agencies, especially in relation to recruitment and promotion. Some of the decisions made by these bodies have been the target of vigorous and successful judicial review applications.

Economic change

Economically, the visible successes of some Indians have generated concerns in some quarters about rising Indian hegemony. The 1970s witnessed an economic boom as a result of sharp increases in the price of crude oil, which was Trinidad's leading export. Some Indians were well placed to exploit the opportunities which this windfall presented. Rising real estate prices enabled some of them to use family landholdings as collateral to secure loans for business ventures in small-scale manufacturing and artisan enterprises, but also as retailers and contract service providers. These ventures were sometimes assisted by the Indian tendency to pool family resources, though some sibling rivalry and internal squabbling also existed. The offspring of these families followed their parents into business, but some opted for professional careers as doctors, lawyers, accountants and engineers. At the same time, rising educational achievements among Indians, facilitated by the local campus of the University of the West Indies, saw growing numbers of Indian graduates entering the teaching profession and competing for positions in state employment.

A brief economic downturn in the 1980s caused by a drastic fall in oil prices stimulated a wave of migration to North America. This was a normal Caribbean-wide response to harsh times at home and beckoning prospects abroad, so much so that in the Caribbean as a whole, remittances from the US and Canada are an important source of funds. What was new in the case of Indians in the 1980s was that a sizeable share of the migrants was from rural areas. They now form significant communities in the suburbs of Toronto and in some localities in New York. This group shares the enterprising spirit of their indentured forebears. Today, a few generations after that first exodus, they are facing some of the same challenges of adaptation and adjustment to a new homeland. Their influence in reshaping attitudes in the villages in Trinidad, only a few hours away by air, cannot be underestimated.

The Hon. Basdeo Panday, the first prime minister of Trinidad and Tobago who was of Indian descent.

A procession celebrating the centennial of the Indian presence in Trinidad, 1945.

Krishna Deonarine (Adrian Cola Rienzi)

Krishna Deonarine—barrister, trade unionist and politician—was born on 19 January 1905. In the early 1920s, he was a member of the East Indian National Congress and the Young Indian Party. He was also the founder of the East Indian Friendly Society. From 1925 to 1930, he was chairman of the Trinidad Workingmen's Association, San Fernando branch. During the late 1920s, he developed a keen interest in India and the independence struggle there. It was around this time that he adopted the name Adrian Cola Rienzi. From 1930 to 1934, he pursued studies abroad, first at Trinity College, Dublin, then at the Middle Temple in London. In both places he was involved in political activity. He returned to Trinidad in 1934, was admitted to the Bar, and once again focused on assisting the Indian population and on reaching out to the larger, national working class. He successfully pressed for the liberalisation of trade union regulations and formed the Trinidad Citizens League, the Oilfield Workers Trade Union, and the All Trinidad Sugar Estates and Factory Workers Trade Union. At his suggestion, the East Indian Advisory Board was appointed in 1937. In addition, he was the first president of the Trade Union Council (1938–44). He was an elected member of the San Fernando Borough Council (1937–42); mayor of San Fernando (1939–42); a member of the Legislative Council (1938–44); and the first Indian member of the Executive Council (1943–44). He also served on the Franchise Committee of 1941; his minority report condemned the proposal to impose an English-language test as a qualification for the right to vote. In 1941 as well, he formed the Socialist Party. However, his career as a trade unionist and politician ended abruptly in 1944 when he joined the civil service as second Crown counsel. He subsequently rose to the position of assistant solicitor-general. He died on 19 July 1972.

None of them are keen to see their parents continue as workers in the sugar industry, an attitude also shared by their siblings in Trinidad. This was one of the reasons why the entire workforce of the state-owned sugar company, amounting to some 9000 workers, more than 90 per cent of whom were Indian, accepted a separation package in 2003, and why, although it caused hardship in some quarters, it did not generate the kind of turmoil which some had predicted. Cane growing in Trinidad is now mainly in the hands of private Indian farmers, some of whom complained about a shortage of field labour during the 2005 harvest period and suggested to the authorities that the shortage be met by recruiting workers from Guyana. This is one indication of how far the Indian community has moved from their first moorings on the sugar plantations.

CONTEMPORARY CONCERNS

A further indication of the ground covered by Indian migrants lies in the fact that many of the contemporary concerns facing Indians in Trinidad are shared by their fellow citizens of all ethnicities. These include increasing rates of criminal activity, arising in part from Trinidad's geographical location on the drug route to the US; an overburdened judicial system, especially at the level of courts of first instance; fears about the competence and efficiency of the police; and doubts over the government's ability to handle the provision of services such as health, water and education. The irony is that these concerns are flourishing at a time when the country is engaged in exploiting its hydrocarbon resources.

There is, however, one area in which Indians often regard themselves as positioned in a category of their own, and this pertains to equality of treatment from the government and its agencies. This calls into question constitutional text as well as state practice. There are no constitutional provisions which explicitly discriminate against Indians. On the contrary, the constitution establishes merit as the basis

Siewdass Sadhu, a plantation labourer, took 25 years to build the Waterloo Temple, a temple in the sea, as he was not allowed to build it on sugar cane land.

for determining treatment from the state, and there are specific provisions about equality before the law, respect for private and domestic life, religious belief and observance, and freedom of expression. The highest offices of the state—president, prime minister and chief justice—have all at one time or another been held by Indians. It is the actual working of these provisions which cause concern. One reason is that competitive ethnic politics generates its own compulsions, so that parties in power are tempted to design policies which skirt around the guarantees enshrined in law. For example, more generous state attention to urban Trinidad with regard to the location of health, sporting and cultural facilities, or other state-provided services such as power and water, implicitly disadvantage rural areas, which are more heavily populated by Indians. Policies designed to assist single-parent families, favour new business entrants, related to the resettlement of the urban homeless, or even work programmes for the urban unskilled—all of which carry a gloss or more of affirmative action—disadvantage Indians.

Another reason behind the grievances of the Indian community can be traced to the circumstances surrounding the 'construction' of the state. The constitution under which Trinidad and Tobago became independent in 1962 reflected a compromise between the main political parties, but it was one in which Indian misgivings were not fully assuaged. A new constitution providing for a republic was enacted in 1976 and, since then, increasing Indian confidence and assertiveness have prompted questions about the fairness of some of the constitution's provisions. For example, electoral politics are based on geographical constituencies, the boundaries of which have been adjusted from time to time by a supposedly neutral Elections and Boundaries Commission, but most Indians think that a system of proportional representation would provide fairer provisions. Another example that is perhaps more subtle, though no less indicative of an emphasis on the notion of full citizenship and belonging, is the attitude of many Indians to the country's highest award, the Trinity Cross. Both Hindus and Muslims claim that this decoration is not sufficiently neutral, and that, like laws related to Sunday trading and blasphemy, it betrays the Christian bias which underlay the original construction of the state, and is now ready for reassessment.

This list of grievances is short and it would be misleading to suppose that non-Indians are unsympathetic to Indian aspirations in these areas. This is an indication of the depth of integration of Indians into Trinidad society, but more telling is the overriding tenor of life in Trinidad, which is more embracing and celebrates the country's diversity. This was not always so. For a considerable period after their first arrival, Indians in Trinidad were regarded as sojourners, outsiders and aliens. Now, they are an essential part of the fabric of society, giving Trinidad a unique quality. This is symbolically captured, perhaps, in the emergence of the country's dance, the soca, a name derived from the last syllable of 'calypso' and the first letter of the Hindi alphabet.

Kusha Haraksingh

GUYANA

Guyana has always been a land of fantasy. It was the land of El Dorado...

V. S. Naipaul, *The Middle Passage*, 1991

Although Guyana—known as British Guiana until 26 May 1966—is situated on the northeastern shoulder of South America, it is considered a part of the Caribbean because of stronger historical links with the archipelago of islands to the north. Monumental efforts were required to colonise Guyana, which was occupied by the Dutch in the late 16th and early 17th centuries. They had tried to circumvent the necessity for onerous hydraulic works by establishing the early settlements upriver, away from the flat coastland and the mangrove swamps below sea level. That proved futile: the fertility of the soil diminishes rapidly away from the coast, in the hilly sand and clay belt. Only the Dutch, with their mastery of empoldering—the reclaiming of land through a complex drainage and irrigation system—and access to enslaved African labour could have initiated the labyrinthine system of dams, embankments, canals, drains, ditches and *kokers* (sluices) without which the coastland is uninhabitable. For this reason, Guyana never became a mature slave society like Jamaica, Barbados and the Leeward Islands.

Map 8.42

Due to its relative underdevelopment, when emancipation came in the 1830s, freed Africans were able to buy land adjacent to the sugar plantations and create their own villages. The estimated total cost of this land was G$1 million; another G$1 million was expended on the construction of houses. Some freed Africans continued to work on the plantations at harvest time. It was against this background that African militancy grew in the 1840s as the people sought to enhance their bargaining position with the planters. In 1842, in the counties of Demerara and Essequibo, they struck when wages were reduced unilaterally. The planters were desperate; the labour supply was erratic and many plantations could not handle the free labour environment. The workers were therefore able to force a reversal of the wage slash. In 1848, however, when African workers took similar action against another reduction in wages, the planters successfully resisted their demands. They had been strengthening their position since 1845, having introduced over 11,000 indentured labourers from India and more than 10,000 from Madeira. The planters resolved to halt the capacity of Africans to negotiate wage rates on their terms.

Indentured Indian labour, therefore, was introduced to enable the sugar plantations to retain a pool of contracted workers, or bound coolies. The fact that one-third of the funding for indentureship came from general revenue, to which Africans contributed through high indirect taxation on foodstuffs, meant that they were subsidising a system designed to curb their fledgling assertion of rights. The Africans quickly perceived Indian indentureship as undermining their welfare. Their situation was aggravated by floods, alternating droughts and chronic malaria, in an environment dominated by the order, size and power of the stable, drained and irrigated sugar plantations. Every perceptible advance by the Indians would kindle and reinforce African apprehension.

CONDITIONS AND FEATURES OF INDIAN MIGRATION

Of the 238,909 Indian labourers taken to British Guiana between 1838 and 1917, 193,154 (81 per cent) arrived between 1851 and 1900; and 75,808 (31.7 per cent) were repatriated between 1843 and 1955. Only 9668 (12.7 per cent) returned after 1917, when the last batch of indentured labourers left India. About 85 per cent of the immigrants to British Guiana originated from the same region, the eastern United Provinces (contemporary Uttar Pradesh or UP) and western Bihar. The impoverished eastern districts of UP alone contributed 70.3 per cent, and 15.3 per cent were from the contiguous western districts of Bihar. Only 5–6 per cent were South Indians from the Madras Presidency (primarily contemporary Tamil Nadu). Most Madrasis had arrived before 1863, when attitudes rooted in slavery still lingered.

Indentureship was not a just system, and assertions that it was a continuation of slavery were fundamentally flawed. A definitive instrument for rejecting this common

An indentured man and woman in their Indian outfits, c. 1890s.

The immigration pass of a male Indian indentured labourer.

Georgetown: the Public Buildings (Parliament) are in the centre and the Demerara River is in the background.

characterisation was the contract—the 'conditions of service and terms of agreement' which all indentured labourers were required to sign in India before departing for the plantation colonies. It is arguable that those terms were often more honoured in the breach, and that it took decades for the contract in its most refined form to evolve. However, implicit in the signing of a contract was the notion of Indian indentured labourers as free agents with rights. Enslaved Africans received no such concession: they were 'property', deprived of the fruits of their labour and their autonomy as individuals, for life, with no recourse to law or any statutory 'protector'. African resentment of coolies on the basis that they were pampered usurpers of material benefits which rightfully belonged to the Africans was not put to rest.

EVOLUTION OF INDENTURE

The contract for indenture evolved progressively, but the basic terms were established by the 1870s. The immigrant had to work every day, except on Sunday or authorised holidays, with seven hours spent in the field or 10 hours in the factory. Able-bodied males aged 16 and over were paid 1 shilling (12 pence) per day; adult males who were not able-bodied, minors aged 10 to 15 and female adults were paid 8 pence per day, but were entitled to extra pay when working overtime. The contract legitimised child labour.

Indentured labourers also had the option of task work, with higher remuneration computed ostensibly on the basis of wage rates obtained by unindentured workers. This was one of the most contentious issues, as workers continually disputed the basis on which earnings from task work were calculated. The alleged grievance was that the vagaries of differing tasks were often not given due recognition. Unlike enslaved Africans, however, Indians had recourse to the immigration agent general, or district agents authorised to visit plantations and investigate specific complaints. In reality, indentured labourers tended to leave the plantations and march to the office of the protector to seek redress of grievances. This often resulted in labourers being prosecuted for breach of contract. In comparison with the rights of employers, those of Indian labourers were breached consistently, even within the judicial system. Between 1874 and 1895, only 208 employers were prosecuted successfully, whereas 65,084 indentured labourers were convicted.

After completing five years of work with a registered employer—and a total of 10 years of continuous residence in the colony—and having procured a 'certificate of exemption from labour', Indians were entitled to free return passage to India (after 1908, men paid half of their repatriation costs and women paid one-third).

Raymond Smith states that the high-caste Brahmins and Kshatriyas formed 13.6 per cent of Indian migrants to British Guiana; middling agricultural and artisan castes accounted for 38.8 per cent; low castes and outcasts made up 31.1 per cent; and Muslims covered 16.3 per cent. Low-caste Chamars constituted the largest single component (12.9 per cent), but the assumption that only the lowest castes went to the plantation colonies is not corroborated by the records. Brij V. Lal argues that in the latter half of the 19th century, the impoverished districts of eastern UP and western Bihar were immersed in a culture of migration: to tea plantations in Assam, jute and textile mills and other industrial enterprises in Bengal (particularly Calcutta), and even to textile mills in Bombay. Migration to the plantation colonies was, in fact, another manifestation of the resolve by an enterprising minority to escape perennial poverty, famine, disease and the stultifying ascription of caste.

The hunger for land was chronic. The best agricultural castes—the Kurmis, Koeris and Ahirs—owned very little. Landownership was monopolised by the high-caste Brahmins and Kshatriyas. By the late 1880s, they owned 79.8 per cent of the land in Basti, the district of origin for the highest number of indentured labourers to British Guiana. Brahmins alone owned 19.3 per cent of the cultivated area, although they were deemed 'inferior agriculturalists because of their prejudice against handling a plough.' The best farmers, consequently, were often indebted to high-caste landlords. Among the lowest castes, indebtedness was so entrenched that some families existed in a state of virtual slavery. Chronic debt passed from one generation to the next, perpetuated poverty and killed ambition among large sections of a potentially enterprising people. Weakened bodies were a haven for violent epidemics such as cholera and smallpox. In Gonda, for example, the source of many migrants to British Guiana, cholera accounted for 11.5 per cent of deaths between 1872 and 1881.

Genuine social and economic reasons impelled a minority of imaginative men and women to flee. Indian indentureship to British Guiana lasted over 75 years. Most migrants were not kidnapped or tricked by the infamous recruiters—the *arkatis*—into bondage; but these were desperate people and they must have been seduced by the blandishment of recruiters. The element of deception cannot be discounted. Young men seeking escape from the yoke of acquired family debts or the macabre spectre of an early grave caused by famine and disease were especially vulnerable. Many girls and young women were in the same boat: 82.6 per cent of the women taken to British Guiana were between the age of 10 and 30, with 30 per cent between the age of 10 and 20, and 52.6 per cent between 20 and 30 years old. Of the male immigrants, 85.6 per cent were in the 10–30 age bracket. This corroborates what Brij V. Lal unearthed in Fiji, and so his findings with regard to the marital status of indentured workers are arguably applicable to British Guiana. He found that 86.8 per cent of the adult male immigrants to Fiji were reportedly single and, surprisingly, 63.9 per cent of the adult females were reportedly single. Moreover, of the

36.1 per cent of women who were reportedly not single, only 73 per cent were accompanied by their husbands. The rest were people on a mission, largely unencumbered by spouses, siblings or children, seeking a new beginning.

As 90 per cent of girls between the age of 10 and 14 were married, according to the UP census of 1891, it is highly likely that most of the female indentured labourers who declared themselves 'single' were, in fact, widowed because of the high mortality rate of child-husbands in the late 19th century. Others had probably been deserted by husbands who went to Assam and Bengal to work and never kept in touch.

HISTORICAL EXPERIENCE

The Indo-Guyanese universe was permeated by the mythical. The 'India' of the Ramayana—reinforced by Ram Lila festivals—and the dramatisation of the text fed the imagination: this was the real 'homeland'. Like the images of Bollywood from the 1930s onwards, it was escapism. The real India was too evocative of recent traumas, such as a terminal break with all relatives, including children, the neglect of communal responsibilities, and the experience of all-consuming poverty. The appeal of the Ramayana is rooted in its narrative of exile, redemption, triumphal return and the dawn of an age of splendour. The loyalty and utter selflessness of Lord Rama's wife, Sita, the epitome of Indian womanhood, also enthrals. The tale is the antithesis of the impoverished, caste-ridden districts of eastern UP and western Bihar in the late 19th and early 20th centuries, but its theme of exile and return was cathartic. It kept the illusion of impermanence on the plantations of British Guiana alive, while the dream of Ram Rajya, the benevolent rule of Lord Rama, offered hope of redemption from the perceived 'new slavery' in the new land.

When Indians on the plantations resisted, this was met by brutal reprisal. They combined passive forms of resistance with active ones. Due to poor wages and the general perception that their contracts were not being honoured, desertions were common: between 1876 and 1910, 20,058 were recorded. In July 1869, at Plantation Leonora, a tradition of militancy was born: about 40 workers of the shovel gang complained that their wages had been unjustly withheld and assaulted the deputy manager. The next year, violence was more widespread, enveloping the plantations Hague, Uitvlugt, Mon Repos, Non Pareil, Zeelugt, Vergenoegen and Success.

A strike at Devonshire Castle (Essequibo) in October 1872 would prove fatal (five were killed and seven wounded), establishing a pattern in Indo-Guyanese resistance. Workers would complain about inadequate earnings and seek redress by marching to the office of the immigration agent general or a district agent; the police would be called in to stop the march; and tempers would flare, culminating in workers being fatally shot by the police. Both men and women were part of the resistance activities. Resistance to perceived injustices, especially after a prolonged depression between 1884 and 1905, was a fact of Indian life on the estates. Between 1886 and 1889, no less than 100 strikes were recorded. In October 1896, five workers were killed and 59 wounded at Non Pareil, East Coast Demerara; in May 1903, at Friends, East Bank Berbice, six were killed and seven wounded; in April 1913, 14 were killed at Rose Hall, East Canje, Berbice; and in April 1924, 13 were shot dead at Ruimveldt, East Bank Demerara. There were strikes on the sugar plantations

This painting shows Sita garlanding the victorious Rama. The epic Ramayana, with the narrative of triumphal return, offered the hope of redemption to indentured labourers.

virtually every year: in 1916 there were 23 strikes, and in 1920, 15 strikes were recorded. There would be more killings at Leonora in 1939 and Enmore in 1948. This was a culture of resistance. It is therefore arguable that by the 1920s and 1930s a predilection for radical change had permeated Indian plantation workers.

SOCIAL, CULTURAL AND ECONOMIC CHANGE

Hinduism has no ultimate source of ecclesiastical authority, and in Guyana in the latter half of the 19th century, freed from the constraints of custom and the tyranny of village ways, Brahmins (no more than 2 per cent of all indentured labourers) were challenged by subversion. Confronted with rampant Christian proselytising, Brahmin priests responded by ministering, even to those known to be of the lowest castes, in their homes. They also partook of their food; this was sacrilegious in India. Self-interest precipitated the Brahmins' radical stance. The plantation regime allocated leadership roles on the basis of secular criteria, thus, Brahmins were often under the supervision of men ('drivers') of lower caste. By facilitating the entry of low-caste people into the mainstream of Hinduism in British Guiana, Brahmins had created a vast body of devotees who reciprocated by paying obeisance to them—a massive ritual compensation for their diminishing status on the estates, but equally a lucrative source of livelihood.

An inclusive Hinduism emerged in British Guiana and Trinidad with the admission of the lowest castes—Chamars, Dusadhs, Doms and Bhangis—into the orthodox mainstream Sanatan Dharma. As Chandra Jayawardena observes, 'Since it was a "higher class cult" it was an attraction to the low castes who had traditionally belonged to cults and sects with distinctive gods and rites because they had been excluded...The redefinition of Hinduism as one religion common to all Indians led to the acceptance of Sanatan Dharma by the smaller groups.'

Orthodox Hinduism has retained its appeal, in spite of the missionary zeal of the reformist Arya Samaj since the late 1920s, because it was not preoccupied with austerity or philosophical and exegetical nuances. The accessible Ramayana engenders more popular empathy than the Mahabharata or the Vedas. Moreover, the accessibility of the god(s) in people's homes, the evocative *murtis* (so-called idols), the carnival of rituals, the exposition of the text accompanied by the infectious rhythm of the music (*at yajnas*), the bacchanalian spirit of festivals (the spring festival of Holi and the harvest festival of Diwali especially), all invested orthodox Sanatan Dharma with a lightness of touch; a chaotic and consuming spontaneity.

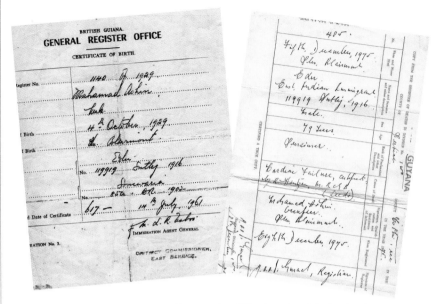

The birth and death certificates of Muhammad Ashim, the son of an indentured migrant.

Rice farmers preparing the padi field for planting. Bullocks were used for this purpose until the late 1950s.

Due to the difficulty of reclaiming land, many more Indians in British Guiana—Hindus and Muslims—remained on the plantations than in Trinidad. This fostered an unprecedented solidarity between them. A sense of community transcended ancient religious differences and inspired the development of secular purpose. This was a pillar of the Indo-Guyanese aspiration to mobility and gave rise to a middle class formed by a focus on rice cultivation, cattle farming, commerce and Western education.

Wet rice cultivation was transplanted from India. By 1903, 7082 hectares were being cultivated. Most of the rice was grown in villages near the plantations. The gradual reform of laws relating to the purchase of Crown land during the 1890s, when the sugar industry faced a prolonged crisis, facilitated a significant rise in landownership among Indians. Predominantly Indian villages emerged in all three counties: Essequibo, Demerara and Berbice. However, Indian acquisition of some land formerly owned by Africans in the villages aggravated the latter's fear of Indian ascendancy.

It was during World War I, when rice could not be imported from India and Burma, that Indian farmers in British Guiana hastened to fill the vacuum. The amount of land under rice cultivation increased from 13,714 hectares in 1913 to 23,508 hectares by 1917, while exports increased from 7709 tons to 14,367 tons. The value of exports rose from G$519,544 in 1913 to G$1,422,806 in 1917. This achievement was accompanied by the impressive expansion in cattle-rearing by Indians. The figures are not reliable as Indians tended to deliberately underestimate the size of their herds in order to elude taxation; but of the cattle reared on the coastland in 1917, was conservatively estimated at 87,000, a very high percentage belonged to Indians.

By the mid-1930s, the area under rice cultivation had risen to 34,609 hectares. Rice cultivation, however, was a precarious business. Droughts and floods could cause very serious damage or total ruin. A drought in the latter part of 1930 and floods in 1934 wreaked havoc on the rice industry. In 1930, the harvested area of rice amounted to 26,001 hectares, but in 1931, with adequate rainfall, this rose to 31,736 hectares. In 1934, it declined to 22,303 hectares, rising yet again to 34,609 hectares in the mid-1930s. In spite of these perennial hazards, the dream of the landless 'bound coolies' from India's UP had been substantially realised by many Indians in British Guiana by 5 May 1938, the centenary of their arrival.

The Indo-Guyanese middle class had its origins in the rice and cattle industries, and was bolstered by the advancement of those who had progressed further in commerce in Georgetown, the capital, and New Amsterdam, the main town in Berbice. Crucial to the rise of the entrepreneurial elite was the consolidation of the joint family as a corporate economic unit by World War I. The labour of sons and daughters-in-law, occasionally even daughters and sons-in-law, could be mobilised within the patriarchal family, facilitating economies of scale in the embryonic stages of a business. It is noteworthy that having some wealth was a prerequisite to being a good Hindu or Muslim: both religions, as practised by Indians in British Guiana, required lavish expenditure on religious functions, marriages and life-cycle rites. Communal ritual feasting sponsored by families were a demanding feature of being a good Hindu or Muslim. Among Hindus, Lakshmi, the goddess of wealth, was revered. Religious and commercial imperatives thus intersected.

THE INDIAN MIDDLE CLASS

An Indian middle class was established by the 1920s. They were pioneers in education, funding the professional pursuits of at least one son, initially, in law and medicine. They were aided by the Canadian Presbyterian Mission (also known as the Canadian Mission), which started in Trinidad in 1868 exclusively among Indians; a similar mission in British Guiana was initiated in 1885. Their manipulation of key Indian cultural symbols gave Western education an unprecedented allure among Indians in both colonies, the latter's general resistance to Christianity notwithstanding. The Canadian Mission encouraged the wearing of the dhoti and sari, the use of Hindi, the singing of *bhajans* (Christian hymns in Hindi), and the holding of cottage meetings in Indian homes, where *Yisu katha* (the story of Jesus) was narrated. Canadian missionaries were expected to speak Hindi. Interesting Bible stories were told in the language. Also, Indian catechists were trained in the colony and tutored to cite the Bhagavad Gita as 'the authority for the claims for Jesus Christ', thus rendering him worthy of worship by Indians. Yisu Masih (Jesus Christ) was lauded as *Ishwari-ji* (the Lord) and *Shri Bhagwan* (God). The principal architects of mission work in British Guiana were Reverend J. B. Cropper and Reverend J. A. Scrimgeour.

The Canadian Mission, more than any other, accelerated the education of Indian boys in the colony. Scrimgeour in particular, a gifted teacher, even resisted the inclination of Cropper to prioritise the saving of souls over the educational component. Scrimgeour had unimpeachable credentials in the education of Indians in Trinidad. In the 1920s, at the Berbice High School for boys in British Guiana (opened in 1916), he replicated that achievement. Equally imaginative was the pioneering work of the Berbice Girls' High School, opened in 1920. It produced several bright Indian girls: Marie Khan, Katie Kowlessar, Helen Khan, and the sisters Irene and Clara Ramdeholl. Clara qualified as a lawyer in London in 1939. Returning to British Guiana the next year, her ship, the *Simon Bolivar*, was torpedoed by the Germans.

Credit is due also to the Canadian Mission primary schools in villages and on plantations, which offered many Indian children basic education. In 1933, with the withdrawal of the obscurantist 'Swettenham Circular' (passed in 1902), which had sanctioned the non-attendance of Indian girls—ostensibly a religious concession—these schools quickly experienced higher female enrolment. As the director of education observed on that momentous occasion, 'it is an advance desired by the Indians themselves, and an acknowledgement of the position they hold in the community today.' Indian educationist J. I. Ramphal was the principal architect of the demise of the 'Swettenham Circular'.

DEMOGRAPHIC CHANGES AND GENDER RELATIONS

Although 238,909 indentured labourers from India went to British Guiana between 1838 and 1917 and only 75,808 (31.7 per cent) were repatriated, the Indian population in the colony did not reach 239,000 until 1956. British Guiana was chronically malarial until the late 1940s, and Indians were the most vulnerable to the disease. With the eradication of malaria by the late 1940s, the next census in 1960 revealed a remarkable demographic change among Indians there.

Attributed principally to the great malariologist Dr George Giglioli (1897–1972), the eradication of malaria is among the most significant events in the social history of Indians in the colony. As Jay R. Mandle observed, whereas the crude birth rates of Indians and Africans between 1911 and 1920 were 31.9 and 30.1 respectively, between 1946 and 1950 these had improved to 46.1 and 35.1. Between 1956 and 1960, the birth rates were 49.4 and

38.6 respectively. This continuing disparity fuelled the escalating political rivalry of Indians and Africans. The comparatively positive economic and social indices identified earlier for Indians were enhanced by these demographic advantages in the 1950s and 1960s, and dramatised by the mastery of the great Indo-Guyanese cricketer, Rohan Kanhai, born in 1935, himself a beneficiary of better health and housing on the plantations. Indeed, the political pendulum had been swinging progressively in favour of Indians since the late 1940s, but the ethnic balance was disrupted as a result.

Another important feature of the Indian population was its distribution. Although the proportion of Indians residing on sugar plantations had declined from 48 per cent in 1911 to 38 per cent in 1946, they still constituted 85.6 per cent and nearly 90 per cent of the estate population in 1911 and 1946 respectively. The urban Indian population had hardly changed (5.8 per cent in 1911 and 5.9 per cent in 1946), but the figures for those living in villages had increased from 46.2 per cent in 1911 to 56.1 per cent in 1946.

The 40 to 100 female/male ratio of recruitment under indentureship had resulted in a chronic shortage of women. This bred prolonged instability in the family structure, especially on the plantations. The freedom women had sought by migration was reflected, in part, in a tendency for them to choose their own partners or leave them if they so wished for a variety of reasons: lack of financial stability, alcoholism, violent behaviour and sexual inadequacy. This was possibly aided by the fact that Hindu and Muslim weddings were not legally recognised. A minority who were possibly prostitutes in India capitalised on the shortage of women in British Guiana to augment their earnings.

The virtual elimination of caste taboos meant that women could marry men of a higher caste. Moreover, women were workers in their own right, thus expanding their freedom to choose. British Guiana was markedly freer for them than the UP and Bihar, but this ostensibly freer state was fraught with danger, especially when wives deserted their husbands, whose wealth was concentrated in the gold jewellery in their possession, for other men. Even amidst the early gender imbalance of the plantations, the 'honour' of men was deemed sacrosanct: the murders of many wives, especially before the 1920s, were rooted in the shame occasioned by the desertion or perceived infidelity of these wives.

Sexual freedom was tenuous and ambiguous for Indian women on the plantation as it went against the Brahminic patriarchal ideal. The latter had reasserted itself in the resistance to evangelical Christianity after the 1870s. The ideal of Sita, as featured in the Ramayana and with a focus on loyalty to mothers-in-law, husbands and sons, permeates the Indian imagination, and most women could not escape its web. Meanwhile, the virtual equalisation of the gender ratio by the 1920s enhanced the reasserted patriarchal ideal: the proportion of Indian women to men in the villages was about 84 to 100; on the plantations it was 76 to 100, improving to 82 to 100 at the end of the decade. Land ownership was crucial to livelihood, so families on the sugar plantations were

The marriage of Rama and Sita. Sita, who maintained the ideals of Hindu womanhood even in exile, was seen as a model for Hindu women in Guyana.

Figure 8.6

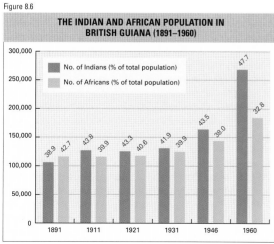

THE INDIAN AND AFRICAN POPULATION IN BRITISH GUIANA (1891–1960)

No. of Indians (% of total population)
No. of Africans (% of total population)

Source: British Guiana, census reports, 1891–1960.

Cultural continuity: young Indian girls in ethnic attire at a religious ceremony.

H.V. P. Bronkhurst's Among the Hindus and Creoles of British Guyana. *The Anglo-Indian missionary's celebration of Indian civilisation in his writings was crucial in the formation of Indian consciousness in British Guiana.*

inclined to arrange marriages for their daughters with the sons of landowning families in the villages.

The tenuous freedom of women on the plantation was superseded by status, however circumscribed, within the Hindu or Muslim joint family. The woman now belonged to the husband's family, which functioned as a corporate economic unit. It was fundamental to exploiting diverse niches in British Guiana's coastal environment. The paterfamilias sought to mobilise family labour for a range of seasonal economic activities. In the villages especially, family labour (both female and male) was deployed in rice cultivation, cattle rearing, coconut growing, market gardening and, to a lesser extent, rural commerce—running a general store and/or a rum shop or rice mill. In poorer families, work in the village was supplemented with employment on the sugar estates during the cane harvest.

This regime necessarily entailed curbing the fledgling freedom of women; but the status conferred by a stable marriage and a degree of financial security within the joint family were more attractive in an agrarian society than the capricious freedom on the plantation.

V. S. Naipaul says that the joint family 'protects and imprisons'. With the reconstitution of the Brahminic code in British Guiana, the sanction against female rebels was reinforced. Divorce was reprehensible. The few who dared to flee desperately unhappy arranged marriages became rudderless, often drifting into prostitution. Though marginalised and maligned, prostitutes played an ambiguous role in Indo-Guyanese society. Sexual services provided a degree of stability on the plantations under indentureship. The Brahminic code sanctioned early arranged marriage: boys aged 17 or 18 would marry girls aged 13 or 14. Female virginity was an imperative. Bereft of sexual experience, even basic social competence with women beyond the immediate family, many young men on the verge of marriage were prone to feelings of anxiety. So although prostitution was not condoned, the brothel, as an institution, paradoxically was a ballast of the Brahminic sexual code, and patriarchal assumptions quietly accommodated it.

However, the options thrown up by Christianity allowed a few Indian women to move away from the mould and beyond the domestic sphere: a secondary education, followed by a job as a schoolteacher in a Canadian Mission school. A few would discover leadership skills within the context of family businesses. However, it would take several decades before a few reached the university level. A new persona for women was taking shape: it accommodated substantially greater exposure to the public sphere than in India, even if it was still heavily circumscribed by patriarchal assumptions. Today, there are thousands in Guyana and in the massive Guyanese diaspora in Canada and the US who have charted successful careers in diverse fields such as law, medicine, business, the academe and the international civil service.

MAJOR EVENTS AND EPISODES

Intellectual resistance was seminal in the making of the community. Reverend H. V. P. Bronkhurst (1826–95), an Anglo-Indian missionary and writer, was the pioneer. In books such as *The Colony of British Guyana and its Labouring Population* (1883), *The Ancestry or Origin of our East Indian Immigrants* (1886) and *Among the Hindus and Creoles of British Guyana* (1888), he documented the magnificent secular legacy of ancient India. He was establishing that the coolie experience in British Guiana was 'a microscopic episode' in the longevity and opulence of Indian civilisation: its art, languages, philosophy, architecture, cave paintings, sculpture, poetry and other manifestations of refinement.

Joseph Ruhomon (1873–1942), the first Indian intellectual born in British Guiana, attributed his position to Bronkhurst. His seminal pamphlet, 'India: The Progress of Her People at Home and Abroad' (1894), the first publication by an Indian born in the Caribbean, was influenced profoundly by Bronkhurst's lofty idea of India, and celebrated her ancient legacy of learning. Bronkhurst and Ruhomon were able to provoke a rudimentary Indian consciousness in British Guiana at the end of the 19th century.

In this pantheon of Indo-Guyanese pathfinders, Bechu, the 'bound coolie radical' and an unremitting critic of the indenture system, has also earned a place. Between November 1896 and February or March 1901, when he apparently left British Guiana, his provocative letters to *The Daily Chronicle* helped to develop embryonic democracy in a society where the franchise was very limited and the power of planters to shape policy was still immense. Bechu's letters in defence of Indian rights were a catalyst for debates on the key issues of the day. He was uncompromising. Ruhomon considered Bechu 'the redoubtable, invincible...champion of his race', and commended his 'fearless and straightforward' articulation of his people's grievances.

The intellectual rehabilitation of 'Mother India' brought pride to the Indo-Guyanese middle class after World War I. They founded three organisations: the British Guiana East Indian Cricket Club (1915), the British Guiana East Indian Association (1916) and the Wesleyan East Indian Young Men's Society (1919), of which Peter Ruhomon (brother of Joseph) was, for nearly two decades, the leading light. The latter two organisations were most prolific in the 1920s and 1930s. They promoted the educational and intellectual elevation of Indians while celebrating India's ancient and modern achievements. The membership of all three bodies comprised Christians, Hindus and Muslims.

The Colonisation Scheme of the 1920s, however, had bred fear among Africans that British Guiana would be flooded by Indians. Promoted by the plantocracy and some prominent Indo-Guyanese, the scheme was an attempt to revive free immigration from India after its termination in 1917. The definite source of African foreboding was a meeting of the multiracial British Guiana Colonisation Deputation with officials of the India Office in London in 1919. Chaired by the Undersecretary of State for India, Lord Sinha (an Indian from India), J. A. Luckhoo, the first Indo-Guyanese legislator, advocated the creation of an

'Indian colony' in British Guiana. In the presence of the African-Guyanese delegates, Luckhoo stated:

> ...although we form 40 per cent of the population [in British Guiana], we feel and we have always felt that we are scattered sons of India, and that India should stretch her hands across to us and lift us up. The only way of doing this is to increase our numbers in the colony...We hope that in [the] future British Guiana will become a great Indian Colony...We appeal to the Head of the India Office, and to the leaders of Indian authority and opinion to give us their help. We feel that you have our destiny in your hands, and we ask you to remember [that] those people who emigrate to British Guiana will have the same rights, and that if they will come in sufficient numbers, we shall be able to build up an Indian Colony which will be a credit to India and the Empire.

Luckhoo and Dr William Hewley Wharton, the Indian members of the deputation, also issued a pamphlet in London, the 'British Guiana Imperial Colonisation Scheme', which restated their case for an Indian colony. They met Mahatma Gandhi in India in 1919–20 but failed to persuade him to support the scheme. When they tried to resurrect it in 1923–24, the principal African organisation in British Guiana, the Negro Progress Convention (NPC), dispatched a memorandum to the Colonial Office in February 1924 denouncing the scheme as 'a distinct act of discrimination' against Africans, who should have been offered first consideration to recruit African immigrants as they were the pioneer settlers of British Guiana. The NPC feared for the future of Africans if the Indian population was augmented inordinately by the scheme.

The contours of Guyanese politics were already ominously discernible. Race would become the bedevilling force after World War II. Indians were in the ascendancy, but the journey to independence would be fraught with many imponderables.

THE NATURE AND ROLE OF POLITICAL PARTICIPATION

Escapism, the El Dorado fantasy, has always had its use in coping with the harsh Guyanese reality. Indians were doubly fortified by the golden age of the Ramayana, which deepened the mythical proclivity of the Indian mind. An element of Aryanism had seeped into the thoughts of Joseph Ruhomon in the 1890s. In the 1920s, Luckhoo's idea of an Indian colony was permeated by the Messianic. This would be followed in the mid-1930s by the fantastic ideals of the first Indian trade unionist in the colony,

Ayube Edun (1893–1957). After World War II, Indians would put their faith in the greatest dreamer of them all, the implacable Marxist, Cheddi Jagan.

In British Guiana, the sugar plantation was ever evocative of enduring hurts. In 1939 and 1948, at Leonora and Enmore respectively, Indian workers were again gunned down. The formation of the first trade union by Ayube Edun had begun to politicise many Indian workers by the end of the 1930s. The intransigence of the plantocracy had stirred the workers' wrath. The shootings in 1939, while the Moyne Commission was sitting in Georgetown investigating social and economic conditions in the British West Indies, hastened the recognition of Edun's Manpower Citizens' Association (MPCA). Through *The Guiana Review* Edun unleashed a searing critique of colonial society in general, and the institution of the plantation in particular. Permeating Edun's philosophy for change was a Utopian strand that would be repeated even more extravagantly in the thoughts of Cheddi Jagan. In his book of 1935, *London's Heart-Probe and Britain's Destiny*, Edun advocated the reforming of the British Empire through the creation of a 'Rational-Practical-Ideal' state, the 'inviolable controller' of production and distribution that would 'mobilise the citizens' in order to cater for 'each citizen's equal needs'. This ideal state would also have sole responsibility for the education of children, taking the place of parents.

The characterisation of the plantation as irredeemably exploitative laid the foundation for the rise of the Marxist

Cheddi Jagan at a PPP rally in March 1953, with his wife Janet on his right and Jai Narine Singh (with the dotted tie) on his left. Forbes Burnham stands at the microphone. The three-finger sign used by Jagan indicates the PPP: the People's Progressive Party.

Cheddi Jagan (1918–97)

Born at Plantation Port Mourant on 22 March 1918 to parents who were taken to British Guiana as babies in 1901 by their mothers (unaccompanied by their fathers), Cheddi Jagan absorbed the abstemiousness of his Kurmi ancestors (from Basti, Uttar Pradesh). The eldest of 11 children, he trained as a dentist in the US between 1936 and 1943. In late 1946, he founded a Marxist study group in British Guiana, known as the Political Affairs Committee.

He was elected to the colonial legislature in late 1947 at the age of 29. Jagan was seen as a fearless champion of the Guyanese working class, whatever their race. In January 1950, he founded the first mass-based political party in the colony, the People's Progressive Party (PPP). Jagan and Forbes Burnham (1923–85), an African, were the leaders of the short-lived multiracial government of 1953, which was rejected after 133 days by the British, who were apprehensive that the PPP was on the verge of creating a communist state. Burnham, who had challenged him early for the leadership of the party, left the PPP in 1955. A man of legendary oratorical skills, Burnham was unencumbered by Marxist dogmas. He would 'tack and turn as the occasion dictated', with drastic consequences. He became embroiled in the Cold War on the side of the Soviet Union. Burnham later formed his own predominantly African party—the People's National Congress (PNC). Jagan's PPP was re-elected in 1957 and 1961 because of overwhelming support from the larger Indian electorate. The bifurcated nationalism between Africans and Indians was so entrenched that elections in the country were ethnic censuses, and are still so today. It would take monumental political blunders for Jagan's predominantly Indian PPP to lose.

Buoyed by the Cuban revolution in 1959, Jagan declared Castro 'the greatest liberator of the 20th century', and by doing so, took British Guiana into the Cold War. The Americans saw him as a communist, subversive of hemispheric security. Jagan's defeat in December 1964 was a consequence of President John F. Kennedy's machinations. He pressured the Macmillan government in 1963 to delay independence and change the electoral system to proportional representation. While Jagan had won easily under the first-past-the-post system, his popular support, at around 45 per cent, was not sufficient to ensure his victory under proportional representation. Burnham's PNC won the 1964 elections with the help of a small right-wing party. The PNC remained in office for 28 years, rigging elections with impunity.

With the collapse of the communist bloc, Americans no longer deemed Jagan a security risk. He returned to power in October 1992. Honest and passionately dogmatic, he died on 6 March 1997.

Jagan at a rally on 23 January 1968.

Cheddi Jagan visits President John F. Kennedy at the White House, 25 October 1961.

leader, Cheddi Jagan. His crusade against the evils of 'bitter sugar' would sustain his mission for over 50 years. Jagan was an industrious, honest man. He was a fighter for the working class against those whom he defined as the 'sugar gods'—capitalist 'exploiters' epitomised by the Booker Company, which owned most of the sugar plantations. Jagan's long-term political failure, however, stemmed from African and Indian racism in British Guiana; his political inflexibility, especially after Castro's revolution of 1959; his inability to cultivate strategic allies (such as Jock Campbell, the head of the Booker Company and a reformer, and Iain Macleod, the liberal Tory secretary of state for the colonies); and his incapacity for clear thinking, marked by a doctrinaire propagation of his beliefs.

This flaw led to the saddling of the country with the dictatorial regime of the African leader Forbes Burnham and his successor, Desmond Hoyte, between 1964 and 1992. After 1976, Burnham took a radical stand in order to consolidate and prolong his dictatorship. By claiming to embrace Marxism and Castro's Revolution—the core of Jagan's creed—he stole Jagan's thunder. Moreover, conscious that elections in Guyana were ethnic censuses, Burnham rigged them all: in 1968, 1973, 1980 and 1985 (the latter by Hoyte). Rigging was deemed necessary to stall the political and economic ascendancy of Indians. The latter was triggered by old fears: loss of land to Indians; the 'Indian colony' idea; Indian commercial success; and their cultural resilience and triumphal identification with 'Mother India'. Astounding advances in education made by Indians after World War II exacerbated that fear as it threatened the last citadel of African superiority, the professions and the civil service, as did their demographic leap following the eradication of malaria in the late 1940s and the granting of universal suffrage in the early 1950s.

Jagan's People's Progressive Party (PPP) won the elections in 1953 and 1957; but in March 1960, although the British granted Jagan internal self-government, with independence virtually assured in a couple of years, he renounced the 'imperialists' for not giving immediate freedom to British Guiana. He knew that independence was there for the taking and that internal self-government was an established precursor. Yet, he denounced the new constitutional proposals: 'They [the British] were prepared to adorn me with the title of Premier and I threw it back in their faces, because I was not asking to become Premier but to have cabinet status as in Trinidad.'

He promptly announced that he was going to Cuba to learn how Fidel Castro was doing things. Buoyed by what he saw there, Jagan alluded sarcastically to Prime Minister

Harold Macmillan's 'Winds of Change' speech, proclaiming his renewed faith in the communist creed: 'The East wind was blowing over the West and because of this the West is forced to liberate colonial peoples. The British are breaking up fast, not because they want to make us free...Two years from now there will be no more colonies.'

Jagan infuriated the British with his rhetoric after 1960 and was tactless in repudiating Iain Macleod, who granted him internal self-government against the reservations of many in the Conservative Party. Yet, when Macleod met US President John F. Kennedy in early 1961 and was cautioned against moving too quickly in granting independence for British Guiana, Macleod responded, 'Do I understand, Mr President, that you want us to decolonise as fast as possible all over the world except on your own doorstep?' Kennedy laughed and said, 'Well, that's probably just about it.' Macleod replied that while he appreciated the President's concern, the policy of taking British Guiana to independence was irreversible.

After the Cuban missile crisis in October 1962, Kennedy's pressure on the British to get rid of Jagan before independence was granted was so relentless that they reluctantly agreed to comply. Kennedy had visited Macmillan in the UK during the summer of 1963 specifically for that purpose. The US Central Intelligence Agency (CIA) had been subsidising a regime of violence by Burnham's African supporters and others, including the trade unions, in 1962–63. Jagan was a broken man and he was vulnerable. This was when Duncan Sandys, the right-wing secretary of state for the colonies, tricked him into signing a document empowering him to change the electoral system to proportional representation in the summer of 1963. This brought Burnham's People's National Congress (PNC) to power in December 1964—in a coalition with the anti-communist party, the United Force—and paved the way for the destruction of the Guyanese economy, its democratic institutions, including the judiciary, as well as its rich educational heritage.

The British Guiana Independence Conference, held in London on 2 November 1965, discussed the country's constitution following independence.

In 1969, out of office, Jagan felt emboldened to embrace his ideological beacon, the Soviet Union: he called it 'a kind of homecoming.' His rigid Marxism would guarantee Burnham's survival in spite of his own flirtation with the communist bloc.

It is ironic that it took the collapse of the Soviet system for Jagan to return to office after 28 years. With the end of the Cold War, the US no longer saw him as a threat. Through the intervention and moral authority of former US president Jimmy Carter, the PNC government was prevailed upon to hold free elections in October 1992. Jagan's undiminished support from Indians combined, for the first time, with that of the indigenous Amerindians, and ensured his victory.

THE CONTEMPORARY SITUATION

This was a pyrrhic victory for Jagan's PPP. Free and fair elections were restored, but Burnham's dictatorship left a dark shadow over the country. Guyana's best and brightest had long fled overseas, and its democratic institutions had been gravely undermined. The means for reconstruction were absent. A new set of party hacks, whose poor intellect was compounded by their moribund Marxist creed, had come to power.

It is believed that the official economy, based on sugar, rice, forestry, bauxite and gold, is now dwarfed by drug-based activities. Guyana is a key location for the trans-shipment of drugs from Brazil and Colombia to North America. A small minority, comprising both Africans and Indians, have become rich, and their money-laundering comprises a major part of the capital invested in the country. People at the highest levels are tainted with corruption. Escalating crime also has its roots in the drug trade. In this respect, the society is even more lawless than during Burnham's regime, as armed criminals frequently terrorise vulnerable people with impunity.

Guyana's problems are compounded by racial bigotry. Indians have the numbers to win elections but they harbour deep-seated fears, vastly more than Africans, of being victims of violence. The African PNC has been out of office since 1992, and they may never be elected even if they could win over the Amerindian minority. Their alienation from the political process is palpable. Yet, Africans dominate the army and police force, and comprise a sizeable portion of the public service. It is conceivable, therefore, that they may resort to violence unless constitutional guarantees are provided so that the winner—Indians for the foreseeable future—does not automatically take all. There was violence after the last two elections in 1997 and 2001 as despairing African supporters of the PNC burnt several Indian businesses in Georgetown. They erroneously alleged that the elections were rigged. Africans believe that they cannot win in free and fair elections. Most are desperate and hence susceptible to those who contend that Indian political domination would be halted only by a violent challenge. The constitutional road is deemed closed. Moreover, the fact that Indians also dominate the commercial sector inflames the African sensibility: Indian businesses are the instinctive target of black rage.

Another grave problem is the massive decline in educational standards since the 1970s. The colonial education system was deemed incompatible with a socialist Guyana. Elsewhere, in the Anglophone Caribbean less prone to fantasy, it has been adapted to meet the needs of modern democratic states. In Guyana, however, many leave school barely literate, some teachers are only marginally less incapacitated, and the best have fled. The University of Guyana once produced many fine scholars, most of whom are now in North America. According to a recent survey, 85 per cent of young people do not see a future in Guyana. This is a culture of migration.

Such problems are aggravated by the susceptibility of the country to floods and droughts. Economic and political decay bred chronic neglect of the complex hydraulic system. Catastrophic floods in January 2005 undermined the system further, increasing Guyana's vulnerability to a capricious climate, apparently a result of the relentless destruction of the Amazon rainforest. Meanwhile, there are no signs of a speedy alleviation of Guyana's economic woes. The preferential prices under the sugar protocol of the European Union are eroding rapidly as those countries disengage from guarantees grounded in residual post-colonial sympathies. Moreover, the corrosion of the society by the drug trade, money-laundering and the corruption of officials render prospects for economic regeneration remote. Nothing illustrates the hopelessness more eloquently than the stark fact that the population of Guyana, estimated at 815,000 in 1974 had declined to 751,000 in 2002.

MAJOR CHALLENGES

There is a frozen sea of suspicion and fear between them.

Stabroek News, 3 May 2005

If Guyana is to avert a race war that Indians are not likely to win, the PPP government must seek a modus vivendi with the African opposition to devise constitutional guarantees for power-sharing. Similar efforts in the past have not been successful: the PPP does not want to share power, having been the victim of so many elections rigged by the PNC. The latter may therefore decide that the military option is the only way for them to gain power. The army is over 95 per cent African, and the police force over 70 per cent. The armed forces could take over the country in a few hours as the ruling PPP has no military capability of its own.

The main deterrent against this is the US, which is still in favour of the constitutional road that is now the highway to governance in Latin America and the Caribbean, Cuba notwithstanding. A number of left-leaning governments have come to power in the region; Guyana's oil-rich neighbour, Venezuela, being the most unpalatable to the US. Efforts by the opposition to destabilise the regime of President Hugo Chávez have failed, but if the leftward trend in the region is compounded by Chávez's alleged 'nuclear ambitions', America may sanction the military option once again.

An Indian family in Guyana. The iron gate is an indication of upward mobility.

Table 8.25			
POPULATION OF GUYANA BY ETHNIC BACKGROUND (1980–2002)			
	1980	**1991**	**2002**
African/Black	234,094	233,465	226,861
Amerindian	40,343	46,722	68,819
Chinese	1864	1290	1395
Indian	394,417	351,939	326,395
Mixed	84,764	87,881	125,669
Portuguese	3011	1959	1496
White	779	308	476
Other	294	107	112
Total	759,566	723,671	751,223

Based on Guyana Census Report, 2002.

If the PNC lose the next elections in Guyana for the fourth consecutive time, as most anticipate, they may resort to violence to destabilise the PPP government. This could bring the army and drug-based paramilitary African gangs into the political sphere. Indians will have no means to defeat them even if similar emerging Indian gangs are recruited. It is therefore imperative that the PPP challenge the PNC into responsible action by agreeing to power-sharing in the short-run, with a long-term programme for promoting African entrepreneurship. If the commercial sector is still monopolised by Indians, even power-sharing will prove of limited use in allaying deep-seated African insecurity.

The biggest challenge for Indians now is to achieve a stable government and national unity. They must explore areas of cultural and political cooperation with Africans in order to stimulate an environment that boosts confidence; become engaged in a long-term programme for protecting a fragile environment; and promote an anti-drug/anti-corruption culture that facilitates the restoration of law and order and normal economic activity. These problems cannot be resolved without a comprehensive programme of national development that engages African youths in the political and economic rehabilitation of Guyana.

Indians are a majority in Guyana, accounting for 44 per cent of the population, but Africans (including those identified as 'mixed') form a substantial minority (estimated at 40–42 per cent). However, the Indian population has declined by 8.4 per cent since 1980, largely through migration. Power-sharing is becoming inescapable, but Indian distrust of Africans is so entrenched that even a little book by an African-Guyanese academic—Kean Gibson's *The Cycle of Racial Oppression in Guyana* (2003), which locates perceived Indian prejudices against Africans in ancient notions of caste, does not provoke a debate on the validity of her case, but immediately evokes assertions of racism.

The country is ungovernable without a culture of compromise. Africans consider Indians to be in the political and economic ascendancy. The latter, therefore, must be viewed as adopting a conciliatory attitude towards Africans, as they are demonstrating towards Amerindians, in order to retain their strategic support. This is not happening. This land of fantasy is sitting on a volcano.

Clem Seecharan

Thirty years ago, a few months after I first arrived in Guyana (1955), I met an impressive Indian man during a visit to the Corentyne. He was a senior civil servant. One of his brothers was a doctor, another was a famous lawyer, and the youngest sister was away at university. But their father had started in the fields of Port Mourant long ago cutting cane. This distinguished civil servant recounted a story I have always remembered as fresh as if told this morning. When he was a little boy an old man, it may have been his grandfather, used to tell him about the time he came over the 'black water' from India. It seems like months, if not years the voyage lasted. And the one clear memory the old man had was that each night on deck he looked at the stars blazing in the sky and gradually, as night succeeded night, his eyes, coached by the imagination, gradually picked out the shape of a tiger leaping in the star amidst the constellations. That is what he recalled in the hardship and the monotony and the homesickness of the journey—a tiger leaping amid the stars. And he told it to his grandson and his grandson told it to me and during that Corentyne weekend traced himself for me that tiger-shape still blazing in the sky. And now at nights, at certain times of the year, I still look up and I think of the old man on his long voyage, and the generations who have done well after him, and it seems to me the tiger leaping in the stars must have become for him a sort of symbol of pride and strength and beauty which he could not then hope to possess but which perhaps he could yearn for in his new land one day. And it seems to me, also, that the generations have not misplaced the symbol or the old man's yearning.

Extract from Ian McDonald, 'Tiger in the Stars', in Joel Benjamin, Lakshmi Kallicharan, Ian McDonald and Lloyd Seawar (eds.), They Came in Ships: An Anthology of Indo-Guyanese Prose and Poetry, 1998.

Ian McDonald was born in Trinidad in 1933 and educated at Cambridge. He has lived in Guyana since 1955. He is a poet, distinguished writer and broadcaster, and editor of *Kyk-over-al*, the oldest surviving literary journal in Guyana.

SURINAM

ON 5 JUNE 1873, the ship *Lalla Rookh* dropped anchor in the Surinam River. Fourteen weeks after leaving Calcutta, 399 indentured Indian immigrants, most often called Hindustanis in Surinam, had almost reached their destination: the colonial plantations of the Dutch colony. The timing was no coincidence. On 1 July 1863, the Dutch government had abolished slavery in its Caribbean colonies. Three weeks before the end of a 10-year transition period in which more than 30,000 of the formerly enslaved were to work under the supervision of the state, the *Lalla Rookh* arrived.

In many Caribbean colonies, the planters resorted to hiring supposedly cheap and docile immigrants to replenish the labour pool. The Surinamese planters introduced Portuguese, Madeirans, Chinese, West Africans and inhabitants of other Caribbean territories to work in the fields and factories. Their numbers, however, were not enough to boost the industry; instead, they increased the heterogeneity of an already diverse population. Immigration really got off the ground with the importation of Indian labourers.

The recruitment of labourers from British India was not a first in Caribbean history. In fact, Indians had already arrived in neighbouring British Guiana some 35 years earlier. It was, however, an important moment in the history of Surinam. Ultimately, 34,304 Indians would come to the colony. The bulk of these immigrants settled in Surinam and soon formed a considerable part of the population. Initially, their impact on society at large was mainly demographic and economic, but in the 20th

A street by the harbour in Paramaribo, c. 1950.

century their cultural influence and political power came ever more to the fore. The arrival of Indian contract labour and its aftermath markedly shaped the (recent) past and present of Surinam.

THE EXPERIENCE OF INDENTURE

The possibility of Indian immigration initiated intense discussions. The Dutch colonial minister finally supported state-supervised migration in the hope that a revival of large-scale agriculture would render Surinam less dependent on the Dutch exchequer. The administration was then confronted with another issue: where to recruit the immigrants? Post-emancipation experiences in the French and British Caribbean helped the Dutch decide where to focus their search for labour. Britain had already set up a recruitment system in India, so the Dutch did not have to bear the full expense of establishing their own depots and emigration administration there. However, as the British administration forbade the recruitment of labourers in India by private enterprise, the intervention of the Dutch government was necessary.

The Dutch opened negotiations with the British government, yet India, rather than London, caused lengthy delays. The government in Bombay argued that emigration would drive wages up and impede material progress in India. In addition, Bombay expected that the supposedly unhealthy climate in Surinam would lead to disease and a high mortality rate. In the end, London agreed with the governments of Madras and Bengal that Surinam was not unhealthier than British Guiana, and that the liberty to import indentured labour, which had been conceded to the French, could not be refused to the Dutch. In 1870, the Dutch and British signed an agreement on the emigration of Indians to Surinam. The Dutch parliament ratified the treaty in 1872.

According to the treaty, the Dutch government entrusted an agent, approved by Britain, with the management of operations in every centre of recruitment. Recruitment would conform to regulations for the recruitment of labourers for the British colonies. At no

A 1920 photograph of Bhoodia, an Indian lady in Surinam.

Map 8.43

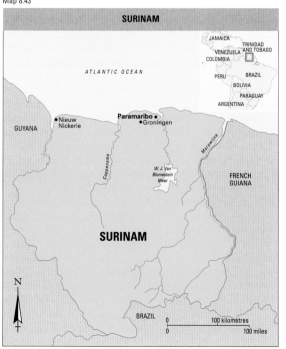

SURINAM

ATLANTIC OCEAN

JAMAICA
TRINIDAD AND TOBAGO
VENEZUELA
COLOMBIA
PERU
BRAZIL
BOLIVIA
PARAGUAY
ARGENTINA

GUYANA

• Nieuw Nickerie

Paramaribo •
• Groningen

Coppename

W. J. Van Blomestein Meer

Marowijne

FRENCH GUIANA

SURINAM

N

BRAZIL

0   100 kilométres
0   100 miles

Indian indentured labourers at the coolie depot in Surinam.

An Indian woman in Surinam washes clothes the traditional way.

time or place would the Dutch government enjoy any special privileges with respect to emigration that were not available to the British colonies. The Dutch agent and his employees enjoyed the same facilities and advantages afforded to their counterparts for British colonies.

In every port of embarkation, the British Crown charged a special agent with the care of the immigrants' interests. This agent was to ensure that all engagements were voluntary and that the emigrant had 'perfect knowledge of the nature of his contract and of the place of his destination, of the probable length of his voyage, and of the different obligations and advantages connected with his engagement.' Each shipment of emigrants was to include a proportion of women equal to at least half of the number of men, i.e. at least 33 per cent were to be female. This was one of the few provisions that the governor-general of India could change. It was prohibited to separate married couples, or parents from their children under the age of 15.

The British-Dutch agreement required having the following provisions stated in the contracts of emigrants: the duration of the engagement and the regulations concerning the return passage; the number of days and hours of work; the amount of wages and rations; and a guarantee of free medical treatment. The length of the contract was not to exceed five years; however, if it could be duly proved that the immigrant had absented himself from work, he would be bound to serve the number of days equal to the time of his absence. At the expiration of that period, the emigrant, plus his wife and all children who had left India under the age of 10 years, as well as those born in Surinam, would receive a return passage to India at the expense of the Dutch government. If the emigrant chose to forgo the return passage, he could reside in Surinam without any contract, provided that his conduct had been regular and he had a means of subsistence. Another option was to sign a re-indenture contract, which entitled him to a bounty and the retention of his right to a return passage.

The rules regarding lodging and transportation were quite specific. Emigrants had the right to leave the depots at the ports of embarkation to consult the British agents, who could also visit the places where the emigrants were collected and lodged. The voyage could be made in British as well as in Dutch ships. After departure, supervision was undertaken by consular agents. Article XIX stated that all Indian emigrants were free to consult, communicate with or claim the assistance of the British consul.

When the planters and officials in Surinam asked for government intervention to provide the colony with Indian labourers, they also requested financial assistance to meet the cost of recruitment and transportation. However, it was not until 1879 that an immigration fund was set up. The fund was to cover the transportation costs of the migrants to Surinam and back to India. It would also include payment for migration agents, premiums for the recruiters, and Dfl. 20 a year for labourers who signed a new contract, along with the cost of the management of the fund. It would reimburse the planters if a migrant should die within three months of arrival or prove to be totally incapable of doing field or factory work. If a migrant was ill upon arrival, the fund would provide medical treatment and pay for living expenses during the period of convalescence. In addition, it would issue loans to the planters to meet the costs of housing, food and medical care for the migrants. The expenses covered by the fund were to be two-fifths of the total cost involved in recruiting, transporting and contracting labourers.

Conditions

Despite improvements, particularly concerning hygiene, the conditions under which indentured migration took place did not change drastically over time. The European migration agent, appointed by the governor of Surinam, was in charge of recruitment in India. He resided in Calcutta at Garden Reach, a few miles from the city, where the Central Depot was sited. The agent nominated the sub-agents, doctors, interpreters and other personnel in the depots. He received a fixed yearly payment plus a premium for each migrant leaving for Surinam. Sub-agents, usually Indians belonging to minority groups, supervised various sub-depots, mainly in the United Provinces (UP), Bengal and Bihar. The law did not recognise these sub-agents, but they were crucial to the system. Their remuneration consisted of the gratuities paid per head for every suitable migrant recruited—Rs. 25 for a man and Rs. 35 for a woman, since female migrants were harder to find. In order to reach the quota for women, the premium paid to the sub-agent often had to be raised. Sub-agents were only on the payroll when the Dutch were involved in a recruiting operation. The recruiting agency of British Guiana, however, operated continuously and thus was able to attract the best sub-agents. In 1885, the Dutch decided to maintain the best sub-agents, even during a recruiting lull, by paying them Rs. 100 a month.

Licensed Indian recruiters, hired by the sub-agents, conducted the actual recruiting and received Rs. 5–10 per migrant. If recruiters violated the regulations, their licences could be revoked. The licensed recruiter would get most of his candidates through the services of an unlicensed collaborator, the *arkati*. He targeted people looking for jobs in the industrial areas in and near Calcutta. Economic factors such as land scarcity, unemployment, indebtedness and bad harvests made many people in North India look for new economic opportunities, and yet deception was a necessary part of recruiting enough candidates for migration. Potential recruits would be told about the attractions in another country, but not of the long sea voyage to get there. Also, recruiters sometimes pronounced Surinam as 'Sri Ram', suggesting that the trip was a pilgrimage in honour of Rama. The deceptive picture painted by the recruiters was one of the main problems of the indentured migration programme—a problem that could not be solved through laws or increased inspections. High officials in British India noted that the great majority of desertions were probably a result of illegal recruitment and 'deceptions practised by unscrupulous recruiters', and that the increased difficulty of obtaining labourers led to an even greater number of irregularities. There was fierce competition to find suitable recruits for the British, French and Dutch Caribbean colonies, exacerbated by the additional demand for labour in Assam, Bengal, Natal and Fiji. The task of the recruiters was not easy; opposition to emigration existed nearly all over the country.

Although Calcutta was the main port of embarkation in the early years of immigration to Surinam (1877–89), most migrants came from the UP and the Bengal Presidency. In fact, over the entire period, 80 per cent of the migrants in Surinam came from the UP. A commonly held view was that the migrants came from the lowest and most undesirable strata of society. In Surinam this opinion was probably even more strongly held because most people asserted that the Dutch recruited the 'scum

of the earth', whom even the British rejected. Yet the data regarding the social and caste origins of indentured labourers leaving from Calcutta show that the migrants represented an average sample of the population.

Before they undertook the journey to the ports of embarkation, the migrants would gather in a closed warehouse under the control of a licensed recruiter and sign a preliminary contract. When a sufficient number of migrants had gathered in the sub-depot, they were transported by train to Calcutta. Upon arrival at the depot, the official indenture process began. The depots were walled, and over the years many improvements had to be made to the ventilation system and the supply of drinking water. In the early years of migration, the prospective recruits for Surinam experienced much longer waiting periods— an average of 42 days—than fellow recruits leaving for other colonies, who waited an average of 28 days. In later years, the waiting period was reduced to just one to three weeks. Ships bound for Surinam usually left between May and September.

When ships were being readied for departure, there were always more people in the depot than were actually dispatched. Men had to show their ability to wield agricultural tools, and nurses would superficially examine the women. Initially, the agent waived more rigorous medical standards in order to recruit more women, but by the end of the 19th century, a more adequate examination process was established.

Recruitment for and migration to Surinam on average compared unfavourably with recruitment and migration to other colonies. In addition to longer waiting periods, the percentage of recruits actually shipped off was lower due to a higher percentage of rejections and desertions, more migrants being unwilling to leave, and more opposition from families. All Surinam had in common with the other colonies was the death rate of migrants.

The migration agent dispatched the bonded migrants as soon as they had signed the final labour contracts. The voyage to Surinam could take up to three months by sailing ship or five-and-a-half to eight weeks by steamship. Only four out of 64 passages were casualty free. The average number of deaths per ship ranged between five and 10. Sometimes an outbreak of measles or cholera led to considerably higher mortality rates.

Problems

In 1873, the first year of Indian migration to Surinam, 2449 migrants arrived. The initial enthusiasm of the planters and authorities cooled when the first shiploads of Indians failed to live up to expectations. Problems with language and customs complicated the incorporation of new migrants into the plantation system. In addition, the planters did not give the new migrants enough time to adapt, and heavy work in the fields took its toll in the form of illness and death. Medical care for sick migrants was insufficient, and in his first dispatch the British consul threatened to suspend emigration. The planters and the administration largely blamed these problems on the physical condition and character of the migrants and the method of recruitment in India. The first recruitment had to be done in a hurry since the planters wanted the first shiploads to arrive in Surinam before the end of state supervision. The agent general in Surinam complained that seven out of eight of the British Indians 'had never done fieldwork before, a great many were beggars, Brahmins and city people good for anything but field and factory work.'

The followers of a Hindu sect. The distinctive U-shaped marks on the foreheads of the men tell us that they are probably members of a Vaishnava sect.

An Indian family in Surinam photographed in front of their early 20th-century thatched-roof hut.

Table 8.26

POPULATION OF INDIAN DESCENT IN SURINAM (1925–70)	
1925	28,807
1935	36,331
1945	51,530
1955	77,550
1965	121,162
1970	142,049

Source: Government of Surinam, Encyclopedie van Suriname, *1977. Note: Since 1972, censuses have not recorded ethnic background.*

Following several complaints by the consul in Paramaribo concerning the health of the migrants and the system of justice, the Indian administration decided in 1875, after eight shipments of Indians to Surinam, to suspend emigration to that colony. However, they failed to notify the Dutch government about this decision, and so, in neither Surinam nor the Netherlands was the administration aware of this decree, especially since no new labourers were requested in 1874 or 1875. Improvements in medical care led to the resumption of immigration in 1877. After 1880, when the immigration fund was instituted, a more regular supply of Indian indentured labourers arrived in the colony.

The resumption of immigration did not immediately lead to better relations between the authorities in Surinam and British representatives. The main problem was that the Indian immigrants remained British nationals. This had two serious drawbacks. First, if immigration were to proceed continuously and rapidly, a considerable proportion of the population in Surinam would very soon be British. Second, these British subjects could appeal against the decisions of the highest Dutch authority and request the assistance of the British consul. The authorities in Surinam could not be sure about the inclinations of the consul. More importantly, this right of appeal would not enhance the submissiveness of the labour force. These were the main reasons why more and more voices called for the import of indentured labourers from the Netherlands East Indies (modern Indonesia). This idea gained even more ground when it became clear that the political climate in India was changing and that the abolition of indentured labour from that colony was becoming a distinct possibility.

Towards the end of the 19th century, serious opposition to the export of Indians mounted, and both Viceroy Lord Curzon and the young lawyer M. K. Gandhi in Natal mobilised Indian public opinion against indentured labour. Following political pressure, an investigative trip was made by James McNeill and Chimman Lal to Fiji, British Guiana, Trinidad, Jamaica and Surinam in 1913.

Their report listed problems such as low wages, harsh punishments, inadequate government supervision and high suicide rates. Yet, while observing that most immigrants were excessively poor and without much hope of betterment, the investigators argued that 'the advantages of the system far outweighed its disadvantages.' The 1914 report of McNeill and Lal came at the wrong time. Viceroy Lord Hardinge judged it better to respond to the charged atmosphere in India and wrote in 1915 that indentured labour resembled slavery and urged the abolition of the system. In 1920, indenture was legally abolished.

The government was responsible for the recruitment, transportation, allocation and protection of the indentured Indians. Once on the plantations, the state had to ensure that employers and labourers fulfilled the terms of the contract. Legal mechanisms were of great importance in controlling the indentured. The so-called penal sanction made neglect of duty or refusal to work punishable by jail sentences. In Surinam, protection of the contracted Indian labourers was the responsibility of the agent general, the British consul and local officials. A structural problem eroding this protection was the discrepancy between theory and practice. The legal system did not work in favour of the Indians because of their inability to communicate effectively with the magistrates, their lack of knowledge of the law, and the class and racial prejudices of many of the magistrates and officials.

The labour and legal systems restricted the freedom and mobility of the indentured. Social control was exercised by physically confining workers to the estates through the use of a pass system, estate housing and plantation shops. The subjugation of indentured labourers went further than that of free workers as high-handedness and legalised elements of force permeated labour relations. This is demonstrated in the continuous conflict over tasks and wages. According to the guidelines, a task was work that an average male labourer could complete in one working day. The imprecision of this policy induced arbitrariness: frequently, the definition of a task was not based on any average performance, but rather on the workload of

An 1898 photograph of a parade in Paramaribo, celebrating the crowning of Queen Wilhelmina of the Netherlands at the age of 18, who succeeded her mother, Queen Emma.

a few selected men. This was of great importance as the contracts stipulated a set wage for a day's work. As a result, many labourers did not earn this fixed wage.

The planters' domination was limited by the state, external pressures such as the nationalist movement in India, and political and social criticism by a number of officials who were sympathetic to the migrants. Such criticism was levelled at the very existence of the indenture system, the legal loopholes and abuses of the system, or the 'quality and character' of the migrants. During the period of indenture, the quality of labour relations remained virtually unchanged, yet amelioration was noticeable in the social and medical conditions of the workers. However, not only external forces but the labourers themselves protested existing conditions. The responses of the indentured to the system were multifaceted and ranged from resignation to open and violent resistance, and from defeatism to entrepreneurism.

SETTLEMENT

In the last decade of the 19th century, the Surinam government accepted that the Indians had come to stay and even actively promoted their permanent settlement. In the 1890s, the government offered plots of land to labourers who had fulfilled their contractual obligations, and if they renounced their right to a free return passage, they received Dfl. 100. Between 1878 and 1920, 33.9 per cent (11,623) of the Indian migrants were repatriated: 62 per cent of the repatriated migrants were men, 20 per cent women, and the rest were children. The return rates in British Guiana and Trinidad were 32 per cent and 22 per cent respectively. Thus, a majority of the Indian migrants chose to settle permanently in Surinam.

After indenture, most Indians became smallholders in districts outside the capital. Smallholdings rapidly gained importance: in 1900, 90 per cent of Surinam's produce came from the plantations, but 40 years later 90 per cent was produced by smallholders. In 1903, 2000 Indians owned or leased 14,000 hectares of land; less than 10 years later, both these figures had doubled. The smallholders produced rice, vegetables, meat, milk and fruit.

In 1923, Hindustanis made up 23 per cent of the colonial population, and in 1939 this figure had risen to 29 per cent. One-tenth of the Indians lived in Paramaribo, comprising about 8 per cent of the town's total population, but the great majority settled in the coastal districts of Nickerie and Saramacca. This geographical concentration led to social and cultural isolation once again, but also made it easier to maintain traditions.

World War II brought about great socio-economic changes in Surinam as the economic base of the country shifted from agriculture to bauxite. The expansion of the bauxite industry, the growing mechanisation of

agriculture and new employment opportunities in the service and construction sectors led to urbanisation and Westernisation. Paramaribo used to be an Afro-Surinamese city dominating an 'Asian' countryside, but the ethnic composition of the capital gradually changed as increasing numbers of Hindustanis and Javanese migrated to the city in search of work or education. In 1964, more than a quarter of Paramaribo's population was of Indian descent.

In the districts, agricultural producers profited from rising prices. Indians became increasingly involved in all economic sectors, including trade and commerce, construction, transport, industry and the public service sector. Consequently, the emergent socio-economic differentiation within the Hindustani group became more pronounced, and after the war, a middle class and a wealthy Indian elite that cooperated economically with other ethnic groups arose. This elite also included individuals who had profited from the expansion of large-scale agriculture, which promoted the mechanised production of rice in particular.

By the 1970s, the Hindustanis had closed the gap in education and economic development compared to the Afro-Surinamese population, but had not overtaken this group. In recent years, it has seemed more appropriate to consider the economic differences within a population group rather than between ethnic groups. Among Hindustanis, the gap between the wealthy and the poor is greater than in any other ethnic group.

Urbanisation, Westernisation and the shift of the economic base away from small agricultural holdings also undermined the existing joint family system that structured the relations between husband and wife, and mother-in-law and daughter-in-law. Demographically, the high fertility rate led to an absolute and relative growth of the Hindustani population. Between 1930 and 1950 this rate hovered between 45 and 50 per thousand. After 1965, a gradual decline in the fertility rate set in. In 1965, Hindustanis became the largest ethnic group in Surinam. The Indian share of the total population continued to grow until the 1970s. Since that time, the number of Hindustanis has stabilised at 37 per cent. In 2004, about 136,000 people of Indian descent lived in Surinam, with a third of them residing in greater Paramaribo.

Migration and indenture had an acute impact on the social and cultural life of the migrants, especially initially. The new conditions in Surinam led to cultural renewal and adaptation on the one hand and isolation and cultural conservatism on the other. The migrants had to adjust to a new environment, a situation made more difficult by the unequal sex ratio and relative youth of most migrants, which disrupted the formation of traditional social and cultural structures. The initial scarcity of women led to conflict, and there were few experienced elderly migrants to guide the younger generation towards common traditions and values. Furthermore, contact with other population groups, however limited, led to hybridisation or creolisation.

The special legal position of migrants during indenture, their sense of displacement, social marginalisation, low standard of living, geographical isolation, ethnic distinctiveness, and their limited interaction with other population groups encouraged them to recreate, as far as possible, their own little 'India' as a means of holding on to their social and cultural practices. Criticisms of their customs voiced by the Europeans and Afro-Surinamese,

A 1933 postcard shows Indian girls living in a charitable missionary home in Surinam. The caption at the back reads 'We little girls warmly thank our benefactors in the Netherlands.'

Indian barbers were a common sight on the streets of Paramaribo in the early 20th century.

Matrons take charge of the children of Indian labourers at a plantation in Surinam.

and the influx of newcomers with more current information about India, reinforced this tendency.

Most migrants originated from northern India, yet there was no clear majority from any particular district. For this reason, there existed great variations in social, cultural and religious backgrounds. Yet these sociocultural differences do not seem to have had a significant impact on the life of migrants in Surinam: several cultural traditions merged into a single 'Indian' one, which strengthened the ethnic identity of the Hindustani population. Consequently, cultural traditions practised by Indians in Surinam may not exist in India itself. The Hindustanis have, however, to the present day, relied on pre-migration traditions. In addition, the social and geographical isolation of the migrants compelled the newcomers to bridge previously existing cultural and religious divides.

SARNAMI

Possibly the clearest example of this process is the development of what was later called the Sarnami language. The Indian migrants spoke a number of different but closely related languages. During recruitment and transportation to Surinam, the migrants communicated in a new language based on the merger of languages and dialects of central-northern India. Sarnami is a mixture of several Indian languages but is not identical to any Indian language. Moreover, Sarnami adopted words from the Dutch language and especially Sranan Tongo, the lingua franca of Surinam. In Surinam, Hindi became the language of prestige for Hindus, while Urdu holds that position for Muslims.

The development and use of Sarnami is unique in the Caribbean. Elsewhere, migrants soon dropped their Indic languages. A reason for this unusual development might be the different educational and cultural policies pursued by the Dutch and British colonial governments. In the British colonies, the superiority of the English civilisation and language was emphasised; in Surinam, the government conducted no consistent cultural and educational policy for decades, and during certain periods even encouraged instruction in Indic languages.

Post-war urbanisation, education and assimilation diminished the use of Sarnami in favour of Dutch, but this changed in the late 1950s and 1960s when, as a reaction to Afro-Surinamese cultural nationalist movements promoting Sranan Tongo, Sarnami once again became the language of choice for many Hindustanis, at least at home. There has also been a tendency to 'Hindinise' Sarnami words. Since Hindi is valued more than Sarnami, which is sometimes considered a Hindi 'dialect', Hindi schools have grown in popularity. Hindi or Urdu is also the language used in religious matters, while Dutch is the medium of instruction in schools subsidised by the government. Consequently, Sarnami is largely used at home, in the political arena or during cultural festivals. In 1992, 60 per cent of Hindustanis spoke Sarnami at home. Since the 1950s, Sarnami poetry has been published in Surinam, India and the Netherlands. Short stories and novels have also been published in Sarnami.

RELIGION

Similar processes of adaptation and the creation of a unique Indian identity can be found in religious practices. These practices played an important role in the lives of most immigrants since they reinforced cultural and ethnic ties. The two main religious groups among the

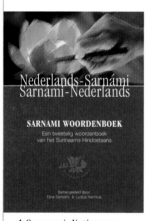

A Sarnami dictionary by Eline Santokhi and Lydius Nienhuis.

British Indians in Surinam were the Hindus and Muslims (20 per cent of the migrants).

Caribbean Hindu traditions are the product of decades of inadvertent as well as deliberate transformations. Out of a profusion of religious traditions, a homogeneous Caribbean Hindu religion was forged. Probably the most decisive socio-religious factor in the growth of a unitary religion was the demise of the caste system. Migration and plantation life led to the breakdown of the caste system, even though the shadow of caste remained. The castes gave up their individuality to form a new kind of national Indian caste which was closed to other population groups. The sense of sharing a common fate proved to be a stronger bond than segregation based on caste distinctions. Yet, culturally, some notion of caste persisted. This was the case of Brahmins, who retained their special status, though it differed slightly from India. Some even managed to strengthen their position in Surinam from the start. Originally, *karam kandis* (ritual experts), Brahmins or pandits often monopolised not only ritual expertise but also sacred religious knowledge. In India, the latter had been the exclusive domain of the gurus, who were absent in Surinam. The pandits were instrumental in preserving and promoting traditional religious and cultural knowledge. The gradual adoption of only one repertoire of rites for all ritual occasions characterises this process of 'Brahminisation'.

In the 19th century, the organisational development of Brahminised Hinduism was modest. Practices throughout the Caribbean were not standardised even though there did possibly exist some sort of regular contact between Brahmin priests in Surinam, British Guiana and Trinidad. In the 1920s and 1930s, however, the attack by the reformist Arya Samaj on the position of the Brahmins strengthened the organisation of Brahminic Hinduism.

The Arya Samaj, a reformist sect founded in 1875, considered the Vedas the only source of knowledge and rejected polytheism, idolatry, the veil, widow burning, infant marriages and also the supremacy of the Brahmins. Arya Samaj missionaries from India travelled to the Caribbean to call for a return to the Vedas and for the glorification of Vedic traditions. These missionaries preached that any man could become a Brahmin on the basis of learning and correct behaviour. By way of British Guiana, the first Arya Samaj representative reached Surinam in 1912.

The religious and social reformism of the Arya Samaj was coupled with nationalism as it stressed the significance of Indian heritage and ethnicity. By repudiating Christianity and Christian education, the movement also initiated a cultural renaissance for the Hindus. The new lives of Indians in Surinam explained the appeal of the progressive Arya Samaj movement. Individualism had become more predominant, even in religion. The Arya Samaj found many followers among the Hindus born in Surinam. The leaders of the Surinaamsche Immigranten Vereeniging (Surinam Immigrants' Association, or SIV) were often linked to the movement.

The effect of the Arya Samaj was, however, contrary to its goals. Despite its many converts, it strengthened the Brahminisation of Caribbean Hinduism. In British Guiana, Trinidad and Surinam, the role of the Brahmins was institutionalised in the late 1920s and early 1930s. The national Hindu association in Surinam was named the Sanatan Dharm (Eternal Religion). Founded in 1929, it was to act as the official authority on doctrine and ritual, and fight the Arya Samaj. The Sanatan Dharm attracted the largest following and is considered the most authoritative voice of the Surinamese Hindus. In the 1990s, about 27 per cent of the Surinamese were Hindus.

The socio-religious transformations brought about by migration reduced the number of religious celebrations and rites practised. However, life-cycle rites observing birth, marriage and death were maintained. Important religious festivals were, likewise, still observed. The two most important and most popular festivals are Holi (or Phagwa) and Diwali; Holi has been a national holiday since 1970. In the post-war era, Indian *bhakti* (devotional) films on the Puranas, religious programmes on Hindu radio stations and, later, television programmes on the Ramayana and Mahabharata, greatly influenced the religious experience of Hindus, and Sanatans in particular.

The first Muslims in Surinam came from Punjab. The Hanafi *shariah* (law) of the Indian Muslims oriented them towards their home country. Their mosques pointed to the East, and their literature and ritual language was based on Urdu. The Javanese Muslims in Surinam, on the other hand, adhered to the Shafi *shariah*, used Arabic and built their mosques facing Mecca (as in Java), thus westward. Other tensions also separated the Indian from the Javanese Muslims. In the 1930s, the Ahmadiyya reform movement reached Surinam via Trinidad. This modernist movement started in India around 1880 and was based on a reinterpretation of the Quran to adapt Islam to modern life. The new doctrine heavily influenced the Surinam Islamic Association, the oldest Muslim organisation, founded in 1919. The orthodox camp disputed the reformist views and thus further split the Muslims into different sections.

The most popular and spectacular festival of the Indian Muslims in Surinam is Muharram. Everywhere in the Caribbean, festivals acquired a secular character and underwent a process of creolisation through the participation of non-Muslims. Id-al-Fitr was made a national holiday in 1970. In the 1990s, approximately one-fifth of the Surinamese were Muslim.

Muslims and Hindus were targets for Christian missionaries, who gradually wanted to integrate Asians into the Christian Surinamese community while still respecting their customs and practices. Conversion and education in missionary schools were the first steps on this road to Westernisation. However, conversion to Christianity seldom occurred because of the intimate connection between religion and nationalism, and the cultural strength of Hinduism and Islam. Over the years, the resistance of the Indians to Christian conversion grew with the increase in their numbers. The government's policy of using Christianity as one of the main pillars of its assimilation policy in Surinam came under great pressure following the large influx of Asian immigrants and was finally abandoned in the 1930s.

ASSIMILATION

The administration in Paramaribo did not have a clear idea as to whether Asian immigrants should be treated as temporary or permanent residents. As a result, policies vacillated between attempts to integrate the newcomers fully and the implementation of different rules and laws for the Asian population.

The introduction of compulsory education in Dutch in 1876 was an important facet of the assimilation policy. This law was applied to Indian children two years later. The education of Asian children in Surinam was closely linked to the evolution of the indenture system. Some authorities thought that the colony had a moral obligation to provide some form of primary education for the children of Indian immigrants. In addition, they hoped that such efforts would impress the British government and thus induce it to grant more favourable immigration conditions. In Surinam, the education of immigrant children was a government concern, whereas in British Guiana, this task was left to missionaries.

In 1890, the first so-called coolie school was opened. An Indian teacher instructed the pupils in at least Hindi and Urdu. This was largely due to the belief that these children would only remain in Surinam for five years and knowledge of the Dutch language would be useless if they were repatriated to India. The children would learn to read, write and do some simple arithmetic. Unlike the situation in the Anglophone Caribbean colonies, the administration in Paramaribo did not initially impose Dutch and Christian values upon migrant children.

In 1907, the government abolished the coolie schools in order to promote the integration of Asian children into

A Hindu wedding in Surinam, 1965.

A Muslim mosque situated next to a Jewish synagogue in Paramaribo.

tion difficult for Hindustanis living in non-urban areas. The number of female students also increased during this period. From the late 1950s, Hindustani students also went to the Netherlands to get an education. Since the 1990s, there has been a marked increase in the number of Hindustani students, particularly women, attending colleges and university. In the 1960s, religious organisations, including Sanatan Dharm, the Surinamese Muslim Organisation and Arya Dewaker founded government-subsidised schools, as well as Hindi and Urdu schools in and outside Paramaribo. Another step in this process of assimilation was the law of 1927 that made all Indians born in Surinam Dutch subjects.

However, during the administration of Governor John C. Kielstra (1933–44), the emphasis was no longer on assimilation but on ethnic diversity. The so-called marriage laws marked the definitive break in the assimilation policy. The great majority of immigrants did not have a civil marriage and their religious unions did not have any legal validity. One of the consequences was that children of an 'illegal union' could not inherit their parents' property if the latter had not made a will. In 1913, the SIV requested the legal recognition of marriages solemnised by acknowledged pandits or *pengulus*. The association noted that most Indians favoured marriages conducted according to the customs and rites of their nation and religion. Yet it was only in 1937 that Governor Kielstra proposed to legalise marriages which had been solemnised according to Islam or Hinduism. This draft bill ran into strong political opposition as Afro-Surinamese feared the dissolution of Surinamese society into different cultural and ethnic communities. Nevertheless, the Asiatic marriage decrees came into effect in 1941, but were revoked in the 1970s.

Surinam society and to instil the values of the colonisers, since so many Asians remained beyond five years in the colony. Accordingly, Indian teachers (largely unqualified) would teach Hindi in addition to education in Dutch, the language of social mobility. A year later, the Surinam Teachers' Association opposed the existing educational system and pleaded for Dutch-style education in integrated schools in order to Westernise Asian settlers. It warned against establishing 'colonies within the colony'. The SIV, however, pressed for continued education in Hindi language and culture, but lost the argument when the administration abolished the institution of the Hindi teacher in 1929. Despite the high rate of absenteeism, especially among girls, integrated schools played an important role in the assimilation of children after the abolition of the coolie schools.

The number of Hindustani students at secondary schools and teacher-training schools remained relatively low until the 1970s, when the percentage of graduates was almost equal to the percentage of Hindustanis in Surinam's total population. This may partly be explained by the concentration of educational institutions in the capital, which made attaining secondary or higher educa-

According to the ordinance of 1907 relating to the marriage of Asians, the minimum age for an Asian groom was 15 years, while the bride could be no younger than 13. The minimum ages for non-Asians were 18 and 15 years respectively. Immigrants who were already married upon arrival were immediately registered at the office of the agent general. Most of the registered marriages between immigrants were recorded upon arrival, and not many legal weddings among immigrants took place in Surinam. Interracial marriages were a rarity. Among both Hindus and Muslims, parents often arranged marriages. After the war, urbanisation, Westernisation and better education also changed marriage patterns. The average age of marriage went up; until the 1950s, the majority of brides were below the age of 17. Choosing one's own partner became more and more accepted, especially in Paramaribo, even though there existed strong social pressure to marry a person from the same ethnic and religious group.

The immigrants themselves undermined assimilation by organising themselves into unions to promote their ethnic interests and to become more politically active. The first decades of immigration saw little coordinated action among the Indian labourers. This changed in the 20th century, when migrants started to organise themselves to defend the immediate interests of their own ethnic group. A lack of radicalism characterised the dozens of unions founded during this period.

The largest and most important association, the SIV, was founded in 1910. Its goal was to promote the moral, intellectual and material interests of the Indian population in Surinam. Much of the rest of its energy was spent promoting immigration from India after the abolition of

Jagernath Lachmon (1916–2001)

Jagernath Lachmon was the foremost politician of Indian descent in Surinam and a paragon of Indian emancipation. He was born in the district of Nickerie in western Surinam, which was largely settled and developed by Indian smallholders. Both his parents were indentured immigrants from Uttar Pradesh. Lachmon was one of the first Indians in the colony to practise law. He entered politics in the 1940s, and the founding of the Hindustani-Javanese Political Party (HJPP) took place in his office in 1947. He soon became its chairman, and two years later the HJPP merged with several other parties to form the United Indian Party (VHP). Lachmon was elected chairman and held this position until his death. The VHP and Lachmon soon became prominent players in the political arena. Lachmon and his Afro-Surinamese counterpart, J. A. Pengel, forged a political alliance in the name of *verbroedering*, or ethnic fraternisation. They shared power from

Lachmon was a prominent politician and lawyer.

1958 to 1967. To Pengel, fraternisation meant gradual integration, while to Lachmon it meant unity through non-assimilation, or unity in diversity. Not surprisingly then, Lachmon was one of the most vocal opponents of Surinam's independence, emphasising the importance of the mediating role of the Netherlands in the multi-ethnic society. However, Surinam became independent in 1975 under the leadership of his Afro-Surinamese opponent, H. A. E. Arron. Subsequently, political and socio-economic developments deteriorated. Following military dictatorship (1980–87), Lachmon's VHP forged an alliance with Javanese and Afro-Surinamese parties and quickly regained power. Lachmon was elected as leader of the parliament, an office he would hold for many years.

Lachmon died in The Hague, the Netherlands, during a working visit in 2001. He was the longest serving parliamentarian in the world.

indenture there, and on persuading Indians planning to repatriate to remain in Surinam. In 1922, the membership made the significant move of changing the association's name to Bharat Uday (The Rise of Hindustan) to express the growing ethnic consciousness of the Indians. They rejected the term 'immigrant' with its connotation of being an 'outsider'. The literature, often published by the Arya Samaj movement, came mostly from South Africa and was nationalist, anti-European and anti-Christian in tone. The political awareness of its members was deliberately not fostered. Despite the South African propaganda having an anti-European character, relations with the colonial government were good. The most important goals of the organisation were the promotion of communal interests and the forging of a Hindustani ethnic identity. To achieve this, the preferred strategy called for cooperation, and not confrontation, with colonial authorities. Only during the period of change after World War II did Asian groups gain real power in Surinam's political arena.

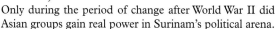

POLITICAL CHANGE

The Dutch queen promised the colonies in the East and the West autonomy during the war. In Surinam, several movements for autonomy, particularly among Afro-Surinamese, soon blossomed. Indian parties in the early period were the Surinaamse Hindoe Partij (Surinamese Hindu Party), the Moeslim Partij (Muslim Party) and the Hindostaans-Javaanse Politieke Partij (Hindustani-Javanese Political Party, or the HJPP), which was dominated by Hindustanis. In 1948, universal suffrage was introduced in the colony despite the opposition of the Muslim Party. In anticipation of the first general elections in 1949, three Hindustani parties, including the HJPP, founded the VHP, which first stood for Verenigde Hindostaanse Partij (United Hindustani Party) and later Vooruitstrevende Hervormingspartij (Progressive Reform Party). Despite the latter name, political parties, and politics in general, were based on ethnicity rather than political ideology. The VHP and its leader, Jagernath Lachmon, quickly gained importance in Surinamese politics.

The period 1958–67 was characterised by political stability, economic progress and ethnic cooperation at the government level. The cooperation between the Hindustanis and Afro-Surinamese was termed 'fraternisa-

Women participating in a Hindu ceremony at the Shri Shiv Mandir in Paramaribo.

tion', which for the Hindustanis meant not integration, but the emancipation of their own ethnic group in a plural society, or, as it was also called, 'unity in diversity'. The VHP's policy and the leadership of Lachmon were challenged by a group of young Hindustani intellectuals, the so-called Actie Groep (Action Group), who feared that fraternisation would lead to dominance by the Afro-Surinamese population.

Lachmon's VHP was the most vocal opponent of Afro-Surinamese plans for Surinam's independence. They considered it a ploy for Afro-Surinamese dominance and called for the Netherlands to continue its role as a 'neutral mediator' in multi-ethnic Surinam. Yet, the Afro-Surinamese political leadership and the Netherlands went ahead with their plans for independence. Once the date was set, there were widespread fears of ethnic violence. This panic caused more than 100,000 Surinamese, the majority of whom were Hindustani, to migrate to the Netherlands.

Hindu women by the Corantijn river offer flowers as part of their ritual prayers in Nickerie.

After independence in 1975, political and socio-economic conditions deteriorated, ultimately leading to a military takeover in 1980. When the military went back to the barracks in 1987, the VHP joined with Javanese and Afro-Surinamese parties to win the elections. Yet, internal disagreements and Lachmon's autocratic style continued to evoke opposition, leading to the formation of splinter movements and parties such as the Basispartij voor Vernieuwing en Democratie (Basic Party for Renewal and Democracy, or BVD), thus weakening the dominant position of the VHP. However, most Hindustanis continue to vote along ethnic lines for one of the Hindustani parties.

Ethnic identity was a key factor in determining the migrants' position in society. Ethnicity in Surinam has definite socio-economic, cultural and political dimensions, and ethnic networks provide access to resources. Ethnicity is the basis of groups that defend the interests of its members. This includes political parties that are of great importance in the allocation of government jobs. Many cultural organisations, including radio and television stations, are also founded on the basis of ethnicity. Moreover, ethnicity plays a leading role in the private sphere—at home, in the choice of partners and friends, and in religion, language, housing and clothing.

The question for Surinam is whether the country will evolve into a unitary multicultural state or disintegrate along ethnic lines. Is creolisation or Surinamisation a process of contention, strengthening ethnic diversity based on culture, rather than a process of inclusion and integration, leading to ethnic and cultural homogenisation? This development will be influenced by external forces such as cultural globalisation and transnationalism. India looms large in the background: family contacts with India are limited, yet the Indian embassy actively promotes 'pure' Indian culture. The mass media—Internet, DVDs and videos—bring the most recent Bollywood films and the latest news from India to Surinam. The role of the transnational communities, particularly in the Netherlands and ancestral countries will affect developments in Surinam.

Rosemarijn Hoefte

JAMAICA

THE ABOLITION OF chattel slaves in the Caribbean between 1794 and 1886 led to a new mobility among the freed people, which caused landholders to complain increasingly that they had a 'labour problem' and needed workers brought in. Most of the migrants imported to Jamaica were Asians, especially Indians, contracted under the system of indenture. Historically, the two most prevalent types of labour systems in the Caribbean involving exploited labourers were slavery and indenture. These systems shared the common characteristics of involving coerced labour and being expressions of social dishonour and humiliation. The differences were equally evident for, unlike the indentured worker, the enslaved were defined as chattels, whose lives and working hours were owned by others.

HISTORICAL ORIGINS

Between 1845 and 1945, approximately 38,000 Indians went to Jamaica through Indian labour migration. The first batch of 261 immigrants arrived in 1845 on the *Blundell Hunter*. Table 8.27 provides an idea of the quantitative dimensions of the labour trade and places Jamaica's import figures in a regional perspective.

Jamaica never developed a large, densely settled Indian community because irregular importation and repatriation (perhaps also combined with a low fertility rate initially and a high mortality rate) kept the population small and scattered. The Indian population in Jamaica in 1911 stood at only 17,380.

Indian immigration to Jamaica was meant to provide landholders with labourers who would return to India upon the expiration of their contracts. By the 1880s, however, Indian immigration had developed into a form of settler colonisation as fewer and fewer indentured workers returned. Voluntary return via the state repatriation scheme, along with involuntary settlement as a result of

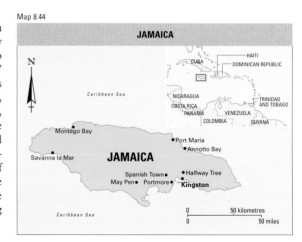

Map 8.44

coercion on the part of the planters, and lack of finances when state-assisted repatriation was discontinued in 1930, resulted in close to 62 per cent of the Indian immigrants settling permanently in Jamaica. The last return ship sponsored by the government in Jamaica was the SS *Sutlej*, which repatriated 425 Indians in 1929.

THE MIGRATION

Indians came to the Caribbean for various reasons. Some left to escape economic distress, others in the hope of earning higher wages or to escape debts, and many because they had lost their land due to unfavourable British land policies in India. A number were also affected by industrialisation, which had destroyed cottage industries such as cloth-making. Women emigrated to escape marital or domestic problems and to seek an independent life. For some, emigration was an adventure.

The main recruiting areas in the late 19th century were the North-Western Provinces and the United Provinces of Agra and Oudh, Bihar, Orissa and Rajputana. The districts of recruitment included Faizabad, Lucknow, Gonda, Basti, Sultanpur, Allahabad, Sitapur, Benares, Gorakhpur and many others. Indians also came from Nepal, Central India and Punjab.

On the ships, single women were placed in the aft, followed by married people, with the single men in front. Attempts were made to ensure that the ships had adequate crew, medical personnel, sweepers (*topazes*) and cooks to look after the welfare of the migrants. In the early years of Indian emigration, the *topazes* were black people. By the 20th century, they had been replaced by Indian *topazes* because of racial tensions between black *topazes* and Indians. Surgeon Superintendent Comins noted, 'I found the West Indian Topazes very useless, indolent and subordinate,' and that 'the prejudices and dislike of East and West Indians to each other, offer a great bar to their acting well together on board ship.'

Interaction between the crew and migrants was forbidden, though not strictly enforced. There were complaints that some of the white crew sexually abused

Table 8.27

NUMBER OF INDIANS IMPORTED TO THE CARIBBEAN (1838–1917)		
	Period	No. of Indians
British Guiana	1838–1917	238,909
Trinidad	1845–1917	143,939
Surinam	1873–1918	34,024
Guadeloupe	1854–87	42,595
Jamaica	1845–1916	38,681
Martinique	1848–84	25,509
St. Lucia	1858–95	4354
Grenada	1856–85	3200
St. Vincent	1860–80	2472
St. Kitts	1860–61	337
French Guiana	1853–85	19,296

Sources: K.O. Laurence, Immigration into the West Indies, *1971; G. Eisner,* Jamaica 1830–1930, *1961; C. Seecharan,* Tiger in the Stars, *1997; and V. Shepherd,* Transients to Settlers, *1994.*

female migrants. Attempts were made to make the journey bearable by paying attention to the migrants' medical care, accommodation and entertainment; musical instruments were allowed on board.

In the 19th century, comparatively slow sailing ships were used to transport Indian migrants to the Caribbean. The route took them across the Indian Ocean, around the Cape of Good Hope and into the Atlantic, entering the Caribbean from the south. The journey on sailing ships could take up to three months, while steamships could make the voyage in one or two months. The *Humber* took a record 163 days to reach Jamaica from Calcutta in 1872, and the barque *Silhet* took 96 days in 1878. By contrast, the steamship *Indus* left Calcutta on 27 November 1912 and arrived in Jamaica, via Trinidad, on 12 January 1913, a journey of only about one and a half months.

Up to the early 1870s, the mortality rate onboard was at times above 17 per cent. A statistical survey of voyages from India to the British Caribbean between 1858 and 1873 revealed a crude average of 17.8 per cent over the entire period, ranging from a high of 52.5 per cent in 1865 (14 voyages) to 5 per cent in 1870 (17 voyages). By the first decade of the 20th century, when steamships owned by Messrs Nourse Ltd were being used, both the length of the journey and the mortality rate onboard the ships were reduced. By the 1890s in fact, the mortality rate for Jamaica ranged from 1 per cent to 4 per cent, but was rarely over 3 per cent.

CONDITIONS UNDER INDENTURE

Life was regimented and harsh for the majority of those under indenture, who often found themselves exploited. Indentured Indians were located on sugar plantations initially, but were later also employed for other types of agricultural production. In 1911, 47 per cent of Indian agricultural labourers were located on banana plantations, compared to 39 per cent on sugar plantations. A few of the livestock farms, called 'pens' in Jamaica, also employed Indian labourers, though not more than 2 per cent in 1911. By the 1850s, three-year contracts with the first employer were the norm, and by 1862 five-year contracts took over. The labourer could choose to buy himself out of the contractual obligations, but few were financially able to do so. Indeed, a weak economic base often forced some of those whose contracts had expired to re-indenture. They would sign a new five-year contract with the same employer or a different one.

Under indenture, Indian men, women and children engaged in day labour or task labour, earning wages ranging from 4 pence to 1 shilling 6 pence a day or per task. Male labourers of 16 years and over were paid 1 shilling 6 pence per day, women and children of 12–16 years were

paid 9 pence, and children under 12 years of age received 4 pence. Like enslaved Africans, they worked mostly in gangs, supervised by African or Indian headmen, and both tasks and wages were gender discriminatory. In all cases, men earned a higher wage than women and children. Men were also more likely to get skilled and supervisory positions, which paid more.

The Immigration Ordinances and Law of 1870 stipulated that all wages had to be paid in cash rather than in kind, and that employers could not make any deductions, except for rations. Failure to adhere to the law could result in the employer being fined a sum not exceeding £5. Even so, regulations were flouted regularly. There is also evidence that workers did not always receive the minimum wage. In 1909, Ramadhin of the Bog Estate in Jamaica wrote to the Protector of Immigrants, complaining, 'I send to make you know that I can't even make 3/-per week. Then how must we live dear sir?' He warned that an investigation must be undertaken and improvements made, otherwise, 'it will bring some great trouble.'

The social and living conditions of indentured labourers also left much to be desired and improved only gradually between 1845 and 1921. While some lived in detached huts, many others were housed on the estates in barracks—long buildings divided into rooms of 11 sq m each, with a covered verandah 1.5 m wide. The buildings had dirt floors and clothes rations were minimal. The immigration law stipulated that employers should provide each male with a shirt and trousers of Osnaburgh and each female with a jersey with sleeves and a petticoat. Even though there were laws to control the health of Indian migrants, poor conditions kept the death rate high. The major causes of death were malaria and ulcers; many also suffered from hookworm. Public hospitals in rural and urban areas, built to replace the old estate hospitals, alleviated the situation somewhat.

Indian men and women were subject to the abusive control of estate managers and efforts to control their mobility, but they did not accept infringements of the immigration laws meekly. They resented the almost total control which employers had over them: the stringent pass law system; the criminalisation of breaches of what should have been a civil contract between two equal parties; the late payment of wages; sexual and physical abuse; and inadequate provisions for their welfare. Consequently, they adopted various strategies to register their

A typical Indian village showing the distribution of homes in which some migrants lived. At the end of their contracts, many Indians opted for land grants instead of return passage to India.

Indians ploughing the field to prepare for the planting of crops, a way of supplementing their income.

Table 8.28

NUMBER OF INDIANS IMPORTED TO JAMAICA (1896–1916)	
1896–98	N.A.
1899	648
1900	N.A.
1901	N.A.
1902	N.A.
1903	662
1904	N.A.
1905	800
1906	799
1907	589
1908	408
1909	1106
1910	N.A.
1911	796
1912	1922
1913	287
1914	N.A.
1915	348 (includes three months of 1916)
1916	250
1917	N.A.

Source: C.O. 871/5, 'Minute Paper 9760', 22 February 1917.

An Indian woman and her child on a plantation in Jamaica. The 1870 immigration law required that employers provide every female immigrant with a jersey with sleeves.

disaffection. These included undermining production on the plantation through strikes and demonstrations, deserting the estates, feigning illness, buying themselves out of their contracts, and committing suicide. Eighteen strikes were recorded in Jamaica between 1847 and 1921, one of which occurred in 1907 on the Moreland Estate in St. James as a result of employers illegally deducting money from workers' wages. At times, the labourers took their employers to court, but it was unlikely that the employers would be convicted. Between 1903 and 1910, only one employer in Jamaica was fined—£3 for assaulting an Indian worker.

There may not have been a direct correlation between the abuses of the indenture system and the cessation of labour migration to Jamaica in 1916, but such abuses were relevant to the anti-emigration/immigration discourses of the early 20th century, which, combined with high shipping costs and the opposition of nationalistic elements in India, eventually led to the discontinuation of Indian immigration schemes to all Caribbean territories by 1917.

LAND ACQUISITION, PEASANTRY AND THE MOVE OUT OF ESTATE WAGE AGRICULTURE

The descendants of formerly indentured Indians have experienced dramatic changes in their socio-economic position. Derek Gordon's analysis of the 1943 and 1984 census data found that while only 4 per cent of Indians were among the middle class in 1943, with almost two-thirds of their population being agricultural wage workers, by the 1980s, 47 per cent could be classified so. Clearly, the Indian segment of the Jamaican population has shown economic gains. The first factor that assisted the upward social mobility of Indian settlers in Jamaica was access to land. Many employers believed that the repatriation provision defeated their attempts to transform Indian immigration into a form of settler colonisation, and so they pressed for land grants in lieu of repatriation. Indians were given the choice of accepting 4 hectares of Crown land or £12 in cash instead of a return passage. Up to 1879, most migrants accepted the cash. Between 1845 and 1848, 1467 accepted land or cash instead of the return passage. The choice of a cash grant was removed in 1879, followed by the removal of the land grant in 1906, because the cost of the land grant, at £12 per head, was becoming just as expensive as the cost of the return passage, £15 per head. By 1895, those who were not sick or disabled were asked to pay a part of the cost of the return passage, which was more than most Indians could afford.

However, much of the land which was granted was too mountainous and arid to be cultivated, and was abandoned; but some of the land provided rural folk with

a base, allowing them to either move out of the plantation labour force altogether, or supplement plantation wages with their own farming of sugar cane, vegetables, rice and other food crops. A few became substantial landowners, even buying entire sugar estates, such as the 596-hectare Dover sugar estate in St. Mary. By 1943, Indians made up 1.4 per cent of the total population of Jamaica and they owned 28 per cent of the land over 4 hectares.

Still, up to the 1940s, the majority of Indians in Jamaica remained agricultural workers. The 1943 census showed that 56 per cent of the female agricultural labour force was Indian, compared to 28 per cent black, 13 per cent of mixed race or 'coloured', 1 per cent Chinese and 1 per cent Lebanese.

COMMERCE

While agriculture was the dominant occupation of rural Indians up to the mid 20th century, an increasing number were engaged in non-agricultural activities. In fact, 14 per cent of those deemed 'productive' in 1921 were engaged in non-agricultural pursuits, specifically the retail trade. Indeed, rural Indians were the main shopkeepers until the Chinese later came to dominate the retail trade. In 1891, several of the ex-indentured Indians were already business people, sales clerks, bankers and jewellers. An index of participation in the retail trade is provided by the number of spirit and petroleum licences granted, a figure which increased steadily from 1872. In that year, 18 licences were granted to Indian men in three parishes alone.

EDUCATION AND PROFESSIONAL OCCUPATIONS

When immigration first started, employers showed very little interest in educating workers or their children. Gradually, estate schools were established in British Guiana, Trinidad and Tobago, and Jamaica. Later, the Quakers and Presbyterians opened schools for the Indians. Jamaica experimented with special Indian schools from 1916 to 1930, but schooling eventually became integrated. As educational opportunities were seized, some Indians entered the industrial and professional fields. However, in 1943, 49 per cent of the Indian population were still recorded as 'illiterate'.

Today, the increase in educational opportunities and levels has resulted in an increase in Indian-Jamaicans—commonly referred to as Indo-Jamaicans—who are skilled workers, business people and professionals (e.g. lawyers, medical doctors, nurses, engineers and educators). Among them, Ivan Parboosingh, G. V. Harry and Haihar Pershadsingh were three of the earliest Indian-Jamaicans to become medical doctors in the 1930s and 1940s; Harold Ballysingh became a Crown prosecutor; Raam Pershadsingh, a lawyer; the late Samuel Carter, an archbishop; Beryl Wiliamsingh was a chief personnel officer in the Services Commission; and Mahadev Dukharan, a judge. Others are justices of the peace, notaries public and university lecturers.

RURAL TO URBAN MIGRATION

Urban settlement, especially in Kingston and St. Andrew, became significant by the mid-20th century. By 1943, according to the population census, 1279 Indians resided in Kingston and 2769 in St. Andrew. This represented only 3 per cent of the total population of Kingston and St. Andrew, which was predominantly black, and 19 per cent of the total Indian/Indian-Jamaican population on the island. Currently, approximately 40 per cent of the

Pictured here is New Market in Elizabeth, probably one of the most ethnically diverse parts of the island.

Indian population live in Kingston and St. Andrew, and about 15 per cent in Spanish Town, Portmore and other urban and peri-urban areas.

In 1891, several ex-indentured Indians were already business people, teachers, bankers and jewellers. Indians who migrated to Kingston and St. Andrew also bought land: Dhanukddhari Tewari bought the 26-hectare Kingston Pen (now Tivoli Gardens) in the 1920s. The chief contributions that urban Indians made to Kingston and St. Andrew were in the areas of floriculture and market gardening. Others, for example in the Mona and Papine areas, grew tobacco and reared cattle. In urban areas, women found employment as domestic/household workers: 5 per cent of the Indian population were said to be in this field in 1921.

SOCIAL AND CULTURAL LIFE

Indian immigrants brought their religious traditions to the Caribbean and further diversified the already rich cultural life of the region. They added to the number of Muslims and Christians in Jamaica and introduced Hinduism and Buddhism. The cultural power exercised by the ruling class threatened to eliminate aspects of Indian culture which the elites found 'strange and barbaric' (e.g. cremation using the pyre system, and religion-, language- and ethnic-specific marriage and divorce practices). The 1943 census indicated that fewer than 20 per cent of the Indian population in Jamaica identified with non-Christian religions. Nevertheless, Indians and Indian-Jamaicans held on to their cultural traditions in the area of cuisine, music, religious customs and festivals (Hussay, Puja, Diwali, Phagwa or Holi, Id, Moulad Shareef, Ramadan, Ram Naumi, Krishna Jayanti and Dussehra). In 1968, the first Hindu organisation, the Sanatan Dharma Mandir (SDM), which is no longer active, was founded. It built a temple on Hagley Park Road in Kingston, which was opened in 1976. An offshoot of the SDM, the Prema Satsangh, was formed in 1973. There is just one aging Hindu pandit to carry on the tradition, but others are invited from overseas to preside over pujas in private homes. The Islamic Society of Jamaica was founded in the early 1950s. Two mosques were built on the island, one in Westmoreland and the other in St. Catherine. The Islamic Council of Jamaica also offers leadership to the Muslim community.

A few members of the older generation and keen younger people still speak Hindi at home, and some women dress in ethnic attire (the sari or *shalwar kurta*) on occasion. The priests who preside over pujas wear the dhoti and kurta when performing religious functions.

Indian cuisine (especially *roti*, dhal, ethnic vegetable dishes and curried dishes) is now popular and there are several Indian restaurants on the island, though in fewer numbers than Chinese restaurants. Indian utensils and food-processing appliances—such as the *dhenki, janta, chakrij, sil batta, tawa, chimta* and *horsa belan*—are not commonly used but still exist.

Arranged marriages and the joint family (or 'yard') system are on the wane, and many marry out of their caste and ethnic group. Thus, there is a fairly large population of mixed Indian-black people. Indian music, musical instruments and dance forms have been preserved, though they have not been uninfluenced by the creolising tendencies of the new society. The tazza drummers of Clarendon, the Raja Sarangi Band and the Indo-Jamaican Cultural Society, formed in 1978 (now operating under

the umbrella National Council for Indian Culture in Jamaica), have contributed to the renaissance of Indian culture since the 1970s. Aspects of this Indian culture can be experienced in August during the Clarendon Hussay festival and the cultural programmes that mark Independence Day celebrations, in keeping with the motto 'Out of Many, One People'.

In terms of sports, Indian-Jamaicans have contributed to the development of cricket and horse-racing in Jamaica. The best known Indian-Jamaican-owned stud farm is that of Henry Jaghai in Bushy Park, St. Catherine.

DEMOGRAPHIC CHANGES AND GENDER RELATIONS

Indian men outnumbered Indian women in the shipments to the Caribbean. By 1855, the usual ratio set by the authorities in India and England was 33 to 100. After 1860, this was increased to 40 to 100. Despite this, Indian women were grossly outnumbered. A survey of the ships which arrived in Jamaica after 1845 reveals that, except in rare cases, the percentage of female Indians shipped to Jamaica ranged from 22 per cent to 30 per cent of the total number of immigrants.

As the recruiters had a hard time filling the required quota of Indian women, they resorted at times to tricking women into migrating. Recruiters were paid more for female than male migrants. In the 19th century, recruiters supplying the British Caribbean territories were paid Rs. 45 for each man and Rs. 55 for each woman recruited. By 1915, as opposition to Indian emigration grew and supply became more scarce, recruiting rates increased to Rs. 60 for men and as high as Rs. 100 for women.

Planters instructed recruiters to obtain married women or young women who were emigrating as part of families. They did not want single women, whom they considered too independent. The minimum age for children to be recruited independently was 16 and the maximum age for men ranged from 30 to 35.

The gender disparity which characterised the migration process up to 1916 was slowly overcome during the period of settlement. The 2500 Indian women in Jamaica in 1871 were 31.5 per cent of the total Indian population of 7793. By 1943, the number of women in the Indian population had risen to about 10,500, which represented 49 per cent of the community. The number continued to

African-Jamaicans often participate alongside Indian-Jamaicans in celebrating the Muslim festival of Hussay. The tabernacles blessed in a religious ceremony would be carried and set adrift in the sea.

Indian jewellers in Jamaica are renowned for their designs and standard of craftsmanship.

rise and, in 1960, there were some 15,000 Indian women. The disparity affected gender relations. There was competition among Indian men for Indian women and incidents of domestic violence against women who asserted their independence occurred. The gender disparity also led to mixed marriages along ethnic, caste and religious lines, which was often frowned on by purists. Today, however, Indian females outnumber Indian males.

MAJOR EVENTS IN THE LIFE OF THE COMMUNITY

There have been several significant episodes in the history of the Indian community in Jamaica: in 1916, indentured labour migration was abolished; in 1921, the indenture system came to an end; between 1930 and 1940, several ethnic organisations emerged to represent the community; and after India's independence in 1947, the High Commission of India was established on the island. This last point gave the Indian community a vital link with India and provided a trigger for the revival of Indian culture in Jamaica. The longest-surviving organisation was the East Indian Progressive Society (EIPS), which celebrated its silver jubilee in 1965.

Of particular note was the achievement of non-quota immigration status to the US. When Jamaica became independent in 1962, the government approached the US about non-quota migration status for Jamaicans. The EIPS kept an eye on the negotiations on behalf of the Indian community because, up to 1962, they were included in the quota for Asians. They wanted to be included as Jamaicans and thus be accorded non-quota status. It was a tough fight, but they won in the end.

The declaration of an annual Indian Heritage Day on 10 May (which also marks Indian Arrival Day) by the government of Jamaica and the establishment of the National Council for Indian Culture in March 1998 were other major achievements.

ENTERING POLITICAL LIFE

The village panchayat, the traditional political institution of Indians, has long disappeared in Jamaica. Yet so long as the Protector of Immigrants and the various Indian organisations represented the Indian community, few among the Indian population participated directly in the political life of the island, except as protestors. The main Indian communal organisations and associations were the East Indian Association of Jamaica (EIAJ, 1930), the East Indian National Union (EINU, 1937) and the EIPS (1940). Still, participation by Indian men in local government and as voters was noted from the late 19th century.

The 1895/96 report of the Protector of Immigrants indicated that an Indian landowner in Trelawny with 1052 hectares had been elected to the Trelawny Parochial Board. Gidhari Singh, a justice of the peace in Clarendon, was a parish council member until his death in the 1980s. In 1920, Ram Rattan Singh, a wealthy landlord, won the election to the Westmoreland Parish Council. Before 1944, the numbers who voted were fairly low. In the fiscal year 1911–12, only 206 (4 per cent) of the adult Indian male population were registered voters. This increased to 1043 (5.2 per cent) on the eve of universal adult suffrage in 1944, the year in which women could also vote. Illiteracy and lack of property disqualified many men from registering as voters. Participation as candidates in general elections and in the central government dates from 1944. In that year, Deosoran Tewari ran as an independent candidate in the general election for the Southern

O. D. Ramtalli of the People's National Party has held numerous posts in the Jamaican Cabinet.

Clarendon constituency. He lost to the Jamaica Labour Party's H. C. Cork. Cheddi Singh from Little London in Westmoreland (1972–76), Enid Bennett from Linstead, St. Catherine (1976–97), O. D. Ramtalli and Ryan Peralto have been members of parliament (MPs). Today, the ruling People's National Party has one Indian MP, Morias Guy, a medical doctor from St. Mary, .

THE CONTEMPORARY SITUATION AND CHALLENGES FACING THE COMMUNITY

Currently, Indians comprise a mere 1.3 per cent of Jamaica's population of 2.7 million, but people of Indian descent—referred to in the 1943 census as 'East Indian Coloureds'—make up a larger percentage. However, Table 8.29 shows that Indians are the largest ethnic minority on the island.

The challenges facing the Indian community in Jamaica are not different from the challenges facing other ethnic groups and are related to unemployment, crime and rural and urban poverty. Those who live in Portland Cottage are also trying to recover from the effects of Hurricane Ivan, which ravaged the area in October 2004. There are also challenges related to funding for skilled training to equip young people for life in the globalised world and the Caribbean Single Market and Economy. Emigration to the US, Canada and the UK continues to be an attractive route for upward social mobility.

The Indian community is fully integrated into Jamaican society. The majority are Christians and are creolised in terms of dress, food and language. The majority also express a sense of belonging to Jamaica, but they maintain a certain diasporic consciousness of India. This marks a change from the mid-20th century, when many had a feeling of not belonging. Even up to the 1940s, members of the Indian/Indian-Jamaican community showed a desire to maintain ethnic exclusiveness. In his report to the Moyne Commission, which gathered evidence in Jamaica in the aftermath of labour protests in 1938, Emmanuel Raout of the EINU stated that 'the majority of Indians regard themselves as a separate community...Only a very minor proportion...feel that they are Jamaicans.'

In some ways, this feeling of isolation and not belonging was often a reaction to the attitudes of the host society, which treated all newcomers as foreigners. There were several letters to the editors of the major newspapers of the day from people who competed with each other to give the 'correct' definition of a 'Jamaican'. Some supported the view that local birth was not enough. On 3 February 1950, the *Jamaica Times* published a letter from the organiser-general of the Afro-West Indian League (AWIL), formed in 1940, which stated that 'simply being born in Jamaica does not make one a

Table 8.29

ETHNIC COMPOSITION OF CARIBBEAN POPULATIONS IN 2002 (%)							
	Black	**Indian**	**Mixed**	**White**	**Amerindian**	**Chinese**	**Other**
Guyana	36.0	50.0	N.A.	N.A.	7.0	N.A.	7.0
Jamaica	90.9	1.3	7.3	0.2	N.A.	0.2	0.1
Surinam	10.0	37.0	31.0	1.0	2.0	2.0	17.0
Trinidad	39.5	40.3	18.4	0.6	N.A.	N.A.	1.2

Source: www.geographic.org/people/people.html, 'Population by Country', 2002 update. Notes: For Guyana 'Other' includes Whites, Chinese and people of mixed heritage. For Surinam, no figures were given for 'Blacks' per se, but 10 per cent are Maroons. 'Other' includes 15 per cent Javanese. For Trinidad, 'Other' includes the Chinese.

In 1940, the illiteracy rate among Indo-Jamaicans girls was high. The appearance of a letter written by a young Indian woman in the island's major daily newspaper was regarded as a remarkable event:

It has been and still is a custom among the Indian parents in this island to betroth their daughters in their teens, at a time even prior to puberty, to husbands of solely their, the parents' choice...If the intention of arranged marriages at an early age is to prevent illegitimate births, a more enlightened path would be to educate Indian girls about sex and its possible consequences.

Extract from a letter by Nora Bedasee, written to the editor of the Daily Gleaner, 21 November 1940.

Jamaican...in the same way that a chicken hatched in an oven cannot be called a bread.'

Since the 1950s, while not forgetting India and their cultural roots, few Indian-Jamaicans have defined themselves as 'Indian', as opposed to 'Jamaican'. At the same time, Jamaica is a multicultural society with the motto, 'Out of Many, One People'. In Jamaica, there is no perceived dichotomy between being a Jamaican citizen and supporting a culture that has historic roots in another homeland, be that homeland India, Africa or Europe. In Khal Torabully's words, 'Negritude', Eurocentrism and 'Coolitude' are all acceptable in multi-ethnic settings.

THE NATIONAL COUNCIL FOR INDIAN CULTURE IN JAMAICA (NCICJ)

The NCICJ was established on 1 March 1998. It is an umbrella organisation for Indian associations in Jamaica, and its aim is to preserve and promote Indian culture. Its member organisations are: Prema Satsangh of Jamaica, Sanatan Dharma Mandir, Club India, Indo-Jamaican Cultural Society of Jamaica, Indian Cultural Society of Jamaica, Friends of the Indian Community and the Ananda Marga Society. The Indian high commissioner is an honorary member and the Brahma Kumaris Raja Yoga Centre is an affiliated organisation. The organisation's founding members were Pandit Lochan Nathan

Sharma, Dr Sitaram Poddar, Hon. Justice Mahadev Dukaran, Barbara Persaud and Lloyd Persaud. The current president is Beryl Williamsingh, who was secretary of the EIPS.

The council provides opportunities to promote Indian music, fashion, culinary arts and the Hindi language. It encourages the celebration of major Indian festivals throughout the year. For example, on the occasion of Diwali, a *mela* is held. An annual awards banquet and cultural show honours those who have made significant contributions to the community. The NCICJ gives financial aid to needy children for education and also gives generously to several charities. A free monthly medical and dental clinic is run by the Prema Satsangh of Jamaica. Recreational facilities are available at Club India, which has Hindi language classes taught by Dr Poddar. The council participates in national celebrations such as National Heroes' Week, contributes equipment to local hospitals and continues to support The Wortley Home, established in 1918 by Canon Wortley to assist young girls (initially, young Indian girls).

The council has a diasporic consciousness and also contributes to relief efforts after major disasters affecting Indian communities, such as the floods in nearby Guyana in 2005 and the Indian Ocean tsunami in 2004. To promote awareness of the work of Mahatma Gandhi, it hosted a function to mount his bust, donated by the government of India, in the newly constructed Park of World Heroes in Kingston.

Verene A. Shepherd

A mid-20th century portrait of Harbour Street in Kingston. In the 19th century, Harbour Street was one of the main areas for trade and commerce in the Jamaican capital.

THE FRENCH CARIBBEAN

An early postcard shows a group of East Indian women in Martinique dressed in all their finery. While most migrants in the Caribbean were recruited from North India, Indians in Martinique and Guadeloupe were largely drawn from South India, where the French had a presence in Pondicherry and Karaikkal.

THE HISTORY OF the Indian diaspora in the French Caribbean is closely tied to the abolition of slavery in the region in 1848. The main source of income on the Caribbean islands was sugar cane and its products, and the plantations had been worked almost exclusively by slaves. After the abolition of slavery, planters tried to employ liberated slaves as wage labour, but they were either reluctant to go on working in sugar plantations, which carried for them memories of misery and forced labour, or they asked for higher wages than the planters were willing to pay. The new law, therefore, left the planters without a cheap workforce in the fields, and this led to a decline in sugar production by almost 50 per cent between 1849–53.

The British had already put an end to slavery in their Caribbean colonies in 1834 and had successfully introduced people from colonial territories in India to the Caribbean sugar producing-islands through the indenture system. The French Caribbean territories also adopted this policy and began to organise Indian immigration, mainly to Martinique and Guadeloupe. The first ship to arrive from India was the *Aurelie*, which docked in St. Pierre, Martinique, on 6 May 1853, and again a year later in Guadeloupe. Indian immigration to Martinique continued until 1883 and to Guadeloupe until 1889. Its end was brought about by the increasing industrialisation of sugar production from sugar beets in Europe, which brought world sugar prices down, thus weakening the economic base of planters in the Caribbean islands considerably.

RECRUITMENT

The main ports of embarkation in India for the journey to the Caribbean islands were Calcutta, Madras, Karaikkal and Pondicherry. Whereas in the non-French Caribbean region Indian migrants were primarily from North India, in the French Caribbean, the picture was different: 60 per cent of the Indian population in Guadeloupe and up to 100 per cent on the other French islands were from South India. Although the main ports of embarkation for the French islands were those located in the French enclaves of India (Pondicherry and Karaikkal), the recruitment of labourers took place largely beyond French territories—initially in a clandestine manner designated by Madras newspapers as 'kidnapping'. In 1861, a more regular process was instituted following a convention between British and French authorities in India. Labourers who embarked at French ports came from a wide range of districts in the Madras Presidency, and from the French colonies of Yanam, Karaikkal and Pondicherry.

Recruitment was done in a rather negligent manner. Little care was taken to find labourers with the necessary skills for the agricultural work they were meant to carry out. No detailed information about the labourers' backgrounds and castes is available except for those from North India. The situation was further aggravated by certain groups consciously providing the wrong information about their backgrounds. On the one hand, many *dalits* claimed to belong to agricultural castes of the middle range in the caste hierarchy, in the hope of being able to start a new life in a better position on the social scale of the new land to which they were migrating. On the other hand, many Brahmins claimed to belong to higher-range agricultural castes in order to be recruited at all, since Brahmins were classified by the Caribbean planters as 'bad workers without value.'

In order to attract workers, recruiters gave them an idealistic picture of what was in store for the migrants: a short journey, easy agricultural work in sugar cane plantations and good remuneration. Many recruits were thus drawn to the idea that after the contract period of five years, they would return home with pockets full of money. The reality was quite different. The journey was

A Hindu temple in Guadeloupe. The tall gopuram at the front of the temple shows the influence of South Indian temple architecture.

Map 8.45

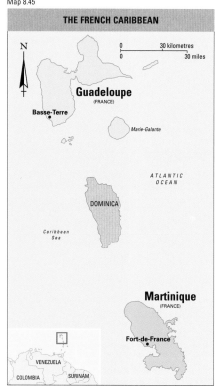

THE FRENCH CARIBBEAN

N

0   30 kilometres
0   30 miles

Guadeloupe
(FRANCE)

Basse-Terre

Marie-Galante

ATLANTIC OCEAN

DOMINICA

Caribbean Sea

Martinique
(FRANCE)

Fort-de-France

VENEZUELA

COLOMBIA   SURINAM

much longer—100 days on average—and more difficult to endure than expected. Although it was in the interest of recruiting companies to ensure that their recruits were in good health upon arrival, the mortality rate during the journey over was high, especially during the first decade of Indian emigration. During the worst season, 1856–57, the median mortality rate on the ships was as high as 17.3 per cent. Upon arrival, the migrants' working and living conditions depended largely on the owner of the plantation.

The process of adaptation set in quite quickly among Indian workers. With regard to language, for example, soon after their arrival the workers picked up Creole, the lingua franca of the Caribbean islands. Indian workers from different backgrounds would even use Creole to speak with each other.

SETTLEMENT

Initially, Caribbean planters were not inclined to support the immigration of families. Women and children were perceived as unnecessary costs who, though needing to be fed, did not contribute significantly to labour on the plantation. This view was later modified. Instead of repatriation, which the planters had to organise for workers and required more financing, Indian immigrants were encouraged to settle permanently once their contracts were fulfilled. This was when the migration of entire families and also of single women started to gain support. A large percentage of Indians, indeed, chose to stay in the French Caribbean. With the money they had saved, initially for the purpose of improving their lives when they returned to India, they now bought land and settled on the islands.

One issue arose from the settlement of migrants. Many of the workers who had been recruited in the British territories of India were considered British subjects, not French citizens, although they had settled permanently in the French Caribbean. To resolve this problem, Henri Cidambaram, a settler of Indian origin, successfully filed a case against the French state in 1921, in which he demanded French citizenship for all Indians in Guadeloupe and Martinique.

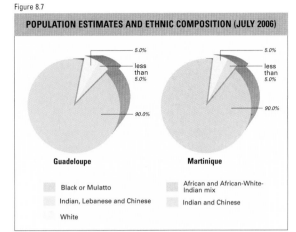

Figure 8.7

POPULATION ESTIMATES AND ETHNIC COMPOSITION (JULY 2006)

Guadeloupe: 5.0%, less than 5.0%, 90.0%

Martinique: 5.0%, less than 5.0%, 90.0%

Legend:
- Black or Mulatto
- Indian, Lebanese and Chinese
- White
- African and African-White-Indian mix
- Indian and Chinese

Source: www.cia.giv/cia/publications/factbook/geos.

THE CONTEMPORARY SITUATION

Records show that between the mid-1850s and the late 1880s nearly 68,000 indentured Indian labourers were brought to the French Caribbean. Descendants of those indentured workers now constitute a significant part of the islands' population. In 2005, the population of Guadeloupe was estimated at 449,000, and that of Martinique at 433,000. 'East Indians' on both islands constitute less than 5 per cent of the population, but people of Indian descent have also assimilated with 90 per cent, or the majority, of the population, which is of mixed ancestry, and these people are predominantly Roman Catholic. Both islands have a community of Hindus, and in Guadeloupe, there is also a small Muslim population.

The islands still have agricultural sectors producing some sugar cane—often for the production of rum—and growing fruit and flowers, but on both islands, tourism and service industries, including those associated with tourism, have become the most important sectors of the economy. People of Indian origin are well represented in all economic sectors of the French Caribbean: transport and construction, vegetable trade, higher education and professional positions.

Ulrike Niklas

An Indian woman in Martinique. By the early 20th century, the migration of women and of entire families was encouraged in an effort to foster the permanent settlement of Indians in the French colonies of the Caribbean.

A postcard at the turn of the 20th century shows a busy market street in Guadeloupe.

313

UNITED STATES OF AMERICA

'East Indian' workers of the
Calapooia Lumber
Company, Oregon, 1909.

THE UNITED STATES is today home to one of the largest Indian populations in the world, as well as to substantial diasporic Indian communities from places such as Fiji, Trinidad and Guyana. Though the early history of Indian Americans can be traced as far back as to about 1900, the contemporary history of most Indian American communities extends back to the passage of new legislation in 1965 that lifted restrictions on the entry of Indians into the US. From a community then numbering a few thousand, the Indian population grew to over 1.71 million in 2000. Few ethnic groups have registered such phenomenal growth. However, for a community that commands the highest per capita income of any racial or ethnic group, as well as the highest rate of college graduates, Indian Americans have not played a significant role in American politics so far, though signs of Indian involvement in community affairs as well as local and national politics are growing. While in the past Indians had made known their presence most visibly in the professions, particularly in medicine and engineering, extending in recent years to computer-related industries and investment banking, today the community is far more diversified, with large number of Indians entering the taxi business, fast food franchises and hospitality industries. The growth and visibility of the Indian American population is also evident in the rapid proliferation of Indian restaurants, the emergence of a complex and sensitive Indian literature and an Indian print media, the rapid increase in the number in places of worship (especially Hindu temples), the demarcation of 'Little Indias' in major metropolitan areas, the annual culture shows staged by Indian student unions across a wide spectrum of colleges and universities, the frequent tours of American cities by Bollywood movie stars and entertainers, and the myriad signs of an emerging familiarity on the part of the wider American population with such diverse aspects of Indian culture as bharatanatyam, yoga, Ayurveda, Hindustani instrumental music and tandoori cooking.

EARLY HISTORY: PEASANTS, STUDENTS AND REBELS

Peasants from Punjab first began appearing on the west coast around 1898–99, seeking work in Washington's lumber mills and California's vast agricultural fields. Though predominantly Sikhs, they were described as 'Hindus', or more commonly, 'Hindoos'. Indeed, the US Immigration Commission of 1911 held that any native of India was, for immigration purposes, to be viewed as a Hindu. The trickle of some 20–30 emigrants annually between 1898 and 1902, rising to 271 emigrants in 1906, some of whom had fled from inhospitable Canada, must have appeared to white America as a deluge, since calls for their removal were already surfacing in the press and among American labour leaders. From the outset they were seen as unassimilable, possessed of 'immodest and filthy habits', and regarded as the 'most undesirable, of all the eastern Asiatic races.' In two separate incidents in 1907, both in the state of Washington, Indians were subjected to racial attacks and compelled to seek protective custody. Samuel Gompers, the president of the American Federation of Labor, declared in 1908 that 'sixty years' contact with the Chinese, twenty-five years' experience with the Japanese and two or three years' acquaintance with Hindus should be sufficient to convince any ordinarily intelligent person that they have no standards... by which a Caucasian may judge them.' Concerted attempts would henceforth be made by the Asiatic Exclusion League and other associations to prevent further immigration from India into the US, to intimidate those already in the country into abandoning the US, and to restrict their capacity to own property. The white lumbermen of the town of Saint John, Oregon, succeeded in driving out its Hindu workers. Greater alarm bells were sounded by the *San Francisco Chronicle*, which warned that reports of Hindu men sending for their wives in India could not be ignored. In these circumstances, the new immigrants, whose difficulties were compounded by their high illiteracy rates and their poor knowledge of English, undoubtedly imbibed their first political lessons, acquiring the skills and tenacity necessary to combat racism, pursue a livelihood, and, as shall be seen, work the courts to gain reprieve.

Meanwhile, two other classes of Indians had begun to make their way to the US. The first Indian student arrived

Map 8.46

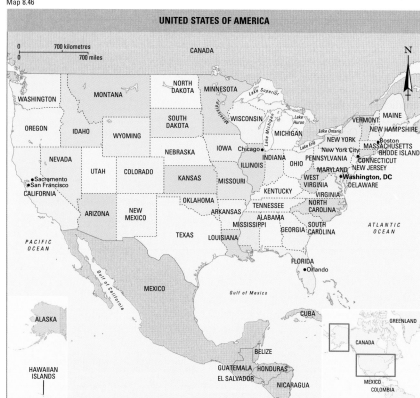

in 1901, and in less than a decade, a small body of Indian students had congregated at the University of California, Berkeley, the polytechnic at San Luis Obispo, and a few agricultural colleges. They could not have been unaware of political developments in India, where a nationalist movement, centred in Bengal, Maharashtra and Punjab, was beginning to pose considerable difficulties for the British. The renowned nationalist leader, Lala Lajpat Rai, visited the US in 1905 and addressed the Boston Anti-Imperialist League to awaken Americans to the realities of British oppression in India and gain worldwide recognition for India's quest for home rule. Political dissenters whose advocacy of Indian independence from British rule had made them wanted men began to arrive in the US, the more prominent ones being Lala Har Dayal, Tarkanath Das, Barkatullah, Ram Chandra and Bhai Parmanand. In 1913, the Hindi Association of the Pacific Coast or, more commonly known as the Ghadar Party, was founded in Oregon, with a weekly newspaper, *Ghadar*, conceived as a vehicle for the expression of seditious ideas.

Adherents of the Ghadar Party, headquartered in San Francisco, set for themselves the goal of liberating India by all means at their disposal. Some returned to India from the US after the outbreak of war, as a British colonial official might have put it, to foment trouble, consort with the Germans and inspire the peasantry to rebel. An early attempt to influence political events in India in 1915 was foiled when a large shipment of guns, ammunition and propaganda literature destined for India was intercepted by the British. America's entry into the war in 1917 sealed the fate of the Ghadarites: acting under pressure from the British, an intensive and successful prosecution was launched against them for conspiring with the Germans to drive the British out of India. Though at least some of its adherents had fled India to seek greater political freedom in the US, they had to contend with openly racist sentiments and even racial violence in the American West. The Ghadar movement drew into its fold political rebels, students, intellectuals, workers and farmers, and it was ecumenical enough to attract Sikhs, Hindus and Muslims.

Canada had closed its doors to Indians in 1909, but the need for migrant labour in the west, especially on railway tracks, meant that American officials were prepared to resist the calls to keep out the Hindus. The commissioner of immigration at San Francisco issued strict orders in 1910 that an Indian seeking admission into the US was to be denied entry if he was likely to become a public charge or if he could not pass an 'exacting physical examination'. Between 1911 and 1920, nearly 1460 Indians were admitted, but 1782 Indians were prevented from entering the

US during the same period. The aspirations of Indians were to receive further setbacks with the passage of the Immigration Act of 1917, which barred all immigrants from areas east of the 50th meridian and west of the 110th meridian—effectively all Asians—from entering the US. Naturalised citizenship was reserved for whites only, though the conflation of the categories of 'White', 'Aryan' and 'Caucasian' had by no means been resolved. In a decision by a Federal Court of Appeals on the citizenship status of Bhicaji Franji Balsara, a Parsi from Bombay settled in the US, it was held that 'Congress intended by the words "free White persons" to confer the privilege of naturalization upon members of the White or Caucasian race only.' The court ruled that Parsis were to be construed as white, and a 1913 ruling, in the case of Ahkoy Kumar Mozumdar, extended the meaning of 'Caucasian' to include 'high-caste Hindu[s] of pure blood'.

The Supreme Court's November 1922 decision in the Ozawa case, where it was ruled that 'White' ought to be interpreted to mean 'Caucasian', appeared to confirm earlier rulings and was received with much jubilation by Indians who viewed themselves as Caucasians, indeed as representatives of the oldest branch of the Aryan family. Less than four months later, however, the Supreme Court declared that in the 'understanding of the common man', which the Court declared to be consonant with the thinking of the founding fathers, 'White' clearly denoted a person of European origin. Thus the émigré from Amritsar, Bhagat Singh Thind, though a Caucasian of 'high-caste Hindu stock' who had lived in the US since 1913, and even served in the US army, was not entitled to naturalisation. *The Sacramento Bee* wrote in an editorial in March 1923 that the Supreme Court's decision 'that Hindus are not eligible to American citizenship, is most welcome in California.' Further, it stated, 'Hindu holders of land' were evidently to be brought 'within the mandatory provisions of the California anti-alien land law.' Thus, the immediate consequence of the Thind decision was that it rendered Indians stateless, and the Immigration and Naturalization Service (INS) moved to cancel the American citizenship of all Indians, including some 45 naturalised Indians, over the next three years. Indians were also placed under the jurisdiction of the Alien Land Law (1913; amended 1920–21), which prevented non-citizens from owning or leasing land. One response was to transfer land into the hands of friendly Anglo farmers and business associates.

Studio portrait of early Sikh migrants based in California, c. 1910.

The revolutionary ideas of the Ghadar movement were often expressed in poetic form.

'Hindoo Smoking Tobacco', produced by the Strater Brothers Tobacco Company of Louisville, Kentucky, in the late 19th and early 20th century. The figure on the tin cover represents one of the ways in which 'Hindoos' were perceived in the US at the time.

Rabindranath Tagore (seated, centre) with Indian students at the University of California, Berkeley, in the late 1920s.

In 1956, Dalip Singh Saund (seated, centre), an advocate of Asian Indian political rights, became the first Indian American to be elected to Congress. He is pictured here with his wife Marian (seated, right) and family.

Indian nationalism was a popular cause among Indians in the US. The handbill informs of a mass meeting at Golden Gate Avenue, San Francisco, on 20 April 1923.

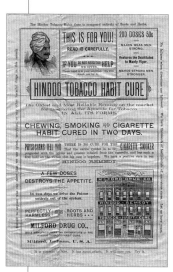

'Hindoo Tobacco Habit Cure', produced by the Indiana-based Milford Drug Co., c. 1890.

The outcome was sometimes tragic. Vaisho Das Bagai, who had immigrated to the US in 1915 and had become a naturalised citizen, committed suicide in 1928: the note he left behind stated that he had tried to become 'as American as possible'. In the late 1930s, the India Welfare League and the India League of America renewed efforts to obtain citizenship for Indians, and similarly fought to increase the support for Indian demands for independence from British rule. None of these challenges could counter the dramatic decline in the size of the Indian community from 1924. The 1940 census found only 1476 Indians in California, a sharp drop from the 10,000 Indians estimated to be resident there around 1914. At least 3000 Indians were to return to their homeland between 1920 and 1940.

The Indian population in the US might have disappeared altogether but for the altered circumstances arising out of World War II. The joint declaration by Winston Churchill and Franklin Roosevelt in 1941 about the Atlantic Charter, which recognised the right of all peoples to self-government, as well as the American perception that Indian assistance in the war might be critical in preventing the formation of a Japanese-German military axis in Asia, were both conducive in advancing the claims of Asian Indians. 'America cannot afford to say that she wants the people of India to fight on her side', wrote one Asian Indian demographer, 'and at the same time maintain that she will not have them among her immigrant groups.' Indian lobbying, led by the charismatic Sikh merchant J. J. Singh, resulted in Congressional approval of the Act of 2 July 1946, which gave Indians the right to naturalisation and allowed a small number of Indians, exclusive of non-quota immigrants (such as spouses and minor children of citizens), to enter the US every year. At this time, a mere 1500 Indians remained in the US. Between 1948 and 1965, 7000 Indians were to migrate to the US and nearly 1780 Indians, many of whom had been American residents for two decades or more, acquired American citizenship. Among the latter was Dalip Singh Saund, who was active in the struggle for Asian Indian political rights. A mathematician by training, Saund also earned higher degrees in agricultural science and went on to become a farmer. Elected to Congress in 1956, Saund spent six years in the House of Representatives.

1965 ONWARDS: THE EMERGENCE OF A DIASPORIC COMMUNITY

The present phase of the history of Indians in the US begins with the Immigration and Naturalization Act of 1965, which set a quota of 20,000 for each country in the 'Eastern Hemisphere'—though most immediate family members of US citizens were not subject to numeric limits—and devised immigrant visas according to seven preferential categories. This system of immigration, with some modifications, such as the abandonment of the hemispheric quotas, is still largely in place. The greater number of Indians, at least in the first 15 years, were to arrive as professionals, and the 1975 census revealed that an astonishing 93 per cent were classified as 'professional/technical workers'. More than anything else, they thought principally of their economic and professional advancement. With the passage of time and as they settled down, family reunification became a prime consideration. By 1975, the number of Indians had risen to well over 175,000, and it is around this time that the question of self-representation first surfaced among members of the Indian community. Maxine P. Fisher, who in 1980

published a study of Asian Indians in New York City, the first monograph of its kind, reported that her informants variously described themselves as Aryan, Indo-Aryan, Caucasian, Oriental, Indian, Asian, Dravidian and Mongol, and she implied that as Indians could be 'very fair', 'very dark' or anywhere in the 'middle', race and skin colour had no necessary association. The earlier and quaint nomenclature of 'Hindu' to designate everyone from the Indian subcontinent had long been abandoned; but the designation of 'Indian' was scarcely more acceptable, since those who are now known as 'Native Americans' were also known as 'Indians'. The confusion between 'Red Indians' and 'Indians' might sound absurd, but as a scene in Mira Nair's *Mississippi Masala* suggests, to some Americans this confusion was real. The term 'Asian American' was not much in vogue and, in any case, referred primarily to those from the Far East (and later Southeast Asia); and unlike in Britain, where Indians perhaps tolerated being grouped with Africans and Caribbean people under the generic category of 'black', and even derived new political coalitions and formations in the common interest of combating oppression, in the US, the designation 'black' was seen as condemning one to membership in a permanent underclass.

Distribution and growth of the Indian population

Efforts at preserving the minority status of Indians while allowing them a distinct identity were to bear fruit when the Census Bureau agreed, from 1980 onwards, to reclassify immigrants from India as 'Asian Indians'. By then, some of the demographic patterns which continue to characterise the Indian community to the present day were well-established. Unlike other Asian ethnic groups, which are to be found in disproportionately large numbers on the west coast, the Indian population is more evenly distributed throughout the US. For many years, there was a heavy density of Indians in the northeast, particularly in the New York–New Jersey area, but by 1990, large Indian communities had emerged in Chicago and its western suburbs, the Bay Area in northern California, and in southern California around Los Angeles and Orange County. More so than other ethnic groups, Indians have largely gravitated towards urban areas, a pattern confirmed by the 2000 census, which shows significant Indian communities, besides those enumerated, in the Washington, DC area (over 50,000 Indians) and in the urban belts of Texas, where Indians are now the third largest Asian American group after the Vietnamese and

Chinese. The exponential growth of the Asian Indian community shows no sign of abating. Between 1980 and 1990, the annual growth rate of the community was 8.5 per cent: nearly half a million Indians were added, taking their number to over 815,000. From 1990 to 2000, the Indian population again more than doubled to 1.71 million, by far the greatest jump for any large Asian American ethnic group. Constituting 16.4 per cent of the Asian American population, the Asian Indian community is exceeded in size only by the Filipinos (18 per cent) and Chinese (23 per cent).

Education and employment

The educational level of Indians continues to be very high, though the percentage of those who earn their living as professionals has declined. According to the 2000 census, 24.4 per cent of Americans had earned at least a bachelor's degree; however, among all Asian Americans, the figure rises to 44.1 per cent, and to an astounding 63.9 per cent among Asian Indians. In a report on Asian American students in 1997, the Educational Testing Service (ETS), which administers standardised exams, found that the percentage of South Asian high school seniors who scored above the 50th percentile was substantially higher than for all other Asian American communities in reading, and between 4–11 per cent higher in mathematics in comparison to the Koreans, Chinese and Japanese.

Between May 1998 and July 1999, the US government issued 134,000 new H-1B visas, which are granted for a period of six years to highly-skilled foreigners seeking employment in the US. Of these, 63,900 were granted to Indians, and in 2003, according to reliable estimates nearly 400,000 Asian Indians were holders of H-1B visas. Though the H-1B is not an immigrant visa and its holders are not counted as residents of the US, typically a very large percentage of H-1B visa-holders eventually acquire

permanent residency. Even among permanent residents and citizens, however, the continued preponderance of Indian professionals is easily estimated by a survey of doctors, engineers and computer specialists. The prestigious Indian Institutes of Technology (at Kharagpur, Kanpur, Chennai, Mumbai, Delhi and more recently Guwahati and Roorkee) have sent as much as 40 per cent of their graduating class in some years to the US, and nearly 20,000 of their graduates are estimated to have made the US their home. Constituting about 0.6 per cent of the US population, Indian students typically grab 5–10 per cent of major awards, such as the Presidential Scholarship and Intel Science Talent Search award.

Such broad demographic patterns may disguise as much as they reveal, apart from the fact that they say little about the politics of the category 'Asian Indian'. Indians had once attempted to be assimilated into the category of 'White' or 'Caucasian'. In the 1970s, however, claiming to be white was a scarcely desired political strategy, and not only because it meant disowning the civil rights movement and the gains that African Americans had won for all minorities. Whereas minorities were once subjected to open discrimination, 50 years after the Thind decision the designation of 'minority' was also calculated to earn one certain entitlements, whatever prejudices might still exist against minorities. Writing to the US Civil Rights Commission in 1975, the recently formed Association of Indians in America (AIA) said that it was undeniably true that 'Indians are different in appearance; they are equally dark-skinned as other non-White individuals and are, therefore, subject to the same prejudices.'

However opportunistic the position of the AIA, there was something of a case to be made for the disadvantages suffered by Indians: as the 1980 census showed, US-born Asian Indians, whose numbers were very small but growing, had an unemployment rate 'five times that of other

A parade on 11 May 1945 in Stockton, California, honouring Jawaharlal Nehru's sister, Vijaya Lakshmi Pandit (front, centre), who was the leader of the Indian delegation to the UN from 1946–61 and was elected president of the 8th session of the General Assembly.

The Swami Vivekananda memorial at the Hindu Temple of Greater Chicago. The city of Chicago is especially significant as it was here that Vivekananda received widespread acclaim for his speech at the World Parliament of Religions in September 1893.

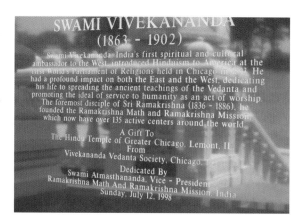

The Mahatma Gandhi memorial in Washington, DC. In September 2000, former Indian prime minister Atal Bihari Vajpayee (front, centre) dedicated the memorial in the presence of former US president Bill Clinton (front, left).

Gandhi Marg designates a portion of Devon Avenue in Chicago. Nearly eight blocks of Devon are filled with Indian restaurants and stores specialising in Indian groceries, saris, 200-volt appliances, Hindi films and music, and that perennial favourite of middle-class Indians, 24K gold jewellery.

Asian American groups.' A comprehensive study conducted by the University of California, published in the *Pacific Rim States Asian Demographic Data Book*, suggested that 15 years later, large pockets of poverty still persisted among Indian Americans in California. In 1995, the mean per capita household income of Indians in California was US$18,472, below the US$20,676 per capita income of the population as a whole and more than US$3000 below the per capita income of white Americans. A report released in March 2005, 'The Diverse Face of Asians and Pacific Islanders in California', still bears out the earlier findings: 14 per cent of Indians in the Central Valley, where agricultural work predominates, are living below the poverty level; 39 per cent have little or no proficiency in English; and 35 per cent have not completed high school. This belies the image of Asian Indians as people who are invariably well-educated and placed in professional positions. In the same state of California, 40 per cent of the 2000 dot.com businesses in Silicon Valley in 1999 were started by Indians. What AIA would not have been unaware of in the late 1970s, when it commenced its agitation to have Asian Indians declared a distinct minority, was that with every passing year, the number of Indians employed as taxi drivers, gas station owners and attendants, subway newsagents, and in other working-class jobs, would continue to grow, and that employment prospects for Indians might diminish.

Moreover, the apprehension that Indians, whose success rendered them vulnerable, might soon have to bear the brunt of racial prejudice and ethnic jokes was not entirely misplaced. In the mid-1980s, this racism acquired a systematic patterning: in New Jersey, a number of Indians were attacked by young white men who described themselves as 'dotbusters', the 'dot' being a reference to the *bindi* placed by some Hindu women on their forehead between the eyebrows. Indian businesses were vandalised; women were molested; and 30-year-old Citicorp executive Navroze Mody was bludgeoned to death.

Professional organisations in the US

Among Indian professionals, the sense that discrimination for a generation or two might stare them in the face began to acquire some urgency in the early 1980s. As the laws governing the admission of doctors from overseas into the American medical profession were tightened, the Association of American Physicians from India (AAPI) was formed to represent this constituency. According to a 1993 estimate, Indian doctors constituted 4 per cent of all doctors in the US, thereby forming the largest ethnic group of doctors in the country. The high profile of the AAPI, which established a permanent legislative office in Washington, DC in December 1995, can be gauged by the fact that its annual convention that same year was addressed by the president, Bill Clinton. Other broader-based organisations also emerged to enhance and safeguard Indian interests. Prominent among these are the Federation of Indian Associations (FIA), the National Federation of Indian American Associations (NFIA), and the National Association of Americans of Asian Indian Descent (NAAAID). The NFIA, together with the American Indian Forum for Political Education and the AAPI, agitated against the proposed legislation in 1985 that would have deeply cut Medicare funding to hospitals employing doctors with foreign medical degrees. It was under the auspices of the Association of Indians in North America, later to be transformed into the NFIA, that the Indian community first convened a national meeting in 1980. In subsequent years, the NFIA was to lobby, along with other Asian American organisations, to defeat a Congressional bill that would have drastically reduced the number of relatives allowed into the US.

The NFIA showed how Asian Indians might further the interests of the Indian nation state when it mobilised the Indian community in 1987, with apparent success, to persuade Congress to withdraw the sale of sophisticated AWACS planes to Pakistan. The NFIA, NAAAID and other organisations also gave their assistance on numerous occasions to the Indian government to help defeat legislation—perceived to be inimical to India's welfare and interests—sponsored by congressmen who were considered hostile towards India, such as the Republican Dan Burton (Indiana), who is also the co-founder and co-chair of the Pakistan Caucus in the House of Representatives.

It is at the local level, however, that Indian community activists and organisations have done some of their most intense lobbying, though they have not been uniformly successful. The Little India Chamber of Commerce, which represents the interests of Indian merchants who own Indian shops and restaurants across several blocks in Artesia in the metropolitan Los Angeles area, has vainly sought for over a decade to persuade the municipality to put up signs guiding visitors to 'Little India'. Allegations have surfaced that Indian shopkeepers, by keeping their stores open on 4 July, have ruffled feathers. On the other hand, it is argued that unjustified stereotypes about Indians as penny-pinchers abound and even influence policy-makers and politicians. Indians, and apparently others, are not likely to forget the accent-laden Apu, the Indian owner of a convenience store in *The Simpsons*, an immensely popular television programme. In one episode, Apu informs a customer, 'I'll sell you expired baby food for a nickel off.'

In what is perhaps its most frequent form, lobbying constitutes attempts to have 'great' Indians memorialised by way of naming streets after them or having their statues installed at prominent public places. Indian communities have lobbied to place public statues of Mahatma Gandhi in numerous cities, among them Atlanta, New York, St. Louis, San Francisco, Salt Lake City, Denver and Washington, DC. Gandhi is one person whose name is considered to earn Indian Americans cultural capital and goodwill, even though in private many of them lean towards the view that the saintly old man is entirely irrelevant to a world of global capitalism. Using Gandhi as an example, Indian Americans can put a different spin on Indian religions and on Hinduism as the quintessential religion of non-violence, inner harmony and tolerance.

The Religious Life of Indian Communities

Though Indians generally numbered in the few thousands before the extensive overhaul of immigration regulations in 1965, they left an impression on American life, and as a miniscule minority, they sought only to assimilate seamlessly into the dominant culture. Several examples of their contribution to American life readily come to mind. One that inescapably confronts any student of Indian religions in the US is Swami Vivekananda's electrifying address at the World Parliament of Religions in 1893, and the subsequent appeal that Vedanta came to have for a small but significant portion of the American elite. Swami Vivekananda established the Vedanta Society of New York in 1894, and another branch in San Francisco in 1900 on his second visit to the US. More arresting, however, is the history of the Vedanta Society of Southern California, where the young monk, Swami Prabhavananda, who had been sent to Hollywood by the Ramakrishna Order in 1929, eventually gathered a renowned group of British writers and intellectuals around him, including Aldous Huxley and Christopher Isherwood.

Indian intellectuals who had been settled in the US since the 1920s and 1930s, such as Krishnalal Shridharani and Haridas Muzumdar, created something of a niche with their staunch advocacy of Gandhian non-violence, while others, such as Sudhindra Bose and R. K. Das, were equally ardent spokespersons for Indian independence. These men were among the first generation of Indians to find academic positions at American universities.

Finally, in the face of blatantly discriminatory legislation as well as anti-miscegenation laws, drafted to protect the honour and dignity of white women and not repealed until 1948, Indians showed considerable, if not always successful, ability to innovate in their social life. Punjabi men took Mexican women as wives, adapted to differences in language, cuisine, dress and religion, and together they created an unusual bi-ethnic community.

Increasing activity

The religious, cultural and social life of diasporic Indian groups took on a new vibrancy in the post-1965 period,

most particularly after the community had found its feet. Hazrat Inayat Khan, a renowned Sufi teacher from India, made his way to the US in 1912, and three years later, the Sikhs, who comprised the bulk of the Indian immigrant community at that juncture in history, had established a gurdwara in Stockton, California. The greater majority of Indians who have arrived in the US since 1965, however, are Hindus, and it is not surprising that Hinduism's growth has perhaps been the most spectacular. Swami A. C. Bhaktivedanta, a Bengali Vaishnava who claimed to be in the direct spiritual lineage of Chaitanya Mahaprabhu, arrived in the US in 1965 and established the International Society of Krishna Consciousness (ISKCON). He acquired a very considerable following, and the 'Hare Krishnas', as his followers were dubbed, were soon a ubiquitous presence at airports and university campuses. Any systematic history of vegetarianism in the US would have to take into account the part played by the Hare Krishnas in popularising vegetarianism, and it is an indisputable fact, though not one that has ever received sustained sociological inquiry, that Indian restaurants, including those managed by the Hare Krishnas, remain the mainstay of the slowly growing number of Americans who are attracted to vegetarianism.

In the incipient years of the Hare Krishna movement, when temples built by immigrant Hindus were few and far between, Indians frequented the ISKCON temples, though few Hindus joined the movement. By the mid-1970s, the Indian population had registered considerable growth and put down roots, and the community could now think of commissioning new temples or converting existing unused structures, such as churches, into temples and community centres. Comprised largely of professionals who had little experience in, or inclination towards, philanthropic activities, the Indian community began to direct much of its affluence towards the construction of new temples. The growth of temples in the Chicago area, particularly in the 1980s, illustrates amply the history of Hinduism in the US.

The 1980 census recorded 33,541 Indians in the Chicago metropolitan region; in 1990, the number had

Members of the International Society of Krishna Consciousness, known commonly as 'Hare Krishna', can be found in many metropolitan cities in the US. The movement was founded in July 1966 by A. C. Bhaktivedanta Swami Prabhupada while he was in the US.

A Sikh temple in California, 1915.

grown to 56,462; and by 2000 it had increased to 125,208. Indians have now surpassed Filipinos as the largest ethnic Asian community in the Chicago area. In December 1977, the Hindu Temple of Greater Chicago (HTGC) was founded as a non-profit organisation. Over the next few years, its members, many of whom were wealthy doctors and other professionals, raised funds for the construction of a temple, and in 1981 they purchased a seven-hectare site for US$300,000 in Lemont. The complex has two separate temples: a Ganesh temple inaugurated by Lata Mangeshkar in 1985 and subsequently expanded to house the deities of Shiva and Durga; and a larger Rama temple, for which the *kumbhabisekham*, or formal dedication, was held on 4 July 1986. The Rama temple 'is built to specifications in the authentic style of the Chola dynasty,' while the Ganesh–Shiva–Durga temple emulates the architecture of Bhubaneshwar in Orissa.

By the early 1980s, Telugu professionals in the Greater Chicago area had committed themselves to the construction of a Sri Venkateswara or Balaji temple in Aurora, also in the western suburbs. The groundbreaking ceremony in 1985 was attended by former Indian prime minister Morarji Desai, Muttaialstapathy, an expert on temple construction in South India, and the Chicago-based architect Subhas Nadkarni. The latter two have since worked together on the recently opened Hindu Temple of Central Florida (Orlando). A handsome structure, which has to date cost more than US$4 million, the Balaji temple, housed on a sprawling 29-hectare site, has shrines to Lakshmi, Andal, Ganapati, Subrahmanyam, Shiva and Parvati. Its opulence is, nonetheless, exceeded by the magnificent Shri Swaminarayan Mandir which opened in Bartlett, some 64 km from Chicago, in August 2004. This temple, which cost over US$30 million, features limestone from Turkey and marble from Italy and Makrana (India), and required nearly 500 craftsmen from India who laboured over the 108 marble pillars which support 15 domes. One might argue that the Bochasanwasi Shri Akshar Purushottam Swaminarayan (BAPS) Sanstha, one of the three groups of the Swaminarayan sect to whom the temple belongs, is prone to ostentatious temple architecture, and that the Bartlett temple follows on the heels of monumental BAPS temples at Akshardham (outside Ahmedabad) and Neasden (in north London), which have become major tourist attractions; but the indisputable fact remains that as the Indian community acquires more

influence and gains self-confidence, it has sought to mark its presence with grand religious edifices. The Chicago region is now served by nearly 20 temples as well as three gurdwaras, several mosques, at least one major Jain temple, and even a church affiliated with the Malankara Orthodox Syrian Church of India. A mosque in Schaumburg serves the Indian Muslim community, and a new gurdwara has opened up in Palatine.

Hindu temples in the US and the practice of the Hindu faith reveal certain marked characteristics. Increasingly, temples are built to conform to the specifications encountered in the *shilpa sastras*, or manuals of temple architecture. Specialists versed in temple architecture are likely to be hired as consultants. This is a reflection not merely of the affluence of Indian communities, but of the tendency, which has become more pronounced, to embrace a textbook view of Hinduism. The temples are decidedly grander, but communities seem much less disposed to innovate or negotiate with other communities. A proposed BAPS temple in Chino Hills, an affluent portion of San Bernadino County in southern California, was the subject of much dispute at the city council meeting, where it was demanded that the height of the proposed temple spires, ranging from 16 m to 24 m, be reduced so that they would not exceed the 13-m height limit stipulated in the city code. However, BAPS representatives refused to entertain the suggestion, arguing that the proportions specified in the *sastras* could not be violated.

Furthermore, not only are temple images carved in India, as one would expect, but priests continue to be drawn to this day from the subcontinent. There are notable exceptions: the priests at the Shri Lakshmi Narayan Mandir in Richmond Hill, New York, which services the largely Indo-Guyanese community now settled on the east coast, are themselves drawn from this community. When some members of the community moved to Orlando, where a branch of the temple was opened in 1992, the priests followed in their wake. The history of this temple is illustrative of a third marked tendency, namely the fact that many temples are associated with distinct Hindu communities. The clientele at the various Sri Venkatesvara temples is largely of South Indian origin, just as the Swaminarayan temples are patronised overwhelmingly by Gujaratis. Murugan temples, likewise, attract mainly Tamils.

Pluralism

At the same time, it is possible to speak of three distinct though related forms in which Hinduism's history in the US is most productively written in the idiom of pluralism. A large metropolitan centre such as Los Angeles is home to a Murugan temple, at least two Radha Krishna temples, a Kali Mandir, a Devi Mandir, a Sanatan Dharma Mandir, a Lakshmi Narayan Mandir, a Sri Venkateswara temple, and close to a dozen other temples. The nondescript Valley Hindu Temple (Northridge) is in some respects more representative of Hindu temples in the US, insofar as the non-sectarian temple houses a diverse array of deities—Shiva, Ram, Krishna, Durga and Lakshmi among others—and welcomes Hindus of all persuasions. It has sometimes been suggested that, mindful of their own minority status, Hindus in the diaspora may be less attentive to distinctions which hold sway in India, such as those between north and south, Vaishnavites and Saivites, and so on. At the brand new Hindu Temple of Central Florida (Orlando), where a substantial portion of the

The Shri Swaminarayan Mandir in Bartlett, Illinois.

pan-Indian Hindu pantheon is to be found, one *gopuram* (gateway) is described as being in the Chola style, and the other in the 'Naga' or northern Indian style. The temple's board of trustees claims that Hinduism is synonymous with diversity, and that Hindu temples in the US must attempt to meet the varying requirements of Hindu communities and their styles of worship. The claim is more far-reaching than it appears, since the supposition is that the practice of Hinduism in the US more likely approximates the ideal of Hinduism than is encountered in India. Secondly, though some have often commented on the social aloofness of Indians (e.g. Indian shopkeepers have been criticised for keeping their stores open on 4 July, which is Independence Day), Hindu and Sikh communities are more cognizant of American mores and customs, and indeed even of the country's physical geography, than is commonly recognised. If the Rama shrine at the Hindu Temple of Greater Chicago was consecrated on 4 July, we can be certain that the temple's trustees and devotees held to the view that Hindus not only share in the (purported) blessings of American 'freedom', but that Hinduism enables a more enriched and spiritual conception of freedom with its stress on spiritual emancipation and self-realisation. The Sri Venkateswara temple in Penn Hills, Pennsylvania, for which construction began in 1976, the bicentennial of the American revolution, stands at the confluence of the Allegheny, Monongahela and 'the subterranean river', according to temple literature—an unmistakable allusion to Prayag, where the Yamuna, Ganga and the underground Saraswati rivers are commonly believed to converge. As one scholar has written of the Penn Hills temple, while it does not ignore the Hindu festival calendar, 'it tries as far as is astrologically possible to plan big events around the holidays of the American secular calendar.'

The expanding scope of religion

Finally, while religion never occupies the space merely marked as 'religion', Hinduism, Sikhism and Jainism in the US have begun to radiate outwards to embrace a much wider array of sociocultural forms. The actual space of the temple complex allows an array of activities that in India are very unlikely to be tolerated under a single roof. Among the definitions of Hinduism widely prevalent in Hindu communities, none is perhaps as frequently encountered as the claim that 'Hinduism is a way of life rather than a religion.' The cultural centres associated with many temples seem designed to vindicate that worldview. Thus, the Hindu temple, with or without a formally designated 'cultural centre' alongside, might very well offer

bharatanatyam classes, instruction in yoga and Indian languages (especially Hindi), and lessons in Indian instrumental music (particularly the sitar and tabla). The concept of 'Sunday school' has enthusiasts among Hindus, and children are enrolled to learn Hindu values or 'the dharmic approach to life', familiarise themselves with religious texts, and embrace the rich culture and heritage of India. Hindu temple societies typically conduct a Bal Vihar (children's class) on Sundays, and often the cultural centres offer senior citizens a public forum for conviviality. Hindu temples and cultural centres often also mobilise resources when natural disasters have struck India.

INDIAN 'CULTURE' IN THE DIASPORA

There are multiple spaces, of course, in which what is taken to be Indian culture not only thrives but is reified; just as how a new generation of Indian Americans have embraced literature, art and music to combat racism, gender discrimination and neo-imperialism, forge solidarities with other, generally less privileged, minorities, and give expression to their perception of politics, public life and social activism.

Indian Americans who, like most people, are accustomed to a traditional view of political life, where politics is construed to mean enrolment in one of the two political parties, running for public office, and taking an interest in America's relations with India and Pakistan, are only now beginning to recognise that political participation can take many forms, and that there is something that might be called cultural activism. While Urvashi Vaid, an Indian American who served as the media director and then the executive director of the National Gay and Lesbian Task Force (NGLTF), is far from being a household name in middle-class Indian American families (who eagerly watch for signs showing that Indian participation in the electoral process is increasing), it is clear that the perception of politics among some Indian communities has shifted and is fundamentally informed by identity politics, multiculturalism and a concern about the geopolitics of culture.

Similarly, while the 'coming out' stories of homosexuals may not interest everyone, and many will view such stories as intensely personal narratives about sexual freedom, the participation of Trikone, a homosexual South Asian group, in the annual San Francisco Gay Pride Parade was viewed by its members as a demonstration of the maturation of South Asian political culture. The apparently seamless shift of homosexual culture from 'Indian' to 'South Asian' reflects not ignorance about the complex politics of being 'Indian' in the US, but rather an awareness of the historical contingencies under which

A poster advertising the annual India Festival held in Columbus, Ohio, which 'offers a place for people to embrace diversity and learn more about the people of India.'

Anurag Kashyap, winner of the National Spelling Bee in 2005.

An Indian family and their friends in New Jersey gather for the Hindu ceremony of Ayush Homam, for long life, often performed on a child's first birthday.

culture operates as a sign of the political. Many South Asian homosexuals have written about how South Asians are not quite viewed as 'Asian' even in gay and lesbian groups and organisations: when Indian, Pakistani and other Asian homosexuals sought to march at the India Day Parade in New York in 1994 as members of the South Asian Lesbian and Gay Association (SALGA), the Federation of Indian-American Associations (FIA) denied them a permit, ostensibly on the grounds that the parade was only open to Indian, not South Asian, groups. One suspects, of course, that the FIA was inclined to view Indian homosexuals as an embarrassment to the Indian community, indeed as not quite 'Indian'.

Negotiating culture

Whatever the negotiations that always take place whenever culture is evoked, no matter how imperceptible, there is a tendency among many Indian Americans to reify Indian culture as something that is almost eternal, rooted to timeless traditions, operative within certain parameters, and observant of moral values—in short, something that is a rather good thing. The complaint most frequently encountered among Indian teenagers and even college students is that their parents forbid them to date before marriage, and the argument to the effect that such behaviour is not countenanced by 'Indian culture' is put forward. Many Indian American students who were often taken to India during their childhood and have some familiarity with the country remark that their parents' notion of Indian culture has little correspondence to the culture of youth at colleges and universities in India. Most Indian students in the US keep their premarital sexual relationships an absolute secret from their parents, and the taboo on interracial relationships is, if anything, even more strictly observed. Those who are inclined to the study of literature, history or the performing arts, rather than engineering, medicine or business administration, are similarly apprehensive about discussing their plans with their parents, though here, few would be prepared to advance the claim that Indian culture rather than practical considerations is likely to make Indian parents fume at their children's choices. Yet, the obvious desire to see their children succeed in some profession that brings both pecuniary success and status to its practitioners notwithstanding, one cannot but wonder whether culture is implicated in the stereotypical representation of Indians as doctors, engineers and computer professionals.

It is widely recognised that Indians dominate the National Spelling Bee, producing the national champion in five of the last seven years, but is there anything specifically in Indian culture that is conducive to such success? Indian parents of winners and other contestants attribute the success of their children to hard work, discipline, high motivation, the premium placed on educational achievements, and even on the desire of recent immigrant communities to partake in the American dream and show that they have arrived; but much of this is also true of Korean Americans, Chinese Americans and some other ethnic groups. Here is one instance among many of how a minority may subscribe to the notion of being a 'model minority'. A somewhat more sociological explanation would perhaps stress the fact that Indian students—to a disproportionately high degree—come from highly educated families, and that knowledge of English, which is almost a native tongue to many Indians in the US, confers advantages on Indians which are denied to other ethnic

groups. One might also take the view that all immigrant communities attempt to create particular niches for themselves, and that Indians excel in spelling bees just as Dominicans dominate American baseball and Kenyans appear to have monopolised the 10,000-m race. When a particular community is viewed as having a stranglehold over some profession, trade or cultural phenomenon, other communities might be inclined to direct their resources elsewhere. Thus, success breeds more success. It can well be argued, however, that all these interpretations fall quite short in their explanatory power, and that many Indians themselves might not have an adequate understanding of the manner in which they are able to call upon certain cultural resources. Indian intellectual traditions persist in emphasising memorisation and mnemonic devices are still deployed in various Indian traditions for the retention of texts. Thus, 'Indian culture' may well be a potent factor in understanding why Indian Americans have monopolised the spelling bee, though this is not the Indian culture that students and their parents have in mind when they are probed by outsiders.

In private conversations, some Indians, particularly of the first generation, have been known to suggest that America is sadly wanting in culture, and that American youth culture, in particular, can only have a detrimental effect on the lives of the young. Indian culture, in this scenario, is visualised as something of an anodyne that counters American culture's corrosive influence on the young. The activities of Indian student unions, which can be found at virtually every college and university where a sizable body of Indian students exist, provide a good illustration of what is perceived to be wholesome Indian culture. At two such institutions, the University of California, Los Angeles (UCLA) and the University of Chicago, the union's agenda is driven largely by an annual culture show. Year after year, the pattern is pretty much the same and loosely follows a tripartite structure. There is a large component focused on the folk and classical dances of India: bharatanatyam and kathak are complemented by a fisherman's folk dance from Kerala, the Gujarati garba, a Rajasthani dance, the Punjabi bhangra, perhaps an instrumental piece, and so on. One can think of this exercise as a miniature version of the Indian Republic Day parade, showcasing the diversity and variegated culture of India. Then there are the Bollywood numbers, a mix of old and new songs, the new ones generally in remix, as well as one specimen each of hip hop and 'fusion'. The dance and music numbers are interspersed by one long skit, or several short ones; but invariably, the subject of the humorous skits is the identity of Indian Americans and the conflict between the first and second generations over dating, marriage and lifestyle choices. Politics, even in the narrowest

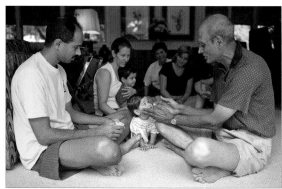

perception of the term, is never allowed to intrude into this world of healthy, insulated Indian culture. Though hate crimes against South Asians, particularly Sikhs (whose turbans were taken by some to mean that they were Muslims, even followers of Osama bin Laden), rose dramatically after 11 September 2001, the 2002 and 2003 culture shows at UCLA, where there may be close to 1000 students of Indian origin, offered not the slightest hint of this violence or the aggressively anti-immigrant sentiments that were openly on display in the wider society.

Not only is Indian culture perhaps more stable in the US than it is in India, it also revolves around fewer phenomena that are supposedly emblematic of Indian and especially Hindu culture. An astounding number of daughters from middle-class and professional Indian American families are tutored in Indian dance, predominantly in bharatanatyam—the dance (*natya*) form around which a manual was penned by the ancient writer Bharat, not, as is commonly rendered, 'the dance of India'. Some bharatanatyam teachers have become an institution unto themselves. The dance company, Natyakalalayam, founded by Hema Rajagopalan in the mid-1970s, undertook 121 performances in the US in 1999, including some at major venues such as the Kennedy Center in Washington, DC. Another famous teacher in Los Angeles reportedly has 250 students: this teacher requires each student to attend the *arangetram*, or first public recital, of all other students in the same cohort. The students' families put on a lavish show and reception, with costs commonly reaching as high as US$40,000. Though these families may not be paying dowries for their daughters, they are now running up '*arangetram* debts'. Such is the view of bharatanatyam as the supreme symbol of refined Indian culture that even a few Pakistani and Bangladeshi Muslim families, oblivious to vicious gossip and innuendo among more orthodox Muslims, have been known to expose their daughters to its charms. Bharatanatyam remains a staple at Indian student culture shows, Diwali *melas* (fairs), Indian Independence Day festivities, and the state-sponsored Festival of India. The other mainstay of all cultural events is bhangra, which is as boisterous as bharatanatyam is staid and elegant. Bhangra's popularity has increased dramatically in recent years, as if Indians wanted to remind themselves and show everyone else that a 'model minority' and nerdy Silicon Valley types can also have fun.

A more aggressive and consequently narrower perception of Indian culture is championed by the Hindu Students Council (HSC), the youth division of the Vishwa Hindu Parishad (VHP), an organisation founded in 1964 to promote Hindu culture worldwide. The VHP is more commonly thought of as the vanguard of Hindutva, the purportedly cultural wing of militant Hindu nationalism. A considerable body of scholarship has focused on the VHP's activities in the US, its recruitment drives and its bold lobbying for funds used to support its activities in India, but much less work has been done on the Hindu Students Council. A consequence of the growing Indian population in the US is the increased visibility of Indian American students on American college and university campuses. These 'heritage students', as they are known to the faculty, have sometimes been vocal in their demand for courses on Indian history, religion and culture, and often, a more enhanced course focused on Hinduism is their most immediate concern. Over the last decade, many have moved into the HSC, which was established in 1990 and now claims to be the largest Hindu student group outside India. Though the HSC aims to bolster the faith of Hindu students on campus, it has frequently sponsored campus visits by advocates of Hindutva ideology, such as David Frawley and Koenrad Elst. The organisational strengths of the HSC can reasonably be surmised from the fact that in 1993, on the centenary of Vivekananda's address to the World Parliament of Religions, it held a 'Vision 2000 Global Youth Conference', attended by 2000 Hindu students from the US, India and nearly 20 other countries. Vivekananda is arguably the patron saint of the HSC, the figure from the relatively recent past who is most admired as someone who evokes the idea of a resurgent India conquering the world with its rich spiritual inheritance.

THE POLITICS OF CULTURE: LANDSCAPES OF REPRESENTATION AND RESISTANCE

The Indian American landscape has, in many respects, vastly changed over the last two decades. Sometime in late 1978 or early 1979, *The Washington Post* carried an article detailing the entrepreneurial acumen and networks of the Patels, who were then described as having descended on the motel business and making it their own. In 1999, the Asian American Hotel Owners Association (AAHOA) stated that 50 per cent of motels were owned by Indian Americans, a figure estimated to have risen to 70 per cent. The vast bulk of these are owned by Gujaratis with surnames such as Patel, Desai and Shah, and it is said that in small towns and rural areas of America 'patel' is thought to be the Hindi word for motel. If all this appears to represent continuity rather than change, then it is also necessary to add that 25 years ago, indeed even 10 years ago, the AAHOA, which is in effect an Indian American association, would not have sought to meddle in politics or have had the self-confidence to associate with an openly political figure. Yet the AAHOA sought to invite Narendra Modi, the chief minister of Gujarat, to its annual meeting in March 2005 as its principal guest. Modi is viewed with contempt and loathing by human rights advocates as it is believed he permitted, perhaps even instigated, a pogrom in 2002 against Muslims in Gujarat which took the lives of at least 2000 Muslims and left 150,000 or more homeless.

The AAHOA describes itself as a non-political organisation, and its chief officials, when queried about their invitation to Modi, described him as a man who has

The Natyakalalayam dance group, based at the Massachusetts Institute of Technology, showcases classical dance forms from various parts of India.

Young Indian dancers in costume at the Festival of India in New Jersey, 1996.

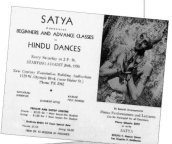

Posters for Hindu dance classes and performances in Los Angeles, 1950.

323

The acclaimed novelists Raja Rao and G. V. Desani were colleagues at the University of Texas at Austin in the late 1960s.

Salman Rushdie is one of the foremost Indian writers of the diaspora, with a string of important—and often controversial—novels.

opened up Gujarat to foreign investment from NRIs (non-resident Indians). They consider the invitation to Modi to address the annual convention as a good business proposition for themselves and the state of Gujarat; but the AAHOA did not envision that the invitation to Modi would be seen as an endorsement of a man accused of mass murder and crimes against humanity, or that there would be Indian American constituencies who could marshal resources in defence of radical politics. Once the word had spread through the Internet, and academic and activist networks had been energised, the pressure upon AAHOA to retract the invitation mounted. Days before Modi was scheduled to arrive in the US, the American government took the unprecedented step of revoking his US visa with a press release stating that American legislation did not permit the entry into the country of a person against whom there are serious allegations of criminal conduct.

One of the many organisations that spearheaded the drive against Modi, and perhaps rightly claimed a hand in the US State Department's decision to revoke his visa, is the Campaign Against Genocide (CAG). This organisation, founded in early 2005, has no office and only a few core members, and its support base is comprised largely of Indian American academics, the vast majority of whom

hold professorships in history, anthropology, literature, cultural studies and other disciplines in the humanities and softer social sciences. A few of CAG's members and supporters, all academics who have combined activism with their intellectual work, whipped up a storm in November 2002 when they published an independent report on the activities of the Indian Development and Relief Fund (IDRF), a non-profit Indian American organisation. They claim that the IDRF supports the work of organisations committed to Hindu nationalism and its pet projects, including religious education, *shuddhi* (purification and reconversion) and the Hinduisation of tribal populations. Twenty years ago, there would have been few such Indian American academics, as the tendency was for Indians to gravitate towards the physical sciences, engineering, medicine and other well-paying professions. While the inclination to enter into one of these professions has scarcely disappeared, the ranks of Indian American graduate students and faculty who are strongly committed to humanistic education and to the university as the twin site of intellectual practices and a space for dissent have steadily grown. There is hardly a department of English at a major liberal arts college or state or private university which does not have in its faculty at least one Indian American. Academics such as Arjun Appadurai, Homi Bhabha and Gayatri Chakravorty Spivak are not only among the most prominent Indian Americans in the country, but are also holders of endowed professorships at the country's most elite universities and they occupy the most pivotal place in their own disciplines.

Indian American literature

In the more public sphere, writing in idioms and genres more congenial to a wider audience, an analogous space is occupied by Indian American writers. For decades, the only modern Indian or Indian American writers known to American audiences were R. K. Narayan, Ved Mehta and V. S. Naipaul (who, at any rate, was an Indo-Trinidadian who wrote with seething contempt about 'Third World' societies). Only two Indian writers of any great distinction were settled in the US, Raja Rao and G. V. Desani: the former, a novelist's novelist, had only a small following, while Desani, whose *All About H. Hatterr* (1948) suggested a dexterity and playfulness with the language that few postmodernists have been able to emulate, similarly died in obscurity. No writer had written about the Asian Indian experience or penned a novel on American society. In contrast, contemporary Indian writers command recognition and advances from publishers that would make Silicon Valley entrepreneurs envious. Though it is debatable whether any contemporary Indian American writer, with the possible exception of Salman Rushdie, is as brilliant a stylist of the English language as either

A. K. Ramanujan

Attipat Krishnaswami Ramanujan was born in Mysore, in what is now the state of Karnataka, on 16 March 1929. He earned degrees in English literature from the University of Mysore and arrived in the US in the late 1950s to pursue a doctorate in folklore and linguistics at Indiana University. In 1963, Ramanujan commenced teaching at the University of Chicago, where eventually he held joint appointments in the departments of South Asian Languages and Civilizations, Linguistics and the Committee on Social Thought until his untimely death at the peak of his powers on 13 July 1993. In those three decades, Ramanujan came to acquire an unsurpassed reputation as a scholar, writer, poet, folklorist and translator, and his intellectual gifts did not go unnoticed. He was honoured by the government of India with a Padma Shri in 1976, and he was among the earliest recipients, in 1983, of a MacArthur 'genius' grant. He was elected to the American Academy of Arts and Sciences in 1990.

Raman, as he was known to his friends and colleagues, was a man of unusual intellectual acuity, poetic sensitivity, immense erudition and prolific output. Though he published poetry in English, Kannada and Tamil, he became rather more renowned for his translations from Kannada and Tamil. Speaking of Siva (1973) introduced readers to Virasaiva literature, while Hymns for the Drowning (1981) offered brilliant translations of poems to Vishnu by the 9th-century poet Nammalvar. The Collected Essays, published posthumously in 2000, are nothing short of a dazzling demonstration of Raman's wide reading in Indian and European literature, his ease with structuralism, psychoanalysis, hermeneutics and semiotics, and the nuanced understanding that he brought to bear upon texts. Folklore was Raman's first love, and in a score of essays and two collections he breathed new life into the study of folktales. The 'same' story told by a man and a woman, as Raman showed, could appear to be anything but the same. Though perhaps not widely known outside academic, intellectual and literary circles, Ramanujan became a legend to those who had the good fortune to know him, as well as a mentor to countless students and scholars. He was, arguably, the most influential scholar of South Asian studies in the US during the 20th century.

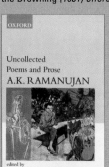

Ramanujan was an accomplished academic and poet.

Extract from Vinay Lal, 'Establishing Roots, Engendering Awareness: A Political History of Asian Indians in the United States', in Live Like the Banyan Tree: Images of the Indian American Experience (exhibition catalogue), 1999.

Rao or Desani, the indubitable fact is that Asian Indian writers now play a prominent role in shaping American literature. However, one would be justified in asking whether they should be viewed as Asian Indian writers or as Indian writers who deploy a near global language in a world of complex transnational exchanges and interconnected histories. Rushdie has only recently been settled in the US; in the novels of Amitav Ghosh, America has only a marginal existence, and often none at all; and Vikram Seth, after his magisterial attempt at the great California novel, *The Golden Gate* (1986), written as 690 tetrameter sonnets, quit America, both as an abode and in his writings. Asian Indian writing is nonetheless much more variegated than was possible even a decade ago. Shishir Kurup, a talented playwright in the Los Angeles area, has sought to understand how the worldview of the Indian epics might be introduced in a secular society; the doctor, Abraham Verghese, has penned a poignant narrative on AIDS in small-town America; and the late Agha Shahid Ali skilfully juxtaposed American and Indian landscapes.

It is perhaps not accidental that the writings of female Asian Indian writers, among them Meena Alexander, Jhumpa Lahiri, Bharati Mukherjee and the largely young members of the Berkeley South Asian women's collective who co-authored *Our Feet Walk the Sky* (1993), speak more directly of the condition of being an Indian in the US. As has been the case with many immigrant groups, the men came first, both in the first phase of immigration from 1900 to 1924, and in the first couple of decades following the passage of INS legislation in 1965. Whereas the men could create a niche for themselves outside the home, particularly in the professions, the women came largely as brides. Chitra Divakaruni has acquired a huge following among young Indian women with her stories of arranged marriages and repressed sexuality, the pressures placed upon women to conform to notions of Indian culture and family, the loneliness of the home-bound wife, and the desire of Indian American women to create lives of their own. Many critics charge Divakaruni with playing up the stereotypes of Indian women as submissive, which predominate in the wider culture, and it is certainly true that a surprisingly monolithic view of Indian American women emerges from her writings. However, if Alexander, Lahiri and Divakaruni resonate so strongly with Indian American women, they do so partly because of a profound unwillingness in the community to question the sanctimonious pieties about allegedly model Indian American families. The rate of heterosexual marriage is higher in the Indian American community than for any other racial or ethnic group; but social workers have amply documented that Indian American women are more likely to be subjected to domestic violence, sexual abuse and other forms of exploitation. Over the last 15 years, numerous women's help groups and shelters—Apna Ghar, Saheli, Narika, Sahara and Maitri—have sprung up in metropolitan centres. If Indian Americans stood to profit from the hard-won achievements of the civil rights movement, then one should expect, as well, that the feminist movement in the US has been inspiring for some Indian American women.

POLITICS AND THE FUTURE OF INDIANS IN THE US

Scholars of diasporic communities have long been cognizant of the fact that an immigrant community generally retains a complex, even torturous, relationship with its homeland. The term 'non-resident Indian', was originally

An Indian couple cross Devon Avenue in Chicago's Indian district. The neighbourhood attracts a significant number of Chicagoans, who are drawn to it by over 30 Indian restaurants.

devised to refer to Indians settled in the US, and more broadly in the affluent industrialised nations, even though older and larger Indian communities were to be found in Mauritius, Trinidad, South Africa and other nations. It was always understood, though never formally acknowledged, that NRIs were to be placed in a different category than the descendants of indentured labourers, and the government of India foolishly ratified this openly discriminatory understanding when it proposed, in 2004, to confer the right of dual citizenship only upon Indians settled in countries of the newer Indian diaspora. For their part, Indian Americans have displayed an increasing interest in exercising their influence to make India more hospitable to foreign investment, and over the years they have successfully prevailed upon the Indian government to rescind regulations that forbid NRIs from owning property in India. One is now beginning to see even more complex manifestations of the Indian American encounter with the homeland. The brain drain, it has been suggested, is now being reversed: not only do several thousand Indian Americans return to India each year, they also take back capital, entrepreneurial skills and technical know-how. Among the beneficiaries in India of American philanthropy have been the famous Indian Institutes of Technology, some of whose millionaire graduates, even when they do not return to the homeland, have laid their wealth at the mother's bosom.

What is rather more striking, perhaps, is the manner in which the internal politics of the Indian subcontinent is echoed in the politics of South Asian communities in the US. When a portion of Chicago's Devon Avenue, a six-block stretch which houses the usual assortment of Patel Brothers grocery stores, jewellers, Indian restaurants, Bollywood music and film outlets, and 220-volt appliance and sari stores, was renamed after Gandhi, Pakistani businesses successfully applied pressure to have an adjoining section named after M. A. Jinnah, the founder of Pakistan. Much more dramatic and rife with consequences is the support rendered to various political movements in India from their adherents in the US. The Sikh separatist movement in Punjab, aimed at creating an autonomous homeland for the Sikhs, to be known as Khalistan, received much institutional and financial support from Sikh militants in the US, Canada and Britain, and the demand for Khalistan flourished among certain Sikh communities in the US even after it had calmed down in India itself. Today, there is more awareness among American Sikhs, greatly enhanced after 9/11, that its principal engagements must be with other communities in the US, and the Sikh Media Advisory and Research Taskforce (SMART) seeks to sensitise all Americans, and in particular state agencies, about Sikh faith and history, the right of Sikhs to wear a turban to work, and the use of the *kirpan*, or ceremonial dagger.

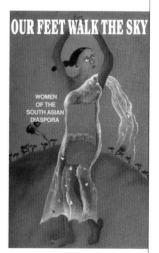

Our Feet Walk the Sky, published in 1993, is a compilation of personal histories and critical essays by women of South Asian descent.

Houston Sikhs and Hindus paying tribute to astronaut Kalpana Chawla, who was a member of the ill-fated space shuttle Columbia, *2 February 2003.*

Samar, a progressive periodical published for the Indian community in the US.

Bobby Jindal is an India-born, conservative Republican, and only the second person of Indian descent elected to the US Congress, in 2004.

Indian American Muslims have not, perhaps, been similarly vocal in stating their views on the political turmoil in Kashmir, nor are they a major source of material support to the insurgents, but on the question of the pogrom directed against Muslims in Gujarat they rightfully took a strong stand and insistently pressed for the perpetrators of the violence to be brought to trial.

Support for Hindu militancy and, more broadly, the vigorous, even aggressive, affirmation of pride in Hindu culture has taken many forms. A few instances might be enumerated, though many more easily come to mind. It is a matter of public record that some Hindus took out full-page advertisements in Indian American publications praising Hindus in India who were firmly committed to the agitation surrounding the Babri Masjid, a 16th-century mosque in Ayodhya which was eventually destroyed by Hindu militants on 6 December 1992, and claimed by the militants to have been built on the foundations of a Hindu temple. Indian American Hindus have poured much money into the construction of a new Hindu temple in Ayodhya and contribute generously to the activities of the Vishwa Hindu Parishad (VHP) and Rashtriya Swayamsevak Sangh (RSS), though often this money is channelled into sister organisations that claim non-profit status. The Chicago chapter of the VHP unabashedly celebrated the 'thunderous successful culmination' of the 'liberation' of Ayodhya and welcomed 'the dawn of Hindu Rashtra' (nation).

That the ossified Hinduism of some Hindus in the US, who are far removed from the complexities of the faith and its rich engagement with the multiple strands of Indian civilisation, has unsavoury political ramifications is nowhere better illustrated than in the activities of the Los Angeles-based Federation of Hindu Associations (FHA). Instituting a 'Hindu of the Year' award in 1994, the FHA conferred it jointly upon Bal Thackeray and Sadhvi Ritambara, two stalwarts of the Hindutva movement who have warned Indian Muslims that they must be prepared to live in India on terms dictated by the Hindu community. The Gujarati Hindu community in the US is so heavily communalised that few of its members had the courage to condemn unequivocally the killing of Muslims in Gujarat. In contrast, Hindutva websites based in the US, often set up by engineering students and Silicon Valley software programmers, offer boldly revisionist accounts of Indian history, claiming that the largest genocide in history was perpetrated against Hindus over 800 years of Muslim rule. Meanwhile, a new organisation, American Hindus against Defamation (AHAD), which describes itself as a staunch defender of the Hindu faith, has been aggressive in compelling American companies to recall from the market products such as beer bottles, underwear, dolls and flip-flops that use logos of Ganesh or other Hindu deities.

Asian Indians continue to occupy a marginal place in American political life. Some members of the community see in the 2004 election of Bobby Jindal to the US House of Representatives a great ray of hope. Jindal is only the second Indian American to have a seat in Congress, and his supporters have sought to minimise the fact that, as an ultra-conservative Republican, he embraces positions with which the Indian American community (which votes for Democratic candidates by a substantial margin) is generally not in agreement. Jindal has never expressed any interest in South Asian affairs and he has never promoted himself as anything other than a proponent of staunchly Christian, conservative and free market values.

Certainly, no Asian Indian liberal or critic of establishment politics has exercised the kind of nearly incalculable influence on American public policy wielded by someone such as Dinesh D'Souza, who has succeeded remarkably well in presenting Asians (including Indians) as 'model minorities' for African-Americans in particular to emulate. It is not altogether surprising that Asian Indian conservatives should have risen to such public prominence: not only are their views in consonance with those of the ruling elites, but their professional status and a narrow perception of a meritocratic society have prevented them from entertaining thoughts about coalitions with Hispanics, African Americans and other working-class minorities. There is also more than a grain of truth in W. E. B. DuBois's observation in 1938 that,

India has also had temptation to stand apart from the darker peoples and seek her affinities among Whites. She has long wished to regard herself as 'Aryan', rather than 'colored' and to think of herself as much nearer physically and spiritually to Germany and England than to Africa, China or the South Seas. And yet, the history of the modern world shows the futility of this thought. European exploitation desires the black slave, the Chinese coolies and the Indian laborer for the same ends and the same purposes, and calls them all niggers.

Still, as one considers the gamut of Indian political activity in the US, there is also reason, as previously suggested, to be hopeful. Asian Indians have partaken of the various movements which offer a strong affirmation of the rights of cultural, religious and ethnic minorities, and *pari passu* a principled critique of American domination and arrogance. Alongside numerous Asian Indian newspapers, there are progressive periodicals such as *Samar* and *Little India*. At the institutional level, while apolitical organisations such as the Network of Indian Professionals (NETIP) and The Indus Entrepreneurs (TiE) have garnered more attention among Indian Americans, it is encouraging to think that the greatest political success of the Indian community was achieved by progressive South Asian activists who formed the Leased Drivers Coalition (LDC) in 1992 to represent Indian, Bangladeshi and Pakistani taxi drivers in New York City. A large strike in 1993 was followed by a city-wide taxi drivers strike in 1998, which ground the city's taxi services to a halt and offered a visceral demonstration of the ability of South Asian working-classes to organise across religious and ethnic lines. There is some reason to believe that the multiple legacies of the Ghadar movement, the struggle for Indian independence and the civil rights, women's and anti-racism movements will stir Asian Indians to a greater political awareness.

Vinay Lal

CANADA

INDO-CANADIANS, OR East Indians whose ancestry can be traced back to India, comprise one of the largest, most diverse, best educated and entrepreneurial ethno-cultural minorities in Canada. Statistics Canada 2001 identifies East Indians as approximately 75 per cent of the nearly 1-million-strong population originating from the countries of South Asia, with whom East Indians are identified in official records, the media and public perception.

Indo-Canadians are deeply spiritual, family oriented and have a positive sense of self worth. While retaining their own ethno-cultural identity, they have learned to appreciate 'difference'. They have a reputation for hard work, tenacity, respect for the law, disciplined pursuit of financial stability, and high professional achievement.

Five Indian languages—Punjabi, Gujarati, Urdu, Hindi and Tamil—are among the top 25 languages spoken in Canada. However, an estimated 80 per cent of Indo-Canadians speak English. They share a democratic value system and are familiar with Western culture. Given these resources, they can readily integrate into Canadian society.

DEMOGRAPHICS

Since the 1901 census, data on ancestral origins has been collected to capture the changing character of Canada's growing pluralistic society. Immigrants with immediate and distant origins in India largely identify themselves as 'East Indian' for census purposes, where they are grouped with those from other South Asian countries. They are further classified by their 'visible minority' status with immigrants from other non-Western countries. Visible minorities are defined, according to the Employment Equity Act (1986), as 'persons, other than Aboriginal peoples, who are non-Caucasian in race and non-white in colour.' The intent of such information is to support programmes that promote equal opportunity for all to share in the social, cultural and economic life of Canada.

Map 8.47

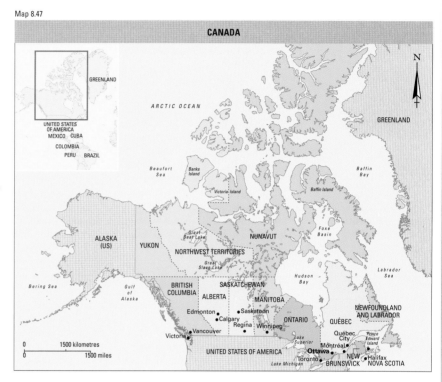

India has remained among the top 10 source countries for permanent residents in Canada since 1994. Although India is likely to continue being a major source country for immigrants, presently, Indo-Canadians are a small fraction of the total Canadian population (see Table 8.30).

The 713,330 East Indians are spread across Canada, with the largest groups based in the provinces of Ontario and British Columbia (see Table 8.31). Ten cities account for 640,530 East Indians (see Figure 8.8), most of whom live in Toronto or Vancouver.

Between 2001 and 2004, East Indian immigration directly from India continued at an average of 26,725 per year, with 70 per cent going to Ontario, 18 per cent to British Columbia, 6 per cent to Alberta, 4 per cent to Québec and 1.4 per cent to Manitoba. Over the same four-year period, the immigration of Indo-Fijians continued at an average of 586 per year, with 70.3 per cent going

Figure 8.8

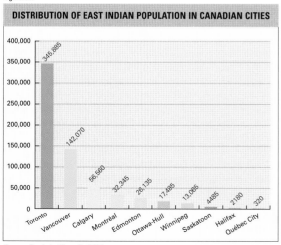

DISTRIBUTION OF EAST INDIAN POPULATION IN CANADIAN CITIES

Table 8.30

SOUTH ASIAN POPULATION CATEGORIES USED IN CANADIAN STATISTICS (2001)		
	Number of persons	% of total population
Country of birth India	314,690	1.06
South Asian	963,190	3.25
East Indian	713,330	2.41
Total no. of immigrants	5,448,480	18.38
Total population of Canada	29,639,035	100

Source: Statistics Canada 2001.

Source: Statistics Canada 2001.

Table 8.31

PERCENTAGE OF EAST INDIANS IN CANADA BY PROVINCE	
Ontario	57.95
British Columbia	25.74
Alberta	8.58
Québec	4.78
Manitoba	1.70
Saskatchewan	0.45
Nova Scotia	0.40
New Brunswick	0.19
Newfoundland and Labrador	0.13
Yukon	0.03
Northwest Territories	0.02
Prince Edward Island	0.01
Nunavut	0.00 (25 people)

Source: Statistics Canada 2001.

Sikh and fellow lumber workers at a Sikh funeral service at Todd Inlet, British Columbia, c. 1909.

to British Columbia, 17.8 per cent to Alberta and only 11.6 per cent to Ontario. From 2001 through to 2004, the immigration of Indo-Guyanese continued at an average of 1453 per year, with 94 per cent going to Ontario, 2.1 per cent to Québec, 2 per cent to Alberta and 1.2 per cent to Manitoba. East Indians do not form a homogeneous community in Canada. Those coming from the same country have more in common with each other than with those from another country. This is one reason why East Indians from specific countries have tended to settle in clusters in Canada. However, all East Indians in Canada still share a common culture based on their ancestral roots in India.

HISTORICAL ORIGINS

Sikhs in India first heard about British Columbia (BC) from British Indian troops, primarily Sikhs from Punjab stationed in Hong Kong. In 1902, these Hong Kong regiments travelled through Vancouver and across Canada to the coronation celebrations of Edward VII. They brought back stories of the rich soil and favourable climate of BC, similar to Punjab, and high earnings for work in lumber yards. Between 1903 and 1908, about 5000 East Indians, almost all male Sikhs from Punjab, came to BC to work on the railroad, in lumber mills or in forestry.

Although these Sikhs were unskilled and uneducated, initially employers favoured them because they were industrious and reliable, and willing to work for low wages. However, in 1907, a downturn in the BC economy produced significant numbers of unemployed whites. They formed the Asiatic Exclusion League to pressure the BC government for action and threatened violence against all Asians. That same year, the BC government disenfranchised East Indians. As a result, they lost the federal vote, were unable to run for public office, serve on a jury or be employed in the professions, and were not eligible for public service jobs or labour on public works.

The Canadian federal government had taken steps to control Chinese immigration through the use of a head tax. Similarly, it wanted to curb the sudden growth in East Indian immigration, but the British government was opposed to a head tax on, or specific regulations against, East Indians, fearing this would increase East Indian opposition to the colonial government in India. On 8 January 1908, the federal government announced legislation that eliminated East Indian immigration without specifically targeting the group. The Order-in-Council which was issued imposed a 'continuous journey' rule on

all immigrants, prohibiting the entry of those who did not come to Canada by continuous journey from their country of origin. Since at the time all steamships travelling from India, China or Japan to Canada stopped at Hawaii, there were no direct trips to Canada for East Indians that satisfied the 'continuous journey' rule.

In 1914, a clever and affluent Sikh leader, Gurdit Singh, set out to test the 'continuous journey' rule as it applied to East Indians. He hired a Japanese ship, the *Komagata Maru*, and arranged for it to make a non-stop voyage from Hong Kong to Vancouver carrying 376 East Indian immigrants. On 23 May 1914, the *Komagata Maru* steamed into Burrard Inlet, Vancouver. The East Indian passengers were legally British subjects, with the right to travel freely within the British Empire, which included Canada. Having satisfied the 'continuous journey' rule, the East Indian passengers should have been allowed to land in Vancouver as legally arrived immigrants. However, for the next two months Canadian immigration officials did everything in their power to prevent any of the passengers from setting foot on Canadian soil, while the local Sikh community argued the legality of the case in the courts. Canadian officials also tried to prevent food and medicine from reaching the ship: some passengers got sick and one passenger died. By 21 July 1914, all legal channels were exhausted. Armed conflict was close, but finally a negotiated settlement was reached. The *Komagata Maru* was reprovisioned with food, medicine and water, 21 passengers who could prove they were returning residents were allowed to disembark, and on 23 July 1914, the *Komagata Maru* steamed out of Burrard Inlet headed for Asia, escorted by the armed cruiser H. M. C. S. *Rainbow*.

LATER DEVELOPMENTS

Because of the 'continuous journey' rule, there was little East Indian immigration to Canada between 1908 and 1947, when the restriction was lifted. Between 1914 and 1920 only one East Indian immigrant was admitted to Canada. The population of 5000 in 1908 decreased rapidly after 1914 as many returned to India or moved to the US. By 1918, there were only 700 Sikhs left in BC. In 1919, the Canadian federal government lifted the restrictions on Indians bringing their wives and children under 18 years of age to the country. The ban against East Indians voting and other restrictions arising from the 1907 law were removed in 1947.

Before 1961, there were just 3360 Indo-Canadians in the country. Between 1961–70 their numbers jumped, with large spurts occurring throughout the 1980s and 1990s. This new pattern of growth can be attributed to the liberalisation of the immigration policy in the mid-1960s by the Liberal government of Pierre Trudeau in response to the economic needs of the country and the introduction of non-discriminatory criteria for entry. Canada's immigration policy evolved from the Immigration Act of 1952, which permitted the refusal of immigrants on several grounds, including nationality, ethnicity, geographic area and citizenship, to the 1966 'White Paper on Immigration', which ushered in the fairer 'point system'. In 1976, the 'Green Paper on Immigration' tightened entry using the

The Komagata Maru *anchored in Vancouver Harbour, 1914.*

A meeting in the Vancouver Sikh Temple during the 1946 campaign to secure the vote for Indians settled in Canada.

'independent class' of immigration, but opened up the 'family reunification' and 'refugee' classes.

In addition to immigration to Canada directly from India, Canada has received immigrants from the Indian diaspora. Approximately 25,000 Indo-Fijians came to Canada from Fiji between 1971 and 1991 due to recurring conflicts between the Indo-Fijians and indigenous Fijians. In 1972, Canada opened its doors to 7000 Ugandan Asians, mostly Ismaili Muslims of Indian background, expelled from their adopted country by the African dictator Idi Amin. Approximately 80,000 Indo-Guyanese also emigrated to Canada from Guyana between 1966 and 1996 due to oppressive conditions in the country after independence.

The pattern of settlement of these three groups in Canada is quite different. Initially, the Indo-Fijians settled around Vancouver. Later, 1000 Indo-Fijians moved to Alberta, another 1000 to Ontario, and only 75 per cent of the original number were left in Vancouver; about 10 per cent of them later emigrated to Australia or New Zealand. Almost all of the Indo-Guyanese immigrants initially settled in Ontario. Only in the late 1970s did 1000 Indo-Guyanese move to Alberta. The Ugandan Asians were distributed roughly equally among the cities of Vancouver, Edmonton, Calgary and Toronto.

Between 1998 and 2002, migrants from India entered Canada primarily in the 'skilled worker' and 'family reunification' classes. Over the past five years, Indian immigration has undergone a major shift, with an estimated 75 per cent of Indians entering in the 'skilled worker' class and a smaller proportion in the 'family reunification' class, except for the Punjabi Sikhs migrating to BC. Between 1996 and 2000, 81 per cent of them were in the 'family reunification' class. The average household income of Indians, at US$41,748, is almost 16 per cent higher than the national median household income of US$35,966. English is the

mother tongue of 35 per cent of Indo-Canadians and 51 per cent of them use English most often at home. While 61 per cent identify a non-official language as their mother tongue, only 41 per cent speak it at home. In 2001, Punjabi was among the top five non-official languages for Ontario, Alberta and BC. Only about 0.5 per cent of Indo-Canadians speak French, Canada's other official language. Of the population aged over 15 years, 26 per cent hold university degrees and 1 per cent hold a doctorate.

Vancouver, Surrey and Abbotsford have dense pockets of Sikhs. In the 1980s, militant Sikhs in India were intent on creating Khalistan, a homeland for Sikhs, independent from India. The 1984 invasion of the Golden Temple in Amritsar by Indian troops, ordered by Prime Minister Indira Gandhi, inflamed the Khalistan movement further. Militant Canadian Sikh supporters began to fund-raise in gurdwaras in Canada.

In 1985, Air India Flight 182, originating in Toronto, blew up over the Atlantic Ocean near Ireland, killing all 329 mostly Indo-Canadian passengers aboard. Canadian

The 46-cent stamp issued by Canada Post on 19 April 1999 features the khanda, *a double-edged sword which appears on the Sikh flag. The* khanda *is a metaphor for divine knowledge, its sharp edges cleaving truth from falsehood.*

East African refugees in the mid-1970s boarding a plane for a flight from Uganda to Canada upon Idi Amin's expulsion orders.

In New Delhi on 18 January 2005, the Canadian prime minister, Paul Martin (centre) is joined by the Indian prime minister, Dr Manmohan Singh (right). With them are Canadian MPs of Indian descent. CLOCKWISE FROM TOP RIGHT: *Gurbax Malhi, Ruby Dhalla, Ujjal Donsanjh, Deepak Obhrai and Navdeep Singh Bains.*

Ujjal Dosanjh has served as the premier of British Columbia and as the federal minister of health.

security investigations led officials to believe that this crime had been orchestrated by militant Sikh supporters of Khalistan in Vancouver. Twenty years and a US$130-million investigation evaporated with the acquittal of the prime co-accused, Ripudaman Singh Malik and Ajaib Singh Bagri in June 2005. The Air India disaster reflected poorly on the reputation of Canadian Sikhs as a peaceful people. The Sikhs grew determined to show that they are law-abiding citizens and not extremists. Over the years they have become highly involved in the political life of Canada by running for public office. It is ironic that the Air India disaster has resulted in the flowering of Sikh participation in the Canadian politics.

POLITICAL PARTICIPATION

Canada is an independent sovereign democracy and a federal state, with ten largely self-governing provinces and three territories controlled by the central government. The national (federal) parliament has the power 'to make laws for the peace, order and good government of Canada,' except for 'subjects assigned exclusively to the legislatures

of the provinces.' Certain powers (e.g. national defence) are exclusively federal; other powers (e.g. higher education) are exclusively provincial; and yet other powers (e.g. medicare) are shared, with the federal government being responsible for setting and enforcing national standards and transferring funds to the provinces to help pay for the programme, while each provincial government is responsible for operating and administrating medicare in its own province.

There are four main political parties in the Federal Parliament. The Conservative Party is the party of big business and higher income individuals, and those who aspire to become wealthy. Its supporters would like to minimise taxes and reduce the amount of government. The Liberal Party is the party of small business and middle-income individuals. Its supporters favour middle-of-the-road solutions to problems. The New Democratic Party (NDP) is a socialist party. It favours increasing opportunities for working-class people and the underprivileged, and is not opposed to raising taxes on the wealthy or on big business. The Bloc Québécquois (BQ) is a separatist party that would like to see Québec become a country, independent of Canada. In the meantime, they are in parliament to look after the interests of Québec.

East Indians have been criticised for being more interested in politics back 'home' than in Canadian politics, but it is becoming harder to support such a contention given recent developments in East Indian participation in Canadian federal politics.

In the Federal Parliament elected in the year 2000, there were a total of five members of parliament (MP) of East Indian origin: two Liberal MPs (Gurbax Malhi and Herb Dhaliwal) and three Conservative MPs (Rahim Jaffer, Deepak Obhrai and Gurmant Grewal). In the federal parliamentary election of 2004, there were 26 candidates of East Indian origin running for election as MPs: 11 for the Conservative Party, 11 for the Liberal Party and four for the NDP. Out of a total of 308 MPs, nine MPs of East Indian origin were elected: four Conservative MPs and five Liberal MPs.

The nine MPs of East Indian origin elected in the federal parliamentary election of 2004 were: Deepak Obhrai (Conservative; Calgary East, Alberta), Rahim Jaffer (Conservative; Edmonton-Strathcona, Alberta), Gurmant Grewal (Conservative; Newton-North Delta, BC), Nina Grewal (Conservative; Fleetwood-Port Kells, BC), Gurbax Malhi (Liberal; Bramalea-Gore-Malton, Ontario), Ruby Dhalla (Liberal; Brampton-Springdale, Ontario), Yasmin Ratansi (Liberal; Don Valley East, Ontario), Navdeep Singh Bains (Liberal; Mississauga-Brampton South, Ontario), and Ujjal Dosanjh (Liberal; Vancouver South, BC).

Ujjal Dosanjh is undoubtedly the federal politician of East Indian origin with the highest profile in Canada. Dosanjh comes from Dosanjh Kalan, near Phagwara, India. He emigrated to England at the age of 17, and four years later, in 1968, moved to BC. He worked in a mill while taking evening classes at a local community college. Later, he attended Simon Fraser University and graduated with honours in political science. He completed his law degree with the University of British Columbia in 1976 and started his own law practice in Vancouver in 1979. He has been involved in community work with many organisations, including the British Columbia Civil Liberties Association and the Vancouver Multicultural Society. In 1991, after two previous unsuccessful attempts, he finally

Outstanding East Indian businessmen in Canada

Shan Chandrasekar

Shan Chandrasekar came to Canada in 1967 from India. In 1971, he and some Indian friends formed an Indian music group as a hobby and eventually launched it as a television show on Rogers Cable, where in 1975 it became the first Asian programme produced as a series for a North American television station. In 1977, Chandrasekar was involved in launching a multicultural television station, Channel 47. He is now the president and CEO of ATN-Asian Television Network International, a publicly traded company which provides television programming in English and several South Asian languages. In 2004, Shan Chandrasekar was inducted into the Canadian Association of Broadcasters Hall of Fame for outstanding achievements and contributions to private broadcasting and Canada.

Bob Dhillon

Bob Dhillon is a Calgary-based real estate entrepreneur and president and CEO of Mainstreet Equity Corp. On 19 June 2004, the Indo-Canada Chamber of Commerce gave Dhillon their 2004 Business Man Award. Part of their citation states that Mainstreet Equity is a Canadian real estate company focused on acquiring and managing multi-family residential rental properties. The company buys undervalued residential units and enhances their value through renovations and improved operating efficiencies. Founded in 1997, Mainstreet owns, operates and maintains its entire portfolio of more than 2600 properties, which are located throughout Vancouver, Calgary, Edmonton, Red Deer, Alberta, Toronto and Mississauga.

Asa Johal

Asa Johal is a prominent Indo-Canadian businessman in Vancouver. In 1991, the government of BC awarded him the Order of British Columbia. Part of the citation stated that in the time since migrating to Canada in 1924, he had become one of the province's most prominent businessmen and outstanding citizens. His Terminal Sawmill Group consists of two mills, two manufacturing plants and a logging camp. Johal has also served as a member of the University of British Columbia Board of Governors and as a director of the Children's Hospital.

won election to the BC Provincial Legislature as a member of the NDP. During his 10 years in the Provincial Legislature, he held cabinet posts as the minister for government services, multiculturalism, human rights and sports, and as the attorney general of BC. On 24 February 2000, Dosanjh was sworn in as the 33rd premier of BC. This made him Canada's first Indo-Canadian premier. After serving as premier until May 2001, he returned to practising law. Dosanjh switched from provincial to federal politics when he ran for Vancouver South as a Liberal and was elected an MP in 2004. He was then appointed minister of health on 20 July 2004.

ECONOMIC LIFE

When the first 5000 East Indians came to Canada between 1903 and 1908, they were almost all Sikh males and settled in BC, and they had primarily only three types of jobs open to them: construction work for a railroad, cutting down trees and working in a lumber mill.

The 2001 census shows that there are 319,045 Canadians over 15 years old who identify their ethnic origins as 'East Indian' and 311,445 of them are employed in a range of industries. These contemporary East Indians comprise a number of different groups of Indians besides Sikhs. Furthermore, they are located in specific concentrations across Canada: in Toronto and the Greater Toronto Area in Ontario; in Vancouver and the region around Vancouver in BC; in Edmonton and Calgary in Alberta; and to a lesser degree in Montréal in Québec and Winnipeg in Manitoba. There are no industries or occupations that are predominantly peopled with East Indians. Instead, just like mainstream Canadians, they are distributed across a wide range of industries and occupations.

The industry with the highest percentage of employed East Indians, however, is manufacturing (21.5 per cent). The industries with the next five highest percentages of employed East Indians are retail trade (11.3 per cent); healthcare and social assistance (8 per cent); transportation and warehousing (7.3 per cent); professional, scientific and technical services (7.2 per cent); and accommodation and food services (6.9 per cent).

The occupations with the highest percentage of employed East Indians are sales and service occupations (22 per cent). The next five occupations with the highest percentage of employed East Indians are business, finance and administrative occupations (19.4 per cent); occupations unique to processing, manufacturing and utilities (14.2 per cent); trades, transport and equipment operators and related occupations (12.7 per cent); management

occupations (9.5 per cent); and natural and applied sciences and related occupations (8.4 per cent).

The census data draw a picture of the economic life of East Indians in Canada in general, showing which industries and occupations are more important than others. However, the East Indian community has a number of outstanding individuals who have used their talent and efforts to make significant contributions to the economic life of Canada.

RELIGIOUS LIFE

The diverse religious traditions of India are represented in Canada and have added to its religious pluralism. Zoroastrianism, Hinduism, Sikhism, Islam, Buddhism, Jainism, Judaism and Christianity have all found a 'home' in Canada. Religious beliefs, philosophical concepts and rituals emanating from these ancient traditions lie at the core of Indo-Canadian existential life. Canada's introduction to the religious traditions of India came at the turn of the last century with the initial presence of a few Sikhs. Temples, gurdwaras, mosques and churches serve as centres for the re-enactment of shared concepts of faith and ritual, and reinforcement of ethno-religious identity, providing communities with social and emotional unity and empowerment with others who are similarly in a new host environment.

In 2001, Hindus comprised 1 per cent of the total Canadian population and Sikhs 0.9 per cent. Both groups are among the 10 major religions for the provinces of Ontario, BC, Alberta and Québec. In addition, both groups have relatively young adherents of their faiths, with a median age of 31.9 for Hindus and 29.7 for Sikhs, which is below the median of 37 years for the overall population. Ontario is home to 73 per cent of Hindus and 38 per cent of Sikhs; most Sikhs are concentrated in British Columbia. Toronto, Vancouver, Calgary, Montréal and Ottawa-Hull host sizable, active, strong communities of these faiths. Sikhs have traditionally maintained a high religious and ethnic consciousness. Their communities are close-knit and their institutions are strong. They have successfully preserved their religion in Canada.

For Indo-Canadian women, the migration experience increases the saliency of religion by 'sacralising' identity. As they acculturate to their new environment, their ethno-religious consciousness is revitalised by membership in

Members of the Baba Fathea Singh Gatka team demonstrate gatka, an Indian martial art, in celebration of Baisakhi, in Vancouver, 2004.

Gurnam Multani's Toronto-based Skylark Restaurant has become a neighbourhood institution.

Lahore Tikka House on Gerrard Street East, Toronto, has an Indian three-wheeler on display.

Young Indian patrons having a drink at a restaurant on Gerrard Street.

their respective ethno-religious institutions. These institutions also provide an avenue for transmitting religious and philosophical beliefs to children, whom they expect to continue practising traditional religions, albeit on more liberal terms.

There are some 70 Hindu temples in Canada, of which 39 are in Ontario. Some are shared with Hindus from many parts of the world. There are more than 20 gurdwaras serving Sikh communities. The first Sikh gurdwara was founded in 1908 in BC, and the largest gurdwara, seating 15,000 people, was opened in 1990 in Malton, Ontario. Often, these centres of worship combine religious, language, educational and cultural activities. Many place the word 'Canada', or the name of respective provinces or cities in the title of the religious institution, expressing the aspiration to belong.

Islam has shown exponential growth since 1961 due to immigration from many countries, of which India is a modest source. The gains in Eastern religious affiliations are concomitant with changing immigration patterns from Asia and the Middle East. In 2001, there were 579,640 Muslims in Canada, representing 2 per cent of the Canadian population. An estimated 167,000 or 29 per cent are of East Indian origin. Ontario has 61 per cent of the entire Muslim population and Toronto has the highest concentration in the country (5 per cent).

Muslim–Christian relations in Canada have positive features. Within the Canadian Council of Churches, mostly Protestant, there is a Christian–Muslim dialogue group. There is also an interfaith division within the Canadian Conference of Bishops. The Canadian Council of Muslim Women handles issues such as employment equity and family violence.

Muslims from India predominantly follow the Sunni branch of Islam. The Ismaili Muslims are one significant group that follows the Shiite tradition. The first Ismailis arrived in Canada in the mid-1960s, followed by a few entrepreneurs, but the largest influx arrived in 1972, when Indians were expelled from Uganda. Many of these refugees were traders and entrepreneurs; they were well

The Nanak Sar Sikh temple in Richmond, British Columbia.

educated, with wide professional and work experience. They have prospered in Canada.

Ugandan Ismaili ancestry is mostly rooted in Gujarat and Kutch on the west coast of India. For Ismaili Muslims, spiritual leadership and inherent authority lies with His Highness, Prince Karim Aga Khan, the 49th imam (spiritual leader) of the group, believed by Ismailis to be a direct descendant of the Prophet Muhammad. Ismailis have a long history of scholarship, intellectual pursuit, volunteer work and support for humanitarian causes. The Aga Khan Development Network (AKDN) contributes to social, economic, and cultural development in many countries and for people of all faiths and origins. In Canada, the AKDN works in partnership with the Canadian International Development Agency (CIDA), several Canadian universities and Toronto's Hospital for Sick Children.

Close adherence to religion impacts on people in two ways. It binds them with shared beliefs and provides an avenue for these beliefs to be transmitted to the next generation. It may also create stress, conflict and even disputes with people of other faiths. It has now been almost a half century since mainstream Canadians of Judaeo-Christian background have had contact with the many and diverse religions and philosophies of Indian and Eastern traditions. Much accommodation, respect, tolerance and appreciation for these traditions has developed during this period. Church halls are used by people of other faiths, newspapers announce their services, report teachings of visiting swamis, gurus and imams, and articles are published on festivals such as Deepavali, Holi, Ramadan, Id-al-Fitr and Guru Nanak's birthday. Conferences on world religions are periodically held, exploring common themes in the spirituality of the major religions as well as their unique features. There is interest in traditional medicine, attention paid to dietary customs, sensitivity shown to minority differences in the law and medicine, and there are educational programmes in schools and on television. Attitudes of inclusiveness and the joy of diversity of faiths has created marked religious harmony in the country.

GENDER ISSUES

Adolescent dating, romantic 'love' marriages and interracial marriages pose challenges for Indo-Canadian families. While arranged marriages remain the preferred norm in highly conservative families, mostly there has been a distinct shift towards more liberal marriages of choice, with varying degrees of parental participation. The focus on religion and caste as core criteria for marriage has given way to choices based on more individualistic and personal attributes. The close link between religion and cultural identity creates problems for some, especially fathers, where a daughter's romantic relationship is deemed unacceptable. Mostly, families resolve interracial marriages in personal ways. An elaborate Hindu wedding followed by a Christian church ceremony is not unusual. Locating desirable partners through matrimonial advertisements in ethnic newspapers and on the Internet are commonplace. There is, however, a growing pool of young women choosing to remain single into their 30s for reasons of higher education, career development or finding the right person to marry.

In the acculturation process, Indo-Canadian women exhibit selectivity towards the values of the host society, gradually attaining a dualistic view of life characterised by the retention of traditional family and religious values and

the adoption of contemporary values of personal development. The strain of adapting to bi-cultural realities in a Western country like Canada is problematic for some women. East Indian psychiatrists report clinical cases of women who experience guilt, loss, mourning and identity crises from tensions created by Hindu beliefs relating to *Sita-Shakti* (passivity versus power) or *pativratya* (deference to spouse). As women gain more resources in their Canadian setting and are exposed to egalitarian ideologies, androcentric *pativratya* will decline and relationships between men and women will become more equal.

Two traditionally taboo subjects that have surfaced in recent years are elder abuse and domestic violence, mostly against women. Abused women have been reluctant to speak out in the past because of notions of *izzat* (honour) or *sharam* (shame), but in recent years they have felt more empowered because of the support services now in place. In 2005, there were 22 domestic violence organisations across the country.

HUMAN RIGHTS AND RACIAL ATTITUDES

Historically, Canada has not welcomed people of different races, cultures, religions and values. Early Sikhs, dubbed 'Hindoos', were victims of blatant prejudice, discrimination and racism. Asians, in general, were viewed as inferior, alien and unassimilable.

The world view of the Canadian government and its attitude towards 'visible minorities', 'people of colour', and 'racialised immigrants'—basically people originating in non-Western countries, including India—has changed drastically over the last few decades. The establishment of legal strategies for combating racism at both the federal and provincial levels attest to Canada's commitment to principles of equality, justice and rights for all its peoples. Given the varied racial, cultural and religious background of the country's immigrants, Canada has chosen cultural pluralism as its model of integration. Thus, various ethnic groups are permitted to maintain their unique identities in the belief that they all have something to contribute to the country's larger society.

Indo-Canadians share in the rights, privileges and protection of the Charter of Rights and Freedoms (1982), the Multicultural Act (1988), the Employment Equity Act (1986), human rights legislation and official race relations programmes. Heritage and language rights for all Canadians are entrenched within sections 15 and 27, respectively, of the charter. The enactment of the Canadian Bill of Rights (1960) expanded the concept of human rights to include equality rights, and in the 1960s, the provinces started to consolidate fair-practice statutes into comprehensive human rights codes, administered and enforced by permanent human rights commissions. By 1975, every province in the country had done so.

The federal Canadian Human Rights Act was passed in 1977 and promulgated in March 1978. The province of Ontario, home to most Indo-Canadians, took an early initiative in revising and updating its human rights legislation. The Ontario Human Rights Code was passed in 1981. The Race Relations Division of the Ontario Human Rights Commission was officially created to inquire into, mediate and resolve community tensions.

The Employment Equity Act was proclaimed on 14 August 1986 following the recommendations of the report 'Equality Now' (1984) and the Abella Commission on Equality in Employment (1984). The act addresses the issue of under-representation of target groups, such as the visible minority East Indians, in the workforce. Overall, visible minorities are proportionately represented at the lower levels of the workforce, but they remain under-represented at senior management and higher echelons. Furthermore, it is widely recognised that human and equality rights education must begin at the school level. Unfortunately, many school programmes are wanting. The University of Toronto has recently established a Centre for Integrative Anti-Racism Studies devoted to anti-racism research and teaching in the educational system.

Today's government in Canada, at all levels, recognises the urgency of addressing and taking action on issues of racism and racial discrimination. Thus, the Multicultural Act, the first of its kind in the world, provides a framework for the pursuit of further legislation, programmes, research, public education and funding to support initiatives for combating racism. In 1988, as part of the restitution arrangement between the Canadian government and Japanese Canadians who had been illegally incarcerated during World War II, a US$24-million grant was put in place for the establishment of the Canadian Race Relations Foundation. Canada also honours the United Nations Day for the Elimination of Racial Discrimination (March 21) and Human Rights Day (December 10).

Within the spirit of liberal and enlightened legislation emanating from the government, mainstream white attitudes towards Indo-Canadians and other visible minorities have evolved markedly. Between the mid-1970s and mid-1980s, instances of blatant racism, stereotyping and rejection of cultural symbols deemed acceptable within the terms of official Canadian multicultural policy were commonplace. White perceptions of East Indian women indicated a rejection of traditional dress (the sari), the dot on the forehead of Hindu women (the *tikka*), jewellery on the face (nose ring) and the perceived subservience of the women to their spouses. A mid-1970s national survey of ethnic/racial preferences showed a clear preference for white groups over non-white ones, with East Indians in the lowest-ranking position. Today, overt racism is mostly passé and attitudes towards ethnic minorities are more positive. There

Indian children perform at a multicultural festival in Canada.

NO FOOD, DRINKS CORN or KULFI

Indian kulfi *(ice cream) is popular enough to be banned in a sari shop in Toronto.*

Traditional representations of Indianness, such as the bindi, *were once rejected by Canadians.*

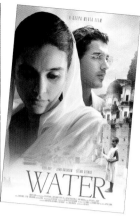

Posters for Deepa Mehta's three best-known films— Fire *(1996), which was controversial because of its discussion of lesbian relations;* Earth *(1999), which was based on Bapsi Sidhwa's novel* Ice-Candy-Man; *and* Water *(2005), which discussed the position of widows in Indian society.* Earth *won the grand prize at the Deauville (France) Pan-Asian Film Festival in 2000.*

An effigy of Mehta is burned in protest against her film Water.

Menaka Thakkar, a renowned dancer, choreographer and teacher of Indian dance.

is a new interest in diversity. Traits liked about East Indian women include their gentle and graceful manner, family-orientedness and high aspirations.

In the interim period, first- and second-generation Indo-Canadians have moved forward. Their adaptation, sharing of culture, investment in education, achievements and loyal law-abiding citizenship have won them a measure of respect. However, they share with other visible minorities the experiences of systemic, covert racism that continue to undermine the fullest development of their high potential.

Sociological literature identifies barriers experienced by new immigrants to their optimal integration into Canadian society. New Indo-Canadians and others are affected differently by these barriers, which include racial discrimination in the employment market; wage discrimination for the foreign-born; lack of formal, official accountability by employers to the government for providing opportunities in the workplace; limited or no recognition of work experience outside Canada; difficulty getting accreditation for foreign medical training, university degrees and trade certificates; and lack of Canadian work experience.

Covert and systemic racism continue to have an adverse impact on 'people of colour'. The reality of Canada is that it is still a country of racial hierarchies. A 2005 poll indicates that 4 million Canadians believe they have been victims of racism. Almost 2 million say they would not welcome someone of another race as a next-door neighbour. Race, class and gender biases interact to marginalise women of East Indian origin and others from fullest participation in larger society and the feminist movement.

CULTURAL LIFE, MEDIA AND LITERARY WRITING

Performances of dance, music and song, whether classic, contemporary, a fusion of East and West, or folk, are always popular among Indo-Canadians. The appeal of Indian dance is cutting across cultures, evoking new styles and fresh expression. Exceptional artists include Menaka Thakkar, Rina Singha, Sudha Khandwani, Lata Pada, Joanna Das, Janak Khendry, Aaloka Mehndiratta and Anne-Marie Gaston (Anjali). Most of them are based in Toronto. The much acclaimed Thakkar, a recipient of many awards, is an internationally renowned dancer, choreographer and teacher of classical bharatanatyam, odissi and kuchipudi. She founded Nrtyakala, the Canadian academy of Indian dance, in Toronto 27 years ago.

Sudha Khandwani is the artistic director and curator of the Kala Nidhi Fine Arts of Canada, dedicated to the promotion of Indian dance as an integral part of the

Canadian dance world. Lata Pada Sampradaya Dance Creations envisions dance as a mirror of society; Pada's dance work, *Revealed by Power*, addresses the empowerment of women.

The creative and entrepreneurial spirit of Indo-Canadians is breaking new ground in the world of film. The India-born Canadian director Deepa Mehta has made moving, if controversial, films such as *Fire*, *Earth* and *Water*. Srinivas Krishna's 1991 film *Masala* was voted best film by a non-resident Indian in a 2002 British Film Institute (BFI) poll for South Asian cinema. Ali Kazimi, raised in India, is a multi-award winning documentary film-maker based in Toronto. Nisha Pahuja has produced a lively documentary, *Bollywood Bound*, and Mitra Sen produced and directed the empathic short film, *Red Dot*, about cultural understanding. Sen is involved in the Peel World film festival, while Mohit Rajhans created the film festival, Filmi, both of which are Toronto-based. Sugith Varughese, Cochin-born but raised in Saskatoon, has been writing, acting and directing for film and television since 1979. He wrote and starred in the first Indian film made in Canada, a television drama for CBC titled *Best of Both Worlds* (1985). Canadian films with Indian themes are increasingly being filmed in India and India-based film-makers are filming in Canada.

Second-generation Indo-Canadians are contributing their pulsating rhythms to Canadian music. These include groups such as Riksha and Lal in Toronto and the Mantraboys in Vancouver. Acclaimed Canadian *ghazal* artist, Kiran Ahluwalia, won a 2004 Juno Award in the 'Best World Music Album' category for her release *Beyond Boundaries*. Desh Pardesh, or Home Away From Home, an Indo-South Asian festival for the arts and political activism, was first held in Canada in 1989 and flourished for a decade until its demise in May 2001 due to lack of financial viability.

Media personalities Ian Hanomansing, Suhanna Meharachand and Monika Deol broke into the television industry at a time when seeing an ethnic face on prime time news was highly unlikely. Today, there are an estimated 30–40 South Asian radio programmes, some with interactive call-in segments in Punjabi, Tamil, Urdu and Hindi. Canadian Multicultural Radio, designated exclusively for ethnic communities, includes many Punjabi, Hindi and Urdu programmes.

For Indo-Canadians in general, preservation of culture and extended cultural bonding continues through dance, cultural festivals, ethnic newspapers and magazines, ethnic organisations and shopping areas. Greater Toronto boasts 250 South Asian organisations, to which Indians have multiple affiliations. The city's estimated 30 South Asian publications include 16 Punjabi newspapers: two in Urdu and a few in Hindi and Gujarati. Colourful Gerrard Street in Toronto has become a 'Little India', with its sari, jewellery, grocery and Indian snack/sweets shops, and Indian eateries intermingled with similar facilities from other parts of South Asia.

Canada's literary world has witnessed a remarkable surge in fictional writing and poetry by authors of Indo-Canadian origin in the past few decades. Some originate directly from India, such as authors Anita Rau Badami, Ashok Mathur and Rahul Varma, and poets Uma Parameswaran and Bal Sethi; others have distant roots in India, such as Guyanese-born Cyril Dabydeen, and Neil Bissoondath and Rabindranath Maharaj, both born in Trinidad. A new Canadian-born generation is represented by playwright Sunil Kuruvilla.

Two highly acclaimed authors are India-born Rohinton Mistry and Africa-born M. G. Vassanji. Mistry came to Canada from Bombay in 1975. His first book, *Tales from Firozsha Baag*, a selection of short fiction, was published in 1987, followed by his very fine novels, *Such A Long Journey* (1991), *A Fine Balance* (1995) and *Family Matters* (2002). His many honours and awards include the Giller Prize (1995), Commonwealth Writers' Prize (1996) and the Governor-General's Literary Award (1991). With the complex characters created in his novels operating in the tumultuous political settings of modern India and set against the backdrop of its ancient history, Mistry touches the core of the human condition with rare sensitivity.

Vassanji, born in Nairobi, Kenya, came to Canada in 1978 and won the 1990 Commonwealth Writers' Prize for his first novel, *Gunny Sack* (1989). His stories give unusual insight into the Asian Indian experience in Africa in the context of colonialism and the rising tide of the fight for freedom in East Africa in the 1950s. Vassanji's most recent prize-winning novels include *The In-Between Life of Vikram Lall* (2003), *Amriika* (1999) and *The Book of Secrets* (1994). Vassanji is also a recipient of the Giller Prize (2003 and 1994) and the F. G. Bressani Prize (1994). He is the founding editor of a literary magazine, *The Review of Contemporary Writing Abroad*, which strives to give a voice to immigrant Canadians. In February 2005, Vassanji was named a Member of the Order of Canada for his contributions to the arts and writing.

Pioneer journalist and Hyderabad-born Haroon Siddiqui, who came to Canada in 1967, may be singled out for his unique editorial writing. He has brought fresh perspectives, sometimes contrary, to matters pertaining to immigration, multiculturalism, and national and international issues as the editorial page editor emeritus of *The Toronto Star*, Canada's largest newspaper. He has

challenged stereotypical thinking about minorities and encouraged dialogue and understanding. Siddiqui joined *The Toronto Star* in 1978 after working for 10 years at the *Brandon Sun* in Manitoba, the last four years as its managing editor. From 1990–98, he was *The Toronto Star's* editorial page editor. In December 2000, Siddiqui was awarded the Order of Ontario and in February 2002, the Order of Canada.

Reflecting the diversity of South Asia and of Greater Toronto, the Little India stretch on Gerrard Street bustles on an ordinary week night.

CHALLENGES IN THE 21ST CENTURY

The newest immigration projections are that visible minorities, the Indians and Chinese in particular, will double by the year 2017, when Canada marks the 150th anniversary of confederation. An urgent challenge for the future is for immigrants to obtain ready recognition for their education and expertise, and to find employment commensurate with their qualifications and skills. Presently, newcomers, including graduates from the celebrated Indian Institutes of Technology, confront a wall of resistance. In addition, established immigrants who have worked their way through the system, reaching relatively high-ranking positions, find they have hit the 'glass ceiling', preventing further upward mobility. Socio-political analysts point out that despite Indo-Canadian economic, professional and political successes, Canada has been slow to capitalise on their potential.

The downside of the much lauded Canadian multicultural policy is its tendency to create ethnic 'solitudes'. Each community develops its own organisations and social networks, and focuses on the interests of its particular constituency. To enter fully into Canadian society, Indo-Canadians must invest in the country's other official language, French, and become knowledgeable about the histories and cultures of First Nations' aboriginal peoples, and the founding French-English charter pioneers. Importantly, they must assume leadership roles in mainstream organisations crucial to the operation of the country. In short, Indo-Canadians must reach beyond ethnic boundaries. Only then will Indo-Canadians attain the opportunity for equity in the corridors of power.

Josephine C. Naidoo and James D. Leslie

A scene from Mitra Sen's acclaimed short film, The Peace Tree.

UNITED KINGDOM

JUST OVER 1 million people of Indian origin were living in the United Kingdom in 2001. This represents just under 2 per cent of the total population of the British isles. It was during the British colonial era in India that the first Indians found their way to the 'imperial motherland'; and it is this connection that accounts for the intimate ties that continue to exist between the two countries. While this bond is often perceived as one-sided, with British institutions and values viewed as continuing to have an effect on India, there is now growing acknowledgement that the Indian presence in Britain has also had a wide-ranging impact on British politics, culture and the economy.

COLONIAL BRITISH INDIANS

The British presence in India formally began with the arrival of the East India Company (EIC) in Calcutta in the 17th century. As the British began to assert imperial rule in the region, the flow of people travelling between Britain and India began. At first this took the shape of Indian servants and ayahs: EIC minutes from as early as 1690 record the passage of these people on ships from Calcutta and Madras. Rozina Visram documented such movements in *Ayahs, Lascars and Princes: Indians in Britain (1700–1947)*. Lascars were Indian sailors initially employed to solve the recruitment problems the EIC was facing in England. They increasingly became an essential part of commercial shipping to and from India and often 'jumped ship'. The Marine Department Records contain many documents which detail the generally poor conditions endured by these sailors who, after a long time at sea, ended up in a place that to them was plagued by inclement weather. These servants and workers of the British elite were found in small numbers in London and the port towns of England.

At the other end of the social hierarchy, the most notable travellers were the princes and elites of the Raj. As more princely states came under British rule, the imperial motherland became a natural source of curiosity as well as a place for the ruling class to further their education.

Map 8.48

Perhaps the most established of these figures, though not by choice, was Maharaja Duleep Singh, son of the deposed ruler of Punjab. Though his presence in England takes us rapidly up to the time of Queen Victoria's rule (r. 1837–1901), it is during this period that a diverse and sizeable population of Indians made their presence felt in the UK. From 1857 onwards, the number of ayahs and lascars travelling back and forth from Britain to India grew into the tens of thousands. Student numbers also increased exponentially from a mere four in 1845 to 207 in the 1890s, and by 1910, around 700 Indians were studying in Britain's universities.

The most notable and important social and political figures in India's colonial and post-colonial history spent some time at Britain's educational institutions. Mohandas Karamchand Gandhi was a law student at the Inner Temple, an affiliate of London University. Jawaharlal Nehru was educated first at Harrow—an elite private school—and then at Trinity College, Cambridge. The Memorial Trust in Nehru's name continues to sponsor the education of Indian students at Trinity College. Student movements were central to the development of the independence movement in the subcontinent. Figures such as Vinayak Damodar 'Veer' Savarkar, Muhammad

A group of Indian lascars photographed relaxing at East India dock in London prior to their journey, c.1908. After spending lengthy periods at sea, many were known to have 'jumped ship' upon their arrival at ports in England and elsewhere to seek employment ashore.

This 1842 image shows a young European woman seated at her dressing table assisted by an Indian maid (ayah), while an older Indian woman pours water in a bowl. Indian maids were some of the earliest Indians to arrive in the UK.

Ali Jinnah, Shapurji Saklatvala and Mancherjee Bhownagree—who later went on to become a member of the British House of Commons—all spent time in the country as students.

The movement of the elite classes between India and Britain was thus represented by students. In addition, the two world wars saw the movement of British Indian soldiers throughout the Empire. During World War II, many injured Indian soldiers were brought to Brighton, where a temporary hospital in the Indian-designed pavilion was set up. Along with sailors from the merchant navy, particularly stokers from Bombay and Sylhet, single men found their way from the port towns to the cities of London, Manchester and Birmingham. These pioneer migrants were often transitory and most returned to India; but those who remained, and even those who returned, came to know of the opportunities that were available in Britain. It was these pioneers who would pave the way for subsequent post-colonial migration.

Both the princes and the labourers were British Indians, and their travel documents and citizenship were an outcome of being a part of the British Empire. During the period of the Raj, there was relatively free movement to many parts of the Empire for these subjects of the Crown. Hence, those who came to Britain, whether as students or ayahs, did not require any visas or entry permits. This situation changed in 1948 with the passing of the first British Nationality Act, which distinguished those citizens of other countries who had the right to enter and settle in Britain (ostensibly white settlers in the dominions of Canada and Australia) from those in the newly independent former colonies.

POST-COLONIAL INDIAN BRITISH

The end of the Empire and the formal independence of India meant that the free movement of people throughout the colonies ended. However, the legal move to restrict travel could not undo the legacy of Indo-British connections. Colonial ties became the basis upon which the mass migration of Indians to Britain occurred. The post-war years in Britain were bleak times; a generation of men had been lost to the war effort and the country's economic outlook was grim. The war losses, coupled with the return of female labourers to the domestic front, meant that there was a labour shortage in agriculture, mining and heavy industries. This was first filled by European refugees displaced by the war, but by the 1960s, as the economy recovered and there was buoyancy both culturally and economically, the demand for labour became acute in public industries such as the National Health Service (NHS), London Transport and other bus companies throughout the country. Industrial labour was also desperately needed in the mill towns of the north, the foundries of the Midlands, the hosiery industry of the shires as well as the newer white goods industries of the south. These geographical references are crucial because they mark the terrain upon which Indian settlement took place and put down roots.

The Indo-British connection in terms of sojourners was strongest in Punjab. Army recruitment as well as membership of the colonial police force was heaviest in

A nationality and identity certificate for lascars issued in 1932.

this region. Soldiers returning from service in Hong Kong and other parts of the Empire would recount their adventures, inspiring other family members to migrate and providing the crucial capital needed. While Punjab was the main region from which labour migration took place, the largest number of migrants in the British Indian diaspora probably came from the district of Jalandhar. The reason behind this was the process of migration itself, which can be termed chain or network migration, where each person who migrates is linked through kinship or friendship to another. This social network reduced the cost of migration by enabling immediate access to housing and the labour market. This was the case for Gurbachan Singh Gill, who had both a job and a place to stay organised by his wife's family, who had migrated earlier. In this way, many of the able-bodied men from a number of villages in a district moved to England, meeting the demand for manual labour.

Stringent emigration laws were instituted in 1962 with the first Commonwealth Immigration Act, and the primary migration of manual labour to the UK from India ended in 1967. A small stream of people continued migrating as part of 'family reunification' and 'dependent elder' schemes, or for marriage, but the era of mass migration from India was over.

The rationale for much of the immigration control in the 1960s was to limit the number of people entering Britain. However, these acts seemed to have the reverse effect as they created a situation where people tried to 'beat the act' and ensure entry before the rules changed. It could be argued that if the British government had not enacted any legislation, many of the men who came as temporary economic migrants would have returned to India as they had originally intended. However, the legislation restricted the entry of young men over the age of 18 and thus gave incentive to the migration of women and children. In this way, family reunions took place in the 1960s which would eventually lay the foundation for the migration of extended families.

Jawaharlal Nehru at Harrow. After completing his education there in 1907, Nehru went on to study at the University of Cambridge. Like him, several Indian political icons were educated at British institutions.

A voucher issued under Section 2 of the Commonwealth Immigrants Act, 1962. The act was passed by the Conservative government in an effort to restrict the number of immigrants from India, Pakistan and the Caribbean, and required all citizens of the Commonwealth to have a government-issued employment voucher to settle in the UK.

I was born on 16 May 1919, in the village of Gandia-kheri in Patiala district [Punjab]. All the men in our household were in the military. In fact during the First World War, my father was in Brighton. He was injured in the fighting and like many other Indian soldiers, he was hospitalised in Brighton. I was married in 1935. A year later in 1936, my father-in-law obtained a passport and migrated to the UK. Then in 1939, I got recruited as a soldier. My regiment was the Hong Kong Singapore Royal Artillery. In 1941, Japanese forces attacked Hong Kong and shot down all our planes. We were taken as prisoners of war and our detention lasted for five years till the war ended in 1945. After the war I returned to the village. I was appointed to look after ex-soldiers. After partition I was given the additional duty to look after refugees also. I spent some four to five years on this job.

My father-in-law returned from England in June 1951. On his return to England he died suddenly. My mother-in-law then suggested I join them in Britain. I left Punjab and arrived in the UK on 29 October 1951. I was employed in various factories and for a number of years had many different labouring jobs. I had a job briefly in Woolf Rubber Factory in Southall, for a while we also worked at Key Glass, Alperton. After leaving factory work, I started my hand at a string of businesses. I first went into the property business and then started my own company, Gill & Co, providing small loans to people. My son, Manjit, joined me taking over the property and development side. Now, we own some twenty five properties in the West London area. We also have some property in the US. Our business is estimated to be worth over £50 million.

Extract from Darshan S. Tatla, Gurbachan Singh Gill: A Short Biography and Memoirs, *2004.*

The third wave of migrants began in 1967 and surged in 1972. These were the so-called 'twice migrants', or perhaps more accurately, 'multiple migrants', from East Africa. In the early 1970s, led by such political figures as Idi Amin in Uganda, a process of Africanisation followed in the footsteps of decolonisation. This led to an exodus of Indians from East Africa to new homes all over the world. Indeed, in small towns in many parts of northern Europe there are pockets of East African refugees who were relocated as part of the United Nations' co-ordinated refugee dispersal programme.

The majority of Indian migrants from East Africa, however, sought refuge in the UK. East African Gujaratis had maintained close links with India and had economic and social links with England long before the process of Africanisation began. There were a number of other Indian groups in East Africa, notably the Punjabis and Khojas, with small numbers from many parts of India. Britain became a natural port of call for these refugees since many of them had British passports. Their mass arrival in the early 1970s—estimated at around 50,000—caused a stir in Britain, leading to the passing of a new immigration law which prevented an automatic right of entry for those from former British colonies and protectorates. While some had left Africa before the expulsion, those who departed during the exodus lost their homes, belongings and livelihoods. Unlike the male migrants who came directly from India, East African Asians came as whole families, which may have offset some of their material losses. Indeed, the social capital of the East African Asians proved resilient and useful in the new context, as they have rapidly become the business elite of the Indian community. East African Gujarati businessmen have re-established themselves in a rags-to-riches story that is repeated in almost all the parts of the world where they resettled.

These various phases of migration have led to specific areas of settlement in Britain for particular groups. This can be usefully summarised in terms of the highways that

Indian and Pakistani children receiving English lessons at a school in Walsall.

Young Indians protesting against racial discrimination outside India House in London, 1952.

While manual labour was propping up the heavy industrial sector in Britain, there was another group of Indian emigrants who were doing the same thing for the NHS: Indian doctors. These migrants were famously satirised by Peter Sellers in the role of Dr Ahmed in the film, *The Millionairess*. The British established medical colleges in India whose graduating doctors spoke impeccable English, so it was natural that they would be recruited for the NHS. However, in the same way that opportunities for manual labour were restricted to those sectors of the economy where locals did not want to work, the NHS also recruited Indian doctors for those positions which were not considered prestigious and were thus unable to attract local candidates. Indeed, at both ends of the class hierarchy, from labourers to doctors, Indians were treated like coolies.

While Punjab more than fulfilled Britain's need for manual labour, the rest of India met the country's need for doctors. Indian elites arrived to take up other professional jobs as well, including teaching, another area with a shortfall. Due to the nature of their postings, Indian doctors were dispersed throughout the country. They were either offered jobs in areas where there was a dense population of migrants or in remote areas of the country. Indian doctors were often the first contact that many white Britons had with a non-white person. These encounters were often negative. More distressingly, there was considerable difficulty for Indian doctors to gain recognition and promotions, a problem that still has resonance in the NHS.

link the major towns of Indian settlement—the M1 and M6. It is along these corridors that the major towns of Bradford, Leeds, Manchester, Birmingham, Coventry, Leicester and, of course, London lie; but it is also the smaller towns and peripheries of these areas that are now home to Indians as they have become more prosperous and ventured into new areas. An estimated 85 per cent of the Indian population still live along this corridor and it remains to be seen if future generations will move on from these traditional locations given that Indian community centres, places of worship and facilities such as shops for food, clothes and jewellery are located in the urban areas. It is likely that even as the population disperses, these towns will remain the hub of activity for some time to come.

Indian migrants continue to come to Britain to work in professional occupations which are experiencing shortages. In the 1990s, the dot.com boom brought with it many IT professionals. The NHS is again recruiting doctors from India and immigration laws have made it easier for young people to come and work for a limited period and then return home. This ongoing migration is why the English language continues to be important as a medium of instruction in Indian schools, and is also why Britain is 'known' in the mental map of would-be Indian travellers. Nonetheless, new migrants are drawn from the urban elite rather than from rural peasant backgrounds and form part of a more mobile professional class than the settled diaspora of old.

Indian doctors

Many doctors, some of whom arrived from India already qualified and others who trained in the UK, ended up working in the poor areas of Britain. Perhaps it is a bias of historical records, which have highlighted the contributions of doctors who worked in deprived areas and made a significant contribution through their involvement in local politics, but it is likely that many avenues were closed to these doctors because the financially lucrative areas were almost certainly taken up by white doctors.

There are many general practitioners included in this group. Dr Baldev Kaushal (1906–92), who worked in Bethnal Green, was awarded an MBE in 1945 for his gallant conduct during the Blitz over East London. Dr Jainti Saggar (1898–1954) was the only Indian doctor in Dundee in the 1920s and was one of the longest serving members of the Dundee Town Council. Dundonians' esteem for Dr Saggar is so great that in the 1970s, 20 years after his death, a street was named Saggar Street by the Dundee Corporation; and in 1974, a public library was opened in memory of him and his brother. There was also the Boomla 'dynasty,' who practised in Plumstead from 1928 and endured for nearly 60 years. One of the grandsons of this dynasty, Kambiz Boomla, is currently working as a general practitioner in East London and is active in local politics. Dr Dharam Sheel Chowdhary (1902–59) practised as a doctor in London for over a quarter of a century and was hugely popular with his patients. It was said that upon his death, patients paid their last homage by standing perfectly still on the pavement, and that no one had ever seen a church so full. Chowdhary County Primary School, built in 1966, was named after him by popular demand. Dr Harbans Gulati (1896–1967), the pioneer of the 'meals on wheels' service, worked as a general practitioner in the working-class district of Battersea for over 40 years. He resigned from the Conservative Party in 1947 on principle over its hostility to the creation of the NHS.

Aneez Esmail

ECONOMIC TIES

The defining feature of the Indian diaspora is probably the determining role that economics has played in the movement and settlement of Indians. Indeed, the story of migration, especially in its post-colonial context, is certainly marked by different demands for certain types of labour that India, due to its colonial past, was able to provide. From manual labour to highly qualified professionals, Indians have played a role in Britain's economic life, spanning the class divide but remaining marginal. Within each strata of the workforce, they have almost always fulfilled roles that have been spurned by the local population. What is equally critical about the various phases of migration is that it created an Indian diaspora which was differentiated by class from the outset—working men, doctors and East African business communities. Other South Asian migrants to the UK during this period were almost exclusively working class.

Indian economic success has become part of the public discourse about Indians in recent years. The 1991 census showed that the Indian community had done well in education and in the labour market, particularly in self-employment. Both academic and public explanations have been offered for this apparent success. The weekly English-language paper *Eastern Eye* has published annually since 1996 a list of the top 200 wealthiest South Asians in the country. Every year, the minimum amount of wealth required to enter the list has increased, and in 2004 it stood at around £10 million.

This idea of success against the odds provides a positive self-image for the Indian community but poses some problems when in-depth analysis is carried out. Even in the list of the top 200 wealthiest South Asians,

Map 8.49

THE INDIAN CORRIDOR

Based on information drawn from the South Asian Development Partnership's UK–Asian Population Report, 1992.

The map of the Indian corridor shows the counties and metropolitan boroughs with the largest concentration of Indians in England.

BRICK LANE   E1

ব্রিক লেন

Brick Lane (note that the street name is translated into Bengali) in East London, also known as 'Bangla Town', has a large Bangladeshi population and dozens of curry houses (see picture below).

Female workers at the United Biscuits factory in Isleworth, Southwest London, on their way home from work, 1972.

Business success

The story of Perween Warsi, the multi-millionaire owner of S & A Foods Ltd and one of Britain's top 100 Asian entrepreneurs, clearly shows how social capital can convert into actual capital.

Unlike the mass of immigrants who left the subcontinent for Britain, Warsi's husband was a medical doctor who came to Britain for further study from Patna, Bihar. Having set himself up as a general practitioner, his wife joined him in 1975. They lived in the northern Welsh town of Rhyll, quite a distance from the majority, working-class Indian communities of Neasden and Handsworth. It was social occasions in the home that exposed her husband's 'English colleagues' to Indian food, and it was these colleagues who told Warsi that there was a market for her food. She began her business by selling a few samosas to a local fish and chips shop. Other outlets followed, and a fortuitous move to Derby meant that Warsi was able to recruit local Indian women to make the samosas with her. She then invested in a factory and the number of all-female employees increased to 12. By 1999, the business employed 650 people and had a turnover of £50 million, supplying a million meals a week to major supermarkets. This meteoric rise typifies the rise from humble beginnings to great things.

Neighbourhood grocery shops owned by Indians, such as Taj Stores in London, are a common sight in many of the larger cities in the UK.

there is a concentration in certain sectors such as clothing, jewellery and food. Indeed, these are the business people who have expanded their enterprises from supplying smaller retailers in immigrant areas, which represent the vast majority of Indian businesses. These enterprises are largely small-scale, heavily reliant on family labour and have low costs of entry but demand intensive inputs. Emerging from providing services for the Indian and wider South Asian community or from taking over small convenience stores in various parts of Britain, these businesses are still engaged in a struggle for economic survival. Media hype and the community's self-perception spotlight the business sector as a source of economic success, but the majority of Indians remain employees in various sectors of the labour market.

One other facet of the Indian success story in Britain has been entry into the professions. The shift into accountancy, law, medicine and to some extent teaching, again indicates the social capital that many migrants had but could not fully realise. For many teachers, solicitors and other professionals who migrated in the 1960s, the need for work and the belief that this was a temporary

Family fortune

Avtar Bansi came to England in 1951 and his wife joined him three years later. He worked in a steel foundry in Birmingham for 30 years until it closed down. He was not an educated man and could not read or write in English or his native language. He had four sons and one daughter; his eldest was in India and the remainder in England. Three of his sons joined him at work in the foundry but also began to work on Saturdays as market traders. His youngest son went to university, as did his daughter. The three sons, between them, managed to buy a shop and establish a chain of supermarkets in the Midlands. His daughter went on to qualify as a solicitor and is now head of a successful practice. His son is a principal social worker for local government in the Midlands. Bansi is now over 75 years old and spends his retirement in India and Birmingham, with six months a year in each location.

experience meant that they took the first available jobs in the factories. Furthermore, the barriers to entry into the professions were substantial, especially outside of London. The children of these migrants have reversed the downward mobility and excelled in the professions. Their parents had both the understanding of what a university education offered and an inclination towards vocational jobs, such as what are often satirised as the 'DEAD' (doctor, engineer, accountant, dentist) professions, referring to the steady income and relatively sanitised lifestyles they afforded. In both business and the professions, the resources that migrants brought with them were never fully utilised because of the barriers to entry; these have now been fully realised by the British-born generation.

If there are any truly remarkable stories of upward mobility in the Indian community, they are from the manual labourers. With the decline of manufacturing, which led to a 50 per cent loss of jobs in all industries, and almost 90 per cent in heavy industrial work, the earlier Indian migrants were left on the scrapheap. Working in jobs where they developed little aptitude in the English language or in the soft skills that the new economy required, a generation of working men and women became permanently unemployed. These families struggled on to ensure that their children would have some economic stability.

Despite stories of success, statistical data reveal that as far as unemployment rates and the economic activity of women are concerned, the Indian diaspora has more unemployed members and fewer economically active women than the white population (see Table 8.32).

Unemployment among young Indians is greater than it is for whites, and graduates find it harder to get employment than their white peers. Even those who have reached the top levels of British institutional life and are more likely to be better qualified than their white counterparts, have taken longer to get to that same position. The glass ceiling in many walks of economic life means that there is a growing population of well-qualified and experienced people from the Indian community who are not fully appreciated or valued.

Table 8.32

EMPLOYMENT STATISTICS FOR THE INDIAN COMMUNITY, 2001–02 (%)

	Employed		Unemployed	
	Male	Female	Male	Female
White	85.0	74.0	5.0	4.0
Indian	79.0	62.0	7.0	7.0

Source: Annual Local Area Labour Force Survey, 2001/02.

POLITICAL INFLUENCE

The integration of India into the British Empire under Queen Victoria led to the migration of various members of the newly formed Indian elites. Many of them, such as Gandhi, Jinnah and Nehru, were educated in England. Other Indians played a more active role in British politics, some at the parliamentary level and others in more revolutionary and activist ways. Dadabhai Naoroji was the first Indian to be elected to the House of Commons (in 1892 as a Liberal). This was his second attempt at entering parliament and was his only term of service as a member of parliament (MP). Known as the 'Grand Old Man of India', Naoroji's main desire was to influence parliamentary and public opinion about Indian self-rule and to demonstrate the negative impact of colonialism. In complete contrast was Mancherjee Bhownagree, who became a Conservative MP for Bethnal Green in 1895 and was re-elected in 1900. Bhownagree was a supporter of the British presence in India and opposed the campaign for home rule. Perhaps the most noteworthy Indian parliamentarian of this time was Shapurji Saklatvala, who became the MP for Battersea in 1922, for the Labour party. Saklatvala played a significant role in British politics at home and was active in the Indian independence movement.

Sixty-five years passed before the next Indian was to take a seat in the House of Commons. Keith Vaz, of Goan heritage, became an MP in 1987. Subsequently, there have been a few Indian representatives in each general election, but nowhere near proportionate to the population. The House of Lords has seen a more sizeable presence of Indians, but this is due to the process of patronage that allows entry into the Lords. Since 1997, the Labour Party in particular has made a conscious effort to diversify the make-up of the House of Lords, and this has seen the inclusion of such notables as Lord Meghnad Desai, an economist at the London School of Economics. While the position of MP is clearly more significant in terms of influence and prestige, there have been Indians in the European Parliament and large numbers in local

PARLIAMENTARY ELECTION, 1922.
WEDNESDAY, NOVEMBER 15th,
8 a.m. to 9 p.m.
NORTH BATTERSEA DIVISION.
VOTE FOR
3 SAKLATVALA, SHAPURJI ☒
THE LABOUR CANDIDATE.
And Sack Your Capitalist Oppressors.

authorities. Indeed, local representation is viewed as a much more attainable target and a desirable goal by the politically active. The Indian population has always been more likely to vote than the whites in local elections, and holding the position of local councillor is seen as having status both within the diaspora and among the wider public.

Historically, post-war Indian migrants have voted for the Labour Party, reflecting both their status as workers and their opposition to the Conservative Party's anti-immigration policy. Labour remains the party with the greatest number of Indian MPs and peers, but the class differentiation which now divides the Indian community shows itself in greater involvement with the Conservative (the main opposition) and Liberal Democratic parties. In fact, at a local level there are Indian council representatives throughout the country belonging to all the main parties. The Labour Party's immediate connection to and reliance on the Indian vote has come to an end. This diversity also illustrates the increasing awareness of the ideologies of the various parties and how these can relate to promoting the needs and demands of the Indian community.

If parliamentary politics has not been able to respond to the presence of the Indian diaspora in any serious way, the field of political activism has seen a much richer engagement. The brothers Rajani and Clemens Palme Dutt were born in Britain to an Indian father and Swedish mother. Rajani went on to become a central pillar of the Communist Party of Great Britain (CPGB) and a key figure in left-wing politics in the country. In contrast to the great divide between colonial parliamentary figures and those elected to parliament in the post-colonial period, activist politics shows continuities between the two periods. The best example of this is the Indian Workers

Dadabhai Naoroji was elected as president of the Indian National Congress in 1886. He went on to become the first Indian MP in the UK parliament.

A leaflet in support of Labour candidate Shapurji Saklatvala during the 1922 general election.

A demonstration in Trafalgar Square organised by the Movement for Colonial Freedom against the 'Colour Bar' immigration bill. In the 1960s, South Asians formed alliances with other ethnic groups in an effort to challenge racist immigration laws.

Shapurji Saklatvala

Shapurji Saklatvala—grand-nephew of Nusserwanji Tata, the father of Jamsetji, who was the founder of the Tata industrial empire—was first elected to the British parliament in 1922 as a member of the Labour Party. He married Sally Marsh in Oldham after being sent to England in 1905 and became a friend of the Marxist politician Sylvia Pankhurst. By 1907, he was a member of the Marxist Social Democratic Foundation, a forerunner of the Communist Party of Great Britain (CPGB). He was imprisoned in 1926 for sedition, at the time of the general strike. As the Labour Party expelled him, the Tories chanted 'send him back to India' as well as 'send him back to Moscow'. Saklatvala departed for a successful tour of India and was greeted by well-wishers wherever he spoke as he was seen as a fighter against the imperialist power. Interestingly, he was criticised by the founder of the Indian Communist Party, M. N. Roy, for speaking with Gandhi during the visit. However, Saklatvala's support of Gandhi was never uncritical and he questioned the Mahatma's promotion of *khaddar* (handspun cloth). Amusingly, in a letter to Gandhi, Saklatvala said that it seemed contradictory to encourage people to spin so as to make more clothes, and at the same time set an example by wearing less and less himself. Saklatvala's visits to India were curtailed when the government revoked his passport. Secretary of State for India William Wedgewood Benn confirmed the ban in 1929 in what has come to be known as the 'ghastly imperialist mode'. Saklatvala's call for the CPGB to organise at the ports among Asian seamen was ignored in much the same way as the white Left today has failed to take up the cause of asylum seekers and refugees. Yet, his influence upon the rank and file cadre was immense. Bengali workers celebrated Saklatvala Day in 1937, and British communists fought in the Saklatvala Battalion in the Spanish Civil War. When Saklatvala died in January 1936, George Padmore paid tribute to him along with Nehru and Palme Dutt.

Saklatvala was an MP for Battersea from 1922–29.

John Hutnyk

The Sunrise Radio (Yorkshire) studio in Bradford. This award-winning community-based radio station broadcasts programmes relevant to the local South Asian population.

Association (IWA), founded in 1938 in Coventry by Udham Singh, the Indian freedom fighter who came to England to avenge the Jallianwala Bagh massacre. The organisation grew rapidly with the arrival of new migrants from Punjab and its centre shifted to Birmingham. The IWA found a natural base among the foundry and factory workers from Punjab. Their demands as workers were not being met by unions, which saw them—incorrectly—as undermining the situation and wages of local workers. The IWA took up issues of racism, immigration law and trade unionism, and was aided by the Pakistani Workers Association and the Kashmiri Workers Association. The white Left in Britain in the 1970s had to take seriously the presence of South Asians.

The relationship of Indians in Britain to Indian politics was shaped by the success of most Indian political parties. When the Congress Party was in power, the fortunes of the Indian National Congress (Overseas) were in good stead. When the Bharatiya Janata Party (BJP) rose to power in India, it also secured overseas branches in cities throughout Britain. Regional parties in India, such as the Akali Dal of Punjab, had an extensive following too. Britain has also been home to radical movements which have, from the relatively safe space of the diaspora, launched scathing critiques of the Indian nation state. Most notable in this regard are Sikh separatists, who demand the formation of a separate state of Khalistan. There has also been support in Britain for an independent Kashmir.

It is perhaps because of the critical stance of many diasporic Indians towards India that there has been an awkward relationship between the two. Unlike Pakistan, which offered its diaspora dual nationality and extended a range of facilities for investment and ownership of property from the time of migration, the British Indian diaspora has always encountered difficulties when dealing with Indian bureaucracy. The problems of passport renewal, for example, were compounded by the requirements

of visas, for which the same rates were paid as all other nationalities. Though relations improved considerably under High Commissioner Kuldip Nayar in 1990, the diaspora and India have had a fraught relationship. This has changed for the better since the late 1990s with the introduction of the 'person of Indian origin' (PIO) card and the availability of dual nationality for British citizens of Indian heritage. Indeed, there seems to be a concerted effort by the Indian government to woo its diaspora, perhaps recognising that the capital in both financial and social terms can be of use to the country.

CULTURAL EXCHANGE

The enrichment of the English language by Indian words such as 'shampoo', 'verandah' and 'pukka' does not compare to the huge impact English has had on the subcontinent. However, the influence of writers—Arundhati Roy, Salman Rushdie and Amitav Ghosh, to name but a few—on the English language has been profound. Indians writing in English have become a fashionable part of the global literary circuit, but their writings do not sit well with a definition of diaspora that requires us to focus on the communities of migrants who become settlers, rather than the footloose literary elite. To fully appreciate the fiction writing of the diaspora we need to turn to the vernacular languages of the migrants themselves. Indeed, it is in Urdu, Gujarati, Hindi, Bengali and Punjabi that we see a range of literary output, primarily of poetry, but also short stories and the occasional novel that presents the life stories of migrants from their own perspective. These texts serve as a kind of ethnographical repository of the experience of migrants, their concerns, worries and joys in their new home. In the early phase, writing these stories often took the form of travelogues, explaining various things about British life to a perceived Indian audience; but as outlets for poetry and stories developed in Britain and temporary migration turned into settlement, the emphasis shifted to social issues.

It was the advent of vernacular media that gave great impetus to poets and writers working as postmen and bus drivers in Britain to take up the pen. The establishment of a viable vernacular press with weekly publications, such as *Garavi Gujarat* and *Des Pardes* (Punjabi), provided a ready outlet for these writers. This print media provided news from back home, which was difficult to access in the era before the Internet and instant communication technology. Indeed, most of the content of these papers was copied directly from regional language papers or translated from English papers where the news was about Britain. In this way, the vernacular press kept people informed about home and in touch with the news in Britain. This dual role overcame the problem that many migrants had in

A concert organised in Wembley in aid of the South Asian earthquake in 2005.

Today there was a lot of excitement at Dr Sharma's house. He had invited about twenty English couples for dinner to his palatial home...Dr Sharma was very happy and it was to share his pleasure that he had organized this party. His name had come in the Queen's honours list and he was to be awarded an O.B.E. [Order of the British Empire]...Dr Sharma came to England twenty years ago to study. His father was a religious man who spent a lot of time in the mandir [temple]. His main prayer was that his son would become a doctor one day and serve the sick and weak.

Dr Sharma got his degree from abroad, but as he finished his studies, the seed that western education had planted in his mind, grew like a fast vine. Englishness became his way of life and all things Indian seemed worthless. He started to measure all things in terms of pounds. In the end he married an English girl and started his medical practice. He began to think England was a heaven that you can reach without dying. Whenever his parents sent him a letter, he would send them the cold comfort of money when they were asking for consideration. Whenever his father sent a letter asking his son to visit them, Dr Sharma would think to himself: 'He does not understand that just like a child, once born, cannot return to its mother's womb, leaving England and going to India is impossible.'

Dr Sharma kept his English friends happy by telling them jokes about how smelly Indians were. He made sure that he had no Indian patients and went at great lengths to tell people how there was no racism in England, rather it was the land of great opportunity. In this way he developed a circle of White friends who cherished him very much.

Today's party was in full swing when Dr Sharma was called to attend to an emergency call. He apologized to his guests and hurried to his patient. In fact Mrs Whitehouse was not on his list, but because he was covering for other doctors he had to go...When Dr Sharma arrived at her flat, he found a ninety year old lady who was on her death bed. When he saw her the doctor asked, 'What can I do for you?' The old English lady with some difficulty opened her eyes and said 'Doctor, it would have been better if you had not come. I am at death's door and it is my bad luck that the last face I will see is that of a black man.' These words she said with her last breath.

Extract from Surjit Singh, 'At the time of Dying', adapted and translated from the original 'Punjabi, Marn Vele', in the collection Baar Praiye *('Strange Outsiders'), 1980.*

achieving proficiency in the English language, which, compared to harsh working conditions and few hours of leisure, was less of a priority.

The Indian-language press has been joined by many English-language papers serving both the Indian community and a wider South Asian audience. These have slowly increased their circulation and have a larger readership than the vernacular media, but the Indian-language papers maintain a close-knit and loyal readership. Even with the advent of instant access to news from India, the overall sales of these papers has not dropped much, though some have adopted an English-language section in an attempt to appeal to British-born English-only readers.

While it is probable that vernacular literature, as well as media, will slowly decline, this does not mean that the languages themselves will cease to have any function. The attraction of Bollywood cinema, with its concomitant language requirements, and perhaps more extensively the linkage of life-cycle rituals with religion and associated language are factors that are likely to protect against total linguistic extinction. The continued importance of celebrating marriages and births, and commemorating deaths in a traditional manner, necessitates participation in religious activities that are predominantly held in vernacular languages. Urdu and Hindi hold religious significance for Muslim and Hindu communities. For Sikhs, Punjabi remains welded to their religious traditions, and even where literacy has declined, the use of Roman letters to transliterate Punjabi remains. This is most often seen in the popular bhangra music industry, where many British-born artists are unable to read Punjabi but sing the lyrics by reading the transliterated script.

In institutional terms, it is the temples, gurdwaras and mosques which have been the most successful markers of the Indian presence in Britain. The landscape of urban Britain has been transformed, with domes and minarets replacing spires and chimneys. These places have also served as community centres, meeting places for families and sites of community conflict. Their histories have yet to be written but the material investment in them is undeniable. The Swaminaryan Temple in Neasden is an architectural masterpiece which took three years to construct, involved 1500 artisans working in Gujarat on the decorations of the interior, and required the import of 60 tonnes of stone from various parts of the world. Less ornate but equally imposing is the Gurdwara Nishkam Sevak Jatha on Soho Road in Birmingham, whose dome dominates the landscape for miles around. Even as the Indian community becomes increasingly integrated into British life, the importance and popularity of religious sites remains, and in some aspects the attention paid to

the design of these buildings is growing. Adopting the outward symbols of religious piety and dressing in traditional garb has become a prominent identity marker for British-born Indians. The interest in the accommodation of Indic religions with a Western lifestyle is a source of much debate and continues to frame the way in which the community views itself.

Gurdwara Nishkam Sevak Jatha on Soho Road in Birmingham. The four-storey building contains five main halls and 100 rooms.

TRANSNATIONAL FUTURES

Migration was once viewed as a one-way, one-off process. This vision has been seriously disrupted by the dramatic reduction in the cost of travel and the rapid development of communication technologies. For those Indians who travelled to the UK as ayahs and lascars in the 18th century, the trip by boat could have taken up to three months, with correspondences taking a similar amount of time. For the immigrants who came after World War II, air travel reduced the journey time to nine hours. Now, with so many flights leaving for India every day from many cities in the UK, air-traffic has grown exponentially.

Vaishnava Hindu sects in the UK have grown in popularity since the 1990s, especially with the twice-displaced Gujaratis.

Music and the mainstream

British mainstream music has had an often difficult relationship with bhangra artists. Punjabi lyrics and the constant mixing of dance-hall rhythms with the sound of the *dhol* (drum) led to a musical form often not appreciated by the Western ear. This musical barrier was coupled with the fact that South Asian music had developed a separate production and distribution industry, which nurtured artists such as Malkit Singh and Nusrat Fateh Ali Khan. These artists have often recorded sales of their audio tapes and CDs in excess of those in the mainstream. However, due to the way in which sales are registered, they have never appeared on the mainstream charts. This situation began to change in the mid-1990s with the signing of Bally Sagoo, arguably the most prolific music producer and arranger in the bhangra industry, by Sony Records. His subsequent entry into the charts signalled the potential of selling bhangra music to a wider audience. However, Sagoo left Sony after they demanded he also produce English-language records, an attempt to harness his talent in a direction he did not want to go. It took another eight years for record companies to take British Asian music seriously again: this marked the advent of the Rishi Rich Project, who took the world of pop by storm. Rishi Rich is a music producer directly influenced by Bally Sagoo, but who has worked with leading pop stars such as Britney Spears, Mis-teeq and Craig David. One of the artists to come out of the Rishi Rich camp is Jay Sean, or Kamaljit Jhutti, who gained acclaim in 2004, registering two Top 20 chart hits—the first time any South Asian artist has managed to achieve this level of commercial success. Mixing urban sounds with Punjabi lyrics and Indian instrumentation, Jay Sean has created a sound that appeals to both South Asian and mainstream audiences. His image as a good-looking, stylish young man also goes down well with pop audiences.

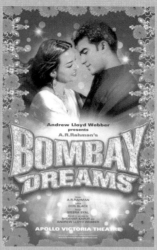

Tamasha's musical love story, Fourteen Songs, Two Weddings and a Funeral, *adapted from the Bollywood film* Hup Aap ke Hain Kaun, *and Andrew Llyod Webber's* Bombay Dreams, *reflect the impact of Indian cinema on British theatre.*

COOL BRITANNIA

Britain markets itself as 'Cool Britannia' on the back of its diverse diasporas. The contribution of the Indian diaspora to this refashioning of Britain has been considerable. Bollywood cinema has the drawing power (though not the universality) of West End musicals and curry is celebrated as a British dish. Note the impact on British Asian bhangra—derived from a Punjabi folk form—of Caribbean reggae and the soul and hip hop styles of Black Africa, which are in themselves highly complex hybrid musical forms, and of Bombay film music. The music of Apache Indian combines rap with Bollywood, as in *Pyar mujhse pyar tum kyun itna karte ho* ('Lovin' [let me love you]'; 1997). Asian bands such as K K Kings, Fun'Da'Mental, Panjabi MC and Kaliphz are further evidence that cultural commodities travel swiftly, criss-crossing geographical boundaries and creating new and vibrant forms. In Nitin Sawhney's album *Beyond Skin* (Outcaste; 1999), the accompanying pamphlet declares: 'I believe in Hindu philosophy. I am not religious. I am a pacifist. I am a British Asian. My identity and my history are defined only by myself—beyond politics, beyond nationality, beyond religion and beyond skin.' Sawhney and Indian music in the diaspora generally demonstrate levels of imagination and creativity absent, in their immediacy, in literature, because music can be so much more mobile and more readily translated into social and cultural practice.

The case of Cornershop may be viewed as symptomatic of the Indo-British music scene generally.

Begun in 1988 by Tjinder Singh and Ben Ayers as The General Havoc, the band changed its name to Cornershop in 1992, after perhaps the stereotype of the Asian cornershop-keeper in Britain. ('Why can't Asians in Britain play football?' 'They'll open a shop whenever they get a corner kick.') Cornershop shows all the characteristics of a fusion band that freely combines music and politics. There is the political statement of the song *Hanif Kureishi Scene*—'Your life is so pristine, mine's like the Hanif Kureishi scene'—and a much more joyful celebration of Bollywood in *Brimful of Asha*, which alludes to the successful remixing of many of Bollywood playback singer Asha Bhosle's songs in the British Asian pop scene.

Nitin Sawhney, Cornershop and Badmarsh and Shri, according to *Time* magazine, 'belong to a generation of young British Asian acts...who have emerged from the ethnic underground to make music that blends—and transcends—traditional pop categories.' With their albums, *Dancing Drums* (Outcaste; 1998) and *Signs* (Outcaste; 2001), Badmarsh and Shri (Mohammed Akber Ali, a Yemeni-Indian, and Shrikanth Sriram, originally from Mumbai) moved away from the Bollywood-influenced, highly artificial compositions of the Asian club and underground music scene in London to a vibrant and mixed form that combines traditional drums, strings and winds (tablas, sitars and flutes) and connects with garage, funk, reggae and Bollywood. The transformation also indicates a shift away from the 'ethnic' to the global, as Nitin Sawhney's appeal clearly demonstrates. Recently in the British Indian-Pakistani diaspora, even classical forms such as the Sufi *qalandari* dance and singing have been mixed with contemporary music. The best example of this is the late Nusrat Fateh Ali Khan's extraordinary *qawwali Dam Mast Qalandar Mast Mast* ('Carry on, O merry Qalandar').

Three instances of cultural translation may be taken up here and all refer to the British South Asian (Indian) diaspora. The first is a musical adaptation of the well-known Bollywood film *Hum Aap ke Hain Kaun* ('Who am I to you'; 1994), the second is Andrew Lloyd Webber's *Bombay Dreams*, and the third is Akram Khan's fusion of Indian kathak and Western modern dance forms in *MA* ('Mother'). When the Indian diaspora began to intervene in British cultural productions with an eye to its own distinctive artistic traditions, Bollywood became the indispensable form to imitate (as in Mira Nair's *Monsoon Wedding*), parody (Kaizad Gustad's *Bombay Boys*), deconstruct (Gurinder Chadha's *Bhaji on the Beach*) or creatively rewrite (Gurinder Chadha's *Bride and Prejudice*). With the impact of Bollywood cinema, there has been a decisive shift to the popular

musical, which is why *Fourteen Songs, Two Weddings and a Funeral*, based on *Hum Aap ke Hain Kaun*—and echoing through its English title *Four Weddings and a Funeral*—is so important. *Fourteen Songs, Two Weddings and a Funeral* adapts a popular genre—Bollywood melodrama—and retains the characteristics of that genre to the extent that the songs, although rendered in English, are sung to the tunes of the Hindi original. What is created is not a hybrid of British 'fusion' music but a different kind of aesthetic assertiveness which, in adapting Bollywood, allows the diaspora to connect with a popular form and make it its own. With Andrew Lloyd Webber's *Bombay Dreams*, the art form that has the highest currency in the Indian diaspora—Bollywood cinema—is repackaged for a much wider audience because the form itself is seen as another element in Western aesthetic modernity: for Western culture always adapts artistic forms on the ascendant, and in doing so liberates art from its own inherently quotidian tendencies.

When Akram Khan's *MA* had its world premiere in Singapore in May 2004, commentators were immediately struck by a daring choreographic style shaped by the fusion of Indian and Western dance forms. *MA*, in this respect, is an ideological statement as much as a creative triumph of multicultural dance: it locates culture with a space of free play that guards not a pristine, hallowed, received form (whether Indian or Western modern), but designates a field out of which anything might emerge. In this respect, even as *MA* is a triumphant art form of diasporic hybridity, it insinuates an ideological imperative: diasporic difference is not an aberration to be gradually transformed into national norms but a statement that the 'other' is to be treated as if it were the 'self'.

To these examples should be added the extraordinary trilogy of theatre group Indian Ink, by the Indo-New Zealander Jacob Rajan—*Krishnan's Dairy, The Candlestickmaker* and *The Pickle King*. These designate three aspects of the diaspora in a multicultural nation. The first suggests self-representation but shows the impossibility of capturing that which is lost; the second is the appropriation of diasporic forms for mainstream, capitalist ends; and the third, the aesthetic possibilities of combining tradition with modernity, as in the highly controlled and rigorously defined movements of kathak, synergising with the fluidity and energy of modernism.

Cool Britannia, therefore, becomes a new, creative, cultural space open to many influences, voices and forms of artistic production.

Vijay Mishra

Birmingham-born and raised, Apache Indian is a reggae legend and has recorded with The Israelites and Desmond Dekker.

Cornershop, the popular British rock band from Leicester.

Birmingham, for example, is directly linked to Amritsar, and Leicester to Ahmedabad. These flights cater exclusively to the diaspora and have provided a link between Britain and India that previously did not exist.

Information and communication technologies have also played a major role in increasing the links between India and Britain. The reduction in the cost of telecommunications allows for instant access with cellular phones, whereas, before, calls had to be booked through several operators, lasted for only three minutes and were exorbitantly priced. This increased communication and connectivity has had a major impact on economic and cultural spheres in particular. Economically, the outsourcing of the workforce of many British companies has led to a situation where it is not possible to tell where a routine telephone call for a financial or other service may lead. Customer service call centres for many leading British companies are now in India. Many British Indian entrepreneurs are engaged in establishing outsourcing businesses in India and act as go-betweens for British companies. Indeed, what was once considered a liability (being of Indian origin) has become beneficial as the diasporic Indian can act as an intermediary in what is deemed difficult terrain.

Increasing connectivity is also apparent in the crossover of Indian culture into the mainstream. The brief relationship between Indian culture and England blossomed during the 1960s with The Beatles and other pop stars following the hippie trail to sitarist Ravi Shankar, after which the complex cultural output of India was neglected by the British mainstream. This has changed in the 21st century, and diasporic Indian culture has become a fashionable commodity. Ever since pop icon Madonna donned a *bindi* and henna painting, body adornment and nose rings have become the height of fashion. Bollywood films, that most popular of Indian art forms, now feature regularly in the British national box office attendance charts. The thirst for Bollywood has grown among the general population as well as British-born Indians with the advent of subtitling and the screening of films in mainstream cinema halls. Beyond Bollywood, films such as *Bride and Prejudice* and the worldwide hit *Bend It Like Beckham* have introduced the world to the lives of diasporic Indians. This impact has also been felt in the world of music, where bhangra artists, mixing Punjabi lyrics with dance-hall rhythms, have entered mainstream British charts. Public institutions, such as the BBC, have also led the way in providing a platform for a new generation of British Asian comics with comedy television such as *Goodness Gracious Me* and *The Kumars at No. 42*. These cultural forays indicate the impact that the Indian diaspora is having on spheres which are far outside the narrow confines of immigrant life, with a relentless concentration on vocational achievement and success measured by standards of wealth and prestige.

Perhaps the most striking cultural impact on the British way of life comes from Indian food, which, in the mainstream, is not produced by the Indian diaspora but in Bangladeshi-owned restaurants. The first recorded Indian restaurant opened in London in 1809: The Hindoostanee Coffee House was designed to give customers a taste of the Raj. It was not a great success, and while others opened later on in the 19th century, most notably Veeraswamy's, it was not until the arrival of the lascars and cooks from the merchant ships that a number of Indian cafés started to appear. These were set up to serve the single men migrating to the UK, and later came to add spice to the British diet. In the 1990s, the availability and mass consumption of Indian food became a central part of the British culinary landscape. Ready-made meals and the infamous 'chicken tikka masala' are a central part of culinary enjoyment in the UK, where Britons partake of Indian food at least once a week on average.

In 2001, 6 per cent of the Indian population were registered as being of mixed parentage; those with one parent of Indian ethnicity and another parent of a different ethnic group. This relatively small number of interracial relationships means that the idea of a melting pot is not in the future of the British Indian diaspora. Rather, it is more likely that we will see increasing cultural fusions of the type reflected in fashion, music and film. While retaining Indian languages is unlikely, the expansion of religious traditions, with white converts and people from other ethnic backgrounds taking an interest in Indic faiths, is an increasing possibility. These cultural interactions are premised on a continuing integration with the economic life of the country. As Indian economic activity diversifies out of the traditional professions and narrow confines of small-scale business activity, it is likely that the culture industries will become an increasing source of employment for the diaspora. A wider occupational profile will also offer the potential for the Indian diaspora to spread geographically outside of the traditional areas of settlement and into the smaller towns and shires of the country. This will increase the visibility of the community, but will also lessen its political clout as the demand of electoral politics is for the concentration of groups in geographical proximity. Nonetheless, increased affluence also leads to the potential for lobbying, and this is the most likely means of political influence that British Indians will have in the future.

Virinder S. Kalra

Many British companies have call centres based in India.

George Harrison (left) of The Beatles, with sitar maestro Ravi Shankar (right). Harrison's attraction to Indian culture ushered a phenomenal interest in Indian music and spirituality in the West.

Kirtan in the Park, a musical recital to celebrate Sikh cultural heritage, held at Gunnersbury Park, London, on 28 August 2004.

THE NETHERLANDS

New arrivals from Surinam wait at the baggage carousel in Amsterdam's Schiphol airport.

INDIANS IN THE Netherlands are the descendants of indentured labourers shipped to the former Dutch colony of Surinam between 1873 and 1914 to work on plantations. Most of these immigrants were recruited from eastern Uttar Pradesh and western Bihar. One-third of the original 34,000 immigrants who went to Surinam returned to India. Later, labourers were encouraged to settle down as farmers since the colony was sparsely populated and needed part-time agricultural workers. According to a persistent myth among the Hindustanis, they lived as joint families for decades. This is impossible given the overwhelmingly male character of the population, its dispersion across vast and highly inaccessible areas, the small plots of land available, and the low productivity of the farmers.

During their integration into Surinamese society, Indians began referring to themselves as Hindustanis. Over the years, large numbers migrated to the capital, Paramaribo. Already active in agriculture, the Hindustanis moved into domestic trade, the import-export business and government service. They established their own temples and mosques, political parties, schools and social clubs. Their progress was met with jealousy from the Creoles—the descendants of African slaves and the Hindustanis' main economic and political competitors. Although complete demographic data are not available, in 2005, 160,000 Hindustanis accounted for approximately 35 per cent of Surinam's population and constituted the largest ethnic group. Other major ethnic groups included the Javanese, Chinese and Brazilians.

Hindustani migration to the Netherlands started in the early 1960s and peaked around the transfer of sovereignty to Surinam in 1975. After the 1973 election, the largest Hindustani party, the United Hindostani Party (VHP), was excluded from the Creole-dominated government. The main issue in the election that year was achieving constitutional independence, a goal the VHP had opposed for years. The party feared that the Creoles would come to power after independence and suppress the Hindustanis. They pointed to neighbouring Guyana, where Creoles and Indians had engaged in violent clashes. When it became clear that constitutional independence could no longer be delayed and violent ethnic clashes loomed, many Surinamese emigrated to the Netherlands. Hindustani emigration was proportional to their percentage of the population and, as a result, Hindustani communities in the Netherlands and Surinam are very similar, although their distribution across economic sectors differs.

The Dutch government was forced to set up emergency centres to deal with the massive immigration. Most of these centres were located in less populated parts of the Netherlands, away from the major cities. However, by the 1960s and early 1970s, a small number of Hindustanis had settled in The Hague and to a lesser extent in Amsterdam, Utrecht and Rotterdam. Over the years, Hindustanis living in remote parts of the country moved to these thriving communities, often because they had found a marriage partner there. While Hindustanis can be found in every part of the Netherlands these days, most still live in the major cities.

Dutch authorities do not register people according to ethnicity. Based on data provided by the Central Bureau of Statistics and a number of surveys, however, the number of first-generation and second-generation Hindustanis in the Netherlands was between 110,000 and 140,000 in 2002. This figure presumes that the percentage of Hindustanis among the Surinamese community in the Netherlands is slightly higher than that of the general population in Surinam. It is generally assumed that about 20 per cent of Hindustanis are Muslim and the remaining 80 per cent, Hindu. These percentages are likely to be lower since an estimated 10 per cent of the Hindustani population is Christian and an unknown number have no religious affiliation. The Indian population in the Netherlands also comprises small groups from India (14,000), Pakistan (17,500), Sri Lanka (10,000) and Uganda (1100).

INTEGRATION

The Surinamese are one of the most integrated and largest ethnic minorities in the Netherlands. Government policy is geared towards the integration of ethnic minorities and ensuring that their level of participation in the labour market, education and politics is similar to that of the population as a whole. Participation in other areas of life, such as recreation and art, is strongly encouraged. Moreover, Dutch policies promote assimilation. Their insistence on living in mixed neighbourhoods and attending mixed schools, and the generally held belief that interracial marriages and maintaining a diverse circle of friends are markers of successful integration, bear this out. The Surinamese community has produced a middle class

Map 8.50

THE NETHERLANDS

NORWAY
SWEDEN
Frisian Islands
UNITED KINGDOM   DENMARK
IRELAND   POLAND
GERMANY
FRANCE

• Amsterdam
THE NETHERLANDS
Leiden •   • Utrecht
The Hague • • Rotterdam
Maas
GERMANY

N

BELGIUM

0   40 kilometres
0   40 miles

of small businessmen, academics, medical practitioners and politicians. While other ethnic minorities are less integrated, according to official Dutch standards, Hindustanis are thought to be among the best integrated, while at the same time successfully maintaining their cultural identity. The same can be said when Hindustanis are compared to other ethnic Surinamese in the Netherlands.

The most important markers of integration in the Netherlands are performance in education, work and politics. The level of education among Hindustanis is increasing rapidly. The community has established four primary schools—three Hindu and one Muslim—in The Hague, Rotterdam and Amsterdam. A training college for pandits (priests) has also been set up. In 2004, about one-fifth (18 per cent) of the adult population (15–65 years old) had a college or university education, more than a quarter (27 per cent) had a mid-level education, and the remainder had a lower level of education. The level of education among Hindustanis is slightly lower than that of the white population as a whole, but higher than that of other ethnic minorities. While the second generation is better educated than the first, the most remarkable strides have been made by second-generation Hindustani women. In 2004, 25 per cent of Hindustani women were enrolled in vocational colleges, compared to 18 per cent of Hindustani men. At universities, the percentages were 12 and 18 respectively.

The Hindustani presence in the labour market is also impressive, although the gender difference in education is not reflected in the labour force. In 2002, about 70 per cent of the male labour force (15–65 years old) were employed, roughly the same percentage as the white male population. Employment rates for women were about 50 per cent. Notably, 11 per cent of men were in school or at a college or university, compared to 16 per cent of women. Figure 8.9 summarises the distribution of the potential labour force.

In 2004, 78 per cent of Hindustani men between 15 and 64 years of age were either employed or looking for work, compared to 81 per cent of the white male population; the percentage of Hindustani women employed or looking for work (53 per cent) was slightly lower than that of white women (59 per cent). The rising level of education among Hindustani women is reflected in their participation in the labour market but not in the unemployment rate. Although on average Hindustanis have an income only slightly lower than the white population as a whole, one-third of the men and half of the women complain of financial problems. This is probably due to different spending patterns as a result of a more active family life and transnational obligations and activities.

Hindustanis are less politically active than their white neighbours. The community is not large enough to establish a political party along ethnic lines, nor is there any desire to do so. They participate in politics through the established white parties. In recent decades, no more than two Hindustanis have been elected to the 150-seat national parliament at any given time. Participation at the municipal level has been much higher. Hindustanis are far more active in community organisations. In 2002, there were almost 400 Hindustani organisations, ranging from Hindu and Muslim schools to sports, social and cultural clubs. One-third of the men and almost a quarter of the women were members of an organisation or club. Half of these memberships were in exclusively Hindustani organisations, one-third were in mixed organisations and

Figure 8.9

DISTRIBUTION OF THE HINDUSTANI LABOUR FORCE (2002)

Source: Unpublished survey results, Institute of Social and Economic Research, SPVA, Erasmus University of Rotterdam, the Netherlands, 2002.

one-fifth in predominantly white ones. Such data do not, however, adequately reflect interaction with the white population: one-third of Hindustanis interact predominantly with their own community, 50 per cent maintain contacts inside and outside their community, and the remainder interact solely with the white population.

COMMUNITY LIFE

Most Hindustanis live in major cities in the western part of the Netherlands and also live close to one another. This is due partly to the fact that housing corporations in the Netherlands tend to take their tenants' preferences into account when distributing apartments, and is also a result of deliberate choice. However, this need to live in close proximity is diminishing. Modern communication technologies—the telephone, mobile phone, email and the Internet—have decreased the need for face-to-face contact. Moreover, increased levels of education have led to greater social and spatial mobility. The strong emphasis placed on schooling and having a career has also led to smaller family units, heralding a change in traditional Hindustani family life.

The Hindustanis' language is Sarnami, a variant of Hindi that developed in Surinam and was influenced by Dutch, English and Surinamese. Since Dutch is the official language in both Surinam and the Netherlands, it should come as no surprise that the majority of Hindustanis speak Dutch at home. An Internet survey determined that only 5 per cent of second-generation Hindustanis speak Sarnami with family members and partners, a quarter switch between Dutch and Sarnami,

A family in Holland of Indian and Dutch heritage.

Sikhs gathered at the Shri Nanak Dev Ji Gurdwara in Rotterdam.

The logo of the Hindoe Raad Nederland.

Indians celebrating the Phagwa festival in Amsterdam. Phagwa, commonly known as Holi, is celebrated on the last day of the Indian lunar month of Phagun.

and about one-tenth encounter problems when speaking Dutch. In cities with large concentrations of Hindustanis, such as The Hague, the use of Hindi among youngsters is a symbolic way of strengthening their ethnic identity.

As is the case in Surinam, the Hindu community in the Netherlands is divided into two main religious groups. About 80 per cent of Hindus are thought to belong to the orthodox Sanatan Dharma movement and the remaining 20 per cent to the reformist Arya Samaj. Both figures are probably inflated, however, since the Hindustani community also comprises a small number of Christians and atheists. Rituals are an important feature of Surinamese Hinduism. Yet, the way Hinduism is practised and how religion is experienced are undergoing major change.

RELIGIOUS CHANGE

One conspicuous change is the diminishing relevance of religious adherence to the second generation. What is more important to the younger generation is the philosophical explanation of symbols and rituals, something that some pandits are hard-pressed to provide. Pandits are increasingly asked to perform services in Dutch and to provide a more rational approach. More is expected of them: not only do they need to perform rituals, they are also asked to act as counsellors and social workers. This move away from ritual and towards a more philosophical approach that addresses the vagaries of life requires different skills, which contemporary pandits do not possess. The result is that his religious authority is undermined.

The role of the *mandir* (temple) is another important issue. Unlike *mandirs* in India, which are visited by Hindus of all persuasions, those in Surinam serve specific communities, not unlike the myriad Christian denominations in Surinam and the Netherlands. However, the *mandirs* have lost much of their appeal as many Hindus prefer to worship at small shrines at home. Despite this focus on home worship, Hindus have long demanded the establishment of large temples in major cities in the Netherlands. This request has not been met in full because Dutch authorities are hesitant when it comes to allowing overt manifestations of non-Western religious—and especially Islamic—symbols in the public domain.

Caste has never been a major factor among Surinamese Hindus because for various reasons, the caste system could not be reproduced in Surinam. It has, however, remained relevant to the pandits of the Sanatan

Dharma and a negligible number of Brahmin families. In the Netherlands as well, caste remains a marginal issue and appears to play no role for the second generation, which welcomes emancipation movements like that of the Karmavadis, which challenge the authority and superiority of the Brahmins and appoint their own lower-caste priests. Another development is the ordination of women as *panditas*. Finally, yoga and other new forms of meditation, vegetarianism and Ayurvedic medicine have also become popular in recent years.

At the organisational level, the Hindustanis' record in the Netherlands is poor. They have been granted a licence to operate a radio and television station (the Organisation for Hindu Media, or OHM), with limited funding and airtime. The licence is part of the Dutch government's policy of organising non-Western minorities along ethnic and religious lines. This policy also resulted in the establishment of the Hindu Council Netherlands (Hindoe Raad Nederland, or HRN), although it took more than 10 years of quibbling among Hindustani leaders before it was actually set up. It is exactly these differences and rivalries that keep the Hindustanis from formulating a swift response or consistent policy.

As mentioned earlier, a small minority of the Hindustani community is Muslim. An estimated one-third of this religious minority belong to the liberal Ahmadiyyas, while the remaining two-thirds are Sunnis. The Muslims have also been granted a licence to operate a radio and television station, the National Muslim Organisation for Broadcasting (NMO). Surinamese Muslims have a low profile and, like the Hindus, are generally thought to be successfully integrated. This perception contrasts favourably with that of other Muslim minorities, such as the Turks and Moroccans, who are often portrayed as culturally and socially backward, and as potential terrorists with international connections.

The sense of community among Hindustanis is strengthened by a number of other media. Commercial radio stations are to be found in every major city in the Netherlands, together with local, non-religious Hindustani television, which broadcasts in both Sarnami and Dutch. Indian movies and songs are popular and the availability of satellite television and the Internet has strengthened the impact of Indian (film) culture. The choice has been further expanded by the advent of the British-Indian Zee-TV.

TRANSNATIONAL RELATIONS

This last point underlines the increasing importance of transnational Indian relations. While the older generation

tends to keep in touch with Surinam, younger Hindustanis are increasingly detached from their parents' homeland and instead reconnect with India through Bollywood and religious affiliations. The worldwide reach of Bollywood culture through DVDs, CDs, magazines, radio and television, plus the availability of Indian apparel, jewellery and more enables Hindustanis—and this is also true for those in Surinam—to identify with Indian culture. In fact, it has become customary to buy wedding outfits, for example, in India. These transnational relations, the communication technologies that facilitate them, and the increased purchasing power of Hindustanis has made it easier for them to establish contacts with Indian communities elsewhere. Transnationalism has boosted travel to India and other diasporic Indian communities. Conversely, Indian movie stars, scholars and religious leaders increasingly visit Western countries—most often the UK, and occasionally the Netherlands.

The number of Hindustani glossy magazines and websites dedicated to Bollywood is also on the rise. There is a wide variety of venues where young Hindustanis can meet, and many opportunities for them to do so, such as beauty contests, singing and costume contests, and conferences on political and religious issues. The most popular leisure activity is dancing and listening to music at weddings. Hindustanis also celebrate the annual Milan festival, with its fair-like atmosphere, and the annual Hindustani film festival, both centred in The Hague but also organised in other major Dutch cities. Religious festivals such as Diwali, Holi and Ramadan are publicly celebrated in most major Dutch cities. In short, Hindustanis have successfully managed to set up and maintain a community.

While these points indicate a reaffirmation of ethnicity, assimilation is also visible. The change in the language spoken at home and the demands made of pandits prove this. Other changes that reflect cultural assimilation include changes in the family structure and gender roles; increased acceptance of Western dress, recreation, music and dance; the gradually increasing number of interracial marriages; and the decreasing size of families. Of a more fundamental nature is the process of individualisation: in allowing women and children to play a greater role, traditional family ties have changed. In most cases, however, assimilation and the reaffirmation of ethnicity go hand in hand, with one or the other being more dominant depending on the context.

THE CONTEMPORARY SITUATION

Despite this positive picture, Hindustanis face some serious social and medical problems. For example, more than one in three marriages end in divorce, which is usually initiated by the woman. The divorce rate is slightly higher than that of the white population. A number of factors are relevant here: individualisation, rising levels of education, the fact that the community is scattered across the country (resulting in a certain anonymity), the availability of unemployment benefits, and probably most of all, the relatively strong position of women in Dutch society.

The divorce rate is likely to drop over time, yet it remains a serious concern since family ties tend to be

Indians in the Netherlands awaiting the arrival of popular Bollywood stars on their way to the 11th International Indian Film Academy Awards (IIFA) which were held in Amsterdam in June 2005.

strong in the Hindustani community and the emotional cost of divorce is felt more acutely. A related problem is the high incidence of alcoholism and the abuse of women and children. This can be attributed to the inability, especially of men, to adjust to changes in gender roles and patterns of communication. The most alarming problem is the high rate of suicide among the Hindustani population compared to the whites. Between 1996 and 2001, suicide was the cause of death among 24 per cent of Hindustani men and 18 per cent of Hindustani women between 18 and 27 years of age. The figures for white men and women are 17 and 14 respectively. The relatively high incidence of diabetes and cardiovascular disease among Hindustanis is another source of concern for the medical establishment in the Netherlands.

Hindustanis in the Netherlands are successfully integrated. Their performance in the labour market, education and politics is remarkably positive. Unlike many other ethnic minorities in the Netherlands, second-generation Hindustanis—like second-generation Chinese—are not considered a problem group. Institutions in the fields of religion, education and leisure serve a community that takes pride in its cultural identity. These institutions enable and reaffirm the growth of Hindustani culture in the Netherlands. However, two developments have modified the kind of Hindustani culture that has emerged in the Netherlands. First, Dutch society drives the community to modernise and adapt to the democratic culture that typifies Western nations. Second, the increased interaction of the Dutch Hindustani community with India and the Indian diaspora has strengthened the sense of ethnic identity.

Still, the Hindustani community faces a number of problems. The first is the balance between the process of assimilation and the emphasis on ethnic identity. Integration allows for a stronger emphasis on individual freedom and development, but also erodes community ties. Managing this balance requires leadership, the lack of which is another problem facing the community. These problems are exacerbated by social and medical problems such as high divorce and suicide rates, and the high incidence of diabetes and cardiovascular diseases. A community-wide debate on these issues is needed. Tackling these problems adequately is essential if the Hindustani community is to survive as an ethnic minority in the decades to come.

Ruben Gowricharn and Chan Choenni

Hindorama features articles concerned with the Hindustani community in Holland and is aimed at fostering the development of multiculturalism in the Netherlands.

Bollywood superstar Shah Rukh Khan played host at the IIFA Awards in 2005.

FRANCE

Indian influences and motifs are important in the Palais Idéal du Facteur Cheval in Hauterives, which was built between 1879 and 1912. In 1969 it was listed as a Monument Historique by the French minister for culture, André Malraux.

THE INDIAN PRESENCE in France has a long history. The Pondicherians are the most prominent Indian community in France—numerically and in terms of social importance and impact. They comprise people from the former French colonies in India who were given the option of French nationality when the subcontinent became independent. Other Indians have arrived in France in small numbers as well, among them Sikhs, some of whom were refugees escaping riots against their community following Indira Gandhi's assassination.

EARLY CONTACTS IN THE 17TH–18TH CENTURY

In 1664, during the reign of King Louis XIV, the French East India Company was established by Jean Baptiste Colbert. It soon established trade links between France and India, importing Indian commodities, mainly textiles, which were popular in Europe. The volume of imports was so great that the French market was soon overrun by these goods and restrictions had to be imposed.

The company was also instrumental in establishing a strategic base in India for the French. This was achieved in 1697 through the Treaty of Ryswick, which ended the Nine Years War, also known as the War of English Succession. The treaty enabled the redistribution and regulation of European and overseas territories between France and Britain. Consequently, Pondicherry and the other small French enclaves in India, such as Karaikkal, Mahé, Yanam and Chandernagore, were officially declared French territories.

The popularity of Indian commodities explains the French public's early attitude towards India, which was

viewed as a flourishing country of beauty and affluence, and gained a phantasmal presence in French literature and art. More significantly, the establishment of French bases in India provided the foundation for the development of an Indian community in France. As age-old British–French discord manifested on Indian soil, French territories, both in India and Europe, would come to serve as a refuge for anti-British activists and freedom fighters. Hence, while these early contacts did not immediately lead to an Indian community establishing itself in France, they paved the way for different forms of migration in the future.

In Chandernagore, a small enclave north of Calcutta, the French presence enabled educated Bengali elites and intellectuals to become acquainted with French literature and philosophy. The growing interest in French language and culture among the 18th-century Bengali elite would later spread to the educated elite of Bombay, and especially to Parsi families. As a result, students who wanted to study French language and literature formed the earliest Indian group in France. Their affluent and educated backgrounds ensured that they socialised almost exclusively with the French intellectual elite.

DEVELOPMENTS IN THE 19TH CENTURY

The opening of the Suez Canal in 1869 shortened travel time between India and Europe by several weeks. Not only was this beneficial to France's trade with India, it also meant that France, with Marseilles as its main Mediterranean port, became an important stopover in the journey between Britain and India. The express train connection between Marseille and Calais, the connecting port to the British Isles, came to be called the 'Bombay Express' as its predominant function was the regular transport of passengers between Britain and India.

The new travel facilities and the considerable reduction in travel time encouraged the Indian elite to study in Europe. During the 19th century, France received an increasing number of Indian students due to the continued interest in French language and literature among the elite in Bengal and Bombay. In Chandernagore, Indian students were encouraged through public speeches to study in France; and in Bombay, the Cercle Franco-Parsi (quickly renamed the more general Cercle Littéraire) was inaugurated by students (predominantly Parsi) in 1886. These efforts were so successful that British authorities soon began to feel uneasy about the increasing interest in their rival's language and culture, and tried to restrict the learning of French. The Cercle Littéraire nevertheless succeeded in keeping such restrictions away from Bombay University, where French was taught continuously.

Besides students, a number of Indian merchants, predominantly pearl traders, came to settle in France during the 19th century. Among them was R. D. Tata, the cousin of Jamsetji Nusserwanji—founder of what was to become the Tata empire. Tata was among the young Bombay Parsis who took an interest in French language

Map 8.51

FRANCE

NORWAY
UNITED KINGDOM   SWEDEN   DENMARK
IRELAND   GERMANY   POLAND
UNITED KINGDOM
SWITZERLAND
ITALY
SPAIN

N

• Calais
GERMANY
BELGIUM
LUXEMBOURG

Channel Islands
Le Havre
Seine

• Paris

Loire

SWITZERLAND

FRANCE

Bay of Biscay

ITALY

Rhône

Nîmes •
Fréjus •   • Marseille

0   300 kilometres
0   300 miles

Corsica

and culture, and was a member of the Cercle Littéraire before he came to France. In 1902, he married Suzanne Brière, a French national, and it was claimed that he had taken French citizenship. Their second child, J. R. D. Tata, would become the fourth chairman of the Tata empire.

The 19th century also saw the development of an entirely different field that would become important in the history of the Indian community in France. In the latter half of the 18th century, Indian literature—mainly in Sanskrit, India's 'classical' language—had become popular among scholars in Europe. From the early 19th century onwards, European universities began to establish departments for Indian or Oriental philology, later known as 'Indology', and Paris became one of the centres of this new academic discipline.

Preceding this development was the study of Parsi texts, highlighted by Abraham Hyacinthe Anquetil-Duperron's translation of the Zend Avesta, the sacred book of the Parsis, which was published in 1771. Anquetil-Duperron had studied the religion and text with Parsi scholars in India. His work was regarded as authentic in Parsi circles and many Parsis who were no longer able to read and understand their original language learnt about their religion from Anquetil-Duperron's work. The high regard he has maintained among the Parsis, even in the contemporary period, is apparent in websites such as www.zoroastriankids.com, where the publication date of his translation is part of the Zoroastrian timeline. Anquetil-Duperron's work on Parsi literature was further pursued by French scholars of the 19th century. These activities in turn encouraged Parsi scholars from India to settle in Paris to learn European scholarly methods and to apply these when dealing with their own culture and literature.

French Indology in the 19th century attracted a still wider body of Indian scholars, who found in Paris a fertile ground for discussion and scientific exchange regarding the roots of Indian culture and science. Some of them stayed on in France for some time and formed a small group of academics who made a distinctive contribution to the diaspora. At the end of the 19th and the beginning of the 20th century, Sylvain Lévi, one of the greatest French Indologists, kept a regular 'open house' which became a meeting place for European and international students and scholars interested in Indian subjects. Indian travellers, including princes and maharajas, famous artists (e.g. Rabindranath Tagore), politicians and distinguished personalities, or whoever else had a connection to or an interest in India and was present in Paris, often frequented Lévi's house, making it one of the centres where the still miniscule and largely elite Indian community met.

Improvements in communications intensified the links between France and India but the development of France's Indian community in the 19th century continued along lines similar to what had been established during the previous century. The community remained small but began to expand, not only in number, but also in fields of interest, although in terms of social composition, it still appeared to be limited mainly to the Indian elite.

THE EARLY 20TH CENTURY

The beginning of the 20th century saw the growth of nationalism and the freedom movement in India, and among sections of the Indian community in Britain. French territories in India and Europe became places of refuge for anti-British activists. From 1905 onwards, important personalities linked to the Indian nationalist

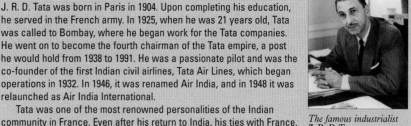

J. R. D. Tata (1904–93)

J. R. D. Tata was born in Paris in 1904. Upon completing his education, he served in the French army. In 1925, when he was 21 years old, Tata was called to Bombay, where he began work for the Tata companies. He went on to become the fourth chairman of the Tata empire, a post he would hold from 1938 to 1991. He was a passionate pilot and was the co-founder of the first Indian civil airlines, Tata Air Lines, which began operations in 1932. In 1946, it was renamed Air India, and in 1948 it was relaunched as Air India International.

Tata was one of the most renowned personalities of the Indian community in France. Even after his return to India, his ties with France, the country of his mother and where he had spent his entire youth, remained very close. When he died in 1993, his funeral was held in Paris and he was laid to rest in the city's most famous burial ground, the Père Lachaise.

The famous industrialist J. R. D. Tata.

movement began to settle in France. Among them were such illustrious names as Madame Cama and Vinayak Damodar 'Veer' Savarkar, who stayed there for a while and published nationalist pamphlets, books and journals.

Indian activists living in Paris had first come to the attention of the British Director of Criminal Intelligence (DCI) in London in 1907. When revolutionaries tried to derail the train of Sir Andrew Fraser, the lieutenant-governor of Bengal, evidence pointed to the participation of activists stationed in Europe. Following enquiries, the French police, who were generally reluctant to cooperate with the DCI, stated that in Paris, a Russian anarchist had taught bomb-making to Bengali students. The British Intelligence Service went into high alert: from 1909, Paris was labelled the 'main centre of Indian agitation in Europe.'

In 1910, one incident led to greater formal cooperation between France and Britain. 'Veer' Savarkar, who had been arrested in England, managed to escape from the ship which was meant to take him to India during a brief stop at Marseilles. Nevertheless, he was arrested by the French police. England demanded his extradition. The French authorities did not immediately respond to this demand, claiming that clear legal procedures were necessary for such a step to be taken; but when the incident threatened to affect diplomatic relations between the two countries, France gave in. Following the incident, France officially disapproved of anti-British activities on its soil. As a result, the Indian community in France came under tighter control, but this did not stop the activists.

The advent of World War I saw the British and the French working closely together against a common enemy, Germany. As a result of this alliance, France complied readily with British requests for the extradition of activists. Paris was no longer the safe refuge for Indian activists that it once was, but French territories in India continued to offer shelter to anti-British freedom fighters.

THE 'PONDICHÉRIENS'

French colonial policy differed from that of the British with regard to the treatment of indigenous populations. The policy adopted, generally called 'assimilation', sought to integrate indigenous peoples as far as possible with the culture of their rulers, and thus, turn them into real French subjects. The assimilation process included education in French, cultural integration (although the French colonial masters respected indigenous cultures, in India at least, to an astonishing degree) and general suffrage, albeit with certain conditions.

Before 1884, different voters' lists were kept for French and Indian voters. In 1884, a new category of

These Indian soldiers were part of the British expeditionary force in France in 1914.

In the annual Chariot Festival at the Ganesha temple in Paris, Sri Manikka Vinayakar, kavadis are taken through the 10th and 18th arrondissement of the city by devotees.

people was introduced in the French Indian territories, the *renonçants*—people who had renounced their legal status as Hindus or Muslims and embraced French civil law. This was originally seen as an important step on the way to an individual becoming a French citizen, although it was of little consequence in the final phase of French colonial rule, when everyone in the territories was free to choose French nationality. Before the French Revolution in 1789, everyone on French territory anywhere in the world, regardless of whether they were French or indigenous, was a subject of the king of France. However, following the creation of the French Republic, questions of citizenship and nationality arose that proved to be difficult to deal with in the colonies. The creation of the *renonçants* was one attempt to cope with such questions.

Most of the French territories in India gained their independence in three stages between 1954 and 1962 (Chandernagore was handed over to India in 1949). In 1954, France withdrew physically from the territories. In 1956, a treaty with the Indian government, which France ratified in 1962, concluded the process of withdrawal. Part of the treaty dealt with the regulation of the nationality of people residing in former French territories. The text stated that the hitherto French nationals in these territories would become citizens of the Indian union. However, it provided the opportunity for individuals to opt to retain French nationality during the first six months after the ratification of the treaty (15 August 1962–15 February 1963). The option even left the decision open for individuals who, at this time, had not yet attained legal maturity, and who might exercise their option at a later stage.

Initially, relatively few people (approximately 2 per cent of the population in these territories) opted for French nationality. Following the increase in birth rates and the exercise of the option at a later stage, the numbers increased considerably. Many families also consciously retained different nationalities, distributing French and Indian nationalities in a balanced manner so that the family could profit most from the Indian and the French social welfare system. This allowed families to gain numerous advantages: Indian nationals in the family could join the Indian government service, an option which was closed to non-Indians; French nationality allowed for settlement and employment in France; and French nationality also meant the individual could receive a French pension, thus ensuring a regular inflow of 'hard currency' to the family.

Contemporary 'Pondichériens'

French colonial policies thus resulted in the formation of an Indo-French community made up of native Indians who kept French nationality and were free to settle and work in France. Since Pondicherry—the largest of the

French territories in India—is the origin of the majority of France's Indo-French population, the people have generally been known as Pondichériens or, more precisely, Franco-Pondichériens. The migration of Pondichériens to France began in 1954 and it has continued to the present. However, Pondicherry is not the birthplace of all Pondichériens: many who served in the French army had been posted to Indo-China (Vietnam) and had settled, married and started families there. A number of Franco-Pondichériens include those who were born and grew up in Indo-China and who might have visited Pondicherry for the first time during their journey from Vietnam to Europe. Still, they share their culture and roots with the 'Indian' Pondichériens who migrated directly and no distinguishing line is drawn between these two groups.

While by far the dominant group among Indians in France today, the Pondichérien identity is not easy to define. In fact, these people form a double diaspora: in France they are generally regarded as Indians (regardless of whether they are French nationals), whereas in India, they are regarded as French. On the one hand, they proudly exhibit and celebrate their French background and, on the other, they nostalgically recall cultural elements of their Indian roots and take great care to retain and manifest their identity as Tamils—a contrast to other groups (mainly North Indian) in their diasporic neighbourhood. In fact, Pondicheriens have three distinct identities—Tamil, Indian and French—any of which become relevant according to circumstance, occasion and surrounding. Since the 1980s, a further need to distinguish their identity has arisen following the influx of Sri Lankan Tamils to Europe. As Pondichériens and Sri Lankan Tamils do not mix, both find it necessary to distinguish themselves from each other. Hence, a fourth identity for the Pondichériens in France is that of 'Tamils from India', or, more precisely, 'from Pondicherry'.

In 1992, an estimated 48,000 Pondichériens lived in France. Although the largest group among them are real Franco-Pondichériens (the term that is used to refer to those of French nationality), the number also includes other Pondichériens who have come to France on scholarships, work permits or even tourist visas (these offer possibilities for people from the former French territories in India who have missed the chance to 'opt' for French nationality to acquire it by establishing their residence in France, often with the help of French family members, and then applying for 'restoration' of French nationality).

Pondichériens can be found in various regions in France. Those who are employed by the army are

Sikhs in France

Among Indians in France there is a small community of Sikhs, numbering not more than a few thousand. Most of them arrived in France after 1984, fleeing the anti-Sikh agitation in India which followed the assassination of Indira Gandhi. This small Sikh community lived largely in anonymity—even French government officials were unaware of Sikhs living in France—until it went public with a protest against a recently introduced law (September 2004) against the wearing of religious symbols in schools. This law directly affected Sikh boys, who were no longer allowed to wear turbans and other religious symbols in school. The issue is a subject of ongoing public debate in France, as it is in other parts of the world.

French Sikhs protesting against the draft law.

generally settled with their families in the *villes de garnison* in the south (e.g. Nîmes and Fréjus), and those in administrative service settle wherever they are posted. However, the vast majority, about 28,000, live in Paris and the surrounding region known as Île-de-France. This is where Pondichérien communities are conspicuous and specific cultural activities can be observed.

Of the Pondichériens in France, approximately 40–45 per cent are Hindu, as is the case for Roman Catholics, while 10–15 per cent are Muslim. The Hindus mainly worship Murugan and Mariamman, two deities who are considered specifically Tamil. The Sri Manikka Vinayakar Temple has been in existence in the 18th *arrondissement* (district) of Paris since 1985. In general, however, Hindu temples are rare in France. (Elsewhere in Europe, Tamil Hindu temples have been established in recent years through the initiatives of the Sri Lankan Tamil diaspora. The same development can be expected in France.)

Roman Catholic Pondichériens worship St. Mary in the form of Arokkiya-Mata of Velankanni, the most important Christian pilgrimage centre in the Tamil-speaking area of South India. In this sense, Arokkiya-Mata is also a specific Tamil deity, the worship of whom contributes to the Tamil identity of Christians, just as the worship of Murugan contributes to that of the Hindus. Arokkiya-Mata icons have been installed in several Catholic churches in the region around Paris and in those parishes where Catholic Pondichériens gather. Sunday mass is regularly conducted in Tamil.

The general lifestyle of the Pondichériens in France is changing under the influence of modern developments, especially among third-generation Pondichériens who have limited connections with India and Indian culture. The first generation consisted mainly of male French citizens who were mostly employed by the army or the administration. They generally arrived in France alone, leaving their wives and children in India, and visiting their families on an average of once in two years. Only after they had established a reasonable economic base and adjusted to life in Europe were they joined by their families. Soon, the sons—and on rare occasions, daughters—of relatives in India would follow in order to profit from better educational facilities and job opportunities.

Nevertheless, even today, the preferred manner of marriage is still to look for a bride or groom in India. Young Pondichériens in France—boys more than girls—appear willing to accept arranged marriages, and they often leave the choice of partner to their parents or other relatives back home in India. Although the traditional Tamil marriage between cousins is no longer appreciated by Pondichériens, they still look for partners whose families match theirs in social status, an important element of which is the caste the families originate from.

French nationality is still a great asset for a marriage partner, and it can be one of great value, especially in the case of a girl: when a France-based female French national marries an India-based male Indian national, he is given the opportunity of gaining French nationality and migrating to France. In such situations, the girl's family does not have to pay any dowry. In recent times, inter-cultural marriages (between Pondichériens and French partners) have increased, which implies major changes in the life patterns of the community.

EVIDENCE OF 'ACCULTURATION'

Other aspects of everyday life, such as food and dress, show growing signs of 'acculturation'. School and work schedules in France require working members of the family (primarily men) and children to eat outside the home during the day, thus getting accustomed to French food. The only Indian meal they may have is dinner. Increasingly, Indian food is reserved for the weekends and festive occasions. However, this change in diet is not extraordinary, given that French food, or at least a blend of Indian and French dishes, is common in Pondicherry among families with French nationality, and also among affluent families who try to exhibit a European lifestyle in order to gain prestige.

While the men generally dress in a European style, and only on very rare occasions wear the traditional Indian *veshti* and *tundu*, older women generally stick to wearing saris, at least when going out. The younger generation has adapted more to the European style, and skirts—never too short, though—and jeans are as common for Pondichérien girls these days as is the *salwar kamiz* or Punjabi suits.

In France, women in Pondichérien families are generally still confined to the house. In accordance with social rules in India, a family with an employed female member loses prestige and status. However, this is changing with the new generation, and a growing number of young women have entered the workforce. These developments have been accelerated by the fact that links to the extended family back in India have become increasingly tenuous. While in the first, and to some extent, the second generation, the general practice was to work in France and return to India upon retirement to live on a French pension, more families now settle in France permanently. They are no longer interested in keeping houses and land in India, which is for them nothing more than a holiday destination.

While the Pondichériens in France have increasingly adapted to French ways in their daily lives, they are still anxious to retain their cultural identity; to have their children learn the Tamil language and adhere to their traditional religious practices, including the celebration of customary 'rites of passage'. In fact, today these celebrations have become more common in France. About 15 years ago, a family would postpone the rituals until their next journey to India, where they would conduct these rites in the original cultural setting. One reason for this change is the availability of various kinds of Indian products in France, so that all the required implements and ingredients needed for rituals are at hand.

Ulrike Niklas

A 'sea of coloured turbans' swamp a French boulevard as Sikhs from across Europe defend the right to wear their traditional headgear in state schools.

A photo exhibition on Pondicherry held in Paris in 2006. Organised by the Indian National Trust for Art and Cultural Heritage (INTACH), the exhibition sought to sensitise visitors to the strategies implemented for preserving Pondicherry's inheritance and its environment, and to point out the tourism potential of the town.

Smashing coconuts at the Ganesh festival in France.

PORTUGAL

A statue of Gandhi
and his wife,
Kasturba, at the
Hindu temple
in Lisbon.

Map 8.52

PORTUGAL

N

0   70 kilometres
0   70 miles

PORTUGAL

ATLANTIC
OCEAN

• Coimbra

• Fatima

SPAIN

Loures
•
Lisbon
•

PORTUGUESE COLONIALISM WAS predominantly centred in Goa, the capital of *Estado da Índia* (State of India), a domain whose Asian boundaries were Melaka in Malaya and Timor in the Indonesian archipelago. Portuguese colonialism in Goa differed from other forms of colonialism in India and also from Portuguese colonialism in other parts of the world. Its distinctiveness resulted from a systematic attempt to reproduce in India a metropolitan culture through conversion and by unifying conflicting interests under the imperial construct of *Goa Dourada* (Golden Goa). Portuguese was imposed as the official language and Konkani, the local vernacular, was downgraded to a dialect of the low castes. Cultural and religious differences were discouraged, when not repressed. From a social perspective, *Goa Dourada* was idealised as a harmonious society without remarkable ruptures between individuals and groups, following the Christian principle of equality. This practice, however, was incompatible with the Indian caste system that was paramount among Hindus and Catholics. Consequently, the system was retained in education and administration, where high-caste Catholics were favoured, and in the church hierarchy, where it was held by Brahmans to guarantee the superiority of the priesthood and ecclesiastical control.

Although this ideology was enforced on all Portuguese territories on the subcontinent, its impact on Províncias do Norte (Northern Provinces, the term used by the Portuguese to identify Daman and Diu in western India) was far less significant when compared to Goa. Even if conversion was enforced and Catholicism was ingrained in local populations to a considerable extent, the Hindu cult was too close and the Episcopado do Oriente (Central Church) in Goa was too distant to prevent the profound appeal of Hinduism among the converted. Furthermore, Gujarati, the local vernacular, was the language of a millenarian civilisation, and not as easily discarded as Konkani, the dialect of fishermen. Not to be neglected is the fact that Daman and Diu were encapsulated within the broader boundaries of the British Empire and, more specifically, within the former Bombay Presidency, which, after Indian independence, would become the state of Gujarat. The distance between Goa and Províncias do Norte was more than geographical; they were separated by the vast region of Maharashtra, whose capital, Bombay, was an essential centre for political, artistic and intellectual debate that would host some of the foremost Goan nationalists.

The more important newspapers printed in Goa during the first half of the 20th century—the more expressive one being *Correio da Noite*, sponsored by the colonial government and used as a tool to propagate colonial ideology—provide evidence of the conflicting positions of the Portuguese and the British, the former blaming the latter for collaborating with anti-colonial individuals from Daman and Diu who would turn to British Indian territories, particularly the Bombay Presidency, to escape Portuguese persecution and to organise the struggle against it. This opposition became even clearer during the nationalist movement, when *satyagrahis* inspired by the Mahatma supported Goan resistance to Portuguese rule. In 1946, a year before India's independence, Gandhi wrote eloquently in *Harijan*:

It is ridiculous to write of Portugal as the motherland of Indians of Goa. Their mother country is as much India as mine. Goa is outside British India but it is within geographical India as a whole. And there is very little, if anything, in common between the Portuguese and the Indians of Goa.

However, Gandhi's voice did not immediately reverberate in post-independence India, and in spite of strong pressure from the Congress Party and African-Asians, it took Prime Minister Jawaharlal Nehru 14 years to bring Goa, Daman and Diu into the Indian Union, thus leading to the collapse of the colonial regime in December 1961.

Notwithstanding the disparity between Goa and the Províncias do Norte, the Portuguese promoted in all their territories the apparatus of their colonial policy: the imposition of Portuguese law and way of life, with the subsequent repression of the native one; and the favouring of Catholics over Hindus and Muslims when it came to positions in administration and education, clerical jobs, economic opportunities and social improvement. Although discrimination in the territories decreased after Portugal became a republic in 1910, during the 40 years

Map 8.53

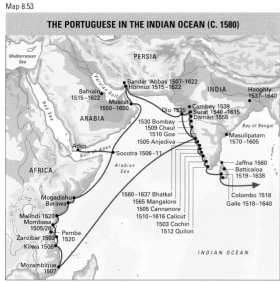

THE PORTUGUESE IN THE INDIAN OCEAN (C. 1580)

Source: Patrick K. O'Brien (ed.), Atlas of World History, 1999.

Chronology: Portuguese India	
1498	Vasco da Gama arrives in India.
March–May 1510	Portuguese occupation of Goa.
November 1510	Goa becomes a Portuguese colony.
December 1535	Diu acquired by Portugal.
1558	Daman acquired by Portugal (occupied since 1531).
1779	Dadra, Nagar and Haveli acquired by Portugal.
July–August 1954	Dadra, Nagar and Haveli occupied by Indian nationalists.
December 1961	Goa, Daman and Diu occupied by India.
March 1962	Goa, Daman and Diu formally annexed by India.
December 1974	Annexation recognised by Portugal; re-establishment of diplomatic relations between Portugal and India.

Based on www.worldstatesmen.org/India.htm.

Map 8.53 shows the linkages between the Portuguese possessions of Goa, the Províncias do Norte (Daman and Diu) and Mozambique, which were an important part of the structure of the Portuguese Empire in the Indian Ocean in the 16th century.

of dictatorship in Portugal (1933–74), anti-Portugal political activity was repressed and transgressions punished with either deportation or imprisonment.

In the early decades of the 20th century, the metropolis fell into a severe economic recession, the effects of which dramatically impacted the colonies. For many Indians, migration was the only way out, with British and Portuguese Africa the main destinations. Mozambique was a major destination for migrants from Goa and the Províncias do Norte. The Portuguese had constructed a network between the two colonies at the edge of the Indian Ocean, shifting government institutions and employees from Goa to Mozambique, the more important being the Escola Medica, a colonial medical school whose physicians would become an elite in the metropolis, both in colonial and post-colonial times.

Portuguese colonialism in India ensured that when the process of migration arose, it reflected the more evident divisions in Portuguese India. Travelling mainly from Daman and Diu and from nearby cities in Gujarat, Hindus and Muslims began to form social and economic systems in Mozambique that would set a precedent for the two main Indian communities in Portugal by the end of the 20th century. In addition, Ismaili migration from Gujarat is particularly noteworthy for its participation in multinational capital and its inclusion in the contemporary West African political agenda.

Muslims living in Portugal have distinguished themselves in finance and have achieved remarkable social recognition. The Indian Muslim community's size is difficult to determine given that this community includes Muslims from other former Portuguese colonies, such as Guinea-Bissau and, more recently Bangladesh, Pakistan, Morocco, Senegal and Mauritania. The community, which is mostly Sunni, assembles in the large mosque in central Lisbon—an indication of the economic power of some of its members. The Ismailis, who gather in their own mosque, are wealthy but politically and socially less prominent than the Sunnis.

TRAVEL, MIGRATION AND THE DIASPORA

Indian groups in Portugal came in distinct migrant streams and embraced different patterns of adaptation and assimilation. The first group to consider comprises those who had participated in colonial networks and who

were, to a large extent, privileged because of their religion and having been sanctioned by the colonial authority. This was mostly the case with the Catholics, who had established solid family and professional networks between Goa and Lisbon throughout the colonial period. By speaking the same language, having skills that would sometimes outshine those of the Portuguese administrators and clergy, sharing the same religion and nationality, and standing out in such professions as medicine and law (gaining both national and international praise), Goan Catholics were absorbed into metropolitan society to such an extent that the formation of an Indian Catholic community in Portugal was inhibited, or unnecessary. (Curiously enough, such a community is on its way to being formed by Catholics from Daman and Diu, and

The Portuguese introduced Christianity to Goa, leading to the establishment of numerous churches, such as The Church of Our Lady of the Immaculate Conception in Panaji.

355

Portugal may have left its mark on the subcontinent, but India has influenced Portugal too, as evidenced by the architecture of this building in Montserrat.

In 1998, members of the Comunidade Hindu de Portugal (Hindu Community of Portugal) built a large temple in Lisbon dedicated to Radha-Krishna, Shiva and Rama.

Gujarati women in Portugal reciting the Bhagavad Gita.

Goans of lower social status who have migrated to Portugal over the last few years). In late 1987, after Goa achieved statehood, a group of prominent Catholics born in Goa created the Casa de Goa (Goan House), a cultural association that brought together the Goan elite (who, to a large extent, are a Portuguese elite) and Portuguese intellectuals and artists linked to Goa. As caste affiliations were sustained within the Casa de Goa, the group was eventually disbanded to form another association by the end of the 1990s.

The experience of the Hindu colonial elite as a component of Portuguese society parallels to a large extent that of the Goan Catholics. This is further endorsed by their leading role in national politics. As a result, there was no socialisation with the wider Hindu community of Portugal, which formed in the 1980s following global transformations and the makeover of the political economy in the late 20th century.

As opposed to the Catholic and Hindu colonial elite, the wider Hindu community originated primarily from Gujarat and arrived either directly or indirectly via Mozambique. Most of its members left Mozambique after the country's independence in 1975 due to civil war and the economic breakdown of the country. Many of them were less familiar with Portugal than with India, and even then, sometimes found themselves at odds with their Indianness since the Partition left those who migrated to Mozambique before 1947 affiliated to two different countries, India and Pakistan.

An increasing number of Hindus from Gujarat also travel to Lisbon to get to other European countries, mainly the UK; a situation which has led to growing pressure from the European Union to decline visas to these migrants, who they view as threatening the unstable European labour market.

The idea of a homogeneous Gujarati Hindu community in Portugal is questionable. Stratification among its members follows lines of economic power, allowing for status reassertion, negotiation and the reconfiguration of caste. This has seen the emergence of a leading economic minority dealing in commerce and acquiring considerable influence in Portugal, ensuring official political representation (especially in the Câmara Municipal de Lisboa, or the Municipality of Lisbon), social acknowledgement and

growing distance from the wider Gujarati community. This larger group mainly consists of manual and unskilled workers, and people engaged in small trade, or working in or running small family shops. Other people from South Asia (mostly male Pakistanis and Bangladeshis), many of whom struggle for economic survival and are haunted by the prospect of repatriation as they lack permanent visas to Portugal, are also labelled as Hindus.

The centre of the Hindu community's commercial activity is Centro Comercial da Mouraria, an enormous shopping centre located in a traditional quarter of downtown Lisbon. The centre speaks volumes about the power held by the community when it comes to intervening in urban cultural configuration and the political agenda. The centre has become more cosmopolitan with the inclusion of the Chinese diaspora.

The community congregates in the large Hindu temple in Lisbon which hosts both Hindus and non-Hindus, the latter frequently encouraged to participate in non-religious ceremonies. The temple has become a centre for socialisation and the reconstruction of cultural beliefs and practices, and sponsors cultural events according to the Hindu annual calendar, thus affirming regional and linguistic identities specific to Gujarat. Caste discrimination is alleged by some Hindus, who are supposedly disallowed from performing roles in some religious rituals. In such situations, private religious groups tend to substitute public ones in daily spiritual observances. These Hindus who were denied a full religious life in Lisbon's main temple have built a new temple in Loures, a city 15 km from the capital with a large Hindu population.

Significantly, this split has reversed religious gender divisions by attributing to women the role of performing ceremonies traditionally ascribed to men. The redistribution of religious gender roles has occurred at a time when traditions are being strengthened through the reproduction of religious texts and growing connections with conservative, and sometimes nationalistic, Hindu organisations—a connection that is not uncommon in many overseas Indian communities. As migrants without the extended family networks they had in India, women have created for themselves alternative networks that offer a supportive female environment. Many of these women cannot speak Portuguese and are kept apart from Portuguese society. Their inability to speak the official language thus excludes them from public and political spheres, keeping them under traditional male authority. Even in families where conventional gender roles are challenged, communitarian traditions end up supporting the patriarchal ideology.

The desire for Indian culture—food, attire, music and yoga—in urban Portugal has created a cosmopolitan intra-social and intra-community web that would be hard to achieve under other circumstances. This offers the younger generation, many of whom have never been to India, an identifiable cultural 'space'.

STRATEGIES OF ADAPTATION

Strategies of adaptation are diverse and complex, and depend on both the country of origin and the new home. A specific example which accurately illustrates the capacity for adaptation relates to Our Lady of Fatima, to whose Catholic sanctuary Hindus travel on pilgrimage. The event

Partout où je vais ('Everywhere I go')

Everywhere where I go
I carry with me this red ground like blood
The quiet sob of the covered hills of smoke
The lachrymose waves of the Zuari river

Everywhere where I go
I carry with me
The anger of the forest of Satari
Deep wounds of the pickaxes
On the bodies of the Gods and Goddesses

Everywhere where I go
I carry on me the signs of the blows of whips
Black spots of blood
On delicate hands and thighs.

Everywhere where I go
I carry with me
The striking down cry of June 18
And my Heart howls like the lion
Prisoner in the cage of Aguada

My firm spirit, my blood boils
My heart is burst like the rice grain
On the burning stove

Everywhere where I go
I carry on me the wounds of my native soil
Without your love, far from your life
O Goa, I do not know how to live

Everywhere where I go
I carry with me
The spark of the Revolt

Translation of a poem by Goan poet Manohar Rai Sardessai, available at www.iatf-inde.com/poet.htm.

has now become part of the sanctuary's religious calendar. It is believed that Hindus in Portugal see Our Lady of Fatima as Mata, the Mother Goddess. At the level of ritual, too, changes have occurred, this time showing adaptation and adoption by the host community. A decade ago, grieving Hindus faced problems caused by the lack of crematoriums. In time, not only were new crematoriums built, but cremation became a practice adopted by the Portuguese themselves.

For many Hindus, India remains the 'old country'. The distinctive history of Indian migration to Portugal has dramatically transformed the migrants' sense of belonging and nationality. New technologies in production, distribution and communications have allowed the community to assert their identity within the broader context of Hindus in the diaspora. To those Indians who never lived in India (having been born in Africa or in Portugal), the subcontinent is a wonderland constructed by films, music and second-hand stories. To those who do not have regular contacts with India, media broadcasts (at a local level through Swagatam: Som do Oriente, broadcasting news through radio from Portugal and Gujarat; and at a global level by Zee-TV, a pan-Indian television channel), Bollywood movies and Indian popular music further reinforce diasporic connections and attachments.

Portuguese colonialism led to the deterioration of bilateral relations between Portugal and India. These gradually improved in the late 1980s through the initiatives of a socialist prime minister who returned territory claimed by India after 1961. Coincidentally, this was when the Indian economy was liberalised and overseas Indians were recognised as potentially influential partners in investment and technology. However, this was not the case with Indians living in Portugal, whose economic status did not make them potential participants in multinational opportunities—the exception being a limited number of families engaged in business. As a consequence, despite the fact that Portuguese colonialism nurtured among the Hindus a deep sense of Indianness and subsequent lack of enduring loyalty to Portugal, the Hindu community is not as divided as one would expect when it comes to national identity: while India is unquestionably the 'old country', where tradition and values are asserted, Portugal is the country that provides for their economic livelihood.

Rosa Maria Perez

Thousands of pilgrims gather at the statue of Our Lady of Fatima during the traditional procession at her sanctuary. Some Hindus in Portugal see her as a manifestation of the Hindu Mother Goddess.

The Centro Comercial da Mouraria, situated at the Martim Moniz square, is popular with the Indian community in Portugal. The enormous shopping complex boasts a large number of Indian, Chinese and African shops.

GERMANY

During World War II, this building at 2A Lichtenstein Street in Berlin housed the Free India Centre led by Subhas Chandra Bose.

IN 2003, 43,566 INDIAN CITIZENS and an estimated 17,500 persons of Indian origin (PIOs) lived in Germany. Due to their small number and their particular migration history, Indians are hardly noticed as an ethnic group by the larger community. Most PIOs live in mainly German neighbourhoods, spend most of their time with Germans, and only occasionally meet other people from the subcontinent.

Even before World War I, some Indian students and freedom fighters were found in Germany. It was an attractive destination as it played no part in the colonisation of India and its universities were famous. The Indians founded an organisation to coordinate the activities of Indian nationalists abroad and gained the support of the German government in their endeavour. As Germany approached defeat in the war, however, support for these activities was withdrawn, resulting in a temporary hiatus for Indian political activism in Germany. In the 1920s, Indian nationalist political activism resumed when M. N. Roy opened an office in Berlin with the support of new Indian students. Antipathy towards their socialist ideals and, more significantly, growing racism against 'coloured' foreigners worsened their position in Nazi Germany. Some were imprisoned and a number fled the country.

NETAJI

In 1941, a major change occurred when Subhas Chandra Bose arrived in Germany to gain Adolf Hitler's support for

Pro India, edited by Chempakaraman Pillai, was a newspaper produced by a small number of Indian freedom fighters and students based in Germany during WWI.

Map 8.54

the Indian freedom struggle. Although Hitler thought that India should be ruled by Europeans, he supported Bose for strategic reasons. German support led to the establishment of a Free India centre, a magazine and a broadcasting station known as Azad Hind (Free India). Following its formation, the Free India centre adopted four key resolutions: '*Jai Hind*' ('Victory to India') would be the official form of salutation (this remains a common greeting among many Indians); Rabindranath Tagore's famous patriotic song *Jana Gana Mana* would be the national anthem of independent India; Hindustani was to be the national language; and Subhas Chandra Bose would thereafter be addressed as 'Netaji', the Indian equivalent of 'leader'. Bose also managed to convince Germany to form an Indian legion, which became the 950th regiment of the German army. The Indian legion consisted largely of the Indian prisoners of war (POWs), who had been captured by the German army while serving the British Indian army in North Africa and Europe. At its largest, it had some 3500 soldiers. Although Bose left for Japan in 1943, the legion remained in Germany, serving at various times in the Netherlands, France and northern Italy. Following the German surrender in May 1945, members of the Indian legion were captured by American and French units while attempting to cross over to the British.

STUDENTS AND WORKERS

Soon after the end of the war, the first students began to arrive again in the Federal Republic of Germany (West Germany) and in the German Democratic Republic (East Germany). In the West, the post-war economic miracle had created a need for qualified workers, the universities were open to foreign students, and Indians could enter the country without a visa. Most of them were single men who, after completing their studies, either went back, migrated to other countries or remained in West Germany. Of the latter, many married German women, while some married in India and brought their wives to Germany. The Indian migrants entered the labour market in the highly-skilled sector, were able to get good jobs and were socially and economically well integrated into the middle class, to which they also belonged in India. Even as students they started to form societies where they met others from the subcontinent. They did not form any religious institutions, choosing to perform religious rituals in private, if at all. A Hindu temple in Frankfurt am Main existed for only a short time, and since then no other temple has been established. Developments in East Germany were similar, although on a much smaller scale.

As a result of the West German economic miracle, there was a shortage of staff in the health sector in the 1960s. Catholic institutions started to recruit young Christian women in Kerala to work as nurses in Germany. In contrast to student migrants, the young Malayalis came in groups and were provided with their own religious and social infrastructure. The nurses lived together and spoke Malayalam. There were also Indian priests and social workers. Due to the economic recession in the 1970s, some of the German states stopped extending the work permits of Indian nurses. Many had to return to India, but some stayed on as they were married to Germans. Others migrated to less restrictive states in Germany or to other countries. Thus, the state of Nordrhine-Westphalia, which was more liberal than others in extending work permits, became the centre of Malayali settlement. Most of the nurses who remained in West Germany had an arranged marriage in India in the 1970s and brought their husbands—most of whom were graduates—back with them. Due to the restrictive immigration policy, these men did not get permission to work for the first years of their stay. A few used this forced break to gain further qualifications, but most of them stayed at home. Thus, among the Malayali families there was a change of gender roles, with the wives more comfortable in their surroundings, earning money and speaking the German language, while the husbands stayed at home and felt alienated. They escaped boredom by establishing sports and theatre groups as well as Malayalam schools for their children, thus developing the Malayali infrastructure in Germany further. When they finally got work permits, most of them could only enter the labour market in the less-skilled sector, which was often below their Indian academic qualifications and also below their wife's position. This led to many problems, and in extreme cases, gave rise to alcoholism and violence in families. The specific migration history of the Malayalis did, however, encourage the development of Malayali communities in Germany, which were mostly defined by their various Christian affiliations. This was quite unlike earlier migrants who, in contrast, had only formed networks but not communities.

The increasingly restrictive immigration policy from the 1970s onwards resulted in a considerable decrease in the number of Indians arriving in West Germany. Only spouses and some students were allowed to enter legally, and all others who wanted to migrate had to apply for asylum. In the 1980s, many young Punjabis, most of them Sikhs, did seek asylum in West Germany. Whether they were genuinely fleeing political persecution, looking for a better life, or both, cannot be easily determined. The German state, in any case, did not grant them asylum as it argued that they could find refuge within India. Thus, these Punjabi migrants were only able to stay legally during their asylum process or if they married Germans.

Many of them settled in the area around Frankfurt am Main and established Sikh institutions, including gurdwaras. Few were able to enter the skilled labour force due to their precarious legal position in Germany; many were forced to do unskilled work.

CHANGES IN THE 1990S

The end of the 1990s once again saw a change in the immigration rules of the now unified Germany. Due to the re-emergence of a scarcity of healthcare workers, Malayali nurses, whose work permits had not been extended in the 1970s, were allowed to return to Germany. The major change, however, came in 2000, when the German chancellor announced a 'green card' for IT specialists, which encouraged the migration of many young Indian IT professionals, who brought their families with them. Hence, the number of Indian citizens living in Germany increased from about 35,000 at the end of the 1990s to more than 43,000 in 2003. The new migrants live mainly in urban centres such as Munich and have developed their own networks, suited to their particular needs. As they are allowed to stay only for five years, their residence is not permanent. These IT professionals are regarded as sojourners and see themselves as such too. Their time in Germany is largely focused on their work, the networks which they have formed and, given their temporary position, in seeking career opportunities in other countries.

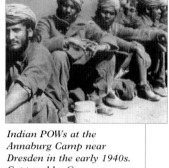

Indian POWs at the Annaburg Camp near Dresden in the early 1940s. Captured by German forces while serving the British Indian army in Europe and North Africa, some would join the 950th regiment of the German army, known as the 'Indian legion'.

The Berlin Mosque, located on Brienner Road in Wilmersdorf, was built by the Lahore Ahmadiyya Movement in 1926.

Devotees of the Hindu god Murugan gather at the Thiru Nallur Sri Arumuka Velalakan temple in the northern German town of Hamm for its annual procession. Many Hindu temples in Europe and the US, like the one pictured here, are built within what were formerly large houses.

Few have learned the German language and their interaction with Germans is limited.

The advent of IT professionals has had repercussions on the image of Indians in Germany. Before the debate about the green card, the image of India in Germany was one of poverty, suppressed women and spiritual superiority. As a result of the debate, a new image has emerged, that of the technologically advanced Indian. While this can be seen as a positive development, it is also a source of irritation for many Germans. Following the emergence of Indian IT professionals in the German workforce, the conservative Opposition launched a political campaign aimed against the liberalisation of immigration, using the slogan '*Kinder statt Inder*' ('Children instead of Indians'), for the first time mentioning Indians in a xenophobic context.

THE SECOND GENERATION

Meanwhile, the second generation of established Indian migrants has now developed into a new group of Indians in Germany. Some of them still retain Indian citizenship, although many do not. Their links to and knowledge of India differ considerably. Some travel there regularly, but others do not. Few speak an Indian language fluently or practise an Indian religion strictly. They live, like their parents, in a predominantly German environment, where they differ in terms of skin colour, name and some family traditions. Yet, they also differ from their parents in that Germany is their first home. Due to this additional sense of 'otherness', both in the family and in the German environment, they have sought to develop their own way of dealing with their status in Germany. In attempting to achieve this, they have established their own 'spaces', organising parties and building Internet portals for information and networking with individuals in a similar situation. Regional and even national distinctions have less importance among the second generation than the first. There have been instances of second-generation Pakistani, Bangladeshi or Afghan migrants considering themselves Indian as they equate Indianness with a common culture

The website www. theinder.net provides information on entertainment and events pertinent to the Indian community in Germany.

*The ultra-nationalist Republican Party in Germany employed the xenophobic slogan '*Kinder statt Inder*' ('Children instead of Indians') as part of its political campaign to restrict immigration.*

from the subcontinent. Regional differences within India, in particular between the north and south, which still are very marked among first-generation networks, are often overcome by the second generation as they network on the basis of their common language, German.

Even more than their parents, the second generation is part of German society: they were brought up and socialised there; German is their first language; and Germany is the place they know best.

Coming from economically well-off middle-class families with a high level of education, second-generation Indians can access the skilled workforce much better than those of many other ethnic minorities. This, however, does not hold true for many children of the later Punjabi migrants as their parents, due to their particular migration history, cannot offer them starting conditions which are as favourable.

Although PIOs have founded many associations in Germany, these are too few, too geographically scattered and too different in their interests to form an umbrella organisation. In fact, several such attempts have failed. Political participation is pursued through German institutions. Apart from two members of parliament at the federal level—Sebastian Edathy and Josef Winkler in 2005—there are some elected politicians at the municipal level as well: one of the few East German Indians, Ravi Gujjula, became the mayor of a small town outside Berlin.

Among the Indians in Germany there are rich businessmen as well as people depending on social welfare. The chances an individual migrant had in life depended largely on his particular migration history, the German immigration rules at the time and the state of the German labour market. Students and nurses have tended to distance themselves from the later Indian migrants, who have had to apply for asylum and have not achieved the same social status as them.

The challenge faced by Indians in Germany is to cope with the consequences of their migration. On the one hand, they have to deal with xenophobic structures in German society and, on the other hand, they have to accept that migration changes their lives and the way their children think and want to lead their own lives.

Urmila Goel

In Merle Kröger's thriller *Cut* the main character, Madita, searches for her Indian father. In her pursuit, she not only travels to Mumbai, but also discovers the dark side of the Indian legion within the SS (Schutzstaffel). A scene at the beginning of the book captures succinctly the daily experiences of second-generation Indians in Germany.

Cut! Merle Kröger's first novel.

...Suddenly you feel the impact of voices and music. A few people leave the cinema and scrutinise you with a fleeting look: a woman in jeans and running shoes with short hair. As always you feel the glare of their eyes, that unspoken, 'Where are you from?' Not necessarily hostile. Just inappropriate. How often have you heard these questions? Whenever you meet someone for the first time the question will come up in the first half hour, you can bet on it. You used to refuse to answer it, embarrassed, as if someone had inquired about the colour of your underwear. Later you learned to turn the embarrassment back on to your interrogator. 'From Hamburg. Why do you ask?' Now it's the other person who has to search for words and attempt to avoid the trap of political incorrectness, which you have set for them. And you have done nothing more than tell the truth.

Merle Kröger, Cut, 2003 (translated from German).

SCANDINAVIA

INDIAN COMMUNITIES IN Denmark, Norway and Sweden are part of the larger South Asian diaspora. The largest groups of South Asians in this region are Pakistanis and Tamils from Sri Lanka. In 2005, approximately 28,500 Indians lived in the Nordic countries. Norway, the country with the largest South Asian population, has about 50,000 persons from the subcontinent, of whom more than half are Pakistanis and a quarter are Tamils from Sri Lanka. Indians are not the largest group of the diaspora in the Nordic countries, but they have contributed considerably to their host societies.

The history of Indian immigration to the Nordic countries can be divided into three periods: early visitors (till 1950), labour migration (1950–80), and family reunions (1980–2000). The first period is characterised by individual movements; the second by educated Indians coming to the Nordic countries for further education, postdoctoral employment and professional work; and the third, by the arrival of wives, children and relatives, alongside the professionals.

EARLY VISITORS

The first Indians to arrive in the Nordic countries were Tamils from Tranquebar (Tarangampadi), a Danish colony from 1620 to 1845. These Tamils went to Denmark

Map 8.55

Map 8.55

SCANDINAVIA

for various reasons. Some were slaves and servants who were brought to the country by Danes returning from India; others went because the court in which lawsuits were heard for Tranquebar's Indians was in Copenhagen; and yet others went there to study or were seamen (European sailors who perished on the trip to India were replaced by Tamils during the return trip to Europe).

In 1706, the first Protestant mission in India began in Tranquebar. Its first missionary, the German Bartolomaes Ziegenbalg, who arrived that same year, took a great interest in the Tamil language and culture. Although the missionaries were German, the mission was a Danish one. Several Tamils were sent to Denmark and Germany by the mission for education. Timotheus (b. 1696), a young Tamil, arrived in Copenhagen in 1713, where he was trained as a bookbinder between 1714 and 1716. While there, he became acquainted with a Tamil girl by the name of Sahra, who was already living there. A Dane returning from Tranquebar had taken her to Copenhagen. After marrying Sahra in Denmark, Timotheus returned to Tranquebar in 1720.

Another Tamil, Peter Maleiappan, arrived in Denmark in 1715 and was then sent to Germany where he worked on the printed edition of Ziegenbalg's translation of a Tamil grammar. Maleiappan returned to Tranquebar in 1716. At Ziegenbalg's suggestion, Tamil studies were introduced at the Martin-Luther-University in Halle: a Tamil was among the first teachers of the language at the university. It took another century before Sanskrit was offered at a European university. However, these events did not create a lasting community of Tamils in Denmark.

The first Indian to settle permanently in Norway was Surendranath Boral, also known as Swami Sri Ananda Acharya from Hooghly, Bengal, who arrived in Europe in 1911. His aim was to spread the message of Hinduism, and more specifically the Advaita Vedanta system of religious thought. Over the next few years following his arrival, Ananda Acharya gave lectures in London, Norway

Ananda Acharya and the famous Norwegian author Arne Garborg working on the first translation into Norwegian of the Ramayana. Garborg spent the summers of 1921 and 1922 on Ananda Acharya's Gaurisankar Saeter at Tronsvangen.

Map 8.56

SOUTH INDIA: THE LOCATION OF TRANQUEBAR (C. 1800)

Based on information in Patrick K. O'Brien (ed.), The Atlas of World History, 1999.

Tranquebar was a small possession in South India which Denmark controlled from 1620–1845.

Figure 8.10

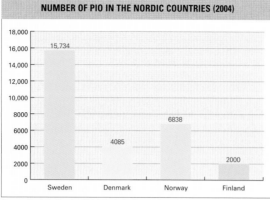

NUMBER OF PIO IN THE NORDIC COUNTRIES (2004)

	Sweden	Denmark	Norway	Finland
	15,734	4085	6838	2000

Source: Statistics Sweden 2004; Statistics Denmark 2004, Statistics Norway 2004; and Statistics Finland 2004.

Chatto was so impressed with the free political atmosphere in Sweden that he thought it would be beneficial to have a Stockholm branch of the Berlin India Committee.

Garborg and Ananda Acharya's translation of the Ramayana, Rama-Kvaedet, was published in 1922.

(at the University of Oslo in 1915) and Stockholm (1916). His lectures influenced many intellectuals, such as Swedish author Dan Andersson. Ananda Acharya grew fond of the Norwegian mountains and in 1917 acquired a house on the slopes of Mount Tron, near Alvdal in eastern Norway, which he called Gaurisankar. In 1924 he wrote, 'A person who has not lived alone in the mountains, has not yet discovered his soul.' He wrote more than 35 books between 1913 and 1928, many of which were published in both Norwegian and English. Ananda Acharya also worked with Norwegian author Arne Garborg on a translation of parts of the Ramayana from Sanskrit to Norwegian. He lived in Alvdal until his death in 1945, following which a memorial was erected on Tronfjell, where he was buried. A group of Norwegian supporters have worked to establish a University of Peace there. The small ashram in Alvdal maintained its religious connection to Bengal, and specialists from there have often visited the site.

VALMIKI: RAMAYĀNĀ

RAMA-KVÆDET

UMSETT FRÅ UPPHAVLEGT SANSKRIT OG MED EI UTGREIDING AV SWĀMI SRĪ ANANDA ĀCHĀRYA

PÅ NORSKT VED ARNE GARBORG

KRISTIANIA
FORLAGT AV H. ASCHEHOUG & CO. (W. NYGAARD)
1924

One of the early immigrants to Sweden was the Indian revolutionary Virendranath Chattopadhyaya (1880–1937), or Chatto, who worked in Europe for India's struggle against British rule. From 1917 to 1920 he was active in Stockholm, where he established a branch of the Indian Nationalist Revolutionary Committee. However, the Swedish government did not approve of his political activities and though he had been allowed to stay in Sweden as a refugee, he was denied re-entry after a visit to Germany in 1920.

Another of the earliest visitors to Sweden, Dinshah Malegamvala, arrived from Bombay in 1939 to work as an engineer at ASEA (Allmänna Svenska Elektriska Aktiebolaget) in Västerås. He was interested in Swedish culture and mastered the language, publishing a book of poetry—*Livet: Lyriska övningar*—in Swedish in 1946. He returned to India soon thereafter.

LABOUR MIGRATION AND FAMILY REUNIONS

Indian labour migration to the region began in the late 1950s and 1960s, but most migrants arrived after 1970. Only one Indian citizen lived in Sweden in 1930, nine in 1950 and 92 in 1960. However, by 1970 the number had increased to 492, and in 1980, to 1624. In addition, by 1979, 2452 Indians living in Sweden had been naturalised. This number increased to 9592 in 2002, and by 2004, 11,900 had acquired citizenship. Denmark and Norway tell a similar story. Most of the migrants came from Northwest India: Delhi, Punjab and Haryana.

While the first Indians in the Nordic countries were brought there by religion or politics, those arriving in the second half of the 20th century wanted to take advantage of new opportunities for economic prosperity through education and professional work. A number of Indians also arrived as a result of discrimination and persecution. These included Indian 'twice-displaced' migrants from Uganda/East Africa between 1971 and 1972 (over 1000 Indian refugees arrived in Sweden and about 160 in Norway), and Sikhs from Punjab after 1984.

Of the more than 28,500 persons of Indian origin (PIOs)—those born in India or born in the Nordic countries to parents of Indian origin—living in the Nordic countries in 2005, the largest number can be found in Sweden (15,734 at the end of 2004) and Norway (6838 at the end of 2004). In addition, several thousand children from India have been adopted by Nordic parents: in Sweden the number exceeds 6000. These children do not figure in the statistics as Indians since their adopted parents are considered their real parents.

About 70–80 per cent of the Indian population have become Swedish, Norwegian or Danish citizens. This indicates that a large portion of the Indian population have been living in the region for several decades or were born there. The balanced gender ratio among Nordic Indians supports this as well. In Finland, where Indian immigration began only recently, there are 2000 persons from India, of whom around 60 per cent are men, most (89 per cent) are of working age (15–64 years), and there are fewer children and elderly among them.

In economic terms, the Indian community can be classified as part of the middle class or upper middle class. Many of them are professionals working with

Swami Sri Ananda Acharya

Many Indians who have settled in Norway have been surprised to learn about Swami Sri Ananda Acharya (1881–1945). That a Hindu guru, early in the 20th century, chose to settle in this cold country in the far north, and chose a mountain here as his Himalaya, has added some significance to their own choice of living in Norway.

Ananda Acharya lived in Norway from 1917 to 1945. He was a religious teacher and author, and wrote more than 35 books which were published in English, Norwegian or Swedish. He had a Master's degree in philosophy from Calcutta University, and in 1910 became a professor at Mahraj's College at Burdwan. In 1911 he went to Europe and in 1914 arrived in Norway, where he gave a series of lectures. In 1917, a Norwegian devotee bought a house for him on the slopes of Mount Tron in eastern Norway, where he lived for the rest of his life. He was popular among the locals, had some influence on Swedish and Norwegian intellectuals, and attracted a few devotees. These devotees published collections of his writings and talks, and kept his memory alive with new editions of his older books. A small ashram at Mount Tron is devoted to his teachings.

Ananda Acharya preached the message of Advaita Vedanta. His literary works were in the field of religious thinking and poetry. His poetry reveals a fondness for nature and his teachings focused on the idea of unity, harmony and peace. He had a vision of a 'University of Peace', and his Norwegian devotees have kept this vision alive. Architectural drawings of the university have been prepared for a building on Mount Tron, next to Ananda Acharya's memorial.

Ananda Acharya's grave on Mount Tron.

various well-known Nordic multinational corporations, such as Hydro, Statoil, Ericsson, Electrolux, SKF and Volvo, among others. Several are professors and occupy high academic positions in leading universities and research institutes. Some work in the government, while others are artists and authors, and a number are leading industrialists and businessmen. A growing number of Indians are in the IT sector or involved in business between India and the Nordic countries.

ORGANISATIONS

Indians in the Nordic countries have established and participated in many organisations over the last few decades, of which three types predominate: Indian cultural organisations, religious organisations and friendship associations.

The organisations founded in the early 1970s were meant to provide an avenue for bringing Indians together. The Indian Association in Sweden was established around 1970. Similar organisations were established in Norway and Denmark, along with several others. Common events include the annual Sikh Sports Mela for youth and children, held in Norway since 1990, an important occasion which brings the Sikh community together and helps to maintain their identity.

Many of the organisations founded in the 1980s and 1990s were religious in orientation. Their main task was to arrange the weekly puja and annual festivals, and their main concern was inculcating the value of Indian identity and religious traditions in the next generation. An important function of religion in the Nordic Indian diaspora is to sacralise and thus assist in conserving aspects of Indian culture.

Indian Christians and Muslims are few in number and have not established separate religious organisations. Indian Christians have mostly joined churches already established in the Nordic countries. Due to the large presence of Tamils from Sri Lanka, a significant number of whom are Christians, Catholic churches offer a monthly mass in Tamil. A considerable number of Indian immigrants are Sikh, and in Norway they constitute as much as 50 per cent of the total Indian population. Though the number is small, many of the refugees from Uganda are Muslim.

Although religious organisations were established in the 1980s, it was only in the 1990s that buildings were bought and transformed into temples and gurdwaras. Most of the men arriving in the 1960s and 1970s had originally planned to work for a few years and then return to India. Restrictions on labour migration in the early 1970s, however, convinced many to stay permanently, which led to the migration of families. The establishment of religious organisations, temples and gurdwaras was a result of the arrival of wives and children, and signified the permanent presence of Indian communities in Nordic societies.

None of the Indian communities has built a temple or gurdwara in accordance with the architectural styles of South Asia. However, plans for such buildings exist and, in 2004, the application to build a gurdwara outside of Oslo was approved. Buying and transforming houses built for secular purposes into temples initially brought diverse religious communities together because it involved

the pooling of economic and other resources. However, disagreements over leadership and finance led to divisions between the communities and the establishment of separate temples. The first Indian Hindu temples built in Sweden, Denmark and Norway were the Hindu Mandir in Stockholm (1998), Bharatiya Mandir in Copenhagen (1996) and Sanatan Mandir in Oslo (1997). The Sikhs have set up a number of gurdwaras, including Gurdwara Sri Guru Singh Sabha and Gurdwara Sangat Sahib in Sweden; Gurdwara Sri Guru Singh Sabha in Denmark; and Gurduara Sri Guru Nanak Dev Ji and Gurduara Sri Guru Nanak Niwas in Norway. The Indian Muslims have not established separate mosques. The majority of Hindus in Scandinavia are not Indians but Tamils from Sri Lanka, who constitute a separate community and have set up separate temples.

Many Indians also participate in organisations founded by Nordic people with an interest in India. Before the advent of Indian immigration, interest among Scandinavians had led to the establishment of organisations aimed at bringing together people with an interest in India and informing the public about Indian culture. Such friendship associations were founded in all the Nordic countries. Norsk-Indisk Forening was founded in 1959 by researchers with an interest in India. The Indian Cultural Club in Sweden, the Finland-India-föreningen, and several others served the same purpose. With the arrival of migrants from India, membership gradually changed to include more Indians, and Indians also became the leaders of many of these groups. Celebrations of events such as India's Independence Day and Republic Day, and Hindu festivals such as Holi and Diwali, are regularly organised by such groups. The Indian communities of the Scandinavian countries have separate identities—Swedish-Indian, Norwegian-Indian, and so on—and so, there are no Scandinavian-Indian organisations.

Knut A. Jacobsen

The Sikhs have established a number of gurdwaras in the Nordic countries. One of the first to be established was the Gurduara Sri Guru Nanak Dev Ji in Oslo. Around 50 per cent of the Indian population in Norway are Sikhs.

A memorial stone erected in honour of Ananda Acharya on Tronfjell.

RUSSIA AND UKRAINE

A Russian poster for an Indian magic show.

RUSSIA AND UKRAINE remain the two most important successor states of the former Soviet Union. The Soviet Union itself had as its predecessors the Russian Empire, the Moscow Rus and the Kiev Rus. While Indians constitute a miniscule proportion of the population of modern-day Russia and Ukraine, they can claim at least four centuries of presence in these countries.

According to the 2002 census, approximately 2000 Indians live in Russia. The report of the High Level Committee on Indian Diaspora notes that there are 16,000 non-resident Indians in the country. At least 10,000 Indians study in Moscow, St. Petersburg, Nizhniy Novgorod, Kazan, Kursk and other Russian cities. A further 10,000 illegal migrants from South Asia also live in Moscow. Factoring in all these elements as well as persons of Indian origin (PIOs) not directly from India, an estimated 40,000 Indians currently live in the Russian Federation, of whom about half stay on a temporary basis. Ukraine has at least 10,000 Indian students and a small number of Indian professionals.

Since the 1950s, Russian society has been enchanted by Indian cinema and music, and Indo-Russian relations have remained warm since Indian independence. It is, therefore, possible that Russians are more likely to accept Indians as part of an emergent multicultural mosaic in post-Soviet Russia. The economic potential of these countries for Indian businessmen is considerable. The political turmoil and administrative chaos, coupled with the complicated business atmosphere, has given South Asians a competitive edge over Western investors in the Russian and Ukrainian markets. The increase in contemporary Indian migration to Russia and Ukraine can also be attributed to the fact that these countries are key transit regions en route to Western Europe. The porous borders of the Russian Federation with Asian countries of the former Soviet Union and new members of the European Union make the Russian Federation and neighbouring

Ukraine ideal stepping stones for Indian migrants seeking to migrate to Western Europe.

EARLY RELATIONS

It is probable that Indian traders used to visit Kiev even before the Mongol invasion of Rus. By the 10th century AD, the main area of Indian trading activity was the region of Bulgar, the capital of the Volga Bulgar kingdom. Both Indian traders and Brahmin advisers were reported to be present there. In the 12th century, the Mongol invasion interrupted Indo-Russian trade contacts, and the Golden Horde, one of the successor states of the Mongol Empire in the Russian steppes and the Volga region, blocked the direct movement of Indian merchants to Rus. Indians went to Sarai, the Tatar capital on the Volga river, but did not go further westwards; as did Russian merchants who were prevented from moving east beyond the Horde capital.

The collapse of the Golden Horde resulted in the emergence of the Tatar Khanate in Astrakhan, not far from the ruins of Sarai, where both Indians and Russians had their trading sites. From there, Indian traders visited Moscow occasionally. The 1532 Nickon *letopis* (chronicle) mentions the Indian ambassador of Sultan Babur (1525–30) of Agra and Kabul. By the time of the ambassador's arrival in Moscow, Babur was dead, and we may assume that the ambassador was either a merchant with some ambassadorial task or an adventurer who used Babur's name as a pass to Moscow. The acquisition of the Astrakhan Khanate by the Moscow tsar Ivan the Terrible in 1556 resulted in the incorporation of the existing trading colony of Indians in the city into the Russian state. By then, Indian enterprise extended as far as Isfahan in Persia and Kizlyar in the North Caucasus.

The first Indians from Multan arrived in Russian Astrakhan between 1615–16. In 1624, a special trading court (Gostiniy Dvor) for Indian merchants, along with separate courts for Armenian and Persian merchants, had been erected in Astrakhan. More than 100 Indian merchants and their servants lived there, trading in jewellery and medicines. From 1632, Russians kept a special file on India and Indians, thus acknowledging their importance. In 1645, an Indian merchant ventured as far as Kazan and Moscow and sold his goods there with great success. Following his accomplishment, an additional 25 Indian traders came to Astrakhan from Persia. In 1650, Indian merchants sold their goods in Yaroslavl on the Volga, not far from Moscow. They often travelled from Astrakhan to Moscow, Kazan, Nizhniy Novgorod and the site of the famous Makarievskaya Fair nearby. By that time, Indians mostly sold textiles and precious stones, and bought furs. They also established themselves as important moneylenders in Astrakhan. The Indian colony there included not only merchants, but several sadhus, a Brahmin priest, a Brahmin cook, beggars and servants. Russian tsar

Map 8.57

RUSSIA AND UKRAINE

Alexei Mikhaylovich invited Indian artisans to Moscow to establish a textile industry there.

English adventurer George Forster mentions Indians who travelled from India to Astrakhan specially to teach their religion—probably Hinduism, Jainism or Sikhism. These 'teachers' were the gurus of Indians traders and possibly also Brahmin priests of the Astrakhan Hindu temple. References to these Indians as 'cow worshippers' by Russian merchants and officers, and by an Armenian merchant, suggest that among the Indians were Hindus. Mentioned among the Hindu *murtis* (idols) in the Indian colony in Astrakhan were Rama, Sita and 'Thakur', the latter probably referring to Vishnu, or the Bengal saint-god known as Chaytanya or Nityanand. Reports on Indian Muslims and Sikhs are also present in the Russian archives, which contain information indicating that Indians had living quarters and a temple along with a trading centre in Astrakhan.

The international trade of the local Indian colony was interrupted with the worsening of political relations between Mughal India and the Persian Empire. While Indian traders survived the political turmoil during the establishment of a new political power in southern Russia and maintained control of the East–West trade, their links with India itself became irregular. This made them concentrate more on trade with Persia via Kizlyar and Derbent, and saw moneylending gain popularity as an occupation. They also tried to enter the horse trade from the Volga region to Moscow. The lack of constant contact with India also resulted in marriages between Astrakhan Indians and Tatar women.

Although Moscow allowed Indian traders to practise their religion and maintain a Hindu temple in the city, the number of Hindus diminished as some converted to Russian Orthodox Christianity and Islam. Following a ceremony where water from the Ganges was poured into the Volga, the Hindus who remained considered this Russian waterway their Ganges. They were free to pray to Hindu gods and cremate their dead despite hostility from Muslims and Christians, who considered them pagans. Despite several petitions to Moscow to remove the *murtis* from the Indian trading centre, the local administrative

head (*voevoda*) was given instructions from Moscow to allow Hindus to continue practising their rituals.

In the 1670s, Indian, Armenian and Persian merchants lobbied to further their trade to Europe via Moscow. This was prevented by Russian merchants, who opposed any Indian economic activity outside Astrakhan. In 1665, Russian merchants demanded that all Indians not involved in trade be expelled from Moscow and, in 1684, Moscow merchants demanded that the state not allow Indians to leave Astrakhan for other Russian cities. During this period, Indians became the main merchants and moneylenders in Astrakhan, and they owned the largest stone trading line in the city.

In spite of opposition from Russian merchants, in the early 18th century Indian merchants were settled not only in Astrakhan but also in Moscow. In 1723, a group of Hindu traders left Moscow in protest against the local administration's objection to the sati (burning of the widow) of a rich Hindu merchant. While records indicate the presence of Hindu traders in Moscow in 18th century, it is also evident that the locals were less aware of Hindu traditions. Furthermore, rituals such as sati often alienated Hindus from the locals.

With the expansion of Indian trade to central Russia and to the capital city of St. Petersburg, many Hindu traders converted to Orthodox Christianity and were given Russian Christian names and surnames. From the 1740s, there are several records of 'Russian Indians' with surnames such as Ivanov and Feodorov. The 18th century also witnessed the incorporation of Kizlyar and Derbent in the North Caucasus, where Indian trading colonies already existed, into Russia. The Kizlyar colony of Indians grew under Russian rule but its fate depended on the major centre for trade, Astrakhan.

Following the halt of direct trade with India and the conversion of Astrakhan Indians to Christianity and

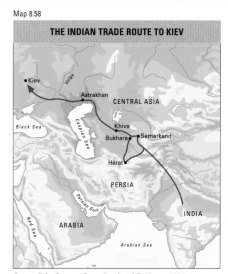

Map 8.58

THE INDIAN TRADE ROUTE TO KIEV

Source: *John Lawton*, Samarkand and Bukhara, *1991.*

Eighteenth-century Indian trading centres in Central Asia were part of the network which linked India with Russia.

Kirov Square in Astrakhan. In the 17th century, a significant Indian colony existed in Astrakhan and included merchants, religious personnel and servants. In Astrakhan, these merchants were able to engage in moneylending in addition to the trade in goods such as textiles and precious stones.

Islam, the Indian community in Astrakhan lost its prominence. By 1799, the famous Indian trading lines were dilapidated and the governor of Astrakhan ordered their demolition. By the early 19th century, Russians attempted to establish their own companies for trade with India. Russian Indians were invited as advisers to Orenburg in the Urals region, where such companies were set up. However, by the early 19th century, Indians as a separate ethnic community or trading colony had all but disappeared from Russia. They had been assimilated into the Russian and Tatar population.

During the latter half of the 19th century, Moscow and St. Petersburg saw the arrival of several Indian adventurers, including the Sikh maharaja Duleep Singh (1838–93), who arrived in Moscow in 1887 disguised as an Irishman. While there, he met the popular Russian publisher and politician Mikhail Katkov.

Indians from Central Asia, where their numbers by the early 20th century were estimated at 6000–8000, visited Moscow and participated at the famous Makarievskaya Fair in Nizhniy Novgorod. Yet, it is impossible to speak of the continuity of the Indian presence. Astrakhan Indians had dispersed to Kazan, Moscow and St. Petersburg. Their descendants assimilated with the population, though it is possible that some families of Russian Indians still have memories of their South Asian ancestors.

THE SOVIET ERA

The Soviet era witnessed the emergence of an Indian communist community in Moscow and Leningrad during the 1920s and 1930s. Abani Mukherji (1891–1937), a prominent communist in Moscow at the time, studied in Japan and Germany, escaped from the British police in Singapore, went to the Netherlands via Indonesia, and from there to Berlin, before ending up in Soviet Russia. Another prominent communist, M. N. Roy (1887–1954), joined the ranks of Indian revolutionaries at the beginning of the 20th century as a member of an underground terrorist group in Bengal. He went to Indonesia to secure arms and from there travelled to the US. He eventually fled the country for Mexico, where he helped to establish a communist party. Roy arrived in Moscow as Mexico's representative at the Second World Congress of the Communist International in the summer of 1920. From Moscow he went to Tashkent, where he was joined by

Mukherji. Both were eager to accept Russian support in organising a revolution in India.

Other revolutionaries arrived in Russia mainly via Afghanistan and Turkestan. Most were Muslim nationalists who were trying to escape British rule. They also wanted to defend the Khalif, the Ottoman sultan, regarded as the leader of the Muslims, but were stopped at the Afghan border with Russia. Many of them attended military courses in Tashkent. However, due to their dissatisfaction with the Anglo-Russian trade negotiations that began in 1920, many expressed their desire to leave Tashkent for Turkey. The British, in turn, demanded that Russia stop any anti-British activity in Central Asia. Under pressure, the Politbureau of the Comintern decided to stop its work with the Indian political immigrants in Turkestan and sent them to Moscow. In May 1921, Indian military courses in Tashkent were stopped and the cadets were sent to Moscow to study at the Communist University of Toilers of the East. That same year, the students of the university, including former *muhajirs* Shaukat Usmani, Gohar Rehman Khan, Rafiq Ahmad, Mohammed Akbar Shah, Sultan Zahid, Fazl-I-Illahi Kurman, Abdulla Safdur, Mukherji and Roy, established the Communist Party of India in Moscow.

The early 1930s witnessed the disenchantment of the Soviet leadership with the Comintern. Famous Indian revolutionaries such as V. Chattopadhyaya and Mukherji continued their careers as academic functionaries in Moscow and Leningrad and ended up in prisons, as did many other academics and politicians in the 1930s. Some of the remaining Indians found jobs as teachers of Indian vernaculars and experts on Indian affairs. Their numbers, though, were negligible. From the mid-1950s, significant numbers of Indian students joined major educational institutions of Moscow, Leningrad, Sverdlovsk and Kursk. Yet, few remained in Russia after completing their education. They did not form a diaspora and the temporary presence of Indians in major Russian cities was not threatened despite strict immigration and residence rules.

INDIANS IN POST-SOVIET RUSSIA AND UKRAINE

The situation changed with the collapse of the Soviet Union. Although economic hardship temporarily made post-Soviet Russia unattractive for foreign students depending on stipends, the better-off students and

An advertisement for the Indian beer, Cobra. The beer was officially launched in Russia in November 2004.

The Kazan Fortress on the Volga river. In the mid-17th century, Indian traders travelled up to Kazan and Moscow to trade their wares.

The elaborate altar and kalasas *at the Moscow Krishna Temple and Cultural Centre.*

'adventurers' found Russian conditions suitable. As Russian immigration and residence rules had been neglected for a decade by the authorities, the 'adventurers' included those attempting to use Russia as a transit point to other parts of Europe. As a result, a new wave of Indians arrived in Russia, consisting mainly of students, although only about half (mostly medical students) made study abroad their main aim. The rest of them found it a good opportunity to combine study abroad with a small business, often in retailing, which they continued after graduating or dropping out. As a result, the number of Indian businessmen in the Russian Federation almost matches that of Indian students. Some of them are successful and rich, others are just petty traders.

Wealthy Indian businessmen are involved in the tea and garments trade and the construction industry, and recently some have invested in breweries in St. Petersburg and Moscow. A brand of Indian beer—Cobra, or Nag, of Sun Breweries—has secured a prominent position in the Russian beer market. Another field of success is the diamond industry.

Moscow is currently experiencing a growth in Indian firms, with a wide clientele in India and Western Europe. Recently, Indian businessmen in the Russian Federation have also been involved in large projects, such as investing in Russian oil fields, particularly at Sakhalin Island in the Russian Far East, and in steel production, where, as a competitor or partner is the steel empire of Lakshmi Mittal. Cheaper jewellery, garments, tea and spices are also sold by Indians in Russia. The infamous Sevastopol Hotel in Moscow seems to have become an 'Indian row', with dozens of small Indian businesses setting up shop there with apartments for their owners and servicemen.

Although Indians cannot be dubbed an invisible minority in the Russian Federation, their small number has ensured that they remain in the shadow of such minorities as the Azeris (Transcaucasian Shia Muslims) and the Chechens. However, Indians continue to be mentioned in the media in relation to a number of key issues. One such issue concerns transit migration. At the Russian–Ukrainian border alone, nearly 1000 Indians are stopped annually. Their aim is to enter Ukraine from Russia and then travel further to Western Europe. Other key Russian borders used for transit into Western Europe are Belarus, Estonia and Latvia. It is estimated that at least half of the migrants manage to cross these borders safely. The total number of such transit migrants, as estimated by the Ukrainian border service, is nearly 10,000 annually. According to the Russian Federal Bureau of

Investigation (FSB), about 40 Indians enter Russia every week in the hope of sneaking to the West.

After a decade of negligence, Russia is taking steps to curb the multi-million-dollar business of human trafficking from India. The FSB has begun screening potential illegal migrants from India. A few years ago, the entire staff of the Russian consular section in Delhi was replaced to stem the smuggling tide. Although these measures have helped to reduce the flow of illegal immigrants, they have not stopped it entirely. The human-trafficking mafia has its men in embassies, at customs and in the police force. Even ministerial staff, educational institutions and travel companies are involved in this business.

The situation for legal migrants from India to Russia, particularly students, has deteriorated as Russian educational institutions often do not have direct representatives in India. On 11 June 2004, the *St. Petersburg Times* reported the sudden disappearance of the Dubai-based Sailan International Firm, which used to be a partner of the St. Petersburg Mechnikov Medical Academy. As the academy did not have a representative abroad, students paid their fees to the school via Sailan International. The disappearance of the firm, along with the fees of some 300 Indian students, has made the future of these students uncertain.

Another concern for Indian nationals in Russia is the rising level of crime. Illegal immigrants of Indian origin often fall victim to abuse and violence. Some are forced into drug trafficking and selling their organs for transplant by members of international gangs, among whom are Indians, Pakistanis, Bangladeshis, Chechens and Russians. In May 2004, a Moscow court sentenced Pakistani traffickers to long-term imprisonment for kidnapping nine Indians.

The rise of racism in Russia is another issue of importance to Indian migrants. Although Azeris and Chechens have been the main victims of racists, attacks on Indians, one of whom was killed in St. Petersburg, show the threat to South Asian students as well. Since racists do not make distinctions based on nationality, Indians and PIOs alike have been subjected to such violence. A recent case, which received national attention, was the murder of Atish Kumar Ramgoolam, a 23-year-old medical student from Mauritius. When the *St. Petersburg Times* reported the incident on 4 February 2003, readers' comments suggested that Indians are often seen as easy victims, unlike Azeris or Arabs. A medical student from the same institution, who signed his letter to the newspaper as 'Jatt Punjabi', suggested that foreigners are often victims of racist offences. Rajesh Jeewon, the brother-in-law of a victim of racism in Russia, and a resident of Portsmouth

President Vladimir Putin and his Indian counterpart Abdul Kalam enter the Catherine the Great Hall during a meeting at the Kremlin, 24 May 2005.

The proposed Krishna temple and Vedic centre in Moscow. In 2005, the archbishop of the Russian Orthodox Church asked the mayor of Moscow, Yuri Luzhkov, to ban the construction of the proposed temple.

The front page of the St. Petersburg Times *reports the murder of Atish Kumar Ramgoolam, a 23-year-old Indo-Mauritian student at the St. Petersburg Mechnikov Medical Academy in 2003.*

A procession by the International Society for Krishna Consciousness (Hare Krishna) in Russia, 1998.

in the UK, recommended the introduction of police patrols in areas of Asian concentration in the city.

The development of Indian cultural institutions in Russia has also been highlighted in the local media. On 17 October 2003, Sanjit Kumar Jha, leader of the Association of Indians in Russia, announced the construction of a Centre of Vedic Culture alongside a Hindu temple in Hodinskoye Pole, Moscow. The plan for the Hindu temple led to a heated debate. The centre was intended to imitate the success of the Swaminaryan Temple in Neasden, London. The task of building the centre was left to local Indian businessmen and Hare Krishna activists. Alfred Ford, of the Ford automobile company, also promised to support the project. However, although support from Ford was welcomed by Indians, it was viewed by Russian Orthodox clerics as another attack on Russia from the West. Pressure was exerted on Moscow city head Yuri Luzhkov not to allow the planned construction.

Part of the reason for the hostility stems from the prominent position of the Hare Krishna movement in Russia. Russian churches seem to be particularly opposed to this movement, which is considered unrepresentative of 'orthodox' Hinduism, but rather is seen as a Western evangelistic variation of Hinduism.

The Indian business elite in Russia are no longer interested in remaining an invisible minority. The Asian Business Club and the Association of Indians in the Russian Federation have lobbied for the allocation of land for a future temple. Concerned by the threatened demolition of the Hare Krishna temple, the delay in constructing a new one, and public dissatisfaction with the project, Jha said, '…this is our sacred thing. The demolition of the temple will be a hard blow towards the Indian community of Moscow and a direct insult to the feelings of Hindus all over the world, the insult that can have far-reaching consequences.'

Jha was among the organisers of several high-profile visits of Indians to Moscow, including that of Murli Manohar Joshi (the former Speaker of the Indian parliament), who offered a prayer in the old Krishna temple on Begovaya Street in Moscow. Atal Bihari Vajpayee, who was then the prime minister of India, promised to inaugurate the new temple and Vedic centre. The failure to construct the temple coincided with the defeat of the Vajpayee government. Another important supporter of the project, the Congress chief minister of Delhi, Sheila Dikshit, remains in power in the Indian capital. The incumbent Indian gov-

ernment is interested in promoting Indian culture in Russia while not emphasising the Hindu religion. Jha also lobbied for the foundation of Indian cultural centres in Saratov, Volga, Nizhniy Novgorod and Yaroslavl. The Indo-Russia business network, close to the Association of Indians in the Russian Federation, supports the collection of money for the Shiva temple initiated by the Indian cultural group Rishikesh, as well as the establishment of a Sikh temple, Gurdwara Guru Nanak Darbar, initiated by the Sikh Cultural Centre in Moscow.

The establishment of a Sikh temple and a cultural centre in Moscow have been approved by mainstream churches. Although often dubbed as a branch of 'traditional Hinduism', Sikhism was considered a traditional religion and the construction of the shrine was supported by clerics of the Russian Orthodox Church as well as Muslims, Buddhists and Jews. Approval of the Sikh shrine seems to support the view that resistance to the construction of the Hindu temple in Moscow arose not due to a generic opposition to Indian religions, but because of the heterodox nature of the Hare Krishna group.

Igor Y. Kotin

EASTERN EUROPE

SINCE THE 1990s, the countries of Eastern Europe have become an increasingly important destination for Indian migrants. The break up of the Soviet Union in 1991 and the collapse of the Warsaw Pact opened the borders of Poland, the Czech Republic, Hungary and Romania, which, like the newly independent Baltic states, have expressed their desire to join the European Union (EU) rather than the Commonwealth of Independent States, the amorphous successor to the Soviet Union.

For more than a decade, immigrants from Asia have used these countries as a stepping stone to the West. Following the bloody war in Yugoslavia and the tragedy on Christmas Day in 1997, when a decrepit Greek craft sank in the Ionian Sea off Malta, killing 280 illegal immigrants from South Asia, Indians seeking to migrate to Western Europe now prefer to make their way to Eastern Europe by air and to the West by road. While this route is more expensive, it is safer than travelling by sea or via Yugoslavia. The tragedy in the Ionian Sea provides revealing statistics on the composition of Indian illegal immigrants. Of the 280 victims of the catastrophe, 166 were from Punjab. Punjabi travel agencies and criminal rings are the leaders in human trafficking from India to Eastern Europe and further to the West.

The inclusion of the Baltic states and other Eastern European countries into the EU has made the western borders porous. Thus, many Indians who managed to enter Eastern Europe were likely to reach their final destination (i.e. the welfare states of Western Europe, particularly the UK, France and Germany). Attempts by Western European countries to dismantle their welfare system diverted the flow of immigrants to Northern Europe.

Not all immigrants, however, have the West in sight. Due to their own expanding economies, Hungary, the Czech Republic and Poland are no longer just mere transit points, but have attracted their fair share of Indian immigrants. The main stepping stone to the European Union is now Belarus: Indians depart for Moscow, travel by bus to the Smolensk region, and from there cross the Russian border with Belarus and Ukraine. From there, Indian migrants move on to Poland and the Czech Republic.

Illegal Indian immigrants are mostly fortune-seekers, but fortune is also sought in Eastern Europe by Indians who can get to the region legally and set up businesses. Both big business and professionals from India look with interest to the rise of this region. The India-based Tata family has investments in the Eastern European automobile industry: the recent purchase of a car factory in Poland resulted in the production of Polish-made 'Indica' cars. In 2005, the UK-based Mittal family, owners of Mittal Steel (LNM Holdings), acquired the Polish steel giant Huta Czestochowa, Romania's Galaz, and others in Kazakhstan. Indian firms also look to Eastern European markets, especially the Czech Republic, for the production of munitions. A number of these firms have invested in local economies and their representatives have settled in Warsaw, Krakow, Prague and Budapest. Poland has seen the largest number of both legal businessmen from India and illegal Indian immigrants. The kidnapping of Indian businessmen in Poland and the media coverage of the incident revealed mixed feelings towards Indian newcomers. Despite claims of adherence to European human rights laws, Poland adopted a tough stance on illegal Indian immigration and the entry of Indian businesses in Polish territory.

Seemingly, the country most welcoming of Indian businessmen is Lithuania. The Lithuanians have one of the oldest cultures in Europe and their language has many similarities with Sanskrit. Despite their strong Roman Catholic affiliations, Lithuanians still honour their pagan gods who, in some ways, are similar to those of the Vedic pantheon. Consequently, Indo-Lithuanian cultural links are a subject of national pride. As the result, during the Soviet period, Indians were warmly accepted as students in universities in Lithuania. These days, Indian IT specialists and businessmen are welcome guests and investors in Vilnius and Kaunas.

Eastern Europe remains a transit area for Indian migration. The Czech Republic, Poland, Hungary and Lithuania attract economic migrants as well as asylum seekers from India. Although the majority of these Indian migrants hold Indian passports, their outlook remains uncertain.

Igor Y. Kotin

A crowd assembles to watch a Hare Krishna-led gathering in Moldova. A small community of Hare Krishna members can be found in the capital Chisinau.

Map 8.59

EASTERN EUROPE

FIJI

Indians on board an indentured immigrant ship. Sailing ships could take up to three months to reach Fiji from India. With the introduction of steamships, the journey was reduced to one month.

Sir Arthur Gordon, the first governor of Fiji (1875–80), was responsible for introducing Indian indentured labour to Fiji.

THE FIJI ISLANDS lie in the southwest Pacific Ocean, south of the Equator, some 1770 km north of Auckland, New Zealand, and 2730 km northeast of Sydney, Australia. About 300 islands, covering 18,333 sq km make up the group, but the bulk of the islands' population live on four main islands: Viti Levu, Vanua Levu, Taveuni and Kadavu. Viti Levu accounts for about 70 per cent of the total and about 80 per cent of the Indo-Fijian population. In 2004, the total population of Fiji was 840,201, comprising 456,207 Fijians, 320,659 Indo-Fijians and 63,335 people of other races.

ORIGINS

Indians were brought to Fiji as a direct consequence of the cession of the islands to the UK on 10 October 1874. The British expected the reluctantly acquired (it was remote and showed few bright prospects) colony to become economically self-sustaining quickly, but the conditions for rapid economic development were absent. Capital was lacking, with local European planters reeling from the effects of the collapse of the local cotton boom following the end of the Civil War in the US. Fiji's first substantive governor, Sir Arthur Hamilton Gordon, decided on sugar as the crop to drive the engine of the colonial economy and invited the Australia-based Colonial Sugar Refining Company (CSR) to Fiji. The CSR came to Fiji in 1882 and remained there until 1973, three years after Fiji became independent.

The choice of the plantation economy as the preferred mode of economic development raised the problem of labour supply, which indenture was meant to resolve. Gordon's 'native policy', as it came to be known, effectively prohibited the commercial employment of Fijian labour so that the Fijian people could develop at their own pace in the subsistence sector under the guidance of their hereditary chiefs, shielded from the corrosive effects of modern influences. The Pacific Islands labour trade was deemed too blood-stained, morally tainted and meagre to meet the projected labour needs of the nascent colony.

Before coming to Fiji, Gordon had been the governor of Trinidad and Mauritius, where he had seen first-hand the success of the Indian indenture system. It was,

therefore, to India and the indenture system that he turned for his labour needs. Negotiations for indentured labourers were completed in 1878 and the first batch of 479 Indians arrived aboard the *Leonidas* on 14 May 1879. By 1916, when importation ceased, some 60,963 men, women and children had been transported to the islands. Like indentured migrants elsewhere, Fiji's migrants came under an agreement—which they termed *girmit*, and those who came under it, *girmitiyas*—which stipulated the terms and conditions of service (in English, Hindi and Urdu in North India, and Tamil and Malayalam in South India). The *girmit* was for five years, during which time the *girmitiyas* would be expected to perform tasks connected to the manufacture of sugar and related jobs. They would work for nine hours daily, for five-and-a-half days a week, Sunday being free. The *girmitiyas* could either do 'time work' or 'task work', the latter defined as six hours of steady work that could be accomplished by an able-bodied man. Men would receive a shilling a day, and women 9 pence. Rations would be provided for the first six months, along with hospital care. On paper, the terms looked reasonable, but the gap between the rhetoric and the reality on the ground was considerable. *Girmitiyas* could return to India at the end of five years at their own expense, or at the government's after a second five-year period of 'industrial residence'. Altogether, 24,000 Indians and their families returned to India after spending various periods in the colony.

Of Fiji's indentured migrants, 45,000 came from modern-day Uttar Pradesh and 15,000 from South India, (when emigration began there in 1903) from such districts as Chingleput, Coimbatore, Godavari, Nellore, North Arcot, Salem and Tanjore. The principal destinations for South Indians under the *kangani* system were neighbouring Southeast Asian countries. In Uttar Pradesh, the majority of migrants came from moth-eaten, impoverished eastern districts such as Basti, Gonda, Gorakhpur, Bahraich, Azamgarh, Faizabad, Sultanpur and Jaunpur. In the latter half of the 19th century, these migration-prone

Map 8.60

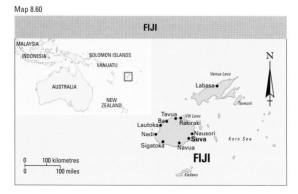

FIJI

MALAYSIA
INDONESIA
SOLOMON ISLANDS
VANUATU
AUSTRALIA
NEW ZEALAND

N

Vanua Levu
Labasa
Taveuni
Tavua Viti Levu
Ba
Lautoka Rakiraki
Nadi Nausori
Suva Koro Sea
Sigatoka Navua

FIJI

0   100 kilometres
0   100 miles

Kadavu

districts were sending large numbers of labourers to the tea gardens of Assam, jute mills in Calcutta, coal mines in Bihar and the textile mills of Bombay as well as to colonies abroad. Indeed, they experienced a population decline during that period which officials attributed partly to emigration. 'The extent of this migration is astonishing, and its economic influence is of the highest importance,' one official wrote, 'since these labourers earn high wages and remit or bring back with them large sums of money to their homes.' The claim about high wages is open to contention—how high was high?—but the importance of migration is beyond doubt.

Fiji's indentured labourers and those heading to other places came from this mass of uprooted humanity. Most of them registered for the programme in their own provinces rather than in distant large cities. In Gonda and Basti, nearly 50 per cent of those recruited did not migrate, while elsewhere, a third remained behind either because they refused to go or were deemed unfit for labour. This is not to deny that unscrupulous recruiters and their sub-agents snared the gullible, needy and unwary. They did, but perhaps not to the extent alleged. The indentured recruits were simple people from simple backgrounds, but they were not simpletons.

It was widely believed (and in some quarters still is) that the indentured labourers came from the lowest rungs of Indian society, and this was used by the colonial government and the European planters to remind the Indians of their proper place in the colonial hierarchy. But the migrants to Fiji and other places came from a representative section of rural India. Nearly 60 per cent were from middling agricultural and higher castes such as the Ahir, Kurmi, Brahmin, Khattri and Rajput. Muslims comprised 15 per cent of the migrants. Lower and menial castes—the Chamars, for example—and tribal groups were also represented in proportion to their population size. These groups were the first to bear the brunt of changes that swept through rural India in the 19th century, caused by the introduction of new notions of private ownership, increasing fragmentation of landholding, increasing debt among the peasantry, and the effects of natural calamity. As employment opportunities diminished, people moved elsewhere for a better life. It was the natural thing to do.

Men left as well as women. The government of India insisted, from the 1870s onwards, that 40 women accompany 100 men on each shipment. In the case of Fiji, and many other colonies, this quota was met, though in some cases barely. Most women enlisted individually, but more than 4500 came as members of families, sometimes with their husbands, sometimes with their children. Most of them probably came from dislocated and desperate backgrounds: widows, young brides and wives of migrants who had not returned and who were regarded as a burden on the meagre resources of the extended family. Perhaps there were others who had never married but worked as domestics, or *kamins*. Supported and sustained during times of prosperity, they were tossed out during times of scarcity or because they had invited someone's displeasure. No doubt there were some who were tricked or terrorised into migrating by the recruiters. There is something deeply moving about these *girmitiya* women who shouldered their little bundles, huddled their children and with quivering hope, left a life of drudgery and desperation for worlds and futures unknown.

The dislocation which had pushed people out from their villages was repeated in different ways as the recruits proceeded to the local depot and from there, by foot or train, to Calcutta (or Madras). The finely tuned, ritually sanctioned social distinctions which were the hallmark of Indian villages were shaken as unfamiliar castes shared cramped conditions in the depots, did their ablutions together and ate food cooked by unknown hands. The disruption continued on the voyage out, which could take up to three months by ship, and after 1904, one month with the advent of the steamship. But whether one month or three, the voyage was a traumatic experience for a landlocked people, most of whom had never seen the sea before. The journey was a great social leveller. The shared ordeals of a long journey in confined cabins produced the bond of *jahaji bhai*, the brotherhood of the crossing, which in time would become as emotionally powerful as real kinship, enduring well into the twilight years of the *girmitiyas*, cushioning them against the alienations and asperities of the outside world.

Once in Fiji, the indentured labourers were allocated to planters—overwhelmingly the CSR—after a brief quarantine for medical check-ups. Care was taken not to allocate *girmitiyas* from one ship or one district to the same plantation for fear that they might unite in protest or strike. To prevent just that, the government passed an ordinance in 1886, which remained in force throughout the period in which indenture operated, making it unlawful for more than five labourers employed on the same plantation to absent themselves for any purpose (such as making complaints) without the authorisation of the employer. There were sanctions for all manner of offences: 'unlawful absence', 'lack of ordinary diligence' and 'neglect', among others. On paper, the law was neutral; in practice, it was anything but. Labourers lodged complaints against overseers for violence or for non-payment of wages, overtasking or falsifying the pay roll; the justice they got was painfully disproportionate to the seriousness of the offence reported. The agent general of immigration, A. R. Coates, noted in 1910 that 'improper penalties being awarded for minor breaches of the Ordinance' were not 'in accordance with the letter or the intention of the law.' It is no wonder then that so few strikes occurred on the plantations: there were a few

Carting cane by bullocks to the tram line. Bullocks are still used in parts of Fiji, but tractors are becoming more common.

minor ones in the 1880s and one by Punjabis and Pathans in 1907. For the most part, the *girmitiyas* consciously adopted the strategy of accommodation rather than active or overt resistance, knowing that their time on the plantations was limited. Indenture, they understood very well, was a limited detention, not a life sentence.

The 1890s were the darkest days of *girmit* in Fiji, a time of distressing mortality rates caused by diarrhoea, dysentery, hookworm, anaemia and other such ailments; of excessive discipline and repressive legislation; and of general unwillingness on the part of the government to guard the rights of the indentured workers. Things improved over time in response to internal pressures and external demands for change. Life in the lines, as the living quarters of the *girmitiyas* were called, was generally sorrowful, especially in the early years. Family life was unstable, quarters were crowded and privacy was almost non-existent. As K. L. Gillion wrote, 'With three bunks and firewood, field tools, cooking utensils cluttered about, smoke, soot, spilt food, flies, mosquitoes, perhaps fowls, or a dog as precaution against theft, and until separate kitchens were required in 1908, a fire place as well, living conditions were neither comfortable nor sanitary.' South Indians, as new arrivals, were sent to remote, newly opened plantations and experienced the same trials as the pioneer *girmitiyas*.

Perhaps the most vulnerable people in the lines were women. Presumed by outsiders to be of low moral character—'unstable and mercenary', according to the agent general of immigration in 1902, 'as joyously amoral as a doe rabbit', according to an Australian overseer, or a 'rudderless vessel [without any] controlling hand', according to C. F. Andrews—they were traded by their own men, abused by overseers and sirdars, and blamed for all manner of ills afflicting the Indian community. Sexual assaults on them were common and frequently ignored by the authorities. No burden, however, was as serious for them as the widespread belief that they were responsible for the high suicide rate among Indian men in Fiji: at the turn of the century, the rate was the highest among Indian labour-importing colonies. 'Sexual jealousy' was the phrase used: women, so it was said, traded on their scarcity and deserted their marriages or relationships for men who offered more comfort or luxury, leaving the jettisoned, jilted

partner to end his life. The truth was more complex; women were as much the victims of indenture as men, and sometimes more victimised, as has been said, 'not just by actions, hostilities, or indifferences of men, but by the institutions of law, invested as they were with the majesty of the state, the formidability of the male jurists and lawyers, and the unbroken faith of the public', in the words of Bertram Wyatt-Brown, an American scholar. No doubt, some women were unscrupulous, but the harshness of plantation life and the anxiety associated with the realisation that there was no going back to India sufficiently account for most suicides. It is worth noting that 22 per cent of the suicides occurred within six months of the deceased's residence in Fiji, 30 per cent within the first year, and 75 per cent within the first five years. Whatever the truth about these suicides, the publication of reports in India of the ill-treatment of Indian women in the archipelago led to the abolition of indentured emigration to Fiji.

Fiji had been receiving attention from India since the turn of the century. The Sanderson Committee, appointed by the government of India, reported in 1910 that emigration was beneficial to India, to the emigrant and, above all, to the colonies. The committee noted some problems, especially the ill-treatment of migrants by overseers or law enforcement agencies, but concluded, with respect to Fiji: 'The system appears to have worked well, to have been productive of excellent results, and the local conditions all seem to point to the expediency of its continuance.' Four years later, another Indian government-sponsored enquiry into Indian indenture, led by J. S. McNeill and Chimman Lal, ended with a sanguine note about the importance as well as the advantages of the system wherever it was properly administered.

Such views, however, were in the minority and were, under the circumstances, necessarily unpopular. This was not because indenture had brought no economic amelioration to many who had left India, for it obviously had, but rather because the moral argument prevailed. C. F. Andrews made the first of three visits to Fiji in 1916 and wrote scathing reports of moral collapse and social ills on the plantations. Andrews wrote in a typical passage: 'Though there are beautiful and stately rivers in Fiji, no women are seen making their morning offerings; no temples rise on the banks. There is no household shrine. The outward life, which Hindu women in the "lines" lead in Fiji appears to be without love and without worship—a sordid round of mean and joyless tasks.' The story of Kunti and her narrow escape from rape by an overseer, and of women 'serving' several men, outraged Indian public opinion. The Kanpur newspaper *The Pratap* expressed the widespread feelings:

Behold, full of sorrow
Surcharged with grief
From Beyond the ocean borne
On the wings of wind
Comes the wail of their weeping.

Indentured Indian women in front of the 'lines' or living quarters of the workers. Government regulations required that every shipment of workers should have at least 40 women for every 100 men.

Indenture was doomed despite pleas from Fiji that the colony faced certain ruin without the continued importation of Indian labour and despite the promise of reforms if the system was allowed to continue. As Pandit Madan Mohan Malviya said, 'When India is asking for a rightful place in the Empire, this badge of helotry ought not to remain and ought to be completely swept away.' The last ship carrying indentured labourers, the *Sutlej IV*, arrived in Fiji on 1 November 1916; all remaining indentures of Indian labourers in the colony were cancelled with effect from 1 January 1920.

SOCIAL CHANGE UNTIL 1920

Working on plantations and living in the crowded lines changed people's lives. Old values and social practices, and institutions which had been an integral part of life in rural India lost their meaning in Fiji. The caste system was among the earliest casualties of migration. Taboos, rituals and observances associated with food, marriage and personal relations could not be maintained. The depots in Calcutta and Madras struck the first blow, and then the long voyage out; but it was on the plantations that the system crashed. Occupational hierarchy based on caste distinctions and notions of purity—with priests at the top and tanners and scavengers at the bottom—could not be maintained, for everyone performed the same tasks in the field and was paid according to the amount of work accomplished, not caste status. Work by itself did not damage caste status, as Adrian Mayer points out, 'but it dealt a blow to the differentiation by occupation, as well as dependence on several other castes for services.' People continued to play at caste, but it was just that, play. It would go with the *girmitiyas*.

In Fiji, *girmitiyas* lived and worked on the plantations for only five or at the most 10 years. Unlike slavery, indenture was, to repeat, a temporary detention, not a life sentence. Once their indentures expired, people settled wherever they could obtain land. Scattered homesteads on individually leased parcels of land, rather than the clustered villages characteristic of India, became the pattern of Indian settlement in Fiji, increasing the emphasis on individual enterprise and initiative. Expediency, contingency and tolerance born of need or circumstance rather than status or prestige determined relations among the settlers. They cooperated on projects requiring a reciprocal exchange of labour, such as building and maintaining temples, roads and cemeteries, and planting and harvesting crops. In the absence of government, they devised their own mechanisms for regulating behaviour or enforcing conformance to the norms of the society they were creating. To this end, they resurrected the traditional village-based panchayat to resolve conflicts and disputes in the community. This declined as the community expanded, as money and education came to the village and as Western institutions took root. The gradual evolution of Indo-Fijian settlements on the fringes of the sugar mills was a strong beacon of hope to those still under indenture, and was also a powerful reminder of the transience of *girmit*.

The Indo-Fijian community developed in cultural and social isolation from other communities. The English, being English, kept themselves apart from everyone else. More damaging to Fiji's long-term future was the complete lack of interaction between Fijians and Indians. The government frowned upon fraternisation between Fijians and Indians, and punished those who crossed boundaries.

Table 8.33

INDIAN OCCUPATIONS IN 1911 AND 1921		
	1911	1921
Agricultural	10,357	19,433
Commercial	530	854
Industrial	1896	3179
Professional (including clerks)	20	54
Domestic (including housewives)	3846	13,492
Sundry	106	336
Unemployed	7731	20,078
Unstated occupation	1491	3139
Total	25,977	60,565

Based on Fiji census reports, 1911 and 1921.

There were many cases of Fijian villagers accepting Indo-Fijians as part of their community, but the Indo-Fijians were expelled when the government found out and the offending Fijians were fined. Indo-Fijians were discouraged, and in some cases prohibited, from settling close to Fijian villages for fear of 'contaminating' the 'natives' with alien ideas. Government policy compounded the pre-existing problem of race relations with cultural prejudice. The two communities lived warily side by side, mutually uncomprehending each other's fears and aspirations in what was fast becoming a plural society.

From the beginning, some enterprising Indians tried their hands at occupations other than agriculture. In 1916, for example, there were 1508 shopkeepers, 974 hawkers, 21 bakers, 80 jewellers and 129 watermen. Some became cane planters themselves, competing with European planters. In Navua in 1898, Indian planters produced 10,519 tonnes of sugar cane valued at £5974, compared to 9447 tonnes worth £5586 produced by Europeans. There were a few prosperous people in the Indian community, but the majority, as Table 8.33 shows, depended on agriculture.

Until the early 1900s, the CSR produced practically all its sugar cane with indentured labour. From 1909 it began leasing some of its plantations to independent contractors, mostly former officers. That practice collapsed when indentured emigration ended in 1916. After a brief experiment with Indo-Fijian planters on 20–32 hectare

A typical rural Indian thatched house in Fiji, common until the 1960s. Thatched huts have now been replaced with modern wood-and-corrugated-iron structures.

parcels of land, the CSR decided to get out of cane cultivation altogether. It divided its extensive holdings—53,776 hectares of freehold land—into 4-hectare parcels and leased them to Indo-Fijian tenants. The conversion occurred rapidly. Within a decade, some 97 per cent of all cane acreage was in smallholdings, with CSR tenants accounting for 52 per cent of the total and independent growers, Indo-Fijians producing cane on native leased land, accounting for 45 per cent. The 4-hectare farm remained the pattern throughout the period of CSR's operations in Fiji.

Dependence on agriculture and on the 4-hectare plot set the pattern for Indo-Fijian economic activity, as did the dispersed settlement. It was here that the Indian community began to put down its roots, building farms, raising families, educating their children and establishing Indian cultural and social institutions. The latter were not as difficult as might be imagined. Indians in Fiji never quite lost touch with their cultural roots in the way they did in other places. As early as the 1890s, the basic literature of Indian folklore and religion were circulating within Fiji's Indian community. Totaram Sanadhya, a remarkable *girmitiya* who came to Fiji in 1893, compiled a list of this literature: the Ramayana, Danlila, Sukh Sagar, Sapt Puran, Indrajal, Sigrabodh, Satyanarayan ki Katha, Alaha Khand, Ekadashi Mahatm and Devi Bhagwat.

These and other texts were read or recited communally so that they became instruments of entertainment as well as spiritual instruction and they kept Indian culture alive. By the early 1900s, a number of sects of folk Hinduism were established in the major centres of Indian settlement, including the Kabir Panth, Nath and Dadu, Jagjivandas and Satnami sects. The Arya Samaj was founded in 1904. Muslims built a mosque in Navua

The Indian Settler was a bilingual periodical started in c.1916 by Manilal Maganlal Doctor, a lawyer who was prominent in the Indian community's affairs from 1912–20.

around 1900 and another in Rewa soon after. Mirza Khan arrived in Fiji from India in 1898 as a missionary to the Muslims. Relations between Hindus and Muslims, cordial during *girmit*, remained so afterwards, surviving the occasional clash when Hindus played loud music near mosques or during Ramadan, or when Muslims slaughtered cattle in the vicinity of Hindu homes. The circulation of religious texts and the creation of cultural institutions kept the Indian community relatively close to its cultural roots and discouraged conversion to Christianity. The number of Christian converts was miniscule despite the presence of missionaries such as J. W. Burton.

Until 1916, Indian concerns were represented in government by the agent general of immigration. Political activity in the Indian community was restricted to acts of supplication; a petition here, a mild demand there. For the most part, emerging Indian leaders were preoccupied with the internal affairs of the community, but by the 1910s, the need for educated and articulate leaders was felt, leaders who could represent Indo-Fijian concerns to the government. A group of Indians wrote to Mohandas Karamchand Gandhi requesting an English-speaking Indian lawyer to help them get organised. Gandhi dispatched Manilal Maganlal Doctor, who arrived in Fiji in December 1912 and immersed himself in the community's affairs. He petitioned the government in 1915 to amend an 1892 law to allow Indian girls between the ages of 12 and 15 to marry without parental consent. His aim in doing so was not to encourage early marriage but to prevent mercenary parents from trafficking in their daughters. He also petitioned for a relaxation of divorce laws to take 'account of the prevalent disproportion of the sexes and its attendant evils.' He also wanted Hindi-speaking court interpreters appointed. In 1916, he even urged the government to establish a platoon of Indian soldiers to 'take part in the responsibilities of the Empire at such a critical time as the present.' He started a bilingual periodical called *The Indian Settler* and, in 1918, he formed the Indian Imperial Association of Fiji.

Manilal's activities, intelligence and standing in the Indian community were noted unfavourably by the government. To the consternation of most in the Indo-Fijian community, the government nominated Badri Maharaj, a wealthy but illiterate Indian, to the Legislative Council in 1916. Manilal was to be marginalised at any cost. He was a native of Baroda and technically, therefore, not a British subject. Using the excuse of the 1920 strike, in which Manilal played an important organising role, the government deported him. Until his deportation, Manilal Maganlal Doctor was the most significant political leader of the Indian community in Fiji.

GROWTH AND DIVERSIFICATION (1920–40)

The period 1920–40 witnessed the rapid growth of the Indo-Fijian population, which signalled a profound social, cultural and psychological transformation of the community. Before the 1920s, the Indo-Fijians tended to be socially isolated, economically dependent, culturally disoriented and politically disorganised and voiceless.

Totaram Sanadhya

Totaram Sanadhya was born in the Ferozabad *thana* of Agra and came to Fiji as an indentured labourer at the age of 16. After indenture, he became a wealthy cane planter. He was passionately concerned about the social welfare of his people. He threw himself into cultural and social activities and defended Hinduism against Christian proselytising. In 1914, he returned to India and, while there, related his Fiji experience to the Hindi journalist Benarsidas Chaturvedi. From that came *Fiji Dvip Men Mere Ikkis Varsh* ('My Twenty One Years in the Fiji Islands'), which became an important tract in the struggle to abolish indenture.

Totaram Sanadhya, pictured here with his wife.

Why do you go to such lengths to convert others to your faith? Religion is something unchanging, unchangeable. True religion is about selfless social service, not about outward appearance or rituals. People may believe in different sects but that for me is not true religion. Religion cannot be divided into compartments such as Islam, Christianity or Hinduism. For me religion means righteousness. I readily accept some of Christ's teachings in the Bible, such as not inflicting pain on others, being benevolent towards others, and the like. For me these are some of Christ's main messages in the Bible. But I don't believe in Baptism...You call them [overseers] Christians. How can that be when these people treat their workers like animals and skin them alive? Their cruelty knows no bounds. They pay them a pittance. Look at the atrocities they commit against our women. And in a court of law they take the oath on the Bible and deny their evil deeds. Does baptism wash away all their evil deeds?

Extract from Totaram Sanadhya's conversation with Reverend J. W. Burton, in Brij V. Lal, Chalo Jahaji, 2000.

Perceived and treated by other groups as coolies, the Indo-Fijians were told to accept as permanent and proper their place at the bottom of the Fijian social hierarchy. This began to change after the 1920s. Fiji-born Indians were different from their indentured forebears. As one official put it in 1927, the Fiji-born 'possess a superior physique to that of his immigrant parents, [exhibits] greater intelligence, practises a higher morality and demands a more advanced standard of living.' The differences in outlook and social organisation arose in part because of the new competitive environment in which the people found themselves and because the policies of the colonial government served to undermine the possibility of reconstituting the social order the Indian immigrants had known in their homeland. A part of the reason for their assertiveness, too, was the realisation among Indo-Fijians that Fiji was their permanent home and that they wanted to live there with dignity and self-respect; this involved obtaining equal political rights in the colony.

Not all Indo-Fijians in this period were descended from *girmityas*. In the 1920s and 1930s, small but steady numbers of free Indians migrated to Fiji. Among them were some repatriates who had returned to India from Fiji only to become disenchanted with life there. Most new immigrants were enterprising agriculturalists from Punjab (principally from the migration-prone districts of Ludhiana and Hoshiarpur) and artisans and petty traders from Gujarat (especially from Surat and Navsari). In 1921, there were 449 Punjabis and 324 Gujaratis in Fiji, and in 1936, 3600 and 2500 respectively. Most of these migrants were single males, who, after establishing themselves in Fiji, returned to India to get married. Their social isolation from the rest of the community produced friction and adverse comment, and still does. The Gujaratis lived in towns and engaged in business activities such as hawking, tailoring, laundering, boot- or jewellery-making, or merchandising. The most successful commercial houses in Fiji today—Punjas, Motibhais and Tappoos—are the product of such humble beginnings. Gujarati dominance in the Indo-Fijian wholesale and retail business continues.

The Gujaratis were strongly nationalistic and avid followers of Gandhi and his non-violent approach to freeing India from British rule. On a few occasions, much to the annoyance of the colonial government, they organised partial hartal, or work stoppages, in protest against British policies on the subcontinent. Besides bringing greater awareness of subcontinental politics to Fiji, new immigration saw the arrival of two young London-trained Gujarati

Manilal was deported by the Fiji government in 1920 to break his influence on the island's Indian community.

If the true destiny of man is divine, one man or one race cannot, morally speaking, enslave, dominate, or even exploit another for mere private gain. If the political and economic conditions of today have not yet permitted a fulfillment of this principle in practice, there is no reason to believe...that the secret forces of the worked are not in fact tending towards the invisible ideal by an unnoticed and unnoticeable march of human development.

Manilal Maganlal Doctor, The Indian Settler, *1917*.

lawyers, S. B. Patel and A. D. Patel (no relation of the former). S. B. Patel, a quiet, reflective and scholarly man, remained in the background, advising, listening and mediating. A. D. Patel, on the other hand, was a gifted orator, a brilliant lawyer and an intellectual; he was a man of action who would become a major public figure in Fijian politics after World War II.

Growth and diversification brought many changes to the Indo-Fijian community. Religious and cultural organisations were established. The Fiji Muslim League was established in 1926, as was the Then India Sanmargya Ikya Sangam, an umbrella organisation of the South Indians. The insistence of religious leaders on adopting proper conduct and following the proper ways of doing things resulted in conflict and tension as Sanatanis and Arya Samajis, and Sunni and Shiites clashed. Occasionally, there was Hindu–Muslim tension as well, reflecting political developments in India; but common sense and overarching common interests prevented an escalation. Cultural organisations gave their communities a sense of purpose and cohesion. They organised festivals and public recitals of sacred texts, which kept their ancestral cultures alive. Perhaps most importantly, especially when the government lagged in providing educational facilities to the Indo-Fijians, preferring to see them remain in the agricultural sector, the organisations started community schools, as they viewed education as the best way to escape the vicissitudes of rural poverty on 4-hectare sugar cane plots. 'No one can help noticing the eagerness, amounting to a kind of hunger, for education among the Indians of Fiji,' wrote an observer. In time, children from these schools would fill the professions and assume leadership positions in the community and in the nation at large.

Indian political representation in the Legislative Council became an important issue in the 1920s. The government of India wanted to protect the political interests of the Indo-Fijians. Its Colonies Committee had raised the issue in 1924, protesting that the two proposed representatives for a large and growing community were not enough. How could they be, it reiterated in 1927, when 3878 Europeans had seven seats in the Legislative Council while 60,634 Indo-Fijians, who cultivated 17,959 hectares of land and owned 36,000 heads of stock, were to have only two? The proposal, it said, was unfair and 'intended to assign an inferior status to Indians as compared with their British fellow subjects, and to limit the growth of their political influence in the Colony.' The government of India wanted a minimum of three seats for the Indo-Fijians, which the colonial government reluctantly conceded.

A. D. Patel, a Gujarati lawyer who became a major figure in Fijian politics after World War II.

Figure 8.11

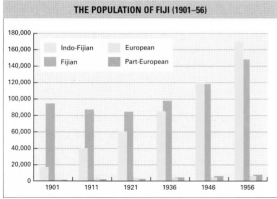

THE POPULATION OF FIJI (1901–56)

Indo-Fijian | European
Fijian | Part-European

Source: Fiji census report, 1956.

Increased Indian representation in the Legislative Council was one issue. The other was the nature of the franchise itself. From the beginning, the franchise in Fiji was communal. The government of India wanted this to be replaced with a non-racial system of voting (one person, one vote, one value). The colonial government opposed this demand, stating its commitment to protecting the Fijian people and seeing that their interests remained paramount. This commitment was cited by the government to oppose a change it had not authorised. European numbers in the Legislative Council were reduced from seven to six, and Indo-Fijians and Fijians had three members each: an artificial parity between Europeans on the one hand and Fijians and Indo-Fijians on the other. On being elected to the Legislative Council, Indian member Vishnu Deo moved a motion on 5 November 1929 that, 'political rights and status granted to Indian settlers in this Colony on racial lines are not acceptable to them', and that 'Indians in Fiji should be granted common franchise along with other British subjects in the Colony.' Predictably, the motion was defeated. S. B. Patel explained the rationale for the Indian stand on the common roll: 'It is the recognition of the principle of the common franchise for all His Majesty's subjects in the Colony that we are looking for. We stand for the Colony as a whole and not for any one section of it. We do not wish or desire to dominate.' A deep sense of *izzat* and *insaf*, or honour and justice, underpinned the Indo-Fijian struggle for political equality, but the colonial government saw this as little more than a challenge to the European-dominated order.

LAND, THE CSR AND WAR

The rapid growth of the Indo-Fijian community and the expansion of agriculture in the 1930s and 1940s brought to the fore the question of land tenure. The ownership of Fijian land was not in question—Gordon's land policy had ensured that 83 per cent of all land in Fiji remained inalienably in Fijian hands; leasing the land, however, was. In the early years, the Indo-Fijians leased land either from the CSR or from the Fijians with the assistance of the government. In 1934, 4100 farmers leased 18,413 hectares from the CSR, while 4600 leased 14,164 hectares

from the Fijians. The leases were for a limited period only, after which the landowner could repossess the land. In 1935, the government of India expressed its concern that the limited lease 'creates insecurity of tenure which leaves the Indian leasee very much at the mercy of the Fijian landlord,' and urged the government to devise a 'satisfactory adjustment of [Indo-Fijian] rights and opportunities in relation to agricultural land.' This sort of external pressure and the realisation that the well-being of the economy depended on resolving the land question led to the creation of the Native Land Trust Board in 1940, which assumed all responsibility for leasing Fijian land while providing for the reservation of sufficient land to meet the needs of the Fijians. With that, the land question was settled for a generation.

So, too, were relations between the Indo-Fijian cane growers and the CSR after a crippling strike in the sugar industry in 1943. As the sole miller of cane in Fiji, the CSR wielded enormous power. As the *mai-bap* (mother-father) of the industry, it knew what was best for the farmers. It regulated all aspects of the industry. Strike leader A. D. Patel observed, 'The relation between the Company and the growers was strongly reminiscent of the relationship of barons and serfs during the medieval ages. They had to take what was given to them and be thankful for the small mercies whether they liked it or not.' The farmers' grievances coalesced around a number of issues: the land-leasing agreement between the company and its Indo-Fijian tenants, which left the latter completely at the mercy of the company; the low wage it paid its workers; and, most importantly, its method of paying for cane, which was a flat rate per tonne, based on the percentage of cane sugar—something the farmers did not understand; they wanted a flat minimum rate of 16 shillings and 6 pence per tonne. The CSR refused, saying the cause of the farmers' poverty was their profligacy. The heart of the matter, A. D. Patel said, was 'not on how little the farmer can manage to live, but how much at the present price of sugar and other products of cane, the Company can afford to pay, after making a due allowance for a margin of profit which can be considered fair and just during wartime.'

The strike lasted several months, wrecking the economy and impoverishing the farmers even further (they lost over £1 million in income). But its long-lasting effects were psychological and political. The Indo-Fijian cane growers had drawn a line in the sand, indicating that they would be prepared to stand up for their rights and fight. The strike also alienated the Indo-Fijians from other communities, who accused them of treachery and selfishness. Their fears of Indian domination were exaggerated by the fact that during the war, the Indo-Fijians had become an absolute majority of the population.

Feelings were also inflamed over the Indo-Fijians' lack of enthusiasm for the war effort. The conventional view is that the Indo-Fijians refused to enlist because the government refused to grant them the same conditions of service and pay as were provided to European soldiers. Equal pay, equal risk, equal worth was certainly a demand, but it was not the only, nor even the prime reason for non-Indian participation. Supported by Fijians and Europeans and with a keen eye on developments in India (for instance the Quit India Movement and Subhas Chandra Bose's Japanese-supported Indian National Army), the government did not want Indo-Fijians as soldiers. Indo-Fijians were implicated in events on the subcontinent which neither the Fijians nor the Europeans fathomed, but which

Loading a truck with cane which would be carted to the sugar mills by diesel trains. Lorries are also used to cart cane to the mills.

Fijian and Indo-Fijian boys engaged in a friendly game of football.

they detested intensely. An Indian platoon formed in the early 1930s was disbanded on the eve of the war. The government had also refused to take up Manilal Maganlal Doctor's offer to assist with the war effort during World War I. A number of Indians did volunteer but were turned down by European officers. Some Indo-Fijian Muslims offered their services unconditionally as the 'mercenary spirit', they said, was alien to Islam, but they, too, were refused enlistment. The government wanted the Indo-Fijians to remain on the farm and to contribute to the war effort through increased agricultural production. Governor Sir Phillip Mitchell told the Indian Central War Committee, 'I assure you and I ask you to carry that assurance back to your Districts when you return that the effort of the Indians in Fiji in response to Government appeals for the growing of foodstuff and the maintenance of essential agricultural interests have been not one of the least important contributions made to the prosecution of the war.' Indo-Fijians told the Governor that they would defend Fiji with their blood if it was attacked, but they wanted the principle of equality recognised if they were to fight for the empire elsewhere. The Indo-Fijians were neither disloyal nor treacherous. It was European propaganda and the exuberant Fijian enthusiasm for the Empire and its causes that made them appear so.

The emotions caused by the strike and by the differential war effort coloured race relations for a long time. In debates about political change in the 1940s, these issues were dredged up again and again. Europeans aligned themselves politically with the Fijians to check the political aspirations of Indo-Fijians. In 1946, A. A. Ragg moved a motion in the Legislative Council for the terms of the Deed of Cession to be reaffirmed, placing Fijian interests at the forefront, but many Fijian and European members turned the debate into an Indo-Fijian 'beat-up' session. A few years later, Ragg and a number of other Europeans—including A. W. Macmillan, a member of the London Missionary Society and inspector of Indian schools in Fiji—argued for the systematic repatriation of Indo-Fijians to New Guinea, where, it was suggested, they would turn native bush into productive farmland, 'help hungry Asia and regulate immigration so as to prevent New Guinea from falling into the hands of Communist China or Japan.' Such a colonisation plan,

they boldly suggested, would be carried out under Commonwealth supervision!

Away from politics, the Indo-Fijian community concentrated on social and economic improvements. By the 1950s, each sizeable Indo-Fijian settlement had a modest primary school of its own, often run by social and cultural organisations such as the Fiji Muslim League, Sangam, Sanatan Dharma, Arya Samaj and the Ramakrishna Mission. In 1946, there were 438 schools with 36,000 pupils. A decade later, there were 479 schools with 60,000 pupils. The number of Fijian schools (that is, schools which admitted only indigenous Fijian students) increased from 306 in 1946 to 310 in 1955, while the number of Indo-Fijian schools (not racially exclusive by policy but in practice, reflecting the distribution of population) increased from 106 to 149. Even though Fijian schools outnumbered Indo-Fijian schools by almost three to one, most Fijian schools did not offer education beyond grade five (only 32 of the 300 schools did). Among Indo-Fijian schools, 84 of the 141 primary schools took their students up to the final year, grade eight.

The disparity between the two communities was evident in other fields as well. In 1958, for example, there was no professionally qualified Fijian lawyer and only one dentist and one medical doctor. In contrast, there were 38 Indo-Fijian lawyers, 12 medical doctors and eight dentists practising in Fiji. The contribution the community made to the education of its children is one of the most inspiring aspects of its history.

Newspapers—*Jagriti, Shanti Dut, The Fiji Samachar, Jai Fiji, Kisan Mitra* and *Sangam*—connected the community to the outside world, breaking the monopoly on news controlled by the government or published by the demonstrably anti-Indian *Fiji Times* under its New Zealand-born editor Leonard Usher. Hindi films were also screened in cinemas around the country, connecting the community to India: *Alam Ara, Anarkali, Baiju Bawra, Awara, Shree 420, Jagte Raho, Pyasa* and *Mother India*. Radio came to most Indo-Fijian homes in the 1950s, as did regular transport and, in areas close to urban centres, paved roads, piped water and concrete buildings. By the 1950s too, a working class had begun to organise. There was a major strike against European oil companies in Suva in 1959, shaking the colonial establishment to its foundations because it was multiracial in character. The sight of Fijian and Indo-Fijian working classes joining hands against expatriate companies was not one that the government nor the Fijian chiefs had expected to see. And the following year, there was a strike in the sugar industry against the CSR, this time because of the refusal of the company to negotiate a mutually acceptable contract with the growers. By the end of the 1950s, the world of *girmit*, with its expectations of subservience to the will of the sahibs, was a remote memory for most Indo-Fijians.

TOWARDS INDEPENDENCE

By the late 1950s, Harold Macmillan's 'Winds of Change' were blowing all over Africa and were on the verge of reaching the Pacific. Samoa became independent from New Zealand in 1962, and the Cook Islands in 1965. The

The Fiji Samachar was one of a number of Hindi newspapers published in Fiji to bring news and information to the Indian community.

The campaigning style of the late 1940s and early 1950s. The vehicles depicted here were left behind in Fiji by the departing US army after World War II. Note the left-hand drive sign on the bus.

question for Fiji was not if but when Fiji would become independent. On this question, opinion was sharply divided. In 1961, the governor informed the Legislative Council that its size would be increased from 15 to 18 unofficial members, comprising six Europeans, six Fijians and six Indians. Four members from each community would be elected from communal (that is, racial) rolls and two nominated by the governor. These proposals were intended to pave the way for greater self-government, eventually leading to independence over the next decade or so.

The proposals elicited different responses from the three communities. Europeans and Fijians rejected any change that took Fiji towards independence and which did not entrench Fijian political dominance; and they wanted the full and complete retention of the racial system of voting. Indo-Fijian leaders disagreed. For them, the pace of change, which the other two feared was too fast, was not rapid enough. They wanted a non-racial common roll system of voting and they saw any constitutional advance as leading inevitably towards full independence in the near future. These contrasting attitudes dominated political debate in Fiji in the 1960s. Party politics was soon to

arrive. In 1963, A. D. Patel formed the Federation Party, attracting the support of the majority of Indo-Fijians. A small number, reflecting fractures and fissures within the community, joined the Fijian-dominated Alliance Party when it was launched in 1966.

In July 1965, Britain held a conference to frame a new constitution for Fiji. Ratu Mara, the leader of the Fijian delegation and the first prime minister of Fiji, spoke warmly of his and his people's 'trust and abiding loyalty in the British Crown and British institutions', saying that independence was not his goal at all. Europeans expressed satisfaction with the status quo and gratitude for all that Britain had done for Fiji. Patel predictably took a completely different line. He hoped that the conference would produce a constitution which would lead Fiji to 'complete independence in the not distant future.' At the conference (and in Fiji before the conference), Patel pressed his case for a non-racial common roll, which he had been advocating since the 1930s. Adopting the common roll was the only way of building a genuinely non-racial political culture in Fiji. Communal rolls stood for divided loyalties and inhibited national consciousness among people. Communalism would inhibit the 'formation of secular parties' and would be 'a serious obstacle to the successful operation of parliamentary democracy', as 'the elected representatives of a racial or religious sub-community cannot afford to subordinate the interests and prejudices of their people to those of the larger community.'

Patel's plea fell on deaf ears. London was more attuned to the fears and anxieties of the Fijians and had a prudent appreciation of their strength. As Julian Amery, the parliamentary under-secretary of state for the colonies, said in 1960, with Fijians comprising 75 per cent of the colony's armed forces, 'the islands could hardly be governed without them let alone against them.' Many in both Suva and London felt that it was morally right to hand Fiji back to the indigenous Fijians who had ceded their islands to the UK in the first instance and who had, in war and peace, remained steadfastly loyal to the

Ratu Mara, Fiji's first prime minister after independence, addressing a Fijian rally at Albert Park in Suva, 1959, at the height of Fiji's first multiracial strike against European commercial houses. He advised his people to disassociate themselves from the strikers.

British Crown. Both Suva and London wanted an outcome that was nominally democratic in nature, but which put the Fijians on top.

Such a constitution was in fact devised. In an expanded Legislative Council, Fijians had 14 seats, Indo-Fijians 12 and Europeans 10. The principle of parity between Fijians and Indo-Fijians was jettisoned and the communal roll was maintained, with the addition of cross-voting seats where the ethnicity of the candidate was specified but everyone voted. The 1966 elections, held under the new constitution, produced a huge majority for Ratu Mara's Alliance Party. When London spoke of the contested constitution, which the Federation Party had accepted under protest, as a long-term solution for Fiji in September 1967, the party walked out of the Legislative Council. The by-elections the following year returned the Federation Party candidates with increased majorities. Threats were issued not to renew leases to Indo-Fijian tenants and to deport Indo-Fijian leaders, but emotions soon subsided and dialogue resumed among the principal leaders, Patel and Mara. Confidential talks were in progress regarding a new constitution when Patel died suddenly in October 1969.

He was succeeded by his deputy, Siddiq Koya, a Malayali Muslim from the large sugar cane-producing district of Ba. Koya struck up a cordial working relationship with Mara, whom he said he trusted, and privately told the governor, Sir Robert Foster, on the eve of the penultimate constitutional conference in London, that for him, as for Mara, the common roll was a long-term objective. Some party delegates in London cavilled at this characterisation of their party's founding platform, but London knew where the party leader stood. If no agreement was reached on the method of election to parliament, all leaders agreed, before proceeding to London, to accept independence under the 1965 constitution—the very one which the Federation Party had rejected. It was also agreed to go into independence without an election, giving Mara a huge political advantage. The constitution negotiated in London essentially preserved the system of communal representation, but in an enlarged form: 25 of the 52 seats in the House of Representatives would be contested from communal rolls and the remaining from cross-voting constituencies. In the Senate, appointees of the Great Council of Chiefs would exercise the power of veto. In his last dispatch as governor, Foster reflected on the transition to independence, its suddenness and

amicability, the cordial atmosphere in which negotiations had taken place, and the concessions which the Indian leaders had made. He told London that none of the deep-seated problems had been resolved. The land problem—not ownership but leasing arrangements—remained as intractable as ever. Another major problem, unresolved at the conference, shelved, and to be confronted after independence, was the electoral system. 'A calm search for a just solution to the problem of representation has in the past proved virtually impossible: feeling ran far too deep. One is therefore bound to regret that in effect a time bomb will lie buried in the new Constitution and to pray that it may be diffused before exploding. The two parties have however publicly committed themselves to an act of faith which must give reasonable ground for hope.' Reasonable hope: that was all that could be hoped for as Fiji took its first tentative steps into an independent future.

Issues associated with independence dominated the 1960s, but there were other changes which would affect the life of the Indo-Fijian community in profound ways. None was more significant than the opening of the University of the South Pacific (USP) in Suva in 1968. It was a regional institution, but Fiji dominated with student numbers as well as with financial contributions. Before the establishment of the USP, the Fiji government sent a select number of students on bonded scholarships to universities in New Zealand and Australia. Tertiary education was the preserve of the brightest and the best-connected. The USP changed that pattern. With its founding, university education was within the reach of most students who passed their secondary school examinations; and on the verge of independence, Fiji needed as much trained manpower as it could get. Indo-Fijian students dominated the student population. They would go on to play an important role in the life of post-independent Fiji.

INDEPENDENCE AND ITS AFTERMATH

Fiji became independent on 10 October 1970, exactly 96 years to the date that it had become a British Crown Colony. The early years after independence were a time of rapid social and economic change, which affected all communities, including Indo-Fijians. Commercial agriculture expanded and pine plantations were established. Tourism increased from about 15,000 visitors annually in the 1960s to 186,000 in the 1970s. The GDP per capita increased from F$369 in 1970 to F$1415 in 1980. Urbanisation increased too. In 1966, only 88,979 (36.9 per cent of the Indo-Fijian population) lived in urban areas. By 1988, the number had increased to 144,533 (42.4 per cent). In the 1980s, Fijians surpassed the Indo-Fijian population, reversing a 40-year trend. Improved communications, airstrips on the outer islands, upgraded roads girdling the two major islands, and better inter-island shipping reduced isolation and enhanced contact among people. The introduction of electrical infrastructure in rural areas brought modern amenities and technology to areas that had long remained untouched by contemporary forces of change.

The result was a growing gulf between the politics based on race that the constitution promoted and the realities of everyday life. It was frustration with the politics of race that led to the formation of the Fiji Labour Party (FLP) in 1985; that, and the failure of the Indo-Fijian based National Federation Party (NFP). Koya's leadership of the party was challenged, his authority undermined by internal dissent. Divisions appeared over crucial

'Change is a fact of life. We must all be willing to accept change when it comes. Throughout our struggles, we have always worked to liberate people from the bondage of racial compartmentalisation and create one nation and one people.' S. M. Koya, leader of the Opposition, extract from a speech in 1977.

Jai Ram Reddy became leader of the Opposition in 1977.

Mahendra Chaudhry, Fiji's first prime minister of Indo-Fijian descent (1999–2000). He was deposed on 19 May 2000 and held captive for 56 days by George Speight and his rebels.

The Fiji flag flying on 10 October 1970, when the islands became independent after 90 years of British colonial rule.

policy issues, such as land tenure, that split the party. In April 1977, the NFP narrowly won the election, but internal divisions prevented it from forming a government, although it has to be said that Governor General Ratu Sir George Cakobau had used the party's procrastination to pre-empt the issue by appointing Mara as prime minister. In the September elections, the NFP was trounced by the Alliance, the division in the party now out in the open. Koya was replaced by Jai Ram Reddy as the Opposition leader, who then set about healing wounds and bringing the warring factions together. In 1982, the party did well but not well enough to win government. Disenchantment with the NFP and frustration with the World Bank-inspired policies of the Alliance government improved Labour's prospects, but not enough for it to fight the election alone. This it did in coalition with the NFP, with Labour leader Dr Timoci Bavadra at its head. The coalition won the election, ending the Alliance party's reign of 21 years.

THE 1987 COUP

The NFP-FLP coalition government, exceptionally talented and for the first time with fair Indo-Fijian representation in the Cabinet, challenged the underpinnings of the race-based political culture spawned by Alliance rule. The long-reigning Fijian provinces which had benefited from British patronage sensed a threat from hitherto neglected areas, such as western Viti Levu, from which Dr Bavadra came. Some defeated ministers feared investigation for corruption and mismanagement of public coffers by the incoming government, and there were many Fijians who were unwilling to accept the verdict of the ballot box and wanted Fijian control of government at any cost. 'Fiji for Fijians' was their motto. They organised themselves into an indigenous nationalist group, calling it the Taukei Movement (People of the Land), and began an active campaign of destabilisation, erecting roadblocks and torching property belonging to Indo-Fijian leaders. Sitiveni Rabuka, the third-ranking officer in the Fiji Military Forces, was approached to execute a coup, with the blessing and foreknowledge, he now says, of some of the leading Fijian chiefly politicians. On 14 May 1987, after a month in office, the coalition government was deposed in the South Pacific's first military coup in

modern times. Ironically, the date also marked the 108th anniversary of the arrival of the Indians in Fiji.

Unable to control the forces he had unleashed, Rabuka severed links with the British Crown and declared Fiji a republic in October that year. When his military administration continued to flounder, however, he handed power back to Mara and Ganilau (his paramount chief, governor general at the time of the coup and the republic's first president) in December 1987. By then, much harm had been done. The period of military rule was a time of wanton disregard for human rights. Many Indo-Fijian supporters of the coalition were publicly humiliated and brutalised. The leaders themselves had to go into hiding briefly to escape the terror of the Taukei. Queues before foreign embassies lengthened as people applied for visas to migrate. The economy teetered on the brink of collapse. A Sunday Ban, a strict observance of the Sabbath, was imposed. Hindu and Muslim places were torched or otherwise desecrated. For most Indo-Fijians, up to that point, it was the darkest period in their lives.

The major task of the Interim Administration was to devise a new constitution to replace the abrogated independence one. The Indo-Fijian community had no meaningful say in its formulation. The constitution was decreed into law on 25 July 1990 by President Ganilau. It was a draconian document and discriminated against their community, the Indo-Fijian leaders argued. The Senate comprised 34 members, 24 of whom would be Fijians. In the House of Representatives, all seats were to be contested from racial electorates. Comprising 46 per cent of the population, Indo-Fijians were allocated 27 seats in the 71-member House, while Fijians (48 per cent) were given 37. The president and the vice-president would be appointed by the Great Council of Chiefs, while chairs of the Police Services Commission and the Public Service Commission were to be Fijian. The Cabinet could authorise affirmative action policies in favour of the indigenous community. Most people in Fiji, including its architects, realised that the constitution was a flawed document, but necessary to return the country to a semblance of democracy. For that reason, the constitution stipulated a review within seven years of its promulgation.

That review took place between 1995–96 by an independent commission chaired by the former governor general of New Zealand, Sir Paul Reeves, with its two other members being Tomasi Vakatora, government nominee, and Brij V. Lal, the nominee of the Opposition. The commission's wide-ranging report recommended fundamental changes, including, especially, moving away from race-based to non-racial politics; forming multi-ethnic

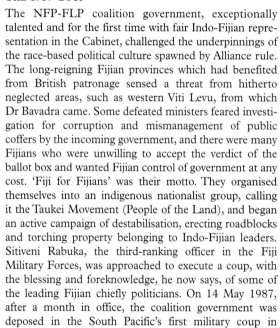

coalitions or genuinely multi-ethnic political parties. It recommended that two-thirds of the seats in the House of Representatives be contested from non-racial rolls and the remaining ones from racially reserved seats (for the time being). The parliament reversed the order, thereby entrenching race back into the constitution. The constitution was approved unanimously by parliament and blessed by the Great Council of Chiefs. Two years later, in the general elections held under the new constitution, the FLP, headed by long-time trade unionist Mahendra Chaudhry, won. Jai Ram Reddy, a key architect of the constitution and a man widely respected across the nation as a statesman of rare integrity, lost because he had formed a coalition with Sitiveni Rabuka's party. In a career marked by inexplicable transformation, Rabuka was the other key figure in the promulgation of the multiracial constitution. Rejected by his people, whom he had led for nearly two decades, Reddy retired from politics, and after a period as president of the Fiji Court of Appeal, was appointed a judge of the International Criminal Tribunal for Rwanda by the United Nations.

The Chaudhry government moved quickly to deliver on its expansive promises to set up commissions (education and human rights), institute inquiries (into corruption), and staff statutory organisations (such as the Housing Authority) with competent people, among others. The economy picked up, employment increased and foreign investment flowed in. In the process, Chaudhry made errors of judgement which his opponents exploited. He appointed his son, a non-public servant, as his personal secretary, spawning unjustified fears of nepotism. His tussle with the media, particularly the local television station, provided further fodder to his critics, who accused him of arrogance and insensitivity. His agriculture minister sacked George Speight as chairman of the Fiji Hardwood Corporation, a statutory organisation overseeing the country's lucrative timber industry. Chaudhry's assured performance as prime minister caused tremors in circles hoping for his early political demise. The issue which galvanised Fijian opinion against Chaudhry was his attempt to set up a Land Use Commission to open up idle native land to productive agricultural use. Always a sensitive issue in Fiji, land was used to whip up Fijian emotion even though many Fijians privately thought the idea was a good one. The Taukei Movement resurfaced and protest marches began in urban areas, culminating in the overthrow of the government on 19 May, exactly a year after it had won office.

As events unfolded, it became clear that the overthrow was not about indigenous rights; George Speight, part-European, was hardly credible as a Fijian nationalist. Nor was it about race; nothing the Chaudhry government did adversely affected Fijian interests. Indeed, the Chaudhry government had more Fijians in it than Indo-Fijians. It was a tussle for power within Fijian society, in particular among its three traditional confederacies. It was about

Fiji's parliament in session on the eve of the military coup of 14 May 1987, which removed the month-old multiracial government from power. Dr Timoci Bavadra, the prime minister, is closest to the camera. To his immediate right is the deputy prime minister, Harish Sharma.

the Kubuna confederacy staking its claim for national leadership against the long dominance of the Tovata, headed by Ratu Mara. There were corrupt businessmen who were alleged to have supported the anti-government camp. Defeated politicians, out of office and out of sorts, without their perks and their expensive Pajeros, lurked in the background. Speight, a failed businessman, was the frontman for other interests. He is now serving time in jail.

In the 2001 elections, Chaudhry's party regained considerable ground, but it was a Fijian party, led by former merchant banker Laisenia Qarase and aligned to George Speight's party, which won. A power-sharing provision of the constitution entitles any political party with more than 10 per cent of the seats in the House of Representatives to be invited to be taken into Cabinet. Prime Minister Laisenia Qarase at first refused to invite Labour (which was entitled to nearly half of the Cabinet portfolios given the closeness of the results), citing fundamental policy differences, but when the courts upheld Labour's right to be represented in Cabinet, Qarase offered Labour ministries of no significance, which the party called 'insulting'. The courts have often been called upon to intervene, but in the end the problem is not constitutional: the constitution is clear on power-sharing; the problem is political. Unless there is a genuine desire to work together, power-sharing will remain an idea on paper, little more.

Political uncertainty and a sense of marginalisation and exclusion from power then constitute one source of anxiety for the Indo-Fijians. The future of the sugar industry, for which Indian indentured migrants were brought to Fiji in the first place, and in whose growth the Indo-Fijians have played a pivotal role, is another.

The threat comes from the expected change in the Sugar Protocol of the Lome Convention, under which Fiji (and other countries) has sold sugar to the European Union at stable prices of two to three times the world market price with guaranteed quotas. When the Lome Convention expired in 2000 (it first came into being in 1975), the original terms of the Sugar Protocol were retained in the Cotonou Agreement, but with the acknowledgement that trade between the EU and the African, Caribbean and Pacific (ACP) countries would have to be liberalised. This places the livelihood of Indo-Fijian cane growers (in 1998 numbering 16,710, or 78.1 per cent of the total number of growers, compared to 4579, or 21.4 per cent of Fijian

> *It is possible that the people of Fiji will still be under the present decadent, divisive and dictatorial administration. It is our aim and hope, however, that the people of Fiji will instead be living under an honest, fair and democratic government working not only for the welfare of all people but seeking to give them one identity. This is the goal and promise of the Fiji Labour Party.*
>
> *Mahendra Chaudhry, extract from a speech at H. V. Evatt Memorial Foundation, Sydney, 1988.*

George Speight being led out of court on 18 February 2002 after being sentenced to death for treason. However, President Ratu Josefa Iloilo commuted the sentence to life imprisonment.

A Hindu temple at Nabila, a rural Indian settlement near Nadi, the site of Fiji's international airport. Temples such as this one are common in Indo-Fijian settlements throughout Fiji.

growers) at risk and threatens the lifeblood of the national economy. The sugar industry, despite years of non-investment in its infrastructure, is the most important export commodity earner and the largest employer in Fiji. A far greater threat to the industry than an uncertain or competitive market, however, is the non-renewal of leases to Indo-Fijian tenants. The 30-year leases granted under the Agricultural Landlord and Tenant Act began expiring in 1997. Between 2001 and 2002, 44 per cent of all native leases expired; this figure is expected to reach 91 per cent by 2009. Fijian landlords refuse to lease land (as political retribution or because, in a few instances, they themselves want to enter cane cultivation) or lease them on conditions too onerous for tenants. Many formerly productive farms have reverted to bush, while the evicted tenants, often poor and unskilled and without connections, start all over again, growing vegetables and doing menial jobs. The emotional turmoil caused by political and economic uncertainties has taken its toll on the community, with an increase in suicides, domestic violence, poverty and bourgeoning squatter settlements around towns and cities.

Indo-Fijians who have skills, money or relatives who have settled abroad emigrate. It is often said that there is hardly a single Indo-Fijian family in Fiji which does not have at least one member or someone close already living overseas. Indo-Fijians had been migrating in small numbers since before independence, but the trickle turned into a torrent after the coups of 1987. Since then, an estimated 120,000 have left, twice the number who originally came to Fiji. About 40 per cent of the migrants leave for Australia, followed by New Zealand, the US and Canada. It is the best and the brightest who leave: architects, engineers, technicians, accountants, teachers, doctors, dentists, veterinarians

Sitiveni Rabuka holding a copy of Fiji's new constitution, 23 May 2000.

A letter from Sushma's mother in Labasa, December 2003

Fiji ke halat bahut kharab ho gai hae
(The situation in Fiji is very bad now)
Hindustani par bahut museebat aahi rahi hae
(Indians are facing a lot of problems)
Jameen le lete hain, ghar men se nikal dete hai
(Their land is taken away, they are forced to leave their homes)
Atyachar karte hain
(They commit atrocities [against us])
Girmit se kamti nahi hae ye time
(Today is no less than girmit)
Naojawan bhagte hai
(Young people are leaving)
Budhe log rahi jate hain, inhi ke gulami karte hai...
(Older people are left behind, slaving for them [Fijians])
Kuch samajh me nahi ata age kya bite gi
(Don't know what will happen in the future)
Sushma Devi bhul chuk sudhar le, bahut ache nahi likh pati hu
(Sushma, pardon any mistakes, can't write too well)
Meri aankh kharab hae
(My eyes are bad)
Bacho ko asirvadh, sabko namaste
(Blessings to the children and greetings to everyone)

Mai hu aap ki mataji
(From your *mataji* [mother])

John Cornell and Sushma Raj, 'A Passage to Sydney', in Brij V. Lal (ed.) Bittersweet, 2004.

and other professionals. Those who remain in Fiji expect their migrating relatives to assist them. They often do, with remittances playing an increasingly important part in the economy. Migrants help with scholarships, meet the medical expenses of close relatives, and raise funds to help hurricane, flood and drought relief efforts.

Official response to Indo-Fijian emigration is mixed. Some express genuine regret at the loss of valuable skill and talent, while there is quiet satisfaction among those who see the decline in the Indo-Fijian population as the first essential step in the 'Fijianisation' of their country, reclaiming its indigenous soul back. Indo-Fijians are caught between the proverbial rock and a hard place. They are accused of being disloyal to Fiji because they emigrate; and those who remain find it difficult to find a place at the Fijian table. The government is reluctant to invest in its citizens whom it knows it will lose in the end, while the denial of opportunity only strengthens the Indo-Fijians' resolve to migrate.

Indo-Fijians once comprised half the population of Fiji. In a few years time, their numbers will decline to about a third because of low birth rates and migration. Their history in Fiji has been a tragically ironic one. They were brought to the islands so that the Fijians could be spared the ordeal of plantation work and thus preserve their way of life, their land and their labour, all under threat from European encroachment. The Fijians prospered in their subsistence environment because Indians toiled on the plantations, but they came to view Indians as their nemesis. After more than a century, Indo-Fijians still struggle for political equality in the land of their birth. The deeply felt but often unacknowledged need of the human soul to belong, to have a place of one's own, to be rooted, is denied them. How long, they ask, should a people live in a place before they are allowed to call it home? 'From Immigration to Emigration'; that may in time come to be the epitaph of Fiji's Indo-Fijian community.

Brij V. Lal

AUSTRALIA

Although the history of migration from India to Australia dates back to the early 19th century, large numbers of people of Indian origin began arriving only after the 1980s. Despite its short history in Australia, the Indian community has become significant not only in numbers but also in its contribution to the economic sector, education and sociocultural life of the 'host' country.

THE EARLY 19TH CENTURY

Indians first arrived in Australia soon after the British established the penal colony of New South Wales in 1788. Trading ships leaving the Bay of Bengal for Australia had Indian crews, some of whom stayed at least for a time in Australia. Between 1800 and 1860 Indians were brought to Australia to work as labourers or domestic help, and between 1800 and 1816, a small group of Indian convicts were sent to New South Wales by British colonial authorities. In 1816, a group of nine Indian workers were brought over as 'free' immigrants by William Browne, a large landowner in New South Wales. Most of these labourers were recruited by British subjects living in India who later resettled in Australia.

Following the abolition of slavery in the British Empire in 1833, a small number of Indians were recruited as labourers for Australia. Records from the mid-1830s show that employers, such as Mr Bruce from Calcutta, arranged for a small group of Indians to be sent over when they settled in South Australia.

With the development of the hinterland, demand for labour increased and Indian indentured workers were introduced by pastoralists in the 1830s and 1840s. In 1837, John Mackay recruited about 40 Indian labourers to work in New South Wales. They were mostly Dhangars, a hill tribe of Chota Nagpur. More Indian men arrived over the next 10 years and were dispersed into neighbouring colonies. The threat of a violent reaction from European settlers forced the Indian government to restrict the

emigration of Indian coolie labour. In 1839, the Indian Emigration Act, enforcing restrictions on Indian indentured labour to Australia, came into effect.

However, a sponsorship scheme was allowed, which assured a return passage to India for young married couples with up to two children. A few Indians took advantage of this scheme and migrated as itinerant merchants. Similarly, 200 Anglo-Indians (of 'mixed' European and Indian origin) arrived, many to work as compositors for Henry Parkes's printing press. In 1840, Edward Gleeson employed Indians on the sheep station he had established along the Hutt River in Western Australia. In 1843, Major Alexander Davidson, who came from India, brought with him 14 Indian servants and settled in Port Phillip. One year later, P. Friell, also formerly a resident of India, brought 25 domestic workers to Sydney, including women and children. In 1846, the ship *Orwell* brought 51 Indian coolies under private indenture for three landowners.

Between 1843–50, attempts were made to recruit Indians on a large scale, but this failed due to strong opposition in Australia against non-European migration. A few Indians migrated independently, some of whom became domestic servants. In 1857, the Victoria census recorded 277 persons of 'Indian or Hindoo race'—race was a common classification used during the period to register colour and religious roots. In this census, Hindus outnumbered Muslims and Sikhs from Punjab.

THE LATER 19TH CENTURY

The period 1861–1901 marked the second phase of Indian immigration to Australia. The 1860s saw the arrival of migrants who were commonly described as 'Ghans' (short for 'Afghans') and 'turban-wearing Pathans'. Other common terms used to identify groups among them included 'Hindoos', 'Syrians', 'Punjabis' and 'Baluchis'. Notwithstanding such descriptions, these migrants originated variously from Punjab, Sind, the North-West

Map 8.61

AUSTRALIA

The first signs of public reaction to the presence of Indians in Australia are depicted in illustrations such as these printed in The Illustrated Australian, *1893. Some of the stereotypes included the 'niggardliness' of Hindus and Muslims, who were said to hoard money to take back to their country. They were also shown as beggars and as being less frugal with drinks.*

Camels being unloaded from the steamer SS Bengal *at the Port Augusta Wharf, 1893. Most of these camels were imported from Punjab, Sind, the North-West Frontier Province, Baluchistan and Afghanistan.*

Frontier Provinces, Baluchistan and Afghanistan. In Australia, they were officially classified as 'Indians' and were racially identified as such. The majority were Muslims who spoke Pashto, Baluchi or Urdu-Punjabi, while some were Sikhs and Hindus.

Employed as cameleers (camel drivers), their arrival followed the development of a new mode of transport (camels) that was considered well suited to the harsh desert terrain in the interior of Australia, where horses and bullocks had proven unsuccessful. These cameleers participated in expedition and pastoral enterprises in the Australian outback. Three of them were enlisted to accompany the camels for the Burke and Wills expedition to the outback. Later, these cameleers began camel breeding stations or caravanserais. Some worked as agricultural labourers, others as hawkers or pedlars and traders in rural and outback Australia. Liberalised licensing provisions in Victoria in the 1890s attracted many of these people and, over time, a number ventured out to work in the gold mines of Victoria.

In addition to the arrival of the cameleers, the period also witnessed the coming of immigrants who worked as crew on liners calling at Australian ports and as horse grooms, and yet more arrived upon hearing of opportunities in Australia from families already there. The introduction of the Indian Coolie Act in 1862 in northwest Queensland facilitated the introduction of Asian labourers to cotton and sugar cane plantations. This was extended in 1882. Some settled in small towns and rural areas in New South Wales, Victoria and Queensland. Others found work as cane-cutters in northern New South Wales and northern Queensland. The majority of immigrant Punjabis settled in Queensland or northern New South Wales. Today, the Sikh settlement in Woolgoolga remains one of the largest rural Indian communities in Australia.

During this period, the Indian population rose steadily from 300 in 1857 to 2000 in 1871 (58 were recorded as Ceylon-born) and 3000 by the end of 1880. The increase in the number of Indians bred resentment among the local population. Following violent opposition to the continued immigration of Indian coolie labour, the acts of 1862 and 1882, which enabled Indian migration, were repealed in 1886. However, free immigrants continued

Many of the camel hawkers were Sikhs, like Kan Singh, shown here standing proudly beside his camels.

to arrive, including some 500 Sinhalese Buddhists who came to work on the banana plantations.

In the 1890s, the hysteria surrounding imported coloured labour resurfaced. In 1895, articles with derogatory references to the presence of 'black and turbaned heathens' appeared in the New South Wales press. The final decades of the 19th century saw further legislative measures introduced by the colonial government in Australia to restrict or prohibit coloured or Asian immigration. At the turn of the 20th century, the presence of about 4500 ethnic Indians alongside other non-white ethnic groups was enough to fuel apprehension in the dominant white population, leading to the birth of the 'White Australia policy'.

At a meeting of colonial premiers in 1896, the call to exclude the entry of all 'coloured races' was reaffirmed. These prohibitions also extended to Indians despite their status as British subjects at the time. In spite of these prohibitions, at the beginning of the 20th century more than 7000 India-born persons were present in Australia, of whom about 58 per cent were thought to be 'ethnic Indians'. Most were labourers in sugar cane and banana plantations, hawkers and pedlars, although some moved about as free traders and entrepreneurs and a handful joined the skilled labour force.

1901 AND AFTER

The year 1901 was a vital year in the history of Indian migration to Australia as it saw the inauguration of the Federation and the passing of the Immigration Restriction Act (otherwise known as the White Australia policy). Following the enactment, Asian entry to Australia became very difficult and there was virtually no further Indian immigration over the next 50 years. The number of India-born Indians in Australia fell initially and then stabilised at around 6500 or 7000 until after the end of World War II. Even so, some Indians, as British subjects, were allowed to enter when their labour was needed. Indians who migrated prior to 1901 were also permitted to stay, although they continued to be the focus of discriminatory laws and restrictions.

New requirements were placed on those who stayed, which had to be met before they could be employed. In 1913, Queensland passed a law restricting the participation of coloured labour in the production of sugar unless they were exempted by 'certificates to say they had passed a dictation test in such a language as the Secretary for Agriculture might direct.' A few years later, similar

Legends of early Indian contact

Pre-19th century Indian contact with Australia is shrouded in legend. P. Bilimoria has narrated two such stories in his account, *The Hindus and Sikhs in Australia* (1996). The first legend refers to Indian merchants arriving at the northern tip of Australia from the trading ports of Java and Sumatra in the early centuries of the last millennium. In Melaka, from where Indian goods were shipped to remote islands such as the Moluccas and Timor, South Asian merchants had settled in small numbers. There was speculation by Hindus about a vast inhabited land mass further to the south of Indonesia, 'beyond the moving sea'. However, fear of the formidable abyss of 'Pausengi', a mythic demonic tree, prevented contact with this 'barbaric' world.

The second legend appears less credible. It relates to Tamil Hindus who had sailed a long way southwards on outrigger boats, establishing commercial and cultural links with inhabitants of the Polynesian, Melanesian and Austral islands. According to anthropologist A. P. Elkin, there may be connections between the occult-yoga practices of Tibet and India and the psychic practices of 'Aboriginal men of high degree'. The Australian Aborigines seem disposed to this linkage with their own ancestry. Many Aboriginal stories refer to the coming of 'our people' from India back in antiquity, contrasting it with the more recent invasion of the 'white men'. Similarly, one of Australia's greatest historians, Professor Manning Clark, has suggested that one of the three groups of Aborigines (who scientists and historians call Carpentarians) travelled to Australia from Ceylon, just south of India, between 20,000 and 40,000 years ago. According to this theory, the Carpentarians forced other groups of Aborigines further south and became the Aborigines of Northern Australia.

provisions were applied to the banana industry, although qualifications to these provisions were introduced subsequently to exempt Indians classified as British subjects.

The next significant period of immigration from India began in 1950 and mainly involved India-born British citizens and Anglo-Indians who had left India after independence. The relaxation of the Immigration Restriction Act in 1966 facilitated the immigration of Anglo-Indian and ethnic Indian professionals from India. The population of India-born Indians increased to 15,754 in 1966, 41,657 in 1981, and 77,689 in 1996. The new arrivals included many professionals such as doctors, teachers, computer programmers and engineers. Unlike earlier settlers, those who arrived after the 1950s came from many parts of India and belonged to various religious, linguistic and cultural groups.

Their numbers, however, do not account for Australian migrants of Indian origin, born in countries other than India, and second-generation Australian Indians. The number of Indo-Fijians who have migrated following the two coups in Fiji is estimated to be over 40,000, and migrants from Malaysia, Mauritius and Singapore have contributed as well to the number of people of Indian origin in Australia. For example, 3440 Malaysians and 2240 Singaporeans have stated their ancestry as Indian, and 390 Mauritians have stated their religion as Hindu, thus linking their ancestry to India.

Thus, the combined figure for people of South Asian origin makes this group one of the largest ethnic minority communities in Australia. Furthermore, given that the rate of population increase for South Asian communities in Australia (see Table 8.34) is greater than most other groups, it appears that the population of this community is set to grow at a much faster rate than most other large ethnic minority communities in Australia. The Italian and Greek communities in Australia, for example, have experienced a negative growth of 8 per cent, and the Lebanese and Vietnamese communities have experienced growth of only 2 per cent. Only the Chinese community has experienced a significant growth of 29 per cent between 1996 and 2001.

Sushma Raj

INDIAN CULTURAL IDENTITY IN AUSTRALIA

A distinguishing feature of Indians in Australia is their diversity, both in terms of geographical origin and their expression of cultural identity. Indians in Australia often identify themselves through their particular cultural or linguistic associations. Differentiation on the basis of religion is also marked since not all Indians in Australia profess Hinduism, which is followed by an overwhelming majority of people in India. Among India-born Indians there are large numbers of both Hindus and Christians, and relatively small numbers of Sikhs, Muslims and others. Even ancestry differentiates Indians because a minority of those born in India claim British ancestry. In view of this heterogeneity, the notion of a singular cultural identity is arguable. Paradoxically, heterogeneity and unity coexist.

Cultural heterogeneity does not negate a sense of being Indian or identifying in myriad ways with India. For some, the identification is derived from close personal and social connections such as birthplace, family and property in India. For others who are not born in India, the links are perhaps less tangible, more affective and imagined. Thus, for Indians from the diasporic communities outside the Indian subcontinent, identification with India is based upon any one or a combination of factors such as

Figure 8.12

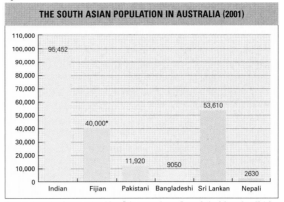

THE SOUTH ASIAN POPULATION IN AUSTRALIA (2001)

*Source: Australia Census, 2001. Note: *An approximate figure derived from the official 'Fijian' population of 44,040, which comprised approximately 10% who can be classified as native Fijians (i.e. not Indo-Fijians). This figure was arrived at after examining census data of Fiji-born Australians in categories such as language, ancestory and religion.*

language, food, kinship through marriage, religion, music and the consumption of Bollywood products and other regional (non-Hindi) celluloid productions. For those diasporic and non-diasporic Indians engaged in business between Australia and India, commercial ties are also a significant contributor to institutional and professional engagement with India.

ORGANISING THE COMMUNITY

A major source of heterogeneity among Indians in Australia is language, which in India corresponds to regional differences. Though Hindi is the common language in northern India, in regions or states such as West Bengal, Tamil Nadu and Punjab for example, identification and cultural pride associated with Bengali, Tamil and Punjabi languages respectively are particularly strong. The extensive network of language-based associations demonstrates the replication of regional identities in the Australian context. For the Sikhs in Australia, religion, region (Punjab) and language all combine to shape a distinct identity. These associations, however, are not exclusive in their membership and casual participants in their activities are welcome regardless of regional, religious or other differences. In the case of the Gujarati Association in Melbourne, for example, people of Gujarati origin from various parts of the world come together to

Table 8.34

POPULATION INCREASE OF SOUTH ASIANS BETWEEN 1996 AND 2001	
Indian	23.0%
Fijian (90% Indo-Fijian)	19.0%
Bangladeshi	79.0%
Nepali	77.0%
Pakistani	43.0%
Sri Lankan	14.0%

Source: Australia Census, 1996 and 2001.

Harmohan Singh Walia

The crowd roared with applause when Harmohan Singh Walia carried the Olympic torch through Greenacre in Sydney on 12 September 2000. The atmosphere became electric when the local bhangra team joined in with drums. Swaying to the bhangra beat, the crowd shouted 'Bole So Nihal, Sat Sri Akal'.

Walia migrated to Australia on 1 February 1991 with his family. An engineer by profession, he began serving the Indian community through the multicultural community station, SBS Radio, and Sikh religious institutions. Walia was the first Indian to be unanimously pre-selected as the Federal Labour candidate for Mitchell in the October 2004 elections. Though he lost, he brought about a 1 per cent swing towards Labour in Mitchell. He was able to unite all Indian communities—and earned their cooperation—along with other ethnic and Australian communities. 'My objective to contest the Federal election was to let Australians know who we are and that we are a part of their society. My Labour candidature is showing our existence in the region,' he said.

Mr Singh realising his Olympic dream.

The 2001 distribution by state and territory shows that New South Wales, with 37,930, had the largest number of India-born migrants to Australia, followed by Victoria (30,690), Western Australia (13,120) and Queensland (7190).

celebrate important religious occasions such as Navarathri and Diwali. For a few Gujarati Muslims who may irregularly attend these functions, the opportunity to speak the Gujarati language, enjoy the food and socialise with people who share a similar cultural background is an important attraction.

When it comes to Bengali-speakers, cultural identity assumes a radically heterogeneous or hybrid character because it transcends national borders and religious distinctions that were historically marked by violence and trauma associated with the partition of India. Thus, the Bengalis from India and Bangladesh participate jointly in cultural activities such as the staging of the *jatra*, which is a genre of popular drama. Bengalis from India and Bangladesh also mingle freely at other functions hosted by their respective associations. Similarly, younger Bengalis belonging to the two national groups socialise with each other, though to some extent this depends upon their parents' predilection for interaction with people from one or the other community.

These associations are important sites of cultural expression and provide communicative and social spaces where the heterogeneity and multiculturalism of both India and Australia are represented. The celebration of seasonal festivals such as Onam in Kerala and Poila Baishakh in West Bengal are organised by their respective associations. Similarly, religious celebrations such as Navarathri and Durga Puja are organised by the Gujarati and Bengali associations respectively. Occasions commemorating the birthdays of local heroes such as Shivaji in Maharashtra and the poets Rabindranath Tagore and Kazi Nazrul Islam in Bengal are also celebrated by these associations. National celebrations such as Independence Day and Republic Day are generally hosted by the federal umbrella organisations with which many of the cultural and linguistic groups are associated.

These umbrella organisations provide a space where interface with the broader Australian society is established in the various states. They represent the interests of Indians in Australia at an official level and host members of the government and opposition parties during occasions commemorating national events. At functions celebrating India's Independence Day in Melbourne, for example, key Australian political figures at both state and Federal levels have been invited to attend. During functions celebrating significant Indian national events,

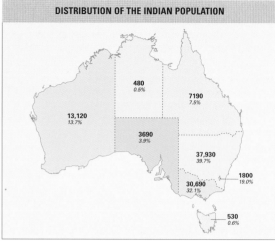

Map 8.62

DISTRIBUTION OF THE INDIAN POPULATION

480
0.5%

7190
7.5%

13,120
13.7%

3690
3.9%

37,930
39.7%

1800
19.0%

30,690
32.1%

530
0.6%

Source: Australian Bureau of Statistics Census of Population and Housing, 'Community Information Summary', 2001. Note: These figures are for the India-born community.

Indian children participate in Diwali celebrations in Sydney.

these organisations project their Indian identity through cultural performances, attire and food.

However, on other occasions involving Australian national events, the participation of Indians expresses their identification with both Australia and India. Thus, in 2005, the Federation of Indian Associations of Victoria (FIAV) marched with other ethnic communities in a parade marking Australia Day. A noteworthy expression of their dual identity was the chanting of both Australian and Indian national rallying calls, namely, 'Aussie Aussie Aussie' and '*Bharat Mata Ki Jai*' ('Long Live Mother India') respectively. Significantly, the unity of Indian identity in the parade was fractured by The Sikh Council of Victoria, which attended the parade in an independent capacity with a placard proclaiming its distinct presence.

The interface between Indians and Australians also occurs through various Indian business associations in the major cities. Though they are not specifically engaged in cultural activities, they are very important in forging an Indian identity that coalesces around commercial issues that bind Australia and India. Through these associations, Indian business people publicise the growing global economic significance of India and bring into their fold business people of Indian and non-Indian origin who are already involved in trade with India or have an interest in promoting commercial ties. The alliance between individuals from these associations and certain university academics interested in furthering Indian (and South Asian) studies within schools and tertiary institutions in Australia attests to contacts that extend beyond business and spill over into fields such as education, which is significant in a broader cultural sense.

Music and dance

An important point of contact and a source of lively cultural interaction between Indians, Pakistanis and Bangladeshis as well as other Australians is Indian music and dance of both classical and popular genres. Music is the medium through which Indian cultural identity is both projected and elevated at the broader national level. Performances of classical Indian music and dance have significant appeal among Australians of Anglo-Celtic and European origin. Many of these Australians have been attracted to performances by world-renowned Indian classical musicians who have visited the country over the years. Schools teaching Indian classical dance have also

The Sikh community in Woolgoolga

Woolgoolga and Griffith are towns populated by Sikhs and they resemble villages in Punjab. Sikh families own 95 per cent of the banana plantations in Woolgoolga. The Punjabi community in the Woolgoolga–Coffs Harbour area of New South Wales is the most residentially concentrated and probably the best-known Sikh community in Australia. Their ancestors arrived in the early decades of the 20th century. The story of how they, as Indians (a restricted race), entered and ultimately settled in 'White Australia' is unique. Their migration was the result of the political, social and economic changes that took place in both Australia and India, and because of the link that these two countries had as members of the British Empire. Significantly, the Sikh community's settlement in Woolgoolga reflects an important step in Australia's development from 'White Australia' to a nation embracing Australian multiculturalism as an ideology and policy.

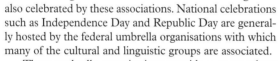

A farmer spraying insecticide at his banana plantation in Woolgoolga, an area known for its Sikh population.

attracted students of both Indian and Western origin. Some Europeans and Anglo-Celtic Australians have dedicated themselves to studying classical Indian music in both Australia and India. Adrian McNeil, an Australian ethnomusicologist of Anglo-Celtic origin who studied with guru Pt Ashok Roy in India and later in Australia, is now an accomplished *sarod* player who gives public performances in Australia as well as India.

Beyond classical Indian music, Bollywood dancing and popular Indian music have captivated many in the Australian community. The movie *Monsoon Wedding* was widely viewed by audiences in major Australian cities and generated considerable curiosity and awareness of Indian popular culture. An Australian television series featuring competition dancing in styles such as funk, hip-hop, rap, Latin and more, also presented Bollywood dancing in one of its programmes. At a fund-raising function for the victims of the Indian Ocean tsunami, which was held by university students and a local music group in Melbourne, a Bollywood dance workshop preceding the main programme attracted many young Australians of different ethnicities, the majority of whom were of Western background. In Sydney, Australia's largest city, the popularity of Bollywood dancing has spread rapidly through the efforts of Indian teachers. Several dance schools in Melbourne also offer classes in classical and Bollywood dancing. Similarly, nightclubs catering to the younger generation regularly feature Bollywood music and a fusion of bhangra (Punjabi folk dance and music), reggae, rap and other genres.

In Melbourne and Sydney there are many formal and informal Indian music groups founded by Indians from different parts of the subcontinent which provide a cultural space where people of Indian ethnicity can mingle with those from other parts of South Asia to enjoy classical, semi-classical and popular music. Through music they identify themselves with aspects of culture that transcend the national differences that divide India. The multicultural character of musical performances was vividly portrayed at a private classical music soirée in Melbourne that was hosted by a Sikh family from Malaysia. The artist playing the sitar was an Afghan resident of Melbourne, and was accompanied by a Sikh tabla player from Sydney. The audience included Indians from Melbourne who originated from different parts of the world, as well as a few Australians of Western background.

Marriage and integration

While Indian dance and music of various genres are part of the rich tapestry of multicultural Australia, the same can-

not be said as far as marriage is concerned. Among the first generation of people claiming Indian ancestry, intermarriage with those of non-Indian ancestry is low, especially compared to people of Western European and American origin in Australia. Cultural identity among first-generation Indians is therefore more strongly retained through endogamous relations. This may be due in part to the fact that many Indians have immigrated to Australia in more recent years. It is quite common for first-generation unmarried Indian migrants in Australia to find a partner from India or from among Indian diasporic communities across the world. This ensures that they are able to marry someone from the same cultural background as far as caste and religion are concerned. Though differences in regional origin may be accommodated, the same does not apply where religion is concerned. Marriage between Hindus and Muslims is both rare and fraught with tension, particularly where the families of the partners are concerned. Even some second-generation Indians report pressure from their parents to secure partners of similar cultural and religious backgrounds. Generally, marriage across religious boundaries is most likely to be accommodated where individuals come from families that are liberal-minded.

The trend favouring endogamous relations has, however, shifted with the second and third generations, as in the case of Europeans from Mediterranean countries such as Greece and Italy. Statistics indicate that second- and third-generation people of Indian descent have married outside their ancestral group to a very substantial extent compared to those of the first generation. In the case of third-generation Indians, a very large majority of both males and females have intermarried with non-Indians. The shift to an increased incidence of exogamous relations among the second and third generations indicates that Indian cultural identity is not rigidly fixed but prone to inter-generational changes in attitudes and cultural practices. It also reflects the integration of later generations of Indians into the multicultural fabric of Australian society.

Other important indicators of integration include the use of English and the acceptance of Australian citizenship. Of those Indians born in India, over 47 per cent have reported speaking English at home. The fluency of the younger generation in English is especially high as many of them have professional middle-class parents who have been educated in English-medium schools and have high aspirations for their children's future. India-born Indians have also enthusiastically embraced Australian citizenship, as evidenced by the rate at which they take up citizenship, which is above 79 per cent, compared to just over 75 per cent for those born elsewhere. Despite the relatively recent immigration of Indians to Australia and their strong cultural identity, they are very much a part of Australian society.

Salim Lakha

Posters advertising Indian cultural performances in Australia. Performances by Indians based in Australia or artistes from India have become increasingly popular since the 1990s, and Indian dance has also become a major component of youth culture in Australia.

Deepavali celebrations at the Sydney Olympic Park Athletic Centre, organised by the Hindu Council of Australia on 23 October 2005.

INDIAN BROADCAST AND PRINT MEDIA

Radio broadcasts

The development of Indian broadcast and print media in Australia has played a crucial role in the maintenance of Indian culture and values. While the earliest migrants encountered a vacuum in both these fields, this void was partly filled by Radio 2EA in Sydney and 3EA in Melbourne in 1975. The multilingual and multicultural radio set up by the Commonwealth government initially as an experiment has gone a long way in helping Indians articulate their identity and maintain their language and culture. Now known as SBS (Special Broadcasting Service), it can be heard in all major Australian cities. Aired in Hindi, Gujarati, Punjabi, Bengali, Urdu, Tamil and Kannada, the programme includes local news as well as news from India, and the service also runs special features, interviews and music.

Gradually, over the years, a number of other local community-based radio programmes in Hindi and other regional languages emerged in the major cities. Numerous community radio programmes can be heard in Sydney. Most of these local radio programmes have frequencies limited to a few suburbs. Darpan, which started in 1992 as a part of the multicultural Radio Association, broadcasts the news, *bhajans* and interviews with religious figures and community leaders. Monika Geet Mala, which began in 1998, is currently on air for four hours every Sunday. Mehak, which started in 1990, airs Hindi programmes on Sunday between 3 pm and 4 pm. Dhanak, which can be heard on Sunday between

3 pm and 6.30 pm, promotes language, popular culture and topics of interest to women. Navtarang, which broadcasts songs, stories, cooking programmes and film gossip is a subscription-based service. Amrit Kalash broadcasts devotional songs from Monday to Friday between 7 am and 8 am. Radio Jhankar can be heard between 6 am and 9 am, while Indian Link Radio is available to subscribers and broadcasts between 8 am and 10 pm daily.

Brisbane has a couple of radio stations, of which the most popular is Brisvaani, established in 1997 by Jatish and Anjali Puran, who originally hail from Fiji. Their radio station is a fully-fledged Asia Pacific commercial broadcaster. It provides a voice for the Indian community and keeps a finger on the pulse of the cultural values and needs of people of Indian background. Their aim is to promote Hindi and use it as a means of 'educating, informing, preserving and developing cross-culture and foster mutual understanding between the different Indian communities settled in Brisbane.' Despite its small size, the Indian population of Adelaide has its own radio programme in Hindi on 5EBI. The chairman of the Indian radio committee Akashvaani Adelaide, Raymond Sardhana, says, 'This one hour programme has grown to become an important icon of Indian music and culture.' The format of these programmes has been created on the basis of the rich cultural heritage of India. They air historical features, news and interviews.

Print media

In 1987, Neena and Vijay Badhwar of Sydney began a newspaper entitled *The Indian Down Under*, with a view to 'bringing India closer to Australia'. The nationally circulated newspaper covers community events and issues, profiles high achievers in the Indian community, and includes a page for children, cookery, Bollywood, spirituality and sports. The year 1994 saw the launch of another free publication targeting Indians, *Indian Link*. Its editor, Pawan Luthra, claims it is also read by mainstream Australians with an interest in India. *Indian Link* has a total readership of 50,000. *The Indian Post*, a monthly newspaper which is circulated Australia-wide, covers news and issues pertinent to the Indian diaspora. Sydney also has publications such as the *Fiji Times*, which fulfils the needs of the Indo-Fijian migrant community. The only Hindi newspaper in Australia, *Samachar Patrika*, which is also published in Sydney, enjoys good readership as well.

Popular Indian publications in Melbourne include *Bharat Times* and the *Indian Voice*. *Bharat Times*, established in 1997, has a very wide readership, with readers accessing its website as well. *Bharat Times* covers news from India and local Australian stories, and also profiles personalities.

In the wider print media, sports writer Kersi Meher Homji writes for the *Sydney Morning Herald* and other publications.

Kumud Merani

Kersi Meher Homji is a sports journalist and passionate writer about cricket.

NEW ZEALAND

INDIAN COMMUNITIES IN New Zealand date back to the late 19th century. They came from Gujarat and Punjab. Most Gujaratis migrated from villages in the Navsari and Bardoli sub-districts in the Surat district and former Baroda state, while Punjabi pioneers were predominantly from Jullundur and Hoshiarpur districts. By the late 1980s, these established patterns changed radically, with substantial Indian migration from Fiji and India, and to a lesser extent from other branches of the Indian diaspora.

The first contacts between Indians and the Maori, the indigenous people of Aotearoa/New Zealand, were brought about by ships of the British East India Company. Vessels crewed by lascars and carrying sepoys landed in New Zealand during the late 18th century. In 1814, six Indian sailors deserted at Otago Harbour. Of these, three survived and taught the Maori strategies for fighting Europeans. One survivor later took the *moko* (tattoo) and was reported to be living on Stewart Island with his Maori family in 1844. Another Bengali deserted in 1809 to live with his Maori wife in the Bay of Islands. 'Black Peter' (Edward Peters), a pioneer gold prospector from Goa, arrived in New Zealand in 1853 and facilitated Otago's 'gold rush', although a European was credited with the find. The few Indians recorded in late 19th-century Canterbury were probably servants of wealthy English settlers who had lived in India.

GUJARATI AND PUNJABI SETTLERS

The origins of the Indian diaspora in New Zealand lie with the Punjabi brothers Bir Singh Gill and Phuman Singh Gill, who arrived in 1890 via Australia. Phuman settled in New Zealand, married an English nurse and set up a confectionery business. Among the Gujaratis seeking work in New Zealand by 1903 were Narotum Barber, Keshav Chhiba, and Gulab and Makan Jivan.

During the late 19th and 20th centuries, rural Punjab and Gujarat were undergoing substantial transformations which encouraged migration. British imperialism and the monetary economy had substantially affected these

Sikh soldiers from India who were members of the New Zealand contingent at Gallipoli in 1915.

regions, with the increasing commercialisation of agriculture and customary services, taxation demands and land shortages leading to more rural debt, among other things. Families were unable to meet their subsistence needs, and an increased dependence on cash and the commodification of goods and services promoted a greater desire for material goods. This was reinforced by cultural practices, such as expenditure on weddings to enhance family and caste status. By the early 20th century, emigration was an accepted practice in the villages of Punjab and Gujarat. This was especially so among the Koli and Kanbi, the two main Gujarati castes which settled in New Zealand (where many later adopted the surname Patel), and the Jat Sikhs, a dominant landowning caste in Punjab. Some migrants to New Zealand were also from artisan castes and some were Harijans.

Global and local immigration policies, political and economic pressures and discrimination against Asians also shaped the character of Indian emigration to New Zealand. Indians did not face immigration restrictions in New Zealand until the passing of the 1899 Immigration Restriction Act. This imposed an English language test for immigrants not from Britain or Ireland. Although few Indians were resident in New Zealand around that time (the 1896 census put the figure at 46), there was still an outcry in parliament about itinerant 'Hindoo' hawkers. Despite the 1899 act, the number of Indian immigrants in New Zealand increased, partly because of exclusionist policies towards Indians in other white settler countries. The increase can be partly attributed to a reluctance on the part of immigrants to follow their families to South Africa after reports of discrimination there. Shipping routes to the South Pacific brought some Indians to Australia, but by 1901, this destination was closed to Indians, and so they sailed on to New Zealand. The possibility of migration to New Zealand was also of interest to Indians in Fiji. 'Cramming schools' there prepared migrants for New Zealand's immigration test.

The increasing migration of Indians to New Zealand prompted demands to exclude them. This was ostensibly justified by fears of economic competition and

Edward Peters came to New Zealand from Goa in 1853.

The first known Punjabis in New Zealand were Sikh brothers Phuman Singh Gill (above) and his brother Bir Singh Gill, who arrived in 1890.

Map 8.63

NEW ZEALAND

AUSTRALIA

Auckland

North Island

Nelson Wellington

South Island

Christchurch

NEW ZEALAND

Dunedin

0   500 kilometres
0   500 miles

N

exaggerated representations of the moral and sexual threat of Asians. The 1920 Immigration Restriction Amendment Act introduced a permit system for prospective migrants not of British birth and parentage, but exceptions were granted to the children, wives and fiancées of Indians resident in New Zealand before 1921. It became virtually impossible for Indians not related to the Gujarati and Punjabi pioneers to emigrate to New Zealand before the immigration policy changed in 1974.

Few Indian women migrated to New Zealand before World War II. Most of the early Indian male migrants regarded their time in New Zealand as temporary, but several had their sons join them there. Many of these young men attended school in New Zealand and worked in family businesses. Daya Kaur was probably the first Indian woman to settle with her family in New Zealand, arriving in 1907. She became known as Nellie Singh, the only Indian woman in a coal mining community on New Zealand's remote West Coast. In 1951, Asian residents who temporarily left New Zealand were only allowed a re-entry immigration permit valid for 18 months. One reason for this was to encourage family migration. Four-year immigration re-entry permits were reintroduced in 1957, but mothers had to accompany sons under the age of 15 who were joining their fathers in New Zealand.

Besides immigration restrictions, Indians faced other forms of discrimination in New Zealand. In 1925, the White New Zealand League, formed in the vegetable-growing centre of Pukekohe, with the support of other organisations, including the Returned Soldiers' Association, drummed up fears of an impending Asian invasion and the dangers of racial miscegenation. This was despite the 1921 census recording only 671 Indians in the country. These organisations wanted Asians repatriated and excluded from business and buying or leasing land. Submissions to a government committee in 1929 accused Indian market gardeners of economically and sexually exploiting Maori women. Discrimination against Asians continued in some centres but was successfully challenged by Indian organisations. In 1927, the Wellington City Council attempted to insist that Indian bottle collectors wear identifiable armbands, and during the 1950s, tried not to employ Indian bus drivers. The Fruit and Vegetable Committee requested the compulsory registration of

Traditional Indian products which found a growing market in New Zealand: medicinal 'Root Pills' and 'Bombay Chutney'.

A contingent of Indian Imperial troops in New Zealand's capital city, Wellington.

Asian fruiterers' thumbprints in 1937. Barbers in Pukekohe refused to serve Asians, who were also banned from first-class cinema seats there during the 1950s.

Examples of such hostility, however, detract from support shown by other New Zealanders towards Indians. In particular, many female Indian migrants, often speaking very little English and lacking the support of female kin, formed close relationships with their non-Indian female neighbours. Some Indians learned to speak Maori and were accepted by rural Maori communities. In fact, the 1945 census declared 125 births of Indian and Maori parentage. These children were raised predominantly by the Maori, although some of them identified more with the Indian community.

Regular visits to villages back in India were important, especially when female family members remained there. Some Indian pioneers retired to India, but most of their children did not. Links with villages were sustained through remittances and visits to see to the construction of houses or the purchase of land, to make marriage arrangements, or for ceremonial and religious obligations. Caste remained a significant consideration when selecting marriage partners for children. Although caste—identification with endogamous sub-groups (*jati*)—was partially reproduced among Gujaratis in New Zealand, the 'caste system' was not a feature of Indian society here.

ECONOMIC AND OCCUPATIONAL CHANGE

Throughout their history in New Zealand, a high proportion of Indians, especially Gujaratis, have been involved in retail at various periods, including hawking or running fruit and grocery shops and, later, supermarkets. The Gujaratis established fruit and vegetable businesses and general stores in remote rural areas. Their other early occupations included collecting bottles and rags for recycling, domestic work in hotels or boarding houses, and labouring in brick factories. A few Punjabis worked in coal mines in Westland during the early 20th century. Until World War II, the most common occupations for Punjabis were flax cutting, farm work, drain digging and the arduous clearing of scrub and weeds on remote hilly farms on the North Island. When unemployment increased during the 1930s economic depression, some Indians returned permanently to their villages in India.

In the early 20th century, very few Indians were professionally qualified. The two exceptions were medical doctors: Dr Baldev Singh Share, who was educated in Europe, emigrated to New Zealand in 1920; and Dr Mutyala Satyanand, who arrived as a secondary school student in 1927 from Fiji, went on to graduate from Otago University. Both were also prominent leaders of New Zealand's Indian community. The first president of the New Zealand Indian Central Association was Sadanand N. Mahraj, who studied law at Auckland University in the 1920s before working as a solicitor. He later returned to his home in Fiji and became a member of the Executive Council.

After World War II, employment and business opportunities shifted to urban New Zealand. Many Gujaratis set up grocery shops in the expanding suburbs. These businesses relied heavily on female and family labour. The deregulation of the New Zealand economy after 1984 also enabled many New Zealand Indians to invest in grocery stores—known as dairies.

While the image of the Indian as a shopkeeper has been dominant in New Zealand, occupations have become more diverse. Despite opposition, from the 1920s some Indians began to purchase or lease land in areas such as Franklin, the county where the White New Zealand League was based. By the 1950s, several Punjabis had established successful dairy farms in the Waikato and Thames valleys. Mangal Singh developed the acclaimed Mount Cosy Jersey Stud Farm on property purchased in 1935. Auckland, Wellington and Hamilton attracted the most Indians. With the exception of Christchurch, few Indians settled on the South Island.

After World War II, increasing numbers of New Zealand Indians worked in factories. Although during the 1980s many faced redundancy with factory closures, unemployment among New Zealand Indians was minimal, as has always been the case. From the 1970s, a growing number of Indians were employed in clerical, professional and technical positions, and other services. The 2001 census revealed these occupational changes and also the continuation of traditional work patterns: 24 per cent of New Zealand Indians were employed in retail compared to 11 per cent of the total population, but 44 per cent were in white-collar occupations compared to 40 per cent of the general population. This reflected a marked occupational shift among New Zealand Indians during the 1990s, with a dramatic decline in the proportion of self-employed Indians. Greater tertiary education among second- and third-generation New Zealand Indians and the global immigration of skilled workers, especially from Fiji, accounted for the shift to management, professional and technical positions. Changes to New Zealand's immigration policies after 1984 promoted the entry of skilled and business migrants. Indians could also visit New Zealand with an offer from a sponsor and then apply for permanent residence, or they could temporarily reside on study or work permits. (In 2001 as well, Indian participation in the workforce was higher, at 77 per cent, than that of the general population, which stood at 67 per cent.)

Between 1967 and 1987, Indo-Fijians were contracted by the Fijian and New Zealand governments to work in New Zealand under various schemes. They laboured in scrub cutting and low-paid, demanding agricultural work on the North Island, and in tussock grubbing in North Canterbury. The schemes extended to fruit picking, tobacco, vegetable and forest cultivation, and halal slaughtering. Some of these workers remained illegally in New Zealand to become permanent residents. Since the late 1980s, employers there have turned to South Asia for low-paid guest workers, particularly for fruit and vegetable harvesting.

REFUGEES AND RESETTLEMENT

New Zealand has accepted a small number of Indian refugees since 1972, when 243 Ugandan Indians were relocated there. Later refugees included small numbers of Pakistanis and Bangladeshis. Although not officially refugees, the sudden resettlement of thousands of Indo-Fijians since 1987 dramatically increased the size and diversity of New Zealand's Indian population.

A more liberal Immigration Act in 1987 encouraged more applications from Indo-Fijians wanting to settle in New Zealand, but this was suspended when thousands lodged applications to migrate following military coups in Fiji in May 1987. After a second coup and during the subsequent military rule, more Indo-Fijians fled the violence and discrimination, heading for New Zealand and other

destinations such as Australia, Canada and the US. The violence of a civilian coup in 2000 prompted thousands of Indo-Fijians to migrate to New Zealand. Some Indo-Fijians had kinship links with New Zealand's established Gujarati and Punjabi communities, though most Indo-Fijians were descended from indentured labourers. There were also some ties with the small number of Indo-Fijians who had originally emigrated to New Zealand as guest workers, students or professionals. The post-1987 influx of Indo-Fijians caused a tremendous upsurge not only in the number of Indians in New Zealand, but also in the availability and diversity of South Asian products, services and cultural facilities in New Zealand.

In 1981, about 46 per cent of the country's Indian population was born in New Zealand, 31 per cent in India, 13 per cent in Fiji and 10 per cent in other countries. By 2001, the proportion of New Zealand-born Indians had fallen to 29 per cent, while the proportion of Indians born in Fiji had risen to 31.3 per cent, and the proportion of those born elsewhere stood at 40 per cent. Those born in India included not only Gujaratis and Punjabis who were linked to the original Indian community, but also a rapidly growing proportion of recent arrivals from other regions in India.

INDIAN CULTURE IN NEW ZEALAND

The discrimination faced by Indian settlers in New Zealand was a catalyst for them to form Indian associations. In 1918, the Auckland Indian Association was established to oppose racism. The New Zealand Indian Central Association was formed in 1927 in response to the threat from the White New Zealand League. Indar Singh Randhawa served as its first general secretary. Indian associations emerged in other centres as well. These associations also provided crucial social and cultural support. Their branches collected funds to establish community halls and buildings for religious and cultural activities, including weddings. The Pukekohe association opened

The Pukekohe branch of the New Zealand Indian Central Association, founded in the late 1920s to provide social and cultural support for the Indian community, built New Zealand's first Indian community hall in 1953.

Nehru Hall in 1953, the Auckland branch built Gandhi Hall in 1954, and the Wellington Indians established Bharat Bhavan in 1959.

Indo-Fijians have formed separate organisations, beginning in 1977 with the Fiji Association in Auckland. It hosts sporting and cultural events, and also sponsors Indian dancers and musicians from Fiji and India. Indo-Fijians of South Indian descent established the first branch of the Then India Sanmarga Ikya Sangam (TISI) in Auckland in 1989. This association is closely affiliated with its original counterpart in Fiji and promotes South Indian culture and languages, offers community support, oversees the Thiri Subramaniyar Temple, and in 2002 constructed the Harish Chandra Kovil in Auckland for Hindu funeral rites.

Indians in New Zealand established many sports clubs during the 1930s. Here, the Wellington Indians are playing the Victoria University of Wellington. The Indians won 1–0.

Several other Indian organisations have emerged following the post-1980s waves of Indian migration to New Zealand, including the New Zealand Tamil Society, New Zealand Telugu Association, Fiji Indian Satsang Mandal, Marathi Association, New Zealand Kannada Koota, Goan Overseas Association New Zealand, Probasee Bengalee Association, Pakistani Association, Bangladesh New Zealand Friendship Society and the Ramayan Sanstha. Some of these organisations are secular, but many have links to religious groups. Some provide social and cultural networks, while others offer new migrants support and contact with the host community. From the 1970s, women formed their own groups, including Mahila Samaj within the Auckland, Wellington and Pukekohe Indian associations. The Mahila Samaj has taken a leading role in organising religious festivals and fund-raising activities. The New Zealand Maathar Sangam, for South Indian women, is part of the TISI. Crucial support for Indian women facing domestic violence has come from the Shakti Asian Women's Support Group, founded in 1995, and New Zealand's first Asian women's refuge in 1998. Shanti Niwas is another welfare initiative; it caters to the rising number of older Indian women and men in New Zealand.

Indian communities have sought to preserve their mother tongues in New Zealand. Gujarati language classes began during the 1950s in Wellington and Auckland and, later, the New Zealand Sikh Society taught Punjabi and Urdu. By the 1980s, other groups had established Hindi language classes. Since the 1990s, many newly established Indian associations have offered language classes in Fiji Hindi, Tamil, Telugu, Bengali, Kannada and Malayalam, among others.

Several groups offer regional Indian dance classes, while institutions such as the New Zealand Academy of Bharata-Natyam and the New Zealand Carnatic Music Society offer classical training and performances. Indian popular culture has been present in New Zealand since the 1950s, when Indian associations screened Hindi movies. These events were important social occasions that were later eclipsed by movie-viewing at home. By the 1990s, Indian movies were being filmed in New Zealand as well with the support of local people. The Internet has become a medium for the spread of popular culture for New Zealand Indians, and news about the local and global Indian diaspora circulates widely. The most successful local Indian website, www.indiannewslink.co.nz, launched in 1999, began as a print publication. Gujarati newspapers were locally published and in circulation much earlier—*Aryodaya* in 1921 and *Uday* between 1933–35.

Sports has been an extremely popular activity among New Zealand Indians. Participation in hockey and cricket has been a key means through which New Zealand Indians have come together as a community and interacted with other New Zealanders. In the late 1920s in Wellington and Auckland, Indians played hockey and cricket on Sundays, sometimes using the lids of banana boxes as bats. Inspired by the All-India Hockey Team's New Zealand tour, Indians formed sports associations in Auckland and Wellington during the 1930s. In the early 1960s, the New Zealand Indian Sports Association was established. In the 1970s, women formed their own teams. Indian hockey players and cricketers such as Ramesh Patel, Mohan Patel and Dipak Patel have achieved national and international success. Since the 1980s, the range of sporting activities has diversified. Soccer and netball have been popular among Indo-Fijians in New Zealand, and international tournaments are held between New Zealand, Fiji and Australia.

Diet is a fundamental aspect of the Indian lifestyle that has undergone profound change in New Zealand. The early pioneers faced considerable problems in sustaining an Indian diet because of the scarcity of appropriate ingredients until the 1980s. Many Gujaratis were vegetarians but found it extremely difficult to adhere to

The circumstances prevailing at present are such in New Zealand that speak for themselves the need of organising the scattered Indian Community. To bring the matter to a close consideration a meeting of the Indians was arranged in Taumarunui on the 17th of April 1926.

Thoughts at the meeting were freely exchanged from all sides. Pukekohe menace was a top subject in the debate. The words of Queen Victoria were once again recalled with condemn the present menace frankly offered against us by the selfish white people. The declaration of Queen Victoria is treated as null and void. She was Queen Victoria who said, 'There shall not be in the eye of the law any distinction or disqualification whatever founded on mere distinction of colour, origin, language or creed but the protection of the law in letter or substance shall be extended impartially to all alike.' The Indian Community notes with regret that these words of great honour are treated as a mere scrap of paper. It was argued at the meeting that Indians being the British subjects deserve all protection in the eye of the law as those of the whites. It was appreciated that equality is God's gift to human beings and this principal is as sacred to the Indians as souls to them. The white New Zealand league's action were wholeheartedly condemned as they are not in the right spirit. The white New Zealand league is issuing vague and misleading statements to cause misunderstandings in the minds of the peaceful New Zealanders to give growth to racial hatred was the opinion of every Indian attending the meeting.

The meeting regarded it as of great importance to carry on a propaganda in face of the white N.Z. League to supply with correct information to the N.Z. public to promote good understandings. The Indian hearts were very sore on the point that there was a time when we threw our lot with the whites in the hour of need but now it the time when we are regarded as unfit to live on their sides in times of peace. It was agreed upon that a man is known by his deeds. Justice and fairplay stand equally for the whites as well as the black. Different colour is due to living under different atmosphere. So a unanimous demand for forming as Association was created at the meeting. [sic]

Report by Indar Singh Randhawa at the inaugural meeting of the Country Section,
New Zealand Indian Central Association, 1926,
at which a decision was made to form a New Zealand Indian Association.

During the late 20th century, temples were built in New Zealand. Pictured here is the Bharat Bhavan Indian Cultural Centre, opened in Wellington in 1992.

this during the early years of residence in New Zealand. Male migrants assumed domestic duties, including cooking, that would have been avoided in India. When Indian women joined them, they painstakingly reinvented ways of sustaining a regional diet that accommodated religious rules. Most of these first-generation Indian women also continued wearing the sari or *salwar kamiz* in their new home. Men abandoned wearing Indian dress in public, including some Sikhs, who discarded their turbans. Indians travelling between India and Fiji were vital suppliers of dried ingredients, utensils and clothing. By the 1990s, however, such items had become widely available throughout New Zealand with the establishment of Indian speciality stores and restaurants.

CHANGING RELIGIOUS PRACTICES

Religious practices were informal in the early days, when the small number of Indians in New Zealand were predominantly men working in itinerant occupations. Nevertheless, prayer meetings or Bhagavad Gita classes began in Wellington in 1926 and Auckland in 1935. In 1964, the Sanskara Kendra, a centre for religious instruction, was established in Auckland. Religious activities became more common with the participation of women. Most Hindu homes had a small *mandir* for puja. With greater Indian family settlement after World War II, the Indian associations staged more religious celebrations. Of special importance were Diwali, Navarathri for the Gujaratis, and Baisakhi for the Punjabis. For those who had lived through India's independence struggle, celebrations on India's Independence Day and Mahatma Gandhi's birthday were community highlights.

Hindu practices functioned in New Zealand without temples and Brahmin priests until the late 1980s. The subsequent growth of the old and new Indian communities produced a demand for religious specialists and *mandirs*, which facilitated the overt expression and institutionalisation of religious practices. Globalisation also boosted religious enthusiasm for older Hindu sects and new syncretic movements. Since the 1980s, an increasing number of religious swamis, devotees and yogis have visited New Zealand. This was partly a reflection of the growing

affluence of Hindus there, who could support such visits and ceremonies, but also an indication of the interest in these activities and beliefs. When the established Indian associations built large multi-purpose complexes in the early 1990s, they included a *mandir*, such as the Radha Krishna Temple at the Mahatma Gandhi Centre in Auckland. Other early temples were the Bharatiya Mandir in Auckland, opened in 1993, the Kurinji Kumaran temple, started in 1992, and a Murugan temple erected by the New Zealand Hindu Association in 1995, both in Wellington. Since the late 1990s, there has been a relative boom in the building of temples in New Zealand. Hindu centres of worship and study are maintained by the Hindu Council of New Zealand, the New Zealand Hindu Temple Society, the Vedic Trust of New Zealand (Arya Samaj), the Bochasanwasi Shri Akshar Purushottam Swaminarayan Sanstha, regional Ramayan Sanstha communities and TISI. Many New Zealand Indians have long supported Sathya Sai Baba, the Brahmakumaris, Gayatri Parivar and in lesser numbers, the International Society for Krishna Consciousness. Hindu religions have attracted the bulk of Indians in New Zealand, with 32,964 Indians identifying themselves as Hindus in the 2001 census.

Sikh religious activities have been organised by the New Zealand Sikh Society, founded in 1964. Until then,

Indians in New Zealand established 'Sunday Schools', where children could learn Indian languages. Pictured here is Auckland's Gandhi Gruh Gujarati School in 1984.

Sukhi Turner, mayor of Dunedin, was the first person of Indian descent to hold such a position in New Zealand.

Indians run many neighbourhood shops, known as 'dairies' in New Zealand. Here, Naliniben N. Patel (left), the manager of the dairy at Shalimar Four Square in Wellington, is seen with Naginbhai Neil Patel and two migrants from Fiji, Bala and Viren Lingappa.

Sikh organisation was through the Country Section of the New Zealand Indian Central Association. In 1977, New Zealand's first gurdwara was opened at Te Rapa in Waikato. The Takanini gurdwara, opened in 2005, is the largest in the southern hemisphere, while the gurdwara in Wellington is the world's southernmost. The post-1984 global resurgence of Sikhism provoked an assertion of religious and ethnic identity among New Zealand Sikhs. The first Amrit Sanskar ceremony (for entry into the Khalsa) was held in New Zealand on 4 January 1987, and by 1989, a *jatha* (team) of members of the Khalsa was established. The number of Sikhs officially recorded in New Zealand increased from 2061 in 1991 to 5196 a decade later.

The global resurgence of Islam during the late 20th century has also been reflected in New Zealand. Records of Indian Muslim hawkers date back to the 19th century. Mohammed Suliman, a Punjabi Muslim, arrived around 1903–04, but until the 1970s, the majority of Muslims in New Zealand were Gujarati Sunni Bohras descended from the pioneers Mohamed Kara, Ismail Bhikoo and Joseph Musa. Gujarati Muslims were instrumental in establishing the New Zealand Muslim Association in 1950 and the Islamic Centre in Auckland in 1957. Emigration from Fiji after 1965 boosted the number of Muslims, and other Islamic associations were started. The first mosques were established in Auckland by 1980 and Christchurch in 1985. Indo-Fijians have been proactive in New Zealand Muslim organisations in sending aid to displaced farmers in Fiji after 2000, and to flood victims there in 2004. In the early 21st century, Indo-Fijians comprised around one-third of over 42 Muslim nationalities in New Zealand.

A major religious change among New Zealand Indians has been the significant increase in those belonging to the Christian faith. In 2001, 9618 Indians declared themselves Christian. Of these, approximately one-third were Catholic. Some Indo-Fijians in New Zealand are members of the Assemblies of God, and the Indian Christian Life Centre had centres in New Zealand by 2004.

POLITICAL PARTICIPATION

Indian settlers in New Zealand retained an interest in political developments in India, especially during the nationalist independence movement. Mahatma Gandhi's Gujarati origins guaranteed support from the Gujaratis, and many of the early migrants from Gujarat to New Zealand remitted money for nationalist schools. Some migrants were also freedom fighters in India's nationalist movement. After World War II, New Zealand Indians raised money for the Punjabi Refugees' Relief Fund. Active interest in politics on the Indian subcontinent has dwindled among later generations of New Zealand Indians. Some New Zealand Chamars have given financial support to the Ad Dharm movement and identify themselves as Ad Dharmis, rejecting the term 'Chamar'. By the 1990s, many preferred to identify themselves as Ravidasi Sikhs.

Indo-Fijians in New Zealand have maintained ambivalent political ties with Fiji. After the 1987 coup, some Indo-Fijian politicians and activists fled to New Zealand. Many Indo-Fijians, along with sympathetic indigenous Fijians and other New Zealanders, established political lobby groups, such as the Coalition for Democracy in Fiji. The Fiji Movement for Justice and Freedom's branches in New Zealand have raised funds and lobbied for international compensation for displaced Indo-Fijian cane farmers in Fiji.

Almost all Indian residents have been Labour Party supporters. This was generally because they identified with the working class (including those who were self-employed) and due to the close relationship some Labour politicians fostered with leaders of the Indian community. The Labour Party's immigration policies and attitudes to ethnic minorities have also gained Indian support, although Indian numbers have always been too small to offer an ethnic vote. There has not been any cohesive Asian electorate in New Zealand either, despite the growing Asian population in Auckland. Since the 1990s, more Indians have supported the National Party. Indian associations have lobbied the government over immigration and human rights issues, but this has been low-key. Since the 1980s, New Zealand Indians have been actively involved in a wide range of local bodies and voluntary

Jelal Kalyanji Natali (1899–1993)

Jelal Kalyanji Natali, a pioneer of the New Zealand Indian community who became a very successful entrepreneur, is remembered for his contribution to the New Zealand Indian Central Association and his articulate defence of the rights of Indian people in New Zealand, India, South Africa and Fiji.

Natali was born in 1899 at Rander in Surat, India. His father, a dhobi, migrated to Natal and assumed the surname Natali. His son, however, followed other Gujaratis and sailed to Auckland in 1920. He became active in the local Indian community, partly because in India he had received an English education and worked as a clerk. By 1921, he was the editor of *Aryodaya*. He served as the Auckland Indian Association's president in 1923 and during the 1950s. As president (1939–40, 1948–51 and 1954–59) and spokesman of the New Zealand Indian Central Association, Natali made several representations against racial discrimination in New Zealand. He condemned the White New Zealand League, New Zealand's anti-Asian immigration policies, and anti-Indian employment and business practices. Natali also criticised discrimination within Indian culture and promoted modernity among New Zealand's Indian community.

Natali was intensely patriotic to his adopted country. He donated generously to collections during World War II and encouraged the Indian community to contribute to charities. In 1986, he was awarded the Queen's Service medal for service to the Indian community and for assistance to the Maori and Pakeha during his years as a storekeeper. In recognition of his contributions, the New Zealand Indian Central Association and the Auckland Indian Association conferred upon him a life membership.

Natali attributed his material success to the view that New Zealand was a land of opportunity. He first worked in a hotel in Rotorua, where he met Kate Beasley, an English immigrant. They married, and purchased and operated a general store in the King Country, and over the years invested extensively in property and land. After World War II they settled in Auckland. Natali died in 1993.

Natali laying the foundation stone for Gandhi Hall in Auckland, 1954.

Bollywood comes to Queenstown in the South Island: the filming of scenes for Mother, Father and a Tamil Girl *featured members of the Queenstown Maori Performance Group, 2003.*

organisations. Sukhi Turner, who emigrated to New Zealand in 1973, was elected as Dunedin's first mayor of Indian descent in 1992. In 2004, she was the first New Zealander to receive the Pravasi Bharatiya Samman from the Indian government. At the national level, Dr Ashraf Choudhary, a Muslim, became New Zealand's first parliamentarian of South Asian descent in 2002.

CHALLENGES IN THE EARLY 21ST CENTURY

New Zealand's ethnic make-up has radically changed since Indians first arrived. Then, Europeans dominated, with an indigenous Maori minority, but in the 21st century, New Zealand is increasingly multi-ethnic. The country's Maori, Asian and Pacific Islander populations are projected to grow faster than the European population, so that by 2021, the proportion of people of Asian ethnicity is estimated to reach 15 per cent, compared to 7 per cent in 2001. Indians constituted the second-largest Asian group in the 2001 census and are likely to increase in size as a result of closer economic and educational ties with India. The extent to which New Zealanders embrace multiculturalism is uncertain. The Maori and Pakeha are still contesting the implications of a bicultural society and a crucial issue here is the acceptance and positioning of other groups. Although a few politicians would like to curb Asian immigration and there remains some anti-Asian discrimination, contemporary New Zealanders have a positive degree of tolerance towards Indians. A high percentage of the country's growing Asian population will increasingly be New Zealand-born and of multi-ethnic descent.

Future challenges also come from within New Zealand's Indian communities. Tensions between the secular and religious aspirations of Indian communities may create internal and external rifts. New Zealand's Bill of Rights (1990) guarantees freedom of observance and conduct grounded in religion, but how acceptable is this when religious minorities engage in controversial practices? In 2005, for example, the New Zealand Sikh Society petitioned the prime minister for exemption from laws which stipulate that a licence is required to carry a weapon. Gender relations are also a source of friction. Unlike their mothers, many Indian women in New Zealand in the 21st century are a part of the formal workforce and are strongly represented in professions. For some years, young adults within the older Indian communities have questioned marriage traditions, especially arranged marriages. Ironically, marriage expenditure is probably much higher than before.

Indians are inclusive of various Indian groups and the general public though they have exclusive ethnic and religious identities. The New Zealand Indian Central Association is responding to the proliferation of new Indian organisations by facilitating their affiliation, although it is likely that many groups will prefer to remain independent. The most overt display of an inclusive identity has been the elevation of the status of Diwali as the premier Indian festival in New Zealand. The Asia New Zealand Foundation has been the principal sponsor of Diwali since 2002. The celebration of national Indian secular anniversaries such as Independence Day and Gandhi's birthday have become less popular. This is only one indicator of inter-generational changes towards what is valued from an Indian heritage.

Indians may be more visible in contemporary New Zealand but as a community they are more fragmented than in the past. Indians with several generations of residence in New Zealand have worked hard to be accepted as 'Kiwis' and have a different historical legacy and identity than the 'newcomers' from Fiji, India and elsewhere. The ties with Fiji have loosened for Indo-Fijians but links remain, especially among those who have relatives in Fiji. It is unlikely that Fiji Hindi will continue to be widely spoken by descendants in New Zealand. The identity of Indo-Fijians as Pacific Islanders is also ambivalent. While many Indo-Fijians see themselves as a distinct category, most of them tick the Asian ethnic box for official purposes. In 2001, approximately one-third of New Zealand Indians were born in Fiji, but only around 2000 declared their ethnicity as Fiji Indian. This suggests that in New Zealand, Indo-Fijians identify themselves as Indians. Ethnic divisions from Fiji may be overlooked when Fijians of different ethnicities interact in New Zealand, but formal networks are usually along ethnic and religious lines. As the proportion of New Zealand-born Indians increases, it may be that a new New Zealand Indian identity will develop. Increasing intermarriage, both between Indian communities and with other groups, may enhance the local Indian culture and also contribute to the making of a more hybrid New Zealand population.

Jacqueline Leckie

A young flower-girl at a contemporary Indian wedding celebrated at the Mahatma Gandhi Centre, Auckland.

Diwali celebrations in Wellington.

THE PACIFIC ISLANDS

Workers at a phosphate mine in Nauru.

L ABOUR AND MOBILITY are two words that perhaps best encapsulate the history of Indians in the Pacific. The first wave of Indians to arrive on the shores of islands in the Pacific were sailors. As early as 1811, an Indian sailor deserted the *Hunter* in Fiji and lived with European beachcombers and Fijians for about two years. He then went to the Solomon Islands and lived on the islands of Anuta and Tikopia for many years. While such incidents were frequent, they were rarely considered historically significant as Indians constituted a small proportion of the ships' crews and did not hold positions of power.

The demand for plantation workers following the French colonisation of New Caledonia in 1853 led to the recruitment of some 454 indentured Indian labourers between 1864 and 1875 from the island of Réunion. As a consequence of being a minority community in a relatively large and diverse population, Indians easily assimilated into the colony. Indian languages and other cultural idioms were soon replaced by a new cosmopolitan culture. Between 1879 and 1916, 60,533 Indian indentured workers were recruited to work in Fiji for the Colonial Sugar Refining Company. This marked the arrival of the second wave of Indians in the Pacific. Today, Fiji is home to the largest proportion of Indians in the Pacific Islands.

The third phase of Indian migration to the Pacific followed the post-World War II reconstruction period, which saw Indian mechanics and builders from Fiji move to the Solomon Islands, Vanuatu, Tonga and Kiribati for work. Indians from Fiji were also recruited in their capacity as pilots and engineers to work for the colonial government, and were employed by companies such as

The Prasads, an Indo-Vanuatu family, at Santo, Vanuatu, 1978.

Burns Philip. Following the departure of Vietnamese artisans and many skilled Tongan workers to New Zealand, Australia and the US, Indians from Fiji have filled that void both in Vanuatu and Tonga. Some churches also employed Indian Christians in other Pacific Island countries. While many of them chose to return to their home countries upon the expiration of their work contracts, a few decided to stay and participate in the commercial sector. Citizenship was granted to the few Indians who married locally in Vanuatu and the Solomon Islands.

More recently, Indians (mainly from India) in Papua New Guinea, Samoa, Nauru and Guam have served in professional positions (as academics at the University of Papua New Guinea, for example), have been providing expertise in the medical and judicial sectors, and are consultants to various international institutions, including agencies of the United Nations, the World Bank and the Asian Development Bank.

Aside from Fiji, Indians constitute less than 1 per cent of the population in the Pacific Islands. Unlike Indians in the Solomon Islands and Vanuatu, who maintain close ties with relatives in Fiji, there is no significant contact between those in Papua New Guinea and elsewhere in the Pacific. Despite the extremely heterogeneous character of their population, many Indians in the Pacific Islands still have a sense of shared culture, experienced through institutional and cultural practices, such as participation in religious festivals.

While Indians have achieved much economically and socially, cultural assimilation between Indians and other Pacific Islanders is kept at a minimum. Though their numbers are waning, Indians continue to play a crucial role in the development of the Pacific Islands.

Ashwin Raj

Map 8.64

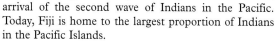

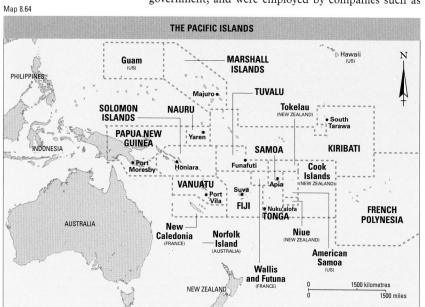

THE PACIFIC ISLANDS

PHILIPPINES

Guam
(US)

MARSHALL
ISLANDS

◊ Hawaii
(US)

N

Majuro ●

TUVALU

SOLOMON
ISLANDS

NAURU

Tokelau
(NEW ZEALAND)

● South
Tarawa

INDONESIA

PAPUA NEW
GUINEA

Yaren ●

SAMOA

KIRIBATI

● Port
Moresby

Honiara ●

Funafuti ●

Cook
Islands
(NEW ZEALAND)

VANUATU

Suva
●

Apia

AUSTRALIA

● Port
Vila

FIJI

● Nuku'alofa
TONGA

FRENCH
POLYNESIA

New
Caledonia
(FRANCE)

Norfolk
Island
(AUSTRALIA)

Niue
(NEW ZEALAND)

American
Samoa
(US)

Wallis
and Futuna
(FRANCE)

NEW ZEALAND

0   1500 kilometres
0   1500 miles

THE FRENCH PACIFIC

THE MALABARS, WHO were the descendants of Indians living on the west coast of the Caledonian Grande-Terre, came from two of the five French *comptoirs* of India (Pondicherry and Karaikkal), or from the region of Madras. The Franco-British convention of 1 July 1861 authorised only Indian volunteers to settle in Réunion and Antille-Guyana. The departure of the Madras Indians to the Pacific Ocean could thus happen only at the time when they were renewing their indenture contracts.

After France took possession of New Caledonia in 1853, the colonial administration sought to populate this South Pacific island. When growers from Réunion who were hit by the sugar crisis complained in Paris about the disastrous consequences, the ministry encouraged them to turn to New Caledonia and develop sugar cane plantations there instead.

A delegation of growers from Réunion thus came to visit New Caledonia in 1864. As early as the end of that same year, colonists from the region of Bourbonnais settled on the west coast of the Grande-Terre, gradually bringing to the island the first group of Indian volunteers between 1864 and 1875. These 454 Indians, the majority of them single, were regarded as excellent farm labourers. They were called 'Malabars' in Réunion as a number of them came from India's Malabar Coast, and this term was retained in New Caledonia.

The Malabars settled along the coast—Ouaménie from 1864 and La Foa from 1875—either to cultivate sugar cane or to operate the sugar factories. Daily life was harsh because their employers seldom respected the agreed conditions regarding hours of work, food rations or clothing. The practice of corporal punishment was extreme, as the murder of a foreman on the Kerveguen station in 1870 showed.

The failure of sugar cane as a commercial crop due to the lack of water, the invasion of grasshoppers, poor market conditions and insufficient manpower caused the eventual dispersion of the Malabars. The administration forced the workers who came from British India and the most deprived to immigrate to the plantations of Fiji or Queensland (in Australia) instead.

The other French citizens who wished to remain in the colony were gathered around the colonial centre of La Foa, which had been confiscated from the *kanak* (native) insurgents of 1878. On the 'Plain of the Malabars', French citizens were granted land concessions of 3.5 to 12 hectares. At the time of the census of 1884, only 173 Indians remained on the island, almost all gathered in the La Foa village, including 26 women and 23 children. Overall, they profited from the distribution of 395 hectares, part of which was repurchased quickly by Mr Camouilly, the director of land administration at that time.

This community was a target of discrimination, especially with regard to voting rights. When a municipal commission was established in La Foa in 1883, there were 15 European voters and 70 Malabar voters—former convicts were not authorised to vote. However, the governor introduced a clause granting only one vote for each group of 10 Malabars. As foreigners, Indians from Madras did not have voting rights. They were also forbidden from consuming alcohol and owning weapons.

In the 1890s, some Indians settled in Nouméa. One of them, Jolimont Kabar, born in Réunion in 1818, arrived with his wife in 1868 and settled on the east coast, close to Houaïlou. He gradually acquired a 100-hectare property on which he raised 18 children. Jolimont, who died at the age of 96, had more than 975 descendants over eight generations by the early 21st century.

In the late 19th and early 20th centuries, some groups of Indian volunteers arrived directly from French-controlled areas of India. They contributed to agricultural colonisation and worked in the nickel mines. Almost all of these unqualified workers returned to their country of origin, partly because they found it difficult to adapt and also because their employers preferred other Asian workers. One of them, born in Pondicherry in 1880, settled under the franchised name of Ducoin in La vallée des Colons. He married a young Paillandi lady from La Foa, with whom he had 12 children.

As for the Indians of the west coast who went to Nouméa, they settled in La vallée du Tir, where a number of them worked for the factory of the Nickel Company. Here, a small Indian temple existed between 1900 and 1936, founded by Mr Ramin.

Their disadvantaged conditions, along with mixed marriages with the European population, have led to 'Caledonian' Indians losing their cultural identity. Due to the prevalence of large families, some surnames are reminders of the existence of a community which is now integrated: Arsapin, Carpin, Condoya, Kabar, Kamatchi, Paillandi, Tandrien, Velayoudon and Waintilingon.

Frédéric Angleviel

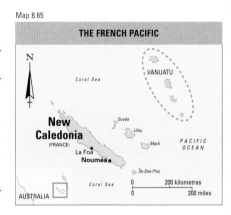

Map 8.65

THE FRENCH PACIFIC

The Marist mission house at Hienghène on the northeast coast of New Caledonia. The Society of Mary was founded in 1816 in France to extend the role of the Catholic Church in the Pacific.

A parade of Indian and Vietnamese migrants in Nouméa to celebrate the golden jubilee of French rule in New Caledonia, 1903.

ACKNOWLEDGEMENTS

The development, management and fulfilment of a project such as this encyclopedia cannot be carried through without the encouragement and guidance of a large group of colleagues, friends, supporters and experts in the many fields that come within the purview of the project and that go into the final research, writing and editing on which the volume depends. As editors, we are very conscious of the strain that we have put on our families and colleagues to bring this project to a successful conclusion. Our first round of appreciation, therefore, goes to them for their forbearance and continued support. In addition, there is that large group of people whose contributions to the project we wish to acknowledge, especially all the writers of articles for the volume who worked in such a timely and dedicated fashion to meet deadlines, answer queries and help with details and the endless requests that come with a project of this size. We thank them most sincerely: it can be very truly said that the encyclopedia would not have been possible without them and both their expertise and goodwill. Finally, we wish to specifically acknowledge the following people and institutions:

- The President of the Republic of Singapore, Mr S. R. Nathan, for his constant encouragement and unfailing belief in the project.

- Our sponsors, Citibank, Warburg Pincus, Jet Airways (India) Ltd, Kewalram Ltd Singapore, Amtel Investment Holdings Pte Ltd, Temasek Holdings, Singapore Buddhist Lodge and Mr Sat Pal Khattar, for their financial support.

- The Chairman of the Editorial Management Board, Associate Professor Tan Tai Yong, and the board's distinguished members, Mr Sat Pal Khattar, Mr S. Dhanabalan and Mr K. Kesavapany, for their guidance and strength of purpose.

- Our Editorial Consultants, Professor Judith Brown, Emeritus Professor Anthony Low, Professor Dipesh Chakrabarty, Professor Emeritus Frank Conlon, Professor Robin Jeffrey, and Professor Brian Stoddart, for their advice and endorsement of the project.

- Mr Didier Millet and the staff of Editions Didier Millet, Singapore, especially Mr Charles Orwin, Mr Timothy Auger, Ms Laura Jeanne Gobal and Ms Nelani Jinadasa for guidance and advice.

- Professor Shih Choon Fong, President, National University of Singapore (NUS), for his encouragement.

- The Division of Pacific and Asian History, Research School of Pacific and Asian Studies, The Australian National University, for support given to the General Editor.

- Professor Lily Kong, Vice-Provost (Education), NUS, for her support and encouragement.

- Associate Professor Tan Tai Yong, Dean, Faculty of Arts and Social Sciences (FASS), NUS, whose interest and involvement with the project was important throughout.

- All staff and faculty of FASS for their sustained and invaluable support.

- The Director, NUS Libraries, and the staff of the Central Library, NUS, who were very generous with their assistance. Our very special thanks to the staff members of the Inter-Library Loans Department who dealt with all our special requests very graciously.

- All faculty members of the South Asian Studies Programme—Dr Ulrike Niklas, Dr Gyanesh Kudaisya, Dr S. P. Thinnappan, Associate Professor Shapan Adnan, Dr Faizal Yahya, Dr Assa Doron, Dr Robina Mohammad, and Dr Rajshree Jetly—who were invaluable as sources of information and encouragement.

- The graduate students in the South Asian Studies Programme—Mr Torsten Tschacher, Ms Carol Thirumaran, Ms Sathiavathi Chinniah, Ms Yamini Vasudevan, Mr Ranajit Dastidar, Mr Sujoy Dutta, Mr Tabarez Neyazi, Mr Din Muhammad—who helped and encouraged us throughout.

- Ms Catherine Lee and Mdm Nur Jannah, Management Support Officers, South Asian Studies Programme, FASS, NUS, for their cheerful and unstinting administrative support.

- Our Research Assistants, who did a wonderful job in meeting almost constant demands: firstly, Mr Terenjit Sevea; then, Ms Wajihah Hamid, who also handled the photo research requirements with great persistence and commitment; and Dr Nandita Khadria who worked with dedication on the glossary.

- The project was supported by those who attended the 'International Workshop on the Feasibility of an Encyclopedia of the Indians Overseas', which was convened in Singapore in December 2001. The report which was produced sustained the project. International speakers who participated were Professor Amarjit Kaur (New England), Dr Marina Carter (Edinburgh), Professor Ravindra Kumar Jain (JNU), Professor Vijay Mishra (Murdoch), Dr Lance Brennan (Flinders) and Professor Frank Conlon (Washington). We also wish to thank Dr Marina Carter for her valuable assistance later on, particularly with illustrations.

- Professor P. Ramasamy and Professor A. Mani, Senior Research Fellows at the Institute of Southeast Asian Studies, Singapore, and Professor Bidyut Chakrabarty of Delhi University, an Isaac Menassah Meyer Fellow in South Asian Studies at NUS, who read and commented on particular chapters and provided valuable advice.

- We also would like to thank all who assisted us in acquiring pictures: Dr Jacqueline Moore, Director, Asian Studies, Austin College; Dr Shompa Lahiri; Ms Sara Wajid; and Mr Karim Sahai. Special thanks also go to Mr Scott Henderson, Mr T. S. Sibia, Mr Stephen Williamson, Mr Carl Haarnack and Mr Mohamad Asgarallie who so generously allowed us to use their rare postcards and pictures.

- Our thanks also go to the many publishers around the world who offered their invaluable and speedy assistance when it was needed: Ms Gabrielle White and Ms Catherine Trippett from Random House UK; Mr Peter Mendelsund and Ms Jenny Pouech from Knopf USA; Ms Rebecca Fish from McClelland & Stewart; and Mr Jonathan Williams from Picador Africa.

- Kinokuniya in Singapore graciously allowed us to photograph a section of their bookshelves on which there were important 'diaspora' books.

- For help with picture research we are grateful to: Mr Aaron White from the Pluralism Project; Dr Martin Baumann and Dr Clare Sisisky; Mr Dusty Mancinelli from Hamilton Mehta Productions Inc.; Ms Alexandra Eveleigh from the West Yorkshire Archive Service, Kirklees; Mr Michael Callaghan from Bradford Museums, Galleries and Heritage; Ms Joanna Petterson from the Nobel Foundation; Ms Beth Thomas from the Museum of London; Mr Hugh Alexander from The National Archives; Ms Sara Grove from the National Maritime Museum; Mr Justin Hobson from the Royal Geographical Society; Ms Rachel Lloyd from the Victoria and Albert Museum; Mr Younis from Birmingham Picture Library; Ms Sue Barber from Wandsworth Museum; Ms Elsie Leung from The University of Hong Kong; Mr Bernard Hui from the Public Records Office of Hong Kong; Mr Charles J. G. Verge, President of the Royal Philatelic Society of Canada; Mr Robert Valliant from the Centre for Southeast Asian Studies, University of Hawaii at Manoa; Mr A. K. Katiyar, Principal, Embassy of India School, Moscow; Mr Rui Miguel Leal; Mr Chris Barton from Photographers Direct; Mr Abdul Kareem from Gulf News; and Ms Lea Tzimoulis from Bose Corporation.

- In the final stages, we had timely and strong support from a group of our students at NUS: Ms Sadhana Rai, Mr Ganga Nirmal Kumar, Ms Kevina Jerrine, Ms Smita Singh and Mr John Paul Foenander.

- Finally, Brij Lal and Peter Reeves would like to commend Rajesh Rai for the sustained excellence of his editorial work, which far exceeded what might be thought of as the role of an 'assistant' editor; well done, Rajesh.

Brij V. Lal, Peter Reeves and Rajesh Rai

LIST OF FIGURES, TABLES AND MAPS

GLOSSARY

adat: 'custom' in Southeast Asia; religious ritual practices in Bali; 'habit' in Hindi.

Adi Dravida: a term used in South India by some 'untouchable' groups to provide a more positive identity.

Advait Math: the institution imparting spiritual instructions on the non-dualist system of the Advait Vedanta philosophy of Hinduism.

agama: religion; in Indonesia, under President Sukarno, five *agamas* were recognised as world religions.

agamic: 'great tradition' in Hinduism.

Ahir: a mid-level caste from North India traditionally associated with dairy farming.

aliyah: 'going up'; a commitment among Jews to emigrate to Israel to build a Jewish homeland.

aqsaqal: a senior representative of a trading firm in Central Asia, responsible for supervising the local Indian community and acting as a mediator with the host country.

arkati or *arkatia*: an unlicensed sub-contractor recruiting Indian indentured labour.

ashram or **asram**: abode; the residence of a hermit or religious scholar.

ata or *atta*: flour; usually refers to coarse brown wheat flour or wholemeal flour.

ayah: a maid or nursemaid in India, who mainly looks after children.

Ayurveda: 'knowledge of life'; a comprehensive Indian system of medicine.

azad: free or emancipated.

badam: almond

baitkas: literally 'sitting places'; places of congregation; Hindu socio-religious institutions.

Bapa Pekerja: 'Father of Workers' in Malay.

bhai: brother

bhajan: Hindu and Sikh devotional song.

bhakti: devotion; Hindu devotional worship of a deity.

bharat: India

bharatiya: Indian

bhavan: abode or dwelling.

bhumi or *bhoomi*: land or earth.

bidesh: foreign land

bidesia: a genre of folk songs about migration and longing; part of a foreign land.

bindi: a decorative mark in the middle of the forehead, worn mostly by Hindu women.

Brahman, *brahmana* or **Brahmin**: member of the highest division of the Hindu caste system; the priestly caste.

chacha: paternal uncle; sometimes used when addressing elders or prominent national leaders.

Chamar: 'untouchable' caste in northern India; traditionally associated with leather work.

chappati: an Indian bread usually made from wheat flour.

chimta: a pair of tongs.

crore: an Indian numerical unit equivalent to 10 million.

dai: midwife

dalit: one who is oppressed, formerly an 'untouchable'.

Deepavali: the Hindu festival of lights in southern India, usually celebrated in the month of October or November.

desi: native, homemade or local.

dhal: lentils; used widely in Indian cuisine.

dhal-puri: an Indian bread stuffed with lentils.

dharma: a term with various meanings, often used by Hindus, Sikhs and Buddhists to refer to righteous conduct and religious and moral duty.

dharma sabha: religious assembly or association.

dharmshala or *dharamshala*: charitable guest house, usually near Hindu places of pilgrimage.

dhenki: a wooden apparatus for pounding or grinding grain.

dhimmi: people of 'the Book', used by Islamic law to denote Jews and Christians.

dhobi: washerman or laundry shop.

dhol: an Indian drum.

dhow: a traditional Arab sailing vessel with one or more triangular lateen sails.

divas: day

Diwali: the Hindu festival of lights in northern India; *see* Deepavali.

Diwan: chief administrator

doodh or *dudh*: milk

doodhwallah: milkman

durgah: a Muslim shrine; the grave of a Muslim saint.

Eid: *see* Id.

gazal or *ghazal*: an important Urdu poetic form consisting of couplets which share a rhyme and refrain.

ghadar: mutiny or rebellion; the name of an anti-British revolutionary movement, the Ghadar Party, formed in 1913 by Indians on the west coast of the US and Canada, with headquarters in San Francisco.

ghee: clarified butter; used in cooking and in Hindu rituals and ceremonies.

girmit or *girmitiyas*: derived in Fiji from 'agreement'; used by Indian indentured migrants to describe their indenture experience.

gopuram: the gateway to Hindu temples in South Indian architecture.

gumashta: an agent, superintendent, manager or commissary; usually of the mercantile class.

gurdwara, *gurudwara* or *gurduara*: a Sikh place of worship.

guru: teacher or guide; a trusted counsellor, adviser or mentor.

Harijan: 'Children of God'; Mahatma Gandhi used this term for the people commonly referred to as the 'untouchables'.

hartal: a strike or public protest.

hawala: transfer, trust or custody; traditionally an informal value transfer system used in East Africa and the Middle East, which developed into a fully-fledged money market system in South Asia; often used by migrant workers to remit funds to their country of origin.

henna: a dye extracted from the leaves of *Lawsonia inermis*; used by women for decorating hands and feet, particularly during wedding ceremonies or religious festivals, and for dyeing hair.

Hindutva: Hinduness; a term coined by V. D. Savarkar in 1923.

Holi: the Hindu festival of colours, celebrated during spring; *see* Phagwa.

Hossay or **Hussay**: The Shia festival of Muharram, which commemorates the martyrdom of Hasan and Husain, sons of Ali, the son-in-law of the Prophet Muhammad.

hundi: bills of exchange or letters of credit used in trade and credit transactions and as remittance instruments for the transfer of funds during the medieval and early modern periods.

hundial: a promissary note; commonly used in the remittance trade.

Id: festival; a short form for the Muslim festivals Id-al-Fitr and Id-al-Adha. Id-al-Fitr, meaning 'the festival of fast breaking', is celebrated by Muslims at the end of Ramadan, the month of fasting. Id-al-Adha is 'the festival of sacrifice'.

insaf: justice, fairness or redress.

izzat: dignity or honour.

Jagapati: 'Lord of the Universe'; an epithet for Vishnu and Shiva.

jahaj: ship or vehicle.

jahaji bhai: the 'brotherhood' forged between indentured men during their sea voyage to the colonies.

janta: a stone hand-mill.

jatha: a band or movement; a company of fully initiated Sikhs.

jati: relates to the birth group and is the term used to denote localised caste groups.

jatra: a genre of popular drama staged by peripatetic theatre groups of Bengal; a variant of *yatra*, which means travel or journey.

Jawi-Pekan: the Indo-Malay community in the Malay peninsula.

jhandi or *jhanda*: flag

jizya: a tax levied on non-Muslim adult males in an Islamic country in return for protection by the state.

kalantar: a senior representative of a firm in Iran, responsible for supervising the local Indian community and mediating with the host country.

kalapani: dark waters; an epithet for the ocean, the crossing of which traditionally led to the loss of caste; a term associated with indentured and convict migration.

kamiz or *kameez*: a long shirt worn by men and women from the Indian subcontinent.

kampong or *kampung*: 'village' in Malay and Bahasa Indonesia.

kangani: overseer or foreman; a labour recruitment system in the late 19th and early 20th century, used primarily in Ceylon and Malaya.

kavadi: an ornamental piece made of bent wood or metal, carried by a devotee with skewers piercing his body, cheek or tongue, usually during the festival of Thaipusam.

kedai jahit: 'tailoring shop' in Malay and Bahasa Indonesia; also used in Brunei.

keramat: a shrine built at the grave of a Muslim saint.

khaddar or *khadi*: handspun and hand-woven cotton cloth; may also refer to handspun and hand-woven silk fabric.

Khalistan: a movement seeking a separate Sikh homeland in Punjab that came to the fore in the 1980s.

khalsa: pure; used by Guru Gobind Singh to refer to all initiated Sikhs.

khanas: an assembly hall.

kirtan: the singing of devotional songs; in the Sikh context, this refers to the singing of hymns from the Guru Granth Sahib.

kisan: peasant, cultivator, agriculturist or farmer.

Koeri: a mid-level peasant caste community from North India.

Kshatriya: a member of the second division of the Hindu caste system; the warrior caste.

Kurmi: a mid-level caste community from North India, traditionally associated with agricultural work.

kurta: a long shirt, waistcoat or jacket worn by both men and women from the Indian subcontinent.

lakh: an Indian numerical unit equivalent to 100,000.

langar: an alms house; a term used by Sikhs for free vegetarian food served from the community kitchen in a Sikh shrine.

lascar: a member of a ship's crew, mostly from India, so it often referred to Indian sailors.

madrasah or *madrassah*: a Muslim college for higher Islamic studies of law, science and religion.

Mahabharata: the Indian epic which tells the story of the conflict between two groups of cousins, the Pandavas and the Kauravas.

mai-bap: literally 'mother-father'; a guardian, benefactor or protector.

maistry: supervisor; a system of labour recruitment in the late 19th and early 20th century, used primarily in Burma.

makkal thondam: a Tamil phrase relating to someone who works in the service of people; refers to V. David in the Malaysian context, who was known as 'the Champion of Workers'.

mandir: a Hindu temple.

mantra: incantation; a form of prayer.

mela: a fair; usually held in conjunction with a religious, cultural or seasonal festival.

muhajir or *muhajjir*: an Arabic word for Muslims who have emigrated from one place to another; in early Islam it was used to denote the Muslim companions of the Prophet Muhammad, who accompanied him from Mecca to Medina.

Muharram: the first month of the Muslim calendar.

murti: idol or image.

mushaira: a gathering of Urdu poets at which they recite their works.

namaskar or *namaste*: a respectful or reverential salutation or address; a gesture of greeting, usually with folded hands.

Pallan: 'untouchable' low-caste communities from South India.

panchayat: 'assembly of five'; the traditional political institution of village India, comprising the village elders.

pandit: a Hindu priest; it is also used to refer to a learned person or a scholar.

panth: literally 'path'; religious belief; the community of baptised Sikhs is known as the Khalsa Panth.

Paraiyan: 'untouchable' low-caste communities from South India.

pardes: foreign land or abroad; a remote or 'other' land.

pardesi: a foreigner or one who has settled abroad.

pengulu or *penghulu*: a village headman in Malay and Bahasa Indonesia; sometimes used for priests in Surinam.

Phagwa: another name for Holi, the festival of colours.

pravasi or *pravaasi*: residing abroad; emigrant or immigrant.

puja: Hindu worship or a ceremonial offering.

pujari: a Hindu priest who officiates the puja.

puraan or *purana*: Hindu devotional and mythological scriptures.

purohit: a Hindu priest who conducts religious ceremonies.

qadi: a Muslim 'judge', whose duties and responsibilities are outlined in the Sharia.

qawwali: Sufi devotional songs.

Ramadan: the ninth month of the Islamic calendar, marked by a month of daytime fasting for Muslims.

Ramayana: the Indian epic which tells the story of Rama, his banishment from his kingdom, the abduction of his wife Sita by Ravana and her rescue, and the restoration of his throne in Ayodhya.

Ramleela, Ramlila or **Ram Lila**: a popular pageant-play depicting the story of the Ramayana.

rashtra: nation or country.

rath: chariot

riba: an Arabic term for interest on loans, which is forbidden by the Quran.

roti: bread

ryot: peasant, tenant or cultivator.

salafi: originally used to refer to companions of the Prophet Muhammad who learned Islam directly from him; it also refers to those returning from the Hijaz, who are believed to have a pure understanding of Islam.

salwar or *shalwar*: traditional trousers; worn by both men and women from the Indian subcontinent.

sangat: a meeting, assembly or association working towards the enrichment of society.

sangh or *sangha*: an assembly or congregation.

sari: a dress worn by Indian women; a long piece of cloth wrapped around the body and passed over the shoulder.

sastra: rules or precepts based on the Hindu scriptures.

satsang: 'the company of truth'; a religious assembly.

sham-e-gazal or *sham-e-ghazal*: an 'evening of gazals (ghazals)'.

shroff: a banker or money-changer; by implication, a comprador.

shuddhi: purification; a purificatory rite in Hinduism; re-conversion to Hinduism.

sirdar or *sardar*: foreman or labour superviser; usually an intermediary between the employer or management and the indentured workers.

stupa: large semi-circular mounds usually containing the relics of either the Buddha or Buddhist monks.

Sufi: a follower of an Islamic mystical order (Sufism).

Suvarnabhumi: 'Land of Gold'; a historical term used in India to refer to a region which comprised parts of present-day Thailand and Malaysia.

swadeshi: indigenously made goods; a movement to boycott British products during the anti-colonial struggle in India.

Swaraj: self-rule; one of the demands of the Indian anti-colonial movement from the early 20th century.

tadja: representations of the tombs of Hasan and Husain, the sons of Ali, taken out in procession during Muharram.

tawa: a flat pan heated to make *roti* or Indian bread.

tazia or *tazza*: *see tadja*.

Thaipusam or **Tai Pucam**: a Hindu festival popular with Tamils, celebrated on the day of the full moon in the Tamil month of Thai, which commemorates the birth of Lord Murugan.

tikka or *tika*: a mark on the forehead, usually of vermillion; applied in connection with Hindu religious functions.

tindal: Indian petty officer in charge of lascars; sometimes the head of a gang of labourers in public works.

toddy: an indigenous liquor fermented from coconut and palm sap, particularly in Kerala and Tamil Nadu.

ulama or *ulema*: Muslim scholars trained in Islamic law; the plural of *alim*.

Vande Mataram: 'Hail to the Motherland'; the national song of India.

yuvak sabha: youth association

zakat: 'to grow (in goodness)'; the contribution for social welfare that a Muslim is required to make during the month of Ramadan.

BIBLIOGRAPHY

THE INDIAN CONTEXT

Allchin, B., and Allchin, F. R., *The Rise of Civilisation in India and Pakistan*, Cambridge University Press, Cambridge and New York, 1982.

Basham, A. L., *The Wonder That Was India*, Sidgwick and Jackson, London, 1954.

Bayly, C. A., *The Raj: India and the British, 1600–1947*, National Portrait Gallery, London, 1990.

Johnson, G., *Cultural Atlas of India*, Facts on File, New York, 1996.

Ludden, D., *India and South Asia: A short history*, Oneworld, Oxford, 2002.

Metcalf, B. D., and Metcalf, T. R., *A Concise History of India*, Cambridge University Press, Cambridge, 2002.

Reat, N. R., *Buddhism, A History*, Asian Humanities Press, Berkeley, 1994.

Robb, P., *A History of India*, Palgrave, London and New York, 2002.

Schmidt, Karl J., *An atlas and survey of South Asian history*, M. E. Sharpe, Armonk, N.Y., 1995.

Spate, O. H. K., and Learmonth, A. T. A., *India and Pakistan: A General and Regional Geography* (3rd edition), Methuen, London, 1967.

Thapar, R., *Early India: From the Origins to AD 1300*, Penguin, London, 2002.

THE AGE OF MERCHANTS

Abraham, M., *Two Medieval Merchant Guilds of South India*, Oxford University Press, Delhi, 1988.

Alam, Muzaffar, 'Trade, State Policy and Regional Change: Aspects of Mughal–Uzbek Commercial Relations, c.1550–1750', in *Journal of the Economic and Social History of the Orient*, 37, 1994, pp. 202–227.

Bayly, S., *Caste, Society and Politics in India from the 18th Century to the Modern Age*, Cambridge University Press, Cambridge, 1999.

——, *Saints, Goddesses and Kings: Muslims and Christians in South Indian Society, 1700–1900*, Cambridge University Press, Cambridge, 1989.

Bouchon, G., *Regent of the Sea: Cannanore's Response to Portuguese Expansion, 1507–1528*, Oxford University Press, Delhi, 1988.

Chaudhuri, K. N., *Trade and Civilisation in the Indian Ocean: An Economic History from the Rise of Islam to 1750*, Cambridge University Press, Cambridge, 1985.

——, *Asia Before Europe: Economy and Civilisation of the Indian Ocean from the Rise of Islam to 1750*, Cambridge University Press, Cambridge, 1990.

Dale, Stephen, *Indian Merchants and Eurasian Trade, 1600–1750*, Cambridge University Press, Cambridge, 1994.

Das Gupta, A., *Indian Merchants and the Decline of Surat*, Harassowitz, Wiesbaden, 1979.

——, and Pearson, M. N. (eds.), *India and the Indian Ocean 1500–1800*, Oxford University Press, Delhi, 1987.

Dhavalikar, M. K., '4000 Year Old Merchant Traders of Western India', in *Indian Ocean Review*, 4, 4, December 1991, pp. 10–13, 20.

Ghosh, A., *In An Antique Land*, Vintage, New York, 1994.

Gorakshkar, Sadashiv, 'An illustrated Anis al-Haj in the Prince of Wales Museum, Bombay', in Skelton, Robert (ed.), *Facets of Indian Art*, Victoria and Albert Museum, London, 1986, pp. 158–67.

——, 'Anis al-Haj', in Khandalavala, Karl (ed.), *An Age of Splendour, Islamic Art in India*, Marg Publications, Bombay, 1983, pp. 132–135.

Kumar, D., *Land and Caste in South India* (2nd edition), Manohar, New Delhi, 1992.

Lahiri, N., 'Harappa as a Centre of Trade and Trade Routes, A Case-Study of the Resource-Use, Resource-Access and Lines of Communication in the Indus Civilisation', in *Indian Economic and Social History Review*, 27, 1990, pp. 405–444.

Levi, Scott C., *The Indian Diaspora in Central Asia and its trade, 1550–1900*, Brill Academic Publishers, Leiden, 2002.

McPherson, K., *The Indian Ocean: A History of People and the Sea*, Oxford University Press, Delhi, 1993.

——, 'Chulias and Klings, Indigenous Trade Diasporas and European Penetration of the Indian Ocean Littoral', in Borsa, Giorgio (ed.), *Trade and Politics in The Indian Ocean: Historical and Contemporary Perspectives*, Manohar, New Delhi, 1990, pp. 33–46.

——, 'Traditional Indian Ocean Shipping Technologies', in Bandaranayake, Senake (ed.), *Sri Lanka and the Silk Road of the Sea*, UNESCO, Colombo, 1990, pp. 261–265.

——, 'Anglo-Portuguese Commercial Relations in the Eastern Indian Ocean from the Seventeenth to the Eighteenth Centuries', in *South Asia XIX*, Special Issue, 1996, pp 41–57.

——, 'Paravas and Portuguese: A study of Portuguese strategy and its impact on an Indian seafaring community', in *Mare Liberum*, June 1997, pp. 69–82.

——, 'Trade and Traders in the Bay of Bengal, Fifteenth to Nineteenth Centuries', in Mukherjee, R., and Subramanian, L. (eds.), *Politics and Trade in the Indian Ocean World*, Oxford University Press, Delhi, 1998, pp. 183–209.

——, '*Uma Historia de Dues Conversões, a Cobiça e o Desenvolvimento de Novas Communidas na Região do Oceano Índico*' (A Tale of Two Conversions, The Evolution of New Christian Communities in the Indian Ocean region), in *Oceanos*, April/June 1998, pp. 74–87.

——, 'Staying on, Reflections on the Survival of Portuguese Enterprise in the Bay of Bengal and Southeast Asia from the Seventeenth to the Eighteenth Century', in Borschberg, Peter (ed.), *Iberians in the Singapore–Melaka Area, 16th to 18th Century*, Harassowitz, Wiesbaden, 2004, pp. 63–91.

Markovits, Claude, *The Global World of Indian Merchants, 1750–1947: Traders of Sind from Bukhara to Panama*, Cambridge University Press, Cambridge, 2000.

Metcalf, Barbara D., 'The Pilgrimage Remembered, South Asian accounts of the Hajj', in Eickelman, Dale F., and Piscatori, James (eds.), *Muslim Travellers, Pilgrimage, Migration and the Religious Imagination*, University of California Press, Berkeley and Los Angeles, 1990, pp. 85–107.

Pearson, M. N., *Merchants and Rulers in Gujarat*, University of California Press, Berkeley and Los Angeles, 1976.

——, 'Littoral Society, The Case of the Coast', in *The Great Circle*, 7, 1, April 1985, pp. 1–8.

——, *The Indian Ocean*, Routledge, London, 2003.

——, *Pilgrimage to Mecca, the Indian Experience*, Markus Wiener, Princeton, 1996.

——, *Pious Passengers, The Hajj in Earlier Times*, C. Hurst, London, 1994.

Qaisar, Jan A., 'From port to port, life on Indian pilgrimage ships in the sixteenth and seventeenth centuries', in Das Gupta, Ashin, and Pearson, M. N. (eds.), *India and the Indian Ocean, 1500–1800*, Oxford University Press, Calcutta, 1987, pp. 331–349.

Ratnagar, S., *Encounters: The Westerly Trade of the Harappan Civilisation*, Oxford University Press, Delhi, 1981.

Ray, H. P., *Monastery and Guild: Commerce Under the Satavahanas*, Oxford University Press, Delhi, 1986.

——, *The Winds of Change: Buddhism and the Maritime Links of Early South Asia*, Oxford University Press, Delhi, 1994.

Subrahmanyam, S., *Improvising Empire: Portuguese Trade and Settlement in the Bay of Bengal 1500–1700*, Oxford University Press, Delhi, 1990.

——, *The Portuguese Empire in Asia 1500–1700*, Longman, London, 1993.

Yang, A. A., 'Peasants on the Move, A Study of Internal Migration in India', *Journal of Interdisciplinary History*, X, 1, Summer 1979, pp. 37–58.

THE AGE OF COLONIAL CAPITAL

Alavi, S., *The Sepoys and the Company: Tradition and Transition in Northern India, 1770–1830*, Oxford University Press, Delhi, 1995.

Anderson, C., '"The Ferringees are Flying—the Ship is Ours!" the Convict Middle Passage in Colonial South and Southeast Asia, 1790–1860', *Indian Economic and Social History Review*, 41, 3, 2005, pp. 143–186.

Anderson, C., *Legible Bodies, Race, Criminality and Colonialism in South Asia*, Berg Publishing, Oxford, 2004.

Chatterjee, I., *Gender, Slavery and Law in Colonial India*, Oxford University Press, Delhi, 1999.

Christophe, Guilmoto, 'The Tamil Migration Cycle, 1830–1950', in *Economic and Political Weekly*, January 16–23 (1993), pp. 112–120.

Federation of Indian Chambers of Commerce and Industry, *Footprints of Enterprise: Indian Business Through the Ages*, Oxford University Press, Delhi, 1999.

Gillion, K. L., *Fiji's Indian Migrants, A History to the End of Indenture in 1920*, Oxford University Press, Melbourne, 1962.

Jain, Prakash, *Racial Discrimination Against Overseas Indians: A Class Analysis*, Concept Publishing Company, New Delhi, 1990.

Jayawardena, C., 'Migration and Social Change, A Survey of Indian Communities Overseas', in *Geographical Review*, LVIII (1968), pp. 426–449.

Kondapi, C., *Indian Overseas, 1838–1949*, Indian Council for World Affairs, New Delhi, 1951.

Kuper, Hilda, *Indian People in Natal*, Oxford University Press, Cape Town, 1960.

Lal, Brij V., *Girmitiyas: The Origins of the Fiji Indians*, Journal of Pacific History Monograph, Canberra, 1983.

Lal, Brij V., *Chalo Jahaji: On A Journey of Indenture Through Fiji*, Fiji Museum, Suva, 2000.

Lunt, J. (ed.), *From Sepoy to Subedar: Being the Life and Adventures of Subedar Sita Ram, a Native Officer of the Bengal Army*, Macmillan, London, 1988.

Mahadevan, Raman, 'Entrepreneurship and business communities in colonial Madras, 1900–1929', in Tripathi, D. (ed.), *Business Communities in India: A Historical Perspective*, Manohar, New Delhi, 1984.

Mahajani, Usha, *The Role of Indian Minorities in Burma and Malaya*, Vora, Bombay, 1960.

Markovits, C., *The Global World of Indian Merchants, 1750–1947: Traders of Sind from Bukhara to Panama*, Cambridge University Press, Cambridge, 2000.

Sandhu, Kernial S., *Indians in Malaya, Immigration and Settlement 1786–1957*, Cambridge University Press, London, 1969.

Satyanarayana, Adapa, 'Birds of Passage, Migration of South Indian Laborers to Southeast Asia', in *Critical Asian Studies*, 34, 1, 2002, pp. 89–115.

Tinker, Hugh, *A New System of Slavery: The Export of Indian Labour Overseas, 1830–1920*, Oxford University Press, London, 1974.

Visram, R., *Ayahs, Lascars and Princes, Indians in Britain, 1700–1947*, Pluto Press, London, 1986.

THE AGE OF GLOBALISATION

BBC, *Viewpoints on Migration*, Online News Series, views of eight commentators, 22 March 2004. *www.news.bbc.co.uk/1/hi/in_depth/3512992.stm*

Bates, Crispin (ed.), *Community, Empire and Migration: South Asians in Diaspora*, Palgrave, New York, 2001.

Ballard, Roger (ed.), *Desh Pardesh: The South Asian Presence in Britain*, C. Hurst, London, 1994.

Brown, Judith M., and Foot, Rosemary (eds.), *Migration, the Asian Experience*, St Martin's Press, New York, 1994.

Cohen, Robin (ed.), *The Cambridge Survey of World Migration*, Cambridge University Press, Cambridge, 1995.

Clarke, C., Peach, C., and Vertovec, S. (eds.), *South Asians Overseas: Migration and Ethnicity*, Cambridge University Press, New York, 1990.

'Diaspora Gives India an Edge in Outsourcing', *The Hindu Business Line*, 1 October 2004. *www.blonnet.com/2004/10/02/stories/2004100200920300. htm*

Federation of Indian Chambers of Commerce and Industry, 'About Us', *www.ficci.com/about-us/about-us.htm*

Gordon, James, and Gupta, Poonam, *Nonresident Deposits in India, In search of Return?* (Working Paper 04/48), IMF, Washington, 2004.

Gulati, I. S., and Mody, Asoka, *Remittances of Indian Migrants in the Middle East, An Assessment with Special Reference to Migrants from Kerala*, (Working Paper No. 182), Centre for Development Studies, Thiruvananthapuram, 1983.

International Organization for Migration, *Return Migration, Policies and Practices in Europe*, IOM, Geneva, 2004.

Issac, Thomas, 'Economic Consequences of Gulf Migration', in Zachariah, K. C., and Rajan, S. Irudaya (eds.), *Kerala's Demographic Transition, Determinants and Consequences*, Sage Publications, New Delhi, 1997, pp. 269–309.

Jensen, Joan M., *Passage from India – Asian Indian Immigrants in North America*, Yale University Press, New Haven, 1988.

Kannan, K. P., and Hari, K. S., 'Kerala's Gulf Connection, Remittances and their Macroeconomic Impact', in Zachariah, K. C. , Kannan, K. P., and Rajan, S. Irudaya (eds.), *Kerala's Gulf Connection: CDS Studies on International Labour Migration from Kerala State in India*, Centre for Development Studies, Thiruvananthapuram, 2002.

Khadria, Binod, *The Migration of Knowledge Workers, Second-Generation Effects of India's Brain Drain*, Sage Publications, New Delhi, 1999.

——, 'Of Dreams, Drain, and Dams – Metaphors in the Indian Emigration of Talent', *India International Centre Quarterly*, 26, 3, Monsoon 1999, pp. 79–90.

——, *Skilled Labour Migration from Developing Countries, Study on India*, (International Migration Papers no. 49), International Labour Office, Geneva, 2002.

——, *Migration of Highly Skilled Indians: Case Studies of IT and Health Professionals*, (STI Working Papers, 2004/6, April), OECD, Paris, 2004.

——, *Human Resources in Science and Technology in India and the International Mobility of Highly Skilled Indians*, (STI Working Paper, 2004/7, May), OECD, Paris, 2004.

——, 'Skilled Labor Migration from India', in Oda, Hisaya (ed.), *International Labor Migration from South Asia*, (ASEDP 70), Institute of Developing Economies, JETRO, Chiba, Japan, 2004.

——, 'Tracing the Genesis of Brain Drain in India through its State Policy and Civil Society', in Green, Nancy, and Weil, François, (eds.), *Citizenship and Those Who Leave, The Politics of Emigration and Expatriation*, University of Illinois Press, Illinois, 2005.

Nair, Gopinathan P. R., 'Incidence, Impact and Implications of Migration to the Middle East from Kerala (India)', in Amjad, R. (ed.), *To the Gulf and Back, Studies on the Economic Impact of Asian Labour Migration*, ILO/ARTEP, New Delhi, 1989.

Organisation for Economic Cooperation and Development, *Trends in International Migration*, (Annual Report 2003 edition), OECD, Paris, 2004.

Rajan, S., Irudaya 'From Kerala to the Gulf, Impacts of

Labour Migration', in *Asia Pacific Migration Journal*, 13, 4, 2004, pp. 497–510.

Robinson, V., *Transients, Settlers and Refugees: Asians in Britain*, Clarendon Press, Oxford, 1986.

Saxenian, AnnaLee, *Silicon Valley's New Immigrant Entrepreneurs*, (CCIS Working Paper No. 15), Center for Comparative Immigration Studies at University of California, San Diego, 2000.

Spencer, I. R. G., *British Immigration Policy Since 1939: The making of multi-racial Britain*, Routledge, London, 1997.

Srivastava, Ravi, and Sasikumar, S. K., *An Overview of Migration in India, its Impacts and Key Issues*, Department for International Development, London, 2004.

'FICCI to be Nodal Agency for Diaspora Business Associations', *The Hindu*, January 11, 2004. *www.hindu.com/2004/01/11/stories/2004011101371300.htm*

The Indus Entrepreneurs, 'About TiE', *www.tie.org/Home/AboutTie/index_html/view_document*

The Indus Entrepreneurs–UK, 'Charter Membership', *www.tieuk.org/Home/Membership/Charter%20Membership/ index_html/view_document*

Tripathi, D., *The Oxford History of Indian Business*, Oxford University Press, New Delhi, 2004.

World Bank, *Global Development Finance, Mobilizing Finance and Managing Vulnerability*, World Bank, Washington, 2005.

Zachariah, K. C., Mathew, E. T., and Rajan, S. Irudaya, 'Impact of Migration on Kerala's Economy and Society', in *International Migration*, 39, 1, 2001, pp. 63–88.

Zachariah, K. C., Prakash, B. A., and Rajan, S. Irudaya, *Gulf Migration Study, Employment Wages and Working Conditions of Kerala Emigrants in United Arab Emirates* (Working Paper No.326), Centre for Development Studies, Thiruvananthapuram, 2002.

Zachariah, K. C., Mathew, E. T., and Rajan, S. Irudaya, *Dynamics of Migration in Kerala: Dimensions, Determinants and Consequences*, Orient Longman, Hyderabad, 2003.

Zachariah, K. C., and Rajan, S. Irudaya, *Gulf Revisited*, (Working Paper No.363), Centre for Development Studies, Thiruvananthapuram, 2004.

INDIAN LEADERSHIP AND THE DIASPORA

Chaturvedi, Bernarsidas, and Sykes, Marjorie, *Charles Freer Andrews, A Narrative*, Allen and Unwin, London, 1949.

Government of India, Ministry of External Affairs, Annual Reports 1947–1995, Central Secretariat Library, New Delhi.

Lall, Marie-Carine, *India's Missed Opportunity: India's Relationship with the Non-Resident Indians*, Ashgate, Aldershot, 2001.

Reports of Annual Sessions of the Indian National Congress and Proceedings of the All India Congress Committee, 1885–1947, Nehru Memorial Museum and Library, New Delhi.

Shukla, Sandhya, *India Abroad: Diasporic Cultures of Postwar America and England*, Princeton University Press, Princeton, 2003.

LIFE IN THE DIASPORA

Afroz, Sultana, 'The Moghul Islamic Diaspora, The Institutionalization of Islam in Jamaica', in *Journal of Muslim Minority Affairs*, 20, 2, 2000, pp. 183–201.

Agnihotri, Rama Kant, *Crisis of identity – the Sikhs in England*, Bahri, New Delhi, 1987.

'An Ugly Day at Lord's Cricket Ground', *www.jewishcomment.com/cgibin/news.cgi?id=11&command =shownews&new*

Appadurai, Arjun, 'How to Make a National Cuisine: Cookbooks in Contemporary India', in *Comparative Studies in Society and History*, 30, 1, January 1988, pp. 3–24.

Arasaratnam, Sinnappah, *Indians in Malaysia and Singapore*, Oxford University Press, Kuala Lumpur, 1970.

Ballard, Roger, 'The Growth and Changing Character of the Sikh Presence in Britain', in Coward, Harold (ed.), *The South Asian Religious Diaspora in Britain, Canada and the United States*, State University of New York Press, New York, 2000, pp. 127–144.

Basu, Anuradha, 'Immigrant Entrepreneurs in the Food Sector, Breaking the Mould', in Kersher, Anne (ed.), *Food in the Migrant Experience*, Ashgate, Burlington, 2002, pp. 149–171.

Basu, Indrajit, *India a Wrap for Global Fashion Designers*, UPI, 28 January 2005.

Basu, Shrabani, *Curry in the Crown: The Story of Britain's Favourite Food*, Harper Collins India, New Delhi, 1999.

Bhachu, Parminder, 'Designing Diasporic Markets, Asian Fashion Entrepreneurs in London', in Niessen, Sandra, Leshkowich, Ann Marie, and Jones, Carla (eds.), *Re-orienting Fashion: The Globalization of Asian Dress*, Berg, Oxford, 2003, pp. 139–158.

Bhat, Chandrashekar, and Sahoo, Ajaya Kumar, 'Diaspora to Transnational Networks: the Case of Indians in Canada', *www.uohyd.ernet.in/sss/cinddiaspora/occ7.html*

Bilimoria, Purushottam, 'The Australian South Asian Diaspora', in Hinnells, John R. (ed.), *A New Handbook of Living Religions*, Blackwell Publishers, Oxford, 1997.

Birbalsingh, Frank, and Seecharan, Clem, *Indo-Westindian Cricket*, Hansib, London, 1988.

'Brief History of Hockey in Hong Kong', *www.hockey.org/hk/hkha/eng/hkhockey/main.html*

Chaudhuri, Nupur, 'Shawls, Jewelry, Curry and Rice in Victorian Britain', in Chaudhuri, Nupur, and Stroebel, Margaret (eds.), *Western Women and Imperialism: Complicity and Resistance*, Indiana University Press, Bloomington and Indianapolis, 1992, pp. 231–246.

Commission for Racial Equality, *Goal: Racial Equality in Football, Summary of Research Findings and Action Plan*, CRE, London, 2004.

Coney, Judith, 'New Religious Movements Led in the West by South Asians', in Coward, Harold (ed.), *The South Asian Religious Diaspora in Britain, Canada and the United States*, State University of New York Press, New York, 2000, pp. 55–73.

'Cricket, Some Memorable Events in Kenya Cricket History', *www.kenyaweb.com/sports/cricket/index/html*

'Cricket in Little India, How's That?' *www.haverfors.edu/library/cricket/CCMA0001.htm*

Curiel, Jonathon, 'Chadha's Homage to Bollywood', *www.sfgate.com/cgi-bin/article.cgi?file=/c/a/2005/02/13/ PKGPGB688S1.DTL&type*

Dangor, S. E., 'Negotiating Identities, The Case of Indian Muslims in South Africa', in Jacobsen, Knut, and Kumar, Pratap (eds.), *South Asians in the Diaspora: Histories and Religious Traditions*, Brill, Leiden, 2004, pp. 243–269.

Devers, Sean, 'I Don't Support Anything That Divides', interview with Ramnaresh Sarwan, *www.caribbeancricket.com/modules.php?name=Nes&file=a rticle&sid=1079*

Dudrah, R. K., *Bollywood: Sociology Goes to the Movies*, Sage, New Delhi, London and Thousand Oaks, 2006.

——, 'Zee TV, Diasporic Non-Terrestrial Television in Europe', *South Asian Popular Culture*, 3, 1, 2005, pp. 33–47.

——, 'Zee TV in Europe, Non-Terrestrial Television and the Construction of a Pan-South Asian European Identity', in *Contemporary South Asia*, 11, 1, 2002, pp. 163–181.

——, 'Drum N Dhol, British Bhangra Music and Diasporic South Asian Identity Formation', in *European Journal of Cultural Studies*, 5, 3, 2002, pp. 363–383.

——, 'Cultural Production in the British Bhangra Music Industry, Music-Making, Locality, and Gender', in *International Journal of Punjab Studies*, 9, 2, 2002, pp. 219–251.

Eriksen, Thomas Hylland, 'Indians in New Worlds: Mauritius and Trinidad', in *Social and Economic Studies*, 41, 1, March 1992, pp. 157–187.

Gambhir, S. K., 'The East Indian Speech Community in Guyana, a Sociolinguistic Study with Special Reference to Koine-formation', Ph.D. thesis, University of Pennsylvania, 1981.

Gaston, Anne-Marie, *Bharata Natyam: From Temple to Theatre*, Manohar, New Delhi, 1996.

Gautam, M. K., 'The Construction of the Indian Image in Suriname, Deconstructing Colonial Derogatory Notions and Reconstructing Indian Identity', in Gosine, M., and Narine, D. (eds.), *Sojourners to Settlers, Indian Migrants in the Caribbean and the Americas*, Windsor Press, US, 1999, pp. 125–179.

Gorringe, Magdalen, 'South Asian Dance in U. K.', Khokar, Ashish Mohan (ed.), in *Attendance 2001, The Dance Annual of India*, EKAH-Printways, Bangalore, 2001.

Gosine, Mahin, 'The Forgotten Children of India: A Global Perspective', in Motwani, Jagat K. (ed.), *Global Indian Diaspora, Yesterday, Today and Tomorrow*, Global Organization of People of Indian Origin (GOPIO), New York, 1993, pp. 11–28.

Hinnells, John R., 'The Zoroastrian Diaspora in Britain, Canada and the United States', in Coward, Harold (ed.), *The South Asian Religious Diaspora in Britain, Canada and the United States*, State University of New York Press, New York, 2000, pp. 35–54.

Hinnells, John, R., 'The Zoroastrian Diaspora', in Jacobsen, Knut, and Kumar, Pratap (eds.), *South Asians in the Diaspora: Histories and Religious Traditions*, Brill, Leiden, 2004, pp. 313–336.

'History of Cricket in Hong Kong', *http://usa.cricinfo.com/db/national/icc_members/history/chronolo*

Howe, Leo, *Hinduism and Hierarchy in Bali*, School of American Research Press, Santa Fe, 2001.

'Indian Look has become an Integral Part of World Fashion, Says Selfridges Rep', *Hindustan Times*, 2 November 2005.

'Introduction, Hockey', *www.kenyaweb.com/sports/hockey/index/html*

Jain, Prakash C., 'Five Patterns of Indian Emigration', in Motwani, Jagat K. (ed.), *Global Indian Diaspora, Yesterday, Today and Tomorrow*, Global Organization of People of Indian Origin (GOPIO), New York, 1993, pp. 29–33.

Jaffrey, Madhur, *Madhur Jaffrey's Ultimate Curry Bible*, Ebury, London, 2003.

———, *A Taste of India: The Definitive Guide to Regional Cooking*, Pavilion, London, 1985.

'Jasmer Singh Grewal', *www.kenya63.homestead.com.JasmerSingh~ns4.html*

Joseph, Clara A. B., 'Rethinking Hybridity, The Syro-Malabar Church in North America', in Jacobsen, Knut, and Kumar, Pratap (eds.), *South Asians in the Diaspora: Histories and Religious Traditions*, Brill, Leiden, 2004, pp. 220–242.

Kent, Alexandra, 'Creating Divine Unity, Chinese Recruitment in the Sathya Sai Baba Movement of Malaysia', *Journal of Contemporary Religion*, 15, 1, 2000, pp. 5–27.

Khan, Aisha, 'Migration Narratives and Moral Imperatives, Local and Global in the Muslim Caribbean', *Comparative Studies of South Asia, Africa and the Middle East*, XVII, 1, 1997, pp. 127–144.

Knott, Kim, *Hinduism in Leeds*, Department of Theology and Religious Studies, University of Leeds, Leeds, 1986.

Lal, Vinay, 'The Politics of History on the Internet, Cyber-diasporic Hinduism and the North American Hindu Diaspora', in *Diaspora*, 8, 2, 1999, pp. 137–172.

Linda, Mary, 'Constructing Identity, Hindu Temple Production in the United States', in Rukmani, T. S., and Manoharlal, Munshiram (eds.), *Global Perspectives*, New Delhi, 2001, pp. 387-396.

Mahabir, Noor Kumar, *Caribbean East Indian Recipes*, Chakra, San Juan, Trinidad, 1992.

Mankekar, Purnima, '"India Shopping", Indian Grocery Stores and Transnational Configurations of Belonging', in Watson, James L., and Caldwell, Melissa L. (eds.), *The Cultural Politics of Food and Eating*, Blackwell, Oxford, 2005, pp. 197–214.

Mann, Gurinder Singh, 'Sikhism in the United States of America', in Coward, Harold (ed.), *The South Asian Religious Diaspora in Britain, Canada and the United States*, State University of New York Press, New York, 2000, pp. 259–277.

Marquesee, Mike, 'Two Cultures of English Cricket', *www.carf.demon.co.uk/feat23.html*

McDonough, Sheila, 'The Muslims of Canada', in Coward, Harold (ed.), *The South Asian Religious Diaspora in Britain, Canada and the United States*, State University of New York Press, New York, 2000, pp. 173–190.

Meduri, Avanthi, 'Bharatha Natyam – What are you?', in *Asian Theatre Journal*, 5, 1, Spring 1988, pp.1–22.

Muman, Sat Pal, 'Caste in Britain', *www.ambedkar.org/Worldwide_Dalits/caste_in_Britain.htm*

Murphy, Anne, 'Mobilising *Seva* (Service), Modes of

Sikh Diasporic Action', in Jacobsen, Knut, and Kumar, Pratap (eds.), *South Asians in the Diaspora: Histories and Religious Traditions*, Brill, Leiden, 2004, pp. 337–376.

'New Cricket Magazine has a particular focus on Asians', *www.asiansinmedia.org/news/article.php/publishing/823*

Nielsen, Jorgen S., 'Muslims in Britain, Ethnic Minorities, Community or Ummah?', in Coward, Harold (ed.), *The South Asian Religious Diaspora in Britain, Canada and the United States*, State University of New York Press, New York, 2000, pp. 109–126.

O'Connell, Joseph, 'Sikh Religio-ethnic Experience in Canada', in Coward, Harold (ed.), *The South Asian Religious Diaspora in Britain, Canada and the United States*, State University of New York Press, New York, 2000, pp. 191–210.

O'Shea, Janet, '"Traditional" Indian Dance and the Making of Interpretive Communities', in *Asian Theatre Journal*, 15, 1, Spring 1998, pp. 45–63.

Panayi, Panikos, 'The Spicing-Up of English Provincial Life, The History of Curry in Leicester', in Kersher, Anne (ed.), *Food in the Migrant Experience*, Ashgate, Burlington, 2002, pp. 42–76.

Pluss, Caroline, 'Constructing Globalized Ethnicity: Migrants from India and Hong Kong', *International Sociology*, 20, 2, 2005, pp. 201–224.

Puwar, Nirmal and Nandi, Bhatial et al.(eds.), *Fashion and Orientalism*, Berg, Oxford, 2003.

Radford, Mikal Austin,'(Re) Creating Transnational Religious Identity with the Jaina Community of Toronto', in Jacobsen, Knut, and Kumar, Pratap (eds.), *South Asians in the Diaspora: Histories and Religious Traditions*, Brill, Leiden, 2004, pp. 23–51.

Rai, Amit S., 'India On-line, Electronic Bulletin Boards and the Construction of a Diasporic Hindu Identity', *Diaspora*, 4, 1995, pp. 31–57.

Ramanathan, K., 'The Hindu Diaspora in Malaysia', in Rukmani, T. S. (ed.), *Hindu Diaspora: Global Perspectives*, Munshiram Manoharlal, New Delhi, 1993, pp. 81–122.

Rampton, Ben, *Crossing: Language and Ethnicity Among Adolescents*, Longman, London, 1995.

Ramyead, L. P., 'Hindi in Mauritius, a Perspective', in Barz, R. K., and Siegel, J. (eds.), *Language Transplanted: The Development of Overseas Hindi*, Harrassowitz, Wiesbaden, 1988, pp. 23–40.

Rayfield, J. R., *The Languages of a Bilingual Community*, Mouton, The Hague, 1970.

Reddy, E. S., 'Sports and the Liberation Struggle', *www.scnc.ukzn.ac.za/doc/sport/sportram.htm*

Roy, Sanjoy, 'Dirt, Noise, Traffic, Contemporary Indian Dance in the Western City: Modernity, Ethnicity and Hybridity', in Thomas, Helen (ed.), *Dance in the City*, St. Martin's Press, New York, 1997, pp. 68–86.

Roy, Parama, 'Reading Communities and Culinary Communities, The Gastropoetics of the South Asian Diaspora', in *Positions*, 10, 2, 2002, 471–502.

Rukmani, T. S. (ed.), *Hindu Diaspora: Global Perspectives*, Munshiram Manoharlal, New Delhi, 2001.

Sandhu, Kernial Singh, *Indians in Malaya, Some Aspects of Their Immigration and Settlement Patterns (1786–1957)*, Cambridge University Press, London, 1969.

Singh, Savinder, 'Sikhs In Sport', *www.bsingh.dsl.pipex.com/khalsa.sikhsports.htm*

Sinha, Vineeta, 'Modern Religious Movements, Religious and Counter-religious', unpublished academic exercise, Department of Sociology, National University of Singapore, 1985.

———, 'Merging "Different" Sacred Spaces, Enabling Religious Encounters through Pragmatic Utilization of Space?', in *Contributions to Indian Sociology*, 37, 3, 2003, pp. 459–494.

Sridhar, Kamal K., 'Language Maintenance by Asian Indians in the U.S., Kannada Speakers in the New York area', in *International Journal of the Sociology of Language*, 69, 1988, pp. 73–87.

———, 'South Asian Diaspora in Europe and the U.S.', in Kachru, Braj B., and Sridhar, S. N. (eds.), *Language in South Asia*, Cambridge University Press, Cambridge, forthcoming.

Sumbly, Vimal, 'NRIs To Set Up Sports Academy', *www.tribuneindia.com/2004/20041104/ldh3.htm*

'Sunny Kanwal', *www.southall-punjabi.com/sports/sikh_union.html*

'The Rise of Indian Billionaire(s) in Canada', *www.despardes.com/Diaspora/newsbriefs/102904.htm*

Thomas, D., 'Curry on the Catwalk', *Newsweek*, 3 December 2001.

Vallely, Anne, 'The Jain Plate, The Semiotics of Diaspora Diet', in Jacobsen, Knut, and Kumar, Pratap (eds.), *South Asians in the Diaspora; Histories and Religious Traditions*, Brill, Leiden, 2004, pp. 3–22.

Van der Avoird, Tim, 'Determining Language Vitality: the Language use of Hindu Communities in the Netherlands and the United Kingdom', Ph.D. thesis, University of Tilburg, 2001.

Van der Veer, Peter and Vertovec, S., 'Brahmanism Abroad: On Caribbean Hinduism as an Ethnic Religion', *Ethnology*, 30, 1991, pp. 149–166.

Venkat, 'Hashim Amla, South Africa's New Indian Son', *www.cricketfundas.com/hashimamlaprofile.html*

Verma, Mahendra K., 'The Hindi Speech Community', in Alladina, Safder, and Edwards, Viv (eds.), *Multilingualism in the British Isles*, Longman, London, 1991, pp. 103–114.

Vertovec, Steven, *The Hindu Diaspora: Comparative Patterns*, Routledge, London and New York, 2000.

Waters, Chris, 'Row Over MP's County Cricket Racism Claims', *www.muslimnews.co.uk?news/news.php?article=8312*

Werbner, Pnina, 'Stamping the Earth with the Name of Allah, Zikr and the Sacralizing of Space among British Muslims', *Cultural Anthropology*, 11, 3, 1996, pp. 309–338.

Williams, Raymond Brady, 'South Asian Christians in Britain, Canada and the United States', in Coward, Harold (ed.), *The South Asian Religious Diaspora in Britain, Canada and the United States*, State University of New York Press, New York, 2000, pp. 13–34.

Zelinsky, Wilbur, 'The Roving Palate, North America's Ethnic Restaurant Cuisines', *Geoform*, 16, 1, 1985, pp. 51–72.

Voices from the Diaspora

Akhil, Shalini, *The Bollywood Beauty*, Penguin Books, Camberwell, Victoria, 2005.

Ankur, 1.1, Spring 1991, and 2.2, Winter/Spring 1992/1993, Vancouver, British Columbia, Canada.

Birbalsingh, Frank (ed.), *Jahaji: An Anthology of Indo-Caribbean Fiction*, TSAR Publications, Toronto, 2000.

Butlin, Ron (ed.), *Mauritian Voices, New Writing in English*, Flambard, Newcastle-upon-Tyne, 1997.

Chandra, Vikram, *Border Dialogues: Journeys in Postmodernity*, Routledge, London, 1990.

Dabydeen, Cyril, *My Brahmin Days and Other Stories*, TSAR Publications, Toronto, 2000.

Dabydeen, David and Samaroo, Brinsley (eds.), *Across the Dark Waters: Ethnicity and Indian Identity in the Caribbean*, Macmillan, Basingstoke, 1996.

———, *India in the Caribbean*, Hansib, London and University of Warwick, Centre for Caribbean Studies, 1987.

de Verteuil, Anthony, *Eight East Indian Immigrants*, Paria Publishing, Port-of-Spain, 1989.

Dhondy, Farrukh, *Bombay Duck*, Picador, London, 1991.

Essop, Ahmed, *Noorjehan and Other Stories*, Ravan Press, Johannesburg, 1990.

———, *Hajji Musa and the Hindu Fire-Walker*, Readers International, London, 1988.

———, *The Emperor*, Ravan Press, Johannesburg, 1984.

Fluderlink, Monika (ed.), *Diaspora and Multiculturalism*, Rodopi, Amsterdam, 2003.

Ghosh, Amitav, *The Imam and the Indian: Prose Pieces*, Ravi Dayal and Permanent Black, Delhi, 2002.

Ghosh-Schellhorn, Martina (with Vera Alexander), *Peripheral Centres, Central Peripheries: India and its Diaspora(s)*, Lit Verlag, Berlin, 2006.

Kumar, Amita, *Bombay London New York*, Routledge, London and New York, 2002.

Khoyratty, Farhad, 'Compass', in Coetzee, J. M. (ed.), *African Compass*, Kenilworth New Africa Books, South Africa, 2005, pp. 7–15.

Kunzru, Hari, *The Impressionist*, Dutton, New York, 2004.

Ladoo, Harold Sonny, *No Pain Like This Body* (reprint 2003), Anansi, Toronto, 1972 .

Lal, Brij V., *Chalo Jahaji: On A Journey of Indenture Through Fiji*, Fiji Museum, Suva, 2000.

Lionnet, Françoise, 'Transcolonial Translations: Shakespeare in Mauritius', in Lionnet, Françoise, and Shih, Shu-mei (eds.), *Minor Transnationalism*, Duke University Press, Durham and London, 2005, pp. 201–221.

Maniam, K. S., 'The New Diaspora', in McMillen, Donald H. (ed.), *Globalisation and Regional Communities: Geoeconomic, Sociocultural and Security Implications for Australia*, University of Southern Queensland Press, Toowoomba, 1997, pp. 18–23.

Manicka, Rani, *Touching Earth*, Sceptre, London, 2004.

Mehta, Suketu, *Maximum City, Bombay Lost and Found*, Alfred A. Knopf, New York, 2004.

Mehta, V. (ed.), *Sound-Shadows of the New World*, W. W. Norton, New York, 1985.

Mishra, Sudesh, *Diaspora Theory*, Edinburgh University Press, Edinburgh, 2006.

Mishra, Vijay, 'The Diasporic Imaginary and the Indian Diaspora', occasional lecture, Asian Studies Institute, Victoria University of Wellington, Wellington, 2005.

——, *Bollywood Cinema: Temples of Desire*, Routledge, New York and London, 2002.

Mooneeram, Roshni, 'Theatre in Development in Banham, Martin, Gibbs, James, and Osofisan, Femi (eds.), Mauritius', in *African Theatre in Development*, James Currey, Oxford, 1999, pp. 24–37.

Myers, Helen, *Music of Hindu Trinidad: Songs from the Indian Diaspora*, University of Chicago Press, Chicago, 1998.

Nelson, Emmanuel S. (ed.), *Reworlding: The Literature of the Indian Diaspora*, Greenwood Press, Westport, 1992.

Poynting, Jeremy, '"You Want to be a Coolie Woman?": Gender and Ethnic Identity in Indo-Caribbean Women's Writing', in Cudjoe, Selwyn R. (ed.), *Caribbean Women Writers*, Calaloux Publications, Wellesley, 1990, pp. 98–105.

Puri, Shalini, *The Caribbean Postcolonial: Social Equality, Post-Nationalism, and Cultural Hybridity*, Palgrave Macmillan, New York, 2004.

Radhakrishnan, Rajagopalan, *Diasporic Meditations: Between Home and Location*, University of Minnesota Press, Minneapolis, 1996.

Rushdie, Salman, *Imaginary Homelands: Essays and Criticism 1981–1991*, Granta/Viking, London, 1991.

——, *Shalimar the Clown*, Jonathan Cape, London, 2005.

Spivak, Gayatri Chakravorty, 'Diasporas Old and New: Women in the Transnational World', in *Textual Practice*, 10, 1996, pp. 245–269.

Srikanth, Rajini, *The World Next Door: South Asian American Literature and the Idea of America*, Temple University Press, Philadelphia, 2004.

Virahsawmy, Dev, 'Toufann' (playscript), in *African Theatre: Playwrights and Politics*, translated by Walling, Nisha, and Walling, Michael, James Currey, Oxford, 2001, pp. 217–254.

SOUTH ASIA

Sri Lanka

Heidemann, Frank, 'Die Hochland-Tamilen in Sri Lanka und ihre Repatriierung nach Indien', thesis, Göttingen, 1989.

——, *Kanganies in Sri Lanka and Malaysia: Tamil Recruiter-cum-Foreman as a Sociological Category in the 19th and 20th Century*, Anacon, Munich, 1992.

Chattopadhyaya, H. P., *Indians in Sri Lanka: A Historical Study*, O. P. S. Publishers, Calcutta, 1979.

Fries, Yvonne and Thomas, Bibin, *The Undesirables: The Expatriation of the Tamil People of recent Origin from the Plantations in Sri Lanka to India*, K. P. Bagchi, Calcutta, 1984.

Peebles, Patrick, *The Plantation Tamils of Ceylon*, Continuum International Publishing Group, London, 2001.

Russell, Jane, *Communal Politics under the Donoughmore Scheme, 1931–1947*, Tisara Prakasayo Ltd, Dehiwala, 1982.

Sahadevan, P., *India and Overseas Indians: The Case of Sri Lanka*, Kalinga Publications, Delhi, 1995.

Vanden Driesen, Ian H., *The Long Walk: Indian*

Plantation Labour in the 19th Century, Prestige Books, New Delhi, 1997.

Weerasooriya, W. S., *The Nattukottai Chettiar Merchant Bankers in Ceylon*, Tisara Prakasakayo, Dehiwala, 1973.

Nepal

Burkert, Claire, 'Defining Maithil Identity: Who is in Charge?', in David Gellner et al. (eds.), *Nationalism and Ethnicity in a Hindu Kingdom: The Politics of Culture in Contemporary Nepal*, Harwood, Amsterdam, 1997, pp. 241–273

Kansakar, Vidya Bir Singh, 'Nepal–India Open Border: Prospects, Problems and Challenges', Nepal Democracy, *www.nepaldemocracy.org/documents/treaties_agreements/nep_india_open_border*

Manchanda, Rita, 'Whose Nepal, Whose India: Of Diasporas and Transnational Identities', in Ghosh, Lipi, and Chatterjee, Ramkrishna (eds.), *Indian Diaspora in Asian and Pacific Regions: Culture, People, Interactions*, Rawat, Jaipur, 2004, pp. 53–63.

Muni, S. D., *India and Nepal: A Changing Relationship*, Konarak, Delhi, 1992.

Parmanand, 'The Indian Community in Nepal and the Nepalese Community in India: The Problem of National Integration', *Asian Survey*, 26, 9 (September 1986), pp. 1005–1019.

Pemble, John, *The Invasion of Nepal: John Company at War*, Clarendon Press, Oxford, 1971.

Upreti, B. C., *Indians in Nepal: A Study of Indian Migration to Kathmandu*, Kalinga, Delhi, 1999.

Weiner, Myron, 'The Political Demography of Nepal', *Asian Survey*, 13, 6, June 1973, pp. 617–630.

Whelpton, John, *A History of Nepal*, Cambridge University Press, Cambridge, 2005.

Maldives

Bell, H. C. P., *The Maldive Islands: Monograph on the History, Archaeology and Epigraphy*, Ceylon Government Press, Colombo, 1940; NCLHR, Male, 1985; Novelty Printers Publishers, Male, 2004.

Hockley, T. W., *The Two Thousand Islands: A Short Account of the People, History and Customs of the Maldives Archipelago*, Witherby, London, 1935.

Rosset, C. W., 'The Maldive Islands', *The Graphic*, 16 October 1886, pp. 413–416.

'Sketches in the Maldive Islands, Indian Ocean', *The Graphic*, 4 June 1881, p. 548.

'Sketches in the Maldive Islands', *Harper's Weekly*, 7 May 1881, p. 296.

SOUTHEAST ASIA

Malaysia

Jain, R. K., *South Indians on the Plantation Frontier in Malaya*, Yale University Press, New Haven, 1970.

Kaur, A., 'Indian Labour, Labour Standards, and Workers' Health in Burma and Malaya, 1900–1940', *Modern Asian Studies*, 40, 2, 2006, pp. 425–475.

——, *Wage labour in Southeast Asia since 1840*, Palgrave Macmillan, Basingstoke, 2004.

——, 'Crossing Borders, Race, Migration and Borders in Southeast Asia', in *International Journal on Multicultural Societies* (IJMS), 6, 2, 2004, pp. 111–132.

——, 'Economy and Society', in Kaur, Amarjit and Metcalfe, Ian (eds.), *The Shaping of Malaysia*, Basingstoke, Macmillan, 1999, pp. 121–173.

——, 'Working on the Railway: Indian Workers in Malaya, 1880–1957', in Rimmer, Peter J., and Allen, Lisa M. (eds.), *Pullers, Planters, Plantation Workers: The Underside of Malaysian History*, Singapore University Press, Singapore, 1990.

——, 'Hewers and Haulers, a History of Coal Miners and Coal Mining in Malaya', in *Modern Asian Studies*, 24, 1990, pp. 75–113.

Rai, Rajesh, '"Race" and the Construction of the North-South Divide Amongst Indians in Colonial Malaya and Singapore', in *South Asia*, XXVIII, 2, 2004, pp. 245–264.

Ramachandran, Selvakumaran, *Indian Plantation Labour in Malaya*, S. Abdul Majeed & Co., Kuala Lumpur, for the Institute of Social Analysis (INSAN), 1994.

Sandhu, K. S., *Indians in Malaya: Some Aspects of Their Immigration and Settlement*, Cambridge University Press, Cambridge, 1969.

Saw, Swee Hock, *The Population of Postwar Malaysia*, Singapore University Press, Singapore, 1988.

Thompson, V., *Labour Problems in South-east Asia*, Yale University Press, New Haven, 1947.

——, *Post-mortem on Malaya*, Macmillan, New York, 1943.

Voon, Phin Keong, *Western Rubber Planting Enterprise in Southeast Asia 1876–1921*, Penerbit Universiti Malaya, Kuala Lumpur, 1976.

Myanmar

Chakravarti, N. R., *The Indian Minority in Burma: The Rise and Decline of an Immigrant Community*, Oxford University Press, London, 1971.

Desai, W. S., *India and Burma: A Study*, Orient Longman, Calcutta, 1954.

Kyi, Khin Maung, 'Indians in Burma, Problems of an Alien Subculture in a Highly Integrated Society', in Sandhu, K. S. and Mani, A. (eds.), *Indian Communities in Southeast Asia*, Institute of Southeast Asian Studies, Singapore, 1993.

Mahajani, Usha, *The Role of Indian Minorities in Burma and Malaya*, Vora, Bombay, 1960.

Taylor, Robert H., 'The Legal Status of Indians in Contemporary Burma', in Sandhu, K. S. and Mani, A. (eds.), *Indian Communities in Southeast Asia*, Institute of Southeast Asian Studies, Singapore, 1993.

Than, Tin Maung Maung, 'Some Aspects of Indians in Rangoon', in Sandhu, K. S. and Mani, A. (eds.), *Indian Communities in Southeast Asia*, Institute of Southeast Asian Studies, Singapore, 1993.

Yegar, Moshe, *The Muslims of Burma: A Study of a Minority Group*, Otto Harrassowitz, Wiesbaden, 1972.

Singapore

Ampalvanar, Rajeswary, 'Politics and the Indian Community in West Malaysia and Singapore', 1945–1957, Ph.D. thesis, University of London, 1978.

Arasaratnam, Sinnappah, *Indians in Malaysia and Singapore* (revised edition), Oxford University Press, Kuala Lumpur, 1979.

Brown, Rajeswary Ampalavanar, *The Indian Minority and Political Change in Malaya, 1945–1957*, Oxford University Press, Kuala Lumpur, 1981.

Chew, Melanie, *Leaders of Singapore*, Resource Press, Singapore, 1996.

Mani, A., 'Indians in Singapore Society', in Sandhu, K. S. and Mani, A. (eds.), *Indian Communities in Southeast Asia*, Institute of Southeast Asian Studies, Singapore, 1993.

——, 'Tamils in Singapore: Yesterday, Today and Tomorrow', in Sankaran, C., Thinappan, S. P., and Arasu, V. T. (eds.), *Tamil in An International Arena: First Step*, UniPress, Singapore, 2004.

Netto, Leslie, *Passage of Indians: Singapore Indian Association, 1923–2003*, Singapore Indian Association, Singapore, 2003.

Purushotam, Nirmala, *Negotiating Language, Constructing Race, Disciplining Difference in Singapore*, Mouton de Gruyter, Berlin, New York, 1998.

Rajesh Rai, 'Positioning the Indian Diaspora: The Southeast Asian Experience', in Maharaj, Brij, Narayan, K. Laxmi, and Sangha, Dave (eds.), *Indian Diaspora: Retrospect and Prospect*, Sage, New Delhi, (forthcoming).

——, '"Race" and the Construction of the North-South Divide Amongst Indians in Colonial Malaya and Singapore', in *South Asia*, XXVIII, 2, 2004, pp. 245–264.

——, 'Sepoys, Convicts and the "Bazaar" Contingent: The Emergence and Exclusion of "Hindustani" Pioneers at the Singapore Frontier', in *Journal of Southeast Asian Studies*, 35, 1, 2004, pp. 1–19.

——, 'The Attrition and Survival of Minority Languages: The Development of Non-Tamil South Asian Languages in the Singapore "Indian" Diaspora', (conference paper), Asian Diasporas: Re-visiting the Chinese and South Asian Experiences, Singapore, 5–7 April 2004.

Sandhu, Kernial Singh, *Indians in Malaya: Some Aspects of their Immigration and Settlement (1786–1957)*, Cambridge University Press, London, 1969.

Siddique, Sharon, and Puru Shotam, Nirmala, *Singapore's Little India: Past, Present, and Future*, Institute of Southeast Asian Studies, Singapore, 1990.

Swinstead, Gene and Haddon, George, *Singapore*

Stopover, Times Books International Singapore, Singapore, 1981.

Tan, Tai Yong and Major, Andrew J., 'India and Indians in the Making of Singapore', in Yong Mun Cheong and Rao, V. V. Bhanoji (eds.), *Singapore–India Relations, a Primer*, Singapore University Press, Singapore, 1995, pp. 1–28.

Walker, Anthony R. (ed.), *New Place, Old Ways: Essays on Indian Society and Culture in Modern Singapore*, Hindustan Pub. Corp., Delhi, 1994.

Thailand

Hussain, Zakir, *The Silent Minority: Indians in Thailand*, Asian Studies Institute, Chulalongkorn University, Bangkok, 1981.

Netnapit, Nagawachara, 'Indian Community in Thailand: Phahurat and Sii Yaek Baan Khaek', paper presented at the workshop on 'Ethnic Group Studies Survey in Thailand', organised by the Thai Studies Institute, Chulalongkorn University, Bangkok, 1985.

Sidhu, Manjit S., *Sikhs in Thailand*, Asian Studies Institute, Chulalongkorn University, Bangkok, 1992.

Mani, A., 'Indians in Thailand', in Sandhu, K. S. and Mani, A. (eds.), *Indian Communities in Southeast Asia*, Institute of Southeast Asian Studies, Singapore, 1993.

Phongthada, Wuthikarn, and Phoonket, Janthakanon, 'Indian–Thai Community in Amphoe Muang, Chiangmai: A Case Study in Economy, Society and Culture', report submitted to the Institute of Research and Development, Payap University, 1990.

Inthira Sahi, 'The Network of Indian Garment Merchants in Thai Society between the Year 2400–2490', Ph.D. thesis, Department of History, Chulalongkorn University, Bangkok, 2002.

Indonesia

Arora, B. D., *India Indonesian Relations (1961–1980)*, Asia Educational Services, New Delhi, 1981.

Bachtiar, H. W., 'Indians in Indonesia, A component of Indonesian National Integration', in Sandhu, K. S. and Mani, A. (eds.), *Indian Communities in Southeast Asia*, ISEAS and Times Academic Press, Singapore, 1993, pp. 131–150,

Howe, L., *Hinduism and Hierarchy in Bali*, School of American Research Press, Santa Fe, 2001.

'Gandhi Memorial International School (GMIS)', *www.indoindians.com/education/gmis.htm*

'Indian traders feel at home in Pasar Baru', *Jakarta Post*, *www.thejakartapost.com/community/India2.asp*

Kurniawan, H., 'IndoIndians.com brings Indians in Indonesia together', *Jakarta Post*, *www.thejakartapost.com/community/India4.asp*

Mani, A., 'Indians in North Sumatra', in Sandhu, K. S. and Mani, A. (eds.), *Indian Communities in Southeast Asia*, ISEAS and Times Academic Press, Singapore, 1993, pp. 46–97.

Mani, A., 'Indians in Jakarta', in Sandhu, K. S. and Mani, A. (eds.), *Indian Communities in Southeast Asia*, ISEAS and Times Academic Press, Singapore, 1993, pp. 98–130.

Picard, M., 'Cultural Tourism, Nation Building, and Regional Culture: The Making of Balinese Identity', in Picard, M., and Wood, E. R. (eds.), *Tourism, Ethnicity, and the State in Asian and Pacific Societies*, University of Hawaii Press, Honolulu, 1997.

Ramstedt, M., (ed.), *Hinduism in Modern Indonesia: A minority religion between local, national, and global interests*, Routledge Curzon, London, 2004.

———, 'Modern Hinduism', *International Institute for Asian Studies News Letter Online*, IIAS, Leiden, October 2000.

Thompson, V., *Minority Problems in Southeast Asia*, Stanford University Press, Stanford, 1955.

Vertovec, S., 'Three Meanings of "Diaspora", Exemplified among South Asian Religions', *Diaspora*, 6, 1997, pp. 277–299.

Vickers, A., *Bali: A Paradise Creat(ed.)*, Penguin, Ringwood, 1989.

The Philippines

Gosine, Mahin, 'Sojourner to Settler', (introduction), *www.saxakali.com/indocarib/introduction.htm*

Mukhi, Sunita S., interview of Michelle Caswell, June 2000, *www.asiasource.org/arts/Writers/Sunitainterview.cfm*

Naqvi, Saeed, 'Little India in Philippines,' *Indian Express*, 20 April 2001.

———, 'Arroyo as Philippina Indira,' *Indian Express*, 4 May 2001.

Thapan, Anita Raina, *Sindhi Diaspora in Manila, Hong Kong and Jakarta*, Ateneo de Manila University Press, Quezon City, 2002.

Indo-China: Vietnam, Laos and Cambodia

Abdoule-Carime, Nasir, 'Les Communautés Indiennes en Indochine', Association d'échanges et de Formation pour les Etudes Khmeres, *www.aefek.free.fr/lecture.htm*

Chanda, Nayan, 'Indians in Indochina', in Sandhu, K. S. and Mani, A. (eds.), *Indian Communities in Southeast Asia*, ISEAS and Times Academic Press, Singapore, 1993.

Coedes, George, *The Indianized States of Southeast Asia*, East-West Center Press, Honolulu, 1968.

Delval, Raymond, *Musulmans Français d'origine Indienne*, Centre des Hautes Etudes sur l'Afrique et l'Asie Modernes (CHEAM), Paris, 1987.

Marius, Claude, 'Les Pondicheriens dans l'Administration Coloniale de l'Indochine', paper presented at 'Les relations entre la France et l'Inde, 1673-2000', Nantes, 8–9 June 2001.

Markovits, Claude, *The Global World of Indian Merchants, 1750–1947: Traders of Sind from Bukhara to Panama*, Cambridge University Press, Cambridge, 2000.

More, J. B. P., 'Indians in French Indochina', in Mathew, K. S. (ed.), *French in India and Indian Nationalism (1700 AD–1963 AD)*, B. R. Publishing Corporation, Delhi, 1999.

More, J. B. P., 'Pathan and Tamil Muslim Migrants in French Indochina', *Pondicherry University Journal of Social Sciences and Humanities*, 1, 1 and 2, 2000.

Pairaudeau, Natasha, 'Other Frenchmen: Indian *Renonçants* in the Colonial Service in Cochinchina', paper presented at the Euroviet Conference, St. Petersburg, Russia, May 2002.

Vidy, G., 'La Communauté Indienne en Indochine', *Sud-Est*, Paris, no. 6, 1949, pp. 1–8.

Brunei

Mani, A., 'A Community in Transition: Indians in Negara Brunei Darussalam', in Sandhu, K. S. and Mani, A. (eds.), *Indian Communities in Southeast Asia*, Institute of Southeast Asian Studies, Singapore, 1993.

EAST ASIA

Hong Kong

Pluss, Caroline, 'Constructing Globalised Ethnicity: Migrants from India in Hong Kong', *International Sociology*, 20, 2, 2005, pp. 203–226.

Vaid, K. N., *The Overseas Indian Community in Hong Kong*, Centre of Asian Studies, The University of Hong Kong, Hong Kong, 1972.

Weiss, Anita, 'South Asian Muslims in Hong Kong: Creation of a "Local Boy" Identity', *Modern Asian Studies*, 25, 3, 1991, pp. 417–453.

White, Barbara-Sue, *Turbans and Traders: Hong Kong's Indian Communities*, Oxford University Press, Hong Kong, 1994.

China

Government of India, 'Report of the High Level Committee on the Indian Diaspora', GOI, New Delhi, 2002.

Government of India, 'Economic Survey 2004–05', GOI, New Delhi, 2005.

Government of India, 'Indian Tourism Statistics 2003', GOI, New Delhi, 2004.

Ray, Haraprasad, 'Indian Diaspora in China', in Ghosh, Lipi, and Chatterjee, Ramkrishna (eds.), *Indian Diaspora in Asian and Pacific Regions: Culture, People, Interactions*, Rawat Publications, New Delhi, 2004.

Stalker, Peter, *The Work of the Strangers: A Survey of International Labour Migration*, International Labour Organisation, Geneva, 1994.

Thampi, Madhavi, *Indians in China, 1800–1949*, Manohar Publishers, New Delhi, 2005.

Japan

Ghosh, Lipi, and Chatterjee, Ramakrishna et al. (eds.), *Indian Diaspora in Asian and Pacific Regions: Culture, People and Interactions*, Rawat Publications, New Delhi, 2004.

Government of India, 'Economic Survey 2004–05', GOI, New Delhi, 2005.

Hiroshi, Komai, 'Improving the position of Immigrants and Foreign Residents in Receiving Countries: Social and Cultural Issues, Migrants in Japan', paper presented at the Technical Symposium on International Migration and Development, The Hague, United Nations, 1998.

Philips, L. Martin, 'Labour Migration in Asia', *International Migration Review*, 25, 1, 1991.

Stalker, Peter, *The Work of Strangers: A Survey of International Labour Migration*, International Labour Office, Geneva, 1994.

CENTRAL ASIA

Afghanistan, Central Asia and Iran

Alam, Muzaffar, 'Trade, State Policy and Regional Change: Aspects of Mughal–Uzbek Commercial Relations, c. 1550–1750', *Journal of the Economic and Social History of the Orient*, 37, 1994, pp. 202–227.

Dale, Stephen, *Indian Merchants and Eurasian Trade, 1600–1750*, Cambridge University Press, Cambridge, 1994.

Levi, Scott C., *The Indian Diaspora in Central Asia and its Trade, 1550–1900*, E. J. Brill, Leiden, 2002.

Markovits, Claude, *The Global World of Indian Merchants, 1750–1947: Traders of Sind from Bukhara to Panama*, Cambridge University Press, Cambridge, 2000.

MIDDLE EAST

Saudi Arabia, Oman and the Gulf States

Abella, Manolo, *Sending Workers Abroad*, International Labour Organisation, Geneva, 1997.

Allen, C., 'The Indian Merchant Community of Masqat', *Bulletin of the School of Oriental and African Studies*, 64, 1, 1981, pp. 37–53.

Awad, I., 'Trends and Prospects of Labour Migration to Kuwait, Saudi Arabia and the UAE', *International Labour Migration Statistics and Information Networking in Asia*, ILO/ARTEP, New Delhi, 1993.

Birks, J. S., and Sindair, C.A., *International Migration and Development in the Arab Region*, AWEP Study, ILO, Geneva, 1980.

———, *National Policies in the GCC States: 1985 to 2010*, Birks and Sindair Ltd, Durham, 1989.

Choueri, Nazil, 'The Hidden Economy: A New View of Remittances in the Arab World', *World Development*, 14, 6, 1986.

El-Shalakuni, Mostafa, 'Determinants of Migration to Kuwait', *Demography India*, 17, 1, 1988.

Ministry of External Affairs, 'Report of the High Level Committee on Indian Diaspora', Government of India, New Delhi, 2001.

Naidu, Lakshmiah K., 'Indian Labour Migration to Gulf Countries', *Economic and Political Weekly*, 16 February 1991.

Nayyar, D., *Migration, Remittances and Capital Flows: The Indian Experience*, Oxford University Press, New Delhi, 1994.

Rahman, Anisur, 'Indian Labour Migration to West Asia: Trends and Effects', *Manpower Journal*, 35, 2, July–September 1999.

Rajan, S. Irudaya, 'From Kerala to the Gulf, Impact of Labour Migration', *Asian and Pacific Migration Journal* 13, 4, 2004.

Richards, Alan, 'The Laissez-Faire Approach to International Labour Migration: The Cases of the Arab Middle East', *Economic Development and Cultural Change*, 9, 1, 1983.

Russell, Sharon Stanton, 'International Migration and Political Turmoil in the Middle East', *Population and Development Review*, 18, 4, December 1992, pp. 719–727.

Saith, A., 'Absorbing External Shocks: The Gulf Crises, International Migration Linkages and the Indian Economy, 1990', *Development and Change*, Sage, London, 1992.

Sasikumar, S. K., 'Trends, Patterns and Characteristics of Indian Labour Migration to the Middle East during the Twentieth Century', *Indian Journal of Labour Economics*, 2, 1995.

Sehuurman, Frans J., and Salib, Raoulf, 'Labour Migration to the Middle East, A Review of its Contexts, Effects and Prospects', *Social Scientist*, 18, 5, May 1990.

Shah, N. M., 'Emigration Dynamics From and Within South Asia', *International Migration*, 23, 3/4, 1995.

Seteney, Shami, 'The Social Implications of Population Displacement and Resettlement: An Overview with Focus on the Arab Middle East', *International Migration Review*, 27, 1, 1993.

Tinker, H., *The Banyan Tree: Overseas Emigrants from India, Pakistan and Bangladesh*, Oxford University Press, London, 1977.

Weiner, Myron, 'International Migration and Development: Indians in the Gulf', *Population and Development Review*, March 1982.

World Bank, *World Development Indicators – 2000*, International Bank for Reconstruction and Development, Washington, 2000.

World Bank, *World Development Report 2005, A Better Investment Climate for Everyone*, World Bank and Oxford University Press, New York, 2005.

United Nations Population Fund, *State of World Population 2004*, United Nations Population Fund, New York, 2004.
Also at: *www.unfpa.org*

Yemen

Aziz Al-Thalebi, *Mohammed Jumaa Khan: the Eternal Hadhrami Song*, Ministry of Culture, Republic of Yemen, Sanaa, 2005.

Das Gupta, Ashin, 'Gujarati Merchants and the Red Sea Trade, 1700–1725', in Kling, B. B., and Pearson, M. N. (eds), *The Age of Partnership*, University of Hawaii Press, Honolulu, 1979, pp. 123–158.

———, 'Indian Merchants and the Trade of the Indian Ocean c. 1500-1750' in Das Gupta, Ashin, *Merchants of Maritime India, 1500–1800*, Ashgate Publishing, Norfolk, 1994.

Gavin, R. J., *Aden under British Rule, 1839–1967*, C. Hurst, London, 1975.

Israel

Katz, Nathan, *Who are the Jews of India?*, University of California Press, Berkeley and London, 2000.

Katz, Nathan and Goldberg, E. S., *The Last Jews of Cochin: Jewish Identity in Hindu India*, University of South Carolina Press, Columbia, 1993.

———, 'Leaving Mother India, Reasons for the Cochin Jews' Immigration to Israel', *Population Review*, 39/1–2, 1995, pp. 35–53.

Kushner, Gilbert, *Immigrants from India in Israel: Planned Change in an Administered Community*, University of Arizona Press, Tucson, 1973.

Roland, Joan G., *Jews in British India: Identity in a Colonial Era*, University Press of New England, Hanover, NH, 1989.

Scaria, Zacharia, and Johnson, Barbara C., *Oh, Lovely Parrot! Jewish Women's Songs from Kerala*, Jewish Music Research Center, Hebrew University of Jerusalem, Jerusalem, 2004.

Yitzhak, Nissim, *Benei Yisrael, Piskei Halakhah* (Bene Israel, Halakhic Decision and the Sources for the Investigation of their Laws and the Question of their Origins), Chief Rabbinate of Israel, Jerusalem, 1962 (in Hebrew).

Turkey

Government of India, 'Report of the High Level Committee on Indian Diaspora', GOI, New Delhi, 2001.

AFRICA AND THE INDIAN OCEAN

South Africa

Bhana, S., *Gandhi's Legacy: The Natal Indian Congress 1894–1994*, University of Natal Press, Pietermaritzburg, 1997.

———, *Indentured Indian Emigrants to Natal, 1860–1902: A Study Based on Ships' Lists*, Promilla, New Delhi, 1991.

Bhana, S., and Brain, J., *Setting Down Roots: Indian Migrants in South Africa 1860–1911*, Witwatersrand University Press, Johannesburg, 1990.

Bhana, S., and Vahed, G., *The Making of a Political Reformer: Gandhi in South Africa, 1893–1914*, Manohar, New Delhi, 2005.

Brain, J., *Christian Indians in Natal, 1860–1911*, Oxford University Press, Cape Town, 1983.

Dhupelia-Mesthrie, Uma, *Gandhi's Prisoner? The Life of Gandhi's Son, Manilal*, Kwela Books, Cape Town, 2004.

Diesel, Alleyn, 'Hinduism in Kwa-Zulu Natal, South Africa', in Parekh, Bhikhu, Singh, Gurharpal, and Vertovec, Steven (eds.), *Culture and Economy in the Indian Diaspora*, Routledge, London, 2003.

Diesel, Alleyn, and Maxwell, Patrick, *Hinduism in Natal*, University of Natal Press, Pietermaritzburg, 1993.

Freund, Bill, *Insiders and Outsiders: The Indian Working Class of Durban, 1910–1990*, Heineman, Portsmouth, NH, 1995.

Goonam, K., *Coolie Doctor*, Madiba Publishers, Durban, 1991.

Meer, Fatima, *The Ghetto People: A Study of the Uprooting of the Indian People of South Africa*, Africa Publications Trust, London, 1975.

———, *Portrait of Indian South Africans*, Avon House, Durban, 1969.

Mesthrie, R., *Language in Indenture: A Sociolinguistic History of Bhojpuri-Hindi in South Africa*, Witwatersand University Press, Johannesburg, 1991.

Mikula, P. et al. (eds.), *Traditional Hindu Temples in South Africa*, Hindu Temple Publications, Durban, 1982.

Naidoo, T., *The Arya Samaj Movement in South Africa*, Motilal Banarsidass Publishers, Delhi, 1992.

Pachai, B., *The International Aspects of the South African Indian Question, 1860–1971*, C. Struik, Cape Town, 1971.

Padayachee, Vishnu, and Hart, Keith, 'Indian Business in South Africa after Apartheid: New and Old Trajectories', *Comparative Study of Society and History*, 2000, pp. 683–712.

Padayachee, Vishnu, and Morrell, R., 'Indian Merchants and Dukawallahs in the Natal Economy, c. 1875–1914', *Journal of Southern African Studies*, 17, 1, 1991, pp. 73–102.

Padayachee, Vishnu, Vawda, S., and Tichmann, P., *Indian Workers and Trades Unions in Durban, 1930–1950*, Institute for Social and Economic Research, University of Durban-Westville, Durban, 1985.

Raman, Parvathi, 'Being an Indian Communist the South African Way: The Influence of Indians in the South African Communist Party, 1934–1952,' Ph.D. thesis, School of Oriental and African Studies, University of London, 2002.

Swan, M., *Gandhi: The South African Experience*, Ravan Press, Johannesburg, 1985.

Tayob, A., *Islam in South Africa: Mosques, Imams and Sermons*, University of Florida Press, Orlando, 1999.

Vahed, Goolam, 'Constructions of Community and Identity Among Indians in Colonial Natal, 1860–1910: The Role of the Muharram Festival', *Journal of African History*, 43, 2002, pp. 77–93.

East Africa

Gregory, R. G., *India and East Africa: A History of Race Relations Within the British Empire 1890–1939*, Oxford University Press, London, 1971.

———, *South Asians and East Africa: An Economic and Social History 1890–1980*, Westview Press, Boulder, Colorado, 1993.

Oonk, G., *Asians in East Africa: Images, Histories and Portraits*, SCA productions, Arkel, Netherlands, 2004.

———, 'The Changing Culture of the Hindu Lohana Community in East Africa', *Contemporary Asian Studies*, 13, 1, 2004, pp. 7–23.

———, 'After Shaking His Hand, Start Counting Your Fingers: Trust and Images in Indian Business Networks, East Africa 1900–2000', *Itinerario*, 18, 3, 1994, pp. 70–88.

Salvadori, C., *We Came in Dhows* (three volumes), Paperchase Kenya Ltd, Nairobi, 1996.

Tandon, Y., *Problems of a Displaced Minority: The New Position of East Africa's Asians*, Minority Rights Group, London.

Tinker, H., *A New System of Slavery: The Export of Indian Labour Overseas, 1830–1920*, Oxford University Press, London and New York, 1974.

———, *The Banyan Tree: Overseas Emigrants from India, Pakistan, and Bangladesh*, Oxford University Press, New York, 1977.

———, *Separate and Unequal: India and the Indians in the British Commonwealth, 1920–1950*, C. Hurst & Co., London, 1976.

Mauritius, the Mascarenes and Southwest Indian Ocean

Anderson, C., *Convicts in the Indian Ocean: Transportation from South Asia to Mauritius, 1815–53*, Palgrave Macmillan, New York, 2000.

Blanchy, Sophie, *Karana et Banians: Les Communautés Commerçantes d'origine Indienne à Madagascar*, l'Harmattan, Paris, 1995.

Carter, M., *Voices from Indenture: Experiences of Indian Migrants in the British Empire*, Leicester University Press, London, 1996.

Chane-Kune, S., *Aux Origines de l'Identité Reunionnaise*, l'Harmattan, Paris, 1993.

Jahangeer-Chojoo, A., *La Rose et le Henné. Une etude des Musulmans de Maurice*, MGI, Mauritius, 2004.

THE CARIBBEAN AND SOUTH AMERICA

Trinidad and Tobago

Carter, M., *Voices From Indenture: Experiences of Indian Migrants in the British Empire*, Leicester University Press, London, 1996.

Dabydeen, David, and Samaroo, Brinsley et al. (eds.), *India in the Caribbean*, Hansib Publishing Limited, London, 1987.

Klass, Morton, *East Indians in Trinidad: A Study of Cultural Persistence*, Waveland Press Inc, Illinois, 1961.

La Guerre, John (ed.), *Calcutta to Caroni: The East Indians of Trinidad*, Extra Mural Studies Unit, University of the West Indies, St. Augustine, 1985.

Laurence, K. O., *A Question of Labour: Indentured Immigration into Trinidad and British Guiana 1875–1917*, Ian Randle Publishers, Kingston, 1994.

Look, Lai Walton, *Indentured Labour, Caribbean Sugar: Chinese and Indian Migrants to the British West Indies, 1838–1918*, Johns Hopkins University Press, Baltimore, 1993.

Malik, Yogendra K., *East Indians in Trinidad: A Study in Minority Politics*, Oxford University Press, London, 1971.

Mohammed, Patricia, *Gender Negotiations Among Indians in Trinidad, 1917–1947*, Palgrave, New York, 2002.

Niehoff, Arthur, and Niehoff, Juanita, *East Indians In The West Indies*, Milwaukee Public Museum Board of Trustees, Wisconsin, 1960.

Singh, Kelvin, *Race and Class Struggles in a Colonial State: Trinidad 1917–1945*, University of the West Indies Press, Mona, Jamaica, 1994.

———, *Bloodstained Tombs: The Muharram Massacre 1884*, Macmillan Caribbean, Basingstoke, 1988.

Seecharan, Clem, *'Tiger in the Stars': The Anatomy of Indian Achievement in British Guiana 1919–29*, Macmillan Education Ltd., London, 1997.

Vertovec, Steven, *Hindu Trinidad: Religion, Ethnicity and Socio-Economic Change*, Macmillan Education Ltd, London, 1992.

Guyana

Adamson, Alan H., *Sugar without Slaves: The Political Economy of British Guiana, 1838–1904*, Yale University Press, New Haven, 1972.

Benjamin, Joel, Kallicharran, Lakshmi, McDonald, Ian and Searwar, Lloyd et al. (eds.), *They Came in Ships: An Anthology of Indo-Guyanese Prose*, Peepal Tree Press, Leeds, 1998.

Birbalsingh, Frank, *From Pillar to Post: The Indo-Caribbean Diaspora*, TSAR, Toronto, 1997.

———, *Guyana and the Caribbean: Reviews, Essays and Interviews*, Dido Press, Chichester, 2004.

Birbalsingh, Frank, and Seecharan, Clem, *Indo-West Indian Cricket*, London, Hansib, 1988.

Bisnauth, Dale, *The Settlement of Indians in Guyana, 1890–1930*, Peepal Tree Press, Leeds, 2000.

Burrowes, Reynold, *The Wild Coast: An Account of Politics in Guyana*, Schenkman Publishing Company, Cambridge, Massachusetts, 1984.

Despres, Leo, *A Cultural Pluralism and Nationalist Politics in British Guiana*, Rand McNally and Company, Chicago, 1967.

Edun, Ayube M., *London's Heart-Probe and Britain's Destiny*, Arthur H. Stockwell, London, 1935.

Jagan, Cheddi, *The West on Trial: My Fight for Guyana's Freedom*, Michael Joseph, London, 1966.

407

Jayawardena, Chandra, *Conflict and Solidarity in a Guianese Plantation*, The Athlone Press, London, 1963.

——, 'Religious Belief and Social Change: Aspects of the Development of Hinduism in British Guiana,' *Comparative Studies in Society and History*, 8, 2, 1966.

Laurence, K. O., *A Question of Labour: Indentured Immigration into Trinidad and British Guiana, 1875–1917*, Ian Randle Publishers, Kingston, 1994.

Look, Lai Walton, *Indentured Labour, Caribbean Sugar: Chinese and Indian Immigrants to the British West Indies, 1838–1918*, Johns Hopkins University Press, Baltimore, 1993.

Mandle, Jay R., *The Plantation Economy: Population and Economic Change in Guyana, 1838–1960*, Temple University Press, Philadelphia, 1973.

Mangru, Basdeo, *Benevolent Neutrality: Indian Government Policy and Labour Migration to British Guiana, 1854–84*, Hansib, London, 1987.

——, *Indenture and Abolition: Sacrifice and Survival on the Guyanese Sugar Plantations*, TSAR, Toronto, 1993.

——, *A History of East Indian Resistance on the Guyana Sugar Estates*, The Edwin Mellen Press, Lewiston, NY, 1996.

Moore, Brian L., *Race, Power and Social Segmentation in Colonial Society: Guyana after Slavery, 1838–91*, Gordon and Breach Science Publishers, Philadelphia, 1987.

——, *Cultural Power, Resistance and Pluralism, Colonial Guyana, 1838–1900*, McGill-Queen's University Press, Montréal, 1995.

Nath, Dwarka, *A History of Indians in Guyana* (2nd edition), D. Nath, London, 1970.

Rodney, Walter, *A History of the Guyanese Working People, 1881–1905*, Johns Hopkins University Press, Baltimore, 1981.

Seecharan, Clem, *Bechu: 'Bound Coolie' Radical in British Guiana, 1894–1901*, The University of the West Indies Press, Kingston, 1999.

——, *British Guiana*, Oxford University Press, London, 1962.

——, (ed.), *Joseph Ruhomon's India*, The University of the West Indies Press, Kingston, 2001.

——, *Sweetening 'Bitter Sugar': Jock Campbell, The Booker Reformer in British Guiana, 1934–66*, Ian Randle Publishers, Kingston, 2005.

——, 'The Shaping of the Indo-Caribbean People: Guyana and Trinidad to the 1940s', *Journal of Caribbean Studies* 14, 1 & 2, 1999–2000.

——, 'Tiger in the Stars': The Anatomy of Indian Achievement in British Guiana, 1919–29*, Macmillan, London, 1997.

Spinner, Thomas J., *A Political and Social History of Guyana, 1945–83*, Westview Press, Boulder, Colorado, 1983.

St. Pierre, Maurice, *Anatomy of Resistance: Anti-Colonialism in Guyana, 1823–1966*, Macmillan, London, 1999.

Surinam

Azimullah, E. G. et al. (eds.), *Van Brits-Indisch Emigrant tot Burger van Suriname, 1873–75 juni–1963: Gedenkboek, uitg. t.g.v. het feit, dat het op 5 Juni Negentig jaar Geleden was dat de Eerste Hindoestanen uit het Toenmalige Brits-Indië Voet op Surinaamse Bodem Zetten*, Surinaamse Jongeren Vereniging "Manan", The Hague, 1963.

Bakker, Freek L., *Surinaams hindoeïsme: Een Variant van het Caraïbisch Hindoeïsme*, Kok, Kampen, The Netherlands, 2003.

Choenni, Chan E. S., and Adhin, Kanta Sh. et al. (eds.), *Hindostanen: van Brits-Indische emigranten via Suriname tot burgers van Nederland*, Communicatiebureau Sampreshan, The Hague, 2003.

Comins, D. W. D., *Note on Emigration from the East Indies to Surinam or Dutch Guiana*, Calcutta, 1892.

Damsteegt, Theo, 'Sarnami as an Immigrant Koin', in Carlin, Eithne B., and Arends, Jacques (eds.), *Atlas of the Languages of Suriname*, KITLV Press, Leiden, 2002, pp. 249–263.

Hassankhan, Maurits S., and Sandew, Hira, *Grepen uit 125 jaar maatschappelijke ontwikkeling van Hindostanen: van Gya tot Lachmon en Djwalapersad*, IMWO/Naugyuga, Paramaribo, Amrit, The Hague, 1998.

Hoefte, Rosemarijn, *In Place of Slavery: A Social History*

of British Indian and Javanese Laborers in Suriname*, University Press of Florida, Gainesville, 1998.

van Kempen, Michiel, *Een Geschiedenis van de Surinaamse Literatuur* (two volumes), De Geus, Breda, The Netherlands, 2003.

de Klerk, C. J. M., *De Immigratie der Hindostanen van Suriname*, Urbi et Orbi, Amsterdam, 1953.

Lamur, Humphrey E., *The Demographic Evolution of Surinam 1920–1970: A Socio-Demographic Analysis*, M. Nijhoff, The Hague, 1973.

McNeill, James, and Lal, Chimmam, 'Report on the Condition of Indian Immigrants in the Four British Colonies, Trinidad, British Guiana or Demerara, Jamaica and Fiji, and in the Dutch Colony of Surinam or Dutch Guiana', His Majesty's Stationary Office 7744, London, 1915.

Mitrasingh, Benjamin S., and Harpal, Marita S., *Hindostanen van Contractarbeiders to Surinamers 1873–1998*, Stichting Hindostaanse Immigratie, Paramaribo, 1998.

Sewradj-Debipersad, Roekmienie, *Emancipatie van Hindoestaanse vrouwen, een Beschrijving van de Veranderingen in het Leven van Hindoestaanse Vrouwen in Surinam Vanaf 1873*, CERDES, Paramaribo, 2001.

Speckmann, J. D., *Marriage and Kinship among the Indians in Surinam*, Van Gorcum, The Netherlands, 1965.

Vertovec, Steven, '"Official" and "Popular" Hinduism in the Diaspora: Historical and Contemporary Trends in Suriname, Trinidad and Guyana', *Contributions to Indian Sociology*, 28, 1, 1994, pp. 123–147.

Jamaica

Bolland, O. Nigel, *On the March: Labour Rebellions in the British Caribbean, 1934–39*, Ian Randle Publishers, Kingston, 1995.

Brathwaite, Edward, *The Development of Creole Society in Jamaica, 1770–1820*, The Clarendon Press, Oxford, 1971.

——, *Contradictory Omens: Cultural Diversity and Integration in the Caribbean*, Savacou Publications, Mona, 1974.

Bryan, Patrick, 'The Creolization of the Chinese Community in Jamaica', in Reddock, Rhoda (ed.), *Ethnic Minorities in Caribbean Society*, Institute of Social and Economic Research, Trinidad and Tobago, 1996, pp. 173–271.

Burton, Richard, *Afro-Creole: Power, Opposition and Play in the Caribbean*, Cornell University Press, Ithaca and London, 1997.

Caldecott, Alfred, *The Church in the West Indies*, Frank Cass & Co. Ltd., London, 1970.

Carter, M., and Khal, Torabully, *Coolitude: An Anthology of the Indian Labour Diaspora*, Wimbledon Publishing Company, London, 2002.

Chatterjee, Partha, 'Nationalism as a Problem', in Ashcroft, Bill, Griffiths, Gareth, and Tiffin, Helen (eds.), *The Post-Colonial Studies Reader*, Routledge, London and New York, 1995, pp. 164–165.

Eisner, Gisela, *Jamaica, 1830–1930: A Study in Economic Growth*, University of Manchester Press, London, 1961.

Gordon, Derek, *Class Status and Social Mobility in Jamaica*, Institute of Social and Economic Research, The University of the West Indies, Kingston, 1986.

Great Britain, Reports and Papers, Colonial Office, P. P. Vol. XVI, 'Papers Relating to the West Indian Colonies and Mauritius', Pt. 1, 1859, Enc. signed by Baptist Minister J. E. Henderson in Gov. Darling to Lord Stanley, 29 March 1858.

Gregg, Veronica, '"Yuh Know Bout Coo-Coo? Where Yuh Know Bout Coo-Coo?" Language and Representation, Creolization and Confusion in Indian Cuisine', in Shepherd, Verene A., and Richards, Glen L. (eds.), *Questioning Creole: Creolization Discourses in Caribbean History*, Ian Randle, Kingston, 2002, pp. 148–164.

Hart, Richard, *Rise and Organize: The Birth of the Workers' and National Movements in Jamaica, 1936–1939*, Karia Press, London, 1989.

Hintzen, Percy C., 'Race and Creole Ethnicity in the Caribbean', in Shepherd, Verene A., and Richards, Glen L. (eds.), *Questioning Creole: Creolization Discourses in Caribbean History*, Ian Randle, Kingston, 2002, pp. 92–110.

Laurence, K. O., *Immigration into the West Indies*, Caribbean Universities Press, Barbados, 1971.

Mangru, Basdeo, *Benevolent Neutrality: Indian*

Government Policy and Labour Migration to British Guiana 1854–1884, Hansib Publishing Ltd, Hertford, 1987.

Mansingh, Laxmi, and Mansingh, Ajai, *Home Away from Home: 150 Years of Indian Presence in Jamaica, 1845–1995*, Ian Randle Publishers, Kingston, 1999.

Mohammed, Patricia, 'The "Creolization" of Indian Women in Trinidad', in Shepherd, Verene A, and Richards, Glen L. (eds.), *Questioning Creole: Creolization Discourses in Caribbean History*, Ian Randle, Kingston, 2002, pp. 130–147.

Nettleford, Rex, *Caribbean Cultural Identity: The Case of Jamaica*, The Institute of Jamaica, Kingston, 1978.

Seecharan, Clem, *'Tiger in the Stars': The Anatomy of Indian Achievement in British Guiana, 1919–29*, Macmillan Education, London, 1997.

Shepherd, Verene, 'The Other Middle Passage?', in Shepherd, Verene (ed.), *Working Slavery, Pricing Freedom*, Ian Randle, Kingston, 2002.

——, 'Indians and Blacks in Jamaica in the 19th and early 20th Centuries, A Micro-Study of the Foundations of Race Antagonisms', in Johnson, Howard (ed.), *After the Crossing, Immigrants and Minorities in Caribbean Creole Society*, Frank Cass, London, 1988, pp. 95-112.

The French Caribbean

Singaravélou, *Les Indiens de la Guadeloupe*, Etude de Géographic Humaine, Université de Bordeaux, Bordeaux, 1974.

——, *Les Indiens de la Caraïbe* (three volumes), L'Harmattan, Paris, 1987.

NORTH AMERICA

United States of America

Das Dasgupta, Shamita (ed.), *A Patchwork Shawl: Chronicles of South Asian Women in America*, Rutgers University Press, New Brunswick, 1988.

Fisher, Maxine, *Indians of New York City*, Heritage, New Delhi, 1980.

Jensen, Joan M., *Passage from India: Asian Indian Immigrants in North America*, Yale University Press, New Haven, 1988.

Khandelwal, Madhulika S., *Being American, Being Indian: An Immigrant Community in New York City*, Cornell University Press, Ithaca and London, 2002.

Kumar, Amitava, *Passport Photos*, University of California Press, Berkeley, 2000.

Prashad, Vijay, *The Karma of Brown Folk*, Minneapolis, University of Minnesota Press, 2000.

Rangaswamy, Padma, *Namaste America: Indian Immigrants in an American Metropolis*, Pennsylvania State University Press, University Park, 2000.

Shankar, Lavina, and Srikanth, Rajini et al. (eds.), *A Part, Yet Apart: South Asians in Asian America*, Temple University Press, Philadelphia, 1998.

Shukla, Sandhya, *India Abroad: Diasporic Cultures of Postwar America and England*, Princeton University Press, Princeton, 2003.

Srikanth, Rajini, *The World Next Door: South Asian American Literature and the Idea of America*, Temple University Press, Philadelphia, 2004.

Williams, Raymond Brady, *Religions of Immigrants from India and Pakistan: New Threads in the American Tapestry*, Cambridge University Press, Cambridge, 1988.

Canada

Buchignani, N., Indra, D. M., and Srivastiva, R., et al. (eds.), *Continuous Journey: A Social History of South Asians in Canada*, McClelland and Stewart Ltd, Toronto, 1985.

Fleras, A., and Elliott, J. L., *The Challenge of Diversity: Multiculturalism in Canada*, Nelson Canada, Toronto, 1992.

Israel, M. (ed.), *The South Asian Diaspora in Canada: Six Essays*, The Multicultural History Society of Ontario, Toronto, 1987.

Li, P. S. (ed.), *Race and Ethnic Relations in Canada*, Oxford University Press, Toronto, 1990.

Magocsi, P. R. (ed.), *The Encyclopedia of Canada's Peoples*, Multicultural History Society of Ontario, University of Toronto Press, Toronto, 1999.

Naidoo, J. C., 'South Asian Canadian Women: A Contemporary Portrait', *Psychology and Developing Societies*, 15, 1, 2003, pp. 51–67.

EUROPE

United Kingdom

Ali, N., Kalra, V. S., Sayyid, S. H. et al. (eds.), *A Postcolonial People: South Asians in Britain*, C. Hurst & Co., London, 2006.

Fisher, Michael H., *Counterflows to Colonialism: Indian Travellers and Settlers in Britain 1600–1857*, Permanent Black, New Delhi, 2005.

Lahiri, Shompa, *Indians in Britain: Anglo-Indian Encounters, Race and Identity, 1880-1930*, Frank Cass, London, 2000.

Visram, Rozina, *Asians in Britain: 400 Years of History*, Pluto Press, London, 2002.

——, *Ayahs, Lascars and Princes: Indians in Britain 1700–1947*, Pluto Press, London, 1986.

The Netherlands

van der Avoird, T., 'Determining Language Vitality: The Language Use of Hindu Communities in the Netherlands and the United Kingdom', dissertation, Tilburg University, 2001.

Bhagwanbali, R., *Contracten voor Suriname*, Amrit, The Hague, 1996.

Choenni, C., 'Hindostaanse Organisaties in Nederland, een Historische Schets', *OSO*, nr 2, Utrecht, 2004, pp. 305–321.

Choenni, C., and Mathura, C., *Hindoe Jongeren in Beeld*, OHM, Hilversum, 1998.

Choenni, C., and Adhin, K. (eds.), *Hindostanen, van Brits-Indisch emigrant via Suriname tot burger van Nederland*, Sampreshan, Den Haag, 2003.

Dabydeen, D., and Samaroo, B. (eds.), *Across the Dark Waters: Ethnicity and Indian Identity in the Caribbean*, MacMillan, Caribbean, London, 1996.

Dijk, A. M. G., van Rambaran, H., and Venema, C. (eds.), *Hindoeïsme in Nederland*, Garant, Apeldoorn, 1999.

Gowricharn, R. S., *Staat en Accumulatie, Over Agrarische Modernisering en Economische Ontwikkeling in Suriname*, Ruward, Den Haag, 1990.

——, 'Hindoeïsme in Nederland,' in Vroom, H., and Woldring, H. (eds.), *Religies in het Publieke Domein*, Zoetermeer, Meinema, 2002, pp. 105–128.

——, 'De Emancipatie van Hindostanen,' in Choenni, C., and Adhin, K. Sh. (eds.), *Van Brits Indisch Immigrant via Suriname tot Burger van Nederland*, Sampreshan, Den Haag, 2003, pp. 90–105.

——, 'Bollywood in de democratie', in Molenaar, L. (ed.), *Ex Pluribus Unum, 675 Jaar Erasmiaans Gymnasium*, Elmar, Rijswijk, 2004, pp. 401–410.

——, 'De Duurzaamheid van het Transnationalisme, De Tweede Generatie Hindostanen in Nederland', *Migrantenstudies*, 20, 4, 2004, pp. 252–268.

de Klerk, C. J. M., *De Immigratie van Hindostanen in Suriname*, Amrit, Den Haag, 1998.

Mungra, G., *Hindoestaande Gezinnen in Nederland*, COMT, Leiden, 1990.

Schudel, W. et al. (eds.), 'Suïcidaal Gedrag en Etnisch-culturele Afkomst Den Haag, 1987–1993', *Epidemiologisch bulletin*, 33, 44, 1998, pp. 7–13.

France

Miles, William F. S., *Imperial Burdens: Countercolonialism in Former French India*, Lynne Rienner Publishers, London, 1995.

Popplewell, Richard J., *Intelligence and Imperial Defence: British Intelligence and the Defence of the Indian Empire 1904–1924*, London, Frank Cass, 1995.

Sébastia, Brigitte, *Les Pondichériens de l'Ile de France: Etude des Pratiques Socialist et Religieuses*, EHESS (Mémoire présenté en vue du D. E. A.), Toulose, 1999. (unpublished; used with the permission of the author.)

Berthet, Samuel, 'Indian Diaspora in France: A Historico-Cultural Perspective' in Singh, Sarva Daman, and Singh, Mahavir (eds.), *Indians Abroad*, Maulana Abul Kalam Azad Institute of Asian Studies, Kolkata, 2003, pp. 133–152.

Lewis, Marti Deming, 'One Hundred Million Frenchmen: The "Assimilation" Theory in French Colonial Policy', *Comparative Studies in Society and History*, 4, 2, January 1962, pp. 129–153.

Portugal

Perez, Rosa Maria, 'Portuguese Orientalism: Some Problems on Sociological Classification', in de Souza, Teotónio (ed.), *The Portuguese and the Socio Cultural Changes in India*, Manohar, Delhi, 2002.

Gilroy, Paul, 'Diaspora, Utopia, and the Critique of Capitalism', in Gelder, Ken, and Thornton, Sarah (eds.), *The Subcultures Reader*, Routledge, London and New York, 1997.

de Souza, Teotónio (ed.), *The Portuguese and the Socio-Cultural Changes in India*, Manohar, Delhi, 2002.

Germany

Brosius, Christiane, and Goel, Urmila et al. (eds.), *Masala, de Menschen aus Südasien in Deutschland*, Draupadi Verlag, Heidelberg, forthcoming 2006.

Goel, Urmila, 'Fatima and theinder.net – A Refuge in Virtual Space', in Fitz, Angelika, Kröger, Merle, Schneider, Alexandra, and Wenner, Dorothee (eds.), *Import Export – Cultural Transfer – India, Germany, Austria*, Parhas Verlag, Berlin, 2005, pp. 201–207.

Guenther, Lothar, and Hans Joachim, Rehmer, *Inder, Indien und Berlin – 100 Jahre Begegnung Berlin und Indien*, Lotus Verlag, Berlin, 1999.

Jan Kuhlmann, *Subhas Chandra Bose und die Indienpolitik der Achsenmächte*, Verlag Hans Schiler, Berlin, 2003.

Kröger, Merle, *Cut*, Hamburg, 2003.

Scandinavia

Andersson, Daniel and Åke, Sander et al. (eds.), *Det Mångreligiöse Sverige – Ett Landskap i Förändring*, Studentlitteratur, Lund, 2005.

Hemmilä, Olavi, *En Yogi Kommer till Stan, Indisk Religiositet i Svensk Skönlitteratur med Särskild Tonvikt på Dan Anderssons Författerskap*, Almquist og Wiksell International, Stockholm, 2002.

Jacobsen, Knut A. (ed.), *Verdensreligioner i Norge* (2nd edition), Universitetsforlaget, Oslo, 2005.

Kjeldstadli, Knut (ed.), *Norsk Innvandringshistorie* (three volumes), Pax, Oslo, 2003.

Liebau, Kurt, 'Die Ersten Tamilen aus der Dänisch-Halleschen Mission in Europa, Vom Object zum Subject kultureller Interaktion', *Fremde Erfahrungen, Asiaten und Afrikaner in Deutschland, Österreich und in der Schweiz bis 1945*, Studien 4, Verlag Das Arabische Buch, Berlin, 1996.

Russia and Ukraine

Gopal, S., *Indians in Russia in the 17th and 18th Centuries*, South Asia Books, New York, 1989.

Kemp, P. M., 'Early contacts between India and Russia', *Journal of Indo-Soviet Cultural Society*, May 1954, pp. 32–34.

——, *Bharat-Rus: An Introduction to Indo-Russian Contacts and Travels from Medieval Times to the October Revolution*, Delhi, 1958.

Government of India, 'Report of the High Level Committee on Indian Diaspora', GOI, New Delhi, 2002.

Vorobyev-Desyatovski, V. S., 'Concerning early contacts between India and Russia,' *Journal of Indo-Soviet Cultural Society*, 2, 1955.

Eastern Europe

Government of India, 'Report of the High Level Committee on Indian Diaspora', GOI, New Delhi, 2002.

AUSTRALASIA AND OCEANIA

Fiji

Ahmed, Ali, *From Plantation to Politics: Studies on the Fiji Indians*, The Fiji Times, Suva, 1980.

Gillion, K. L., *Fiji's Indian Migrants: A history to the end of indenture in 1920*, OUP, Melbourne, 1962.

——, *The Fiji Indians: Challenge to European Dominance, 1920–1947*, Australian National University Press, Canberra, 1977.

Lal, Brij V., *Girmitiyas: The Origins of the Fiji Indians*, Journal of Pacific History Monograph, Canberra, 1983.

——, *Chalo Jahaji: On A Journey of Indenture Through Fiji*, Fiji Museum, Suva, 2000.

——, (ed.), *Bittersweet: The Indo-Fijian Experience*, Pandanus Books, Canberra, 2004.

Mayer, A. C., *Indians in Fiji*, Oxford University Press, London, 1961.

——, *Peasants in the Pacific: A study of Fiji Indian Rural Society* (2nd edition), University of California Press, Berkeley, 1973.

Moynagh, Michael, *Brown or White? A History of the Fiji Sugar Industry, 1873–1973*, Australian National University Press, Canberra, 1981.

Naidu, Vijay, *The Violence of Indenture*, Fiji Institute of Applied Studies, Lautoka, 2004.

Sanadhaya, Totaram, *Fiji Dvip Mere Ikkis Varsh* (2nd edition), privately published, Kanpur, 1919.

Australia

Australia, Department of Immigration and Multicultural and Indigenous Affairs, *The People of Australia, Statistics from the 2001 Census*, DIMIA, Canberra, 2003.

Khoo, Siew-Ean, 'Intermarriage in Australia: Patterns by ancestry, gender and generation', *People and Place*, 12, 2, 2004, pp. 35–44.

Lakha, Salim and Stevenson, Michael, 'Indian identity in multicultural Melbourne: Some preliminary observations', *Journal of Intercultural Studies*, 22, 3, 2001, pp. 245–262.

Voigt-Graf, Carmen, 'Indians at home in the Antipodes, Migrating with Ph.D.s, bytes or kava in their bags' in Parekh, Bhikhu, Singh, Gurharpal, and Vertovec, Steven (eds.), *Culture and Economy in the Indian Diaspora*, Routledge, London and New York, 2003, pp. 142–164.

New Zealand

Leckie, Jacqueline, 'The Southernmost Indian Diaspora: From Gujarat to Aotearoa', *South Asia*, 21, 1998, pp. 161–180.

——, 'South Asians, Old and New Migrations,' in Greif, S. (ed.), *Immigration and National Identity in New Zealand; One People, Two Peoples, Many Peoples?*, Dunmore Press, Palmerston North, 1995, pp. 133–160.

——, 'From Race Aliens to an Ethnic Group – Indians in New Zealand,' in Howard, M. C. (ed.), *Ethnicity and Nation Building in the South Pacific*, United Nations University, Tokyo, 1989, pp. 169–197.

——, 'In Defence of Race and Empire; the White New Zealand League at Pukekohe', *New Zealand Journal of History*, 19, 2, 1985, pp. 103–129.

McLeod, W. H., *Punjab to Aotearoa: Migration and Settlement of Punjabis in New Zealand, 1890–1990*, New Zealand Indian Association Country Section, Hamilton, 1992.

——, *Punjabis in New Zealand: A History of Punjabi Migration, 1890–1940*, Guru Nanak Dev University, Amritsar, 1986.

Tiwari, Kapil (ed.), *Indians in New Zealand: Studies in a Subculture*, Price Milburn for the Central Indian Association, Wellington, 1980.

The Pacific Islands

Ahmed, Ali et al. (eds.), *Pacific Indians: Profiles in 20 Pacific Countries*, Institute of Pacific Studies, University of the South Pacific in association with the Hanns Seidel Foundation, Suva, 1981.

The French Pacific

Amiot, Isabelle, '*Kabar Jolimont*', *Une Histoire en cent Histoires*, Bambou edition, Nouméa, 2004, p. 14.

Angleviel, Frédéric, 'De l'engagement comme Esclavage "Volontaire", le cas des Océaniens, Kanaks et Asiatiques en Nouvelle-Calédonie (1853–1963)', *Journal de la Société des Océanistes*, 110, 2000, pp. 65–81.

Cacot, Jean, 'Des Calédoniens Prolifiques, la Famille Kabar', *Bulletin de la Société d'Etudes Historiques de la Nouvelle-Calédonie*, 71, Nouméa, 1987, pp. 65–66.

Delathière, Jerry, 'Métissage Forcé ou Volontaire? Un Exemple d'acculturation Rapide, les Indiens de Nouvelle-Calédonie', *La Nouvelle-Calédonie, Terre de métissages*, Annales d'histoire calédonienne 1, Les indes savantes, 2004, pp. 107–114.

Roux, Jean-Claude, *New Caledonia, 'The First Settlement' of Pacific Indians*, University of the South Pacific, Suva, 1981.

——, '*Les Indiens de Nouvelle-Calédonie (une Ethnie Disparue par Assimilation)*', *BSEHNC*, 58, Nouméa, 1984, pp. 3–11.

INDEX

Note: Page numbers in *italic* refer to illustrations; page numbers in **bold** refer to maps.

PICTURE CREDITS